The Elements of

BOAT STRENGTH

for Builders, Designers, and Owners

▼

DAVE GERR

INTERNATIONAL MARINE / McGRAW-HILL
Camden, Maine • New York • San Francisco • Washington, D.C. • Auckland
Bogotá • Caracas • Lisbon • London • Madrid • Mexico City • Milan
Montreal • New Delhi • San Juan • Singapore • Sydney • Tokyo • Toronto

Also by Dave Gerr

Propeller Handbook
The Nature of Boats: Insights and Esoterica
    for the Nautically Obsessed

To Honor and Clare, who prove
that the future must be bright.

International Marine

A Division of The McGraw·Hill Companies

10

Copyright © 2000 International Marine
All rights reserved. The publisher takes no responsibility for the use of any of the materials or methods described in this book, nor for the products thereof. The name "International Marine" and the International Marine logo are trademarks of The McGraw-Hill Companies. Printed in the United States of America.

Library of Congress Cataloging-in-Publication Data
Gerr, Dave.
    The elements of boat strength : for builders, designers, and owners / Dave Gerr.
        p. cm.
    Includes bibliographical references and index.
    ISBN 0-07-023159-1 (alk paper)
    1. Boatbuilding. 2. Boats and boating—Maintenance and repair. I. Title.
    VM321.G44 1999
    623.8'17—dc21   99-28949
                                                        CIP

Questions regarding the content of this book should be addressed to
    International Marine
    P.O. Box 220
    Camden, ME 04843
    www.internationalmarine.com

Questions regarding the ordering of this book should be addressed to
    The McGraw-Hill Companies
    Customer Service Department
    P.O. Box 547
    Blacklick, OH 43004
    Retail customers: 1-800-262-4729
    Bookstores: 1-800-722-4726

This book is printed on 60# Finch smooth
Printed by Quebecor, Fairfield, PA
Drawings, charts, and photographs by Dave
    Gerr, unless otherwise noted
Design by Faith Hague
Production by Janet Robbins
Edited by Jonathan Eaton, Alex Barnett,
    Constance Burt, and Pamela Benner

NOTE: Although every effort has been made to present rules and procedures that will produce strong, safe, and long-lasting hulls, the builder uses the information in this book at his or her own risk. The author and International Marine make no representations as to the suitability of these rules and procedures for determining the scantlings of any vessel. If a builder needs any further information regarding the use of a scantling rule or engineering boat structures, he or she is urged to consult a qualified naval architect or marine engineer. The author welcomes information regarding any suggestions, corrections of errors or omissions, and other improvements readers may suggest.

Aquamet 22, Bakelite, Bondo, Cor-Ten, Formica, Kevlar, Monel, Spectra, and Vectra are registered trademarks.

CONTENTS

FORMULAS, TABLES, AND CHARTS

ACKNOWLEDGMENTS

*T*his book, like any other, is the result of many solitary hours of hard work. No book, however, could be successful without outside aid. Indeed, many individuals and companies provided assistance to me throughout my writing and in my office's ongoing design work, which needed completion at the same time. Without their help, *The Elements of Boat Strength* simply could not have been finished.

In particular, Jon Eaton, at International Marine, was an unflagging source of support and guidance, and a pillar of patience throughout this all-consuming project. Pat Kearns, of the American Boat & Yacht Council (ABYC), provided far more assistance than I think she ever realized. And the ABYC itself has proven, time and time again, to be the most invaluable resource for technical information—perhaps the finest association in the industry.

Captain Bill Brogdon undertook the Herculean task of checking each and every formula, as well as reading through the entire manuscript. His corrections, suggestions, insights, and additions were invaluable and mightily appreciated.

My ever-trusty staff of design engineers kept work flowing through the office while I was—more often than I had planned—otherwise occupied with writing and research. Alan Salisch and Mark Kunz, your efforts made a tremendous difference.

Kanter Yachts, Covey Island Boatworks, Kortchmar & Willner, Cape Dory/Newport Shipyards, Westbourne Custom Yachts, American Dream Makers, North River Boatworks, Hills Marine, and Sutherland Boat and Coach all have built some of my designs, and were generous in sharing know-how and experiences—a source of much lore and insight. The Lund Boat Company, Derecktor Shipyards, Topper Hermanson Boats, and Treworgy Yachts each took time from their busy schedule to provide valuable photographs and information. Paul Fleury and Michael Charters selflessly shared their electrical know-how.

And then there are the many friends and clients who have kept me going and shared their experiences so generously: Spyros Garbis, Chris Wentz, Herb Gliick, Frank MacLear, Carol and Gene Montgomery, Paul and Anne Cohen, David Raskin, Paul and Linda Bremer, Tom Reinertson and Arlah Alley, and Sam and Judy Haigh—just a few of the many wonderful individuals who have helped make my work so rewarding.

INTRODUCTION

*T*his book was not written for specialists looking for the latest arcane developments in structural engineering; rather, it was written for the average boatbuilder (amateur or professional), mechanic, marine surveyor, serious yachtsman, and naval architect. *The Elements of Boat Strength* is intended to be an easy-to-use reference for calculating reliable, practical, and solid scantlings for boats of differing types and service. (*Scantlings* are the sizes, shapes, materials, and weights of the structural components of a boat.)

It is necessary to take the time to make sense of a few tables and graphs; however, all the calculations in this book can be done by anyone with a basic understanding of high-school math and every formula can be solved using an inexpensive, student-grade scientific calculator.

Boats are packed with odd, complex, and interesting structures and assemblies. To make things plain, I've included many photos—so many that they've spilled over into a photo gallery, which begins on page 332.

Why *The Elements of Boat Strength*?

As I write this, I'm working on a case in which a production boat's hull flexed so much in ordinary weather that one of its windows literally blew out underway. I've seen vessels that had engine mounts cracked from inadequate engine beds and a transmission that split open at sea due to improper engineering and installation. There was the aluminum charter boat with 80 percent of its underwater welds burned away by corrosion, and the aluminum ocean-racer with its hull stove in in just 30 knots of wind and 6-foot (2 m) seas. I've seen hulls with gallons of water in their foam or balsa cores, and vessels whose keels fell off. Boats have sunk because bulkheads popped loose or masts snapped or chainplates ripped out or steel plates rusted to nothing.

This is the reason for *The Elements of Boat Strength*—the need for well-engineered and well-built boats. Boats carry sailors to sea. Their first, last, and most important job is to take their crew out and bring them back safely, come what may. If your vessel's structure isn't up to snuff—sooner or later—a day of reckoning will come. With luck, this day will be merely expensive and inconvenient. Without luck, lives may be lost. The procedures and recommendations in *The Elements of Boat Strength* will help ensure that your next boat is up to its most important job . . . without needing luck at all.

Boat-Structure Calculations and Practices

The construction of boats—until the last 150 years or so, almost always wooden boats—dates back to the ancient Phoenicians and beyond. The ensuing three or four millennia of cut-and-try, experiment-and-discard, test-and-retest have gradually taught us how to build vessels that will hold together . . . most of the time. It wasn't, however, until the last 150 or so years that the art of building boats strong enough—but no stronger than needed—was formalized. Indeed, there are two standard methods for determining the scantlings of a vessel: The first method—and by far the oldest—is rule-of-thumb; the second is engineering analysis. Rule-of-thumb is considerably quicker and easier to apply; however, simple rule-of-thumb can be unreliable and limiting—especially when you stray from the norm or when you use new or different materials.

Scantling Rules

The most reliable and most practical rules-of-thumb are formalized "scantling rules." These rules are based on engineering analysis cross-checked against a database of successful vessels. The results are then condensed and simplified for quick application using easily determined factors. This is the subject of this book. Such rules establish the required construction materials and dimensions based on a few easily obtainable numbers, such as length overall, displacement, and boat speed. Scantling rules have been one of the principal methods of specifying boat construction for well over a hundred years. They have been used by classification societies, such as the American Bureau of Shipping (ABS) and Lloyds, and by many of the finest designers and builders, such as Herreshoff and Nevins. Because of their ease of use—as compared with a detailed engineering analysis—many builders and designers prefer to work with scantling rules. It is important to keep in mind, however, that scantling rules work *only* for the specific type and size of boat intended by the initial rulemaker.

The scantling rules in this book were developed by the author and are intended to cover all monohull vessels between 10 and 120 feet (3 and 37 m) in length overall, power and sail, displacement and planing, up to about 45 knots top speed. For larger and smaller vessels, for multihulls, and for higher speed, builders must do a more detailed engineering analysis.

Determining Scantlings by Engineering Analysis

Engineering analysis—although considerably more time-consuming than scantling rules—frees the builder to use unusual combinations of materials; to push the performance envelope; to employ unique structural solutions, unusual hull forms or deck structures, and experimental fittings and gear; and to design any specific component of a boat sensibly and with reasonable certainty. Engineering boat structures is a relatively modern approach (compared to rule-of-thumb and scantling rules). The concept of systematic, detailed engineering of a boat structure is not much over 150 years old. In most cases, smaller craft—under 100 feet (30 m) or so—have been built by rule-of-thumb almost exclusively until shortly after World War II. Nevertheless, if you're involved in cutting-edge boatbuilding, you should gain a basic understanding of engineering, thus acquiring the tools to solve the unusual construction questions that you are sure to encounter.

I'm pleased to offer this book, with its easy-to-use scantling rules and detailed discussions of materials and building techniques for the most common standard forms of fiberglass, wood, aluminum, and steel construction. Throughout the book are worked examples to make the processes clear and straightforward. The appendices contain reference material such as bolt-strength tables, unit-conversion tables, and the like.

Alternate Building Methods

I wouldn't even begin to claim that the methods and approaches in *The Elements of Boat Strength* are the only means to build strong, safe boats. I wouldn't even claim that these methods are necessarily the best methods. Indeed, there are so many ingenious and clever alternatives for creating objects as complex and wonderful as boats that no single book could hope to include even a small fraction of them. You should, however, find that the scantlings given here will produce safe, sound, cost-effective vessels. I would even claim that—if the methods given are followed carefully and with common sense—the result will be a superior boat.

Decimal Exponents

Decimal exponents are used extensively throughout this book. If you "don't like math," decimal exponents can seem a little technical. Don't let them put you off, however. Decimal exponents are easy to master; it takes just a few moments. For instance, in

Formula-, Table-, and Chart-Numbering System

The formulas and tables in this book are numbered sequentially together, for each chapter. For example, Formula 4-2 is the second formula in the fourth chapter. Table 4-9 follows Formula 4-8, even though there is no Table 4-8. In almost all cases, the charts (or graphs) are associated with a specific formula. Thus, Chart 4-3 is a graphic representation of Formula 4-3. All such charts have the same number as their formula. Of course, not every formula has a corresponding chart; Formula 4-2 does not, for instance. Accordingly, there will be gaps in the numbering for either formulas, charts, or tables taken separately. Taken as a whole, they run in order in each chapter. This should help you locate specific items. For example, if you're searching for Chart 4-10, and happen to flip open to Formula 4-16, you simply page back through the formula and table numbers until you reach Chart 4-10 (and its related formula) in sequence.

Formula 9-1 for plank thickness (Plank Thickness, in. = $0.74 \times Sn^{0.4}$), 0.4 is the decimal exponent.

It is quite easy to solve this on a pocket scientific calculator (an inexpensive one from any local stationery store or Radio Shack); but it is important to understand what decimal exponents are

$X^{0.5}$ *is the same as* $X^{1/2}$ *is the same as* $\sqrt{X}$ *or* $\sqrt[2]{X}$ *, the square root of X*

$X^{0.334}$ *is the same as* $X^{1/3}$ *is the same as* $\sqrt[3]{X}$ *, the cube root of X*

and so on.

You can see that a decimal is just another way of writing a fraction and that it makes no difference whether we use a decimal or a fraction as the exponent. (The decimal, of course, is easier to enter in a calculator.)

You also can see that a decimal or fractional exponent is the same as taking the root of a number, and the root is always the same as the inverse (or reciprocal) of the decimal. Thus, raising a number to the 0.5 power is the same as taking the square root of that number. (The inverse or reciprocal of 0.5 = 1 ÷ 0.5 = 2, and $\sqrt{X}$ is the same as $\sqrt[2]{X}$.) Raising a number to the 0.334 power is the same as taking the cube root of that number. (The reciprocal of 0.334 = 1 ÷ 0.334 = 3, giving $\sqrt[3]{X}$.)

The nice thing about decimal exponents is that they allow quick manipulation of formulas with exponential relationships that don't happen to fall exactly on even powers or roots, such as square or cube roots. In the case of Formula 9-1, the data showed that plank thickness did not vary as the square root of the scantling number (Sn), but as the Sn to the 0.4 power. This could be rewritten a number of ways:

$$Sn^{0.4} \text{ is the same as } Sn^{4/10} \text{ is the same as } \sqrt[10]{Sn^4}$$

Not only is the 0.4 exponent easier to enter into a calculator, it is also easier to write by hand or to type. Try it yourself. Take your calculator and punch in the number for the Sn. Then, hit the exponentiation key (usually the X^y key). Now enter the exponent and finally press the equal key. That's it, there's your answer. For example, if you raise an Sn of 2.5 to the 0.4 power, the answer would be 1.44; an Sn of 8.7 raised to the 0.4 power would equal 2.37.

ONE

Scantling Rules and the Scantling Number

*T*he principal reference point for all the scantling rules in *The Elements of Boat Strength* is the scantling number (Sn). To determine the dimensions, weights, and shapes of structural components for a boat, it is first necessary to determine the Sn for the vessel being considered. The system laid out here has been designed so that the Sn is the same for all the rules (for each material), for any given boat, so that the resulting Sn value is numerically the same whether calculated in English or metric units. Only length, beam, and depth of hull are required for the basic Sn calculation.

FORMULA 1-1

The Scantling Number (Sn)

Sn = LOA (ft.) × Beam (ft.) × Depth of Hull (ft.) ÷ 1,000 (English)

Sn = LOA (m) × Beam (m) × Depth of Hull (m) ÷ 28.32 (Metric)

Where

LOA = Length overall of the hull proper, not including bow pulpits, false stems

on clipper bows, rails, stern platforms, boomkins, and bowsprits

Beam = Beam overall of the hull proper, not including rub strips, guards, and rails

Depth of Hull = Depth of hull at midships from the sheer down to the top of the keel inside the boat; depth of hull is not draft

NOTE: Midships is at exactly half the waterline length, not half the LOA.

Example:

If our new vessel, *Fish 'n Squish,* had the following dimensions,

LOA	40.00 ft.	12.19 m
WL	37.20 ft.	11.34 m
Beam	12.56 ft.	3.83 m
Depth of Hull	5.91 ft.	1.80 m

it would have an Sn of 2.97.

40 ft. LOA × 12.56 ft. Beam × 5.91 ft. Depth of Hull ÷ 1,000 = 2.969; use 2.97

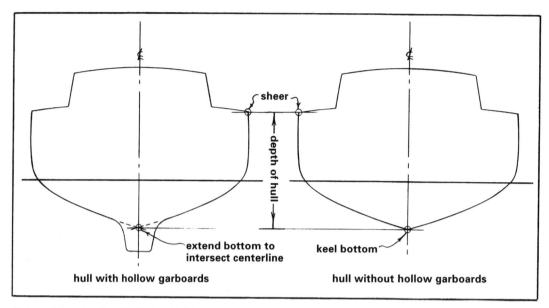

Determining depth of hull at midships

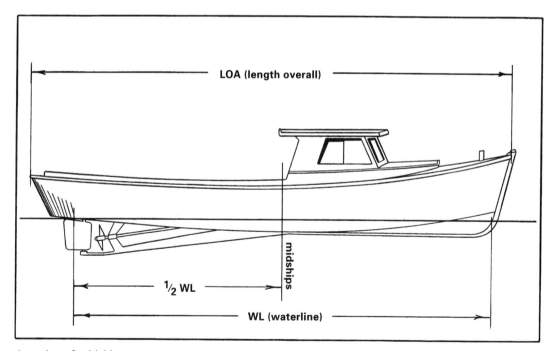

Location of midships

*12.19 m LOA × 3.83 m Beam × 1.80 m
Depth of Hull ÷ 28.3 = 2.969; use 2.97*

Adjusting for Long Overhangs

When the LOA divided by Waterline Length (WL) is greater than 108 percent, find the corrected LOA to use in the Sn calculation:

FORMULA 1-2
Long-Overhang Correction for Formula 1-1

Corrected LOA = (LOA + WL) ÷ 2

Adjusting for Hollow Garboards and/or a Deep Sump

In vessels with pronounced hollow garboards and/or a deep sump, the depth-of-hull measurement will be proportionately too large. For such craft, a sketch of the midships section should be made, and the hull bottom—port and starboard—should be extended down and in to intersect the centerline. Take the depth-of-hull measurement from sheer down to this intersection.

Adjusting for Pronounced Flare

As with depth of hull, vessels that have pronounced flare amidships (i.e., outward slope to their topsides) will have large beams overall in proportion to their volume. This too will generate an excessively large Sn. When beam overall is more than 1.12 percent of beam on the waterline, find the corrected beam to use in the Sn calculation.

FORMULA 1-3
Pronounced-Flare Correction for Formula 1-1

Corrected Beam = (Beam Overall + Beam Waterline) ÷ 2

NOTE: When a vessel has extreme tumblehome (i.e., the opposite of flare), use the maximum beam overall without any correction.

Additional Adjustment Factors

The Sn is the starting point for entering and using the rules that follow. Speed, type of service, and displacement-length (D/L) ratio will be used in specific instances (in the following rules) to adjust the scantling results. The Sn itself, however, applies consistently to all standard hull forms because it approximates total hull volume, which is closely linked to displacement, and required power for a given speed—the two principal factors determining the loads on a vessel. Because the Sn is closely tied to true weight or displacement, no adjustment for displacement is necessary for vessels with D/L ratios between 275 and 100. This range covers the majority of ordinary craft. Adjustments for higher or lower D/L ratios are covered in each specific rule as they apply.

Scantling Rules Apply to Standard Construction Methods and Materials

The scantling rules that follow are intended for use with normal or standard construction methods and materials. High-modulus materials (e.g., carbon fiber, Spectra, and Kevlar) are not generally covered; nor are what are currently somewhat exotic techniques such as prepreg laminates, glued rather than welded aluminum, and foam-cored cold-molded wood. If you wish to build with such materials and methods, you must do a detailed engineering analysis.

Types of Vessels Covered by *The Elements of Boat Strength*'s Scantling Rules

It is critical to note again that the scantling rules in this book were developed by the author, to cover *only*

- standard monohull vessels (i.e., power and sail, displacement and planing)
- vessels between 10 and 120 feet (3 and 37 m) length overall
- vessels with a maximum speed of 45 knots

To determine scantlings for larger or smaller vessels, for multihulls, and for higher-speed craft, builders must do a detailed engineering analysis or consult a qualified naval architect or marine engineer.

TWO

Fiberglass Construction Materials and Methods

*I*t is necessary to understand fiberglass itself before we describe the scantling-rule calculation for fiberglass boats: what is fiberglass? What are its constituents? How was it developed? How is it fabricated and handled? What special considerations must be accounted for in its design and construction?

History and Development of Fiberglass Construction

Modern fiberglass boat construction is based on an ancient principle: adding just 2 percent of a fiber-like impurity to something like clay or plaster of Paris will dramatically increase its strength—especially its resistance to cracking on impact or in bending. This is why, for instance, you can't make bricks without straw—at least not strong, usable bricks. The more fiber you add in proportion to the binder (the fiber-to-binder ratio or fiber content), the stronger the combination—the composite. As you can see, the first "composite material" application is several thousand years old. Of course, if you try to combine much more than 2 percent fiber (straw or whatever), things get too stiff to mix or work properly. Instead, you have to add the binder to the fiber rather than the other way around.

PAPER "HIGH-TECH" COMPOSITES

Papier-mâché, for example, is nothing more than this, and it's another "high-tech" composite that has been with us for three or more millennia. The ancient Egyptians used it to make sarcophagi (i.e., highly molded and brightly painted coffins); eighteenth-century Europeans utilized it to make jewelry boxes and furniture; and during World War II, it was even employed—in a big way, believe it or not—to make airplane fuel tanks! Papier-mâché has its drawbacks—it's not especially strong; it's not at all fire-resistant; and, worst of all, it's unable to stand up to moisture. As long as it is kept well painted or varnished and in a reasonably dry environment, fine; get it wet, though, and it's finished.

BAKE-A-LITE?

Strangely, it was largely the pressures of the newfangled electronics industry that encouraged improved composites. The old insulators—gutta-percha, waxed paper, shellac, and ceramics (which had been adequate for the ordinary telegraph-line voltages)—weren't up to the job as we began using higher currents. The Belgian chemist Leo Baekeland found in 1906 that reacting phenol and formaldehyde would produce a reasonably tough and somewhat water-resistant resin. It wasn't until many months later that he realized that adding fibers (in this case, in powdered form) to his brittle resin would generate superior strength. The result was Bakelite, the first "modern" high-tech composite and the beginning of our contemporary plastics revolution. Between the two world wars, many household appliances and a vast amount of electric equipment were fitted or equipped with Bakelite handles, knobs, cases, and insulators.

ASBESTOS, ANYONE?

From here on, it was a regular, ongoing process to increase strength, stiffness, and weather resistance in these new, highly moldable composite wonder goos. All sorts of binder/chemical combinations were tried along with all manner of fibers—everything from wood pulp to asbestos. Indeed, asbestos-phenolic composites seemed to have all the answers at the end of World War II. Known largely as Durestos, this material was tough, strong, and quite stiff, rivaling even modern laminates in some respects. Back then, no one was much concerned with asbestos health risks, so I guess we can consider ourselves lucky that Durestos didn't gain wide acceptance. Think of the multimillion-dollar

Plug for deck and hull for the author's 72-foot (21.9 m) charter schooner design.

Durestos cleanups that would be underway today if it had!

Modern Fiberglass Construction

Today, we've settled on fiberglass fibers (nothing more than modern-day straw) in polyester resins (modern-day clay) as the most suitable and cost-effective combination for building large, waterproof, composite structures—boats. The process most builders use is almost precisely identical to the application of papier-mâché, employed by the ancient Egyptians. For ancient papier-mâché sarcophagi, a hollow female mold was made from clay or plaster of Paris. It was coated with a mold-release agent (the Egyptians used soap or linseed oil) so the layup wouldn't stick. Alternating layers of paste or glue and paper then were laid in and pressed tightly down until the desired thickness was built up.

The majority of modern production hulls are built up exactly this way. If you were building a new boat, *Glass Slipper,* you would build a hollow female mold (the shape of the hull), which then is coated with a mold-release agent (today, a wax). Next, alternating layers of polyester resin and fiberglass cloth (of varying styles and weights) are laid in until the desired thickness is reached. Maybe "modern" technology isn't quite as modern as we think it is!

HAND LAYUP, VACUUM-BAGGING, OR CHOPPER GUN

What was described previously is commonly known as *hand layup*. It is the most widely used and one of the most successful methods of forming a hull. There are, however, two standard alternatives. The first is really a hand-layup enhancement: the entire hand-layup process on *Glass Slipper* is performed as described, but—after the layup and before the resin cures—a vacuum bag (really a sheet of plastic) is taped in place over the fiberglass in the hollow female mold. Some of the air is sucked out by a pump, causing the outside air to press down evenly on the entire plastic sheet—and thus the laminate—with great force. The result is extremely dense, strong, even layups—considerably stronger than hand layups. This is because vacuum-bagged layups have more glass in proportion to the resin. (Remember, the more fiber you use—if properly applied—the stronger the laminate.)

Atmospheric pressure, by the way, is about 14.7 pounds per square inch (psi) (101 kPa). Using *Glass Slipper*'s builder's trusty vacuum pump, if pressure were reduced by just 25 percent to 11 psi (76 kPa), the resulting force on and through the vacuum bag would be 3.7 psi (25.5 kPa). Doesn't sound like much? Well, 3.7 psi equals 533 pounds per square foot (25.5 kPa equals 2,600 kg/m²). And if *Glass Slipper* were an average 28-footer (8.5 m), it would have about 480 square feet (44.6 m²) of hull surface. Net result: 255,800 pounds (115,900 kg) total pressure—about

equal to a 115-ton hydraulic press! (In practice, pressures of 7 to 9 psi [48 to 62 kPa] are common.)

At the other end of the spectrum is the chopper-gun layup (see photo on p. 332). With a special gun, the builder blows small, short glass fibers mixed with liquid resin onto the surface of the mold. This is then rolled down by hand. (The short fibers are called *chopped fibers*; hence the name *chopper gun*.) Because the fibers are short, run in random direction, and laid down without precise thickness control, a chopper-gun-layup *Glass Slipper* hull is less dense and less strong than a hand-laid-up hull, and far less strong than one that is vacuum-bagged. But chopper-gun layup is very quick and low cost.

We know chopper-gun hulls are cheap. Does this mean they are bad? It doesn't, but—as always—you get what you pay for. Clearly, chopper-gun layups have to be thicker and thus heavier for the same approximate strength. Even so, they don't quite reach the reserve of strength and longevity that a good hand-laid-up hull has. Still, if cutting-edge performance is not a major factor and getting boats out on the water inexpensively is, a properly engineered chopper-gun hull can fill the bill.

ADVANTAGES AND DISADVANTAGES OF THE THREE STANDARD METHODS

Knowing all this, we can assess the pros and cons of the three standard laminating methods. Generally, hand layup is the industry standard. A properly hand-laid-up hull has a smooth, even surface inside and out, and has constant thickness throughout each specific region of the hull. The mechanical properties of the hull will be more than adequate for the majority of average vessels.

Vacuum-bagged laminates are denser, with less resin in proportion to the glass-fiber reinforcement. Such laminates have higher mechanical properties for the same thickness. Although not required for sound hulls, designers and builders can reduce weight or increase performance (or both) by using vacuum-bagging. The vacuum-bagging procedure can add construction costs (often less than expected), and skins on sandwich construction may become too thin for safety on smaller craft or high-speed vessels.

Chopper-gun layups are low cost and—because they have the highest resin content per weight—are the weakest, or have the lowest mechanical properties. Chopper-gun layups are suited to mass production of hulls where weight and performance are not critical. Chopper-gun layups can also be used effectively to fabricate internal and secondary components on otherwise hand-laid-up hulls. Of course, these same parts would be lighter if hand-laid-up or vacuum-bagged, but the cost savings in production applications may be well worth this compromise.

Considerations in Sandwich Fiberglass Construction

Contrary to some common conceptions, fiberglass is neither particularly strong for its weight nor particularly stiff—indeed, fiberglass is rather bendy. To compensate, these days many boats are laid up using *sandwich construction*. Such vessels have cores of end-grain balsa; closed-cell foam; plastic honeycomb or plastic-impregnated paper honeycomb; or, in areas of high loads, plywood or solid wood, with thin fiberglass skins inside and out. This is excellent construction practice if properly engineered and properly fabri-

cated. It increases stiffness without adding weight and—as a bonus—adds built-in insulation.

PROPER CORE INSTALLATION
While on the subject of cores, it is important to note that any of the closed-cell foams from major manufacturers is acceptable. End-grain balsa core is also extremely good. Indeed, it currently provides the highest stiffness for the lowest cost of any core. It is critical that the balsa core be presaturated with resin before layup. If it isn't, when the first layer of fiberglass mat is applied against the new *Glass Slipper's* core, the dry balsa will wick away the resin and ultimately lead to a core-bond failure. This is a really big—frequently uncorrectable—problem.

GETTING GOOD CORE-TO-LAMINATE BOND
The proper core-installation procedure is to lay up the outside skin (inside the female mold), then lay down a wet, resin-rich layer of chopped-strand mat, and squish down the precoated (or presaturated) core onto the still-wet, resin-soggy mat.

Because hulls have compound curvature, almost all cores (balsa and foam) come in sheets cut with *kerfs* (i.e., slits or notches) into numerous little squares, which in turn are bonded to a thin, flexible (usually thin, light fiberglass) binder sheet. The kerfs are necessary for the core sheet to bend and mold into the hull shape. When installed, however, the kerfs also spread open, leaving small voids running along the core. It is *critical* that the kerfs be filled with as much resin as possible. For both balsa and foam, the best procedure is to drape the core sheets over the corner of an upturned barrel, for example. This spreads the kerfs so the builder can spray (hot-coat) the core with resin with maximum penetration into the open cuts (i.e., the kerfs).

Prepared and precoated like this, the core must be rolled down hard by hand while both the core and soggy mat are still wet. The purpose of the resin-rich squishy mat in conjunction with the precoated core is to ensure a good bond between the skin laminate and the core, and to squish as much resin up into the core's kerfs as possible. Properly done, this procedure will produce a very sound, long-lasting hull.

Some companies manufacture special core-bond putties to be used in place of the wet mat. These putties are applied or troweled onto the hull and the precoated core is again rolled down hard on it. Next, a vibrator is used on top of the core to help further press the core down on the putty and to work as much putty up into the core kerfs as possible. Core-bond putties can be used instead of the resin-rich mat, as and when specified by the core manufacturer. Correctly applied, such putties are excellent, but the builder absolutely must use either resin-rich mat or a proper dedicated core-bond putty between the core and the skin laminates to ensure a proper bond. You cannot use ordinary Bondo or some home-brewed putty for core-bonding.

In a female mold, the core kerfs are almost always laid down (facing outward); however, the builder must still use either resin-rich mat or putty between the core and the inside skins as well. It cannot be overemphasized how critical careful attention to detail in bonding and installing cores is to a successful hull.

The best method of bonding a core to a hull is to vacuum-bag it—even if the rest of the laminate is not vacuum-bagged. Most builders report virtually no additional labor in vacuum-bagging cores. At the same time, vacuum-bagging presses the core down onto the skins with the maximum pressure attainable and also sucks up resin to fill all the kerfs nearly 100 percent with resin.

PEA-SOUP CORE FAILURES

Virtually the opposite of high-quality hand-layup, fiber-reinforced plastic (FRP) with foam core, or presaturated balsa core, is inexpensive chopper-gun boats with balsa cores. Frequently, these are installed in, say, their transoms as stiffening for the outboard mount.

Again, the only way to get a good bond between the fiberglass layers and the balsa core is to press down hard—hand-rolling fabric styles or vacuum-bagging. Chopper-gun spraying, even after rolling, applies less reliable and predictable pressure. What's worse, such boats—built in small shops—are often constructed on a lean budget and tight schedule. The builder will be tempted to skimp on (or even ignore totally) presaturating the core.

With the engine-mount fastening gear and the continuous engine and prop vibrations, it is not a question of *if* the transom and core will fail, but rather *when*. I've seen boats in the shop for repairs with such construction. When the transoms were taken apart—often you could peel them open with your fingertips—the rotten balsa inside resembled congealed, decaying pea soup. It is this kind of third- or fourth-rate construction that has given balsa a questionable reputation in some circles, which is totally undeserved. Balsa is one of the best cores when installed correctly. (The proper chopper-gun transom core, by the way, is marine plywood carefully presaturated with three coats of polyester resin *before* it's laid in and sprayed up or chopped over.)

WATER-FILLED CORES

Similarly, I've seen boats that were hand-laid-up with foam cores using ordinary auto-body Bondo as core putty, with no mat and no core presaturation or hot-coating. One of these vessels, a 34-foot (10.4 m) fishing boat, leaked through an improperly bedded spray strip. Water was forced, under pressure, so effectively through the screw holes and into all the open channels left by the unfilled kerfs that nearly the entire hull shell—from keel to sheer—was filled with water (see photo on p. 332). When this boat was hauled out of the water, water literally shot out of holes drilled in the bottom. One hole alone filled a 1-gallon (3.8 l) coffee can three-quarters full in just a few minutes. This was a new boat and it was never fully reparable. This would not have happened with proper core-bonding procedures.

AVOID EXCESS RESIN

Although the mat layers between the cores and the skins should be resin-rich and squishy, this is the *only* place a layup should be soggy. The *sole* way to get a strong, light layup is to use just enough resin to get a thorough wet-out and a good bond—*not one whit more*. Again, the more fiber (i.e., fiberglass) used in proportion to the binder (i.e., resin), the stronger the laminate. Any additional resin actually reduces strength. Strangely, some builders don't know this. Whether you're designing or building, it is vital to keep this principle in mind.

Components of Traditional Fiberglass Laminates

Since fiberglass was introduced for hull construction in the late 1940s and early 1950s, there have been just three "standard" fiber-

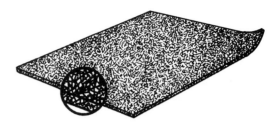

Mat consists of short chopped fibers running in all directions. Squashed together (usually in a binder), these fibers generate relatively low strength. (Courtesy Brunswick Technologies, Inc.)

glass materials, all commonly composed of E-glass (ordinary, electrical-, or construction-grade fiberglass).

CHOPPED-STRAND MAT

Chopped-strand mat (CSM)—frequently known simply as *mat*—is literally that: strands of glass fibers are chopped into short pieces (about $1/2$ inch to 2 inches [12 to 50 mm] long) and mashed together with a temporary binder called a *seizing*. The result is a mat-like material. Because the mat's fibers are short and run every which way, it is not particularly strong. However, it is fairly easy to wet-out, and—because it is soft, thick, bulky, and somewhat sponge-like when wet—it is good for bonding to layers of other types of glass and cores. For this reason, the most common way to lay up a hull is with alternating layers of mat and woven roving.

WOVEN ROVING

Woven roving is a heavy, coarse fabric literally woven from bundles of glass fibers. Because the fibers run for long lengths in two specific directions (at right angles to each other), woven roving forms a strong reinforcement. In fact, an all-roving laminate can be nearly twice as strong, for the same weight, as the

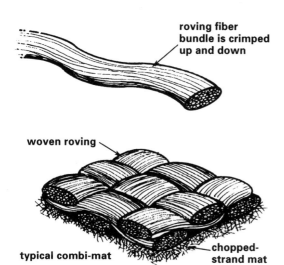

roving fiber bundle is crimped up and down

woven roving

typical combi-mat

chopped-strand mat

Woven roving is much stronger than mat because the fiber bundles are aligned in neat rows at right angles to each other. The crimping of the roving bundles does weaken them some, and the small gaps made by the thick bundle's weave makes for a higher resin content than with a uni-di (see p. 20). Nevertheless, roving and is the "standard" layup reinforcement, and is excellent for most ordinary vessels. (Courtesy Brunswick Technologies, Inc.)

standard combined-roving-mat laminate. It takes great skill and attention to detail, however, to produce a high-quality, all-roving layup. Without soft, spongy mat between the roving layers, it is difficult to make the comparatively hard, flat plies of roving stick to each other reliably. Because the combined-roving-mat layup has proved adequate for ordinary boats, few builders go to this extra expense.

FIBERGLASS CLOTH

True fiberglass cloth is also quite strong. It is used almost exclusively in small boats and for finish work, though, because it is fairly expensive. Unlike woven roving, glass cloth has a very fine weave, not dissimilar to the fiberglass, fireproof curtains you can buy in department stores. Glass cloth is often used as a surface layer to smooth out the roughness of mat and woven roving. For instance, a simple single layer of glass cloth on the inside of the hull makes a nice smooth finish. Accordingly, lightweight fiberglass cloth is sometimes termed *finishing cloth*.

STANDARD POLYESTER RESIN

The most common resin for fiberglass construction is ortho-polyester resin. (Fiberglass is also known as FRP for *fiber-reinforced plastic* or GRP for *glass-reinforced plastic*.) The liquid polyester is mixed with a catalyst and an accelerator to produce a chemical reaction chemists call *polymerization*. Boatbuilders—being practical—just call it *curing*. This means that the molecules in the plastic interlock with each other to form a very rigid unit. Ideally, the whole hull (or at least its plastic part) is just one long-chain (i.e., interlinked) molecule. If you visualize this giant "molecule" wrapped around all that glass reinforcement, you get an idea of why glass boats work so well.

MEKP: THE CATALYST

Although there are a number of catalysts available, the most frequently used is methyl ethyl ketone reacted with hydrogen peroxide, or MEKP. MEKP is tricky stuff. It is highly corrosive and, if it touches your skin, you better wash pretty darn quick. Even more exciting, MEKP is rather volatile—yes, it can explode. In fact, if the accelerator used to speed up the curing process were to come in direct contact with the MEKP, an explosion and certainly a fire could result. Accordingly, most polyester resins used in boatbuilding come with an accelerator already mixed in.

THE STANDARD FIBERGLASS LAYUP

During the past 40 years or so, the standard, plain-vanilla hull layup has become alternating layers of woven roving and CSM. As with the core, the mat between roving layers produces better adhesion between layers (a better interlaminar bond); however, except at the core, the mat shouldn't be any wetter than absolutely necessary. Most frequently, builders will purchase this combination already stitched together: a woven roving with a mat stitched or glued to it. Such fabrics are often referred to as *fab-mat*, *bi-ply*, or *combi-mat*. They save labor in construction by allowing the builder to apply the two layers as one.

The fiber-to-binder ratio is called the *glass-to-resin ratio* or *glass content*, and for a standard hand-layup using alternating layers of woven roving and CSM, it is about 35 percent by weight. For an all-mat layup, the glass content is about 28 percent by weight; for an all-woven-roving layup, the glass content or ratio is about 40 percent by weight. Again, it is important to note that the higher the glass content (the glass-to-resin ratio), the higher the laminate's mechanical properties (i.e., the greater its strength).

Plywood Bottom Framing

The internal structure/framing described in chapter 5 is not the only method of reinforcing the interior of a hull; it would be impossible to cover all possible approaches. One fairly common alternative, however, is to install a framework of longitudinal and transverse plywood panels across the hull bottom. These plywood bottom stiffeners and frames are sprayed with several coats of resin. Then they are tabbed in place to the bottom of the hull, and both the tabbing and ply are usually sprayed with a finish coat of gelcoat. This method is proven and works. It is common on many smaller-production powerboats.

I prefer cored framing (described in chapter 5) because its wider form spreads loads and reduces stress concentrations. Furthermore, there is no partially exposed plywood (i.e., not covered all around with FRP laminate) in the bilge, where small scratches and cracks can permit water penetration and potential long-term degradation. The plywood bottom-framing method is not covered in detail in this scantling rule; however, the method itself is basically safe and workable.

PLYWOOD FLOORS

For plywood floors—as opposed to the cored floors recommended in Formulas 5-7 and 5-8—you can use plywood that totals 1.15 times the thickness of the recommended cored-floor laminate, both sides, but not less than $1/2$ inch (12 mm); see photo on p. 332. A 0.32-inch laminate would be 0.64-inch both sides, and 0.64-inch × 1.15 = 0.74; use $3/4$-inch (8.1 mm laminate would be 16.2 mm × 1.15 = 18.6 mm; use 20 mm). These ply floors should otherwise be shaped and proportioned as described in Formulas 5-7 and 5-8. The ply floors should be tabbed in place with tabbing exactly as for bulkheads (see Formula 5-5); however, the ply floor tabbing should be 10 percent thicker.

PLYWOOD ENGINE BEDS AND BOTTOM STRINGERS

For solid plywood engine beds and bottom stringers, find the core thickness from Formula 5-1 and multiply it by 0.75. Determine the height of the cores from Formula 5-1 and increase it by 10 percent. The tabbing should be 1.3 times heavier than for the bulkhead tabbing found in Formula 5-5.

THREE

Fiberglass Design Considerations, Modern Laminates, and One-Off Construction Methods

Fiberglass Design Considerations

AVOIDING HARD SPOTS

Because fiberglass is quite flexible or bendy and most fiberglass layups are also fairly thin, they can flex repeatedly, especially at hard spots, tight bends, machinery mounts, and bolt and fastening holes. Thus, it is vitally important that large backing plates are employed to spread out loads; large extended tabbing/bonding areas are used to fasten stringers, bulkheads, and other attachments; and all transitions in laminate thickness are gradually tapered throughout.

It is also critical that all corners in the laminate and in secondary bonds be made with a radius or fillet. Fiberglass laminates do not work well with hard, sharp corners. The builder must use foam or balsa fillets or putty-grout fillets to round over any layup making a sharp inside turn. This is equally true for a transom corner, a stem, tabbing a bulkhead or stringer in place, or bonding in machinery or tank flats.

CORE TAPERING

Because the skins of cored fiberglass laminates are even thinner than solid laminates, spreading loads and avoiding hard spots is—if anything—more important. Indeed, the U.S. Coast Guard and the American Bureau of Shipping (ABS) *require* that the transition from a cored area of the hull to a solid, uncored area be done gradually with an angle or slope in the core.

THE NOT-SO-SECONDARY "SECONDARY BOND"

On properly manufactured fiberglass craft, the hull is laid up in one continuous process, with no more than 16 hours (fewer is better) between applying layers.

FORMULA 3-1
Time between Laminate-Layer Application

A still better rule is that no more than twice the resin's gel time should be permitted between the application of

(continued)

17

each successive layer. The resin in each subsequent layer then forms cross-linked chemical bonds with the preceding layer.

If this is done, all of the layers (more or less) cure together to form a single unit locked together in a *primary bond*. Of course, bulkheads, stiffeners, and interior structure have to be added later—after the hull proper has fully cured. The tabbing that attaches such items to the inside of the hull makes a *secondary bond*, which is never as strong as any primary bond. (There is little significant chemical cross-linking.)

Clearly, this is unavoidable. Happily, it is also perfectly okay; however, the builder must take proper steps to get a good secondary bond. The area to be bonded must be ground slightly (i.e., roughed up to produce a good "tooth" to which to glue), vacuumed clean, and then wiped down and rendered oil-free with acetone or styrene. (Styrene is preferable when bonding to laminates that are more than three months old; it softens the old resin more for better secondary adhesion.) Only then can the tabbing/bonding be wet-out, rolled, and pressed down. Most builders use ordinary polyester resin for all laminating, including critical secondary bonds. Again—if done with care—this is fine; however, a few of the finest builders use vinylester resin for all structural secondary bonds. Vinylester yields still stronger, longer-lasting secondary bonds.

What if these basic secondary bonding steps aren't taken? The photograph on page 333 shows a boat that came to one of my builder's shops for repairs. This vessel literally had started to come apart in a storm. The bulkhead/stiffener panel, shown in the photograph, pulled out when it was yanked on with one hand. Not only had this builder neglected to prep for good secondary bond, but—as you can see—he also didn't use foam spacers or even fillets to ease the radius at the corner of the tabbing.

AVOIDING NAKED WOOD

Solid-wood or solid-plywood cores are frequently used in fiberglass hulls. Also, wood cleats and panels are almost always found in the interior, whether for supporting machinery or joinerwork. For structural woodwork (as opposed to interior cabinetry), there must be no bare wood in the boat—period! Every single piece of wood simply must be sealed (see photo on p. 333). If it isn't, not only can it rot, but worse still, it also will expand and contract from the constant moisture changes found on any boat. In time—sometimes an amazingly short time—this will cause the wood to split and to separate from the FRP structure—bad news, indeed. Usually, wood that is otherwise exposed but is in contact with the glass structure should be coated liberally with resin and sprayed with gelcoat. Unless you've got a good eye, it can even be hard to spot timber that has been so treated. If the wood is not partially laminated or structurally fastened to the glass structure, it's okay to set it in marine bedding compound and seal it with Cuprinol, or to paint it—but coat it with something, coat it all around, and coat it well.

GELCOAT AND AVOIDING PRINT-THROUGH

Print-through is the term used to describe a smooth-finished surface that has been marred by the weave of the underlying fiberglass reinforcement, showing as distinct ridges. The usual layup procedure is to wax the inside of the female mold, then spray it evenly with a gelcoat 20 to 30 mils (i.e., 20 to 30 thousandths of an inch) thick (0.5 to 0.76 mm).

(A gelcoat more than 30 mils [0.75 mm] thick is prone to crack; less than 20 mils [0.5 mm] thick is too thin for adequate coverage and surface quality.) *Gelcoat* is high-quality resin pigmented to the color desired for the surface finish. The gelcoat is allowed to reach partial cure (about three to four hours, depending on the resin system). Next, a layer of mat is laid down on the partially cured gelcoat; this is known as the *skin coat.*

For most vessels more than 25 to 30 feet (7.5 to 9 m), the skin coat is from 1- to 1^1/$_2$-oz./sq. yd. (305 to 457 g/m^2) mat. For boats less than 25 feet (7.5 m), the skin coat is usually ^{3}/$_4$- to 1-oz. mat (228 to 305 g/m^2). The mat skin coat is allowed to cure (usually overnight), then the remainder of the structural laminate is applied. Again, on vessels more than 30 feet (9 m) or so, this next layer is usually another 1- to 1^1/$_2$-oz. (305 to 457 g/m^2) mat; on vessels less than 25 feet (7.5 m), the next layer is usually ^{3}/$_4$-oz. (228 g/m^2) mat. The purpose of the mat is to eliminate the print-through—that is, showing the rough weave or the structural reinforcing cloth behind it (usually roving). Mat accomplishes this because it is soft and squishy, and has a high resin content (or low glass content—same thing).

Most builders will try for a total of 2 oz. (610 g/m^2) of mat (or a little more) between the gelcoat and the balance of the structural laminate (^{3}/$_4$ to 1 oz. [228 to 305 g/m^2] on vessels less than 25 feet [7.5 m]). This is necessary but unfortunate because—as discussed previously—the mat is relatively heavy and weak. However, you must allow for this mat skin on most average design laminates. Another factor to keep in mind is that the finer the weave of the structural cloth, the less it will print-through. Thus, some of the light stitch-mat styles (discussed later in this chapter) can use somewhat less mat in the skin coat. Alternately, if most of the laminate is standard 24-15 fab-mat (i.e., 24-oz. [813.6 g/m^2] roving plus 1.5-oz. [457 g/m^2] mat), you could make the layer immediately under the skin coat of 14-oz. (474.6 g/m^2) roving. This too would help reduce print-through.

When the resin cures, it generates heat. This is a natural product of the *exothermic* chemical reaction, which means that it gives off heat. Many builders refer to the heat as *exotherm*. The greater the heat or exotherm during cure, the more the laminate will shrink when it cools down after cure. This shrinkage aggravates print-through. Accordingly, print-through also can be reduced by using the slowest-cure resin mixture practically permissible; by keeping the internal layup skins thinner; and by keeping the entire shop cool to reduce temperature overall. All this is a truly delicate balancing act, and it is critical that the resin manufacturer be consulted regarding the best procedure for the exact resin system and formulation to use.

RESIN MIXING AND STORAGE

Although the fiberglass-cloth reinforcement has essentially unlimited shelf life, the resins used are quite volatile chemical mixtures. I am frequently astonished by how little care some builders give to storing and preparing their resin. Keep track of the ages of your resin drums, and don't try to use them after they're too old—you'll be sorry if you do. All resins must be stored in a cool environment, out of direct sunlight. The drums must be kept sealed airtight and watertight, and even condensation in partly used but resealed drums must be kept to a minimum. Also—most important—the resins must be stirred in their storage drums *before* distribution and use. Many an inexplicable laminating failure has been a result of ignoring these simple precautions.

Modern Laminates: Fibers and Resins

In the past 15 years or so, new, more advanced fabric styles and materials and new resins have become more common. These new approaches give the designer and builder the opportunity to produce stronger, stiffer, lighter hulls. Usually, though, such laminates cost more—sometimes significantly more.

As we discussed previously, traditional or standard fiberglass is available in CSM, woven roving, and cloth. All these are of E-glass—standard marine- or construction-grade fibers. S2-glass or S-glass is identical in chemical composition to E-glass, but it is aircraft-grade fiberglass. The individual fibers are spun finer and are of higher purity with fewer defects. This dramatically improves the strength of individual fibers and, thus, the resulting laminate.

Similarly Kevlar, Spectra, and carbon fiber can be used in place of E-glass. These fibers can have anywhere from 3 to 10 times

Directional fabric has all the bundles of fibers aligned neatly, running in the same direction. There is no crimping and few gaps to hold resin. (Courtesy Brunswick Technologies, Inc.)

the strength and stiffness of ordinary E-glass, giving much stronger laminates. All these modern fibers have higher stiffness as well as higher strength characteristics. Stiffness is measured in a unit known as the *modulus* (modulus of elasticity), so these fibers are often referred to as *high-modulus* fibers or *high-modulus* reinforcement.

MODERN FABRIC STYLES: UNI-DI, BI-AXIAL, AND STITCH-MAT

Uni-Di Fabric Styles

Another way to increase the mechanical properties of a laminate is to remove kinks or bends in the individual fibers and to align the fibers in the direction needed for strength. To do this, the builder applies layers of fibers all running in the same direction. These fibers are held together in a cloth roll with a very light stitching and/or some binder or seizing. This fabric style is called *uni-directional*, or *uni-di*. Because the fibers are not bent by being woven in and out, over and around each other, they are stronger even than woven roving (which is composed of woven bundles of fibers). The fibers all lay in the same direction, so they have maximum strength in that one direction. Additionally, the neatly aligned fibers pack together very closely and wet-out easily. This means that they will have a very low resin or binder content in proportion to their weight. (They will have a high glass-to-resin ratio.) Pure, vacuum-bagged, uni-di laminates will have glass contents as high as 55 to 60 percent—under the very best conditions, as high as 65 to 70 percent.

Bi-Axial Fabric Styles

Unfortunately, there are two practical problems with using pure uni-di fabric styles. The first and most obvious is that strength only runs in one direction. To counteract this, the builder has to apply uni-di styles in multiple layers running at opposing angles. The first layer will be laid on at, for example, 45 degrees to the fore-n-aft line, then the second layer will be laid on, crossing the first at 45 degrees to the fore-n-aft line, like double-diagonal planking. This is known as ±45 degrees, +45 degrees, −45 degrees, or simply 45,45. Alternately, the layers could run transversely and straight fore-n-aft. This is 0 degrees, 90 degrees, or 0,90.

Just as with *combi-mat* or *fab-mat* (i.e., CSM stitched to woven roving), glass suppliers make fabric styles that combine uni-di layers for the builder. Again, this allows the builder to apply two layers as one. These fabric styles are commonly known as *bi-axial* (even when they are 0,90). There are even *tri-axial* and *quadra-axial* styles. A tri-axial might have three uni-di layers: +45, −45, and 0 degrees, all prestitched together in a single roll of cloth. By combining +45,−45 bi-ax with 0,90 bi-ax styles, the builder can generate even strength in all directions; however, although stronger than woven roving, this isn't as strong as the pure uni-di along its one-strength direction.

Stitch-Mat Fabric Styles
The second problem with uni-di fabric styles is that there is no mat

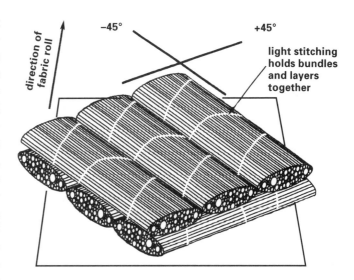

Plus/minus 45-degree bi-axial fabric style, in both diagonal directions across the fabric roll. If a mat were stitched to one side of this fabric, it would be a plus/minus 45-degree stitch-mat. (Courtesy Brunswick Technologies, Inc.)

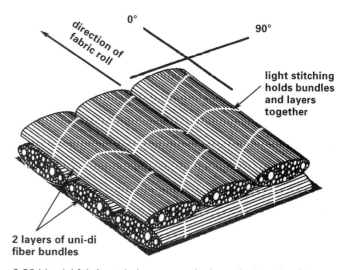

0,90 bi-axial fabric style has strength along the length of the fabric roll and across the roll. If a mat were stitched to one side of this fabric, it would be a 0,90 stitch-mat. (Courtesy Brunswick Technologies, Inc.)

between the layers to ensure a good interlaminar bond. If great attention to detail is used and if the hull or component is vacuum-bagged in a high-elongation, gap-filling resin system, this can work. For most applications, however, some mat is desirable. This, again, is a delicate balance. First, mat is comparatively weak and heavy, so you want to use as little as possible. Second, many mat products are not compatible with high-strength resin systems. To solve this difficulty, glass manufacturers make fabric styles that are bi-axial with a light or thin layer of mat stitched to it. These are known as *stitch-mat* styles. A typical stitch-mat is Hexcel Knytex DBM1708. This is a +45,−45 bi-axial (the "DB"), built from two layers of 8.5-oz./sq. yd. uni-di (totalling 17 oz./sq. yd.—the "17"), with a single layer of $^3/_4$-oz./sq. ft. (0.75-oz.) mat stitched to it. (The "08" is for the 0.75-oz. mat, rounded off.) In metric units, this is two bi-ax uni-di layers 288.1 g/m², with a 25.4 g/m² mat. Additionally, this mat is specifically made without the chemical binder or seizing that can be incompatible with high-strength resin systems.

Stitch-mat reinforcements are available in a wide variety of styles, both 0,90 and +45,−45, and with differing thicknesses and weights of mat. This is an excellent way to make the best use of higher-strength fabrics and resin systems without excessive labor. Applying a stitch-mat is like applying three layers at once: two uni-di and one mat.

Even with ordinary E-glass, stitch-mat bi-axial fabric styles can offer a substantial increase in strength. The flexural strength of DBM1708, for instance, is 63,000 psi (434 mPa), while a standard E-glass fab-mat (mat/roving) layup has a flexural strength of just 30,000 psi (206 mPa).

ALTERNATE RESIN SYSTEMS

Polyester Resin

There is little point in using any of the modern fabric styles or high-modulus materials with standard orthophthalic-polyester resins. This is the plain-vanilla resin that has remained the industry standard for years. Its drawback is that it tends to be rather brittle; it cracks under high load rather than stretching, giving, and then returning to its original shape. Ortho-polyester resin elongates about 2 percent of its length before cracking, with tensile strength of 9,400 psi (65 mPa). This means that when the thinner high-modulus fibers and modern fabric styles flex in ortho-polyester, the resin cracks before the fibers develop their full usable strength.

The next step up in resin systems is isophthalic-polyester. Isos have somewhat better elongation and much better resistance to chemical attack—blistering or degradation by oil or pollutants. Isos elongate 2.5 percent before cracking and have roughly the same tensile strength of ortho resins. A vacuum-bagged E-glass iso-polyester laminate using bi-axial stitch-mat fabric styles will generate a fairly strong hull—stronger than the standard mat/roving layup. The increase in cost over a mat/roving ortho-polyester layup is modest.

Vinylester Resin

To make full use of the greater strength of the modern fabric styles and high-modulus fibers, you need to utilize a high-strength, high-elongation resin system. The two commonly used in boatbuilding are vinylester resins and epoxy resins. Vinylesters have much greater elongation than any of the polyester resins—they stretch farther before cracking and breaking. On average, vinylesters elongate fully 5 percent before cracking, with a tensile strength of 11,800 psi (82 mPa).

This means that laminates using vinylesters are much tougher than polyester laminates. It also means that interlaminar bonds (the bonds between layers and to the core) are stronger, because it is harder to peel the layers apart. Imagine the cured resin stretching like taffy and springing back if you try to peel the layers apart. This is known as having high *peel strength*. Vinylesters, furthermore, have even higher resistance to chemical attack and to blistering than do any of the polyesters.

Another nice feature of vinylester is that it is compatible with standard mat chemical binders and with standard polyester shop equipment and methods. Builders used to polyesters have little difficulty switching to vinylesters, or switching back and forth between the two. Furthermore, vinylester has the unique property of forming a good bond to polyester; polyester, in turn, will bond well to it. This also makes for great flexibility in the production shop. In most cases, a vinylester-resin system using bi-axial stitch-mat fabric styles with either E-glass or high-modulus reinforcement fabric will produce about as strong a laminate as reasonable, practical, and necessary.

Epoxy Resin

The resin system still stronger than vinylester is epoxy. Epoxy resin not only fills relatively large gaps (helping to avoid small-void defects in fabrication), but it also is both stronger and has even higher elongation than vinylester. Elongation is usually more than 5 percent, and tensile strength is 12,500 psi (86 mPa). Epoxy has still higher resistance to chemical attack and blistering than vinyl-

ester's already high resistance. Because of its gap-filling and very high elongation, epoxy has the highest peel strength of any ordinary resin system. Accordingly, epoxy layups can be made successfully without using mat at all (an epoxy-compatible mat or core-bond putty must be used to bond to cores). When the mat is eliminated completely, the highest glass or fiber content is possible and, thus, the highest mechanical properties. A carefully vacuum-bagged bi-axial S-glass epoxy laminate, for instance, can have a flexural strength of nearly 85,000 psi (586 mPa). This is as strong as stainless steel, although the S-glass epoxy laminate weighs just one-fifth as much and will never corrode. Laminates like this are quite expensive, both in materials and in skilled labor and design. Application equipment and methods are not readily compatible with polyester. Epoxies are usually best suited to and most practical for the cutting edge in racing performance and military or rescue-craft applications.

One-Off FRP Construction Methods

All of the foregoing discussion is based on the standard production-shop method of fiberglass construction in a female mold. For one-off or limited-run production, or for special components like tanks, other methods may be used. These methods dramatically reduce the labor involved in building the female mold in the first place; however, they usually require considerable additional labor in finishing the exterior surface.

All the basic materials, considerations, and approaches described previously still apply, but one-off methods do not use gelcoat because there is no prepared smooth finished

Close-up view of Baltek's DuraKore showing how it fits together to form a complex curved form. (Courtesy Baltek Corporation)

Thirty-six-foot (10.9 m) fishing-boat hull under construction at "Pettegrow" using Baltek's DuraKore strip technique. (Courtesy Baltek Corporation)

exterior surface. Instead, the builder has to engage in the painstaking, time-consuming process of fairing the surface by repeatedly filling and sanding—using ever finer grits and filling smaller and smaller voids—until the desired surface quality is obtained. The exterior is then painted for the final finish surface.

The most common methods of one-off FRP construction are foam core over a disposable wooden male-skeleton mold; foam core or solid FRP over a male mold or plug; Baltek DuraKore, a proprietary balsa-core strip-plank process; and C-Flex, a proprietary solid (single-skin) FRP process. Refer to chapter 6 for foam-core construction and to standard books on fiberglass boatbuilding and/or the manufacturers for detailed descriptions. For DuraKore, refer also to *Boatbuilding with Baltek DuraKore*, by David Brown, and to *The Baltek DuraKore Scantling Handbook*, by the author.

C-FLEX ONE-OFF METHOD

Seemann Fiberglass, Inc.'s C-Flex consists of bundles of thin fiberglass rods bound together into "planks" with a light, transverse fiberglass weaving holding the rods in place. These planks can be bent around a male mold to form a fair substrate for a solid-glass (single-skin) FRP hull. To use C-Flex, you can use the standard scantling rule given in chapter 4, and simply replace the interior portion of the laminate with the equivalent thickness of C-Flex. Currently, C-Flex is available in two thicknesses:

| C-Flex | CF-39 | 0.080 in. | 2.03 mm |
| C-Flex | CF-65 | 0.125 in. | 3.17 mm |

The thinner C-Flex is suited to smaller boats with closer mold-station spacings. It is also critical that a very slow-cure, low-shrink

The Westbourne-44 high-speed Express Cruiser designed by the author. Constructed entirely of Baltek DuraKore and balsa-core panels, this boat came in under its predicted weight and has a top speed of 36 knots. (Courtesy Bob Grieser)

resin be used with the C-Flex to avoid shrinkage distortion. This is commonly called a *casting resin*. Consult with the manufacturer for details before building a C-Flex hull.

Mass-Production Tooling

FIBERGLASS TOOLING/MOLDS

Mass-production fiberglass boats have an additional structural element—the tooling or molds. Although it can be helpful to have hull and deck molds fairly light to keep them manageable, neither lightness nor great strength is important—low cost and ease of construction are. Almost all molds are made up entirely of mat layups braced with external core and stiffeners. The following is a good guide to standard practice:

> Small components and canoes:
> 8 layers $1^1/_2$-oz. (457 g/m^2) mat
> Boats 20 to 50 feet (6 to 15 m):
> 12 layers $1^1/_2$-oz. (457 g/m^2) mat

Boats more than 50 feet (15 m):
> 16 to 18 layers $1^1/_2$-oz. (457 g/m^2) mat

Where tight bends and creases are molded in, the buildup can be made from an equivalent layup of $^3/_4$-oz. (228 g/m^2) mat.

EXTERNAL STIFFENING OR PIPING

External stiffeners often were made of steel pipes welded and bolted into a framework surrounding the outside of the hull or deck mold. These pipes were then tabbed onto the mold exterior. Properly configured, the entire mold and pipe framework would be supported on two pivots—one at the bow and one at the stern—which permits rotating the tooling so all layup can be down-handed work. Because of this practice, mold-stiffening is sometimes generically termed *piping*.

Although pipe-mold stiffening works, I don't care for it. The piping rusts and cor-

Another use for core. Here it stiffens the Gerr 34 hull mold. This is a lighter and easier-to-handle structure than a solid-glass mold reinforced with piping.

rodes when the tooling is stored outside. Also, the coefficient of expansion for metal is very different than for fiberglass, which leads to distortion and separation of the piping's tabbing over time.

TABBED-ON PLYWOOD STIFFENING
Instead of pipe stiffening, I recommend tabbing on external plywood stiffening webs. These webs can be of low-grade exterior B-B or B-C ply, and of about the same thickness as the bulkheads that would be installed inside the hull, but not less than 1/2 inch (12 mm). The depth of the ply stiffener webs should be 12 times the thickness or more. Tabbing is of all mat, roughly similar in weight and in tabbing run out to that used for bulkheads of the same thickness; however, only rudimentary corner-filleting is required. A good rule-of-thumb is to arrange and space the ply stiffening so there is no panel on the mold that is more than 12 feet (3.6 m) unsupported fore-n-aft and no more than 5 feet (1.5 m) unsupported *athwartships* (i.e., along the girth or transverse surface of the mold).

For longevity, all the plywood and other wood-reinforcing used on the mold should be sprayed/sealed with three coats of gelcoat or resin.

BALSA-CORE MOLD STIFFENING
I recommend installing balsa core under the outer two or three layers of mat, over most of the central 70 to 80 percent of the mold—extending it farther fore-n-aft can't hurt. The core should be roughly the thickness of the core to be used on the hull topsides. Install the core first and the ply web stiffeners over it.

PLYWOOD TURNING RINGS
A nice trick is to make transverse turning rings of plywood that double as part of the web stiffeners. These rings rest on pipes set in a ply-and-timber frame secured on rollers on the shop floor. They are an efficient and inexpensive way to rotate the tooling. The ply-turning rings should be located about 20 percent aft of the bow and forward of the stern. Molds more than 50 feet (15 m) should have a third midships turning ring, and more than 75 feet (22 m) should have two rings equi-spaced between the end rings. Turning-ring ply thickness should be twice the standard bulkhead thickness for the hull, and fore-n-aft webs should be tabbed to both sides of the rings and onto the hull for a considerable length to hold the turning rings rigid. The circular perimeter of the rings should be banded with steel or aluminum strapping. This strapping forms the metal "tire" that bears on the rotating pipes in the timber frame. A little grease makes rotation a surprisingly easy operation even for large tooling. Ropes should be set up to turn the mold and to hold it set at the desired working angle.

FOUR

Fiberglass Scantling Rule: Basic Solid-Glass Hull Shell

*H*aving explored the fundamentals of FRP construction, we can now determine the scantlings for a fiberglass vessel. The following rule will permit calculation of complete scantlings for most ordinary types of fiberglass boats with solid-glass (uncored) hulls, also known as *solid* or *single-skin construction*.

Materials

There are four basic materials used in this rule:

1. fiberglass or other reinforcing cloth or fiber
2. low-density core: usually foam or balsa
3. resin system: polyester, vinylester, or epoxy
4. high-density core, solid wood: timber block, laminated wood, or plywood

FIBERGLASS

As discussed in chapter 3, fiberglass comes in a wide array of styles. The basic FRP rule applies to the most common layup of alternating layers of woven roving and CSM. Hand-laid-up in polyester resin, this laminate has an average density of 96 lb./cu. ft. (1,538 kg/m³). Average glass (or fiber) content is 35 percent by weight.

FOAM OR BALSA CORE

For sandwich construction, either closed-cell foam cores or end-grain balsa cores may be used. Take great care to bed, bond, and pre-saturate or coat all cores with resin, as described in the previous chapter. Standard structural foam cores are about 5.5 lb./cu. ft. (88 kg/m³) density, while standard balsa is 6.5 lb./cu. ft. (104 kg/m³). (Other densities are available for special applications.)

Although there are significant differences between the mechanical properties of foam and balsa cores, this rule treats them as being roughly the same. Keep in mind, however, that balsa cores are generally the stiffest, with the highest sheer strength. A slightly thinner laminate will give a stiffer hull than with standard foams. A highly elastic foam, on the other hand, will require somewhat thicker skins for the same stiffness, but will deflect farther without cracking or breaking.

RESIN SYSTEM

The basic rule assumes standard ortho- or iso-polyester resin, formulated for marine structural applications. It is the resin system that actually holds the boat together; follow the manufacturer's recommendations and instructions rigorously.

SOLID WOOD

Wood cores and reinforcement are used—in some form or another—on the majority of fiberglass vessels. All wood, without exception, must be presealed with resin before applying the fiberglass laminate. All wood that is not covered with laminate must be sealed with a minimum of three coats of resin. Plywood is frequently used as core for engine beds, transoms, and high-load hardware attachments. All plywood *must* be fabricated from a glue rated waterproof (not simply water-resistant) by boil test (see chapter 12). The ideal plywood is rated marine grade; however, ordinary exterior grade is usually acceptable for core construction.

Solid-timber core should be from softwoods such as fir, pine, or larch. Hardwoods—like oak or locust—have greater expansion rates with changes in moisture and are thus more likely to split away from the fiberglass structure.

Wherever wood cores are penetrated by fasteners, great care must be taken to seal the edges with resin and/or a marine bedding compound.

Standard Solid (Single-Skin) Fiberglass Scantlings (Roving/Mat/Polyester)

FORMULA 4-1

Calculating Basic Shell Thickness

FRP shell thickness (lower topsides), inches = $0.25 \times \sqrt[3]{Sn}$

FRP shell thickness (lower topsides), mm = $6.35 \times \sqrt[3]{Sn}$

Where

Sn = Scantling Number

This lower-topsides shell thickness is the "basic thickness" for this rule. Other areas of the laminate are based on this basic thickness.

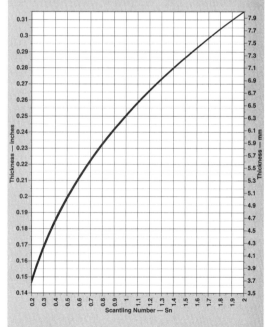

Solid-Glass Hull Thickness (Lower Topsides): Small Boats

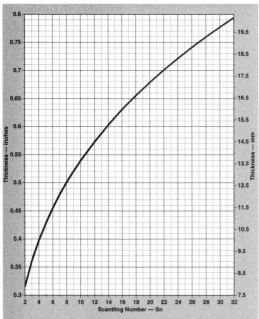

Solid-Glass Hull Thickness (Lower Topsides):
Large Boats

Example:

Let's return to our example boat, *Fish 'n Squish*, from chapter 1, which had the following characteristics:

LOA	40.00 ft.	12.19 m
WL	37.20 ft.	11.34 m
Beam	12.56 ft.	3.83 m
Depth of hull	5.91 ft.	1.80 m

This gave an Sn of 2.97 (see Formula 1-1). Accordingly, the solid fiberglass thickness for the boat's lower topsides would be 0.36 inch (9.2 mm).

$$0.25 \times \sqrt[3]{2.97 \ Sn} = 0.36 \ in.$$

$$6.35 \times \sqrt[3]{2.97 \ Sn} = 9.19 \ mm$$

This is the thickness for the lower topsides only. Other regions on the hull and deck are determined as follows.

FORMULA 4-2

Hull-Regions Laminate Thickness

Hull bottom extends from bottom laminate height (BLH) (see Formula 4-3) and down: multiply lower topsides thickness by 1.15

Lower topsides extends from BLH up to half the distance to the sheer: no thickness adjustment

Upper topsides extends from half the distance up the sheer to the sheer: multiply lower topsides thickness by 0.85

Keel Region: multiply lower topsides thickness by 1.5

Deck and Cabin: same thickness as upper topsides

FORMULA 4-3

Bottom Laminate Height

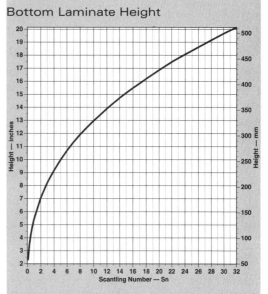

Bottom Laminate Height (BLH) Above Waterline

The height above the design waterline (DWL) at which the topsides laminate starts is derived from

(continued)

BLH in. = 5.4 × $Sn^{0.38}$ (English)

BLH cm = 13.71 × $Sn^{0.38}$ (Metric)

This height can be constant from bow to stern; however, for higher-speed craft, workboats, and serious cruising boats, the BLH height should be increased evenly from midships forward to the stem, so that—at the stem—the BLH is twice the formula height above. This provides additional impact resistance at the forefoot.

Example:

For *Fish 'n Squish,* the bottom laminate should extend from 8 inches (20 cm) above the DWL down to the keel.

$$5.4 \times Sn\ 2.97^{0.38} = 8.12 \text{ in.; use 8 in.}$$

$$13.71 \times Sn\ 2.97^{0.38} = 20.7 \text{ cm; use 20 cm}$$

Adjusting Laminate Thickness at Hull Bottom for Boat Speed

The previous thicknesses are suitable for both the bottom and topsides of vessels with a top speed of 10 knots or less. This same thickness should be used on the topsides of higher-speed craft, but the bottom thickness (from the BLH down) should be adjusted as follows.

FORMULA 4-4

Speed-Adjusted Bottom-Laminate Thickness

Increase laminate thickness 1 percent for every knot over 10 knots.

Example:

Our 40-foot (12.19 m) *Fish 'n Squish*'s Sn is 2.97; thus, its under-10-knot bottom thickness should be 0.41 inch (10.5 mm) (i.e., 15 percent greater than the upper topsides). If, however, *Fish 'n Squish* were a 25-knot planing hull, then

25 knots – 10 knots = 15,
or increase thickness 15 percent

$$0.41 \text{ in.} \times 1.15 = 0.47 \text{ in.}$$

$$10.5 \text{ mm} \times 1.15 = 12.1 \text{ mm}$$

Adjusting Laminate Thickness for Heavy Displacement

The basic scantling rule assumes the vessel has D/L ratios between 100 and 275 or less. For D/L ratios outside this range, make the following adjustments. Heavy-displacement boats—with D/L ratios greater than 275—place additional strain on their hulls. All the laminate thicknesses should be adjusted as follows.

FORMULA 4-5

Heavy-Displacement Laminate Increase

Percent increase of laminate thickness for heavy displacement = 0.89 + (D/L Ratio ÷ 2,500)

Where

D/L Ratio = Displacement-Length Ratio

D/L Ratio = Tons ÷ (0.01 × WL ft.)^3 (English)

D/L Ratio = (Mtons ÷ 1,267) ÷ (WL m ÷ 328)^3 (Metric)

Tons = full-loaded displacement, in long tons of 2,240 lbs.

Mtons = full-loaded displacement, in metric tons of 1,000 kg (2,204 lbs.)

WL = Waterline length, in feet or meters

Example:

Up to now, our *Fish 'n Squish* has had an average D/L ratio under 275. If, however, *Fish 'n Squish,* with a waterline of 37.2 feet (11.34

m), had a displacement of 18 long tons (18.28 metric tons), the D/L ratio would be 349. This would increase the boat's laminate thicknesses as follows:

Increase = 0.89 + (349 D/L Ratio ÷ 2,500) = 1.029; use 3 percent thicker

Vessels with D/L ratios under 100 also require an increase in skin thickness over the standard rule. This is because their hulls are either long and slender or wide and shallow, and thus are subjected to proportionately higher bending or slamming loads. For craft with D/L ratios under 100, increase the laminate thickness as follows.

FORMULA 4-6

Light-Displacement Laminate Increase

Increase of laminate thickness for light displacement = 1.13 – (D/L ratio ÷ 770)

Example:

If *Fish 'n Squish*, with a waterline of 37.2 feet (11.34 m), had a displacement of 3.5 long tons (3.56 metric tons), the D/L ratio would be 68. This would increase the laminate thickness as follows:

Increase = 1.13 – (68 D/L ratio ÷ 770) = 1.04; use 4 percent thicker

Combining Speed Adjustment and Displacement Adjustment for Hull-Bottom Laminate Thickness

On larger heavy workboats (e.g., an offshore crewboat), both the speed and displacement adjustments might apply. First, find the increase for displacement and apply that to all the laminates.

Next, find the increase for the speed and multiply the displacement-adjusted bottom-laminate thickness by that to get the final bottom thickness.

Weight of Dry Glass Cloth (Alternating Roving-Mat Laminate) for Required Thickness

Refer to manufacturer's style sheets for laminate thickness per layer; however, the following formula gives close estimates for layups of alternating layers of woven roving and CSM.

FORMULA 4-7

Chopped-Strand Mat Weight vs. Thickness

(English)

NOTE: Mat is usually specified in oz./sq. ft., not the more customary oz./sq. yd.

Weight of Dry Mat (oz./sq. ft.) = Laminate Thickness (in.) × 31.25

Laminate Thickness (in.) = Weight of Dry Mat (oz./sq. ft.) ÷ 31.25

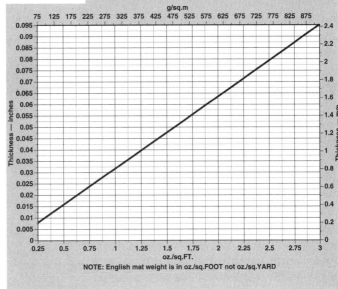

Mat: Dry Fabric Weight vs. Laminate Thickness

(continued)

Density of Finished Layup, with Resin = 85 lb./cu. ft.

Glass Content of Finished Layup with Resin, by Weight = 28 percent

(Metric)

Weight of Dry Mat (g/m²) = Laminate Thickness (mm) × 375.3

Laminate Thickness (mm) = Weight of Dry Mat (g/m²) ÷ 375.3

Density of Finished Layup, with Resin = 1,360 kg/m³

Glass Content of Finished Layup with Resin, by Weight = 28 percent

FORMULA 4-8

Woven Roving and Bi-Axial Uni-Di Weight vs. Thickness

(English)

Weight of Dry Roving (oz./sq. yd.) = Laminate Thickness (in.) × 580

Laminate Thickness (in.) = Weight of Dry Roving (oz./sq. yd.) ÷ 580

Density of Finished Layup, with Resin = 99 lb./cu. ft.

Glass Content of Finished Layup with Resin, by Weight = 38 percent

(Metric)

Weight of Dry Roving (g/m²) = Laminate Thickness (mm) × 774

Laminate Thickness (mm) = Weight of Dry Roving (g/m²) ÷ 774

Density of Finished Layup, with Resin = 1,585 kg/m³

Glass Content of Finished Layup with Resin, by Weight = 38 percent

NOTE: For bi-axial styles, this formula is less accurate; consult manufacturer's data whenever possible.

You can use these formulas to determine the laminate specification, or you can refer to the following table. The table is drawn up for stock cloth weights.

Remember that laminate thicknesses are not exact numbers. The actual thickness obtained will vary up or down by ±8 percent. This variation is caused by differing shop procedures, different application styles among workers, how easy or difficult it is to get at and press down on the part being laminated, and many similar factors. Use the thicknesses and specifications given here for calculating laminates, but keep the limits of real-world accuracy in mind.

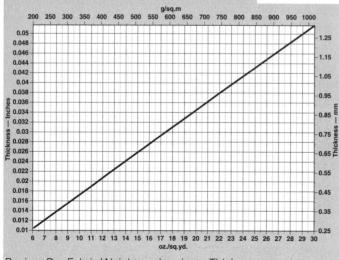

Roving: Dry Fabric Weight vs. Laminate Thickness

TABLE 4-9 Fabric Weight vs. Thickness Table

Fabric Weight, oz./sq. ft. (g/m²)	Thickness, in. (mm)
Mat Weight vs. Thickness	
0.75 (228.75)	0.024 (0.61)
1.00 (305.00)	0.032 (0.81)
1.50 (457.50)	0.048 (1.22)
2.00 (610.00)	0.064 (1.63)
Roving Weight Thickness	
14 (475)	0.024 (0.61)
16 (542)	0.028 (0.70)
18 (610)	0.031 (0.79)
24 (814)	0.041 (1.05)

NOTE: Two of the most common combi-mat styles are as follows:

- 24-15 Combi-Mat = 24 oz./sq. yd. (814 g/m²) woven roving with 1.5 oz./sq. ft. (457 g/m²) chopped-strand mat; 0.089 in. (2.26 mm) thick
- 18-10 Combi-Mat = 18 oz./sq. yd. (610 g/m²) woven roving with 1.0 oz./sq. ft. (305 g/m²) chopped-strand mat; 0.063 in. (1.60 mm) thick

FORMULA 4-10

To Convert from Oz./Sq. Yd. to g/m², and Vice Versa

(Conversion for most fabric styles)

Multiply oz./sq. yd. by 33.9 to get g/m².

Divide g/m² by 33.9 to get oz./sq. yd.

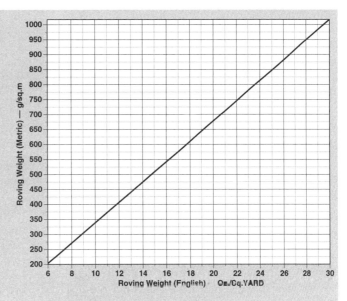

English-to-Metric Roving Weight Conversion

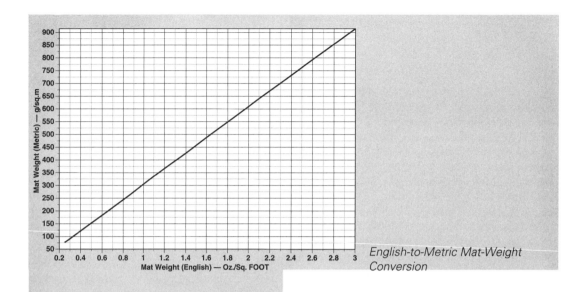

English-to-Metric Mat-Weight Conversion

FORMULA 4-11

To Convert from Oz./Sq. Ft. to g/m², and Vice Versa

(Conversion for standard English chopped-strand mat)

Multiply oz./sq. ft. by 305 to get g/m².

Divide g/m² by 305 to get oz./sq. ft.

Example:

We found that *Fish 'n Squish*'s lower topsides require a 0.36-inch-thick (9.2 mm) laminate. You can calculate the thickness of any combination of roving and mat weights from the tables or formulas, but assuming a standard 24-15 combi-mat, we find that four layers of 24-15 combi-mat (i.e., four layers 24-oz. roving, four layers 1.5-oz. mat) are required (0.36 in. ÷ 0.089 in. 24-15 = 4.04 layers; 9.2 mm ÷ 2.26 mm 24-15 = 4.07 layers).

FORMULA 4-12

Additional Laminate on Keel and Stem

To protect from grounding, impact, and hauling damage, and to provide added longitudinal strength, the rule increases the thickness of the laminate on the keel and stem over the above outside bottom laminate. The keel and stem region should have a laminate 1.5 times that of the bottom laminate, after the adjustments to thickness for speed and displacement. The additional laminate should extend transversely to protect the projecting portions of the keel and skeg, or for 8 percent of the beam, whichever is greater.

FORMULA 4-13

Additional Laminate on High-Stress Areas

High-speed planing powerboats should increase the laminate above the propellers on the hull-bottom underside to 1.1 times the thickness of the standard hull-bottom layup. The area of additional thickness should run from the struts aft to the transom, and should extend for a width of 2 times the propeller diameter, centered over the propeller shaft.

Deck-Hardware Areas

Sailboats should increase the laminate thickness at the chainplates and under and around the mast step by 1.25 times the surrounding or local laminate—usually the upper topsides and deck layup. This increase should be at least 3 times the width of the chainplate attachment, and 1.5 times the length.

All vessels should increase the laminate thickness at high-load hardware (e.g., bollard, mooring and docking cleats, davit bases, and winches) by 1.25 times the surrounding or local laminate—usually the upper topsides and deck layup. The buildup should extend around the base of the hardware and be at least 2 times the hardware footprint in all directions.

FORMULA 4-14

Adjusting Thickness for Type of Service

Racing boats and light trailerable day boats can use just 95 percent of the glass or laminate thickness given previously. Workboats such as patrol and pilot boats, fishing vessels, passenger vessels, and charter boats should increase all laminate and core thicknesses by 5 to 10 percent.

Working through a Full Laminate Specification

Using our example boat, *Fish 'n Squish*, we can now work through a complete hull- and deck-laminate specification. We will assume that *Fish 'n Squish* has a standard D/L ratio between 100 and 275, and—for the moment—that it's a 25-knot planing vessel, for yacht use. Using the dimensions given previously, we found that *Fish 'n Squish* has an Sn

of 2.97, which gives a basic or lower topsides laminate thickness of 0.36 inch (9.2 mm).

FIND THICKNESS

Deck: 0.36 in. × 0.85 = 0.30 in.

Deck: 9.2 mm × 0.85 = 7.82 mm

Upper Topsides: same as deck

Lower Topsides: 0.36 in. (9.2 mm)

Hull Bottom: 25 knots is 15 knots over 10 knots; increase bottom thickness 15 percent

Hull Bottom: 0.36 in. × 1.15 × 1.15 (for knots over 10 knots) = 0.47 in.

Hull Bottom: 9.2 mm × 1.15 × 1.15 (for knots over 10 knots) = 12.16 mm

Keel and Stem: 0.36 in. × 1.5 × 1.15 × 1.15 (for knots over 10 knots) = 0.71 in.

Keel and Stem: 9.2 mm × 1.5 × 1.15 × 1.15 (for knots over 10 knots) = 18.24 mm

Hull-Bottom High-Stress Areas: 1.10 × 0.47 in. = 0.52 in.

Hull-Bottom High-Stress Areas: 1.10 × 12.16 mm = 13.37 mm

Deck-Hardware-Mounting Areas: 1.25 × 0.30 in. = 0.375 in.

Deck-Hardware-Mounting Areas: 1.25 × 7.82 mm = 9.77 mm

SPECIFY LAMINATE (ENGLISH)
Use 24-15 combi-mat 0.089-inch thick for the majority of laminate.

Deck: 0.30 in. ÷ 0.089 in./layer = 3.37 layers 24-15 combi-mat

3 layers 24-15 combi-mat: 0.267 in.

1 layer 1.5-oz. mat: 0.048 in.

Deck Laminate Total Thickness: 0.315 in.

Upper Topsides: same as deck

Lower Topsides: 0.36 in. ÷ 0.089 in./layer = 4.04 layers 24-15 combi-mat

NOTE: A 1.5-oz.-mat skin coat is needed under the gelcoat, with a total of 2 oz. (or a little more) between the gelcoat and the roving, so add a layer of 1.5-oz. mat outside.

4 layers 24-15 combi-mat: 0.356 in.

1 layer 1.5-oz. mat: 0.048 in.

Lower Topsides Laminate Total Thickness: 0.404 in.

Hull Bottom: 0.47 in. ÷ 0.089 in./layer = 5.28 layers

5 layers 24-15 combi-mat: 0.445 in.

1 layer 1.5-oz. mat: 0.048 in.

Hull-Bottom Total Thickness: 0.493 in.

Keel and Stem: 0.71 in. ÷ 0.089 in./layer = 7.97 layers

8 layers 24-15 combi-mat: 0.712 in.

1 layer 1.5-oz. mat: 0.048 in.

Keel and Stem Region Total Thickness: 0.760 in.

Hull-Bottom High-Stress Areas: 0.52 in. ÷ 0.089 in./layer = 5.8 layers

Add 1 layer 24-15 combi-mat over propellers and at struts.

Deck-Hardware-Mounting Areas: 0.375 in. ÷ 0.089 in./layer = 4.2 layers

Add 1 layer 24-15 combi-mat plus 1 layer 1.5-oz. mat at chainplates, mooring cleats, etc.

SPECIFY LAMINATE (METRIC)
Use 24-15 combi-mat (814 g/m^2 roving plus 457 g/m^2 mat; 1,271 g/m^2 total) 2.26 mm thick for the majority of laminate.

Deck: 7.82 mm ÷ 2.26 mm/layer = 3.4 layers 24-15 combi-mat

3 layers 24-15 (1,271 g/m^2) combi-mat: 6.78 mm

1 layer 457 g/m^2 mat: 1.22 mm

Deck Laminate Total Thickness: 8.00 mm

Upper Topsides: same as deck

Lower Topsides: 9.2 mm ÷ 2.26 mm/layer = 4.04 layers 24-15 combi-mat

NOTE: A 457 g/m^2 mat skin coat is needed under the gelcoat, with a total of 610 g/m^2 (or a little more) between the gelcoat and the roving, so add a layer of 457 g/m^2 mat outside.

4 layers 24-15 (1,271 g/m^2) combi-mat: 9.04 mm

1 layer 457 g/m^2 mat: 1.22 mm

Lower Topsides Laminate Total Thickness: 10.26 mm

Hull Bottom: 12.16 mm ÷ 2.26 mm/layer = 5.38 layers

5 layers 24-15 (1,271 g/m^2) combi-mat: 11.30 mm

1 layer 457 g/m^2 mat: 1.22 mm

Hull-Bottom Total Thickness: 12.52 mm

Keel and Stem: 18.24 mm ÷ 2.26 mm/layer = 8.0 layers

8 layers 24-15 (1,271 g/m^2) combi-mat: 18.08 mm

1 layer 457 g/m² mat: 1.22 mm

Keel and Stem Region Total Thickness: 19.30 mm

Hull-Bottom High-Stress Areas: 13.37 mm ÷ 2.26 mm/layer = 5.9 layers

Add 1 layer 24-15 (1,271 g/m²) combi-mat over propellers and at struts.

Deck-Hardware-Mounting Areas: 9.77 mm ÷ 2.26 mm/layer = 4.3 layers

Add 1 layer 24-15 (1,271 g/m²) combi-mat plus 1 layer 1.5-oz. (457 g/m²) mat at chainplates, mooring cleats, etc.

NOTE: All the laminates have been arranged with 3 oz. (915 g/m²) of mat outside, under the gelcoat. In a female mold, the gelcoat is sprayed on, followed by the skin coat of 1.5-oz. (457 g/m²) mat, then the first layer of 24-15 (1,271 g/m²) combi-mat, with the mat down—facing out. This is to eliminate print-through (see chapter 3).

NOTE: Wherever we've spec'd combi-mat, we could also use a layer of roving and a layer of mat of the indicated individual weights. This will yield precisely the same thickness and strength; it's simply more labor.

COMMENTS ON THE LAMINATE SPECIFICATION

The laminate specified previously contains a number of features that are helpful but not required. First, by specifying the entire hull laminate out of all the same fabric styles and weights (i.e., 24-15 combi-mat and a 1.5-oz. mat; 814 g/m² roving stitched to 457 g/m² mat, and a 457 g/m² mat), there is minimum waste and the maximum fabric quantities can be ordered for the best pricing. Second, the construction/layup process is most straightforward: the gelcoat and skin coat are applied,

followed by three layers of 24-15 combi-mat on the entire hull. A fourth layer is run inside (from halfway up the topsides down) to form the lower-topsides thickness. A fifth layer is run from the BLH down, forming the hull bottom. Finally, two additional layers are added inside at the keel region. All layers go on mat down, so a layer of mat bonds each ply of combi-mat to the exposed (i.e., upturned) roving below.

Try to produce uniform laminates of this pattern whenever practical. There are other considerations, however, that may make this less convenient or desirable. Smaller, lighter hulls may be too thin for this approach. You can, perhaps, try to do the same with a lighter combi-mat, for example an "18-10" (i.e., 18-oz. roving plus 1.0-oz. mat; 610 g/m² roving plus 305 g/m² mat). Some weights and styles may not be obtainable, or sticking with one style throughout may cause some specific region (e.g., the deck or topsides) to be either too light or too heavy. In these cases, it's usually best to adjust the laminate by changing the inner layers to a different fabric style.

Another consideration is lowering the number of layers at thick sections of the hull shell to reduce labor. In these areas, it might be worth going to, perhaps, a 24-20 combi-mat.

FORMULA 4-15

Shell Laminate Overlaps

The rolls of fiberglass should be laid on with overlaps for continuous strength in each layer, as follows:

Each Overlap = 2 in. (5 cm)

Overlap Stagger = 4 in. (10 cm) or more

If butting some plies is unavoidable, the overlap stagger must be at least 8 inches (20 cm).

Weight of Laminate

The weights of fabric—in oz./sq. yd. or g/m²—to which we are referring are the weights of the dry glass cloth, as specified by the manufacturer. For structural calculations and stability calculations, you need the weight of the finished laminate with resin, in pounds per square foot or in kilograms per square meter. This is a fairly simple matter; if you know the density of the material, multiply by the thickness. Our standard mat/roving layup is 96 lb./cu. ft. (1,538 kg/m³). For more accuracy, however, you can refer to Table 4-16.

Example:

Take the lower topsides of our *Fish 'n Squish*. The laminate we called for was 0.404-in.-thick (10.26 mm) mat/roving combination. Multiply 0.404-in. thick × 8.00 lb./sq. ft. 1-in. thick = 3.23 lb./sq. ft. (10.26 mm thick × 1.53 kg/m² 1 mm thick = 15.67 kg/m²). Use the same approach for each region of the laminate.

You can also determine the weight of dry glass and resin required. Because the laminate is 35 percent glass by weight, just multiply the laminate weight by 35 percent to get the dry-glass content, and by 65 percent to get the resin content (or as appropriate for the laminate). For *Fish 'n Squish*'s lower topsides, this would be 1.13 pounds of dry glass cloth for each square foot and 2.1 pounds of resin for each square foot for the lower topsides (or 5.48 kg of dry glass cloth for each square meter and 10.19 kg of resin for each square meter for the lower topsides).

Multiplying these values out for the entire hull structure gives you purchase quantities. (Be sure to add in a wastage allowance.) For an even more detailed purchase breakdown, subdivide each laminate section into its respective thickness of mat, combi-mat, and roving only. Then, determine weights and quantity for each fabric style and its resin, per square foot or per square meter.

Alternative for Building Bulk in Laminate

The bottom and keel laminate we called for on *Fish 'n Squish* is fairly thick. The boat's bottom, for instance, is five layers of 24-15 (1,271 g/m²) combi-mat, 0.493 inch (12.52 mm) thick. An alternative to laying down five layers of combi-mat would be to replace the combi-mat in the center of the laminate (where the fibers are stressed the least) with a bulk material. These are mat-like products available under various trade names such as

TABLE 4-16 Hand-Layup Polyester Laminate Densities (Weights)

	Glass Content by Weight	Density, lb./cu. ft. (kg/m³)	lb./sq. ft. (kg/m²), 1-in. (1 mm) thick
Mat only	28%	85 (1,360)	7.08 (1.36)
Mat/Roving	35%	96 (1,538)	8.00 (1.53)
Roving only	38%	99 (1,585)	8.25 (1.58)

CoreMat and Tiger Core. They are usually manufactured in dry thicknesses ranging from 1.5 to 10 mm (0.059 to 0.39 inch). After wet-out and roll-down, these finish to between 1 and 9 mm (0.039 and 0.35 inch).

For *Fish 'n Squish*'s hull bottom, we could replace the interior three layers of 24-15 with a single layer of 9 mm (0.35 inch) bulk-mat, with a finish of about 8 mm (0.31 inch). This would leave a single layer of 24-15 to make essentially inside and outside skins over a bulk-mat core, plus the external-mat skin coat. The advantage is that the labor of applying the three interior 24-15 layers has been reduced to one layer—not insignificant. Our new bulk-mat hull bottom would finish 13.74 mm (0.54 inch) thick—an increase of 9 percent in thickness.

All-mat laminates (which also can be used for bulking) and materials like bulk-mat are not as strong as mat/roving laminates. This drawback to bulk-mat (or to mat-laminate bulking) is largely overcome by using it in the laminate interior, where the fibers do the least work. Another drawback, however, can't be easily overcome. Bulk-mat laminates are relatively brittle. When they are loaded heavily enough to flex, they have a greater tendency to crack.

FORMULA 4-17
Bulk-Mat Laminates
For this reason, bulk-mat or all-mat-bulked laminates should total at least 5 percent thicker than the equivalent mat/roving laminate. Furthermore, no more than 70 percent of the laminate, at the center, should be of bulk-mat or mat-bulk, and the inner and outer skins (of mat/roving) should be a minimum of 0.90 and 1.0 inch (22.8 and 25.4 mm) thick, respectively.

We're just skirting these limits with the bulk-mat laminate we spec'd previously. Bulk-mat or all-mat-bulk is workable and safe. It is an excellent way to reduce labor cost and production time. In the final analysis—for really rugged use—the standard mat/roving laminate originally specified has slightly greater resistance to severe impact damage. The mat/roving laminate can take greater deflection (thus absorbing more energy) before failure.

Some builders use bulk-mat under the skin coat to further reduce the chance of print-through. I don't recommend this application because the external bulk-mat is brittle and subject to extensive cracking on sharp impact.

Bulk-mat is, however, a superb material for laminating up interior, trim, and detail components quickly, especially when weight is not critical. Intelligent use of bulk-mat to fabricate components such as instrument panels, bridge moldings, deck boxes, fish wells, and trim moldings is a very economical way to make relatively stiff FRP parts quickly.

FIVE

Fiberglass: Internal Structure

Longitudinals

The hull shell we specified in chapter 4 is only part of the picture. The shell requires internal structure for adequate strength. The principal components of this internal structure are engine beds, longitudinal stringers, bulkheads and/or ring frames, and floors.

Longitudinal Stringers

FORMULA 5-1

Number of Longitudinal Hull Stringers

For single-skin (solid FRP) hulls, this rule requires five continuous longitudinal stringers on each side of the hull inside (10 stringers total). The underside of the deck requires similarly spaced stringers as well.

Working up one side of the hull, two stringers—usually engine beds—are located roughly equidistant between the keel and the chine (or the turn of the bilge). One stringer is either a stringer proper at the turn of the bilge

or is the reinforced chine itself. Two additional stringers are located roughly equidistant between the sheer and the chine (or the turn of the bilge). Without this stringer system, the solid FRP hull shell will be too bendy.

ENGINE BEDS/STRINGERS

Engine beds/stringers are the principal fore-n-aft (longitudinal) members in most FRP hull bottoms. They should run continuously and unbroken over the bottom inside for nearly the full length of the vessel. Single-engine craft will have two engine beds and twin-engine craft will have four (two for each engine). On single-engine planing vessels, it is recommended that four "engine beds" still be used. The outer beds act simply as longitudinal stringers about midway between the inner engine bed and the chine (or the turn of the bilge).

Engine beds are foam or balsa cores cut to shape—with vertical sides and the top (upper) corners well rounded—and covered with an FRP laminate that runs off onto the hull bottom on both sides of the stringer. This runout is usually referred to as *tabbing*. At the engine mounts, the top third of the core—at the engine-mount-bolt area—must be solid wood. Engine-bed/stringer dimensions should be as follows (see also chapter 2).

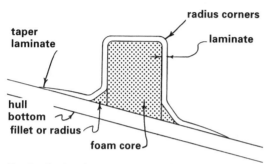

Engine-bed stringers not at engines

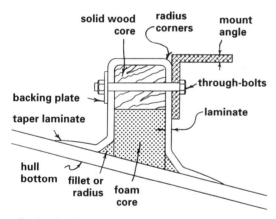

Engine-bed stringers at engines

FORMULA 5-2

Engine-Bed/Stringer Dimensions

Height and width of engine-bed/stringer core (foam or balsa core), not at the engines:

$in. = 3.1 \times Sn^{0.3}$ *(English)*

$mm = 78.7 \times Sn^{0.3}$ *(Metric)*

Height of cores at the engines = 1.5 × the width, with roughly the top third of solid wood

Where

Sn = Scantling Number

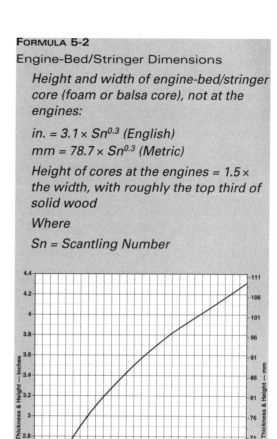

At Engines Core Height Is 1.5 x Width

Engine-Bed Core Dimensions: Small Boats

(continued)

Engine-bed/stringer laminate thickness, not at engine mounts:

(English)

in. = 0.18 × Sn⁰·⁴ × % increase for speed × % increase for displacement

Engine-bed/stringer laminate thickness, not at engine mounts:

(English)

$in. = 0.18 \times Sn^{0.4} \times \% \text{ increase for speed} \times \% \text{ increase for displacement}$

(Metric)

$mm = 4.6 \times Sn^{0.4} \times \% \text{ increase for speed} \times \% \text{ increase for displacement}$

Laminate thickness at engine mounts = 1.4 × laminate not at the engine mounts

Laminate tabbing runoff = 10 × laminate thickness, on both sides of the engine bed/stringer

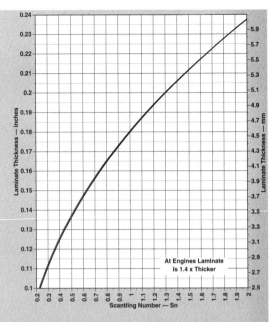

Engine-Bed Laminate Thickness: Small Boats

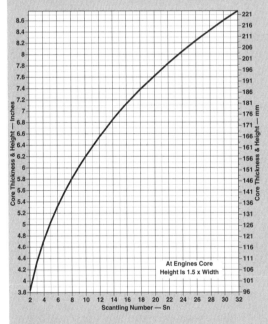

Engine-Bed Core Dimensions: Large Boats

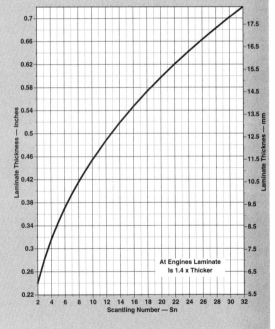

Engine-Bed Laminate Thickness: Large Boats

Example:

Our 40-foot (12.19 m) *Fish 'n Squish,* with an Sn of 2.97, would require foam or balsa cores 4.3 inches thick and 4.3 inches high (109 × 109 mm) not at the engine mounts; and 4.3 inches wide and 6.45 inches high (109 × 164 mm) at the engine mounts.

Adding the 15 percent increase for the boat's 25-knot speed, the laminate should be 0.32 inch (8.1 mm) thick, not at the engines, and 0.45 inch (11.3 mm) thick at the engines. A layer of 1.5-oz. mat plus three layers of 24-15 combi-mat (457 g/m² mat plus 814 g/m² roving) will generate this away from the engine mounts.

Five layers of 24-15 combi-mat would be sufficient at the engine mounts. It is best to use a layer of 1.5-oz. (457 g/m²) mat against the core. This makes for better adhesion to the core, so you should add another layer of 1.5-oz. (457 g/m²) mat to the engine beds at the engine mounts.

The laminate should be tabbed onto the hull for 3.2 inches (81 mm) and, at the engine mounts, 4.5 inches (113 mm) on either side of the engine beds/stringers.

The engine beds can be higher and/or wider than called for previously if necessary to mount the engine properly, but never lower or thinner. In all cases, there must be a foam or balsa fillet strip or a putty fillet in the corners of the stringer where it meets the hull. The laminate must run smoothly over this fillet onto the hull inside to ensure proper strength.

NOTE: Some builders have installed hollow- or partially hollow-core engine beds/stringers. They reason that the core is really just a former and does no work, so they can save weight. Although many fine craft are constructed this way, hollow stringers worry me, because any small cracks or leaks into the hollow stringer will turn it into a rather long water tank. Not only could this add considerable weight, but—should it freeze—it also will burst open the stringer and destroy its strength. It is accurate, however, that the core is a nonstructural former. You can use any low-cost foam that is convenient, as long as it is compatible with the resin and cannot absorb water. (Solid-wood core at the engine mounts is *always* required.)

FORMULA 5-3

Longitudinals or Hull and Deck Stringers

Hull stringers are determined as follows:

Stringer Core Width, in. = 3.12 × Sn$^{0.28}$ (English)

Stringer Core Width, mm = 79.2 × Sn$^{0.28}$ (Metric)

Stringer Core Height = half core width

Stringer Laminate Thickness, in. = 0.17 × Sn$^{0.38}$ (English)

Stringer Laminate Thickness, mm = 4.32 × Sn$^{0.38}$ (Metric)

Stringer Laminate Tabbing Runout on Hull: 10 × laminate thickness, on both sides of the stringer

Deck Stringer Spacing: no greater than the maximum distance—center to center—of the widest separation between the hull stringers on the upper topsides, or 32 inches (80 cm), whichever is less

(continued)

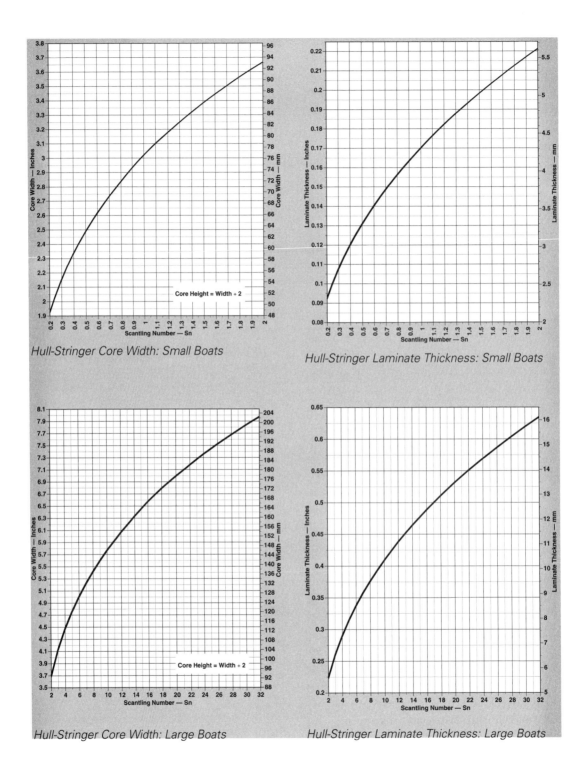

Hull-Stringer Core Width: Small Boats

Hull-Stringer Laminate Thickness: Small Boats

Hull-Stringer Core Width: Large Boats

Hull-Stringer Laminate Thickness: Large Boats

The stringer cores should be roughly trapezoidal in section, with their sides angled in at 15 to 20 degrees from the base (against the inside of the hull). The top (inside) corners of the core must be well rounded off to allow the laminate to drape over it properly.

Example:

Fish 'n Squish, with an Sn of 2.97, would require hull stringers with cores 4.25 inches wide and 2.25 inches high (108 mm wide and 54 mm high). The laminate thickness should be 0.25 inch (6.5 mm). This could be made of three layers of 24-15 combi-mat, totalling 0.267 inch (6.7 mm). The tabbing should extend 2.67 inches (6.7 cm) onto the hull.

FORMULA 5-4

Chine Reinforcing

On hard-chine craft, the corner of the chine itself forms a stiffening member. This eliminates the need for the bilge stringer; however, chine reinforcing should be added longitudinally along the inside of the chine, as follows:

Chine Reinforcing Thickness = 35 percent of the hull-bottom thickness

Chine Reinforcing Width = 70 times the reinforcing laminate thickness

Example:

We found that *Fish 'n Squish* would have a hull-bottom thickness of 0.493 inch (12.52 mm). Accordingly, the chine reinforcing would be 0.17 inch (4.38 mm) thick, and it should be 11.9 (use 12) inches wide—6 inches along the bottom, and 6 inches up the topsides (310 mm; that is, 155 mm along the bottom and 155 mm along the topsides).

As with all tabbing and reinforcing, the chine reinforcement should be tapered away from maximum thickness at the chine to just one or two layers of cloth at the edges.

Transverse Members

BULKHEADS AND RING FRAMES

Bulkheads and/or ring frames provide most of the transverse strength in FRP hulls. Bulkheads must be tabbed into the hull along both front and back faces and around their entire perimeter (see photo on p. 334). Bulkheads should be—very roughly—evenly spaced; strive to make them closest together between Stations 2 and 6, where slamming and rigging loads are maximum on both powerboats and sailboats (see photo on p. 333).

NOTE: Where bulkheads will intrude on the interior, ring frames can be substituted (discussed later in this chapter). Standard bulkheads are slightly stiffer than ring frames, however, so use as many true bulkheads as practical.

On sailboats, there should be ideally two bulkheads at the mast—one in front of the mast step and one aft. At least one bulkhead/ring frame at the mast is required. There must also be at least one bulkhead/ring frame at or near the shroud chainplates.

The tabbing that holds the bulkhead in place may be of combi-mat, but it is best made of a bi-axial-style stitch-mat, which more efficiently transmits the loads into the hull. The light mat on the stitch-mat provides a more reliable bond between layers and to the hull and bulkhead than bi-ax alone.

FORMULA 5-5

Bulkheads—Number, Thickness, and Tabbing

Minimum Number of Bulkheads and/or Ring Frames: 0.5 × Scantling LOA$^{0.7}$ (English)

(continued)

Minimum Number of Bulkheads and/or Ring Frames: 1.15 × Scantling LOA$^{0.7}$ (Metric)

NOTE: Use the scantling length overall, not the Sn.

For Workboats: Increase the number of bulkheads or ring frames by at least one.

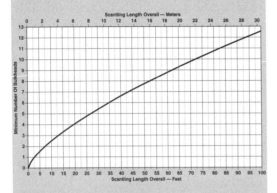

Minimum Number of Bulkheads

Minimum Bulkhead Thickness (for Solid Plywood): in. = 0.45 × Sn$^{0.3}$ (English)

Minimum Bulkhead Thickness (for Solid Plywood): mm = 11.43 × Sn$^{0.3}$ (Metric)

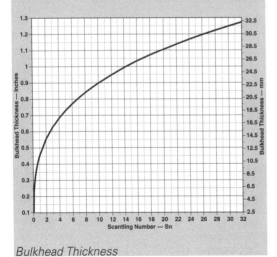

Bulkhead Thickness

Minimum Cored-Bulkhead Thickness: 1.1 × minimum solid-plywood thickness

Weight of Bi-Axial Glass Tabbing, oz./sq. yd. = 22 × Sn$^{0.3}$ (English)

Weight of Bi-Axial Glass Tabbing, g/m^2 = 746 × Sn$^{0.3}$ (Metric)

Tabbing Runout on Hull and on Bulkhead, in. = 0.6 × (oz./sq. yd.)$^{0.56}$ (English)

Tabbing Runout on Hull and on Bulkhead, mm = 2.1 × (g/m^2)$^{0.56}$ (Metric)

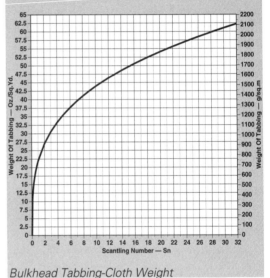

Bulkhead Tabbing-Cloth Weight

Example:

Our trusty *Fish 'n Squish* doesn't have extreme overhangs, so its scantling length overall is simply 40 feet (12.19 m). It would require

- 6.6 (use 7) bulkheads minimum (if a workboat, add 1 for 8 bulkheads minimum).
- 0.62-in.; use $^5/_8$-in. solid-ply bulkheads, or
- 15.8 mm; use 15 mm solid-ply bulkheads, or

0.68-in.; use $5/8$- or $3/4$-in. balsa-cored or foam-cored bulkheads, or

17.4 mm; use 18 mm balsa-cored or foam-cored bulkheads

30.4-oz./sq. yd. tabbing, use two layers Hexcel/Knytex DBM1708 (35.5 oz./sq. yd.)

1,030 g/m^2 tabbing, use two layers Hexcel/Knytex DBM1708 (1,204 g/m^2)

4.3-in. tabbing run out onto the hull and the bulkhead

109 mm tabbing run out onto the hull and the bulkhead

Alternately, 24-15 combi-mat of approximately this weight can be used, but will not be quite as strong. Do not use mat only for tabbing.

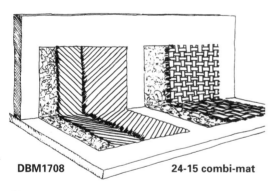

DBM1708   **24-15 combi-mat**

Plus/minus 45-degree bi-axial stitch-mat is superior to 24-15 combi-mat for tabbing in bulkheads and panels. It has a higher proportion of roving to mat and the fibers are better aligned to take torsional loads. Plus/minus 45 bi-axials are not superior for laying up stringers. Here, combi-mat or 0,90 stitch mat places 50 percent of the fibers along the working axis. Plus/minus 45 bi-axial would have all the fibers working at an angle (along the bias), which is weaker.
(Courtesy Hexcel/Knytex)

NOTE: DBM1708 is a bi-axial style E-glass with 0.75-oz. (228 g/m^2) mat attached (thus the final "08," a rounding of 0.75). The "17" stands for 17-oz./sq. yd. bi-ax fabric—an 8.5-oz. layer running diagonally one way, and a second 8.5-oz. layer running diagonally across the first layer (576 g/m^2 bi-ax fabric of two 288 g/m^2 diagonal layers).

In all cases, there must be a putty fillet or a foam or balsa fillet strip in the corner of the bulkhead where it meets the hull. The fillet should be formed to approximately a 2-inch (50 mm) radius.

Bulkheads thinner than $5/8$ inch (15 mm) are somewhat bendy and can be inconvenient to work with; accordingly, many builders use $5/8$-inch (15 mm) or thicker bulkheads even on smaller hulls. The alternative is to install either temporary or permanent cleats on thinner bulkheads to help hold them rigid until they are fully tabbed in place.

WATERTIGHT/COLLISION BULKHEADS

Use Formula 9-29 for watertight bulkheads. Except when the bulkheads are to be tabbed into the hull, use tabbing 1.3 times heavier than for standard bulkheads (above); tabbing runouts 1.1 times longer on both the bulkheads and on the hull. Stiffeners should end about 2 to 3 inches (50 to 75 mm) inboard from the tabbing on the bulkhead.

FORMULA 5-6

Bulkhead Backing Strip

Where the bulkhead contacts the hull, it leaves a hard spot. This can cause the bulkhead line to form a crease, clearly visible from outside, and it can cause stress concentrations that weaken the hull. Before installing the bulkhead or

(continued)

its tabbing and fillets, a backing strip (like a ring running transversely around the hull) should be installed for the bulkhead to land on.

Backing Strip Weight = tabbing weight

Backing Strip Width = 8 × solid plywood bulkhead thickness

ELASTOMETRIC FOAM SPACERS AT BULKHEAD-TO-HULL JOINT

The U.S. Coast Guard requires a trapezoidal foam spacer between the edge of the bulkhead and the inside of the hull shell on FRP vessels intended for passenger-carrying as Subchapter-T boats (see photo on p. 334). The purpose of the spacer is, again, to avoid hard spots on the hull and to distribute the loads over the width of the tabbing. You must install the spacers to comply with the Code of Federal Regulations and obtain certification.

RING FRAMES IN PLACE OF BULKHEADS

More bulkheads are better than fewer bulkheads. If possible, it is best to use one or two additional bulkheads over the minimum specified previously. Frequently, even using the minimum number of bulkheads is difficult or inconvenient, however, because the bulkheads would interfere with the machinery, tanks, or accommodations. Where a bulkhead can't be used, a ring frame can be substituted (see photo on p. 334). The ring frame should be exactly the same dimensions and construction as the engine beds/stringers, not at the engine mounts, but—of course—running transversely.

FLOORS

Floors provide additional transverse strength at the hull-bottom inside. They spread the loads of ballast-keel bolts and the mast step.

In cored-FRP construction, floors are principally used on sailboats; however, high-speed planing craft (more than 30 knots) should have at least one floor midway between each bulkhead, between Stations 1 and 6, where slamming loads are highest. Floors should be foam- or balsa-cored FRP, similar to the engine beds/stringers.

FORMULA 5-7

Floors for Powerboats

Fore-n-aft Thickness of Floor Core (Foam or Balsa):

in. = 3.1 × Sn^{0.3} (English)

$$in. = 3.1 \times Sn^{0.3} \text{ (English)}$$

$$mm = 78.7 \times Sn^{0.3} \text{ (Metric)}$$

Minimum Height of Floor Cores = 2.5 × the fore-n-aft thickness

Where

Sn = Scantling Number

(See also chapter 2)

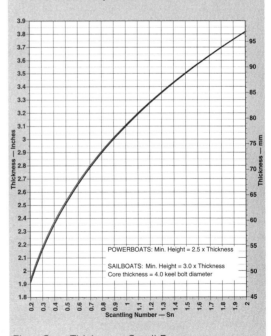

Floor-Core Thickness: Small Boats

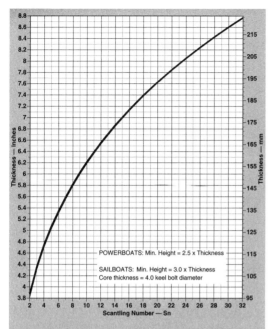

Floor-Core Thickness: Large Boats

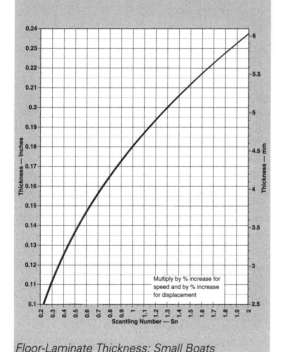

Floor-Laminate Thickness: Small Boats

Powerboat Floor-Laminate Thickness

in. = $0.18 \times Sn^{0.4} \times$ % increase for speed $\times$ % increase for displacement (English)

mm = $4.6 \times Sn^{0.4} \times$ % increase for speed $\times$ % increase for displacement (Metric)

Laminate Tabbing Runout: fore-n-aft core thickness, on both sides of the floors

Floor-Laminate Thickness: Large Boats

Example:

Our 40-foot (12.19 m) *Fish 'n Squish,* with an Sn of 2.97, would require foam or balsa cores 4.3 inches thick, fore-n-aft, and 10.75 inches high (109 × 273 mm). The tabbing runout would be 4.3 inches (109 mm).

Once again, adding the 15 percent increase for the boat's 25-knot speed, the floor laminate should be 0.32 inch (8.1 mm) thick. As with the engine beds, a layer of 1.5-oz. mat plus three layers of 24-15 combi-mat (457 g/m² mat plus 814 g/m² roving) will accomplish this. Use a layer of 1.5-oz. (457 g/m²) mat against the core for best drape and adhesion.

In both cases, the laminate should be tabbed onto the hull for 4.3 inches (109 mm) on either side of the engine beds/stringers, and the same distance transversely on the end of the floors athwartships.

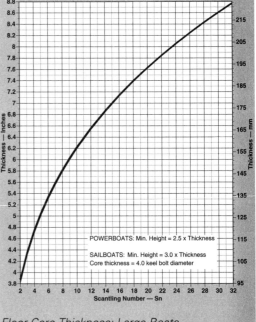

Floor-Core Thickness: Large Boats

FORMULA 5-8

Floors for Sailboats: Cores

Floor-Core Thickness: same as for powerboats or 4 × keel-bolt diameter, whichever is larger

Minimum Floor Height: = 3 × wood core thickness

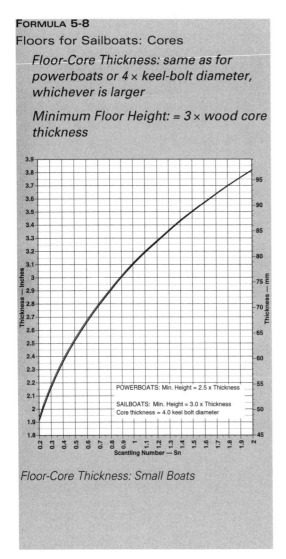

Floor-Core Thickness: Small Boats

Cores for floors with keel bolts and floors at the mast step should be solid wood sawn and/or laminated to shape (not plywood, and not foam or balsa core). Special care must be taken to seal the wood with at least three coats of resin before installation, and then to reseal the keel bolt and any other fastening holes with resin after boring. Finally, great care must be taken to seal and bed the keel bolts in marine bedding compound, inside and out.

The top corners of the floors must be well rounded-off for proper drape of the fiberglass without hard spots, and a foam, balsa, or putty-grout fillet must run along the floor joint at the hull.

Floors at keel bolts and mast steps take very large loads; their laminate needs to be quite heavy.

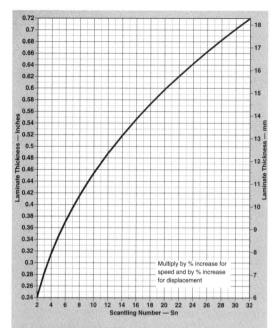

Floor-Laminate Thickness: Large Boats

FORMULA 5-9

Sailboat Floor-Laminate Thickness and Maximum Spacing

Floor-Laminate Thickness = same as powerboat floor laminate

Laminate Tabbing Runout = 12 × laminate thickness

Maximum Floor Spacing at Ballast Keel, in. = 16 × $Sn^{0.2}$, on center (English)

Maximum Floor Spacing at Ballast Keel, mm = 406 × $Sn^{0.2}$, on center or centered on each keel bolt (Metric)

Minimum Number of Floors at Mast Step = 3 × $Sn^{0.2}$

Where

Sn = Scantling Number

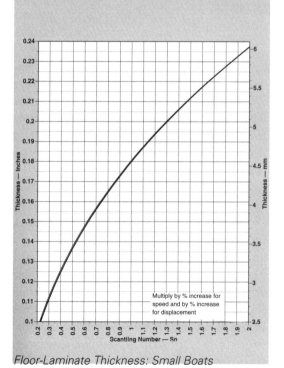

Floor-Laminate Thickness: Small Boats

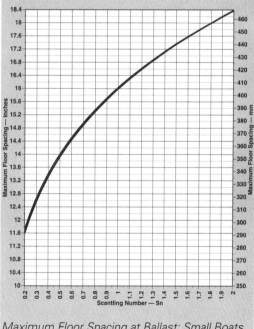

Maximum Floor Spacing at Ballast: Small Boats

(continued)

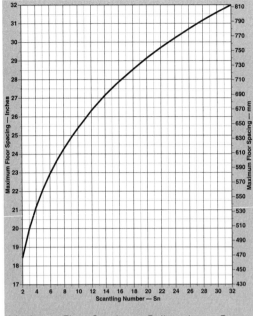

Maximum Floor Spacing at Ballast: Large Boats

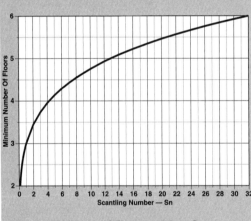

Minimum Number of Floors at Mast Step

Example:

If our *Fish 'n Squish* is a 40-foot (12.19 m) sloop with an Sn of 2.97, we would find

Minimum Wood-Core Floor Thickness = 4.29; use 4.25 in.

Minimum Wood-Core Floor Thickness = 108.9; use 110 mm

Minimum Wood-Core Height = 12.87; use 13 in.

Minimum Wood-Core Height = 326.7; use 325 mm

Laminate Thickness = 0.28 in.

Laminate Thickness = 7.1 mm

Laminate Tabbing Runout on Hull = 3.34; use 3.5 in.

Laminate Tabbing Runout on Hull = 85.2; use 90 mm

Maximum Floor Spacing at Ballast Keel = 19.9 (use 20 in.) on center

Maximum Floor Spacing at Ballast Keel = 532 (use 530 mm) on center

Minimum Number of Floors at Mast Step = 3.73; use four floors

NOTE: The mast step should land on, be notched over, and be fastened to the floors. Floors must extend at least 30 percent of beam-overall athwartships (a span of 30 percent of beam or more); a 40 to 45 percent span is better where possible. On the inside of hulls without hollow garboards, the minimum heights given will usually automatically create floors of sufficient athwartships span. With hollow garboards or on very steep deadrise hulls, it may be necessary to increase floor height to get sufficient athwartships span.

If this intrudes too much on the interior arrangement or machinery, the floor height amidships can be limited to the minimum given previously and the floor extended athwartships with a laminated "half-frame" top of solid laminated timber, the same width as the floor and the same height as the floor width (square in section). This laminated half-frame floor top is screwed and glued to the top of the standard floor core. It is run athwartships up the hull-bottom inside until the required span is reached. The laminated "partial-frame" floor top should be tapered away at the ends, port and starboard, by reducing the number of laminations in steps. The entire standard floor core plus the laminated half-frame floor top forms the complete solid-wood core, and it is then entirely glassed over with the recommended floor laminate.

Additional Structures

HULL-TO-DECK JOINT
The hull-to-deck joint is critical, yet there are so many variations of hull construction, boat type, construction method, and desired finished appearance that it is difficult to give a comprehensive rule. The following discussion will serve as a general guide.

There are three common hull-to-deck joint configurations: out-turned flange, in-turned flange, and shoebox. Each works well structurally.

Out-Turned Flange Hull-to-Deck Joint
My personal preference is for the out-turned flange because it is easier to assemble with good quality control. The topsides are turned outboard to form a flat shelf at the sheer, and the deck is extended outboard to form a matching flange above. During assembly, the deck can be rested on the hull and maneuvered around until you get a proper fit. The parts are then clamped in place, marked, and drilled for the vertical through-bolt fasteners. If you lay up excess flange width (which you should), it's not difficult to get a good fit, and the excess is now trimmed back to the finished flange-width dimension. Then the deck is lifted off, bedding compound is applied, and the whole is reassembled and bolted together permanently.

All the bolts are easy to install, tighten securely, and inspect—a great advantage, in addition to the ease of overall fit. The whole is finished off with a vinyl, aluminum, or wooden molding/rubstrip. This not only hides the joint, but also acts as a very effective chafe guard. Some surveyors have developed a poor opinion of the out-turned flange joint because they have inspected cheaply made vessels with improper scantlings and machine-screw fastenings rather than proper through-bolts. Correctly fabricated, I believe the out-turned flange, however, is the most rugged and the easiest to build. Proper construction requires through-bolts, never pop rivets or machine screws. Heavy FRP flanges and rugged, rigid vinyl or wood molding cover caps are also a must.

In-Turned Flange Hull-to-Deck Joint
The in-turned flange is common on sailboats in particular, but can be found on all types of vessels. In this case, the hull-side laminate is turned in, not out, at the sheer. The deck simply rests on this in-turned shelf, as with the out-turned shelf of the out-turned flange. Fitting and installation are roughly the same for both in-turned and out-turned flanges; however, the vertical bolts are not as readily accessible inside the hull for easy assembly and checking as they are with the out-turned flange. Another drawback is that—for fabrication—the in-turned flange requires that a removable shelf be built onto the hull mold. This complicates not only initial tooling, but also the layup of every hull and the process of pulling the hull from the mold each time. Again, the exterior of the joint is covered and protected by a rubstrip.

Some people believe that the in-turned flange presents a sleeker appearance than the out-turned flange, but this depends on how the flange-covering rubstrip is treated in each case, overall styling considerations, and personal taste.

Shoebox Hull-to-Deck Joint

The shoebox hull-to-deck joint is similar to its namesake. The topsides are bent in slightly to vertical with a slight knuckle so it forms a flange exactly straight up and down at the joint (i.e., the upper inch or two [25 to 50 mm]). The deck is fabricated with a flange turned down roughly at right angles to the deck (parallel to the vertical topsides above the knuckle). Then the deck is lowered onto the hull, with the down-turned deck flange surrounding the outside of the hull topsides at the knuckle.

There are many successful hulls with the shoebox hull-to-deck joint, but I don't understand its popularity. On most larger craft, by the time some of the interior machinery, tanks, and rough joinerwork have been installed (usually before the deck is attached), it is totally impossible to reach some portions of the interior to fasten through-bolts. In all these areas, then, sheet-metal screws or the like must be used; this forms a weak joint. Furthermore, the fit between the down-turned deck flange and the vertical topsides, above the knuckle, must be quite precise. Not only does this present initial tooling problems, but it also can add alignment and fitting time during assembly. Where—in the final event—the gap turns out too large, the builder has no choice but to fill with putty-grout on a vertical surface; again, bad practice.

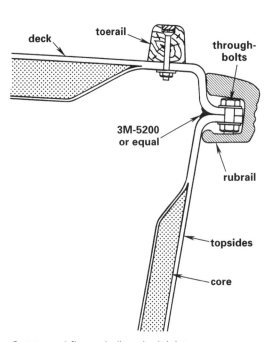

Out-turned flange hull-to-deck joint

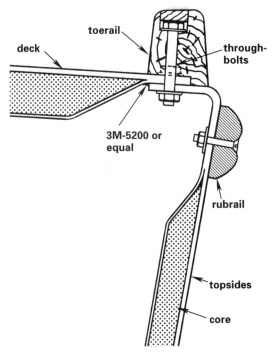

In-turned flange hull-to-deck joint

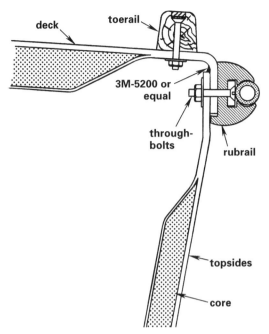

Shoebox hull-to-deck joint

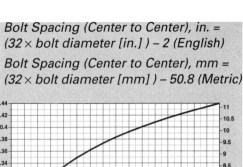

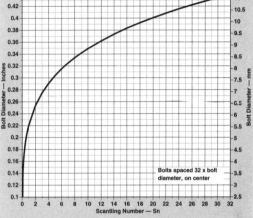

Hull-to-Deck-Joint Bolt Diameter

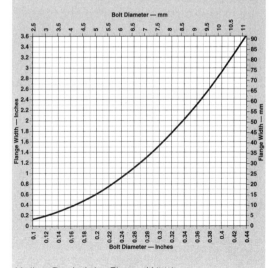

Hull-to-Deck-Joint Flange Width

All types of hull-to-deck joints must be carefully bedded for watertightness and additional strength. You can use a soggy, resin-rich mat strip, 1.5 to 2 oz./sq. ft. (457 to 610 g/m²), laid between the two flanges. Alternately, you can use an adhesive sealant, such as 3M-5200. Both methods work, but I believe the adhesive sealant to be somewhat longer-lasting and—being more elastic—less likely to leak in the event of local damage.

The following formula gives the required through-bolt and flange dimensions for each of the three hull-to-deck joints.

FORMULA 5-10

Hull-to-Deck Joint

Bolt Diameter, in. = 0.22 × Sn$^{0.20}$ (English)

Bolt Diameter, mm = 5.58 × Sn$^{0.20}$ (Metric)

Example:

For our trusty *Fish 'n Squish* with an Sn of 2.97, we would find

Bolt Diameter = 0.27; use 0.25-in. diameter

Bolt Diameter = 6.9; use 7 mm diameter

Bolt Spacing = 6 in.

Bolt Spacing = 174; use 170 mm

Flange Width = 1.016; use slightly over 1 in. (e.g., 1¹/₁₆ in.)

Flange Width = 31.8; use 32 to 35 mm

HULL-TO-DECK-JOINT BONDING ANGLE

The conventional interior treatment for the hull-to-deck joint is to finish it with a molded-in-place fiberglass bonding angle. This angle is made by laminating fiberglass strips inside the hull-to-deck joint. Although this is the standard method, I've come to believe that this bonding angle is not required. For instance, one of my designs is a 34-foot, FRP, 20,000-pound (9,090 kg), twin-diesel Sportfisherman. A number of these vessels have been in hard service for several years. They routinely cruise at 25 knots in Force 5-plus conditions, and not infrequently run at 33 knots in such weather. These craft have the out-turned flange hull-to-deck joint and have no internal bonding angle. None of these vessels has shown the slightest sign of weakness, flexing, or leaking at the hull-to-deck joint. Additionally, installing the bonding angle is often awkward and time-consuming. Nevertheless, the bonding angle is considered standard practice. You may also be required to install it if building to a classification-society rule. If you plan to use

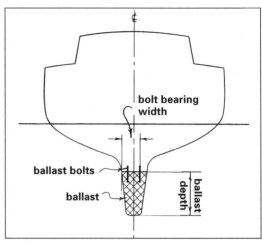

Ballast bolts

a bonding angle, it should be sized using the following formula.

FORMULA 5-11

Bonding Angle

Bonding-Angle Laminate Thickness = 0.7 × upper-topsides laminate thickness

Bonding-Angle Width = 16 × bonding-angle laminate thickness

FORMULA 5-12

Keel-Ballast Bolts

To find the diameter of the keel-ballast bolts,

Load per Bolt, in Pounds or Kilograms = (S.F. 8 × ballast depth × ballast weight) ÷ (2 × bolt-bearing width × number of bolts on one side)

Where

Ballast Depth = distance from hull bottom, or keel-bolt attachment level, to the underside of the ballast, in. or mm

Where

S.F. 8 = a safety factor of 8

Ballast Weight = total weight of ballast, pounds or kilograms

Bolt-Bearing Width = average distance from one row of ballast bolts to the opposite side of the top edge of the ballast keel. (If the keel has a single row of bolts down the centerline—not recommended—all bolts are used, NOT half on one side.)

NOTE: Neglect all bolts on the centerline for keels fastened with most bolts running down two sides of the ballast.

Refer to the bolt-tensile-strength table in appendix 3 to find the bolt diameter.

Example:

Our reliable old *Fish 'n Squish* is a 40-foot (12.19 m) cutter with 8,300 pounds (18,290 kg) of ballast. The bottom of the ballast keel is 45.6 inches (1,158 mm) below the keel-bolts attachment point, and the average bolt-bearing width is 10.5 inches (267 mm). The boat has 18 ballast bolts. Two bolts on the centerline are neglected, leaving 16—8 on each side. Then

Load per Bolt, lb. = S.F. 8 × 45.6-in. ballast depth × 8,300 lb. ÷ 2 × 10.5 in.-bolt width × 8 bolts = 18,020 lb. per bolt

Load per Bolt, lb. = S.F. 8 × 1,158 mm ballast depth × 3,765 kg ÷ 2 × 267 mm bolt width × 8 bolts = 8,165 kg per bolt

Referring to the bolt-breaking-strength table, we would fit *Fish 'n Squish* with ³/₄-inch-diameter (20 mm) silicon bronze bolts, with an ultimate tensile strength of 20,068 pounds (9,100 kg) or higher.

The floor's wood core must be at least four times the bolt diameter or 3 inches (80

mm). Accordingly, the 4.25-inch (110 mm) floor thickness found previously is acceptable.

FORMULA 5-13
Keel-Bolt Backing Plates

Backing plates must be placed under each keel-bolt nut, on top of the floors. The backing plates should be equal to the floor's core width in diameter and one-third the thickness of the keel-bolt diameter. Usually, the backing plates are simply square, the same width as the floor width. Even better is a continuous plate on top of the floor from the port-to-starboard keel bolt.

Stainless-steel bolts should have either stainless or mild-steel backing plates; bronze bolts must use bronze backing plates. (Mild-steel backing plates should be hot-dip galvanized and/or well painted all around with an epoxy-based paint.) The use of stainless-steel keel bolts should be avoided whenever possible. Stainless-steel can suffer from severe pitting corrosion over time. For this reason, Type 302 or 304 alloys are not acceptable for any keel bolts; only 316L ("L" for low carbon) and Aquamet 22 (also known as Nitronic 50) have sufficient resistance to pitting. Neither is as resistant as bronze. If stainless-steel bolts are used, aluminum backing plates can be used; however, they should be 1.5 times thicker than the thicknesses given for steel and bronze. Monel is also an excellent keel-bolt material. Use either bronze or Monel backing plates with Monel bolts.

Example:

For *Fish 'n Squish's* ³/₄-inch-diameter keel bolts, the backing plate should be ¹/₄ inch thick and 3 inches in diameter. For *Fish 'n*

Squish's 20 mm diameter keel bolts, the backing plate should be 6.6; use 8 mm thickness and 80 mm diameter.

The best procedure would be to use a single plate 3 inches (80 mm) wide, fore-n-aft, and running athwartships continuously under both keel bolts in the floor.

FORMULA 5-14
Laminate at Chainplates

There are several methods of attaching chainplates to the hull. They may be attached to bulkheads, internal knees, special framing, or tie-rods. The common "traditional" method, however, is to bolt the chainplates to the hull topsides. Where this is done, the topsides laminate must be increased as follows:

Chainplate-Region Topsides Laminate = 1.3 × topsides laminate thickness

Fore-n-Aft Length of Chainplate Region = beam overall at chainplates

Height of Chainplate Region = from sheer down to lowest chainplate bolt, plus a distance equal to 20 times the lowest bolt diameter down beyond the lowest bolt

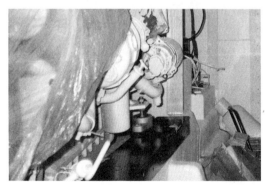

Proper steel engine mounts. These angles have been placed on top of the beds. They impart tremendous rigidity to the structure.

Improper engine mounts. These plywood mounts impart no rigidity. They aren't even sealed. It's only a matter of time before they soften or split, causing vibration, misalignment, or worse.

As we saw in Formulas 5-1 and 5-2, the engine beds are critical structures. Continuous, unbroken longitudinal strength is vital. In addition, the engine itself must be fastened to the beds with great strength and rigidity. The engine mounts must be bolted to a steel or aluminum angle. This angle must be through-bolted to the wood-core portion of the engine bed with a metal backing strip on the opposite side.

Most commonly, the angle is bolted to the side of the engine bed, with the flange projecting out from the side to accept the engine mounts. The angle can be installed with the flange facing up or down, as required. Alternately, the angle can be placed on top of the engine bed, and flush against one side. The engine mounts are then bolted to a weldment on top of the angle, or through-bolted down into a transverse insert bar, and run across the wood core, port to starboard, which is drilled and tapped to receive the mount bolts. The top-mounted angle should not only be bolted through the side of the engine bed, but also lag-bolted from the top down into the wood core. The lag bolts should be roughly centered between each pair of transverse through-bolts.

Engine Mounts

The engine-mount angles should extend at least 1.3 times the length of the distance between the engine-mount centers, with the engine roughly centered on the angles.

Use five transverse through-bolts in each bed. Use four lag bolts, in addition to transverse bolts, through the top (if angle is placed on top of bed).

Bolt Diameter (Lag and Transverse), in. = engine weight, lb. ÷ 4,000 (English)

or

Bolt Diameter (Lag and Transverse), in. = 0.012 × hp$^{0.66}$ (English)

Use whichever is larger.

Bolt Diameter (Lag and Transverse), mm = engine weight, kg ÷ 70 (Metric)

Bolt Diameter (Lag and Transverse), mm = 0.37 × kw$^{0.66}$ (Metric)

Use whichever is larger.

Steel angles should be 0.75 times the bolt-diameter thickness. Aluminum angles should equal the bolt diameter in thickness. Both flanges should be at least 10 percent wider than the maximum width of the engine mount's base plate.

Angles that are bolted to the side of the engine beds, with bolts 0.5 inch (12.5 mm) or more in diameter, require two tripping brackets. The brackets should be welded in place approximately 4 inches (100 mm) forward of the aft engine mount and 4 inches (100 mm) aft of the forward engine mount. The tripping brackets should be the same thickness as the angle.

Backing-Strip Length = angle length

Backing-Strip Width = 0.8 × height of angle

Backing-Strip Thickness = 0.6 × angle thickness, but not less than $^3/_{16}$-in. (5 mm) steel or $^1/_4$-in. (6 mm) aluminum

Insert-Bar (if used) Thickness = bolt diameter

Insert-Bar (if used) Width = 3 to 4 times bolt diameter

NOTE: Like all penetrations into a wood core, great care must be taken to seal the slot for the insert bar with resin and to bed the bar very well in marine bedding compound.

SIX

Fiberglass Sandwich or Cored Construction

*A*s discussed in chapter 2, fiberglass is neither a particularly strong nor stiff material. Again, contrary to common belief, solid FRP structures tend to be somewhat heavy when built for adequate stiffness. The best way to reduce weight while increasing stiffness and—to some degree, reducing internal-structure complexity—is to employ *sandwich construction*. It is, however, absolutely vital that you follow the core-installation and bedding procedures outlined in chapter 2. Double-check these procedures with your core and resin manufacturers to get their specific installation/bedding recommendations. Don't let potential core problems scare you away from sandwich construction. Cored hulls and decks are rugged, safe, reliable, and long-lasting. In fact, they are my preference for most FRP structures, including hull bottoms. You simply must take proper care during construction.

WHY CORES WORK

Fundamentally, the way to make a structure stiffer is to make it thicker. Of course, you can't just double the thickness as you would double the weight—too heavy. Instead, use a core material (for this rule, foam or balsa). This way, you have an FRP outer shell and an FRP inner shell bonded (glued) to a tough but very light sandwich material in between. The increase in stiffness is huge. If you had,

An assortment of standard core products: end-grain balsa, rigid panels, and kerfed Contour-kore; pre-manufactured fillet strips and Ribkore; DuraKore strips and center-bottom Baltekmat bulk. (Courtesy Baltek Corporation)

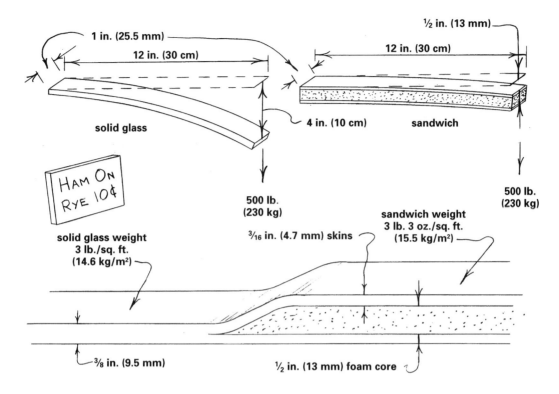

Sandwich anatomy: bending with a 500-pound (230 kg) load

for example, a 3/8-inch-thick (9.5 mm) strip of ordinary solid glass about 1 inch (25.5 mm) wide and a foot (30 cm) long, you would find that a 500-pound (230 kg) load hung on one end would bend it about 4 inches (10 cm). If you took that same strip and slit it in half to make two layers 3/16 inch (4.7 mm) thick and 1 inch (25.5 mm) wide, you would have the beginnings of a sandwich-construction hull laminate.

If you add a core—for example, a 1/2 inch (13 mm) of closed-cell foam or end-grain balsa—between the two layers and glue it in place firmly, you would have a much different story. The same 500-pound (230 kg) weight would deflect it barely a 1/2 inch (13 mm)—an eightfold increase in stiffness. Note that you've increased thickness from 3/8 inch (9.5 mm) to 7/8 inch (22.5 mm)—230 percent thicker. In return, you got an 800 percent increase in stiffness, but with only the slight additional weight of the core in between. This is the principle of cored or sandwich construction. Indeed, the increase in stiffness is so marked that you can decrease the total thickness of the fiberglass—the two (i.e., inner plus outer) FRP skins—to less than that of the entire solid-hull laminate. Weight savings are substantial.

Sandwich Hull Shell

FORMULA 6-1
Sandwich Fiberglass Scantlings

To determine the scantlings for cored or sandwich FRP construction—using the standard layup of alternating layers of mat and woven roving, in polyester resin—calculate the solid-hull-shell thickness as described in chapter 4, then proceed as follows:

Basic Hull-Core Thickness = 2.2 × solid FRP thickness at lower topsides, for entire hull—bottom and topsides— except on planing hulls, where the bottom core is thicker

Planing Hull-Bottom Thickness = 2.2 × solid FRP thickness of hull bottom

Deck-Core Thickness = 1.5 × basic hull-core thickness

Total FRP Laminate Thickness = 0.70 × the solid FRP thickness

For most boats more than 20 feet (6 m), the following is recommended:

Outer-Skin Laminate = 0.40 × the solid FRP thickness

Inner-Skin Laminate = 0.30 × the solid FRP thickness

The additional thickness outside adds abrasion and impact resistance where it is needed most. On small vessels, convenient and practical laminate styles may force you to use roughly the same thickness both inside and out. This is acceptable although not quite as tough as having the thicker outer skin. Sometimes having equal thicknesses in and out is referred to as having a "balanced" laminate or having "balanced" skins.

FORMULA 6-2
Core Density

For vessels with Sns under 3.0, all the cores should be closed-cell foam, 5.5-lb./cu. ft. (88 kg/m³) density, or end-grain balsa, 6.5-lb./cu. ft. (104 kg/m³) density—or slightly greater. For the bottoms and topsides of boats with Sns more than 3.0, and in the bottoms of all craft with top speeds more than 25 knots, the core density is to be closed-cell foam, 8.0-lb./cu. ft. (128 kg/m³) density, or end-grain balsa, 9.5-lb./cu. ft. (152 kg/m³) density—or slightly greater. (The deck cores can be the lighter density.) This is because both sheer and compressive strength of the core is directly proportional to its density. Higher-density cores are required to handle these greater loads and the bigger panel sizes in larger and/or faster hull laminates. Deck cores on workboats and charter vessels, for example, with Sns more than 3.0 are to be closed-cell foam, 8.0-lb./cu. ft. (128 kg/m³) density, or end-grain balsa, 9.5-lb./cu. ft. (152 kg/m³) density—or slightly greater. Higher-density cores can always be used in place of the minimum required lower density; however, they are more expensive.

ALTERNATE CORES AND DENSITIES
There are types of cores other than closed-cell foam and end-grain balsa; plastic-impregnated paper-honeycomb, all-plastic honeycomb, and aluminum-honeycomb cores (some filled with foam, some open-cell) are the most common. Each is excellent and has specific advantages; however, they are not covered in this rule. Both closed-cell foam and end-grain balsa are available in other densities besides the two "standards" men-

tioned previously. The higher densities are useful on larger, faster boats and in areas of very high loading, such as at the attachments for cranes, hoists, and windlasses. The lower densities can be used for internal-framing cores like stringers. This rule does not cover application of these other densities, except as mentioned for internal stiffeners in chapter 5.

Example:

Let's return to our salty, 25-knot *Fish 'n Squish*: 40 feet (12.19 m) LOA, beam 12.56 feet, Sn 2.97. We found its solid FRP hull shell in chapter 4. Using this, we can apply Formulas 6-1 and 6-2 to find the sandwich fiberglass scantlings as follows.

Find Laminate and Core Thickness (English)

Outer Deck: solid glass was 0.30 in. × 0.40 = 0.12 in.

Inner Deck: solid glass was 0.30 in. × 0.30 = 0.09 in.

Deck Core: basic core thickness = 0.75 in. × 1.5 = 1.12 in.; use 1.25-in. core

Upper Topsides: laminate same as deck

Upper-Topsides Core: basic core thickness = 0.75-in. core

Outer Lower Topsides: solid glass was 0.36 in. × 0.40 = 0.14 in.

Inner Lower Topsides: solid glass was 0.36 in. × 0.30 = 0.11 in.

Basic Core Thickness: Lower Topsides Core = solid glass was 0.36 in. × 2.2 = 0.79; use 0.75-in. core. (NOTE: On a displacement hull, the 0.75-in. basic core thickness would be used for the bottom core as well.)

Core Density: Sn less than 3.0; use 5.5-lb./cu. ft. foam or 6.5-lb./cu. ft. balsa

Outer Hull Bottom: solid glass was 0.47 in. × 0.40 = 0.19 in.

Inner Hull Bottom: solid glass was 0.47 in. × 0.30 = 0.14 in.

Planing Hull-Bottom Core: solid glass was 0.47 in. × 2.2 = 1.03 in.; use 1-in. core

Planing Bottom-Core Density: 8-lb./cu. ft. foam or 9.5-lb./cu. ft. balsa

Keel and Stem: 0.71-in. solid glass, DO NOT USE CORE

Outer Hull-Bottom High-Stress Areas: solid glass was 0.52 in. × 0.40 = 0.21 in.

Inner Hull-Bottom High-Stress Areas: solid glass was 0.52 in. × 0.30 = 0.15 in.

Deck-Hardware-Mounting Areas: See Formula 6-3.

Find Laminate and Core Thickness (Metric)

Outer Deck: solid glass was 7.82 mm × 0.40 = 3.13 mm

Inner Deck: solid glass was 7.82 mm × 0.30 = 2.34 mm

Deck Core: Basic Core Thickness = 20 mm × 1.5 = 30 mm core

Upper Topsides: laminate same as deck

Upper-Topsides Core, Basic Core Thickness: 20 mm core

Outer Lower Topsides: solid glass was 9.2 mm × 0.40 = 3.68 mm

Inner Lower Topsides: solid glass was 9.2 mm × 0.30 = 2.76 mm

Basic Core Thickness: Lower Topsides Core = solid glass was 9.2 mm × 2.2 = 20.24; use

20 mm core (NOTE: On a displacement hull, the 20 mm basic core thickness would be used for the bottom core as well.)

Core Density: Sn less than 3.0; use 88 kg/m³ foam or 104 kg/m³ balsa

Outer Hull Bottom: solid glass was 12.16 mm × 0.40 = 4.86 mm

Inner Hull Bottom: solid glass was 12.16 mm × 0.30 = 3.65 mm

Planing Hull-Bottom Core: solid glass was 12.16 mm × 2.2 = 26.75; use 25 mm core

Planing Bottom-Core Density = 128 kg/m³ foam or 152 kg/m³ balsa

Keel and Stem = 18.24 mm solid glass, DO NOT USE CORE

Outer Hull-Bottom High-Stress Areas: solid glass was 13.37 mm × 0.40 = 5.35 mm

Inner Hull-Bottom High-Stress Areas: solid glass was 13.37 mm × 0.30 = 4.0 mm

Deck-Hardware-Mounting Areas: see Formulas 6-2 through 6-5

Specify Laminate (English)

(Refer to Formulas 4-7 and 4-8 and Table 4-9, or manufacturer's data sheets.) One of the difficulties with sandwich construction—particularly acute for vessels 50 feet and less—is that the inner and outer skins are too thin to use multiple layers of 24-15 combi-mat and still include sufficient mat to avoid print-through and for core bedding. This will cause the actual laminate to be thicker than required by the rule. Instead, we can use 18-10 combi-mat, 0.063 inch thick (i.e., 18-oz./sq. yd. roving stitched to 1.0-oz./sq. ft. mat) for the majority of the laminate (see photo on p. 335).

Deck Outer Skin: 0.12 in. ÷ 0.063 in./layer = 1.9 layers 18-10 combi-mat

1 Layer 0.75-oz. Mat	0.024 in.
2 Layers 18-10 Combi-Mat	0.126 in.
1 Layer 1.5-oz. Mat (Skin Coat)	0.048 in.
Outer Deck-Laminate Thickness	0.222 in.

Deck Inner Skin: 0.09 in. ÷ 0.063 in./layer = 1.4 layers 18-10 combi-mat

1 Layer 18-10 Combi-Mat	0.063 in.
1 Layer 1.0-oz. Mat	0.032 in.
Inner Deck-Laminate Thickness	0.095 in.
Total Laminate Thickness	0.320 in.

Deck Core: 5.5-lb. foam or 6.5-lb. balsa	1.250 in.
Total Deck Thickness	1.570 in.

Upper-Topsides Outer Skin: 0.12 in. ÷ 0.063 in./layer = 1.9 layers 18-10 combi-mat

1 Layer 0.75-oz. Mat	0.024 in.
2 Layers 18-10 Combi-Mat	0.126 in.
1 Layer 1.5-oz. Mat (Skin Coat)	0.048 in.
Upper-Topsides Outer-Laminate Thickness	0.198 in.

Upper-Topsides Inner Skin: 0.09 in. ÷ 0.063 in./layer = 1.4 layers 18-10 combi-mat

1 Layer 18-10 Combi-Mat	0.063 in.
1 Layer 1.0-oz. Mat	0.032 in.
Upper-Topsides Inner-Laminate Thickness	0.095 in.
Total Laminate Thickness	0.290 in.

Upper-Topsides Core: 5.5 lb./ft.³ foam or 6.5 lb./ft.³ balsa	0.75 in.
Total Upper-Topsides Thickness	1.04 in.

Lower-Topsides Outer Skin: 0.14 in. ÷ 0.063 in./layer = 2.2 layers 18-10 combi-mat

1 Layer 0.75-oz. Mat	0.024 in.
2 Layers 18-10 Combi-Mat	0.126 in.
1 Layer 1.5-oz. Mat (Skin Coat)	0.048 in.
Lower-Topsides Outer Laminate	
Thickness	0.198 in.

Lower-Topsides Inner Skin: 0.09 in. ÷ 0.063 in./layer = 1.4 layers 18-10 combi-mat

1 Layer 18-10 Combi-Mat	0.063 in.
1 Layer 1.0-oz. Mat	0.032 in.
Lower-Topsides Inner-Laminate	
Thickness	0.095 in.
Total Laminate Thickness	0.290 in.
Lower-Topsides Core: 5.5 lb./ft.³	
foam or 6.5 lb./ft.³ balsa	0.75 in.
Total Lower-Topsides Thickness	1.04 in.

(NOTE: The upper and lower topsides are the same in this case because the thickness of the necessary mat skin coat increases the laminate thickness over the rule requirements.)

Hull-Bottom Outer Skin: 0.19 in. ÷ 0.063 in./layer = 3.0 layers 18-10 combi-mat

1 Layer 0.75-oz. Mat	0.024 in.
3 Layers 18-10 Combi-Mat	0.189 in.
1 Layer 1.5-oz. Mat (Skin Coat)	0.048 in.
Hull-Bottom Outer-Laminate	
Thickness	0.261 in.

Hull-Bottom Inner Skin: 0.11 in. ÷ 0.063 in./layer = 1.74 layers 18-10 combi-mat

2 Layers 18-10 Combi-Mat	0.126 in.
1 Layer 1.0-oz. Mat	0.032 in.
Hull-Bottom Inner-Laminate	
Thickness	0.158 in.
Total Laminate Thickness	0.42 in.

Hull-Bottom Core: 8.0 lb./ft.³ foam	
or 9.5 lb./ft.³ balsa	1.00 in.
Total Hull-Bottom Thickness	1.42 in.

Solid-Glass Keel and Stem (see Formula 6-10): 0.71-in. thick – 0.395 in. sandwich hull-bottom FRP laminate = 0.315 in., and 0.315 ÷ 0.089 in./ply (24-15 combi-mat) = 3.54 layers

1 Layer 0.75-oz. Mat	0.024 in.
(outer laminate)	
3 Layers 18-10 Combi-Mat	0.189 in.
1 Layer 1.5-oz. Mat (Skin Coat)	0.048 in.
2 Layers 18-10 Combi-Mat	0.126 in.
(inner laminate)	
1 Layer 1.0-oz. Mat	0.032 in.
1 Layer 18-10 Combi-Mat	0.063 in.
(added buildup)	
3 Layers 24-15 Combi-Mat	0.267 in.
Total Keel and Stem Thickness	0.75 in.

Hull-Bottom High-Stress Areas: Use same as standard hull bottom; standard hull bottom is thicker than required by rule, and is as thick as required by rule for high-stress areas.

Specify Laminate (Metric)
(Refer to Formulas 4-7 and 4-8 and Table 4-9, or the manufacturer's data sheets.) One of the difficulties with sandwich construction—particularly acute for vessels 15 m and under—is that the inner and outer skins are too thin to use multiple layers of 24-15 combi-mat (814 g/m² roving by 457 g/m² mat; 1,271 g/m² total) and still include sufficient mat to avoid print-through and for core bedding. This will cause the actual laminate to be thicker than required by the rule. Instead, we can use 18-10 combi-mat, 1.6 mm

thick (610 g/m² roving stitched to 305 g/m² mat; 915 g/m² total) for the majority of the laminate.

Deck Outer Skin: 3.13 mm ÷ 1.6 mm/layer = 1.9 layers 18-10 combi-mat

1 Layer 228 g/m² Mat	0.61 mm
2 Layers 18-10 (915 g/m²) Combi-Mat	3.20 mm
1 Layer 457 g/m² Mat (Skin Coat)	1.22 mm
Outer Deck-Laminate Thickness	5.03 mm

Deck Inner Skin: 2.34 mm ÷ 1.6 mm/layer = 1.4 layers 18-10 combi-mat

1 Layer 18-10 (915 g/m²) Combi-mat	1.60 mm
1 Layer 305 g/m² Mat	0.81 mm
Inner Deck-Laminate Thickness	2.41 mm
Total Laminate Thickness	7.44 mm

Deck Core: 88 kg/m³ foam, or 104 kg/m³ balsa	30.00 mm
Total Deck Thickness	37.44 mm

Upper-Topsides Outer Skin: 3.13 mm ÷ 1.6 mm/layer = 1.9 layers 18-10 combi-mat

1 Layer 228 g/m² Mat	0.61 mm
2 Layers 18-10 (915 g/m²) Combi-Mat	3.20 mm
1 Layer 457 g/m² Mat (Skin Coat)	1.22 mm
Upper-Topsides Outer-Laminate Thickness	5.03 mm

Upper-Topsides Inner Skin: 2.34 mm ÷ 1.6 mm/layer = 1.4 layers 18-10 combi-mat

1 Layer 18-10 (915 g/m²) Combi-Mat	1.60 mm
1 Layer 305 g/m² Mat	0.81 mm

Upper-Topsides Inner-Laminate Thickness	2.41 mm
Total Laminate Thickness	7.44 mm

Upper-Topsides Core: 88 kg/m³ foam or 104 kg/m³ balsa	20.00 mm
Total Upper Topsides Thickness	27.44 mm

Lower-Topsides Outer Skin: 3.68 mm ÷ 1.6 mm/layer = 2.2 layers 18-10 combi-mat

1 Layer 228 g/m² Mat	0.61 mm
2 Layers 18-10 (915 g/m²) Combi-Mat	3.20 mm
1 Layer 457 g/m² Mat (Skin Coat)	1.22 mm
Lower-Topsides Outer-Laminate Thickness	5.03 mm

Lower-Topsides Inner Skin: 2.76 mm ÷ 1.6 mm/layer = 1.4 layers 18-10 combi-mat

1 Layer 18-10 (915 g/m²) Combi-Mat	1.60 mm
1 Layer 305 g/m² Mat	0.81 mm
Lower-Topsides Inner-Laminate Thickness	2.41 mm
Total Laminate Thickness	7.44 mm

Lower-Topsides Core: 88 kg/m³ foam or 104 kg/m³ balsa	20.00 mm
Total Lower Topsides Thickness	27.44 mm

(NOTE: The upper and lower topsides are the same in this case because the thickness of the necessary mat skin-coat increases the laminate thickness over the rule requirements.)

Hull-Bottom Outer Skin: 4.86 mm ÷ 1.6 mm/layer = 3.0 layers 18-10 combi-mat

1 Layer 228 g/m² Mat	0.61 mm
3 Layers 18-10 (915 g/m²) Combi-Mat	4.80 mm

1 Layer (457 g/m²) Mat (Skin Coat) 1.22 mm
Hull-Bottom Outer Laminate
Thickness: 6.63 mm

Hull-Bottom Inner Skin: 3.65 mm ÷
1.6 mm/layer = 1.74 layers 18-10 combi-mat

2 Layers 18-10 (915 g/m²)
Combi-Mat   3.20 mm
1 Layer (305 g/m²) Mat   0.81 mm
Hull-Bottom Inner-Laminate
Thickness: 4.01 mm
Total Laminate Thickness   10.64 mm

Hull-Bottom Core: 128 kg/m³
foam or 152 kg/m³ balsa   25.00 mm
Total Hull-Bottom Thickness   35.64 mm

Solid-Glass Keel and Stem (see Formula
6-10): 18.24 mm thick – 10.03 mm Sandwich
Hull-Bottom FRP Laminate = 8.21 mm, and
8.21 ÷ 2.26 mm/ply (24-15, 1,271 g/m²
combi-mat) = 3.6 layers

1 Layer 228 g/m² Mat   0.61 mm
                             (outer laminate)
3 Layers 18-10 (915 g/m²)
Combi-Mat   4.80 mm
1 Layer 457 g/m² Mat
(Skin Coat)   1.22 mm
2 Layers 18-10 (915 g/m²)
Combi-Mat   3.20 mm
                             (inner laminate)
1 Layer 305 g/m² Mat   0.81 mm
1 Layer 18-10 (915 g/m²)
Combi-Mat   1.60 mm
                             (added buildup)
3 Layers 24-15 (1,271 g/m²)
Combi-Mat   6.78 mm
Total Keel and Stem Thickness   19.02 mm

Hull-Bottom High-Stress Areas: Use same
as standard hull bottom; standard hull
bottom is thicker than required by rule and
is as thick as required by rule for high-
stress areas.

COMMENTS ON THE LAMINATE SPECIFICATION

In all cases, the necessary skin-coat and core-bedding mat increased the practically necessary laminate thicknesses beyond that required by the rule—a common difficulty with the thin laminates in sandwich construction. The 1.5-oz. (457 g/m²) mat skin coat is laid in the mold first, followed by the 18-10 (915 g/m²) combi-mat, mat down (facing out). The 0.75-oz. (228 g/m²) mat is applied on top of that, under the core as bedding, followed by the core itself.

You could elect instead to apply the 0.75-oz. (228 g/m²) mat on top of the skin coat followed by the 18-10 (915 g/m²) combi-mat, mat up. In this case, there would

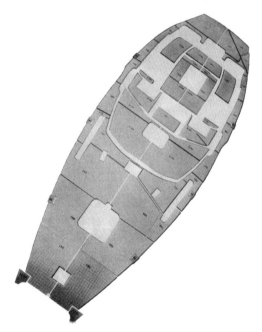

Complete deck-core kit for a 34-foot sailboat.
(Courtesy Divinycell/Barracuda Technologies)

be additional mat on the surface to prevent print-through, and the upturned mat face of the combi-mat would be laid on wet as the core bedding. It is slightly stronger to have the roving closer to the outside (farther from the core center), however. And, the 1.5-oz. (457 g/m^2) mat skin plus the 1.0-oz. (305 g/m^2) mat on the 18-10 yields 2.5 oz. (762 g/m^2) total, which should be enough to prevent print-through with the finer weave of the 18-oz. (610 g/m^2) roving—as opposed to 24-oz. (814 g/m^2).

On the inner skin, the 18-10 (915 g/m^2) combi-mat could have been applied directly to the inside of the core, mat down. In this laminate for our *Fish 'n Squish*, however, the additional 1.0-oz. (305 g/m^2) mat was added to build up the required inner-skin thickness. Again, the 1.0-oz. (305 g/m^2) mat is placed against the core so the roving will be farther out from the core center, which is slightly stronger.

Although the laminate we've come up with is somewhat thicker than required by rule, it has a higher proportion of mat in it than the nearly balanced roving-mat the rule assumes. Because mat is weaker than roving, the extra thickness is not much overkill.

Always keep in mind the principle that there should be a fresh, wet mat layer between each layer of roving and against both faces of the core to ensure proper interlaminar bonds.

OPTIONS FOR REDUCING EXCESS LAMINATE THICKNESS

There are many fabric styles, and—as long as you follow the basic rules for skin coat and interlaminar mat—you can use any combination or style of fabric to bring the individual skin thickness closer to the minimum spec'd by the rule. Finer styles give you more flexibility—a 14-07 combi-mat, for instance (475 g/m^2 roving times 228 g/m^2).

The best fabric styles for light, thin sandwich laminates are the knitted stitch mats such as Brunswick's 1603—a 0,90 bi-axial with two layers of 8-oz. uni-di, stitched to a 0.25-oz. mat. Alternately, you could use Knytex's 1208—a 45,45 bi-axial with two layers of 6-oz. uni-di, stitched to a 0.75-oz. mat (1603 is 0,90 bi-ax with two layers of 271 g/m^2 uni-di, plus 76 g/m^2 mat; 1208 is 45,45 bi-ax with two layers of 203 g/m^2 uni-di, plus 228 g/m^2 mat).

The stitch-mat styles have a higher proportion of uni-di-to-mat than most woven-roving combi-mats and are thus stronger. The uni-di bi-ax is also less prone to print-through than the coarser-weave rovings. Furthermore, the fabrics themselves are thinner, giving you more flexibility in adjusting skin thickness. Brunswick's 1603 totals just 0.035 inch (0.89 mm) thick; 1208 is 0.045 inch (1.14 mm) thick. The drawback is that bi-axial stitch-mat fabric styles are somewhat more expensive.

Sandwich Construction Details

DECK-HARDWARE-MOUNTING AREAS

Sandwich cores have low compression strength. They can't transmit the loads from high-strength deck fittings, such as cleats, chocks, sail track, and winches, from the inner to the outer skins. The three standard methods for transmitting these compressive loads are solid-plywood core (or very high-density foam), stainless-steel or aluminum compression tubes (sleeves around the fastener through-bolt), and epoxy annuluses.

Solid-Plywood Cores

Solid plywood has extremely high compression strength compared to standard low-density foam or balsa cores. In the region around the deck hardware, solid plywood is installed instead of the normal core. Care must be taken to presaturate the ply with resin, seal all fastener holes, and bed the fittings well or water can get at the ply core, causing decay.

FORMULA 6-3
Solid-Plywood-Core Dimensions

Solid-Plywood-Core Thickness: Same thickness as the standard core

Solid-Plywood-Core Dimensions: Extend at least 1.1 times the footprint of the mounted hardware in all directions

Solid-plywood cores can be practically installed only in advance. If the deck-hardware layout is known, ply cores are a reliable method and—if the solid-ply areas are made a little oversize—they make locating fittings fairly easy. Numerous solid-plywood cores can add significant weight, however.

Some manufacturers make very high-density foam cores for use in place of solid plywood for this application. These high-density foams save weight over the plywood and cannot rot. Consult your core supplier for information on its products.

Compression Tubes

Where plywood cores aren't used, you can simply drill a slightly oversize hole and install a compression tube between the underside of the hardware and the backing plate, under the deck. This frees you to install deck hardware at any location; however, it requires careful fitting of the tube length to ensure a tight, snug, watertight joint.

Epoxy Annuluses

A recommended alternative to metal compression tubes is epoxy annuluses. These are simply compression tubes formed of poured-in-place epoxy grout.

FORMULA 6-4
Epoxy-Annulus Diameter

Epoxy Annulus = 2.0 × bolt diameter

Locate the deck hardware and mark the fastener holes. Drill holes two times the bolt diameter. Fill the holes with high-density, high-strength epoxy grout. Back the underside of the holes with plastic that doesn't stick to epoxy, held in place with duct tape until cure. After the epoxy has hardened, remove the plastic and tape; relocate the fastener; rebore for the correct through-bolt size (through the center of the epoxy annuluses); and fasten the hardware permanently in place.

Any grout protrusions can be knocked off quickly with a disk sander, and any small surface gaps can be filled with a dab of grout filler. The advantage of the epoxy annulus is that it can be inserted anywhere without pre-planing. The fit is easy, and added weight is virtually nil.

Some builders find it quicker to "pot" the through-bolt and the curing epoxy grout in place in one step. They use the backing plate and the hardware base to retain the epoxy. This too is acceptable as long as the grout can be kept from running out.

DECK-HARDWARE BACKING PLATES

In all cases, the deck hardware requires a backing plate under the deck. Backing plates are usually aluminum, even for bronze hardware. Well above the waterline, with the backing plates inside and out of the weather, galvanic corrosion is not a problem.

Lightly loaded hardware, such as an awning cleat and flagpole socket, does not require a backing plate, but large washers must be used under the nuts inside.

DECK-HARDWARE-MOUNTING PRECAUTIONS

Never fasten any hardware to a cored deck or exterior with screws. You absolutely must use through-bolts every time, for every fitting.

Take great care to bed all hardware with a marine bedding compound. It is vital to keep water from seeping into the core. Even small amounts of water (which do little harm at first) can freeze. The frozen water bursts open the core and laminate slightly, which leads to more water penetration. The result is a self-perpetuating destructive cycle. Bed well, bed everything, bed carefully.

SOLID GLASS (NO CORE) AT HIGHLY LOADED HULL PENETRATIONS

Where there are holes or fasteners through the hull carrying large loads or substantial running gear, the core must be locally removed and replaced with a solid-glass laminate that equals the standard solid-glass hull laminate at high-stress areas or at the chainplates (see Formulas 4-13 and 5-14).

The principal items requiring core removal are as follows:

- Ballast-bolt region in the hull bottom, if the bolts do not run through the floors as recommended
- Penetrations for rudder ports
- Penetrations for shaft logs and stern tubes
- Strut bases and their mounting bolts
- All chainplate bolts and attachments
- Towing eyes and hoisting rings

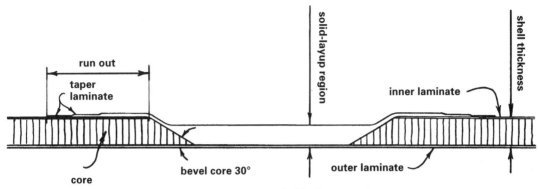

Solid glass at highly loaded hull penetrations

- Trim tabs
- Steering-gear mountings and fastener penetrations
- Around installation cutouts for surface-propeller drives and for jet drives. NOTE: Additional solid-plywood cores or similar reinforcing is also required for propulsion units; follow the manufacturer's recommendations.

In these areas, the core is not installed. Surrounding core edges are carefully beveled back to approximately a 30-degree slope. The required additional inner laminate is run down off the core onto the inside of the outer laminate and built up until the specified thickness is achieved.

FORMULA 6-8
Solid-Glass-Region Specifications

Tabbing (On Top of the Remaining Inside Core, Around the Removed-Core Area): 10 × the thickness of the added inside laminate or 6 in. (15 cm), whichever is greater

Tabbing Thickness: 30 percent of the interior solid-glass layup used to build up the total required solid-glass thickness

Tabbing should taper away gradually, to just one or two layers of glass at its outermost edge.

INTERNAL STRUCTURE: NO DECK OR TOPSIDES STRINGERS

One of the nice things about cored FRP construction is that the required internal structure is simpler. No deck or hull-topsides longitudinal stringers are required. This can represent considerable time savings, both when building the hull and in installing bulkheads and joinerwork later. Engine beds/stringers, bulkheads, ring frames, and floors are all required exactly as determined in chapter 5, however.

Chine Reinforcement

Hard-chine planing craft should have chine reinforcement installed as described in Formula 5-4. This can be done by applying the additional laminate required to the inside only of the cored chine structure. Preferably, I recommend that the core be stopped some distance back from the chine, and the chine region be made of a solid-glass laminate in the thickness specified in Formula 5-4.

Improper strut mounting. This simple plywood pad is badly deteriorated. There was no backing plate—only washers—which repeatedly compressed into the ply, causing loose struts and vibration.

Proper strut mounting through solid-glass bottom-laminate region with heavy backing plate.

FORMULA 6-9

Solid-Glass Chines

Distance Between Chine Corner and Core: 8 × core thickness, both up along topsides and across bottom

Solid-Glass-Laminate Chine Thickness: same as in Formula 5-4

Hard chines take concentrated abrasion abuse. Solid-glass laminate is superior in this one regard. Installing it along the chine adds only little weight, but increases toughness where needed. Furthermore, most builders find it is easier to lay up solid-glass corners.

Solid-Glass Keel and Stem (Use No Core)

For the same reason that chines are recommended to be solid glass, the keel and stem region must be solid glass. The keel and stem take the most continuous and severe impact and abrasion abuse.

FORMULA 6-10

Solid-Glass Keel

Solid-Glass-Keel Width: 0.125 × scantling beam (see Formula 1-3)

Solid-Glass Keel-Laminate Thickness: keel-region laminate, as determined in chapter 4

The solid-glass-keel region can decrease in width toward the stem, but not to less than 6 inches (15 cm).

Internal Ballast

Where internal ballast is fitted in a sailboat (instead of external bolted-on ballast), the hull must be all solid glass (no core).

FORMULA 6-11

Internal-Ballast-Laminate Thickness

Internal-Ballast-Laminate Thickness: 1.1 × keel-region laminate thickness

Tapering of Core at Transition from Solid Glass to Cored Areas

As discussed in chapter 3, it is important to avoid hard spots in FRP construction. Accordingly, wherever there's a transition from a cored to a solid-glass region of the hull or deck, you must use a tapered core fillet to make a sloping, gradual change. (Again, these

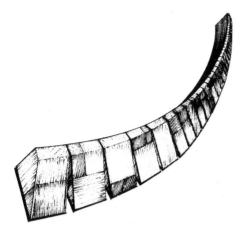

Typical premanufactured fillet strip, for tapering transition from cored to solid laminate. (Courtesy Baltek Corporation)

are required by ABS and U.S. Coast Guard requirements for Subchapter-T boats.) Most core manufacturers sell core fillet strips specifically designed for this use.

Alternately, you can make your own fillet strips by cutting pieces of standard core to shape. Still another option is to knock down the edge of the core with a grinder, but don't forget to presaturate the ground-off area with resin before continuing with the layup. Some builders leave the core untapered and trowel-in a fillet of putty grout. This is not recommended; not only is the grout heavier than the core fillets, but it is also brittle. If the structure is flexed by a heavy load, the putty fillets will crack; the core fillets would not. Cracked putty-grout fillets can work loose, causing stress concentrations and/or small leaks in the laminate.

FORMULA 6-12
Core-Fillet Angle
Ideal Core-Fillet Angle: between 18.5 and 30 degrees, or a slope between 3:1 and 1.76:1

This is the ideal fillet angle. Some off-the-shelf fillet strips have a steeper angle. These are generally adequate, but be leery of using angles steeper than 30 degrees.

Laminate Corners

There are two ways to make corners in laminates for transoms, chines, trunk-cabin to deck joints, and cockpit corners. One method involves making *butted-core corners*: Install the cores covering the entire interior, with each core (from either surface) butting tight to the other at the corners. The second method is to make *solid-glass corners*: Stop the cores back from the corner and simply run the inner laminate down off the core (over the fillet-strip edge), down onto the inside of the outer laminate (without core), and then up again onto the other core inside. Both methods are entirely acceptable and can be used interchangeably on the same hull.

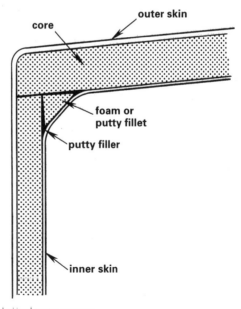

Butted-core corner

Butted-Core Corners

With butted cores, you must take great care to fill all gaps in the corner and between the cores with putty grout. You must also apply either a putty-grout fillet on the inside corner or a foam-core fillet, before applying the inside laminate. Although I use them whenever it seems convenient, butted cores usually require slightly more work. In addition, cores at sharp exterior corners are more easily subject to exposure from abrasion than solid glass.

Solid-Glass Corners

Solid-glass corners are usually slightly easier to fabricate than butted cores. The corners are thicker solid glass, so they are more resistant to abrasion and easier to repair if damaged. Also, using solid-glass corners throughout (in conjunction with the solid-glass keel) segregates the core into distinct regions. If there should ever be a core water-penetration problem, this isolates it to one region. Solid-glass corners are roughly the same as recommended in Formula 6-9.

> **FORMULA 6-13**
> Solid-Glass Corners
>
> *Distance Corner and Core: 4 to 8 × core thickness*

Hull-to-Deck Joint

Hull-to-deck joints for sandwich hulls and decks are fabricated exactly as for solid-glass hulls, as described in chapter 5. The core is stopped back from the hull to deck joint, on both the topsides and the deck, exactly as with a solid-glass corner. The core cut-back distance is the same as in Formula 6-13.

High-Modulus Laminates

Up to this point, we've stayed with industry-standard, plain-vanilla FRP laminates; all the reinforcing fibers employed have been ordinary E-glass, while all the resin has been polyester. Chapter 3 discussed the advantages of high-modulus fiber reinforcement combined with vinylester or epoxy-resin systems. For most common applications, these high-modulus laminates offer only a modest advantage with single-skin construction. In sandwich construction, however, such laminates come into their own. They offer greater strength with thinner (and thus lighter) skins, and they are available in light fabric styles that offer more flexibility in specifying sandwich layups. The following rules can be used to determine a high-modulus-reinforcement cored hull and deck structure.

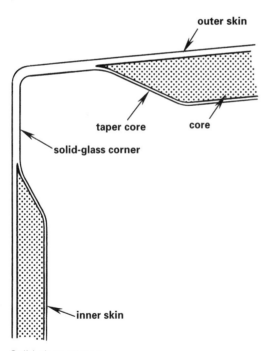

Solid-glass corner

Conversion for S-Glass Vinylester Skins

Use S-glass (aircraft-grade fiberglass cloth) in uni-di, bi-axial, and tri-axial stitch-mat styles. To use S-glass, calculate thickness and glass weights using the standard sandwich rule, then reduce skin thickness (not the core) by 10 percent. Vacuum-bagging both the laminate and core is recommended, but high-quality hand layup is acceptable. Vinylester or epoxy resin must be used.

FORMULA 6-15

Kevlar Inner Skin

Use Kevlar on the inside skin only. Kevlar is highly abrasion-resistant, so there's a tendency to place it outside. Unfortunately, Kevlar has high tensile strength but relatively modest compressive strength. On impact, exterior skins are placed in compression, so Kevlar shouldn't be used there—unless it's in addition to the standard laminate thickness, and for abrasion resistance only.

To use Kevlar on the inside skin (the inside skin is in tension—Kevlar's real strength), calculate the laminate using the standard sandwich-construction rule and reduce the Kevlar skin thickness (not the core) by 15 percent. Again, vacuum-bag both laminate and core, and use only vinylester or epoxy resins.

Note that Kevlar is not only costly, but is also difficult to work with. It requires special cutting techniques and equipment, and it's more difficult to wet-out evenly and consistently than most other types of reinforcement.

S-GLASS OUTER SKIN, KEVLAR INNER SKIN

The highest strength to lightest weight will be achieved by using S-glass exterior and Kevlar interior laminates that are vacuum-bagged.

FORMULA 6-16

Vacuum-Bagged E-Glass Stitch-Mat Vinylester Laminates

S-glass and Kevlar fabric styles are considerably more expensive than E-glass fabrics. Most ordinary vessels (even extremely light ones) will find cored hulls—using standard uni-di (bi- and tri-axial) E-glass stitch-mat laminates in vinylester resin—to be as light as required and still strong and serviceable, especially if vacuum-bagged. Use the same scantlings as given in the standard sandwich rule. Determine the weights of glass cloth in the usual way. The actual finished thicknesses will be slightly less after vacuum-bagging (i.e., tighter layup and less excess resin). The resulting laminate will be lighter as well as stronger (see photo on p. 336).

FIBER ORIENTATION AND STITCH-MAT STYLES

Standard mat/roving laminates have roughly the same strength in all directions. Whatever the resin system, the +45,−45 and 0,90 bi-axial fabric styles have maximum strength only along their two respective axes. The strength on the diagonal (along the "bias") is lower. Accordingly, you should try to alternate +45,−45 and 0,90 styles. This produces a finished laminate with close to uniform strength in all directions.

GRAPHITE AND CARBON FIBER

This rule does not cover graphite or carbon-fiber reinforcements (really the same material—carbon—but graphite is, by convention, purer and somewhat stronger). Although carbon-fiber laminates have very high stiffness properties, they also have quite low elongation (i.e., they don't stretch much before they break). This makes carbon-fiber laminates brittle and subject to sudden, violent failure. Carbon/graphite laminates and reinforcement can offer real advantages at the cutting edge of design and construction. These laminates must, however, be carefully engineered and, again, are *not* covered in this rule.

FORMULA 6-17

The Hammer Puncture Test

Sandwich laminates, whether standard E-glass/polyester or S-glass/ Kevlar/ vinylester, all share one real problem: the thin skins are subject to puncture. It's easy to forget this and to play games with thin skins that seem otherwise strong enough. You must not do this. Always keep puncture resistance in mind. Small, light pleasure craft and high-performance racing vessels can skirt the edges of safety here—as long as the designer, the builder, and the boat's future crew are fully aware of the trade-offs. For all other boats, the bottom laminate—at least up to the bottom-laminate height (see Formula 4-2)—must be able to withstand the following puncture test. If it fails, you must increase skin thickness.

Make a sample of the bottom laminate panel you've specified. Use an ordinary carpenter's curved claw hammer, between 20 and 24 ounces (including handle) and from 12 to 13 inches long (0.57 to 0.68 kg and 304 to 330 mm). An average man (145 to 180 pounds [66 to 82 kg]) should be able to strike the outer skin of the panel fairly hard, repeatedly, with the round (nail-driving) end and see no penetration, no crushing of the core, and no delamination. (Surface marring/denting and crushing of the outer layers of glass is normal and acceptable.) The hammer should then be turned over—clawside down. With the sharp claw, strike the panel (in a previously untested area) with moderate force (less than fairly hard, but not lightly—a firm strike). The claw should not penetrate more than $\frac{1}{16}$ inch (1.6 mm) into the core. The skin should show no delamination from the core around the impact area. The inner skin and the core directly below the penetration must be unaffected. Laminates for workboats and for serious voyaging cruisers should allow no penetration into the core at all.

NOTE: Small boats with Sns under 1.0 will have outer-bottom laminate thicknesses of roughly 0.10 inch (2.5 mm) or less. Skins much thinner will usually not pass the hammer test. Here, you're squarely up against the puncture limits of sandwich construction. You must make the decision for each boat whether the type of craft and intended service can tolerate lower puncture resistance safely, or if you should pay the weight and cost penalty of additional thickness to the outer-bottom skin.

Weight of Sandwich Laminate

The weights of hand-laid-up sandwich laminates can be determined by referring to Table 4-16 and the method described in chapter 4. For vacuum-bagged layups and bi-axial style fabrics, and for standard balsa and sandwich cores, refer to the following tables.

TABLE 6-18 Vacuum-Bagged Laminate Densities (Weights)

Material	Glass Content by Weight	Density, lb./cu. ft. (kg/m³)	lb./sq. ft.. (kg/m²), 1-in. (1 mm) thick
Stitch-mat with balanced mat/bi-ply like CDM1815	40%	101 (1,618)	8.42 (1.62)
Stitch-mat with light mat like CM1603	45%	107 (1,714)	8.92 (1.71)
All bi-ply with no mat* like DB120	50%	112 (1,794)	9.33 (1.78)

*Must be used with epoxy resin only; vacuum-bagging strongly recommended.

TABLE 6-19 Standard Core Densities (Weights)

Material	Density, lb./sq. ft. (kg/m²)	lb./cu. ft. (kg/m³), 1-in. (1 mm) thick
Closed-cell foam	5.5 (88)	0.46 (0.088)
Closed-cell foam	8.0 (128)	0.66 (0.128)
Balsa	6.5 (104)	0.54 (0.104)
Balsa	9.5 (152)	0.78 (0.152)

FORMULA 6-20

Laminate Density (Weight) vs. Glass Content

You can estimate the density of any laminate from its glass content by weight:

lb./cu. ft. = 57.97 + 108.3 × percent of glass content, by weight (English)

kg/m³ = 917.3 + 1,754.4 × percent of glass content, by weight (Metric)

Or, you can estimate the glass content of a sample by measuring its specific gravity, as follows (see also appendix 4):

Percent of Glass Content, by Weight = (lb./sq. ft. – 57.97) ÷ 108.3 (English)

Percent of Glass Content, by Weight = (kg/m³ – 917.30 ÷ 1,754.4 (Metric)

Example:

If you made a sample of your proposed laminate and measured its specific gravity as 1.57, then its density is (1.57 × 62.4 lb./cu. ft.) or 97.9 lb./cu. ft. (1,570 kg/m³).

(97.9 lb./cu. ft. – 57.97) ÷ 108.3 = 0.368; use 37 percent glass content, by weight

(1,570 kg/m³ – 917.3) ÷ 1,754.4 = 0.372, use 37 percent glass content, by weight

SEVEN

Wood Construction Materials and Methods

*T*raditional wood construction—known as *plank-on-frame* or *carvel plank*—is the underpinning of almost every other method of boatbuilding. We'll use traditional plank-on-frame construction as the starting point for other more modern variants of wooden-boat construction. Before we can delve into the details of a plank-on-frame scantling rule, however, we have to know what this construction is. We also have to understand what that deceptively simple and common material, wood, is: what makes it up, how best to employ it, and how it's formed and fastened.

History and Development of Plank-on-Frame Construction

For more than 4,000 years, boats were fashioned of wood and virtually nothing else. Metal hulls are barely 150 years old; fiberglass goes back a mere 50 years or so. By comparison, we know the ancient Phoenicians and Egyptians were systematically building sizable vessels of wood in 2000 B.C. We can be

sure that boats were being formed from hollow logs or from logs lashed together for thousands of years before that. Indeed, the hollow-log boat or dugout canoe can be quite a handsome and sophisticated vessel. Even today, indigenous peoples around the world are still fabricating such craft using the same methods that were almost certainly employed during the Stone Age. As recently as 1992, a client stopped by my office with photos he had taken a few weeks before of an outrigger dugout canoe under construction in Micronesia. This boat was beautifully finished off, carefully crafted, and proven capable of long ocean passages.

LOG BOATS
If it will serve, it's still hard to improve on a log canoe. Log canoes are solid, can't leak, and—if large trees are available—can be sizable. Of course, here you run into one of the log boat's drawbacks. You can't very well make a 90-footer (27 m) with a 22-foot (6.7 m) beam from a single tree. Even if you

A log canoe starts with a single felled tree hewn to shape with hatchet and adz. It's been done just this way for more than 5,000 years. (Courtesy Stephen J. Winter)

The log canoe body takes shape. After that massive trunk is shaved down to this form, it's not so big. The builder is hewing the bow piece separately, which will be sewn in place. (Courtesy Stephen J. Winter)

The Polynesian outrigger log canoe finished, before paint or rig. If you look closely at the bow, you can make out the two lashings that hold this separate piece in place. (Courtesy Stephen J. Winter)

A log canoe's first sail. (Courtesy Stephen J. Winter)

could find a large enough tree for a 40-footer (12 m), think of the waste of lumber and the limitations of shape. Modern planked-up hulls are—I believe—a direct logical outgrowth of the log canoe and the centuries of effort that have gone into overcoming its limitations. You can only make a log boat substantially larger if you take a second log, split

it in half, shape it properly, and add it to the top of the sheer running full length. This is, in fact, just how the Chesapeake log canoes (still being raced today) evolved. Originally, these craft were based on ordinary American Indian dugout canoes. As the European settlers required larger vessels, they added second, third, and even fourth logs to build up the sides and to extend the length along the stem. Fifty- and sixty-footers (15 to 18 m) were fashioned this way, with individual logs fastened to each other along their edges with iron drift bolts or wooden dowels.

ANCIENT BOATS

The amazing thing is that this closely approximates the construction technique employed in ancient Greek vessels around 1000 and 1500 B.C. These craft were fashioned—in principle—exactly as the Chesapeake log canoes of today. The greatest difference in construction is that square tenons were used at the joints between logs (planks) rather than iron pins or dowels. As these ancient boats grew larger, they added internal framing as well to further strengthen the structure. Of course, the larger Chesapeake log canoes do much the same.

PLANK-ON-FRAME

All this works and—obviously—has worked for 4,000 years. Still, the drawbacks are obvious too: Boats built up from several carved-out logs need quite large trees, they're labor-intensive, there's considerable waste of timber that is simply hacked or chiseled away and burned, the larger boats need internal stiffening anyway. From here, it's easy to see how "modern" *plank-on-frame* or *carvel* construction came into being. The original single log—of the multilog boat—shrank in proportion to become the keel-stem-sternpost/backbone, the stiffening structure became regular frames or ribs, and the side logs became straightforward planks.

CARVEL AND CLINKER

This describes the standard plank-on-frame or carvel plank hull to a tee. Certainly, all manner of vessels have been constructed in exactly this fashion for at least 2000 years. There are essentially two main variants of the plank-fastened-to-frame method of hull construc-

tion. These depend on the approach taken to the planking itself. The most common now is smooth or carvel plank. Here, planks are neatly fitted over the frames (also called *ribs*) so that each plank butts smooth, tight, and even to its neighboring planks or to the keel. The alternative—and a most successful one, at that—is *lapstrake* or *clinker-built* hulls. In these craft, the planks are fastened to the frames shingle-fashion, overlapping and fastened to the plank below by a small percentage of the plank width. Both lapstrake and smooth plank-on-frame (carvel) construction work excellently and are employed regularly all over the world today. Smooth-plank, however, is the most common method and virtually the standard for most yachts longer than 20 feet (6 m). We will examine smooth-plank construction in detail in the following chapter (see photo on p. 337).

FIRST FASTENINGS

Another interesting consideration in traditional wooden-boat construction is the method of fastening used throughout the structure. We take metal fastenings for granted today; they're cheap and plentiful. This was not the case just 300 years ago, and was much less so the farther back you go. As a result, boats were fastened together with wooden dowels, mortise-and-tenon joints, and even sewn. Some of the most rugged and seaworthy vessels ever built had sewn planks and partially sewn framing. The fabled Viking ships were clinker-built, often with planks sewn to each other along the plank laps and sewn to the frames. Cord of carefully prepared animal sinew lasted well in this application. These oceangoing vessels were very light and flexible. They bent and gave in response to the forces imposed on them and so could take incredible punishment.

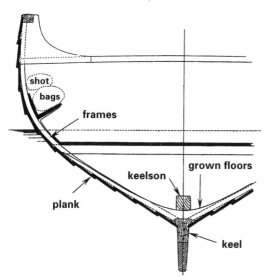

Typical lapstrake construction

Square-cut galvanized-iron boat nail. (Courtesy Tremont Nail Company)

NAILS FROM TREES

Nevertheless, sinew lashings and stitching need attention and renewal; they're also finicky and labor-intensive. Combine this with the gradually developing preference for smooth-planked boats (in larger sizes especially) and you can see how we arrived at what we would consider today more conventional fasteners. These were dowels hammered into holes of just the right diameter. Such dowels were largely employed to fasten planks to frames, but also could be used in most places metal screws and bolts are used today. Such dowel fastenings were called *trunnels* (literally, *tree nails*). After being driven home, a small wedge was hammered into a slot in the trunnel's top, locking it in place. Once the wood structure had swelled with water, these trunnels could only be removed by boring them out. The fact is that trunnels don't corrode and are inexpensive. If you want to take the time and learn how to use them, they make quite excellent fasteners to this day.

IRON SPIKES AND NAILS

For larger timbers (in larger boats particularly), iron spikes called *drifts* or *drift bolts* were preferred and are still used frequently in the built-up keel/backbone structure. With the advent of mass-produced galvanized-iron nails, trunnels were gradually replaced for planking. These old-fashioned, square-cut, hot-dip galvanized-iron boat nails still make strong, reasonably long-lasting fasteners. As far as I know, they are only available now from Tremont Nail Company in Wareham, Massachusetts.

BRONZE SCREWS

Today, almost all wooden boats are fastened with bronze (or Monel) wood screws, bronze keel bolts, and bronze strapping. Bronze, with its extremely high corrosion resistance in the marine environment, was always the fastener of choice whenever enough of it could be acquired inexpensively. It was, however, Captain Nat Herreshoff who invented the bronze wood screw as we know it today and first employed it for fastening planks to frames, as well as for fastening other structural components in the hull.

COPPER RIVETS, CLENCH NAILS, AND BOLTS

The alternative to the bronze (or Monel) wood screw (and to the trunnel) was the copper rivet. These are still used by some traditional builders, but they are not as long-

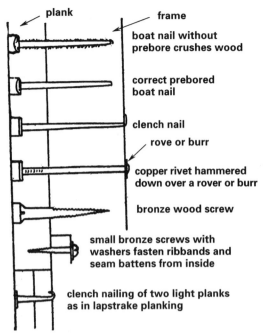

Labels in figure:
- plank
- frame
- boat nail without prebore crushes wood
- correct prebored boat nail
- clench nail
- rove or burr
- copper rivet hammered down over a rover or burr
- bronze wood screw
- small bronze screws with washers fasten ribbands and seam battens from inside
- clench nailing of two light planks as in lapstrake planking

Plank fasteners

lasting as bronze wood screws. This is because as the wood in the plank and frame swells, it stretches the rivet slightly and/or compresses the wood under the rivet's heads. Consequently, when the wood dries out and shrinks again, the rivet is a little loose. Repeated cycles exacerbate the situation. Furthermore, the softer copper required for proper heading of the rivet and the somewhat more slender diameter (compared to bronze screws) are less effective at restraining the plank from sliding on the frame (resisting shear)—one of the plank fastener's chief functions. Accordingly, the rule we use here generally applies to bronze wood screws as fasteners. (Copper rivets do make one of the best fastenings for plank laps in clinker construction.)

Another alternative is clench nails. These are similar to rivets but, rather than headed over a rivet ring, the clench nail is simply long enough to project through the inside of the frame or plank. The projecting inside end is bent over and hammered flat down inside, making it act much like a rivet. Again, this method is acceptable but suffers from all the drawbacks of copper rivets (although also excellent for fastening clinker plank laps).

Some builders advocate through-bolts for plank fastening. These too suffer from the wood expansion/contraction problems experienced by rivets and clench nails. Such bolts are the same diameter as bronze screws and are usually made of bronze. Accordingly, they're just as strong in shear. Although bronze through-bolts are workable for fastening planks to frames, I don't see any great advantages that would justify the extra work required to fit them.

ANNULAR-RING BOAT NAILS

There is a modern alternative to the bronze or Monel wood screw: the *annular-ring* (or *barbed-ring*) bronze or Monel boat nail. Often sold under trade names like Anchorfast or Gripfast, annular-ring boat nails are nearly as strong and long-lasting as bronze or Monel wood screws. The boat nail is usually somewhat less expensive and somewhat quicker and easier to install. We examine these as alternate fastenings.

Wood, the Wonder Material

Wood is a high-tech composite material. The fact that it was invented by nature and not humans, and that it's been around several hundred million years longer than we have, doesn't alter the fact that it's one of the strongest and most tenacious materials known—period. Stronger in tension and in bending than even high-tensile steel, wood is also just plain tougher than steel; pound for pound, it will absorb more energy or abuse before failure than even the best steels. A structure built of good-quality, dry, straight-grained wood will be lighter and stiffer than the same structure fabricated from nearly any other material—even including most modern, manmade, high-tech composite laminates like Kevlar/epoxy and carbon-fiber/epoxy. (The best carbon composites can exceed wood in strength in stiffness, pound for pound, but at considerably higher cost.)

AS STRONG AS SUGAR

Wood's secret is its internal structure. It is formed of fairly regularly aligned tubules of cellulose—literally, cells made up of sugar. (The suffix -ose means sugar.) These cellulose-fiber tubules account for about half of the wood by weight. They are formed of a linear polymer of high molecular weight in quite long chains, all of ordinary sugars. The individual cells are joined in fibers (usually averaging about $1/25$ inch [1 mm] long) held together with *lignin*, a tough resin-like binder that acts, in many ways, not unlike manmade resin in FRP construction. Lignin constitutes about one quarter to one third of the weight of wood. Interestingly, a large portion of the cellulose in wood is crystallized, which is what gives wood's polymers their high molecular weight. This also makes wood surprisingly water-resistant because the crystals do not absorb water.

The aligned tubule/fiber structure of wood is what makes it so light and stiff—it's a uni-directional composite. Most boatbuilding woods have densities between 24 and 44 lb./cu. ft. (384 to 706 kg/m³). On average,

this is half as dense as water. By comparison, steel is about 500 lb./cu. ft. (8,000 kg/m³), and even the relatively light metal, aluminum, is 168 lb./cu. ft. (2,690 kg/m³). Yet wood's individual fibers are nearly as strong as steel in tension, and are stronger than aluminum. What's more, the fibers in wood are arranged in patterns that resist crack propagation during high-load conditions. The hollow cellular structure of wood creates creases rather than cracks when local cell walls buckle. What's more, the individual tubules (bound in lignin) form crack-stoppers, which resist the spread of cracks during high stresses. Generally, compression creases in wood (rather than the cracks formed in metal or many manmade laminates) run a short way in from the surface and stop, which tends to be self-stabilizing. If more load is applied, new creases form, and often previous creases are not enlarged or extended. The result is that wood is exceptionally tough for its weight. It can absorb far more energy, pound for pound, before fracturing than metal or laminates.

STRUCTURE OF WOOD
The Outer Layer

The larger structure in wood is created by the way trees grow. In a mature tree, the outer bark is a layer of somewhat corky dead cells that protect the trunk from abrasion and that form an insulating layer. Just inside of the outer bark is—not surprisingly—the inner bark, which carries the nutrients prepared by the leaves to the living parts of the tree. Then, inside this layer is the *cambium,* a microscopic layer that gives birth to new cells in the bark and in the timber that form the majority of the core of a tree. Every year, as new cells form in the cambium, a new layer of wood, called an *annual ring,* is formed. The tree trunk grows outward, forming successive layers each year (or each growing season).

The Core

The core of the trunk is made of what we generally think of as ordinary wood. It too, however, is subdivided. The outermost layer (under the bark and cambium) is the *sapwood*. In fully grown softwood trees, this layer is roughly 1.5 inches thick. In hardwoods, however, the sapwood can encompass as much as 50 percent or more of the trunk's diameter. The sapwood is a mixture of dead and living cells that form tubes that store nutrients and transport sap. The *heartwood* is the balance of the core of the trunk. It's composed almost entirely of dead cells. Every year a new layer of sapwood gradually becomes heartwood, while a new layer of sapwood is born under the cambium. Broadly speaking, the sapwood and heartwood have the same physical strength. The problem with sapwood is that the living cells and the sap they contain are more prone to decay in moist environments, such as on boats.

INSULATING QUALITIES

Yet another advantage of wood's hollow-tubule structure and consequent low density is that it is an excellent insulator. Wood does not transmit heat or—of course—electricity. Wood, in and of itself, is also a fairly good insulator of sound. Metal, laminates, and even water transmit sound's compression waves far faster and with less energy loss. Thin, hard, dry membranes of any substance, however, can make excellent sounding boards. Wood is so good for this purpose that it is the material of choice in nearly all musical instruments. In modern, monocoque laminated hulls, this sounding-board effect can cause noise

difficulties. Additional sound-deadening insulation may be required in some areas, such as on the hull-bottom inside, over the propeller.

WOOD TYPES

Trees are subdivided into two major groups of species: *hardwoods* and *softwoods*. These names can be deceptive because some softwoods—such as Douglas fir and yellow pine—are physically harder than some hardwoods, such as basswood and cottonwood. In spite of this paradox, both the difference between and the definition of hardwood and softwood are precise.

Hardwoods

Hardwoods are trees that lose their leaves once a year in the fall—they are *deciduous*. Their leaves are generally broad and flat. Most hardwoods are *deliquescent*; that is, they have pronounced branching and forking in their trunks and main branches. This makes hardwoods excellent for finding and getting out natural crooks and bent timbers with the grain running along the curve for maximum strength. The botanical term for hardwood is *angiosperm*.

Softwoods

By contrast, softwoods are cone-bearing trees (*coniferous*) with needle- or scale-like leaves. Almost all softwoods keep their leaves throughout the year, with a few exceptions, such as the larch (also known as hackmatack or tamarack). Most softwoods are highly *excurrent*, which means that they grow with tall, straight, single trunks with minimal branching and forking. Even the main branches that support the smaller branches and leaves are proportionately thinner than main branches on hardwoods. Softwood-tree branches also project out from the trunk at sharper angles. Softwoods are generally poor sources for natural crooks, but their long straight trunks are excellent for spars, long planks, and long framing timbers, such as clamps and bilge stringers. The botanical term for softwood is *gymnosperm*.

Proper Structural Use of Wood

SLASH-SAWN TIMBER

Because of the annual-ring structure of uncut timber, cut boards and timbers behave very differently depending on how they're sawn. The wood grain you see in a plank is essentially the run of the wood-fiber tubules along the annual rings. If a log is placed in a sawmill and simply cut lengthwise from end to end in successive slices, the majority of the resulting plank will have hooked or curved grain. Such timber is called *slash-sawn* or *plain-sawn*. Slash-sawn lumber—although inexpensive—is inferior in strength because the grain does not run straight along its length. Worse still, slash-sawn lumber has an unavoidable tendency to cup and warp with changes in moisture content. Slash-sawn lumber should be used as little as possible (best not at all) in traditional wooden-boat construction. You can recognize it easily because of the clear hooked or swirled appearance of the grain on the face of the board.

RIFT-SAWN TIMBER

If care is taken with the cutting sequence and the rotation of the log as it is run through the sawmill, most of the lumber can be cut so that the grain runs fairly even and straight along its length. Essentially, this lumber is cut so that the resulting boards are

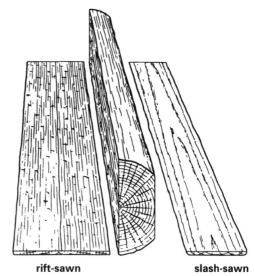

rift-sawn   **slash-sawn**

Rift- and slash-sawn boards

at roughly right angles to the center of the trunk (i.e., to the *pith*). Such lumber is called *rift-sawn* or *quarter-sawn* (from one of the standard methods of cutting up the log in quarters). This is proper boatbuilding lumber. You can recognize it easily because the grain will run fairly straight along the surface of the board. Not only is rift-sawn lumber stronger because of its straight grain, but it also has much less tendency to cup or warp. Swelling and contraction with changes in moisture content generally occur at approximate right angles to the board faces. Rift-sawn lumber is so useful that it goes under other names as well as quarter-sawn; the most common are *edge-grain*, *vertical-grain*, and *vertical-cut*.

TANGENTIAL AND RADIAL GRAIN DIRECTION

Even in a rift-sawn board, the orientation of the grain is critical. The *fiber direction* essentially runs along the length of the board, corresponding to up and down on the tree. The *radial direction* is the direction across the grain in the plank: if you returned the plank to the place in the log that it came from, the direction across the grain would point radially either directly in or directly out from the log's center. The *tangential direction* in the board runs with the grain across the tree—more or less tangent to the average of the annual rings in that board. Again, if you put the board back into the log that it came from, the tangential direction would be at right angles to the radial line and roughly along the annual rings.

There are three important things to keep in mind about the tangential and radial directions in a rift-sawn board. First, the board will swell and contract more in the tangential direction than in the radial direction. In most average woods, the change will be approximately twice as much in the tangential direction. Second, fasteners hold better when driven in at right angles to the tangential direction, or along the radial-axis direction. Third, the board will be considerably stiffer when the load is applied in the radial direction.

Considering these factors explains why steam-bent (and laminated) frames should be installed so that the radial direction of the frame stock's grain is at right angles to the hull. This makes it easier to bend the frame to begin with; it allows the frame to flex and give more before breaking; and the plank fasteners hold best driven in at right angles to the tangential direction as well. By the same token, planks are installed so the radial direction faces inboard and outboard and the tangential direction runs along the surface of the hull. Again, this ensures strong fastening as well as a tighter caulked joint between planks when the wood swells more in the tangential direction, squeezing the planks together.

NO FASTENING INTO ENDGRAIN
Of course, you can and will fasten into both sides or all sides of some framing in a hull. This is fine as long as you keep in mind the difference between the tangential and radial directions in each component. What you can never do is fasten into endgrain—into the end of a plank in the same direction as the grain/fibers. Not only would such fastenings have virtually no strength, but they will also accelerate water penetration into the timber, weakening it and creating rot pockets.

WOOD GRAIN IN THE REAL WORLD
Of course, wood is a natural material; it's not geometrically regular. Many boards, even though carefully rift-sawn, will have some hook or angle in the grain; sometimes in large timbers, straight edge-grain will actually be appar-

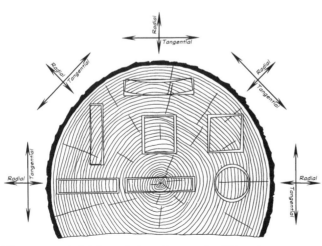

Warpage and shrinkage in boards sawn in different ways

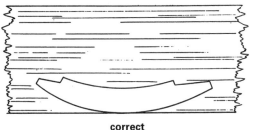

**correct
grain running roughly
along sawn timber**

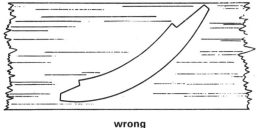

**wrong
grain running across
sawn timber**

Grain in sawn timbers

ent on two adjacent sides. Large timbers, such as keels in larger boats, will essentially be hewn from a substantial cross section of a single log. Such timbers can't properly be classified as either rift- or slash-sawn. The important thing is to try and use relatively clear straight-grained wood throughout, ideally from lumber that shows minimal hook in the board's surface and in which you can generally determine the radial and tangential directions.

UNI-DIRECTIONAL WOOD

It's also critical to remember that wood is a true uni-directional material. All significant strength runs along the grain. Strength across the grain is—as a rule—merely between 2 and 4 percent of the strength along the grain. Even a relatively small angle in the wood

grain, relative to the board it's in, will result in reduction in strength. For example, if you had a rift-sawn Douglas-fir board with an average grain angle of 4 degrees, the effective strength of the board would be 9,500 psi (65.5 mPa) in bending.

Grain angles of 4 and 5 degrees are quite common, and have notably less strength. You can see that it is important to employ the straightest-grain lumber practical (increasingly difficult in the current lumber economy), and to make allowances for the decrease in strength due to grain angle.

SMALLER TIMBERS LAST LONGER

It's a curious thing, but it seems clear to most people that larger, heavier framing members would be stronger and last longer than thinner lighter ones. This is, however (more often than not), incorrect when applied to boat structures. A 12.5-inch-square (300 mm) keel timber may well be physically stronger (in the absolute sense) than an 8-inch-square (200 mm) keel timber. Unfortunately, larger timbers usually have more defects (both from their sheer volume to contain such defects and because of their necessarily longer and more uneven drying/seasoning process). Additionally—and most important—timbers swell and contract in direct proportion to their dimensions.

Broadly speaking, timbers swell and contract about 1.2 percent of their radial dimension and 2.4 percent of their tangential dimension, cycling between 15 and 10 percent moisture content. Thus, the dry 12.5-inch (300 mm) keel timber will swell radially to 12.8 inches (307 mm); the 8-inch timber will swell to just 8.2 inches (205 mm). The larger changes in dimension (in larger timbers) inflict greater distorting loads on the structure as a whole. Furthermore, repeated swelling-shrinkage cycles open cracks in the timber itself and between other members fastened to that timber. This causes loose fastenings (structural weakness), and opens potential rot pockets. Wherever there are knots or sharp changes in grain direction, swelling-shrinkage-cycle crack creation within the timber is further aggravated.

For this reason, it's important to use the smallest timbers that are strong enough to stand up to the required loads. Larger structural members—although seemingly stronger in the short term—will actually weaken the structure over the long haul. Such unnecessarily heavy timbers will also accelerate decay.

WINTER-CUT LUMBER

Even considerations as subtle as the time of year a tree is cut affect longevity. Lumber that is felled in the winter or late fall has less sap in it than lumber felled at other times of the year. This means that there are fewer potential microorganisms in the wood (when it's cut) to promote decay. Furthermore, the relative humidity in cold weather is lower, which promotes faster drying in weather that's too chilly for much fungal action to begin. These factors make winter-cut wood less prone to decay and superior for boat construction.

MOISTURE CONTENT, SEASONING, AND STRENGTH

All wood in the atmosphere contains some small amount of water. This is measured as *moisture content*. Moisture content is taken as a percentage of weight of water relative to the weight of the wood bone dry—with no water at all. ("Bone dry" can only be achieved by heating in an oven.) For structural use, wood should be dried to well below 20-percent moisture content. The ideal average is 12 percent, the moisture-content standard for testing the properties of wood samples. The drying, also known as *seasoning*, can't be permitted to take place too quickly. If it does, the lumber dries unevenly, causing it to check, split, warp, and crack.

Essentially, as green fresh-cut lumber dries, all the free water in the cell cavities evaporates first. Only when this stage is reached does the water bound in the cell walls themselves just begin to dry out. This stage—the *fiber saturation point*—is around 30 percent moisture content. It is important to use timber that has been gradually and carefully dried or seasoned below the saturation point, to well under 20 percent moisture content. Not only does low moisture content reduce the chance of decay, but drier timber is also stronger than moisture-laden timber.

Although well-seasoned timber in a dry environment has a moisture content of about 12 percent (to a low of about 6 or 8 percent in extremely dry conditions), wood in traditional plank-on-frame boats has a moisture content of about 15 percent. This is a fair average for well-painted wood in the underwater planking and framing of a hull. At 15 percent moisture content, strength in bending is roughly reduced to about 65 percent of strength at 12 percent moisture content. Strength in compression is reduced to about 78 percent of strength at 12 percent moisture content.

KILN-DRYING AND BOG SEASONING

Kiln-dried lumber is perfectly acceptable, but only if the kiln-drying has been done gradually and at relatively low temperatures, under properly controlled conditions. Air-dried lumber usually takes longer to dry (to season) than kiln-dried; consequently, air-dried lumber develops fewer checks and cracks. If you can get it, air-dried lumber seasoned slowly is superior; but again—in the current lumber economy—such timber is difficult and expensive to obtain.

Interestingly, some of the finest boat lumber is from logs that have been "pickled" in the bottom of swamps and bogs. These logs—aged in the swamp for years—have all their natural sap and fluids leached out. When they're dredged up, sawn, and air-dried, the result is timber that is as strong, hard, and rot-resistant as it's possible to get.

THE BEST LUMBER SPECIFICATIONS

The best lumber you can use in a boat is clear (knot-free), straight-grained (no swirls or bends), rift-sawn, winter-cut, air-dried heartwood. Some hardwoods obtained to these specifications—like white oak and hickory—are so hard and tough that they will literally bend heavy iron spikes driven into them with sledges. There was a time when a sizable industry revolved around harvesting and seasoning such timbers. Today, however, wood like this is nearly impossible to locate. Usually, if you want this degree of quality in your lumber, you have to go and get it out yourself, which means finding and selecting the best trees; paying the property owners for permission to cut and transport the felled trees (cut in late fall or winter); arranging for a good sawmill to rift-saw the logs to your specifications (and making allowance for the smaller size of these boards after drying-shrinkage); and finding a proper location to air-dry your lumber for the required months or years. All this can be a satisfying undertaking, but is not generally commercially realistic. In practice, you'll simply have to compromise on the best commercially available lumber you can locate. Today, ideal boat lumber is a dream; you simply have to make do with what you can find.

HAND-HEWN TIMBERS LAST LONGER

Another factor that has changed over the years is that timbers hand-hewn with chisel, axe, and adze are less prone to decay than sawn timbers. In the old days, most large timbers were only roughly sawn to size and then trimmed to shape by craftsmen with well-sharpened hand tools. The power saws and grinders used today chew up the woodgrain at the cut, leaving the mangled tubules and cell edges much more prone to fungal attack. Again, except in rare instances where old-time shipwrights can be employed, this is not a practical approach for most modern builders.

DECAY AND BORERS

Because wood is basically sugar, it makes quite a delectable treat for numerous forms of life. The most common of these are the varied fungal growths that live off the wood, digesting it as they grow. Such decay is generally (and inexplicably) termed *dry rot*, even though there's nothing dry about it. (It can only occur in wood with a fairly high moisture content—generally more than 20 percent; at the same time, it can't occur in wood wholly submerged in salt water, which is poisonous to fungus.) The other common form of attack is from marine borers, such as teredo worms, and other boring insects, such as carpenter ants and termites.

A third, less well-known form of attack is a byproduct of galvanic action. If, for instance, too much zinc is installed on a bond-

Decay caused by stray current at a through-hull fitting.

ing system, it can raise the negative potential of any attached metal hardware to more than 400 millivolts. This overprotection produces ions in seawater that can manufacture alkaline byproducts that destroy the lignin holding wood fibers together. It is sometimes termed *alkali rot*. Most often, it shows up as a whitish or yellowish, foamy, soapy gunk around metal fittings.

PRESERVATIVES AND SEALERS

Extensive use of preservatives in traditional boat construction is not common. Among other things, most preservatives contain toxic chemicals that are subject to government regulation. Nevertheless, the U.S. Navy and several production builders found—during and immediately after World War II—that preservatives can effectively reduce decay. Lumber that has been pressure-treated with preservative gives the best results here; however, painted-on preservatives are still useful. Copper-based formulations are most common. Copper-naphthenate solutions such as Cuprinol seem to offer the best trade-off between price, effectiveness, and ease of application. These preservatives accept most paints without discoloration or adhesion problems.

Kerosene and Linseed Oil

A moderately effective traditional preservative is one or two coats of painted kerosene. This is slightly toxic to fungal growth and helps seal the wood to moisture. Large timbers also can be coated with a couple of coats of boiled (not raw) linseed oil. Probably the best treatment is a coat or two of kerosene followed by a brushed-on coat of a 50/50 mixture of kerosene and boiled linseed oil, finished with a coat of boiled linseed oil only. This procedure seems to drive some of the remaining moisture out of the wood, kill some remaining fungal spores, and slow down water penetration and evaporation, thereby slowing changes in moisture content. The greatest benefit is to reduce swelling and contraction in larger timbers, thus reducing cracks and checks. Such cracks—as we've seen—weaken the timber and form vulnerable points for fungal attack. Some builders, for the same reason, paint all the large backbone timbers (e.g., keel, stem, and horn timber) and floor timbers with red lead as well.

The old standby for coating, protecting, and treating unpainted wood on deck, in the cabin, and wherever other coatings were not used is (by volume) equal parts turpentine, linseed oil, and carnauba wax (also known as Brazil wax). Mix the ingredients thoroughly and shake well before every application. Simply rub this into the wood with a soft cloth and, after an hour or two, wipe off any excess. Repeat as necessary to saturate thoroughly. Larger timbers can be painted with a brush and then rubbed down.

BEDDING JOINTS: LUTING

The mating or *faying* surfaces of all bolted joints in timbers (and between structural members) must be sealed and bedded. This was formerly referred to as *luting*, and was traditionally done using red- or white-lead paint, hot tar, marine glue, or—most commonly—a luting mixture. Luting mixture was created from one-part oil-based bedding putty and half-part white lead (by volume). This was stirred together with a few drops of boiled linseed oil until it had about the same consistency as soft butter or very heavy cream. Finally, a small amount of turpentine or a sprinkling of red lead was stirred in (just enough to turn the mixture a faint pink). Instead of traditional luting compound, today I would recommend using a highly elastic adhesive-sealant marine bedding compound, such as 3M-5200.

Care should be taken to seal the heels (i.e., exposed endgrain) of all framing everywhere. Red lead alone works, but brushing on a few coats of kerosene/linseed-oil mixture before the red lead is even better.

Seams and joints in cabin, cockpit, and other deck structures were usually bedded on white lead or additionally on cotton caulking strands saturated with white lead. Again, for permanent structures, I recommend 3M-

Luting a deadwood timber before installation. 3M-5200 is my preferred modern method. Traditional luting mixture can be used. Another traditional method is Irish felt bedded in roofing cement (tar). Luting is also sometimes termed "gacking up." (Courtesy Kortchmar & Willner)

5200 today. If the item is to be unbolted and removed occasionally, use one of the polysulfide, nonadhesive polyurethanes or other non-adhesive sealants.

MODERN SEALANTS AND CAULKING COMPOUNDS

These days, sealants and caulking compounds abound. Most of the common brands work well, but there are differences—different types, different purposes. Boat Life-Caulk is a polysulfide-based sealant that will cure under paint or water. It gets fairly tacky in about two days and cures totally in about five. Sikaflex is a polyurethane—No. 231 is primarily a bedding compound with low adhesive properties; No. 420 is primarily an adhesive; No. 241 is both a sealant and an adhesive. All the Sikaflexes cure under paint or water. 3M-5200 is also an adhesive sealant and it, too, cures under water. Although not truly a glue, it has the highest adhesive prop erties of the sealants—so high, in fact, that (with bolts pulled for removal) 12,000-pound

(5,400 kg) keels have been temporarily held in place by 3M-5200 alone! This is the drawback to 5200: heaven help you if you have to remove a fitting bedded in it!

Woolsey's Dolphinite is the flip side of the coin. Dolphinite won't cure under paint or water, it's not a good adhesive, and it never really cures at all (it is always soft or tacky). It is, however, a fine bedding and sealant with the great plus that you can remove the fittings you used it on fairly easily. All these products are suited for use under water as well as on deck. Silicone sealants won't cure under paint or water and they're *not* intended or suitable for *any* underwater work. They are good, however, for sealing ports, edgings, deck hardware, and the like.

INTERIOR PAINTING?

One of the great controversies in traditional boat construction is whether to paint the hull interior. Some builders and many reference sources strongly advise that you leave the interior of planking and frames unpainted, except for a possible coat of kerosene and/or boiled linseed oil. Other builders and references advocate painting every surface in the interior as well as the exterior. I don't know which school of thought is correct. I have personally owned two plank-on-frame hulls (both more than 20 years old) that had been painted inside; they showed no more evidence of rot than unpainted hulls of similar age. I suspect it is not too important one way or the other, as long as good building practice has been followed throughout, and as long as the interior wood has been otherwise coated with preservative or with kerosene and boiled linseed oil.

SALTING

Salt water is unfriendly to dry rot. Wood submerged in salt water will not rot, although it can be attacked by borers. With this in mind, many traditional craft (e.g., coasting schooners, wooden tugs, and heavy yachts) were fitted with *salt boxes* or *salt bags*. These receptacles were sited at strategic locations along the inside of the hull with the intention that they provide a continual salt-water drip, thus discouraging decay. Although salting has adherents, I don't believe it is markedly effective, and it can cause problems with electrical systems and metal fittings. I don't recommend it.

VENTILATION

Finally, it is important to consider ventilation of the structure when building any wooden boat. Where air can pass freely, the moisture content of wood will remain under 15 percent and rot has great difficulty taking hold. The most common locations for so-called dry rot are under the corners of the sheer, behind the clamp, under and behind the coach roof and cockpit carlins, and in the under-deck corners of stems and transom knees. All these locations are fairly high up and under the deck. The heat of the sun warms the wood, while condensation (freshwater) collects in cracks and crevices. If air can't circulate, this warm, moist, freshwater environment is heaven for fungus. During construction, you must take every step possible to promote free circulation of air in these areas and to build in avenues for collected water to drain away into the bilge.

EIGHT

Wood Design Considerations

*A*ll traditional plank-on-frame construction has fundamentally the same structure. A keel forms the backbone of the hull. This backbone curves up forward to form a *stem*, and projects up aft in a *sternpost*. The sternpost is the simplest form of aft-end backbone extension. On a deep-keel boat, where the hull sweeps aft in a longer run to a transom, the sternpost runs roughly vertically up from the keel, for a relatively short distance, to a *horn timber*, which in turn runs horizontally aft to the transom. The transom itself is fastened to the horn timber with a *transom knee*.

Keel and Backbone

PLANK KEELS

Keels come in a wide variety; the possibilities are as endless as the hull forms they serve. Small boats may have simple plank keels, literally from a single plank. Quite large powerboats can have relatively thin flat keels, built up from multiple timbers. These too are called plank keels (because they resemble a flat plank, even though they are built up from several). Even fair-sized sailboats can have plank keels, either penetrated with a centerboard case or with a ballast keel and deadwood bolted to its bottom.

DEEP KEELS AND KEELSONS

Deep keels are commonly found on larger, heavy-displacement workboats, as well as other vessels. These keels are considerably deeper in cross section than they are wide and also are usually built up of several timbers. Still larger displacement vessels usually have an additional keel/backbone member called the *keelson*. This is a longitudinal member running along the keel, bolted down on top of the floors and into the keel. The keelson is used on heavy boats with Sns of 9 or higher.

DEADWOOD

Where the keel projects far down into the water, below the body of the hull, it is built up to great depth with numerous timbers called the *deadwood*. The deadwood is usually

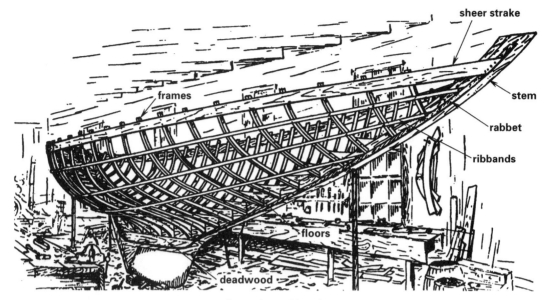

Bow view of framing

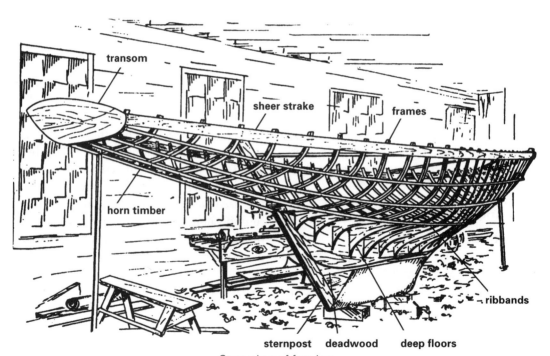

Stern view of framing

roughly the same thickness as the rest of the keel, unless it is a separate component bolted onto the bottom of a wide-plank keel.

RABBETS AND KEEL BATTENS

Deep keels are usually rabbeted to take the *garboard strake* (i.e., the planks running along the keel), as is the stem. Alternately, it is common practice to make up the keel of two pieces: the lower external piece is called the *keel*, the upper internal piece is called the *keel batten*. (Sometimes—and confusingly—this is also referred to as the *keelson*, the *keel apron*, or the *hog* or *hog timber*.) In this case, the keel batten and the keel, as a unit, together form the keel proper. Plank keels are usually fabricated this way, with a keel and keel batten. The keel batten may well be a larger and heavier timber, with a cross-sectional area greater than the external keel in this construction.

LAMINATED KEELS

Large keel timbers (and large timbers in general) are a problem because of the substantial dimensional changes with variations in moisture content. Although some classification societies' scantling rules call for very heavy timbers in the keel, I believe this is counterproductive. An excellent way to avoid the problem of swelling in large timbers, however, is to laminate the keel from smaller stock using epoxy glue. Then coat and seal the entire keel structure with epoxy. The individual smaller timbers generate fewer dimensional changes; they are

easier to work with and are less expensive to obtain; any size and shape required can be built up; and coating with epoxy holds the moisture content almost perfectly stable—thus, there is no expansion or contraction problem. Laminated keels should not be made of oak, which contains acids that don't bond as well to epoxy as some other woods. Yellow pine and Douglas fir are excellent for laminated keels and stems.

THIN TIMBERS FOR EPOXY LAMINATIONS

It is important not to epoxy-laminate large timbers from individual layers that are too thick themselves. Such larger timbers—even saturated with epoxy—will swell and shrink enough to cause structural and glue-bond

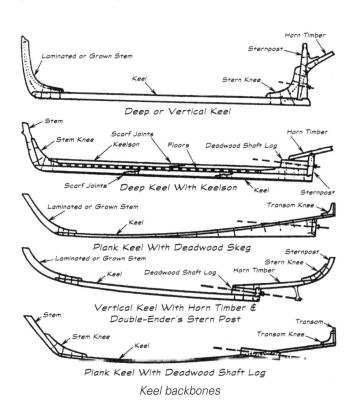

Keel backbones

problems. Generally, you should not laminate wood thicker than $2^{1}/_{2}$ inches (60 mm). The most stable structure and the longest life will be achieved if lumber no thicker than $1^{1}/_{2}$ inches (38 mm) is used.

HEAVY KEEL TIMBERS ADD LITTLE STRENGTH

It is important to keep in mind that a large heavy keel, in and of itself, does not add any great strength or rigidity to the hull as a whole. The strength and stiffness of the entire hull is generated by the rough box-section girder, which is formed by *the entire hull as a unit*. The deck, sheer clamp and shelf, planking, bilge stringers, and keel all work in concert. Doubling or tripling the cross-sectional area of a keel adds no more strength to the structure as a whole than, say, arbitrarily doubling or tripling the deck thickness or the plank. Avoid the common tendency to use massive keel timbers.

LEAD BALLAST STRUCTURAL KEELS

Another option for large keels in sailboats with lead outside ballast is to form part of the keel/backbone structure out of a long, shallow lead keel-ballast casting. No wooden keel structure at all is required in this area. Fore and aft of the ballast keel, the wood keel and deadwood can be fastened and scarfed to the lead keel just as if it were timber. These structural ballast keels should be cast from lead with about 2 percent antimony content. This is stronger than a solid-oak keel of the same dimension, without any of timber's dimensional instability. The lead can be carved and machined for the plank rabbet and drilled and taped for floor bolts. This is an exceptionally strong and long-lasting arrangement.

The Stem

The stem almost always has a pronounced curve to it, often approaching a 90-degree bend at the forefoot. There are several ways to build up such a timber.

NATURAL CROOK STEMS

In small craft, the traditional method is to find a grown natural crook that would approximate the desired stem shape in size and curvature. The stem is then hewn from the crook as a single piece. Somewhat larger hulls can have their stems fashioned from two or three natural crooks sawn to shape and bolted together.

BUILT-UP STEMS

Natural crooks are difficult to locate (more so with every passing year, it seems). Accordingly, most medium- to large-sized boats have built-up stems fabricated from several sawn timbers; usually two or three timbers are sufficient. If two timbers are used, the lower stem timber with the maximum bend is called the *stem knee* or *anchor stock*. When three timbers are used, the lowest and aftermost timber is called the *gripe*. The next timber up (usually with the maximum curvature) is the *stem knee*. In all cases, the uppermost timber is termed the *stem*, even though all these timbers together form the stem proper.

These timbers are notched together with carved hook joints or locking keys and are carefully through-bolted. Bolt diameter, key, and nib size should be proportioned approximately the same as for scarfed timbers of similar dimensions (see chapter 10). All are trimmed and dressed to the exact cross-sectional shape of the stem, which frequently varies along its length. For these built-up stems, be sure to cut each individual timber so the woodgrain runs along the majority of its length, not across it.

LAMINATED STEMS

Built-up stems are excellent but require heavy and labor-intensive construction. My preference is for laminated stems, made using epoxy glue and coated with epoxy. Traditionally, such laminated stems were built up with the laminations running longitudinally athwartships (like a laminated frame rotated to face the bow). Theoretically, this is the correct and strongest method. Such laminating jobs are time-consuming, however. A jig has to be formed, numerous clamps prepared, and the whole procedure requires several hands and much wood.

Alternative Laminated Stems

I have had very good results using stems that were laminated up from layers running fore-n-aft, made approximately like a sawn frame that has been rotated around to face forward, only with more layers. These fore-n-aft laminated stems are fashioned from three to six layers each, sawn to shape, with butts well staggered. The advantage here is that sawing the flat plank stock to shape is quick, simple work. The clamping job is also easier, with most of the clamping pressure coming from annular-ring boat nails and bronze screws that are left in place, unless they interfere with finishing off the timber. The folks at Covey Island Boatworks introduced me to this stem construction. Although theoretically weaker than standard horizontally laminated stems, I have found these fore-n-aft laminated stems to be more than strong enough.

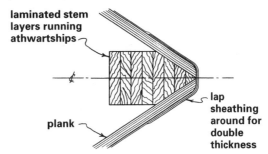

Traditional stem of a plywood boat with exterior hull sheathing

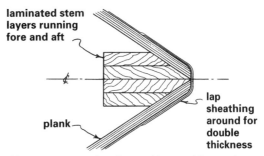

Alternate stem of a plywood boat with exterior hull sheathing

Frames and Floors

FLOORS

Frames are fastened to the keel, stem, horn timber, and sternpost with floors. First, floors are cut from fairly heavy plank and are bolted down into the top of the keel. The floors are then fastened fore-n-aft into the frames. Floors also can be bolted down centered on top of the frames. Such floors are screw-fastened into the frames from above, as well as bolted to the top of the keel. On vessels with hollow garboards, floors may be quite deep, especially in the run—at the deadwood, sternpost, and horn timber. These floors are often notched around the backbone timbers, and may fasten into the sides of the sternpost and deadwood. Floors like this are often made in two sections. The lower section is really three separate, roughly triangular pieces, each fastened into the side sternpost or horn timber. The upper section is a crosspiece like a normal floor or frame across the bottom. It runs from port to starboard and is fastened to the frames. This upper crosspiece is sometimes referred to as the *strongback*.

Floors can also be made of metal, see pages 172–74.

STEAM-BENT FRAMES

Steam-bent frames are generally superior for round-bilge hulls. This is because the grain in the frame runs smoothly and evenly in the direction of the frame throughout its length. (Laminated frames are nearly as strong and resilient as steam-bent frames, but they require more labor.) By contrast, the grain in sawn frames almost always runs at off angles to the direction of the frame itself. As a consequence, sawn frames in round-bilge hulls are only about half as strong as steam-bent or laminated frames.

Large Steam-Bent Frames

Steam-bent frames more than 2 inches (50 mm) thick athwartships are quite difficult to bend, however. The common solution is to split the frame athwartships and to bend it in place in two sections. For example, a 3-by-3-inch (76 × 76 mm) frame would be bent in two layers 3 inches (76 mm) fore-n-aft and $1^1/_2$ inches thick (38 mm) athwartships. It is not necessary to glue the two layers together; they are simply clamped in place to the ribbands and screwed together, just enough to hold them when the clamps are removed. The

Steamed-oak frames can literally be twisted in knots. (Courtesy North River Boatworks)

regular plank-fastening screws are long enough to pass through both frame layers, thus ensuring that the double frame acts as a unit.

Some people worry about rot occurring between the two layers of a steam-bent frame. However, this does not seem to be a problem. I have inspected several vessels more than 50 feet (15 m) long that were built with split-bent frames. These boats were all more than 30 years old and, although they had rot in several locations, the one place there wasn't any was between the split frame halves!

Steam-Bent Frame Bevels

Another advantage to steam-bent frames is that they can be twisted against the ribbands at the same time they are bent in place. This means steam-bent frames can be cut square all around and still take the correct bevel automatically during the bending process (if the bevel is not too severe). Such twisted-in-place bent frames make an angle where they meet the floors, which are flat and run square athwartships. Accordingly, the floors are beveled and/or shimmed out where they meet these frames to make a tight fit.

SAWN FRAMES IN BOW AND STERN OF ROUND-BILGE HULLS

There are places where sawn frames make sense and can save labor in round-bilge hulls. In the bow, where the hull is roughly vee-shaped, the frames are nearly straight. Here, sawn frames can be cut so the grain runs close to lengthwise along the frame. Ideally, you would get these frames from boards with grain that had a natural sweep similar to the desired curvature. Such frames are almost as strong as steam-bent frames. At the same time, up in the bow, the bevel is most severe and it may not be possible to bend it in here. Sawn frames can be cut and then dressed to the exact bevel, making a better fit and still mating the floors at right angles. Similarly, at the transom in hulls with pronounced reverse curve (particularly on hulls with wine-glass transoms), sawn frames can be gotten out

more easily than bent frames. In this application, though, the sawn frames are weaker than bent frames would be. Still, it is nearly impossible to bend in frames near the transom on a hull with tight hollow garboards, deep deadwood, and tumblehome in the upper portion of the transom. Sawn frames may be the only practical solution (and a perfectly acceptable one). Usually, single-sawn frames are used.

Sawn Frames on Round-Bilge Hulls

When sawn frames are used throughout on a round-bilge hull, they should be double the size—fore-n-aft—of bent frames and essentially made up of two frames side by side, with the butt joints in each sawn section or *futtock* well staggered. Such frames are called *double-sawn frames*. Very large heavy craft with Sns over 10 often use sawn frames of the same

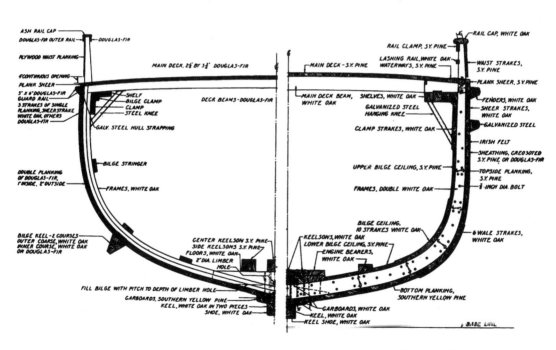

Section through steam-bent frame workboat

Section through double-sawn frame tug

doubled fore-n-aft dimension, but divided into three fore-n-aft layers or subframes (i.e., *triple-sawn frames*). With all the futtock butts well staggered, this is slightly stronger still, and the individual timbers are smaller and easier to handle during fashioning.

Sawn Frames on Hard-Chine Hulls

On hard-chine hulls, sawn frames work well all around. Compared to round-bilge hulls, hard-chine hulls have fairly straight frames from keel to chine and from chine to sheer. As a result, the grain in a sawn frame on hard-chine hulls runs fairly straight along its length. Hard-chine hulls almost always are built with sawn frames, although some hard-chine hulls can have pronounced curve in the forefoot and in the topsides at the bow. In these locations, it is occasionally sensible to use bent frames. In hard-chine hulls, the sawn frames need only have joints at the chine. Here, the bottom and topsides futtocks are joined with gussets. Frames like this are called *single-sawn frames*.

MORTISING FRAMES INTO THE KEEL

One of the oddest practices in wooden-boat construction is mortising the heels of frames into the keel. Mortising is exacting work and—if done at all—must be performed on both sides of the keel for each frame. The mystery is that some of the finest builders throughout history have followed this practice. All I can tell you is that it is always wrong! Never notch the keel for the heels of frames—ever! The drawbacks are numerous:

- The notches weaken the keel.
- The notches form pockets for fungal growth and decay to start.
- The notches create numerous small corners that can split during swell/contraction cycles.

- The notches add absolutely no strength to the frame or to its attachment to the keel.
- The construction of the notches interferes with proper drainage, through the limbers in the bilge.
- The notches consume substantial amounts of time in fabrication—wasted time.

The floors and the floors alone transmit the loads from the frames to the keel (and across the boat). Indeed, it is possible to cut the frames off completely above the keel, fastening them to the floors alone. This, in fact,

Garboard strake removed reveals frames notched into the keel—bad! Many rot pockets were found. Note the feeble little notches in each frame bottom. These were to form limbers but were quickly clogged.

is excellent construction practice. The frames can be cut off at a height of one frame siding (see chapter 9) above the keel. The limber can then be cut into the very outside corner of the floor, where it meets the garboard. This ensures the best possible drainage in the bilge.

Planking

Planking presents more options and varieties than any other portion of the hull structure, including single-carvel; double-carvel (usually called double-plank); strip-plank; lapstrake-, clinker-, or clench-plank; double-diagonal; Ashcroft; batten-seam; and herringbone-bottom. The scantling rule that follows primarily applies to carvel plank; however, adjustments are given for other planking methods.

CARVEL PLANK
Carvel plank is traditional single-plank-on-frame construction, with the planking made watertight by caulking and by the natural swelling of the planks themselves. The planks are laid on running fore-n-aft. This method requires moderate skill. Carvel plank is one of the easiest planking methods to repair because each plank can be unscrewed, removed, and replaced without disturbing other planks or the interior.

DOUBLE PLANK OR DOUBLE-CARVEL PLANK
Double plank is two layers of fore-n-aft carvel plank laid on so that the seams of the inside layer fall approximately in the middle of the plank on the outside layer. Double-plank construction requires high levels of skill because all the planks on both layers must fit very closely. The benefit is that double-plank

hulls tend to be tighter and smoother (to show fewer seams) than single plank. Traditionally, the two plank layers were laid on each other with a thick layer of shellac. This forms a somewhat flexible adhesive that is also reasonably water-resistant.

STRIP-PLANK
Strip-plank construction is strong and tight. It has almost no tendency to open up and leak when dried out. It is similar in principle to ordinary plank-on-frame, but individual planks are much narrower—square or almost square strips that are edge-nailed and glued to each other along their full length. Ordinary, traditional strip-plank construction requires less skill than any other planking method; however, the numerous edge-fastened strips are tedious and laborious to install. The solution is to arrange for a large, well-organized strip-plank crew. A team of seven (i.e., three on each side and one supervisor) can strip up a 40-footer (12 m) in just a few days. Modern wood-epoxy strip-plank construction is—by a slim margin—my construction method of choice for one-off hulls. It is even easier than

Stripping up a wood-epoxy strip-plank hull.
(Courtesy Alan Salisch)

traditional strip-planking and is dimensionally stable and exceptionally rot-resistant (nearly but not quite rot-impervious). Strip-planking is not as easy to repair as carvel planking, but it is easier than lapstrake and repairs usually can be made without disturbing the interior.

LAPSTRAKE (CLINKER- OR CLENCH-BUILT) PLANK

Lapstrake hulls are generally lighter than comparable hulls made single- or double-plank or strip-planked. The lapstrake seams have much less tendency than carvel plank to leak when the hull dries out and is subsequently relaunched. This combination of lightness and staying tight when dry made lapstrake the favorite choice for small launches (see photo on p. 338).

Lapstrake takes more skill than carvel plank. It takes great patience, especially to form the plank-lap joints as they run into the stem and sometimes into the transom or sternpost. Another drawback is that the wide planking stock required for larger hulls is nearly impossible to find today. For this reason, plywood lapstrake planking is used on

Lapstrake fishing vessels on the beach in Kittery, Maine. (Courtesy Alan Salisch)

some larger powerboat hulls. It is important, however, to keep in mind the lower longitudinal strength of plywood in this application.

DOUBLE-DIAGONAL PLANK

Double-diagonal plank is two layers of plank laid on the hull at roughly between 35 and 45 degrees to the fore-n-aft axis. In both traditional and cold-molded construction, it is one of the strongest constructions for its weight; however, it is labor-intensive and more difficult to repair than carvel. In traditional construction, double-diagonal planking requires great skill.

Cold-Molded Double- (or More) Diagonal Plank

The modern variant of double-diagonal plank is two *or more* layers of plank laid on at 35 to 45 degrees to the horizontal axis. If three or more layers are used, every third layer will run fore-n-aft. All the layers are glued together and coated with epoxy. This forms an exceptionally light, stiff, monocoque hull shell that is totally watertight. Although somewhat less skill is required to build cold-molded double-diagonal than traditional double-diagonal, it still requires considerable know-how and patience. When three or more layers are used, labor can be very time-consuming indeed. Unlike cold-molded strip-plank, multiple-diagonal planking does not lend itself as well to large planking crews working quickly.

ASHCROFT PLANK

Ashcroft plank is double-diagonal planking with both diagonal layers running the same way, but overlapped as in double-carvel planking. The planking starts at the keel and angles up and back to the sheer at roughly 40 degrees to vertical. This planking system had great popularity for a time in Great Britain, but I don't see any advantages to it with modern construction materials and methods.

BATTEN-SEAM PLANK

Batten-seam plank is ordinary carvel plank with small backing strips—the *battens*—running behind each seam. This helps reduce leaking in dried-out hulls on relaunching. Batten-seam plank is almost universally used on hard-chine hulls. The individual battens must be carefully lined up and notched into the frames so the planks can lie smooth and flush on top of them and the frames together. A fairly high level of skill is required. As with Ashcroft planking, batten-seam construction has been outdated by modern materials and methods. If the hull sections are suitable, plywood can be used. If not, then the hull can be planked in either ordinary carvel-plank or strip-plank.

PLYWOOD PLANK

Plywood plank is very attractive to the amateur. It offers rapid planking of large surfaces with minimum measuring and fitting. Plywood planking is neither a magic bullet nor a cure-all, however. Plywood cannot be made to take compound curvature. Accordingly, most traditional hulls *cannot* be planked up with sheet plywood. Hulls must be specifically designed (or specially modified in shape) to accept sheet plywood. The hull surface must be cylindrically or conically developed, which avoids compound curvature.

Furthermore, plywood is made up of layers of veneer with the grain running at right angles. This drastically increases plywood's strength across the grain because there is no true "across the grain." Unfortunately, only half the grain runs in any given direction,

which roughly halves the strength of plywood in the fore-n-aft direction. For instance, Douglas-fir plank has a tensile strength along its length (a modulus of rupture) of 12,200 psi (84 mPa); however, Douglas-fir plywood has a strength of just 5,570 psi (38.3 mPa).

When subject to repeated high strain (i.e., deflection) in a wet environment, internal defects—in the individual layers and between the layers—can cause local internal delamination, which is often undetectable from the outside. However, these defects substantially reduce the strength of the plywood planking. When highly loaded again, this region can fail dramatically. Accordingly—and contrary to common belief—plywood planking should not be made too much lighter than ordinary carvel planking would be on the same hull.

HERRINGBONE-BOTTOM PLANK

On hard-chine hulls, the bottom planking can be made of relatively heavy boards laid on diagonally, herringbone fashion, with the planks starting at the keel and angling back at about 45 to 55 degrees aft. Herringbone planking is usually nailed in place and is quick and easy to install. It will work with most hull surfaces, including those with compound curvature (unlike plywood). Herringbone bottoms are excellent for traditional hard-chine hulls. The topsides of such hulls are usually carvel-plank or strip-plank; however, they also can be lapstrake, which looks quite handsome and saves weight. On cold-molded hard-chine hulls, strip-planks on the bottom can be laid on herringbone fashion. This is sometimes easier and quicker than laying the strips on longitudinally along the bottom, and is just as strong. Some builders cross-plank V-bottom hulls with no angle—with the planks running square athwartships.

Decks

Decks and deck beams must be quite strong. Not only do they have to support the weight of crew and gear, but they also have to be able to withstand the weight of green water breaking aboard in rough weather. Even more important, the deck forms the upper portion of the hull-structure box-girder. If the deck is too weak, the entire hull will flex or pant.

LAID DECK

Traditional decks either were constructed of laid planks carefully caulked or were strip-planked, edge-nailed, and glued, often with caulking run into grooves in the upper third of the plank seams. Both of these systems were prone to leaks because the individual planks still shrink and expand repeatedly with changes in moisture—these changes are regular, pronounced, and frequent on decks. Decks can be exceptionally dry after just a few rain-free days at anchor in the hot sun. A day later, the same deck will be fully wetted with fresh water from a rainstorm. On the day after, the deck will be saturated with salt

A laid-pine deck. Each strake is edge-nailed to its neighbor and toe-nailed into the deck beam below. A bead of 3M-5200 is between each plank. (Courtesy Kortchmar & Willner)

water while driving hard to windward in rough seas.

CANVAS DECKS

The other traditional deck treatment was to plank up the deck normally—smooth carvel plank—but cover it with canvas laid in paint. This resulted in very clean, tight, waterproof decks, which were also quite light. (It is still the best non-skid deck surface.) The painted canvas expands and contracts with the expansion and contraction of the planks beneath it. Properly built, these decks will last for years without leaking.

PLYWOOD DECKS

Today, there is no better deck than marine plywood covered with a layer or two of glass cloth set in epoxy. Plywood decks are as light as canvas decks, are dimensionally far more stable, and also have diagonal (torsional) stiffness, which planked decks do not. Plywood decks are generally much quicker and easier to build and install than any traditional decking.

The layer of glass cloth is strongly recommended to protect and seal the grain of the surface veneer of the plywood. In the past, the fiberglass was often laid on in polyester resin. Although this can work if everything is done just right, polyester does not have the tenacity, elongation, and peel strength required to ensure a permanent watertight bond in such applications. Epoxy is the proper answer. If the plywood deck is also sealed and coated with epoxy on the underside and around all the edges, it will be virtually rot-proof, as well as highly stable dimensionally.

DECK BEAMS

For the same reason that the decks themselves must be strong, so must the deck beams. Deck beams are frequently heavier timbers than the frames. The deck beams must be securely fastened to the heads of the frames in traditional construction, and be well fastened to the shelf and/or clamp.

Shelf, Clamp, and Bilge Stringer

In addition to the keel, there are several other critical longitudinal members required for proper strength.

SHELF AND CLAMP

Up at the sheer—running along the inside of the frames, just under the deck beams—are the shelf and the clamp. These longitudinal members tie the frames together fore-n-aft at the sheer, and provide a strong foundation for the deck beams. The clamp is a longitudinal generally higher than it is wide athwartships. The shelf is usually roughly square, and is bolted to the inboard upper edge of the clamp. On small boats, sometimes only the clamp is used. Even on larger craft and on cold-molded hulls, the shelf can be dispensed with, but—in this case—the clamp must be made somewhat heavier, and is more difficult to fit unless laminated in place. The clamp and shelf, port and starboard, should be tied together at the stem with a large athwartships knee, called the *breasthook*. The breasthook is bolted to the inside face of the stem, and the clamp and shelf are screwed and bolted to the breasthook. Both the shelf and clamp should be tied similarly into the transom with *quarter knees*.

BILGE STRINGER

At the turn of the bilge, a longitudinal member called the *bilge stringer* is run inside of and fastened to the frames. The bilge stringers, port and starboard, also should be tied together and to the stem with a breasthook and to the transom with quarter knees.

Other Structural Components

In addition to the principal ones already discussed, numerous other structural components comprise a hull, including hanging and lodging knees, mast steps and partners, engine beds, butt blocks, diagonal strapping, caulking, cabin and cockpit structures, and ballast keels. These are discussed in detail in the scantling rules in the following chapters.

NINE

Plank-on-Frame Scantling Rule

*I*n the preceding chapters, we reviewed the principles behind and standard structures employed in traditional wooden-boat construction. In this chapter, we discuss the scantling rule that will enable you to calculate the scantlings for most ordinary plank-on-frame wooden boats.

Recommended Woods

The wood used for each specific application—floors, frames, plank, knees—is critical. Boatbuilding woods are discussed in detail in chapter 12. Wherever possible, you should attempt to use the woods recommended in that chapter for the uses labeled "excellent" or "good." Woods listed as "acceptable" will be just that. You can employ them as required, but they will not last as long as those rated excellent or good for that specific application.

Molded and Sided Dimensions

Before we delve into the plank-on-frame scantling rule, however, we need to establish more precise terminology for describing scantling dimensions. Up until now, we have referred to planks, frames, and keels as being "so thick," "so wide," "so high," or "so deep." This can be imprecise because it's not always clear which direction is the "width," "depth," or "height." The correct terms are *molded* and *sided* dimensions, or *molding* and *siding*.

The molded dimension of any piece is its dimension measured in from the outside toward the interior of the hull. Thus, for a keel timber, the molding is the vertical dimension (the up-and-down direction points into the interior). Conversely, for the sheer clamp, the molding is the horizontal dimension (the side-to-side direction points into the interior). The siding is the direction at right angles to the molded dimension that is *not* running along the length of the woodgrain. A deck beam's molding, for example, is the up-and-down direction; its siding is in the fore-n-aft direction. It's worth taking a moment to make sure you understand this nomenclature because it eliminates much potential confusion.

For instance, a bilge stringer could be described as 4 inches (100 mm) wide and 2 inches (50 mm) high. This is vague, though, because as the bilge stringer runs forward to the bow, it twists nearly 90 degrees. Amidships, the bilge stringer is roughly horizontal on the frames, but forward it will lie nearly vertical against them. Where the 2-inch (50 mm) dimension would be approximately vertical (high) amidships, it will be more or less horizontal (wide) near the stem. By contrast, if we described the stringer as sided 4 inches (100 mm) and molded 2 inches (50 mm), there would be no possibility for error. The molded 2-inch (50 mm) dimension would always be the dimension measured in or out from the interior. We use molded and sided dimensions almost exclusively throughout the wood scantling rule.

For constancy and convenience in comparing materials, we'll stay with our example boat, the trusty *Fish 'n Squish*. In honor of the boat's new wood construction, however, we are renaming it *Logger Bobber*.

Logger Bobber has the following characteristics:

LOA	40.00 ft.	12.19 m
WL	37.20 ft.	11.34 m
Beam	12.56 ft.	3.83 m
Depth of Hull	5.91 ft.	1.80 m

This gave an Sn of 2.97 (see Formula 1-1).

Plank, Frames, and Floors

FORMULA 9-1

Plank Thickness

(Refer also to Formula 9-34.)

Plank Thickness, in. = $0.74 \times Sn^{0.4}$
(English)

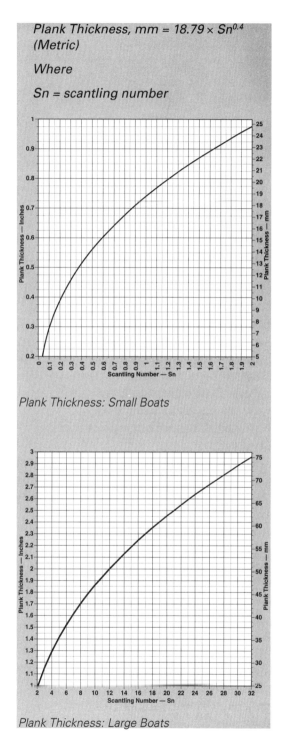

Plank Thickness, mm = $18.79 \times Sn^{0.4}$
(Metric)

Where

Sn = scantling number

Plank Thickness: Small Boats

Plank Thickness: Large Boats

- Increase the bottom-plank thickness only—from the chine or from the turn of the bilge down to the keel—by 1 percent for every knot over 25 knots.
- Increase the plank thickness (including speed-adjusted bottom plank) by 5 to 10 percent for hard-service workboats.
- Workboats and heavy offshore cruising boats will often increase the thickness of the garboard strake and the sheer strake by 10 percent over the neighboring planks.
- All boats can reduce plank thickness—from the BLH up—by 10 percent (see Formula 4-3).
- Light high-performance yachts can reduce plank thickness by 10 percent but at some cost in longevity.
- Strip-planking should be the same thickness as carvel-planking. The strips must be edge-nailed and glued along their entire length (see Formula 10-4).
- For sheet-plywood planking, calculate as before, then use the same thickness for the bottom plank and 90 percent of the thickness for the topsides plank. Note that plywood hulls are hard-chine, so use hard-chine frames and frame spacing.
- Lapstrake planks are 85 percent of the thickness for carvel planks.

For our *Logger Bobber*, this gives

Plank Thickness = 0.74 × 2.97$^{0.4}$ = 1.14; use 1$^{1}/_{8}$-in. plank

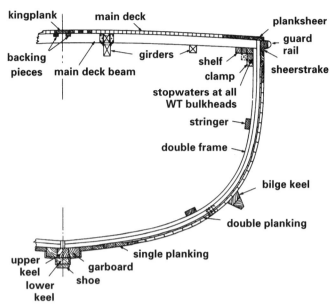

Section through heavy double-planked hull. Note extra-heavy garboards and single planking near keel and sheer. The large frames are bent double.

Plank Thickness = 18.79 × 2.97$^{0.4}$ = 29; use 28 mm plank

If *Logger Bobber* were a 30-knot boat, the bottom-plank thickness would be increased by 5 percent to 1.19 inches, say 1$^{3}/_{16}$ inches (30.45 mm, say 30 mm). Old *Bobber*, however, runs at 20 knots, so we don't have to make any speed adjustment.

FORMULA 9-2

Frame Siding and Molding

Standard steam-bent frames are square in section—they have the same siding and molding.

Frame Siding and Molding, in. = 1.37 × Sn$^{0.36}$ (English)

Frame Siding and Molding, mm = 34.79 × Sn$^{0.36}$ (Metric)

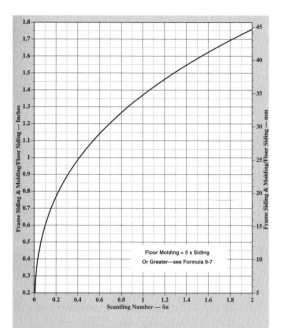

Frames and Floors: Small Boats

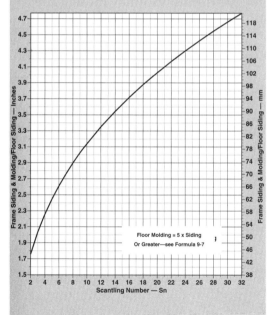

Frames and Floors: Large Boats

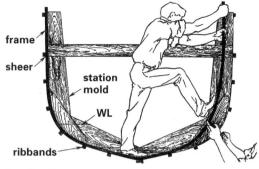

Bending frames

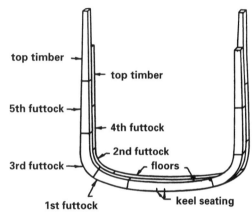

Double-sawn frame futtocks

- Double-sawn frames for round-bilge hulls should be twice the siding and the same molding as the single-bent frames.
- Single-sawn frames on hard-chine hulls should have the same siding as the square-bent frames, but the molding on the bottom futtock should be 3 times the siding. Molding on the topsides futtock should taper from 3 times the bent-frame siding at the chine to 1.3 times the bent-frame siding at the sheer.
- Gussets on hard-chine single-sawn frames are best made from marine plywood, through-bolted (or screwed and glued on

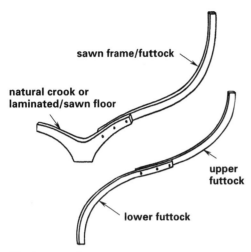

sawn frame/futtock

natural crook or
laminated/sawn floor

upper
futtock

lower futtock

Single-sawn frames

smaller craft) to both the front and back faces of the frame. Each gusset is sided one-third the frame siding, and extends for a distance of at least 3 times the frame molding along the side of the frame—measured both up and athwartships—from the inside of the plank at the chine (see photo on p. 338).

- An alternative to plywood gussets is simply to have the topsides futtock overlap the bottom futtock, bolting them together. This is somewhat quicker and easier than installing plywood gussets, but the joint is not quite as strong.
- Single-sawn frames used for ease of construction in the bow and stern of round-bilge hulls are sided and molded about the same as the standard bent frame; however, it is good practice to increase

the molding by 25 to 30 percent.
- On sailboats, it is recommended that the molding and siding of the frames immediately ahead and abaft of the partners be increased by 20 percent. This is a requirement on boats with Sns over 8.
- Lapstrake frames are molded slightly thinner, or 90 percent of the molding given previously, but use the same siding (see photo on p. 338).

Logger Bobber would require the following:

Bent Frames Sided and Molded, in. =
$1.37 \times 2.97^{0.36} = 2.03$ in.; use 2 in.

Bent Frames Sided and Molded, mm =
$34.79 \times 2.97^{0.36} = 51.48$ mm.; use 50 mm

If old *Bobber* were a hard-chine hull, its bottom-frame futtock would be molded 6

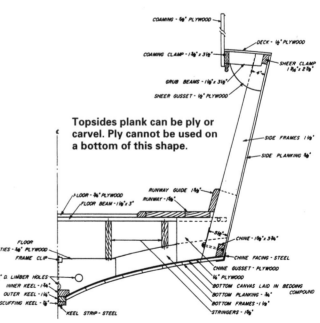

Topsides plank can be ply or carvel. Ply cannot be used on a bottom of this shape.

Section through a V-bottom workboat

inches (150 mm) and sided 2 inches (50 mm). Its topsides futtock would be sided 2 inches (50 mm), with molding tapering from 6 inches (150 mm) at the chine to 2.6, say $2\frac{5}{8}$ inches (66 mm), at the sheer. Gussets would be $\frac{5}{8}$-inch (15 mm) ply, extending a minimum of 18 inches (457 mm) along each futtock. (In the bow and stern, it is sometimes necessary to reduce the length of the gussets.)

FORMULA 9-3

Frame Spacing

Bent-Frame Spacing, in. = 10.14 × Sn$^{0.27}$, center to center (English)

Bent-Frame Spacing, mm = 257.5 × Sn$^{0.27}$, center to center (Metric)

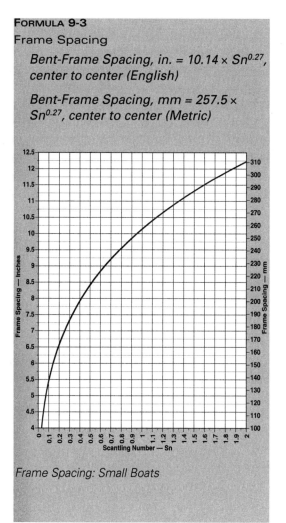

Frame Spacing: Small Boats

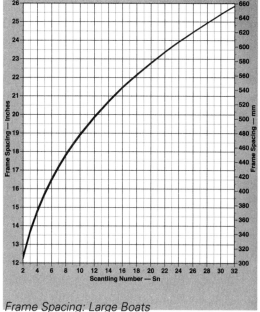

Frame Spacing: Large Boats

- Decrease frame spacing by 1 percent for every knot over 25 knots.
- Double-sawn frames on round-bilge hulls have the same spacing as standard bent frames.
- Single-sawn frames on hard-chine hulls are spaced 2.5 times farther apart than bent-frame spacing.
- No frame spacing on any hull is to exceed 36 inches (900 mm).
- Bent frames on lapstrake hulls are spaced closer, or 90 percent of the spacing given previously (see photo on p. 339).

Returning to *Logger Bobber*, we would use

Bent-Frame Spacing = 10.14 × 2.97$^{0.27}$ = 13.6 in., center to center

Bent-Frame Spacing = 257.5 × 2.97$^{0.27}$ = 345.5 mm, center to center

For a hard-chine *Bobber*, we would multiply by 2.5 to get 34-inch (864 mm) frame spacing.

Adjusting Frame Siding and Molding for Convenient Frame Spacing

Frames can be spaced farther apart or closer together, as convenient, by increasing or decreasing frame siding and molding 3.2 percent for each inch or millimeter of increase or decrease in frame spacing.

Say you wanted *Logger Bobber*'s bent frames to fall evenly on 16-inch centers (or O.C., for *on center*). This is an increase in spacing of 2.4 inches. Accordingly, we would increase *Bobber*'s frame siding and molding from 2 to $2^1/_{16}$ inches (2.4-inch increase × 0.032 = 0.077, and 2.03 inches + 0.077 = 2.10 inches; use $2^1/_{16}$ inches).

or

If we wanted to increase *Bobber*'s frame spacing to an even 400 mm, we would find a frame siding and molding increased to 54 mm from the original 51.48 mm (400 mm − 345.5 mm = 54.5 mm increase, and 54.5 mm × 0.032 = 1.74 mm, so 51.48 mm + 1.74 mm = 53.2 mm; use 54 mm).

If you wish to decrease the frame spacing, frame siding and molding is decreased in the same way.

FORMULA 9-5

Strip-Plank Frame Spacing

Because of the more rigid nature of edge-nailed and glued strip-plank, the frame spacing (including the associated floors) can be substantially increased.

Strip-Plank Frame Spacing =
4 × bent-frame spacing

- Frame spacing may exceed 36 inches (900 mm).
- Calculate frame spacing and frame size, including all adjustments for speed, per the previous formulas, then multiply the spacing by 4 to get the strip-plank spacing.
- Hard-chine hulls with sawn frames may increase frame spacing over the bent-frame spacing (not the sawn-frame spacing) by 4.6 times.

FORMULA 9-6

Flat (Non-Square) Frames

It is sometimes desirable to use frames that are not square in section. In this case, use the standard square-section frames from Formula 9-2, and adjust as follows.

For every percent of reduction in molding, increase the siding:

Percent Siding Increase = 1 ÷ percent molding reduction

Or, if you know the new larger siding you wish, decrease the molding:

Percent Molding Reduction = 1 ÷ percent siding increase

- Siding may not be greater than 1.7 times the molding.

Say we wanted to reduce *Logger Bobber*'s frame molding from 2 inches (50 mm) to just $1^5/_8$ inches (40 mm). This is a reduction of about 80 percent of the square-section molding. The new flat-frame siding would be

1 ÷ 0.80 Molding Reduction = 1.25 siding increase

so

1.25 × 2 in. = 2.50; use 2½-in. siding

1.25 × 50 mm = 62.5; use 62 mm siding

2.5-in. siding ÷ 1.625-in. molding = 1.53, less than 1.7, okay

or

62 mm siding ÷ 40 mm molding = 1.55, less than 1.7, okay

- Heavy floors are used under the mast steps and on planing hulls or on displacement workboats, with heavy slow-turning diesel engines, under the engine beds at and between the engine-mount bolts.
- Heavy floors also may be used at ballast-keel bolts.

Say we stick with the 16-inch O.C. frame spacing; this means that *Logger Bobber*'s floors will be $2^1/_{16}$ inches thick and $10^3/_8$ inches high, minimum. Or, for the 400 mm O.C. frames, the floors would be sided 54 mm and molded 270 mm, minimum. (Higher floors or floors with deeper molded dimensions are stronger, but usually take up too much interior room.) Note that as a practical matter, it is acceptable for a few widely scattered floors to have lower moldings. This is sometimes necessary to work in tanks, machinery, or accommodations. There should never be more than two such low floors on adjacent frames, and no more than 10 percent of the floors in the hull should be lower than the ideal minimum given.

Where heavy floors are used, they would be sided $2^3/_4$ inches or 70 mm. The minimum height molding of the heavy floors is the same as that on the standard floors: $10^3/_8$ inches (270 mm).

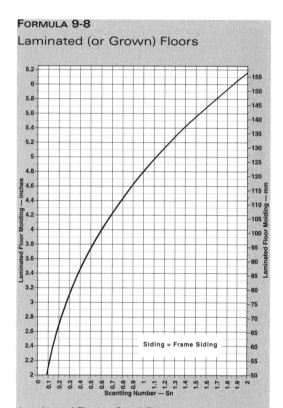

to starboard on top of the keel, as a continuous member, the bolts into the keel will naturally pass through the frame as well.

Laminated Floor Siding = frame siding

Laminated Floor Molding, in. = 4.8 × $Sn^{0.36}$ (English)

Laminated Floor Molding, mm = 122 × $Sn^{0.36}$ (Metric)

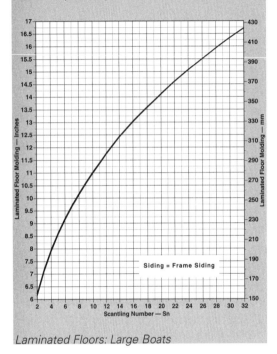

Laminated Floors: Large Boats

- Athwartships width of floor is to be 30 percent of the beam at that frame.
- Molding is to taper to 80 percent of frame siding at the port and starboard ends of the floors.
- An alternate composite metal-strap floor also can be used (see Formula 11-16).

If *Bobber* were to be built with laminated floors installed on top of its $2^1/_6$-inch-square frames (54 mm), we would use

Laminated Floor Siding = $2^1/_6$ in. (54 mm)

Laminated Floor Molding = 4.8 × $2.97^{0.36}$ = 7.1; use 7 in.

Laminated Floor Molding = 122 × $2.97^{0.36}$ = 180.5; use 180 mm

Molding tapers to $1^3/_4$ in. (44 mm) at ends

In the days when natural crooks were readily available, the laminated floors we described would have been hewn from these.

FORMULA 9-9

Limbers

Limber-Hole Radius = floor siding, but not less than $3/_4$ in. (20 mm)

Limber holes in each floor, port and starboard, are vital to permit drainage of water to the lowest point in the bilge, where it can be pumped out efficiently. In the narrow bow near the stem and in the narrow bilge of a deep hollow-garboard hull, a single limber will be used on the centerline.

Keel/Backbone, Longitudinals, Web Frames, and Ceiling

FORMULA 9-10

Keel

Plank-Keel Molding, in. = 2.6 × $Sn^{0.4}$ (English)

Plank-Keel Molding, mm = 66 × $Sn^{0.4}$ (Metric)

Plank-Keel Siding = 1.75 × molding

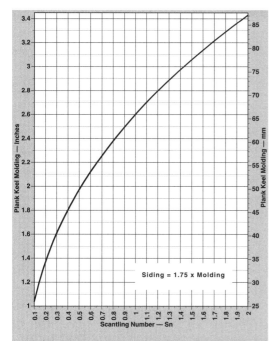

Plank Keels: Small Boats

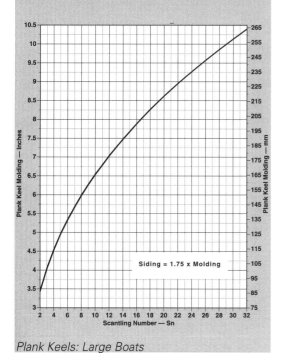

Plank Keels: Large Boats

Our *Logger Bobber* would use

Plank-Keel Molding = 2.6 × 2.97$^{0.4}$ = 4 in.

Plank-Keel Molding, mm = 66 × 2.97$^{0.4}$ = 102 mm; use 100 mm

Plank-Keel Siding = 7 in. (175 mm)

If *Bobber* were faster than 25 knots, you would add the suitable speed-adjusted increase for sided and molded dimensions. These dimensions are for the keel and keel batten combined—if this construction is used rather than a one-piece rabbeted keel. In this case, the keel batten might be approximately 2-inch (50 mm) siding by 8-inch (200 mm) molding and the keel 2-inch (50 mm) molding by 6-inch (150 mm) siding.

Keel shapes vary dramatically with hull type and construction method. The plank-keel dimensions from Formula 4-6 can be rotated 90 degrees to give minimum deep-keel dimensions. Usually, you'll find that hull shapes naturally tend to generate deep keels with somewhat fatter dimensions (i.e., wider moldings) than this rule indicates. This is acceptable and often unavoidable. Additionally, sailboats with external ballast often require considerably greater molding than indicated, especially if a deep-keel configuration is employed.

On most traditional hull forms, the keel is sided widest amidships and tapers away toward the ends, where it mates with the stem and the sternpost. This is not a requirement in any way, however, and the keel can have constant siding from stem to stern. Of course, *Logger Bobber*'s plank keel of 7-inch (175 mm) siding would be too wide at the stem for most normal 40-foot (12 m) hull forms; how-

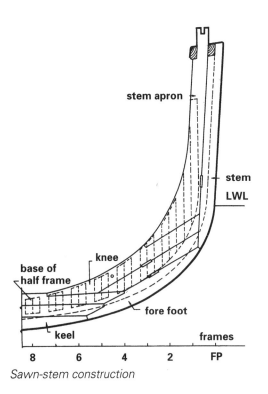

ever, the deep keel sided 4 inches (100 mm) could be kept at constant width from stem to sternpost on a 40-footer (12 m) like our trusty *Bobber*.

FORMULA 9-11

Stem and Sternpost

> *Stem and Sternpost Siding = plank-keel molding*
>
> *Molding = 1.25 × the siding, or more*
>
> • *Increase siding and molding by 1 percent for every knot over 25 knots.*

Note that the keel siding will be greater than the stem and sternpost; however, the keel should taper down to the stem and sternpost formula siding (or close to it) at the stem and sternpost. Alternately, the stem and sternpost can be sided somewhat fatter to mate with the keel.

Sawn-stem construction

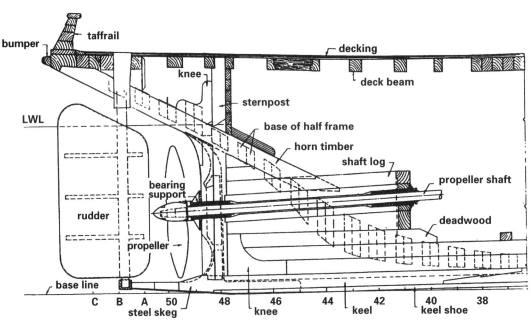

Deadwood, sternpost, horn-timber construction on harbor tug

Built-up stems usually have molding much greater than given here to allow for proper joints, keys, or hooks; long-enough faying surfaces; and proper through-bolting (refer to chapter 10). Stem siding must also be adjusted as necessary to mate with the keel. Laminated stems can come very close to the scantling dimensions. The sternpost may often be exactly as specified in the formula. Again, however, it must be adjusted in size and shape to mate with the keel and the deadwood.

FORMULA 9-12
Horn Timber

$Horn\text{-}Timber\ Molding,\ in. = 1.85 \times Sn^{0.4}$ (English)

$Horn\text{-}Timber\ Molding,\ mm = 47 \times Sn^{0.4}$ (Metric)

$Siding = 1.2 \times molding$ (or to mate with keel)

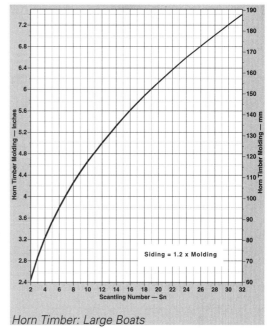

Horn Timber: Large Boats

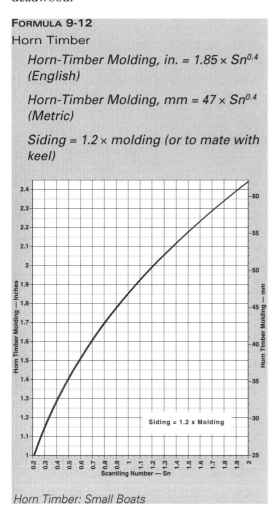

Horn Timber: Small Boats

Logger Bobber's horn timber would be

$Horn\text{-}Timber\ Molding = 1.85 \times 2.97^{0.4} =$ 2.86 in.; use 2⅞ in.

$Horn\text{-}Timber\ Molding = 47 \times 2.97^{0.4} = 72.6;$ use 72 mm

$Siding = 3.45\ in.\ (86\ mm)$

FORMULA 9-13
Ceiling

Ceiling Thickness = 0.4 × plank thickness

Ceiling is a layer of "planking" fastened to the inside of the frames. Although it is common on many traditional designs, I recommend against installing structural ceiling except when unavoidable. Ceiling adds surprisingly little strength compared to its weight and cost. The other scantlings given in this chapter are sufficient without the additional strength of ceiling for most boats.

More important, the ceiling greatly reduces air circulation around the inside of the planks and frames, thereby promoting decay.

On yachts and light commercial craft, the ceiling's principal purpose is cosmetic. It makes a nice smooth-wall surface on the inside of the plank on the topsides, and it can help keep gear from rolling into the bilge water when a boat is heeled and driving hard. Ceiling also permits using joiner bulkheads that don't fall on the frames. Install the joiner ceiling sparingly, only in locations that it is required. If used for these purposes, I recommend that the ceiling be installed with $1/8$- to $1/4$-inch (3 to 6 mm) gaps between each ceiling plank; this greatly enhances ventilation. In many instances, ceiling like this can be screwed into the frames with oval-head screws set in finish rings. So installed, the ceiling planks can easily be removed and replaced for maintenance and repairs.

On cargo and fishing vessels, the ceiling protects the planking in the hold from being strained outward by the weight of the cargo or the catch. On such craft, ceiling must be used and should be installed tight without gaps. Such ceilings should have a gap of one strake left open, for full length under the clamp, for ventilation. The ceiling should end several frame bays short of the stem and of the transom, again to promote ventilation.

FORMULA 9-14

Belt Frames (Web Frames)

Belt Frames = 0.75 × frame siding and molding

When employed, belt frames are bent in and fastened down on top of the ceiling over a frame (fastened into the frame below) and are also bolted to the floor. Hanging knees attach the belt frame to the deck beam.

Belt or web frames are employed only on round-bilge hulls with extensive ceiling. Because this rule does not require ceiling, belt frames are seldom required in practice, except in heavy cargo and fishing vessels that have ceiling.

Belt frames are not required at all on vessels with Sns under 3. On vessels with Sns between 3 and 5, two belt frames are used—roughly one-third of the way aft of the bow and one-third of the way forward of the transom. On craft with Sns over 5, four belt frames are used—approximately one-quarter of the way aft of the bow to about one-quarter of the way forward of the transom. The purpose of the belt frames is to add strength at highly loaded areas, so they should be installed about athwartships from the mast, crane, main engine, and cargo hold.

FORMULA 9-15

Clamp and Bilge Stringer

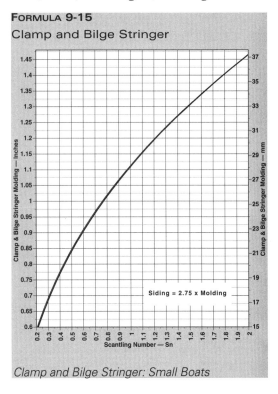

Clamp and Bilge Stringer: Small Boats

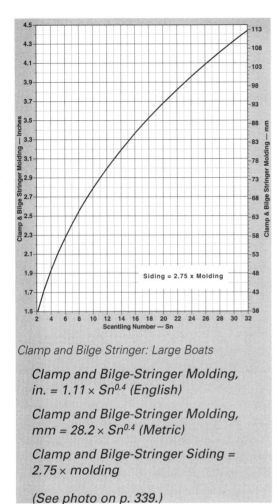

Clamp and Bilge Stringer: Large Boats

Clamp and Bilge-Stringer Molding, in. = 1.11 × Sn^{0.4} (English)

Clamp and Bilge-Stringer Molding, mm = 28.2 × Sn^{0.4} (Metric)

Clamp and Bilge-Stringer Siding = 2.75 × molding

(See photo on p. 339.)

- Both the clamp and the bilge stringer can taper in siding, at the bow and stern, to 60 percent of their maximum siding. The middle third of the clamp and bilge stringer should have maximum siding, with no taper. Such taper makes it easier to bend these members into place and saves some weight in the ends.
- Increase siding and molding by 1 percent for every knot over 25 knots.
- If no shelf is used, increase clamp molding by 30 percent.

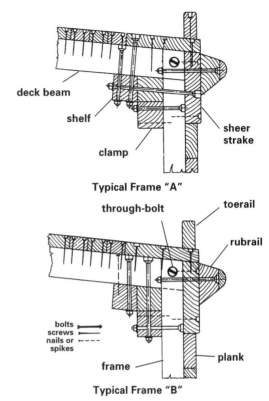

Sheer clamp and shelf, heavy boats

- Hard-chine boats do not use bilge stringers at the chine.
- Boats with Sns under 0.5 may omit the bilge stringer.

Our trusty old *Logger Bobber* would use the following:

Clamp and Bilge-Stringer Molding = 1.11 × 2.97^{0.4} = 1.71; use 1¾ in.

Clamp and Bilge-Stringer Molding = 28.2 × 2.97^{0.4} = 43.58; use 45 mm

Clamp and Bilge-Stringer Siding = 4⅞ in. (124 mm), tapering to 3 in. (75 mm)

If *Bobber* had no shelf, the clamp's molding would increase to 2¼ inches (57 mm).

edit, can you loose a line from this column?

Such heavy clamps are more difficult to bend in, especially in the bow where there is often combined edge-set and twist. In such cases, the heavy clamp should be laminated in place, from thinner stock.

The bilge stringer and clamp are screw-fastened to each frame, and should be fastened to each other and to the stem at the bow with a breasthook and to the transom with quarter knees, port and starboard. On vessels with Sns greater than 4, the clamp and bilge stringers are better through-bolted to the frames.

FORMULA 9-16
Strip-Plank Bilge Stringer

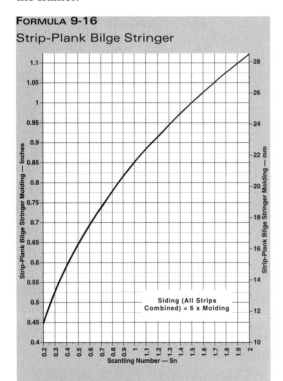

Strip-Plank Bilge Stringer: Small Boats

The bilge-stringer dimensions given by the previous formula are for standard traditional bilge stringers. Although these work well, they can produce a hard spot in the frames. I prefer to use a strip-plank bilge stringer. This is molded thinner and sided considerably wider than the standard bilge stringer. As a result, it makes less of a hard spot in each frame. It is like a narrow width of very heavy ceiling.

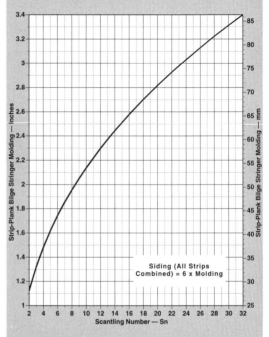

Strip-Plank Bilge Stringer: Large Boats

Strip-Plank Bilge Stringer:

Molding, in. = $0.85 \times Sn^{0.4}$ (English)

Molding, mm = $21.6 \times Sn^{0.4}$ (Metric)

Total Siding, All Bilge-Stringer Strip Planks Combined = $6 \times$ molding

- Increase siding and molding by 1 percent for every knot over 25 knots.
- The bilge stringer can taper in siding, at the bow and stern, to 60 percent of its maximum total siding at midships. The middle third of the bilge stringer should have maximum siding, with no taper.

This would give *Bobber* a strip-plank bilge stringer of

$$Molding = 0.85 \times 2.97^{0.4} = 1.31 \text{ in.;}$$
$$use\ 1\tfrac{3}{8}\ in.$$

$$Molding = 21.6 \times 2.97^{0.4} = 33.4 \text{ mm;}$$
$$use\ 34\ mm$$

Total Siding All Strip-Planks = approximately 8¼ in. (210 mm), tapering to 5 in. (125 mm)

The strip-plank bilge stringer is built up of strip planks edge-nailed together, inside the frames at the turn of the bilge. Every other strip is screw-fastened to a frame, alternating each frame. Strips are square to sided, approximately 1.2 times the molding.

FORMULA 9-17

Shelf

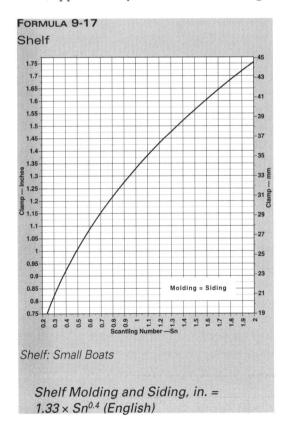

Shelf: Small Boats

Shelf Molding and Siding, in. = 1.33 × Sn⁰·⁴ (English)

Shelf Molding and Siding, mm = 33.8 × Sn⁰·⁴ (Metric)

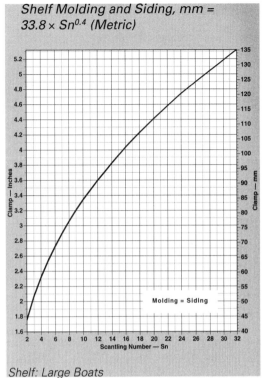

Shelf: Large Boats

Bobber would be fitted with

Shelf Molding and Siding, in. = 1.33 × 2.97⁰·⁴ = 2.05 in.; use 2 in.

Shelf Molding and Siding, mm = 33.8 × 2.97⁰·⁴ = 52.2 mm; use 50 mm

The shelf is through-bolted to the top inside of the clamp—flush with the clamp's top edge—to form a foundation for the deck beams. The through-bolts should run right through the frames. On vessels with Sns of 2.5 or less, it may be more practical to screw-fasten the shelf to the clamp only. Both the shelf and clamp together form the landing for the deck beams, and they must be beveled and smoothed off to match the varying angles the underside of the deck beams make, due to the deck crown.

FORMULA 9-18
Chine or Chine Log

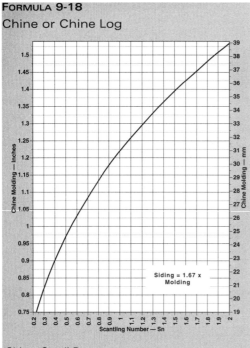

Chine: Small Boats

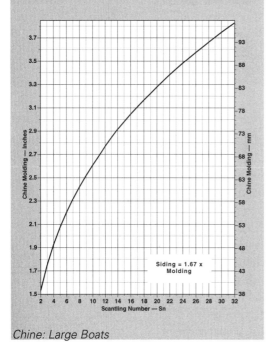

Chine: Large Boats

Chine Molding, in. = 1.22 × $Sn^{0.33}$
(English)

Chine Molding, mm = 31 × $Sn^{0.33}$
(Metric)

Chine Siding = 1.67 × molding

- Add 1 percent to siding and molding for every knot over 15 knots.

The chine forms a prominent projecting corner. Even on displacement hulls, it can take quite a beating. On planing boats, the chine needs to be exceptionally strong for impact and abrasion resistance. The chine or *chine log* can be formed from a single piece, beveled and rabbeted to mate with the plank, or it can be from two pieces—an interior chine or *chine batten*, and the external chine, called the *chine proper*. Like the keel batten, the chine batten is often a heavier timber than the outer chine. Because of abrasion considerations, if chine-batten construction is used, I recommend making the chine batten the full siding and molding specified for the chine, with the chine batten added on to fair out the plank intersection, as required.

On boats with herringbone-bottom planking, it is usual to run the bottom plank out along the underside of the chine log and the underside of the topsides plank. No rabbeting or outer chine is required. Similar construction is used on plywood hulls. Plywood chines should be glassed on the outside (glass cloth laid in epoxy). Often, planing plywood hulls have a shallow external chine and spray-knocker installed, which further protect the outside corner of the chine and help throw spray flat and wide.

Our 20-knot *Logger Bobber* would require

Chine Molding = 1.22 × $2.97^{0.33}$ = 1.75 in.

Chine Molding = 31 × 2.97$^{0.33}$ = 44.4 mm

Chine Siding = 2.92 in. (74.1 mm)

Add 5 percent for 5 knots over 15 knots:

*Chine Molding = 1.75 in. × 1.05 = 1.83;
use 1^7/$_8$ in.*

*Chine Molding = 44.4 mm × 1.05 = 46.6;
use 47 mm*

Chine Siding = 3^1/$_8$ in. (80 mm)

Deck and Cabin

FORMULA 9-19
Deck

*Laid-Deck-Plank Thickness = hull-
topsides plank thickness*

*Canvas-Covered-Deck Plank Thickness =
0.9 × hull-topsides plank thickness*

*Plywood-Deck-Plank Thickness (FRP-
Covered) = 0.75 × topsides-plank
thickness*

*• Plywood decks may be of a single
layer scarfed together or joined with
butt straps underneath. The best
practice, however, is to make the deck
of two layers of plywood with the
butts well staggered.*

Returning to *Logger Bobber*, we find

*Laid-Deck-Plank Thickness =
1^1/$_8$ in. (28 mm)*

*Canvas-Covered-Deck Plank Thickness =
1 in. (25 mm)*

*Plywood-Deck-Plank Thickness (FRP-
Covered) = ^{7}/$_8$ in. (20 mm), better two layers
^{7}/$_{16}$ in. (two layers 10 mm)*

FORMULA 9-20
Deck Sheathing

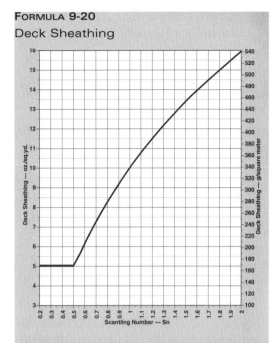

Deck Sheathing: Small Boats

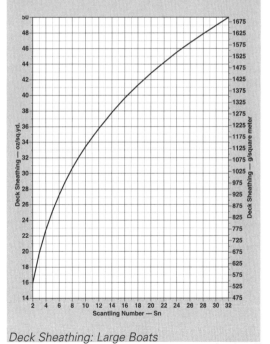

Deck Sheathing: Large Boats

(continued)

> Plywood decks should be sheathed in fiberglass cloth laid in epoxy, as follows:
>
> *Deck-Sheathing Fabric Weight, oz./sq. yd. = (40 × Sn$^{0.2}$) – 30 (English)*
>
> *Deck-Sheathing Fabric Weight, g/m^2 = (1,356 × Sn$^{0.2}$) – 1,017 (Metric)*

- On small boats, glass cloth is used. Larger craft, with heavier deck sheathing, can use a bi-axial uni-di glass fabric style. This may be covered with finishing cloth if desired.
- On small boats, with Sns under 0.5, deck sheathing is optional but recommended. The minimum deck sheathing used should be 5 oz./sq. yd. (169 g/m^2).
- Increase sheathing weight by 10 percent on workboats and offshore cruisers.
- 4 oz./sq. yd. (135 g/m^2) of Dynel, Vectra, or Xynole polyester may be substituted for every 8 to 10 oz./sq. yd. (270 to 339 g/m^2) of glass cloth.

Logger Bobber's $^7/_8$-inch (20 mm) plywood deck would be sheathed with

Deck-Sheathing Fabric Weight = (40 × 2.97$^{0.2}$) – 30 = 19.7; use 20 oz./sq. yd.

Deck-Sheathing Fabric Weight = (1,356 × 2.97$^{0.2}$) – 1,017 = 668; use 670 g/m^2

FORMULA 9-21

Deck Beams and Carlins

> *Deck-Beam Molding, in. = 1.85 × Sn$^{0.34}$ (English)*
>
> *Deck-Beam Siding, in. = 0.92 × Sn$^{0.4}$ (English)*
>
> *Deck-Beam Molding, mm = 47 × Sn$^{0.34}$ (Metric)*
>
> *Deck-Beam Siding, mm = 23.3 × Sn$^{0.4}$ (Metric)*
>
> *Strong Deck-Beam Siding = 1.5 × standard deck-beam siding*

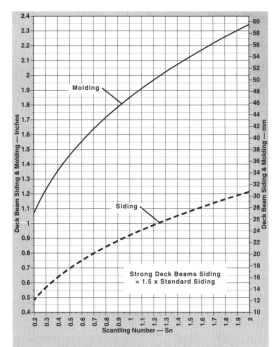

Deck Beams: Small Boats

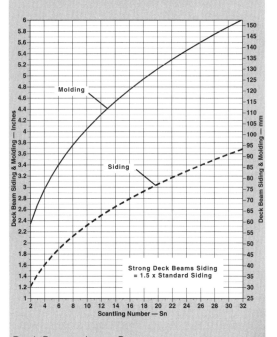

Deck Beams: Large Boats

- Strong deck beams are used at the fore-n-aft end of all major deck openings, such as at the fore-n-aft ends of the cabin and the cockpit, and at the frames immediately fore-n-aft of each mast.
- Deck carlins frame out the fore-n-aft sides of deck openings, such as along the cabin sides and the cockpit sides. Deck carlins are usually the same siding and molding as standard deck beams except at large re-movable hatch openings, such as cargo hatches and removable cockpits.

Our *Bobber* would be fitted with

Deck-Beam Molding = 1.85 × 2.97$^{0.34}$ =
2.67 in.; use 2⅝ in.

Deck-Beam Siding = 0.92 × 2.97$^{0.4}$ =
1.42 in.; use 1⁷⁄₁₆ in.

Deck-Beam Molding = 47 × 2.97$^{0.34}$ =
68.05 mm; use 68 mm

Deck-Beam Siding = 23.3 × 2.97$^{0.4}$ =
36.04 mm; use 36 mm

Strong Deck-Beam Siding = 2⅛ in. (54 mm)

Deck beams are fastened to the side of each frame. Where standard floors are used—through-bolted to the side of the frame—the deck beam is on the same side as the floor (above the floor). It is very important that each deck beam be through-bolted to the head of its frames, as well as down into the shelf and/or clamp. The bolt through the frame holds the frame heads from springing outward. On small boats, with Sns less than 1, the deck beams can be screw-fastened into the side of the frames.

FORMULA 9-22

Cabin Sides

Cabin-Side-Plank Thickness, in. = 1.1 ×
Sn$^{0.24}$ (English)

Cabin-Side-Plank Thickness, mm = 27.9
× Sn$^{0.24}$ (Metric)

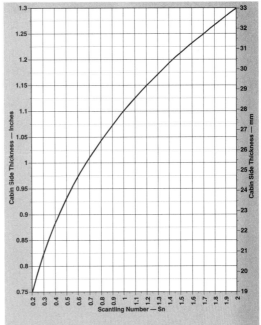

Cabin Sides: Small Boats

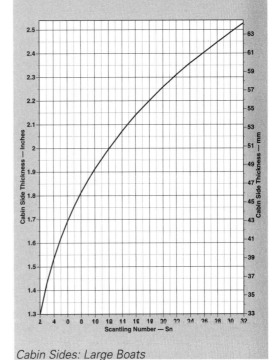

Cabin Sides: Large Boats

- Use 70 percent of plank thickness for plywood cabin sides.

Cabin sides were traditionally of planks edge-bolted together and notched into rabbeted cornerposts. Marine plywood is superior for this use, however. Single layers are acceptable, but double layers of plywood with the scarfs well staggered are better.

Bobber's cabin sides are as follows:

Cabin Sides (Plank) = 1.1 × 2.97$^{0.24}$ =
1.42 in.; use 1⅜ in.

Cabin Sides (Plank) = 27.9 × 2.97$^{0.24}$ =
36.2 mm; use 36 mm

Cabin Sides (Plywood) = 1 in. (25 mm);
better: two layers ½-in. ply
(two layers 12 mm ply)

FORMULA 9-23

Cabin-Side Reinforcement

Cabin sides form a weak point in hull construction. If a boat is knocked down in breaking seas (or if heavy seas break aboard), the cabin side can be stove open. This is dangerous and can lead to foundering. All offshore boats must have their cabin sides strongly reinforced, as follows:

Cabin-Side Braces (Hanging Knees) Spaced, ft. = 8 × Sn$^{0.2}$ (English)

Cabin-Side Braces (Hanging Knees) Spaced, m = 2.43 × Sn$^{0.2}$ (Metric)

Cabin-Side Braces (Hanging Knees) Siding, in. = 0.82 × Sn$^{0.36}$ (English)

Cabin-Side Braces (Hanging Knees) Siding, mm = 20.8 × Sn$^{0.36}$ (Metric)

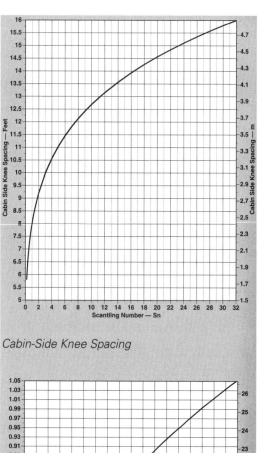

Cabin-Side Knee Spacing

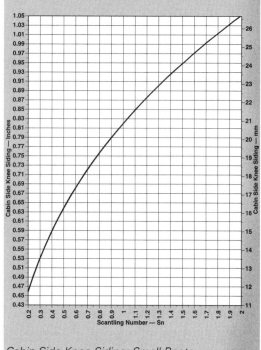

Cabin-Side Knee Siding: Small Boats

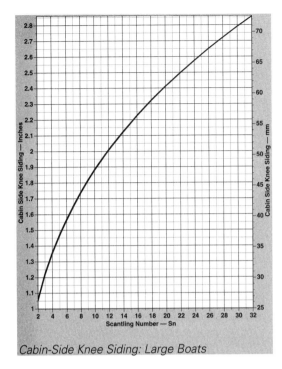

Cabin-Side Knee Siding: Large Boats

- Cabin hanging knees should extend at least 70 percent of the height of the cabin sides down from the underside of the roof beams. Extending all the way down to the cabin-deck carlin is better. The knees should extend approximately 14 times the cabin-roof thickness inboard from the roof carlin, or more.
- Bulkheads of the thickness recommended in Formula 5-5 may be used instead of hanging knees. Such bulkheads must be securely screwed and glued to the roof beams, as well as to cleats that fasten to the inside of the cabin sides.
- Tie rods should be installed just fore-n-aft of the cabin corners from the cabin carlin horizontally under the deck outboard to the shelf or clamp under the deck. Tie rods should also be installed vertically, bolted through the roof carlin, and run

down through the cabin-deck carlin just fore-n-aft of each cabin corner.

For *Bobber*, we would install

Cabin-Side Braces (Hanging Knees)
Spacing = 8 × 2.97$^{0.2}$ = 9.9 ft.

Cabin-Side Braces (Hanging Knees)
Spacing = 2.43 × 2.97$^{0.2}$ = 3.0 m

Cabin-Side Braces (Hanging Knees)
Siding = 0.82 × 2.97$^{0.36}$ = 1.21; use 1¼ in.

Cabin-Side Braces (Hanging Knees)
Siding = 20.8 × 2.97$^{0.36}$ = 30.7; use 30 mm

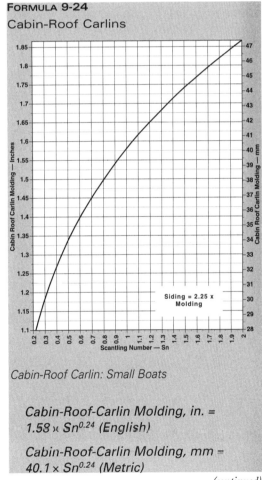

FORMULA 9-24
Cabin-Roof Carlins

Cabin-Roof Carlin: Small Boats

Cabin-Roof-Carlin Molding, in. =
1.58 × Sn$^{0.24}$ (English)

Cabin-Roof-Carlin Molding, mm =
40.1 × Sn$^{0.24}$ (Metric)

(continued)

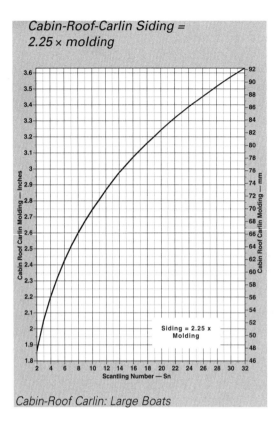

Cabin-Roof-Carlin Siding = 2.25 × molding

Cabin-Roof Carlin: Large Boats

The cabin-roof carlins form the support for the cabin-roof beams, and strengthen the upper corner of the cabin roof. Roof carlins are screwed and glued to the inside of the cabin side. On boats with Sns over 4, the roof carlins are better through-bolted to the cabin side.

Our example, *Logger Bobber*, would have carlins as follows:

Cabin-Roof-Carlin Molding = $1.58 \times 2.97^{0.24}$
= 2.05 in.; use 2 in.

Cabin-Roof-Carlin Molding = $40.1 \times 2.97^{0.24}$
= 52.07 mm; use 50 mm

Cabin-Roof-Carlin Siding = 4½ in. (110 mm)

The roof-carlin dimensions here are sided high and molded moderately thin. This can interfere with the top edge of cabin windows on some boats. When this occurs, you can reduce the carlin height (siding) by increasing the width (molding) proportionally. The cross-sectional area should be the same on the modified carlin as for the standard carlin given by the formula.

FORMULA 9-25
Cabin Roof and Roof Beams (Small Cabin Roofs) (Also Standard Cabin Soles)

It is important to keep weight high up to a minimum. Cabin roofs (also called coach roofs) should be built as light as possible. Additionally, the roof must be as thin as possible to maximize headroom in the accommodations. For cabin roofs with an athwartships span of 8 feet (2.4 m) or less, select the roof thickness and beam spacing from the following table.

TABLE 9-25A
Cabin-Roof Construction

Maximum Cabin-Roof Beam 8 ft. (2.4 m)

Roof Thickness		Beam Spacing O.C.	
Inches	mm	Inches	mm
¼	6	5.75	140
⅜	9	8.00	200
½	12	10.00	250
⅝	15	12.00	300

All with roof beams molded ¾ inch (20 mm), sided 2 inches (50).

Cabin roofs built to this table will support crew weight ruggedly, and will withstand severe weather.

- Cabin roofs are all to be of marine plywood. A single layer is adequate but double layers are superior.

- Cabin-roof beams may be steam-bent, but—if the cabin-roof crown is constant—it is usually best to make a jig and laminate them.
- The cabin roof should be covered with one layer of 10 to 12 oz./sq. yd. (339 to 407 g/m²) of glass cloth laid in epoxy.
- 4 oz./sq. yd. (135 g/m²) of Dynel, Vectra, or Xynole polyester may be substituted for every 8 to 10 oz./sq. yd. (270 to 339 g/m²) of glass cloth.
- Workboats and vessels with Sns over 4 should increase the roof-beam molding to 1 inch (25 mm). These craft should also use a total of 20 to 24 oz./sq. yd. (678 to 814 g/m²) of glass cloth laid in epoxy.

Cabin soles for most boats can be proportioned from the previous table, with the following notes:

- Height under the sole is not usually a problem, so the sole beams can be $1^3/8$ inches (35 mm) square, or alternately sided 1 inch (25 mm) and molded $1^3/4$ inches (45 mm).
- Because cabin soles are low in the boat, it is seldom worth going to great lengths to save small amounts of weight here.
- The standard cabin sole for small boats is $1/2$-inch (12 mm) ply covered with $1/4$-inch teak and holly-veneer ply.
- For almost all boats with Sns over 2, the standard sole is $3/4$-inch (18 mm) ply covered with $1/4$-inch (6 mm) teak and holly-veneer ply.
- For these 1-inch-thick (25 mm) soles, the sole beams should be approximately 2 inches (50 mm) square, or sided $1^1/2$ inches (38 mm) and molded $2^1/2$ inches (64 mm), from 16- to 18-inch centers (400 to 460 mm).

- If great added weight savings is required, substitute 1-inch (25 mm) balsa-cored panels for the $3/4$-inch (18 mm) ply.

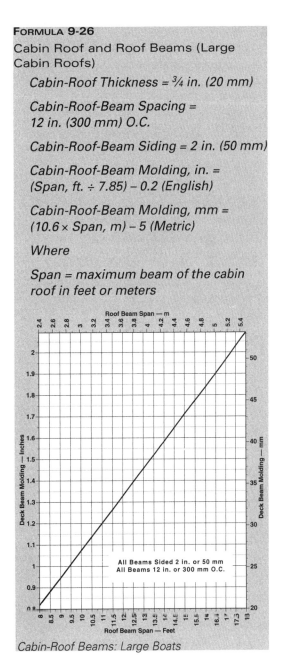

FORMULA 9-26

Cabin Roof and Roof Beams (Large Cabin Roofs)

Cabin-Roof Thickness = $3/4$ in. (20 mm)

Cabin-Roof-Beam Spacing = 12 in. (300 mm) O.C.

Cabin-Roof-Beam Siding = 2 in. (50 mm)

Cabin-Roof-Beam Molding, in. = (Span, ft. ÷ 7.85) – 0.2 (English)

Cabin-Roof-Beam Molding, mm = (10.6 × Span, m) – 5 (Metric)

Where

Span = maximum beam of the cabin roof in feet or meters

Cabin-Roof Beams: Large Boats

- Cabin roofs are all to be of marine plywood. A single layer is adequate, but double layers are superior.
- The cabin roof should be covered with a total of 20 to 24 oz./sq. yd. (678 to 814 g/m²) of glass cloth laid in epoxy.
- 4 oz./sq. yd. (135 g/m²) of Dynel, Vectra, or Xynole polyester may be substituted for every 8 to 10 oz./sq. yd. (270 to 339 g/m²) of glass cloth.
- Workboats and vessels with Sns over 4 should increase the roof-beam molding by 10 percent. These craft should also use a total of 30 to 36 oz./sq. yd. (1,017 to 1,220 g/m²) of glass cloth laid in epoxy. Alternately, a bi-axial uni-di glass fabric style of this weight may be used, covered with finishing cloth or equivalent.

If *Logger Bobber* had a maximum cabin-roof beam of 9.8 feet (2.98 m), then its cabin-roof beams would be molded as follows:

Cabin-Roof-Beam Molding = (9.8 ft. ÷ 7.85) − 0.2 = 1.04; use 1 in.

Cabin-Roof-Beam Molding = (10.6 × 2.98 m) − 5 = 26.5; use 26 mm

Transom and Bulkheads

FORMULA 9-27
Transom

Transom-Plank Thickness (Planked Up) = 1.2 × hull-topsides plank

Transom-Plank Thickness (Plywood) = hull-topsides plank (Carvel plank)

Logger Bobber's transom is then

Planked Up = 1⅜ in. (33 mm)

Plywood = 1⅛ in. (28 mm)

(See photo on p. 339.)

FORMULA 9-28
Bulkheads

Bulkheads are not main structural members in traditional plank-on-frame hulls as they are in FRP and in some cold-molded and strip-plank construction methods. However, bulkheads can be used to increase strength and stiffness in the way of the masts and other highly loaded regions. This can be in addition to or sometimes instead of using hanging and lodging knees. Most bulkheads in plank-on-frame construction are simply interior partitions (joiner panels), dividing up the arrangement, engine spaces, forepeak and lazarette, and cargo holds. The exception is for bulkheads used to brace and stiffen the cabin sides; these are structural. For bulkhead thickness, use Formula 5-5.

FORMULA 9-29
Watertight/Collision Bulkheads

Watertight/collision bulkheads must be fastened to the face of a frame, with substantial filler blocks fastened as required to close any gaps at floors, futtocks, or gussets. At least one collision bulkhead in the bow is recommended for all vessels longer than 50 feet (15.2 m). As a general guide, this bulkhead should be neither less than 0.10 times nor more than 0.25 times the LOA aft of the bow. Where collision bulkheads are required by government agencies or classification societies, their requirements must be followed.

Watertight-Bulkhead Thickness = standard topsides-plank thickness

Watertight-Bulkhead-Stiffener Siding = standard frame siding for hull topsides

Watertight-Bulkhead Molding (fore-n-aft dimension) = 2 × standard frame siding for hull topsides

Watertight-Bulkhead-Stiffener Spacing = 2.5 × standard frame spacing

Watertight-Bulkhead-Stiffener Fastening = plank fastening

- Watertight bulkheads should be made of two layers of plywood glued and screwed (or Anchorfast-nailed) together.
- The stiffeners are screwed and glued to either face of the bulkhead, as convenient. The stiffeners may stop approximately 6 to 10 inches (150 to 250 mm) inboard from the plank. They need not be fastened to the frames, floor, or deck beams. Usually, stiffeners are installed running vertically.
- Where strong interior joinerwork, cleats and panels, or chain lockers are fastened to the watertight bulkhead, they can replace stiffeners in those locations.

Mast Steps, Partners, and Engine Beds

FORMULA 9-30
Mast Step

Mast-Step Siding, in. = 6.2 × Sn$^{0.34}$ (English)

Mast-Step Siding, mm = 157.5 × Sn$^{0.34}$ (Metric)

Mast-Step Molding = 0.7 × siding

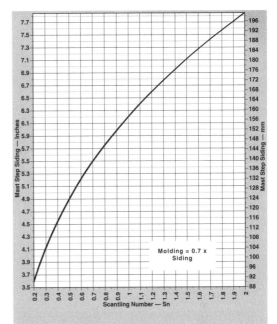

Mast Step: Small Boats

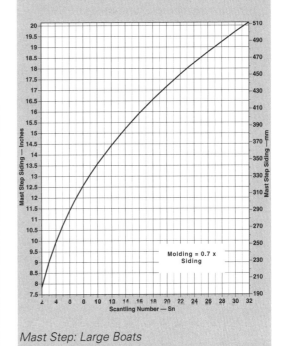

Mast Step: Large Boats

- The mainmast step must land on and be fastened to at least three floors—four or more floors are better.
- If a traditional wooden-mast heel is set into a mortise in the top of the step, the mast-step mortise must be provided with a drainhole.
- On schooners, both the mainmast and foremast steps should be approximately identical in size.
- On ketches and yawls, the siding and molding of the mizzenmast step may be reduced to 70 percent of the mainmast step. The mizzenmast step must land on and be fastened to at least two floors—three or more are better.
- Mast steps should be notched over each floor to keep them from sliding fore-n-aft. The notch cannot be deeper than 10 percent of the mast-step molding.
- The middle third of the step should be of constant molding. The fore-n-aft thirds should taper down to approximately 50 percent of the maximum molding.
- Mast steps must not make contact with the planking.

If *Logger Bobber* were a graceful yawl, it would be fitted with

$$Mainmast\text{-}Step\ Siding = 6.2 \times 2.97^{0.34} = 8.97\ in.;\ use\ 9\ in.$$

$$Mainmast\text{-}Step\ Siding = 157.5 \times 2.97^{0.34} = 228.04\ mm;\ use\ 230\ mm$$

$$Mainmast\text{-}Step\ Molding = 6\tfrac{3}{4}\ in.\ (160\ mm)$$

$$Mizzenmast\text{-}Step\ Siding = 6\tfrac{3}{4}\ in.$$

$$Mizzenmast\text{-}Step\ Siding = 160\ mm$$

$$Mizzenmast\text{-}Step\ Molding = 4\tfrac{1}{2}\ in.\ (112\ mm)$$

FORMULA 9-31

Mast Partners

Mast-Partners Molding = 0.8 × deck-beam molding

- The partners are solid-wood blocking, immediately under the deck, that fill the space between the strong deck beams just fore-n-aft of the mast.
- The partners are through-bolted fore-n-aft through each of these strong frames, fore-n-aft of the mast. Use two bolts port and two bolts starboard (four bolts total) on all boats with Sns of 2 or more. Vessels with Sns less than 2 may use just one bolt port and one bolt starboard (two total).
- The partners extend athwartships for 22 percent (or more) of the beam on deck at the mast step.
- On boats with Sns over 4, a tie rod should be installed athwartships under the deck, running from the mast partners outboard to the sheer clamp.

Logger Bobber's mast partners would be $2\tfrac{1}{8}$ inches (54 mm) thick.

Mast partner installed. Note tie-rod/through-bolt port and starboard. (Courtesy Kortchmar & Willner)

Inboard engine beds end abruptly. This is poor practice. On this boat, the heavy diesels cracked all the frames near the engine bed's end in its first few years of life. Engine beds should extend as far fore-n-aft as possible and taper in molding toward their ends.

FORMULA 9-32

Engine Beds

Engine-Bed Siding, in. = $3.1 \times Sn^{0.3}$
(English)

Engine-Bed Siding, mm = $78.7 \times Sn^{0.3}$
(Metric)

Engine-Bed Molding = $1.5 \times$ siding, or more

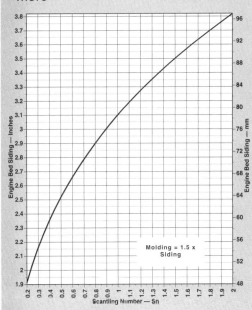

Engine Beds: Small Boats

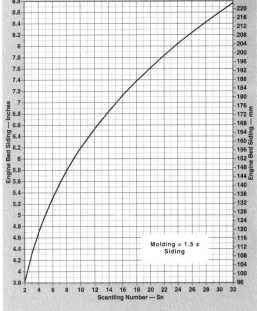

Engine Beds: Large Boats

- Increase both siding and molding by 1 percent for every knot over 15 knots.
- Engine beds may have deeper moldings than indicated, as required, to mount the engine, but not the lower molding.
- On displacement hulls, engine beds must extend at least two floors forward and two floors aft of the fore-n-aft engine-mount bolts—extending the bed six or more floors fore-n-aft is better.
- On displacement hulls—starting the distance of one engine-bed siding fore-n-aft of the fore-n-aft engine-mount bolts—the engine-bed molding should taper until the molding equals the siding at each end, fore-n-aft.
- On planing hulls, engine beds must extend at least six floors forward and six floors aft of the fore-n-aft engine-mount bolts. If the engine beds reach the transom before

six floors' distance, the engine bed will simply stop at the transom.

- On planing hulls, it is strongly recommended that the engine beds be extended for 50 to 60 percent of the hull bottom or more. If this is done, the engine-bed molding should continue to taper to 60 percent of siding at each end, fore-n-aft.
- Engine beds should be notched over and fastened to each floor to keep them from sliding fore-n-aft. The notches cannot be deeper than 10 percent of the engine-bed molding.
- Engine beds must not make contact with the planking.
- Engine beds are to have two cross braces—one just forward and one just aft of the fore-n-aft engine-mount bolts. The cross braces are to have the same siding and molding as the engine bed. Each cross brace is to be notched into the inside of the face of the engine bed, in a notch 10 percent of the bed's siding deep. Each cross brace is to be through-bolted from the outside face of each engine bed with two tie rods.

Assuming *Logger Bobber* were a 20-knot boat, the engine beds would be as follows:

Engine-Bed Siding = 3.1 × 2.97$^{0.3}$ = 4.29 in.

Engine-Bed Siding = 78.7 × 2.97$^{0.3}$ = 109.1 mm

Engine-Bed Molding = 6.43 in. (163.6 mm)

Increase scantling for speed:

20 knots – 15 knots = 5 knots, and 5 knots × 1 percent increase per knot over 15 knots = 5 percent increase

Engine-Bed Siding = 4.29 in. × 1.05 = 4½ in.

Engine-Bed Siding = 109.1 mm × 1.05 = 114 mm

Engine-Bed Molding = 6¾ in. (170 mm)

On the boat's 37.20-foot (11.34 m) waterline length, our 20-knot *Bobber* is planing. This means that the engine beds should extend at least six frames forward and six frames aft of the fore-n-aft engine-mount bolts. Better still would be to run the engine beds for as much of the length of *Logger Bobber*'s bottom as possible. In this case, the bed molding should taper down to 2^3/$_4$ inches (68 mm) at the ends (60 percent of siding).

FORMULA 9-33
Engine Mounts

Engine mounts are the same as described in Formula 5-15.

FORMULA 9-34
Herringbone-Bottom Planking (Cross-Plank Bottom)

An alternative method for planking hard-chine hulls is to lay on the bottom plank athwartships rather than fore-n-aft. On flat-bottom boats, the plank is literally run exactly athwartships from chine to chine, usually continuous under the keel. On V-bottom hulls, the cross-planking is usually (although not always) installed at an angle raking aft and outboard from the centerline, at roughly 45 to 55 degrees. This looks vaguely like the bones in a fish, hence the name herringbone bottom.

Herringbone planking is usually simply nailed down over the keel and the chine. It is often installed with no caulking, with the planks just touching each other so that they take up and become watertight when wet. Indeed, some builders recommend leaving a space about equal to the thickness of a piece of ordinary writing paper between the planks of larger cross-plank boats, so that the swelling of the planks doesn't strain the bottom or the plank fasteners.

Herringbone-bottom (or straight cross-plank-bottom) structure should be sized as follows:

- Plank thickness should be 1.4 to 1.5 times the standard plank thickness (use 1.5 for workboats).
- Bottom frames are not usually used on vessels with Sns less than 3, and are often omitted on even larger craft. Vessels with Sns greater than 5 must use standard bottom framing and floors in addition to longitudinal bottom girders.
- The chine-log molding should be increased 10 percent. On workboats, increase molding 12 percent and siding 10 percent.
- Where the unsupported athwartships width or span from the outside face of the keel to the inboard edge of the chine log exceeds 4 feet (1.2 m), additional longitudinal hull-bottom girders must be installed inside the bottom plank—running straight fore-n-aft—to reduce the athwartships span between girders to 4 feet (1.2 m) or less. If bottom frames are used, their undersides are notched for the girder, which runs continuous just above the bottom plank. The girders must run the full length of the hull bottom and be fastened to the chine and transom.
- The bottom girder should be the same as the engine beds (see Formula 9-32), which they should double as. Accordingly, even small boats usually have bottom girders, which are fastened directly to the bottom plank.

Big-Boat Structural Members

Large offshore vessels and workboats often require additional structure in addition to that previously mentioned. The keel and keel batten are reinforced with a *keelson*, the deck is strengthened with longitudinal *deck girders*, and the hull itself may be further stiffened with added bilge stringers.

FORMULA 9-35
Keelson

Heavy workboats and offshore vessels with Sns larger than 15 should further reinforce their keel with an internal keelson. Yachts and high-speed vessels with diagonal hull-strapping need not fit a keelson unless their Sns are greater than 20.

The keelson is roughly a second internal keel bolted down through the top of the floors and into the keel below. In smaller sizes (for these large craft), the keelson may be from a single centerline timber. Larger craft, however, traditionally build up the keelson from several pieces: the *keelson proper* immediately above the keel on the centerline; *sister keelsons* bolted to either side of the keelson and down

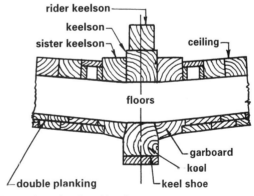

Large-boat keel and keelson

to the floors, and—on very large craft—a *rider keelson* bolted down on top of the centerline keelson. Building up the keelson structure from multiple pieces in this way keeps the timber dimensions smaller, which reduces problems with swelling and shrinkage.

Most boats under 90 feet (25 m) will not require a rider keelson. Also, in my opinion, it is better practice to laminate up a single centerline keelson from small stock than to hew and bolt together a keelson and sister keelsons. Whichever approach is used, the cross-sectional area of the keelson should equal approximately 80 percent of the cross-sectional area of the keel or of the keel and keel-batten combined.

FORMULA 9-36
Deck Girders

Large workboats that can experience substantial deck loads should install longitudinal deck girders running under and through-bolted to the deck beams. Vessels with Sns between 15 and 20 should install two girders about one-third and two-thirds of the way inboard from the maximum beam, and running straight fore-n-aft. Vessels with Sns over 20 should install four equi-spaced girders. Yachts with Sns under 20 do not require deck girders, nor do high-speed vessels (i.e., Sns less than 20) that have been diagonally strapped.

Deck girders should be molded the same as the heavy deck beams, and sided 1.1 times the siding of the heavy deck beams. The deck girders should be tied into the sheer clamp and shelf forward with knees or joining plates, and into the transom aft with knees. Where large cargo or fish-hold hatches are installed, it is best to adjust the girder spacing or the hatch dimensions so that the deck girders—running uninterrupted fore-n-aft—form the side structure of the hatch opening.

FORMULA 9-37
Multiple Bilge Stringers

Workboats and heavy offshore cruisers with Sns greater than 15 should further reinforce their hulls by adding additional bilge stringers (see Formula 9-15). Again, yachts and high-speed vessels that are diagonally strapped do not require these added stringers unless their Sns are greater than 20. A vessel like a tug or pilot boat that is expected to lie against other boats frequently would add a second bilge stringer midway up the topsides, between the standard bilge stringer and the sheer clamp. A vessel expected to take ground regularly should add a bilge stringer midway between the standard bilge stringer and the keel. Vessels with Sns greater than 20 should install both.

TEN

Fasteners, Straps, Knees, and Details

*T*raditional plank-on-frame wooden boats are only as strong as the fasteners that hold them together. Using the proper size and type of fastener and the correct joint is critical to a successful hull. In this chapter, we examine the standard fasteners and joints used throughout most wooden hulls.

Glue Joints

Glue was not traditionally used as a primary fastener on plank-on-frame boats; therefore, this section does not discuss glue joints in detail. However, Resorcinol waterproof glue was the standard for gluing plank scarfs and laminating timbers, such as laminated floors and stems. Although Resorcinol works well, modern two-part epoxy-adhesive systems are superior. Epoxy has exceptional gap-filling abilities and tremendous strength and elasticity. I recommend that epoxy be used for all structural gluing and laminating.

One important warning about epoxies, as well as other glues: They will not stick to anything with oil or grease (or any other petroleum-based product) contaminating the surface. Kerosene, regular motor oil, tallow, vegetable oil—all will destroy a glue's ability to form a reliable bond. Keep your joints oil-free. Similarly, some woods contain acids and/or oils that do not work well with some glues, particularly epoxy; oak and teak are two examples. Before making any glue joints or doing any laminating, read the glue manufacturer's literature carefully.

Scarf Joints

LONGITUDINAL JOINTS IN LARGE TIMBERS

The keel, stem, and other backbone timbers often must be made up of two or more lengths of timber joined together longitudinally. It's rare to find good clear stock sufficient to get out, for example, a 42-foot-long (12.8 m) keel in a single piece. The joints used to build up such longer timbers are called *scarf joints* (also spelled *scarph*). Scarf

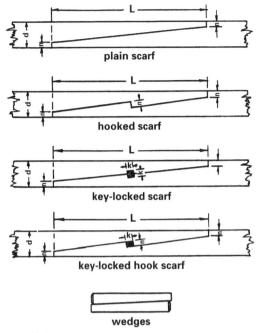

plain scarf

hooked scarf

key-locked scarf

key-locked hook scarf

wedges

Scarf joints

joints allow you to connect two short timbers together end-to-end to form a long one, while transmitting most of the full strength of the timbers across the joint.

A sloped faying surface is made on each of the two timbers (in mirror image) so they can be mounted together and through-bolted over a substantial length. The standard rule is that the slope runs six times the depth of the timber. In large timbers, the sloped surfaces aren't allowed to run out to a feather edge; instead, they are cut off vertically or *nibbed* at the ends. The nibs are 25 percent of the depth of the timber high. Nibbed ends avoid feather edges where cracks can start, and they help keep the joint from sliding if the fastening-bolt holes elongate.

TYPES OF SCARF JOINTS

Because the two nibs together total half the depth of the timber, the actual faying surface is at a 12:1 slope. This simple joint is used for most construction; it is called the *plain scarf*. If additional resistance to sliding is required, a *hooked-scarf* joint or a *key-locked scarf* joint (sometimes called a *key scarf*) can be used, as shown. The key-locked hooked-scarf joint provides maximum resistance to sliding, with maximum longitudinal joint strength as well. Generally, the plain scarf will be adequate for smaller longitudinal members (e.g., clamps and stringers), while the key-locked scarf should be used in the principal keel timbers. The hooked scarf is as strong as the key-locked scarf, but harder to fashion. The key-locked hook scarf is only called for in large vessels that will experience extreme service loadings, such as minesweepers or harbor tugs.

SCARF KEYS AND HOOKS

The key is square and each side is 25 percent of the depth of the timber. If a hook is used, its height is 25 percent of the timber depth. In timbers under 6 inches (150 mm) deep, the key is usually fashioned from a single solid block. In deeper timbers, the key is made of two wedges, each with a 12:1 slope. The wedges are driven in from opposite sides after the joint has been bolted together. Any excess is cut off. A hard dense wood such as locust or oak should be used for keys. The fastening bolts should be snugged up again after driving in the key.

TIMBERS TO BE SCARFED

On vessels with Sns over 3, nibbed scarf joints should be used on other longitudinal members in addition to the keel, including the shelf, clamp, bilge stringer, and deck carlins.

SCARF-FASTENING BOLTS

The plain scarf should be fastened with bolts equally spaced along the length of the scarf in timbers. For timbers with cross-sectional areas less than 20 square inches (130 cm²), use four bolts; between 20 and 100 square inches (130 and 650 cm²), use five bolts; for more than 100 square inches (650 cm²), use six bolts. The end bolts should be 25 percent of the timber depth in from the nib. The bolt diameter should be as shown in the following formula.

FORMULA 10-1

Scarf-Bolt Diameter and
Keel/Deadwood-Bolt Diameter

$Bolt\ Diameter\ (in.) = (sq.\ in.)^{0.4} \div 12$

$Bolt\ Diameter\ (mm) = 0.88 \times (cm^2)^{0.4}$

Where

sq. in. = timber sectional area, in square inches

cm² = timber sectional area, in square centimeters

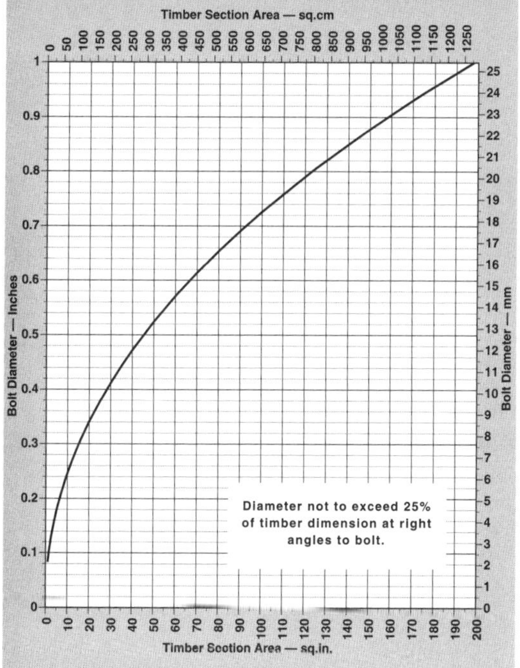

Scarf-Bolt Diameter

- Bolt diameter must not exceed 25 percent of the timber thickness measured at right angles to the bolt axis.
- Hooked- or keyed-scarf joints on timbers between 20 and 100 square inches (130 and 650 cm²) use only four through-bolts.
- Hooked or keyed scarfs are seldom called for on timbers less than 20 sq. in. (130 cm²).
- The bolt line should be staggered (not in line) on all but the narrowest timbers. Bolts must be at least four diameters in from the side of the timber.
- Heavy washers are required under the heads and nuts of all bolts.

Keel/backbone bolts for fastening the stem, horn timber, and deadwood should be sized using either this formula or Formula 10-6, whichever gives the larger diameter (as long as the bolt diameter is not larger than 30 percent of the keel siding). Generally, the joints between backbone components should be fashioned to be similar to keyed- or hooked-scarf joints for timbers of the dimensions being joined. Where practical, through-bolts are best; however, drift bolts work excellently for fastening keel timbers. Drift bolts are fashioned from a rod that is hammered to a slight conical point at the leading end and to a mushroom head at the driving end. A hole slightly smaller than the drift diameter is bored in the timbers to be joined and the drift bolt is hammered home with a large washer under the mushroom head. Drift bolts should be driven in at slightly opposing angles to each other; this locks the backbone timbers from sliding. Drift bolts used to be of hot-dip galvanized wrought iron. Today hot-dip galvanized mild steel is the common substitute. Bronze is good but doesn't rust to lock in place as tightly. Some builders use a

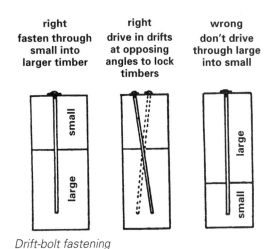

right	right	wrong
fasten through small into larger timber	drive in drifts at opposing angles to lock timbers	don't drive through large into small

Drift-bolt fastening

chisel to nick "barbs" into the sides of bronze drifts to increase holding power.

SCARF JOINTS IN PLANKS AND SMALLER TIMBERS

Smaller planks must also frequently be joined end to end to get sufficient length. Hull planks can be joined with butt blocks, but it's even better to scarf the planks into a single length. Ideally, plank scarfs are cut to a 12:1 slope just as in large timber scarfs. Because the planks are much thinner, however, no nibs are used. Glued scarfs are run out to a feather edge. These plank scarfs are glued together with no other mechanical fasteners. A well-made glued scarf joint, with a 12:1 slope, will have 90 percent of the strength of a continuous board without a joint.

Bilge stringers, clamps, shelves, and deck beams on small craft with Sns of 2 or less should also be made with the glued 12:1 plank scarf, without nibs.

Scarfs in planking should be separated fore-n-aft by at least three frame bays and vertically by a minimum of six strakes. Al-

Driving in a drift bolt to fasten deadwood and sternpost. The timbers are sealed with red lead. (Courtesy Kortchmar & Willner)

though 8:1 scarfs can be used, they are weaker; however, they are standard for scarfing plywood plank and other plywood panels.

Hull Fasteners

FASTENER MATERIAL

Metal fasteners are best made from the following metals, in order of preference:

1. Monel
2. Silicon bronze, phosphor, or aluminum bronze

3. Aquamet 22 or Nitronic 50 (chrome/moly stainless-steel alloys)
4. Stainless steel, Type 316L or 316
5. Stainless steel, Type 304 or 302
6. Galvanized mild steel (hot-dip galvanized only)
7. Brass screws—do not use

Monel is the best material for any marine fastening; it has high strength and very high corrosion resistance. Silicon bronze (occasionally phosphor or aluminum bronzes are available) is excellent for fastening. These bronzes have high corrosion resistance and high strength. They are not quite as strong as Monel; however, bronze is *the* standard marine-fastening alloy. Aquamet 22 and similar chrome/moly stainless-steel alloys are customarily used for propeller-shafting and rod-rigging. These alloys have exceptionally high tensile strength and corrosion resistance; they make ideal tie rods and bolts. Chrome/moly stainless is somewhat more prone to pitting corrosion than bronze or Monel, however.

All other stainless steels are subject to potentially severe pitting-corrosion attack when immersed in salt water, without free-oxygen (exactly the conditions of keel bolts and such). Thus, these stainless steels are less reliable than bronze, Monel, or chrome/moly stainless (in that order). Use stainless-steel fasteners under water only as a second choice. Stainless, however, makes fine internal bolts and tie rods. Type 316L ("L" for low carbon) is the most resistant to pitting corrosion and thus the first choice among stainless, followed by standard 316. The 302 and 304 stainless (even in low-carbon alloy) are still more liable to pitting attack than 316, and should not be used under water at all.

Galvanized mild-steel bolts have been employed for years. They are tolerable if you are willing to accept their shorter life expectancy and rust weeps. Only true *hot-dip* galvanized fasteners should be used.

Brass, with its high zinc content, has no place as a structural fastener on any boat. Brass is weaker than bronze or stainless steels, and it is also eminently prone to extreme brittle failure through corrosion called *dezincification*. Brass is, however, ideal for interior joinerwork.

FORMULA 10-2

Plank Fasteners

Plank-Fastener Diameter, in. = 0.09 + (plank thickness, in. ÷ 7.2) (English)

Plank-Fastener Diameter, mm = 2.29 + (plank thickness, mm ÷ 7.2) (Metric)

Screw Length = 2 × plank thickness

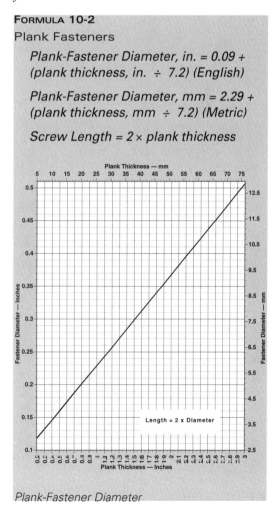

Plank-Fastener Diameter

TABLE 10-3 American Screw Gauge Screw Dimensions

No.	Shank Diameter, in. (mm)	Shank, Diameter, Nearest Fraction, in.	Head Diameter, in. (mm)
0	0.060 (1.52)	$^1/_{16}$	0.109 (2.78)
1	**0.073 (1.85)**	$^5/_{64}-$	**0.141 (3.57)**
2	0.086 (2.18)	$^5/_{64}+$	0.172 (4.37)
3	**0.099 (2.51)**	$^3/_{32}$	**0.138 (3.51)**
4	0.112 (2.84)	$^7/_{64}$	0.219 (5.56)
5	**0.125 (3.18)**	$^1/_8$	**0.250 (6.35)**
6	0.138 (3.51)	$^9/_{64}$	0.281 (7.14)
7	**0.151 (3.84)**	$^5/_{32}-$	**0.297 (7.54)**
8	0.164 (4.17)	$^5/_{32}+$	0.328 (8.33)
9	**0.177 (4.50)**	$^{11}/_{64}$	**0.359 (9.13)**
10	0.190 (4.83)	$^3/_{16}$	0.375 (9.53)
11	**0.203 (5.16)**	$^{13}/_{64}$	**0.406 (10.32)**
12	0.216 (5.49)	$^7/_{32}$	0.438 (11.11)
14	0.242 (6.15)	$^{15}/_{64}$	0.484 (12.30)
16	0.268 (6.81)	$^{17}/_{64}$	0.531 (13.49)
18	0.294 (7.47)	$^{19}/_{64}$	0.594 (15.08)
20	0.320 (8.13)	$^{21}/_{64}$	0.656 (16.67)
24	0.372 (9.45)	$^3/_8$	0.750 (19.05)

NOTE: Sizes in bold are usually special order items, not in regular stock.

In returning to our example boat, *Logger Bobber*, we found that it would require $1^1/_8$-inch (28 mm) plank. Accordingly, *Bobber*'s plank screws should be as follows:

0.09 + (1.125 in. ÷ 7.2) = 0.24-in. diameter; use No. 14 wood screws (0.242-in. diameter)

2.29 + (28 mm ÷ 7.2) = 6.17 mm diameter; use 6 mm wood screws

Screw Length = $2^1/_4$ in. (56 mm)

- Use three fasteners in each frame for wide planks and two fasteners per plank for narrow planks.
- On strip-planking, every other plank is fastened to the frame, alternating each frame bay.
- Annular-ring boat nails (i.e., silicon bronze or Monel) can be used instead of screws. The nails should be sized using Formula 10-12 and Tables 13A and 13B.
- In all planks over $^5/_8$ inch (16 mm) thick, the screws should be counter-bored and bunged.
- Copper rivets, clench nails, and galvanized boat nails are not covered by this formula.

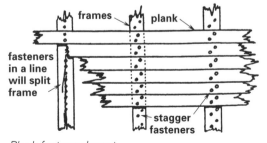

Plank-fastener layout

FORMULA 10-4
Butt Blocks

Where planks are too short to run the full length of the hull (which is common), the short planks are joined from a single long strake. This can be done with scarf joints or butt blocks.

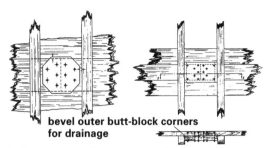

**bevel outer butt-block corners
for drainage**

**bolts shown are for large vessels; most boats use
wood screws**

Two butt-block arrangements

*Planks can never be butted at a frame.
A full butt block must be installed
between frames. Butt blocks should be
sized as follows:*

*Butt-Block Molding (Thickness) = plank
thickness*

*Butt-Block Height = 1.125 × plank height
at the butt block*

*Butt-Block Width (Fore-n-Aft) = 12 ×
plank height at the butt block*

*Butt-Block-Fastener Diameter = plank-
fastener diameter*

*Butt-Block-Fastener Length = 1.5 × plank
thickness (See photo on p. 339.)*

- Butt blocks must be screw-fastened, not nailed.
- Use five fasteners in each plank end, 10 total for each butt block.
- Planks less than 5 inches (127 mm) wide can use four fasteners; planks less than 3.5 inches (89 mm) wide can use just three fasteners.
- Counter-sink, counter-bore, and bung on all planks more than ⅝ inch (16 mm) thick.

- Planks over 9 inches (228 mm) must use six fasteners.

FORMULA 10-5

Strip-Plank Edge Nails

*Nail Diameter, in. = (plank thickness,
in.)$^{0.34}$ ÷ 10.3 (English)*

*Nail Diameter, mm = 0.2 + 0.8 × (plank
thickness, mm)$^{0.34}$ (Metric)*

*Nail Length = 1.75 × plank-siding
minimum to 2.25 × plank-siding
maximum*

*Nail Spacing = approximately 6 × plank
thickness*

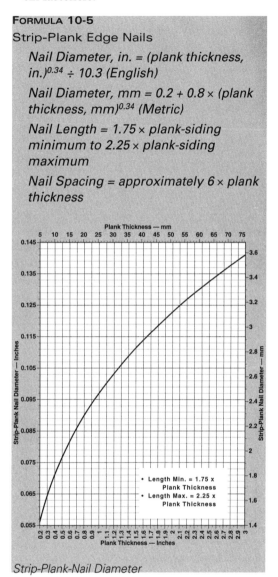

Strip-Plank-Nail Diameter

- Bronze or Monel annular-ring boat nails are preferred; stainless-steel nails are acceptable; and galvanized boat nails can be used, but may weep rust and begin to fail after 10 years or so.

- Nail spacing can be as much as 10 to 12 times plank thickness where there is little curvature, and should be as close as 4 times plank thickness where the hull is highly curved.
- Nails are staggered. For example, if the spacing is 6 inches, then the centers of the edge nails on the plank above will be offset 3 inches fore-n-aft from the plank below it.
- The planks must be edge-glued as well as nailed, although a high-strength adhesive sealant like 3M-5200 may be used instead of glue.

Say we strip-planked *Logger Bobber* with 1¹⁄₈-inch-thick (28 mm) plank. The average plank siding would be about 1.2 times the thickness or 1³⁄₈ inches (34 mm). Accordingly, we would use the following:

Nail Diameter = (1.125 in.)^{0.34} ÷ 10.3 = 0.10-in. diameter

Nail Diameter = 0.2 + 0.8 × (28 mm)^{0.34} = 2.67 mm diameter

Nail Length = 1.75 to 2.25 × 1³⁄₈ in. = 2³⁄₈ to 3 in.

Nail Length = 1.75 to 2.25 × 34 mm = 60 to 77 mm

Nail Spacing = approximately 7 in. (180 mm)

FORMULA 10-6

Floor-to-Frame Fasteners

Fastener Diameter, in. = 0.24 × Sn^{0.36} (English)

Fastener Diameter, mm = 6.1 × Sn^{0.36} (Metric)

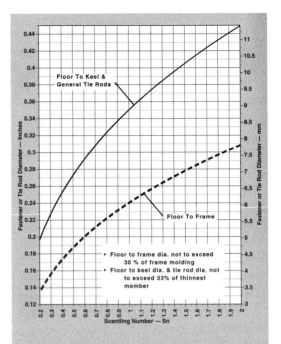

Floor Fasteners and General Tie Rods: Small Boats

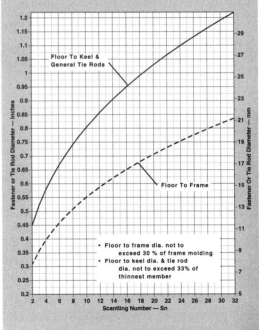

Floor Fasteners and General Tie Rods: Large Boats

- Vessels with Sns higher than 2 should use through-bolts.
- Vessels with Sns of 2 or less can use wood screws.
- Fastener diameter must not exceed 30 percent of frame molding.
- Washers must be used under the heads and nuts of all bolts.

Reliable old *Logger Bobber*'s floors should be fastened with the following:

Fastener Diameter = 0.24 × 2.97$^{0.36}$ = 0.36; use ⅜-in. diameter

Fastener Diameter = 6.1 × 2.97$^{0.36}$ = 9.02; use 9 mm diameter

0.375-in.-Diameter Bolt ÷ 2.125-in. frame siding = 17 percent; okay

9 mm diameter bolt ÷ 54 mm frame siding = 17 percent; okay

FORMULA 10-7

Floor-to-Keel Fasteners and General Tie Rods

The bolts fastening the floors down to the keel and the general tie rods used in places such as the mast partners and cabin sides are generally the same diameter.

Fastener Diameter, in. = 0.35 × Sn$^{0.36}$ (English)

Fastener Diameter, mm = 8.9 × Sn$^{0.36}$ (Metric)

- Bolt diameter may not be larger than 33 percent of the floor siding.
- Two bolts should be used in each floor (i.e., one port and one starboard). At the bow near the stem and at the narrow deadwood aft, a single bolt on the center-

line may be used where this is unavoidable.
- For general tie-rod use, the bolt diameter may not be larger than 33 percent of the thickness of the thinnest member it penetrates.
- Where diameter exceeds 33 percent, reduce diameter until a 33 percent ratio is achieved.
- Heavy washers must be used under the heads and nuts of all bolts.

Logger Bobber's floors would be fastened with the following:

Fastener Diameter = 0.35 × 2.97$^{0.36}$ = 0.52; use ½ in. diameter

Fastener Diameter = 8.9 × 2.97$^{0.36}$ = 13.16; use 12 mm diameter

0.5-in.-Diameter Bolt ÷ 2.125-in. floor siding = 23 percent; okay

12 mm Diameter Bolt ÷ 54 mm floor siding = 22 percent; okay

Most of the other structural tie rods at the mast, engine beds, cabins, and sides should be of this same diameter.

MAST-STEP TIE RODS

On sailboats with keel-stepped masts, the compression load on the mast is trying to drive the mast step through the bottom of the boat. This forces the keel down, which in turn pulls down the frames attached to the floors. In response, this pulls the frames together, which pinches the deck together athwartships. Finally, this causes the deck to bulge up at the centerline. To counteract these forces, a tie rod should be installed from the partners vertically down through the mast step. The tie rod can be installed just forward or just aft of the mast at the partners. It is surprising to me how many boats I see without a mast-step tie rod. I inspected one such vessel in which the plywood deck had lifted a full $1/4$ inch (7 mm) off the deck beams at the centerline near the mainmast. This boat was just 20 feet (6 m); even small vessels should be fitted with a mast-step tie rod.

Of course, when a mast is stepped on deck, the resulting forces are very different and a mast-step tie rod is not appropriate.

FORMULA 10-8

Mast-Step Tie Rods

Tie-Rod Breaking Strength, lb. = 3,200 × $Sn^{1.2}$ (English)

Tie-Rod Breaking Strength, kg = 1,450 × $Sn^{1.2}$ (Metric)

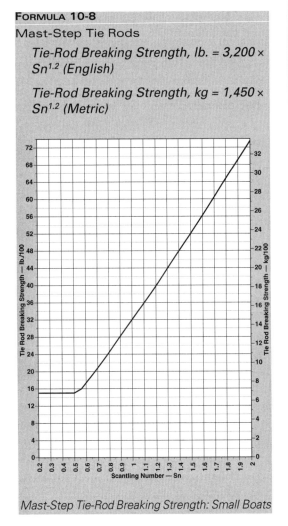

Mast-Step Tie-Rod Breaking Strength: Small Boats

Mast-Step Tie-Rod Breaking Strength: Large Boats

- The minimum breaking strength for small boats with Sns less than 0.55 should be 1,500 lb. (680 kg), which equals the breaking strength of $1/8$-in.-diameter (3 mm) 1 × 19 stainless-steel rigging wire. Anything lighter will be to liable to damage from being stepped on and knocked about.
- Find the breaking strength and then refer to the bolt-tensile-strength table to find the diameter (see appendix 3).
- Mizzenmast tie rods can be 70 percent of the mainmast tie-rod diameter.
- Foremast tie rods on schooners should be the same diameter as the mainmast tie rod.
- The tie rod may best be made from 1 × 19 wire with a turnbuckle for tensioning. The 1 × 19 wire should have the same tensile strength as the tie rod.

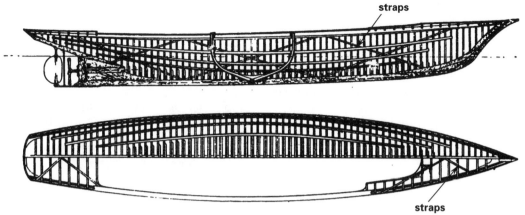

straps

straps

Diagonal strapping

- On larger boats, two tie rods can be used—one forward and one aft of the mast, at the partners. The combined breaking strength of the two tie rods should equal the strength of a standard single tie rod.

If *Logger Bobber* were a cutter, its mast-step tie rod would be

$$\text{Tie-Rod Breaking Strength} = 3{,}200 \times 2.97^{1.2}$$
$$= 11{,}816 \text{ lb.}$$

$$\text{Tie-Rod Breaking Strength} = 1{,}450 \times 2.97^{1.2}$$
$$= 5{,}354 \text{ kg}$$

Diameter in Silicon Bronze
(from the Bolt-Strength Table) = ⁹⁄₁₆ in.

Diameter in Silicon Bronze
(from the Bolt-Strength Table) = 16 mm

FORMULA 10-9
Keel-Ballast Bolts
Use Formulas 5-12 and 5-13.

- Ballast bolts must pass through the center of the floors.
- The floors must be sided at least four times the ballast-bolt diameter.

DIAGONAL STRAPPING

One of the reasons the frigate *U.S.S. Constitution* was so strong, could carry such heavy cannon for her size, and has survived as long as she has is her diagonal bracing. The use of diagonal bracing was fairly new in the late eighteenth century, and it put *Old Ironsides'* designer, Joshua Humphreys, at the cutting edge of marine technology. It also meant that Yankee know-how—and the strength of live oak—gave so substantial an advantage that the *Constitution* never lost a battle. It's indicative of how little diagonal bracing is understood, however, that over a hundred years later—when the *Constitution* was rebuilt—these diagonals were left out. It wasn't until the 1997 restoration that the missing members were refitted and the *Constitution* was again fit to sail.

The fact is that traditional plank-on-frame construction is quite strong and efficient, with one exception: Plank-on-frame hulls are not torsionally stiff; they can wrack or twist. In the broadest sense, the stem twists clockwise, the transom twists counterclockwise. This lack of torsional stiffness can also lead to *hogging*, where the bow and stern droop. The fix: Diagonal braces or strapping—ruggedly screwed and through-bolted to the plank and frames—distributes torsional loads into the structure giving the necessary torsional strength. Humphreys used wood diagonals on *Old Ironsides*; the modern standard—as far as I know, pioneered by Captain Nat Herreshoff—is bronze strapping.

It is astonishing to me just how few plank-on-frame boats are built with diagonal strapping. It's not particularly difficult or costly, and it will add years to the life of any plank-on-frame boat. Diagonal straps should be proportioned as follows.

Width (Siding), in. = $1.65 \times Sn^{0.4}$ (English)

Width (Siding), mm = $41.9 \times Sn^{0.4}$ (Metric)

Thickness (Molding) = width ÷ 22

Fastener Diameter = width (siding) ÷ 14 (but not less than ⅛ in. [3.2 mm])

Fastener Spacing = width (siding) ÷ 2.5 (along both edges of strap)

Fastener in from Edge = 3.5 × fastener diameter

Fastener Length = 0.75 × plank thickness

- Small boats and inshore boats don't require diagonal strapping; however, all boats with an Sn greater than 2.5 will benefit markedly from diagonal straps. All larger offshore boats and workboats with Sns over 4 should have diagonal strapping.
- Strapping must be of silicon bronze or the equivalent, with a minimum tensile strength of 60,000 psi (413 mPa).
- Straps of somewhat differing proportions may be used, as long as their net cross-sectional area equals that of the strap recommended by the formula.
- Strapping is installed over the frames and under the plank. The frames are mortised just enough at the strap so the top of the strap lies flush under the plank.
- Screw-fasten the strap to the inside of each plank, using round-head screws. On very large boats, lag bolts may be used. Use two rows of fasteners along each edge of the strap. Where straps cross, fasten down through the inner strap, through the outer strap, and into the plank. Use one standard plank fastener to hold the strap to each frame. Fasten standard plank fas-

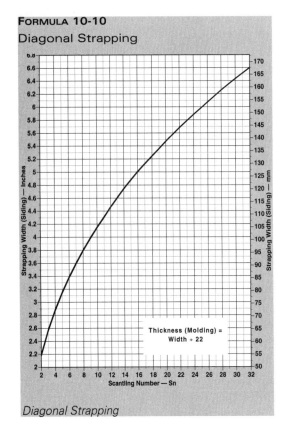

FORMULA 10-10

Diagonal Strapping

Diagonal Strapping

teners through the plank and the strap.

- Straps are installed at approximately a 45-degree angle to the fore-n-aft axis.
- There should be a pair of diagonal straps (running at approximately right angles to each other) at each mast, on the hull sides, and on the deck. Additional straps are used on larger hulls.
- The hull straps start together at the sheer and angle 45 degrees fore-n-aft.
- Deck straps form an X on the deck, with the center of the X either immediately in front or aft of the mast at the partners. The deck straps should be through-bolted to the partners.
- On boats with Sns higher than 6, three pairs of straps (six total) should be used on each side.
- All boats, power and sail, should use straps per side (and on deck) equal in number to the Sn rounded up to the nearest whole number, but not to exceed six straps per side and not less than two.
- Plywood decks have torsional rigidity and do not require diagonal strapping.
- Because of the edge-nailing and gluing of the planks on strip-plank hulls, the planks will not slide fore-n-aft relative to each other. This introduces torsional stiffness. Strip-plank hulls do not require diagonal strapping. For the same reason, lapstrake hulls do not require diagonal strapping.

In *Logger Bobber*'s case, its Sn is under 4, so straps are optional but recommended. With an Sn of 2.97, we would round up to three straps per side. If it were a cutter or a sloop, we would install a pair of straps on each side of the hull, starting at the sheer athwartships from the mast. The third strap would start aft near the cockpit and angle for-ward. If, however, *Bobber* were a ketch, we would use four straps per side: two at the foremast and two at the mizzenmast. Alternately, if *Logger Bobber* were a powerboat, we would use three straps, with a pair starting at the sheer, a little forward of midships; the third strap would start at the sheer, aft near the cockpit, and angle forward. Dimensions would be as follows:

$$Width\ (Siding) = 1.65 \times 2.97^{0.4} = 2.55;$$
$$use\ 2\tfrac{1}{2}\ in.$$

$$Width\ (Siding) = 41.9 \times 2.97^{0.4} = 64.7;$$
$$use\ 65\ mm$$

$$Thickness\ (Molding) = \tfrac{1}{8}\ in.\ (3\ mm)$$

$$Fastener\ Diameter = 0.17\ in.;\ use\ No.\ 9\ or$$
$$No.\ 10\ screws\ (4.5\ mm\ screws)$$

$$Fastener\ Spacing = 1\ in.\ (25\ mm)$$

$$Fastener\ in\ from\ Edge = 0.59\ in.;\ use\ \tfrac{9}{16}\ in.$$
$$(1.25\ mm)$$

$$Fastener\ Length = \tfrac{7}{8}\ in.\ (20\ mm)$$

FORMULA 10-11
Breasthook and Quarter Knees

Molding = deck-beam molding

Breasthook Length = approximately 1.75 × frame spacing

Quarter-Knee Length = approximately 1.3 × frame spacing

The quarter knees and breasthook are bolted down onto the shelf and clamp, and to the inside face of the stem and transom.

- Fastenings should be the same diameter as the floor-to-frame fasteners in Formula 10-6.
- Metal knees can be substituted; silicon bronze or Monel is the first choice, stainless-steel is the second choice, and hot-dip galvanized steel is a distant third.

correct   incorrect

Driving square-cut boat nails. Square-cut boat nails must be driven so the thin dimension is aligned with the grain. (Courtesy Tremont Nail Company)

- Metal-Knee-Siding Molding = wooden-knee molding ÷ 6
- Metal-Knee Bolt-Flange Length = frame molding

BOAT NAILS, CLENCH NAILS, AND RIVETS

Modern round wire nails should not be used for structural fastenings in a hull. Stainless-steel wire nails can be used, however, for edge-nailing strip-plank and for tacking and clamping together laminated hull components. Bronze or Monel annular-ring boat nails are superior, though, and much preferred.

If square-section, hot-dip-galvanized boat nails can be found, they are acceptable for plank-fastening. Bronze or Monel annular-ring boat nails are excellent. The old rule-of-thumb for sizing U.S. boat nails is as follows:

FORMULA 10-12

Boat Nail Size

- *For hardwood: The penny of the nail equals the number of eighths of an inch in the plank thickness.*
- *For extremely hard woods (e.g., well-seasoned white oak or hickory), the penny of the nail can be one less than the eighths of an inch in the plank thickness.*
- *For softwoods: The penny of the nail should equal the number of eighths of an inch in the plank thickness plus a quarter-inch.*
- *See Tables 10-13A and 10-13B for nail dimensions relative to the penny or length of the nail.*

Clench-nail length should equal the combined thickness of the plank plus the frame, plus a quarter-inch (6.5 mm) if bunged and a half-inch (13 mm) if not bunged. Because clench nails are *turned over* (i.e., hammered back around into a U shape on the inside of the hull), they must be from a soft malleable material. The old standard was soft wrought-iron, hot-dip galvanized. The current alternative is copper or some of the softer bronzes.

Built by the Covey Island Boatworks, the Gerr 42-foot (12.8 m) tunnel-drive motor cruiser Summer Kyle/Belle Marie *cruises the Chesapeake. The boat's construction is wood-epoxy strip-plank with heavy exterior hull sheathing exactly as detailed in the scantling rule. Drawing just 21 inches (53 cm), the boat has repeatedly weathered rough seas offshore and numerous groundings, all without the slightest difficulty.* (Courtesy Starke Jette)

Clench nails can be turned over on the inside without a washer, but a washer is preferable on larger vessels. The washer on a clench nail or rivet is usually termed a *rove* or a *burr*. In lapstrake construction, clench nails and rivets are not counter-bored or bunged, but rather are left flush with the surface even on bright-finished hulls.

Nail diameter is roughly proportional to length, and length—in the English system—is termed penny, which is abbreviated as "d." Tables 10-13A and 10-13B give standard lengths and diameters for U.S. boat nails.

- As a rule, heavy boat nails should be used in hardwood and light boat nails in softwood.
- All nail holes must be pre-bored before driving.

Copper rivets are about the same diameter as boat nails and slightly shorter than clench nails. Copper rivets are always hammered down on the inside over a rove or burr. The rove is a tight fit over the shank of the rivet, and is driven down on top of the plank inside with a roving iron. Excess rivet length is cut off and the remaining interior rivet is hammered down tight on top of the rove, forming the inside head.

Knees and Details

HANGING AND LODGING KNEES

Hanging knees are knees installed vertically, such as between the underside of the deck beams and the side of the frames on the hull topsides. *Lodging knees* are knees that are installed horizontally, usually under the deck. For example, a knee between the strong deck beam ahead of the mast and the sheer clamp would be a lodging knee.

TABLE 10-13A
Heavy Boat Nails

Penny	Length, in. (mm)	Diameter, in. (mm)
4d	1.50 (38)	¼ (6.3)
6d	2.00 (51)	¼ (6.3)
8d	2.50 (63)	¼ (6.3)
10d	3.00 (76)	⅜ (9.5)
12d	3.25 (83)	⅜ (9.5)
16d	3.50 (89)	⅜ (9.5)
20d	4.00 (101)	⅜ (9.5)

TABLE 10-13B
Light Boat Nails

Penny	Length, in. (mm)	Diameter, in. (mm)
4d	1.50 (38)	3⁄16 (4.7)
6d	2.00 (51)	3⁄16 (4.7)
8d	2.50 (63)	3⁄16 (4.7)
10d	3.00 (76)	¼ (6.3)
12d	3.25 (83)	¼ (6.3)
16d	3.50 (89)	¼ (6.3)
20d	4.00 (101)	¼ (6.3)

Hanging knees are sided fore-n-aft; their thickness, however, is up and down, which is their molding.

FORMULA 10-14
Hanging and Lodging Knees

Knee Thickness = frame siding

Hanging-Knee Length Along the Arms = approximately 1.5 × frame spacing

Lodging-Knee Length Along the Arms = slightly less than frame spacing

Hanging and lodging knees present a conundrum: They are common in many traditional plank-on-frame hulls, and they do strengthen the structure; however, they also form crevices and pockets where decay can begin. Generally, vessels built to this scantling rule with Sns of 9 or less do not require hanging or lodging knees. This is particularly so if the hull has been diagonally strapped and tie rods are installed at the mast and partners. Craft with Sns greater than 9 will benefit from installing knees (see photo on p. 340).

Some of these drawbacks can be reduced or eliminated by using cast or welded metal knees. These do not shrink, swell, or decay.

see photo on p. 340

FORMULA 10-15
Metal Knees

- *Metal knees should be silicon bronze or Monel (first choice), stainless-steel (second choice), or hot-dip galvanized steel (a distant third).*

- *Metal-Knee Thickness = wooden-knee thickness ÷ 6*

- *Metal-Knee Bolt-Flange Length = frame molding*

Knees are installed as follows:

- Hanging knees at each strong deck beam.
- Lodging knees facing in opposing directions at every other strong deck beam.

Logger Bobber, with an Sn of 2.97, is not large enough for the added strength of lodging knees to be worth the cost in potential future decay. Again, this is particularly so if *Logger*'s hull is diagonally strapped.

FORMULA 10-16
Backing Blocks

Backing blocks should be installed under all highly loaded deck hardware. The highest loads are experienced by windlasses and sampson posts. The backing blocks for these items should be nearly identical to the mast partners, including the through-bolting to the deck beams. The width of these backing blocks need be no more than 12 percent wider than the width of the windlass base. In the case of sampson posts, the backing block should be at least as wide as the transverse width of the sampson post, on each side of the post. Windlasses must have aluminum, stainless-steel, or bronze backing plates under the backing block. These plates should be at least 5 percent larger in every dimension than the footprint of the windlass. Backing plates should be at least 0.375 times the thickness of the through-bolts and never less than $\frac{3}{16}$ inch (5 mm).

Mooring and docking cleats are best fastened to similar backing blocks; however, they may be fastened through plywood backing blocks instead. These should be at least 75 percent of the thickness of the plywood deck. They should be at least 12 percent larger in footprint than the footprint of the cleat on deck. All fasteners must be through-bolted with large washers.

Special attention must be paid to backing blocks and associated reinforcement for all other highly loaded deck hardware, including davits, fighting chairs, fishing gear, winches, rigging cleats, genoa, and traveler track.

ELEVEN

Modern Wood-Epoxy Construction

*D*uring the last 30 years or so, wooden-boat construction has undergone something of a revolution. As rugged and efficient as traditional plank-on-frame construction is, it still has several significant drawbacks: (1) the structure is no stronger than the individual fasteners holding it together; (2) most importantly, the wood structure is subject to decay; (3) wood is relatively soft, particularly when compared to metal—hulls can be damaged by impact and abrasion; (4) the swelling-shrinkage cycles in the wood lead to loose fasteners and deterioration of the timber; and (5) the very high-quality lumber necessary for first-rate plank-on-frame construction is becoming increasingly difficult to locate and increasingly expensive to buy.

Modern epoxy glues and coatings are so tenacious, elastic, and water-vapor-impermeable that they have solved (or helped to solve) all these drawbacks. A boat that has been entirely glued together with epoxy is not limited in strength by its metal fasteners. The glue joints are far stronger than individual metal

fasteners, and the structure forms a large one-piece assembly—*monocoque* construction.

Sealing and coating every piece of wood all around with epoxy roughly freezes the timber at the moisture content it had at the time of the coating. Neither water vapor nor oxygen pass freely through the sealing barrier. (There is some slight permeability, but it's too slow for decay.) This not only eliminates almost all possibility for rot, but it also stabilizes the structure against swelling/shrinkage cycles—they simply don't occur.

Finally, sheathing the hull with fiberglass laid in epoxy—or other appropriate fibers—vastly increases abrasion and impact resistance. Early attempts at hull sheathing used polyester resin, but these attempts were usually unsuccessful. Polyester simply does not have the elasticity and peel strength required. Epoxy has both and does a splendid job. Furthermore, the sheathing itself is not subject to the extensive shrinkage and swelling on a hull with its wood structure stabilized by epoxy saturation.

Lumber Specification

Epoxy's sealing of the wood and the greater strength achieved by monocoque construction permit a far wider selection of woods to be used in epoxy-saturated hulls. Furthermore, the quality of the lumber need not be as high, nor does the wood have to be a species that is naturally highly rot-resistant. Generally, you can use virtually any conveniently available wood that meets the following requirements.

FORMULA 11-1

Wood-Epoxy Lumber-Density Specifications

- *Planking Wood—Small Boats (Hulls with Sns Less than 2.5): between 24 and 32 lb./cu. ft. (384 to 512 kg/m³)*

- *Planking Wood—Large Boats (Hulls with Sns of 2.5 or Higher): between 32 and 44 lb./cu. ft. (512 to 704 kg/m³)*

- *Frames, Keel, and All Framing Timber (All Size Boats): between 32 and 44 lb./cu. ft. (512 to 705 kg/m³)*

- *Lumber should be relatively clear and straight-grained; rift-sawn is greatly preferred. (If plain-sawn lumber is used extensively, scantlings should be increased by 8 to 10 percent.)*

- *Wood must not contain natural oils or acids that interfere with good epoxy-glue bonds; teak and oak are two such woods. Although you can glue teak and oak successfully with epoxy, longevity is suspect and more extensive joint preparation and practical gluing experience is required—not recommended for structural applications.*

Construction Methods

Almost all types of wooden-boat construction can be built with wood-epoxy-saturated techniques. Even plank-on-frame hulls can be fully saturated (if and only if they're built this way from scratch). A wood-epoxy carvel-plank hull would have individual timbers saturated with epoxy—the frames, floors, keel structure, deck beams, clamp, and stringers would all be glued together as well as metal-fastened. A plywood deck and cabin structure would be fully epoxied together and coated. The planks, however, would be individually installed with normal screws and caulking (not glued). If traditional cotton and oakum caulking is used, the planks must not be epoxy-saturated. This is so the planks will take up properly to make the seams watertight. Alternately, the planks could be individually coated all around with epoxy and installed with screw fasteners, but not glued. In this case, the seams should be sealed with epoxied-in-place *splines* (i.e., slender triangular-section wedges glued into the seam openings).

Epoxy-saturated carvel-plank hulls can be built, but they would be rather labor-intensive. The three standard wood-epoxy hull constructions are strip-plank, sheet-plywood, and cold-molded (i.e., multiple diagonal veneers). We examine each of these in turn.

WOOD-EPOXY STRIP-PLANK CONSTRUCTION

Wood-epoxy strip-plank construction runs the continuum from boats that are completely traditional plank-on-frame strip-plank-built vessels to hulls that are extensively glassed inside and out and devoid of most traditional framing. The latter are really strip-plank, cored-composite hulls and are much more akin to cored FRP than to traditional wooden boats. One of the lightest forms of fiberglass-skin, wood-epoxy, strip-plank construction is Baltek's proprietary DuraKore construction. A complete detailed scantling rule for Dura-Kore—devised by the author—is available in the *Baltek DuraKore Scantling Handbook*.

Conventional Wood-Epoxy Strip-Plank Construction

Conventional wood-epoxy strip-plank construction is identical to traditional plank-on-frame construction. Follow the formulas and recommendations in chapters 9 and 10. The difference is that every component of the entire wooden structure is glued together with marine-epoxy grout. Additionally, every component is coated and sealed with three coats (minimum) of unthickened marine epoxy.

Substantial labor savings can be achieved as follows:

- You don't have to bevel the planks or even make convex/concave edges on the planks to get a tight joint. Cut all the planks square and strip them on the hull, allowing the gaps created in the seams (plank edges) to form as they will. These gaps are simply filled with the thickened epoxy grout/glue as each plank is installed.

- It is not necessary to scarf the planks into long lengths. Simply butt each short length of plank to the next. Edge-nail down into the strip below at each butt. Be sure to stagger each butt by at least six planks vertically, and by at least three frames fore-n-aft. (This butt-only strip-joint may raise eyebrows in some circles. It works because—taken as a whole—the well-staggered individual butts essentially form a "finger join" in the hull shell, which is quite strong.)

- It is not necessary to *spile* (i.e., taper) the strip-planks to get a consistent plank run that harmonizes with the sheer. It is permissible to let the planks simply run out at any angle or curve they naturally take as they are installed from sheer to garboard or vice versa. Alternately—if you want a fair, harmonious plank run in the topsides—you can mark a constant distance on the frames, measured from the sheer down to roughly the turn of the bilge. Then install the bottom strip-planks, starting at the keel, until you reach the marks. Allow these bottom strip-planks to take any angle or curve they want, but cut them off in a neat, smooth, continuous line fore-n-aft at the marks. This cut line will now run parallel to the sheer. Start strip-planking the topsides from this cut plank line up to the sheer. All the topside planks will run parallel to the sheer.

- On many boats, you can use permanent structural bulkheads instead of standard frames. In this case, the bulkheads are structural members similar to their use in FRP hulls. Bulkheads should be sized (but not spaced) according to Formula 5-5. Wherever the bulkhead can be located close to the calculated strip-plank frame spacing—and where the bulkhead is essentially an unbroken ring (molded at least 6.75 times its thickness at the deepest cutout)—a separate frame is not required (see photo on p. 340).

- Watertight/collision bulkheads should be according to Formula 9-29. These may be tabbed in place according to Formula 5-5 or they may be glued and screwed to frames, or some combination of the two. Tabbing should be from a bi-axial stitch-mat-style fabric that is compatible with epoxy.

- Frames may be laminated in place against the strip-planked hull shell. In this case, the sheer clamp may also be laminated in place against the inside of the planking (instead of against the inside of the frames). A shelf is not required, but the clamp should be sized according to the rule for sheer clamps without shelves (see Formula 9-15).

Wood-Epoxy Strip-Plank Exterior Hull Sheathing

All wood-epoxy hulls and decks should be covered with glass cloth or a similar material (e.g., Dynel or Vectra). This enhances abrasion resistance and gives a much thicker outer layer of epoxy-fiber matrix, which further protects the wood from degradation.

The minimum glass layer on hulls and cabin structures that are to be finished bright should use one layer of 8- to 10-oz./sq. yd. (270 to 339 g/m^2) glass cloth laid in epoxy. Very small boats (e.g., canoes and rowing skiffs) would use 5-oz./sq. yd. (170 g/m^2) cloth. For Dynel, Vectra, or Xynole polyester, the minimum is 4 oz./sq. yd. (135 g/m^2) for all size boats.

Decks and cabin roofs should be covered with glass cloth, as specified in Formulas 9-19 through 9-26.

Better abrasion resistance, torsional strength, and longevity is achieved with heavier exterior sheathing on the hull; however, such hulls must be painted because the laminate is too thick to show attractive wood-grain. Even better—as we'll see—the torsional strength and increased abrasion resistance of the sheathing allows the use of thinner strip-plank (see photo on p. 341).

FORMULA 11-2

Heavy Exterior Hull Sheathing for Strip-Plank Hulls

For hulls with Sns of 0.6 or higher:

Hull-Sheathing Fabric Weight, oz./sq. yd. = 30.8 + (8.3 × Sn) (English)

Hull-Sheathing Fabric Weight, g/m^2 = 1,044 + (281.4 × Sn) (Metric)

For Hulls with Sns Less than 0.6:

Hull-Sheathing Fabric Weight, oz./sq. yd. = 0.11 + (59.45 × Sn) (English)

Hull-Sheathing Fabric Weight, g/m^2 = 3.73 + (2,015 × Sn) (Metric)

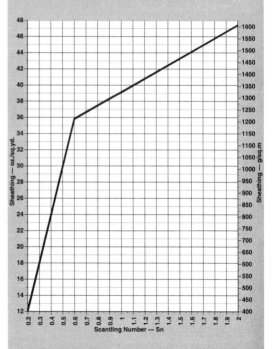

Heavy Exterior-Sheathing-Only Strip-Plank Hulls Sheathing Weight: Small Boats

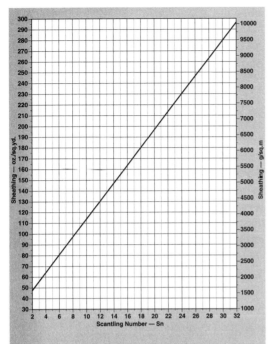

Heavy Exterior-Sheathing-Only Strip-Plank Hulls Sheathing Weight: Large Boats

- Vessels with Sns over 2 should use a sheathing laminate composed of bi-axial uni-di E-glass. With the uni-di layers installed at plus and minus 45 degrees to the fore-n-aft axis, such sheathing acts as diagonal strapping. In this way, the sheathing not only increases abrasion resistance but also torsional stiffness as well.
- Vessels with Sns less than 2 can use glass cloth instead of bi-axial fabric.
- Increase sheathing weight on bottom by 1 percent for every knot over 25 knots.
- Boats with Sns under 1.0 will not see much benefit from this construction method. Standard wood-epoxy strip-plank with lighter sheathing will work well.
- Increase sheathing weight by 10 percent on workboats and offshore cruisers.

- With internal frames, bulkheads, and backbone structure, no internal hull sheathing is required or recommended.

To sheath the exterior of *Logger Bobber*'s hull, we would apply

Hull-Sheathing Fabric Weight = 30.8 + (8.3 × 2.97) = 55.4; use 55 oz./sq. yd.

Hull-Sheathing Fabric Weight = 1,044 + (281.4 × 2.97) = 1,879.7; use 1,880 g/m²

FORMULA 11-3
Exterior-Only Sheathed Strip-Plank Thickness

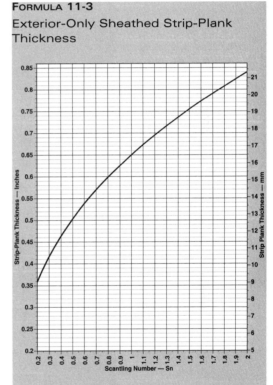

Exterior-Only Sheathed Strip-Plank Thickness: Small Boats

To determine the reduced strip-plank thickness that can be used with wood-epoxy strip-plank hulls that have the heavy exterior bi-axial E-glass sheathing specified in Formula 11-2, we would use the following:

(continued)

Strip-Plank Thickness, in. = 0.65 × Sn^0.3 (English)

Strip-Plank Thickness, mm = 16.51 × Sn^0.3 (Metric)

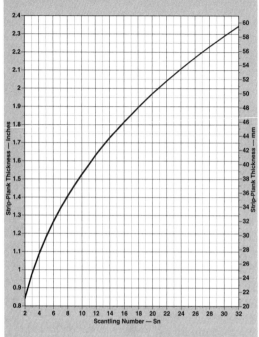

Exterior-Only Sheathed Strip-Plank Thickness: Large Boats

If our *Bobber* were so built, it would have

Strip-Plank Thickness = 0.65 × 2.97^0.3 = 0.97; use 1-in. plank

Strip-Plank Thickness = 16.51 × 2.97^0.3 = 24.7; use 25 mm plank

This is as opposed to the 1⅛-inch or 28 mm plank we specified for unsheathed strip-plank or conventional carvel-plank.

Double-Diagonal Exterior Wood Veneers on Wood-Epoxy Strip-Plank Hulls

An alternative to the heavy FRP exterior sheathing is double-diagonal layers of wood veneer—a layer of double-diagonal cold-molding. The outside of the hull must still be sheathed with a minimum 8- to 12-oz./sq. yd. (270 to 407 g/m²) glass cloth. (For Dynel or Vectra, the minimum is 4 oz./sq. yd. [135 g/m²].) With this construction, the double-diagonal cold-molded layers provide the same torsional stiffness that the heavy exterior hull sheathing provides. Because the veneers add appreciable thickness to the shell, the underlying strip-plank is reduced proportionately.

Boats with Sns less than 2.0 will not benefit much from this construction technique. Standard wood-epoxy strip-plank will serve best.

There are two drawbacks to external-wood diagonal layers on strip-plank hulls: the process of applying the diagonal wood layers is more labor-intensive than the FRP sheathing; and the heavy exterior FRP sheathing provides greater impact and abrasion resistance. Nevertheless, double-diagonal wood veneers over strip-plank is an excellent construction.

Note that although the method specifies two diagonal layers, there is no reason you cannot employ four or six layers, each proportionately thinner, to generate the total veneer thickness specified.

FORMULA 11-4
Strip-Plank Exterior Diagonal Wood-Veneer Thickness

Use the following to determine the thickness of the diagonal layers:

Thickness, Both Diagonal Layers Combined, in. = (0.43 × Sn^0.2) – 0.32 (English)

Thickness, Both Diagonal Layers Combined, mm = (10.92 × Sn^0.2) – 8.13 (Metric)

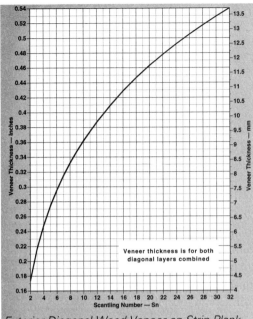

Exterior Diagonal Wood Veneer on Strip-Plank Hulls

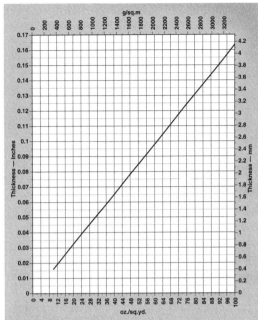

Bi-Axial Stitched Fabric (No Mat) Dry-Glass Weight vs. Laminate Thickness: Small Boats

Thus, *Logger Bobber* would use the following:

Thickness, Both Diagonal Layers Combined = $(0.43 \times 2.97^{0.2}) - 0.32 = 0.21$; use two diagonal layers ⅛-in. veneer, totals ¼ in.

Thickness, Both Diagonal Layers Combined = $(10.92 \times 2.97^{0.2}) - 8.13 = 5.44$; use two diagonal layers 3 mm veneer, totals 6 mm

To determine how much we can reduce the underlying strip-plank thickness, we have to know the thickness of the bi-axial sheathing laminate called for in Formula 11-2.

FORMULA 11-5
Bi-Axial Glass Laminate Thickness vs. Weight of Dry Glass

(English)

Weight of Dry Glass (oz./sq. yd.) = (Laminate Thickness [in.] × 610) – 0.3

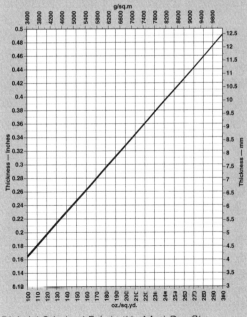

Bi-Axial Stitched Fabric (No Mat) Dry-Glass Weight vs. Laminate Thickness: Large Boats

(continued)

> *Laminate Thickness (in.) = (Weight of*
> *Dry Glass [oz./sq. yd.] – 0.3) ÷ 610*
>
> *(Metric)*
>
> *Weight of Dry Glass (g/m²) = (Laminate*
> *Thickness [mm] × 813) – 9.7*
>
> *Laminate Thickness (mm) = (Weight of*
> *Dry Glass [g/m²] – 9.7) ÷ 813*

We found an exterior sheathing for *Logger Bobber* of 55 oz./sq. yd. (1,880 g/m²). The laminate thickness would then be

> *(55 oz./sq. yd. – 0.3) ÷ 610 = 0.09 in.*
>
> *(1,880 g/m² – 9.7) ÷ 813 = 2.3 mm*

FORMULA 11-6
Reducing Underlying Strip-Plank
Thickness with Diagonal Wood Veneers
> *The thickness of the strip-plank is*
> *reduced relative to the total shell*
> *thickness of the all-strip-plank hull with*
> *heavy hull-exterior sheathing.*

Accordingly, *Logger Bobber*'s underlying strip-plank thickness—with the exterior diagonal wood veneers—can be reduced to ⁷/₈ inch (22 mm).

> *0.97-in. strip-plank + 0.09-in. sheathing =*
> *1.06 in., and 1.06 in. – 0.25-in. veneers =*
> *0.81; use ⁷/₈ in.*
>
> *or*
>
> *24.7 mm strip-plank + 2.3 mm sheathing =*
> *27 mm, and 27 mm – 6 mm veneers = 21;*
> *use 22 mm*

Thus, we have specified a hull shell composed of the following:

- One external layer of 8- to 12-oz./sq. yd. glass cloth (or one 4-oz./sq. yd. Dynel or Vectra layer).

- Two diagonal veneers, ¹/₈ inch each (¹/₄ inch total).
- Strip-plank ⁷/₈ inch.

or

- One external layer of 270 to 407 g/m² glass cloth (or one 135 g/m² Dynel or Vectra layer).
- Two diagonal veneers, 3 mm each (6 mm total).
- Strip-plank 22 mm.

Diagonal-Veneer or External-Glass-Sheathed Strip-Plank Hull Internal Structure

Adding the diagonal veneers or heavy bi-axial sheathing to the strip-plank allows you to eliminate much internal framing. Interior hull structure should follow the rules for FRP internal hull structure for cored FRP construction, as described in chapter 5, with the following comments and adjustments:

- No topsides longitudinals are required.
- Engine beds/stringers should be installed as described. They may be of foam- or balsa-core FRP or they may be of solid laminate, wood-screwed, bolted, and epoxy-glued to the hull. The solid-wood engine beds/stringers should be the same dimensions as the foam or balsa cores.
- Where a chine log is used, no other chine reinforcing is required.
- Alternately, an epoxy-chine may be used. (See the discussion on liquid joinery, page 166.)

- Bulkheads and ring frames do not require elastometric spacers under the CFR (Code of Federal Regulations, for passenger vessels or T-boats).
- Floors should be located as described in

the FRP rule. Solid-wood floors are made to the dimension of the foam or balsa core specified.

- It is possible to omit the keel and stem completely in this form of construction. Instead, the strip-planking and exterior-wood diagonal veneers are run right across the stem and keel. If this is done, the sheathing laminate at the keel and stem must be equal to 1.8 times the standard exterior-hull-sheathing laminate outside and 1.2 times the standard exterior-hull-sheathing laminate inside. A hull like this is really a wood-epoxy/FRP composite hull.

- Another approach to keel/backbone structure is to use a laminated plywood keel (see Formula 11-9C).

NOTE: All laminates and sheathing must be bonded in epoxy, using fabric styles compatible with epoxy (i.e., without binders) —usually stitch-mat bi-axial styles.

Internal/External FRP-Sheathed Strip-Plank

Yet another possibility with wood-epoxy strip-plank construction is to use heavy bi-axial sheathing both inside and outside of the hull shell in conjunction with an ordinary strip-plank core and with no diagonal wood veneers. This also allows you to eliminate the traditional frames and structure. Again, you should use the internal framing for cored FRP hulls described in chapter 5. (Note the comments and adjustments noted for strip-plank construction.)

FORMULA 11-7
Internal/External FRP-Sheathed Strip-Plank Thicknesses

The internal/external strip-plank construction uses a heavy internal sheathing or laminate in conjunction with the heavy external sheathing specified in Formula 11-2. This construction is true cored-composite construction. Because the strip-plank acts as a core, it can be reduced still further in thickness, as follows:

Strip-Plank Thickness, in. $= 0.6 \times Sn^{0.34}$ (English)

Strip-Plank Thickness, mm $= 15.24 \times Sn^{0.34}$ (Metric)

Thus, *Logger Bobber*'s internal and external sheathed strip-plank hull would have

Strip-Plank Thickness $= 0.6 \times 2.97^{0.34} = 0.86$; use $^7/_8$ in.

Strip-Plank Thickness $= 15.24 \times 2.97^{0.34} = 22$ mm

FORMULA 11-8
Interior-Hull Sheathing for Internal/External Strip-Planked Hulls

The internal hull sheathing is also bi-axial E-glass on boats with Sns over 2. On boats with Sns less than 2, the internal sheathing may be of glass cloth. The internal sheathing should be 66 percent of the thickness or weight of the external sheathing found in Formula 11-2.

Returning to *Logger Bobber*,

Internal-Hull-Sheathing Fabric Weight = 0.66×55 oz./sq. yd. = 36 oz./sq. yd.

Internal-Hull-Sheathing Fabric Weight = $0.66 \times 1,880$ g/m² = 1,240 g/m²

Cored-Strip-Plank Construction vs. Cored-FRP Construction

Unlike the very low-strength (low-modulus) cores used in conventional cored-FRP construction, the wood strip-plank core itself provides substantial longitudinal strength, as well as local flexural strength and impact resistance. Furthermore, the wood-strip core has vastly greater sheer strength than the low-modulus cores used in conventional FRP. Additionally, the bi-axial E-glass/epoxy laminates have higher mechanical properties (they're stronger) than standard mat/roving polyester layups. Accordingly, although the total shell thickness of cored strip-plank and cored-FRP construction will work out similarly using the rules in this book, the interior and exterior laminates are thinner for wood-strip-cored construction than they are for cored-FRP construction.

Diagonal (Herringbone) Strip-Plank on Hard-Chine Hull Bottoms

On hard-chine hull bottoms—particularly those that have not been designed for plywood construction—it is sometimes more convenient to strip-plank the bottom diagonally, herringbone fashion. Plank thickness should be the same as given previously, unless the hull was intended for herringbone construction with minimal bottom framing. In this case, increase the bottom strip-plank thickness by 1.5 times.

Lindsay Lord's Ultralight Sheathed Strip-Plank Construction

Up until now, we've been designing conservative rigid-hull shells. Rigidity with safety requires considerable stiffness. There's another approach: allow the shell to flex slightly. If this sounds risky, it's not. Naval architect Lindsay Lord developed what is probably the lightest system of strip-planking (and one of the lightest approaches to boatbuilding ever) in the period after World War II. Although Lord designed and extensively tested several boats ranging from 22-foot (6.7 m) runabouts to 80-foot (24.4 m), 40-knot patrol boats in this method, for some reason his whole approach is little known. This is odd, because the Lord system is inexpensive in both materials and labor, and it's amazingly tough. What's more, Lord wrote about his results at the time.

The Lord-type strip-plank boat is also a cored-composite hull. Its core is strip-planked of softwood (e.g., pine, cedar, or fir). This core serves as just that—a true core—so it can be of quite low-grade lumber. It is simply lightly tacked together as strip-planking (well glued with epoxy grout) over temporary molds. Then it is sheathed on the inside and the outside with Vectra polypropylene or Dynel (a modacrylic) from Union Carbide. All sheathing and gluing is done in marine epoxy, as with standard wood-epoxy strip-plank; no other resin is elastic enough for this application.

The critical point is that ordinary fiberglass is not used. Vectra and Dynel have much higher elongation (i.e., they will stretch much farther before they break) than FRP. When bonded as skins to a moderately thin wood-strip core, the resulting composite panel can deflect to absorb shocks and impacts, and bend and twist with extreme loading. This deflection/flexure is harmless with Dynel or Vectra. In epoxy resin, the skins and the strip-plank core bend together and spring back without any damage. This means that a thinner, lighter structure can absorb as much energy as a thicker, stiffer one.

FORMULA 11-9A

Lord's Sheathed Strip-Plank Core

Modified in format to match the procedures in this book, Lord's rules for determining scantlings are as follows:

Core:

Strip-Plank Hull-Core Thickness, in. = $0.34 \times Sn^{0.44}$ (English)

Strip-Plank Hull-Core Thickness, mm = $8.63 \times Sn^{0.44}$ (Metric)

Core not to be less than $3/8$ in. (9.5 mm).

Strip-plank deck and walk-on roofs to be 1.5 to 2 times the hull-core thickness.

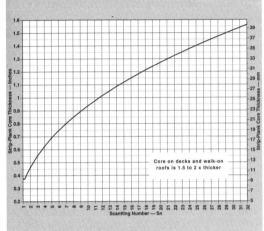

Lord's Strip-Plank Core Thickness

FORMULA 11-9B

Lord's Sheathed Strip-Plank Sheathing

Sheathing:

Both Vectra and Dynel come in 4-oz./sq. yd. (135 g/m²) fabric styles standard. In the following rule, one ply is one layer of either 4 oz./sq. yd. (135 g/m²) of either of these fabric styles. (Don't mix the two—use one or the other.)

Outside Laminate, oz./sq. yd. = $11.1 \times Sn^{0.43}$ (English)

Inside Laminate, oz./sq. yd. = $7.36 \times Sn^{0.36}$ (English)

or

Outside Laminate, g/m² = $376 \times Sn^{0.43}$ (Metric)

Inside Laminate, g/m² = $249 \times Sn^{0.36}$ (Metric)

Reverse the outside and inside layers for decks and cabin roofs.

Round up exterior laminate remainders over 2 oz./sq. yd. (68 g/m²) to one more full ply.

Round down interior laminate remainders less than 3 oz./sq. yd. (101 g/m²) to one ply.

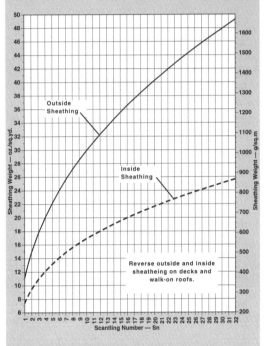

Lord's Strip-Plank Sheathing

To construct *Logger Bobber* using Lord's strip-plank method, we would use the following:

Core:

Strip-Plank Hull-Core Thickness = $0.34 \times 2.97^{0.44} = 0.55$; use $1/2$ in.

Strip-Plank Hull-Core Thickness = $8.63 \times 2.97^{0.44} = 13.9$; use 14 mm

Sheathing:

Outside Laminate = 11.1 × 2.97$^{0.43}$ = 17.7 oz./sq. yd.; use four plies Vectra or Dynel

Inside Laminate = 7.36 × 2.97$^{0.36}$ = 10.89 oz./sq. yd.; use two plies Vectra or Dynel

or

Outside Laminate = 376 × 2.97$^{0.43}$ = 600 g/m^2; use four plies Vectra or Dynel

Inside Laminate = 249 × 2.97$^{0.36}$ = 368 g/m^2; use two plies Vectra or Dynel

Internal Structure:

Lord uses neither regular frames nor much other traditional internal structure; however, he does employ numerous bulkheads: "about every 8 to 10 feet, plus partial bulkheads, on an 80-footer (24.4 m)" (*Naval Architecture of Planing Hulls*). Also, Lord uses well-placed integral tanks, cabin soles, and such as additional hull stiffeners. Basically, you can use the standard internal FRP structure for cored hulls discussed in chapter 5, with the comments and adjustments noted in the previous section on internal structure for cored strip-plank hulls.

Keel/Backbone:

For the keel, stem, deadwood, and horn-timber backbone, Lord uses layers of plywood that are cut to the outline (profile) of the keel and stem, and glued together to the required thickness (siding). Butts between layers must be well staggered. The strip-plank-core garboard (and the planking at the stem) simply lands on a small furring strip tacked and epoxy-glued to each side of the keel at what would be the rabbet. Little beveling and no spiling to speak of are required. Any gaps or voids are filled with epoxy-putty grout or

foam (for large voids). All is tacked and glued in place, and all joints are generously radiused off using epoxy-grout putty and foam fillers of very large radii. Then the entire plywood backbone and strip-core structure is sheathed with the specified laminate inside and out. Really, this keel construction could be described as a keel or backbone core.

FORMULA 11-9C
Lord's Plywood-Keel-Core Siding (Thickness)

Scantling LOA between 20 and 30 feet, use two layers ⅝-in. ply

Scantling LOA between 30 and 40 feet, use two layers ¾-in. ply

Add one layer ¾-in. ply for every 10 feet over 40 feet

or

Scantling LOA between 6 and 9 m, use two layers 15 mm ply

Scantling LOA between 9 and 12.2 m, use two layers 18 mm ply

Add one layer (18 mm) ply for every 3 m over 12.2 m

Thus, an 80-footer (24.4 m) would have six layers of ¾-inch (18 mm) ply comprising its keel/backbone, and would be sided 4½ inches (108 mm).

- If desired—instead of Lord's cored-strip construction—any portion of the decks and cabins can be made of epoxy-sheathed plywood, as described in Formulas 9-19 through 9-26.
- It is important that the internal hull sheathing/laminate run continuous and unbroken inside for the full length of the hull. Standard construction procedure is to

fabricate the permanent plywood-keel core and erect it upside down on temporary station molds. Strip the hull over the molds and permanently attach the strips to the keel core but not (of course) to the molds. Fill all voids and radii, and fill the corner fillets at the garboard, stem, and transom. Apply the outside sheathing and fair. Roll the hull right side up. Install a few temporary *exterior* molds to hold the hull in shape. Remove the temporary molds from inside. Smooth and fillet the hull interior core and its intersection with the keel/backbone. Apply the interior sheathing continuously and uninterrupted from bow to stern and athwartships. Now add the permanent bulkheads and internal structure.

- Unusual shapes, fairings, and nacelles can be built up out of wood core, foam, epoxy, and balsa, as required, and sheathed with the appropriate interior or exterior laminate.
- Lord even fabricates rudders and struts from plywood and/or pine strips, simply tacked together or to the hull, and faired-in with epoxy grout and foam as required. This then is sheathed with appropriate plies of Dynel or Vectra laminate.
- Add additional plies to the keel bottom and stem face as follows:

    Boats under 40 feet (12.2 m), add one ply

    Boats between 40 and 80 feet (12.2 and 24.4 m), add two plies

    Boats over 80 feet (24.4 m), add three plies

- A common problem with Dynel or Vectra layups is that these fabrics are so light (their specific gravity is so low) that they tend to float on the resin during layout.

The Gerr-designed 28-foot (8.5 m) offshore skiff is a good example of tape-seam sheet-plywood construction. (Courtesy Iain Neish)

The trick here is to use as little resin as required to wet-out each ply—no more and no less. Work a few test panels to get the hang of it, and you should have no difficulty. Vacuum-bagging the laminate would be an even better solution.

EPOXY/PLYWOOD CONSTRUCTION AND LIQUID JOINERY

Plywood hulls lend themselves very well to epoxy-saturated and glued construction. The large sheets of plywood are already more dimensionally stable than ordinary planks (although plywood has about half the tensile strength). Furthermore, the large sheets are easy to coat and glue in place.

Plywood planking thickness for wood-epoxy construction should be the same as determined in Formula 9-1. When subjected to repeated flexing, plywood's laminated construction is too prone to internal failures to allow any additional reductions in thickness. Decks and cabins should be sized according to Formulas 9-19 through 9-26.

Epoxy Chines (Tape-Seam Construction)

Plywood lends itself particularly well to tape-seam or epoxy-chine construction; however, tape-seam construction also can be used successfully at chines in epoxy strip-plank hulls, at great labor savings (see photo on p. 341). In tape-seam construction, the intersection between the topsides and the bottom plank is made—to start with—simply by allowing the two plank edges to touch each other. Usually, the bottom plank runs off past the topsides plank and is trimmed back flush. Because of epoxy-grout's gap-filling abilities, little beveling is required (and that of the roughest kind); a moderately sloppy fit is acceptable.

The exterior of the chine corner is radiused off and then an epoxy-grout fillet is applied smoothly, continuously, and evenly over the full length of the inside of the chine. Any exterior gaps or voids are filled with epoxy grout and smoothed off. The whole is then painted and sealed, inside and out, with a layer of unthickened epoxy. Finally, layers of glass-cloth tape are applied to both the inside and outside of the chine, all laid in epoxy. The resulting chine is smooth, fair, and watertight; it is quite strong. Better still, it is quick and easy to make, requiring little skill or painstaking measurements. By comparison, conventional chine logs—formed from solid wood—often require exacting beveling, plus they have edgeset, bend, and twist.

Liquid Joinery

This whole process can be called *liquid joinery* (a term attributed to multihull designer Jim Brown). Although we're discussing chines, the same *liquid-joinery* principle can be applied—with common sense—wherever strong corner joints must be made in wood-epoxy construction; for example, the corner intersection between the transom and the hull sides and bottom; the intersection between the bottom plank (garboard) and the keel (discussed in Lord's strip-plank rule); centerboard trunks; the cabin and coachroof joints; and even the hull-to-deck joint (in place of a clamp). In locations where it is relatively easy to work and to attach and shape solid wood (e.g., at the sheer clamps), the liquid-joinery or tape-seam approach doesn't add up to much time or labor savings and is probably not warranted. Chines and similar complex longitudinal joints, however, will be substantially easier to make in tape-seam.

Applications of Liquid Joinery

Other items that lend themselves well to liquid joinery are integral fuel and water tanks built into wood-epoxy hulls (these fuel tanks can be for diesel only), as well as built-in refrigerator and icebox compartments, shower sumps, bait wells, and even wood-epoxy sinks. In addition to (and on top of) the taped corner joints, fuel tanks must be completely sealed on the inside with a minimum of 8- to 12-oz./sq. yd. (270 to 407 g/m^2) glass cloth or 4-oz./sq. yd. (135 g/m^2) Vectra or Dynel. Twice this amount of sheathing should be used as a minimum on tanks over 100 gallons (455 l).

Laminated-Plywood Keel and Epoxy Sheet-Plywood Hull

A tape-seam sheet-plywood hull can have a laminated-plywood keel per Lord's strip-plank rule (see Formula 11-9C). If this is done, the interior of the keel should be generously filleted and taped to the plywood planking. Additional sheathing should also run athwartships over the plywood keel to completely cover it.

FORMULA 11-10

Tape-Seam Fabric Weight

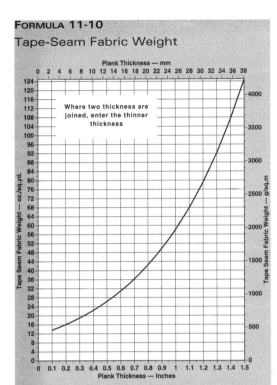

Tape-Seam Fabric Weight

> The total weight of the fabric reinforcement used in a tape-seam chine (or other structural tape-seam joint) should be proportioned according to the plank thickness, as follows:
>
> Fabric Weight, oz./sq. yd. = (1.13 + [plank thickness, in. ÷ 10.5])[20] (English)
>
> Fabric Weight, g/m² = (1.345 + [plank thickness, mm ÷ 220])[20] (Metric)

- Where two planks of different thicknesses are joined, use the thickness of the thinner plank.
- The total fabric weight given is the maximum formed by the overlap of all the layers, inside and outside combined.
- When the individual layers applied are

10 oz./sq. yd. (340 g/m²) or less, it is usually applied as glass cloth. When the individual layers are greater than 10 oz./sq. yd. (340 g/m²), the fabric should be bi- axial E-glass.

- The tape is applied in roughly equal weights inside and out; however, when the total weight does not balance out per ply, the extra layers are installed on the interior because the overall exterior hull sheathing adds exterior strength.

If our old *Logger Bobber* were hard-chine sheet plywood, its topsides plank would be 1 inch (25 mm) thick (see Formula 9-1). Accordingly, its tape-seam chines would require the following:

*Fabric Weight = (1.13 + [1-in. plank ÷ 10.5])[20]
= 58.1; use 60 oz./sq. yd.*

Fabric Weight = (1.345 + [25 mm plank ÷ 220])[20] = 1,900 g/m²

For *Logger*, we would then use

Three plies of 12-oz./sq. yd. (406 g/m²) bi-axial tape on the inside and two plies of 12-oz. (406 g/m²) bi-axial tape on the outside. This happens to total exactly 60 oz./sq. yd. (2,030 g/m²), although such precision is not necessary.

FORMULA 11-11

Tape-Seam Fabric Runout

> The fabric reinforcement is applied to the joint in overlapping layers that build up to the required thickness at the chine and taper away along the plank.
>
> The total tape reinforcement should extend away from the center of the joint at each side for a distance of nine times the plank thickness.

FORMULA 11-12

Epoxy-Fillet Dimensions

The epoxy fillet under the tape reinforcement is very much the heart of the tape-seam joint. It should be proportioned as follows:

Fillet Runout Along Side = 1.5 to 2 × plank thickness

Fillet-Throat Depth = 0.75 to 1 × the plank thickness

- The throat depth necessarily decreases as the angle the two panels make increases. When the angle is 180 degrees, the joint is a butt joint and there can be no throat depth at all.

COLD-MOLDED CONSTRUCTION (MULTIPLE DIAGONAL VENEERS)

Up until now, we've been using diagonal layers of wood as a portion of the hull shell only (when we used them at all). It is quite possible to use nothing but diagonal layers for the hull shell. This construction is usually termed *cold-molding*. Epoxy strip-plank methods could technically fit this term as well; however, it's seldom used in connection with strip-planking. Cold-molding originally referred to laminating up an entire wooden-hull shell (regardless of planking method) using glues that cured at room temperature (i.e., cold temperatures). This was in contrast to early laminated hulls, which were glued and cured in a massive female mold in an autoclave under pressure. Of course, most autoclave-laminated hulls employed some version of diagonal planking; thus—when room-temperature glues arrived on the scene—the term *cold-molding* came to refer to diagonal-veneer hull shells.

Only a light layer of exterior glass sheathing is used with most cold-molded hulls. Its purpose is not structural, but rather simply to add some abrasion and impact resistance. The interior of cold-molded hulls, however, must be reinforced with longitudinal stringers. These give the required fore-n-aft strength, plus they act as a form over which the planking veneers are laid. Widely spaced frames—installed inside the stringers—and/or bulkheads complete the structure. These members supply transverse strength.

Generally, cold-molded hulls are the lightest wooden-boat hulls you can build, except for boats built to Lord's strip-plank rule or of DuraKore. Cold-molded construction has many adherents; however, I usually find the labor required is not justified. Although the hulls are somewhat lighter than standard sheathed- or diagonal-veneer strip-plank, there are considerably more skill and hours required to properly spile, fit, staple down, and glue all the many diagonal veneers. On a larger boat—over 50 feet (15 m)—this can be many layers indeed. In fact, several experienced builders I know tried cold-molding and found it so labor-intensive that they no longer build in epoxy-saturated wood at all. Instead, these yards switched to aluminum for large vessels. This is a shame, because—although aluminum certainly has many excellent points—in contrast to cold-molding, many of the strip-plank building methods are very economical of labor and materials.

My experience has been that—using proper methods—wood-epoxy strip-plank is the most cost-effective way to build a one-off round-bilge hull. Labor considerations aside, however, cold-molded hulls are excellent structures—light, strong, and long-lived. For high-performance boats—race boats, sail and power; high-speed motor yachts; and patrol boats—the extra labor may well be worth the cost for the relatively modest gain in performance at the top end of the envelope.

- Shell thicknesses of $1/2$ inch (13 mm) or less generally consist of just two diagonal layers.
- Shell thicknesses between $1/2$ and 1 inch (13 to 25 mm) should consist of at least three layers. When three layers are used, the outer layer is laid on fore-n-aft.
- Shell thicknesses more than 1 inch (25 mm) should consist of four or more layers. When an odd number of layers is used,

the outer layer is laid on fore-n-aft; however, this is not mandatory.

- Hulls 1 inch (25 mm) and less should be sheathed with a minimum of one layer of 8- to 10-oz./sq. yd. (270 to 339 g/m^2) glass cloth laid in epoxy. Very small boats (e.g., canoes and rowing skiffs) would use 5-oz./sq. yd. (170 g/m^2) cloth. For Dynel, Vectra, or Xynole polyester, the minimum is 4 oz./sq. yd. (135 g/m^2).
- Hulls more than 1 inch (25 mm)—and all boats running over 25 knots—should increase the bottom sheathing to a minimum of 16- to 20-oz./sq. yd. (542 to

FORMULA 11-13
Cold-Molded-Hull Thickness

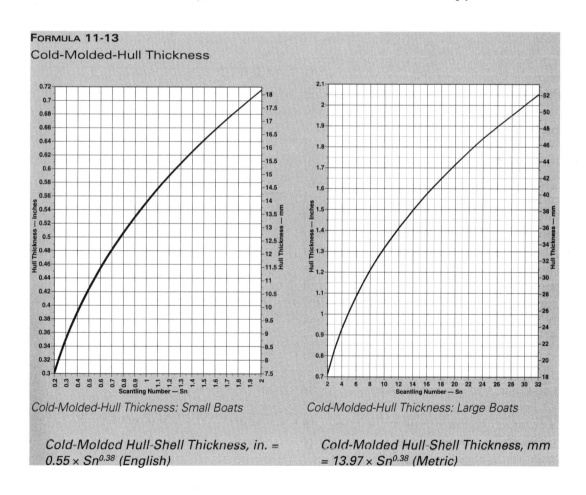

Cold-Molded-Hull Thickness: Small Boats

Cold-Molded-Hull Thickness: Large Boats

Cold-Molded Hull-Shell Thickness, in. = 0.55 × Sn$^{0.38}$ (English)

Cold-Molded Hull-Shell Thickness, mm = 13.97 × Sn$^{0.38}$ (Metric)

678 g/m²) glass cloth laid in epoxy on the bottom. For Dynel, Vectra, or Xynole polyester, the minimum is 8 oz./sq. yd. (271 g/m²) on the bottom. The topsides on these hulls may still use the lighter sheathing employed on hulls under 1 inch (25 mm) thick.

Thus, a cold-molded *Logger Bobber* would have the following shell scantlings:

Cold-Molded Hull-Shell Thickness =
$0.55 \times 2.97^{0.38} = 0.83$; use ⅞ in.

Cold-Molded Hull-Shell Thickness =
$13.97 \times 2.97^{0.38} = 21.1$; use 22 mm

So, we would use four diagonal layers, each ⁷⁄₃₂ inch (5.5 mm) thick.

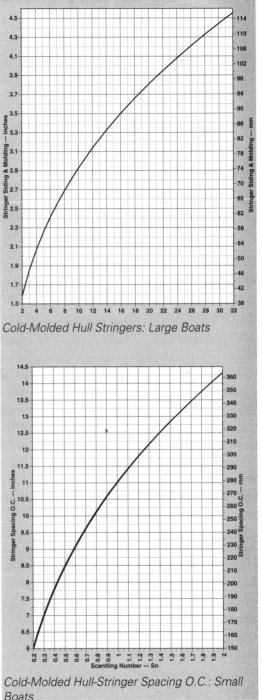

Cold-Molded Hull Stringers: Large Boats

FORMULA 11-14
Cold-Molded-Hull Stringers

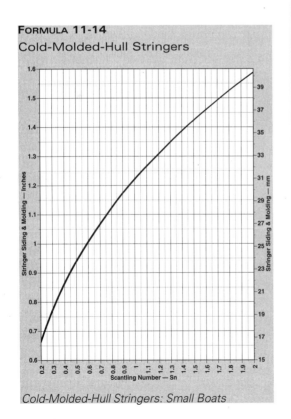

Cold-Molded-Hull Stringers: Small Boats

Cold-Molded Hull-Stringer Spacing O.C.: Small Boats

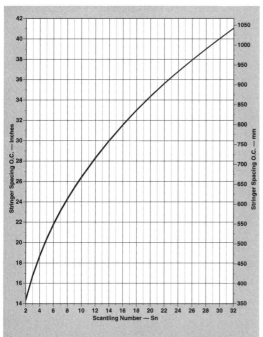

Cold-Molded Hull-Stringer Spacing O.C.: Large Boats

Stringers Sided and Molded, in. = 1.22 × Sn$^{0.38}$ (English)

Stringers Sided and Molded, mm = 31 × Sn$^{0.38}$ (Metric)

Stringers Spaced O.C., in. = 11 × Sn$^{0.38}$ (English)

Stringers Spaced O.C., mm = 279.4 × Sn$^{0.38}$ (Metric)

- Stringer siding may be tapered to 66 percent of the maximum siding, at the fore-n-aft thirds of the stringer's length.
- The stringers must be fastened to each other and to the stem with breasthooks and to the transom with quarter knees (see Formula 10-11).
- Stringers are laid out so that the maximum spacing center-to-center (O.C.) is at midships. The hull shape will naturally bring the stringers closer together as they run toward the ends. This is desirable, at the bow in particular, because the impact loads are greatest here.
- The stringer immediately adjacent to the keel should be spaced only half the standard O.C. distance from the side of the keel.
- Decrease stringer spacing by 1 percent for every knot of boat speed over 25 knots.
- Although not required, it will often work out best to run the stringers along diagonals worked out on the line-drawing section view or body plan and then transferred to the inside of the plank along the length of the hull. This eliminates edgeset in the stringers, leaving only bend and twist to deal with during construction.
- Planing powerboats should install nearly full-length laminated engine beds sized according to Formulas 9-31 and 9-32. The engine beds on cold-molded hulls should be fastened directly to the inside of the hull shell. It is often possible and desirable to eliminate one or two standard bottom stringers where the engine beds perform essentially the same function (see photo on p. 341).

Returning to reliable old *Bobber*, we would find it as follows:

Stringers Sided and Molded = 1.22 × 2.97$^{0.38}$ = 1.84; use 1⅞-in. square

Stringers Sided and Molded = 31 × 2.97$^{0.38}$ = 46.8; use 48 mm square

Stringers Spaced O.C. (at Midships) = 11 × 2.97$^{0.38}$ = 16.6; use 16 in.

Stringers Spaced O.C. (at Midships) = 279.4 × 2.97$^{0.38}$ = 422.5; use 420 mm

If *Logger Bobber* were a 35-knot boat, we would decrease stringer spacing to 14³/₄ inches

(380 mm); (35 knots − 25 knots = 10 knots, so reduce spacing by 10 percent; 0.9 × 16.6 in. = 14.9 in. [422.5 mm × 0.9 = 380.2 mm]).

FORMULA 11-15
Cold-Molded-Hull Frames and Bulkheads

The longitudinal hull stringers are supported transversely on frames and bulkheads. Frames should be sized according to Formula 9-2 and spaced according to Formula 9-3; however, even for round-bilge cold-molded hulls, use the spacing for sawn frames, or 2.5 times the standard round-bilge plank-on-frame spacing. The frames are fastened to the inside of the stringers only; they don't touch the hull shell.

Bulkheads and watertight/collision bulkheads should be sized according to Formulas 5-5 and 9-29; however, the rule for spacing the bulkheads does not apply because regular frames are used. Wherever the bulkhead can be located close to the calculated frame spacing—and where the bulkhead is essentially an unbroken ring (molded at least 6.75 times its thickness at the deepest cutout)—a separate frame is not required. If as many bulkheads as specified in Formula 5-5 are used, then many of the frames can often be eliminated. Again, the bulkheads usually fasten only to the inside of the stringers; they need not touch the inside of the hull shell. Bulkheads can do so, however, wherever a watertight or vaportight seal is needed.

FORMULA 11-16
Cold-Molded-Hull Floors/Composite Metal-Strap Floors

Floors on cold-molded hulls with longitudinal stringers should end on top of one of the hull-bottom stringers.

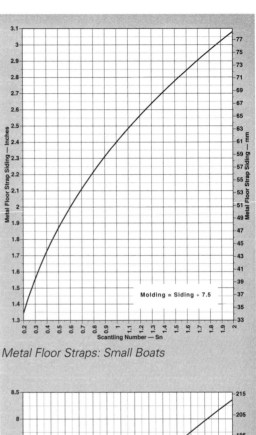

Metal Floor Straps: Small Boats

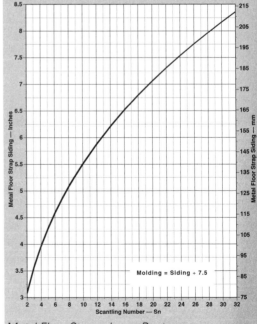

Metal Floor Straps: Large Boats

This avoids hard spots and distributes the stress from the floor ends longitudinally into the stringer. On powerboats, the floors should extend athwartships to at least the second stringer out from the keel, port and starboard. On sailboats—at the ballast keel and at the mast steps—the floors should extend out at least to the third stringer out from the keel. In other regards, the floors should be as described in Formulas 9-7 and 9-8.

An excellent alternative floor construction for use with cold-molded and longitudinal-stringer hulls is a composite floor (wood and metal combined), with a metal-strap floor plate bolted down on top of the stringers athwart-ships and wood blocking underneath, between the stringers. These floors are low in molding, easy to fabricate, and can be installed easily, either at a frame or where there is no frame.

The principal transverse strength is in the metal strap, which should be dimensioned as follows:

Metal-Strap Floor Siding, in. = 2.4 × $Sn^{0.36}$ (English)

Metal-Strap Floor Siding, mm = 60.9 × $Sn^{0.36}$ (Metric)

Molding = siding ÷ 7.5

- Silicon bronze and 316 stainless steel (second best) are the proper materials for metal-strap floors. Hot-dip galvanized mild steel, primed and painted all around before installation, can be used; however, it seems a poor economy after adding in the cost of galvanizing and painting and its lower life expectancy.
- Through-bolt the metal-strap floor into each stringer and into the keel.

- Through-bolt the metal-strap floor through the wood blocking and into the plank. On hulls with Sns less than 2, it may be easier to screw-fasten the blocking to the plank from outside, and then to screw-fasten (or lag-bolt) the metal strap down into the blocking from inside.

Install wood blocking under the metal strap at the same height, or a little higher, then the keel top athwartships. The blocking should be sided the same as the metal strap. Run the blocking out over the first stringer, out from the keel, and then taper the blocking height until it reaches the second stringer out and butts against it, flush with the stringer's top. The metal-strap floor runs on top of the blocking continuously from port to starboard. On sailboats, at the ballast keel and the mast steps, the blocking should be extended out to the third stringer out from the keel (or farther). The blocking height—outboard of the second stringer—will be the same height as the stringers, and the metal strap will extend out over the third stringer.

If *Logger Bobber* were fitted with metal-strap floors, we would install

Metal-Strap Floor Siding = 2.4 × $2.97^{0.36}$ = 3.55; use 3½ in.

Metal-Strap Floor Siding = 60.9 × $2.97^{0.36}$ = 90.1; use 90 mm

Molding = $7/16$ in. (12 mm)

The Metal Floor Option

In Formulas 9-7 and 9-8, we described traditional wooden floors. Formula 11-16 details the metal-composite alternative to the grown or laminated wooden floor. There is also an

An interesting and unusual variation of metal floors. Note the double-sawn frames alternating with every two steam-bent frames. (Courtesy Kortchmar & Willner)

Metal floors installed by Larry and Lin Pardey on their Taleisin. (From *Details of Classic Boat Construction: The Hull,* by Larry Pardey, reproduced with permission.)

excellent metal-composite alternative to the wooden sawn floor described in Formula 9-7. In this case, floors can be cast or welded up from bronze plate with angles to fasten or bolt down to the keel. In other respects, the

overall dimensions and arrangements are similar to the Formula 9-7 sawn floors. Silicon bronze and Monel are the best materials for metal floors of this type, with stainless steel second best. Hot-dip galvanized steel can be used, but doesn't seem to be worth the slight economy in the long run.

FORMULA 11-17
Standard Metal Floors

Metal-composite floors should be dimensioned and fashioned exactly as described for standard sawn floor, with the following exceptions:

- *Siding = sawn-floor siding ÷ 6*

- *The length of the angle (i.e., bolt flange) along the keel to receive the keel bolts should be 1.1 times the standard sawn-floor siding.*

Metal floors can be formed to extend higher up along the frames' sides than sawn wooden floors because the metal can be trimmed back in the center, so that only the upper half of the floor continues up along the frames. The area between the frames thus opens and does not intrude on interior space. The metal floor can be cut down to 40 percent of the minimum molding for a standard sawn floor amidships to increase interior room, as long as the arms project up along the frames at least as high as the minimum sawn frame height (molding), or higher.

Metal floors can be used on either completely traditional plank-on-frame construction or on wood-epoxy construction. They do not shrink, swell, or decay. They provide more usable interior space and they are as strong or stronger than the best sawn floors. Labor is slightly greater than for sawn floors, but the added expenditure would be well justified.

TWELVE

Wood: Species, Type, and Application

Selection of Wood Species

In traditional wood hulls, the wood itself is subject to great variations in moisture content and temperature, and to complete immersion for extended periods. Therefore, to obtain long life and reliability, the wood species employed is critical. Generally, in the United States, the most common, plain-vanilla boat-building woods are as follows:

Small Boats to 20 Feet (6 m):

Keel/Backbone: Douglas fir, white oak, yellow pine
Frames: white oak, Douglas fir, elm
Deck-Beam Stringers, Carlins, etc.: cedar, spruce, Douglas fir, yellow pine
Planking: white cedar, Port Orford cedar, Honduras mahogany, Philippine mahogany (second-best)

Medium-Size Boats, 20 to 45 Feet (6 to 14 m):

Keel/Backbone: white oak, yellow pine, western larch, Douglas fir
Frames: white oak, elm

Deck-Beam Stringers, Carlins, etc.: Douglas fir, yellow pine, white or red oak
Planking: Honduras mahogany preferred, Philippine mahogany second-best, white cedar, Port Orford cedar, teak, yellow pine

Large Boats More Than 45 Feet (14 m):

Keel/Backbone: white oak, yellow pine, western larch
Frames: white oak, elm
Deck-Beam Stringers, Carlins, etc.: white or red oak, Douglas fir, yellow pine
Planking: Douglas fir, yellow pine, Honduras mahogany, white or red oak

These are, however, only the most common woods for these applications; many other wood species are suitable. Still other species, such as locust or lignum vitae, have specialized applications. Following is an alphabetical list of many of the common woods available in the United States and Europe. This list will serve as a general guide; however, many other local and imported species are suitable. It pays to investigate locally available woods.

Wood Species

Afromosia: *Afromosia spp.*, hardwood, 45 lb./cu. ft., 721 kg/m³. Acceptable for planking and deck trim, good for small-boat keel/backbone, reasonably rot-resistant, tends to split.

Agba: *Gossweilerodendron balsamiferum*, hardwood, 30 lb./cu. ft., 481 kg/m³. Acceptable for planking, decks, cabin sides, and joinerwork; fairly reliable all-around wood for boats with Sns less than 3.5 to 4.

Aptong: *Sipterocarpus spp.*, hardwood, 44 lb./cu. ft., 705 kg/m³. Not well suited to boat use except for interior joiner cleats, etc.

Ash, White: *Fraxinum americana*, hardwood, 42 lb./cu. ft., 673 kg/m³. Excellent deck beams, internal framing, and laminated frames; good for sawn frames, acceptable for bent frames; very strong for its density; not particularly rot-resistant; and it stains and discolors easily—not recommended for brightwork or deck trim.

Blue Gum (Eurrabbie): *Eucalyptus globulus*, hardwood, 56 lb./cu. ft., 897 kg/m³. Good for sawn frames and keel/backbone parts that are reasonably straight.

Butternut: *Juglans cinera*, hardwood, 26 lb./cu. ft., 416 kg/m³. Beautiful interior joiner wood but somewhat soft so mars easily; excellent thwarts and transoms on skiffs and rowboats.

Cedar, Port Orford: *Chamae cyparis*, softwood, 28 lb./cu. ft., 449 kg/m³. Excellent planking for boats with Sns up to 3.5 or 4; aromatic, rot-resistant; good for scrubbed decks, light longitudinals.

Cedar, Red (Western Red): *Thuja plicata*, softwood, 23 lb./cu. ft., 368 kg/m³. Good planking and secondary structure for boats with Sns up to 3; not especially strong for its density and swells more than most average woods.

Cedar, Spanish: *Thuja spp.*, softwood, 24 lb./cu. ft., 384 kg/m³. Excellent small-boat planking; hard and strong for its density.

Cedar, White (Juniper): *Thuja occidentalis*, softwood, 21 lb./cu. ft., 336 kg/m³. Excellent small-boat planking, rot-resistant, absorbs water and becomes heavier with long-term immersion.

Cedar, Yellow (Alaskan Cedar): *Chamaecyparis nootkatensis*, softwood, 31 lb./cu. ft., 496 kg/m³. A rot-resistant, strong, and moderately hard cedar, more resistant to denting than other cedars; good for planking and general framing; sometimes hard to paint well.

Cypress, Bald: *Taxodijim distichum*, softwood, 34 lb./cu. ft., 545 kg/m³. Good for ceiling and secondary structures, acceptable for planking, highly rot-resistant, can have a strong smell.

Douglas Fir: (see Fir)

Elm, English: *Ulmus campestris*, hardwood, 37 lb./cu. ft., 593 kg/m³. Excellent small-boat planking, light and flexible.

Elm, Rock: *Ulmus thomasii*, hardwood, 44 lb./cu. ft., 705 kg/m^3. Good for steam-bent frames, deck beams, keel/backbone; tough, hard, and abrasion-resistant; does not absorb much water so makes excellent bottom planking.

Elm, White (American): *Ulmus americana*, hardwood, 37 lb./cu. ft., 593 kg/m^5. Good for deck beams, bent frames, table and counter tops; excellent for grates; gets whiter as it is scrubbed; does not bend well; not as strong as ash or fir; acceptable for small-boat frames.

Eurrabbie: (see Blue Gum)

Fir, Douglas (Oregon Pine): *Pseusdotsuga menziesii* (previously *taxifolia*), softwood, 36 lb./cu. ft., 577 kg/m^3. Excellent planking wood, particularly for boats with Sns over 2; excellent for longitudinals, stringers, clamps, shelves; good for heavier spars; acceptable for keel/backbone; very good all-around structural wood; pronounced grain can be hard to paint.

Gabon: (see Okoume)

Green Heart: *Ocotea rodiaei*, hardwood, 61 lb./cu. ft., 977 kg/m^3. Hard and dense, similar to locust, but with still higher strength.

Hackmatack: (see Larch)

Iroko (Bang, Tule, Odum, Nigeria Teak, Kambala, Intuile, Mareira): *Chlorophora excelsa*, hardwood, 41 lb./cu. ft., 657 kg/m^3. Acceptable as a substitute for mahogany but not as durable or as strong; still available in wide boards; resistant to borers.

Ironbark: *Eucalyptus sp.*, hardwood, 64 lb./cu. ft., 1,025 kg/m^3. Excellent for ice sheathing and similar abrasion protection.

Juniper: (see Cedar, White)

Khaya: (see Mahogany)

Larch, Eastern (Hackmatack, Tamarack): *Larix laricina*, softwood, 38 lb./cu. ft., 609 kg/m^3. Roots make excellent grown knees, floors, and frames, as well as stems and sternposts with curvature.

Larch, European: *Larix decidua*, softwood, 35 lb./cu. ft., 561 kg/m^3. Good for frames and beams; acceptable for planking; a popular all-around wood; sometimes termed *Scots boatbuilder's timber*.

Larch, Western: *Larix occidentalis*, softwood, 39 lb./cu. ft., 625 kg/m^3. Good general boatbuilding lumber; good for keel/backbone; similar to Eastern Larch.

Lignum Vitae: *Guaiacum sp.*, hardwood, 78 lb./cu. ft., 1,249 kg/m^3. Excellent for fairleads, deadeyes, lizards, pulley blocks, sheaves; the old standard for water-lubricated propeller-shaft bearings; contains oils that resist rot and act as a lubricant; extremely tough and abrasion-resistant; hard but brittle if longer lengths are bent.

Locust, Black: *Robina pseudacacia*, hardwood, 51 lb./cu. ft., 817 kg/m^3. Excellent for cleats, tillers, butts, sampson posts, chafing boards, belaying pins, stanchions, deck trim; hard, dense, and abrasion-resistant.

Lauan: (see Mahogany)

Mahogany, African (Khaya and many other species): *Khaya ivorensis*, hardwood, 37 lb./cu. ft., 593 kg/m³. Excellent planking; good for coamings, cabin sides; good for joinerwork; hard to plane; can stain at metal fasteners.

Mahogany, Honduras (Mexican): *Swietenia macrophylla*, hardwood, 35 lb./cu. ft., 561 kg/m³. Excellent for planking, coamings, cabin sides; good for joinerwork.

Mahogany, Philippine (Red Lauan): *Shorea negrosensis*, hardwood, 31 lb./cu. ft., 496 kg/m³. Acceptable for planking, coamings, cabin sides; does not take large bends; tendency to split; good for joinerwork. NOTE: White Lauan, *Pentacame contorta*, is not as strong or as rot-resistant as Red Lauan, and should not be used for structural work, but is acceptable for joinerwork.

Mahogany, Philippine (Tangile): *Shorea polysperma*, hardwood, 41 lb./cu. ft., 567 kg/m³. Similar to Red Lauan, but somewhat denser and stronger; slightly superior for planking. NOTE: Tiaong, *Shorea teysmanniana* (also called Philippine mahogany) is not as strong or as rot-resistant as Tangile, and should not be used for structural work, but is acceptable for joinerwork.

Meranti, Red (Red Seraya): *Shorea*, hardwood, 42 lb./cu. ft., 673 kg/m³. Good for planking and frames (in smaller boats); a reasonably useful all-around wood, but must be carefully selected for quality and grain.

Oak, Black: *Quercus velutina*, hardwood, 43 lb./cu. ft., 689 kg/m³. Similar to white oak, but not quite as strong and not as rot-resistant.

Oak, European: *Quercus spp.*, hardwood, 46 lb./cu. ft., 737 kg/m³. Good for frames, keel/backbone, beams, stringers; hard and durable; not as rugged as white oak.

Oak, Red: *Quercus rubra*, hardwood, 43 lb./cu. ft., 689 kg/m³. Similar to white oak, but not quite as strong and not as rot-resistant.

Oak, White: *Quercus alba*, hardwood, 48 lb./cu. ft., 769 kg/m³. Excellent for keel/backbone and bent frames; crooks in roots make best knees; may be used for almost any part of a larger boat; expands and contracts greatly; prone to rot if not seasoned with great care. White oak is *the* standard all-around structural boat wood.

Okoume (Gabon): *Aucoumea klaineana pierre*, hardwood, 25 lb./cu. ft., 400 kg/m³. Acceptable for plywood and for laminated (cold-molded) planking; acceptable for secondary joiner cleats, etc.; neither strong for its weight nor rot-resistant.

Pine, Eastern White: *Pinus strobus*, softwood, 27 lb./cu. ft., 432 kg/m³. Excellent for scrubbed decks; good for planking; durable; good for joinerwork and secondary structures.

Pine, Oregon: (see Fir, Douglas)

Pine, Pitch: *Pinus spp.*, softwood, 40 lb./cu. ft., 641 kg/m³. Acceptable all-around wood for longitudinals, deck beams, decking, cabin sides, and framing; resin makes gluing, finishing, and painting difficult.

Pine, Ponderosa: *Pinus ponderosa*, softwood, 28 lb./cu. ft., 449 kg/m³. Rot prone, not good for boat use.

Pine, Scots (Scots Fir, Redwood, Red Deal): *Pinus sylvestris*, softwood, 32 lb./cu. ft., 513 kg/m³. Not strong or rot-resistant; not suitable for boat use, except for interior joiner cleats and similar light use.

Pine, Sugar: *Pinus lambertiana*, softwood, 27 lb./cu. ft., 432 kg/m³. Excellent for carving casting patterns and half models; similar to white pine.

Pine, Yellow (Longleaf Yellow): *Pinus palustris*, softwood, 44 lb./cu. ft., 705 kg/m³. Excellent planking for boats with Sns higher than 2.5; high resin content resists water absorption and rot; excellent all-around structural wood for longitudinals, deck beams, and all heavy framing; good for keel/backbone when white oak is unavailable; believed to be more rot- and borer-resistant than white oak in tropical waters.

Red Meranti: (see Meranti)

Redwood: *Sequoia sempervirens*, softwood, 28 lb./cu. ft., 449 kg/m³. Good for planking and cabin framing.

Spruce, Eastern: *Picea spp.*, softwood, 29 lb./cu. ft., 465 kg/m³. Not decay-resistant; seldom used in boats.

Spruce, Sitka: *Picea sitchensis*, softwood, 27 lb./cu. ft., 432 kg/m³. Excellent for masts and spars; good for beams, stringers, and secondary framing on light boats; prone to decay.

Tamarack: (see Larch)

Tangile: (see Mahogany)

Teak: *Tectona grandis*, hardwood, 45 lb./cu. ft., 721 kg/m³. Excellent for planking, cabin sides, coamings, transoms, and joinerwork; not as strong as commonly believed; high oil content makes it very rot- and check-resistant; does not glue well.

Plywood

PLYWOOD WATERPROOF BOIL-TEST

All plywood used in boats *must* be laminated with glues rated waterproof by the boil test. The standard test to establish a glue as truly "water*proof*" (not simply water-resistant) is a complete cycle of boiling fully immersed for 4 hours, drying at 140°F (60°C) for 20 hours, boiling again for 4 hours, allowing to cool in the water, and then sheer-testing wet. This roughly duplicates the extreme swings in moisture content all boats experience repeatedly throughout their service life. Plywood that doesn't withstand this boil test can't be used *anywhere* onboard. No amount of coating or sealing, with any wonder material, can *ever* make up for nonwaterproof glue. Plywood rated "exterior grade" is waterproofed by the boil test.

MARINE PLYWOOD FOR HULL PLANKING

In almost all cases, plywood used for hull planking should be American Plywood Association (APA) marine plywood, with A-A, A-B, or B-B face veneers, five plies minimum. It is made only from Douglas fir or western larch, with solid jointed cores and strict limitations on gaps and defects in the core veneers. Indeed, all the interior plies must be at least B-grade, with no gaps over 1/8 inch (3.1 mm). An A-grade surface is the highest grade—smooth with no knots or knotholes—but it may have wood or synthetic patches. B-grade surfaces are the next step down—

they may have knots but no knotholes. Marine ply is sanded on both surfaces.

Such marine ply is quite expensive. As a result, some builders use ordinary APA Exterior A-A- and A-B-grade ply for hull planking. Although there are success stories, I recommend against compromising on the integrity of the hull planking in this way. The defects permissible in the interior plies of exterior grade form hidden danger zones. Decay and localized glue-line failures can develop undetected until a catastrophic failure occurs. For example, APA-exterior-ply cores can have knotholes up to $1^{1}/_{2}$ inches (38 mm) across, and can have gaps between veneer butts as much as 1 inch (25.4 mm) wide. The cores only need to meet C-grade requirements, and they can be from other, less tough species of wood than Douglas fir or western larch.

EXTERIOR-GRADE PLYWOOD FOR BOATS

Throughout the remainder of the boat's structure (i.e., any place but the hull planking), you need not use true marine plywood; ordinary exterior A-A or A-B plywood can be employed safely. Decks, cabins, bulkheads, floors, interior joiner panels, solid cores on FRP-laminated stringers, and engine beds can all be fabricated from exterior ply. This is, of course, a cost-saving option and all marine ply throughout is the best.

OVERLAY PLYWOOD

One of the drawbacks to fir plywood—in any grade—is that the fir-veneer surface (even in A-grade) shows ripple and grain unless there is extensive surface preparation before paint-

ing. An apparently little-known but excellent solution is to use a medium-density overlay plywood (MDO). APA MDO exterior ply is identical to exterior B-B, but with a laminated surface of opaque resin-treated fiber sheet. This is tough, abrasion-resistant, highly weather-resistant, and provides a very smooth, clean painting surface, with virtually no preparation. MDO ply is substantially less expensive than marine grade. It can be used at will, anywhere but for the hull planking. Of course, MDO is not warranted where the ply will be sheathed with glass laid in epoxy, such as decks; however, it can still be used to advantage with the MDO side down. This makes a very smooth, easily painted overhead between the deck beams. MDO usually comes with the overlay on one side only, but can be found with the overlay on both sides, which saves even more time on interior finish. High-density overlay (HDO) is also available, and is even more abrasion- and weather-resistant. APA marine-grade plywood is also available with MDO and HDO overlays on either or both sides. Overlay marine-grade ply can be used for hull planking. The reduction in finish time may well be worth the added cost.

NON-APA "BOAT PLIES"

Various manufacturers produce non-APA plywood for the marine industry under product names like "Boat Ply." These plies generally fall somewhere between APA marine and exterior grade in quality. Hulls should not be planked with this unless heavily sheathed; however, it is excellent for all other applications on a boat.

THIRTEEN

Aluminum and Steel Construction Materials and Methods

*I*n this and following chapters, we examine metal-boat construction. As a practical matter, this means steel or aluminum. Bronze is too expensive and wrought iron, although it makes a long-lasting (if heavy) hull material, has long been unavailable. There is really only one other suitable modern boatbuilding metal; this little-known alternative is copper-nickel. It is very expensive like bronze, but it has the remarkable advantage of being totally nonfouling and virtually inert in a marine environment. Copper-nickel hulls have been built quite recently, and—under some circumstances—may make good economic sense. We take a brief look at copper-nickel in chapter 19.

Development of Metal Boats

EARLY METAL BOATS

Although older than fiberglass, metal boats are quite a modern development compared to wood construction. The first known all-metal boat was a riveted-iron barge built in 1787 by J. Wilkinson, Ironmaster. Although this barge was successful, when Richard Trivithick and Robert Dickenson later proposed all-iron ships in 1809, they were met with incredulity and mirth. After all, everyone knew that iron was heavier than water and would sink!

It was nine years later—as best as can be determined—in 1818 that the first all-metal commercial self-propelled boat, the *Vulcan*, was constructed at Faskine, near Glasgow. Despite being a new concept and built of a radical material, it was stout enough to remain in active service through 1875—a good run for a commercial boat of any material or era. Finally, the *Aron Manbu* was built by the Horsely Iron Works, near Birmingham, in 1821. At 106 feet (32.3 m) with a 17-foot (5.18 m) beam, a newspaper described the boat as the "most complete specimen of workmanship in the way of iron that has ever been witnessed." Metal hulls were now fully accepted, particularly for craft over 200 feet (60 m), because they were stronger than nailed, screwed, and bolted wooden structures could ever hope to be.

STEEL TAKES CHARGE

Of course, all the early metal boats were entirely of iron. Iron was an improvement on wood for large boats and for supporting the incredible weight of the colossal steam-boilers of the day, but iron isn't particularly strong for its weight. Steel has much higher tensile strength and greater elongation. Probably the earliest steel boat was the *Ma Robert*, constructed in 1858 for David Livingstone's expedition to the Zambezi, in Africa. The tensile strength of her puddled steel was about 51,000 psi (351 mPa), which is approximately the same as the steel used on the liners *Mauritania* and *Lusitania*. Today, standard mild steel is about 60,000 psi (413 mPa).

The *Ma Robert* and another contemporary steel boat both went off to Africa, where they were out of sight of the public and made little impression on European boatbuilders. Accordingly, it wasn't until 1879, when the *Rothomahana*, built by W. Denny and Bros. for service in New Zealand, was launched that the age of steel ships really began in earnest. By 1891, more than 80 percent of the new steamers under construction were made of steel rather than iron or wood. Wooden ships would soon be, well . . . history.

EARLY ALUMINUM

Perhaps surprisingly, experiments with aluminum vessels started not long after steel. The first all-aluminum boat is believed to be a leeboard sailboat built in 1890. Probably the first all-aluminum powerboat was the *Mignon* (see photos on p. 342). Constructed in Switzerland in 1892, it was driven by a 2-hp (1.5 kW) naphtha engine. In 1894, several 18-foot (5.48 m) surfboats were built of aluminum in the United States for a polar expedition. Weighing in at 375 pounds (170 kg)—compared to 1,700 pounds (773 kg) for the equivalent screw-fastened wood—they were the first aluminum boats built in North America.

PROBLEMS WITH CORROSION

Naturally, there were problems. Even in the 1890s, there was more than just iron, steel, and aluminum to choose from; bronze, brass, and lead—the traditional boatbuilding metals—were still available as well. This opened all sorts of interesting possibilities in construction, but it also presented new and little-understood pitfalls. Indeed, the best designers could run into difficulty.

One of these was none other than the Wizard of Bristol, Captain Nat Herreshoff. Using his considerable high-tech expertise, he designed an all-metal boat for the America's Cup defense of 1895. Herreshoff's construction for his 123-foot (37.5 m) *Defender* was truly remarkable. The foundation was the heavy-bulbed lead keel, on top of which was a cast-brass keel plate in three sections, joined by bronze bolts through flanges on the upper side; this keel plate was fastened by bronze lag screws to the lead keel. The stem and sternpost were of cast bronze, as was the frame of the rudder. The plating, down from a little above the water, was of manganese bronze. The topsides were of aluminum, with a 4 percent alloy of nickel, $5/16$ and $3/8$ inch thick (7.9 and 9.5 mm), with a steel plate in the way of the chainplates. The rivets were bronze and the frames were steel.

Well, you get the idea—a lot of different metals all mixed together in salt water. Not good! In fairness to Captain Nat, all-metal hull construction was such a new concept that the corrosion problems just weren't fully understood. More important, *Defender* not only held together through her entire racing campaign, she also won it. Still, her problems were—to say the least—severe. The U.S. Navy inspected *Defender* to see about using aluminum in shipbuilding:

the topsides in bad condition, with the paint peeling and corrosion visible at the juncture of the aluminum and bronze. In spite of a special paint prepared by a local painter after the usual yacht paints had failed, it was difficult to maintain a satisfactory surface.

After a later inspection, the report continued:

In June, she showed more serious corrosion and the heads of many bronze rivets had fallen off. . . . The cast fittings about the deck were so corroded that many might be broken by hand.

Fully a hundred years have passed, and we have at last gained a firm understanding of how to build boats of metal and how to employ metal fittings. (There was a time when even ordinary metal fittings were nearly unheard of, and most cleats, chocks, brackets, and even rudder stocks were of wood.) The key is to keep dissimilar metals separated, which we take a closer look at in chapter 14.

Aluminum and Steel Materials

TYPES OF STEEL

Iron is no longer competitive (or available) for boat construction and bronze, which could make a fine boat hull, is far too expensive. This leaves steel as the only practical ferrous material; however, steel comes in many flavors; that is, alloys. Basically, steel is iron alloyed with carbon and other trace elements to adjust its characteristics. Generally, the higher the carbon content, the stronger and harder the steel. Too much carbon, though, makes the steel brittle and difficult to weld, particularly in a marine environment where carbide byproducts in the weld can cause corrosion. Steels are thus divided into categories based on their carbon content.

- Low-carbon steel has no more than 0.15 percent carbon.
- Structural carbon steel, or "mild steel," has between 0.15 and 0.30 percent carbon.
- Medium-carbon steel has between 0.30 and 0.50 percent carbon.
- High-carbon steel has between 0.50 and 1.00 percent carbon.

Medium- and high-carbon steels require pre- and post-heat treatment and/or low-hydrogen welding. They aren't suited to boatbuilding. Mild steel is most commonly used, with the exception of Cor-Ten steel, which at 0.09 percent carbon is a low-carbon steel.

The most common boatbuilding steel alloys are listed in Table 13-1.

An Eckold machine for rapid, precise bending of metal shapes and plate. A MIG welder is to the left and a grinder to the right.

TABLE 13-1 Steel Boatbuilding Alloy Physical Properties

Alloy	UTS, psi × 1,000 (mPa)	Yield, psi × 1,000 (mPa)	Elongation	Endurance Limit, psi × 1,000 (mPa)
A242 (Cor-Ten)	70 (482)	50 (345)	19%	35 (241)
A373	58 (400)	32 (221)	24%	28 (193)
A36	60 (414)	36 (248)	23%	28 (193)
ABS/A	58 (400)	34 (234)	21%	28 (193)
A440	75 (517)	50 (345)	18%	39 (269)
A441	70 (482)	50 (345)	18%	42 (289)

Note: Modulus of elasticity E = 29,000,000 psi (199,862 mPa)

UTS = Ultimate Tensile Strength

Elongation is a percent of an 8-inch (200 mm) sample.

A242 is manufactured by U.S. Steel under the trademark name Cor-Ten.

A36 is the most common standard structural steel or mild-steel alloy.

STEELS USED IN THE SCANTLING RULE

In general, the steel scantling rule assumes that A36, ABS/A, or A373 alloys will be used. It is intended for steels with a tensile strength between 58,000 and 60,000 psi (400 and 414 mPa) and a yield strength between 32,000 and 36,000 psi (221 and 248 mPa). These are *mild steels,* a term that originally indicated that these steels were not brittle.

Endurance Limit

All materials lose strength when they are flexed repeatedly. The more times and the farther they are bent, the weaker they get, until—eventually—they break. (This applies to elastic bending, where the material is not bent so much that it won't naturally spring back to its original shape. Plastic bending stretches the material so far that it deforms permanently and won't snap back. Plastic bending causes even more severe weakening, but it follows different rules than the endurance limit and fatigue strength considered here.)

Imagine bending a thin steel plate back and forth. It will be stiff at first, then grow easier to bend, and finally snap. Vibration and repeated slamming by waves cause just such repeated bending or flexure. Over time, all materials (including wood, fiberglass, and aluminum) grow gradually weaker from continued bending. This is measured as their *fatigue strength,* and it decreases with the number of cycles or the "age" of the structure. Of course, the weakening process can take a long time. For example, after 100,000 cycles of bending, an average aluminum alloy will lose about 15 percent of its original strength; after 200,000 cycles, 25 percent; after 400,000 cycles, 32 percent. Although 400,000 cycles might correspond to more than 50 years of hard use, this loss of strength continues indefinitely.

Steel is a unique exception to this rule. At some point, it ceases to lose any more strength no matter how many additional flexures it experiences. This is the "endurance limit"; obviously, it applies only to steel. The higher the endurance limit of the alloy, the stronger the hull will be many years in the future, all other things being equal. Unfortunately, steel's corrosion is a much bigger factor than its fatigue strength or endurance limit in small-craft applications.

Handbooks list "endurance limits" for other materials; however, read the fine print. These nonsteel "endurance limits" are really the fatigue strength after an arbitrarily defined number of cycles of testing—usually around 500,000 cycles.

HIGHER-STRENGTH STEELS

A440 and A441 steels have higher strength but lower elongation than the more common steels. They also have a higher endurance limit. However, in the thin plate used on boats under 100 feet (30 m), there is little to be gained by employing these steels. Their increased strength cannot be used to reduce thickness because the thinner plate will still corrode at the same rate as the standard structural steels; therefore, it would corrode away too fast. Because A440 and A441 are somewhat more expensive and a little harder to work (because they're stiffer), there's little advantage in using them for hulls. (However, certain high-strength fittings might benefit from these alloys.) Nevertheless, you can certainly build with them if convenient, using the same thickness specified in the standard scantling rule.

Cor-Ten (A242) Steel: Thinner Plate

Cor-Ten steel has strength properties similar to A440 and A441, but it also has improved corrosion resistance. You can reduce the plate thickness from the scantling rule that follows. Calculate the plate thickness and multiply by 0.88 for Cor-Ten. If, for example, the rule called for a $^3/_{16}$-inch (4.76 mm) topsides plate, you could reduce that to 0.165-inch (4.19 mm), which is equal to 8-gauge plate.

Don't be misled by its somewhat improved corrosion properties—Cor-Ten steel is not a stainless steel. It requires the same intensive paint and anodic protection against rust and corrosion that ordinary mild steel does. If not properly maintained, it will weep rust stains at about the same frequency, and can rust away nearly as rapidly as mild steel. Cor-Ten's corrosion advantage is that the rust—once it starts—progresses more slowly on well-maintained hulls, and tends to seal itself against further penetration (for a time).

TYPES OF ALUMINUM

Pure aluminum is not very strong. To increase its mechanical properties, it is alloyed with other elements. There is a wide assortment of aluminum alloys. Only true marine aluminum alloys will stand up to corrosion in salt water. You absolutely cannot use, for example, aircraft or cooking-utensil alloys for marine applications. Serious corrosion will destroy such a hull in short order.

Almost all marine aluminum alloys are in the 5000 series, which is aluminum alloyed with magnesium. The 6000 series—aluminum alloyed with magnesium and silicon—is used for spars and is suitable for some extrusions and structural shapes in hull construction.

ALUMINUM ALLOYS USED IN THE SCANTLING RULE

The temper of an alloy plays a significant role in determining its physical properties, and

TABLE 13-2 Aluminum Boatbuilding Alloy Physical Properties

Alloy	Temper	Form	UTS, psi × 1,000 (mPa)	Yield, psi × 1,000 (mPa)	Elongation
5083	H111	extrusions	40 (276)	24 (165)	16%
	H321	sheet & plate: U.S. Coast Guard now advises against marine use			
	H323	sheet	45 (310)	34 (234)	
	H324	sheet	50 (345)	39 (269)	
	H321	plate: U.S. Coast Guard now advises against marine use			
5086	H111	extrusions	35 (241)	21 (145)	
	H112	plate	35 (241)	16 (110)	14%
	H32	sheet & plate	40 (276)	28 (193)	12%
	H34	drawn tube	44 (303)	34 (234)	10%
5054	H111	extrusions	33 (227)	19 (131)	14%
	H112	extrusions	31 (214)	12 (83)	18%
	H32	sheet & plate	36 (248)	26 (179)	10%
	H34	sheet & plate	39 (269)	29 (200)	10%
5456	H111	extrusions	42 (289)	26 (179)	18%
	H112	extrusions	41 (283)	19 (131)	22%
	H321	sheet & plate	46 (317)	33 (227)	16%
	H323	plate	48 (331)	36 (248)	
	H324	sheet	53 (365)	41 (283)	
6061	T6	sheet & plate	42 (289)	35 (241)	17%
	T6	extrusions	38 (262)	35 (241)	17%
	T6	rod & bar	42 (289)	35 (241)	17%
	T6	drawn tube	42 (289)	35 (241)	17%
	T6	pipe	42 (289)	35 (241)	17%

Note: Modulus of elasticity E = 10,000,000 psi (68,918 mPa)

UTS = Ultimate Tensile Strength

Elongation is a percent of a 2-inch (50 mm) sample.

temper varies with the way the alloy is worked to form it into the shapes you purchase. Allowing for this, 5083, 5086, and 5456 are the alloys applicable to the scantling rule that follows. The 5054 alloy is somewhat weaker. It can be used, but—when given the choice—round up on the thickness given in the rule.

6061 Aluminum and Heat- Versus Non-Heat-Treatable Alloys

Aluminum 6061-T6 is the standard material for masts and spars, and is perfectly acceptable for specialized extrusions and stanchions. However, avoid 6061-T6 for hull construction whenever possible. It can be used for framing but not for plating at all, for two rea sons: 6061 contains 0.25 percent copper and the 5000 series has no copper, so the 6061 is somewhat less corrosion-resistant; and 6061 is a heat-treatable alloy, again compared to the 5000 series alloys, which are non-heat-treatable. Therefore, 6061 is stiffer and more difficult to bend into complex shapes without heating it first—although it can be done effectively and frequently is. The sweeping curves of longitudinals are little or no problem for 6061, for instance.

Even with these two drawbacks, however, in the real world it is often either too hard to find specific shapes in the 5000 series or too expensive. In this case, use the 6061; it will give acceptable service for internal hull framing—it is simply the second choice. For the deck, superstructure, and interior framing (e.g., sole beams), there is no practical difference, and 6061 can be considered interchangeable with the 5000-series alloys. However, on the exterior or where water can collect, it is still marginally more prone to corrosion.

Isotropic Materials for Uniform Strength

Both wood and fiberglass are similar in that they are made up of individual fibers held together by some binding agent and run in clearly defined directions. Wood fibers run with the grain; fiberglass fibers run according to the weave and construction of the cloth, but are clearly directional. The strength of steel and aluminum is uniform in every direction. No matter which way you orient a plate, it has the same strength up or down, fore-n-aft, diagonally, and even through the thickness of the plate. This is called *isotropy*, and steel and aluminum are both *isotropic* materials.

The nice thing about this is that you don't have to pay special attention in design or construction to the alignment of the fibers.

As we've seen, this takes much careful thought in wood and fiberglass.

Comparing Aluminum and Steel

ADVANTAGES OF ALUMINUM

Frankly, of the four standard boatbuilding materials covered in this book—fiberglass, wood, aluminum, and steel—steel is my least favorite. Aluminum has many advantages over steel, which we examine later. Before steel aficionados condemn me for this view, let me say clearly that steel is still a fine material from which to build a boat (or it wouldn't be included in this book). I have designed boats in steel and will continue to do so. In fact, as I write this, my office is designing a 65-foot (19.8 m) steel dinner/cruiser charter boat (see illustration on p. 193, top).

Nevertheless, aluminum has several significant advantages over steel:

1. **Light aluminum.** Aluminum is lighter than steel for the same strength. For example (roughly speaking and neglecting corrosion allowance in steel), aluminum plate should be between 1.25 and 1.5 times thicker than steel for the same strength. Aluminum, however, weighs 168 lb./ft.^{3} (2,691 kg/m^3) versus steel's 490 lb./ft.^{3} (7,849 kg/m^3)—only 34 percent of steel's weight. Even taking the larger thickness's multiplier of 1.5, this means that aluminum is about half the weight for the same strength—a huge difference (i.e., 1.5 times thicker × 0.34 lighter = 0.51, or 51 percent)! Indeed, aluminum structural weight compares favorably to wood or fiberglass. Steel hulls in vessels under 100 feet (30 m)

are nearly impossible to make both really light and long-lasting. Aluminum hulls, in contrast, can even be built extra heavy, resulting in a hull that is literally stronger than steel and still weighs significantly less.

2. **More stable and faster aluminum boats.** The light weight obtainable from aluminum construction lowers the center of gravity of a boat, making it more stable and thus more seaworthy. Less weight also means you can go faster with the same power or sail area, or have a higher ballast ratio in a sailboat for more sail area and improved performance. Alternately, you can use less power for the same speed or get greater range with the same tankage. Of course, you have more cargo capacity or allowable weight for joinerwork and auxiliary machinery with aluminum construction.

3. **Aluminum superstructures on steel hulls.** It is so difficult to make steel light enough that most vessels with Sns under 8 (roughly under 60 feet [18 m]) must use wood, FRP, or aluminum superstructures rather than steel. If they don't, it is nearly impossible to keep the boat's center of gravity low enough for adequate stability. Even larger steel craft benefit from lighter superstructures and frequently use this approach.

4. **Light weight equals labor-saving.** The lighter weight of the components makes building in aluminum less labor-intensive than steel. A $^3/_{16}$-inch, 400-sq. ft. (4.7 mm, 37.1 m²) steel plate would weigh 3,000 pounds (1,363 kg) and would require careful

handling and heavy gear. Roughly equivalent $^1/_4$-inch, 400-sq. ft. (6.3 mm, 37.1 m²) aluminum plate would weigh just 1,408 pounds (640 kg)—again, a vast difference.

5. **Easier to work in aluminum.** Aluminum is softer and easier to bend, cut, and form. It cuts about three times faster than steel. Aluminum bends so easily, in fact, that round-bilge hulls in aluminum are little problem. It can be cut with ordinary woodworking equipment, and quickly and easily drilled, sanded, and filed to exact dimensions. Steel, by comparison, takes heavy grinders and specialized cutting and bending tools. Larger building yards, of course, have specialized machinery for either aluminum or steel, but for aluminum it is simply to make the work go faster still.

6. **No compromise on hull shape.** The freedom to build inexpensively nearly any hull shape in aluminum means that the hull form doesn't have to be compromised with developable surfaces or chines when they're not wanted (see photo on p. 343). This translates into more efficient hydrodynamics for better performance and increased seakindliness.

7. **Faster welding.** Welding aluminum is roughly three times faster than welding steel. Even allowing for somewhat heavier welds (i.e., more passes) for the comparably thicker aluminum plate of the same strength, the total hours in welding aluminum should be about half that for a similar steel hull.

8. **No rust, lower maintenance.** Aluminum doesn't rust at all. Yes, alu-

minum can corrode when in contact with dissimilar metals or from stray electrical currents, but so can steel. Aluminum is so corrosion-resistant and totally rust-free that it doesn't even have to be painted above the waterline or on the inside. (Antifouling bottom paint is still a must.) Many workboats are routinely left bare above the waterline, but most vessels are painted for appearance. The net savings in maintenance over the life of the boat as a result of freedom from rust and generally reduced corrosion is substantial.

9. **No added plate thickness to allow for corrosion.** Even more important, rusting wastes away the steel so the plates get thinner with age. This is why on small craft you can't make effective use of most higher-strength alloys. Indeed, the plate thicknesses for small-boat steel hulls are somewhat heavier than required for basic strength to allow for corrosion—the *corrosion allowance*.

A good rule-of-thumb is that a steel hull will lose about 0.004 inch (0.1 mm) of thickness every year. A well-maintained and properly built steel boat will do a little better than this in most places. Still, in those hard-to-reach areas—such as inside the bilge at the base of bulkheads, near stiffeners and other obstructions—this rule is close.

Another old saying is that steel boats rust from the inside out. This is because it's just these hard-to-reach areas, which are difficult to inspect and maintain, that waste away fastest.

All this means is that in 25 years, $^3/_{16}$-inch (4.7 mm) shell plate would be reduced to 0.09 inch (2.2 mm) thick in several areas, approaching just $^1/_{16}$ inch left. To get adequate life in small craft, steel plates must be made heavier than needed for strength, with a corrosion allowance to accommodate this *wastage*.

10. **Aluminum is nonsparking and nonmagnetic.** Being nonsparking makes aluminum safer both in the building shop and in operation. Fires can't be ignited by the friction spark of some heavy object falling or scraping against the aluminum structure. The lack of magnetic interference is a great plus for navigation and electronics.

11. **Aluminum deforms to absorb more energy.** Aluminum deforms or stretches beyond its elastic limit more than steel before rupturing. This is why dents in aluminum canoes and runabouts seldom split open, and can usually be hammered out again. Such plastic deformation accords aluminum still more energy absorption for its weight than steel.

12. **Aluminum is less sensitive to stress risers.** Aluminum's plastic deformation offers another benefit as well. Steel is particularly sensitive to sharp corners in construction. This is called *notch sensitivity*; the notches or sharp corners are called *stress risers*. Although it is still recommended practice to radius corners and avoid hard spots on aluminum, in fact, aluminum is much more resistant to stress concentrations caused by stress risers than steel. Before the aluminum can fail at

such a hard corner, it deforms—absorbing some of the energy and relieving the stress.

Steel, on the other hand, develops cracks that further increase the stress concentration, which then, in turn, extends the crack and generates new ones as well—a progressively worsening downward spiral in strength. Large ships have literally broken in half and sunk at sea from small stress-riser cracks propagated at a sharp-corner hatch opening on deck. A World War II liberty ship, with square-corner deck openings, broke in half at its loading berth!

13. **Custom extrusions.** Custom dies are possible for aluminum to make specialized shapes. This is generally too costly for small one-off projects; however, production yards often find it economical and practical to have a few specialized extrusions made up for standard rubrails and similar details. This is not possible in steel.

14. **No attack by bacteria.** Aluminum hulls are not subject to attack by sulfate-reducing bacteria. These little-known bacteria can accumulate in bilges, ballast tanks, and fuel tanks—usually in commercial vessels—and eat their way through $5/16$ inch (8 mm) of steel plate in a year! Colonies of microorganisms, sulfate-reducing bacteria speed up corrosion by digesting sulfates and producing sulfides. They can cause catastrophic corrosion quickly if not detected.

15. **Higher scrap value.** Aluminum has higher scrap value than steel, recouping some of its added initial material cost.

16. **Reduced labor costs compensate for increased material costs.** The much greater ease of working with and forming aluminum substantially reduces labor costs. Usually, the labor-cost reduction—combined with the lower total weight of metal purchased—can be enough to offset the substantially higher cost of the aluminum itself.

DISADVANTAGES OF ALUMINUM

No material is perfect and, in spite of the many pluses listed previously, aluminum does have some drawbacks compared to steel.

1. **Aluminum is considerably more expensive.** Recently, I got prices for steel at around 29 cents and aluminum at $1.50 per pound. Although the relationship shifts with commodity-market vagaries, aluminum will always be significantly more costly. Still, it's not quite what it seems. Remember that an aluminum structure weighs only half as much as a steel structure of comparable strength. So, for proper boat-to-boat comparison, you need to cut the total weight of aluminum purchased to half that of steel, or—for convenience—figure on the same weight of metal for both, but half the price for aluminum. At today's prices, this is 29 cents versus 75 cents.

2. **Less abrasion-resistant.** Aluminum is softer than steel. This is a big plus for working and forming, but aluminum hulls are less resistant to abrasion. Still, aluminum is considerably more abrasion-resistant, however, than standard wood or fiberglass construction,

so this isn't much of a drawback for most boats. In fact, aluminum runabouts are routinely run up on rough concrete launching ramps on their bottom. Although not the best practice, aluminum hulls can survive such abuse, which most wood and FRP vessels could not. Still, when it comes to pure abrasion abuse, it's impossible to beat steel. For tugs, canal boats, barges, and dredges, steel becomes more attractive.

3. **Aluminum can melt and burn in a fire.** For a structural metal, aluminum has a low melting point, at approximately 1,080°F (592°C). It can even burn in an exceptionally intense fire. Steel, with a melting point of approximately 2,600°F (1,427°C), is the only truly fireproof boatbuilding material. Once again, aluminum is vastly more fire-resistant than wood or FRP; however, steel is clearly superior in this regard.

4. **Welding equipment is more expensive.** The gas-shielded welding equipment required for aluminum is more expensive than the stick/electrode welding used for steel. What's more, aluminum really should be welded in an enclosed building. If not, breezes will blow the gas shield away from the arc, causing defective welds. Builders have had good success setting up temporary windscreens for outdoor construction, but this is second-best for aluminum construction compared to having a properly enclosed building shed.

5. **Qualified workers and equipment are harder to find.** There are fewer yards

and welders qualified for and experienced in welding aluminum than steel. Especially when voyaging to out-of-the-way corners of the globe, it may be difficult to find places to make repairs. Of course, most damage to aluminum can be temporarily patched by hammering the holed area as smooth as possible, drilling holes in the surrounding shell, and then bolting on a patch sealed with bedding compound.

6. **Aluminum alloy is harder to locate.** Aluminum alloys are frequently tough to find in many regions outside of North America and Europe. Even where aluminum suppliers and manufactures are common, it can be difficult to purchase the sizes and quantities of material necessary for a small-boat project.

Larger building yards will not have too much difficulty with this through their regular suppliers, due to their high annual purchase volume. Small yards and home builders, however, often have to expend great amounts of effort searching for adequate supplies at reasonable cost, and they may be compelled to import materials from distant sources. Even with this extra effort, compromises on more readily available sizes and shapes may become unavoidable. Steel, by comparison, is obtainable quickly and inexpensively—in small and large quantities—all over the world.

Construction Considerations

WELDING VERSUS RIVETING

Until the 1930s, virtually every part of every metal boat was fastened together with rivets and occasionally with bolts or screws. Riveting is labor-intensive and slow compared to welding, and leaves seams that can start and leak on impact. Probably the most structurally complicated and most carefully engineered boats anywhere are submarines. The stress that their hulls experience exceeds anything surface ships encounter, and even the smallest failure can be deadly. Naturally, the very finest and newest technology is used throughout.

It is interesting so see how, at the beginning of World War II, U.S. fleet subs were of nearly all-riveted construction, but by the end of the war they were entirely welded. Not only could they be built faster, but the extra strength from both all-welded construction and newer high-strength steels also enabled them to dive to deeper depths than had ever been possible before. All-welded boat construction really came into its own in the early 1940s, barely 15 years before the beginning of modern fiberglass boat construction.

WELDING DISTORTION

For all its advantages, welding does have some drawbacks. The most important of these is distortion. Every time you weld, you melt a portion of the structure, which then recools and resolidifies. This tremendous fluctuation in temperature distorts and warps the hull. Controlling and limiting weld distortion is critical to good boat construction. (More about this in chapter 18.)

Minimum Practical Plate Thicknesses for Welding

Another consideration, however, is that the thinner the plate, the more prone it is to distortion during welding. Generally, the thinnest aluminum plate that can be welded with standard gas-shielded equipment—

without distortion or burn-through—is $3/16$ or 0.1875 inch (4.75 mm). For steel, the minimum is 10-gauge (0.1345 inch [3.4 mm]). Using pulse-arc welding, aluminum down to $1/8$ inch (3.2 mm) and steel down to 11- or even 12-gauge (0.1196 to 0.1046 inch [3.0 or 2.7 mm]) can be welded. However, such thin plates take very careful attention to detail by experienced welders.

Except where both experienced welders and pulse-arc equipment are available (with the increased cost they represent), you're largely limited to a minimum of $3/16$ inch (4.75 mm) for aluminum and 10-gauge (3.4 mm) for steel.

In the scantling rules that follow—where the results give thinner plate than can be welded—simply round up to the $3/16$ inch in aluminum or 10-gauge in steel.

RIVETING THIN PLATE FOR SMALL BOATS

This is where riveted construction is still useful. Airplanes are made of aluminum rather than steel because aluminum offers so much lighter a structure. Even so, the plate in airplane shells must be well under $3/16$ inch (3.4 mm) and can't be effectively welded—instead, it's riveted.

It isn't practical to make small boats under 30 feet (9 m) light enough in steel, but it certainly is possible—even superior—in aluminum. Such small runabouts and skiffs are nearly universally riveted. Larger, high-performance aluminum sail and powerboats can also benefit from thin plate on their superstructure. There's an overall savings in weight (thus an increase in speed) and improved stability. Light, riveted superstructures are practical where performance is an overriding criterion—but it adds cost.

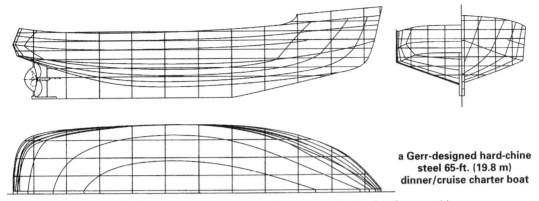

**a Gerr-designed hard-chine
steel 65-ft. (19.8 m)
dinner/cruise charter boat**

*This hull's lines show the characteristic convexity in the forefoot resulting
from conic development for easy plating in steel.*

Hull Shapes and Metal Construction

STEEL HULL SHAPES

Whereas aluminum can be bent into virtually any hull shape, steel hulls usually require compromise. Most small U.S. yards aren't familiar with the techniques required to build true round-bilge hulls with full compound curvature in steel. This is a shame because it is not as difficult as many believe. The standard steel hull is hard chine with *developable surfaces*, which can be rolled along the surface of a theoretical cone or a cylinder, or a series of cones and cylinders, joined smoothly together. Because the lines radiating along the surface of a cone—from its tip to its base—are straight, these *conic surfaces* curve only in one direction and are easy to plate up. (The lines are referred to as *radians*.)

In practice, steel plate can be bent, hammered, and heated into considerable curvature on a hard-chine hull—curvature that is not developable. More complex shapes (which usually occur at the forefoot) can be made up by installing the plate in smaller wedge sections. The only drawback here (besides the added labor) is some further distortion from the extra welding.

Even without any special torturing of the plate, steel can be bent in compound curvature on a hard-chine hull as long as the depth of the transverse curve is less than $1/40$ of the width of the plate athwartships. The fact is that such slight compound curvature actually makes the hull shell stiffer, and also keeps it fairer, reducing the tendency to get that hungry-horse look between frames. Furthermore, it looks nicer than pure slab-sided hulls.

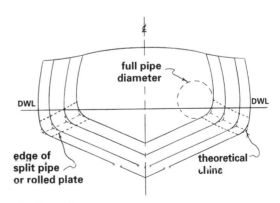

Radius chine

RADIUS-CHINE STEEL CONSTRUCTION

This leads us to an extremely useful intermediate path between true hard-chine and round-bilge construction. The hard corner, where the topsides and the bottom plate meet, can be replaced with a split pipe or a large-radius rolled plate. Such plates can be rolled to spec at a mill with rolling equipment, cut to moderately short lengths fore-n-aft, and then trucked to the building site, where they are welded in place to form the soft chine. Also, the slight convexity or concavity can be worked into steel along the topsides and bottom without special forming equipment using the $1/40$ rule and—properly faired—such a hull is essentially true round bilged specifically designed for easy construction in steel. Not surprisingly, this method is called *radius-chine construction*.

The pre-rolled bilge (chine) plates cannot be bent in the fore-n-aft direction, so they must be installed in many small segments, usually starting midships and working alternately fore-n-aft.

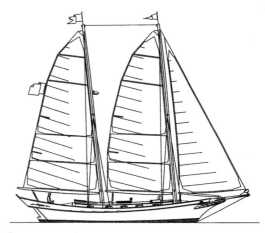

Papoo, *a 51-foot (14.4 m) radius-chine steel pinky schooner*

A Radius-Chine Example

The drawings show the author's radius-chine steel design, *Papoo*, a 51-foot (14.4 m) length-on-deck steel pinky schooner displacing 30 tons. Her sections show what a sweet round-bilge hull shape can be achieved with radius-chines combined with small amounts of convexity elsewhere. You can also see how the hard-chine hull design is converted to a radius-chine hull. On this hull, portions of the forefoot and after-end of the underbody do have considerable twist to the plate—it's not at all developable. In these regions, plate will need to be fitted in several triangular wedges of steel, heated as required and pulled in to the frames.

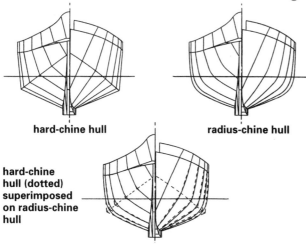

hard-chine hull   radius-chine hull

hard-chine
hull (dotted)
superimposed
on radius-chine
hull

Radius chine and hard chine compared

Developable and Radius-Chine Aluminum
Of course, any hull form that makes construction easier in steel makes it easier still in aluminum. Hard-chine, developable-surface hulls are common in aluminum but are far less necessary. Remember that usually a developable- or conic-surface hard-chine hull is somewhat less than the ideal form for best performance or seakindliness; however, with good design, the losses can be slight indeed. Still, for aluminum hard-chine planing hulls, it makes good sense to design substantial portions of the hull topsides and superstructure developable simply to reduce labor. Here, there is no compromise in performance, although occasionally there can be in appearance. Even the entire underbody can be developable, but again, often at some slight performance loss.

LINE-HEATING OF STEEL: FULL COMPOUND CURVATURE IN STEEL

The general belief is that true round-bilge steel construction requires heavy bending and forming equipment, furnaces, and other expensive machinery. Although such equipment can be used, it is not required and may not even be the quickest way to form compound-curved shell plates. Instead, a technique known as *line-heating* can be employed.

Line-heating uses the distortion caused be the heat of welding or by a welding torch to deliberately shrink the plate into exactly the compound curvature required. Basically, when you heat a portion of steel and it cools, it shrinks at that location. If you take a welding torch and pass it in a line down the length of a plate fairly quickly, it will heat the surface considerably, but—because you were moving fast—the heat will not penetrate fully through the plate. A section cut instantaneously through the hot plate would show a triangle of heat perhaps 1 inch (25 mm) wide at the torch surface, tapering to nearly zero at the opposite side. When the heated line cools, it shrinks, drawing the plate together. (Actually, it puckers in the top—surface—center, which draws the surface material together.)

Because a wider band was heated at the surface, it draws together more than does the side opposite the torch, which experienced little heat. The result is that the plate has bent or curled up slightly at right angles to the torch line. Repeating the process in parallel lines—closer together or farther apart as required—can introduce a great amount of controlled curvature into the plate with no force or heavy equipment. The depth of the curve in the plate is termed *backset*.

Compound Curvature with Line-Heating

If you ran the torch at right angles, in a cross, the plate would curl in both directions and give you compound curvature. If you wanted a plate curved convexly around the fore-n-aft axis and concavely around the transverse axis (e.g., at a garboard), you would turn the plate over and run the torch at a right angle to the curve direction on the opposing side. These

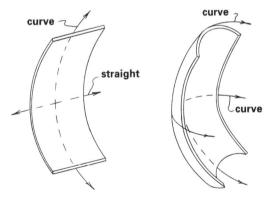

Single curvature, compound curvature

plates are called *saddle plates* because they vaguely resemble saddles.

Shrinking Plates with Line-Heating

Running the torch slowly along the plate allows the heat to penetrate evenly through its thickness. This contracts the plate at right angles to the torch line with little curvature. With practice—using varying torch speeds and directions, running lines closer together and farther apart and at differing orientations—a good fitter can make a steel plate match virtually any odd compound-hull shell with amazing precision.

Line-Heating to Curve Frames and Twist Plate

You can run up to four passes over exactly the same line to maximize curvature. You get less effect on each pass, and more than four passes generates virtually no additional bend. Curved frames can also be formed using line-heating. In this case, an equilateral triangle is marked on the web with the wide triangle base at the inside of the curvature. Start the torch at the apex until it gets cherry red, then cool off the apex end; weave the torch back and forth, heating the triangular area in widening passes to the wide edge of the triangle. Running your torch in diagonally crossing lines on opposite sides of a plate generates twist, which will help bend in the forefoot of nondevelopable forefoot plating, as on *Papoo*. For those knowledgeable in line-heating, this would be quicker and fairer than fitting the plate in several smaller triangular sections.

Using Heat and Restraint to Amplify Line-Heating Effects

Combining cold with heat and restraining the edges can further amplify the effects of line-heating. For example, it will help increase the difference in temperature between the torch side and the opposite side of the plate by spraying water on the opposite side during heating. This amplifies the resulting curvature.

Templates for Line-Heating Complex Plates

For relatively simple plates, experienced craftsmen will work to the hull framing, and then pull in the edges to fit. More complex steel hulls require wooden fitting molds made of widely spaced wooden mold frames called *sight-line templates*. The plate can be line-heated to the approximate shape, then placed on the fitting mold to check. Fine adjustments can be made conveniently and accurately on these light molds to get the best possible fit. Yards that do much of this work may fabricate adjustable sight-line templates that can be used repeatedly on different boat projects.

Line-Heating to Remove Distortion

Just as line-heating can form compound-curved plates deliberately (and help with making tight curves even in a single-curved plate), it can also be used to remove distortion from installed plating. Even a basic understanding of line-heating will help you build better, fairer steel hulls. To learn more about line-heating, refer to naval architect Chris Barry's excellent articles published in *Boatbuilder Magazine*.

Line-Heating Cannot Be Used on Aluminum

Aluminum is easy enough to form without line-heating, which is a good thing. Heating aluminum plate in this way causes stresses and weakens the grain structure of the metal. You cannot use line-heating on aluminum.

Structural Arrangement of Metal Hulls

MAKING THIN PLATE RIGID

Although aluminum and especially steel are very stiff—having high moduluses of elasticity compared to wood or FRP—they are so dense or heavy compared to wood and FRP that the hull shell or plating must be very thin to reduce weight. This is acceptable because both aluminum and steel are quite strong and abrasion-resistant, but it sets the background for the design of metal-boat structures. The aim is to create a structure that is strong enough to withstand the loads of service with plate thin enough to keep the boat light. The problem is that such thin plates are bendy. As we've seen, repeated bending reduces strength over time and will cause failure. It is also unsightly, uncomfortable, and noisy.

What we need to do, then, is support the thin hull-shell plate with a framework that divides the plate into panels small enough not to bend excessively under the expected loads. For example—using the identical $^3/_{16}$-inch (4.75 mm) aluminum plate—a panel, say 10 by 30 inches (250 by 760 mm), will support a pressure loading of 12 psi (82.7 kPa), deflecting just 0.16 inch (4.0 mm) at its center.

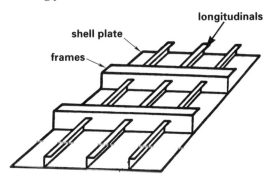

Plate stiffening

A larger panel, say 15 by 40 inches (380 × 1,000 mm), would deflect 0.78 inch (19.8 mm) with the same 12 psi (82.7 kPa) load.

TRANSVERSE FRAMING

Most early metal boats used simple transverse framing. This is exactly analogous to the ribs on traditional plank-on-frame hulls. A welded keel/stem backbone structure (most commonly, a vertical plate called the *centerline vertical keel* [*CVK*]) is laid down and numerous closely spaced transverse frames are attached to it. Transverse deck beams run athwartships at each frame, bulkheads are built in where required, and longitudinal sheer bar and a few longitudinal engine beds/girders round out the principal structure.

Transverse framing works and is covered in the scantling rule that follows. It has the advantage of defining the shape of the hull very tightly with the closely spaced frames, and the numerous frames are molded smaller than more widely spaced frames need to be. This gains some usable volume in the interior for accommodations, machinery, and cargo.

Welded metal-hull construction is, however, a monocoque construction. Transverse framing with few longitudinals is not as structurally efficient in such structures as extensive longitudinal stiffening. Also, longitudinal stiffening produces a fairer hull than all-transverse framing, which has a much greater tendency to get the hungry-horse ripple effect in the shell at each frame.

LONGITUDINAL FRAMING

The alternative to transverse framing is longitudinal framing. Here, widely spaced but deeper molded ring frames (or web frames) support numerous closely spaced longitudinal stringers. This is structurally the most effi-

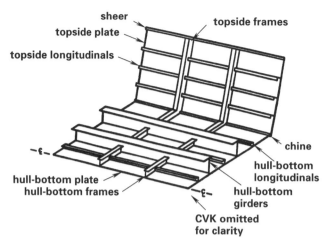

sheer
topside plate
topside longitudinals
topside frames
chine
hull-bottom longitudinals
hull-bottom plate
hull-bottom frames
hull-bottom girders
CVK omitted for clarity

Longitudinally framed chine-hull bottom and topsides

cient framework for a monocoque structure like a welded-boat hull. It is considerably easier to get a smooth, fair shell, and the framework goes together more quickly than using numerous transverse ring frames.

This is because fewer frames have to be cut exactly to shape. The many longitudinals are notched into the ring frames, and are simply bent and swept into place around the hull. The ring frames themselves are set on the same CVK as the transverse-framed hulls. Again, longitudinal en-

Magic Moment, *built by Kanter Yachts. This Gerr-designed 52-foot (15.8 m) aluminum ketch clearly shows the transverse frames, flat-bar longitudinals, and CVK.*

gine beds/stringers and secondary girders finish off the principal structure. The only disadvantage to full longitudinal framing is that the widely spaced ring frames must be molded quite deep, which steals some valuable volume from the interior.

Another disadvantage for longitudinal framing—for some larger vessels—stems from legal tonnage admeasurement considerations. On such craft, the legally admeasured tonnage must be kept low to ensure that the vessel meets the most economical commercial regulations—under 100 tons; under 300 tons; and the like. The depth of hull for admeasurement is defined to the top of the floors; however—as the rule is interpreted—floors penetrated by longitudinals don't count here. Accordingly, on large boats, when it's necessary to reduce admeasured tonnage, transverse framing may be the best approach.

TRANSVERSE FRAMING WITH LONGITUDINALS

To get the best combination of fairness with maximum interior volume, some builders use closely spaced transverse framing in combination with light longitudinals. The goal of this approach is to reduce the molding (depth) of the frames to increase usable interior volume, while simultaneously achieving the improved fairness and increased structural efficiency offered by the longitudinal stringers. The transverse frames in this construction can be slightly farther apart than if there were no longitudinals at all.

My personal preference is for true longitudinal framing as a first choice, falling back on transverse with longitudinals if the extra volume is necessary. Although perfectly good hulls can be crafted with all transverse framing, I think the drawbacks of slightly reduced longitudinal strength, somewhat increased labor, and a less fair hull make it generally the least attractive.

MIXING FRAMING TYPES

Although it is not common, it is permissible to mix framing types. For example, a trawler might use longitudinal framing in the fore-n-aft thirds of the hull, but all transverse or transverse with longitudinals in the middle third of the boat to maximize the fish-hold volume. If this approach is used, the transitions between the two types of framing must be at essentially full transverse metal bulkheads. In the case of our trawler, these bulkheads would likely form the fore-n-aft walls of the fish hold itself.

TORSIONAL STIFFNESS IN METAL HULLS

Because welded metal hulls are monocoque and because metal is isotropic, metal-hull plating has equal strength fore-n-aft, athwartships, and along the diagonal; this means that they have built-in torsional stiffness. Unlike wood and FRP—where special consideration has to be given to torsional strength either with diagonal strapping or by aligning some fibers or planks at plus and minus 45 degrees—this is not an issue for metal hulls.

FOURTEEN

Aluminum and Steel Design Considerations

*F*or both aluminum and steel boats, the details and procedures used to prevent corrosion, attach hardware, and insulate the hull are critical to longevity and usefulness. These factors must be kept in mind during design and construction, and throughout the process of determining the scantlings.

Corrosion Prevention

Corrosion in metal hulls occurs as three principal types: galvanic corrosion, stray-current corrosion, and rust.

GALVANIC CORROSION/DISSIMILAR METALS

When you connect two different metals or metal alloys together electrically and through an *electrolyte* (in this case, seawater), the electrons from the *less-noble* (i.e., *anodic*) metal will try to flow into the *more-noble* (i.e., *cathodic*) metal. This flow of electrons generates a real measurable force, exactly as you could measure, for example, the force in a stream of water flowing through a pipe from a tank with a high water level (the *anode*) to one with a low water level (the *cathode*). Where electrons are concerned, the force of flow is measured not in pounds but rather in volts, and is often referred to as *potential* (because it measures how great the potential is for a flow to occur).

The Galvanic Series

Of course, this potential is relative. Mild steel holds onto its electrons more strongly than marine aluminum, for example. If these two materials were in contact in seawater, the aluminum would corrode (too fast by half), but not nearly as fast as if the aluminum were in direct contact with silicon bronze, for example. Relatively speaking, silicon bronze holds more tightly to its electrons than mild steel, and far more tightly than marine aluminum.

The key word is *relative*, and the best way to keep tabs on these relative potentials is by listing the voltages of all materials with reference to a single test metal (electrode) in

TABLE 14-1 The Galvanic Series

Anodic or Least-Noble End (Active)	Millivolts (mV)
Magnesium (Mg)	−1,730
Magnesium (2% Manganese [Mn])	−1,670
Magnesium (9% Aluminum [Al], 1% Mn, 1.5% Zinc [An])	−1,580
Galvanized Iron (hot dip)	−1,140
Zinc Electroplating	−1,130
Cadmium (Cd) Zinc Solder (71%/29%)	−1,120
Zinc (Zn)	−1,050
Cadmium (Cd)	−860
Cadmium-Plated Steel (Cd 0.001 in.)	−860
Aluminum (Marine Alloys 5086, 5083, 6061)	−820
Mild or Structural Steel (A36)	−790
Alloy Steel	−740
Aluminum (forged alloy)	−730
Stainless Steel (316, 314, 304, 303, 302; active, oxygen-starved)	−550
Tin (Sn)	−500
Manganese Bronze, CA-464 Naval Brass (58% Cu, 39% Zn, 1% Aluminum, 0.25% Mg)	−450
Naval Brass (60% Copper, 39% Zinc)	−450
Yellow Brass	−450
Admiralty Brass (70% Copper, 29% Zinc)	−360
Copper CA-110 (Cu)	−340
Brass (60% Copper, 40% Zinc)	−330
Gunmetal (88% Copper, +Tin)	−310
Silicon Bronze (96% Cu, 1.5% Silicon)	−260
Tin Bronze	−260
Lead (Pb)	−240
Copper/Nickel (CA-715; 70% Cu, 30% Ni)	−200
Aluminum Bronze (90% Cu, 10% Aluminum)	−150
Stainless Steel (316, 317, 321, 347, 302, 304; passive, oxygenated)	−150
Monel 400 & 500	−110
Titanium (Ti)	−100
Silver (Ag)	−80
Graphite and Carbon Fiber (C)	(+250)
Platinum (Pt)	(+260)
Cathodic or Most-Noble End (Passive)	**Millivolts (mV)**

the electrolyte that you're concerned with—seawater, for our purposes. (The most stable and sensitive electrode material for this use is silver/silver chloride [Ag/AgCl]). The list of relative potentials generated this way comprises the *galvanic series* (see Table 14-1). (Electrical activity increases with temperature, so this is specified as well. Standard galvanic tables usually give voltages at 77°F or 25°C.)

- All measurements taken relative to an Ag/AgCl electrode, at 77°F (25°C).
- The sign of potential applies with the negative (black) probe of the voltmeter connected to the reference electrode, and positive (red) terminal connected to the fitting being tested.
- If using a zinc reference electrode, add 100 mV to the potential. For example, silicon bronze is −260mV; then + 100 mV = −160 mV.
- Average variability of potential is ±40 mV for alloys with iron and/or nickel; ±20 mV for copper-based alloys without nickel.
- Readings 200 to 400 mV more negative (i.e., more anodic) than given indicate the material is protected.
- Readings at or near those given up to 200 mV above those given indicate the material is unprotected and freely corroding.
- Readings over 400 mV more negative than given indicate over-protection.
- Stray-current corrosion is indicated by metals reading more cathodic (i.e., more positive) than indicated on the table.

Selecting Fittings and Alloys Using the Galvanic Series

There are two critically important uses for the galvanic series. First, you should refer to it when installing hardware and selecting alloys.

Make sure the voltage difference between any two metals—in direct contact in seawater—is less than 0.20 volt or 200 millivolts (mV). Metals that are less that 200 mV apart corrode each other fairly slowly and need little additional protection. If you must use two metals farther apart than 200 mV, you need to take steps to protect them, either by insulation or isolation (so they're not in contact) or by using anodes.

In metal hulls, the key is to have no dissimilar metals touching anywhere on the hull, and virtually nowhere in the rest of the boat structure. Stainless-steel hardware can mount directly to aluminum and steel on deck and in the cabin, for example. You can barely get by with some small brass joiner hardware in contact with aluminum on the interior (if and only if it doesn't contact any portion of the principal hull structure) and when there's absolutely no other choice. (Of course, brass, bronze, and stainless are all ideal for joiner hardware that is not in contact with aluminum at all.)

Isolating Bronze Seacocks and Fittings

This means that bronze seacocks must be isolated *exceptionally* well from the hull. In fact, these days, glass-fiber-reinforced-nylon plastic seacocks (sold by Forespar under the Marelon trade name) are approved for use by the ABS and Lloyds, and are recognized by the U.S. Coast Guard. I recommend using these exclusively to avoid any possibility of corrosion. Marelon is currently available in diameters up to 2 inches (50.8 mm) and, being a plastic, it can melt and burn in a fire. Some commercial regulations may demand metal seacocks.

Large engine-water intakes and other high-volume seawater pumps may require

3- or 4-inch (75 or 100 mm) diameters. You must not use ordinary PVC or similar alternate plastic valves for seacocks. Only plastic (and metal, for that matter) valves specifically certified for use as seacocks by Underwriters Laboratories, ABS, or Lloyds are rugged enough. A broken seacock can sink a boat fast. Accordingly, for such large-diameter inlets, solid-bronze seacocks are the only option. (Stainless is too subject to pitting corrosion, and aluminum is too soft.) The bronze seacocks must be insulated from the hull on a plastic or fiberglass pad, and bolted to the hull with stainless through-bolts. The bolts themselves must be isolated from the bronze by spacer tube/sleeves that completely surround each bolt, as well as with a plastic washer/spacer under the stainless washer under the nut on the seacock's interior flange. Similarly, cutless bearings must have fiberglass or plastic shells rather than brass or bronze.

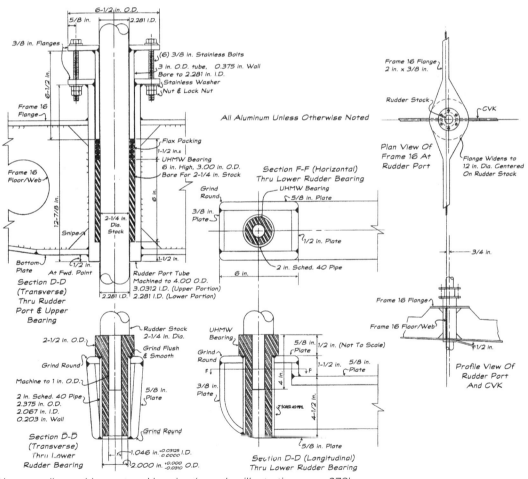

Noncorroding rudder port and bearing (see also illustration on p. 278)

Check Design and Fittings for Potential Corrosion

Careful thought must be given to rudder bearings and all other fittings that may contain dissimilar metals. I recently reviewed the plans of a 60-foot steel motor cruiser that had a dangerous detail for a lower rudder bearing in the rudder skeg. It contained a brass sleeve bearing with stainless-steel ball bearings under the end of the rudder stock to take the axial load. The combination of mild steel, brass, and stainless-steel balls rolling about would create a galvanic nightmare that would destroy this assembly in months, or less. Thordon makes a wide variety of plastic bearings that will not corrode and are water-lubricated. Ultra-high-molecular-weight polyethylene (UHMWPE) also makes an excellent bearing material and a perfect isolator/ spacer material. UHMWPE is strong, tough, very smooth, exceptionally abrasion-resistant, and—of course—totally inert electrically.

Stainless-Steel Hardware and Fittings

Stainless steel is quite useful for both aluminum and mild-steel hulls. Stainless is close enough galvanically not to cause too much of a problem. On aluminum under water, it must still be isolated, but it's the only choice for those rare instances when you must attach fittings or weldments to the aluminum hull below the waterline. (It's far better to fabricate these fittings entirely from aluminum, and usually there's little excuse not to do so.)

On the deck and superstructure, stainless-steel fittings can be bolted directly to the aluminum without problems—using no more than good bedding compounds. Stainless-steel bolts and screws are the standard fas-tener material for hardware attachment on both aluminum and steel vessels. On steel boats, it is also sometimes practical to weld stainless acorn nuts under the deck and inside the cabin to accept stainless through-bolts. Lightly welded all around, these won't leak and will permit easier removal and refastening without the need for a pair of hands below decks.

Stainless-Steel Inserts for Chafe and Corrosion Resistance on Mild-Steel Boats

On mild-steel hulls, stainless steel offers another option: It can be welded directly into the mild-steel structure using the proper welding rod/electrode (e.g., 309L). You must *not* do this anywhere that will be regularly below the waterline; it will lead to serious corrosion. Still, on the deck and cabin, stainless welded into the structure offers many advantages. Insert plates and riser weldments (e.g., winch bases) of stainless can be built in around areas of high chafe, such as at chocks, around winches, windlasses, mast bases, turning blocks, cleats, and hawseholes. You can even weld stainless-steel rod or heavy-wall tube around the interior perimeter of hawsehole openings.

You can also weld in stainless-steel plates or plugs in areas where you may have to fasten and unfasten hardware and fittings fairly regularly. The stainless itself can be drilled and taped for the bolts, which are then far less likely to freeze, and can be removed and refastened numerous times without losing the thread. All these welded-in stainless-steel areas should be painted to match the surrounding surface; however, when chafe occurs, you won't get the corrosion and rust weeps you would get on the basic mild steel of the hull proper.

The Best Stainless-Steel Alloys

All stainless steel is not created equal. For use below the waterline, only 316L (L for low carbon) steel should be used. All other stainless is too prone to localized pitting corrosion. (Even 316L can suffer from this is some cases.) The first choice for all marine stainless fittings is 316L, but it is the most expensive and sometimes hard to locate. On deck, 304 and 302 stainless is acceptable, although 302 is the most prone to light-brown rust discoloration and cosmetic pitting.

Isolate Wood from Metal to Prevent Corrosion

Wood also must be isolated from metal hulls. Moisture will collect under the wood, and the acids and oils in the wood mixed with the salt water generate poultice corrosion that can be quite severe. The solution is to bed the wood very well before fastening, and fasten it over a painted hull surface. At a minimum, the wood also must be painted or varnished on its mating surface before fastening it down. Better still is to saturate the wood with three coats of marine epoxy before fastening it down on bedding compound. Again, stainless is more resistant to this and, on mild-steel hulls, it can make sense to weld in stainless steel under wooden fittings and rails; however, this is expensive and not required.

Anodes Protect by Flooding with Electrons

After a good paint job and avoiding contact of dissimilar metals, anodes are the next line of defense against corrosion. There's a nice feature about anodic metals, if you use them correctly: as long as they're losing electrons, all the other more-noble (i.e., more-cathodic) metals they're connected to are protected from corrosion. For example, our *Aluma-Naught* had bronze seacocks. Even though you took care to isolate the bronze, there remains a possibility of electrical interaction. In this case, electrons would be tumbling from the less-noble aluminum to the bronze. *AlumaNaught's* hull would then quickly waste away near the seacocks. If a zinc anode were attached to the hull, however, its electrons would—roughly speaking—tumble toward both the aluminum and the bronze (it's far more anodic than both). It would flood the system with zinc electrons—again, roughly speaking. (Other anodic metals, such as magnesium and aluminum, are occasionally used as anodes. Zinc, however, offers the best trade-off between cost, reliability, and ease of manufacture. It's the standard marine-anode material.)

> **Making Your Zincs Work**
>
> *It takes some smarts to make zincs work.*
>
> 1. You must install zincs to protect your boat's metal fittings or hull.
> 2. The zincs must be in tight, clean electrical contact with the metal components they're protecting. (If they're not electrically connected to the bonding system or metal hull, they're useless.)
> 3. The surface of the zincs must be exposed to the water. You can't paint a zinc anode—ever! You want it exposed and you want it to corrode. (They're not called "sacrificial zincs" for nothing!)

Anode Installation

Anodes should be installed on all metal hulls to protect for corrosion. They even help protect against rust on steel hulls.

A converted army T-boat, this 60-foot (18.3 m), 100-ton steel tug was gutted and converted to a live-aboard home to the author's design. The numerous anodes are clearly visible. (Courtesy Sam Haigh)

It's possible to weld lugs projecting from some anodes directly to the hull. This, however, makes replacing anodes a difficult business. A better approach is to weld bolts to the hull to mate with the anode's fastener holes. Replacing anodes is then as simple as turning a wrench.

On aluminum craft, the best practice is to weld either a backing or doubler plate to the exterior of the hull, or a thick insert plate into the hull at the anode location. (The doubler or insert plate should be of the same aluminum alloy as the surrounding plate. The doubler thickness should be approximately 1.5 times the fastening-bolt diameter; the insert plate about 2.2 times the bolt diameter. Both should match the footprint of the anode or be slightly larger.) Drill the doubler for stainless threaded inserts and use standard 316-stainless hex-head machine bolts to fasten the anode. Be certain to install lock washers under each nut. Without these, engine vibration and corrosion will loosen the nuts.

To ensure good electrical contact and a firm mounting base, proper anodes are cast around a steel-bar core. Fastening bolts penetrate and land on this core. For aluminum hulls, the best practice is to use anodes with aluminum cores.

Amount of Zinc for Metal Hulls

A good estimate of the anode required can be made from the following formulas.

FORMULA 14-2

Steel Anode Quantity

For one year of protection of a steel hull with an average (i.e., less than perfect) paint job:

Steel-Hull Required Anode Weight (lbs.) = hull wetted surface (sq. ft.) ÷ 16.75

Steel-Hull Required Anode Weight (kg) = hull wetted surface (m²) ÷ 3.43

For two years of protection, use twice as much anode. For one year of protection for bare metal, use 2.5 times as much.

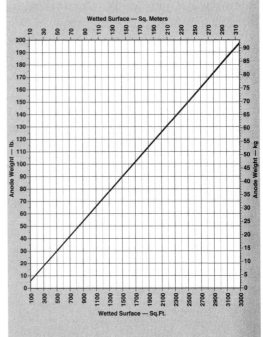

Steel-Hull Zinc Anode Weight

FORMULA 14-3

Aluminum Anode Quantity

For aluminum hulls, anodes are better selected by their surface area than by their weight.

For one year of protection:

Aluminum-Hull Required Anode Surface Area (sq. ft. or m²) = hull wetted surface (sq. ft. or m²) ÷ 220

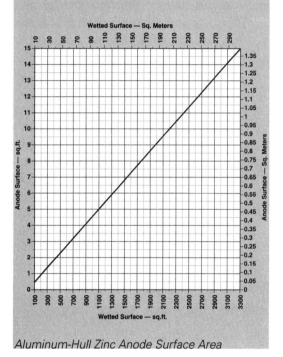

Aluminum-Hull Zinc Anode Surface Area

Remember, these formulas give estimates. Boats that operate in warm or highly polluted water may need more protection. Vessels that operate in cold clean waters can often get by with less.

FORMULA 14-4

Steel and Aluminum Anode Location

Anodes should be roughly evenly spaced on the hull under the waterline starting from the transom. Generally, they should be located about two-thirds of the waterline half-beam out from the centerline, port and starboard. On larger hulls, there is an additional anode pair aft, about one-third of the waterline half-beam out from the centerline, or mounted on the sides of the keel. Find the total amount of anodes you need from the previous formulas, then locate them roughly as follows (again, with all measurements starting at the transom):

25 Feet (7.5 m) and Under:
2: 1 each, port and starboard; one-third of WL

25 to 35 Feet (7.5 to 11 m):
4: 2 each, port and starboard; one-fifth of WL, and then 2 at 55% of WL

35 to 50 Feet (11 to 15 m):
6: 3 each, port and starboard; 2 at one-sixth of WL; 2 at 40% of WL; and 2 at 65% WL

50 to 65 Feet (15 to 20 m):
8: 6 of which are the same as for 35 to 50 feet (15 to 20 m), but with 2 additional closer to the centerline, at 14% of WL

65 to 85 Feet (20 to 26 m):
10: 8 of which are about evenly spaced, port and starboard, at about 17% of WL length O.C.; plus 2 at about 12% of WL, closer to the centerline

85 to 100 Feet (26 to 30 m):
12: 10 of which are about evenly spaced, port and starboard, at about 14% of WL length O.C.; plus 2 at about 11% of WL, closer to the centerline

Additional Anodes

Anodes should be installed on the rudder, sized according to the rudder's surface area.

Smaller rudders can have a single anode on one side; larger rudders should use one each, port and starboard. A collar-type shaft anode should be installed on the propeller shaft. Alternately, a commutator-type internal shaft brush can be used to contact the rudder, and then connect to the through-bolt and external anode on the hull bottom or keel side. Sea chests, bow thrusters, and similar recesses open to the sea each require their own small anode, which must be easily accessible and easy to replace.

Corrosion Monitors and Bonding

Larger metal boats, especially those with extensive electrical systems, should have a corrosion monitor installed. Corrosion monitors allow you to keep tabs on *AlumaNaught*'s hull potential, enabling you to be sure that its zincs are working properly, know when they need replacement, and identify overprotection and stray-current corrosion.

On still larger craft, the isolated fittings (e.g., bronze seacocks) should be connected to their own completely separate and isolated secondary internal-bonding system. The bonding conductors on these secondary systems must be insulated. Even the zinc anodes for this separate system must be completely isolated from the metal hull. Dual-metal corrosion monitors are available to monitor the hull anodes and to monitor the isolated secondary-bonding system. A reliable monitor, such as that made by Electrocatalytic of Union, New Jersey, is important.

STRAY-CURRENT CORROSION

Stray-current corrosion is the most dangerous form of corrosion to which any metal boat can be subjected. The voltages generated by dissimilar metals alone in salt water are measured in millivolts. Stray currents from faulty wiring—on board or from shore power—can reach more than 100 volts. Not only do these high voltages pose a serious electrocution hazard (particularly AC current), but they also can eat away large portions of metal hulls in just weeks, sometimes days (even at just a few volts, as compared to millivolts for galvanic corrosion). It is vital that the electrical system on all metal boats complies precisely with American Boat and Yacht Council Standards. There is just no point in building a strong beautiful hull only to have it eaten away by stray electrical currents.

Vital Isolation Transformer

All metal boats (except small runabouts, canoes, and skiffs) should be fitted with an isolation transformer at their shore-power inlet. If properly wired and installed, the isolation transformer nearly guarantees that faulty shore-side wiring cannot somehow short to the hull. Failure to install an isolation transformer is asking for serious trouble the first time your *AlumaNaught* or *Iron Maiden* spends a few days at an incorrectly wired dock—and there are plenty of those around. Simple galvanic isolators help in this regard, and may be adequate for metal runabouts with shore-side connection to a battery charger, but they're not sufficient insurance for larger metal boats. At this writing, the only *marine* UL-approved isolation transformer being manufactured comes from Charles Marine Products (Rolling Meadows, IL).

Isolate Electric Wiring from Hull

Great care must be taken with the DC system as well to ensure that it's entirely isolated. All wiring, both positive and the return negative wires, must be fully isolated from the hull. The sole exception is that the DC negative bus must be bonded to the hull. This is best accomplished as follows:

For aluminum hulls, weld a $^3/_8$-× 4-in. (10 × 100 mm) aluminum lug to convenient frame or hull stringer. Bolt $^1/_4$-× 4-in. (6.4 × 100 mm) stainless flat bar to this lug, with two $^1/_4$-in.-diameter (6.5 mm) stainless bolts, with lock washers. Attach a 00 DC ground cable, from the negative bus, to the stainless bar (at least 3 in. or 75 mm clear from aluminum), with a stainless bolt, with lock washer. Paint all bolts, the stainless bar, adjacent aluminum, and the terminal fitting of the 00 cable with three coats of marine varnish to seal out moisture. For a steel hull, weld the $^1/_4$-inch stainless flat bar directly to the hull framing.

At first glance, isolation of the DC system seems relatively easy to accomplish, but there are many potential pitfalls and hidden paths to short the negative return to the hull

structure. One of the most commonly overlooked paths is the engine block. Most automotive alternators (commonly found on many marine engines) use the engine block as the negative/ground. This can short the negative to the hull through the engine-mount bolts. Be certain to install isolated-negative-return marine alternators for engines and generators in metal boats. Then, go the next step and float the engine on rubber mounts, with a flexible rubber coupling to the shaft. This further isolates the engine from potential shorts to the hull. Another item often overlooked is engine instruments. Many of the standard senders also use the engine block for negative return. Again, be sure to use only senders that have isolated negative returns. Still another potential path for shorts is hose with embedded wire reinforcement. Should the wires wear through and make contact at both ends, again you have a potential electrical path to the hull.

AC Bonded to DC Bus

Like the DC electric system, the AC system must be completely isolated from the hull and from the DC system itself. Once again there is one, and only one, mandatory exception: The AC system green wire ground—from the isolation transformer (or the galvanic isolator on small boats)—*must* be bonded to DC negative bus. AC wiring must not make electrical contact with any other portion of the hull or the DC wiring.

RUST

Rust and excessive weight are the two central drawbacks to steel hulls. Both can be addressed to some degree, but never eliminated. It is difficult to say which is the more serious problem, but rust is the cause of more maintenance and expense throughout the life of the vessel than any other consideration in steel hulls. (Aluminum, as we've seen, doesn't rust at all.)

Basically, rust is the most common byproduct of the corrosion of most ferrous alloys, including boatbuilding steels. It is principally hydrated ferric oxide, but this varies slightly depending on the conditions and the alloy. Moisture and oxygen are the only two requirements for the rusting process to start. Salt increases the moisture's chemical efficiency at transmitting ions, and so considerably accelerates the oxidation reaction that produces rust, as do warm temperatures, which also encourage chemical activity. In other words, the environment most boats operate in is the best possible for making rust and the worst possible for preventing it! Given the slightest opportunity, rust *will* occur and *will* spread extensively.

Paint: The First Line of Defense against Rust

There is only one real preventative for rust in steel hulls: seal the steel away from the environment—from the moisture, the oxygen, and the salt. A superb paint system is critical. Reducing moisture and humidity in the hull interior also helps. Insulation assists here, as do various spray-on surfacing agents.

Because rust is a chemical reaction involving the exchange of electrons, anodes that flood the steel hull with their own electrons also help prevent rust. The anode's electrons flood the steel and combine with the ions in the salt-water/salt-air environment before the steel's own electrons can. This is the principle behind galvanizing, and hot-dip galvanized iron and steel fittings have a tolerable (although no better) life expectancy on boats.

Simply electroplated or painted-on zinc coatings (a cheap galvanizing) aren't up to marine applications.

Zinc or Aluminum Spraying (Galvanizing) Steel Hulls

Some builders essentially galvanize their hulls by sandblasting them to white metal and then flame-spraying on molten zinc or molten aluminum. A full paint job is applied over this zinc or aluminum surface. This can be effective but does have some drawbacks. First, it adds cost. Second, the flame-sprayed zinc or aluminum surface is roughish, with a faint stipple. You can't grind it smooth because you would remove the protection you just added. Accordingly, such hulls should be finished workboat-rough with matte paint. Third, when the paint and zinc or aluminum coating underneath is scratched through to the bare steel, that location can suffer accelerated local attack that usually shows up first as bubbles or blisters in the paint. On mild steel, sprayed-on aluminum is less reactive than zinc (it's closer on the galvanic series) and, therefore, is somewhat less likely to promote local attack. My opinion is that a high-quality paint finish inside and out, along with good insulation, sufficient anodes, and proper interior drainage, is the best approach. Using welded-in stainless-steel inserts at high-chafe areas helps still more.

Painting

On steel hulls, paint is the most essential barrier to rust. There are many paint systems, and most work well if carefully applied according to the manufacturer's instructions. The key to a long-lasting paint job on new steel construction is preparation. Spare no expense and reasonable labor on this—it will pay back many times over. Sandblast to near-white or pure-white metal, prime immediately—before there's any chance of surface contamination, and paint as soon as possible. Although there are a number of good paint systems available, I believe modern epoxy paints are the best for protecting steel.

For aluminum, the same recommendations apply. Although paint is really optional above the waterline, it is used on the overwhelming majority of boats. Even on aluminum, a good paint surface helps protect against both galvanic and stray-current corrosion by isolating the aluminum from the electrolyte (i.e., seawater) that carries half the "current"; that is, the ions needed for chemical reactions to occur.

Again, sandblasting to bare metal—as with steel—is one approach: Wash with fresh water, blow dry, and prime, followed by the fairing putty and topcoats as soon as possible. This is the key, along with religiously following the paint manufacturer's instructions. However, sandblasting aluminum is tricky. It is soft enough that too much pressure or too much flow will erode a significant thickness of metal. It will also leave a wavy pitted surface. Although you can use regular sand, the best "sandblasting" material for aluminum is crushed walnut shells or plastic beads, which are used in fine auto-refinishing and aren't excessively costly. Being softer, they don't pose the problems that harder silica sand does, although care is still needed with aluminum's soft surface.

Many builders prefer to prep aluminum hulls for paint with grinding rather than sandblasting. They grind the whole surface clean (and to give it tooth) with 24- to 36-grit disks. The bare metal is washed and/or blown clean, and then painted with an etching solution. The prime coat must be applied within an hour or two. Fairing putty follows on top of the primer as needed. During hull fairing—for both aluminum and steel—care must be taken to quickly touch up any bare metal that is exposed through the primer. The topcoats finish off the job.

Mud: Fairing Compound

Most yacht builders will expostulate at length about how little mud or fairing compound they use on their beautifully faired hulls and superstructures. Although there are a few exceptional boats and a few exceptional builders, in general I don't believe these claims and neither should you. I once had the opportunity to examine a damaged portion of a superstructure built by one of the finest luxury-yacht yards in the world. In some places, there was nearly $3/4$ inch (19 mm) of mud on the cabin roof! This was and still is a good builder, and clearly there had been a problem with distortion in this one location. Still, such problems occur—to greater or lesser degree—on most welded boats.

Many workboats, of course, don't bother with fairing. Some visible ripples, kinks, and dents are unimportant—only performance and economy count. On yachts and highly finished workboats—before you finish painting—you will need to fair your hull with mud. This is normal. The best fairing putties, in my opinion, are epoxy-based. Screeding on the mud, letting it cure, sighting along it, and long-boarding and hand-sanding are time-consuming, and these processes must be repeated over and over. If you're after a truly perfect, mirror-smooth finish, the labor involved can almost equal the labor in assembling the hull. You have to plan accordingly. You also need to allow for the weight of the mud. My experience has been that a good builder, obtaining an average but not perfect finish, uses fairing compound about equal to 3 percent of the weight of the aluminum hull structure, and about 2 percent of the weight of a steel hull structure (not the full displacement of the boat and not including deck or superstructure).

Construction Details

THREADED INSERTS FOR REMOVABLE FASTENERS

We previously discussed welded-in stainless-steel plates to accept fasteners and reduce chafe. For both steel and aluminum, stainless-steel threaded inserts are the best way to install bolts and screws of every type. In steel, the stainless threaded insert prevents corrosion and freezing of the fastener. In aluminum, the inserts additionally increase holding power in this softer material. All structural bolts that are not through-bolted should be bolted into stainless threaded in-

Stainless threaded insert. (Courtesy Camloc Fasteners)

serts. Helicoils or coil-thread inserts seem to be the easiest to install and have the greatest gripping power, but other forms of stainless threaded inserts are acceptable.

VOID AREAS IN HULLS

A conundrum on most metal hulls is what to do with the void areas in the keel, hollow rudders, under tanks, and so on. Traditional practice was to fill voids in the keel with bitumastic. It can be spread onto clean surfaces in layers of $1/2$ to 1 inch thick (12.5 mm to 25 mm), and it adheres very well. Massive solid buildups of bitumastic were often used to fill in deep areas of the keel. The buildups were applied in patterns and sloped to create a sump. The solid, hard, tarry mass lasts years and usually sticks tenaciously enough not to allow water to run in and collect between it and the inside of the plating. However, bitumastic is heavy and oily, and can have a noticeable odor. A lighter and more modern alternative is pour-in-place foam and various special filler chemicals.

However, there are difficulties with all these nearly permanent resilient materials in hard-to-get-at spots. You can't inspect under them, and—if you need to make repairs—you can't weld in these areas because the stuff smokes and/or burns. Before any work can be done, you have to get down into these inaccessible regions and remove the tenacious gooey mass—a nightmare.

Empty Voids Are Best

My preference for void spaces in the bilge and keel is to seal them off with a cover plate welded watertight all around. Install an access plate or two in the cover plate, in areas that are relatively easy to get at, using the same details as for a removable tank-manhole cover.

The access hole need only be a 6- or 7-inch (150 or 180 mm) clear opening (larger is better, if there's room). In this way, you can take a flashlight and a small mirror, remove the access panel, and inspect the interior to see if there are any leaks. A further refinement is a screw-in drain plug through the hull at the low point of the void space; this can be added later when any repairs are needed. By keeping the void space empty, you're free to make weld repairs with ease.

Oil-Filled Voids

On steel boats, some argument can be made for filling the void spaces with oil. The idea is that corrosion can't occur. Still, if the void space is sealed watertight (including the access panel—as it should be), the oxygen required for rust and corrosion will be quickly used up and further corrosion will be retarded. Fill and drain plugs should be installed at the high and low points if oil-fill is employed. (To comply with environmental regulations, only biodegradable vegetable oil should be used.) Keep in mind that oil-fill in the void spaces in the keel adds weight. Although this weight is low down, it does sink the boat lower and reduce performance potential to some degree.

A stronger case can be made for filling hollow-steel rudders and similar small fins or appendages with vegetable oil. These areas are difficult to inspect, and the weight of the oil is negligible. Still, no oil and a simple drain plug at the low point are really sufficient. Make it a practice to remove the plug at every haul-out. The void area should be bone dry. If any water leaks out, there is nothing to remove before welding a repair, not even drained oil. The leak can usually be located quickly by screwing an air-hose fitting into the drain-plug opening, pressurizing the void area (1.5 psi [10.3 kPa] is ample), then spraying the exterior with soapy water and looking for telltale bubbles.

On aluminum hulls, I see no reason to use any oil or a more solid void fill. Simple watertight cover plates with watertight inspection-access holes and outside drain plugs handle all eventualities and do not hinder repair.

INSULATION AND INTERIOR COATINGS

Because metal is such a superb conductor of heat and sound, extensive insulation of the hull, deck, and superstructure is required for comfortable interior accommodations. Without insulation, veritable rivers of condensation collect on the inside of the plating and run down into the bilge. The resulting high humidity promotes decay and damages wiring and electrical equipment. Even worse, on steel hulls it greatly accelerates rusting on the inside, where it's most difficult to inspect, locate, and repair. Finally, without insulation, the cabin spaces would be nearly impossible to heat in winter or cool in summer; they'd be noisy too.

Insulating the inside of a metal hull is a laborious and finicky job. Some builders are inclined to skimp here, but it must be done correctly, with patient attention to detail.

TYPES OF INSULATION

Standard insulation is either closed-cell foam, fiberglass batts or panels, or cork sheets. Of these, only fiberglass is truly fire-resistant and, therefore, is my first choice for safety. Nevertheless, foams are acceptable and have been installed in most of my metal designs. Cork is somewhat fire-retardant, especially compared to some of the foams available. It works well but is heavier than most foam or fiberglass. Cork is also a natural material and is subject to degradation from age and fungal attack.

Advantages of Spray-on Foam

The major question with insulating the hull interior is whether to use spray-in-place urethane foam or to apply sheets of material—either foam, fiberglass, or cork. Spray-in foam is difficult to blow onto the hull evenly. For this reason, it should only be installed by a professional with the right equipment and much experience. Its big advantages are maximum coverage and adhesion. If sprayed onto a steel hull correctly, the foam will adhere quite tenaciously and protect it well from both air and moisture—a good rust-inhibitor. You'll practically need a chisel to peel off the foam.

Drawbacks of Spray-on Foam

Spray-on urethane foam does give the maximum insulation effect because it covers every little nook and cranny, and can be built up quite thick. Its drawbacks are considerable, though. Spray-on foam burns fiercely and gives off very toxic gases. It should be coated with fire-retardant paint; however, even with protective paint, it can still burn. It also absorbs odors, which are impossible to eliminate, and can become quite unpleasant. Most intractable of all is that once in place, you can't weld anywhere near the foam without starting a real conflagration. One excellent boatbuilder I worked with lost a boat nearing completion in his shop in just this way. Any future welding repairs will require the difficult and messy job of scraping off this tenacious messy foam—all of which is inside,

behind joinerwork, and nearly impossible to reach.

INSULATION APPLIED IN SHEETS

Because of the drawbacks of spray-on foam, I prefer to insulate the hull with removable sheets/panels of foam or fiberglass. In this case, a steel hull should be blasted to near-white metal inside, primed immediately, and painted with a good epoxy paint. Then the foam or fiberglass sheets are glued in place between the frames and stringers. The stringers themselves should be covered with strips of foam glued over them in a U shape. Stringers with relatively low molding heights can simply be covered by running the sheets over them and pressing down as tightly as possible at the corners. Only the tops of the inside faces of the frames are left exposed. Yes, these bare spots do transmit some heat, but the square footage exposed is very small. (Aluminum hulls are not blasted or painted on the interior; rather, they are simply cleaned to ensure a good glue bond.)

These foam sheets are available from various manufacturers with excellent adhesive systems. They can be peeled off for repairs and—unlike spray-on foam, which is generally applied in one big job—the sheets can be added piecemeal during construction, permitting some portions of the boat to be insulated and finished off while other areas are still undergoing welding work. Fiberglass insulation panels are so fire-resistant that they actually help retard the spread of a blaze. All these insulating sheets/panels are available with mylar or aluminized mylar interior surfaces, which make the insulation much more resistant to absorbing odors and much easier to keep clean.

LOCATION OF INSULATION AND INTERIOR PAINT

In all cases, the insulation should start from the waterline, extend up the topsides, run under the deck, up the inside of the cabin sides, and under the cabin roofs. This should be done wherever there will be accommodations. Forepeaks, lazarettes, and cargo spaces need not be insulated, but—for steel—they must be painted. Aluminum requires no interior paint, although I like to paint the interior of aluminum hulls in the machinery spaces. This protects the aluminum from dropped pieces of copper or steel that might cause local corrosion inside, and it gives the compartment a more finished look. The inside of the hull topsides in the engine compartment should be insulated with foam or fiberglass. This is really a living space; you have to work in it regularly. What's more, without this insulation, the bare metal hull transmits and reflects engine noise fiercely.

ATTACHING THICK SOUND INSULATION

Insulation in machinery spaces also doubles as vital sound insulation. On larger boats, foam 3 to 6 inches (75 to 150 mm) may be used under the sole and along bulkheads to reduce noise. These thicker sheets can be held in place with inexpensive spiked fittings that have small base plates glued onto the hull or bulkhead. The insulation is jammed down on the spikes that penetrate it. Then the spikes are turned down (almost like a clench nail) over interior pads (similar to rivet roves). Again, I prefer fiberglass (mineral wool) insulation for its fire resistance but often end up using foam to please the builder because it's less expensive.

Extensive sound insulation in the engine room (still under construction) of the author's Imagine *design.*

DO NOT INSULATE THE BILGES

Never run insulation below the waterline. Any bilge water—and there's sure to be some eventually—will splash up onto the foam or fiberglass, where it will cause mildew, fungus, and a repulsive stench.

PAINTING THE INTERIOR OF STEEL-HULL BILGES

Except as desired in engine spaces and such, the bilge in aluminum hulls can be left bare. The bilge in steel hulls must be sandblasted, primed, and coated with epoxy paint. A more expensive but even tougher alternative is to paint the bilge, or the most inaccessible portions of it, with Isotrol, POR-15, or Pettit Rustlok 6980. These are thick specialty coatings for steel and usually contain aluminum or zinc powders for anodic protection. Although costly, they are remarkably tenacious and retard rust even better than ordinary paint.

INSTALLING BALLAST

Ballast is installed on almost all sailboats and on many displacement powerboats as well. Lead is—by far—the best material, and the only one acceptable for aluminum (steel or iron would cause corrosion). The ballast is almost always installed inside a hollow keel. Never pour all the lead in in molten form. The tremendous heat will distort any metal hull beyond salvaging. Instead, lay in as much of the ballast as possible in pigs. Then fill the gaps and corners with molten lead poured down around the pigs. On deep ballast keels, it may be necessary to do this in two or three layers to ensure maximum penetration and to reduce heat.

Scrap-Iron Ballast

Steel boats can also be ballasted with scrap iron. This is not as dense as lead, so its center of gravity will be higher, but it is cheaper. A mixture of large scrap bar stock with smaller steel shot and scrap nuts and bolts can be set in the bilge. It can be locked in place with a slurry of cement. Alternatively, you can lock it in place with a low-exotherm epoxy resin or bitumastic, but these have the drawback of being flammable and impeding future welding repairs.

External Bolted-on Ballast

It is possible to bolt cast-iron external ballast to steel hulls with stainless-steel bolts, although all stainless bolts are subject to pitting corrosion, even 316L. Nitronic 50 (Aquamet 22) is the best ballast-bolt material for steel. Bolt diameters should be determined using Formula 5-12. Lead external ballast can also be bolted externally to the bottom of aluminum or steel boats. Great care must be taken to isolate both the ballast and the bolts from the hull.

Use an external isolation pad between the entire ballast keel and hull bottom. It should be made of E-glass laminated in epoxy resin and vacuum-bagged to ensure that it's bubble-free. Similar isolation pads should be installed under the stainless-steel backing plates in the bilge (under the keel-bolt nuts), and sleeve isolation spacers are necessary around the bolts themselves. Except in the case of very high performance sailboats, there's little reason to use external ballast on most metal hulls.

LIGHTER-WEIGHT SUPERSTRUCTURES ON STEEL BOATS

As discussed previously, steel is so heavy that it is quite common to use wood, aluminum, or FRP deckhouses and superstructures fastened to a steel hull and deck. This reduces overall weight, and—more important—lowers the center of gravity for proper stability characteristics. FRP superstructures pose no corrosion problems, and wood only minor ones (nicely handled by proper bedding and fastening). The scantlings of the superstructure—whatever the material—can be determined using the scantling rule appropriate for that material.

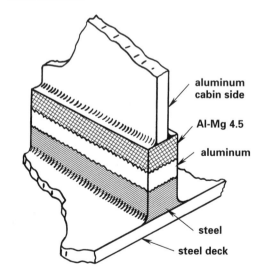

aluminum cabin side

Al-Mg 4.5

aluminum

steel

steel deck

Triclad

JOINING ALUMINUM SUPERSTRUCTURES TO STEEL HULLS

Joining an aluminum superstructure to a steel hull must be done so that the aluminum doesn't corrode, however. The old method was to weld a vertical flat bar of steel to the steel deck and then bolt the aluminum superstructure sides to that, insulating it with neoprene (or something similar), plus insulating each bolt with spacer sleeves. This is time-consuming and subject to degradation when the insulating material ages. This method has not proven very satisfactory over the long term.

The modern method uses a DeltaStrip or DeltaCouple from DuPont, also sold as Tri-Clad in Europe. This special strip is steel on one half and aluminum on the other, explosively bonded to an inert central core. Simply weld the steel lower half to the steel deck and the aluminum superstructure to the aluminum upper portion of the DeltaCouple.

STAINLESS FLAT-BAR JOINT BETWEEN ALUMINUM AND MILD STEEL

Another useful method is to weld a vertical flat bar of steel (just as with the traditional approach) to the deck, but use stainless instead. Then the aluminum superstructure is bolted to the stainless directly with stainless bolts. Ordinary bedding compound is all that is necessary to seal it.

FORMULA 14-6

Stainless Joint between Mild Steel and Aluminum

Stainless Vertical-Flat-Bar Thickness = 1.33 × steel-deck-plate thickness; not less than $^3/_{16}$ inch (4.75 mm)

Stainless Vertical-Flat-Bar Height = 12 × thickness; not less than $2^3/_4$ inches (70 mm)

The aluminum cabin-side plate's bottom edge must be 1 inch (25 mm) above the mild-steel deck for all but the smallest boats, and never less than $^3/_4$ inch (19 mm) even on small boats.

Stainless Through-Bolt Diameter = 1.5 × stainless-bar thickness

Stainless Through-Bolt Spacing, O.C. = 16 × bolt diameter; not more than 10 inches (250 mm)

If, for example, our steel *Iron Maiden* had $^3/_{16}$-inch steel deck plate and we were attaching an aluminum cabin to it, then its vertical stainless bar would be $^1/_4$ inch (6.4 mm) thick and 3 inches (75 mm) high; the through-bolts would be $^3/_8$ inch (9.5 mm) in diameter, spaced 6 inches (150 mm) O.C.

Plate Thickness and Weights

You can select plate thickness only from standard stock. Tables 14-7 and 14-8 give the common stock sizes and weights of steel and aluminum sheet or plate.

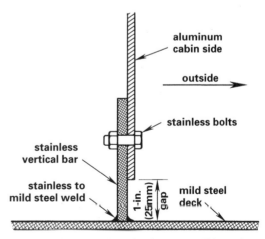

Stainless flat-bar joint: aluminum to mild steel

TABLE 14-7 Plate Thickness and Weights

Designation	Thickness, in.	Aluminum Weight, lb./sq. ft.	Steel Weight, lb./sq. ft.	Thickness, mm	Aluminum Weight, kg/sq. m	Steel Weight, kg/sq. m
16 gauge	0.0598	—	2.44	1.52	—	11.91
1/16 inch	0.0625	0.88	2.55	1.59	4.30	12.45
15 gauge	0.0673	—	2.75	1.71	—	13.41
14 gauge	0.0747	—	3.05	1.90	—	14.88
13 gauge	0.0897	—	3.66	2.28	—	17.87
12 gauge	0.1046	—	4.27	2.66	—	20.83
11 gauge	0.1196	—	4.88	3.04	—	23.82
1/8 inch	0.1250	1.76	5.10	3.18	8.60	24.90
10 gauge	0.1345	—	**5.49**	3.42	—	**26.79**
0.160 inch	0.1600	2.25	—	4.06	11.01	—
8 gauge	0.1644	—	6.71	4.18	—	32.75
7 gauge, 3/16 in.	0.1875	**2.64**	7.65	**4.76**	12.90	37.35
0.190 inch	0.1900	2.68	—	4.83	13.07	—
0.204 inch	0.2040	2.87	—	5.18	14.03	—
1/4 inch	0.2500	3.52	10.20	6.35	17.20	49.80
5/16 inch	0.3125	4.40	12.75	7.94	21.50	62.25
3/8 inch	0.3750	5.28	15.30	9.53	25.80	74.69
7/16 inch	0.4375	6.16	17.85	11.11	30.09	87.14
1/2 inch	0.5000	7.05	20.40	12.70	34.39	99.59
9/16 inch	0.5625	—	22.95	14.29	—	112.04
5/8 inch	0.6250	8.81	25.50	15.88	42.99	124.49
11/16 inch	*0.6875*	*9.69*	*28.05*	*17.46*	*47.29*	*136.94*
3/4 inch	0.7500	10.57	30.60	19.05	51.59	149.39
13/16 inch	*0.8125*	*11.45*	*33.15*	*20.64*	*55.89*	*161.84*
7/8 inch	0.8750	12.33	35.70	22.23	60.19	174.29
1 inch	1.0000	14.09	40.80	25.40	68.79	199.19
1 1/4 inch	1.2500	17.61	51.00	31.75	85.98	248.98
1 1/2 inch	1.5000	21.14	61.20	38.10	103.18	298.78
1 3/4 inch	1.7500	24.66	71.40	44.45	120.38	348.57
2 inch	2.0000	28.18	81.60	50.80	137.57	398.37
2 1/2 inch	2.5000	35.23	102.00	63.50	171.97	497.96

NOTES: Weights in **bold** indicate the thinnest size readily weldable with standard equipment. Sizes in *italic* are nonstandard and not usually stocked. Gaps in the weight columns indicate that material is not normally available in that thickness.

TABLE 14-8 English and Metric Plate Thicknesses

Designation	Thickness, in.	Nearest Metric Thickness, mm	Designation	Thickness, in.	Nearest Metric Thickness, mm
16 gauge	0.0598	1.50	—	0.4331	11.00
1/16 inch	0.0625	1.60	7/16 inch	0.4375	11.25
15 gauge	0.0673	1.70	—	0.4724	12.00
14 gauge	0.0747	1.90	1/2 inch	0.5000	13.00
—	0.0787	2.00	—	0.5512	14.00
13 gauge	0.0897	2.25	9/16 inch	0.5625	14.25
12 gauge	0.1046	2.70	—	0.5906	15.00
11 gauge	0.1196	3.00	5/8 inch	0.6250	16.00
1/8 inch	0.1250	3.20	—	0.6693	17.00
10 gauge	0.1345	3.40	11/16 inch	0.6875	17.50
0.160 inch	0.1600	4.00	—	0.7087	18.00
8 gauge	0.1644	4.20	3/4 inch	0.7500	19.00
7 gauge,			—	0.7874	20.00
3/16 inch	0.1875	4.75	13/16 inch	0.8125	20.50
0.190 inch	0.1900	5.00	—	0.8268	21.00
0.204 inch	0.2040	5.25	—	0.8661	22.00
—	0.2362	6.00	7/8 inch	0.8750	22.25
1/4 inch	0.2500	6.40	1 inch	1.0000	25.00
—	0.2756	7.00	1 1/4 inch	1.2500	32.00
5/16 inch	0.3125	7.90	1 1/2 inch	1.5000	38.00
—	0.3150	8.00	1 3/4 inch	1.7500	45.00
3/8 inch	0.3750	9.50	2 inch	2.0000	50.00
—	0.3937	10.00	2 1/2 inch	2.5000	65.00

FIFTEEN

Aluminum and Steel Shell Plate and Longitudinal Framing

*N*ow that we have reviewed the factors underlying sound metal-boat construction, we can proceed to determine the scantlings for aluminum and steel hulls. Before we can do this, however, we need to discuss the basic structural shapes used and how they are described.

Framing Methods

There are actually two common methods to framing a standard metal hull. I'll call them the old and the new methods.

OLD METHOD

The old method largely (although by no means exclusively) uses standard shapes (usually angles and Ts) to form the frames and deck beams. These off-the-shelf extrusions might be cut or trimmed somewhat where appropriate, but are generally simply bent carefully to the shape of each frame. At their bottom, the frames are welded to floor plates, and at their top to knees that connect to deck beams, which are also made using standard extrusions.

NEW METHOD

The new method has been gaining popularity steadily as plate-cutting has become quicker and more accurate. The advent of *NC cut* (numerically controlled cut, or NCC), computer-driven, automatic cutting machines has accelerated this trend. In this new method, the frame—usually including the deck beams and sometimes even the superstructure—is cut out as a single ring of flat plate from individual pieces as needed. These individual plates are welded together into a single-unit ring. Next, the interior flange of the frame is welded to the inside of its ring. Most commonly, this forms a simple T; however, it can also form an angle, if that's more convenient for some reason. The T-ring frame as a unit is erected on the CVK, and braced in position temporarily until longitudinals and plating lock it permanently in place. Often, the

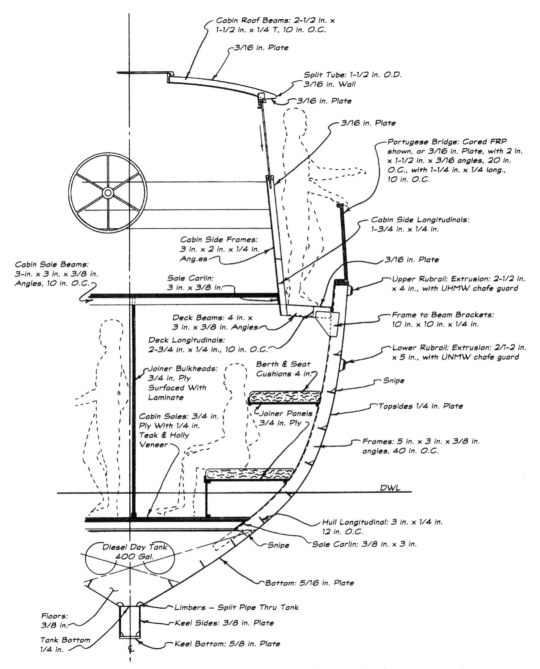

Cabin Roof Beams: 2-1/2 in. x
1-1/2 in. x 1/4 T, 10 in. O.C.

3/16 in. Plate

Split Tube: 1-1/2 in. O.D.
3/16 in. Wall

3/16 in. Plate

3/16 in. Plate

Portugese Bridge: Cored FRP
shown, or 3/16 in. Plate, with 2 in.
x 1-1/2 in. x 3/16 angles, 20 in.
O.C., with 1-1/4 in. x 1/4 long.,
10 in. O.C.

Cabin Side Longitudinals:
1-3/4 in. x 1/4 in.

Cabin Side Frames:
3 in. x 2 in. x 1/4 in.
Angles

3/16 in. Plate

Cabin Sole Beams:
3-in. x 3 in. x 3/8 in.
Angles, 10 in. O.C.

Sole Carlin:
3 in. x 3/8 in.

Upper Rubrail: Extrusion: 2-1/2 in.
x 4 in., with UHMW chafe guard

Deck Beams: 4 in. x
3 in. x 3/8 in. Angles

Frame to Beam Brackets:
10 in. x 10 in. x 1/4 in.

Deck Longitudinals:
2-3/4 in. x 1/4 in., 10 in. O.C.

Lower Rubrail: Extrusion: 2/1-2 in.
x 5 in., with UNMW chafe guard

Joiner Bulkheads:
3/4 in. Ply
Surfaced With
Laminate

Berth & Seat
Cushions 4 in.

Snipe

Topsides 1/4 in. Plate

Cabin Soles: 3/4 in.
Ply With 1/4 in.
Teak & Holly
Veneer

Joiner Panels
3/4 in. Ply

Frames: 5 in. x 3 in. x 3/8 in.
angles, 40 in. O.C.

DWL

Hull Longitudinal: 3 in. x 1/4 in.
12 in. O.C.

Snipe

Sole Carlin: 3/8 in. x 3 in.

Diesel Day Tank
400 Gal.

Bottom: 5/16 in. Plate

Floors:
3/8 in.

Tank Bottom
1/4 in.

Limbers — Split Pipe Thru Tank

Keel Sides: 3/8 in. Plate

Keel Bottom: 5/8 in. Plate

Old framing method, frame at Station 3, 57-foot (17.3 m) aluminum motor cruiser

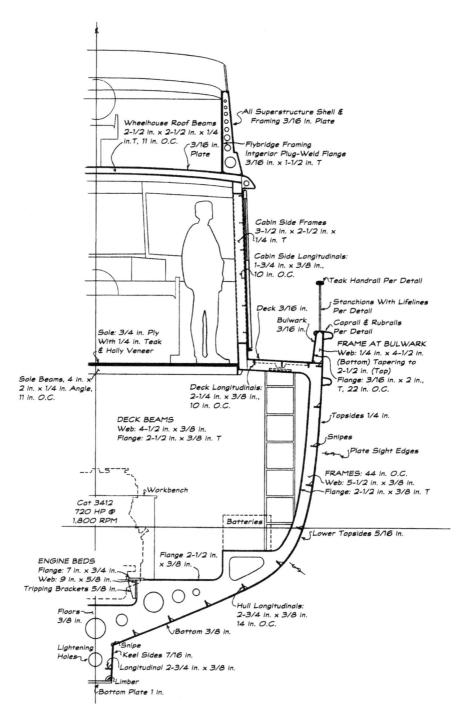

New framing method, midships section, 82-foot (25 m) aluminum motor yacht

frames are prenotched for the longitudinal stringers as well.

NEW FRAMING METHOD IS USED IN THESE SCANTLING RULES

There is no real difference between the scantlings of the two methods. If the frame were to have a web $1/4$ by 4 inches (6.4 by 100 mm), with a flange of $1/4$ by 2 inches (6.4 by 50 mm), then it makes no difference if this is welded up out of cut plate as in the new method or bent out of standard T-bar stock. However, throughout the following rule, we assume that the modern method is being used.

Describing Shapes Used in the Metal Scantling Rule

MANMADE SHAPES

Metal is different from wood and fiberglass in that it comes in a bewildering variety of manmade shapes—not only in plates of varying thicknesses, but also in flat bar, angles with equal and unequal legs, Ts of varying proportions, H- or I-beams, Z sections, channels, square and round tubes, bulb-angles and bulb-Ts, and more. It is necessary to be able to define the dimensions of these shapes.

Ts AND ANGLES

Although they are less common in use with metal-boat structures, I will continue to refer to molded and sided dimensions occasionally, where it helps in clarification (see chapter 9). Still, the standard method of describing metal shapes is by referring to the *flange* and the *web* of the shape. The web of a T or angle is its "vertical" portion that is welded at right angles to the hull, deck, or cabin-roof shell—it extends in the molded dimension and its

siding is small. (Properly speaking, the web is parallel to the direction of load.) The flange is the "horizontal" part of the T or angle. It extends in the fore-n-aft (sided) dimension, and its molding is small. (Again, speaking more precisely, the flange is at right angles to the direction of load.)

SHAPES USED IN THESE RULES

The fact is, there is a nearly endless combination of shapes that can quite properly be employed for framing a hull. To simplify the scantling rule, however, I will almost exclusively use Ts for the frames (angles of the same web and flange dimensions can be substituted at will) and flat bar for longitudinal stiffeners.

There are two reasons for this: these shapes are easy to define and easy to purchase or fabricate; and hulls framed with T or angle frames and flat-bar longitudinal stringers are the most common. There is no reason at all why other shapes of comparable section properties can't be substituted. Indeed, where ultimate weight savings and/or maximum strength are required, shapes like bulb angles or trimmed-flange I-beams can be structurally more efficient.

Some builders also prefer to use Ts (or channels or angles) for longitudinals because they are somewhat easier to control when bending into place. This too is fine—although I personally don't like the large notches such longitudinals cut into a frame. Chiefly, however, almost all the builders I have dealt with recently prefer the modern cut-plate method, using built-up T or angle frames and flat-bar longitudinals. (They employ standard Ts or angles whenever there is little curvature and where little cutting or bending would be required.)

FLOATING-FRAME CONSTRUCTION

The overwhelming majority of metal hulls are built with their longitudinals notched into the frames. In this way, both the longitudinals and the frames lie against the inside of the shell plate, and both are welded to the shell. It is also possible to run the longitudinals over the outside face or edge of the frames without notching them into the frames. Then the shell plate is laid on top of the longitudinals. In this construction, the frames don't touch the shell plate anywhere. Indeed, they are separated from it by the molding of the longitudinal stringers. (These stringers need to be Ts or angles.)

This less-common building method is known as *floating-frame construction*, which is *not* covered in these scantling rules. Properly engineered, it is an acceptable building method, but it requires different proportions than the scantlings given here. It also has the drawback of stealing the more interior volume from a metal hull, because the inside of the frames must be quite far from the plate.

Our Example Boats

In previous chapters, we used *Fish 'n Squish* and *Logger Bobber* as our examples. They were both 40 feet (12.19 m) LOA. Metal boats can be quite small; indeed, aluminum boats can be efficiently built as diminutive as in any other material. Nevertheless, most welded-metal vessels tend to be larger custom or semi-production projects. Accordingly, our metal example boats will be huskier at 64 feet (19.50 m). We've named them *AlumaNaught* in aluminum and *Iron Maiden* in steel.

AlumaNaught and *Iron Maiden* have the following characteristics:

LOA	64.00 ft.	19.50 m
WL	54.42 ft.	16.58 m
Beam	17.67 ft.	5.38 m
Depth of Hull	8.33 ft.	2.54 m

This gives an Sn of 8.71 (see Formula 1-1).

ALUMINUM AND STEEL FORMULA NUMBERS

Generally, both aluminum and steel have the same components and are assembled in the same way in this scantling rule; therefore, we consider them together in the following formulas. To help differentiate between them, I have added the suffix "A" to all aluminum formula numbers and the suffix "S" to all steel formula numbers. Formulas without a suffix apply equally to aluminum and steel.

Small Boats and the Limits of These Scantling Rules

Because steel is such a heavy construction material, all the steel scantling rules apply exclusively to boats with Sns greater than 1.0—approximately equal to 28 feet (8.5 m). I would say that building steel craft with dimensions that generate an Sn of less than 3.0 (around 40 feet [12.2 m]) results in a vessel

Midships in Imagine, looking forward. The integral diesel day tank is in the center of the photo; integral water tanks are port and starboard. The vertical angles are temporary braces and alignment aids.

with either poor performance or low life expectancy.

Using aluminum, really tiny boats—such as canoes and rowing skiffs—can be fabricated quite efficiently. The aluminum rules that follow generally apply to vessels with Sns greater than 0.50—roughly equivalent to boats greater than 20 feet (6 m). For smaller boats, follow the recommendations given in chapter 19 and Table 19-1.

Plate Thickness

FORMULA 15-1A
Aluminum Bottom Plate

Aluminum Bottom-Plate Thickness, in. =
$0.2 \times Sn^{0.2}$ *(English)*

Aluminum Bottom-Plate Thickness, mm
$= 5.08 \times Sn^{0.2}$ *(Metric)*

Where

Sn = scantling number

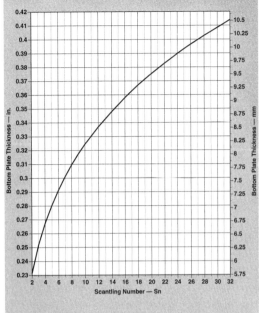

Aluminum Bottom-Plate Thickness: Large Boats

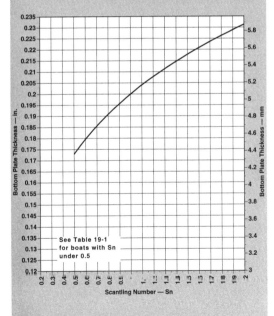

Aluminum Bottom-Plate Thickness: Small Boats

The bottom plate should extend down from the BLH to the keel (see Formula 4-3). This is heavy bottom plate and it is most definitely optional on displacement hulls or boats operating under 15 knots. Even planing hulls operating under 25 knots can opt to go with the lighter topsides plate on the bottom. However, if this is done to save weight (not an unreasonable consideration), the boat will have a shorter life and will sustain more damage on grounding or striking flotsam at speed. Over 25 knots, this heavier bottom plate is required.

On powerboats, it is recommended practice to increase the plate thickness by one standard size in the aft 20 to 25 percent of the hull bottom, over the propellers; the thicker plate is more rigid and therefore vibrates less. The result is a quieter boat and less fatigue in the shell at this location.

Displacement boats that have opted not to go with the heavy bottom plate should use this heavy plate in the aft underbody, but further thickness is not usually called for. High-powered, high-speed planing hulls should use the thicker bottom plate and then go up one standard size over the props. Again, this extra thickness above the heavier bottom plate is optional, but will reduce noise and increase life.

On *AlumaNaught*, we would find

Aluminum Bottom-Plate Thickness =
0.2 × 8.71$^{0.21}$ = 0.315 in.; use ⁵⁄₁₆ in.

Aluminum Bottom-Plate Thickness = 5.08 ×
8.71$^{0.21}$ = 8.00; use 8 mm

For heavy-displacement workboats and ocean voyagers, the heavier bottom plate throughout is recommended. The weight in the hull bottom actually increases stability, in addition to adding strength and corrosion allowance.

In *Iron Maiden*'s case,

Sn of 8.71 is between 3 and 12, so C =
¹⁄₁₆ in. (0.0625 in.) (3.2 mm)

Steel Bottom Plate = 0.0625 in. + 0.206 in. =
0.268; use ¼ in.

Steel Bottom Plate = 1.6 mm + 5.24 mm =
6.84 mm; use 6.4 mm

(See Formula 15-2S for steel shell-plate
thickness.)

FORMULA 15-1S

Steel Bottom Plate

Steel Bottom Plate = C + shell plate

C = 0 for Sns under 3

C = ¹⁄₁₆ in. (1.6 mm) for Sns between 3 and 12

C = ⅛ in. (3.2 mm) for Sns greater than 12

The bottom plate should extend down from the BLH to the keel (see Formula 4-3). Cor-Ten steel can be 0.88 of this thickness. (See Formula 15-2S for steel shell-plate thickness.)

Thicker bottom plate on steel is optional for all boats, including planing hulls. The extra thickness does increase longevity and impact resistance, but it also adds weight. Even if the heavy bottom plate isn't used for most of the hull, it is advisable to use this extra thickness in the aft 20 percent of the hull bottom, over the propellers, on high-powered boats.

FORMULA 15-2A

Aluminum Topsides (Shell) Plate

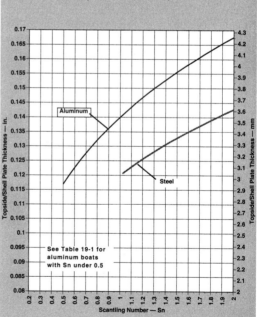

Topsides/Shell-Plate Thickness, Aluminum and Steel: Small Boats

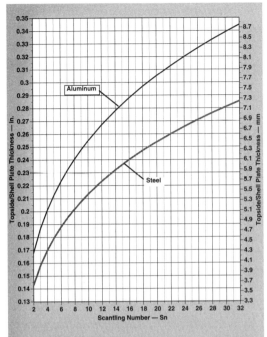

Topsides/Shell-Plate Thickness, Aluminum and Steel: Large Boats

Aluminum Topsides-Plate Thickness, in. = 0.14 × Sn^0.26 (English)

Aluminum Topsides-Plate Thickness, mm = 3.55 × Sn^{0.26} (Metric)

The topsides plate can be run right around into the hull underbody and form the bottom plate, with no additional thickness, as described in Formula 15-1A.

For *AlumaNaught*,

Aluminum Topsides-Plate Thickness = 0.14 × 8.71^{0.26} = 0.245; use ¼ in.

Aluminum Topsides-Plate Thickness = 3.55 × 8.71^{0.26} = 6.23; use 6.4 mm

The upper-topsides plate—the upper third of the topsides below the sheer—can be reduced in thickness to that of the deck plate for maximum weight savings. Aluminum

plate is light enough, however, so this is not necessary and it is seldom done.

FORMULA 15-2S

Steel Topsides (Shell) Plate

Steel Shell Plate, in. = 0.12 × Sn^{0.25} (English)

Steel Shell Plate, mm = 3.05 × Sn^{0.25} (Metric)

Cor-Ten steel can be 0.88 of this thickness.

Iron Maiden would use

Steel Shell Plate = 0.12 × 8.71^{0.25} = 0.206; use ³⁄₁₆ in. (0.1875 in.)

Steel Shell Plate = 3.05 × 8.71^{0.25} = 5.24; use 4.75 mm

Here, we have faced a common question in selecting plate thickness: 0.206 in. (5.24 mm) doesn't correspond to any standard plate or sheet size. In both English and Metric, sizes closest are thinner, so we rounded down. This is preferable in steel to control weight and permissible because steel is so strong. If the boat has great initial stability and is intended for rugged workboat use, you may want to round up instead of down, however. Switching to Cor-Ten for this plate, though, would put thickness in better agreement with the rule and increase its life at this thinner size. If Cor-Ten steel were used, then

Cor-Ten Shell Plate = 0.206 × 0.88 = 0.181; use ³⁄₁₆ in.

Cor-Ten Shell Plate = 5.24 mm × 0.88 = 4.61; use 4.75 mm

Steel is stronger and stiffer than aluminum, so (as described in Formula 15-2A) the topsides plate can be used as bottom plate on all boats, even planing hulls. Accordingly, *shell plate* rather than *topsides plate* is a more accurate name.

Because it is necessary to keep weight low on steel boats, vessels with shell plate over $3/16$ in. (4.75 mm) should reduce the thickness of the shell plate in the upper topsides to the next standard plate size down. The upper topsides are roughly the upper third of the side of the hull, below the sheer. Any plate above the sheer is either bulwark or raised-deck cabin side. It should be reduced to the thickness of the deck plate (see Formula 15-4S).

On *Iron Maiden*, using mild steel, we already rounded down on the shell-plate thickness, so a further reduction in the upper topsides is not recommended. However, on a Cor-Ten-hull *Iron Maiden*,

Cor-Ten Upper Topsides = 8-gauge (0.1644 in.)

Cor-Ten Upper Topsides = 4.20 mm

Obviously, tugs, barges, and other vessels that will experience extensive abrasion and heavy impact loads on their topsides should use the full standard shell plate up to the sheer.

FORMULA 15-3

Aluminum and Steel Transom and Transom Framing

Aluminum Transom Plate = (bottom plate + 1/8 in.) (English)

Aluminum Transom Plate = (bottom plate + 3.2 mm) (Metric)

Steel Transom Plate = (bottom plate + 1/16 in.) (English)

Steel Transom Plate = (bottom plate + 1.6 mm) (Metric)

For boats with Sns less than 2.5, transom plate = topsides plate

Stiffeners on the inside of the transom run vertically. They are the same dimensions as the hull-bottom longitudinals (see Formulas 15-7A and S) without speed adjustment, and are spaced O.C. using the longitudinal spacing for the transom's plate thickness (see Formulas 15-6A and S). Install the stiffeners starting at the centerline, with the centerline stiffener welded to the top of the CVK at the stern and reinforced with a bracket (i.e., knee), with legs about 1.5 times the stiffener height. The knee should be the same thickness as the stiffener.

Except for the centerline stiffener, none of the other transom framing needs to be welded to the hull's longitudinal stiffeners. The stiffeners and the transom frames can end several inches or centimeters in from the hull side. However, it may be convenient to weld some or all of the transom's frames to suitable hull longitudinals. In this way, the curved frames and the centerline stiffener define the shape of the transom. The remaining stiffeners and frames are then added, and the plate scribed to fit and welded in place.

Transom frames run athwartships inside the transom and are notched out for the vertical transom stiffeners. The transom frames are spaced at half the O.C. spacing of the non-speed-adjusted hull frames (see Formula 15-9). This spacing is measured along the face of the transom, which is usually sloped either fore or aft. Transom-frame dimensions should be the same as the topsides frames (at their deepest web) (see Formula 15-10).

FORMULA 15-4A

Aluminum Deck and Superstructure Side Plate

Aluminum Deck- and Cabin-Side-Plate Thickness, in. = $0.14 \times Sn^{0.20}$ (English)

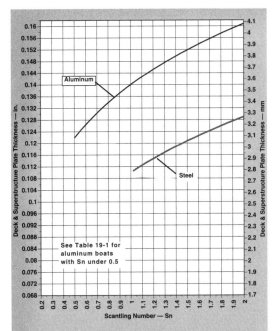

Deck- and Superstructure-Plate Thickness, Aluminum and Steel: Small Boats

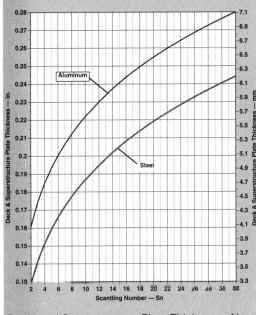

Deck- and Superstructure-Plate Thickness, Aluminum and Steel: Large Boats

Aluminum Deck- and Cabin-Side-Plate Thickness, mm = 3.55 × Sn^0.20 (Metric)

On oceangoing craft, cabin-house fronts in the forward third of the vessel should use the next standard plate size up. Good old *AlumaNaught* would fit as follows:

Aluminum Deck- and Cabin-Side-Plate Thickness, in. = 0.14 × 8.71^0.20 = 0.22; use 3/16 or 7/32 in.

Aluminum Deck- and Cabin-Side-Plate Thickness, mm = 3.55 × 8.71^0.20 = 5.47; use 4.75 (5.55 mm)

Aluminum plate $^{7}/_{32}$ inch (5.55 mm) thick is also difficult to find, although it fits the calculation best. It is better to round down—to the nearest standard plate—to decrease weight high up. Even with the light alloy aluminum, this is still a consideration. Assuming easy availability, ideally, the decks would be $^{7}/_{32}$ inch (5.55 mm) and the cabin sides $^{3}/_{16}$ inch (4.75 mm). Heavy workboats should round up in plate size rather than down.

FORMULA 15-4S
Steel Deck and Superstructure Side Plate

Steel Deck Plate, in. = 0.11 × Sn^0.23 (English)

Steel Deck Plate, mm = 2.79 × Sn^0.23 (English)

Cabins sides to be 90 percent of the deck thickness.

Cor-Ten steel can be 0.88 of this thickness.

Iron Maiden would then have

Steel Deck Plate – 0.11 × 8.71^0.23 = 0.181; use 3/16 in.

Steel Deck Plate = 2.79 × 8.71⁰·²³ = 4.59; use
4.75 mm

Steel Superstructure Side Plate = 0.181 in. ×
0.9 = 0.163; use 8-gauge

Steel Superstructure Side Plate = 4.59 mm ×
0.9 = 4.12; use 4.2 mm

Because we rounded down *Iron Maiden*'s shell-plate thickness, we ended up with the same thickness for both deck and shell plate. Except for the hardest usage, you could slim down deck thickness to 8-gauge (0.1664 in. [4.2 mm]). In Cor-Ten, we would get this anyway, with longer life and higher stiffness:

Cor-Ten Deck Plate = 0.181 in. × 0.88 = 0.159
in.; use 8-gauge (0.1664 in.)

Cor-Ten Deck Plate = 4.59 in. × 0.88 =
4.03 mm; use 4 mm

Cor-Ten Superstructure Side Plate = 0.163
in. × 0.88 = 0.143; use 10-gauge (0.1345 in.)

Cor-Ten Superstructure Side Plate = 4.12
mm × 0.88 = 3.62; use 3.4 mm

You can see that the 8- and 10-gauge (4.2 and 3.4 mm) plates we're getting for *Iron Maiden*'s superstructure are near the limit that can be welded practically. Yet, *Iron Maiden*—at 64 feet (19.5 m) with an Sn of 8.71—is a fairly large vessel, which is why smaller steel craft should usually use wood, aluminum, or FRP superstructures. If they don't, the thicker plate required for welding raises the center of gravity too high. Of course, some smaller boats are built with steel superstructures anyway. These boats must be beamier and heavier than otherwise, however, to compensate for the higher weight distribution.

Note that because we rounded the aluminum deck plate and superstructure plate down some to match stock plate sizes, and

rounded the steel deck plate up a little, we ended up with the same deck-plate thickness for both materials. This is an anomaly. In most cases, aluminum plate will be thicker. Indeed, the Cor-Ten-steel deck and superstructure are thinner than even the rounded-down aluminum, though still heavier.

FORMULA 15-5
Butt and Seam Locations in Plate

Minimum Butt-Joint Distance from
Transverse Frame = 24 × plate thickness

Minimum Seam-Joint Distance from a
Longitudinal = 12 × plate thickness

The smooth joints in the shell plating are all made with butt welds; however, convention calls the vertical or transverse joints *butts* (like butt joints in planks) and the horizontal or fore-n-aft joints *seams*. Where practical, these joints should be separated from frames and longitudinals by the following recommended distance to avoid stress concentrations.

On some transverse-framed hulls and at the bow of some longitudinally framed hulls, it can be nearly impossible to achieve these minimums. In this case, try to locate the butts and seams about midway between each frame or longitudinal.

Longitudinal-Construction Framing

FORMULA 15-6A
Aluminum Longitudinal-Stiffener
Spacing

Aluminum Longitudinal-Stiffener
Spacing O.C., in. = 4 + (plate thickness,
in. × 32) (English)

Aluminum Longitudinal-Stiffener
Spacing O.C., mm = 101.6 + (plate
thickness, mm × 32) (Metric)

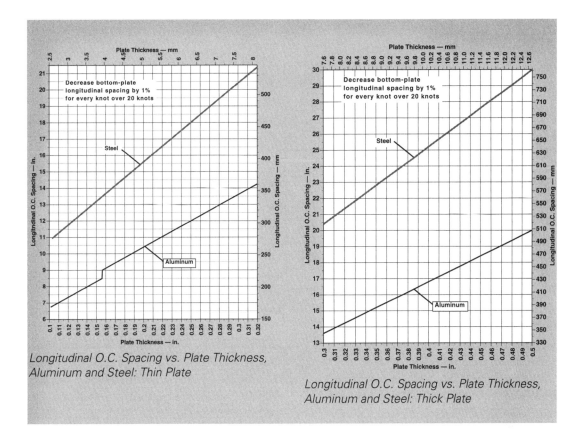

Longitudinal O.C. Spacing vs. Plate Thickness, Aluminum and Steel: Thin Plate

Longitudinal O.C. Spacing vs. Plate Thickness, Aluminum and Steel: Thick Plate

For plate under $^5/_{32}$ inch (4 mm), subtract $^1/_2$ inch (12.7 m) from the O.C. spacing. (Such thin plate should be welded with pulse-arc equipment.) The spacing must decrease to 85 percent of the formula value at the forefoot in the bow, from around Station 3.5 forward.

Use O.C. spacing for the topsides plate on the heavier bottom plate. Use the thickness of the plate actually installed after rounding or other adjustments, not the calculated plate thickness. In the case of *AlumaNaught*, the shell plating we settled on yields the following stiffener spacing:

Aluminum Bottom Plate: $^5/_{16}$ in. (8 mm)
Bottom-plate longitudinals will be spaced the same as the thinner topsides plate.

Aluminum Topsides Plate: $^1/_4$ in. (6.4 mm)

Longitudinal O.C. = 4 + (0.25 in. × 32) = 12 in.

Longitudinal O.C. = 101.6 + (6.4 mm × 32) = 306.4; use 300 mm

Aluminum Deck and Superstructure Plate: $^3/_{16}$ in. (4.75 mm)

Longitudinal O.C. = 4 + (0.1875 in. × 32) = 10 in.

Longitudinal O.C. = 101.6 + (4.75 mm × 32) = 253.6; use 250 mm

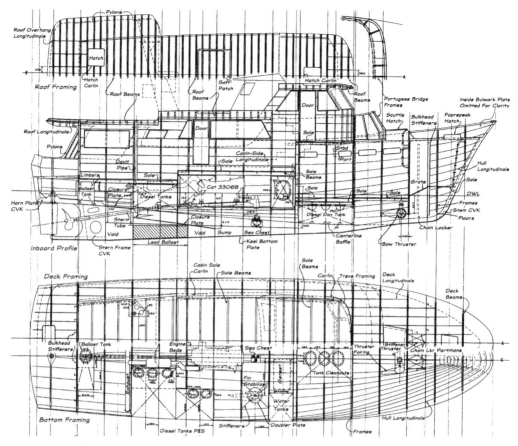

Construction plan of the Gerr 57-foot (17.3 m) aluminum motor yacht Imagine

FORMULA 15-6S

Steel Longitudinal-Stiffener Spacing

Steel Longitudinal-Stiffener Spacing O.C., in. = 6 + (plate thickness, in. × 48) (English)

Steel Longitudinal-Stiffener Spacing O.C., mm = 152.4 + (plate thickness, mm × 48) (Metric)

The spacing must decrease to 85 percent of the formula value at the forefoot in the bow, from around Station 3.5 forward.

Use O.C. spacing for the topsides plate on the heavier bottom plate (when heavier bottom plate is installed). Use the thickness of the plate actually installed after rounding or other adjustments, not the calculated number. In the case of *Iron Maiden*, the shell plating we settled on yields the following stiffener spacing:

Steel Bottom Plate (if used) = ¼ inch (6.4 mm)

Bottom-plate longitudinals will be spaced the same as the thinner topsides plate.

Steel Shell Plate $^3/_{16}$ inch (4.75 mm) Cor-Ten:

Longitudinal O.C. = 6 + (0.1875 in. × 48) = 15 in.

Longitudinal O.C. = 152.4 + (4.75 mm × 48) = 380.4; use 380 mm

Steel Upper Topsides and Bulwark Plate 8-Gauge (0.1644 in. [4 mm]) Cor-Ten:

Longitudinal O.C. = 6 + (0.1644 in. × 48) = 13.89; use 13 in.

Longitudinal O.C. = 152.4 + (4.0 mm × 48) = 344.4; use 340 mm

Steel Deck and Superstructure Plate 8-Gauge (0.1644 in. [4 mm]) Cor-Ten:

Same as previous upper topsides and bulwark.

BOTTOM LONGITUDINAL O.C. SPACING ADJUSTMENT FOR SPEED

Decrease bottom longitudinal O.C. spacing—up to the BLH (or to the chine) (see Formula 4-3)—by 1 percent for every knot over 20 knots. If good old *AlumaNaught* were a 35-knot boat, we would adjust its bottom longitudinals as follows:

Aluminum 35-Knot Bottom Longitudinal O.C., in. = 35 – 25 = 10; therefore, reduce by 10%, or 0.90 × 12 in. = 10.8; use 10 in.

Aluminum 35-Knot Bottom Longitudinal O.C., in. = 35 – 25 = 10; therefore, reduce by 10%, or 0.90 × 300 mm = 270; use 250 mm

For *Iron Maiden*, as a 35-knot boat, we would adjust its bottom longitudinal as follows:

Steel 35-Knot Bottom Longitudinal O.C., in. = 35 – 25 = 10; therefore, reduce by 10%, or 0.90 × 15 in. = 13.5; use 13 in.

Steel 35-Knot Bottom Longitudinal O.C., in. = 35 – 25 = 10; therefore, reduce by 10%, or 0.90 × 380 mm = 342; use 340 mm

NOTES ON ALUMINUM AND STEEL LONGITUDINALS

You can see in this scantling rule that the longitudinal spacing is directly controlled by the plate thickness. Thus, when we round down (or up) on plate thickness, the rule adjusts the stiffener spacing accordingly. Unless otherwise called for, the longitudinal O.C. spacing formulas apply to all panels everywhere on the vessel.

Always round the stiffener spacing *down* to the nearest convenient even distance. Decreasing the spacing from 13.8 to 13 inches (350 to 330 mm), for example, will add at most one or two stringers to the hull. This is little increase in weight, in proportion to the overall structure, while ensuring adequate panel stiffness.

Using the closer spacing of the thinner topsides plate on the heavier bottom plate decreases the panel size in proportion to the plate thickness for further increased strength and stiffness.

HULL LONGITUDINAL LAYOUT

My preferred practice on the hull is to run the longitudinals along the inside surface of the plate, in diagonals laid out on the body plan. The previous O.C. spacing is used as the governing distance between stiffeners at midships. Because the diagonals sweep closer together at the bow and stern, the longitudinal spacing will decrease at the bow and stern, which gives increased stiffness at the bow where slamming loads are greatest, and aft where propeller vibration is a factor. This also automatically gives the 85 percent decreased

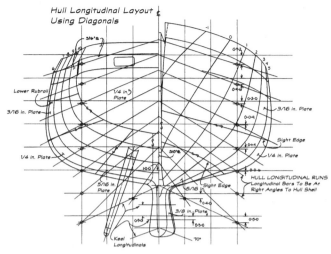

Hull longitudinal layout using diagonals

O.C. spacing at the forefoot. Other advantages to the diagonal stiffener layout is that the longitudinals naturally take smooth fair curves, they are very easy to lay out on the frames, and they experience only bend and twist but no edgeset. This makes flat-bar longitudinals easier to lay in.

DECK AND CABIN LONGITUDINAL LAYOUT

On decks, I most frequently run the longitudinals dead straight fore-n-aft, in plan view, at the specified O.C. spacing. Where the cabin sides meet the deck, they form a very substantial longitudinal-strength member. Adjust the longitudinals somewhat to work around these at close to or slightly less than the formula O.C. Sometimes it is convenient to sweep some of the deck longitudinals parallel to the sheer (or close to that). Again, any arrangement that results in smooth fair runs and O.C. equal to or less than specified is fine.

The same goes for cabin sides. Usually, straight fore-n-aft longitudinals are easiest, but sometimes it's more convenient for some (or all) to run with the curve of the deck or cabin roof in plan view.

OTHER LONGITUDINAL LAYOUTS AND ENDING LONGITUDINALS

It is possible—particularly on hard-chine vessels—to run the longitudinals in other patterns, including at constant-width spacing. Any system of laying out the stringers is acceptable as long as the O.C. spacing is less than or equal to the spacing called for in the formula, including closing together in the forefoot.

Longitudinals that will run out of the hull should be ended at the nearest frame inside the hull, where practical. Don't simply end a longitudinal under the middle of a deck panel; this would cause a hard spot. It sometimes works out best to sweep otherwise straight and parallel deck longitudinals in at their ends to maximize their run, and end them on a frame.

FORMULA 15-7A
Aluminum Hull-Longitudinal Dimensions

Aluminum Flat-Bar Hull-Longitudinal Height, in. = $1.05 \times Sn^{0.4}$ (English)

Aluminum Flat-Bar Hull-Longitudinal Thickness, in. = $0.23 \times Sn^{0.21}$ (English)

Aluminum Flat-Bar Hull-Longitudinal Height, mm = $26.67 \times Sn^{0.4}$ (Metric)

Aluminum Flat-Bar Hull-Longitudinal Thickness, mm = $5.84 \times Sn^{0.21}$ (Metric)

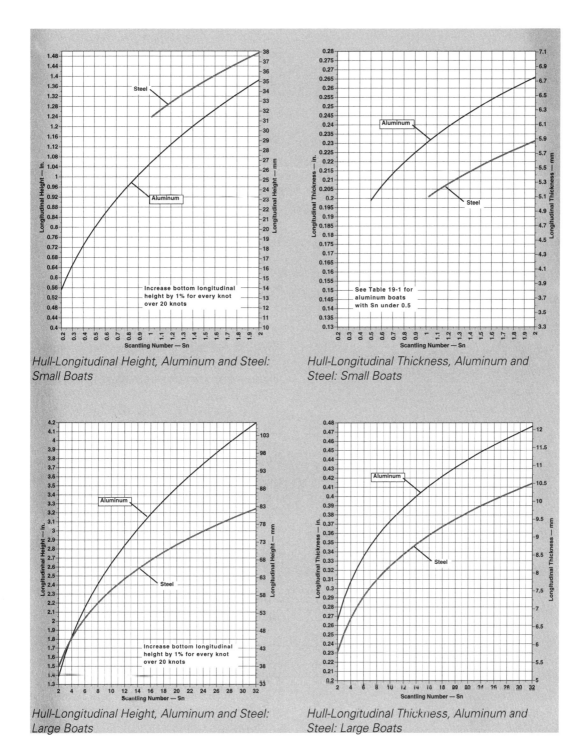

Hull-Longitudinal Height, Aluminum and Steel: Small Boats

Hull-Longitudinal Thickness, Aluminum and Steel: Small Boats

Hull-Longitudinal Height, Aluminum and Steel: Large Boats

Hull-Longitudinal Thickness, Aluminum and Steel: Large Boats

To stiffen *AlumaNaught*, we would employ

Aluminum Flat-Bar Hull-Longitudinal Height
= 1.05 × 8.71$^{0.4}$ = 2.49; use 2½ in.

Aluminum Flat-Bar Hull-Longitudinal
Thickness = 0.23 × 8.71$^{0.21}$ = 0.36; use ⅜ in.

Aluminum Flat-Bar Hull-Longitudinal Height
= 26.67 × 8.71$^{0.4}$ = 63.39; use 65 mm

Aluminum Flat-Bar Hull-Longitudinal
Thickness = 5.84 × 8.71$^{0.21}$ = 9.2; use 9.5 mm

FORMULA 15-7S

Steel Hull-Longitudinal Dimensions

Steel Flat-Bar Hull-Longitudinal Height,
in. = 1.23 × Sn$^{0.28}$ (English)

Steel Flat-Bar Hull-Longitudinal
Thickness, in. = 0.20 × Sn$^{0.21}$ (English)

Steel Flat-Bar Hull-Longitudinal Height,
mm = 31.24 × Sn$^{0.28}$ (Metric)

Steel Flat-Bar Hull-Longitudinal
Thickness, mm = 5.04 × Sn$^{0.21}$ (Metric)

To stiffen *Iron Maiden*, we would employ

Steel Flat-Bar Hull-Longitudinal Height =
1.23 × 8.71$^{0.28}$ = 2.25; use 2¼ in.

Steel Flat-Bar Hull-Longitudinal Thickness =
0.20 × 8.71$^{0.21}$ = 0.315; use ⁵⁄₁₆ in.

Steel Flat-Bar Hull-Longitudinal Height =
31.24 × 8.71$^{0.28}$ = 57.26; use 58 mm

Steel Flat-Bar Hull-Longitudinal Thickness =
5.04 × 8.71$^{0.21}$ = 7.9; use 8 mm

INCREASE BOTTOM-LONGITUDINAL HEIGHT FOR SPEED

Increase bottom-longitudinal height up to the BLH or chine (see Formula 4-3) by 1 percent for every knot over 20 knots.

On a 35-knot *AlumaNaught*, we would use

Aluminum 35-Knot Bottom-Longitudinal
Height, in. = 35 – 20 = 15; therefore,
increase by 15% or 1.15 × 2.5 in. = 2.875;
use 2⅞ or 3 in.

Aluminum 35-Knot Bottom Longitudinal
Height, in. = 35 – 20 = 15; therefore,
increase by 15% or 1.15 × 65 mm = 74.7; use
75 mm

If *Iron Maiden* were driven 35 knots, it would have

Steel 35-Knot Bottom-Longitudinal Height,
in. = 35 – 20 = 15; therefore, increase by
15% or 1.15 × 2.25 in. = 2.58; use 2 ⅝ in.

Steel 35-Knot Bottom-Longitudinal Height,
in. = 35 – 20 = 15; therefore, increase by
15% or 1.15 × 57.26 mm = 65.8; use 68 mm

PRACTICAL MINIMUM LONGITUDINAL THICKNESS

On small boats, the rule generates flat-bar longitudinals that are quite thin. Structurally, these will work fine. As a practical matter, however, such thin flat-bar is difficult to bend and fabricate into smooth fair members. Generally, aluminum flat-bar longitudinals under ¼ inch and steel under ³⁄₁₆ inch will be inconvenient to work with; however, it can be done if weight-saving considerations call for it.

DECREASING LONGITUDINAL HEIGHT ON UPPER TOPSIDES

To maximize weight reduction, you can gradually reduce the topsides longitudinals' height to the height of the deck longitudinals, decreasing each longitudinal from bilge to sheer (see Formulas 15-8A and S). This is seldom done, however, because the weight savings is minimal.

FORMULA 15-8A

Aluminum Deck-Longitudinal Dimensions

Aluminum Flat-Bar Deck-Longitudinal Height, in. = 0.77 × Sn$^{0.32}$ (English)

Aluminum Flat-Bar Deck-Longitudinal Thickness, in. = 0.19 × Sn$^{0.21}$ (English)

Aluminum Flat-Bar Deck-Longitudinal Height, mm = 19.55 × Sn$^{0.32}$ (Metric)

Aluminum Flat-Bar Deck-Longitudinal Thickness, mm = 4.83 × Sn$^{0.21}$ (Metric)

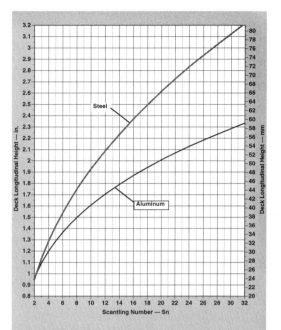

Deck-Longitudinal Height, Aluminum and Steel: Large Boats

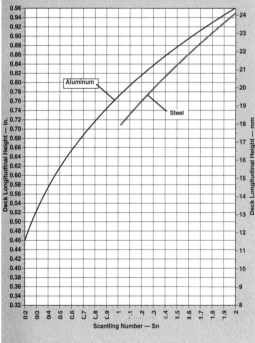

Deck-Longitudinal Height, Aluminum and Steel: Small Boats

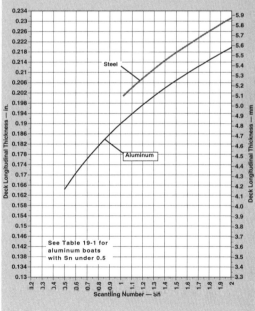

Deck-Longitudinal Thickness, Aluminum and Steel: Small Boats

(continued)

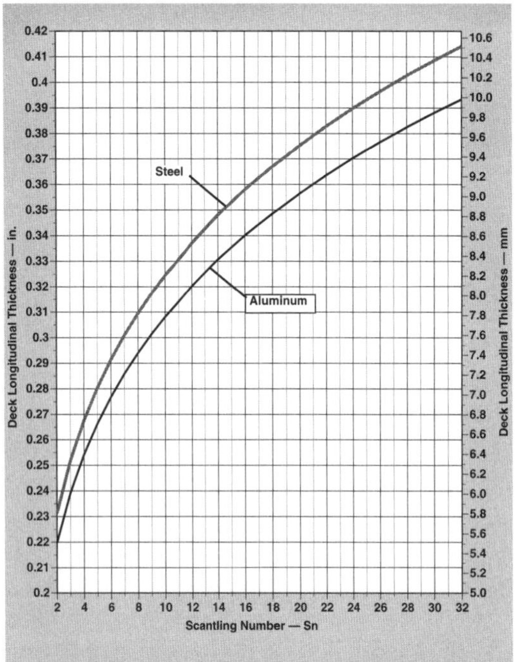

Deck-Longitudinal Thickness, Aluminum and Steel: Large Boats

Applying this to *AlumaNaught:*

Aluminum Flat-Bar Deck-Longitudinal Height = $0.77 \times 8.71^{0.32}$ = 1.53; use 1½ in.

Aluminum Flat-Bar Deck-Longitudinal Thickness = $0.19 \times 8.71^{0.21}$ = 0.29; use 5⁄16 in.

Aluminum Flat-Bar Deck-Longitudinal Height = $19.55 \times 8.71^{0.32}$ = 39.07; use 40 mm

Aluminum Flat-Bar Deck-Longitudinal Thickness = $4.83 \times 8.71^{0.21}$ = 7.63; use 7.9 mm

FORMULA 15-8S
Steel Deck-Longitudinal Dimensions

Steel Flat-Bar Deck-Longitudinal Height, in. = $0.7 \times Sn^{0.44}$ (English)

Steel Flat-Bar Deck-Longitudinal Thickness, in. = $0.2 \times Sn^{0.21}$ (English)

Steel Flat-Bar Deck-Longitudinal Height, mm = $17.78 \times Sn^{0.44}$ (Metric)

Steel Flat-Bar Deck-Longitudinal Thickness, mm = $5.08 \times Sn^{0.21}$ (Metric)

Or, on *Iron Maiden*, this yields

Steel Flat-Bar Deck-Longitudinal Height = $0.7 \times 8.71^{0.44}$ = 1.81; use 1⅞ or 2 in.

Steel Flat-Bar Deck-Longitudinal Thickness = $0.2 \times 8.71^{0.21}$ = 0.315; use 5⁄16 in.

Steel Flat-Bar Deck-Longitudinal Height = $17.78 \times 8.71^{0.44}$ = 46.08; use 48 mm

Steel Flat-Bar Deck-Longitudinal Thickness = $5.08 \times 8.71^{0.21}$ = 8.00; use 8 mm

FORMULA 15-9
Ring-Frame Spacing O.C. (Longitudinal Construction)

Aluminum and steel have the same ring-frame spacing:

Transverse Ring Frames O.C., in. = $33 \times Sn^{0.15}$ (English)

Transverse Ring Frames O.C., cm = $83.8 \times Sn^{0.15}$ (Metric)

We would then build *AlumaNaught* or *Iron Maiden* with the following:

Transverse Ring Frames O.C. = $33 \times 8.71^{0.15}$ = 45.6; use 46 in.

Transverse Ring Frames O.C. = $83.8 \times 8.71^{0.15}$ = 115.9; use 115 cm

ADJUSTING RING-FRAME SPACING FOR SPEED

Decrease Frame O.C. by 1 percent for every knot over 15 knots.

Applying this to a 35-knot *AlumaNaught* or *Iron Maiden* gives the following:

35 knots – 15 knots = 20 knots, so decrease O.C. by 20%

Speed-Adjusted Ring-Frame O.C. = 45.6 in. × 0.80 = 36.48; use 36 in.

Speed-Adjusted Ring-Frame O.C. = 115.9 mm × 0.80 = 92.7; use 90 cm

FORMULA 15-9A

Aluminum Ring-Frame Dimensions: Hull Bottom

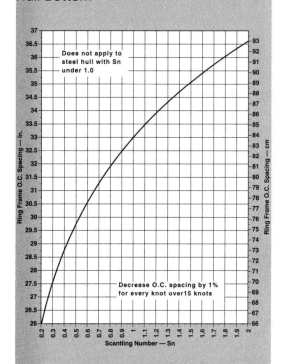

Ring-Frame Spacing and Dimensions for Aluminum and Steel in Longitudinally Framed Hulls
(1) Ring-Frame O.C. Spacing: Small Boats

Aluminum Hull-Bottom Ring-Frame Web Height, in. = 2.33 × Sn$^{0.4}$ (English)

Aluminum Hull-Bottom Ring-Frame Web Thickness, in. = 0.23 × Sn$^{0.21}$ (English)

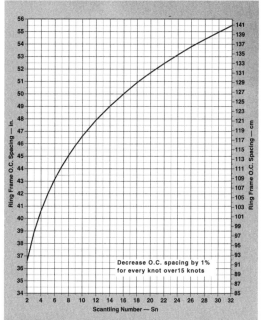

(2) Ring-Frame O.C. Spacing: Large Boats

Aluminum Hull-Bottom Ring-Frame Flange Width, in. = 1.75 × Sn$^{0.4}$ (English)

Aluminum Hull-Bottom Ring-Frame Flange Thickness, in. = 0.29 × Sn$^{0.21}$ (English)

Aluminum Hull-Bottom Ring-Frame Web Height, mm = 59.18 × Sn$^{0.4}$ (Metric)

Aluminum Hull-Bottom Ring-Frame Web Thickness, mm = 5.84 × Sn$^{0.21}$ (Metric)

Aluminum Hull-Bottom Ring-Frame Flange Width, mm = 44.45 × Sn$^{0.4}$ (Metric)

Aluminum Hull-Bottom Ring-Frame Flange Thickness, mm = 7.37 × Sn$^{0.21}$ (Metric)

(continued)

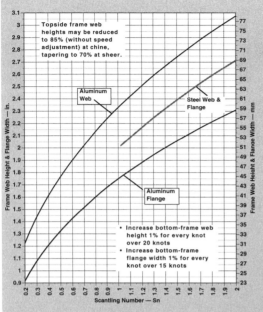

(3) Ring-Frame Web Heights and Flange Widths: Small Boats

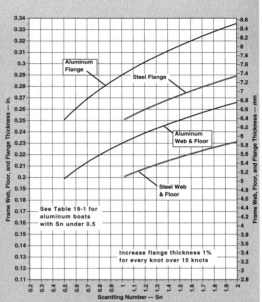

(5) Ring-Frame Web and Flange Thicknesses and Floor Thickness: Small Boats

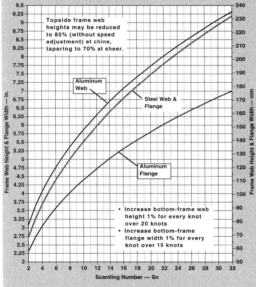

(4) Ring-Frame Web Heights and Flange Widths: Large Boats

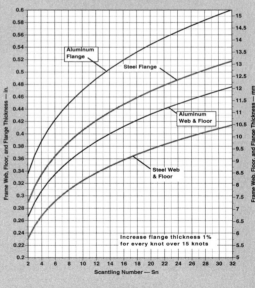

(6) Ring-Frame Web and Flange Thicknesses and Floor Thickness: Large Boats

Note that the flange's thickness is 1.25 times greater than the web. This maximizes the stiffness of the section while reducing its intrusion into the interior volume, and improves access to welding at the "closed bevel" side of the frame. If you prefer to use a flange the same thickness as the web, then increase the flange width 1.25 times.

The hull-bottom ring-frames on our reliable old *AlumaNaught* then work out as follows:

Aluminum Hull-Bottom Ring-Frame Web Height = 2.33 × 8.71$^{0.4}$ = 5.53; use 5½ in.

Aluminum Hull-Bottom Ring-Frame Web Thickness = 0.23 × 8.71$^{0.21}$ = 0.36; use ⅜ in.

Aluminum Hull-Bottom Ring-Frame Flange Width = 1.75 × 8.71$^{0.4}$ = 4.15; use 4 in.

Aluminum Hull-Bottom Ring-Frame Flange Thickness = 0.29 × 8.71$^{0.21}$ = 0.45; use ⁷/₁₆ or ½ in. (Alternately, use a ⅜ × 5 in. flange.)

Aluminum Hull-Bottom Ring-Frame Web Height = 59.18 × 8.71$^{0.4}$ = 140.6; use 140 mm

Aluminum Hull-Bottom Ring-Frame Web Thickness = 5.84 × 8.71$^{0.21}$ = 9.2; use 9.5 mm

Aluminum Hull-Bottom Ring-Frame Flange Width = 44.45 × 8.71$^{0.4}$ = 105.5; use 100 mm

Aluminum Hull-Bottom Ring-Frame Flange Thickness = 7.37 × 8.71$^{0.21}$ = 11.61; use 11.25 mm (Alternately, use a 9.5 × 125 mm flange.)

FORMULA 15-9S

Steel Ring-Frame Dimensions: Hull Bottom

Steel Hull-Bottom Ring-Frame Web Height, in. = 2.0 × Sn$^{0.44}$ (English)

Steel Hull-Bottom Ring-Frame Web Thickness, in. = 0.20 × Sn$^{0.21}$ (English)

Steel Hull-Bottom Ring-Frame Flange Width, in. = web height (English)

Steel Hull-Bottom Ring-Frame Flange Thickness, in. = 0.25 × Sn$^{0.21}$ (English)

Steel Hull-Bottom Ring-Frame Web Height, mm = 50.8 × Sn$^{0.44}$ (Metric)

Steel Hull-Bottom Ring-Frame Web Thickness, mm = 5.08 × Sn$^{0.21}$ (Metric)

Steel Hull-Bottom Ring-Frame Flange Width, mm = web height (Metric)

Steel Hull-Bottom Ring-Frame Flange Thickness, mm = 6.35 × Sn$^{0.21}$ (Metric)

As with the aluminum rule, the flange is 1.25 times thicker than the web. You can use a flange the same thickness as the web by increasing the web's width by 1.25 times. Applying this to *Iron Maiden*, we get the following:

Steel Hull-Bottom Ring-Frame Web Height = 2.0 × 8.71$^{0.44}$ = 5.18; use 5¼ in.

Steel Hull-Bottom Ring-Frame Web Thickness = 0.20 × 8.71$^{0.21}$ = 0.31; use ⁵/₁₆ in.

Steel Hull-Bottom Ring-Frame Flange Width = web height

Steel Hull-Bottom Ring-Frame Flange Thickness = 0.25 × 8.71$^{0.21}$ = 0.39; use ⅜ in. (Alternately, use a ⁵/₁₆ × 6½ in. flange.)

Steel Hull-Bottom Ring-Frame Web Height = 50.8 × 8.71$^{0.44}$ = 131.6; use 130 mm

Steel Hull-Bottom Ring-Frame Web Thickness = 5.08 × 8.71$^{0.21}$ = 8 mm

Steel Hull-Bottom Ring-Frame Flange Width = web height

Steel Hull-Bottom Ring-Frame Flange Thickness = 6.35 × 8.71$^{0.21}$ = 10 mm (Alternately, use 8 × 160 mm flange.)

ADJUSTING HULL-BOTTOM RING-FRAME SCANTLINGS FOR SPEED

Increase web height by 1 percent for every knot over 20 knots.

Increase flange width by 1 percent for every knot over 15 knots. Increase flange thickness by 1 percent for every knot over 15 knots. Only the bottom-frame scantlings are adjusted for speed in this way; the topsides frames and deck beams are unaffected.

In the case of our 35-knot *AlumaNaught*, the bottom frames would be adjusted to the following:

35 knots – 20 knots = 15 knots; therefore, increase web height by 15%

Bottom-Web Height = 1.15 × 5.53 in. = 6.35; use 6⅜ in.

35 knots – 15 knots = 20 knots; therefore, increase flange by 20%

Bottom-Flange Width = 1.20 × 4.15 in. = 4.95; use 5 in.

Bottom-Flange Thickness = 1.20 × 0.45 in. = 0.54; use ½ in.

or

35 knots – 20 knots = 15 knots; therefore, increase web height by 15%

Bottom-Web Height = 1.15 × 140.6 mm = 161.7; use 160 mm

35 knots – 15 knots = 20 knots; therefore, increase flange by 20%

Bottom-Flange Width = 1.20 × 105.5 mm = 126.6; use 125 mm

Bottom-Flange Thickness = 1.20 × 11.61 mm = 13.9; use 14 mm

The same approach would be used on a 35-knot *Iron Maiden*; however, it's rare to have steel hulls this size that are light enough to achieve such speeds efficiently.

VARYING FLANGE DIMENSIONS

The section properties of the combined frame, web, and flange determine its strength and stiffness. For the same web height and web thickness, a flat-plate flange will yield nearly identical section properties (i.e., moment of inertia and section modulus) if its area is the same. In other words—for any of the flat-bar flanges called for in the rule—you can substitute another flat bar that has the same total cross-section area. The resulting flange width, however, cannot exceed 12 times its thickness for aluminum or 15 times its thickness for steel.

For example, we found that *Aluma-Naught*'s speed-adjusted bottom flanges were 4.95 by 0.54 inches, which is 2.67 square inches. If you wanted to use a $^7/_{16}$-inch (0.4375-inch) flange instead of a $^1/_2$-inch flange, you would divide 2.67 square inches by 0.4375 to get the new required flange width of 6.1 inches. Check to be sure this isn't too thin, as follows:

7.12 in. ÷ 0.375 in. = 13.9:1. This is greater than 12:1; therefore, it is too thin and can't be used.

or

For example, we found that *Aluma-Naught*'s speed-adjusted bottom flanges were 126.6 by 13.9 mm, which is 1,759 m². If you wanted to use a 11 mm flange instead of a 14 mm flange, you would divide 1,759 m² by 11 mm to get the new required flange width of 160 mm. Check to be sure this isn't too thin:

160 mm ÷ 11 mm = 14.59:1. This is greater than 12:1; therefore, it is too thin and can't be used.

In this example, you can't go much thinner than the speed-adjusted flange thickness from the rule. You could go thicker, though, reducing the flange width accordingly.

FORMULA 15-10
Aluminum and Steel Ring-Frame Dimensions: Topsides

On displacement and semi-displacement boats, the bottom frames are often carried up and around, unchanged, along the topsides to the sheer. However, you can save weight by reducing the web height as follows:

Web Height at Chine or Bilge = 0.85 × bottom-web height (not speed-adjusted)

Web Height at Sheer = 0.70 × bottom-web height (not speed-adjusted)

The flange can also be reduced in thickness, as follows:

Flange Thickness = Web Thickness

The weight saved here is minor, but well worth doing on high-speed craft; the lower web heights (moldings) gain an extra 1 or 2 inches (25 to 50 mm) of interior space.

CHANNEL AND SQUARE-TUBE HULL FRAMING

Some builders use channels welded open-end down against the inside of the plate, or square tube for hull frames, and even for longitudinals, deck beams, and cabin-roof beams. The sizing of such beams isn't covered in this rule, but I recommend against this practice. Water can get into or behind these shapes where corrosion can take place, but you can't ever see it to inspect.

TOPSIDE FRAMES ON SAIL BOATS NEAR MAST AND CHAINPLATES

On sailboats, additional strength is required at the masts and shroud chainplates. The top-sides frames at the mast and chainplates should be the same dimensions as the hull-bottom frame (not the reduced topsides-frame dimensions). In addition—on boats with Sns greater than 3—the web thickness should be increased to the next standard plate size up. Usually, the two or three frames athwartships from the mast should meet this requirement; however, if shrouds fall at some other location, the topside frame there should be increased as well (see photo on p. 343).

FORMULA 15-11A
Aluminum Deck-Beam Dimensions

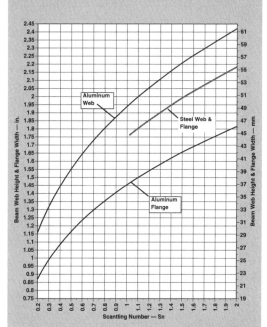

Deck-Beam-Web Heights and Flange Widths in Longitudinally Framed Hulls, Aluminum and Steel: Small Boats

Aluminum Deck-Beam-Web Height, in. = $1.94 \times Sn^{0.32}$ (English)

Aluminum Deck-Beam-Web Height, mm = $49.27 \times Sn^{0.32}$ (Metric)

(continued)

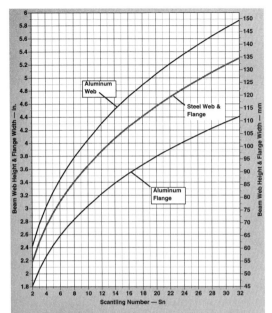

Deck-Beam-Web Heights and Flange Widths in Longitudinally Framed Hulls, Aluminum and Steel: Large Boats

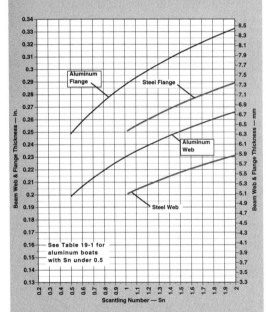

Deck-Beam-Web and Flange Thicknesses in Longitudinally Framed Hulls, Aluminum and Steel: Small Boats

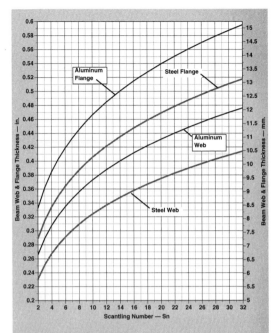

Deck-Beam-Web and Flange Thicknesses in Longitudinally Framed Hulls, Aluminum and Steel: Large Boats

Aluminum Deck-Beam-Web Thickness, in. = same as bottom and topsides web

Aluminum Deck-Beam-Flange Width, in. = 0.75 × web height

Aluminum Deck-Beam Flange Thickness, in. = 1.25 × web thickness

Here again, you can choose a flange that is the same thickness as the web, but then increase the flange width by 1.25 times. *AlumaNaught*'s deck beams then would be

Aluminum Deck-Beam-Web Height, in. = 1.94 × 8.71^{0.32} = 3.87; use 3⅞ or 4 in.

Aluminum Deck-Beam-Web Height, mm = 49.27 × 8.71^{0.32} = 98.49; use 100 mm

Aluminum Deck-Beam-Web Thickness, in. = ⅜ in. (9.5 mm)

*Aluminum Deck-Beam-Flange Width, in. =
3 in. (75 mm)*

*Aluminum Deck-Beam-Flange Thickness, in.
= $^7\!/_{16}$ or ½ in. (11.25 mm) (Alternately, use
$^3\!/_8 \times 4^7\!/_8$ in. or 5 in. flange [9.5 × 125 mm].)*

If you want the flange to be the same thickness as the web, multiply its width by 1.25. This means that our *Iron Maiden* should have

Steel Deck-Beam-Web Height, in. = 1.75 ×
$8.71^{0.32}$ = 3.49; use 3½ in.

Steel Deck-Beam-Web Height, mm = 44.45 ×
$8.71^{0.32}$ = 88.8; use 90 mm

Steel Deck-Beam-Web Thickness, in. =
$^5\!/_{16}$ in. (8 mm)

Steel Deck-Beam-Flange Width =
web height

Steel Deck-Beam-Flange Thickness =
$^3\!/_8$ in. (10 mm) (Alternately, use $^5\!/_{16} \times 4\,^3\!/_8$ in.
flange [8 × 110 mm].)

NOTES ON RING FRAMES

The ring frames in this rule are Ts. It is assumed that they'll be built up in the new method from cut plate welded together. On hard-chine vessels—where the hull curvature of the frames may be slight, or if you prefer to bend standard extrusions—you'll need to use the rule results for a flange with a thickness equal to that of the web. Keep in mind, however, that the formula web height doesn't include the flange thickness. You have to add flange thickness to web height to get the height for an off-the-shelf extrusion.

OPEN- OR CLOSED-BEVEL FRAMES

Angles are also perfectly acceptable for frames. Their webs and flanges should be sized exactly the same as the Ts. An important consideration with angles is that if their flange projects aft from the web forward of midships, and forward of the web aft of midships, then the angles project farther into the hull interior and steal room. At the same time, though, the frame's welds are easier to get at, both during construction and for later

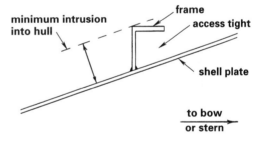

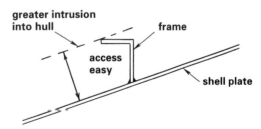

Top: Closed-bevel frame. Bottom: Open bevel frame.

painting, inspection, and repairs. Angle frames installed in this orientation are termed *open–bevel* frames.

Because of the necessity to clean, paint, and inspect under the flanges, open-bevel frames are strongly recommended on steel hulls. On aluminum vessels, though, *closed-bevel* frames (i.e., flanges pointing forward, forward of midships; and pointing aft, aft of midships) will increase interior volume. Be sure there is enough clearance to get a MIG welding gun in to work on the frames up in the bow.

An approach that can help in this regard with Ts is to locate the flange of the T off-center, with either a fourth or a third of the flange either fore or aft of the web. In this way, you can produce open- or closed-bevel Ts. On a steel hull, an open-bevel T aids in painting and inspection; on an aluminum hull, a closed-bevel T increases usable volume.

FORMULA 15-12

Aluminum and Steel Deck-Beam Knees

In frames built using the new method, the deck-beam web is an integral continuation of the topsides web. This should be achieved with a radiused-corner web plate at the sheer. The frame's flange is bent around the inside of the corner and welded to it. When the frames are assembled from off-the-shelf shapes, they're welded together at the sheer and reinforced with a bracket or knee, instead of the integral radiused plate.

Minimum Frame-Web Radius at Sheer = non-speed-adjusted bottom-frame-web height

Minimum Knee Thickness = web thickness

Minimum Knee-Leg Length = 1.3 × non-speed-adjusted bottom-frame-web height

On Ts, the knee is welded to the underside of the flanges; however, on angle frames, the knees are welded to the opposite sides from the flanges. Here, the knee lies on top of the web, forming an overlap.

Minimum Overlap of Knee onto Both Deck-Beam Web and Topsides-Frame Web = 0.3 × non-speed-adjusted bottom-frame-web height

On sailboats, the frames at the mast and chainplates need extra strength. The minimum radius should be 1.3 times the non-speed-adjusted bottom-frame-web height on these frames, or

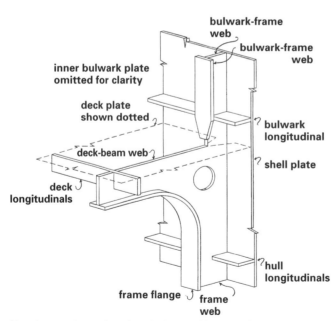

inner bulwark plate
omitted for clarity

bulwark-frame web

bulwark-frame web

deck plate
shown dotted

bulwark longitudinal

deck-beam web

shell plate

deck longitudinals

frame flange

frame web

hull longitudinals

Framing at sheer showing deck, topsides, and bulwark

the knee should be 1.7 times the bottom-web height. Thus, *AlumaNaught* would be fitted with the following:

Minimum Frame-Web Radius at Sheer = 5.5 in. (140 mm)

Minimum Knee Length = 5.5 in. × 1.3 = 7.15; use 7 in.

Minimum Knee Length = 140.6 mm × 1.3 = 182.7; use 180 mm

Minimum Knee Overlap = 5.5 in. × 0.3 = 1.65; use 1⅝ in.

Minimum Knee Overlap = 140.6 mm × 0.3 = 42.18; use 42 mm

Precisely the same approach would be used on our steel *Iron Maiden*.

FORMULA 15-13A

Aluminum Centerline Vertical Keel (CVK) and Stem

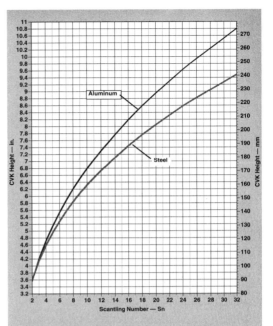

Centerline Vertical Keel (CVK) Height, Aluminum and Steel: Large Boats

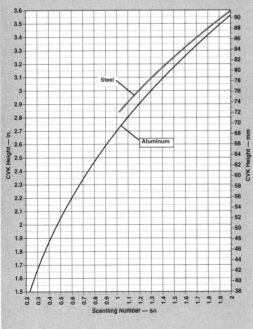

Centerline Vertical Keel (CVK) Height, Aluminum and Steel: Small Boats

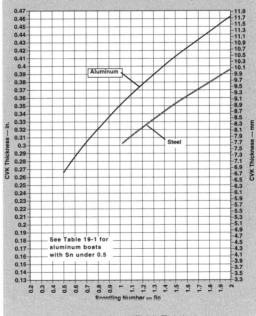

Centerline Vertical Keel (CVK) Thickness, Aluminum and Steel: Small Boats

(continued)

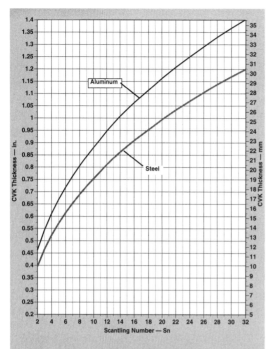

Centerline Vertical Keel (CVK) Thickness, Aluminum and Steel: Large Boats

For standard flat-plate CVKs:

Aluminum CVK Height, in. = 2.7 × $Sn^{0.4}$ (English)

Aluminum CVK Height, mm = 68.58 × $Sn^{0.4}$ (Metric)

Aluminum CVK Thickness = height ÷ 7.7

Horn plates are the same as the CVK—the CVK aft of the deep keel. Stems are the same thickness, but may taper in height (molding) to 60 percent of the CVK maximum at the sheer. *AlumaNaught's* CVK backbone then works out as

Aluminum CVK Height = 2.7 × $8.71^{0.4}$ = 6.41; use 6½ in.

Aluminum CVK Height = 68.58 × $8.71^{0.4}$ = 163; use 165 mm

Aluminum CVK Thickness = 6.41 in. ÷ 7.7 = 0.83; use ⅞ in.

Aluminum CVK Thickness = 163 mm ÷ 7.7 = 21.1; use 22 mm

FORMULA 15-13S
Steel CVK and Stem

For standard flat-plate CVKs:

Steel CVK Height, in. = 2.82 × $Sn^{0.35}$ (English)

Steel CVK Thickness, in. = 0.30 × $Sn^{0.4}$ (English)

Steel CVK Height, mm = 71.62 × $Sn^{0.35}$ (Metric)

Steel CVK Thickness, mm = 7.62 × $Sn^{0.4}$ (Metric)

Horn plates are the same as the CVK—the CVK aft of the deep keel. Stems are the same thickness, but may taper in height (molding) to 60 percent of the CVK maximum at the sheer. The upper 60 percent of the stem CVK can also be 80 percent of the CVK maximum thickness. This means that *Iron Maiden* would have

Steel CVK Height = 2.82 × $8.71^{0.35}$ = 6.01; use 6 in.

Steel CVK Thickness = 0.30 × $8.71^{0.4}$ = 0.71; use ¾ in.

Steel CVK Height = 71.62 × $8.71^{0.35}$ = 152.7; use 150 mm

Steel CVK Thickness = 7.62 × $8.71^{0.4}$ = 18.1; use 18 mm

The upper-stem CVK thickness could be reduced to ⅝ inch (16 mm).

CVKs AS EXTERNAL SKEGS
The CVK can be entirely in the boat or it may extend some distance below the bottom

plate to form an exterior skeg keel. In this case, it is normal for the CVK height to be much greater than the minimum specified by the rule.

FORMULA 15-14
Stern Frame

> The stern frame is the CVK where it is split by the stern tube at the aft end of the keel—on single-screw vessels. It runs roughly vertically from the bottom of the keel or skeg, up the trailing edge of the keel to the horn timber, to which it is welded. Twin-engine craft do not require a heavier stern frame; their CVK is constant thickness along the hull bottom.

> Stern-Frame Thickness = 1.42 × CVK thickness

AlumaNaught's stern frame would then be

> 0.83 in. × 1.42 = 1.17 in.; use 1¼ in.
> 21.1 mm × 1.42 = 29.9; use 30 mm

Iron Maiden's stern frame works out to

> 0.71 in. × 1.42 = 1.07; use 1 in.
> 18 mm × 1.42 = 25.5; use 25 mm

Fore-n-aft, the stern frame should extend to at least a full ring-frame length. It should be welded to a floor for at least twice the height of the CVK, which will butt against and be welded to the forward face of the same floor.

FORMULA 15-15
Floors

> Floors connect the frames from both sides of the vessel across the CVK, just as in wood construction.

> Floor Thickness = same as speed-adjusted bottom-frame webs

> Floor Height = at least the same as the CVK

Floors can be integral with the new-method built-up ring-frame or welded to the faces of frames made of angles. If the frames consist of Ts, the Ts are cropped and the floor butt is welded to them.

Preferably, the floors should extend at least 60 percent of the bottom-frame-web height above the CVK, with the bottom-frame flange extending across the top of the floor. On some boats with deep box keels, this almost happens naturally. Other craft, with shallow bilges and no box keel, may lose too much interior height to such deep floors. In this case, floors the same height as the CVK are acceptable. Run the bottom-frame flange along the top of the floors; in any case, continuously athwartships across the top of the CVK.

BOX KEELS

Most displacement vessels have deep box keels. These deep-section keels are far stronger than the standard CVK plate, so the CVK can be eliminated wherever the box keel exists. The true CVK stem runs down into the box keel at its leading edge, and is welded to the top of the keel-bottom plate and to the floors. The stem should extend at least one full frame bay aft of the front of the box keel.

At the aft end of the box keel, the stern frame is welded to the top of the keel-bottom plate and to the aft floors. The box keel's side plates usually sweep in to join to the stern frame, port and starboard. Aft of the box keel, the CVK reappears as the horn plate, which is welded to the top of the stern frame.

Weight in the keel of displacement hulls is not detrimental, so I usually round up on

Welding on box-keel steel sideplates. (Courtesy Treworgy Yachts)

the keel plate to maximize corrosion and impact resistance. In addition, on sailboats and many voyaging motor cruisers, the weight of the box-keel plating can be deducted from the lead ballast.

FORMULA 15-16A

Aluminum Box-Keel Sides

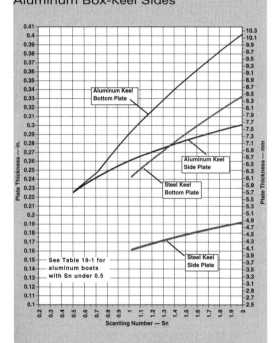

Box-Keel Side- and Bottom-Plate Thickness, Aluminum and Steel: Small Boats

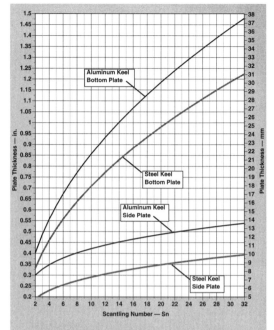

Box-Keel Side- and Bottom-Plate Thickness, Aluminum and Steel: Large Boats

Aluminum Box-Keel-Side Plate, in. = $0.26 \times Sn^{0.21}$ (English)

Aluminum Box-Keel-Side Plate, mm = $6.6 \times Sn^{0.21}$ (Metric)

AlumaNaught's box-keel-side plate should then be

Aluminum Box-Keel-Side Plate = $0.26 \times 8.71^{0.21} = 0.41$; use $7/16$ in.

Aluminum Box-Keel-Side Plate = $6.6 \times 8.71^{0.21} = 10.39$; use 11 mm

FORMULA 15-16S

Steel Box-Keel Sides

Steel Box-Keel-Side Plate, in. = $0.16 \times Sn^{0.26}$ (English)

Steel Box-Keel-Side Plate, mm = $4.06 \times Sn^{0.26}$ (Metric)

Thus, the box-keel-side plate on *Iron Maiden* would be

Steel Box-Keel-Side Plate = $0.16 \times 8.71^{0.26}$ = 0.28; use 5/16 in.

Steel Box-Keel-Side Plate = $4.06 \times 8.71^{0.26}$ = 7.12; use 7.9 mm

BOX-KEEL-BOTTOM PLATE

The bottom plate of the box keel takes all the grounding loads and abrasion imposed by the weight of the entire hull. It should be quite heavy. Again, the weight can be deducted from the lead ballast. On steel hulls, the combined weight of the heavy box-keel-side plate and the bottom plate can make a substantial contribution to the total ballast weight.

FORMULA 15-17A

Aluminum Box-Keel-Bottom Plate

Aluminum Box-Keel-Bottom Plate, in. = $0.29 \times Sn^{0.4}$ (English)

Aluminum Box-Keel-Bottom Plate, mm = $7.37 \times Sn^{0.4}$ (Metric)

Accordingly, *AlumaNaught*'s box-keel-bottom plate would be

Aluminum Box-Keel-Bottom Plate = $0.29 \times 8.71^{0.4}$ = 0.80 in.; use 7/8 or 1 in.

Aluminum Box-Keel-Bottom Plate = $7.37 \times 8.71^{0.4}$ = 20.3; use 20 to 25 mm

Thicker doesn't hurt here, so I might even use a 1 1/4-inch (30 mm) box-keel-bottom plate. The thickness from the formula should be about minimum.

For Sns less than 0.65, the bottom-plate formula gives smaller thicknesses than for the side plate. Use the thicker side plate on the bottom, or refer to the box-keel-thickness chart.

FORMULA 15-17S

Steel Box-Keel-Bottom Plate

Steel Box-Keel-Bottom Plate, in. = $0.24 \times Sn^{0.4}$ (English)

Steel Box-Keel-Bottom Plate, mm = $6.09 \times Sn^{0.4}$ (Metric)

The keel-bottom plate on *Iron Maiden* is then

Steel Box-Keel-Bottom Plate = $0.24 \times 8.71^{0.4}$ = 0.66; use 5/8 in.

Steel Box-Keel-Bottom Plate = $6.09 \times 8.71^{0.4}$ = 16.8; use 17 mm

Once again, thicker bottom plates are usually better (within reason); therefore, 7/8 or 1 inch (22 to 25 mm) would certainly be worth considering. Even thicker bottom plates still could be installed for ballast purposes.

CHINE ROD

On hard-chine craft, some builders use a chine rod or round bar at the corner between the bottom and topsides plate. The argument for this is that it is somewhat easier to make a fair joint and the heavy rod can take more abuse than a sharp welded corner. Still, it is perfectly acceptable to simply weld the topsides and bottom plates together with no chine rod. Indeed, a drawback to chine rods is that they form a narrow crevice (against the inside of the topside plate) where water can collect and corrosion can start—which is particularly troubling in steel.

FORMULA 15-18A

Aluminum Chine-Rod Diameter

Aluminum Chine-Rod Diameter, in. = $0.42 \times Sn^{0.38}$ (English)

Aluminum Chine-Rod Diameter, mm = $10.66 \times Sn^{0.38}$ (Metric)

(continued)

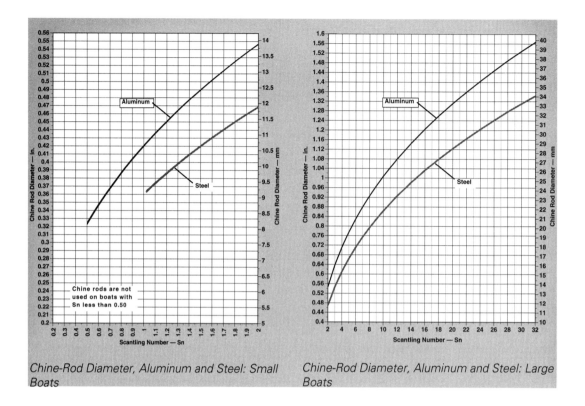

Chine-Rod Diameter, Aluminum and Steel: Small Boats

Chine-Rod Diameter, Aluminum and Steel: Large Boats

The chine rod on *AlumaNaught* is

Aluminum Chine-Rod Diameter = 0.42 × $8.71^{0.38}$ = 0.95; use 1-in. diameter

Aluminum Chine-Rod Diameter = 10.66 × $8.71^{0.38}$ = 24.2; use 25 mm diameter

Chine rods are not used on boats with Sns less than 0.50.

FORMULA 15-18S

Steel Chine-Rod Diameter

Steel Chine-Rod Diameter, in. = 0.36 × $Sn^{0.38}$ (English)

Steel Chine-Rod Diameter, mm = 9.14 × $Sn^{0.38}$ (Metric)

The chine rod on *Iron Maiden* is

Steel Chine-Rod Diameter = 0.36 × $8.71^{0.38}$ = 0.81; use ⅞-in. diameter

Steel Chine-Rod Diameter = 9.14 × $8.71^{0.38}$ = 20.8; use 20 mm diameter

SIXTEEN

Aluminum and Steel Structural Details

*A*lthough the plate and framing discussed in chapter 15 describe the basic hull structure—as we've seen for other materials—there are numerous secondary structures and details required to complete a strong and long-lasting vessel. Bulkheads, cabin roofs, mast partners, engine beds, and more: we examine these items in this chapter.

Bulkheads

Bulkheads fall into one of the following three categories:

- joiner bulkheads (wood, nonstructural)
- metal structural bulkheads, watertight or not (not rated for full head)
- metal watertight collision bulkheads (rated for full head of water to 1 foot [30 cm] above the top of the bulkhead)

JOINER BULKHEADS

These days, joiner bulkheads are almost exclusively from sheet ply (i.e., marine, exterior grade, or MDO). On boats between 35 and 100 feet (10 to 30 m), joiner bulkheads are from $1/2$ to $3/4$ inch (12 to 20 mm) thick, with $3/4$ inch (20 mm) being most common. On vessels under 35 feet (10 m), joiner bulkheads as thin as $3/8$-inch (9.5 mm) ply may be used; however, $1/2$ or $5/8$ inch (12 or 16 mm) are stiffer and easier to hold in plane and fasten to.

Old practice was to fabricate joiner bulkheads out of tongue-and-groove lumber. This still works well, but is more costly and noticeably heavier than ply. The minimum practical thickness is about $1^1/2$ to 2 inches (38 to 50 mm), which also steals a little more interior room.

METAL STRUCTURAL BULKHEADS (WATERTIGHT AND NOT)

Most larger metal hulls have several metal structural bulkheads separating the machinery spaces, the lazarette, and the forepeak. These may or may not be watertight. Although it increases safety to have several fully watertight bulkheads in the hull, it also complicates the bilge piping system and can break up the accommodations unacceptably.

Even nonwatertight structural metal bulkheads help prevent the spread of fire and combustion byproduct gases. A nonwatertight bulkhead between machinery and accommodations spaces, which has a combined opening area of less than 0.01 percent of the area of the bulkhead separating the accommodation and machinery, is considered effective at containing the spread of both noxious gases and fire.

Unlike FRP hulls and some forms of wood-epoxy hulls, even the so-called "structural" bulkheads on a metal boat aren't required for strength. The basic framing and plate alone are quite robust enough by themselves. Bulkheads on aluminum and steel craft are principally to divide the vessel into compartments to separate machinery, accommodations, and cargo spaces, and to increase watertight integrity in case of a hull breach.

For strength purposes, full structural bulkheads are called for under exceptionally heavy-load deck machinery, such as cranes, dredges, and similar heavy lifting equipment.

Common Locations of Metal Bulkheads

On boats under 60 feet (18 m), I usually use a full watertight collision bulkhead at the aft end of the forepeak (between 5 and 15 percent of WL aft of the WL at the bow) and another aft at the forward end of the lazarette, if the arrangement permits (i.e., no aft cabin in the hull). Under 40 feet (12 m), it's difficult even to work in a collision bulkhead forward.

Vessels over 60 or 70 feet (18 or 20 m) can often fit two additional bulkheads, one forward and one aft of the engine compartment.

It's tempting to make these watertight; however, there are drawbacks. All the penetrations through these centrally located bulkheads (including propeller shaft, wires, hoses, and vent ducts) must be made watertight, which is time-consuming and costly. Fully watertight access doors are heavy and cumbersome, and awkward to fit in. This extra investment should be made for serious ocean-voyaging yachts and workboats; however, it's not usually warranted for ordinary yachts.

Bulkhead Stiffeners

Bulkhead stiffeners should not touch the hull. They should end about three to four times the stiffener's web thickness from the hull shell, inside. Their flanges should be sniped back or beveled at their ends to avoid sharp projecting corners. Alternately, the vertical stiffeners can be aligned with and welded to the deck longitudinals. It may not be convenient to do this, though, and the added strength is not required.

Decreasing Weight on Steel Bulkheads

To decrease weight on steel bulkheads, the upper 40 percent of the bulkhead is usually reduced in thickness to the next standard plate size down. This can only be done, of course, when the resulting lighter upper-bulkhead plate won't be too thin to weld. Aluminum bulkheads can be treated the same way, but this is appropriate only on the lightest and highest-performance aluminum vessels.

FORMULA 16-1A
Aluminum Bulkheads (Not Rated for Full Head)

Aluminum Bulkhead Plate = same as deck plate

Aluminum Bulkhead Vertical Stiffeners O.C., in. = 5 + (plate thickness, in. × 38) (English)

Aluminum Bulkhead Vertical Stiffeners O.C., mm = 127 + (plate thickness, mm × 38) (Metric)

Aluminum Bulkhead Stiffener: web height, in. = 15 × plate thickness (does not include flange thickness)

Aluminum Bulkhead Stiffener: flange and web thickness = plate thickness + 1/16 in. (English)

Aluminum Bulkhead Stiffener: flange and web thickness = plate thickness + 1.6 mm (Metric)

Aluminum Bulkhead Stiffener: flange width = web height ÷ 1.4

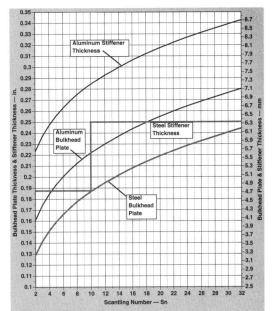

Bulkhead Plate and Stiffener Thickness, Aluminum and Steel: Large Boats (Not Rated for Full Head)

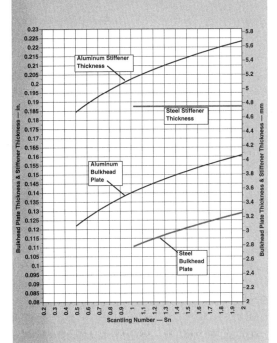

Bulkhead Plate and Stiffener Thickness, Aluminum and Steel: Small Boats (Not Rated for Full Head)

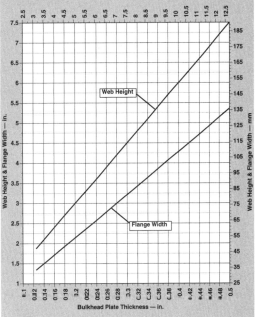

Aluminum Bulkhead Stiffener, Web Heights and Flange Widths (Not Rated for Full Head)

(continued)

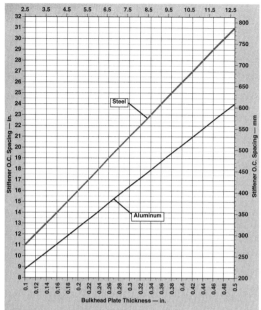

Aluminum and Steel Bulkhead-Stiffener O.C.
Spacing (Not Rated for Full Head)

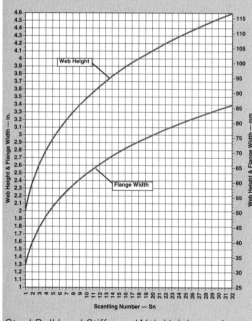

Steel Bulkhead Stiffener, Web Heights and
Flange Widths (Not Rated for Full Head)

In the previous chapter, *AlumaNaught*'s deck plate was ³/₁₆ inch (4.75 mm). Accordingly, its bulkheads would be

Aluminum Bulkhead Plate = ³/₁₆ in.
(0.1875 in.)

Aluminum Bulkhead Vertical Stiffeners O.C.
= 5 + (0.1875 in. × 38) = 12.1; use 12 in.

Aluminum Bulkhead Vertical Stiffeners O.C.
= 127 + (4.75 mm × 38) = 307.5; use 300 mm

Aluminum Bulkhead Stiffener: web height =
15 × 0.1875 = 2.81 in.

Aluminum Bulkhead Stiffener: web height =
15 × 4.75 = 71.2

Aluminum Bulkhead Stiffener: flange and
web thickness = ³/₁₆ + ¹/₁₆ in. = ¼ in.

Aluminum Bulkhead Stiffener: flange and
web thickness = 4.75 + 1.6 mm = 6.35;
use 6.4 mm

Aluminum Bulkhead Stiffener: flange width
= 2.81 in. ÷ 1.4 = 2 in.

Aluminum Bulkhead Stiffener: flange width
= 71.2 mm ÷ 1.4 = 50.8; use 50 mm

Bulkhead stiffeners can be Ts or angles interchangeably. Angles are most common, because—being straight—there's no reason to make these up. It's quicker and less expensive to use off-the-shelf extrusions. We have to add the flange thickness to the web height to get the full extrusion height

2.81 in. web + 0.25 in. flange = 3.06;
use 3 in. height

71.2 mm web + 6.4 mm flange = 77.6; use
78 mm height

Thus, ¼ in. × 3 in. × 2 in. angles, 12 in. O.C.
would fill the bill;

or

6.4 mm × 80 mm × 50 mm, 300 mm O.C.
would fill the bill

Steel Bulkheads (Not Rated for Full Head)

Steel Bulkhead Plate = same as deck plate

Steel Upper-Bulkhead Plate = next standard plate size down on the upper 40% of the bulkhead

Steel Bulkhead Vertical Stiffeners O.C., in. = 6 + (plate thickness, in. × 50) (English)

Steel Bulkhead Vertical Stiffeners O.C., mm = 152.4 + (plate thickness, mm × 50) (Metric)

Steel Bulkhead Stiffener: web height, in. = $(2 \times Sn^{0.24})$ – 0.4 (including flange thickness) (English)

Steel Bulkhead Stiffener: web height, mm = $(50.8 \times Sn^{0.24})$ – 10.16 (including flange thickness) (Metric)

Steel Bulkhead Stiffener: flange and web thickness = ¼ in. for all bulkheads with plate thicker than ³⁄₁₆ in.; ³⁄₁₆ in. for plate ³⁄₁₆ in. or less (English)

Steel Bulkhead Stiffener: flange and web thickness = 6.4 mm for all bulkheads with plate thicker than 4.75 mm; 4.75 mm for plate 4.75 mm or less (Metric)

Steel Bulkhead Stiffener: flange width, in. = (0.81 × web height in.) – 0.33 (English)

Steel Bulkhead Stiffener: flange width, mm = (0.81 × web height, mm) – 8.38 (Metric)

In the last chapter, *Iron Maiden*'s deck plate was ³⁄₁₆-inch mild steel or 8-gauge Cor-Ten (0.1664 in.) (4.75 mm mild steel or 4 mm Cor-Ten). Using Cor-Ten to reduce weight, *Iron Maiden*'s bulkheads work out as

Steel Bulkhead Plate = Cor-Ten 8-gauge (0.1664 in.) (4 mm)

Steel Upper-Bulkhead Plate = Cor-Ten 10-gauge (0.1345 in.) (3.4 mm)

Steel Bulkhead Vertical Stiffeners O.C. = 6 + (0.1664 in. × 50) = 14.3; use 14 in.

Steel Bulkhead Vertical Stiffeners O.C. = 152.4 + (4 mm × 50) = 352.4; use 350 mm

Steel Bulkhead Stiffener: web height = $(2 \times 8.71^{0.24})$ – 0.4 = 2.96; use 3 in.

Steel Bulkhead Stiffener: web height = $(50.8 \times 8.71^{0.24})$ – 10.16 = 75.2; use 75 mm

Steel Bulkhead Stiffener: flange and web thickness = ³⁄₁₆ in.

Steel Bulkhead Stiffener: flange and web thickness = 4.75 mm

Steel Bulkhead Stiffener: flange width = (0.81 × 2.96 in.) – 0.33 = 2.06; use 2 in.

Steel Bulkhead Stiffener: flange width = (0.81 × 75.2 mm) – 8.38 = 52.5; use 50 mm

Bulkhead stiffeners can be Ts or angles interchangeably. Angles are most common, because—being straight—there's no reason to make these up. It's quicker and less expensive to use off-the-shelf extrusions. The rule for steel bulkhead stiffeners *does include* the thickness of the flange in the web height, so we would find that

³⁄₁₆ n. × 3 in. × 2 in. angles, 14 in. O.C. would do the job

or

4.75 mm × 75 mm × 50 mm, 350 mm O.C. would do the job

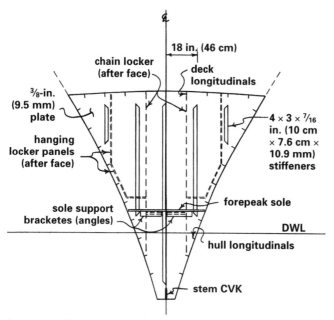

Forward-collision bulkhead, 10-foot (3 m) head, looking aft

WATERTIGHT COLLISION BULKHEADS AND TANK WALLS

The bulkheads from Formulas 16-1A and S may or may not be strong enough to rate as full watertight collision bulkheads. The con-

trolling factor is the head or the height of water that the bulkhead can withstand with adequate safety. Formulas 16-1A and S simply estimate approximate strength based on the Sn. For wide shallow-bodied boats—where the head will be low—it will give over-strength bulkheads in terms of head. For deep bodied hull, Formulas 16-1A and S bulkheads may not be strong enough.

To ensure that a bulkhead can withstand a head of water 1 foot (30 cm) above the top of the deck, use the following tables. The head in feet or meters is the distance from the bottom-most point of that bulkhead on the keel to the underside of the deck at the centerline. Watertight collision bulkheads in the middle of a deep-bodied hull need to be beefier than the shallower bulkheads at the ends of such a hull.

TABLE 16-2A Aluminum Watertight Collision Bulkheads and Tanks (English)

| Head, ft. | Plate Thickness, in. | Stiffener | | | |
		O.C., in.	Web, in.	Flange, in.	Thickness, in.
4	0.1875	12	2.0	1.0	0.1875
6	0.2500	18	2.5	2.0	0.2500
8	0.2500	18	3.5	2.5	0.3750
10	0.3750	18	4.0	3.0	0.4375
12	0.3750	18	6.0	3.0	0.4375
14	0.4375	18	6.0	4.0	0.6250
16	0.4375	18	8.0	4.0	0.6250

See table note on page 260.

TABLE 16-2A Aluminum Watertight Collision Bulkheads and Tanks (Metric)

| Head, m | Plate Thickness, mm | Stiffener | | | |
		O.C., mm	Web, mm	Flange, mm	Thickness, mm
1.22	4.75	300	50	25	4.75
1.83	6.40	450	65	50	6.40
2.44	6.40	450	90	65	9.50
3.05	9.50	450	100	75	11.25
3.66	9.50	450	150	75	11.25
4.27	11.25	450	150	100	16.00
4.88	11.25	450	200	100	16.00

See table note on page 260.

TABLE 16-2S Steel Watertight Collision Bulkheads and Tanks (English)

| Head, ft. | Plate Thickness, in. | Stiffener | | | |
		O.C., in.	Web, in.	Flange, in.	Thickness, in.
4	0.1345	12	1.25	1.00	0.1250
6	0.1644	12	2.00	1.00	0.1875
8	0.1875	18	3.00	1.75	0.2500
10	0.2500	18	4.00	2.50	0.2500
12	0.2500	18	5.00	2.25	0.3750
14	0.2500	18	5.00	4.00	0.3750
16	0.3125	18	6.00	4.75	0.3750

See table note on page 260.

TANKS DESIGNED FOR HEAD (PRESSURE)

The walls of integral tanks need to meet the same criteria for head; therefore, the tables also give wall thickness and stiffeners for tanks. Because large tanks need baffles, every other stiffener should be replaced with an internal baffle so that no area measures more than 36 inches (92 cm) of free surface in any direction. (As much as 44 inches [112 cm] in the fore-n-aft direction is acceptable, as long as there are adequate stiffeners on the walls.) Baffles must have large snipes that double as limbers cut out in all four corners, with a central hole as well. The total cut-out area should be about 18 to 20 percent of the baffle's square area; more would reduce the baffles effectiveness and less could impede fluid flow.

TABLE 16-2S Steel Watertight Collision Bulkheads and Tanks (Metric)

Head, m	Plate Thickness, mm	Stiffener			
		O.C., mm	Web, mm	Flange, mm	Thickness, mm
1.22	3.40	300	32	25	3.20
1.83	4.20	300	50	25	4.75
2.44	4.75	450	75	45	6.40
3.05	6.40	450	100	64	6.40
3.66	6.40	450	130	58	9.50
4.27	6.40	450	130	100	9.50
4.88	8.00	450	160	120	9.50

For fuel tanks—regardless of the height of the plumbing—in no case should a total pressure head of less than 3 psi or 20.7 kPa (6.9 feet or 2.1 m) be used for yachts, and never less than 5 psi or 34.5 kPa (11.5 feet or 3.5 m) for charter vessels and workboats.

Determining Tank Head

The curious and most critical thing about pressure head on tanks is that it is not measured to the top of the tank but rather to the top of the highest plumbing point. For instance, say that you have an integral diesel tank in the bilge. Its top is just 3 feet (0.91 m) "deep" above the keel and 1 foot (0.30 m) below the waterline. However, the fill is on deck 4 feet (1.22 m) above the WL, and the vent is on the cabin roof 5 feet (1.52 m) above that. You need to use the height from the bottom of the tank to the top of the vent for head. (You can't just use the height to the fill because, if the tank were topped up with cold fuel and capped off, the fuel will then warm up on a hot summer day. The fluid will expand and rise to fill a surprising portion of the vent tube.) This works out to the remarkable head of

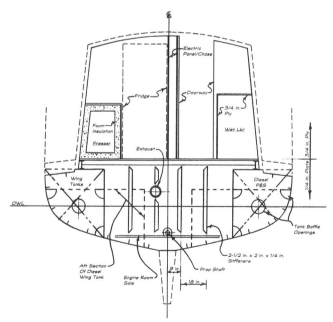

Engine-room bulkhead, 5-foot (1.5 m) head

3 ft. deep tank + 1 ft. to WL + 4 ft. WL to deck + 5 ft. to cabin top vent = 13 ft.!

or

0.91 m deep tank + 0.3 m to WL + 1.22 m WL to deck + 1.52 m to cabin top vent = 3.95 m!

Thin-Plate Bulkheads and Tanks and Structural Penetrations

Small tanks with low heads require plate thickness too thin to weld except with pulse-arc equipment. Usually, you simply use the smallest conveniently weldable thickness. Adequate plate thickness for welding is critical on tanks and watertight bulkheads because the welds must be tight. It's much easier to ensure a proper seal on a heavier weld. Indeed, on penetrations of the watertight bulkhead and tanks—with thinner plate—it's good practice to weld in an insert plate of twice the plate thickness surrounding the penetrating member. This allows quite heavy and, therefore, tight welding around the corners of stringers and pipes. On integral fuel tanks, in particular, my preference is to cut the longitudinal framing at the tank wall and butt-weld these to the tank-wall plate fore-n-aft.

Superstructure Framing and Cabin Roofs

CABIN FRAMING

The cabin and superstructure sides are framed out much like the hull. The ring frames—wherever possible—continue up into the cabin sides, and longitudinal stiffeners are notched into these fore-n-aft.

FORMULA 16-3A

Aluminum Cabin-Side Framing

Aluminum Cabin-Side Plate from Formula 15-4A

Aluminum Cabin-Side-Frames O.C. = hull frame O.C.

Aluminum Cabin-Side-Frame Web Height, in. = $2.1 \times Sn^{0.21}$ (English)

Aluminum Cabin-Side-Frame Web Height, mm = $53.34 \times Sn^{0.21}$ (Metric)

Aluminum Cabin-Side-Frame Web and Flange Thickness = web height ÷ 11.67

Aluminum Cabin-Side-Flange Width = 0.55 × web height

Aluminum Cabin-Side-Longitudinal Height = 0.52 × web height

Aluminum Cabin-Side-Longitudinal Thickness = web thickness

Aluminum Cabin-Side-Longitudinal O.C. from Formula 15-6A

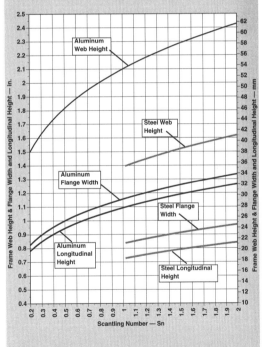

Cabin-Side-Frame Web and Flange Widths and Longitudinal Height, Aluminum and Steel: Small Boats

(continued)

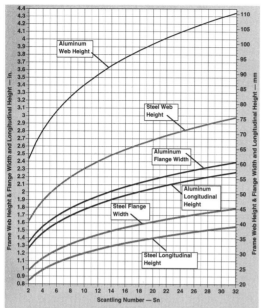

Cabin-Side-Frame Web and Flange Widths and Longitudinal Height, Aluminum and Steel: Large Boats

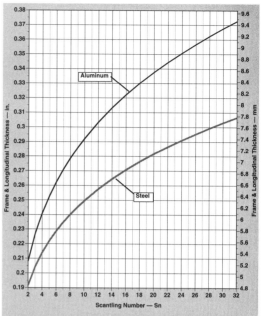

Cabin-Side-Frame and Longitudinal Thickness, Aluminum and Steel: Large Boats

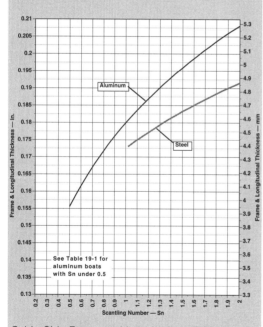

Cabin-Side-Frame and Longitudinal Thickness, Aluminum and Steel: Small Boats

Applying this to our trusty *Aluma-Naught*, we would use the following:

Aluminum Cabin-Side Plate = ³⁄₁₆ in. (4.75 mm) (see Formula 15-4A)

Aluminum Cabin-Side-Frames O.C. = hull frame O.C. = 46 in. for the displacement version and 36 in. for the 35-knot version

Aluminum Cabin-Side-Frame Web Height = $2.1 \times 8.71^{0.21} = 3.3$; use 3³⁄₈ in.

Aluminum Cabin-Side-Frame Web Height = $53.34 \times 8.71^{0.21} = 84$ mm

Aluminum Cabin-Side-Frame Web and Flange Thickness = 3.3 in. ÷ 11.67 = 0.28; use ¹⁄₄ in.

Aluminum Cabin-Side-Frame Web and Flange Thickness = 84 mm ÷ 11.67 = 7.19; use 7.5 mm

Aluminum Cabin-Side-Flange Width = 0.55 × 3.3 in. = 1.81; use $1\frac{7}{8}$ or 2 in.

Aluminum Cabin-Side-Flange Width = 0.55 × 84 mm = 46.2; use 45 mm

Aluminum Cabin-Side-Longitudinal Height = 0.52 × 3.3 in. = 1.71; use $1\frac{3}{4}$ in.

Aluminum Cabin-Side-Longitudinal Height = 0.52 × 84 mm = 43.6; use 45 mm

Aluminum Cabin-Side-Longitudinal Thickness = $\frac{1}{4}$ in. (7.5 mm)

Aluminum Cabin-Side-Longitudinal O.C. = 4 + ($\frac{3}{16}$ in. × 32) = 10 in.

Aluminum Cabin-Side-Longitudinal O.C. = 101.6 + (4.75 mm × 32) = 253.6; use 250 mm

FORMULA 16-3S
Steel Cabin-Side Frames

Steel Cabin-Side Plate from Formula 15-4S

Steel Cabin-Side-Frames O.C. = hull frame O.C.

Steel Cabin-Side-Frame Web Height, in. = $1.39 \times Sn^{0.22}$ = (English)

Steel Cabin-Side-Frame Web Height, mm = $35.3 \times Sn^{0.22}$ = (Metric)

Steel Cabin-Side-Frame Web and Flange Thickness = cabin-side plate thickness (in mild steel) + $\frac{1}{16}$ in. (English)

Steel Cabin-Side-Frame Web and Flange Thickness = cabin-side plate thickness (in mild steel) + 1.6 mm (Metric)

Steel Cabin-Side-Flange Width = 0.6 × web height

Steel Cabin-Side-Longitudinal Height = 0.52 × web height

Steel Cabin-Side-Longitudinal Thickness = web thickness

Steel Cabin-Side-Longitudinal O.C. from Formula 15-6S

In the previous chapter, we settled on 10-gauge (0.1345 inch) (3.4 mm) Cor-Ten plate for *Iron Maiden's* cabin sides. We use the actual thickness of the Cor-Ten plate installed for the longitudinal spacing, but the equivalent thickness of mild-steel plate to determine the cabin-framing thickness. Therefore, we would determine the following:

Steel Cabin-Side Plate = Cor-Ten 10-gauge (0.1345 in.) (3.4 mm) Equivalent mild steel, from Formula 15-4S = 0.163 in. (4.59 mm)

Steel Cabin-Side Frames O.C. = hull frame O.C. = 46 in. for the displacement version and 36 in. for the 35-knot version

Steel Cabin-Side-Frame Web Height = $1.39 \times 8.71^{0.22}$ = 2.23; use $2\frac{1}{4}$ in.

Steel Cabin-Side-Frame Web Height = $35.3 \times 8.71^{0.22}$ = 56.8; use 58 mm

Steel Cabin-Side-Frame Web and Flange Thickness = 0.163 in. (in mild steel) + $\frac{1}{16}$ in. = 0.225; use $\frac{1}{4}$ in.

Steel Cabin-Side-Frame Web and Flange Thickness = 4.59 mm (in mild steel) + 1.6 mm = 6.19; use 6.4 mm

Steel Cabin-Side-Flange Width = 0.6 × 2.23 in. = 1.33; use $1\frac{3}{8}$ in.

Steel Cabin-Side-Flange Width = 0.6 × 56.8 mm = 34.08; use 34 mm

Steel Cabin-Side-Longitudinal Height = 0.52 × 2.23 in. = 1.15; use $1\frac{1}{8}$ in.

Steel Cabin-Side Longitudinal Height = 0.52 × 56.8 mm = 29.54; use 30 mm

Steel Cabin-Side-Longitudinal Thickness =
¼ in. (6.4 mm)

Steel Cabin-Side-Longitudinal O.C. = 6 +
(0.1345 in. Cor-Ten × 48) = 12.45; use 12 in.

Steel Cabin-Side-Longitudinal O.C. = 152.4 +
(3.4 mm Cor-Ten × 48) = 315.6; use 300 mm

CABIN ROOFS

Cabin roofs are the highest large structure on any boat. Accordingly, for both aluminum and steel vessels, it is vital to make these as light as possible to keep the center of gravity low. Usually—even on an otherwise longitudinally framed craft—it is more convenient to fabricate the cabin roofs transversely framed, with no longitudinals at all. In this construction, the transverse frames are quite closely spaced. (Longitudinals are added at fore-n-aft ends to support overhangs here, if required.)

Use the following tables to select the proper cabin-roof scantlings, based on the *span* (i.e., the beam or width athwartships) of the cabin roof at its widest point. In general, there are two somewhat conflicting goals. Thinner plate makes for lighter weight, but deeper cabin beams either steal headroom or force you to raise the roof slightly, thus raising the center of gravity. You need to select the thinnest roof plate you can weld that will give the maximum acceptable roof-beam depth, for headroom.

Keep in mind that even on the largest steel boat, aluminum, wood, or FRP cabin roofs—even when the cabin sides are steel—are lighter and will lower the center of gravity. Such nonsteel roofs are almost a necessity for proper stability on vessels with Sns under 6. Tables 16-4A and 16-4S are based on 200 lb./sq. ft. (976 kg/m²) loading, with a safety factor of 1.5 over yield.

TABLE 16-4A Aluminum Transverse-Frame Cabin-Roof Construction (English)

Cabin Span, ft.	Roof Beams O.C., in.	Beam Height, in.	Beam Flange, in.	Beam Thickness, in.
⅛-in. Roof Plate				
4	7.5	1.50	1.00	0.1250
6	7.5	2.00	1.00	0.1250
8	7.5	2.25	1.50	0.1875
10	7.5	2.50	2.00	0.1875
12	7.5	3.00	2.00	0.2500
⁵⁄₃₂-in. Roof Plate				
6	9	2.00	1.00	0.1875
8	9	2.50	1.25	0.1875
10	9	3.00	1.50	0.1875

TABLE 16-4A Aluminum Transverse-Frame Cabin-Roof Construction (English) *(Cont.)*

Cabin Span, ft.	Roof Beams O.C., in.	Beam Height, in.	Flange, in.	Thickness, in.
5/32-in. Roof Plate (con't.)				
12	9	3.00	2.00	0.2500
14	9	3.50	2.50	0.2500
3/16-in. Roof Plate				
6	10	2.00	1.00	0.1875
8	10	2.00	1.50	0.2500
10	10	2.75	1.50	0.2500
12	10	3.00	2.00	0.2500
14	10	3.50	2.50	0.2500
16	10	4.00	2.75	0.2500
18	10	4.00	3.00	0.3125
1/4-in. Roof Plate				
8	12	2.25	1.50	0.2500
10	12	2.75	1.75	0.2500
12	12	3.00	2.50	0.2500
14	12	3.00	2.75	0.3125
16	12	3.75	2.75	0.3125
18	12	4.00	2.75	0.3750
20	12	4.50	3.00	0.3750
22	12	4.75	3.50	0.3750
5/16-in. Roof Plate				
10	12	2.50	1.75	0.2500
12	12	3.00	1.50	0.3750
14	12	3.50	1.75	0.3750
16	12	3.75	2.00	0.3750
18	12	4.00	2.75	0.3750
20	12	4.50	2.75	0.3750
22	12	4.75	3.25	0.3750
24	12	5.00	3.25	0.4375
26	12	5.25	4.00	0.4375

TABLE 16-4A Aluminum Transverse-Frame Cabin-Roof Construction (Metric)

Cabin Span, m	Roof Beams O.C., mm	Beam Height, mm	Flange, mm	Thickness, mm
3.2 mm Roof Plate				
1.22	190	40	25	3.20
1.83	190	50	25	3.20
2.44	190	60	40	4.75
3.05	190	60	40	4.75
3.66	190	75	50	6.40
4 mm Roof Plate				
1.83	230	50	25	4.75
2.44	230	65	30	4.75
3.05	230	75	40	4.75
3.66	230	75	50	6.40
4.27	230	90	65	6.40
4.75 mm Roof Plate				
1.83	250	50	25	4.75
2.44	250	50	40	6.40
3.05	250	70	40	6.40
3.66	250	75	50	6.40
4.27	250	90	65	6.40
4.88	250	100	70	6.40
5.49	250	100	75	8.00
6.4 mm Roof Plate				
2.44	300	58	40	6.4
3.05	300	70	45	6.4
3.66	300	75	65	6.4
4.27	300	75	70	8.0
4.88	300	100	70	8.0
5.49	300	100	70	9.5
6.10	300	115	75	9.5
6.71	300	120	90	9.5
7.9 mm Roof Plate				
3.05	300	65	45	6.4
3.66	300	75	40	9.5

Table 16-4A Aluminum Transverse-Frame Cabin-Roof Construction (Metric) *(Cont.)*

Cabin Span, m	Roof Beams O.C., mm	Beam Height, mm	Beam Flange, mm	Beam Thickness, mm
7.9 mm Roof Plate (con't)				
4.27	300	90	45	9.5
4.88	300	75	50	9.5
5.49	300	100	70	9.5
6.10	300	115	70	9.5
6.71	300	120	80	9.5
7.32	300	130	80	11.0

Table 16-4S Steel Transverse-Frame Cabin-Roof Construction (English)

Cabin Span, ft.	Roof Beams O.C., in.	Beam Height, in.	Beam Flange, in.	Beam Thickness, in.
⅛-in. Roof Plate				
4	12	1.0	1.00	0.1250
6	12	1.5	1.00	0.1875
8	12	2.0	1.25	0.1875
10	12	2.5	1.75	0.1875
12	12	3.0	2.00	0.1875
14	12	3.0	2.25	0.2500
16	12	3.5	2.50	0.2500
10-Gauge (0.1345 in.) Roof Plate				
6	12	1.5	1.50	0.1250
8	12	2.0	1.25	0.1875
10	12	2.5	1.50	0.1875
12	12	3.0	1.75	0.1875
14	12	3.5	2.25	0.1875
16	12	3.5	2.25	0.2500
18	12	4.0	2.50	0.2500
20	12	4.3	3.00	0.2500
8-Gauge (0.1644 in.) Roof Plate				
6	14	2.00	1.00	0.1250

(continued)

TABLE 16-4S Steel Transverse-Frame Cabin-Roof Construction (English) *(Cont.)*

Cabin Span, ft.	Roof Beams O.C., in.	Beam		
		Height, in.	Flange, in.	Thickness, in.
8-Gauge (0.1644 in.) Roof Plate (con't)				
8	14	2.25	1.25	0.1875
10	14	2.50	2.00	0.1875
12	14	3.00	2.25	0.1875
14	14	3.50	2.75	0.1875
16	14	4.00	3.00	0.1875
18	14	4.00	3.00	0.2500
20	14	4.75	3.50	0.2500
7-Gauge (0.1875) 3/16-in. Roof Plate				
8	15	2.00	1.00	0.1875
10	15	2.50	1.50	0.2500
12	15	2.75	2.00	0.2500
14	15	3.00	2.50	0.2500
16	15	3.50	2.50	0.3125
18	15	4.00	2.50	0.3125
20	15	4.25	3.00	0.3125
22	15	4.50	3.50	0.3125
24	15	4.75	4.00	0.3125

TABLE 16-4S Steel Transverse-Frame Cabin-Roof Construction (Metric)

Cabin Span, m	Roof Beams O.C., mm	Beam		
		Height, mm	Flange, mm	Thickness, mm
3.2 mm Roof Plate				
1.22	300	25	25	3.20
1.83	300	40	25	4.75
2.44	300	50	30	4.75
3.05	300	65	45	4.75
3.66	300	75	50	4.75

TABLE 16-4S Steel Transverse-Frame Cabin-Roof Construction (Metric) (Cont.)

Cabin Span, ft.	Roof Beams O.C., in.	Beam Height, in.	Flange, in.	Thickness, in.
3.2 mm Roof Plate (con't)				
4.27	300	75	60	6.40
4.88	300	90	65	6.40
3.4 mm Roof Plate				
1.83	300	40	40	3.20
2.44	300	50	30	4.75
3.05	300	65	40	4.75
3.66	300	75	45	4.75
4.27	300	90	60	4.75
4.88	300	90	60	6.40
5.49	300	100	65	6.40
6.10	300	110	75	6.40
4.2 mm Roof Plate				
1.83	350	50	25	3.20
2.44	350	55	30	4.75
3.05	350	65	50	4.75
3.66	350	75	60	4.75
4.27	350	90	70	4.75
4.88	350	100	75	4.75
5.49	350	100	75	6.40
6.10	350	120	90	6.40
4.75 mm Roof Plate				
2.44	380	50.00	25.00	4.75
3.05	380	65.00	40.00	6.40
3.66	380	70.00	50.00	6.40
4.27	380	75.00	65.00	6.40
4.88	380	90.00	65.00	8.00
5.49	380	100.00	65.00	8.00
6.10	380	110.00	75.00	8.00
6.71	380	115.00	90.00	8.00
7.32	380	120.00	100.00	8.00
7.92	380	130.00	100.00	9.50

Based on Tables 16-4, if *AlumaNaught* had a trunk cabin with a roof beam 12.2 feet (3.71 m) across the top of the cabin, we could select the following:

³⁄₁₆-in. roof plate, with beams 10 in. O.C., each ¼ in. thick, with 3-in. web and 2-in. flange

or

4.75 mm roof plate, with beams 250 mm O.C., each 6.4 mm thick, with 75 mm web and 50 mm flange

If *Iron Maiden* had a roof beam 12.2 feet (3.71 m) across the top of its cabin, we could use the tables to select the following:

10-gauge (0.1345 in.) roof plate, with beams 12 in. O.C., each ³⁄₁₆ in. thick, with 3-in. web and 1¾-in. flange

or

3.4 mm roof plate, with beams 300 mm O.C., each 4.75 mm thick, with 75 mm web and 45 mm flange

FORMULA 16-5
Longitudinally Framed Cabin Roofs

Occasionally, longitudinal framing makes more sense for cabin roofs. This is most likely for larger boats with wide cabins; for example, cabins that extend the full width of the deck. In this case, the following would apply:

Cabin-Roof Plate = one standard size down from the deck plate

Cabin-Roof-Longitudinals O.C. = use Formula 15-6A or 15-6S for the roof plate used

Cabin-Roof-Longitudinals Height = deck longitudinal height

Cabin-Roof-Longitudinal Thickness = deck longitudinal thickness

Cabin-Roof-Beams O.C. = speed-adjusted hull-frame O.C.

Cabin-Roof-Beam Web Height = 0.88 × deck-beam-web height

Cabin-Roof-Beam Web Thickness = deck-beam web thickness

Cabin-Roof-Flange Width and Thickness = same as deck beams

Engine Beds and Hull Girders

ENGINE BEDS

Displacement hulls and planing hulls require different engine beds and hull-bottom girders. Longitudinally framed displacement hulls don't need the added longitudinal strength of long bottom girders. Although the engine beds can extend down to meet the interior hull plate, this isn't necessary. The engine beds of displacement craft need only be welded to a minimum of three ring frames, or one full frame beyond the forward-most and after-most engine mounts, whichever extends a greater length. Engine beds can be made in many configurations; however, this rule will use made-up T-section beds with heavy vertical plate and still heavier flange plate on top to accept the engine-mount bolts. Tripping brackets are welded between the flange and the web for added rigidity.

FORMULA 16-6A
Aluminum Engine Beds

Aluminum Engine-Bed-Flange Thickness, in. = $0.012 \times hp^{0.66}$ (English)

Aluminum Engine-Bed-Flange Thickness, in. = $0.24 \times Sn^{0.24}$ (English)

Aluminum Engine-Bed-Flange Thickness, mm = $0.305 \times hp^{0.66}$ (Metric)

Aluminum Engine-Bed-Flange Thickness, mm = $6.09 \times Sn^{0.24}$ (Metric)

Whichever is greater, and never less than $\frac{3}{8}$ in. (9.5 mm)

Aluminum Engine-Bed-Flange Width = 9.5 × thickness

Aluminum Engine-Bed-Web Thickness = 0.83 × flange thickness

Aluminum Engine-Bed-Web Height = 14 × web thickness

Aluminum Engine-Bed Trip-Bracket Thickness = same as web thickness

Aluminum Engine-Bed Number of Trip Brackets = 2 + (hp ÷ 330), but not more than 5 (round down all decimals under 0.5; round up all decimals 5.0 and higher)

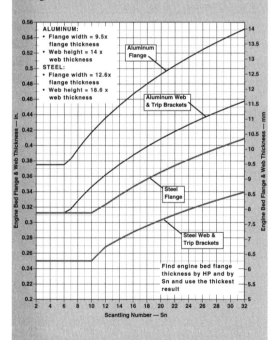

Engine-Bed-Flange and Web Thickness vs. Scantling Number, Aluminum and Steel

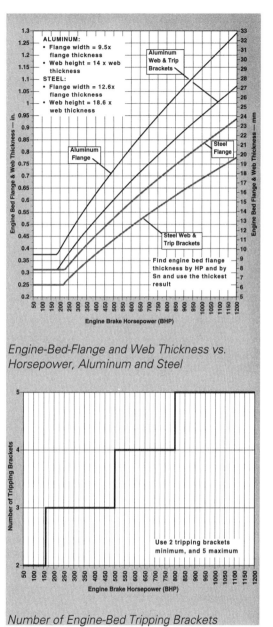

Engine-Bed-Flange and Web Thickness vs. Horsepower, Aluminum and Steel

Number of Engine-Bed Tripping Brackets

Say our reliable old *AlumaNaught* were fitted with a 300-hp (2224 kW) engine. We would then install engine beds as follows:

Aluminum Engine-Bed-Flange Thickness = 0.012 × 300 hp^0.66 = 0.52 in.

Aluminum Engine-Bed-Flange Thickness = 0.24 × 8.71^0.24 = 0.40 in.

Aluminum Engine-Bed-Flange Thickness = 0.305 × 300 hp^0.66 = 13.2 mm

Aluminum Engine-Bed-Flange Thickness = 6.09 × 8.71^0.24 = 10.2 mm

0.51 in. is greater, use ½ in.; or 13.1 is greater, use 13 mm

Aluminum Engine-Bed-Flange Width = 9.5 × 0.5 in. = 4.75 in.

Aluminum Engine-Bed-Flange Width = 9.5 × 13 mm = 123; use 125 mm

Aluminum Engine-Bed-Web Thickness = 0.83 × 0.5 in. = 0.41; use ⁷⁄₁₆ in.

Aluminum Engine-Bed-Web Thickness = 0.83 × 13.1 mm = 10.87; use 11 mm

Aluminum Engine-Bed-Web Height = 14 × 0.41 in. = 5.74; use 5¾ in.

Aluminum Engine-Bed-Web Height = 14 × 11 mm = 154; use 155 mm

Aluminum Engine-Bed Trip-Bracket Thickness = ⁷⁄₁₆ in. (11 mm)

Aluminum Engine-Bed Number of Trip Brackets = 2 + (300 hp ÷ 330) = 2.9; use 3

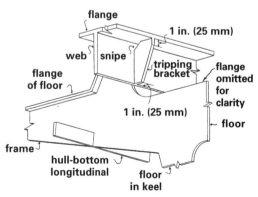

Engine-bed construction

A 35-knot *AlumaNaught* would require heavier engine beds. It would have, for example, twin 1,200-hp (895 kW) engines. In this case, the following would apply:

Aluminum Engine-Bed-Flange Thickness = 0.012 × (1,200 hp)^0.66 = 1.29.; use 1¼ in.

Aluminum Engine-Bed-Flange Thickness = 0.305 × (1,200 hp)^0.66 = 32.8; use 32 mm

Aluminum Engine-Bed-Flange Width = 9.5 × 1.25 in. = 11.8; use 12 in.

Aluminum Engine-Bed-Flange Width = 9.5 × 33 mm = 313.5; use 310 mm

Aluminum Engine-Bed-Web Thickness = 0.83 × 1.25 in. = 1.03; use 1 in.

Aluminum Engine-Bed-Web Thickness = 0.83 × 33 mm = 27.3; use 25 mm

Aluminum Engine-Bed-Web Height = 14 × 1.03 in. = 14.4; use 14½ in.

Aluminum Engine-Bed-Web Height = 14 × 27.3 mm = 382; use 380 mm

Aluminum Engine-Bed Trip Bracket Thickness = 1 in. (25 mm)

Aluminum Engine-Bed Number of Trip Brackets = 2 + (1,200 hp ÷ 330) = 5.6; 5 is maximum, use 5

FORMULA 16-6S

Steel Engine Beds

Steel Engine-Bed-Flange Thickness, in. = hp^0.66 ÷ 115 (English)

Steel Engine-Bed-Flange Thickness, in. = 0.178 × Sn^0.24 (English)

Steel Engine-Bed-Flange Thickness, mm = 0.22 × hp^0.66 (Metric)

Steel Engine-Bed-Flange Thickness, mm = 4.52 × Sn^0.24 (Metric)

Whichever is greater, and never less than ⁵⁄₁₆ in. (8 mm)

Steel Engine-Bed-Flange Width = 12.6 × thickness

Steel Engine-Bed-Web Thickness = 0.83 × flange thickness

Steel Engine-Bed-Web Height = 18.6 × web thickness

Steel Engine-Bed Trip-Bracket Thickness = same as web thickness

Steel Engine-Bed Number of Trip Brackets = 2 + (hp ÷ 330), but not more than 5 (round down all decimals under 0.5; round up all decimals 5.0 and higher)

Fit *Iron Maiden* with a 300-hp (224 kW) engine and the boat would use the following:

Steel Engine-Bed-Flange Thickness = (300 hp)$^{0.66}$ ÷ 115 = 0.375 in.

Steel Engine-Bed-Flange Thickness = 0.178 × 8.71$^{0.24}$ = 0.299 in

Steel Engine-Bed-Flange Thickness = 0.22 × (300 hp)$^{0.66}$ = 9.49 mm

Steel Engine-Bed-Flange Thickness = 4.52 × 8.71$^{0.24}$ = 7.59 mm

0.375 in. is greater, use ⅜ in.; or 9.49 is greater, use 9.5 mm

Steel Engine-Bed-Flange Width = 12.6 × 0.375 in. = 4.73; use 4¾ in.

Steel Engine-Bed-Flange Width = 12.6 × 9.5 mm = 119.7; use 120 mm

Steel Engine-Bed-Web Thickness = 0.83 × 0.375 in. = 0.31; use ⁵⁄₁₆ in.

Steel Engine-Bed-Web Thickness = 0.83 × 9.49 mm = 7.88; use 8 mm

Steel Engine-Bed-Web Height = 18.6 × 0.3125 in. = 5.81; use 5¾ in.

Steel Engine-Bed-Web Height = 18.6 × 7.87 mm = 146.3; use 150 mm

Steel Engine-Bed Trip-Bracket Thickness = ⁵⁄₁₆ in. (8 mm)

Steel Engine-Bed Number of Trip Brackets = 2 + (300 hp ÷ 330) = 2.9; use 3

HULL-BOTTOM GIRDERS

High-speed craft require additional longitudinal strength to stiffen the hull bottom against slamming impacts, and to resist the forces generated by the engine weight due to the accelerations caused by this slamming. The bottom girders should be welded to the inside of the bottom plate and extend from the transom forward to approximately Station 2, where they end aft and are welded to a convenient frame. Because these hull-bottom girders are so much deeper and stronger than the smaller hull-bottom longitudinals, you can eliminate the longitudinals where they run close to and/or cross the bottom girders.

The hull-bottom girders should run continuously over the top of the floors or frames for the minimum height given in Formulas 16-7A and S. Therefore, the hull-bottom girders' vertical webs are notched to fit over the floor's vertical plates, with an unnotched continuous portion above. This is capped with the girder's flange. The floor's transverse-running flange is cut at the girder's web, and then butted and welded to the girder web, port and starboard. Where the frames are from off-the-shelf sections, the minimum height of the girder's web is measured above the top of the floor's flange.

HULL-BOTTOM GIRDERS OR ENGINE-MOUNT FOUNDATIONS/ EXTENSIONS

The bottom girders double as extensions of the engine mounts. In other words, the engine-mount vertical web (see Formulas

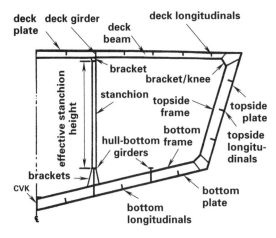

Section through hard-chine hull with stanchions

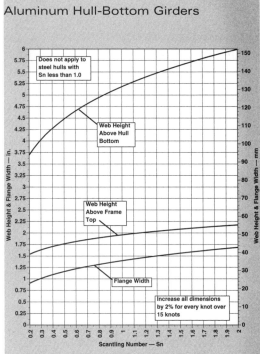

Bottom-Girder-Web Heights and Flange Width, Aluminum and Steel: Small Boats

16-6A and S) is welded into the hull-bottom girder on high-speed craft (in addition to being welded to the floors). Accordingly, at the engine mounts, you'll have the vertical web plate of the hull-bottom girder extending up from the bottom plate. Then welded on edge on top of that, you have the heavier vertical engine-mount web plate, and—on top of all—the still thicker engine-mount flange plate.

The engine's mounting-bolt centers thus govern the transverse location of the hull-bottom girders. On twin-engine vessels, there will necessarily be four hull-bottom girders. On single-engine planing vessels, four hull-bottom girders are still required. The outer girders act simply as longitudinal-strength members about midway between the inner engine-bed/hull-bottom girder and the chine (or the turn of the bilge).

Keep in mind that hull-bottom girders are intended for high-speed craft. The basic Formulas 16-7A and S are really step one in determining their scantlings; step two is to make the speed adjustments given on page 277.

Aluminum Hull-Bottom Girder-Web Thickness, in. = 0.2 × Sn^{0.24} (English)

Aluminum Hull-Bottom Girder-Web Height Minimum, in. = 5.18 × Sn^{0.21} (English)

Aluminum Hull-Bottom Girder-Web Height Above Top of Floor or Frame Minimum, in. = 1.96 × Sn^{0.15} (English)

Aluminum Hull-Bottom Girder-Flange Thickness, in. = 0.24 × Sn^{0.24} (English)

Aluminum Hull-Bottom Girder-Flange Width, in. = 1.4 × Sn^{0.27} (English)

or

Aluminum Hull-Bottom Girder-Web Thickness, mm = 5.08 × Sn^{0.24} (Metric)

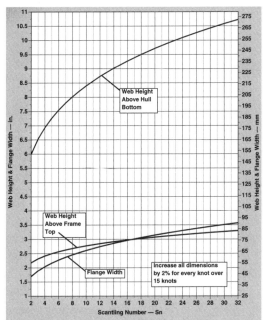

Bottom-Girder-Web Heights and Flange Width, Aluminum and Steel: Large Boats

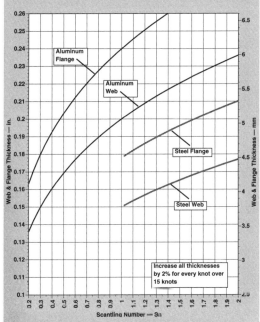

Bottom-Girder-Web and Flange Thickness, Aluminum and Steel: Small Boats

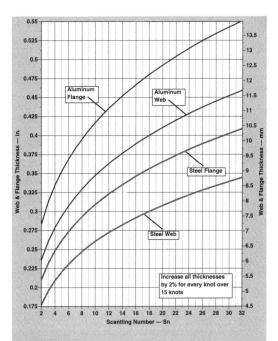

Bottom-Girder-Web and Flange Thickness, Aluminum and Steel: Large Boats

Aluminum Hull-Bottom Girder-Web Height Minimum, mm = 131.5 × $Sn^{0.21}$ (Metric)

Aluminum Hull-Bottom Girder-Web Height Above Top of Floor or Frame Minimum, mm = 49.8 × $Sn^{0.15}$ (Metric)

Aluminum Hull-Bottom Girder-Flange Thickness, mm = 6.09 × $Sn^{0.24}$ (Metric)

Aluminum Hull-Bottom Girder-Flange Width, mm = 35.5 × $Sn^{0.27}$ (Metric)

If *AlumaNaught* were a high-speed planing hull, we would install four hull-bottom girders in line with the engine mounts (which would be welded into the top of them), as follows:

Aluminum Hull-Bottom Girder-Web Thickness, in. = 0.2 × $8.71^{0.24}$ = 0.34; use ⅜ in.

Aluminum Hull-Bottom Girder-Web Height, in. = 5.18 × 8.71$^{0.21}$ = 8.16; use 8¼ in. minimum

Aluminum Hull-Bottom Girder-Web Height Above Top of Floor or Frame, in. = 1.96 × 8.71$^{0.15}$ = 2.71 in.; use 2¾ in. minimum

Aluminum Hull-Bottom Girder-Flange Thickness, in. = 0.24 × 8.71$^{0.24}$ = 0.40; use ⁷⁄₁₆ in.

Aluminum Hull-Bottom Girder-Flange Width, in. = 1.4 × 8.71$^{0.27}$ = 2.51; use 2½ in.

or

Aluminum Hull-Bottom Girder-Web Thickness, mm = 5.08 × 8.71$^{0.24}$ = 8.54; use 8.5 mm

Aluminum Hull-Bottom Girder-Web Height, mm = 131.5 × 8.71$^{0.21}$ = 207.1; use 210 mm minimum

Aluminum Hull-Bottom Girder-Web Height Above Top of Floor or Frame, mm = 49.8 × 8.71$^{0.15}$ = 68.9; use 70 mm

Aluminum Hull-Bottom Girder-Flange Thickness, mm = 6.09 × 8.71$^{0.24}$ = 10.2; use 11 mm

Aluminum Hull-Bottom Girder-Flange Width, mm = 35.5 × 8.71$^{0.27}$ = 63.6; use 64 mm

FORMULA 16-7S

Steel Hull-Bottom Girders

Steel Hull-Bottom Girder-Web Thickness, in. = 0.15 × Sn$^{0.24}$ (English)

Steel Hull-Bottom Girder-Web Height Minimum, in. = 5.18 × Sn$^{0.21}$ (English)

Steel Hull-Bottom Girder-Web Height Above Top of Floor or Frame Minimum, in. = 1.96 × Sn$^{0.15}$ (English)

Steel Hull-Bottom Girder-Flange Thickness, in. = 0.178 × Sn$^{0.24}$ (English)

Steel Hull-Bottom Girder-Flange Width, in. = 1.4 × Sn$^{0.27}$ (English)

or

Steel Hull-Bottom Girder-Web Thickness, mm = 3.81 × Sn$^{0.24}$ (Metric)

Steel Hull-Bottom Girder-Web Height Minimum, mm = 131.5 × Sn$^{0.21}$ (Metric)

Steel Hull-Bottom Girder-Web Height Above Top of Floor or Frame Minimum, mm = 49.7 × Sn$^{0.15}$ (Metric)

Steel Hull-Bottom Girder-Flange Thickness, mm = 4.52 × Sn$^{0.24}$ (Metric)

Steel Hull-Bottom Girder-Flange Width, mm = 35.5 × Sn$^{0.27}$ (Metric)

Our steel *Iron Maiden* would be unusual, indeed, if it could make high-planing speeds; but this can be done on steel hulls. The hull-bottom girders would then be

Steel Hull-Bottom Girder-Web Thickness, in. = 0.15 × 8.71$^{0.24}$ = 0.252; use ¼ in.

Steel Hull-Bottom Girder-Web Height Minimum, in. = 5.18 × 8.71$^{0.21}$ = 8.16; use 8 ¼ in. minimum

Steel Hull-Bottom Girder-Web Height Above Top of Floor or Frame Minimum, in. = 1.96 × 8.71$^{0.15}$ = 2.71; use 2¾ in. minimum

Steel Hull-Bottom Girder-Flange Thickness, in. = 0.178 × 8.71$^{0.24}$ = 0.299; use ⁵⁄₁₆ in.

Steel Hull-Bottom Girder-Flange Width, in. = 1.4 × 8.71$^{0.27}$ = 2.51; use 2½ in.

or

Steel Hull-Bottom Girder-Web Thickness, mm = 3.81 × 8.71$^{0.24}$ = 6.4 mm

Steel Hull-Bottom Girder-Web Height Minimum, mm = 131.5 × 8.71^0.21 = 207.1; use 210 mm minimum

Steel Hull-Bottom Girder-Web Height Above Top of Floor or Frame Minimum, mm = 49.7 × 8.71^0.15 = 68.7; use 70 mm

Steel Hull-Bottom Girder-Flange Thickness, mm = 4.52 × 8.71^0.24 = 7.59; use 8 mm

Steel Hull-Bottom Girder-Flange Width, mm = 35.5 × 8.71^0.27 = 63.6; use 64 mm

SPEED ADJUSTMENT FOR HULL-BOTTOM GIRDERS

Increase hull-bottom girder-web height by 2 percent for every knot over 15 knots. Increase hull-bottom girder-web thickness by 2 percent for every knot over 15 knots. Increase hull-bottom girder-web height above top of floor or frame by 2 percent for every knot over 15 knots.

Increase hull-bottom girder-flange width by 2 percent for every knot over 15 knots. Increase hull-bottom girder-flange thickness by 2 percent for every knot over 15 knots.

NOTE: If the speed-adjusted hull-bottom girder flange thickness is greater than the engine-mount thickness based on horsepower (see Formulas 16-6A and S), use the speed-adjusted flange thickness for the engine mount as well.

Returning to our 35-knot *AlumaNaught*, its hull-bottom girders would be adjusted to the following:

35 knots – 20 knots = 15 knots, then 15 knots × 2% per knot = 30%

Hull-Bottom Girder-Web Height = 1.30 × 8.16 in. = 10.6; use 10⅝ in.

Hull-Bottom-Web Thickness – 1.30 × 0.33 in. = 0.429; use ⁷⁄₁₆ in.

Hull-Bottom Girder-Web Height Above Top of Floor = 1.30 × 2.71 in. = 3.52; use 3½ in.

Hull-Bottom Girder-Flange Width = 1.30 × 2.51 in. = 3.26; use 3¼ in.

Hull-Bottom Girder-Flange Thickness = 1.30 × 0.40 in. = 0.52; use ½ in.

or

35 knots – 20 knots = 15 knots, then 15 knots × 2% per knot = 30%

Hull-Bottom Girder-Web Height = 1.30 × 207.1 mm = 269.2; use 270 mm

Hull-Bottom-Web Thickness = 1.30 × 8.54 mm = 11.1; use 11 mm

Hull-Bottom Girder-Web Height Above Top of Floor = 1.30 × 68.9 mm = 89.5; use 90 mm

Hull-Bottom Girder-Flange Width = 1.30 × 63.6 mm = 82.6; use 85 mm

Hull-Bottom Girder-Flange Thickness = 1.30 × 10.2 mm = 13.2; use 13 mm

For the remarkably fast (for steel) 35-knot *Iron Maiden*, hull-bottom girders would be adjusted to the following:

35 knots – 20 knots = 15 knots, then 15 knots × 2% per knot = 30%

Hull-Bottom Girder-Web Height = 1.30 × 8.16 in. = 10.6; use 10⅝ in.

Hull-Bottom-Web Thickness = 1.30 × 0.524 in. = 0.33; use ⅜ in.

Hull-Bottom Girder-Web Height Above Top of Floor = 1.30 × 2.71 in. = 3.52; use 3½ in.

Hull-Bottom Girder-Flange Width = 1.30 × 2.51 in. = 3.26; use 3¼ in.

Hull Bottom Girder-Flange Thickness = 1.30 × 0.299 in. = 0.388; use ⅜ in.

or

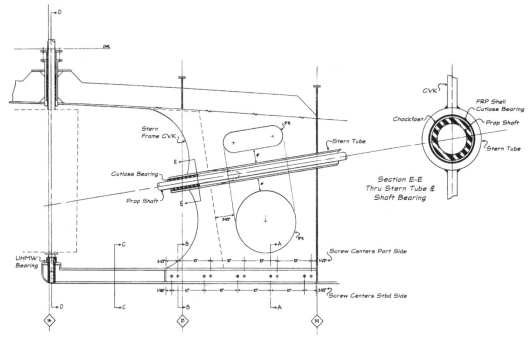

Stern tube and cutless bearing

35 knots – 20 knots = 15 knots, then 15 knots × 2% per knot = 30%

Hull-Bottom Girder-Web Height = 1.30 × 6.4 mm = 8.32; use 9 mm

Hull-Bottom Girder-Web Height Above Top of Floor = 1.30 × 68.9 mm = 89.5; use 90 mm

Hull-Bottom Girder-Flange Width = 1.30 × 63.6 mm = 82.6; use 85 mm

Hull-Bottom Girder-Flange Thickness = 1.30 × 7.59 mm = 9.86; use 10 mm

FORMULA 16-8
Stern Tube

Traditional commercial practice has been to use an exceptionally heavy-wall tube for the stern bearing and line-bore it exactingly for the cutless bearing. My opinion is that this practice is obsolete. It's vastly easier to use Schedule 80 pipe (or tube of roughly equivalent thickness) that has an inside diameter (I.D.) slightly larger that the outside diameter (O.D.) of the bearing housing. (Schedule 80 pipe is also known as "heavy-wall" or "extra-strong" pipe.) The bearing is slipped around the shaft and into the stern tube. Inside the boat, the shaft is run through all intermediate bearings and bolted to the engine coupling. The bearing itself is then set in Chockfast in the end of the stern tube, which—with the small play from the slightly oversize I.D.—takes the proper angle, ensuring perfect alignment when the Chockfast sets. All this, without the lengthy process of precise line-boring. Remember to provide water input to lubricate the bearing. Most commonly, this is accomplished with a water-injected stuffing box.

Deck Girders, Stanchions, and Brackets

DECK GIRDERS

Deck girders strengthen the deck in much the same way that hull-bottom girders reinforce the hull bottom. Such reinforcement is only required on larger vessels or boats that will carry heavy deck loads.

Vessels with Sns over 12 that run at speeds over 20 knots and that carry substantial cargoes or other loads on deck should install two girders each about a third of the way inboard from the maximum beam, and running straight fore-n-aft. All vessels with Sns between 10 and 15 should considered for installation of at least one girder on the centerline of wide decks. Yachts with Sns under 15 do not require deck girders, nor do high-speed vessels that don't carry deck cargo (with Sns less than 12). Boats with Sns under 12 require deck girders only if they are workboats that will routinely haul heavy loads on deck.

It is usually most convenient to adjust the athwartships location of a pair of deck girders to form the sides of cargo hatches and the deckhouse. Because stanchions are used to support the deck girder, it is sometimes more convenient to locate the deck girder directly over the hull-bottom girders, so that the stanchions can land on these.

FORMULA 16-9A
Aluminum Deck Girders

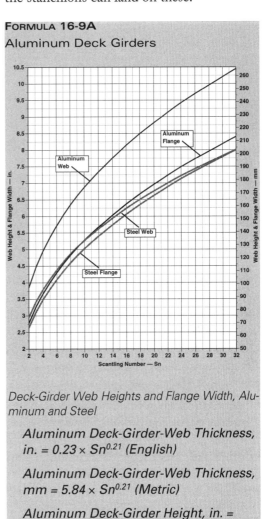

Deck-Girder Web Heights and Flange Width, Aluminum and Steel

Aluminum Deck-Girder-Web Thickness, in. = 0.23 × Sn$^{0.21}$ (English)

Aluminum Deck-Girder-Web Thickness, mm = 5.84 × Sn$^{0.21}$ (Metric)

Aluminum Deck-Girder Height, in. = 3 × Sn$^{0.36}$ (English)

Aluminum Deck-Girder Height, mm = 76.2 × Sn$^{0.36}$ (Metric)

(continued)

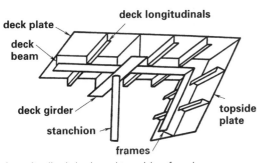

Longitudinal deck and topsides framing

Aluminum Deck-Girder-Flange Thickness = 1.2 × web thickness

Aluminum Deck-Girder-Flange Width, in. = 2.1 × $Sn^{0.4}$ (English)

Aluminum Deck-Girder-Flange Width, mm = 53.34 × $Sn^{0.4}$ (Metric)

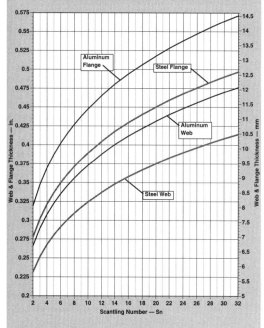

Deck-Girder-Web and Flange Thickness, Aluminum and Steel

At 64 feet (19.5 m) and with an Sn of 8.71, *AlumaNaught* is not large enough to require deck girders for most service. If, however, *AlumaNaught* were a crewboat that would be operating at speeds over 20 knots offshore and carrying deck cargo, that would be a different story. In that case, our boat would require

Aluminum Deck-Girder-Web Thickness = 0.23 × $8.71^{0.21}$ = 0.36; use ⅜ in.

Aluminum Deck-Girder-Web Thickness = 5.84 × $8.71^{0.21}$ = 9.2; use 9.5 mm

Aluminum Deck-Girder Height = 3 × $8.71^{0.36}$ = 6.53; use 6½ in.

Aluminum Deck-Girder Height = 76.2 × $8.71^{0.36}$ = 166; use 170 mm

Aluminum Deck-Girder-Flange Thickness = 1.2 × 0.36 in. = 0.42; use 7/16 in.

Aluminum Deck-Girder-Flange Thickness = 1.2 × 9.2 mm = 11.04; use 11 mm

Aluminum Deck-Girder-Flange Width = 2.1 × $8.71^{0.4}$ = 4.99; use 5 in.

Aluminum Deck-Girder-Flange Width = 53.34 × $8.71^{0.4}$ = 126.7; use 125 mm

FORMULA 16-9S

Steel Deck Girders

Steel Deck-Girder-Web Thickness, in. = 0.2 × $Sn^{0.21}$ (English)

Steel Deck-Girder-Web Thickness, mm = 5.08 × $Sn^{0.21}$ (Metric)

Steel Deck-Girder Height, in. = 2.3 × $Sn^{0.36}$ (English)

Steel Deck-Girder Height, mm = 58.42 × $Sn^{0.36}$ (Metric)

Steel Deck-Girder-Flange Thickness = 1.2 × web thickness

Steel Deck-Girder-Flange Width, in. = 2.0 × $Sn^{0.4}$ (English)

Steel Deck-Girder-Flange Width, mm = 50.8 × $Sn^{0.4}$ (Metric)

A steel crewboat *Iron Maiden* would then have

Steel Deck-Girder-Web Thickness = 0.2 × $8.71^{0.21}$ = 0.31; use 5/16 in.

Steel Deck-Girder-Web Thickness = 5.08 × $8.71^{0.21}$ = 8.0 mm

Steel Deck-Girder Height = 2.3 × $8.71^{0.36}$ = 5.0 in.

*Steel Deck-Girder Height = 58.42 × 8.71^0.36 =
127.3; use 130 mm*

*Steel Deck-Girder-Flange Thickness =
1.2 × 0.31 in. = 0.37; use ⅜ in.*

*Steel Deck-Girder-Flange Thickness =
1.2 × 8.0 mm = 9.6; use 10 mm*

*Steel Deck-Girder-Flange Width =
2.0 × 8.71^0.4 = 4.75; use 4¾ in.*

*Steel Deck-Girder-Flange Width =
50.8 × 8.71^0.4 = 120.4; use 120 mm*

STANCHIONS

The deck girders are supported underneath with stanchions—usually of pipe—that extend down to the bottom framing. All stanchions *must* land on a frame or hull-bottom girder; they can *never* run down and weld directly to the hull plate. Because of this, stanchions pose a problem for interior and machinery layout. If the deck girder doesn't lie directly above the hull-bottom girder, then the stanchions can only be located at a frame. In many cases, this may conflict with the interior arrangement and can be the source of much juggling.

If the deck girders, however, are immediately above the hull-bottom girders, then you can move the stanchions fore-n-aft along the length of the girders to any convenient location along their length. However, deck girders located over the hull-bottom girders may not be ideal for the deck openings and superstructure framing. There's no right or wrong here, simply a set of trade-offs for each vessel.

Solving Stanchion Location Problems

Smaller displacement vessels that carry heavy deck loads may require deck girders but no hull-bottom girders. Again, you're forced to

locate the stanchions on the frames. However, you can simply add hull-bottom girders for convenience. In fact, you can use a partial hull-bottom girder under the stanchions, which should extend between three frames. Its dimensions under the stanchion should be the full height of a hull-bottom girder (see Formulas 16-7A and S); however, the web height can be tapered down to the same height as the bottom frame's web, at the fore-n-aft ends.

In circumstances where there is no way to locate a stanchion over either a hull-bottom girder or a frame (even on a boat's full hull-bottom girders), this same partial girder approach can be used—adding an additional partial girder where it is required for that problem stanchion.

Stanchion Strength Governed by Moment of Inertia

Pipes come in a wide variety of diameters and wall thicknesses. When used as stanchions, however, what we're interested in is the pipe's ability to resist compression loads. Essentially, the deck load above the stanchions presses down on the stanchion, and—if it's not strong enough—it will bend over or buckle. The way engineers determine a member's resistance to buckling is by a section property called *moment of inertia* or *I*. To select the proper stanchions for your *AlumaNaught* or *Iron Maiden*, find the required moment of inertia from the formula, and then select a suitable pipe from the table in appendix 2 or from similar tables found in engineering handbooks and many manufacturers' brochures.

Moment of inertia is in units of in.[4] or cm[4] (i.e., inches to the fourth power or centimeters to the fourth power). To convert in.[4]

to cm⁴, multiply in.⁴ by 41.62. To convert cm⁴ to in.⁴, divide cm⁴ by 41.62.

Stanchions Don't Have to Be Pipe

You're not limited to pipe for stanchions—although it is the most common and usually the most convenient. You can select any shape that provides the required moment of inertia (I). Keep in mind, though, that pipes—being circles—are perfectly symmetrical. An H-beam or an angle, in contrast, will have different moments of inertia relative to different axes. Using such asymmetrical shapes, be certain that its *smallest* I is equal to or greater than the I from the formula.

Brackets Strengthen Stanchions

Most stanchions are reinforced at their top and at their base with brackets welded to the girders and frames. The stanchion rule assumes brackets top and bottom. If no brackets are used, the stanchion's I should be increased by 15 percent. Formulas 16-10A and S are based on a uniform deck loading of 300 lb./sq. ft. (1,465 kg/m²).

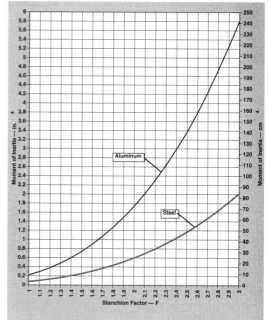

Stanchion Moment of Inertia, Aluminum and Steel

FORMULA 16-10A

Aluminum Stanchions (with Brackets)

Aluminum Stanchion I, in.⁴ = 0.22 × F²·⁹⁸ (English)

Aluminum Stanchion I, cm⁴ = 9.15 × F²·⁹⁸ (Metric)

Where

F = [(depth of hull, ft.)² × beam, ft. × stanchion spacing, ft.] ⁰·³⁴ ÷ 10 (English)

or

F = [(depth of hull, m/3.28)² × beam, m/3.28 × stanchion spacing, m/3.28]⁰·³⁴ × 10 (Metric)

Stanchions are usually spaced about every second or third ring frame. Say our 35-knot *AlumaNaught*'s stanchions are spaced every two ring frames. They are then 2 × 36 inches (6 ft.) or 182.9 centimeters (1.83 m) apart. Our boat's stanchions would be as follows:

$$F = [(8.33 \text{ ft. depth of hull})^2 \times 17.67 \text{ ft. beam} \times 6.0 \text{ ft. stanchion spacing, ft.}]^{0.34} \div 10 = 1.946$$

$$\text{Aluminum I} = 0.22 \times 1.946^{2.98} = 1.599 \text{ in.}^4$$

$$\text{Aluminum I} = 9.15 \times 1.946^{2.98} = 66.53 \text{ cm}^4$$

Referring to the pipe table (see appendix 2), we find that a 2½-in. nominal Schedule 80 pipe (2.875-in. O.D., 0.276-in. wall) has a moment of inertia of 1.92 in.⁴ (79.9 cm⁴), which will do nicely.

Steel Stanchions (with Brackets)

Steel Stanchion I, in.^{4} = F^3 ÷ 13.4 (English)

Steel Stanchion I, cm^4 = 3.1 × F^3 (Metric)

Where

F = [(depth of hull, ft.)^2 × beam, ft. × stanchion spacing, ft.]$^{0.34}$ ÷ 10 (English)

or

F = [(depth of hull, m/3.28)^2 × beam, m/3.28 × stanchion spacing, m/3.28]$^{0.34}$ × 10 (Metric)

If our displacement speed steel *Iron Maiden*'s stanchions are spaced every two ring frames, they are then 2 × 46 inches (7.667 feet) or 233.7 centimeters (2.33 m) apart. Its stanchions would be

F = [(8.33 ft. depth of hull)^2 × 17.67 ft. beam × 7.667 ft. stanchion spacing, ft.]$^{0.34}$ ÷ 10 = 2.12

Steel Stanchion I = 2.12^3 ÷ 13.4 = 0.71 in.^{4}

Steel Stanchion I = 3.1 × 2.12^3 = 29.54 cm^4

Referring to the pipe table (see appendix 2), we find that a 1^{1}/$_2$-inch nominal Schedule 80 pipe (2.375-in. O.D., 0.218-in. wall) has a moment of inertia of 0.868 in.^{4} (36.12 cm^4), which will fill the bill.

BRACKETS

Brackets are angles welded (like knees) to support a structural component. We've already defined tripping brackets welded under the engine mounts and the knees (which are really brackets) at the joint between the topsides frames and the deck beams.

Brackets are also used to reinforce other miscellaneous structures, like generator mounts and stanchions. Brackets can be defined by the length of their legs, which form approximate right triangles—although other convenient proportions are fine. On stanchions, the bracket legs are usually about 1.25 to 1.50 times the stanchion diameter.

Brackets can be flanged or flat. Flanged brackets have a bent-over angle or a welded-on T on their hypotenuse (i.e., long edge). Flanged brackets are suited to heavy-load applications.

TABLE 16-11 Bracket Dimensions (English)

Hypotenuse, in.	Aluminum			Steel		
	Unflanged Thickness, in.	Flanged Thickness, in.	Flange Width, in.	Unflanged Thickness, in.	Flanged Thickness, in.	Flange Width, in.
Under 12	0.2500	0.1875	0.0	0.1875	0.1644	0.0
12 to 18	0.3125	0.2500	1.5	0.2500	0.1875	1.5
18 to 26	0.4375	0.3125	2.0	0.3125	0.2500	2.0
20 to 30	0.5000	0.4375	2.5	0.3750	0.3125	2.5
36 to 54	0.5625	0.5000	3.0	0.4375	0.3750	3.0

TABLE 16-11 Bracket Dimensions (Metric)

Hypotenuse, mm	Aluminum			Steel		
	Unflanged Thickness, mm	Flanged Thickness, mm	Flange Width, mm	Unflanged Thickness, mm	Flanged Thickness, mm	Flange Width, mm
Under 300	6.40	4.75	0	4.75	4.20	0
300 to 450	7.90	6.40	40	6.40	4.75	40
450 to 660	11.25	7.90	50	7.90	6.40	50
660 to 900	13.00	11.25	65	9.50	7.90	65
900 to 1400	14.25	13.00	75	11.25	9.50	75

Unless otherwise specified in a specific rule, bracket thickness can be selected based on hypotenuse length.

The hypotenuse of a triangle is found as follows:

$$hypotenuse = (a^2 + b^2)^{0.5} \ or \ \sqrt{a^2 + b^2}$$

Where

a and b are the length of each leg

In the case of *AlumaNaught*, we found 2.875-inch O.D. (73 mm) pipe stanchions; 1.25 × 2.75 inches = 3.59-inch leg (1.25 × 73 mm = 91.2 mm). It might be that there is only room for a 3-inch-high (75 mm) face along the stanchion, without projecting through the sole. Therefore, we choose a 3-inch-high bracket with a 4-inch base (75 × 100 mm).

The hypotenuse is then

$$(3^2 + 4^2)^{0.5} = 5 \ in.$$

and reading from Table 16-11, we see that a $^1/_4$-inch-thick unflanged aluminum bracket would do.

Or

$$(75^2 + 100^2)^{0.5} = 125 \ mm$$

and reading from Table 16-11, we see that a 6.4-mm-thick unflanged aluminum bracket would do.

The same procedure would be used for the steel stanchion brackets on *Iron Maiden*.

MAST STEPS

The compression loads on masts are immense. On a 52-footer (15.8 m) I have under construction at the moment, the compression load calculated to 21 tons—close to the displacement of the boat. Mast steps must be strong.

The mast step in this rule is a T with a heavy vertical web and flange on top. Usually, the web is a vertical extension of the CVK. This is ideal but not required. If the web is an extension of the CVK, then the mast step must extend fore-n-aft at least between two frames. If the mast step is not an extension of the CVK, then it must extend for at least three frames. (The mizzenmast step can extend to only two frames in either case.)

The mast step is braced underneath with tripping brackets. Be sure to check that the width of the mast section you will actually install against the calculated mast-step width.

Aluminum Mast Steps

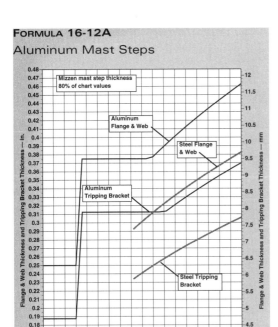

Mast-Step Web and Flange Thickness and Tripping-Bracket Thickness, Aluminum and Steel: Small Boats

Aluminum Mast-Step Web and Flange Thickness = CVK thickness (see Formula 15-13A), but not less than ⅜ in. (9.5 mm) (on boats with Sns less than 0.50, minimum thickness is ¼ in. [6.4 mm])

Aluminum Mast-Step Web and Flange Width and Height = 18 × thickness (on boats with Sns less than 0.50, width may be just 20 percent wider than the mast width)

Number of Tripping Brackets = 2.6 × (thickness, in.)^{0.72} (English)

Number of Tripping Brackets = 0.25 × (thickness, mm)^{0.72} (Metric)

Aluminum Tripping-Bracket Thickness = 0.8 × flange thickness, but not less than ⁵⁄₁₆ in.(8 mm)

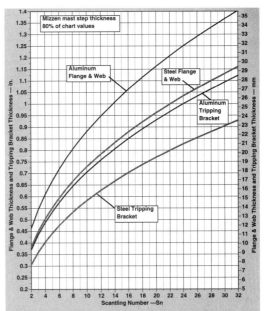

Mast-Step Web and Flange Thickness and Tripping-Bracket Thickness, Aluminum and Steel: Large Boats

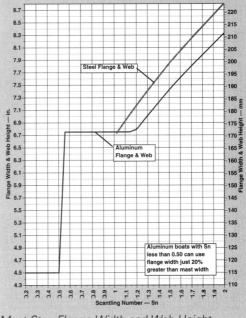

Mast-Step Flange Width and Web Height, Aluminum and Steel: Small Boats

(continued)

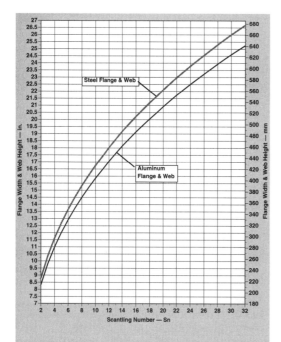

Mast-Step Flange Width and Web Height, Aluminum and Steel: Large Boats

For aluminum mizzenmast step, use 80 percent of this flange thickness and proportion everything else according to the reduced thickness. Schooner foremast steps are the same as mainmast steps.

AlumaNaught's mainmast step would then be as follows:

Aluminum Mast-Step Web and Flange Thickness = 7/8 in. (22 mm)

Aluminum Mast-Step Web and Flange Width and Height = 15 3/4 in. (400 mm)

Number of Tripping Brackets = 2.6 × (0.875 in.)^0.72 = 2.36; use two—one just forward and one just aft of the mast

Number of Tripping Brackets = 0.25 × (22 mm)^0.72 = 2.31; use two—one just forward and one just aft of the mast

Aluminum Tripping-Bracket Thickness = 0.8 × 0.875 in. = 0.7; use 3/4 in.

Aluminum Tripping-Bracket Thickness = 0.8 × 22 mm = 17.6; use 17.5 mm

FORMULA 16-12S

Steel Mast Steps

Steel Mast-Step Web and Flange Thickness = 0.29 × Sn^0.4 (English), but not less than 1/4 in.

Steel Mast-Step Web and Flange Thickness = 7.36 × Sn^0.4 (Metric), but not less than 6.4 mm

Steel Mast-Step Web and Flange Width and Height = 23 × thickness

Number of Tripping Brackets = 2.94 × (thickness, in.)^0.72 (English)

Number of Tripping Brackets = 0.28 × (thickness, mm)^0.72 (Metric)

Steel Tripping-Bracket Thickness = 0.8 × flange thickness, but not less than 3/16 in. (4.75 mm)

For steel mizzenmast steps, use 80 percent of this flange thickness and proportion everything else according to the reduced thickness. Schooner foremast steps are the same as mainmast steps. Fitting a mainmast step into *Iron Maiden* would give us the following:

Steel Mast-Step Web and Flange Thickness = 0.29 × 8.71^0.4 = 0.69; use 5/8 in.

Steel Mast-Step Web and Flange Thickness = 7.36 × 8.71^0.4 = 17.49; use 17.5 mm

Steel Mast-Step Web and Flange Width and Height = 23 × 0.68 in. = 14.96; use 15 in.

Steel Mast-Step Web and Flange Width and Height = 23 × 17.5 mm = 402.5; use 400 mm

Number of Tripping Brackets = 2.94 × (0.68 in.)$^{0.72}$ = 2.22: use two—one just forward and one just aft of the mast

Number of Tripping Brackets = 0.28 × (17.5 mm)$^{0.72}$ = 2.19; use two—one just forward and one just aft of the mast

Steel Tripping-Bracket Thickness = 0.8 × 0.68 in. = 0.54; use ½ in.

Steel Tripping-Bracket Thickness = 0.8 × 17.49 mm = 13.99; use 14 mm

MAST PARTNERS

It is just as important to increase the strength of the deck in the way of the mast on a metal boat as it is on an FRP or wood vessel. A doubler plate should surround the mast hole under the deck. The doubler should extend fore-n-aft to the closest deck beams. A mast collar or ring surrounds the opening, and the partners are usually diagonal stiffeners welded to the underside of the deck between the collar and the deck beams, fore-n-aft.

FORMULA 16-13A

Aluminum Mast Partners

Doubler-Plate Thickness = deck thickness (see Formula 15-4A)

Doubler Width = 2.2 × mast width

Mast-Collar-Ring Thickness = deck plate plus ⅛ in. (3.2 mm)

Mast-Collar-Ring Height = 16 × thickness

Mast Partners = frames the same as the deck beams running diagonally from the mast collar to the nearest deck beams, fore-n-aft, port and starboard

---

AlumaNaught's mast partners are as follows:

Doubler-Plate Thickness = ³⁄₁₆ in. (5.55 mm)

Doubler Width = 2.2 × mast width

Mast Collar-Ring Thickness = ⁵⁄₁₆ in. (8.5 mm)

Mast Collar-Ring Height = 5 in. (135 mm)

Mast Partners = frames the same as the deck beams running diagonally from the mast collar to the nearest deck beams, fore-n-aft, port and starboard

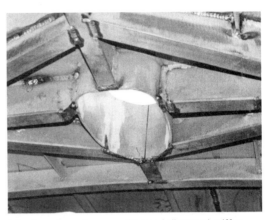

Mast-partner ring or collar and diagonal stiffeners. (Courtesy Topper Hermanson Boatbuilding)

FORMULA 16-13S

Steel Mast Partners

Doubler-Plate Thickness = deck thickness (see Formula 15-4S)

Doubler Width = 2.2 × mast width

Mast-Collar-Ring Thickness = deck plate plus ¹⁄₁₆ in. (1.6 mm)

Mast-Collar-Ring Height = 21 × thickness

Mast Partners = frames the same as the deck beams running diagonally from the mast collar to the nearest deck beams, fore-n-aft, port and starboard

---

Reinforcement at Imagine's stabilizer fin shaft penetrations. Note the doubler plate on the hull shell and the diagonal bracing to the frames.

Imagine's stabilizers installed.

Fitting partners in *Iron Maiden*, we would find

Doubler-Plate Thickness = Cor-Ten 8-gauge (0.1664 in.) (4 mm)

Doubler Width = 2.2 × mast width

Mast-Collar-Ring Thickness = ¼ in. (5.55 mm)

Mast-Collar-Ring Height = 5¼ in. (120 mm)

Mast Partners = frames the same as the deck beams running diagonally from the mast collar to the nearest deck beams, fore-n-aft, port and starboard

FORMULA 16-14
Doubler Plates and Insert Plates

Doubler plates should be installed under winch and windlass bases and at mooring cleats, chocks, and other high-load hardware. Underwater, insert plates should be installed at shaft-log penetrations, sea chests, and the like.

Doubler-Plate Thickness = shell plate thickness

Insert-Plate Thickness = 2 × shell plate thickness

The ends and corners of the doubler plate should be very well radiused, or the ends should be run into the nearest frames.

SEVENTEEN

Aluminum and Steel Alternate Construction Methods

*C*hapters 15 and 16 illustrate how to calculate scantlings for longitudinally framed boats—boats with widely spaced transverse ring frames and closely spaced longitudinals. In chapter 13, however, we saw that there are other standard framing approaches: transverse framing with longitudinals and transverse framing with no longitudinals at all.

Longitudinal Scantling Rules Form the Basis for Alternate Rules

We examine these alternatives—and some lightweight construction methods—in this chapter. Keep in mind throughout that the longitudinal scantling rules form the basis for all the variants that follow. You need to fully understand the longitudinal scantlings before you can use these transverse scantlings. Indeed, unless a change is specifically mentioned, the transverse or lightweight rules simply use the scantlings from the longitudinal rules. For example, the transverse-framing rules don't mention the CVK or the shell-

plating; accordingly, they are the same as specified for the longitudinal rule.

Aluminum Transverse Framing

OPTIONAL LONGITUDINALS

Because aluminum plate is usually between 1.25 and 1.5 times thicker than steel, it has greater stiffness for the same or less weight. As a result, the transverse-frame aluminum scantlings don't require longitudinal framing for strength. You can construct a boat with or without the longitudinals described.

Then why include longitudinals at all? The answer is weld distortion. Longitudinals—properly installed and welded—are the most effective method of reducing this problem. Some builders also find it is easier to fit plate on complex-curved hull surfaces to have both the closely spaced transverse frames and the closely spaced longitudinals. For this reason, most round-bilge yachts—built with closely spaced transverse frames—use the optional longitudinals. On workboats—where fairness is less of a consideration—it's somewhat more common to omit them.

FORMULA 17-1

Aluminum Transverse Frame Space O.C.

Transverse Bottom Frames O.C., in. =
$10.2 \times Sn^{0.24}$ *(English)*

Transverse Bottom Frames O.C., mm =
$259 \times Sn^{0.24}$ *(Metric)*

Decrease frame O.C. by 1% for every knot over 15 knots.

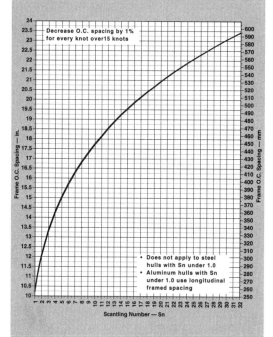

Frame O.C. Spacing in Transversely Framed Hulls, Aluminum and Steel

Hulls with Sns less than 1.0 should be built with longitudinal framing and frame spacing.

FORMULA 17-2

Aluminum Transverse Bottom-Frame Dimensions

Bottom-Frame-Web Thickness, in. =
$0.23 \times Sn^{0.21}$ *(English)*

Bottom-Frame-Web Thickness, mm =
$5.84 \times Sn^{0.21}$ *(Metric)*

Bottom-Frame-Web Height, in. =
$1.23 \times Sn^{0.46}$ *(English)*

Bottom-Frame-Web Height, mm =
$31.24 \times Sn^{0.46}$ *(Metric)*

Bottom-Frame-Flange Thickness =
$1.25 \times$ *web thickness*

Bottom-Frame-Flange Width, in. =
$0.92 \times Sn^{0.46}$ *(English)*

Bottom-Frame-Flange Width, mm =
$23.36 \times Sn^{0.46}$ *(Metric)*

Increase web height by 1% for every knot over 20 knots.

Increase flange width by 1% for every knot over 15 knots.

Increase flange thickness by 1% for every knot over 15 knots.

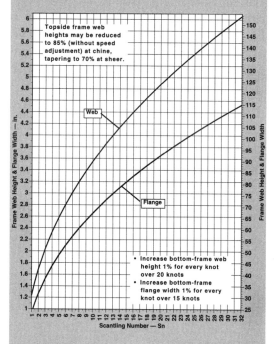

Frame-Web Heights and Flange Widths in Aluminum Transversely Framed Hulls

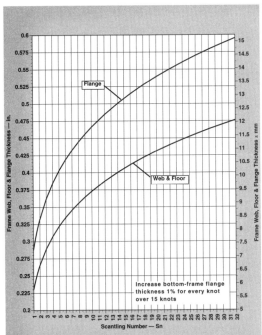

Frame, Deck-Beam and Cabin-Side Frame: Web, Floor, and Flange Thicknesses in Aluminum Transversely Framed Hulls

FORMULA 17-3

Aluminum Transverse Topsides-Frame Dimensions

Bottom frames can extend—unchanged in dimensions—from the bottom, up along the topsides, to the sheer. However, you can elect to save weight by reducing the web heights in the topsides, as follows:

Topsides-Frame-Web Height at Chine or Bilge = 0.85 × bottom web height (not speed-adjusted)

Topsides-Frame-Web Height at Sheer = 0.70 × bottom web height (not speed-adjusted)

On sailboats—at the masts and shroud chainplates—the topside frames should be the same dimensions as the hull-bottom frame

(not the reduced topsides-frame dimensions). In addition, on sailing vessels with Sns greater than 3, the web thickness should be increased to the next standard plate size up from the reduced topsides-frame-web thickness.

FORMULA 17-4

Aluminum Transverse Deck-Beam Dimensions

Deck-Beam-Web Thickness, in. = same as bottom and topsides web

Deck-Beam-Web Height, in. = 1.05 × $Sn^{0.36}$ (English)

Deck-Beam-Web Height, mm = 26.67 × $Sn^{0.36}$ (Metric)

Deck-Beam-Flange Thickness = 1.25 × web thickness

Deck-Beam-Flange Width = 0.75 × web height

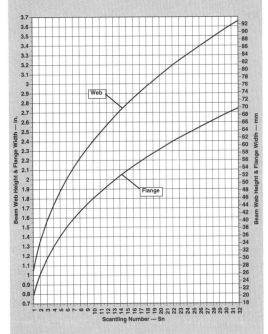

Deck-Beam-Web Heights and Flange Widths in Aluminum Transversely Framed Hulls

FORMULA 17-5

Aluminum Transverse-Framing Optional Longitudinals

Longitudinal-Stiffener-Spacing O.C., in. = 4 + (plate thickness, in. × 32) (English)

Aluminum Longitudinal-Stiffener-Spacing O.C., mm = 101.6 + (plate thickness, mm × 32) (Metric) (same as in Formula 15-6A)

Longitudinal Height = 0.45 × frame or beam-web height

Longitudinal Thickness = plate thickness or one standard size thicker

On vessels with Sns less than 2.5, longitudinals are not usually used.

FORMULA 17-6

Aluminum Transverse-Framed Cabin-Side Frames

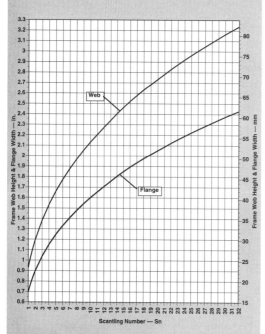

Cabin-Side-Frame Web Heights and Flange Widths in Aluminum Transversely Framed Hulls

Cabin-Side-Frame Web Thickness = same as deck-beam-web thickness

Cabin-Side-Frame Web Height, in. = 0.93 × $Sn^{0.36}$ (English)

Cabin-Side-Frame Web Height, mm = 23.62 × $Sn^{0.36}$ (Metric)

Cabin-Side-Frame Flange Thickness = 1.25 × web thickness

Cabin-Side-Frame Flange Width = 0.75 × web height

FORMULA 17-7

Aluminum Transverse-Framed Stanchion Spacing

Stanchions may be spaced as convenient using Formula 16-10A; however, the usual spacing is approximately every five frames.

FORMULA 17-8

Deck Girders

Deck girders should be proportioned according to Formula 16-9A; however, in addition to the requirements from this formula, deck girders should be installed in all transverse-framed aluminum hulls with Sns greater than 8.

FORMULA 17-9

Aluminum Transverse-Framed Engine Beds and Bottom Girders

The engine beds and bottom girders are the same as in longitudinal construction, except that the engine beds of displacement craft need to be welded to a minimum of four ring frames, or one full frame beyond the forward-most and after-most engine mounts, whichever extends a greater length.

CALCULATING AN EXAMPLE TRANSVERSE-FRAMED ALUMINUM HULL

Returning to our trusty old *AlumaNaught*, we would adjust the boat's structure as follows to frame it out transversely:

Transverse-Framed Hull Frames O.C. = 10.2 × $8.71^{0.24}$ = 17.1; use 17 in.

Transverse-Framed Hull Frames O.C. = 259 × $8.71^{0.24}$ = 435.4; use 430 mm

A 35-knot *AlumaNaught* would use

35 knots–15 knots = 20 knots; therefore, decrease O.C. by 20%

Speed-Adjusted-Frame O.C. = 17.1 in. × 0.80 = 13.68; use 13 in.

Speed-Adjusted-Frame O.C. = 430 mm × 0.80 = 344; use 340 mm

Bottom-Frame-Web Thickness = 0.23 × $8.71^{0.21}$ = 0.362; use $3/8$ in.

Bottom-Frame-Web Thickness = 5.84 × $8.71^{0.21}$ = 9.2; use 9.5 mm

Bottom-Frame-Web Height = 1.23 × $8.71^{0.46}$ – 3.33; use $3\frac{3}{8}$ in.

Bottom-Frame-Web Height = 31.24 × $8.71^{0.46}$ = 84.5; use 85 mm

Bottom-Frame-Flange Thickness = 1.25 × 0.362 in. = 0.45; use $7/16$ in.

Bottom-Frame-Flange Thickness = 1.25 × 9.2 mm = 11.5; use 11 mm

Bottom-Frame-Flange Width = 0.92 × $8.71^{0.46}$ = 2.48; use $2\frac{1}{2}$ in.

Bottom-Frame-Flange Width = 23.36 × $8.71^{0.46}$ = 63.2; use 64 mm

For a 35-knot *AlumaNaught*, the bottom frames would be adjusted as follows:

35 knots–20 knots = 15 knots; therefore, increase web height by 15%

Bottom-Frame-Web Height = 1.15 × 3.32 in. = 3.818; use $3\frac{7}{8}$ in.

35 knots –15 knots = 20 knots; therefore, increase flange by 20%

Bottom-Frame-Flange Width = 1.20 × 2.48 in. = 2.97; use 3 in.

Bottom-Frame-Flange Thickness = 1.20 × 0.362 in. = 0.434; use $7/16$ in.

or

35 knots–20 knots = 15 knots; therefore, increase web height by 15%

Bottom-Frame-Web Height =1.15 × 84.5 mm = 97.1; use 100 mm

35 knots–15 knots = 20 knots; therefore, increase flange by 20%

Bottom-Frame-Flange Width = 1.20 × 63.2 mm = 75.8; use 75 mm

Bottom-Frame-Flange Thickness = 1.20 × 9.2 mm = 11.04; use 11 mm

Topsides-Frame-Web Height at Chine or Bilge = 0.85 × 3.32 in. = 2.82; use $2\frac{7}{8}$ in.

Topsides-Frame-Web Height at Chine or Bilge = 0.85 × 84.5 mm = 71.8; use 72 mm

Topsides-Frame-Web Height at Sheer = 0.70 × 3.32 in. = 2.32; use 2 ⅜ in.

Topsides-Frame-Web Height at Sheer = 0.70 × 84.5 mm = 59.1; use 60 mm

Deck-Beam-Web Thickness = ⅜ in. (9.5 mm)

Deck-Beam-Web Height = 1.05 × 8.71^{0.36} = 2.29; use 2¼ in.

Deck-Beam-Web Height, mm = 26.67 × 8.71^{0.36} = 58.1; use 58 mm

Deck-Beam-Flange Thickness = 1.25 × 0.362 in. = 0.45; use ⁷⁄₁₆ in.

Deck-Beam-Flange Thickness = 1.25 × 9.2 mm = 11.5 mm

Deck-Beam-Flange Width = 0.75 × 2.25 in. = 1.68; use 1⅝ in.

Deck-Beam-Flange Width = 0.75 × 58.1 mm = 43.57; use 44 mm

In chapter 15, we found the following plate thickness for *AlumaNaught*:

Bottom: ⁵⁄₁₆ in. (8 mm)
Topsides: ¼ in. (6.4 mm)
Deck: ³⁄₁₆ in. (4.75 mm)

Accordingly, the optional longitudinals would be spaced as follows:

Hull-Bottom-Longitudinal O.C. = 4 + (0.3125 in. × 32) = 14 in.

Topsides-Longitudinal O.C. = 4 + (0.25 in. × 32) = 12 in.

Deck-Longitudinal O.C. = 4 + (0.1875 × 32) = 10 in.

or

Hull-Bottom-Longitudinal O.C. = 101.6 + (8 mm × 32) = 357.6; use 350 mm

Topsides-Longitudinal O.C. = 101.6 + (6.4 mm × 32) = 306.4; use 300 mm

Deck-Longitudinal O.C. = 101.6 + (4.75 mm × 32) = 253.6; use 250 mm

or

Hull-Bottom-Longitudinal Height = 0.45 × 3.375 in. = 1.51; use 1½ in.

Hull-Bottom-Longitudinal Thickness = ⁵⁄₁₆ or ⅜ in.

Topsides-Longitudinal Height = 0.45 × 2.75 in. at bottom = 1.23; use 1¼ in.

Topsides-Longitudinal Thickness = ¼ or ⁵⁄₁₆ in.

Deck-Longitudinal Height = 0.45 × 2.25 in. = 1.01; use 1 in.

Deck-Longitudinal Thickness = ³⁄₁₆ or ¼ in.

or

Hull-Bottom-Longitudinal Height = 0.45 × 85 mm = 38.2; use 38 mm

Hull-Bottom-Longitudinal Thickness = 8 or 9.5 mm

Topsides-Longitudinal Height = 0.45 × 72 mm at bottom = 32.4; use 32 mm

Topsides-Longitudinal Thickness = 6.4 or 8 mm

Deck-Longitudinal Height = 0.45 × 58 mm = 26.1; use 25 mm

Deck-Longitudinal Thickness = 4.75 or 6 mm

Cabin-Side-Frame Web Thickness = ⅜ in. (9.5 mm)

Cabin-Side-Frame Web Height =
0.93 × 8.71$^{0.36}$ = 2.03; use 2 in.

Cabin-Side-Frame Web Height =
23.62 × 8.71$^{0.36}$ = 51.48; use 52 mm

Cabin-Side-Frame Flange Thickness =
1.25 × 0.362 in. = 0.45; use $^7/_{16}$ in.

Cabin-Side-Frame Flange Thickness =
1.25 × 9.2 mm = 11.5 mm

Cabin-Side-Frame Flange Width = 0.75 ×
2 in. = 1½ in.

Cabin-Side-Frame Flange Width = 0.75 ×
52 mm = 39; use 40 mm

Lightweight Aluminum Scantlings

Both the longitudinal- and transverse-framed scantlings presented so far are generous with heavy plate. Aluminum, however, is so rust-free and tough (it absorbs so much energy by deforming) that both the longitudinal- and transverse-framed scantlings can be reduced still more. This may be done safely for most yachts and high-speed craft. The penalties are less reserve strength and a somewhat shorter operational life expectancy. The reward—and it is an important one—is improved performance: higher speed, longer range, greater cargo capacity, better fuel economy, higher ballast ratio.

On high-performance sailboats and high-speed planing hulls, weight savings is so critical to success that it can be well worth this trade-off in less reserve strength. Indeed, even at these lightweight scantlings, such hulls are still quite tough. Displacement boats (e.g., sailboats) can reduce the scantlings everywhere, including on their underbodies.

Extreme lightweight construction system pioneered by Derecktor Shipyards. Closely spaced ring frames and longitudinals allow very thin plate. Numerous carefully engineered lightening holes further reduce weight. This construction gives hull weights comparable to high-tech composite materials. (Courtesy Derecktor International)

Planing hulls, however, must use the standard bottom framing and bottom longitudinals and the standard heavier bottom plate on their underbodies—from the BLH or the chine down (see Formula 4-3).

Of course, heavy workboats and serious ocean-voyaging vessels would do well to build-in the reserve of strength from the standard scantlings in chapters 15 and 16. In aluminum—in larger, heavier-displacement hulls—the greater weight of the standard scantlings is modest in proportion with overall displacement, and therefore does not significantly affect performance.

The following formulas give the adjustments for lightweight aluminum construction suited to high-performance vessels.

FORMULA 17-11

Aluminum Lightweight Plate

Lightweight-Plate Thickness = 0.88 × standard-weight plate

Because $^3/_{16}$-inch (4.75 mm) plate is the thinnest conveniently weldable with standard equipment, no further reduction should be made below $^3/_{16}$ inch (4.75 mm), unless pulse-arc welding is available and economically viable or unless riveting is practical.

For displacement craft, the standard heavier bottom plate should be determined and then 88 percent of that thickness used. This heavier bottom plate is required—not optional—with the lightweight rule. Again, planing hulls must use the standard heavier bottom plate without reduction.

FORMULA 17-12

Aluminum Lightweight Longitudinals

Longitudinal Spacing, O.C. = use the longitudinal spacing in Formula 15-6A for the plate actually installed

Longitudinal Height = standard longitudinal height × 1.10

Longitudinal Thickness = one standard plate size thicker than the shell plate

FORMULA 17-13

Aluminum Lightweight Frame O.C.

For displacement hulls with the lightweight bottom plate, calculate the standard frame-spacing O.C. and use 90 percent of that. For planing hulls with standard-rule heavy bottom plating, use standard speed-adjusted frame spacing without reduction.

FORMULA 17-14

Aluminum Lightweight Frame Dimensions

Frame-Web Thickness = one standard plate size thicker than the shell plate

Frame-Web Height = standard height × 1.10, where the plate thickness has been reduced

Frame-Web-Flange Thickness = same as standard

Frame-Web-Flange Width = standard × 1.10, where the plate thickness has been reduced

SCANTLINGS FOR A LIGHTWEIGHT ALUMANAUGHT

If our sleek *AlumaNaught* were a 35-knot planing hull, it would make good sense to use lightweight scantlings to ensure we achieved this high speed. Because it's a planing hull, we would keep the same standard heavier bottom plating and the same bottom framing calculated in chapter 15. We would adjust the following scantlings, however, to get a lightweight hull—in this case, longitudinally framed:

Lightweight Bottom Thickness = $^5/_{16}$ in. (8 mm) (same as standard)

Lightweight Topsides Thickness = 0.88 × 0.245 in. = 0.21; use 0.204 in.

Lightweight Topsides Thickness = 0.88 × 6.23 mm = 5.25 mm

Lightweight Deck and Cabin-Side Thickness = $^3/_{16}$ in. (4.75 mm)

These thicknesses were already rounded down and are the thinnest practical for standard welding; do not reduce.

Bottom Longitudinals = same as standard

Topsides-Longitudinal Spacing, O.C. = 4 + (0.21 in. × 32) = 10.72; use 10½ in.

Topsides-Longitudinal Spacing, O.C. = 101.6 + (5.25 mm × 32) = 269.6; use 265 mm

Deck- and cabin-longitudinal spacing will be unchanged as the plate thickness is unchanged.

Topsides-Longitudinal Height = 2.49 in. × 1.10 = 2.73; use 2¾ in.

Topsides-Longitudinal Height = 63.39 mm × 1.10 = 69.7; use 70 mm

Topsides-Longitudinal Thickness = ¼ in. (6.4 mm)

Deck-Longitudinal Height = 1.53 in. × 1.10 = 1.68; use 1⅝ in.

Deck-Longitudinal Height = 39.07 mm × 1.10 = 42.9; use 44 mm

Deck-Longitudinal Thickness = ¼ in. (6.4 mm)

Cabin-Side-Longitudinal Height = The plate is unchanged in thickness (cannot reduce below 3/16 in.); therefore, use standard cabin-side longitudinals.

Frame Spacing, O.C. = same as standard

Bottom-Web-Frame Dimensions = same as standard for AlumaNaught's planing hull

Topsides-Frame-Web Thickness = ¼ in. (6.4 mm)

Topsides-Frame-Web Height = 1.10 × 5.53 in. non-speed-adjusted bottom height × 0.85 for standard topsides = 5.17; use 5.14 in. tapering to 0.75% of bottom or 4½ in. at sheer

Topsides-Frame-Web Height = 1.10 × 140.6 mm non-speed-adjusted bottom height × 0.85 for standard topsides = 131.4; use 130 mm tapering to 0.75% of bottom or 115 mm at sheer

Topsides-Frame-Flange Thickness = same as standard 7/16 in. (11.25 mm)

Topsides-Frame-Flange Width = 1.10 × 4.15 in. = 4.56; use 4½ in.

Topsides-Frame-Flange Width = 1.10 × 105.5 mm = 116; use 115 mm

Deck-Frame-Web Thickness = ¼ in. (6.4 mm)

Deck-Frame-Web Height = 1.10 × 3.87 in. = 4.25; use 4¼ in.

Deck-Frame-Web Height = 1.10 × 98.49 mm = 108.3; use 110 mm

Deck-Frame-Flange Thickness = same as standard 7/16 in. (11.25 mm)

Deck-Frame-Flange Width = 1.10 × 3 in. = 3.3; use 3⅜ in.

Deck-Frame-Flange Width = 1.10 × 75 mm = 82.5; use 85 mm

Steel Transverse Framing with Longitudinals

Like aluminum, steel can be built with closely spaced transverse frames and light longitudinals. Hulls built to these steel-transverse-framing-with longitudinal scantlings can do away with the small longitudinals completely if a pair of longitudinal hull girders are used. Also, in smaller craft (i.e., Sns less than 2.5), no longitudinals are required at all, although such vessels would be quite heavy in steel. Keep in mind that fewer longitudinals means greater difficulty in getting a fair hull.

As with the aluminum-transverse-framing rule, the longitudinal scantlings from chapters 15 and 16 are the basis for the steel-transverse scantlings. Unless a component is specifically changed, it is determined identically to the longitudinal scantlings. You must understand the scantlings selection in chapters 15 and 16 before using the following transverse-framing rules.

FORMULA 17-15

Steel Transverse-Framing with Longitudinals Frame Spacing

Frame Spacing O.C., in. = 10.2 × $Sn^{0.24}$ (English) (same as Formula 17-1)

Frame Spacing O.C., mm = 259 × $8.71^{0.24}$ (Metric) (same as Formula 17-1)

Decrease frame O.C. by 1% for every knot over 15 knots.

FORMULA 17-16

Steel Transverse Bottom-Frame Dimensions

Bottom-Frame-Web Height, in. = 1.25 × $Sn^{0.44}$ (English)

Bottom-Frame-Web Height, mm = 31.75 × $Sn^{0.44}$ (Metric)

Bottom-Frame-Web Thickness, in. = 0.20 × $Sn^{0.21}$ (English)

Bottom-Frame-Web Thickness, mm = 5.08 × $Sn^{0.21}$ (Metric)

Bottom-Frame-Flange Width = 0.75 × web height

Bottom-Frame-Flange Thickness = 1.25 × web thickness

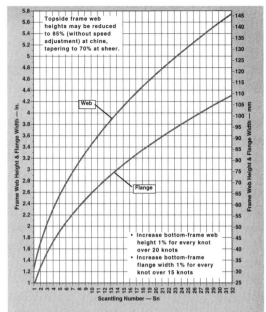

Frame-Web Heights and Flange Widths in Steel Transversely Framed Hulls

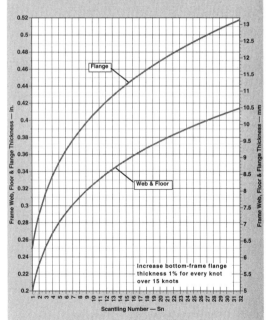

Frame, Deck-Beam, and Cabin-Side Frame: Web, Floor, and Flange Thicknesses in Steel Transversely Framed Hulls

Increase web height by 1 percent for every knot over 20 knots. Increase flange width by 1 percent for every knot over 15 knots. Increase flange thickness by 1 percent for every knot over 15 knots.

FORMULA 17-17

Steel Transverse Topsides-Frame Dimensions

The same as non-speed-adjusted bottom frames, except the web can be 0.85 × bottom-frame-web height at the chine or bilge, tapering down to 0.75 × bottom-frame web height at the sheer.

On sailboats—at the masts and shroud chainplates—the topsides frames should be the same dimensions as the hull-bottom frame (not the reduced topsides-frame dimensions). In addition—on boats with Sns greater than 4.5—the web thickness should be increased to the next standard plate size up from the reduced topsides-frame-web thickness.

FORMULA 17-18

Steel Transverse-Framed Hull Longitudinals

Longitudinal Thickness = frame web thickness

Longitudinal Height = 0.35 × frame web height

Longitudinals are not required on hulls with Sns less than 2.5.

FORMULA 17-19

Steel Transverse-Framed Deck-Beam Dimensions

Deck-Beam-Web Thickness = same as hull-bottom web

Deck-Beam-Web Height, in. = 1.05 × Sn^{0.35} (English)

Deck-Beam-Web Height, mm = 26.67 × Sn^{0.35} (Metric)

Deck-Beam-Flange Thickness, in. = 1.25 × web thickness

Deck-Beam-Flange Width, in. = 0.75 × web height

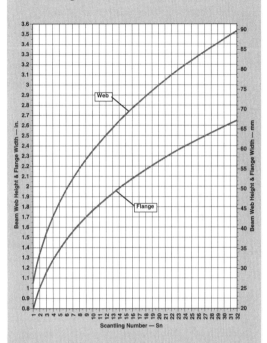

Deck-Beam-Web Heights and Flange Widths in Steel Transversely Framed Hulls

FORMULA 17-20

Steel Transverse-Framed Deck Longitudinals

Deck longitudinals are optional with transverse frames spaced this close; however, they are frequently used to improve fairness.

Deck-Longitudinal Thickness = plate thickness or the next standard size up (based on mild-steel plate, not Cor-Ten thickness)

Deck-Longitudinal Height = 0.35 × deck-beam-web height

FORMULA 17-21

Steel Web Frames or Deep Frames or Transverse-Framed Hulls

Transverse-framed vessels with Sns over 6 should install heavier or deeper frames at every third frame.

Web-Frame Thickness = same as standard transverse frame

Web-Frame Height = 1.8 × standard transverse frame web height (for topsides and bottom web, respectively)

Web-Frame-Flange Thickness = same as standard transverse frame

Web-Frame-Flange Width = 0.5 × web frame web height

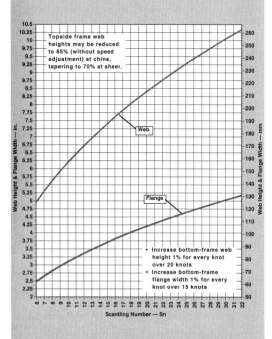

Deep Web Frames, Web Heights, and Flange Widths in Steel Transversely Framed Hulls

FORMULA 17-22

Steel Transverse-Framed Cabin-Side Frames

Cabin-Side-Frame Web Thickness = same as deck-beam-web thickness

Cabin-Side-Frame Web Height, in. = 0.92 × Sn^{0.35} (English)

Cabin-Side-Frame Web Height, mm = 23.3 × Sn^{0.35} (Metric)

Cabin-Side-Frame Flange Thickness = 1.25 × web thickness

Cabin-Side-Frame Flange Width = 0.75 × web height

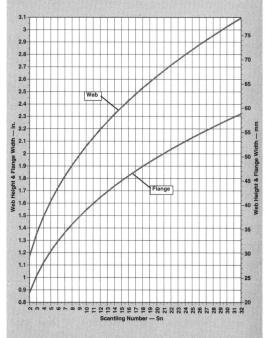

Cabin-Side-Frame Web Heights and Flange Widths in Steel Transversely Framed Hulls

FORMULA 17-23

Steel Transverse-Framed Longitudinal Stringer or Girder Plates in Lieu of Web Frames

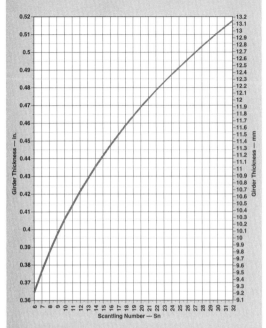

Hull Girder in Place of Deep Web Frame: Thickness in Steel Transversely Framed Hulls

Deep web frames every third frame interfere with one of the advantages of transverse-framed construction: reduced frame molding for increased interior room. The web frames can be dispensed with if two heavy longitudinal stringers or girder plates are installed. These are built in at roughly right angles to the hull plating at: one about half way out from the keel to the bilge or chine on the hull bottom; one about 35 percent of the topside height up from the bilge or chine, on the topside. These longitudinal girders are flat plate, as follows:

$$\text{Girder Thickness, in.} = 0.25 \times Sn^{0.21}$$
(English)

$$\text{Girder Thickness, mm} = 6.35 \times Sn^{0.21}$$
(Metric)

$$\text{Girder Height, in.} = 3.08 \times Sn^{0.36} \text{ (English)}$$

$$\text{Girder Height, mm} = 78.23 \times Sn^{0.36}$$
(Metric)

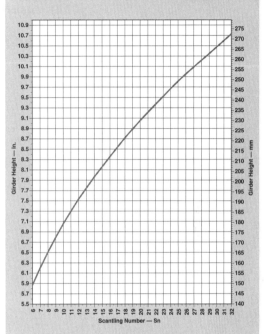

Hull Girder in Place of Deep Web Frame: Height in Steel Transversely Framed Hulls

It is unusual to produce larger steel hulls light enough to operate as high-speed planing craft. If this were done, however, the bottom girders would be the same as the high-speed hull girders from the longitudinal section. In this case, if you wanted to avoid deep web frames, you would only have to add the upper (topsides) girder specified previously.

FORMULA 17-24

Steel Transverse-Framed Stanchion Spacing

Stanchions may be spaced as convenient, using Formula 16-10S;

(continued)

however, the usual spacing is approximately every five frames.

Steel Transverse-Framed Deck Girders

Deck girders should be proportioned according to Formula 16-9S; however, in addition to the requirements in chapter 16, deck girders should be installed in all transverse-framed steel hulls with Sns greater than 8.

Steel Transverse-Framed Engine Beds and Bottom Girders

The engine beds and bottom girders are identical to longitudinal construction, except that the engine beds of displacement craft need to be welded to a minimum of four ring frames or one full frame beyond the forward-most and after-most engine mounts, whichever extends a greater length.

Steel Transverse-Framed Mast Step

Mast steps for transverse framing are the same as for longitudinal construction, except that if the mast step is not an extension of the CVK, then it must extend for at least four frames. (The mizzenmast step can extend to only three frames.)

WORKING THROUGH A TRANSVERSE-FRAMED DISPLACEMENT-SPEED *IRON MAIDEN*

If we decided to use transverse framing on our 10.5-knot (for example) *Iron Maiden*, we would get the following scantlings:

$$Frame\ Spacing\ O.C. = 10.2 \times 8.71^{0.24} = 17.1;\ use\ 17\ in.$$

$$Frame\ Spacing\ O.C. = 259 \times 8.71^{0.24} = 435.4;\ use\ 435\ mm$$

$$Bottom\text{-}Frame\text{-}Web\ Height = 1.25 \times 8.71^{0.44} = 3.23;\ use\ 3\tfrac{1}{4}\ in.$$

$$Bottom\text{-}Frame\text{-}Web\ Height = 31.75 \times 8.71^{0.44} = 82.2;\ use\ 84\ mm$$

$$Bottom\text{-}Frame\text{-}Web\ Thickness = 0.20 \times 8.71^{0.21} = 0.31;\ use\ \tfrac{5}{16}\ in.$$

$$Bottom\text{-}Frame\text{-}Web\ Thickness = 5.08 \times 8.71^{0.21} = 8\ mm$$

$$Bottom\text{-}Frame\text{-}Flange\ Width = 0.75 \times 3.23\ in. = 2.42;\ use\ 2\tfrac{1}{2}\ in.$$

$$Bottom\text{-}Frame\text{-}Flange\ Width = 0.75 \times 82.2\ mm = 61.6;\ use\ 65\ mm$$

$$Bottom\text{-}Frame\text{-}Flange\ Thickness = 1.25 \times 0.31\ in. = 0.38;\ use\ \tfrac{3}{8}\ in.$$

$$Bottom\text{-}Frame\text{-}Flange\ Thickness = 1.25 \times 8.0\ mm = 10\ mm$$

$$Topsides\text{-}Web\ Height,\ at\ Bilge\ or\ Chine = 0.85 \times 3.23\ in. = 2.74;\ use\ 2\tfrac{3}{4}\ in.$$

tapering to

$$Topsides\text{-}Web\ Height\ at\ Sheer = 0.75 \times 3.23\ in. = 2.42;\ use\ 2\tfrac{1}{2}\ in.$$

or

$$Topsides\text{-}Web\ Height,\ at\ Bilge\ or\ Chine = 0.85 \times 82.2\ mm = 69.8;\ use\ 70\ mm$$

tapering to

$$Topsides\text{-}Web\ Height\ at\ Sheer = 0.75 \times 82.2\ mm = 61.6;\ use\ 62\ mm$$

$$Hull\text{-}Longitudinal\ Thickness = \tfrac{5}{16}\ in.\ (8\ mm)$$

$$Hull\text{-}Longitudinal\ Height = 0.35 \times 3.23\ in. = 1.13;\ use\ 1\tfrac{1}{8}\ or\ 1\tfrac{1}{4}\ in.$$

$$Hull\text{-}Longitudinal\ Height = 0.35 \times 82.2\ mm = 28.7;\ use\ 30\ mm$$

Deck-Beam-Web Thickness = $\frac{5}{16}$ in. (8 mm)

Deck-Beam-Web Height = $1.05 \times 8.71^{0.35}$ = 2.24; use $2\frac{1}{4}$ in.

Deck-Beam-Web Height = $26.67 \times 8.71^{0.35}$ = 56.8, use 58 mm

Deck-Beam-Flange Thickness = 1.25×0.31 in. = 0.38; use $\frac{3}{8}$ in.

Deck-Beam-Flange Thickness = 1.25×8.0 mm = 10 mm

Deck-Beam-Flange Width = 0.75×2.23 in. = 1.67; use $1\frac{5}{8}$ in.

Deck-Beam-Flange Width = 0.75×56.8 mm = 42.6; use 42 mm

We found *Iron Maiden*'s deck to be 8-gauge (0.1664 in.) (4 mm) Cor-Ten, which equaled $\frac{3}{16}$-in. (4.75 mm) mild steel.

Deck-Longitudinal Thickness = $\frac{3}{16}$ or $\frac{1}{4}$ in. (4.75 or 6 mm)

Deck-Longitudinal Height = 0.35×2.23 in. $\times$ 0.78; use $\frac{3}{4}$ or 1 in.

Deck-Longitudinal Height = 0.35×56.8 mm = 19.88; use 20 or 25 mm

Web-Frame Web Thickness = $\frac{5}{16}$ in. (8 mm)

Web-Frame Web Height, Bottom = 1.8×3.23 in. = 5.81; use $5\frac{3}{4}$ in.

Web-Frame Web Height, Bottom = 1.8×82.2 mm = 147.9; use 145 mm

Web-Frame Web Height, Lower Topsides = 1.8×2.74 in. = 4.93; use 5 in.

Web-Frame Web Height, Lower Topsides = 1.8×69.8 mm = 125.6; use 125 mm

Web-Frame Web Height, Upper Topsides = 1.8×2.42 in. = 4.36; use $4\frac{3}{8}$ in.

Web-Frame Web Height, Upper Topsides = 1.8×61.6 mm = 110.8; use 110 mm

Web-Frame-Flange Thickness = $\frac{3}{8}$ in. (10 mm)

Web-Frame-Flange Width = 0.5×5.81 in. = 2.9; use 3 in.

Web-Frame-Flange Width = 0.5×147.9 mm = 73.9; use 74 mm

Cabin-Side-Frame Web Thickness = $\frac{5}{16}$ inch (8 mm)

Cabin-Side-Frame Web Height = $0.92 \times 8.71^{0.35}$ = 1.96; use 2 in.

Cabin-Side-Frame Web Height = $23.3 \times 8.71^{0.35}$ = 49.7; use 50 mm

Cabin-Side-Frame Flange Thickness = 1.25×0.31 in. = 0.38; use $\frac{3}{8}$ in.

Cabin-Side-Frame Flange Thickness = 1.25×8.0 mm = 10 mm

Cabin-Side-Frame Flange Width = 0.75×1.96 in. = 1.47; use $1\frac{1}{2}$ in.

Cabin-Side-Frame Flange Width = 0.75×49.7 mm = 37.2; use 38 mm

Girder Thickness = $0.25 \times 8.71^{0.21}$ = 0.39; use $\frac{3}{8}$ in.

Girder Thickness = $6.35 \times 8.71^{0.21}$ = 10 mm

Girder Height = $3.08 \times 8.71^{0.36}$ = 6.7; use $6\frac{3}{4}$ in.

Girder Height = $78.23 \times 8.71^{0.36}$ = 170.5; use 170 mm

---

Steel Transverse-Framing with No Longitudinals

It is possible to construct steel vessels with closely spaced transverse frames using no longitudinals at all. I'm not sure I see much advantage to this. Weld distortion is more difficult to control, which often results in rippled, hungry-horse plating. To minimize this problem, the plating should be thicker than normal. This adds weight, which is detrimental to stability and performance. Still, for heavy workboats such as trawlers, this heavy plate can increase the life of the steel hull, especially when maintenance may be poor. The thicker plate has a higher built-in corrosion allowance. Indeed, the plate for this rule is so thick that it qualifies as light ice-class, which also can be an advantage in some waters.

Because of the heavy plate and the resulting heavy hull, the scantlings from this all-transverse-framed rule are only suited to heavy-displacement vessels with Sns greater than 6.

The transverse-frame-with-no-longitudinal scantlings are based on the previously given standard transverse-frame scantlings.

FORMULA 17-28

Steel Transverse-Framed Hull Plate with No Longitudinals

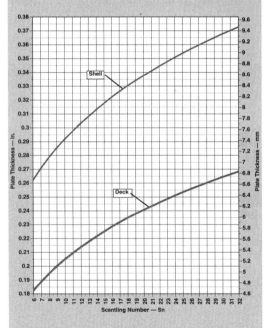

Heavy Shell and Deck Plate in Steel Transversely Framed Hulls

Hull Plate (Bottom and Topsides), in. = $0.18 \times Sn^{0.21}$ (English)

Hull Plate (Bottom and Topsides), mm = $4.57 \times Sn^{0.21}$ (Metric)

FORMULA 17-29

Steel Transverse-Frame Spacing

Transverse Framed Spacing O.C. = same as standard steel transverse-framed spacing (see Formula 17-15), except not to exceed 24 in. (610 mm)

FORMULA 17-30

Steel Transverse-Framed Deep Web Frames

With this construction, the deep web frames are not required.

FORMULA 17-31

Steel Transverse-Framed Deck Plate

Deck Plate, in. = $0.121 \times Sn^{0.23}$ (English)

Deck Plate, mm = $3.07 \times Sn^{0.23}$ (Metric)

(See chart 17-28.)

CONVERTING *IRON MAIDEN* TO TRANSVERSE-FRAMED WITHOUT LONGITUDINALS

Going back to our reliable *Iron Maiden*, we could convert the boat to transverse-framed without any longitudinals as follows:

Hull Plate (Bottom and Topsides) = $0.18 \times 8.71^{0.21} = 0.28$; use ¼ in.

Hull Plate (Bottom and Topsides) = $4.57 \times 8.71^{0.21} = 7.2$; use 7.2 mm

Transverse-Framed Spacing O.C. = same as standard steel transverse-framed spacing (see Formula 17-15), except not to exceed 24 in. (610 mm). The 17 in. (435 mm) that we found previously is acceptable.

*Deck Plate, in. = 0.121 × 8.71$^{0.23}$ = 0.199;
use $^3/_{16}$ in.*

*Deck Plate, mm = 3.07 × 8.71$^{0.23}$ = 5.05;
use 5 mm*

Lightweight Steel

You would expect that—like aluminum—we could make lightweight steel hulls by reducing plate thicknesses from those given for the standard construction method. Unfortunately, because of steel's rust problem, this is not generally a good idea. Such thin-plate steel hulls can lose too large a percentage of their hull thickness to rust and corrosion too quickly. Yes, a perfect construction job, with excellent engineering followed by superb paint and coating and with ongoing excellent and regular maintenance, can make even thin-plate steel last a very long time in saltwater. Achieving all these ideals in one boat—especially continuing the high-level of maintenance for years—is seldom a realistic prospect. In addition, because steel is so heavy to begin with, the standard rule already generates reasonably thin plates.

FORMULA 17-32

Lightweight Steel: All Cor-Ten

So what is the answer to lightweight steel? The best I can come up with is Cor-Ten. We've already seen that using Cor-Ten, you can reduce plate thickness to 88 percent of the standard mild-steel calculated in the rule. Generally, I believe it is better to use mild steel for the interior framing; however, you can go the next step: convert all thicknesses to Cor-Ten by reducing them to 88 percent of mild steel.

True round-bilge steel boats *can be built by yards that know how. Here, one comes together nicely at Treworgy Yachts.* (Courtesy Treworgy Yachts)

Remember, though, that Cor-Ten is not rustproof by any means. These thinner Cor-Ten members can corrode out and, if you lose $^1/_{16}$ inch (1.6 mm) of plate from a $^3/_{16}$-inch-thick (4.75 mm) longitudinal, you have lost a third of its strength. The same $^1/_{16}$-inch (1.6 mm) loss from a comparable $^7/_{32}$-inch (5.5 mm) longitudinal would be 28 percent. Still, Cor-Ten does rust more slowly than mild steel, so converting to all Cor-Ten is acceptable. Remember, reduce only thicknesses; the web and longitudinal heights should all remain the same. You must *increase* the flange widths by 1.13 times. Alternately, leave the flange dimensions unchanged from the standard scantlings.

EIGHTEEN

Welding, Small Openings, and Riveting Aluminum

Welding

TYPES OF WELDING

Except for thin sheet, which is riveted, almost every component of a metal boat is joined or fastened by welding. Originally, welding could be accomplished only on a forge. Not surprisingly, this is termed *forge welding*. Although at least a couple of thousand years old, forge welding is limited to parts small enough for you to heat them to near melting and then hammer together. Clearly, this is labor-intensive and hardly suited to welding a boat hull. Modern welding is either oxyacetylene or electric-arc welding. Oxyacetylene has little application for welding boats; however, the oxyacetylene-torch equipment does have important uses. Electric-arc welding—in one of several standard forms—is the welding method for modern steel- and aluminum-boat construction.

In this chapter, we discuss the different types of welding equipment appropriate to different materials, and we determine how to specify the correct size and frequency of weld bead to join various components; this is akin to determining fastener size in wood construction. We also discuss some of the principles underlying sound welding practice and joint design. This chapter is not a welding manual, however—welding is a craft that takes time, thought, and effort to acquire. No one should undertake building a metal hull without, at the minimum, taking a course in welding from a local technical school. For classed or U.S. Coast Guard–certified vessels, welders must be certified by ABS, Lloyds, or the Coast Guard.

OXYACETYLENE EQUIPMENT AND CUTTING PLATE

Oxyacetylene welding uses the heat of acetylene gas burned in combination with pure oxygen to melt the metal to be welded. Extra filler metal is added to the joint with hand-fed filler rods. Oxyacetylene is not efficient for welding hulls, but the equipment is essential for cutting steel plate and for pre- and post-heating special weldments. It's also useful for heating plate to ease bending and for line heating, brazing, and soldering.

Oxyacetylene torches are the standard method for cutting steel plate. It might seem odd that the same process can both weld and cut. To cut rather than weld, enough extra oxygen is forced through the torch so that the molten metal actually burns. This burning is the "cutting" action. Keep in mind at all times that both the oxygen and the acetylene are dangerously explosive. In many ways, the oxygen is more dangerous than the acetylene. Pure oxygen can transform normally inflammable or slow-burning materials into bombs. For instance, pure oxygen can cause oil or grease to ignite spontaneously. Use great care!

The fastest and most accurate method of cutting plate (aluminum or steel) is with a plasma cutting machine. These are quite expensive, however, and are usually found only in larger building yards.

ELECTRIC-ARC WELDING

The first patent on arc welding was issued to an Englishman named Wilde in 1865. It wasn't until the 1890s, however, that what is known as *carbon-arc* welding became a commercially viable process. In this form of arc welding, a carbon electrode is held close to the metal to be welded to create the hot electric arc that melts the metal, and any filler metal is added manually.

Modern *metal-arc welding* was invented in 1889, when N. G. Slavinoff and Charles Coffin were each granted patents—in Russia and the United States, respectively—on a new process. They replaced the carbon electrode with a metal rod. The rod not only acted as the electrode to generate the hot metal-melting arc, but the rod itself also melted away to form filler metal for the joint at the same time. This is basically the *metal-arc-welding* process, or simply the *arc-welding* or *stick-welding* process, used to fabricate most steel hulls.

ARC-WELDING ELECTRODES (RODS OR STICKS)

Still, there were difficulties. The early metal electrodes (i.e., the metal rods that doubled as electrode and filler metal) were the problem. When you heat metals to melting, they react chemically with oxygen in the atmosphere and with trace elements in the metal and the electrode. These reactions can cause brittleness and corrosion. Special formulations of flux coatings and proper weld-filler metal alloys were the solution. The flux coatings vaporize and shield the arc from oxygen, so this modern-arc or stick-welding is properly termed *shielded metal-arc welding*. Using this method, the first all-welded vessel was built in Charleston, South Carolina, in 1930. As discussed previously, World War II marked the transition. Before the war, almost all steel ships were riveted; by the end of the war, riveted ships were the exception.

Today, metal-arc electrodes come in a wide variety of alloys and flux coverings, each best suited for welding specific alloys, with specific welding equipment, in exact conditions. These shielded-arc electrodes are critical to the success of any metal-arc-welding project. It is vital to follow the recommendations of the rod manufacturer in using exactly the right electrodes for your machine and building circumstances.

WELDING ALUMINUM ALLOY: GAS-SHIELDED ARC WELDING

The flux-coated rods of metal-arc welding do not provide sufficient protection from undesirable chemical reactions when welding aluminum, which is far more chemically active than steel. The solution—which wasn't fully arrived at until the 1950s—is to shield the weld arc with an inert gas such as argon, nitrogen, helium, or carbon dioxide.

Tungsten Inert-Gas Welding

The first of these processes was *tungsten inert-gas (TIG) welding*, which employs a tungsten electrode with a helium-gas shield. A high-frequency, high-voltage AC current is superimposed on the welding current to stabilize the arc. TIG welding is somewhat slower than *metal inert-gas (MIG) welding*, but it generates a smoother weld bead, which minimizes or eliminates grinding on many surfaces. TIG welding is still useful, especially for fabricating small fittings and components; its drawback is that it requires a separate hand-held filler rod.

Metal Inert-Gas Welding

Metal inert-gas welding (MIG) is the process used for assembling most components of most aluminum boats. With MIG welding, the welder holds a gun with a nozzle that blows the shielding gas around the arc struck from a filler-metal wire electrode. This wire is fed continuously and automatically into the weld line through the center of the gun tip. A spool of filler/electrode wire is mounted on the welding machine and runs through to the gun, which is attached by hoses and cables to the welding machine many feet away (as convenient). This is the quickest and easiest welding technique for most aluminum boatbuilding applications.

MIG welding is faster than metal-arc or stick-welding and can be used on steel as well as aluminum. Most steel boats, however, are built entirely with shielded-metal-arc equipment (i.e., stick-welding). Although MIG equipment is considerably more expensive, large boatbuilding shops might well consider the potential economies from faster welding with MIG on steel hulls. A factor often overlooked in this evaluation is that the faster welding speeds with gas-shielded-arc welding such as MIG mean less heat is put into the structure, so there is less distortion. Of course, MIG and TIG welding should both be done indoors (or, less satisfactorily, with windscreens outdoors) to ensure that the gas shield isn't blown away from the weld.

TYPES OF WELDS

There are two basic types of welds: butt welds and right-angle welds. Joints made at right angles are usually made with fillet welds, although heavier plate can benefit from beveled V-groove welds. Welds can also be subdivided into continuous and intermittent welds. A continuous weld on a flange to a web that was 10 feet (3 m) long would run the full 10 feet (3 m), without interruption. An intermittent weld might run for perhaps 2 inches (50 mm), then skip 10 inches (250 mm), followed by 2 more inches (50 mm), and so on.

Fillet-Weld Dimensions

Because fillet welds are so common, most welds are defined with respect to them. A cross section through a standard fillet weld is roughly a section through a right triangle with equal legs. The throat of the weld is the line that slices through the widest portion of the triangle from the center of the hypotenuse to the 90-degree (inside) corner. It is the weld metal in the throat that determines the strength of a weld; however, it's not easy to measure throat size directly. For this reason, in the United States the custom is to specify weld size in terms of leg length—the length of the triangle sides against the welded parts. In Europe, throat size is often specified rather than leg length. We use leg length exclusively in this discussion.

The throat is equal in length to half the hypotenuse, so it is easy to convert leg length to throat size or vice versa.

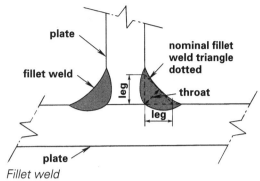
Fillet weld

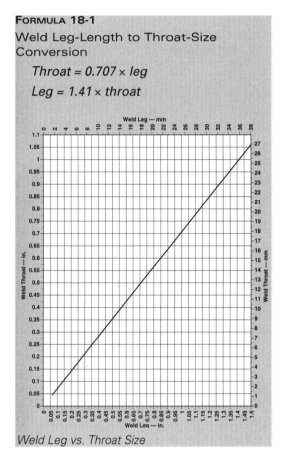

Formula 18-1

Weld Leg-Length to Throat-Size Conversion

$$Throat = 0.707 \times leg$$

$$Leg = 1.41 \times throat$$

Weld Leg vs. Throat Size

Accordingly, a ¼-in. weld has a 0.176-in. throat; 0.25-in. leg × 0.707 = 0.176 in.

or

a 6.4 mm weld has a 45.2 mm throat; 6.4 mm × 0.707 = 45.2 mm

Minimizing Weld: Intermittent and Continuous Welds

There is a common misconception that metal hulls are welded continuously throughout. Nothing could be farther from the case! Because every additional bit of weld introduces extra heat into the structure, each extra weld length increases distortion. It is vital that no more weld be used than is necessary for strength. Excess welding does not make a boat stronger; in fact, the resulting locked-in stresses from distortion can make it weaker. It will also make the vessel lumpy, wrinkled, and unsightly.

Generally, the vast majority of the internal structure is intermittently welded. The exceptions are high-load components such as engine beds, mast steps, chainplates, and butt-joint welds in frame members. Of course, the shell, deck, tanks, and superstructure plate must all be continuously welded to make them watertight. This is naturally unavoidable, but is unfortunate because the continuous welding of all the shell plate is one of the principal sources of weld distortion in a hull.

Chain and Staggered Welds

Intermittent welds are further subdivided into two categories: *chain* and *staggered*. If you

A close-up of the stringers or longitudinals where they notch into the hull. The draining snipes in the frames at the longitudinal slots show clearly. The internal flat bar is temporary bracing. Note the chain weld of frame web to flange.

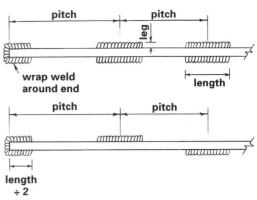

Top: Chain weld. Bottom: Staggered weld.

lay down, for example, 2 inches (50 mm) of weld on both sides of a web-to-flange joint, back to back, then skip 10 inches (250 mm) and lay down another 2 inches (50 mm) back to back, you've been doing chain welding. Staggered welding alternates the welds on opposite sides of the web. In this case, you would put down 2 inches (50 mm) on the left side (with nothing on the right side), skip 10 inches (250 mm) and lay down 2 inches (50 mm) on the right side (with no weld on the left), and so on. Because the pitch is the same for both chain and staggered welds, in this rule staggered welds have twice the total weld of chain welds. Both staggered and chain welding are sometimes referred to as *stitch welding*. My opinion is that this term should be properly applied only to staggered welds (not chain welds), but this convention isn't strictly observed.

The following table gives the type of weld—staggered, chain, or continuous—to be used on various structural components.

TABLE 18-2 Component Weld Selection Table

All standard webs to shell or bulkhead plate:	staggered
All standard longitudinals to shell plate:	staggered
All standard flanges to webs:	chain
Web to shell at mast partner and chainplate frames (for 6 × web height on longitudinally framed hulls, down topsides from sheer, and in from sheer along deck beam; for 8 × web height on transversely framed hulls, down topsides from sheer, and in from sheer along deck beam):	continuous
Floors to shell:	chain
Floors to frame:	continuous
Floors to keel-bottom plate:	continuous
Floors to shell in engine compartment:	continuous

TABLE 18-2 Component Weld Selection Table *(Cont.)*

Floors to shell at stern tube:	continuous
Floors to shell at mast step:	continuous
Floors to CVK:	continuous
CVK to stern frame:	continuous
Bottom girders to floors and frames:	continuous
Bottom-girder web to shell under engine mounts:	continuous
Bottom-girder web to shell:	chain
Frame webs to shell under engine beds (for at least 1.5 times length of engine and gear, or from CVK to chine or bilge, whichever is less):	continuous
Frame webs to shell at shaft logs:	continuous
For at least three longitudinals wide	
Engine-bed flange to web and engine bed to floors and bulkheads:	continuous
Engine beds to bottom girder:	continuous
Deck girder to beams:	continuous
Deck-girder web to shell:	chain
Bulkheads to shell:	continuous
Interior decks to shell (not watertight):	staggered
Stanchion tops and bases:	continuous
Brackets:	continuous
Doubler and insert plates:	continuous

All continuous welds are double continuous; that is, equal fillet welds on both sides. If access to one side is limited, a full-penetration, 60-degree bevel weld can be used instead, from the accessible side.

WELD SIZES

Welds are sized according to the thickness of the plates they join and the loads they will experience. The size of a fillet weld is specified by its leg; the spacing between intermittent welds is termed the *pitch*. Accordingly, to fully define a weld, you have to call out the following:

leg length
weld bead laid down (if intermittent)
pitch (if intermittent)
continuous (if continuous)

For example, the web of a $^1/_4$-inch (6.4 mm) aluminum frame would be fastened to $^3/_{16}$-inch (4.75 mm) shell plate with $^1/_8$-inch (3.2 mm) fillet welds, 1 inch (25 mm) long, with a 10-inch (250 mm) pitch, staggered (not chain).

FORMULA 18-3

Fillet-Weld Sizes

Fillet-weld size is based on the thinnest of the two plates being joined.

Weld Leg = thinnest plate – $^1/_{16}$ in. (for plates up to $^1/_2$ in.) (English)

Weld Leg = thinnest plate – 1.6 mm (for plates up to 13 mm) (Metric)

Weld Leg = thinnest plate – $^1/_8$ in. (for plates $^1/_2$ to 1 in.) (English)

(continued)

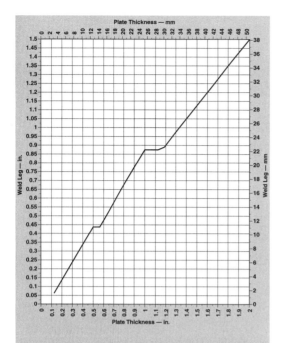

Fillet Weld Leg vs. Plate Thickness

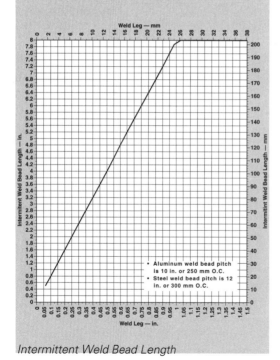

- Aluminum weld bead pitch is 10 in. or 250 mm O.C.
- Steel weld bead pitch is 12 in. or 300 mm O.C.

Intermittent Weld Bead Length

Weld Leg = thinnest plate – 3.2 mm (for plates 13 to 25 mm) (Metric)

Weld Leg = 0.75 × thinnest plate (for plates over 1 in. [25 mm])

Weld Length (Intermittent Welds) = 8 × leg, but not over 6 in. (152 mm)

Pitch O.C. = 10 in. (250 mm) for aluminum

Pitch O.C. = 12 in. (300 mm) for steel

Around the end of a member, say at a frame web at a limber hole, there should be a wraparound weld approximately equal to the standard weld-segment length.

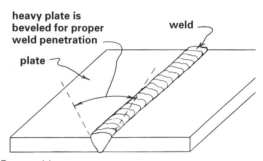

heavy plate is beveled for proper weld penetration

weld

plate

Butt weld

FORMULA 18-4

Butt Welds

For plates ¹⁄₁₆ to ¹⁄₈ in., the gap should be 0 to ¹⁄₁₆ in. (English)

For plates 1.6 to 3.2 mm, the gap should be 0 to 1.6 mm (Metric)

For plates ¹⁄₈ to ³⁄₁₆ in., the gap can be 0 to ³⁄₁₆ in. (English)

For plates 3.2 to 4.75 mm, the gap can be 0 to 4.75 mm (Metric)

Plates ³⁄₁₆ to ⁵⁄₁₆ in. should have a 60- to 100-degree groove in one face penetrating to within at least ⅛ in. of the opposite side (a single-groove butt weld) (English)

Plates 4.75 to 7.9 mm should have a 60- to 100-degree groove in one face penetrating to within at least 3.2 mm of the opposite side (a single-groove butt weld) (Metric)

Plates over 5/16 in. require a 60- to 100-degree groove in both faces with a 1/16- to ⅛-in. flat in the center (a double-groove butt weld) (English)

Plates over 7.9 mm require a 60- to 100-degree groove in both faces with a 1.6 to 3.2 mm flat in the center (a double-groove butt weld) (Metric)

PLUG AND SLOT WELDS

There are usually several places on a hull where it is impossible to reach to weld from inside. Deep keels, hollow rudders and skegs, and enclosed superstructure pylons all have internal stiffeners but are closed in from both sides. To assemble these components, the framework is erected. Then the plate along one side is welded from the inside. Finally, the opposite plate is installed and plug- or slot-welded from the outside. However, you can't plug-weld from the outside to the thin-plate edge of an internal stiffener. Accordingly, the framing on the cover-plate side must have T flanges welded to the stiffener edges. These flanges are fillet-welded to the stiffeners from the side on which the first plate will be installed, before that plate is installed.

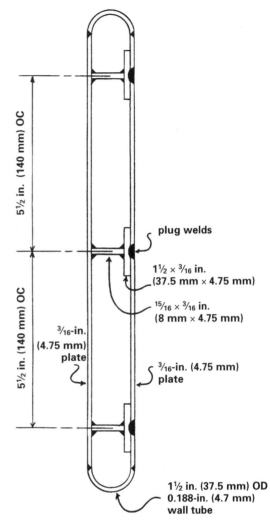

Section through pylon showing stiffeners and plug welds

FORMULA 18-5

Plug and Slot-Weld Sizes

A plug-weld is a round "rivet" weld from an outside plate through to the plate below.

Plug-Weld Diameter at Base = 2 × plate thickness (plate under ½ in. [12.7 mm])

Plug-Weld Diameter at Base = (2 × plate thickness) + ½ in. (plate over ½ in.) (English)

(continued)

Figure labels: 5½ in. (140 mm) OC; 5½ in. (140 mm) OC; ³/₁₆-in. (4.75 mm) plate; plug welds; 1½ × ³/₁₆ in. (37.5 mm × 4.75 mm); ¹⁵/₁₆ × ³/₁₆ in. (8 mm × 4.75 mm); ³/₁₆-in. (4.75 mm) plate; 1½ in. (37.5 mm) OD 0.188-in. (4.7 mm) wall tube

> *Plug-Weld Diameter at Base = (2 × plate thickness) + 12.7 mm (plate over 12.7 mm) (Metric)*
>
> *Plug-Weld Hole Beveled at 45 Degrees (wider at top than at base)*
>
> *Plug-Weld Pitch, Aluminum = 4.5 in. (115 mm)*
>
> *Plug-Weld Pitch, Steel = 5.5 in. (140 mm)*

Slot-welds are rectangular slots with round ends, through the outside plate to the plate below.

Slot-Weld Width = 2 × plate thickness (plate under ¼ in. [6.4 mm])

Slot-Weld Width = 2 × plate thickness with a 45-degree bevel (plate between ¼ and ½ in. [6.4 and 12.7 mm])

Slot-Weld Length = length for fillet weld of the same plate size

Slot-Weld Pitch = pitch of fillet weld for the same plate size

A FULL WELD SCHEDULE FOR ALUMANAUGHT

With this information, we can generate a complete weld schedule using, for example, our longitudinally framed, 35-knot, standard-scantling *AlumaNaught*.

Bottom-Frame Webs to Shell
$5/16$-in. (8 mm) plate, $3/8$-in. (9.5 mm) web: $1/4$-in. weld, 2-in. long, staggered, 10-in. O.C. (6.4 mm weld, 50 mm long, staggered, 250 mm O.C.)

Bottom-Frame Webs to Flange
$3/8$-in. (9.5 mm) floor, $1/2$-in. (14 mm) flange

$5/16$-in. weld, 2.5-in. long, chain, 10-in. O.C. (8 mm weld, 64 mm long, chain, 250 mm O.C.)

Bottom-Frame Webs to Shell under Engine Beds
$5/16$-in. (8 mm) plate, $3/8$-in. (9.5 mm) web: $5/16$-in. (8 mm) double-continuous weld for at least 1.5 times length of engine and gear, or from CVK to chine or bilge, whichever is less

Bottom-Frame Webs to Shell at Shaft Logs
$5/16$-in. (8 mm) plate, $3/8$-in. (9.5 mm) web: $5/16$-in. (8 mm) double-continuous weld, for at least three longitudinals

Floors to Shell
$5/16$-in. (8 mm) plate, $3/8$-in. (9.5 mm) floor: $1/4$-in. weld, 2-in. long, chain, 10-in. O.C. (6.4 mm weld, 50 mm long, chain, 250 mm O.C.)

Floors to Shell in Engine Compartment
$5/16$-in. (8 mm) plate, $3/8$-in. (9.5 mm) floor: $1/4$-in. (6.4 mm) double-continuous weld

Floors to Shell at Stern Tube
$5/16$-in. (8 mm) plate, $3/8$-in. (9.5 mm) floor: $1/4$-in. (6.4 mm) double-continuous weld

Floors to Frame
$3/8$-in. floor to $3/8$-in. frame (9.5 to 9.5 mm): continuous butt weld

Floors to Keel-Bottom Plate
$3/8$- to $7/8$-in. (9.5 to 20 mm)
$5/16$-in. (8 mm) double-continuous weld

Floors to CVK
$3/8$-in. (9.5 mm) floor to $7/8$-in. (22 mm) bottom plate: $5/16$-in. (8 mm) double-continuous weld

CVK to Stern Frame

7/8-in. CVK to 1 1/4-in. stern frame (22 to 30 mm): continuous 60-degree double-groove butt weld

Topsides-Frame Webs to Shell

3/8-in. web to 1/4-in. plate (9.5 to 6.45 mm): 3/16-in. weld, 1.5-in. long, staggered, 10-in. O.C. (4.75 mm weld, 38 mm long, staggered, 250 mm O.C.)

Topsides-Frame Web to Flange

3/8-in. web to 7/16-in. (9.5 to 11.25 mm): 5/16-in. weld, 2.5-in. long, chain, 10-in. O.C. (8 mm weld, 64 mm long, chain, 250 mm O.C.)

Deck-Beam Web to Shell

3/8-in. web to 3/16-in. shell (9.5 to 4.75 mm): 1/8-in. weld, 1-in. long, staggered, 10-in. O.C. (3.2 mm weld, 25 mm long, staggered, 10-in. O.C.)

Deck-Beam Web to Flange

3/8- in. web to 7/16-in. flange (9.5 to 11.25 mm): 5/16-in. weld, 2.5-in. long, chain, 10-in. O.C. (8 mm weld, 64 mm long, chain, 250 mm O.C.)

Hull-Bottom Longitudinals to Shell

3/8-in. longitudinals to 5/16-in. shell (9.5 to 8 mm): 5/16-in. weld, 2.5-in. long, staggered, 10-in. O.C. (8 mm weld, 64 mm long, staggered, 250 mm O.C.)

Topsides Longitudinals to Shell

3/8-in. longitudinals to 1/4-in. shell (9.5 to 6.4 mm): 3/16-in. weld, 1.5-in. long, staggered, 10-in. O.C. (4.75 mm weld, 38 mm long, staggered, 250 mm O.C.)

Deck Longitudinals to Shell

5/16-in. longitudinals to 3/16-in. shell (8 to 4.75 mm): 1/8-in. weld, 1-in. long, staggered, 10-in. O.C. (3.2 mm weld, 25 mm long, staggered, 250 mm O.C.)

Cabin-Frame Webs to Shell

1/4- to 3/16-in. (6.4 to 4.75 mm): 1/8-in. weld, 1-in. long, staggered, 10-in. O.C. (3.2 mm weld, 25 mm long, staggered, 250 mm O.C.)

Cabin-Frame Webs to Flange

1/4- to 1/4-in. (6.4 to 6.4 mm): 3/16-in. weld, 1.5-in. long, chain, 10-in. O.C. (4.75 mm weld, 38 mm long, chain, 250 mm O.C.)

Cabin Longitudinals to Shell

1/4-in. longitudinals to 3/16-in. shell (6.4 to 4.75 mm): 1/8-in. weld, 1-in. long, staggered, 10-in. O.C. (3.2 mm weld, 25 mm long, staggered, 250 mm O.C.)

Cabin-Roof-Beam Webs to Shell

1/4-in. web to 3/16-in. shell (6.4 to 4.75 mm): 1/8-in. weld, 1-in. long, staggered, 10-in. O.C. (3.2 mm weld, 25 mm long, staggered, 250 mm O.C.)

Cabin-Roof-Beams Web to Flange

1/4-in. web to 1/4-in. flange (6.4 to 6.4 mm): 3/16-in. weld, 1.5-in. long, chain, 10-in. O.C. (4.75 mm weld, 38 mm long, chain, 250 mm O.C.)

Hull-Bottom-Girders Web to Shell under Engine Mounts

7/16 in. web to 5/16-in. shell (11 to 8 mm): 1/4-in (6.4 mm) double-continuous weld

Hull–Bottom–Girder Web to Shell

$7/16$-in. web to $5/16$-in. shell (11 to 8 mm): $1/4$-in. weld, 2-in. long, chain, 10-in. O.C. (6.4 mm weld, 50 mm long, chain, 250 mm O.C.)

Hull–Bottom–Girder Web to Flange

$7/16$- to $1/2$-in. (11 to 12.7 mm): $3/8$-in. weld, 3-in. long, chain, 10-in. O.C. (9.5 mm weld, 115 mm long, chain, 250 mm O.C.)

Engine-Bed Web to Hull-Bottom Girder

$7/16$- to 1-in. (11 to 25 mm): continuous 60-degree double-bevel butt weld

Engine-Bed Web to Engine-Mount Flange

1-in. web to $1 1/4$-in. flange (25 to 30 mm): $3/4$-in. (19 mm) double-continuous weld

Bulkheads to Hull

$3/16$-in. bulkhead to $1/4$-, $3/16$-, and $5/16$-in. shell (4.75 mm bulkhead to 6.4, 4.75, and 8 mm shell): $1/8$-in. (3.2 mm) double-continuous weld

Bulkhead-Stiffener Webs to Bulkhead

$1/4$-in. web to $3/16$-in. plate (6.4 to 4.75 mm): $1/8$-in. weld, 1-in. long, staggered, 10-in. O.C. (3.2 mm weld, 25 mm long, staggered, 10-in. O.C.)

Bulkhead-Stiffener Web to Flange

$1/4$-in. web to $1/4$-in. flange (6.4 to 6.4 mm): $3/16$-in. weld, 1.5-in. long, chain, 10-in. O.C. (4.75 mm weld, 38 mm long, chain, 250 mm O.C.)

WELDING ACCESS

In both design and construction, access for welding in general is an important consideration. Boats are a glut of odd shapes and tight corners. An average MIG welding gun is about 15 inches (38 cm) long, with heavy hoses and cables fastened to one end; it can be difficult, even impossible, to get in to weld some areas. Careful thought must be given to the design of the structure so that welding is physically possible; equal thought must be given to the construction sequence to ensure that interior welds aren't made inaccessible.

WELDING SEQUENCE

The sequence or order of structural welding is critical to controlling distortion. There are three aspects to consider:

- Use back-step welding to minimize local distortion.
- Skip around the hull evenly from port to starboard and back, and fore-n-aft and back.
- The actual sequence in which the structural welds are completed must be selected to minimize distortion.

Back-Step Welding

Back-step welding eliminates local distortion. For example, take two plates 5 feet square (0.5 m²) and lay them just touching, parallel, side by side on a flat floor. If you joined them with a butt weld starting at one corner, running along the seam and working straight to the other end without stopping, you would end up with distorted plates. The corners you started at would cool first and shrink together. By the time you reached opposite corners to finish the seam, the once-parallel line between the plates would have spread open into a V shape. Where the plates were just touching to begin with, there might be an inch gap at the finishing corners. You would find it impossible to pull the plates together again; therefore, you would have to fill this gap with weld metal, meaning still more welding. This, in turn, would introduce yet more heat into the gapped-end, warping the plates.

To eliminate this, you must start in the middle of the plate. Weld several inches, with the gun moving in one direction. Then skip over to close to one end and weld several inches, running the welder in the opposite direction. Next, skip back to the opposite end and weld a few more inches, again switching the welding-pass direction. Then go back to an area near the middle for a few more inches still, and so on until the entire seam is complete. In this way, you draw the two plates together evenly without introducing a triangular gap or any warp.

In aluminum, you can weld up to 10 inches (255 mm) in a single pass, then skip about 15 inches (380 mm) away or more, and weld another 10 inches (255 mm), making the pass in the opposite direction. In steel—with the higher heat input required—weld no more than 3 or 4 inches (75 or 100 mm), then skip 12 inches (300 mm) or more, and weld running in the opposite direction.

Spreading Welds around the Boat

The principle of back-step welding applies not only at the local level for each plate, but also for the entire structure. Thus, if you were welding frames to the shell, you would start at the middle of the boat on starboard, and weld several inches. Next, switch to the same location on the port side. When this is done, don't go back to the same frame on the starboard side again; rather, skip forward or aft a few frames and repeat the process. Then go back to another frame next to your first one and do a few inches there. Again, you should spread the welds around in small increments to draw the structure together equally, without causing the same kind of large-scale distortion in the hull as you would by seaming two plates together in a single continuous pass.

Overall Welding Sequence

Keeping both local back-step welding and spreading welds around the boat in mind at all times, it is vitally important to follow a careful weld sequence in the final structural welding.

Except for backbone and framing components that won't be accessible later, all the frame and interior structure and all the plating should just be lightly tack-welded in place. Only when most of this structure is fitted and tacked can final structural welding begin.

Always start with the shell plate. Begin at the bilge or chine midships, gradually skipping your way outward toward the bow and stern and up to the sheer and down to the keel. Weld all the seams in this way, port and starboard (paying careful attention to back-step welding and weld-spreading). At the same time—skipping around as always—weld the shell plate to the backbone (i.e., stem, transom, and keel).

Next, break the longitudinals free from their tack welds to the frames and weld the longitudinals to the shell plating. Finally, weld the transverse frames to the shell plate and then to the longitudinals.

Aligning Plate Seams

To keep the plate seams in alignment (smooth and flush), it is often helpful to drill small holes along the seam and insert stainless steel bolts with heavy washers tightening them down to hold the plates flush and in line. These bolts are removed once most of the seam is welded and the holes are filled with weld metal. The bolts should be slightly larger in diameter than the plate thickness. Alternately, Ts with notches in them can be made up and slid through the seam. Wedges hammered in through the notch from the outside keep the plates aligned and knock out more quickly than unscrewing several bolts.

Clean Welds

Dirt, dust, slag, oil, rust, and scale play havoc with weld integrity. Edges to be welded have to be clean and free of contamination. In aluminum, even greasy handprints can make for local imperfections. Both rust and scale must be totally removed. In aluminum, for example, the oxide has nearly four times the melting point of the clean alloy. If you were to weld over aluminum oxide, you would have unwelded oxide flakes included in the weld and unwelded sections of alloy behind the flakes—not good!

JIGS

Because distortion can be such a serious problem, many yards fabricate on a massive steel strongback or jig. The intention is that the strongback will hold the structure in alignment against much weld distortion. I think this is good practice; however, I've worked with a builder who used virtually no strongback or jig at all. This builder simply hangs the transverse frames in place, attaching the CVK, gradually building up the internal framework including longitudinal stringers, and finally the plating. The result was quite fair. Jigs or strongbacks do help reduce distortion, but only within reason. Nothing on earth can resist the contraction in a metal hull due to poor weld control and planing. Carefully thought-out weld sequences and widely spread back-step welding are the keys to success. Heavy jigs help minimize distortion still further and help reduce problems—to a limited degree—when they occur.

JOINING LIGHT PLATE TO HEAVY PLATE

Heavy welds to light plate is an inconsistency; it can't be done. Still, there are heavy components—like engine beds $5/8$ inch (16 mm) thick—that must be continuously welded in hulls with plate just $3/16$ inch (8 mm) thick. The trick is to build up to the heavier component with gradually thicker ones. The structure specified for bottom girders and engine beds is a good example. In our example 35-knot *AlumaNaught*, we called for $5/16$-inch (8 mm) bottom plate. Fastened vertically to that is the hull-bottom girder, which was $7/16$ inch (11 mm) thick. On top of this is welded the web of the engine bed itself which, for *AlumaNaught*, came to 1 inch (25 mm). On top of all is the engine-bed flange, which is $1 1/4$ inches (32 mm). This same approach should be used whenever possible for heavy components.

When thick plate has to be butt-welded to thin plate, the thick plate must be beveled down to the thickness of the thin plate on a 3:1 bevel. Then a standard butt weld for the thin plate is used.

ROTATING JIGS AND BUILDING RIGHTSIDE UP OR UPSIDE DOWN

Welding is always easiest downhanded. On vertical surfaces, it is fairly easy; overhead, it is comparatively difficult. Some large production builders, fabricating multiple hulls, employ specialized rotating jigs that hold the entire hull and revolve it so almost every weld can be downhanded—much like a rotating fiberglass production mold. Nevertheless, most larger metal hulls are one-off or short-run production operation. All the yards I've worked with on such hulls have elected to build them rightside up. Without the ability to rotate the boat, there's little advantage to building the hull upside down and then righting it to finish. However, there's nothing wrong with building a hull upside down if some special circumstances seem to favor it. Some yards do prefer to build upside down in steel because it's easier to muscle the heavy plate onto the hull bottom.

V-GROOVE WELDS IN PLACE OF FILLET WELDS IN HEAVY PLATE

The majority of welding on boats is on plate under $1/2$ inch (25 mm). Nevertheless, there are a few heavier plates: CVK, horn plate, engine beds, chainplate, and lugs. When welding two plates over $3/4$ inch (19 mm), it is faster to use partial-penetration, double-bevel, V-groove welds. Even better, these welds use less weld metal, so they introduce less heat and less distortion.

The web plate should be beveled to 0.29 times the thickness of the thinner plate at a 60-degree angle on both sides. This is welded flush, and a fillet weld with a base leg of 0.29 thickness is added outside.

Where space is at a premium on heavy plate weldments, fillet welds can be replaced with double V-groove welds that penetrate nearly to the center of the web. Bevel the groove at 45 degrees and fill flush with weld metal. This does not reduce total weld or heat, but it keeps the base plate free of external fillet weld.

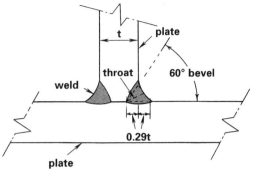

60-degree partial-penetration V-groove weld

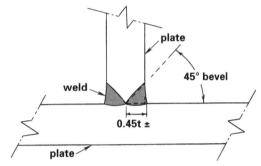

45-degree full-penetration V-groove weld

AVOID WELD GRINDING

On the hull exterior, welds must be ground smooth and flush. Everywhere else, though, weld grinding should be minimized. Grinding welds removes weld metal and weakens them; in tight corners, it can also create new crevices for corrosion.

RIGHT-ANGLE PLATE JOINTS PREFERRED

Where two plates meet at roughly right angles, they are joined with a fillet weld. Fillet welds, in fact, are easiest to make and strongest and close to right angles. In the odd shapes found in boat hulls, sole plates and tank walls often make obtuse or acute angles rather than right angles with the hull shell. Wherever possible, modify the shapes of such components to approximate a right-angle joint for maximum strength and ease of assembly.

Snipes, Rat Holes, and Limbers (Small Openings)

SNIPES

Snipes are cut-out corners where three welded plates meet at right angles so that weld lines don't cross each other. For instance, the CVK is welded to the hull-bottom plate. At right angles to these two are the floors. If the floor were welded continuously to the bottom plate and to the CVK, the longitudinal weld of the CVK to the bottom plate would cross the transverse weld of the floor to the bottom plate and the CVK. This causes tri-axial stress in the weld line and should be avoided as much as possible. (There is no avoiding it at watertight bulkheads, tanks, and such.) Accordingly, the corner of the floor (or any plate where weld lines could cross at right angles) should be snipped away in a snipe.

Close-up of longitudinal slot with snipe in frame. Note the rat hole in the longitudinal and the chain weld of the frame flange to the web.

In the previous example, the snipe doubles as a limber hole, which we need in this location anyway. In fact, snipes double as limber holes throughout, and help avoid areas where water can collect. Almost every right-angle plate intersection in the hull should be installed with a snipe. All the ring frames, for example, should have a snipe where each longitudinal passes through them—except, of course, at tanks and watertight bulkheads. The longitudinal snipe should be on the upper face of the longitudinal. This allows water to drain fore-n-aft along the stringers.

LIMBER HOLES AND RAT HOLES

Snipes are usually simply cropped back in a straight line, making a triangular opening. In the case of main limber holes in the floors—as discussed previously—this triangular opening is not as large in cross section as a quarter-circle cut out of the same height and width (same radius). Principal limber holes in the floors should be true quarter-circle cutouts. These naturally double as snipes.

The longitudinals themselves require limbers to drain the water so it can't pool on top. Limbers in stringers are usually termed *rat holes* because that is what they resemble. They are half-circles cut in the longitudinal against the inside of the shell plate. Stringers that are vertically oriented or overhead (e.g., deck and cabin-roof stringers) don't need rat-hole limbers because they shed water freely.

Rat holes in stringers also serve to avoid tri-axial weld stresses caused by crossing welds. The stringer should have a rat hole centered over any vertical butt seams in the shell plate to avoid weld lines crossing. This is recommended practice, but because the stringers are only welded intermittently to the plate, I find it is enough simply to instruct the

Limbers in floors.

welders to slightly adjust the weld spacing, as required, so that no stringer-to-plate weld crosses a plate's seam weld.

FORMULA 18-6
Snipes, Rat Holes, and Limbers

Snipes—General Applications = roughly right-triangle legs one-fourth the depth of the member or 1¼ in. (32 mm), whichever is less

Snipes—in Frames for Longitudinals = roughly right-triangle legs 0.6 × the longitudinal's height

Limbers to be 1¾ in. (44 mm) radius or radius one-third the depth of the member, whichever is less

Rat-Hole Radius = ¼ × longitudinal height

Rat-Hole Location = one between every frame

LIGHTENING HOLES

Large webs in girders and in floors are usually penetrated by *lightening holes*. This term is a little misleading. Yes, the holes do reduce weight; however, their principal purposes on most vessels are to make it easier to run cables and pipes and to improve access. A rigorous program of extensive lightening holes is required to make a significant impact on total structural weight. This can be done, but is only worth the expense on very lightweight high-performance vessels.

FORMULA 18-7
Lightening Holes

Lightening-Hole Closest Distance to Edge of Web

Hull and Deck: 22.5%

Superstructure: 20%

Upper Superstructure (e.g., flybridge): 17.5%

Lightening-Hole Maximum Height

Hull and Deck: 55% of web

Superstructure: 60% of web

Upper Superstructure (e.g., flybridge): 65%

Lightening-Hole Minimum Distance Between Hole Edges

Hull and Deck: 85% of web

Superstructure: 60% of web

Upper Superstructure: 45% of web

Lightening-Hole Maximum Total Area Removed from Web

Hull and Deck: 55%

Superstructure: 65%

Upper Superstructure (e.g., flybridge): 70%

The length of any individual hole may not be more than the web height. On floors, the bottom outside edge of the lightening holes can't be closer to the shell plate than 85 percent of the frame web height, or the minimum specified previously, whichever is greater.

Lightening holes can be circles, ellipses, or round-end rectangles. They must not have sharp corners anywhere. Engine mounts and mast steps cannot have lightening holes.

We found the 35-knot *AlumaNaught* had bottom-girder webs 8¼ inches high. Thus, lightening holes through the girder web would be as follows:

No closer to the edge than 0.225 × 8.25 in. = 1.85; use 1⅞ in.

Maximum Height = 0.55 × 8.25 in. = 4.53; use 4.5 in.

Minimum Distance between Hole Edges = 0.85 × 8.25 in. = 7.01; use 7 in.

Maximum Length = 8¼ in.

The 35-knot *AlumaNaught*'s frame spacing is 36 inches, so the area of the web between frames is

36 in. × 8.25 in. = 297 sq. in.

Maximum Total Lightening-Hole Area = 0.55 × 297 sq. in. = 163.3 sq. in.

or

The 35-knot *AlumaNaught*'s bottom-girder webs were 210 mm high, so the lightening holes through the girder web would be

No closer to the edge than 0.225 × 210 mm = 47.25; use 46 mm

Maximum Height = 0.55 × 210 mm = 115.5; use 115 mm

Minimum Distance Between Hole Edges = 0.85 × 210 mm = 178 mm

Maximum Length = 210 mm

The 35-knot *AlumaNaught*'s frame spacing is 90 cm, so the area of the web between frames is

90 cm × 21 cm = 1,890 cm²

Maximum Total Lightening Hole Area = 0.55 × 1,890 cm² = 1,039 cm²

Riveting Aluminum

Welding is the fastest and strongest method of fastening metal hulls with sufficient plate thickness. Small boats—under 25 feet or so—only require very thin plate too thin to weld. Using heavier plate on such vessels just to be able to weld it effectively makes for an unnecessarily heavy hull. The answer—and it's a good one—is riveting. (Steel would rust too quickly and is too heavy for efficient small-boat work.)

It's a little odd that some people seem leery of riveted hulls; after all, welding is the new technology and riveted boats have been around nearly 100 years longer. Airplanes are made of aluminum, but—needing to be so light—even giant jumbo jets are fabricated from thin aluminum sheets riveted together. Clearly, these airframes don't leak or fail. Indeed, the Lund Boat Company has been manufacturing small aluminum production boats in Minnesota since 1948. In a recent conversation with its manager, he related that since he had been with the company, they had produced more than 200,000 boats and there hadn't been a single hull-seam failure.

Riveted joints are so tight that no caulking is required, except at joints that might not draw tight together readily, such as hull-to-deck joints in production boats, where 3M sealing tape about ⅛ inch thick may be employed. In the rare event that a rivet or two did loosen, they're either easily hammered back in tight, using a bucking iron inside, or replaced with a slightly fatter rivet.

Although the rivets in a properly designed joint take the load in sheer, the two joint surfaces are clamped so tightly together that they add considerably to the joint strength by resisting sliding from their friction.

Riveted joints on hull seams are usually simple lap joints. Edge-to-edge joints with single backing (doubler) plate on the inside are also acceptable. Where maximum strength is needed in a larger structure, double-backing (doubler) plates—one on each side—can be used. This would be the strongest way to attach a T engine-bed web to a vertical hull-bottom girder, for example.

Rivets must be of the correct diameter for the sheet or plate they are fastening. Use the thinnest of the two plates to be

TABLE 18-8 Rivet Diameter, Sheet or Plate

Thickness, in. (mm)		Diameter, in. (mm)
from	to	
0.025 (0.64)	0.036 (0.91)	¹⁄₁₆ (1.59)
0.036 (0.91)	0.048 (1.22)	³⁄₃₂ (2.38)
0.048 (1.22)	0.064 (1.63)	⅛ (3.18)
0.064 (1.63)	0.080 (2.03)	⁵⁄₃₂ (3.97)
0.080 (2.03)	0.104 (2.64)	³⁄₁₆ (4.76)
0.104 (2.64)	0.128 (3.25)	¼ (6.35)
0.128 (3.25)	0.188 (4.78)	⁵⁄₁₆ (7.94)
0.188 (4.78)	0.200 (5.08)	⅜ (9.53)
0.200 (5.08)	0.250 (6.35)	⁷⁄₁₆ (11.11)
0.250 (6.35)	0.300 (7.62)	½ (12.70)
0.300 (7.62)	0.350 (8.89)	⁹⁄₁₆ (14.29)
0.350 (8.89)	0.400 (10.16)	⅝ (15.88)
0.400 (10.16)	0.550 (13.97)	¾ (19.05)
0.550 (13.97)	0.700 (17.78)	⅞ (22.23)

NOTE: All these are solid (not hollow) rivets.

The old rule-of-thumb for rivet diameter is that the rivet should be between 2.5 and 3 times the plate thickness and never less than the thickness of the thinnest plate.

FORMULA 18-9
Rivet Pitch, Edge Distance, and Row Spacing

Edge Distance, Normal = 2 × diameter

Edge Distance, Minimum = 1.5 × diameter

Pitch, Minimum Allowable = 3 × diameter

Pitch for Watertight Seams, Maximum = 4 × diameter or 10 × the thinnest plate thickness, whichever is less

Pitch for Non-Watertight Joints = 5 to 8 × diameter (6 is average)

fastened. Pitch and edge distance are equally important for a proper joint.

Double rivet rows are recommended on watertight lap seams. The rows should be spaced two times the rivet diameter apart, with the rivets alternating centers between rows.

RIVETED ALUMINUM SUPERSTRUCTURES
In addition to riveting light sheet on small aluminum boats, riveting permits the use of lighter sheets on the superstructure of larger

lightweight high-performance boats. For instance, for the lightweight 35-knot *Aluma-Naught*, we could refer to Table 16-4A and use $^1/_8$-inch (3.2 mm) cabin-roof plate. The best welders could weld this with pulse-arc equipment, but distortion is still likely. This would not be a problem with riveting.

Remember that *AlumaNaught* had a trunk cabin roof with a maximum span (beam) of 12.2 feet (3.71 m). Referring to Table 16-4A, we would use the following:

$^1/_8$-in. plate
beams 7.5-in. O.C.
3-in. web × 2-in. flange × $^1/_4$-in. thick
    beams

or

3.2 mm plate
beams 190 mm O.C.
75 mm web × 50 mm flange × 6.4 mm thick

The beams in this construction need a flange against the underside of the deck plate to accept the rivets. This flange should be four times the rivet diameter. Rivets attaching the $^1/_8$-inch (3.2 mm) plate to the $^1/_4$-inch (6.4 mm) flange would be

$^1/_4$-in. diameter (6.35 mm); the flange under the deck would be 1 in. wide

Because this is not a watertight seam, the rivets would be spaced 1.5 inches (38 mm) pitch. At the edge of the cabin roof, the rivets would fasten down into a $^1/_4$-inch (6.4 mm) boundary bar. This is a watertight seam and rivet pitch would be reduced to 1 inch (25 mm).

On a somewhat smaller *AlumaNaught*, the cabin side too could be reduced to less than $^3/_{16}$-inch (4.75 mm) plate. It could also then be of riveted construction.

NINETEEN

Small Aluminum Boats and Copper-Nickel Hulls

Small Aluminum Boats

Aluminum, unlike steel, is an ideal material for small aluminum hulls. It is light enough so that boats as small as 20 feet (6 m) can be fabricated using welded construction. Most small welded boats are constructed of $^3/_{16}$-inch (4.75 mm) plate for weldability, which makes them heavier than necessary, but—on beefier small craft—this isn't too much of a drawback. Plate as thin as $^1/_8$ inch (3 mm) is welded using pulse-arc equipment by some production builders. This approach yields fairly light small welded hulls. Nevertheless, the very thin sheet necessary to produce really light structure weights on hulls with Sns less than 0.50 (roughly under 20 feet [6 m]) is really not suited to welding. Riveted construction is the best approach.

ALUMINUM SHEET THICKNESS FOR SMALL BOATS
Table 19-1 is a simple guide to proper sheet thickness on small riveted aluminum hulls.

- Planing boats over 15 feet (4.5 m) should increase the bottom plate in the forward third of the hull to 0.90 inch (2.29 mm).
- Planing boats over 15 feet (4.5 m) should use the framing thickness sheet size from the next boat size up on the table.
- Planing boats with Sns under 0.50 should use hull-bottom girders with thicknesses and dimensions as described in chapter 16, except that single-engine and outboard boats require only one girder per side, not two. The deep floors used to support the cockpit sole usually extend over the top of the bottom girder, so the minimum height above floor dimensions does not apply.
- Topside longitudinals are not required on boats with Sns under 0.50. Deck longitudinals are only required for hulls with large walk-on decks. Bottom longitudinals, or stiffeners of some sort, are required on these small hulls only for planing craft.
- Longitudinal spacing is not determined

TABLE 19-1 Aluminum Small Riveted Boat Scantlings (English)

LOA, ft.	Bottom, in.	Topsides, in.	Transom, in.	Deck and Cabin, in.	Keel, in.	Thickness, in.
10	0.050	0.050	0.063	0.050	0.000	0.050
13	0.063	0.050	0.090	0.063	0.075	0.063
15	0.063	0.063	0.090	0.071	0.075	0.063
16	0.071	0.063	0.090	0.071	0.075	0.067
18	0.080	0.063	0.090	0.071	0.075	0.080
21	0.090	0.080	0.090	0.071	0.075	0.085

TABLE 19-1 Aluminum Small Riveted Boat Scantlings (Metric)

LOA, m	Bottom, mm	Topsides, mm	Transom, mm	Deck and Cabin, mm	Keel, mm	Thickness, mm
3.0	1.3	1.3	1.6	1.3	0.0	1.3
4.0	1.6	1.3	2.3	1.6	1.9	1.6
4.6	1.6	1.6	2.3	1.8	1.9	1.6
4.9	1.8	1.6	2.3	1.8	1.9	1.7
5.5	2.0	1.6	2.3	1.8	1.9	2.0
6.4	2.3	2.0	2.3	1.8	1.9	2.2

according to the formulas in chapters 15 and 16. Instead, arrange the combination of longitudinals and frames so that no hull-bottom panel (or walk-on deck) is larger than 3 square feet (0.278 m²). In other words, the area contained between any two frames and their two intersecting longitudinals must be less than 3 square feet (0.278 m²).

- Interior components such as thwarts, engine beds, cockpit sole supports, and cuddy bulkheads should be used in place of frames and longitudinals wherever possible.

Riveted aluminum outboard fishing runabout.
(Courtesy Lund Boat Company)

Riveted aluminum-boat assembly. Note the deep floors to support the cockpit sole. Foam flotation and "belly" fuel tank are installed. (Courtesy Lund Boat Company)

INCREASING SHEET STIFFNESS

On most of these small craft, you can increase panel stiffness by stamping in joggles in the plate, like imitation lapstrake, or as spray rails. Displacement vessels and small boats under 14 feet (4.2 m) benefit only slightly from this—although they do benefit. Planing hulls over this size should employ this technique as much as possible.

FRAMING FOR SMALL ALUMINUM BOATS

The Sn can be used to determine the frame dimensions and longitudinal height for riveted aluminum craft under 21 feet (6.4 mm); however, use the sheet thickness from Table 19-1.

Let's say we wanted to build a riveted aluminum open-cockpit outboard skiff. We'll call it *MiniAlloy*. *MiniAlloy*'s dimensions are

LOA	19.22 ft.	5.85 m
WL	17.02 ft.	5.37 m
Beam	6.83 ft.	2.08 m
Chine Beam	6.00 ft.	1.82 m
Depth of Hull	3.22 ft.	0.98 m

This makes *MiniAlloy*'s Sn 0.41 (see Formula 1-1). Using the formulas in chapters 15 and 16 for a longitudinally framed aluminum hull and using Table 19-1, we would find our riveted *MiniAlloy*'s scantlings to be as follows:

Bottom Sheet = 0.090 in. (2.3 mm)

Topsides Sheet = 0.080 in. (2 mm)

Transom Sheet = 0.090 in. (2.3 mm)

Deck Sheet = 0.071 in. (1.8 mm)

Keel CVK = 0.075 in. (1.9 mm)

Note that the keel is often an external extrusion riveted to the plate, port and starboard, along the centerline.

Keel CVK Height – 1.81; use 1⅞ in. (48 mm)

Framing Thickness (Webs, Flanges, and Longitudinals) = 0.085 in. (2.2 mm)

Frame Spacing O.C. = 28.8; use 29 in. (735 mm)

Bottom-Frame-Web Height = 1.62 in. (41.1 mm)

Riveted aluminum runabouts going together. (Courtesy Lund Boat Company)

If we say *MiniAlloy* is a 28-knot boat, we would increase web height by 1 percent for every knot over 20 knots:

1.62 in. × 1.08 = 1.74; use 1¾ in.

or

41.0 mm × 1.08 = 44.3; use 44 mm

Note that since the floors will be used to support the cockpit sole, they will probably greatly exceed this height.

Topsides-Frame-Web Height = 1 ⅜ in. (35 mm)

Bottom-Frame-Flange Width = 1.21; use 30.7 mm

MiniAlloy is a 28-knot boat, so increase flange width by 1 percent for every knot over 15 knots.

1.21 in. × 1.13 = 1.36; use 1⅜ in.

or

30.7 mm × 1.13 = 34.6; use 35 mm

Topsides-Frame-Flange Width = 1.21; use 1¼ in. (30 mm)

Deck-Beam-Web Height = 1.45; use 1 ½ in. (38 mm)

Deck-Beam-Flange Width = 1.09; use 1 in. (25 mm)

Few if any bottom longitudinals would be required if three deep stamped-in spray rails were formed into the bottom sheet. No longitudinals are required elsewhere; however, stamped-in lapstrake on the topsides will look handsome and make it stiffer.

MINIALLOY'S BOTTOM LONGITUDINALS

Without stamped-in spray rails, bottom longitudinals from angle should be installed on *MiniAlloy*'s planing hull as follows:

Longitudinal Spacing:

Frames are spaced 29 in. or 2.416 ft., so 3 sq. ft. ÷ 2.416 ft. = 1.24 ft., or 14.88; use 15 in.

Frames are spaced 735 mm, so 0.278 m² ÷ 0.735 m = 0.378 m, or 378 mm; use 380 mm

Longitudinal Dimensions:

Height from Formula 15-7A = 0.731 in.

MiniAlloy is a 28-knot boat, so increase height by 1 percent for every knot over 20 knots.

0.731 in. × 1.08 = 0.789; use ⅞ in.

or

Height from Formula 15-7A = 18.56 mm

18.56 mm × 1.08 = 20 mm

Because the longitudinals are riveted to the hull shell inside, they require a flange against the shell that is at least four times the rivet diameter wide.

The bottom sheet is 0.090 inch (2.3 mm) and the framing is 0.085 inch (2.2 mm); 0.085 inch (2.2 mm) is thinner. Thus, from Table 18-8, the rivets for the flange should be ³/₁₆ inch (4.76 mm) in diameter.

The flange to the hull should then be 4 × 0.1875 in. = 0.75 in. wide

(4 × 4.76 mm = 19 mm wide)

This is not a watertight seam in the hull plating, so average pitch is six times the diameter, accordingly,

pitch = 6 × 0.1875 in. = 1⅛ in. rivet O.C.

or

pitch = 6 × 4.76 mm = 28.5 mm rivet O.C.

If we used stamped-in spray rails on *MiniAlloy*'s bottom, we would make them about ⁷/₈ inch (20 mm) deep throughout most of the boat's length.

SMALL-BOAT ALUMINUM FRAMING DETAILS

Usually, the bottom frames are rather deep and straight across the top in small boats like *MiniAlloy*. In this way, the bottom frame is floor, frame, and cockpit sole beam all in one. Standard practice is to fabricate all the components from sheet, cutting them to shape and bending in flanges on a press brake. Cockpit soles, decks, and many joiner components (interior and exterior) are frequently made of marine plywood.

Aluminum thwarts, boxes, bulkheads, and engine wells are normally the same thickness as the topsides sheet. The press brake is used extensively to bend flanges into these components for stiffening.

Keep in mind that the thin plate on these hulls is very sensitive to hard spots. The framing needs to be thought out so that structural loads are dissipated into the structure at floors, frames, and stringers. Components like diagonal braces under thwarts cannot land on the plate; they must land on some framing member.

Copper-Nickel Hulls

There is one very different alloy that offers some significant advantages—at least on larger vessels over 45 feet (14 m) or so: copper-nickel. Copper-nickel is similar in strength to marine aluminum; however, at 530 lb./cu. ft. (8,490 kg./m³), it weighs somewhat more than steel. Therefore, it is not as light a construction material as aluminum, but—unlike steel and like aluminum—copper-nickel doesn't rust at all.

The really remarkable thing about copper-nickel is it requires no bottom paint ever. It's almost completely and totally non-fouling—forever! In fact, if you didn't want to, you wouldn't have to paint *any* part of an all copper-nickel boat. Of course, there must be some reason that you aren't completely surrounded by copper-nickel boats; there is one: they cost dearly. Copper-nickel is expensive, considerably more expensive than almost any other form of construction. Even so, a few commercial vessels—primarily fishing boats and tugboats—have been built of

Alloy	Copper-Nickel %	UTS, psi (mPa)	Yield, psi (mPa)
CA-706	90-10 cu-ni	40,000 (276)	15,000 (103)
CA-706 (¼ Hard)	90-10 cu-ni	55,000 (379)	30,000 (207)
CA-715	70-30 cu-ni	45,000 (310)	18,000 (124)

TABLE 19-2 Copper-Nickel Boatbuilding Alloy Physical Properties, psi (mPa)

Modulus of elasticity E = 18,000,000 psi (124,050 mPa)

UTS = Ultimate Tensile Strength

copper-nickel because the savings in fuel and bottom-cleaning charges, as a result of having a clean bottom all the time, can make it worth their while.

COPPER-NICKEL SCANTLINGS

You can see from Table 19-2 that CA-706 and CA-715 alloys are very close in physical properties to marine aluminum. CA-706 ($1/4$-hard), on the other hand, is closer to steel. Copper-nickel's modulus of elasticity, however, is 80 percent greater than aluminum (it is 80 percent stiffer), while it is only 62 percent of that steel (38 percent bendier). Based on these factors, the following formula can be used to determine the scantlings for copper-nickel hulls.

FORMULA 19-3
Copper-Nickel Scantling Conversions

For CA-706 and CA-715:

Use the aluminum rule to calculate all scantlings.

- *Multiply the plate thickness found by 0.60 for copper-nickel.*

- *Use the same frame-web and flange dimensions and longitudinal heights, but multiply the thickness by 0.88 for copper-nickel.*

- *Because of the tremendous corrosion resistance of copper-nickel, even the lightweight aluminum rule can be used and converted to copper-nickel.*

- *Use the longitudinal spacing according to the aluminum rule based on the actual final copper-nickel plate thickness installed.*

For CA-706 ($1/4$-hard):

Use the steel rule to calculate all scantlings.

- *Use the steel longitudinal spacing rule and multiply the plate thickness by 1.4 to get the copper-nickel plate thickness.*

- *Or use the aluminum longitudinal spacing rule and multiply the plate thickness by 0.60 for copper-nickel.*

WELDING STEEL TO COPPER NICKEL

Note that several copper-nickel vessels have been constructed with copper-nickel hulls and all-steel framing. The goal of this approach is to get the nonfouling and nonrusting/nonwasting benefits of copper-nickel while keeping cost down. On several such commercial vessels, the galvanic corrosion was found to be minimal (although it was present) after more than four years of operation in tropical waters.

These hulls were sandblasted inside and the copper-nickel in the bilge was painted with epoxy paint. The steel (sandblasted as well) was painted throughout the boat. In the bilge—where water can collect from an interior electrolyte—internal zinc anodes were installed on portions of the steel framing.

Although this system of steel framing and copper-nickel plating has worked and is acceptable, it seems counterproductive to me. After all, copper-nickel's big advantage is its total lack of corrosion combined with total nonfouling. Even with a good paint system and anodes, the steel framing will eventually corrode (if slowly). On most craft, much of this corrosion would be difficult to get at to inspect or repair. If at all possible, I would stick to all copper-nickel: framing and hull.

This is how *Miss Rivere* was built. A 45-foot (13.7 m) motor yacht, *Revere* was launched in 1938 and served in the coastal patrol of the U.S. Coast Guard during World War II. Built of CA-715 copper-nickel (hull shell and all framing), its plating was just 0.080 inch (2 mm) thick, yet the boat gave reliable service even in ice conditions.

Conclusion

Not too long ago I received an interesting e-mail from one of my clients. Cruising his *Belle Marie* along the Intracoastal Waterway, he had . . . well, a minor adventure:

I've finally run the boat aground hard! Before, [when I've run aground] I've known that the water was shallow and was drifting or moving at idle speed. We were running down the Intercoastal Waterway, in South Carolina, Saturday, in one of the long ditch-like sections of the ICW. I moved over to the edge of the cut to let a faster boat go by but failed to notice the stream that crossed into the ditch. It had evidently built up a sand shoal out into the channel at the edge. The stern sank suddenly and as I reached to pull power off and turn back into deeper water, we hit the bar at about nine knots. Wham!! As our stern wave caught up to us, the transom lifted and we went over the bar into deeper water again. Although it threw us around inside, nothing flexed, nothing even rattled! I'm sure that it scuffed a couple of feet of bottom paint off the bottom plate. It also scuffed a couple of square inches of skin off Marie, and I haven't heard the end of it yet.

This is what *The Elements of Boat Strength* is all about—fabricating vessels that can take punishment and keep their crews safe. There was some good-natured banter at this boat's builder about "overbuilding." Certainly, *Belle Marie*'s shoal bottom was designed extra strong. After all, she was specifically drawn up to take ground at will. Still—heavily constructed or not—she floats on her lines and makes proper speed. *Belle Marie* has proven a fine seaboat too.

If *Belle Marie* were "overbuilt," she would have been too heavy, or too tender, or too slow, or all of the above. In the final analysis, what can be said for sure is that she is plenty rugged. As a result, we all sleep well at night—designer, builder, and owner. That's what *Boat Strength* is all about.

APPENDIX 1:
PHOTO GALLERY

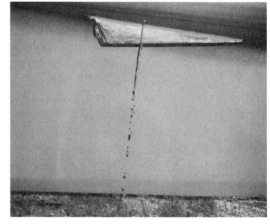

Above right: *No we didn't drill into a tank! This 34-foot (10.4 m) foam core hull was ruined by improper core bedding. All this water was forced in through improperly bedded fasteners for spray strips. More than 20 holes all over the bottom "leaked" like this (see p. 14).*

Above: *Bottom stringers and floors in a 40-foot (12.2 m) planing hull. The well-tabbed-in ply floors are acceptable. The thicker-cored FRP floors called for in the rule are better still (see p.16).*
Right: *A chopper gun in use. This fellow should at least be wearing a facemask and goggles (see p. 11).* (Courtesy Owens-Corning Fiberglass Corporation)

Right: This secondary bond failed when yanked on with one hand. The builder didn't pay attention to getting a good bond and didn't fillet the corners before tabbing (see p. 18).
Below: Numerous bulkheads in the Cape Dory 40 motor yacht. All are well tabbed in and sealed (see p. 45). **Bottom:** Proper treatment of interior wood. Note that all structural members—bulkheads, furring strips, and the like—have been sprayed with gelcoat and sealed. This is a Cape Dory 40 motor yacht (see p. 18).

Left: Clear view of the robust continuous bulkhead tabbing on the Cape Dory 40 (see p. 45). **Below:** Engine-bed stringers and transverse hat-hection ring frame on the Gerr "Westbourne 44" (see p. 48). (Courtesy Westbourne Custom Yachts.) **Bottom:** A well-made elastometric foam spacer at a bulkhead joint (see p. 48).

The Gerr 34-foot (10.4 m) Sportfisherman is of standard cored FRP construction. It is entirely balsa core with stitch-mat and combi-mat style glass. Scantlings and details follow the FRP scantling rule. The boat does a steady 30 knots in Force Six conditions and has proven very rugged (see p. 64). (Courtesy Off Soundings Yachts)

Above: The Gerr-designed 44-foot (13.4 m) catamaran Slipstream *is built of vacuum-bagged balsa core with bi-axial E-glass laid in vinylester resin. All joiner panels, soles, and joiner bulkheads are Decolite (balsa core) and Nida core (plastic honeycomb) panels. The boat's displacement/length ratio is just 70 (see p. 75).* (Courtesy Z Sails). **Right:** *Interior of* Slipstream's *bridge-deck cabin. Every joiner panel is balsa core or Nida core to reduce weight (see p. 75).*

Deck of the Sutherland Runabout (see p. 80).
(Courtesy Sutherland Boat and Coach)

Top: *Sawn frames with plywood gussets for the hard-chine Sutherland Runabout (see p. 110).* **Middle:** *View of interior framing of* Madrigal. *Floors, frames, plank laps, sheer clamp, stem, and plank keel are all plainly visible (see p. 110).* **Bottom:** *The author's canoe-stern lapstrake sloop design* Madrigal *gleaming as she leaves her builder, North River Boatworks, on launching day (see p. 102).*

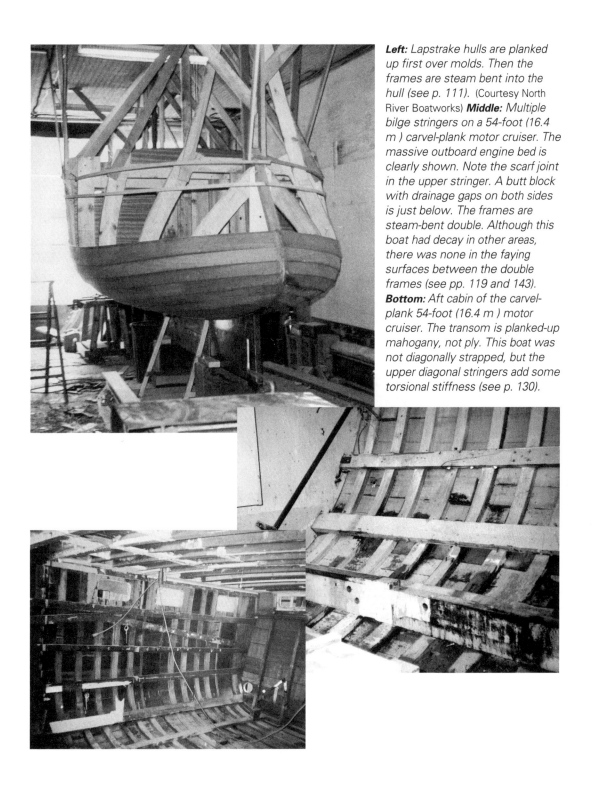

Left: *Lapstrake hulls are planked up first over molds. Then the frames are steam bent into the hull (see p. 111).* (Courtesy North River Boatworks) **Middle:** *Multiple bilge stringers on a 54-foot (16.4 m) carvel-plank motor cruiser. The massive outboard engine bed is clearly shown. Note the scarf joint in the upper stringer. A butt block with drainage gaps on both sides is just below. The frames are steam-bent double. Although this boat had decay in other areas, there was none in the faying surfaces between the double frames (see pp. 119 and 143).* **Bottom:** *Aft cabin of the carvel-plank 54-foot (16.4 m) motor cruiser. The transom is planked-up mahogany, not ply. This boat was not diagonally strapped, but the upper diagonal stringers add some torsional stiffness (see p. 130).*

Above: Notching a double lodging knee for a half-deck beam (see p. 152). (Courtesy Kortchmar & Willner)
Right: Proper bulkhead/ring frames well tabbed in place in a sheathed wood-epoxy strip-plank hull (see p. 155). (Courtesy Alan Salisch)

Top: *The author's 60-foot (18.2 m) Class 1 BOC racer Holger Danske. Wood-epoxy strip-plank construction sheathed with bi-axial S-glass allowed an extremely light but tough hull. D/L ratio is just 40 (see p. 156).* (Courtesy Onne van der Wal)

Middle: *A beautifully finished Gerr-designed 28-foot (8.5 m) tape-seam plywood Offshore Skiff built by Hill's Marine (see p. 166).* (Courtesy Hill's Marine)

Bottom: *Diagonal-veneer cold-molded V-bottom powerboat hull. The closely spaced longitudinal stringers and chine log are clearly visible. Note the treatment of the bottom stringers on the V-bottom (see p. 171).* (Courtesy Alan Salisch)

Top: Photograph of the first all-aluminum boat, a leeboard spritsail sloop built in 1890 (see p. 182). ***Middle:*** Photograph of Mignon, *the first aluminum powerboat (a naphtha launch) (see p. 182).* (Courtesy Kaiser Aluminum) ***Bottom:*** Imagine, built by Kanter Yachts. This Gerr-designed 57-foot (17.3 m) aluminum voyaging motor cruiser has a range of more than 3,500 nautical miles and a top speed of 12 knots at light load (see p. 187). (Courtesy Kanter Yachts)

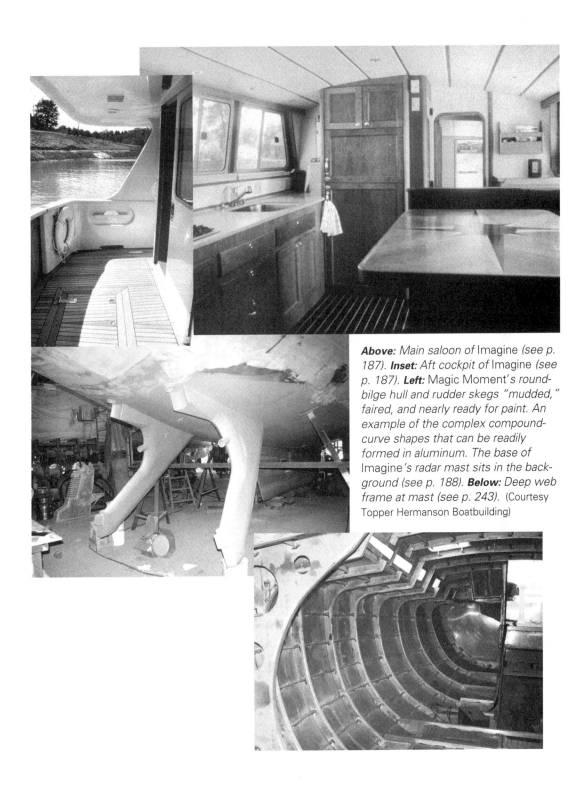

Above: *Main saloon of* Imagine *(see p. 187).* **Inset:** *Aft cockpit of* Imagine *(see p. 187).* **Left:** Magic Moment's *round-bilge hull and rudder skegs "mudded," faired, and nearly ready for paint. An example of the complex compound-curve shapes that can be readily formed in aluminum. The base of* Imagine's *radar mast sits in the background (see p. 188).* **Below:** *Deep web frame at mast (see p. 243).* (Courtesy Topper Hermanson Boatbuilding)

APPENDIX 2: PIPE SIZES AND PROPERTIES TABLE

Nominal pipe size, in	Schedule no.	OD, in	ID, in	Wall thickness, in	Weight per linear foot, lb, plain ends†	Cross-sectional wall area, in²	Inside cross-sectional area, in²	Moment of inertia, in⁴	Section modulus, in³	Radius of gyration, in
⅛	40‡	0.405	0.269	0.068	0.085	0.0720	0.0568	0.0011	0.0053	0.1215
	80§	0.405	0.215	0.095	0.109	0.0925	0.0363	0.0012	0.0060	0.1146
¼	40‡	0.540	0.364	0.088	0.147	0.1250	0.1041	0.0033	0.0123	0.1628
	80§	0.540	0.302	0.119	0.185	0.1574	0.0716	0.0038	0.0139	0.1547
⅜	40‡	0.675	0.493	0.091	0.196	0.1670	0.1909	0.0073	0.0216	0.2090
	80§	0.675	0.423	0.126	0.256	0.2173	0.1405	0.0086	0.0255	0.1991
½	40‡	0.840	0.622	0.109	0.294	0.2503	0.3039	0.0171	0.0407	0.2613
	80§	0.840	0.546	0.147	0.376	0.3200	0.2341	0.0201	0.0478	0.2505
¾	10	1.050	0.884	0.083	0.297	0.2521	0.6138	0.0297	0.0566	0.3432
	40‡	1.050	0.824	0.113	0.391	0.3326	0.5333	0.0370	0.0705	0.3337
	80§	1.050	0.742	0.154	0.510	0.4335	0.4324	0.0448	0.0853	0.3214
1	5	1.315	1.185	0.065	0.300	0.2553	1.103	0.0500	0.0760	0.4425
	10	1.315	1.097	0.109	0.486	0.4130	0.9452	0.0757	0.1151	0.4382
	40‡	1.315	1.049	0.133	0.581	0.4939	0.8643	0.0873	0.1328	0.4205
	80§	1.315	0.957	0.179	0.751	0.6388	0.7193	0.1056	0.1606	0.4066
1¼	5	1.660	1.530	0.065	0.383	0.3257	1.839	0.1037	0.1250	0.5644
	10	1.660	1.442	0.109	0.625	0.5311	1.633	0.1605	0.1934	0.5497
	40‡	1.660	1.380	0.140	0.786	0.6685	1.496	0.1947	0.2346	0.5397
	80§	1.660	1.278	0.191	1.037	0.8815	1.283	0.2418	0.2913	0.5238
1½	5	1.900	1.770	0.065	0.441	0.3747	2.461	0.1579	0.1662	0.6492
	10	1.900	1.682	0.109	0.721	0.6133	2.222	0.2468	0.2598	0.6344
	40‡	1.900	1.610	0.145	0.940	0.7995	2.036	0.3099	0.3262	0.6226
	80§	1.900	1.500	0.200	1.256	1.068	1.767	0.3912	0.4118	0.6052
2	5	2.375	2.245	0.065	0.555	0.4717	3.958	0.3149	0.2652	0.8170
	10	2.375	2.157	0.109	0.913	0.7760	3.654	0.4992	0.4204	0.8021
	40‡	2.375	2.067	0.154	1.264	1.074	3.356	0.6657	0.5606	0.7871
	80§	2.375	1.939	0.218	1.737	1.477	2.953	0.8679	0.7309	0.7665
2½	5	2.875	2.709	0.083	0.856	0.7280	5.764	0.7100	0.4939	0.9876
	10	2.875	2.635	0.120	1.221	1.039	5.453	0.9873	0.6868	0.9750
	40‡	2.875	2.469	0.203	2.004	1.704	4.788	1.530	1.064	0.9474
	80§	2.875	2.323	0.276	2.650	2.254	4.238	1.924	1.339	0.9241
3	5	3.500	3.334	0.083	1.048	0.8910	8.730	1.301	0.7435	1.208
	10	3.500	3.260	0.120	1.498	1.274	8.346	1.822	1.041	1.196
	40‡	3.500	3.068	0.216	2.621	2.228	7.393	3.017	1.724	1.164
	80§	3.500	2.900	0.300	3.547	3.016	6.605	3.894	2.225	1.136
3½	5	4.000	3.834	0.083	1.201	1.021	11.55	1.960	0.9799	1.385
	10	4.000	3.760	0.120	1.720	1.463	11.10	2.755	1.378	1.372
	40‡	4.000	3.548	0.226	3.151	2.680	9.887	4.788	2.394	1.337
	80§	4.000	3.364	0.318	4.326	3.678	8.888	6.281	3.140	1.307
4	5	4.500	4.334	0.083	1.354	1.152	14.75	2.810	1.249	1.562
	10	4.500	4.260	0.120	1.942	1.651	14.25	3.963	1.761	1.549
	40‡	4.500	4.026	0.237	3.733	3.174	12.73	7.232	3.214	1.510
	80§	4.500	3.826	0.337	5.183	4.407	11.50	9.611	4.272	1.477
5	40‡	5.563	5.047	0.258	5.057	4.300	20.01	15.16	5.451	1.878
	80§	5.563	4.813	0.375	7.188	6.112	18.19	20.67	7.432	1.839
6	40‡	6.625	6.065	0.280	6.564	5.581	28.89	28.14	8.496	2.246
	80§	6.625	5.761	0.432	9.884	8.405	26.07	40.49	12.22	2.195
8	30	8.625	8.071	0.277	8.543	7.265	51.16	63.35	14.69	2.953
	40‡	8.625	7.981	0.322	9.878	8.399	50.03	72.49	16.81	2.938
	80§	8.625	7.625	0.500	15.01	12.76	45.66	105.7	24.51	2.878
10		10.750	10.192	0.279	10.79	9.178	81.59	125.9	23.42	3.704
	30	10.750	10.136	0.307	11.84	10.07	80.69	137.4	25.57	3.694
	40‡	10.750	10.020	0.365	14.00	11.91	78.85	160.7	29.90	3.674
	80§	10.750	9.750	0.500	18.93	16.10	74.66	211.9	39.43	3.628
12	30	12.750	12.090	0.330	15.14	12.88	114.8	248.5	38.97	4.393
	‡	12.750	12.000	0.375	17.14	14.58	113.1	279.3	43.81	4.377
	§	12.750	11.750	0.500	22.63	19.24	108.4	361.5	56.71	4.335
Construction pipe										
		2.00	1.900	0.050	0.3602	0.3063	2.835	0.1457	0.1457	0.6897
		3.00	2.900	0.050	0.5449	0.4634	6.605	0.5042	0.3361	1.043
		4.00	3.900	0.050	0.7297	0.6205	11.95	1.210	0.6051	1.397
		5.00	4.896	0.052	0.9506	0.8083	18.83	2.474	0.9896	1.749
		6.00	5.876	0.062	1.360	1.157	2.712	5.098	1.699	2.100
		7.00	6.856	0.072	1.843	1.567	36.92	9.403	2.687	2.450
		8.00	7.812	0.094	2.745	2.335	47.93	18.24	4.561	2.795

* **Aluminum Co. of America.**
† **Weights calculated for 6061 and 6063. For 3003 multiply by 1.010.**
‡ **Also designated as standard pipe.**
§ **Also designated as extra-heavy or extra-strong pipe. All calculations based on nominal dimensions.**

APPENDIX 3:
BOLT-STRENGTH TABLES

Bolt Breaking Strength in Pounds: In Tension

No. or Inches	Decimal Inches	Millimeters	Threads/Inch UNC*	Threads/Inch UNF†	Stainless 85,000 psi UNC*	Stainless 85,000 psi UNF†	Bronze 60,000 psi UNC*	Bronze 60,000 psi UNF†
No. 4	0.112	2.84	40	48	513	561	362	396
No. 6	0.138	3.51	32	40	772	862	545	609
No. 8	0.164	4.17	32	36	1,191	1,252	841	884
No. 10	0.190	4.83	24	32	1,490	1,699	1,052	1,200
No. 12	0.216	5.49	24	28	2,054	2,192	1,450	1,547
¼	0.250	6.35	20	28	2,705	3,092	1,909	2,182
⁵⁄₁₆	0.313	7.94	18	24	4,457	4,936	3,146	3,484
⅜	0.375	9.53	16	24	6,587	7,465	4,649	5,270
⁷⁄₁₆	0.438	11.11	14	20	9,036	10,091	6,379	7,123
½	0.500	12.70	13	20	12,061	13,596	8,514	9,597
⁹⁄₁₆	0.563	14.29	12	18	15,465	17,253	10,917	12,179
⅝	0.625	15.88	11	18	19,210	21,756	13,560	15,357
¾	0.750	19.05	10	16	28,429	31,702	20,068	22,378
⅞	0.875	22.23	9	14	39,247	43,305	27,704	30,568
1	1.000	25.40	8	12	51,488	56,359	36,345	39,782
1⅛	1.125	28.58	7	12	64,878	72,736	45,797	51,343
1¼	1.250	31.75	7	12	82,374	91,200	58,147	64,377
1⅜	1.375	34.93	6	12	98,165	111,751	69,293	78,883
1½	1.500	38.10	6	12	119,446	134,387	84,315	94,861
1¾	1.750	44.45	5		161,454		113,968	
2	2.000	50.80	4½		212,349		149,894	
2¼	2.250	57.15	4½		276,054		194,861	
2½	2.500	63.50	4		339,900		239,930	
2¾	2.750	69.85	4		419,391		296,041	
3	3.000	76.20	4		507,227		358,042	
3¼	3.250	82.55	4		603,407		425,935	
3½	3.500	88.90	4		707,933		499,717	
3¾	3.750	95.25	4		820,803		579,390	
4	4.000	101.60	4		942,018		664,954	

Formula

$P = S \times At$

At = Net effective tensile area

$At = 0.7854(D - [0.9743/n])^2$

n = Number of threads per inch

S = Ultimate fiber tensile strength

P = Ultimate breaking load in pounds

D = Nominal screw diameter in inches

*UNC = Unified coarse

†UNF = Unified fine

Bolt Breaking Strength in Kilograms: In Tension

No. or Inches	Decimal Inches	Millimeters	UNC* Threads/Inch	UNFt Threads/Inch	Stainless 585.8 mPa UNC*	Stainless 585.8 mPa UNFt	Bronze 413.5 mPa UNC*	Bronze 413.5 mPa UNFt
No. 4	0.112	2.84	40	48	233	255	164	180
No. 6	0.138	3.51	32	40	350	391	247	276
No. 8	0.164	4.17	32	36	540	568	381	401
No. 10	0.190	4.83	24	32	676	771	477	544
No. 12	0.216	5.49	24	28	932	994	658	702
1/4	0.250	6.35	20	28	1,227	1,402	866	990
5/16	0.313	7.94	18	24	2,021	2,239	1,427	1,580
3/8	0.375	9.53	16	24	2,988	3,386	2,109	2,390
7/16	0.438	11.11	14	20	4,099	4,577	2,893	3,231
1/2	0.500	12.70	13	20	5,471	6,167	3,862	4,353
9/16	0.563	14.29	12	18	7,015	7,826	4,952	5,524
5/8	0.625	15.88	11	18	8,714	9,869	6,151	6,966
3/4	0.750	19.05	10	16	12,895	14,380	9,103	10,150
7/8	0.875	22.23	9	14	17,803	19,643	12,566	13,866
1	1.000	25.40	8	12	23,355	25,564	16,486	18,045
1 1/8	1.125	28.58	7	12	29,429	32,993	20,773	23,289
1 1/4	1.250	31.75	7	12	37,365	41,368	26,375	29,201
1 3/8	1.375	34.93	6	12	44,527	50,690	31,431	35,781
1 1/2	1.500	38.10	6	12	54,181	60,958	38,245	43,029
1 3/4	1.750	44.45	5		73,235		51,695	
2	2.000	50.80	4 1/2		96,321		67,991	
2 1/4	2.250	57.15	4 1/2		125,217		88,389	
2 1/2	2.500	63.50	4		154,178		108,831	
2 3/4	2.750	69.85	4		190,235		134,283	
3	3.000	76.20	4		230,077		162,407	
3 1/4	3.250	82.55	4		273,704		193,203	
3 1/2	3.500	88.90	4		321,116		226,670	
3 3/4	3.750	95.25	4		372,314		262,810	
4	4.000	101.60	4		427,297		301,621	

Formula

$P = S \times At$

At = Net effective tensile area

$At = 0.7854(D - [0.9743/n])^2$

n = Number of threads per inch

S = Ultimate fiber tensile strength

P = Ultimate breaking load in pounds

D = Nominal screw diameter in inches

*UNC = Unified coarse

tUNF = Unified fine

Bolt Breaking Strength in Pounds: In Shear

No. or Inches	Diameter Decimal Inches	Diameter Millimeters	Area Sq. In. at Root of Thread, UNC*	Stainless Steel and Bronze 45,000 psi At Thread	Stainless Steel and Bronze 45,000 psi Unthreaded
No. 4	0.112	2.84	0.00496	190	443
No. 6	0.138	3.51	0.00745	285	673
No. 8	0.164	4.17	0.01196	457	950
No. 10	0.190	4.83	0.01450	555	1,275
No. 12	0.216	5.49	0.02060	788	1,648
¼	0.250	6.35	0.02690	1,029	2,208
⁵⁄₁₆	0.313	7.94	0.04540	1,737	3,450
³⁄₈	0.375	9.53	0.06780	2,593	4,968
⁷⁄₁₆	0.438	11.11	0.09330	3,569	6,761
½	0.500	12.70	0.12570	4,808	8,831
⁹⁄₁₆	0.563	14.29	0.16200	6,197	11,177
⁵⁄₈	0.625	15.88	0.20200	7,727	13,799
¾	0.750	19.05	0.30200	11,552	19,870
⁷⁄₈	0.875	22.23	0.41900	16,027	27,046
1	1.000	25.40	0.55100	21,076	35,325
1⅛	1.125	28.58	0.69300	26,507	44,708
1¼	1.250	31.75	0.89000	34,043	55,195
1⅜	1.375	34.93	1.05400	40,316	66,786
1½	1.500	38.10	1.29400	49,496	79,481
1¾	1.750	44.45	1.74000	66,555	108,183
2	2.000	50.80	2.30000	87,975	141,300
2¼	2.250	57.15	3.02000	115,515	178,833
2½	2.500	63.50	3.72000	142,290	220,781
2¾	2.750	69.85	4.62000	176,715	267,145
3	3.000	76.20	5.62000	214,965	317,925
3¼	3.250	82.55	6.72000	257,040	373,120
3½	3.500	88.90	7.92000	302,940	432,731
3¾	3.750	95.25	9.21000	352,283	496,758
4	4.000	101.60	10.61000	405,833	565,200

Formula

P – Area at root of thread × Shear stress × 0.85 (for thread stress riser) or

P = Area at full nominal diameter × Shear stress

*UNC = Unified coarse

Bolt Breaking Strength in Kilograms: In Shear

No. or Inches	Diameter Decimal Inches	Diameter Millimeters	Area mm² at Root of Thread, UNC*	Stainless Steel and Bronze 310.1 mPa At Thread	Stainless Steel and Bronze 310.1 mPa Unthreaded
No. 4	0.112	2.84	3.20	86	201
No. 6	0.138	3.51	4.81	129	305
No. 8	0.164	4.17	7.72	208	431
No. 10	0.190	4.83	9.35	252	578
No. 12	0.216	5.49	13.29	357	748
¼	0.250	6.35	17.35	467	1,001
⁵⁄₁₆	0.313	7.94	29.29	788	1,565
⅜	0.375	9.53	43.74	1,176	2,253
⁷⁄₁₆	0.438	11.11	60.19	1,619	3,067
½	0.500	12.70	81.10	2,181	4,006
⁹⁄₁₆	0.563	14.29	104.52	2,811	5,070
⅝	0.625	15.88	130.32	3,505	6,259
¾	0.750	19.05	194.84	5,240	9,013
⅞	0.875	22.23	270.32	7,270	12,268
1	1.000	25.40	355.48	9,560	16,023
1⅛	1.125	28.58	447.10	12,024	20,280
1¼	1.250	31.75	574.19	15,442	25,036
1⅜	1.375	34.93	680.00	18,287	30,294
1½	1.500	38.10	834.84	22,451	36,052
1¾	1.750	44.45	1122.58	30,189	49,071
2	2.000	50.80	1483.87	39,905	64,093
2¼	2.250	57.15	1948.38	52,397	81,118
2½	2.500	63.50	2400.00	64,542	100,146
2¾	2.750	69.85	2980.64	80,157	121,176
3	3.000	76.20	3625.80	97,507	144,210
3¼	3.250	82.55	4335.48	116,593	169,246
3½	3.500	88.90	5109.67	137,413	196,286
3¾	3.750	95.25	5941.92	159,794	225,328
4	4.000	101.60	6845.15	184,084	256,373

Formula

P = Area at root of thread × Shear stress x 0.85 (for thread stress riser) or

P = Area at full nominal diameter × Shear stress

*UNC = Unified coarse

APPENDIX 4:
FINDING SPECIFIC GRAVITY

The Standard Specific Gravity Measurement

Specific gravity (SG) is the difference between the weight of an object and the weight of fresh water that occupies an equal volume

or

SG = weight of sample ÷ weight of displaced water

Where

the weight of displaced water = the weight of water filling a volume equal to the sample's volume

To find the SG of an FRP test piece, for example, you need an accurate scale and two containers open at the top. One container should fit inside the other (open end up) with plenty of room to spare. You also need a supply of clean fresh water (salt water would throw off the results).

- Weigh the sample and record the results.
- Weigh the larger container, empty and dry, and record the results.
- Place the smaller container inside the larger container and set them both on the scale.
- Fill the smaller container carefully all the

way to the brim with fresh water, without spilling a drop.
- Gently ease the FRP sample into the water in the smaller container.
- Water will spill out into the surrounding larger container.
- Use a straw to lower the level of water in the smaller container until you can lift it out without spilling any additional water.
- Remove the smaller container and note the total weight of the larger container with the spilled water in it.
- Subtract the weight of the empty larger container from the total weight to find the weight of the displaced water.
- Divide the sample weight by the weight of the displaced water; the result is the SG.

Example:

Say your FRP sample weighed 3.72 oz. After following the procedure, you find that the water it displaced weighed 2.38 oz. The sample's SG is 1.56 (3.72 oz. ÷ 2.38 oz. = 1.56 SG).

The density of the sample is simply the density of fresh water times the SG, or 97.3 lb./cu. ft. (1.56 SG × 62.4 lb./cu. ft. fresh water = 97 lb./cu. ft.).

or

Say your FRP sample weighed 105.5 g. After following the procedure, you find that the water it displaced weighed 67.5 g. The sample's SG is 1.56 (105.5 g ÷ 67.5 g = 1.56 SG).

The density of the sample is simply the density of fresh water times the SG, or 1,560 kg/m³ (1.56 SG × 1,000 kg/m³ fresh water = 1,560 kg/m³).

Measuring Specific Gravity of Wood

You can determine the SG of materials that float (e.g., balsa or foam) the same way, but the quantity of displaced water is very small and will require either a large sample or many highly accurate measurements tabulated and averaged.

Structural woods are a little easier; they float roughly half in and half out of the water.

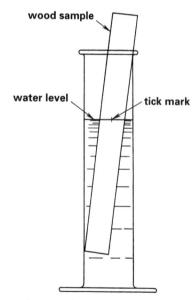

Measuring wood specific gravity

There is a simple method for determining a timber sample's SG. It doesn't even require a scale.

- Cut a sample from a board. Make it long, thin, narrow, and straight, and perfectly square and regular in dimensions; for example, 5 inches long by ¹⁄₄ inch thick and ¹⁄₂ inch wide (125 mm long by 5 mm thick and 12 mm wide).
- Sand the edges lightly to remove roughness or saw-cut strands that can hold air bubbles; wipe clean.
- Float the sample in a tall, narrow, clear-plastic container—filled about half full—so the sample is held more or less vertical by the sides of the container.
- Lift out the sample and make a tick mark in the center of the waterline.
- Measure the distance from the bottom up to the waterline.
- Measure the distance from the bottom to the top.
- To find the SG, divide the distance to the waterline by the distance to the top.

Example:

Say you floated a wood sample 5 inches long and the tick mark at the waterline measured 3 inches up from the bottom. This sample's SG is 0.6 (3 inches ÷ 5 inches = 0.6 SG).

The density of the sample is 0.6 SG × 62.4 lb./cu. ft. fresh water = 37.4 lb./cu. ft.

or

Say you floated a wood sample 125 mm long and the tick mark at the waterline measured 75 mm up from the bottom. This sample's SG is 0.6 (75 mm ÷ 125 mm = 0.6 SG). This is a good average structural wood, say, Douglas fir.

APPENDIX 5:
MEASURE AND UNIT
CONVERSION TABLES

Linear Measure Conversions

	inches	feet	yards	mm	cm	m	
inches	1	0.08333	0.02778	25.4	2.54	0.0254	inches
feet	12	1	0.33333	304.8	30.48	0.3048	feet
yards	36	3.00000	1	914.4	91.44	0.9144	yards
mm	0.03937	0.00328	0.00109	1	0.1	0.001	mm
cm	0.3937	0.03281	0.01094	10	1	0.01	cm
m	39.37008	3.28084	1.09361	1,000	100	1	m

Square Measure (Area) Conversions

	sq. in.	sq. ft.	sq. yd	sq. mm	sq. cm	sq. m	
sq. in.	1	0.00694	0.00077	645.16	6.4516	0.000645	sq. in.
sq. ft.	144	1	0.11111	92,903.04	929.0304	0.092903	sq. ft.
sq. yd.	1,296	9.00000	1	836,127.36	8,361.27	0.836127	sq. yd.
sq. mm	0.00155	0.0000108	0.0000012	1	0.01	0.000001	sq. mm
sq. cm	0.155	0.00108	0.00012	100	1	0.0001	sq. cm
sq. m	1,550.00	10.76391	1.19599	1,000,000	10,000	1	sq. m

Units of Density Conversions

	lb./cu. in.	lb./cu. ft.	g/cu. cm	kg/cu. m	
lb./cu. in.	1	1,728	27.6799	27679.9	lb./cu. in.
lb./cu. ft.	0.0005787	1	0.016018461	16.01846	lb./cu. ft.
g/cu. cm	0.0361273	62.42797	1	1,000	g/cu. cm
kg/cu. m	0.000036127	0.06243	0.001	1	kg/cu. m

Cubic Measure (Volume) Conversions

	cu. in.	cu. ft.	cu. yd.	cu. mm	cu. cm (ml)	cu. m	U.S. gal.	U.S. oz.	Imp. Gal.	Imp. oz.	Liters (l)	ml (cu. cm)
cu. in.	1	0.00058	0.00002	16,387.10	16.3871	0.0000164	0.00433	0.05541126	0.003605	0.57674	0.01639	16.3871
cu. ft.	1,728	1	0.03704	28,316,846.60	28,316.85	0.028317	7.48052	957.50649	6.228835	996.61367	28.31685	28316.848
cu. yd.	46,656	27	1	764,554,858	764,554.86	0.764555	201.97403	25852.67532	168.178557	26908.5692	764.55486	764554.858
cu. mm	0.000061	0.000000035	0.0000000013	1	0.001	0.000000001	0.0000002642	0.000033814	0.0000021997	0.0000351951	0.000001	0.001
cu. cm (ml)	0.061024	0.0000353	0.00000131	1,000	1	0.000001	0.000264172	0.03381	0.00021997	0.03520	0.001	1
cu. m	61,023.74	35.31467	1.30795	1,000,000,000	1,000,000	1	264.17205	33814.0227	219.96925	35,195.0797	1000	1000000
U.S. gal.	231	0.13368	0.00495	3,785,411.784	3,785.41178	0.00379	1	128	0.83267	133.22787	3.78541	3785.4118
U.S. oz.	1.80469	0.00104	0.0000387	29,573.5296	29.57353	0.0000296	0.007813	1	0.00651	1.04084	0.02957	29.5735
Imp. gal.	277.41943	0.16054	0.005946	4,546,090	4,546.09	0.00455	1.200950	153.7216	1	160	4.54609	4546.09
Imp. oz.	1.73387	0.001	0.0000372	28,413.0625	28.41306	0.0000284	0.007506	0.96076	0.00625	1	0.02841	28.41306
Liters (l)	61.02374	0.03531	0.00131	1,000,000	1,000	0.001	0.264172	33.81402	0.21997	35.1951	1	1000
ml (cu. cm)	0.06102	0.0000353	0.000001308	1,000	1	0.000001	0.000264	0.033814	0.00021997	0.0351951	0.001	1

NOTE: cubic centimeters (cu. cm) are the same as milliliters (ml)

Units of Force and Mass Conversions

	oz.	lb.	long ton	short ton	metric ton
oz.	1	0.0625	0.000027902	0.00003125	0.0000283495
lb.	16	1	0.000446429	0.0005	0.000453592
long ton	35,840	2,240	1	1.12	1.01605
short ton	32,000	2,000	0.89286	1	0.90718
metric ton	35,273.96	2,204.623	0.98421	1.10231	1
g	0.03527	0.0022046	0.0000009842	0.0000011023	0.000001
Kg	35.27396	2.20462	0.000984207	0.0011023	0.001
N	3.59643	0.22481	0.000100361	0.0001124	0.000101971
kN	3596.43	224.81	0.100361	0.112405	0.101971
mN	3596430	224810	100.361	112.405	101.971

	g	Kg	N	kN	mN
oz.	28.34952	0.02835	0.27801	0.000278	0.000000278
lb.	453.59237	0.45359	4.448221	0.004448	0.0000044482
long ton	1,016,046.909	1016.04691	9964.0146	9.964015	0.009964015
short ton	907,184.74	907.18474	8896.4416	8.896442	0.008896442
metric ton	1,000,000	1000	9806.64820	9.806648	0.009806648
g	1	0.001	0.00980665	0.0000098067	0.0000000098
Kg	1000	1	9.80665	0.0098067	0.0000098067
N	101.97	0.10197	1	0.001	0.000001
kN	101971	101.971	1000	1	0.001
mN	101971000	101971	1000000	1000	1

NOTE: Newtons are units of force only. Killograms, pounds, or ounces of MASS cannot be converted to newtons. Only killograms, pounds, or ounces of FORCE can be converted to newtons

Units of Pressure and Stress Conversions

	psi	lb./sq. ft.	g/sq. cm (cm water fresh)	kg/sq. cm	kg/sq. m	Pa (N/sq. m)	kPa
psi	1	144	70.307	0.070307	703.0695	6,894.76	6.894757
lb./sq. ft.	0.00694	1	0.4882	0.0004882	4.8824	47.88026	0.04788
g/sq. cm	0.01422	2.0482	1	0.001	10	98.0665	0.0980665
kg/sq. cm	14.22334	2,048.16	1,000	1	10,000	98,066.5	98.0665
kg/sq. m	0.00142	0.2048	0.1	0.0001	1	9.80665	0.009807
Pa (N/sq. m)	0.000145	0.0208854	0.010197	0.000010197	0.10197	1	0.001
kPa	0.14504	20.88543	10.197	0.010197	101.97	1,000	1
mPa (N/sq. mm)	145.03774	20,885.43	10,197	10.197	101,970	1,000,000	1,000
atmosphere	14.69600	2,116.2124	1,033.227	1.033227	10,332.27	101,325	101.325
in. water (fresh)	0.03613	5.2023	2.54	0.00254	25.4	249.079	0.24909
ft. water (fresh)	0.43350	0.0361	30.48	0.03048	304.8	2,989.067	2.98907
m water (fresh)	1.42233	204.8161	100	0.1	1,000	9,806.65	9.80665
hg in.	0.49115	70.7262	34.53155	0.034531	345.3155	3,386.38	3.38638
hg mm	0.01934	2.78446	1.35951	0.00136	13.5951	133.32205	0.13334

Units of Pressure and Stress Conversions

	mPa (N/sq. mm)	atmosphere	in. water (fresh)	ft. water (fresh)	m water (fresh)	hg in.	hg mm
psi	0.006895	0.068046	27.679910	2.30666	0.7031	2.0360	51.7149
lb./sq. ft.	0.00004788	0.00047254	0.192221	0.01602	0.0049	0.0141	0.3591
g/sq. cm	0.0000980665	0.00096784	0.393708	0.03281	0.01	0.02896	0.7356
kg/sq. cm	0.0980665	0.967841	393.700790	32.80839	10	28.9591	735.5592
kg/sq. m	0.0000098067	0.0000967841	0.03937	0.00328	0.001	0.002896	0.0736
Pa (N/sq. m)	0.000001	0.000009869	0.004015	0.00033	0.000102	0.0002945	0.00748
kPa	0.001	0.009869	4.014631	0.33455	0.1020	0.294523	7.4809
mPa (N/sq. mm)	1	9.869	4,014.631	334.5526	101.9718	294.523	7,480.88
atmosphere	0.101325	1	406.782	33.8985	10.3323	29.9213	760
in. water (fresh)	0.00024909	0.002458	1	0.08333	0.0254	0.186832	4.4755
ft. water (fresh)	0.002981	0.0294998	12.00000	1	0.3048	0.88267	22.4198
m water (fresh)	0.00981	0.096784	39.37007	3.28084	1	2.8959	73.2229
hg in.	0.00339	13.594	1.132925	0.345323	535.25364	1	25.4
hg mm	0.000133	0.001316	0.53524	0.044603	0.013595	0.03937	1

NOTE: cm water (fresh) is the same as g/sq. cm

BIBLIOGRAPHY

The Elements of Boat Strength required wide-ranging, intensive research. In addition to my own notes, observations, calculations, and data from my files, copious use was made of numerous references. The principal sources are listed here:

Adams, Jeannette T. *Arco's Complete Woodworking Handbook.* New York: Arco, 1981.

ALCOA Aluminum. *Aluminum Afloat.* New York: ALCOA Aluminum, 1964.

Aluminum Association. *Aluminum Construction Manual: Engineering Data for Aluminum Structures.* New York: Aluminum Association, 1969.

American Boat and Yacht Council (ABYC). *Standards and Recommended Practices for Small Craft.* ABYC, 1998.

American Bureau of Shipping (ABS). *Guide for Building and Classing High-Speed Craft.* Paramus NJ: ABS, 1991.

———. *Guide for Building and Classing Motor Pleasure Yachts.* Paramus NJ: ABS, 1991.

———. *Guide for Building and Classing Offshore Racing Yachts.* Paramus NJ: ABS, 1986.

American Institute of Steel Construction. *Manual of Steel Construction.* 7th ed. New York: American Institute of Steel Construction, 1970.

Attwood, E. L., and Longmans Pengelly. *Theoretical Naval Architecture.* 19th printing. London: Green & Co.

Baltek Corporation. *Care and Use of Contourkore.* Data File #115.

Barnaby, Kenneth C. *Basic Naval Architecture.* 5th ed. London: Hutchinson, 1967.

Breneman, John W. *Strength of Materials.* 3d ed. New York: McGraw-Hill, 1965.

Brockenbrough, R. L., and B. G. Johnston. *USS Steel Design Manual.* Pittsburgh PA: U.S. Steel Corporation, 1968.

Brown, David G. *Boatbuilding with Baltek DuraKore.* Camden ME: International Marine, 1995.

Carrick, Robert W., and Richard Henderson. *John G. Alden and His Yacht Designs.* Camden ME: International Marine, 1983.

Chapelle, Howard I. *The American Fishing Schooners: 1825–1935.* New York: Norton, 1973.

———. *Boatbuilding: A Complete Handbook of Wooden Boat Construction.* New York: Norton, 1941.

———. *Yacht Designing and Planning for Yachtsmen, Students & Amateurs.* Rev. and enl. ed. New York: Norton, 1971.

Cohen, Ghsoh, and Shepard. *Design and Construction of the U.S. Coast Guard's 47-Foot Self-Righting, Heavy Weather Rescue Craft.* Vol. 98. SNAME Transactions, 1990.

Colvin, Thomas E. *Steel Boatbuilding.* Vol. 1: *From Plans to Bare Hull.* Vol. 2: *From Bare Hull to Launching.* Camden ME: International Marine, 1985.

Cooley, R. H. *Complete Metalworking Manual.* New York: Arco, 1967.

Culler, R. D. *Skiffs and Schooners.* Camden ME: International Marine, 1974.

D'Arcangelo, Amelio M. *A Guide to Sound Ship Structure.* Cambridge MD: Cornell Maritime Press, 1964.

Devlin, Samual. *Devlin's Boatbuilding: How to Build Any Boat the Stitch and Glue Way.* Camden ME: International Marine, 1996.

Donaldson, Sven. *Understanding the New Sailing Technology: A Basic Guide for Sailors.* New York: Putnam's, 1990.

DuCane, Peter. *High-Speed Small Craft.* 4th ed., rev. Tuckahoe NY: J. de Graff, 1973.

Du Plessis, Hugo. *Fiberglass Boats.* 3d ed. Camden ME: International Marine, 1996.

Estep, Cole H. *How Wooden Ships Are Built: A Practical Treatise on Modern American Wooden Ship Construction with a Supplement on Laying Off Wooden Vessels.* Ohio: Penton Publishing, 1918.

Faherty, Keith F., and Thomas G. Williamson, eds. *Wood Engineering and Construction Handbook.* 3d ed. New York: McGraw-Hill, 1989.

Farmer, Weston. *From My Old Boat Shop: One-Lung Engines, Fantail Launches & Other Marine Delights.* Camden ME: International Marine, 1979.

Fock, Harald. *Fast Fighting Boats 1870–1945: Their Design, Construction, and Use.* Annapolis: Naval Institute Press, 1978.

Fox, Uffa. *Seamanlike Sense in Power Craft.* London: Peter Davies, 1968.

Friedman, Norman. *U.S. Small Combatants, Including PT-Boats, Subchasers, and the Brown-Water Navy: An Illustrated Design.* Annapolis: Naval Institute Press, 1987.

Garden, William. *Yacht Designs.* Camden ME: International Marine, 1977.

———. *Yacht Designs II.* Mystic CT: Mystic Seaport Museum, 1992.

Gerr, Dave. *The Baltek DuraKore Scantling Handbook.* Northvale NJ: Baltek Corporation, 1995.

———. *The Nature of Boats: Insights and Esoterica for the Nautically Obsessed.* Camden ME: International Marine, 1992.

———. *Propeller Handbook: The Complete Reference for Choosing, Installing, and Understanding Boat Propellers.* Camden ME: International Marine, 1989.

———. *Pocket Cruisers for the Backyard Builder: Thirty Small Sailboats You Can Build for Less than $12,000.* Camden ME: International Marine, 1987.

Gibbs & Cox, Inc. *Marine Design Manual for Fiberglass Reinforced Plastics.* New York: McGraw-Hill, 1960.

Gordon, J. E. *Science of Structures.* New York: Scientific American Library, 1988.

———. *The New Science of Strong Materials or Why You Don't Fall Through the Floor.* Princeton: Princeton University Press, 1984.

———. *Structures, or Why Things Don't Fall Down.* New York: Da Capo Press, 1978.

Gougeon, Meade. *The Gougeon Brothers on Boat Construction: Wood & WEST SYSTEM Materials.* Bay City MI: Gougeon Brothers, 1985.

Graul, Timothy. *Aluminum Planing Boats.* Monograph.

Griffiths, Maurice. *Little Ships and Shoal Waters: Designing, Building and Sailing Shoal Draught Cruising Yachts—With a Cruise or Two in Both Blue and Sandy Waters.* London: Conway Maritime Press, 1972.

Guarino, Salvadore, J. *The PCF, A Patrol Craft Standard.* Vol. 106. Naval Engineers Journal (ASNE), May 1994.

Henderson, Richard. *Philip L. Rhodes and His Yacht Designs.* Camden ME: International Marine, 1981.

Henry, Robert J., and Richards T. Miller. *Sailing Yacht Design: An Appreciation of a Fine Art.* Cambridge MD: Cornell Maritime Press, 1965.

————. *Sailing Yacht Design: A New Appreciation of a Fine Art.* Vol. 98. SNAME Transactions, 1990.

Herreshoff, L. Francis. *Common Sense of Yacht Design.* Jamaica NY: Caravan-Maritime Books, 1974.

————. *Sensible Cruising Designs.* Camden ME: International Marine, 1973.

International Maritime Organization. *SOLAS Consolidated Edition.* International Maritime Organization (U.K.), 1997.

James W. Brown, Inc. *Searunner Construction Manual.* Santa Cruz CA: James W. Brown, 1971.

Kaiser Aluminum. *Aluminum Boats.* Kaiser Aluminum, 1964.

Klingel, Gilbert C. *Boatbuilding with Steel.* Camden ME: International Marine, 1973.

Lambert, John, and Al Ross. *Allied Coastal Forces of World War II.* 2 vols. Annapolis: Naval Institute Press, 1994.

Larsson, Lars, and Rolf E. Eliasson. *Principles of Yacht Design.* Camden ME: International Marine, 1994.

Lincoln Electric Co. *The Design of Welded Structures.* Cleveland: Lincoln Electric Co., 1982.

————. *The Procedure Handbook of Arc Welding.* Lincoln Electric Co., 1973.

Lloyds Register of Shipping. *Rules and Regulations for the Classification of Yachts and Small Craft.* London: Lloyds Register of Shipping, 1983.

Lord, Lindsay. *Naval Architecture of Planing Hulls.* Cambridge MD: Cornell Maritime Press, 1963.

Manzolillo, J. L., Thiele, E. W., and Tuthill, A. H. *CA-706 Copper Nickel Alloy Hulls: The "Copper Mariner's" Experience and Economics.* Vol. 84. SNAME Transactions, 1976.

Marks, Lionel S. *Marks' Standard Handbook for Mechanical Engineers.* 8th ed. Eugene A. Avallone and Theodore Baumeister III, eds. New York: McGraw-Hill, 1978.

Muckle, W. *The Design of Aluminum Alloy Ships' Structures.* London: Hutchinson, 1963.

Najeder, K. W. *Machine Designers' Guide.* 2d ed.

Nicholson, Ian. *Boat Data Book.* Lymington, Hampshire, England: Nautical Publishing, 1978.

————. *Small Steel Craft.* Frogmore, St. Albans, England: Granada Publishing/Adlard Coles, 1978.

Oberg, Jones, Horton, and Ryffel. *Machinery's Handbook.* 24th ed. New York: Industrial Press, 1992.

Parker, Reuel B. *The New Cold-Molded Boatbuilding: From Lofting to Launching.* Camden ME: International Marine, 1992.

Phillips-Brit, Douglas. *Sailing Yacht Design.* Frogmore, St. Albans, England: Adlard Coles, 1971.

————. *Motor Yacht and Boat Design.* 2d ed. Frogmore, St. Albans, England: Adlard Coles, 1966.

————. *The Naval Architecture of Small Craft.* Philosophical Library, 1957.

Pretzer, Roger. *Marine Metals Manual: A Handbook for Boatmen, Builders, and Dealers.* Camden ME: International Marine, 1975.

Rabl, S. S. *Practical Principles of Naval Architecture.* Cambridge MD: Cornell Maritime Press, 1942.

Roark, Raymond J., and Warren C. Young. *Formulas for Stress and Strain.* 5th ed. New York: McGraw-Hill, 1975.

Rogers, Howard T. *The Marine Corrosion Handbook.* Toronto: McGraw-Hill Canada: 1960.

Rossell, Henry E., and Lawrence B. Chapman. *Principles of Naval Architecture.* Vols. 1 and 2. New York: Society of Naval Architects and Marine Engineers, 1942.

Scott, Robert J. *Fiberglass Boat Design and Construction.* 2d ed. Jersey City NJ: Society of Naval Architects and Marine Engineers, 1996.

Shenoi, R. A., and J. F. Wellicome, eds. *Composite Materials in Maritime Structures.* Vols. 1 and 2. New York: Cambridge University Press, 1993.

Sims, Ernest H. *Aluminum Boatbuilding.* 2d ed. Dobbs Ferry NY: Sheridan House, 1993.

Skene, Norman L. *Elements of Yacht Design.* New York: Kennedy Bros., 1938.

———. *Skene's Elements of Yacht Design.* 8th ed. Completely rev. and updated by Francis S. Kinney. New York: Dodd, Mead, 1973.

Smith, Carroll. *Carroll Smith's Nuts, Bolts, Fasteners, and Plumbing Handbook.* Osceola WI: Motorbooks International, 1990.

Steward, Robert M. *Boatbuilding Manual.* 4th ed. Camden ME: International Marine, 1994.

Sucher, Harry V. *Simplified Boatbuilding*: The Flat-Bottom Boat. New York: Norton, 1973.

———. *Simplified Boatbuilding: The V-Bottom Boat.* New York: Norton, 1974.

Traung, Jan-Olan. *Fishing Boats of the World.* Fishing News, 1955.

———. *Fishing Boats of the World.* Vol. 2. Fishing News, 1960.

———. *Fishing Boats of the World.* Vol. 3. Fishing News, 1967.

Union Carbide Corporation. *Oxy-Acetylene Handbook.* 2d ed. New York: Union Carbide, Linde Division, 1960.

U.S. Coast Guard NVIC 7-95. *Guidance on Inspection, Repair, and Maintenance of Wooden Hulls.* Navigation and Vessel Inspection Circular (NVIC), 1995.

U.S. Coast Guard NVIC 8-87. *Notes on Design, Construction, Inspection and Repair of Fiber Reinforced Plastic (FRP) Vessels.* Navigation and Vessel Inspection Circular (NVIC), 1987.

U.S. Coast Guard NVIC 11-80. *Structural Plan Review Guidelines for Aluminum Small-Passenger Vessels.* Navigation and Vessel Inspection Circular (NVIC), 1980.

U.S. Coast Guard NVIC 7-68. *Notes on Inspection and Repair of Steel Hulls.* Navigation and Vessel Inspection Circular (NVIC), 1968.

U.S. Code of Federal Regulations. *Shipping—46.* Washington DC: U.S. Government (GPO).

U.S. Department of the Navy. *Wood: A Manual for Its Use as a Shipbuilding Material.* Vols. 1–4. U.S. Department of the Navy, Bureau of Ships, 1957.

Vaitses, Allan H. *Boatbuilding One-Off in Fiberglass.* Camden ME: International Marine, 1984.

Walton, Keith R. *Designing and Building with Cored Composites.* Northvale NJ: Baltek Corporation.

Warren, Nigel. *Metal Corrosion in Boats.* Camden ME: International Marine, 1980.

White, Gerald Taylor, ed. *Problems in Small Boat Design.* Dobbs Ferry NY: Sheridan House/Society of Small Craft Designers, 1972.

INDEX

WHAT'S THAT SOUND?

AN INTRODUCTION TO ROCK AND ITS HISTORY

FIFTH EDITION

John Covach
**University of Rochester
and the Eastman School of Music**

Andrew Flory
Carleton College

W. W. NORTON AND COMPANY
NEW YORK • LONDON

Copyright © 2018, 2015, 2012, 2009, 2006 by W. W. Norton & Company, Inc.

All rights reserved
Printed in Canada
Fifth Edition

Editor and Digital Media Editor: Steve Hoge
Project Editor: David Bradley
Assistant Editor and Digital Media Assistant Editor: Stephanie Eads
Media Project Editor: Jesse Newkirk
Manuscript Editor: Candace B. Levy
Managing Editor, College: Marian Johnson
Managing Editor, College Digital Media: Kim Yi
Production Manager: Benjamin Reynolds
Ebook Production Manager: Mateus Manço Teixeira

Ebook Production Coordinator: Lizz Thabet
Marketing Manager, Music: Trevor Penland
Design Director: Rubina Yeh
Designer: Anna Reich
Photo Editor: Nelson Colón
Permissions Manager: Megan Schindel
Permissions Clearer: Elizabeth Trammell
Composition: Jouve International—Brattleboro VT
Illustration Studio: Open
Manufacturing: Transcontinental Interglobe

Permission to use copyrighted material begins on page C1.

Library of Congress Cataloging-in-Publication Data

Names: Covach, John Rudolph, author. | Flory, Andrew, author.
Title: What's that sound? : an introduction to rock and its history /
    John Covach, Andrew Flory.
Description: Fifth edition. | New York, N.Y. : W. W. Norton & Company, [2018]
    | Includes index.
Identifiers: LCCN 2017053888 | ISBN 9780393624144 (pbk.)
Subjects: LCSH: Rock music—History and criticism.
Classification: LCC ML3534 .C7 2018 | DDC 781.6609—dc23 LC record available at
https://lccn.loc.gov/2017053888

W. W. Norton & Company, Inc., 500 Fifth Avenue, New York, NY 10110

www.wwnorton.com

W. W. Norton & Company Ltd., 15 Carlisle Street, London W1D 3BS

2 3 4 5 6 7 8 9 0

ABOUT THE AUTHORS

 **John Covach** (Chair and Professor of Music, University of Rochester and Professor of Theory, Eastman School of Music) received his Bachelor of Music (1983), Master of Music (1985) and Ph.D. (1990) in music theory from the University of Michigan. He was also a Fulbright student in Vienna, Austria, in 1987–1988. The recipient of several teaching awards and citations, Professor Covach teaches theory and analysis as well as courses in popular music. Since 1993, he has taught large-lecture courses on rock at the University of North Texas, the University of North Carolina at Chapel Hill, and the University of Rochester and has lectured across North America and Europe. Introduced in 2013, his online rock history MOOCs have enrolled hundreds of thousands of students worldwide. He is co-editor of *Understanding Rock* (Oxford 1997), *American Rock and the Classical Music Tradition* (Harwood 2000), *Traditions, Institutions, and American Popular Music* (Harwood 2000), and *Sounding Out Pop* (Michigan 2010). His extensive writing on twentieth-century music, popular music, and the philosophy of music have appeared in numerous books and journals. Professor Covach also maintains an active career as a performing and recording musician.

 **Andrew Flory** (Assistant Professor of Music, Carleton College) received his Bachelor of Music from the City College of New York (1998), and Master of Music (2003) and Ph.D. (2006) from the University of North Carolina at Chapel Hill. Professor Flory teaches courses in American music, focusing on rock, rhythm and blues, and jazz. Since 2004, he has taught courses on the history of rock to intimate groups, in the large-lecture format, as continuing education, and in the distance-learning environment at the University of North Carolina, Shenandoah University, and Carleton College. He has lectured internationally and written extensively about American rhythm and blues and is an expert on the music of Motown. Working directly with Universal Records, Professor Flory has served as consultant for several recent Motown reissues. He is the author of *I Hear a Symphony: Motown and Crossover R&B* (Michigan 2017).

The 1950s 75

CHAPTER 2

The Birth and First Flourishing of Rock and Roll   79

LISTENING GUIDES

WHAT'S THAT SOURCE? READINGS

WHAT'S NEW IN THE FIFTH EDITION?

The structure and many features of the Fifth Edition will be familiar to users of previous editions. We have made some revisions and additions to the content in order to clarify historical content, expand coverage of areas that seemed to require it, and react to major changes in the music industry during the last decade. As time passes, the 1980s and 1990s have come into clearer focus historically and this is reflected in the text. The music since 2000 is still settling in, but we have made every attempt to capture a responsible survey—even if the subject is something of a moving target.

Among the additions in this new edition is an increased coverage of rock's impact outside the United States. It would take another book at least as long as the current one to provide a comprehensive account of rock's history outside of the United States, and so we make no claims that this new material accomplishes this. It does, however, serve to remind students that there is more to the history of rock music than the particular way it unfolded within the United States. Rock has sounded a wide range of resonances around the globe since the mid 1950s, and these new passages throughout the text provide examples of the ways in which this happened. Another new feature are paragraphs in several chapters called "A Performance That Launched a Career." These provide glimpses into performances that in some cases seemed to forecast a band or artist's future success, and in others serve to emphasize how great things can come from small beginnings.

Those who know the Fourth Edition will notice that a few new Listening Guides have been added throughout the book, providing a more balanced number of guides for each chapter. We have also added dozens of new guides online, as well as included guides from previous editions of the book. Our goal is to provide instructors with the broadest and most varied collection of Listening Guides possible, and we hope this assists them as they use the book and supporting materials to design a course that best fits their individual pedagogical and scholarly emphases. We have retained the What's That Source readings from the Fourth Edition to provide experience in source readings for students. The collection of brief essays by top pop scholars and writers remains an online resource, providing students with other voices than those of the authors in the telling of rock's history.

When John first began writing *What's That Sound?* in the late 1990s, most instructors still taught from CDs and records and depended on print resources for biographical and historical information and data. This new edition marks the first one published at a time when many undergraduates who will use it were born after the first introduction of Napster (1999). File sharing has changed the world of music in such fundamental ways over the almost two decades since that it may be tough for students to imagine a world in which the only music you could hear was either on the radio, television, on a record, tape, or CD, or live. Today's students have more music available to them than at any other time in civilization (that we know of, at least) and it is all accessible with a click or two on a phone, tablet, or other device. The recent resurgence of vinyl, though, seems to reflect an attempt to get back to something more authentic or even somewhat nostalgic. Analog, once the only option, has become a hip alternative to digital ease and convenience. Online reference sources such as Wikipedia have put facts about rock and pop music at students' fingertips. As useful as these technologies are, they also make it all the more important that we work hard to recover the conditions of pop and rock music as they were before the digital revolution. These conditions are now outside of the experience and memory of most college undergraduates. Indeed, one of the themes that runs throughout the book is how technology has played an important role in shaping the development of rock music. For many millennials, the challenge may be to imagine a world with far less access to music and to information about the music and the artists.

DIGITAL MEDIA

digital.wwnorton.com/whatsthatsound5

A talented team of Norton specialists and college instructors has updated the digital media array to accompany the Fifth Edition. Cary Campbell (Weber State University) focused on the new Interactive Instructor's Guide; Joe Gennaro (University of Central Florida) developed the test bank, and Chris Reali (Ramapo College of New Jersey) revised and updated the online practice quizzes.

Elements for the Fifth Edition include:

Playlists. Available from digital.wwnorton.com/whatsthatsound5, **Playlists** provide links to the songs on Spotify, iTunes, Amazon and authorized YouTube videos. Forty-five author videos are also accessed from the Playlists. The videos help students learn what to listen for in a song and address overarching themes.

Chapter Quizzes. Accessible free of charge, **Chapter Quizzes** prepare students for their exams and help them understand the textbook's coverage. Each chapter includes 35–40 questions.

Chapter Resources. Also available free of charge, **Chapter Resources** include *Backstage Pass* articles from a list of prominent rock historians, Chapter Outlines and additional Listening Guides.

For Instructors. A testbank of over 1000 questions is available for download. The NEW Interactive Instructor's Guide (IIG) is an easy-to-use, searchable and sortable online resource that includes topics for classroom discussion, lecture ideas, chapter outlines, video links for each chapter, and a list of additional recordings referenced in the text. All the art from the text is available in PowerPoint and JPEG format.

Ebook. Now integrated with Spotify, the **Ebook** streams music off the page, offering students an immediate listening solution, accessible on laptops, tablets, and mobile devices. An Additional Selections playlist of songs referenced in each chapter is also included to round out the listening experience.

ACKNOWLEDGMENTS

Like most textbooks, the one you are about to read developed over the course of many years—in this case, over twenty years of teaching university-level courses in rock music. As a consequence of this prolonged period of gestation, we owe debts of gratitude to many more people than we can list here. Our apologies in advance to those we may have overlooked.

The genesis of the book occurred during John's time at the University of North Texas College of Music, where Thomas Sovik and David Joyner gave him the chance to teach courses in the history of rock music. At the University of North Carolina at Chapel Hill, John Nadas, James Haar, Jon Finson, and Mark Evan Bonds were especially supportive in helping John to establish a series of rock-music courses there. At the University of Rochester, John is most grateful for the continued support of Tom Leblanc (now at the University of Miami), Peter Lennie, Joanna Olmsted, Kim Kowalke, Jamal Rossi, and the late Doug Lowry. These colleagues have supported his research and teaching in more ways than he can list here. Andy is especially grateful to current and former colleagues at Shenandoah University and Carleton College. At Shenandoah, Tracy Fitzsimmons, Bryon Grigsby, Michael Stepniak, Keith Salley, Adam Olson, and Golder O'Neil were especially helpful in establishing and inspiring courses in rock music, and at Carleton, Justin London, Ron Rodman, Melinda Russell, Hector Valdivia, Alex Freeman, Nikki Melville, Larry Archbold, Lawrence Burnett have provided administrative support, professional inspiration, and personal encouragement.

We owe a significant debt to the thousands of students who have taken our courses over the years. Much of what is contained in this book was tried out on them first, and we have benefited immensely from their feedback. Over the years, many of John's students helped to educate him on a number of the finer points of rock history. This special group of students includes Mark Spicer, David Carson Berry, Tim Hughes, John Brackett, Paul Harris, Marc Medwin, Akitsugu Kawamoto, Sarah Nicholson, Jason Titus, Anna Stephan-Robinson, Martha Bausch, Christina Brandt, Jonathan Hiam, Joel Mauger, Joe Gennaro, Richard Rischar, Trevor deClercq, Crystal Asmussen, David Leblanc, and Christopher Gupta. Several incredibly knowledgeable students provided Andy with administrative assistance during in his early time working on this book; these include including Robbie Taylor, Alan Weiderman, Billy Barry, Miles Campbell, and Jen Winshop.

Many friends and colleagues have also given us wise, helpful, and encouraging advice and support, including Walter Everett, Albin Zak, James Grier, Jocelyn Neal, Mark Butler, Betsy Marvin, Tim Riley, Carl Woideck, Dan Harrison, Lori Burns, Rob Wegman, John Buzby, Paul Cole, Chris Chamis, Stefan Zajic, John Howland, Phil Ford, Travis Stimeling, Annie Randall, Mark Clague, Bob Fink, Daniel Groll, Jason Decker, and Mike Fuerstein.

Thanks are also due to the instructors who reviewed and commented on parts of various editions of the book: Alexandra Apolloni, Robert Bonara, John Brackett, Theo Cateforis, Jerome Camal, Carey Campbell, Diane Cardarelli, David Carlson, John M. Crabtree, Marcus Dickman, Jr., Jeff Donovick, David Englert, marc faris, Roberta Freund-Schwartz, Tom Garcia, Joe Gennaro, Jennifer Gunderman, Lindsay Johnson, Mark Katz, Laura Lohman, Bente Hansen, Steven Maxwell, Michelle McQuade Dewhirst, Heather Miller, Richard Mook, Michael A. Morrison, David M. Moskowitz, Jon Newton, Cora Palfy, Joseph Poshek, Gary Pritchard, Jr., Karl Raudsepp, James Scott, Jerry Skelley, Stephen Slawek, Nick Sullivan, Joseph Taylor, Patrick Warfield, Larry Wayte, Arthur White, and Amy S. Wooley.

We would like to thank Gary Giddins, Albin Zak, John Jackson, Tim Riley, Ben Fong-Torres, Guthrie Ramsey, Graeme Boone, Susan Fast, Robert Bowman, Mark Spicer, Jeff Chang, Norma Coates, Mark Katz, Joanna Love, Maureen Mahon, Elizabeth Wollman, Jocelyn Neal, William Gibbons, and Theo Cateforis for contributing their scholarship to the "Backstage Pass" articles and Tim Hughes for his "Live from . . ." essays.

The excellent staff at Norton also deserve a big thanks, including Michael Ochs and Suzanne LaPlante, who convinced John to write the first edition of this book; Roby Harrington and Maribeth Payne, who offered wisdom and guidance along the way; Peter Lesser, who edited the first two editions of the book; project editor David Bradley; media project editor Jesse Newkirk; production manager Benjamin Reynolds; photo editor Nelson Colón; assistant editor Stephanie Eads; and ebook designer Lizz Thabet. We were thrilled that legendary poster artist Ron Liberti agreed to provide the cover art for this edition. For his wisdom and one-liners, Steve Hoge deserves huge thanks for his work as the main editor of both media and text for this Fifth Edition.

Most of all, we would like to thank our families, Julie, Jonathan, and Ricky Covach, who suffered John's many obsessed moments over the years with grace and loving support, and Kate, Charlotte, Ben, and Alexander Flory, whose love and patience made the Fifth Edition possible.

John Covach
Rochester, New York

Andrew Flory
Northfield, Minnesota

September 2017

WHAT'S THAT SOUND?

FIFTH EDITION

STUDYING ROCK

Rock music was born out of controversy, and its rebellious image has always appealed to fans. In the mid-1950s, many adults accustomed to the fatherly crooning of Bing Crosby and the suave, swinging delivery of Frank Sinatra were shocked by Elvis Presley's emphatic **blues**-influenced singing and suggestive dance moves. Teenagers, of course, loved him. Similarly, the Beatles' moptop haircuts upset a lot of parents in the mid-1960s, while setting a fashion trend among youngsters. Rock continued to push the envelope in later years: artists such as Jim Morrison, Alice Cooper, and David Bowie challenged cultural values in the late '60s and early '70s, while Madonna and Prince did the same in the 1980s. Issues such as payola and obscene lyrics have even been the focus of federal government hearings. While only a small portion of rock has been the source of controversy or cultural struggle, nonconformity and misbehavior are central to the rock movement.

blues

Considering rock's frequent (and sometimes militant) opposition to the status quo, some people are surprised to learn that colleges and universities across the country have been offering courses in rock for many years. As music historians look back on the last century, it is obvious that popular music has played an enormous role in the recent development of the Western musical tradition, and rock music has been dominant among popular styles. Even music historians whose work focuses on other genres and decades must take into account the many and often far-flung effects rock has had on the world of music in general.

Despite the acknowledged importance of rock music, determining exactly what "rock" means is not easy. Some scholars use the term "rock and roll" to describe the first wave of rock from 1954 to 1959 (covered in Chapter 2). Other scholars describe music after 1964 as "rock." Using these two distinct terms preserves what many scholars and fans see as an important difference. This book will employ the term "rock" in a broad sense, however, using the term to designate popular music that is produced specifically for a youth audience. But even this more encompassing usage is still problematic and includes seeming contradictions. Is rock defined by race, or musical style, or specific musical elements, such as instrumentation or lyrical content? Can 1960s soul be considered rock? How about folk or rap? Is all pop also rock, and is all rock also pop? Moreover, how do we think about rock music after its musicians and audience have grown up? While it seems obvious that artists such as Elvis Presley, the Beatles, the Rolling Stones, Jimi Hendrix, Led Zeppelin, the Police, and U2 were central to the rock movement, artists like the Supremes, Madonna, and the Kingston Trio are harder to categorize.

Recorded in 1951 by Jackie Brenston and His Delta Cats, "Rocket '88'" is considered by many to be the first rock and roll record. Though it was first released as a 78-rpm single, this is a photograph of a 1955 pressing—one of only a handful of "Rocket '88'" 45s still in existence.

This book will not completely resolve these kinds of questions. Rather, it will tell a history of popular music that focuses on rock but includes many other styles. The chapters that follow consider rock in an inclusive manner, discussing artists as diverse as the Andrews Sisters, Bessie Smith, Bill Haley and His Comets, the Supremes, Santana, Parliament Funkadelic, Metallica, and Britney Spears. The main purpose of the book is to organize this repertoire—an enormous body of music that covers over sixty years of popular-music history—to make it easier to understand and appreciate. Today there is more popular music available to listeners than at any other time in the history of recorded music. The rock era included a vast amount of music, more than can be covered in a typical university course, which only scrapes the surface of rock music. In the chapters that follow, we organize the music into styles and eras to make the rock repertoire easier to understand and appreciate and to provide broad stylistic and historical perspectives.

ELEMENTS TO CONSIDER

Rock History in the Media. Studying rock is not new, and most fans will have had some exposure to background information on artists and their music. For those who have not studied rock as an academic subject, this historical information will probably have come from general interest publications, radio, television, the Internet, and even biographical movies. Magazines such as *Rolling Stone* and *Mojo* provide readers with useful information about rock musicians, their music, and aspects of the entertainment industry. Books targeted at the general reader—often written by journalists and music critics—are plentiful and varied. Cable networks such as VH1 and MTV regularly offer profiles of artists and styles, frequently taking larger historical patterns into account. The development of the classic-rock radio format in the early 1990s also encouraged a growing sense of rock's history, along with the time-tested oldies format that has existed for decades. All these sources of information about the history of rock can be useful, and many have been employed in the writing of this textbook—a list of some of the best general sources follows this introduction, and references to more focused material are provided at the end of each chapter. Be aware, however, that a scholarly approach to rock will differ significantly from general interest books or media accounts. In many cases, information found in the popular media is designed primarily for entertainment rather than educational or research purposes. Some of this information may be accurate, well researched, and balanced, but some of it is also skewed, gossipy, and unreliable. Remember that magazines and broadcast stations generate revenue through the sale of advertising; the worst thing that can happen in such businesses is for people to put the magazine down, change the radio station, or turn off the TV. It is in the best interests of media outlets to deliver what they believe people want most, which can lead to a focus on the more sensational and titillating aspects of biography, rather than serious consideration of musicians and their music. This can be especially true of biopics.

This textbook will attempt to provide a balanced and fair account of the history of rock music. Many more artists and groups will enter the story than may typically appear in general interest accounts. Some artists or groups were more important in

Rock is difficult to define. Almost any listener would agree that "rock" includes Jimi Hendrix (top left). But what about Taylor Swift (bottom left) or the Supremes (bottom right)?

their day than they have been since. Other artists have become more popular over time. There will be no attempts to convince you to like a style of music, to elevate one style over another, or to dismiss or otherwise discredit any artist or group. The following chapters will provide reliable information, historical context, and informed debate. We hope this book will elicit informed discussion of contested issues in rock, such as the relevance of popularity to historical importance, the role of gender and masculinity in rock's history, and the responsibility of music executives to share profits with musicians.

I Know What I Like: The Fan Mentality. Many fans of rock are passionate about the music they like. But what does it mean to be a fan? Fans of rock music listen frequently to the music of a particular artist, group, or style and gather interesting facts about both the artists and the music. As fans, there is absolutely nothing wrong with ignoring artists, groups, or styles that do not interest us. This is perfectly natural. But as students of rock music, we cannot simply ignore music we do not like. We must strive to be balanced as we study rock's history and development, which often forces us to consider carefully music we probably wouldn't choose to listen to otherwise. If you were studying American history, it wouldn't be acceptable to study only those presidents who shared your political persuasion. An objective history of the last few decades of the twentieth century would consider John F. Kennedy *and* Richard M. Nixon, Ronald Reagan *and* Jimmy Carter, and Bill Clinton *and* George W. Bush. When it comes to studying music, you don't have to suspend your sense of judgment, but you do have to work to keep the fan mentality at bay.

The Ups and Downs of Chart Positions. This book will make frequent reference to chart positions. Almost everyone is familiar with charts that rank hit songs and albums by popularity for a given week, and the best-known American charts appear in *Billboard* magazine. Charts help us draw general conclusions about the popularity of a song or album at the time it was released. It can also be useful to compare how certain songs did on pop charts with the way they fared on rhythm and blues or country charts, or even on the British charts. More important for this book is that charts can help us avoid the fan mentality—in a sense, they keep us honest. Among scholars, charts are viewed with understandable suspicion because little is known about how they have been put together in the past, making them susceptible to manipulation. Clearly, charts are not precision instruments for measuring a song or an album's success or popularity, and they do not accurately reflect the popularity or influence of some songs or albums. A record can chart well and have little influence, or chart moderately well (or even poorly) and have a lot of influence. But in a broad sense, charts are still the best instruments we have available to judge listeners' changing tastes, even if chart measurements are flawed. Ideally, we would have access to comprehensive radio playlists of various eras, or the actual number of records sold of any song or album. However, playlist data are not plentiful and record companies often manipulate sales numbers (a frequent complaint of artists and bands since the beginning of recording). The Record Industry Association of America (RIAA) does award gold records for sales of 500,000 units and platinum records for sales of 1 million units, which can be helpful in measuring the success of an album or single. The RIAA website (www.riaa.com) allows you to look up any hit record and track its award history. The popular Google Books search engine also provides access to an extensive collection of *Billboard* magazines, allowing us to consider aspects of advertising and industry news at a particular date.

The Four Themes. The following chapters each take a three- to ten-year period of rock's history and organize the music along stylistic lines. Some chapters cover the same years from different angles. For example, the mid-1960s are covered in three chapters: Chapter 4, which is devoted to the British invasion; Chapter 5, which discusses the American response to it; and Chapter 6, which focuses on black pop. Each chapter also raises a set of interpretive issues that provide insight into scholarly and critical debates about the music and its historical circumstances or aesthetic impact and value. In the discussion of psychedelia in Chapter 7, for instance, the differences between mainstream popular culture of the mid-1960s and the hippie subcultures in both London and San Francisco are highlighted; the questions that arise in this discussion are representative of the issues that can surface whenever strong subcultures overlap. While interpretive angles change from chapter to chapter, four important themes are pursued throughout the book: social, political, and cultural issues; issues of race, class, and gender; the development of the music business; and the development of technology.

Each of these themes plays an important role in the development of rock music as a musical style and a force in popular culture. The music business has changed dramatically since the early 1950s, as the rock element of the business has grown from small independent upstarts to some of the most successful and dominant corporations of the modern age. In the realm of technology, the rise of radio in the 1920s and the emergence of television after World War II are central factors in rock's explosion into mainstream American culture in the mid-1950s. Just as important is the development of cable television that facilitated the introduction of MTV in the early 1980s and the rise of file sharing and streaming after 2000. Issues of race, class, and gender are also essential to understanding the origins of rock, the constant challenge of stereotypes in this music, and the ever-present struggle for authenticity in a form that blends down-home vernacular sensibilities with public adoration and extreme wealth. As the chapters unfold, you will be urged to examine how these themes fit into the story of rock's development. No style of music exists in a vacuum, and consideration of these broader perspectives will help us identify and appreciate the forces that have shaped the repertoire and the ways it has been interpreted, both by scholars in academia and by writers in the popular media.

Tracking the Popularity Arc. As we study rock's history and progress from the 1950s through the 1990s and beyond, you may notice a pattern of styles and their popularity. In many cases, a specific style will appear within a relatively restricted geographic region and remain unknown to most fans of popular music. For instance, few rock fans were aware of the punk scene in New York during the mid-1970s, and bands such as Television, the Ramones, and Blondie played to small, local audiences. The American punk style, which would morph into new wave by the end of the decade, developed within this small subculture before breaking into the national spotlight in 1978. By the early 1980s, some artists formerly associated with punk embraced styles and commercial strategies of the rock mainstream, while the more die-hard, aggressive groups retreated back into the punk underground. The rise of punk from a small, regional underground scene to mainstream pop culture, and its subsequent retreat, follows a pattern that we might think of as a "popularity arc." Over and over, the stories of specific styles in rock music follow this template. Typically, histories of rock music account for the time each style spends in the pop limelight—the peak of the popularity arc—creating a chronology without examining a style's pre-mainstream roots or existence after the commercial boom years. In a sense, it is difficult to avoid such a historical account, and similar problems arise in histories of other musical styles (such as jazz and classical music). To keep the popularity arc in mind for any given style, ask yourself the following questions: How did this style arise? When did it peak in popularity? Does it still exist in a subculture somewhere? How are elements of this style incorporated into current mainstream pop?

This book will give you the information you need to answer the first two questions. But you will probably need to do your own research to answer the last two. You may be surprised to discover how many older rock styles are still thriving, often long after they have fallen out of the mainstream spotlight.

Jackie Brenston (foreground) is credited with writing "Rocket '88.'" In this poster for a Memphis appearance, Brenston (with saxophone) is shown with Ike Turner (at the piano). Turner and His Kings of Rhythm band played with Brenston on the "Rocket '88'" record.

WHAT TO LISTEN FOR IN ROCK

Throughout this book, Listening Guides will direct your attention to individual songs that illustrate specific musical features of the styles discussed. While the circumstances surrounding a style, band, or song may be interesting, the way the music sounds is the element that attracts most listeners. The analysis of rock music can require a high level of specific music-analytical training. Books, articles, and doctoral dissertations demonstrate the many dimensions of rock's musical structure. The Listening Guides in this book will help you identify the structural features of rock music, with a focus on musical form. In the broadest sense, musical form refers to the structure and organization of different sections in a song or piece. Rock generally uses a limited number of common formal types; once you are familiar with these types, you will notice that most songs fit relatively neatly into one form or another (with certain exceptions). Understanding formal structure will help you hear new things in the music itself and perceive similarities between musical styles that may otherwise seem very different. The basic formal types are introduced here, along with short explanations of rhythm, instrumentation, and recording techniques. Instrumentation, or the types of instruments used in a given recording, can drastically change the way a song sounds and allow for variation within a performance. A familiarity with basic techniques used to record rock music will also help us understand some of the important differences between studio recordings, which form the bulk of the repertoire discussed in this book, and live rock performances. In addition to the sounds of rock, we will also consider the sights of rock, with a special introduction to viewing rock in its multiple contexts.

"Rocket '88.'" Before delving into greater detail, it may be helpful to look closely at some of these features in a brief analysis of a classic track: Jackie Brenston and His Delta Cats' 1951 single, "Rocket '88.'" Recorded in Memphis and produced by Sam Phillips (Elvis Presley's first producer), "Rocket '88'" is considered by many to be the first rock and roll song. While it is legally credited to Brenston, he may have written only the lyrics and lifted the music from an earlier song called "Cadillac Boogie" (such "borrowings" are relatively common in early rock and roll). To **formal diagram** show how the song is laid out, the book provides a **formal diagram** that breaks it into sections and lists them according to music timings. These timings simply give you an idea of where in the song a specific section begins and ends. Each section is also marked by a snippet of lyrics or some other description to help you locate it. The formal diagram for "Rocket '88'" is in the following Listening Guide. "Rocket '88'" is in what we call **simple verse form.** It repeats a single section of music eight times and, as you will see in the diagram, each section is labeled either **"verse"** or **"instrumental verse."** The only exception is verse 2, which slightly alters the structure found in all the other sections. Simple verse form is common in rock music, and we will see many instances of it in the chapters that follow.

In the first section, labeled "Instrumental Verse" in the diagram, note that the description "12 mm." is given. This indicates that the section is twelve **measures** in length ("mm." is commonly used to abbreviate measures in musical writing). You have probably heard musicians begin a song by counting out "one, two, three, four!" Musicians commonly count the **beats** in music in groups of four (though groups of two or three beats can also be found). This simply means that you count "one, two, three, four" and continue counting "one, two three, four" again rather than "five, six, seven, eight." Each group of four beats is called a "measure" or **bar** of music—these terms are synonymous and used interchangeably. Note that each

simple verse form
verse
instrumental verse

measures

beats

bar

Listening Guide

Jackie Brenston and His Delta Cats, "Rocket '88'" Chess 1458

Words and music by Jackie Brenston, produced by Sam Phillips. "Rocket '88'" hit #1 on the *Billboard* "Best Selling Retail Rhythm and Blues" and "Most Played Juke Box Rhythm and Blues" charts in 1951.

FORM: Simple verse.

TIME SIGNATURE: 4/4.

INSTRUMENTATION: Piano, drums, saxophones, solo vocals, distorted electric guitar playing a repeated boogie-woogie pattern.

Timings	Section	Description
0:00–0:19	Instrumental verse	12 mm., piano featured.
0:19–0:38	Verse 1	12 mm., "You women have heard of jalopies . . ."
0:30–0.57	Instrumental verse	12 mm., saxophones featured.
0:57–1:10	Verse 2 (partial)	8 mm., "V-8 motor . . ."; breaks off early.
1:10–1:28	Instrumental verse	12 mm., sax solo.
1:28–1:47	Instrumental verse	12 mm., sax solo continues.
1:47–2:05	Instrumental verse	12 mm., sax solo continues.
2:05–2:23	Verse 3	12 mm., "Step in my rocket . . ."
2:23–2:46	Instrumental verse	12 mm., sax and guitar featured.

verse and instrumental verse (except one) in "Rocket '88'" is twelve measures (bars) in length. You might count it like this:

mm.:	1	2	3	4	5	6	7	8	9	10	11	12
beats:	1234	1234	1234	1234	1234	1234	1234	1234	1234	1234	1234	1234

Verse 2 is the exception and is only eight measures in length; it seems to break off early compared to the twelve-measure pattern shown above. This is likely a mistake, because you can hear the musicians scrambling a bit to come back together as a band. Verse 2 can be counted like this:

mm.:	1	2	3	4	5	6	7	8	9??
beats:	1234	1234	1234	1234	1234	1234	1234	1234	???

Despite the irregularity of verse 2, if you count the measures and watch the music timings, you should be able to follow the diagram as the song plays. If you are having trouble keeping up, try pausing the music at the section boundaries given by the timings; this may help you hear the sections more clearly. When you have followed the form with the diagram, see if you can do so without the diagram. Once you begin hearing form in music, you may find that it can be difficult *not* to hear it!

In addition to form and rhythm in this song, it is also useful to listen for the instrumentation. This particular track uses drums, electric guitar, acoustic piano, two saxophones, and lead vocals. Try to listen to the song all the way through following only one of these instruments; don't let your attention be drawn away by what's happening in another part. Then, play the song again and see if you can follow a different instrument all the way through. Typically, our attention darts from part to part in a song, usually when something new comes in to grab our interest. While listening to "Rocket '88,'" for instance, we may focus on the piano in the first instrumental verse, the vocals in verse 1, the saxes in the next section, and so on. You may be surprised at the difficulty of focusing on one part as you listen, but if you can train yourself to do this, you will hear things in the music that you've never noticed before.

TYPICAL FORMAL TYPES IN AMERICAN POPULAR MUSIC

The analysis of musical form is a study of the way sections are structured in a piece of music and the way these sections combine to produce larger structures. Most musical styles work within the constraints of a small number of formal types, so formal analysis of a single work usually consists of noting its similarities to and differences from some formal design common to the style. Formal types and musical styles are often linked to one another. For our purposes, it will be useful to look at some common formal types that occur in rock music.

12-bar blues

The 12-Bar Blues and the Doo-Wop Progression. Perhaps the best place to begin the study of musical structure in rock is with the **12-bar blues.** This is a common structural pattern found in rhythm and blues, rock and roll, and many styles of

A Note on Rhythm and Meter

Generally, rhythm refers to the ways musical sounds are organized in time and **beat** refers to a regular rhythmic pulse. Most of the music in this book will employ four-beat measures. Measures may also contain two or three beats, and these are counted "one two, one two" and "one two three, one two three," respectively. It is even possible for a measure to contain five, six, seven, or more beats per measure. These ways of organizing rhythm and beats in music are called **meter**. A fuller consideration of a song's meter takes into account not only how many beats are in each measure but also how each beat may be subdivided. A single beat can be divided into either two or three equal parts; in the first case you would evenly count, "one &, two &, three &, four &," and in the second, "one & uh, two & uh, three & uh, four & uh." When each beat is evenly divided into two parts, we call this **simple**, and when each beat is divided evenly into three parts, we call this **compound**. Meters are grouped by combining the number of beats per measure with the way each beat is divided, as shown in the following chart:

	Simple (2 parts)	Compound (3 parts)
Duple (2 parts)	duple simple (2/4)	duple compound (6/8)
Triple (3 beats)	triple simple (3/4)	triple compound (9/8)
Quadruple (4 beats)	quadruple simple (4/4)	quadruple compound (12/8)

When the meter employs two beats per measure, and each beat is evenly divided into two parts, we classify the meter as "duple simple," and this can be seen in the chart. Notice that a time signature is given in parentheses next to each **meter classification**. In each case, the time signature given represents the most common one used to indicate this meter classification in written music. You may have noticed that sheet music almost always has a time signature provided at the beginning of the song or piece; this indicates what the meter classification of the rhythm will be in the song. Meter plays a crucial role in establishing the rhythmic "feel" of a song, though it is not the only element that influences this. In this book, most songs will be in quadruple time, with both simple and compound divisions in play. "Rocket '88,'" for instance, is in quadruple compound time, which many musicians simply think of as a **"shuffle"** in four (4/4).

jazz. A 12-bar blues consists of twelve groups of four-beat measures and is distinctive because of the way its measures fall into three groups of four. These groups can be seen in the measure length, phrasing, lyrics, and chord structure. Once this twelve-measure pattern is in place, an entire song will often repeat the structure several times, with new lyrics and instrumental solos added to make these repetitions fresh. The first four measures, which are called a **phrase,** often feature a lyric that is repeated in the next four measures. The words of the final four measures often complete the thought begun in the repeated initial phrase. Think of this pattern as "question—question—answer" (although the lyrics don't literally have to ask a question). The first line in each verse is repeated in the second phrase, with the third phrase completing the thought with a new line.

phrase

Listen again to "Rocket '88'" and you will find that it uses a 12-bar blues structure. After you have listened to the song two or three times, you should begin to hear the 12-bar blues structure clearly. Notice that eight of the nine phrases in the song are twelve measures long—the only exception is the fourth phrase, which does not complete the structure (the Listening Guide notes that this phrase "breaks off early"). The entire 12-bar blues structure appears in the **introduction,** for example, and begins a second time with the vocals. Phrase one begins with the lyrics, "heard of jalopies"; phrase two, "yes, it's great"; and the third phrase, "ride in style." You will

introduction

notice that, although "Rocket '88'" is constructed using the 12-bar blues, its lyrics do not follow the question—question—answer pattern. For an example of a 12-bar blues that uses this lyrical structure, see Big Joe Turner's "Shake, Rattle, and Roll," which appears in Chapter 1. Other examples of 12-bar blues in the book are Chuck Berry's "Johnny B. Goode" (Chapter 2) and Little Richard's "Tutti Frutti" (Chapter 2).

Roman numerals
chords

key
scale

The following chart illustrates some of the structural properties of 12-bar blues. Notice that **Roman numerals** occur under each measure number. This shows the **chords** that are typically played in those measures. Chords are combinations of notes played together—think of somebody strumming chords on a guitar or banging them out on the piano. Chords in any **key** can be organized by the **scale** for that key, and the Roman numerals show which note of the scale the chord is based on. If we are in C, for instance, the scale goes C – D – E – F – G – A – B – C. The I chord is a C chord, the IV is an F chord, and the V is a G chord, since the notes C, F, and G are the first, fourth, and fifth notes of the scale. Why would musicians bother with arcane Roman numerals when they could just write C, F, and G? The reason is more pragmatic than you might think: this pattern can occur in twelve distinct keys, and the specific labels C, F, and G cover only one of these, while the Roman numerals generalize across all twelve. If a musician knows the Roman numerals, she can play the pattern in any key as easily as in C.

bars:	1	2	3	4	5	6	7	8	9	10	11	12
chords:	I	(IV)	I	I	IV	IV	I	I	V	(IV)	I	(V)

1st phrase (question)   2nd phrase (question)   3rd phrase (answer)

doo-wop
progression

Another musical structure that appears in a lot of rock music is the **doo-wop progression.** Though it can occur in many styles of pop, this chord progression is most often associated with the doo-wop of the 1950s. Moreover, like the 12-bar blues, the doo-wop progression can form the underlying structure for many of the forms that we discuss later. Using our Roman numerals, we can characterize the doo-wop progression as a series of four chords: I – vi – IV – V. In the key of C, this progression would go C – A minor – F – G. This familiar chord progression can be heard in 1950s tracks such as the Five Satins' "In the Still of the Night" and the Del Vikings' "Come Go with Me." The following chart illustrates the doo-wop progression as it appears in the first vocal phrase of the Chords' "Sh-Boom" (labeled "verse 1" in the Listening Guide). Note that there is a new chord every two beats, forming a harmonic pattern (or "progression") that repeats through the entire song, except for the short section labeled **"bridge."** Note as well that "Sh-Boom" employs a common variant of the doo-wop progression, I – vi – ii – V. Like the 12-bar blues, it is not difficult to hear the repeating doo-wop progression that forms the basis for the song's musical content.

bridge

beats:	1	2	3	4	1	2	3	4
chords:	I		vi		ii		V	

Life could be a dream . . .   if I could **take** you up in paradise . . .

Listening Guide

The Chords, "Sh-Boom" Cat 104

Words and music by Jimmy Keyes, Carl Feaster, Claude Feaster, Floyd "Buddy" McRae, and Ricky Edwards. Reached #5 on the *Billboard* rhythm and blues "Most Played in Juke Boxes" chart in 1954. (This recording dropped quickly off the charts after a cover version was released by the Crew Cuts.)

FORM: Simple verse with several **interludes** and a bridge.

TIME SIGNATURE: 12/8.

INSTRUMENTATION: Electric guitar, bass, piano, drums, saxophone, solo vocals, and lead vocals.

0:00–0:06	**Prelude**, 4 mm.	"Life could be a dream . . ."
0:06–0:22	**Verse 1**, 8 mm.	"Life could be a dream . . ."; solo vocal with background harmonies.
0:22–0:29	**Interlude (partial)**, 4 mm.	Nonsense syllables; "De dong e ding dong . . ."
0:29–0:43	**Verse 2**, 8 mm.	"Life could be a dream"; beginning of verse punctuated by vocal harmony.
0:43–0:57	**Bridge**, 8 mm.	"Every time I look at you . . ."; performed by bass vocalist.
0:57–1:11	**Verse 3**, 8 mm.	"Life could be a dream"; performed as harmony throughout (note the high range of the tenor vocalist).
1:11–1:25	**Interlude (full)**, 8 mm.	Nonsense syllables followed by entrance of saxophone.
1:25–1:39	**Instrumental verse**, 8 mm.	Saxophone solo.
1:39–1:53	**Instrumental verse**, 8 mm.	Saxophone solo.
1:53–2:07	**Verse 4**, 8 mm.	Repeat of verse 3.
2:07–2:23	**Interlude**, 8 mm.	Repeat of full interlude.

Simple Verse Form. Repetitive structures like the 12-bar blues and the doo-wop progression often combine to form larger structural patterns. As these patterns repeat, we may think of them differently depending on what aspects are repeated. A verse is defined as a section with repeating music and nonrepeating lyrics. A form that employs only verses is called a simple verse form. Look back at the Listening Guide for "Rocket '88'" and you will see that it is in simple verse form. Elvis Presley's 1956 recording of "Heartbreak Hotel" provides another clear example of simple verse form: each 8-bar verse is based on the same chord progression, which is actually an abbreviated version of the 12-bar blues (though it is not a 12-bar blues). As you listen to "Heartbreak Hotel," notice how the song consists of repetitions of the same music with different words for each verse (and one instrumental verse).

Listening Guide

Elvis Presley, "Heartbreak Hotel" RCA 47-6420

Words and music by Mae Boren, Tommy Durden, and Elvis Presley, produced by Steve Sholes. Reached #1 on the *Billboard* "Top 100" chart, #1 on all three *Billboard* country and western charts (sales, jukebox, and radio), and #3 on the *Billboard* rhythm and blues "Most Played in Juke Boxes" chart in 1956.

FORM: Simple verse.

TIME SIGNATURE: 12/8 (shuffle in four).

INSTRUMENTATION: Electric guitar, piano, acoustic bass, drums, and lead vocals.

0:00–0:22	**Verse 1**, 8 mm.	"Well, since my baby left me . . ."
0:22–0:42	**Verse 2**, 8 mm.	"Oh, though it's always crowded . . ."
0:42–1:01	**Verse 3**, 8 mm.	"Now, the bellhop's tears . . ."
1:01–1:22	**Verse 4**, 8 mm.	"Well, if your baby leaves you . . ."
1:21–1:42	**Instrumental verse**, 8 mm.	Guitar solo for first 4 mm., then piano solo.
1:42–2:05	**Verse 5**, 8 mm.	"Oh, though it's always crowded . . ."

AABA form

AABA Form. The song form most associated with mainstream pop before the birth of rock and roll is **AABA form.** This is one of the most common formal patterns in Tin Pan Alley songs and usually occurs in a 32-bar scheme that combines four 8-bar phrases. We use the designation AABA to show that the first two 8-bar phrases are very similar, the third 8-bar phrase is contrasting, and the last 8-bar phrase is similar to the first two.

A	A	B	A
8 mm.	8 mm.	8 mm.	8 mm.

Among the songs in later Listening Guides that employ the standard 32-bar AABA form are "Over the Rainbow," "All or Nothing at All," "I'm Sittin' on Top of the World," "Hey Good Lookin'," and "Blueberry Hill." As it turns out, most AABA songs would be too short if the song did not repeat some or all of the 32-bar pattern. (In "I'm Sittin' on Top of the World" and "Hey Good Lookin'," the entire AABA form returns, but in "Over the Rainbow," "All or Nothing at All," and "Blueberry Hill," only part of the AABA structure is repeated.) When the entire AABA form is repeated, it is a **full reprise,** and when only part of the AABA form returns, a **partial reprise.** While the 32-bar AABA is common, this form can also be modified to include sections that exceed eight measures. Jerry Lee Lewis's recording of "Great Balls of Fire" provides a good example of this from the rock and roll repertoire. The A sections are eight measures long, but each presentation of the bridge uses twelve measures of music. This extended bridge structure produces a complete AABA pattern of

full reprise
partial reprise

thirty-six measures, not the usual thirty-two. Note that "Great Balls of Fire" employs a full reprise of this 36-bar pattern to form the second half of the song.

Simple Verse-Chorus. A **chorus** is a section that repeats the same music and lyrics intact in each presentation. (Remember that verses use the same music with different words.) When a single musical pattern is used as the basis for both verses and choruses in a song, the resulting form is called **simple verse-chorus.** Note that the melody portion of a song may change from verse to chorus, while the chords underneath stay the same. Hence, the biggest difference between a simple verse and a simple verse-chorus is the presence of a repeating set of lyrics to form a chorus section. Consider "Can the Circle Be Unbroken" as recorded by the Carter Family. The verses and choruses in this song are built on the same 16-bar progression. While the verse and chorus may seem different on the first listen, repeated listenings reveal that the verse and chorus use the same melody and chord progression, with only slight changes made between sections. Listen to this track and see if you can hear the similarity.

In order to count the measures in "Can the Circle Be Unbroken," you will need to keep two things in mind. First, rather than the four-beats-per-measure rhythmic pattern we encountered in the 12-bar blues, this song uses a two-beats-per-measure

chorus

simple verse-chorus

Listening Guide

Jerry Lee Lewis, "Great Balls of Fire" Sun 281

Words and music by Otis Blackwell and Jack Hammer, produced by Sam Phillips. Reached #2 on the *Billboard* "Top 100" chart, #1 on the country and western "Best Sellers in Stores" chart, and #3 on both the "R&B Best Sellers in Stores" and "Most Played R&B by Jockeys" charts in 1958.

FORM: AABA, with full reprise.

TIME SIGNATURE: 4/4.

INSTRUMENTATION: Piano, drums, acoustic bass, and lead vocals.

0:00–0:13	**A-Verse**, 8 mm.	Vocals delivered in stop time, "You shake my nerves . . ."
0:13–0:25	**A-Verse**, 8 mm.	Full band in, "I laughed at love . . ."
0:25–0:43	**B Bridge**, 12 mm	"Kiss me baby . . ."
0:43–0:55	**A-Verse**, 8 mm.	"I chew my nails down . . ."
0:55–1:06	**A-Instrumental verse**, 8 mm.	Raucous piano solo.
1:06–1:18	**A-Instrumental verse**, 8 mm.	
1:18–1:37	**B-Bridge**, 12 mm.	"Kiss me baby . . ."
1:37–1:49	**A-Verse**, 8 mm.	"I chew my nails . . ."

Listening Guide

The Carter Family, "Can the Circle Be Unbroken" Columbia 37669

Words and music by A. P. Carter, recorded in 1935. Released before the era of country charts in the United States. (There were no *Billboard* country charts until 1944.)

FORM: Simple verse-chorus.

TIME SIGNATURE: 2/4, with dropped beats.

INSTRUMENTATION: Acoustic guitar, two female and one male voice, with one female voice taking the lead during verses and choruses sung in three-part harmony.

0:00–0:06	**Introduction**, 3 mm.	Guitar accompaniment.
0:06–0:26	**Verse 1**, 16 mm. (only one beat in m. 12)	Solo vocal, "I was standin' . . ."
0:26–0:44	**Chorus**, 16 mm. (only one beat in mm. 4 and 12)	Choral vocal, "Can the circle . . ."
0:44–1:04	**Instrumental verse**, 16 mm. (no dropped beats)	Guitar solo.
1:04–1:23	**Verse 2**, 16 mm.	As before, "I told the undertaker . . ."
1:23–1:41	**Chorus**, 16 mm.	As before, "Can the circle . . ."
1:41–2:00	**Verse 3**, 16 mm.	As before, "I followed close behind her . . ."
2:00–2:18	**Chorus**, 16 mm.	As before, "Can the circle . . ."
2:18–2:28	**Instrumental verse** (partial), 8 mm.	Guitar solo.
2:28–2:47	**Verse 4**, 16 mm.	"Went back home, Lord . . ."
2:47–3:04	**Chorus**, 16 mm.	"Can the circle . . ."

pattern. You thus need to count "one-two, one-two," and so on. A second aspect of this song involves irregular counting of measures. When you try to count measures during the verses of this song, the twelfth bar contains only one beat, while in the choruses the fourth and twelfth measures contain only one beat. Musicians often refer to this as "dropping a beat," meaning that in each instance the second beat is dropped. The only instance of this 16-bar pattern not to drop these beats is the first instrumental verse on the guitar. In this verse, the group "corrects" the dropped beats from the sung verses and choruses by playing sixteen full measures of two beats.

Contrasting Verse-Chorus. Unlike a simple verse-chorus, in which the verse and chorus sections share the same musical material, when the verses and choruses of a song employ different music, we call this **contrasting verse-chorus.** Forms like contrasting verse-chorus may also include a bridge, or a section that provides a contrasting, nonrepeated section of music and lyrics and returns to a verse or chorus. A rock and roll example of contrasting verse-chorus with a bridge is Buddy Holly's "That'll Be the Day." As you listen to this track, notice the differences between the 8-bar verse and chorus sections, in addition to the instrumental bridge formed out of a 12-bar blues pattern.

contrasting verse-chorus

The diagram below summarizes the four common formal types found in rock music. While we will encounter more complicated formal designs later in this book, these four will apply to a large majority of the songs we study. Listening for form in rock music helps us gain a deeper understanding of how music is structured. It provides fans and students of this music with a glimpse of how musicians, songwriters, producers, and arrangers organize these songs. In many ways, understanding form helps us hear the larger patterns in the music and gives us a sense of the "bigger picture."

Listening Guide

The Crickets, "That'll Be the Day" Brunswick 55009

Words and music by Buddy Holly, Jerry Allison, and Norman Petty, produced by Norman Petty. Reached #1 on the *Billboard* pop "Best Sellers in Stores" chart and #2 on the *Billboard* "R&B Best Sellers in Stores" chart in 1957.

FORM: Contrasting verse-chorus with instrumental bridge.

TIME SIGNATURE: 12/8 (shuffle in 4).

INSTRUMENTATION: Electric guitar, acoustic bass, drums, lead and backup vocals.

0:00–0:04	**Introduction**, 2 mm.	Solo guitar featured.
0:04–0:19	**Chorus**, 8 mm.	"Well, that'll be the day . . ."
0:19–0:34	**Verse**, 8 mm.	"Well, you give me . . ."
0:34–0:49	**Chorus**, 8 mm.	"Well, that'll be the day . . ."
0:49–1:12	**Instrumental bridge**, 12 mm.	Guitar solo over 12-bar blues.
1:12–1:27	**Chorus**, 8 mm.	"Well, that'll be the day . . ."
1:27–1:42	**Verse**, 8 mm.	"Well, when Cupid shot . . ."
1:42–1:58	**Chorus**, 8 mm.	"Well, that'll be the day . . ."
1:58–2:14	**Ending**, 8 mm.	Based closely on chorus, "That'll be the day . . ."

Four Common Formal Types

Simple verse	All verses based on same music, no chorus.
Simple verse-chorus	Verses and choruses based on same music.
Contrasting verse-chorus	Verses and choruses based on different music.
AABA	Verses and bridge based on different music; can employ full or partial reprise.

12-bar blues or the doo-wop progression may occur as the basis for any of the sections in these forms. Simple verse, simple verse-chorus, and contrasting verse-chorus forms may also employ a bridge.

WHO'S PLAYING WHAT: INSTRUMENTATION IN ROCK

Beat It: Drums and Percussion. The musical instruments used in rock music, and especially the ways these instruments are combined, are central to the myriad musical styles discussed in this book. While most rock fans can tell the difference between an electric guitar and a keyboard, or a drum set and a saxophone, far fewer listeners understand exactly how these instruments typically work together in songs. Instruments in rock frequently have specific roles within the music. The task of the **rhythm section** is to establish a solid foundation for singers, instrumental soloists, and other members of the group that focus on melody. At the heart of the rhythm section is the drummer, whose role is to establish not only the tempo and meter but also the "feel" of each song. Most rock drummers employ a set consisting of a snare drum (which sits on a stand between the drummer's legs), a bass drum (played by the right foot), and a high-hat (two cymbals that can be clamped together using a stand controlled by a foot pedal). Most drummers also use medium-size drums called tom-toms. Tom-toms that are mounted on the bass drum are called ride toms; those that stand on the floor are called floor toms. A drummer may also use several cymbals, most often a larger ride cymbal and a smaller crash cymbal. The rhythmic patterns drummers play work something like the gears of a clock, with some gears moving quickly and others moving more slowly. The high-hat or ride cymbal is often used for the fastest notes, played in a regular stream. The bass and snare drums are generally played at slower intervals, and often seem to be in dialogue with one another. A typical drumbeat is shown here; the numbers across the top show how the rhythm would be counted, while the x's show which drums (or high-hat) are used on which beats:

rhythm section

Count:	1	&	2	&	3	&	4	&			1	&	2	&	3	&	4	&		
High-hat	x	x	x	x	x	x	x	x		x	x	x	x	x	x	x	x
Snare			x				x					x				x
Bass	x				x	x				x				x	x

Carl Palmer's extensive drum set is seen here from above. Note that he is playing on the high-hat cymbals, with the snare drum between his legs. Two ride toms (with clear heads) are adjacent to the snare and two floor toms (also with clear heads) are to Palmer's right. He is using two bass drums, striking these with the pedals using his right and left foot. Note the array of cymbals used, as well as the wood blocks (black) to Palmer's left.

The drum set can be enhanced by the addition of other percussion instruments, such as tambourine, cowbell, conga drums, or even hand claps. Most drummers will use one pattern for verses and another for bridges or choruses, and also break the pattern to play "drum fills" that help lead the music from section to section.

The Low Down: Electric Bass. The bass player's job is to "lock in" with the drummer rhythmically, and to provide the important bass notes to the chord progressions played by the guitar and/or keyboards. Within the rhythm section, the bassist is a kind of bridge between the rhythmic and harmonic (or chord-based) dimensions of the music. Often the bass player will create her part around the rhythmic pattern played on the bass drum, stressing those notes rhythmically while filling in other notes to provide an interesting bass line. Much early rock music used the acoustic upright bass, which could be amplified; but by the early 1960s, the more easily amplified electric bass guitar was the preferred instrument for most popular music except jazz and country. The bass (both acoustic and electric) usually has four strings that match the bottom four strings of the guitar. The distance between the tuning of guitar and bass strings is what musicians call an **octave**, a lower or higher version of the same note. If you sing the pattern Do-Re-Mi-Fa-Sol-La-Ti-Do, the two "Do" notes are an octave apart, and represent the distance between the typical tuning of strings on a bass and a guitar.

octave

Harmony in Motion: Rhythm Guitar and Keyboards. While the bass usually provides the foundation for a song's harmony within the rhythm section, the rhythm guitar fleshes out the harmonic dimension by playing full chords. Rhythm

Parliament Funkadelic's Bootsy Collins playing the electric bass in concert. The electric bass plays a prominent part in rock and is central to funk music.

guitar can be played on either acoustic or electric guitar. The electric guitar produces little sound on its own, but can reach high volume levels when connected to an amplifier. In 1950s rockabilly, the acoustic rhythm guitar often replaces the drum set and provides the rhythmic propulsion that drives the song forward. More often, though, the rhythm guitar part complements the bass and drum parts, and these three instruments work together to establish the harmonic and rhythmic basis for the song. The rhythm guitarist also has to be careful to fit his part in with the bass and drums. Sometimes if the bass locks in with the bass drum, the rhythm guitar will lock in with the snare, emphasizing the snare part while filling in the remaining space between beats. Sometimes the piano, organ, or synthesizer is used along with, or even in place of, the rhythm guitar. If keyboards or organs are used with rhythm guitar, they may play the same rhythmic figure as the guitar or simply sustain chords while the guitar plays its more rhythmic part. However the parts are organized, rhythm guitar and keyboard players have to be careful not to conflict musically.

In the Spotlight: Lead Singers and Backup Vocals.
With the rhythmic and harmonic dimensions of the piece firmly secured by the rhythm section, the singer focuses on the melodic dimension of the music. Singers are sometimes very free with the rhythmic placement of their melody notes, which translates into a lively dialectical tension with the tightly structured grid of the rhythm section. The singer's job is to create melodic interest and deliver the lyrics in a convincing manner—one that does not seem contrived or unnatural in comparison with normal speech. Many listeners attend as closely to the lyrics as to the melody that projects them, so a vocal performer has to be sure that the words come across effectively. Many solo vocalists are also accompanied by background vocals. A singer may have no backup vocals (Elvis Presley's "That's All Right [Mama]"), or the singer's melody will be accompanied by harmony vocals that follow the melody (the Beach Boys' "Surfer Girl") or support and echo some part of it (the Beatles' "Twist and Shout"). Like the rhythm section parts described earlier, the vocals are usually coordinated (with one another and with the rhythm section) to avoid conflict between parts.

Steppin' Up: Instrumental Solos.
In order to create contrast in arrangements, an instrumental solo is often introduced somewhere past the midpoint in a song. This might be a saxophone solo (the Coasters' "Yakety Yak"), a guitar solo (Jimi Hendrix's "Purple Haze"), or a piano solo (Jerry Lee Lewis's "Great Balls of Fire"). Sometimes an arrangement can feature several solos, as in Yes's "Roundabout."

Keyboard instruments most common in rock music are piano, organ, synthesizer, and digital piano. Keyboardist Rick Wakeman from the progressive rock group Yes, who uses synthesizers, organ, and electric piano in this photo, was known for his large battery of instruments.

In all of these cases, the instrumental soloist is the central focus of the music for the duration of the solo, taking the place usually reserved for the singer. The job of the rhythm section remains the same as it was during the other sections of the song: to support the soloist. The instrumental solo often makes the return of the vocals sound fresh, since there is usually no singing during the solo. In this regard, the solo is itself subordinate to the sung sections of the track (although with some bands—like Santana—this relationship can be reversed).

Horns and Strings: Sweetening the Sound. Some arrangements use horns or strings to add the finishing touches to a track. Horn sections often consist of a combination of trumpets, trombones, and saxophones used to give a tune a little more "punch." This approach is evident in much of the soul music recorded in Memphis and Muscle Shoals (Chapter 6). Strings can make an arrangement sound bigger and more elegant. Strings are often saved until late in the arrangement and are employed to give the end of the track a convincing lift. An arranger has to be careful that the horns or strings added to sweeten a track stay out of the way of the rhythm section and singers, creating a backdrop that enhances the song without drawing too much attention to itself.

How It All Fits Together: "Smoke on the Water." Now that we have discussed the instruments used in rock music and outlined their respective roles, we will explore an example to observe how instrumentation works. Deep Purple's "Smoke on the Water" is a prime example of how rock music from the mid-1960s (and beyond) is organized in terms of instrumentation. The track follows the contrasting verse-chorus formal pattern: after a lengthy introduction there are four verse-chorus pairs (the third of which is instrumental), with a **coda** rounding the tune off. It is easy to hear each instrument during the introduction, since the band brings them in almost one at a time. The song begins with the electric guitar alone, playing a

coda

riff

four-measure blues-inflected **riff** that is then repeated. Notice the guitar's distorted tone, which is a result of overdriving the amplifier; this tone is used extensively in rock. The third time through the guitar riff, the drums enter (0:17); first the high-hat alone, and on the fourth time through, the snare drum as well. Notice that the guitar is also doubled by the organ here, although the effect is subtle because the organ is also distorted and sounds like a second guitar. With the fifth occurrence of the guitar riff (0:34), the bass guitar is added, and the sixth time through (0:43), the bass is doubled by the bass drum. As the vocals enter for the first verse (0:51), notice that the drummer is primarily playing the high-hat, bass drum, and snare, using crashes on the cymbal and bass drum to mark the beginning and end of vocal phrases. The guitar and bass are playing almost the same part, while the organ takes the "rhythm guitar" role, playing the chords off the drums and bass. As the chorus begins (1:25), note that the organ becomes more sustained, as do the guitar and bass, while more crashes and drum fills and a second vocal harmony are added. The verses and choruses that follow are mostly the same as the first pair, although the verse and chorus during the guitar solo are different (2:58). The bass moves in faster notes during the solo, while the drum part emphasizes the snare on the faster notes rather than the high-hat. The arrival of the chorus during the solo is particularly dynamic (3:30), as is the return to the guitar riff in the passage before the beginning of the last verse (3:40).

Listening to this example analytically helps us focus our attention on the separate elements that make up "Smoke on the Water." Most listeners never really attend to the ways the musical parts in a track work together; they may notice only individual parts when one stands out in some way, and then only for a moment. As we continue our study of rock music, try to listen more carefully to each song's instrumentation to hear how the musicians are working together to make the music sound the way it does. As mentioned earlier, it sometimes helps to follow a single part all the way through a tune, for example listening to the bass only, then playing the song again and focusing only on the drums. While rock music sometimes gives the impression of musical simplicity, there are often layers of complexity waiting to be discovered. The tapestry of musical texture often does not draw attention to itself; a good rhythm section helps the listener focus on the vocals or solos, making the background instrumentation relatively transparent.

IN THE STUDIO: THE ROLE OF RECORDING TECHNIQUES IN ROCK MUSIC

Because of the importance of recordings to the history of rock music, some scholars argue that the rock repertoire is not simply a collection of songs, but a collection of *specific recordings* of songs. There is, for instance, only one recording of *Sgt. Pepper's Lonely Hearts Club Band* that we value: the one made by the Beatles in 1967. Many recordings have what might be thought of as "sonic signatures"—features that distinguish them in terms of where and when they were recorded, as well as by whom.

Elvis's early recordings with Sam Phillips at Sun Records have a distinctive sound that is, in a sense, separable from the songs themselves or the actual performances of them. For scholars with this view, rock is largely a recorded art, and when we talk about rock songs, we are almost always talking about rock *records*, even if we don't realize it.

Is It Live or Is It Memorex? There are two principal approaches to thinking about what a recording represents. The first is to think of the recording as an "audio snapshot." In this case, the recording is meant to reproduce a live performance as faithfully as possible and the listener should be unaware that a recording process is involved. On these types of recordings, the sounds should seem natural and indiscernible from an actual performance. This approach to recording is frequently used in classical, jazz, and folk music. The second approach to recording is to exploit the possibilities offered by the studio. This often produces sounds that would be impossible to re-create in a live setting. The records of Les Paul and Mary Ford (see Chapter 1) are early examples of this second approach. By progressively building up tracks of his guitar and Ford's voice, Paul was able to create a recorded sound that was very much a consequence of the recording technology that produced it. The recording studio also allows instruments to be combined in ways that would not easily work in a natural acoustic setting. Since the early 1970s, live performance technology has made it increasingly possible to combine acoustic instruments with louder electric ones, which is largely a result of sounds that first occurred in the studio. Since the days of Elvis Presley's Sun recordings in the 1950s, rock music has been more dependent on exploiting the possibilities of the studio than creating audio snapshots.

Reverb and Echo. Whether we are aware of it or not, every space we enter has specific acoustic properties. Whenever a sound is made, it is the result of a series of vibrations moving through the air. Some of these vibrations reach our ears directly from the source, while others bounce around the room and reflect back to us. Hard surfaces reflect sound; more porous ones (like carpeting, curtains, or furniture) absorb sound. Architects who design concert halls are keenly aware of this, and they devote considerable energy to determining the balance of harder and softer surfaces in a hall and how these surfaces will be angled. The idea, of course, is to create a space that makes the performances in the hall sound as acoustically rich as possible. If there's too much reflection, the sound can be too bright or boomy; if there's not enough, the music can sound dry and lifeless. When taking the audio snapshot approach, it is crucial to find a space with "good acoustics"—that is, with the right kind of reflected sound for the ensemble or soloist involved. Major record companies have in the past maintained their own studios that have been acoustically engineered for the best natural sound. For them, the task is not only to capture the way the musicians sound but also to commit to tape how those musicians sound in that specific room. Stories abound of vocals that were recorded in bathrooms, or guitar parts that were recorded in hallways or stairwells in order to take advantage of the natural acoustics of those spaces.

It is also possible to artificially create a room sound—often referred to as **ambience**—via electronic means, and this effect is called **reverb**. Most commercially available electronic reverb units (or digital plug-ins) offer settings that reproduce the

ambience
reverb

sound of small rooms, medium-size rooms, large rooms, auditoriums of various sizes, churches, and a number of "unnatural" spaces. When an engineer knows that she will use reverb, she may record the original sounds with as little natural ambience as possible, often called a "dry" recording. This dry sound is then fed through the reverb device to produce the desired sound. Reverb is used on almost all rock recordings, meaning that the "spaces" captured on tape are often not real spaces at all. Different kinds of reverb can also be used on different instruments or voices, producing sounds that are the result of multiple "spaces," none of which could naturally coexist in a world with only three dimensions.

echo   Reverb is different from **echo.** In the natural world, an echo occurs when sound bounces back to our ears to create two sonic images of the same event—we hear the original and then its reflection. This sound can be produced electronically as well, though some recording studios have built their own trademark "echo chambers" (the chamber at Gold Star Studios in Los Angeles—now destroyed—has a mythical standing within the recording world). Echo tends not to be of much concern to those who employ the audio snapshot approach; mostly they try to avoid it. In rock, echo is used extensively and often on voices. Together with reverb, echo can make the singing voice sound much richer and even mask certain imperfections in tone or intonation. The beginning of the Supremes' "Where Did Our Love Go?" offers an example of studio reverb. The clapping (actually two-by-fours being slapped together) is drenched in a rich reverb that creates the sound of a large gymnasium or some other big, reflective space. The most famous echo can be found on Elvis Presley's Sun recordings. For many years after Elvis's success, studio engineers around the world tried to reproduce the distinctive echo found on songs such as "That's All Right (Mama)," in which the quick echo (often called "slap-back echo") gives Presley's voice a quality that he could never have produced live. Reverb and echo provide what might be thought of as the ambient dimension of the music, and these effects can make instruments sound closer to or farther from the listener, depending on how much reverb or echo is employed—the more reverb or echo, the farther away the sound seems to be.

River Deep, Mountain High: Equalization (EQ). Frequency also plays a major role in recording techniques, as **equalizers** are used to affect the quality of most sounds. Each note played by an instrument is called its "fundamental," but along with this note, every instrument also subtly produces other, higher notes that help to form the tone, or **timbre** (pronounced to rhyme with "amber") of the instrument. You may have noticed that if you adjust the treble and bass settings on your music player you can greatly affect the sound—more treble and the sound is brighter, less treble and it sounds muffled. These tone settings adjust the volume of the frequencies in the sounds you hear and affect not only the fundamentals but also the higher notes that are generated in each case (called "upper partials" or "harmonics"). In the process of recording instruments, an engineer has a significant amount of control over the timbre of each recorded sound; for each microphone in use there may be multiple controls that work like the treble and bass on your stereo. Adjusting frequencies of sounds is often called "EQ," which is short for equalization. A good recording is "EQ-ed" to produce a balanced distribution of frequencies. EQ can also help to highlight certain instruments, and keep instruments in a similar range from covering each other up, resulting in a crisper, clearer, more defined sound.

Every Breadth You Take: Stereo Placement. For its first decade or so, most rock music was recorded and released in monophonic sound, **mono,** meaning that there was assumed to be only one speaker for playback and no possibility of stereo imaging. Almost all of the Beatles' records, for instance, were originally released in mono, with later **stereo** versions being prepared mostly (and sometimes hastily) for hi-fi enthusiasts, often without the band participating in the stereo mixes. Among the most successful producers to work in mono was Phil Spector. By the late 1960s, however, stereo was the preferred format for albums and FM radio, and by the mid-1970s complex stereo mixes had become the norm. The development of more and more tracks, greater use of the stereo field, and increasingly ambitious musical projects progressed in tandem throughout the late '60s and '70s, as listeners purchased more sophisticated stereo equipment to get the full effect of the music.

mono

stereo

When we hear sounds in the natural world, we can locate the position of a sound source because the sound enters each of our ears in a different way. Our mind calculates where a sound is coming from on the basis of the "stereo" effect. In music that is recorded in stereo, the engineer can control whether a sound comes out of the right or left speaker, or some combination of the two. In order to hear this clearly, use headphones to listen to a stereo recording and close your eyes: you will notice that there is a kind of "sonic landscape" in the space between the two headphones. Some sounds seem to come from the center, while others seem to come from the right or left, or mid-right or mid-left. It is, of course, impossible for the sounds that seem to be coming from the center to really be coming from there; after all, you are sitting between the headphone speakers and there is no center speaker physically present. Stereo sound is thus an aural illusion that we construct as a result of how we hear. Engineers use this phenomenon to separate sounds so we can hear more detail in the recording. For instance, if a rhythm guitar and an organ are playing almost the same thing in the same frequency range, the listener may not be able to distinguish them from one another—one will cover up, or "mask," the other. If you adjust one to sound like it is coming from the right and the other from the left, each will be much more distinct. So, in a stereo recording, the instruments and voices are arranged across the stereo field and the result is that the recording sounds clearer and more sonically complex.

Mixing. These dimensions of recorded sound—ambience, EQ, stereo placement, and overall volume—are controlled from a mixing board. A mixing board is used in two ways: first, to record the sound to tape (or more recently to a digital recorder), and second, to play the recording back. In classical music, the engineer's job is to capture the sound in the natural ambient space as faithfully as possible; a playback should not color the sound (though it may, and sometimes adjustments are made at this second stage). In rock, sounds are often recorded dry (except when special room effects are desired) and stored for playback. Until the 1960s, most popular music was recorded using a single performance. The use of tape after World War II allowed engineers to begin experimenting with multi-track tape, creating recordings from multiple performances. Early recording tape could store three **tracks** of music (meaning that three performances could be played back simultaneously), but

tracks

as the '60s and '70s progressed, tapes could contain eight, sixteen, twenty-four, forty-eight, or even more tracks. As computer hardware and software have become less expensive, in the last decade more musicians have turned to **digital audio workstations** (or DAWs) to record music, shedding the need for large, expensive recording studios. Although now encased in computer software, modern recording programs such as GarageBand and Pro-Tools still incorporate the same principles as older mixing boards. However, with the advance of digital technology in recent years, the number of tracks available is so large that track space is no longer a technical limitation. Regardless of the process used to capture the sounds (analog or digital), once all the tracks are recorded, the engineer is ready to **mix down** meaning that she will adjust the ambience, EQ, stereo placement, and relative volume of the tracks to produce the final version of the song. (Notice that the word "track" is used in recording to designate a recorded part, but it is also used more generally among fans and writers to mean "song.") Mixing is a complicated and creative process undertaken by highly skilled professionals who are often known for their distinctive "sound." Since the mid-1960s, bands have often spent more time mixing an album than recording the individual tracks.

digital audio workstations

mix down

(left) Phil Spector in the producer's role at the famous Gold Star Studios in California. This 12-input mixing board shows the limited resources of performers and engineers in the recording studio during the early 1960s.
(top right) Members of Yes gather around the recording console at London's Advision Studios with producer Eddie Offord in the early 1970s. Note the increase in channels on the mixing board.
(bottom right) Modern digital audio workstations such as GarageBand and Pro Tools are commonly used to perform the functions of a mixing board and tape machine. This shot of a Pro Tools session shows how digital recording software often directly emulates physical recording equipment.

Putting It All Together: "Josie." Some of the most sophisticated recorded sounds in rock were created by Steely Dan. Taking a closer look at Steely Dan's "Josie" will allow us to observe many of the techniques explained in the preceding sections at work in a single recording. "Josie" is structured according to the **compound AABA form,** meaning that each section of the AABA form is made up of smaller verse and chorus sections. After an angular introduction featuring the electric guitar, there are several measures of vamp before the first verse begins. Two verse-chorus pairs make up the large-scale A sections, followed by an instrumental bridge making up the B section. The return to the verse-chorus pair in this case features a guitar solo over the verse material, with the vocals returning for the chorus. A return to the introduction and vamp close the song as it fades out. In terms of the instrumentation, the track uses a fairly standard rhythm section of rhythm guitars, electric piano, bass, and drums. The vocals are mostly solo, with some backing vocals added during both the verse and chorus sections. Horns, percussion, and synthesizer strings are also added to "sweeten" the mix. The stereo aspect of the record can be heard most readily in the drums: note that the snare and bass drums are in the center, the high-hat is panned right, and tom-toms and cymbals are panned both right and left. As is usual for rock, the lead vocals and bass are in the center. Three electric guitars are involved in the rhythm section: two of these are panned right and left and play a part almost identical to the piano, which is panned center. The third guitar, which plays a funky single-note part, is panned right. When the synthesizer strings enter in the second chorus, they are panned left. Note that the horns and backup vocals are both panned mid-right and mid-left to keep them distinct in the mix. Listen for the reverb and echo that have been added to the lead vocals and the heavy reverb on the synthesizer strings and solo guitar; by contrast, the bass, bass drum, and high-hat are very dry. Thus, in addition to the separation that occurs through stereo placement, ambience is also used to help keep the parts distinct. The distribution of instruments and equalization across the full frequency range makes the recording sound full, with plenty of low end balanced by bright highs.

compound AABA form

VIEWING ROCK

Formal structure, instrumentation, and studio techniques are among the most important aspects of recorded sound. Yet rock music became popular in an age after World War II, when images of musicians were often inextricable from sound. Various forms of video-based media—including television, films, and music videos—have enabled rock musicians to reach audiences visually as well as aurally. Thus, images of rock have been vital to the formation of cultural tastes for dance, fashion, and behavior that would not have been possible without the combination of rock music with the moving image.

Although the average listener often has experience with the visual aspects of rock, when studying rock in an academic setting it is informative to consider the relationship between music and images. For one, when viewing a musical performance on video it is important to observe whether the musicians perform live or lip-synch to a prerecorded audio track. Similarly, knowledge of the original context can change how we might view a video performance. Among television broadcasts, for example,

Listening Guide

Steely Dan, "Josie" ABC Records AB-12404

Words and music by Walter Becker and Donald Fagen, produced by Gary Katz. Reached #26 on the *Billboard* "Hot 100" chart in 1978. Contained on the album *Aja*, which reached #3 in the United States and #5 in the UK in late 1977.

FORM: Compound AABA form, with A sections employing a verse-chorus pair.

TIME SIGNATURE: 4/4.

	0:00–0:32	**Introduction**, 16 mm.	8 mm. guitar figure then 8 mm. vamp.
A	0:32–1:03	**Verse 1**, 16 mm.	"We're gonna break out . . ."
	1:03–1:28	**Chorus**, 12 mm.	8 mm. chorus then 4 mm. link to verse 2.
A	1:28–1:59	**Verse 2**, 16 mm.	As before, "Jo would you love . . ."
	1:59–2:15	**Chorus**, 8 mm.	No link this time, "When Josie . . ."
B	2:15–2:31	**Bridge**, 8 mm.	Instrumental.
A	2:31–3:03	**Instrumental verse**, 16 mm.	Guitar solo.
	3:03–3:19	**Chorus**, 8 mm.	As second chorus, "When Josie . . ."
	3:19–4:24	**Coda**, 32 mm.	8 mm. as intro, then 24 mm. vamp and fade.

INSTRUMENTATION

Rhythm section	Singing	Solos	Sweetening
Electric piano	Solo with some backing	Electric guitar	Horns
Two rhythm guitars	vocals on verse and		Synth strings
"Funky" guitar	chorus		Percussion
Drum set			
Bass			

MIX

Left		Center		Right
Cymbal	Solo guitar	Lead vocal	Backup vocals	High-hat
Rhythm guitar	Backup vocals	Electric piano	Horns	Cymbal
Tom-tom	Horns	Percussion		"Funky" guitar
Synth strings		Snare drum		Rhythm guitar
		Bass		Tom-tom
		Bass drum		

there are noteworthy differences between late-night talk show appearances, prime-time variety shows, and daytime talk shows. Moreover, dramatic feature films starring rock musicians and performances have been popular for decades, and serve a different function than documentaries that compile footage from live performances.

Rock Television. Prior to their demise in the 1980s, variety shows presented compelling rock performances on network television. They featured comedy, skits, dancing, and musical performances, among many other odd acts. Important variety shows in the history of rock included the *Ed Sullivan Show* (officially called *Toast of the Town*) on CBS and *The Hollywood Palace* on ABC. While many readers can easily conjure iconic images of the Beatles appearing on Ed Sullivan's variety hour, many have not considered these performances in the context of the variety show, in which the band performed alongside ventriloquists, acrobats, and magicians that rounded out Sullivan's nightly lineup. Other variety shows in the 1960s, such as *Hullaballoo, Shindig!,* and *Shivaree,* were more youth-oriented, featuring Technicolor sets and go-go dancers. Although rock purists might find it odd to celebrate variety show appearances, the shows are often historically valuable because they included real-time (not lip-synched) musical performances.

While variety shows were often marketed to adults in prime-time slots, teen-oriented dance programs also became extremely popular during the 1950s. These programs were often locally produced, and broadcast in late-afternoon time slots to reach kids at home after school. Early dance shows popular during the 1950s included *American Bandstand* and *The Arthur Murray Party*, both of which became nationally syndicated. Dance-oriented television shows usually featured a room full of young dancers, both professional and amateur, who demonstrated new moves and fashion trends to a soundtrack of popular recordings. In many cases, these shows featured a special guest performance, but most artists did not perform their music live in this context, lip-synching instead. The dance show format maintained popularity well past the 1960s, with *American Bandstand* running until the late 1980s. During the 1970s, disco-oriented shows such as *Soul Train* and *Dance Fever* continued this tradition, while 1980s audiences enjoyed programs like *Solid Gold* and *Dance Party USA*. MTV also played an important role in producing dance-oriented television shows, with *Club MTV* in the 1980s and later with *TRL* (or *Total Request Live*) in the 1990s and 2000s. *TRL* was certainly created out of the same mold as *American Bandstand*: it aired in an after-school time slot, centered on a live studio audience, and featured live performances by the most popular teen-oriented groups of the time.

Television has also been an important forum for artists starring in musical sit-coms. Beginning with *The Monkees* in the mid-1960s, there have been numerous script-based comedies that featured rock musicians or musical performances. The Partridge Family was a fictional musical group, popularized during the 1970s, in a self named television series starring teen heartthrob David Cassidy and his real-life stepmother Shirley Jones. A decade later, the series *Fame* (based on a feature film of the same name) offered a similar musical-dramatic construct that included notable elements of theater and dance. Although no real-life rock stars were featured in this series, much of the music became quite popular, especially in the UK. A modern brand of this same musical sitcom can also be found in *Glee*, which has struck a chord with television audiences while racking up dozens of hit singles and millions of worldwide album sales.

Rock Film. From the beginning of the rock movement, many rock music performances were featured in motion pictures. While early depictions of rock music in films like *Rock Around the Clock* and *Blackboard Jungle* characterized rock musicians and fans as "hoodlums," rock performances were increasingly common in major motion pictures only a few years later. After signing to RCA in the mid-1950s, Elvis Presley made dozens of films, most of which featured musical performances. Some of Presley's most iconic video performances came from his work in films, including the famous "Jailhouse Rock" sequence from 1957. Presley's move into motion pictures helped to usher rock and roll into Hollywood, and during the early 1960s it became common for low-budget teen-oriented films to feature musicians and rock performances. The most popular of these were the "beach party films" produced between 1963 and 1967, many of which starred Annette Funicello and Frankie Avalon. In addition to music performed by the stars, many of these films included a house band (often Dick Dale and the Del-Tones), and various pop and R&B stars of the time.

Throughout the 1970s and 1980s rock musicians continued to star in films. Some of these might be considered serious works, while others simply served as popularity vehicles. KISS famously starred in the cult-classic *KISS Meets the Phantom of the Park* in 1978, a made-for-television film that is best known for its embarrassing and campy acting. The Ramones were central to the plot of the 1979 film *Rock and Roll High School.* Many conceptual rock albums of the 1970s also translated easily into dramatic film, producing rock-oriented movies such as *Tommy* (1975) and *Pink Floyd The Wall* (1982). Prince also starred in a series of films during the 1980s, including *Purple Rain* (1984), *Under the Cherry Moon* (1986), and *Graffiti Bridge* (1990). These are only a few of the many films after the 1960s to blur the line between music video and Hollywood feature, exposing the visual aspects of rock music to a wider audience.

Concert films have also been important to the history of rock music. The first notable film in this genre was *T.A.M.I. Show*, a 1964 feature film shot at the Santa Monica Civic Auditorium that included performances by many of the most popular rock stars of the time, ranging from British invasion groups to James Brown. The tradition of concert films has produced many of the most notable visual images in the history of rock, which include Otis Redding coaxing a newfound audience in *Monterey Pop* (1968), Jimi Hendrix playing "The Star-Spangled Banner" in *Woodstock* (1970), and the Rolling Stones' catastrophic performance at Altamont in *Gimme Shelter* (1970). As rock became more prominent, attracting the attention of Hollywood and the financial clout to secure important directors, the artistic quality of the concert film continued to improve. These include Martin Scorcese's depiction of the 1976 Thanksgiving farewell concert by the Band at San Francisco's Winterland Ballroom portrayed in *The Last Waltz* (1978) and Jonathan Demme's documentary of the Talking Heads' 1983 three-night stand in a Hollywood theater released as *Stop Making Sense* (1984). While films such as these were notable in their time, documentary films and high-quality concert footage are now released frequently, providing fans with ongoing opportunities to experience the visual element of rock without actually attending live performances.

Music Videos. Since the advent of rock, artists have also used films as a vehicle for advancing their careers and increasing their popularity. Short films made to promote singles date back at least to the 1960s, although these were more a part of the European market than the American one. The Beatles created some of the earliest promotional videos, intended to promote their music after they stopped performing live. In 1966, the band made videos for "Rain" and "Paperback Writer." Judged by later standards, these seem unimaginative and bland: the band lip-synchs performances in various scenes shot in the same outdoor garden setting. But because the Beatles were weary of touring, these and later videos—most especially those for "Penny Lane" and "Strawberry Fields Forever"—became important tools in promoting new Beatles releases. The promotional video, which later became called the music video, has an extraordinary history that eventually made a massive impact on the entire popular music industry. The emergence of 1980s music videos and the rise of MTV will be covered in depth later in the text.

Visual and Contextual Aspects of "Nowhere to Run."

For the purposes of this introduction to the video elements of rock, a useful example is a famous performance by Martha and the Vandellas for their hit single "Nowhere to Run." This well-known video footage was filmed for a summer 1965 television special hosted by disc jockey Murray the K and sponsored by the national Office of Economic Opportunity. The lip-synched video features Martha and the Vandellas in a car factory in Detroit, riding down the assembly line in a Ford Mustang as it is being assembled (see the top image on this page). Images taken from this footage have often been associated with Motown, the Vandellas' record company. As the most important record company to emerge from Detroit, historians often associate Motown's creative process with an assembly line, akin to the city's many car factories (middle). This footage might seem like an effort on the part of Motown to create this association, but the video actually comes from a larger television special called *It's What's Happening, Baby*, not created by Motown, that featured many of the most popular acts of the period, including Ray Charles, the Righteous Brothers, Johnny Rivers, and the Ronnettes. The purpose of the special was to get young viewers to mail employment concerns to a government-sponsored organization called New Chance. Moreover, at the end of the Vandellas clip, Murray the K drives the Mustang created during the performance to a beach-oriented setting, segueing into a video featuring Jan and Dean (bottom). From this clip, we learn several things about the connection between video and musical performances during the early rock era. First, we see how the government was attuned to the power of musical performances to inspire youth to action. We also see how specific settings can

enhance regional and cultural stereotypes of musical sounds. Finally, we witness how the larger context of a video performance can be lost over time, and how reconnecting these settings is valuable to the study of rock music and its history.

Throughout the remainder of this book, many notable performances in films, on television, and in music videos are discussed in special Viewing Rock boxes. In addition, many of the online Backstage Pass essays provide commentary on historically significant performances that are available on commercial video, including DVD and Internet media services like Netflix, Amazon, and iTunes. Further study of these performances can be a rewarding experience that enhances the aural consideration of rock recordings.

Now that we have discussed the organization of the book, listened carefully to some music, and considered some visual aspects of rock, it is time to dive in and explore rock music's history and repertoire. Before we consider the emergence of rock and roll, however, we will need to get a clear picture of how the music business was configured in the first half of the twentieth century. Chapter 1 will help us understand what the popular music world was like before the advent of rock and roll.

For Additional Online Resources, visit:
digital.wwnorton.com/whatsthatsound5

FURTHER READING

Mark Cunningham, *Good Vibrations: A History of Record Production* (Sanctuary, 1996).

Simon Frith, *Sound Effects: Youth, Leisure, and the Politics of Rock 'n' Roll* (Constable, 1985).

Theodore Gracyk, *Rhythm and Noise: An Aesthetics of Rock* (Duke University Press, 1996).

David Hajdu, *Love for Sale: Pop Music in America* (Farrar, Straus & Giroux, 2016).

Greil Marcus, *The History of Rock 'n' Roll in Ten Songs* (Yale University Press, 2014).

Howard Massey, *Behind the Glass: Top Record Producers Tell How They Craft the Hits* (Backbeat Books, 2000).

James Miller, *Flowers in the Dustbin: The Rise of Rock and Roll, 1947–1977* (Fireside, 1999).

Robert Palmer, *Rock & Roll: An Unruly History* (Harmony Books, 1995).

Dafydd Rees and Luke Crampton, *Rock Stars Encyclopedia*, new rev. ed. (Dorling Kindersley, 1999).

The Rolling Stone Encyclopedia of Rock & Roll, 3rd ed., eds. Holly George-Warren and Patricia Romanowski (Fireside, 2001).

The Rolling Stone Illustrated History of Rock Music, eds. Anthony DeCurtis and James Henke (Random House, 1992).

Martin C. Strong, *The Great Rock Discography* (Canongate, 2000).

Ed Ward, *The History of Rock & Roll*, Vol. 1: *1920–1963* (Flatiron, 2016).

Nona Willis Aronowitz, ed., *Out of the Vinyl Deeps: Ellen Willis on Rock Music* (University of Minnesota Press, 2011).

Albin Zak III, *The Poetics of Rock: Cutting Tracks, Making Records* (University of California Press, 2001).

The decades of the 1920s, '30s, and '40s in America were to a great extent shaped by three crucial events: the end of World War I ("The Great War"), the stock market crash of 1929, and World War II. Before and after these crushing events, Americans conquered flight, fought for the right to vote, battled for and against Prohibition, danced new dances, and made new music.

When World War I ended, 10 million soldiers were dead. Although American casualties accounted for only 1 percent of the total, the Great War had taken a costly toll on American culture. The war was bloody, fought with gas as well as bullets and with old-world strategies that could not accommodate modern weaponry. The modern world was torn apart and people everywhere were horrified.

With the war finally over, Americans felt simultaneous relief and fear, and the result was a sense of desperate recklessness. Upheaval in world politics was reflected in the arts, with the emergence of riotous new forms of literature, dance, and music. Songs remained the dominant form of popular music in the 1920s, but the radical sounds of Louis Armstrong, Duke Ellington, and others helped define the decade musically. F. Scott Fitzgerald (author of *The Great Gatsby*) dubbed the 1920s "the jazz age," and jazz's strong rhythms, jagged melodies, and big sound made people get up and dance, with young, single, female "flappers" dancing (and smoking and drinking) right alongside their male counterparts.

But the excitement and freedom of the "roaring" twenties were quickly snuffed out in one day, with the stock market crash of October 29, 1929, forever known as "Black Tuesday." The crash sent the American economy into turmoil: 26,000 businesses failed in 1930. By 1932, 11 million Americans—25 percent of the labor force—were out of work. People were forced to move from their homes into shantytowns, and many stood in line for bread every day.

In 1932, with the nation out of work and looking to its government for help, Franklin Delano Roosevelt was elected president. Roosevelt promised Americans a "New Deal" and used the power of the federal government to get people back to work, creating government-paid jobs to improve the nation's roads, bridges, tunnels, and forests and national parks. Roosevelt also established the Works Progress Administration (WPA), which contributed significantly to the arts. With the creation of federal agencies like the WPA, along with the establishment of the Social Security system, Roosevelt defined a new role for the federal government that some argue broke the United States out of its psychological, if not its economic, depression.

No sooner had Americans started to leave the Great Depression behind than a new enemy emerged: Adolf Hitler. Like Roosevelt, Hitler was dealing with a severe economic crisis in his nation. Hitler, however, began to solve Germany's economic problems in a different way. He chose expansion, eventually leading his military forces into Austria, Czechoslovakia, and Poland and pitting the German "master race" against "undesirables," most notably Jews—6 million of whom were killed in Nazi death camps by 1945. Joining forces with Italy and Japan,

States did not join in the fighting, but when Japan attacked Pearl Harbor on December 7, 1941, the country entered the fray in the Pacific, and after Germany declared war on the United States, in Europe as well. The war on the European front ended with Germany's

the United States dropped atomic bombs on Hiroshima and Nagasaki. The war was over, but the world had entered the atomic age.

While war had ravaged Europe and rocked the world, American soldiers returned home as conquering heroes. Optimism reigned at

This cover of *Life* magazine from February 18, 1926. Shows a "flapper" teaching an older man the Charleston, a popular dance of the time. Many women smoked, danced, and drank in public for the first time in the 1920s.

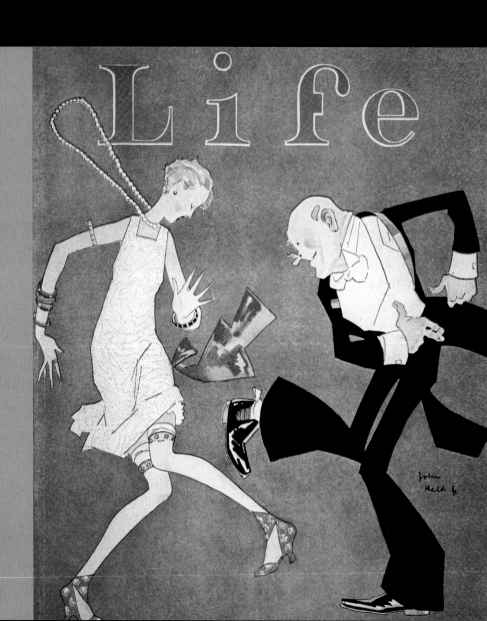

home, signaled by the G.I. Bill, which allowed more Americans to attend college than ever before, and by a dramatically increased birth rate—a "baby boom" that would have long-range consequences for American culture, especially for popular music and its audience. Being such a large (and prosperous) generation had its benefits. There were lots of baby boomers and soon they would have their own money to spend. Many would spend it on music, a music that was also all their own: rock and roll.

During the Great Depression, nearly 25 percent of the American labor force was out of work. Here, hundreds of homeless and unemployed people wait in line seeking shelter in New York in 1930.

CHAPTER 1

THE WORLD BEFORE ROCK AND ROLL

CHAPTER PREVIEW

- Before rock and roll emerged in 1955, there were three prominent markets for popular music: mainstream pop, rhythm and blues, and country and western.

- The music business before 1955 was dominated by music publishers, who sold sheet music as a principal source of revenue.

- A national audience for mainstream pop developed before World War II via national radio and films. After World War II, this national audience migrated to television.

- Bing Crosby, the big bands, Frank Sinatra, and Les Paul and Mary Ford were important figures in mainstream pop before 1955.

- Country and western has its roots in country music (Southeast) and western music (Southwest and West Coast). After 1945 these styles came together in Nashville.

- Jimmie Rodgers is an important star of country and western before World War II and Hank Williams an important songwriter and performer after 1945.

- Bessie Smith was an important star of rhythm and blues before World War II, while Muddy Waters and Big Joe Turner are important figures after 1945.

- The migration of the national audience to television created opportunities for local and regional radio stations playing rhythm and blues in the early 1950s.

Irving Berlin's "White Christmas" is one of the most successful songs in the history of popular music. Originally featured in the 1942 movie *Holiday Inn* starring Bing Crosby and Fred Astaire, the song has been recorded by a wide range of performers, including Crosby, Frank Sinatra, Perry Como, Clyde McPhatter and the Drifters, Elvis Presley, and Al Green. Crosby's version is reported to be the biggest-selling record in history, and it returned to the upper regions of the pop charts during the Christmas season almost every year until 1962, hitting number one in 1942, 1945, and 1946. While the song has come to conjure up nostalgic and warm images of snowy winter nights in front of a crackling fire, the original opening (shown on the previous page) has the singer stuck in sunny Southern California during the Christmas season, lamenting the balmy climate.

I n 1956, a young, slim Elvis Presley appeared on the *Toast of the Town*, a weekly television variety program hosted by Ed Sullivan that aired Sunday evenings on CBS. Presley's appearance on the show was the source of considerable controversy; in an earlier performance of "Hound Dog" on Milton Berle's show, Elvis had launched into an improvised ending to the tune, grinding his hips suggestively as he sang. Such on-stage antics earned the singer the nickname "Elvis the Pelvis," and caused such a public uproar that when Presley appeared on Sullivan's show, the cameras reportedly were not permitted to show his body below the chest. Despite the heated protests of parents—or maybe because of them—Elvis became the central figure in a new kind of popular music intended especially for teenagers: rock and roll.

We'll discuss Elvis and his music in further detail in the next chapter. For now, recognizing the importance of Elvis's early television performances can help us approach the ways rock and roll developed in the mid-1950s. Consider, for instance, that Presley appeared before a national audience, making his performance one that the entire country reacted to. As rock and roll erupted in 1955 and 1956, a new and interesting feature of its success was that it was a national style of music almost from the beginning—it didn't spread gradually from town to town and region to region around the country but rather broke onto the national cultural scene relatively suddenly. How was it possible, then, for this first wave of rock and roll to saturate American culture so quickly and thoroughly? What kinds of cultural conditions and commercial means of production and distribution had to be in place for a new musical style to "catch fire" as rock and roll did? And what were the musical and stylistic sources of this new style?

This chapter will examine these issues as well as outline the world of popular music before rock and roll made its rowdy entrance onto the national scene. Few musical styles emerge fully formed and in isolation from other styles of their time, and rock and roll is no exception. Rock and roll developed out of three principal sources that preceded it: mainstream popular music, rhythm and blues, and country and western. Each of these styles has its own history and development in the decades before rock and roll. This chapter will examine how these styles developed in the 1930s, '40s, and early '50s, providing a historical backdrop and music-stylistic context that will help us understand how and why rock and roll emerged as it did and when it did. It will also explore how the development of new technologies like radio and television played a crucial role in preparing the ground for this critical shift in the pop-music landscape.

BUILDING A NATIONAL AUDIENCE FOR MUSIC AND ENTERTAINMENT

National versus Regional. One of the important changes that took place in popular music in the first half of the twentieth century was the emergence of a national audience. In today's world, in which satellite TV and the Internet provide us convenient and instant access to even remote parts of the globe, it is difficult to imagine an America in which most culture was regional. But at the end of the nineteenth century, the majority of Americans lived in a world very much conditioned by their local and regional surroundings. People tended not to travel nearly as much as we do now, and in many parts of the country there was no quick access to news of national and world events. In terms of popular musical styles, this meant that styles often could be identified with particular regions of the country. Early gramophone cylinders and disks made recorded performances available to many Americans, but the music that people knew still tended to be mostly the music they could either play or hear performed in person, perhaps at a vaudeville show. If someone played the piano and read music—and many Americans did—he or she could purchase the sheet music to a favorite song, often at the local Woolworth's five-and-dime store, where pianists were on hand to personally play the music for customers trying to decide among competing titles. Music was also available through oral tradition, and one could learn to play tunes by ear, without having to read music. The technological and marketing developments in radio and motion pictures played a central role in making the same kinds of popular entertainment available in all parts of the country during the first few decades of the century, in many ways breaking down regional differences. The 1930s and '40s are often thought of as a golden age in the history of motion pictures, as Hollywood churned out a wide variety of films that played movie houses in towns across America. These films helped create a national entertainment culture. Later we will consider the role films played in the music business during those years, but the central role of radio in building this national audience is probably just as crucial.

Radio technology was developed at the end of the nineteenth century and used initially for military purposes and to communicate with ships at sea; the first radio broadcasts of consequence for our story date back to 1920, when KDKA in Pittsburgh and WWJ in Detroit went on the air with a blend of news, local information, and live music. It would be hard to exaggerate the marked effect early radio had on American culture, and especially on the history of popular music. For the first time, listeners within range of a regional radio station could enjoy music that might otherwise be unavailable to them. For instance, listeners way out in farm country could hear performances from far-off big-city nightclubs. When NBC went coast-to-coast with its national radio network in 1928, regional boundaries in popular culture began to blur. Now it no longer mattered as much where one lived: the same news, music, drama, and comedy were simultaneously available to significant portions of the country. Listeners within the transmitting range of stations in Philadelphia, Buffalo, Detroit, Chicago, and Los Angeles, for instance, could all hear the same programming at the same time. Network radio audiences suddenly became national audiences.

Especially important to the history of popular music is the way some pop styles became national while other styles kept their regional identities. To a great extent this can be attributed to the programming of the networks: the mainstream pop music of

Many of the first radio stations developed from modest beginnings. This photo shows the original facilities used to broadcast the results of the 1920 presidential election. This small setup, originally housed in a garage, would soon become Pittsburgh's KDKA.

Today, *Amos 'n' Andy* is considered politically incorrect, but in the heyday of radio, the show was enormously popular nationwide. Amos (Freeman Gosden) and Andy (Charles Correll) are shown here broadcasting their show in 1935.

performers such as Bing Crosby, the Andrews Sisters, the big bands, and later Frank Sinatra were heard frequently on network radio; country and western, and rhythm and blues were not. Because mainstream pop developed a national audience, regional distinctions are not particularly useful when we chart the development of that particular style in the 1930s, '40s, and '50s; instead, experts tend to stress how similar pop was in most markets across the country. Also, the mainstream pop played on network radio during the 1930s and '40s was directed at a white, middle-class listening audience. Music that music-business people thought might appeal to only low-income white or low-income black listeners (rural or urban) was mostly excluded, or at best, given a marginal role in radio programming. Since country and western and rhythm and blues were considered music for such low-income listeners, these styles were not often programmed on network radio; as a consequence, they retained their regional distinctions. We will want to keep track of such regional differences within and among country and western and rhythm and blues styles, and this will be discussed in more detail later in this chapter and in Chapter 2.

The Rise of the Radio Networks in the 1920s (How Did They Work?).

The early years of radio were an exciting time, and as broadcasters worked to get radio into every home in America, they discovered there were two reliable ways of reaching ever-larger audiences. The first was to broadcast the radio signal via a high-power transmitter. Under the most favorable atmospheric conditions, such "superstations" could reach listeners within a radius of several hundred miles of the transmitter. The federal government even licensed a few stations not only for high power but also for exclusive use of a particular frequency. With no local stations to mask the signal, such "clear channel" stations could regularly reach entire multistate regions of the country. Other enterprising broadcasters placed their transmitters in Mexico, just south of the border, where the U.S. government had no licensing authority. These "X-stations" (named after their first call letter) could sometimes be picked up as far north as Chicago.

A more effective way of reaching a large audience was to link a number of local and regional stations together to form a network. NBC used AT&T telephone lines to link up sixty-nine stations across the country for its first coast-to-coast broadcast in 1928. Soon NBC was running two networks, and other networks were getting into the business as well. The network system had a number of distinct advantages: programming could be run from one central location (most often a studio in New York), and it was also possible to run live programming from member stations (called "affiliates"). This gave the networks a tremendous range of programming from which to choose. When networks could get one of the clear-channel stations on board, this offered the best of both worlds. This network system survives today relatively intact in the television industry, where most of the prime-time programming originates from the main studios in Los Angeles or New York, while other shows and newscasts originate locally. Current talk radio also employs this model, as shows originate from many parts of the country but play to a national audience. All of this was first developed for radio in the 1920s.

Perhaps the biggest difference between today's radio and radio before 1945 was that back then it was considered unethical to play records on the air. It was thought that by playing a record you were trying to fool people into believing a performance was live when it really was not, so most music was performed live on the air. Modern radio listeners expect that the music they hear is recorded, but from the first broadcast moments of radio, listeners assumed and expected that what they heard over the airwaves was occurring live and in real time. This was, of course, a happy situation for most musicians, who eagerly took advantage of the opportunities for ample work. Even though affiliates were fed network programming for large segments of the broadcast schedule, most larger stations also employed a studio band for local programming. In addition, stations had to work to fill the remaining on-air time when no network programs were broadcast, and this created plenty of opportunity for entrepreneurial local bandleaders, who were often eager for a chance to promote their groups. In this context, it is not surprising that the musician's union (American Federation of Musicians) took strong political steps in the 1940s to keep records ("canned music") off the airwaves—keeping music live meant keeping musicians (and union members) working.

Network radio programming offered listeners a wide range of entertainment: soap operas, adventure shows, and comedies were all popular, as well as variety shows and feeds from dance clubs across the nation. *The Guiding Light* appeared in 1937, while shows like *The Lone Ranger* and *Superman* entertained listeners throughout most of the 1930s and '40s, but one of the greatest successes of the era was the comedy *Amos 'n' Andy*, which premiered in 1929. Though its use of racial stereotypes, drawn from the minstrel tradition, would be unacceptable by today's standards, during its heyday the adventures and mishaps of Amos and Andy had the undivided attention of the country (not unlike the success later enjoyed by television shows such as *All in the Family*, *M*A*S*H*, *Cheers*, *Seinfeld*, and *Breaking Bad*). Network radio created an audience that stretched from the East Coast to the West Coast, and in so doing, it created a national popular culture in which music played a central role. Once radio came on the scene, a song could become popular almost overnight; no more waiting for word of mouth to spread from town to town and from region to region: with radio, a song could be heard far and wide in a single performance.

Among many of the radio shows that survived the move to television, *The Lone Ranger* became one of the most popular small-screen staples of the 1950s. The Lone Ranger (Clayton Moore, left) is shown here with his faithful sidekick, Tonto (Jay Silverheels).

The Migration of Big Corporate Money Away from Radio to Television.

Network radio helped create a national audience, but by the late 1940s that audience was beginning to move away from radio and toward the newest technological marvel: television. The Radio Corporation of America (RCA), under the direction of David Sarnoff, had been a key player in the development of radio since the beginning. Sarnoff had been the young man decoding radio transmissions from the *Titanic* as she went down in 1912, and as a rising executive in the radio industry, he led RCA in building the NBC networks in the 1920s and '30s. In the 1940s, Sarnoff's attention turned to television, and soon RCA would increasingly redirect its resources from radio to television in the period after World War II, betting that sound with pictures would be even more popular—and profitable—than sound alone. As more Americans could afford to acquire television sets in the late 1940s and 1950s, the national audience migrated away from radio and toward television. This changeover occurred slowly but steadily and could be seen in programming as well; some of the most popular radio shows—*The Guiding Light*, *Amos 'n' Andy*, *The Lone Ranger*, and *Superman*—all made the leap and became popular TV shows. Along with motion pictures, radio had created a national audience, and television now inherited radio's share of that audience.

Our discussion has thus led us back to television in the 1950s and provided us with a greater context for interpreting Elvis's 1956 appearance on *Toast of the Town*. It was crucial to the rapid and broad success of rock and roll that this new style appear before a national audience. Fifteen years earlier, that audience would

Is It Live or Is It Memorex? A Note on Recording Technology

As a result of the popularity of the audiobook format of recent years, recordings of some old radio broadcasts have been released and are readily available. Many assume that these shows are tapes of original broadcasts; it is important to note, however, that recording tape was not widely used in radio until the late 1940s. Most of us are familiar with magnetic tape, which is used in cassette and reel-to-reel formats. This technology was first employed by the Germans during World War II for military purposes and was intended to protect Adolf Hitler from attack by Allied forces. The Germans were concerned that the Allies might detect the exact source of specific radio transmissions, and so could possibly attack the station from which Hitler was delivering one of his many radio speeches to the German people. They refined magnetic tape recording in order to produce the most realistic recorded version of Hitler's voice, and then the tape was broadcast at a later time, while

Hitler was far away from the radio studio. When the Allies conquered Germany, they found that the radio stations all had sophisticated tape machines, and this new technology quickly made its way into the radio business.

For those radio programs that date from before 1945, most of the broadcasts are lost forever. But of those that are preserved, many are "transcription disc" recordings, made on 16-inch discs that resemble LP records and were made for circulation only among stations and not for general sale. It says a good deal about the importance of radio in the lives of Americans in the 1940s that the U.S. government made certain that transcription discs of popular radio shows were shipped to armed forces stations overseas and played for the troops. In addition to letters and packages from home, familiar radio shows helped ease the strain for servicemen of being a long way from home and often in hostile conditions.

have been reached via network radio, but by the mid-1950s they were instead gathered around the television set. Thus, the national audience that television enjoyed had been brought together for the first time by radio. Rock and roll was able to spread as fast as it did because this audience could be reached with a single Sunday evening television broadcast. As television grew in national prominence, however, radio was left out in the cold in many ways. With its national audience dwindling, radio returned to its local and regional audiences. The migration of the networks (and their audiences) toward television, though it might be seen as a major blow to the radio industry, actually opened up new kinds of opportunities for entrepreneurial station owners and managers. The transformation of local and regional radio stations in response to the early age of television played a critical role in the development of country and western and rhythm and blues, and, in turn, figured prominently in the emergence of early rock and roll.

TIN PAN ALLEY

Sheet Music Publishers and Professional Songwriters. The development of radio and television technologies was one influence on the mainstream popular-music business in the decades before rock and roll. A second was music publishing. In the first half of the twentieth century, sheet music was the principal way to sell music. The sheet music business was concentrated in an area of New York City often referred to as Tin Pan Alley, where, about a hundred years ago, songwriters and song producers had clustered to form the geographic heart of the industry. The area apparently got its name because the high concentration of songwriters plunking out their song ideas on rows of pianos sounded to the locals like a bunch of people banging on tin pans. The term "Tin Pan Alley" has now become shorthand not only for the body of music produced at that time but also for a way of doing business in popular music. The body of music consists of the thousands of songs written and made popular, mostly in the first half of the twentieth century, by such professional songwriters as Irving Berlin, Cole Porter, George and Ira Gershwin, and Jerome Kern. The way of doing business has to do with how these songs were sold.

Musically speaking, Tin Pan Alley songs follow a standard, though very flexible, formal pattern. Many of these songs make use of a **sectional verse-chorus** format, in which the **sectional chorus** is the song listeners are likely to recognize, while the **sectional verse** is a kind of introduction that sets the scene for the song. Most listeners, for instance, know only the sectional chorus of the perennial favorite "White Christmas" (sung by many but made famous by Bing Crosby); the song actually has a sectional verse that explains how Christmas doesn't seem the same in California with all the bright sunshine. Sectional choruses are often cast in a 32-measure structural pattern called AABA form. Judy Garland's performance of "Over the Rainbow"—a song featured in the classic 1939 film *The Wizard of Oz*—provides a representative example of how the 32-bar AABA form is structured. While there are some standard variations on this common structural pattern in the Tin Pan Alley repertory—ABAC, for instance—the basic 32-bar sectional chorus length remains intact in most instances. Thus what holds this repertory together musically is a fairly

**sectional
verse-chorus
sectional chorus
sectional verse**

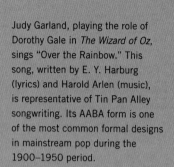

Judy Garland, playing the role of Dorothy Gale in *The Wizard of Oz*, sings "Over the Rainbow." This song, written by E. Y. Harburg (lyrics) and Harold Arlen (music), is representative of Tin Pan Alley songwriting. Its AABA form is one of the most common formal designs in mainstream pop during the 1900–1950 period.

uniform approach to musical form, practiced by a majority of the professional song-writers of Tin Pan Alley, along with a consistent approach to the many other musical elements that are used to help delineate the form. The sectional verse-chorus format is rare in rock music, but the AABA form common to so many Tin Pan Alley sectional verses plays a central role in rock.

This repertory is unified not only in the way it is structured but also in the way it was marketed. In rock music, the basic unit of trade is a specific recorded performance, available on a record, tape, CD, MP3, or other format. But in the Tin Pan Alley era, the basic unit of trade was the song itself, not a specific recording of the song. A successful song was recorded by a series of artists, each trying to tailor the tune to suit his or her personal style, and the more versions, the more money that could be made by the songwriter and his or her publisher. In this practice, professional songwriters composed the songs and publishers then worked to get each tune heard by the public. The songwriters themselves were rarely performers, so publishers needed ways of "pitching" songs to performers who might consider working them into their performances. In the first few decades of the twentieth century, songs were pitched in all kinds of ways—some more ethical than others. The usual way to get a song known was to convince a professional to perform the tune as part of a show. Another more aggressive method was to plant a "song plugger" in the audience who would stand up during the show and offer a rendition of a new song—an action that could land him either in the street, or worse, in jail.

With the rise of musical theater, Broadway musicals became a prime vehicle for getting songs heard, and some early Broadway shows had only the skimpiest of plots, provided merely to give some sense of sequence to the songs themselves (later musicals were far more integrated). The first movies had no sound, though music was in

Listening Guide

Judy Garland with Victor Young and His Orchestra, "Over the Rainbow" Decca 2672

Words by E. Y. Harburg, music by Harold Arlen. Reached #5 on the *Billboard* pop chart in fall 1939.

FORM: This example uses AABA form, which is closely associated with Tin Pan Alley songwriting and is one of the most common of the mainstream pop formal designs used during the 1900–50 period. Typically, an AABA form presents two verses, followed by a contrasting bridge, and a return to the verse. To fill out a particular performance arrangement of an AABA song, verses and the bridge may be repeated. Here two verses are repeated, as well as part of the bridge, after the complete AABA structure has been presented. Note that the verses within the AABA form are not the same as the verse employed in the sectional verse-chorus form.

TIME SIGNATURE: 4/4. Note the frequent speeding up and slowing down of the tempo. These tempo variations help shape the vocal phrases and make them more expressive. Such changes of tempo are not common in dance music or any style that uses a drummer. In this case, a conductor directs the changes of tempo and dynamics.

INSTRUMENTATION: Vocalist with orchestra.

0:00–0:11	**Introduction**, 4 mm.	String melody with pulsating winds accompaniment sets the dreamy mood for the song.
0:11–0:34	**A-Verse**, 8 mm.	Vocal enters, "Somewhere . . . way up high . . ." Listen for the large leap in the melody, which then works its way back to Earth, paralleling the words.
0:34–0:55	**A-Verse**, 8 mm.	As before, "Somewhere . . . skies are blue . . ."
0:55–1:18	**B-Bridge**, 8 mm.	"Some day I'll wish . . ." Notice how the first half of each vocal phrase seems to rush forward, then slow down toward the end.
1:18–1:40	**A-Verse**, 8 mm.	As before, "Somewhere . . . bluebirds fly . . ." Note the melodic support in the orchestra.
1:40–2:01	**A-Verse**, 8 mm.	Vocal gets a rest and the melody is played by clarinet and answered by orchestra.
2:01–2:25	**A-Verse**, 8 mm.	Vocal returns with variations that make the melody seem fresh, "Somewhere . . . bluebirds fly."
2:25–2:46	**B-Partial Bridge**, 4 mm.	Beginning of bridge serves as the basis for the ending, "If happy . . ."

During the 1930s, Fred Astaire and Ginger Rogers enjoyed a string of successful films for RKO. The often innovative and sometimes elaborate dance scenes were choreographed by Astaire and Hermes Pan. Astaire often gets the credit as a superb dancer for these scenes, though many have noted that Rogers did everything Astaire did—but backwards and in high heels. Though Astaire is regarded as one of the great dancers of his era, his vocal performances introduced audiences to many top pop standards.

many instances furnished by local musicians—sometimes even an orchestra—and occasionally musical scores were provided by the film studio for specific movies. When sound films became popular in the 1930s, Broadway musicals were often released in film versions, and new musicals were composed expressly for the movies. Many songs were introduced via films. During the 1930s, for instance, Fred Astaire enjoyed a series of hit songs from his movies with Ginger Rogers, including "Cheek to Cheek," an Irving Berlin song from the 1935 film *Top Hat*. Thus musical theater and movies provided convenient vehicles for promoting Tin Pan Alley songs. Records could also help promote songs, though when we think of recordings during the pre-rock era we have to remember that the central element in a record was the song, not the particular performance of it. By far the best way to get a song out during the 1930s and '40s was to get it on the radio, and radio was dominated during the 1935–45 period by big bands, and then in 1945–55 by star singers. By getting a song performed on national radio, a publisher could expect the best chance of success. In some instances, sales of a recorded version of a song could outsell the sheet music, but the usual mode of success for Tin Pan Alley came in the form of sheet music sales. During the years before rock and roll, songs were seen as entities separable from particular performances of them. For a Tin Pan Alley music publisher, the best thing that could happen to a song was for it to be recorded by a wide variety of artists (this is still true for music publishers today). But until the advent of rock and roll, the heart of the business was squarely in sheet music sales.

THE SINGER STEPS FORWARD

The Singers and the Big Bands. One important objective for all Tin Pan Alley publishers was to get their songs on the radio, and this is where our discussions of radio and Tin Pan Alley come together. Because most radio performances until the late 1940s were live, promoting a song meant much more for music publishers than just getting a record out: bandleaders and singers had to be convinced to perform a song and in the process be persuaded that using the song in their live shows would also serve their own career interests—and for most musicians during that era (much as today), "career interests" meant "future bookings for more money." Publishers thus had to bargain with bandleaders and singers, as well as radio producers, to get their songs included in those live radio broadcasts that the bands and singers were using to prompt future bookings. The radio networks, performers, and song publishers thus needed one another to succeed, and much of the behind-the-scenes action in the music business during those years had to do with which artists would perform on which shows, and which songs they would play or sing.

The era from about 1935 to 1945 is considered the big band era. During this time, dance bands employed a rhythm section of bass, drums, piano, and guitar combined with a horn section of trumpets, trombones, and saxophones to create arrangements of Tin Pan Alley songs designed to provide music appropriate for dancing, while also featuring the instrumental prowess of the musicians and the virtuosity of the arranger. Big bands were led by instrumentalists such as Benny Goodman, Tommy Dorsey, Jimmy Dorsey, and Glenn Miller, and singers were merely featured soloists. Thus, the celebrity in the band was its leader; the musicians and singers could (and did) change frequently. Arrangements during the big band era gave more emphasis to the band, often allotting only one time through the sectional chorus of a song for the singer. Sections of the band, and perhaps instrumental soloists, might also be featured both before and after the singer. Many arrangements, such as the Glenn Miller Band's 1942 number-one hit "A String of Pearls," employed no vocals at all. Such an emphasis on the band may seem strange to many rock listeners. The rock music practice that developed later is exactly the opposite of the big band practice: in rock music, the vocalist is usually the focus of the song and an instrumental solo takes a verse of the song to provide variety. In big band music, the vocalist provides the variety! Perhaps because of the emphasis on instrumental playing in the big bands, there is a close relationship between big band music and jazz, which developed both within and alongside big band music. In fact, many important jazz musicians played in big bands, and several significant bands figure heavily in most accounts of jazz history.

Despite the general focus during the big band era on the bands themselves, a number of performing artists developed careers independent from any particular band. The most important pop singer in the 1930s and 1940s was Bing Crosby, whose relaxed, easygoing crooning made him a favorite in both the United States

Duke Ellington (at the piano) was an important band leader in the swing music scene during the 1930s and '40s. Shown here in a poster for the 1943 movie *Reveille with Beverly*, Duke's band was joined by Frank Sinatra, the Mills Brothers, and the Count Basie Orchestra in a film that gave radio listeners across the country a chance to see and hear performances of these popular artists in the years before the rise of television.

Shown here singing at a club in London during World War II, Bing Crosby was popular not only in North America and England, but also in Germany. Broadcasts of "Der Bingle" were directed at German audiences in hopes of winning them over to Crosby's dulcet tones and markedly American ways. Like Fred Astaire, Crosby also appeared in a series of film musicals throughout his career, winning an Academy Award in 1944 for his performance in *Going My Way*.

and abroad. In fact, Crosby's popularity with German listeners earned him the nickname "Der Bingle." Crosby enjoyed a long string of hit recordings, including "I've Got a Pocketful of Dreams" (1938), "Only Forever" (1940), and "Swinging on a Star" (1944), along with "White Christmas," which topped the pop charts in 1942 and again in 1945. In addition to being perhaps the most successful solo performer of his era, Crosby acted and sang in films (often with comedian Bob Hope) and hosted his own radio variety show (sponsored by Kraft Foods). In contrast to some of the pop singers who would come to fame in the years after World War II, Bing Crosby projected a wholesome, friendly, and paternal image; in many ways, he was America's dad (or favorite uncle). The Andrews Sisters and the Mills Brothers were also important figures in the 1935–45 period, each ringing up a long series of hit records. Both groups made harmony singing their trademark, and in some ways the vocal arrangements of each group owe something to big band horn arrangements. This can be heard especially in the Andrews Sisters' "In the Mood," which is a vocal rendition of a song made popular by the Glenn Miller Orchestra. The Andrews Sisters enjoyed their greatest commercial success with "Bei Mir bist du Schoen" (1938), "Shoo-Shoo Baby" (1943), and "Rum and Coca Cola" (1945), while the Mills Brothers scored biggest with "Tiger Rag" (1931), "Paper Doll" (1943), and "You Always Hurt the One You Love" (1944). The Andrews Sisters' and Mills Brothers' approach to harmony singing served as one precursor to the doo-wop and girl groups that played an important role in rock and roll in the 1950s and 1960s.

Frank Sinatra. To somebody inside the entertainment business in the period before 1945, it would probably have seemed crazy to think that a big band singer could strike out on his own and have a viable career; Bing Crosby had enjoyed considerable success as a solo act, but he was considered more the exception than the rule. Frank Sinatra, however, established a new model for the pop-music singer; building in part on Crosby's accomplishments, Sinatra made the singer, not the band, the star of the show, and thus paved the way for later rock and roll singers like Elvis Presley and Pat Boone. Sinatra came up through the big band ranks as a singer with the Harry James and Tommy Dorsey bands, singing the occasional solo but mostly sitting on the sidelines. He went solo in 1943, enjoying a number-two hit with "All or Nothing at All," a track he had recorded in 1939 with Harry James. Perhaps owing to his good looks and slightly rebellious sensuality, Sinatra became a teen idol almost immediately. In a preview of the rock and roll hysteria to come a decade later, teenage girls mobbed Sinatra performances, fainting or grabbing at him. Although Sinatra enjoyed the fanatical attention and advantages of a successful solo singing career, he continued to think of himself as a musician and frequently acknowledged that he owed much of his vocal phrasing and technique to his study of the musicians with whom he had worked during the big band era. Of Sinatra's many important records from the late 1940s, his rendition of "I've Got a Crush on You" (1948) is a good example of his distinctive singing style, employed in a song that reinforced his teen idol image. Sinatra went on to become one of the most successful singers of the post–World War II era, selling millions of records and playing to packed houses well into the 1980s.

In the wake of his first successes, Sinatra drew many imitators, as singers now replaced the big bands as the focus of the music business and many of the now-former big band vocalists took center stage in the wake of Sinatra's success. At the same time, financial pressures forced many of the big bands to break up; after about 1945 it simply became too expensive to employ so many musicians, and smaller combos became a more cost-effective way of making a suitable living playing dancehall gigs. By the end of the 1940s, the big band era was over, and increasingly, new singers emerged who had no significant previous association with any particular big band. For many involved with the big bands, this was an unfortunate turn of events. As far as Tin Pan Alley was concerned, however, it was a good thing. The new singers continued to depend on Tin Pan Alley for songs, and the focus on singing created a stronger vehicle for song sales. Rock and roll would upset this applecart in 1955, but until then it was business as usual for the New York publishers: the big bands were out and the singers were in.

The Sound of Pop in the Early 1950s. Pop music in the first half of the 1950s is sometimes dismissed as being hopelessly corny and stiff, especially in comparison to the rhythm and blues of the same time. Patti Page's "How Much Is That Doggie in the Window?" might be thought of as representative of the generally wholesome and inoffensive approach found in much early to mid-1950s pop, but there was more to pop in the first half of the decade than hopelessly happy tunes with canine obbligato. Singers such as Eddie Fisher and Tony Bennett scored hit records in the new, more youth-oriented mold cast by Sinatra; Fisher's sentimental "Oh! My Pa-Pa" (1954) and Bennett's swinging "Rags to Riches" (1953) each

Starting out as a featured singer with the Harry James and Tommy Dorsey bands, Frank Sinatra struck out on a solo career in 1942. Sinatra was especially popular with young women, who often swooned when the slim, handsome singer crooned.

WHAT'S THAT SOURCE?

During the mid-1940s Frank Sinatra emerged out of the heavily instrumental swing movement to became a well-known vocalist. This New Yorker profile from October 1946 discusses Sinatra as a vocalist in the lineage of Bing Cosby and how electrical amplification allowed singers to establish a more intimate vocal technique.

In the past three years, there has been a flourishing revival of sentimental type singing originated, mainly by Rudy Vallee, in the twenties. This is known as "crooning," and is largely dependent on mechanical amplification, in the early days by megaphone and now by microphone. Most of the modern crop of crooners admit that Sinatra is single-voicedly responsible for the limelight in which they now bask. Many of them have tried to copy his casual, intimate manner of singing, and the few who have not consciously aped him have been accused of doing so anyway. "All I want to do is sing straight and relaxed," one singer said in self-defense a while ago. "If you do that, you *got* to sound like Sinatra." The most relaxed and most successful of all contemporary singers is Bing Crosby, who sometimes sounds as if he were falling asleep in mid-song. Crosby began singing with bands in 1922, when Sinatra was four. Since Sinatra has grown up, he has occasionally imitated Crosby; at rehearsals, he sometimes shows up wearing a yachting cap and a florid sports shirt and clutching a pipe—all equipment for which Crosby is noted. The two singers, who are casual acquaintances, get along well enough, but their supporters have been known to clash. A twenty-seven-year-old lady admirer of Sinatra had to be taken to a hospital after her roommate, a Crosby fan, had stabbed her with an icepick during a debate. Many of the radio stations that rely almost entirely on recorded music have tried to give a certain variety to their fare by calling any joint recital of Crosby and Sinatra records a Battle of the Baritones or something else equally bellicose. Listeners are often asked to indicate which of the contestants they favor. Crosby wins the majority of them. Sinatra's most noteworthy triumph was beating Crosby, in one of the larger polls, 571,978 to 533,211.

Source: E. J. Kahn Jr., "Phenomenon: The Voice with the Golden Accessories," *New Yorker*, October 26, 1946, 37–38.

placed the musical focus squarely on the singer, with the orchestra in a supporting role. Johnnie Ray took the male vocalist role from suave and controlled to overtly emotional and romantically melodramatic with his ballad, "Cry," creating an international hit in 1951. In addition to the success enjoyed by Page—whose "The Tennessee Waltz" topped the charts for thirteen weeks in 1950—female vocalists were well represented in the pre–rock and roll hit parade: Jo Stafford's "You Belong to Me" (1952) and Kay Starr's "Wheel of Fortune" (1952) both follow the singer-up-front format with the band relegated to an accompanimental role. Rosemary Clooney also enjoyed a string of hits, with "Come On-A My House" (1951), featuring a driving rhythmic feel with an Armenian flair.

The most important aspect of mainstream pop in the years preceding rock and roll is that much of this music was produced for a family audience—teenagers were expected to enjoy this music as readily as their parents and grandparents might. As family entertainment, pop music mostly avoided any topics that might be considered unsuited for general audiences. "I'm Sittin' on Top of the World," a hit in 1953 for guitarist Les Paul and vocalist Mary Ford, is a representative example of the happy, wholesome sound of early 1950s mainstream pop and a showcase of the duo's trademark layering of guitars and vocals.

As discussed in the next chapter, early rock and roll was a style directed primarily at young people, serving as a marker of generational difference. In the first half of the 1950s, however, mainstream pop was designed to appeal to a broad, mostly white middle-class audience. Aspects of this music that might seem corny and naive in retrospect resulted from trying to produce music that would be acceptable to a wide range of listeners. But even within this relatively constrained context, it is possible to detect features that point to the emergence of the rowdier, youth-oriented rock and roll: the sensual appeal of Sinatra and the emotional directness of Johnnie Ray. By the mid-1950s, many of the elements were in place for rock and roll. Singers were dominating pop music, with some placing more emphasis on emotional performances and sensuality, and a national audience for popular music was well established.

Listening Guide

Frank Sinatra with Harry James and His Orchestra, "All or Nothing at All" Columbia 35587

Music by Arthur Altman, lyrics by Jack Lawrence. Recorded in 1939 and rose to #2 on the *Billboard* "Best Selling Retail Records" (national) chart in 1943.

FORM: AABA, with introduction and partial reprise. After an introduction, the AABA form unfolds in a typical manner, though each verse ends in a slightly different way. The last instrumental verse features the horns playing the melody most of the way, with vocal returning only at the end to conclude the song.

TIME SIGNATURE: 4/4, slow tempo.

INSTRUMENTATION: Big band consisting of trumpets, saxophones, trombones, piano, drums, bass, and guitar. The microphone placement makes Sinatra's voice sound close and intimate while the rest of the band sounds distant.

0:00–0:09	**Introduction**, 2 mm.	Begins with pick-up featuring ascending horn melody against a descending bass.
0:09–0:42	**A-Verse 1**, 8 mm.	Vocal enters, notice how close the voice sounds, while the horns and saxes seem distant, "All or nothing . . ."
0:42–1:15	**A-Verse 2**, 8 mm.	As before but with transition in last measure leading to bridge, "All or nothing at all . . ."
1:15–1:48	**B-Bridge**, 8 mm.	"Distant" horns continue in dialogue with vocal melody, "Oh please, don't bring your lips . . ."
1:48–2:21	**A-Verse 3**, 8 mm.	As before but with a more conclusive last measure, "And if I fell . . ."
2:21–2:55	**A-Verse**, 8 mm.	Follows Verse 3 structure, as horns take the melody while saxes answer, vocal re-enters to create an ending in last two bars.

Listening Guide ▪▫▪▫

Les Paul and Mary Ford, "I'm Sittin' on Top of the World"
Capital F2400

Words and music by Sam Lewis, Joe Young, and Ray Henderson, produced by Les Paul. The song reached #10 on the *Billboard* "Most Played in Juke Boxes" chart in 1953 and had been featured in the 1946 film *The Jolson Story*.

FORM: AABA, with three presentations of the complete verse-verse-bridge-verse structure. The first and third presentations are sung, while the second one features a guitar solo. The verses in the second presentation are adapted from the sung verses and do not match these earlier and later verses exactly. During the first two verses in the third presentation, the time signature changes from 2/4 time to 4/4 time, and while the tempo does not change, this creates the impression that the music slows down. The 2/4 time signature returns at the bridge and continues to the end. The change of key that occurs in the last verse helps drive the music toward a big ending.

TIME SIGNATURE: 2/4, with verse in 4/4 as indicated.

INSTRUMENTATION: Layered electric guitars and lead vocals. The highest and fastest guitar lines were recorded at half speed, creating a "chipmunk" sound.

0:00–0:09	**Introduction**, 8 mm.	Layered guitar melody; note the echo effect on the guitar—this is the trademark Les Paul sound.
0:09–0:17	**A-Verse**, 8 mm.	Multitrack harmony vocals, all recorded by Mary Ford, with "chipmunk" guitar lines filling in the gaps, "I'm sittin' . . ."
0:17–0:25	**A-Verse**, 8 mm.	As before, "I'm quittin' . . ."
0:25–0:34	**B-Bridge**, 8 mm.	Harmony vocals continue, layered guitars create a nice descending cascade effect, "Hallelujah . . ."
0:34–0:43	**A-Verse**, 8 mm.	As before, "I'm sittin' . . ."
0:43–0:51	**A-Instrumental Verse**, 8 mm.	Guitar solo, music adapted from earlier verses. Les Paul's skill as a jazz soloist comes to the fore throughout this sectional verse.
0:51–0:59	**A-Instrumental Verse**, 8 mm.	Guitar solo continues.
0:59–1:08	**B-Instrumental Bridge**, 8 mm.	Guitar solo continues, high and fast "chipmunk" guitar lines created as described above.
1:08–1:16	**A-Instrumental Verse**, 8 mm.	Guitar solo continues.
1:16–1:33	**A-Verse**, 8 mm.	As before but now in 4/4 time, creating a sense that the music slows down. Note the addition of new backing vocals, "I'm sittin' . . ."

1:33–1:50	**A-Verse**, 8 mm.	Continues in 4/4, "I'm quittin' . . ."
1:50–1:58	**B-Bridge**, 8 mm.	Music goes back to 2/4, creating a sense that the music is speeding up, "Hallelujah . . ."
1:58–2:06	**A-Verse**, 8 mm.	This last verse changes key and this helps drive the song effectively to its ending, "I'm sittin' . . ."
2:06–2:15	**Coda**, 8 mm.	A showy ending adapted from last verse, "I'm sittin' . . ."

As some aspects of popular music were preparing the way for rock and roll, the Tin Pan Alley part of the music business was caught entirely off guard by the new style, and some of this had to do with the rise of two other styles that the big music publishing houses had previously ignored: rhythm and blues and country and western. Big publishers, along with major record companies like Columbia, Decca, and RCA-Victor, had tended to stay out of the rhythm and blues and country and western markets, partly because they considered their profitability to be limited, and partly because they had tried to work in these markets and found that they were not very good at it. Both rhythm and blues and country and western developed in their own way during the 1930s, '40s, and '50s. To understand clearly how rock and roll was forged from combining these two styles with mainstream pop, we will now need to trace these separate but in many ways parallel developmental paths. We turn first to country and western music.

Les Paul and Mary Ford were among the most popular acts during the first half of the 1950s. The couple is shown here recording at home, using a roomful of Paul's custom modified equipment.

Les Paul, Electric Guitars, and Multitrack Recording

A new role for the electric guitar in pop was pioneered by guitarist and inventor Les Paul, whose innovations in electronics and recording during the 1950s had a lasting impact on popular music. Paul's innovations manifested themselves stylistically and technologically. Some of the most important examples are listed here.

As Guitarist and Arranger for Les Paul and Mary Ford Les Paul was one of the country's leading guitarists during the big band era. While his own musical preference was for up-tempo jazz, he was a master of many styles. In fact, early in his career he posed as the country singer Rhubarb Red, singing traditional "hillbilly" music on a local radio show in his home state of Wisconsin. Paul met country singer Mary Ford in 1945, and in 1949 they married and formed a musical duo that featured spirited husband-and-wife banter and gags on stage. Paul arranged all of the duo's music, playing guitar and employing his latest electronic inventions to create a distinctive pop style that made Les Paul and Mary Ford records unmistakable and enormously successful.

As Inventor of the Solid-Body Electric Guitar Les Paul was one of the first to experiment with this type of instrument. Before Paul's experiments, electric guitars were traditional hollow-body jazz guitars with an electric pickup attached. Paul was convinced that to produce the purest electric sound the pickup must be free from vibrations caused by the guitar body on which it was mounted. In 1941 this led Paul to design a guitar with a solid body that would vibrate less. By mounting a pickup on this guitar—which he con-structed out of a railroad tie and called "the log"—Paul invented one of the first solid-body electric guitars. He later negotiated with the Gibson Guitar Company in 1951 to produce the Gibson Les Paul guitar, which has become one of the most frequently used models in the history of rock music. Leo Fender was experimenting with the same idea in Southern California in the late 1940s, resulting in his Broadcaster and Telecaster guitars. Fender's later Strato-caster design rivals that of the Les Paul in popularity among rock guitarists.

As Inventor of Sound-on-Sound Recording ("Overdubbing") Les Paul was one of the first musicians to experiment with sound-on-sound recording—the process by which a musician records one instrumental part and then another part so that the two parts sound together when played back. By extending this process, one musician can record several parts to an arrangement that would take many musicians to play in real time. Using discs in his first recordings, Paul figured out how to lay one take over the previous one, painstakingly building up the parts according to a method that allowed for no error—a mistake could be corrected only by starting the process all over again. In the early 1950s, Paul developed the first multitrack tape machine by synchronizing several tape machines to produce a more flexible method of "overdubbing." On his hit records with Mary Ford, such as "How High the Moon" (1951) and "I'm Sittin' on Top of the World" (1953), Paul overdubs choruses of guitars and vocals to create complex arrangements that reveal his big band roots. Paul also developed a technique of recording guitar parts at half speed so that when the machine ran at full speed the parts were not only higher but also much faster (the same technique was originally used to record the voices of the cartoon Chipmunks).

The electric guitar is central to rock music, and two models have achieved particularly iconic status. The Les Paul guitar (left) was developed by Paul in collaboration with the Kalamazoo-based Gibson company, while the Fender Stratocaster (right) was developed in Southern California by Leo Fender.

REGIONAL STYLES

"Country" Music in the Southeast in the 1930s. Country and western music generally remained regional until after 1945: unlike the mainstream pop heard on the radio networks, the regional musical styles that would ultimately come together under the umbrella of "country and western" after World War II mostly kept their distinctive regional accents until Nashville was established as the central location for this type of music in the late 1940s. These regional styles can be divided up into folk styles that could be found in the southeast and Appalachia, called "country" music, and styles that were prevalent in the west and southwest, called "western" music. Country music in the southeast can be traced to the folk traditions of the region, which are themselves derived in part from the folk music of the British Isles. Some of the first recordings of country music were made by Ralph Peer, a producer who traveled the south in search of what record companies would soon call "hillbilly music." These early recordings are probably as close as historians will ever get to capturing an authentic, regional folk music unaffected by nonindigenous styles, and Peer recorded many of the earliest country performers, including "Fiddlin'" John Carson and Gid Tanner and His Skillet Lickers. Peer went from small town to small town, setting up his gear as he went; these country musicians then lined up and recorded a few numbers each on his recording apparatus. The Carter Family is a representative example of this down-home country style. Accompanied by an acoustic guitar and an autoharp (played by Maybelle and Sara Carter, respectively), the three voices of Maybelle, Sara, and A. P. Carter sing together in a style very much influenced by white gospel music. "Can the Circle Be Unbroken" (1935) captures both the musical style and the confessional spirit of much of this music, as does "Great Speckled Bird" (1936) of Roy Acuff and His Crazy Tennesseans. The Acuff group also adds the Hawaiian slide guitar to the mix (a more developed version of the slide guitar, the pedal steel guitar, would later play a central role in country and western instrumentation).

"Western" Music in the Southwest and California in the 1930s. If country music is most often associated with the Appalachian Mountains, western music is most closely linked with the wide open prairie of the cowboys—or at least Hollywood's portrayal of it. Gene Autry was the first of the singing cowboys to appear in a long string of movies set in the Wild West. His "Back in the Saddle Again"—complete with a "whoopie ti yi yea"—is representative of the kind of song that he and Roy Rogers sang throughout their careers on the silver screen. Patsy Montana made her mark as the singing cowgirl with "I Want to Be a Cowboy's Sweetheart" (1935) and featured a yodeling style very much under the influence of Jimmie Rodgers (discussed next). Historians may dispute how authentically western some of this music was, but for the national movie-going public, these artists defined "cowboy music."

Perhaps more interesting than the music of the Hollywood cowboys was western swing, a style of music that gave the big band idea a cowboy twist. Made popular by Bob Wills and His Texas Playboys and Milton Brown and His Musical Brownies, western swing sometimes featured not only the rhythm section and horns one

Often considered the first star of country music, Jimmie Rodgers appears here in his "Singing Brakeman" attire. Although Rodgers's career was short, his musical influence was felt for decades.

would expect to find in a radio dance band, but also fiddles, a steel guitar, and even at times mariachi-style trumpet parts, imported from south of the border. Wills's "New San Antonio Rose" (1940) is an example of this eclectic stylistic blend of the urbane dance band of the northeast with the rough-and-tumble western hoedown stompers of the southwest. When this song was redone by Bing Crosby in 1941 and became a national hit, it helped gain western swing far more attention than it might have received otherwise, and Wills's band especially benefited from this. By the 1940s, Wills and the Playboys were appearing in Hollywood films and expanding Americans' sense of western music beyond cowboy songs.

Jimmie Rodgers, the First Star of Country Music. As we think about country and western music, it is important to consider not only how it developed but when and how it began to come to the attention of the mainstream pop audience. The movies helped promote western music, and Gene Autry and Roy Rogers were its biggest stars. The most important figure in the early history of country music is Jimmie Rodgers. Rodgers's music and performances made him a national star, though only for a brief time: he died in 1933 at the age of thirty-six from tuberculosis. His performances were almost always solo, with Rodgers accompanying his singing on the acoustic guitar. His "Blue Yodel" (1927)—often called "T for Texas" and later covered by Lynyrd Skynyrd—is a representative example of Rodgers's style, complete with his trademark yodel. Rodgers's singing style was much imitated by later country and western singers, including Gene Autry, Ernest Tubb, and Eddy Arnold.

During his brief career, Rodgers was known as both "The Blue Yodeler" and "The Singing Brakeman." The Blue Yodeler image cast Rodgers as a kind of rustic backporch guitar picker and singer, while the Singing Brakeman image had Rodgers as something of a roving hobo, wandering the country in the back of a freight car and stopping only long enough to sing a song about his lonely nomadic existence. Neither of these images was an accurate portrait of Rodgers, who, according to many reports, frequently performed in stylish clothes of his day. While Rodgers did work on the railroad before he became a well-known singer, these rustic images played on stereotypes of the time and seem to have been contrived simply to sell sheet music and records. This manipulation of Rodgers's image marks an early awareness in country music of the importance of marketing. Constructing homespun images would increasingly become the specialty of the country barn-dance radio shows, the most successful of which was the *Grand Ole Opry*. Thus Rodgers's legacy to country music is not only his music, but the way in which he and those who represented him crafted its reception.

RECORDINGS AND RADIO FURTHER A NATIONAL SOUND FOR COUNTRY AND WESTERN MUSIC

Superstation Radio Broadcasts in Prime Time. Mainstream pop in the 1930s and '40s played to a national audience, but country and western was limited to mostly regional radio exposure during those years. In 1922, Atlanta's WSB went on the air featuring local country music (including "Fiddlin'" John Carson and Gid Tanner), while WBAP in Fort Worth began a barn-dance program, featuring hoe-down fiddle music. Within a few years, local and regional radio stations across the South were programming country music, especially WSM in Nashville (the *Grand Ole Opry*) and WLS in Chicago (the *National Barndance*). At first broadcasting to the middle Tennessee region, in 1932 WSM became a clear-channel station whose signal reached most of the Southeast and could even be picked up in Texas. This made *Opry* broadcasts available to a significant portion of the country, and when NBC picked up a half-hour version in 1939, the *Opry* could be heard coast-to-coast. As the listening audience for the show increased, so did the clamor from musicians to appear on these broadcasts; performers were happy to make the trip to Nashville to sing and play on the show, since the large radio audience could provide enormous exposure for ambitious performers.

While the *Grand Ole Opry* blanketed southern evenings with country music, the *National Barndance* did the same for the midwest. And although the *Opry* eventually became the more prominent and influential radio venue in country and western music, the *Barndance* enjoyed a national audience much sooner when a one-hour segment of it was programmed on the NBC network in 1933. In addition to hearing country and western music on NBC, listeners in the northeast could tune to the *Wheeling Jamboree* beginning in 1933 from WWVA in Wheeling, West Virginia. Combined with numerous other barn-dance shows that emanated from local and regional stations across the United States, at least some country and western music was readily available to radio listeners, even if the style remained something of a novelty on network radio, receiving far less exposure than mainstream pop of the day.

Country Music during World War II (War Buddies). Other important factors that led to the dissemination of country music among northerners (and those outside the South generally) developed as a result of World War II. Military personnel hailing from all regions of the country found themselves living together overseas during the war, and as people got to know one another they naturally shared their favorite music. Many northerners got their first sustained exposure to country and western music from the southerners with whom they served. Country singers became so popular among the U.S. Armed Forces during the war that Roy Acuff was voted best singer by the troops in Munich (over Frank Sinatra); and hoping to insult American soldiers, Japanese attackers on Okinawa raised the battle cry, "To hell with Roosevelt! To hell with Babe Ruth! To hell with Roy Acuff!" When

With her trademark "Howdy!" Minnie Pearl (left) would launch into one of her stand-up comedy routines on the *Grand Ole Opry*. Like many *Opry* regulars, Pearl played up the idea that country folk are simple and honest, but somewhat backward and naive.

the troops headed home after the war, many took their newfound affection for country and western music with them and sought it out in their hometowns. But soldiers were not the only ones who found themselves among new company because of the war. Stateside, many southerners migrated north to fill the great number of factory jobs created by the war effort. Detroit had long been a popular destination for southerners before the war because of its automobile manufacturing, but during the early 1940s a number of cities—including Baltimore, Washington, D.C., Cincinnati, Chicago, and Los Angeles—became home to southerners from the surrounding regions as they followed wartime production jobs. These relocated country and western fans brought their music with them, and jukebox records in these cities show that in some places country and western music was the most popular style in local bars and clubs.

Nashville Becomes Country and Western Headquarters.
In the years after World War II, Nashville became the center of much professional activity in country and western music. The West Coast also saw growth in this type of music, but Nashville increasingly assumed the role of the capital of country and western. Nashville had been home to the *Grand Ole Opry* since its first broadcast in 1925, and by the late 1940s the *Opry* had become the most highly regarded radio show in country music. But in the postwar years, Nashville also became a center for country music recording and publishing, and to meet the demand created by the nation's new interest in the style, the business of country and western music became more sophisticated. As these musicians increasingly made their way to Nashville to record (especially in the studios of Castle Recording Company), promoters, booking agents, and record company representatives soon moved their offices there as well—it was just more convenient to have everything in one place. The catalyst for this new music industry growth in Nashville was a publishing firm established in 1942 by singer Roy Acuff and songwriter Fred Rose. Acuff-Rose did not rely on sheet music sales the way Tin Pan Alley publishers might; instead, they primarily worked to have the firm's songs recorded and performed by country artists. When Patti Page's version of "The Tennessee Waltz"—an Acuff-Rose song—became a hit pop record in 1950, the resultant financial success allowed the company to expand its operation and extend its influence. And while in some ways country and western publishing in the postwar years differed from mainstream pop publishing, it was the same in needing talented songwriters. In 1946, Fred Rose signed the then-unknown Hank Williams to Acuff-Rose—not as a singer, but as a songwriter.

HANK WILLIAMS, COUNTRY MUSIC SINGER-SONGWRITER IN THE BIG BUSINESS OF COUNTRY AND WESTERN

A Short Career That Cast a Long Shadow. In the minds of many Americans in the early 1950s, Hank Williams stood for country and western music. Though Jimmie Rodgers, Gene Autry, and Roy Acuff had enjoyed considerable commercial success, none matched the popular appeal of this singer-songwriter from rural Alabama. It is therefore surprising that the first of his songs to be recorded was sung by Molly O'Day, a singer Fred Rose was promoting in 1946. But by 1948, Williams was enjoying his first taste of success as a performer in his own right, appearing as a regular on the new *Louisiana Hayride* radio show out of KWKH in Shreveport (a young Elvis Presley would get his start on the same show only a few years later). Williams's first important hit was not one of his own songs, but rather a Tin Pan Alley number titled "Lovesick Blues." On the strength of its popularity, Williams became a regular on the *Grand Ole Opry* in the summer of 1949 and enjoyed tremendous success until his death on New Year's Day, 1953, at the age of twenty-nine. While Williams himself enjoyed fewer than five years of success, his music would be recorded by generations of country singers to follow. The story of the hard-living singer-songwriter who died too young would become a romantic image for future rock singers as well.

Williams's singing style shows the influence of both Roy Acuff and Ernest Tubb, and his many vocal inflections create an impression of sincere emotional expression. He pours out his personal romantic anguish in "Your Cheatin' Heart," "Cold, Cold Heart," and "I'm So Lonesome I Could Cry"; he radiates confident excitement

After 1945, Nashville emerged as the center of country and western music, and Hank Williams became one of its most important and distinctive performers. Williams started out as a songwriter, and many of his songs are considered staples of the country repertoire.

Listening Guide

Hank Williams, "Hey Good Lookin'" MGM-K11000

Words and music by Hank Williams, produced by Fred Rose. Hit #1 on the *Billboard* "Records Most Played by Folk Disc Jockeys" chart in 1951.

FORM: AABA, with three presentations of the complete verse-verse-bridge-verse structure. The arrangement of the song is similar to "I'm Sittin' on Top of the World." But where the Les Paul and Mary Ford track devotes the middle presentation of the AABA to a guitar solo, Williams's track splits the solo between the steel guitar and fiddle, with the steel taking the verses and the fiddle taking the bridge. Note also that Williams composes two sets of lyrics for the AABA structure, turning what was a formal chorus with unchanging lyrics in typical Tin Pan Alley music to a type of verse, with different lyrics for every presentation of the form.

TIME SIGNATURE: 4/4.

INSTRUMENTATION: Acoustic guitars, bass, steel guitar, fiddle, and lead vocal. Note that there are no drums, which were forbidden in the early years of the *Grand Ole Opry*. The piano and steel guitar take turns playing fills behind the vocals, seeming to comment on each vocal line, often echoing some part of it at the ends of phrases.

0:00–0:07	**Introduction**, 4 mm.	The steel guitar is featured, its notes sliding gracefully into one another.
0:07–0:21	**A-Verse**, 8 mm.	Vocal enters, "Hey good lookin' . . ." Note how the rhythm of the accompaniment is driven by the acoustic guitars and piano. The piano echoes the vocal at the ends of phrases.
0:21–0:34	**A-Verse**, 8 mm.	As before, "Hey sweet baby . . ."
0:34–0:47	**B-Bridge**, 8 mm.	"I got a hot-rod Ford . . ." The chords now change more quickly beneath the melody, creating a sense of excitement and anticipation. The steel guitar steps forward.
0:47–1:01	**A-Verse**, 8 mm.	As before, "Hey good lookin' . . ." Piano commentary returns.
1:01–1:15	**A-Verse**, 8 mm.	Steel guitar solo, plays an arrangement of vocal melody.
1:15–1:28	**A-Verse**, 8 mm.	Steel guitar solo continues. This simple solo is considered a classic by fans of the steel guitar.
1:28–1:41	**B-Bridge**, 8 mm.	Fiddle picks up the melody to provide contrast.
1:41–1:55	**A-Verse**, 8 mm.	Steel guitar returns to round off this AABA presentation.
1:55–2:08	**A-Verse**, 8 mm.	Vocal returns, "I'm free and ready . . ." Now steel echoes vocal, instead of piano.

2:08–2:22	**A-Verse**, 8 mm.	Note that the story develops this last time through the AABA form, "No more lookin' . . ."
2:22–2:35	**B-Bridge**, 8 mm.	"I'm gonna throw my datebook . . ." Piano adds new part in its high register.
2:35–2:51	**A-Verse**, 8 mm.	As before, "Hey good lookin' . . ." Steel "commentary" returns as song drives to ending.

in "Hey, Good Lookin'"; and he offers prayerful testimony in "I Saw the Light." His lyrics are direct and simple, and his performances seem to come straight from the heart. Whether Williams's songs really are autobiographical (some are) is less important than the fact that most listeners took them to be so. To most listeners in the early 1950s, Hank Williams was "pure country"—a country boy right down to the bone. His music and performance style thus became an important influence on subsequent country performers and writers.

BLUEGRASS, THE NEW, OLD-TIME COUNTRY MUSIC

Bill Monroe and His Blue Grass Boys. Fans of 1960s television can call to mind the banjo-dominated theme from the popular television show *The Beverly Hillbillies* ("The Ballad of Jed Clampett"). And fans of classic movies may even remember "Foggy Mountain Breakdown" from *Bonnie and Clyde* or "Dueling Banjos" from *Deliverance*. These songs are all in a style of country music called "bluegrass." To most ears, this music sounds as old as the hills, but bluegrass music actually developed during the same post–World War II period that saw the growth of country music in Nashville. The origin of the style can be traced to Bill Monroe and His Blue Grass Boys, whose first performance at the *Grand Ole Opry* occurred in 1939 but who gained far greater popularity in the late 1940s. The group's lineup after 1945 featured Monroe playing mandolin and singing high harmony, Robert "Chubby" Wise on fiddle, Lester Flatt on guitar and lead vocals, and Earl Scruggs on banjo. This version of the Blue Grass Boys cast the musical mold that most other bluegrass groups would imitate.

While bluegrass numbers often feature singing, they also showcase virtuosic instrumental soloing, causing some to compare bluegrass with jazz. Monroe's late-1940s band had three dynamic and technically accomplished soloists—Wise, Scruggs, and Monroe himself—and the solos were frequently more the focus of the group's music than the singing. Banjoist Earl Scruggs's playing is especially noteworthy in this context: Scruggs developed a technique called the "three-finger roll," which allowed him to play passages of greater complexity than banjo players

Starting out as members of Bill Monroe's band, Earl Scruggs (right) and Lester Flatt (left) left to establish their own act. Scruggs's virtuosic banjo playing was a model for many bluegrass musicians who followed.

had done previously. Along with developing other technical innovations, Scruggs raised the level of banjo playing to new heights. In 1948, Flatt and Scruggs left the Blue Grass Boys to form their own group. Many other musicians, inspired by the playing of Monroe's classic lineup, became attracted to bluegrass in subsequent years.

By the early 1950s, country and western music had gone from a mostly regional musical style to one known at least to some extent by most Americans. Building on the exposure of the national audience to cowboy and western swing music in the movies, as well as to a broad range of country and western via the barn-dance shows that played as novelty programs on the network radio stations, and powered by stars such as Gene Autry, Jimmie Rodgers, Roy Acuff, and Hank Williams, country and western began to make its mark as a national style at just about the time that rock and roll was poised to explode. Despite its growth throughout the 1930s, '40s, and '50s, country and western music remained separate from mainstream pop, which still could boast a national market share that dwarfed country and western in terms of sales and profitability. Early rock and roll would challenge the lines that separated pop and country and western, but for the time being that boundary was clear and secure. Rhythm and blues was also seen as a style set apart from both mainstream pop and country and western. While country and western was assumed to be the music of low-income whites, rhythm and blues was assumed to be the music made for and by black Americans. In many ways, the growth of rhythm and blues in the decades before rock and roll parallels the rise of country and western, and so it is to this third stylistic ingredient in the recipe for early rock and roll that we now direct our attention.

RURAL (DELTA) AND URBAN BLUES

Migration Patterns from the Rural South to the Urban North. The music that came to be called "rhythm and blues" in the years immediately after World War II was popular music played by black musicians intended for black listening audiences. In a manner that might be thought of as "separate but not very equal," it developed as an entire music business that remained almost completely outside the world of mainstream pop. While country and western had at least a marginal presence in mainstream American pop in the years leading up to the emergence of rock and roll, rhythm and blues played almost no role: most white listeners had no familiarity with either its artists or their music. This situation was a result of racial segregation in American culture; most white, middle-class Americans were simply unaware of most aspects of black culture. But the same forces that drove white southerners to migrate to large cities in the North were also a factor in the migration of black southerners. Many left their field jobs in the South in hopes of finding better work in the North; and when they arrived in Memphis, Chicago, and Detroit, they brought their music with them.

In the years immediately after World War I, blues had enjoyed several years of popularity with mainstream white pop listeners, partly through the popular sheet music of W. C. Handy, whose "Memphis Blues" and "St. Louis Blues" sold well nationally, and partly through records by female black singers. The historical roots of the blues may be unclear, but the roots of selling blues records can be traced to the 1923 million-selling hit "Down Hearted Blues," sung by Bessie Smith. Originally from Tennessee, Smith enjoyed enormous success in the years following this hit record. Her style is considered more authentically blues-based than some of the other female blues singers of her day, and this is probably because she toured the South as a youngster performing in tent and minstrel shows, where she was undoubtedly exposed to early blues music. Her recordings were made in New York, however, where she was able to use the best jazz musicians of the day, including Louis Armstrong. But by the end of the decade, Smith's career began to fade and the blues fell off the mainstream radar.

As rural blacks began to migrate to urban centers in the 1930s and '40s, many were drawn to Memphis. As a result, the city developed a strong black music scene as musicians adapted their rural blues approach to fit an urban, club environment. Many of the rural blues recordings of the 1920s and '30s are the result of record companies heading into the South in an attempt to find new blues artists who might repeat Bessie Smith's success. Among the many blues artists representative of the rural approach is Robert Johnson, whose recordings of the 1936–37 period became enormously influential on rock guitarists in the 1960s, in large part owing to Eric Clapton's enthusiastic endorsement (discussed in Chapter 5). Like many rural blues singers, Johnson performed solo, and similar to Jimmie Rodgers during a slightly earlier period, he sang to the accompaniment of his own acoustic guitar playing. The rural blues style allowed for tremendous flexibility, and artists could easily add extra beats or measures as the spirit moved them; this can be heard clearly in Johnson's "Cross Roads Blues" (1936), as he alters the regular blues structural patterns whenever it suits his sense of musical expression. But as blues musicians moved into city bars and clubs, they often formed combos, using electric guitars, bass, piano, drums, and harmonica (in addition to microphones to amplify the singer's voice); this arrangement forced them to stick more closely to a prearranged structure. This style of electric blues quickly made its way to other cities, and by the early 1950s Chicago had become

Pictured in the center of this advertisement for "race" records, Bessie Smith was one of the most famous blues singers of the 1920s. Her 1923 recording of Alberta Hunter's "Down Hearted Blues" sold over a million copies. Her style influenced many singers, including Billie Holiday and Janis Joplin.

Legend has it that Robert Johnson (left) made a deal with the devil to acquire his forceful skill as a blues guitarist. Johnson's 1930s recordings were embraced by the 1960s British blues revival, making him a guitar hero decades after his death.

the most important blues center in the country. The scenes in Memphis and Chicago remained relatively isolated from one another, as well as from similar music in other cities across the country. Musicians might move from city to city, but records from one area often remained in that area, creating regional distinctions much like those in country and western music of the time.

While much of the development of rhythm and blues during the 1940s remained regional and outside the pop mainstream, the jump blues of Louis Jordan and His Tympani Five became popular with pop listeners through a series of hit singles, including "G.I. Jive" (1944), "Caldonia Boogie" (1945), and "Choo Choo Ch'boogie" (1946). Jordan adopted the fast tempos of swing dance music but pared down the instrumentation to only a rhythm section and his saxophone, a move that worked both musically and financially, considering the expenses of traveling with a larger band. Jordan's vocal delivery was upbeat and often comical, though his humorous lyrics could lightly touch on pressing social issues such as racism and poverty. Jordan's influence can be seen in the comical hits of the Coasters, as well as in the spirited delivery and clever wordplay of Chuck Berry.

Regional Radio and the Black Experience in 1950s America.

A new approach to radio played an important role in the dissemination of rhythm and blues outside regional black communities, and to understand how radio changed in the years following the introduction of television, it is important to know what makes a radio station work financially. Commercial radio makes its profits by selling advertising time; to reach a particular kind of listener, radio stations program music they hope will attract that specific group. These stations can then offer that audience to sponsors, who often will also have developed an idea of the kind of person who might be most interested in their products. We know from our earlier discussions that by the early 1950s, the national audience for popular music had largely shifted from radio to television. This meant that radio needed to adapt considerably to survive, and many stations opted for a local or regional approach. As black populations began to grow in urban areas, it soon became clear that they constituted a distinctive community with needs for particular goods and services. In 1948, WDIA in Memphis began programming and advertising especially to the local black population, playing rhythm and blues records supported by a roster of sponsors who welcomed a black clientele. Soon black stations—or programs directed to a black audience on otherwise white stations—began to pop up around the country. These programs and stations not only provided black listeners with music they could enjoy; they also informed them of which advertisers would welcome their business. In those days of racial segregation, when black patrons were required to sit only in the back of a bus, often ate in sections of restaurants designated for "colored" customers, and could in many cases not even use the same drinking fountains or bathrooms as whites, this was useful information.

Independent Labels Target Regional Audiences. As radio stations devoted to rhythm and blues arose across the country, so also did record labels specializing in black popular music. Sun Records in Memphis, Chess Records in Chicago, King Records in Cincinnati, and Atlantic Records in New York were just a few of the more successful of these new rhythm and blues labels. Most of the new record companies were independents—that is, they were not one of the few major labels that dominated the music industry at the time: Decca, Mercury, RCA-Victor, Columbia, Capitol, and MGM. Major labels had enormous financial resources, manufacturing plants, and sophisticated distribution networks that allowed them to get their newest records out quickly to most areas of the country; independent labels were sometimes just the owner and perhaps a secretary, driving from store to store, distributing records out of the trunk of a car. This meant that independents had to focus on local or regional markets. But independent labels could prosper precisely because the major labels were so big; and since the rhythm and blues market was not nearly as profitable as the mainstream pop one, the majors tended to devote their resources to pop, leaving room for the independents to survive—and in many cases, to thrive. (Independent labels also played a role in country and western music at the same time, and these labels likewise took advantage of opportunities created by the majors' focus on pop and neglect of almost everything else.)

In both radio and records, then, rhythm and blues in the 1945–55 period was a style of popular music intended specifically for black urban listeners. Nobody expected that white listeners would hear this music; if they did and bought some records, so much the better, but no one within the rhythm and blues industry was counting on that. White teenagers could pick up the black stations on their radios just as well as anybody, however, and when they developed a taste for rhythm and blues, the stage was set for rock and roll to emerge. It is important to understand that rhythm and blues in the decade before rock and roll was not a single musical style; rather, it was a collection of popular-music styles tied together as much by its audience as by its specific musical characteristics. Within the music business, if a record was expected to have a black listening audience, it was rhythm and blues, and this has led to a number of distinctive black pop styles being grouped together under that single label.

RHYTHM AND BLUES AS A MARKETING CATEGORY THAT INCLUDES A BROAD RANGE OF MUSICAL STYLES

The Influence of Gospel Music (Rural Southern Church Traditions). One trait shared by most rhythm and blues styles during this era was a debt to gospel music. Much like the southern whites who sang country music, many of the southern blacks who would eventually sing in secular pop styles learned to sing in church.

The often sophisticated harmony singing that characterized doo-wop also had roots in the mainstream pop vocalizing of the Mills Brothers, the Ink Spots, and the Andrews Sisters, but it was clearly influenced by gospel harmony singing in the black church. The vocal emphases and embellishments that rhythm and blues singers frequently employed, as well as the call-and-response between the soloist and the chorus, were drawn from typical gospel practices. Sometimes—as in the case of Ray Charles's "I Got a Woman"—the religious lyrics to gospel songs were changed to make them pop songs. This borrowing from religious music by pop music was a source of controversy within the black community, as some viewed such stylistic secularization a sacrilege. Sometimes performers who moved from gospel music into pop had feelings of guilt that they might have "sold out," and this ambivalence over popular music would continue to affect both white and black singers after the emergence of rock and roll.

Chess Records and Chicago Electric Blues.

As a talent scout for Sam Phillips's Sun Records in Memphis, Ike Turner would typically search in two types of places for new performers: churches and bars. Gospel was clearly grounded in the sacred, and blues was strongly secular. By the early 1950s, Chicago's electric blues scene had developed into the most important one in the country, a growth due in part to an independent label founded in 1947 by two white fans of black music, Phil and Leonard Chess. Along with its subsidiary label Checker, Chess collected an impressive roster of blues artists: Howlin' Wolf, Muddy Waters, John Lee Hooker, Little Walter, and Bo Diddley, among others. The Chess style emphasized a sometimes rough-edged emotional directness, with vocals that were more expressive than beautiful or technically accomplished, and instrumental playing that blended technical prowess with raunchy bravura. Early Chess recordings were made with the simplest of equipment, producing a raw, technically unsophisticated

Leonard Chess (left) is shown here in the Chess recording studio with three of the most influential artists in electric blues: (from left) Muddy Waters, Little Walter, and Bo Diddley. Chess blues recordings defined the sound of Chicago electric blues. Their style was often rough-edged and direct, with expressive vocals. Early Chess recordings used simple equipment, which produced a raw, unsophisticated sound—contrasting with records released by major labels.

Listening Guide

Muddy Waters, "I'm Your Hoochie Coochie Man"

Chess 1560

Words and music by Willie Dixon, produced by Leonard Chess. Reached #8 on the Billboard "Rhythm Blues Best Sellers in Stores" chart in 1954.

FORM: Simple verse. The verses employ a version of the 12-bar blues that expands the first 4 bars to 8 measures, making for a 16-bar pattern that is repeated in each verse. Except for changing lyrics, the verses are very similar to one another, featuring only minor variations in the accompaniment. The "stop time" feature of the first 8 bars highlights the main riff of the song, as well as creating emphasis on the lyrics.

TIME SIGNATURE: 12/8. Note that the first measure of the song is preceded by a two-beat pick-up initiated by the bass drum on beat 3.

INSTRUMENTATION: Lead vocal, electric guitars, bass, drums, piano, and harmonica. The instruments play the main riff together during the first 8 measures and then break into more independent parts for the second 8 bars. The band for this track features many of Chess's legendary musicians, including Little Walter (harmonica), Otis Spann (piano), and songwriter Willie Dixon (bass).

0:00–0:11	**Introduction,** 2 mm.	Main riff played by the band twice, employing two-beat pickup to measure 1.
0:11–1:04	**Verse 1,** 16 mm.	Lead vocal enters, stop-time riff continues during first 8 bars, "That gypsy woman . . ."
1:04–1:57	**Verse 2,** 16 mm.	As before with only slight variation, "I got a black cat bone . . ."
1:57–2:51	**Verse 3,** 16 mm.	As before, but with the last 2 bars forming an ending, "On the seven' hour . . ."

recorded sound, in marked contrast to the kinds of records the major labels were releasing. This lack of studio polish, combined with the directness of many of the performances, would give Chess records an aura of honesty for many of the white rock and rollers who came along later. But at the time, the Chess brothers were simply doing the best they could with the resources they had. Howlin' Wolf's "Evil" (1954), Muddy Waters's "Hoochie Coochie Man" (1954), and Bo Diddley's "I'm a Man" (1955) are representative examples of Chicago electric blues, with adult-oriented lyrics delivered with more gusto than polish and accompanied by accomplished instrumental playing. Chess also recorded other artists who had the potential to appeal to a white audience, but their electric blues records made few concessions to white, middle-class sensibilities, and it is these records that had the most impact on rock and roll.

Atlantic and Black Pop. One independent label that did at times make some attempt to reach a broader audience was Atlantic Records in New York. Founded in 1948 by Ahmet Ertegun and Herb Abramson, Atlantic worked for a more polished pop sound, influenced by the production practices of mainstream pop and featuring accomplished singers such as Ruth Brown, Big Joe Turner, Clyde McPhatter, and Ray Charles. While Atlantic also offered its share of blues records, in general its most characteristic releases followed the mainstream pop practice of focusing on the singer and the song. Ruth Brown's "Mama, He Treats Your Daughter Mean" (1952) is a good example of this tendency and has clear ties not only to blues and gospel, but also to big band pop. Atlantic singles tended not to focus on instrumental playing; backup arrangements were structured and controlled, with solos occurring only rarely. In comparison with the electric blues records released by Chess, Atlantic singles are cleaner, more vocally oriented, and generally more pop oriented. Taken together, the music of these two labels begins to suggest the wide stylistic range found within 1950s rhythm and blues—and these are just two of many regional labels that produced R&B records during this era, though they were the most prominent.

Doo-Wop (Urban Vocal Music). In the years immediately following World War II, doo-wop groups began to emerge from the neighborhoods of American urban areas. The singers in these groups often could not afford the instruments they needed to accompany themselves, so their vocal arrangements were designed to be completely self-contained and without need of accompaniment ("a cappella"). A common practice was for groups from one block in an urban neighborhood to challenge groups from nearby blocks, leading to group-singing contests in the street. As independent labels sought out local talent to record, many invited these groups into the recording studio. Professional studio musicians would then learn the group's arrangements in order to accompany them on piano, bass, drums, and sometimes guitar. The result of these sessions was a style of music called "doo-wop," named after the nonsense syllables singers would often use in their arrangements. Doo-wop groups would typically feature a solo singer against the vocal accompaniment of the other singers, with one section of the song, usually toward the end, reserved for a sophisticated harmony-vocal rendition of one of the song's verses. The songs were sometimes in the AABA form derived from Tin Pan Alley and cast in a rolling rhythm—called "compound time"—in which the beat is divided into three equal parts and in many instances pounded out as chords on the piano (imagine this as one & uh, two & uh, three & uh, four & uh). The Chords' "Sh-Boom" (1954) is a representative example of doo-wop, with the syllables "sh-boom" used in the vocal accompaniment as a solo singer delivers the initial verses. A contrasting section features different singers from the group, and a last verse features the entire group singing together in harmony (see the Introduction for a Listening Guide for this song). "Sh-Boom" is a bouncy up-tempo number, but doo-wop songs were frequently ballads appropriate for slow dancing; the Five Satins' "In the Still of the Night" (1956) is a good example of this kind of song. Doo-wop is easily distinguished stylistically from Chicago blues or Atlantic pop (though Chicago blues labels and Atlantic also recorded doo-wop groups), but in the eyes (and ears) of the market, it was all rhythm and blues.

RHYTHM AND BLUES AS A "DANGEROUS INFLUENCE" ON AMERICAN (WHITE) YOUTH

Stagger Lee and the Black Male Swagger. As white teenagers were increasingly drawn to rhythm and blues in the early 1950s, their parents worried about the effects this music might have on their children. Much of this concern—which at times ran to fear—resulted from racial stereotypes circulating within the white community that are well known and have been thoroughly discussed by social historians. Of these, the image that seemed the most threatening is one scholars call the Stagger Lee myth: the idea that black men are especially defiant, often driven sexually, and that their greatest conquests are white women. These often supervirile and swaggering black men are thought to be constantly on the lookout for virginal white women, and teenage girls are thought to be especially vulnerable targets. This is not the place to explore the origins of such ugly stereotypes; it is enough to realize that when many white listeners heard Muddy Waters singing "I Just Wanna Make Love to You," it confirmed a certain stereotype for them. Such stereotypes are almost always based on fundamental sociocultural misunderstanding. A song that is understood one way within the black community can be interpreted in an entirely different way by white listeners unfamiliar with that culture. This misunderstanding had the unfortunate consequence of convincing many white parents that rhythm and blues was a dangerous influence on their teenagers, and many worked to have this music, and the later rock and roll that developed out of it, abolished.

Hokum Blues and Fun with Double Meanings. Popular songs with lyrics containing sexual double entendres can be traced back centuries; songs by Elizabethan composer John Dowland (1563–1626), for instance, are full of subtle wordplay designed for adult amusement. Within American popular music, Jimmie Rodgers's "Pistol Packin' Papa" features one line after another about the singer's need to shoot his "gun." Within black culture at mid-century, there was a well-established musical tradition of similar kinds of songs called "hokum blues" that poked fun at various aspects of adult relationships, mostly centered on sexual relations and the many situations that can arise in this context. Earlier hokum blues numbers like "Let Me Play with Your Poodle" took this kind of fun about as far as one can and still have a double meaning, but others were far more gentle in their references. "Hound Dog," recorded by blues singer Big Mama Thornton and written by white songwriters Jerry Leiber and Mike Stoller, features these lines: "You ain't nothin' but a hound dog, snoopin' 'round my door. You

Although rock fans know his 1950s recordings for Atlantic Records, Joe Turner's success in rhythm and blues music dates back to the late 1930s. Turner is often considered the premiere blues shouter of the postwar years, possessing a voice that could rock a club even without the benefit of a microphone.

Listening Guide

Big Joe Turner, "Shake, Rattle, and Roll" Atlantic 1026

Words and music by Jesse Stone (Charles Calhoun), produced by Ahmet Ertegun and Jerry Wexler. Reached #1 on the *Billboard* rhythm and blues "Most Played in Jukeboxes" chart in late 1954.

FORM: Simple verse-chorus. This song is based on 12-bar blues, which appears in both the verse and chorus sections.

TIME SIGNATURE: 12/8 (shuffle in 4).

INSTRUMENTATION: Piano, saxes, guitar, bass, drums, and lead vocals.

0:00–0:07	**Introduction**, 4 mm.	Piano featured. Note the easy, rolling rhythmic feel.
0:07–0:25	**Verse 1**, 12 mm.	Vocal enters and musical focus remains almost entirely on the singing, with the saxes answering the ends of vocal lines "Get out of that bed . . ."
0:25–0:44	**Verse 2**, 12 mm.	The story begins to unfold, "You're wearin' those dresses . . ."
0:44–1:02	**Verse 3**, 12 mm.	"I believe to my soul . . ." New horn lines added.
1:02–1:21	**Chorus**, 12 mm.	This sing-along type chorus uses the same background music as the verses; at this point, it still is not clear how these lyrics relate to the verses, "Shake, rattle, and roll . . ."
1:21–1:40	**Instrumental verse**, 12 mm.	Sax solo.
1:40–1:58	**Verse 4**, 12 mm.	Sexual innuendos increase, "I'm like a one-eyed cat . . ." Simpler sax commentary returns.
1:58–2:17	**Chorus**, 12 mm.	The connection is getting clearer, "Shake, rattle, and roll . . ."
2:17–2:36	**Verse 5**, 12 mm.	This verse almost stops having a double meaning, horn parts from earlier return, "I said, over the hill . . ."
2:36–3:00	**Chorus** with ending, 12 mm.	Now the connection is clear, "Shake, rattle, and roll . . ."

can wag your tail, but I ain't gonna feed you no more." In the context of such a tradition, the words "snoopin' 'round my door," "wag your tail," and "feed you" suggest a more sexual interpretation than they might in isolation.

Big Joe Turner's "Shake, Rattle, and Roll," released on Atlantic Records in 1954, provides a representative example of the hokum blues (the lyrics are provided later). This song was also recorded by Bill Haley and His Comets (a band made up entirely of white musicians). Haley adapts the song to make the lyrics acceptable to white audiences, since Turner's original lyrics would have never been allowed on the mainstream pop airwaves. In Turner's rendition, for instance, a man tells his lover to get out of bed and make him some breakfast. He then casts the reasons for his attraction to this woman in increasingly colorful terms: she looks great in a light cotton dress and nylon hose, though he complains about the way she spends his money. The "one-eyed cat" is definitely a metaphor for something more anatomical, as is the "seafood store." When Turner gets to gritting his teeth in the last verse, any doubt about what "Shake, Rattle, and Roll" of the chorus refers to is dispelled. As innocuous as this song may be by today's standards, it would have been considered obscene in white middle-class culture in the mid-1950s. Accordingly, Haley changes the lyrics enough to make the song seem harmless: the references to bed and sensuality are gone, replaced with more wholesome images. Note that while Haley retains the line about the one-eyed cat, it no longer seems sexual in this new context.

Another aspect of the song that gets changed in Haley's version is the rhythmic feel. While Turner's version projects a laid-back rhythmic feel that comes from not "pushing" the beat, Haley's version is somewhat frantic by contrast, pushing the

Two Versions of "Shake, Rattle, and Roll"

TURNER'S VERSION (Atlantic 1026):

Get out of that bed, wash your face and hands
(well you) get in that kitchen, make some noise with the pots and pans

(well) You're wearin' those dresses, the sun comes shinin' through
I can't believe my eyes, all of this belongs to you

I believe to my soul you're the devil in nylon hose
(well) the harder I work, the faster my money goes

(I said) Shake, Rattle, and Roll
(well) you won't do right to save your doggone soul

I'm like a one-eyed cat, peepin' in a seafood store
(well) I could look at you till you ain't no child no more

(ah) Shake, Rattle, and Roll
(well) you won't do right to save your doggone soul

(I said) Over the hill and way down underneath
you make me roll my eyes, baby make me grit my teeth

(I said) Shake, Rattle, and Roll
(well) you won't do nothing to save your doggone soul

HALEY'S VERSION (Decca 29204):

Get out in that kitchen and rattle those pots and pans
(well) Roll my breakfast 'cause I'm a hungry man

(I said) Shake, Rattle, and Roll
(well) You'll never do nothin' to save your doggone soul

Wearin' those dresses, your hair done up so nice
You look so warm but your heart is cold as ice

(I said) Shake, Rattle, and Roll
(well) You'll never do nothin' to save your doggone soul

I'm like a one-eyed cat, peepin' in a seafood store
I can look at you till you don't love me no more

I believe you're doin' me wrong and now I know
The more I work, the faster my money goes

(I said) Shake, Rattle, and Roll
(well) You'll never do nothin' to save your doggone soul

beat as if the musicians can't wait to get to the next measure. This gives the Haley version a peppier, happier feel and helps in creating the impression that the song is really only about good, clean fun. In many ways, Haley's adaptation is a prototype of the pop adaptation of rhythm and blues that came to define rock and roll in its early years.

The ways white musicians adapted rhythm and blues for the pop market is discussed in more detail in the next chapter. For now, remember that rhythm and blues in the first half of the 1950s was in many ways very different from the mainstream pop of the same period. Like the market for country and western, the market for rhythm and blues was assumed to be quite distinct: industry insiders believed that nobody but black listeners would be interested in this music. But as things turned out, white middle-class teenagers were interested in both rhythm and blues and country and western by the middle of the decade, and because both styles of music were available over the radio, they could hear music from neighborhoods and communities their parents would prefer they avoided. Still, until 1955, the music business remained highly segregated into pop, rhythm and blues, and country and western markets, with most of the media exposure and industry dollars devoted to pop. Pop was deeply invested in Tin Pan Alley music publishing, but this was not the case with rhythm and blues or country and western. Pop was focused on the song; the other two styles were focused on the record. When rock and roll broke out in 1955, it not only challenged the boundaries of style but it also threatened the way the popular music business was run—as well as some white Americans' sense of moral decency. Elvis the Pelvis seemed to assault middle-class sensibilities, and Tin Pan Alley appeared to be under siege by styles and practices that originated in the other two, smaller areas of the music business. The next chapter focuses on the first tumultuous years of this musical and cultural onslaught: rock and roll.

For Additional Online Resources, visit:
digital.wwnorton.com/whatsthatsound5

FURTHER READING

Glenn C. Altschuler, *All Shook Up: How Rock 'n' Roll Changed America* (Oxford University Press, 2003).

Fred Astaire, *Steps in Time: An Autobiography* (Harper & Brothers, 1959).

Gerald Clarke, *Get Happy: The Life of Judy Garland* (Delta, 2000).

Rosemary Clooney, with Joan Barthel, *Girl Singer: An Autobiography* (Doubleday, 1999).

Philip K. Eberly, *Music in the Air: America's Changing Tastes in Popular Music, 1920–1980* (Hastings House, 1982).

Phillip H. Ennis, *The Seventh Stream: The Emergence of Rocknroll in American Popular Culture* (Wesleyan University Press, 1992).

Ross Firestone, *Swing, Swing, Swing: The Life and Times of Benny Goodman* (Norton, 1995).

Gary Giddins, *Bing Crosby, a Pocketful of Dreams: The Early Years, 1903–1940* (Little, Brown, 2001).

Sound Check

Artist	Song	Sound
Judy Garland	Over the Rainbow (1939)	Form: AABA Tempo variations Repetition of two verses and part of the bridge Conversation between voice and orchestra
Frank Sinatra w/ Harry James Orchestra	All or Nothing at All (1943)	Form: AABA Mic placement makes Sinatra's voice sound "close" Horns sound "distant" Each verse ends in a slightly different way
Les Paul and Mary Ford	I'm Sittin' on Top of the World (1953)	Form: AABA Eche effect on guitar Multitracked guitars and vocals Jazz influence
Hank Williams	Hey Good Lookin' (1951)	Form: AABA Piano and lead guitar alternate fills Instrumental solos through an entire AABA cycle No drums
Muddy Waters	I'm Your Hoochie Coochie Man (1954)	Form: Simple verse Stop-time main riff 16-bar verse structure based on 12-bar blues Verses feature only minor variation
Big Joe Turner	Shake, Rattle, and Roll (1954)	Form: Simple verse-chorus Piano featured in introduction 12-bar blues Double entendre in lyrics

Charlie Gillett, *The Sound of the City: The Rise of Rock and Roll*, rev. and expanded ed. (Da Capo, 1996).

Peter Guralnick, *Lost Highway: Journeys and Arrivals of American Musicians* (Back Bay, 1999).

Charles Hamm, *Yesterdays: Popular Song in America* (Norton, 1983).

Tom Lewis, *Empire of the Air: The Men Who Made Radio* (Perennial, 1993).

Bill C. Malone and Jocelyn R. Neal, *Country Music U.S.A.*, 3rd rev. ed. (University of Texas Press, 2010).

Russell Sanjak, updated by David Sanjek, *Pennies from Heaven: The American Popular Music Business in the Twentieth Century* (Da Capo, 1996).

Mary Alice Shaughnessy, *Les Paul: An American Original* (William Morrow, 1993).

Wilfrid Sheed, *The House That George Built, with a Little Help from Irving, Cole, and a Crew of about Fifty* (Random House, 2008).

Nick Tosches, *Unsung Heroes of Rock 'n' Roll: The Birth of Rock in the Wild Years before Elvis* (Da Capo, 1999).

Jerry Wexler and David Ritz, *Rhythm and the Blues: A Life in American Music* (St. Martin's, 1994).

After the roaring 1920s, the depressed '30s, and the war-ravaged '40s, the 1950s seemed to some a kinder, simpler, and more innocent decade. Many of the 1950s' conservative (and, some would say, puritanical) values were reflected in popular TV shows like *Father Knows Best* and *Leave It to Beaver*, and grandfatherly President Dwight Eisenhower. But the decade also saw the birth of the modern civil rights movement, *Playboy* magazine, and rock and roll.

While visible wars erupted in Korea and began to boil in Vietnam, Americans were much more aware of an ideological battle being fought: the Cold War. During World War II, the Americans and Soviets had been allies in the struggle against the Axis powers. But this partnership arose almost entirely out of necessity, and both parties remained acutely suspicious of one another. Many Americans were convinced that communists were trying to infiltrate their culture and overthrow the U.S. government. In 1948, former State Department official Alger Hiss was indicted for smuggling secrets to the Soviets (he was convicted in 1950), and Julius and Ethel Rosenberg were tried and convicted on espionage charges in 1951 (they were executed in 1953). Riding what many viewed as a wave of communist paranoia (often called the "Red Scare"), Senator Joseph McCarthy, chairman of the Committee on Government Operations of the Senate, used his position to lead an anti-communism campaign (some would call it a witch hunt) during the early 1950s. McCarthy's subcommittee undertook a series of well-publicized hearings and private investigations dedicated to exposing communists thought to be lurking among U.S. citizens in politics, film, and labor unions.

The Soviets did have secrets: while the United States had stunned the world with the development and use of the atomic bomb in 1945, the Soviets launched the first satellite into space in 1957. Called *Sputnik*, this satellite reinforced American fears of Soviet ambitions and fueled an intense race for technological superiority between the two countries, which was won when America landed the first men on the moon in 1969.

Out of this strange brew of technology, spaceflight, and communist paranoia came a distinctly American passion for science-fiction stories and movies. Evil aliens seemed to drop out of the skies every night, and films such as *Invasion of the Body Snatchers* (1956) captured the sense that these intruders might well be lurking among us, waiting for the right moment to execute their diabolical plan for domination of the Earth.

Along with communist paranoia, economic prosperity increased after World War II. The American economy boomed, spurred by strong demand for new houses and consumer goods like televisions, home appliances, and cars. Most new homes were constructed in the suburbs, and new highways and automobiles made commuting to and from these towns easy.

Americans spent more time in cars than ever before, and many automobiles were equipped with AM radios. These car radios would play a significant role in the

of this obsession with sexually prudent normality, Hugh Hefner introduced *Playboy*, a magazine devoted to such modern and sophisticated topics as fine wines, clever writing, and naked women, challenging the long-standing notion that consumerism was feminine. Hefner caused a considerable stir in 1953 when he launched the magazine with a calendar featuring nude pictures of case concerning a black child named Linda Brown, who had been denied the opportunity to attend an all-white public school in Topeka, Kansas. In *Brown v. Board of Education*, attorney Thurgood Marshall argued that no one should be kept out of a school on the basis of race; the justices concurred and ruled that the practice of racial segregation in schools was unconstitutional. In 1955

With the rise of the suburbs, many Americans became reliant on the automobile for transportation during the 1950s. This 1958 photo of a Utah drive-in movie theater during a showing of *The Ten Commandment*s depicts the decade's "car culture."

in Montgomery, Alabama, a black woman named Rosa Parks refused to give up her seat on the bus to a white passenger, as was required by law. When Parks was arrested, Martin Luther King Jr. organized a peaceful, citywide bus boycott that held until Parks's case made it to the Supreme Court in 1956. When the court ruled that Montgomery's bus segregation law was unconstitutional, the city's blacks returned to the buses and sat wherever they wanted.

The effects of these antisegregation decisions by the Court extended well beyond Topeka and Montgomery. They strengthened the growing civil rights movement across America, although some people (especially, but not exclusively, in the South) staunchly resisted these new social changes. Racial tensions reached a peak in 1957 when President Eisenhower had to send National Guard troops to Little Rock, Arkansas, to defend nine black students who had won the right in federal court to attend an all-white school. In the early 1960s, folk music aligned itself with the civil rights movement that had developed throughout the mid-1950s racial struggles and by the end of the '60s, civil rights would be widely accepted as an important cause by the country's burgeoning rock-music counterculture. In the context of such racial struggles, it is easier to understand how rhythm and blues might be viewed as a threat to white culture, and how a new style of youth music called rock and roll could become so controversial.

The 1950s were a time of great contradictions. Joseph McCarthy and Martin Luther King Jr., *Leave It to Beaver* and *Playboy*, consumerism and the civil rights movement all existed in the same time and space. Out of these tensions arose a new music that would bring together black and white, urban and rural, and North and South. That music was rock and roll.

Racial segregation was one of the most divisive issues of the 1950s. This picture's original caption says it best: "9/4/1957—Little Rock, AR: Arkansas National Guardsmen turn away Elizabeth Eckford, a Negro girl, as she attempts to enter Central High School here, Sept. 4th. The troops stopped eight Negro students from entering the school. The soldiers, called out to prevent the desegregation of the school because it might set off rioting between Negroes and whites, stopped the students in defiance of a federal judge's order that the school was to be integrated." President Eisenhower eventually sent troops in to enforce the judge's order and integrate the school.

CHAPTER 2

JOHNNY B. GOODE
(C. Berry)

CHESS

Arc Music
BMI 8633
2:30

CHUCK BERRY
1691

MANUFACTURED BY CHESS PRODUCING CORP., CHICAGO, ILLINOIS, U.S.A.

THE BIRTH AND FIRST FLOURISHING OF ROCK AND ROLL

CHAPTER PREVIEW

- The emergence of rock and roll in the mid-1950s is linked with the rise of the "teenager" in the United States and the development of youth culture, which included not only new musical tastes but also distinct fashions, slang, and movies dealing with teen themes.

- Many teens were first exposed to rhythm and blues via local and regional radio programs targeted primarily at black listeners.

- Both records and songs crossed over from the rhythm and blues charts to the pop charts. White covers of songs by black artists often changed lyrics to make the songs less controversial.

- Fats Domino, Little Richard, and Chuck Berry are among the earliest artists crossing from rhythm and blues to rock. Berry wrote songs directed at a white teen audience.

- Elvis Presley signed with the major label RCA in late 1955—an important event that signaled rock and roll's new movement into the pop mainstream.

- In the wake of Elvis's success, other labels signed rock and roll artists such as Buddy Holly, Jerry Lee Lewis, and Gene Vincent.

- The 1950s ended with the payola scandal—a congressional investigation into questionable business practices in the music business.

A fan of both country and western music and rhythm and blues, Chuck Berry came to Chicago to record with Chess Records on the advice of Muddy Waters. Berry's 1955 hit "Maybellene" was followed by a string of crossover hits, including "Johnny B. Goode." Beginning with one of Berry's trademark guitar riffs, the song tells the story of a young country boy who is destined to be a big star, because he can "play the guitar like ringing a bell." Notably, the song steers clear of any suggestive language, eliminating an obstacle that kept many rhythm and blues hits off mainstream pop radio until white artists rerecorded them in cover versions more appropriate for teenage ears. Berry was happy to write about typical topics of teenage life (school, dancing, parents), although he is perhaps most admired for the clever wordplay found in many of his lyrics.

Historians love to define historical periods with specific beginning and end dates. In American history, for instance, we think of 1776 as the year when the United States broke with England to become a country in its own right. Of course, more careful study reveals that many events before and after 1776 influenced how the United States came to be organized as a sovereign nation. Important years and specific dates allow historians to organize the past, but they must be understood as representative markers in the flow of a broad range of historical events. Music historians also use important dates to account for the development of musical styles. While many scholars distinguish 1955 as the first year of rock and roll, there is not a clean dividing line between rock and roll, rhythm and blues, and even some country music until a few years later. However, 1955 is a useful marker and will help us draw a line between the world before rock and roll and everything that follows.

In the preceding chapter, we saw that country and western and rhythm and blues were clearly established styles by the early 1950s and how regional radio made this music available to middle-class white youth. This audience was essential to the emergence of rock into the popular-music mainstream. Before 1955, rhythm and blues and country and western were still mostly outside the mainstream of American popular music, which was dominated by the major record labels and the Tin Pan Alley publishers. But as a youth culture developed in America after World War II, rhythm and blues became the music of choice for young people. When rhythm and blues broke into the mainstream in 1955, rock and roll was born.

Many elements came together to create this eruption of rock and roll in the later 1950s, primarily the rise of a youth culture and the emergence of independent radio and record labels. Rock and roll played a crucial role in challenging Tin Pan Alley's dominance of the music business and removing the divisions between the three industry markets: mainstream pop, country and western, and rhythm and blues. In 1955 and the years that followed, songs and records moved freely among these three markets and astounded the major labels. Since these markets had been divided along racial and socioeconomic lines, the integration of musical styles was bound to have reverberations throughout American culture. But none of this could have happened without the middle-class teenage audience, which created a lucrative market for record companies, radio stations, and others involved in the pop-music business.

This chapter will consider the "first wave" of rock and roll, loosely encompassing the period between 1955 and 1960. During this time, artists such as Fats Domino, Little Richard, Chuck Berry, Bill Haley, Elvis Presley, Jerry Lee Lewis, and Buddy Holly established rock and roll as a distinct style. As mentioned earlier, white teenagers thought of rock and roll as their music—something distinct from the culture of their parents and grandparents. White adult culture mostly viewed rock and roll as a dangerous influence, leading to juvenile delinquency or adoption of unacceptable attitudes and cultural practices. In many cases, adult opinions of rock were either tacitly or explicitly based on its association with black culture.

Due to a variety of factors, most of rock's originators and many of the independent labels they worked for were out of the music business by 1960. But these early years were crucial in establishing rock as a musical style and a central element of youth culture. Later musicians would frequently look back on these years as the Golden Age of rock and roll. Popular music had crossed a line, and in many fundamental ways, the music business would never be the same again.

THE RISE OF YOUTH CULTURE IN THE 1950S

The First Wave of War Babies Reaches Adolescence (This Is Not Your Father's Pop Music).

The end of World War II saw the rise of a new and significant phenomenon in American society: a pop culture devoted exclusively to teenagers. While earlier generations had been expected to assimilate into adult culture as soon as they left high school, in the 1950s white, middle-class teens were allowed to avoid adult responsibility longer than any group in history. They had fashion, music, dancing, movies, magazines, and a bevy of slang terms that belonged exclusively to them. In part, this phenomenon arose from the country's relative political stability and affluence in the post–World War II years: teens had money to spend on leisure activities and luxury items. There was also an attempt within the middle class to return to "normalcy" following the war. Parents, in many cases recovering from the domestic disruption of the war, now focused increasingly on family life, devoting considerable attention and resources to the health, education, and overall happiness of their children. Children born just before the American involvement in the war (December 1941) were the first beneficiaries of this new attention. By 1955, many of them were in high school. In a pattern that has since become familiar, these adolescents wanted music that did not sound like that of their parents or their older siblings. To these kids, rhythm and blues—available via local black radio—seemed exotic, dangerous, and sexual in ways that excited them.

Listening to rhythm and blues was not simply a forbidden pleasure to white teens. It was also an act of social rebellion—a way to resist assimilation into the adult world of responsibilities and commitments. Conversely, juvenile delinquency was a major concern for adults during the 1950s. Several contemporary films reflect this societal conflict. In *The Wild One* (1953), Marlon Brando plays the rebellious young leader of a motorcycle gang. When asked at one point what he's against, he replies simply, "Whaddya got?" *Rebel without a Cause* (1955) features James Dean in a classic portrayal of a tragically misunderstood teenager. Before the film was released, Dean was killed in a car crash, and his untimely death at the age of

In the mid-1950s, several films helped establish the image of restless and rebellious youth that soon would become associated with rock and roll. Directed by László Benedek, *The Wild One* (1953, top) starred Marlon Brando as the charismatic and troubled leader of a motorcycle gang. James Dean also played a troubled youngster in *Rebel without a Cause* (1955, left), becoming a legend after his untimely death in an automobile accident. Also in 1955, *Blackboard Jungle* (right, starring, from left, Vic Morrow, Sidney Poitier, and Glenn Ford) gave rise to adult concerns when teenage viewers got rowdy as the song "Rock around the Clock" was played in the film.

twenty-four made him an icon for misunderstood youth and teenage tragedy. While both of these films directly addressed teen angst and rebellion, neither reflected this musically, relying on traditional orchestrated film soundtracks. By contrast, *Blackboard Jungle* (1955)—a film about the perils of juvenile delinquency in an urban high school setting—featured Bill Haley's "(We're Gonna) Rock around the Clock" over the opening credits. The success of the movie, which actually led to youth riots in some theaters in both the United States and the United Kingdom, catapulted the Haley song to the top of the pop charts. This marked an important moment in the emergence of rock and roll. Not only was "Rock around the Clock" one of the top pop records of 1955, but its inclusion in a film dealing with juvenile delinquency cemented the association of rock music with teenage rebellion and rowdiness. Haley was among a growing number of artists to score pop hits with rhythm and blues records. Once it became clear that such records would sell, the market was flooded with them.

RADIO AND RECORDS

The Rise of the Disc Jockey. Many white teenagers were first exposed to rhythm and blues by hearing it on the radio. During the early 1950s, small and inexpensive tube-driven tabletop radios were common among the white middle class, and the majority of black urban households had at least one radio. Radios were also common in automobiles. By the end of the decade, the development of the transistor had made small portable radios affordable and available to almost everyone.

As radios became more available to teenagers, disc jockeys (DJs) emerged as the most important tastemakers of early rock and roll. In 1951, Alan Freed was an announcer at a radio station in Cleveland, hosting an evening classical-music show sponsored by one of the city's largest record stores—the Record Rendezvous, owned by Leo Mintz. Mintz noticed that teenagers were buying significant numbers of rhythm and blues records, and he offered to sponsor a late-night radio show devoted to this music, with Freed as the host. Freed was reluctant at first, but on July 11, 1951, *The Moondog Show* premiered on WJW, a clear-channel station with a signal that reached far beyond the Ohio state line. Radio programming that had been targeted at a black audience was now being enjoyed by white teens. Freed was among the first of a new wave of disc jockeys to develop rhythm and blues programming, and he is often cited as the most influential DJ in rock and roll's breakthrough to the popular music mainstream.

As it turns out, Freed was not the first disc jockey to play rhythm and blues on the radio. In 1949, Dewey Phillips began his *Red, Hot, and Blue* show on WHBQ in Memphis, while Gene Nobles, John R. Richbourg, and Hoss Allen were playing rhythm and blues at WLAC in Nashville, as were Zenas "Daddy" Sears in Atlanta (WGST), and Hunter Hancock in Los Angeles (KFVD). Freed was reportedly a WLAC listener and modeled his early shows on those from Nashville, even calling occasionally to find out what records were hot there. All of these early DJs were white, though most listeners assumed they were black on the basis of their on-air voices. According to one survey, of the 3,000 or so disc jockeys on the air in the United States in 1947, only sixteen were black. However, during the late 1940s and throughout the '50s black DJs made their mark on radio throughout the country, including Vernon Winslow ("Doctor Daddy-O") in New Orleans, Lavada Durst ("Doctor Hepcat") in Austin, William Perryman ("Piano Red" and "Doctor Feelgood") in Atlanta, Al Benson in Chicago, Jocko Henderson in Philadelphia, and Tommy Smalls ("Jive") in New York. WDIA in Memphis featured an all-black on-air staff, including Rufus Thomas, B. B. King, and Martha Jean ("The Queen") Steinberg. When he debuted his rhythm and blues show in Cleveland in 1951, Freed was simply emulating something that was already going on in other parts of the country.

Freed was enormously successful in Cleveland, and reports of his popularity there drew the attention of WINS in New York. In September 1954, he debuted in the Big Apple, where he repeated his midwestern success on a much larger media stage. Freed renamed his show *The Rock and Roll Party* (after a dispute over the Moondog moniker) and was soon syndicated nationally and eventually in Europe. Thus, in the waning months of 1954 and into 1955, Freed created a considerable buzz over rhythm and blues among white teenagers in one of the country's major markets. He extended his involvement in bringing rock and roll to the masses by promoting concerts, producing films, and eventually working in television, capitalizing on the tremendous success of his radio show. He took his 1958 concert show, *The Big Beat* (which included Jerry Lee Lewis and Buddy Holly), on the road across the United States. Freed starred in hastily produced films like *Rock around the Clock* (1956) and *Don't Knock the Rock* (1957), which had flimsy plots and featured appearances by early rhythm and blues and rock and roll acts, including Bill Haley, Chuck Berry, Frankie Lymon, and the Moonglows. He also hosted a TV dance show from 1958 to 1960. To many teenagers, Alan Freed was the father of rock and roll, so it came as no surprise when the almost continual backlashes against the music were directed at him, and especially his concert shows, which the press often portrayed as teen riots. As Freed enjoyed celebrity on the national level, his popularity was paralleled in every major city by local DJs who were stars in their own communities. These DJs also aggressively promoted the new youth music—now widely known as rock and roll thanks to Freed's influence.

Aggressive Marketing by Independent Labels. Most of the rhythm and blues that teens heard on the radio during the 1950s was recorded by and released on independent labels. In the previous chapter, we noted that these labels were much smaller operations than the major labels, and while the majors were national, the indies were mostly regional. The majors—Decca, Mercury, RCA-Victor, Columbia, Capitol, and MGM—had their own manufacturing plants and national distribution networks; most indies had to farm out manufacturing and improvise distribution systems, at first cooperating with indie labels in other parts of the country to establish reciprocal arrangements ("You distribute my records, I'll distribute yours") until independent distributors were established. This competitive disadvantage was significant and meant that a successful indie

Starting out playing rhythm and blues records on a Cleveland-area radio station late at night, Alan Freed became one of the most important disc jockeys in the early years of rock music. After moving his show to New York in 1954, he dubbed it *The Rock and Roll Party* and took credit for giving the new style its name. While in Cleveland, Freed began to promote rhythm and blues shows for African American audiences, but soon white teens who had also tuned in to his show began to attend these events.

label had to be aggressive about marketing. For independent labels, success was dependent on gaining radio play for their records and getting them into stores and jukeboxes. To get a record played, it was necessary to develop relationships with DJs, who could be influenced by gifts ranging from cash and merchandise to nights on the town and even vacations. Stores might receive extra copies of records to sell at full profit in order to push a particular record. Jukeboxes were a fixture in many bars and restaurants; if a label could get a regional distributor to pick up a record for use in jukeboxes, this constituted significant sales and stimulated jukebox listeners to buy even more records. In this context, the practice of paying disc jockeys to play music on the radio was later called "payola."

Both independent and major labels used payola, but it was most beneficial to the independent labels, who used this practice more readily in order to compete with the greater resources shared by major labels. Employees at a major label were often working with the company's money, but the owner of an indie label often had his own money on the line with a record. In the early 1950s, the conventional wisdom held that an indie could not beat a major label in the pop market, so rhythm and blues and country and western were markets in which independents could make money. In many ways, the emergence of rock and roll in the 1950s can be attributed to the entrepreneurship of both indie labels and DJs, each working on the outskirts of their respective business worlds: indie labels were fighting for a place on the margins of the recording industry, while independent radio stations were battling in regional markets with the local affiliates of the national networks. Rhythm and blues had been largely ignored by the major corporate powers, mostly because these companies found that the profit generated by such music did not justify the effort to develop, record, and market it. All of this occurred, for the most part, outside the powerful corporations and institutions that had shaped popular music in the United States for decades. When rhythm and blues records started showing up on the pop charts in the early 1950s, however, the industry was headed for a significant shake-up.

CROSSOVERS AND COVERS

Hit Records and the Charts. In order to be successful, people who sell music for a living ultimately have to view it as a business. It is great if a record company executive, radio station manager, record store owner, or jukebox distributor likes some of the music they sell, but this is by no means a necessity. Businesspeople need to think in terms of markets, product, distribution, and promotion—especially given the fickle character of many listeners when it comes to popular music—and it is tremendously beneficial to be able to identify trends. If you can spot a trend, your chances are greatly increased for having the right amount of product where it needs to be, timed precisely to meet the peak consumer demand. If your timing is right, your profits soar; if you time it wrong, they plummet. Such "inside" information is usually not very interesting to most listeners, who just want to hear the music, so magazines devoted to the more dollars-and-cents aspect of the business have developed for industry professionals. The most important of these in the history of rock and roll in the United States were *Cashbox* and *Billboard*, both of which contained sales charts that attempted to predict trends in record and jukebox sales.

Doo-wop and Crossover

Doo-wop music played an important role in rhythm and blues before 1955. Doo-wop originated with the vocal quartets of urban areas. The vocal quartet had been a long-standing tradition among African American men that could be traced back decades, and groups like the Mills Brothers and the Ink Spots had brought vocal-group music to the top of the pop charts during the 1940s. One of the first doo-wop records to cross directly over to the pop charts was "Cryin' in the Chapel" by the Baltimore-based Orioles (on the Jubilee independent label). The Chords' "Sh-Boom" was also a crossover hit on Atlantic in 1954, though it was quickly covered for the white market by the Crew Cuts. The success of these records led independent labels to search the streets for vocal groups. In such cases, the label brought a group into the studio, added a rhythm section—often consisting of drums, bass, piano, and guitar—and recorded the tunes the group had worked up, releasing the best of them. Some groups used their own arrangements, giving many classic doo-wop recordings an amateurish quality that fans of the style find especially endearing. Consequently, most doo-wop groups had only one or two hits; follow-up hits were difficult because the first hit was often the best arrangement a group had, and it had developed over months of rehearsing. In some cases a label would work with a group to help them develop material and arrangements, as Atlantic did with Clyde McPhatter and the Drifters, who had a series of rhythm and blues hits, including "Money Honey" (r1, 1953) and "Whatcha Gonna Do?" (r2, 1955). Recording for Mercury, the Platters were among the most successful of the 1950s vocal groups, charting eighteen pop Top 40 hits during the 1955–60 period, including "Only You (and You Alone)" (r1 p5, 1955), "The Great Pretender" (r1 p1, 1955), "My Prayer" (r1 p1, 1956), "Twilight Time" (r1 p1, 1958), and "Smoke Gets in Your Eyes" (r3 p1, 1958).

Based on the most recent issue of *Billboard*, a store owner might have decided to order additional copies of a record that was climbing the charts, while making sure to get rid of extra copies of a record that was falling. Likewise, jukebox owners wanted the most popular songs in their machines; the more jukeboxes were played, the more they paid. Jukebox distributors would use the most recent *Cashbox* charts to decide which records to add and remove on their regular visits to service their regional clients.

The charts in these industry periodicals were divided according to the professionals' assessment of how consumers could most effectively be separated, so they were driven by purchasing patterns. Thus, pop charts listed records that would likely be marketed to white, middle-class listeners. Rhythm and blues (originally called "race" and then "sepia") charts followed music that was directed to black urban audiences, and country and western (originally called "hillbilly" and then "folk") charts kept track of music directed at low-income whites. This system of parallel charts was based on assumptions about markets and audience tastes, not musical style. The arrangement suggests that rhythm and blues listeners would not enjoy country and

Reading the Chart Numbers

Throughout this book, *Billboard* chart positions will be noted and often these numbers will be cited in an abbreviated form. Rhythm and blues positions will be abbreviated with an "r": "r1, 1955" indicates a record that hit the number one slot on the R&B charts in 1955. Pop records will be abbreviated with a "p," and country positions will use the letter "c." Later in the book, British chart positions will be abbreviated with the letters "uk" (these numbers come from *Record Retailer*). Using these abbreviations, a record's chart success might be cited as "r1 p3, 1956," meaning it rose as high as number one on the R&B charts and number three on the pop charts in 1956. Bear in mind that chart numbers are not precision instruments and are subject to manipulation in some cases; they provide only a general indication of a record's success. We are using them here mostly for comparison purposes and to keep the "fan mentality" in check, as discussed in the Introduction.

● **Best Sellers in Stores**

For survey week ending May 2

RECORDS are ranked in order of their current national selling importance at the retail level, as determined by The Billboard's weekly survey of the top volume dealers in every important market area. When significant action is reported on both sides of a record, points are combined to determine position on the chart. In such a case, both sides are listed in bold type, the trading side on top.

Title		Last Week	Weeks on Chart
1. HEARTBREAK HOTEL (BMI)— E. Presley... I Was the One (BMI)—Vic 20-6420		1	10
2. HOT DIGGITY (ASCAP)—P. Como... JUKE BOX BABY (ASCAP)— Vic 20-6427		2	10
3. BLUE SUEDE SHOES (BMI)— C. Perkins... Honey, Don't (BMI)—Sun 234		4	10
4. MOONGLOW AND THE THEME FROM "PICNIC" (ASCAP)— M. Stoloff... Theme from "Picnic" (ASCAP)—Dec 29888		6	4
5. POOR PEOPLE OF PARIS (ASCAP)— L. Baxter... Theme From "Helen of Troy" (ASCAP)— Cap 3336		3	13
6. LONG, TALL SALLY (BMI)— Little Richard... SLIPPIN' AND SLIDIN' (BMI)— Specialty 572		13	6
7. MAGIC TOUCH (BMI)—Platters... Winner Take All (ASCAP)—Mercury 70819		5	7
8. MOONGLOW AND THE THEME FROM "PICNIC" (ASCAP)— G. Cates... Rio Batucada (ASCAP)—Coral 61618		11	4
9. WHY DO FOOLS FALL IN LOVE? (BMI)—Teen-Agers... Please Be Mine, (BMI)—Gee 1002		7	13
10. IVORY TOWER (ASCAP)—C. Carr... Please, Please, Believe Me (ASCAP)— Fraternity 734		14	5
11. A TEAR FELL (BMI)—T. Brewer... BO WEEVIL (BMI)—Coral 61590		9	11
12. LISBON ANTIGUA (ASCAP)— N. Riddle... Robin Hood (ASCAP)—Cap 3287		8	20
13. IVORY TOWER (ASCAP)— O. Williams... In Paradise (BMI)—De Luxe 6093		17	5
14. I'M IN LOVE AGAIN (BMI)— F. Domino... MY BLUE HEAVEN (ASCAP)— Imperial 964		22	2
15. ROCK ISLAND LINE (BMI)— L. Donegan... John Henry (BMI)—London 1650		10	7
16. WAYWARD WIND (BMI)—G. Grant... No More Than Forever (ASCAP)—Era 1013		23	2
17. STANDING ON THE CORNER (ASCAP)—Four Lads... MY LITTLE ANGEL (BMI)— Col 40674		15	3
18. HAPPY WHISTLER (ASCAP)— D. Robertson... You're Free to Go (ASCAP)—Dec 29878		21	2
19. MAIN TITLE (MAN WITH THE GOLDEN ARM)—R. Maltby... Heart of Paris (ASCAP)—Vik 0196		17	7
20. I'LL BE HOME (BMI)—P. Boone... Tutti Frutti (BMI)—Dot 15443		12	14
21. MAIN TITLE (MAN WITH THE GOLDEN ARM) (ASCAP)— E. Bernstein... Clark Street (ASCAP)—Dec 29869		19	6
22. I WANT YOU TO BE MY GIRL (BMI)—Teen-Agers... I'm Not a Know-It-All (ASCAP)—Gee 1012		—	1
23. LONG, TALL SALLY (BMI)— P. Boone... Any Place in Heaven (ASCAP)—Dot 15457		—	1
24. CHURCH BELLS MAY RING (BMI)—Diamonds... Little Girl of Mine (BMI)—Mercury 70835		—	1
25. CAN YOU FIND IT IN YOUR HEART? (ASCAP)—T. Bennett... Forget Her (ASCAP)—Col 40667		23	8

WHAT'S THAT SOURCE?

The leading music industry publication during the 1950s was *Billboard*, which published various charts to alert music business professionals of current trends. This "pop" sales chart was published in May 1956, a period when rock and roll had emerged in the American mainstream alongside more conservative styles of the time. Important early rock numbers such as "Heartbreak Hotel," "Blue Suede Shoes," "Why Do Fools Fall In Love," and "Rock Island Line," appear in this tally together with silly songs like "Hot Diggity," lush instrumentals such as "Poor People of Paris," and the upbeat novelty whistling featured in "The Happy Whistler." With four duplicate titles, including versions of "Long, Tall Sally" by Little Richard and Pat Boone, this chart also reminds us that the song (rather than the recording) was still an important unit of trade during the 1950s.

Source: *Billboard*, "Best Sellers in Stores," May 2, 1956, 82.

western or pop, but all it really tries to predict is who is most likely to buy records or play them on the jukebox. According to this system, if you owned a record store on Main Street that had few black customers and almost none from the country, you would not pay much attention to the rhythm and blues and country and western charts, since most of your customers would have been interested in pop records. Contrary to beliefs about such segregated listening, anecdotal evidence suggests that many black listeners enjoyed pop and country and western, and that many country and western listeners enjoyed pop and rhythm and blues. Young, middle-class white listeners already knew some country and western from network broadcasts, although most white adults were apparently not interested in rhythm and blues. One of the most significant changes to these business practices that occurred during the early 1950s was when middle-class white teens discovered rhythm and blues, which led to the softening of the boundaries between chart classifications.

When a record or song holds a prominent position on more than one of the three types of charts, this is called "crossover." Crossover can occur in many ways. The record itself or the song, recorded by a different artist, may cross over. A new version of a song is called a "cover," and the original recording or a cover version might cross over. Until 1955, chart boundaries were relatively reliable; for the most part, records and songs popular on one chart stayed on that chart and crossovers were more the exception than the rule. From 1950 to 1953, for instance, about 10 percent of the hits appearing on the rhythm and blues charts crossed over. Beginning in 1954, however, a clear trend can be seen, as rhythm and blues records began to cross over onto the other charts; 25 percent of the rhythm and blues hits crossed over that year, and by 1958 the figure increased to 94 percent (See What's That Source? for a 1956 Billboard chart). Sometimes two versions of the same song would appear on the pop charts—the original rhythm and blues performance, most often performed by a black artist, and a cover version, usually performed by a white artist. With only a few notable exceptions, the versions by white artists performed better on the pop charts than the rhythm and blues originals. When the original version appeared on a small independent label, a larger independent label (or a major label) could record a cover and distribute its records faster and more widely; to some extent, this explains the greater success of these versions and why we call them "covers." Race played a significant role in pop listeners' tastes, which was the source of much resentment among the black artists whose records were copied.

THE FIRST ROCK AND ROLLERS CROSS OVER

Fats Domino. Among the first of the early rockers to enjoy consistent crossover success was Antoine "Fats" Domino. Based in New Orleans and recording on the West Coast independent label Imperial, Domino scored a series of rhythm and blues hits in the early 1950s, including "The Fat Man" (r6, 1950), "Goin' Home" (r1, 1952), and "Something's Wrong" (r6, 1953). "Ain't It a Shame" was a number-one hit on the rhythm and blues charts in 1955 and crossed over to the pop charts, rising as high as number ten that summer. Between 1955 and 1963, Domino released thirty-seven Top 40 singles, the most successful of which were "I'm in Love Again" (r1 p3, 1956), "Blueberry Hill" (r1 p2, 1956), and "I'm Walkin'" (r1 p4, 1957). Domino delivered his songs from the piano, gently tapping out repeated triplet chords and singing his often lyrical melodies in a relaxed manner. He projected a warm, friendly image that was unlikely to trigger the kind of racial anxiety in white listeners that Big Joe Turner might. According to Domino's producer, Dave Bartholomew, close musical associates thought of Domino as a country and western singer. His biggest pop song, "Blueberry Hill," had been a hit for Glenn Miller in 1940, and provides a representative example of Domino's easygoing crossover style.

Based in New Orleans, Fats Domino had a series of rhythm and blues hits before crossing over onto the pop charts. His easygoing style is characterized by rolling triplets on the piano and a smooth vocal delivery.

Chuck Berry. Charles Edward Anderson (Chuck) Berry grew up in St. Louis and was introduced to Leonard Chess of Chess Records by blues great Muddy Waters. Berry's first hit for Chess was "Maybellene," his version of a traditional country fiddle tune called "Ida Red," which had been recorded by both Roy Acuff and Bob Wills. There are several stories about how the lyrics and title of the song changed— Chess reported that he got the idea from a makeup case and Berry claimed it was the name of a cow in a book he read as a child. Either way, "Maybellene" became a number-one hit on the rhythm and blues charts and crossed over to reach number five on the pop charts in the fall of

Listening Guide

Fats Domino, "Blueberry Hill" Imperial 5407

Words and music by Al Lewis, Larry Stock, and Vincent Rose, produced by Dave Bartholomew. Reached #1 on all three *Billboard* rhythm and blues charts (best sellers, jukeboxes, and radio) and #2 on the "Most Played in Jukeboxes," pop chart in 1956.

FORM: AABA form, with only the bridge and last verse repeated (BA).

TIME SIGNATURE: 12/8, with a characteristic easy, loping New Orleans feel. Each measure contains four beats, with each beat divided into three parts (compound). Note how the piano chords play these three parts of each beat, creating a rolling one & uh, two & uh, three & uh, four & uh rhythmic undercurrent.

INSTRUMENTATION: Piano, electric guitar, acoustic bass, drums, horns, and lead vocal.

0:00–0:12	**Introduction**, 4 mm.	Piano featured as the New Orleans feel locks in.
0:12–0:33	**A-Verse**, 8 mm.	Vocal enters. Note the repeated chords high on the piano, and the rolling line in the bass and guitar below. Sustained horns support the vocal, "I found my thrill . . ."
0:33–0:53	**A-Verse**, 8 mm.	As before, "The moon stood still . . ."
0:53–1:14	**B-Bridge**, 8 mm.	New horn line enters to emphasize contrast, "The wind in the willow . . ."
1:14–1:35	**A-Verse**, 8 mm.	As before, "Though we're apart . . ."
1:35–1:56	**B-Bridge**, 8 mm.	Supporting horn line returns, "The wind in the willow . . ."
1:56–2:18	**A-Verse**, 8 mm.	As before, "Though we're apart . . ."

1955. Berry followed with several more hit singles, including "School Day" (r1 p3, 1957), "Rock and Roll Music" (r6 p8, 1957), "Sweet Little Sixteen" (r1 p2, 1958), and "Johnny B. Goode" (r2 p8, 1958). His vocal delivery in these early rock hits is heavily influenced by his love of country music. In fact, reports from early personal appearances chronicle a sense of surprise among many audience members who had assumed from his records that Berry was white. Berry had a more showy performance style than Fats Domino, and the iconic "duck walk" he performed during his guitar solos became a Berry trademark. Like Domino, however, there was little about Berry's music or performances that struck white audiences as threatening or menacing.

Unlike the many cover versions that toned down adult-oriented songs, Berry has stated that his intention was not to reach adult black listeners but to write songs specifically geared toward the average teenager. "Roll Over Beethoven" gently celebrates the idea that the practice of teens listening to rhythm and blues music—which is playfully cast as a contagious virus—would probably make Beethoven turn over in his grave. Of course, the real target here is not classical music, but what classical music stands for—conservative and serious adult culture. Early in his professional career Berry developed an affection for what he called "story songs," and "School Day" (originally titled "A Teenager's Day") is one such song, chronicling the daily life of the average teen—off to school in the morning, classes, lunch, and the final bell, after which everyone goes down to the local meeting place to play rock and roll on the jukebox. In this case, the conservative and oppressive institution is not the stuffy world of classical music and culture, but school life, and rhythm and blues (here referred to as "rock and roll") is the music of resistance. The ending chorus of the tune, "Hail, hail, rock and roll," has been an anthem for rock fans ever since.

Such lyrics might have been delivered with an earnestness that could prove tedious or directly rebellious. But Berry's clever allusions and good humor make his songs more of a friendly ribbing of adult culture than a full frontal assault advocating or affecting social change. Later rock musicians such as John Lennon and Bob Dylan, among many others, admired Berry's lyrics and imitated his careful and creative wordplay. Berry's songs do not all deal with teen life, and some can be interpreted on many levels. "Memphis, Tennessee" (1963) is perhaps the best example of a more adult story song that expertly plays on the expectations of the listener. Throughout the song, the listener believes that Berry is trying to reach his estranged wife by telephone, revealing details of his personal life to the operator; in the last line we find out that this is not the case. (Listen to the song to hear its conclusion.) Even "Maybellene," which alternates between seemingly unrelated stories of the singer racing Maybellene's Cadillac in his Ford and a chorus complaining of Maybellene's unfaithfulness, can be read at a second level. The problem with Maybellene is that she is a "fast woman," represented in this case by a fast car (the Cadillac). Trying to keep up with her is like a race, as the allusions follow one after another. The singer begins by "motorvatin' over the hill" but soon they are "bumper to bumper, rolling side to side"; later Berry describes "rainwater flowin' all under my hood, knew that was doin' my motor good," and at the end of the song the Ford catches the Cadillac "at the top of the hill." It is not difficult to interpret this as a thickly veiled song about sexuality, ultimately not much different from "Sixty Minute Man" or "Shake, Rattle, and Roll."

Most of Berry's songs are in simple verse or simple verse-chorus form, often employing a chord structure influenced by the 12-bar blues. His songs are relatively easy to learn, and with their catchy lyrics, they have been favorites with rock bands since the late 1950s. Most of the musicians who created the rock music of the '60s and '70s could have played half a dozen Berry tunes without even thinking about it, and many often did so in live shows. Berry's guitar style became one of the most imitated in rock. His chordal accompaniments often featured a characteristic two-string boogie-woogie pattern on the low strings, and his solos used frequent double stops (playing two notes at the same time) on adjacent high strings. These can be heard clearly on a number of songs, but "Johnny B. Goode" is perhaps the best example.

A consummate showman, Chuck Berry decided early on that he would write and perform songs that didn't need to be changed for white radio. Berry's attention to lyrics provided a model for many songwriters who followed, as did his bursts of lead guitar.

Listening Guide

Chuck Berry, "Johnny B. Goode" Chess 1691

Words and music by Chuck Berry, produced by Leonard and Phil Chess. Reached #8 on the *Billboard* "Top 100" chart and #5 on both rhythm and blues charts (jukeboxes and best sellers) in 1958.

FORM: Simple verse-chorus.

TIME SIGNATURE: 4/4, with a tendency to blend in a shuffle.

INSTRUMENTATION: Electric guitars, piano, acoustic bass, drums, and lead vocal. Note how the drums tend to shuffle, while the guitar stays stubbornly in simple time.

0:00–0:17	**Introduction**, 12 mm.	Famous guitar intro using double stops, with stop time in first 4 mm. and band entering in m. 5.
0:17–0:34	**Verse 1**, 12 mm.	Vocal enters; note the constantly changing piano fills in the background throughout the song, "Deep down in Louisiana . . ."
0:34–0:51	**Chorus**, 12 mm.	Vocal punctuated by characteristic Chuck Berry guitar bursts, "Go, Go Johnny . . ."
0:51–1:08	**Verse 2**, 12 mm.	As before, note Berry's vocal sound—does it sound country influenced? "He used to carry . . ."
1:08–1:26	**Chorus**, 12 mm.	As before.
1:26–1:43	**Instrumental verse**, 12 mm.	(Like Intro), guitar solo, more double stops, full of rhythmic drive but technically simple.
1:43–2:00	**Instrumental verse**, 12 mm.	(Like Intro), guitar solo continues.
2:00–2:18	**Verse 3**, 12 mm.	As before, "His mother told him . . ."
2:18–2:38	**Chorus**, 12 mm.	As before, driving to ending.

Little Richard. The most flamboyant performer in the early years of rock and roll was probably Little Richard, born Richard Wayne Penniman. Recording on the Hollywood-based Specialty independent label, Richard's high-energy "Tutti Frutti" climbed the rhythm and blues charts in late 1955, hitting number two and crossing over to the pop charts, where it peaked at number seventeen. In subsequent years, Richard placed nine hits on the pop Top 40, including "Long Tall Sally" (r1 p6, 1956), "Keep a Knockin'" (r2 p8, 1957), and "Good Golly, Miss Molly" (r4 p10, 1958). With his sometimes-maniacal singing and screaming, aggressive piano pounding (he frequently played with one leg propped up over the piano), and strong driving beat in the rhythm section, Richard provided a remarkable contrast to the gentler Fats Domino. Little Richard was the first rock and roll artist to cultivate the

Richard Penniman (Little Richard) was the most flamboyant figure in rock's first years. He often stood while playing the piano, which allowed him more flexibility to move during performances. Little Richard had a string of crossover hits before quitting rock music to enter the ministry.

"wild man" persona. While this made him attractive to white teens, it also made it more difficult for him to advance his career in the mainstream pop market. A clear country and western influence may have made it easier for white audiences to accept Fats Domino and Chuck Berry, but there was little of that influence evident in Little Richard. Lyrics such as "Good golly, Miss Molly, you sure like to ball" and "I got a girl named Sue, she knows just what to do" were not appropriate for pop audiences. Richard was a prime target for cover versions; if a white artist covered a song and took much of the sexual innuendo out of the lyrics, his record could often outperform Richard's on the charts and in sales, even if it was far less vital and exciting than the original.

The "Whitening" of Rhythm and Blues. As we saw in the previous chapter, Bill Haley's version of "Shake, Rattle, and Roll" removes much of the sexual playfulness from Big Joe Turner's original song. These changes were clearly made so the song would be more appealing to white listeners. Indeed, the resulting record, like much of Haley's music that followed it, exudes a kind of innocent excitement by replacing references to sexuality with references to dancing. Many listeners would not think of it this way now, but when viewed in context, "(We're Gonna) Rock around the Clock" might sound like a song that deals with sexual stamina. Prompted by the success of the Dominoes' "Sixty Minute Man"—a number-one rhythm and blues hit in 1951 that briefly crossed over to the pop charts—a series of songs followed that dealt with this same topic, including Ruth Brown's "5–10–15 Hours" (r1, 1952), the Ravens' "Rock Me All Night Long" (r4, 1952), and "Work with Me, Annie" (r1, 1954) and "Annie Had a Baby" (r1, 1954), both by the Midnighters with Hank Ballard. (In early 1955, Georgia Gibbs had a number-two pop hit with "Dance with Me Henry," a reworked version of "Work with Me, Annie" that also substitutes dance for sex.) Adjustments to both the lyrics and the music of rhythm and blues began to establish a model for rock and roll in the early years, and Haley was an important figure in what might be called the "whitening" of rhythm and blues.

In the early 1950s, William John Clinton Haley Jr. was a disc jockey who also played in a Philadelphia-area country swing band, Bill Haley and His Saddlemen. In 1954, Bill Haley and His Comets signed with the major label Decca and released "Shake, Rattle, and Roll" and "(We're Gonna) Rock around the Clock." "Shake, Rattle, and Roll" was the most popular of Haley's early singles, rising to the top ten of the *Billboard* pop "Best Sellers" chart. In late 1954, Haley released "Dim, Dim the Lights," which crossed over to the rhythm and blues charts. With the release of *Blackboard Jungle*, "(We're Gonna) Rock around the Clock" enjoyed a newfound popularity, rereleased and topping the pop charts for eight weeks in mid-1955, while rising to the upper reaches of the rhythm and blues charts. Even though Haley represented a whitened version of rhythm and blues, he still found popularity in black markets. Haley and the group placed nine more hits in the pop Top 40, including "Burn That Candle" (r9 p9, 1955) and "See You Later, Alligator" (r7 p6, 1956).

Many listeners who associate rock and roll with the raucousness of Chuck Berry and Little Richard might be surprised to learn that Charles Eugene "Pat" Boone (a direct descendant of Daniel Boone) was one of the most successful artists in

Listening Guide

Little Richard, "Tutti Frutti" Specialty 561

Words and music by Richard Penniman, Robert "Bumps" Blackwell, and Dorothy LaBostrie, produced by Bumps Blackwell. Reached #1 on the *Billboard* "Most Played in Jukeboxes" pop chart and #2 on both rhythm and blues charts (jukeboxes and best sellers) in 1956.

FORM: Simple verse-chorus, beginning with chorus.

TIME SIGNATURE: 4/4.

INSTRUMENTATION: Piano, acoustic bass, drums, saxophones, and lead vocal.

0:00–0:18	**Chorus**, 12 mm. + 2 mm.	Vocal intro, "Wop bop . . ."
0:18–0:34	**Verse 1**, 12 mm. (with slight change from chorus)	"I got a girl . . . Sue . . ."
0:34–0:49	**Chorus**, 12 mm.	"Tutti frutti . . ."
0:49–1:04	**Verse 2**, 12 mm.	"I got a girl . . . Daisy . . ."
1:04–1:20	**Chorus**, 12 mm.	"Tutti frutti . . ."
1:20–1:35	**Instrumental verse**, 12 mm.	Sax solo.
1:35–1:50	**Chorus**, 12 mm.	"Tutti frutti . . ."
1:50–2:06	**Verse 3**, 12 mm.	Same lyrics as verse 2.
2:06–2:22	**Chorus**, 12 mm.	"Tutti frutti . . ." ends on vocal intro "Wop bop . . ."

Listening Guide

Bill Haley and His Comets, "(We're Gonna) Rock around the Clock" Decca 9-29124

Words and music by Max C. Freedman and James E. Myers, produced by Milt Gabler. Reached #1 on all three *Billboard* pop charts (best sellers, jukebox, and radio) and #3 on the *Billboard* R&B "Most Played by Jockeys" and "Most Played in Jukeboxes" charts and #4 on the R&B "Best Sellers in Stores" chart in mid-1955. Also reached #17 on the UK pop charts earlier that year (before it found success in the United States!) and later rose as high as #5.

FORM: Simple verse, with introduction. Verses are based on the 12-bar blues structure, with last verse altered slightly to create an ending.

TIME SIGNATURE: 12/8.

INSTRUMENTATION: Electric guitars, acoustic bass, drums, saxophone, piano, steel guitar, and lead vocal.

0:00–0:12	**Introduction,** 8 mm.	Begins with lead vocal, band plays stop-time. "One, two, three o'clock . . ."
0:12–0:27	**Verse 1,** 12 mm.	Haley's lead vocal enters, and the countdown in the lyrics begins, "Get your glad rags on . . ."
0:27–0:43	**Verse 2,** 12 mm.	As before, the countdown continues, "When the clocks strikes two . . ."
0:43–0:59	**Verse 3,** 12 mm.	Guitar solo, displaying the virtuosic skill of Danny Cedrone.
0:59–1:14	**Verse 4,** 12 mm.	As before, more countdown, "When the chimes ring . . ."
1:14–1:30	**Verse 5,** 12 mm.	As before, "When it's eight, nine, ten . . ."
1:30–1:45	**Verse 6,** 12 mm.	Sax featured, as the band locks in together on the same rhythm.
1:45–2:07	**Verse 7,** 14 mm.	As before, though the end of this verse is expanded to create the ending, "When the clock strikes twelve . . ."

the early years of rock and roll. Recording for the independent, Nashville-based Dot Records, Boone scored thirty-two Top 40 hits—sixteen of these in the Top 10—between 1954 and 1959. Boone's cover of Fats Domino's "Ain't It a Shame"— renamed "Ain't That a Shame"—outperformed the original on the pop charts, hitting number one for two weeks in the fall of 1955 (r13), and his covers of Little Richard's "Tutti Frutti" (p12, 1956) and "Long Tall Sally" (p8, 1956) equaled or surpassed the originals in the pop market. Rock historians and critics often consider Boone's contribution to rock and roll only in terms of these cover versions, but he had many other hit records during this period that were not derived from rhythm and blues material, including "Don't Forbid Me" (p1 r10, 1956), "Love Letters in the Sand" (p1 r12, 1957), and "April Love" (p1, 1957). Boone cultivated a polite, clean-cut personal image. His musical approach in many ways continued in the mainstream pop style of Frank Sinatra, but extended it to include the country and western, rhythm and blues, and gospel repertoire. If Little Richard presented a musical and personal image that many white parents found threatening, Boone's music and manner were much more readily assimilated into middle-class white culture. Most important for the history of early rock music, Boone's popularity was both dependent on and fueled by the rise of rock and roll. More than just a singer who covered rhythm and blues records for a white audience, Boone played a crucial role in establishing rock and roll within mainstream pop music.

The Controversy over Cover Versions. With the success of Bill Haley, Fats Domino, Little Richard, Pat Boone, and Chuck Berry, it became common practice in the record business to watch the rhythm and blues charts for hits and then cover these songs for the pop market. This practice significantly reduced the crossover potential for both the original records and the original artists, who were almost always black. In many people's view, black artists were "ripped off." Rhythm and blues artists were often paid a flat fee for recording a number and frequently signed away any rights to future royalties they might be entitled to as songwriters. For musicians in the habit of going from town to town and gig to gig, it was far more prudent to be paid up front than to sign an agreement for future royalties with a small, financially fragile record company. Thus, the only beneficiaries of cover versions were record company people—who were almost always white—and white performers. Early rock and roll cover versions remain a controversial and hotly debated topic among scholars and critics of rock music. It is easy to see how many black rhythm and blues artists could resent white cover versions. In some cases, song arrangements were copied in great detail, the only substantial differences being that the new record was on a different label and the artist was white. Record companies seemed intent on having white cover versions replace the original versions on the charts, in jukeboxes, on the radio, and in stores.

However, the situation was not so clear-cut. The unit of trade within American popular music since the late nineteenth century had been the song, not a particular recording of it. This was still true in 1955, when the top thirty records featured three different performances of the same song, "The Ballad of Davy Crockett." It was a well-established practice among record companies to release a version of the latest popular song on their label to capitalize on its success. In fact, our current understanding of the term "cover version," in the strictest sense, is based on the idea that a particular recording is the primary source of reference. This understanding of the cover version did not develop until the 1960s, as rock musicians and producers explored the possibilities of the recording studio. It seems silly, for instance, to imagine a band covering *Sgt. Pepper's Lonely Hearts Club Band* in the same style as the Beatles only weeks after its release in June 1967. But in 1955, copying someone else's record was common, and the practice went back decades. There is an important difference

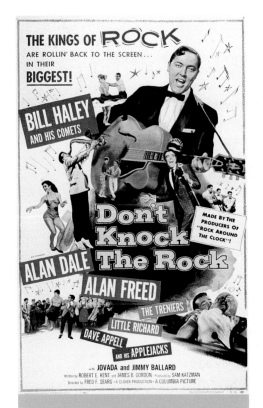

Fueled by the success of "Rock around the Clock," Bill Haley and His Comets became one of the first successful white acts in rock and roll. In addition to recording many popular hits in the early years of rock, the group also appeared in several rock-oriented films.

with the early white covers of rhythm and blues hits, however. Record labels in the prerock music business invested in particular singers whose distinctive approach, it was hoped, set them apart and fostered "brand loyalty." If you liked a song, you might especially want to hear the Frank Sinatra or Tony Bennett version. The formula was largely a matter of matching songs with "song stylists." None of these stylists would dream of closely copying another version of a song, since that would diminish his or her own mark of musical distinction. Many of the white rhythm and blues covers of the 1950s, however, are not distinctive versions but almost note-for-note replications of the originals.

If this seems to further complicate the issue, also consider that most of the Pat Boone and Bill Haley records were distinct versions that would not be confused with the originals; they are not replicas. In fact, the extent to which Haley and Boone's covers can be distinguished from their rhythm and blues models illustrates the important features that will ultimately distinguish rock and roll from rhythm and blues. Pat Boone has remarked that the records he covered would never have been played on white radio anyway; to Boone, the changes were necessary to bring this music to a white pop audience. Haley might have said the same thing. Little Richard would strongly disagree. As we might

If Elvis Presley seemed dangerous to middle-class parents, Pat Boone was the alternative. Boone's cover versions of songs by Fats Domino and Little Richard outperformed the originals on the pop charts, and together with his other hit records made him one of the top-grossing pop artists of the late 1950s.

expect, both Boone and Haley were most popular on the pop charts; however, both artists also placed their songs prominently on the rhythm and blues charts. Our discussion here does not settle the issue, but using the context established by this discussion, consider the issue for yourself: Were black artists ripped off, or were these cover versions understandable within the context of music-business practices of the day?

THE RISE OF ELVIS PRESLEY: IN STEPS CORPORATE AMERICA

Elvis at Sun. If the music of early rock musicians such as Haley, Domino, Boone, Berry, and Little Richard began breaking down the boundaries between pop, country and western, and rhythm and blues, then Elvis Presley would complete the job. He was the first rock and roller to draw intense interest from the major labels and have hits on all three charts simultaneously. When Elvis moved from Sun Records to RCA in November 1955, RCA mobilized its vast resources to support the rising star, which would not only lead to Elvis's success, but firmly establish rock and roll in the pop mainstream.

Born in Tupelo, Mississippi, Elvis and his parents moved to Memphis when he was only thirteen. Raised in a city with a rich and thriving black music scene, Elvis became well versed in both the country music of the South and the rhythm and blues of the black community. As a teenager, he performed around the neighborhood and at school, gaining a reputation as a flashy dresser who seemed to buy much of his wardrobe at Memphis's leading clothing store for blacks, Lansky Brothers. In 1950, radio announcer and technician Sam Phillips opened his Memphis Recording Service, specializing in recording black blues singers (including Joe Hill Louis, B. B. King, Howlin' Wolf, and Roscoe Gordon) and taking whatever other recording jobs might come his way. Phillips initially licensed his recordings to other labels such as the Los Angeles–based Modern and Chicago-based Chess. Among these recordings was Jackie Brenston's 1951 rhythm and blues hit, "Rocket '88,'" which he licensed to Chess. In 1952, Phillips decided to start his own label, Sun Records. He focused his efforts on black blues, releasing records by Rufus Thomas, Little Junior Parker, Little Milton, and the Prisonaires, a group of singing inmates from the Tennessee State Penitentiary. In 1953, a teenage Elvis Presley showed up at Phillips's studio to make a private demo. Phillips decided to try using Elvis as a vocalist on two songs in 1954—"It Wouldn't Be the Same without You" and "I'll Never Stand in Your Way." While Presley didn't ultimately seem right for these songs, Phillips asked guitarist Scotty Moore and bassist Bill Black to work up some other tunes with Elvis to see what he might be able to do.

Phillips had a flair for spotting talent. As a producer, he also had the patience to let performers loosen up and explore in the recording studio. Part of his routine was to roll tape and let the musicians keep working until they hit on something interesting. That was what happened in July 1954 when, after trying several numbers and perhaps feeling a bit tired and slap-happy, Elvis grabbed his guitar and started playing an Arthur "Big Boy" Crudup song called "That's All Right (Mama)." Bassist Black joined right in and Moore began fiddling with a guitar part. Phillips, who was busy doing something else in the studio at the time, asked the group to start again as he hit the record button. Before long, they had recorded the single that would launch Presley's career and establish Sun Records as an independent label of national stature. The band recorded a rocked-up version of Bill Monroe's classic bluegrass number "Blue Moon of Kentucky" as the B-side. Phillips rushed a copy of the recording to DJ Dewey Phillips, who played it on his popular *Red, Hot, and Blue* radio show, making Elvis a local celebrity. Elvis and the group began touring, performed on the *Grand Ole Opry* (which did not go well), and landed a regular spot on the *Louisiana Hayride* out of Shreveport. Despite the strong rhythm and blues influence on his music, Elvis was marketed as a country and western artist, using the moniker "The Hillbilly Cat."

A Performance That Launched a Career. The turning point in Elvis Presley's early career may have been his first performance on the *Louisiana Hayride* on October 16, 1954. Presley and his band were scheduled to perform twice on the show that night. The first set went well enough, much like the performance at the *Grand Ole Opry* had a couple of weeks earlier. But when Presley and company returned for the second set, they seemed filled with more confidence, energy, and excitement than ever before. The audience response to this more dynamic presentation was overwhelmingly positive, and it seemed to many that this performance made it clear—to both the listeners *and* the performers themselves—that something big might be in store.

The Big RCA Deal. As Elvis's success increased and word spread about his dynamic performances, he drew the attention of professionals within the music business.

Listening Guide

Elvis Presley, "That's All Right (Mama)" Sun 209

Words and music by Arthur Crudup, produced by Sam Phillips. Recorded and released on Sun Records in July 1954. Did not chart.

FORM: Simple verse, with measures added and subtracted throughout.

TIME SIGNATURE: 2/4, employing a country two-step feel with alternating bass notes.

INSTRUMENTATION: Electric guitar, acoustic guitar, acoustic bass, and lead vocals. Note that what sounds like a snare drum is actually Bill Black slapping on his bass.

0:00–0:06	**Introduction,** 5 mm.	Note strummed guitar and country feel, and entrance of the slap bass after the guitar begins alone.
0:06–0:26	**Verse 1**, 18 mm.	Vocal enters, note electric guitar fills, "That's all right, Mama . . ."
0:26–0:47	**Verse 2**, 18 mm.	Listen to how Presley swoops and shades the vocal line, sometimes moving from a low chest voice to a higher and thinner head voice. "Mama, she done told me . . ."
0:47–1:10	**Instrumental verse**, 20 mm.	Chet Atkins–influenced guitar solo, 18 mm. verse extended by 2 mm.
1:10–1:30	**Verse 3**, 18 mm.	As before, "I'm leavin' town . . ."
1:30–1:53	**Verse 4**, 20 mm.	Presley improvises using "di" during the first part of the vocal; the previous 18 mm. verse is shortened to 16 mm. then extended by 4 mm. to create the ending.

Among these was Colonel Tom Parker, who had managed Hank Snow (one of the most popular country singers of the early 1950s). Parker began working with Elvis as a promoter and later became his personal manager. In the meantime, Sam Phillips received at least two serious offers to buy out the young singer's contract. Phillips turned these down, but as 1955 wore on he found himself in need of funds to keep Sun afloat. Parker believed that Elvis could never achieve national success with Sun; he felt Phillips did not have the necessary capital to promote Presley. Parker brokered a deal with the country division of RCA records that paid Phillips the unheard-of sum of $35,000 for Presley's contract, while Elvis received an additional $5,000. Phillips had asked RCA for an amount that he thought they would never be willing to pay; to his surprise, they took his offer. Phillips invested the money in Sun and a radio station he had purchased. He went on to produce artists such as Carl Perkins, Johnny Cash, Jerry Lee Lewis, and Roy Orbison.

Presley's first single for RCA was "Heartbreak Hotel," which hit number one on both the pop and country and western charts in early 1956 and rose as high as

TELEVISION IN THE 1950S: ELVIS ON ED SULLIVAN

Viewing Rock

Elvis Presley's first appearance on Ed Sullivan's *Toast of the Town* in September 1956 was a historic moment in television, offering an example of the role of rock performance on a prime-time television variety show during the mid-1950s. A conflict between the "old guard" of prerock entertainment and the youthful exuberance behind Presley's popularity is evident in the program. Because Sullivan had recently been in a serious car accident, the program

trasted sharply with the down-home ways of Presley (1).

Despite an evident cultural gap, Presley's first Sullivan appearance was hardly shocking and controversial. The singer was filmed from Hollywood, where he was working on his first film, *Love Me Tender* (2).

Laughton referred respectfully to Presley's remarkable record sales, and displayed four recent gold records. In response, Presley commented that his appearance was "probably the greatest honor that I've ever had in my life." Presley performed in two segments. The first was remarkably tame. Flanked by the Jordanaires vocal group, Presley performed the mid-tempo "Don't Be Cruel" and the ballad "Love Me Tender" (3).

The second segment included the upbeat "Ready Teddy" and a single chorus of "Hound Dog," which ventured into the dance-oriented rock of the Sun years. These offered only glimpses of the physical movements that we closely associate with Presley's television appearances. Upon returning to host Laughton, he remarked in clear mockery to the laughter of the mostly adult audience in New York, "Music hath charms to soothe the savage breast"(4).

was hosted by stage actor Charles Laughton, whose proper British mannerisms con-

number five on the rhythm and blues chart. Television appearances followed in 1956, including the famous performance on Ed Sullivan's *Toast of the Town* variety show discussed in Chapter 1. Parker also began to work on movie deals for his young star. By the beginning of 1957, Presley had begun to ring up sales and chart numbers that would establish him as one of the most successful entertainers of all time. Tom Parker and RCA had elevated Presley from a regional sensation to an international star.

The importance of Presley's deal with RCA is hard to exaggerate. Before he moved to RCA, most major labels were not interested in rock and roll, considering it a fad. Columbia Records' Mitch Miller even saw his label's lack of involvement in rock and roll as a point of personal pride. But when industry leader RCA paid an enormous sum for a rock and roll singer, it was clear that the game was changing. The other major labels soon began to add rock and roll artists to their rosters, which pushed rock and roll even closer to the center of the pop mainstream. Compared

Why Would Sam Phillips Sell Elvis's Contract?

Sam Phillips benefited from selling Elvis Presley's contract to RCA because of the way independent labels were forced to operate in the mid-1950s. When an independent put out a record, the owner had to pay up front for all manufacturing costs—the businesses making the labels, sleeves, and records were paid before any income from the record was realized. Independent distributors, however, paid for the records that were shipped to them *after* these records were sold. This meant that there was a lag of weeks or months between when labels paid for printing costs, and when they received money from distributors. Once records were being released on a regular schedule, profits and expenses could begin to balance out after the initial expenses were absorbed. Ironically, a hit record could throw everything into disarray. Due to the high upfront cost of manufacturing large numbers of records to meet demand, a label could face great financial jeopardy until the profits were realized. Elvis's fame was increasing around the time his contract was due to expire. Phillips judged that the smart thing to do was to sell Elvis's contract while it was still worth something and use the money to put his label in a better financial position.

with its place at the very margins of the business just a few years earlier, things had changed considerably.

Covers in Elvis's Early Career. Elvis Presley was not a songwriter. He is best thought of as a master song stylist who had an exceptional ability to choose songs and discover engaging ways to interpret them. From the beginning of his recording career, Presley had almost total control over this aspect of his music. If there was a song or version of a song he didn't like, neither Sun nor RCA would release it (since his death in 1977, many of these recordings have been issued). Presley's recording sessions were often a series of experiments with a wide variety of songs. Some songs Presley learned from commercial recordings, while others were supplied on acetates (inexpensive demonstration records not designed for commercial release) by professional songwriters. Among the songs offered to him was "Don't Forbid Me," but Pat Boone recorded it first and had a number-one hit. With his focus on style, Presley joined Boone as a singer in the pop tradition of Bing Crosby, Frank Sinatra, and Tony Bennett. Presley extended this tradition by drawing broadly from folk, country and western, rhythm and blues, and gospel sources for his tunes. His first sessions for Sun featured not only Crudup's "That's All Right (Mama)" and Monroe's "Blue Moon of Kentucky," but also "I Love You Because," which had been made famous by traditional vocalist Eddie Fisher, and "I Don't Care if the Sun Don't Shine," which had been recorded by Patti Page.

The Sun recordings are often viewed as some of Elvis's best, and they helped establish a style that came to be called "rockabilly." These songs were mostly recorded without drums, featuring Presley singing to the accompaniment of his acoustic guitar, Black's acoustic bass, and Moore's Chet Atkins–influenced electric guitar. Warm reverberation and "slapback echo" are sonic features that Sam Phillips pioneered, and this general ambience has been imitated by rockabilly artists since Elvis's first release.

When Elvis (center in background, choosing his uniform from clothing bins) was drafted into the U.S. Army, many predicted his career would be over. However, Elvis's manager, Tom Parker (second from right, talking to two RCA executives), calculated that military service would show that Presley was a good, upstanding American boy. This image would position the singer closer to the center of the entertainment business mainstream. Presley recorded several records before he shipped out to boot camp, and these singles were released while he was away, keeping his career alive until his return.

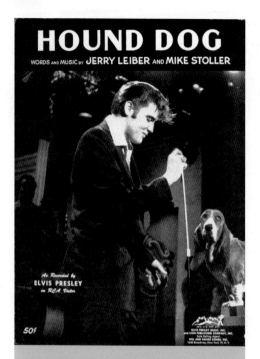

Referred to early in his career as "The Hillbilly Cat," Elvis Presley became one of the biggest stars in show business when RCA bought his contract from Sun Records. The young Elvis was handsome, sexy, and dangerous. Presley scandalized parents and became extremely popular with a wide variety of teenagers.

Although these recordings often featured light percussion, the absence of drums is a clear marker of their country and western roots: drums were important to pop dance music and rhythm and blues generally, but country musicians tended not to use them. The *Grand Ole Opry* even had a long-standing policy against using a drum set in performances. Even in his very first recordings, Elvis's distinctive vocal style is as much a stylistic hybrid as his repertoire. Much of the swooping in his voice can be traced to early '50s pop singers like Dean Martin, while other vocal mannerisms derived from rhythm and blues.

Presley's Move to RCA for Broader Appeal. While Presley's move to RCA signaled the greater involvement of the major labels in rock and roll, the plan almost from the beginning of his tenure with RCA was to broaden his appeal beyond a teenage audience. The movies he made were part of that strategy, but the mainstreaming process can be seen most clearly after 1960. Presley's career was interrupted by a stint in the U.S. Army from 1958 to 1960. While much happened in popular music while he was stationed in Germany, his return to civilian life was celebrated by a television performance hosted by Frank Sinatra and featuring some of Sinatra's Rat Pack buddies, including Sammy Davis Jr. The plan was to turn necessity into a virtue, and Presley was transformed from the hip-swiveling menace to society into a patriotic G.I., doing his part to protect the American way of life. Musically, his three number-one hits from 1960 show this transition. "Stuck on You" (p1 r6 c27, 1960) is a clear continuation of Presley's earlier RCA hits such as "Hound Dog" (p1 r6 c10, 1956), "Too Much" (p1 r3 c3, 1957), and "Teddy Bear" (p1 r1 c1, 1957). But "It's Now or Never" (p1 r7, 1960) is reminiscent of Italian crooner Mario Lanza, while "Are You Lonesome Tonight" (p1 r3 c22, 1960) features a narration in the middle that contrasted sharply with Elvis's bad-boy image. Separating Presley from his close association with rock and roll was a prudent business move at the time. Rock and roll had been viewed by many in the music business as a fad that would pass with time. By the late 1950s (as we'll see later), the first wave of rock and roll was about to enter a new era. Since so much had been invested in Presley, it was important that his popularity was sustained even as the public grew tired of rock and roll. By mid-1960, Presley was a pop song stylist who had established himself in rock and roll but had moved on. Despite an excellent 1968 television special intended to reestablish his rock roots, the music he made before 1960 became the most important to his legacy as a pivotal figure in rock and roll.

ROCKABILLY IN THE WAKE OF PRESLEY

Carl Perkins, Johnny Cash, and Jerry Lee Lewis at Sun. After Presley left Sun, Sam Phillips focused on other artists who would help develop rockabilly. Only weeks after signing over Elvis's contract, Phillips recorded Tennessee guitarist-vocalist Carl Perkins. In one December session in 1955, Perkins laid down four songs, including "Honey, Don't" and his biggest hit, "Blue Suede Shoes." In the first half of 1956, "Blue Suede Shoes" rose to number two on the pop charts; more importantly, the record was a hit on all three charts (r2 c1). While some popular records crossed over from the rhythm and blues charts and others from the country and western charts, it was rare for the same record to climb all three. Beginning with "Heartbreak Hotel," which raced up all three charts neck-and-neck with Perkins's "Blue Suede Shoes," Presley's records did this routinely. "Blue Suede Shoes" was the first million-selling single for Sun and likely served to reassure Phillips that he had acted wisely in selling Presley's contract to RCA. Perkins's career was dealt a severe blow when he and his band were involved in a serious auto accident. Despite the fact that he was unable to capitalize on the success of "Blue Suede Shoes" through live performances, several of his songs were later covered by the Beatles. (George Harrison admired Perkins so much that at one point before the Beatles became famous he adopted the stage name Carl Harrison!)

In 1956, Johnny Cash was another of Sam Phillips's young hopefuls at Sun. Early that year he had become a regular on the *Louisiana Hayride* broadcasts out of Shreveport, barely overlapping with Presley, who was moving into the mainstream market with RCA. Cash's "Folsom Prison Blues" (c4, 1956) was on the country and western charts at the same time as "Heartbreak Hotel" and "Blue Suede Shoes," but it did not cross over. By late 1956, however, "I Walk the Line" did make the leap, reaching number seventeen on the pop charts and becoming the first of four Top 40 pop singles Cash would release on Sun. By the end of 1957, Cash and Perkins had followed Elvis's lead and signed new contracts with the same major label, Columbia.

In July 1957—about a year after Elvis's first provocative national television appearances—viewers of *The Steve Allen Show* tuned in for new Sun artist Jerry Lee Lewis's energetic performance of "Whole Lotta Shakin' Goin' On." Lewis pounded the piano as he belted out the lyrics, at one point tossing the piano bench across the stage only to have Allen toss it back. This performance fueled the record's ascent on all three charts. Lewis's manic style was nothing new—Little Richard had beat him to that punch by two years. Nevertheless, in the following twelve months Lewis would have three additional hits on all three charts: "Great Balls of Fire" (p2 r1 c1, 1957), "Breathless" (p7 r3 c4, 1958), and "High School Confidential" (p21 r5 c9, 1958). Lewis might have turned out more hit records for Sun had he not been involved in a scandal: on a concert tour of Britain, Lewis let it slip that his new bride, Myra Gale Brown, was fourteen years old (she was actually thirteen and also his cousin). The British press picked up on this, also revealing that Lewis had already been married twice before. These stories played into the negative stereotypes of American southerners and rock and roll musicians. Because of public backlash, Lewis was not active in the entertainment business for several years afterward.

After Elvis left for RCA, Sam Phillips invested in a number of other artists, including the blonde-haired, piano-banging Jerry Lee Lewis. Lewis enjoyed a string of hits but was chased briefly from the business when reporters learned that his wife was only thirteen.

Gene Vincent and Eddie Cochran.

While Sam Phillips continued to develop new talent at Sun, new rockabilly artists also emerged on other labels. Bearing a striking stylistic resemblance to Elvis Presley,

Virginian Gene Vincent scored three Top 40 hits for Capitol, the most noteworthy of which was his "Be-Bop-a-Lula," which rose to number seven in 1956 (r8, c5). Guitarist-vocalist Eddie Cochran hailed from Oklahoma City and recorded three Top 40 hits for Liberty, including "Summertime Blues," which hit number eight in 1958 (r11). Both artists appeared in the 1956 film *The Girl Can't Help It*, and Cochran's performance of "Twenty Flight Rock" in that movie made an impression on the teenage Paul McCartney. Both rockabilly stars were very popular in Great Britain, and they were involved in an auto accident during a UK tour in 1960; Cochran was killed and Vincent was seriously injured.

Rockabilly Ladies. Several female performers also made an impact on the rockabilly movement of the late 1950s. Although she is more often remembered for her hit singles from the early 1960s, such as "I'm Sorry" (p1 r4, 1960), Brenda Lee started her career singing rockabilly. Her 1956 single, "Bigelow 6-200," is credited to Little Brenda Lee. Lee was only twelve when the song was recorded in Nashville with experienced session musicians backing her up. Janis Martin was known as "the female Elvis" and enjoyed moderate success in 1956 with her self-penned debut single, "Drugstore Rock 'n' Roll" and "My Boy Elvis." Martin was signed to RCA just weeks after Elvis and used some of the same musicians, though the two met only briefly. Wanda Jackson did know Presley well, however, and credits him with convincing her to sing rockabilly. Jackson released a series of singles in the second half of the 1950s, enjoying her greatest rockabilly success with "Let's Have a Party," which hit the Top 40 in 1960. The rest of Jackson's career was spent in country music, and she was active on the country charts for the remainder of the 1960s.

Buddy Holly. As rockabilly moved into the pop mainstream, new artists emerged who put greater stylistic stress on pop at the expense of the country and western and rhythm and blues influences. Among these were the Everly Brothers and Ricky Nelson, who will be discussed in Chapter 3 since both acts continued to have hits after 1960. Another important figure, Buddy Holly, was killed in a tragic plane crash in early 1959, so his contributions to the history of rock music were complete by the beginning of the new decade.

Charles Hardin (Buddy) Holly was one of the first major figures in rock music who was significantly influenced by the rock and rollers who emerged in 1955 and 1956. Growing up in Lubbock, Texas, Holly was first exposed to the music of Elvis Presley, Little Richard, and Chuck Berry by listening to the radio. Like many teenagers, Holly was glued to the screen when Elvis appeared on *Toast of the Town*. Holly had seen Presley perform in Lubbock in January 1955, and he spent time with both Presley and Little Richard when they passed through Lubbock on tour.

In early 1956, the Columbia and Decca offices in Nashville were searching for young rockabilly artists to compete with Presley on RCA, so Decca signed Holly. The recording sessions did not go well, and when the records from them were not successful, he was dropped by the label. Buddy Holly and his band, the Crickets, began recording for Norman Petty in his independent studio in Clovis,

Signed by Capitol Records to take advantage of Elvis Presley's rising popularity, Gene Vincent made his most lasting mark with a song that almost beats Elvis at his own game. Recorded in Owen Bradley's studio in Nashville, the iconic opening vocal and Cliff Gallup's guitar solos—both drenched in slapback echo—help make "Be-Bop-a-Lula" a rockabilly classic.

Listening Guide ▄▄▄

Gene Vincent and His Blue Caps, "Be-Bop-a-Lula" Capitol F3450

Words and music by Gene Vincent and Bill "Sheriff Tex" Davis, produced by Ken Nelson. Charted heavily in all three industry markets in mid-1956, reaching #7 on the amalgamated "Top 100" pop chart, #5 on the "C&W Best Sellers in Stores" and "Most Played C&W in Jukeboxes" charts, #9 on the "Most Played C&W by Jockeys" chart, #8 on the "Most Played R&B in Jukeboxes" chart, and #11 on the "Most Played R&B by Jockeys" chart.

FORM: Contrasting verse-chorus. The verse and chorus sections are only mildly contrasting: the chorus features the title of the track sung over a standard 12-bar blues structure; the verse introduces new lyrics during the first 8 bars but then returns to the title of the song to create a refrain in the second 8 bars. The two guitar solos are each played over the 12-bar blues structure found in the chorus; they are labeled "chorus" below; the quotation marks indicate their similarity with the chorus, though they stop short of being chorus sections in any usual sense. Although the chorus is sung only twice, it is an interesting feature in that it occurs at the beginning and end of the song, creating a kind of frame around the rest of the music.

TIME SIGNATURE: 12/8, laid-back, "cool" rockabilly feel.

INSTRUMENTATION: Electric guitar, acoustic guitar, acoustic bass, drums, and lead vocal.

0:00–0:25	**Chorus**, 12 mm.	Vocal enters; note heavy echo on voice, use of 12-bar blues structure, "Be-bop-a-lula . . ."
0:25–0:55	**Verse 1**, 16 mm.	First 8 bars feature stop-time, second 8 bars serve as refrain, "She's the girl . . ."
0:55–1:17	**"Chorus,"** 12 mm.	Guitar solo supported by 12-bar blues, also with the strong echo often associated with rockabilly guitar playing.
1:17–1:47	**Verse 2**, 16 mm.	As before, with added vocal mannerisms, "She's the woman . . ."
1:47–2:10	**"Chorus,"** 12 mm.	Guitar solo, as before.
2:10–2:32	**Chorus**, 12 mm.	Sung chorus returns to close out song, "Be-bop-a-lula . . ."

New Mexico. When some of these recordings were shopped around to labels, Coral, ironically a Decca subsidiary, was interested. It was decided that another subsidiary, Brunswick, was a better home for the Crickets. Later, Decca shifted again and released Buddy Holly records on Coral. This explains why some Holly hits are credited to him while others are credited to the Crickets, despite the fact that there is little difference in personnel on the actual recordings.

The Crickets' first hit, "That'll Be the Day," was released on Brunswick and reached number one on the pop charts in the second half of 1957 (r2). Between his emergence onto the national scene in August of 1957 and his death in early February of 1959, Holly had seven Top 40 hits, including "Peggy Sue" (p3 r2, 1957),

"Oh, Boy!" (p10 r13, 1957), and "Maybe Baby" (p17 r4, 1958). Despite being a clean-cut, white performer who wrote his own material, Holly's biggest hits were also very popular in the rhythm and blues market. He also recorded a number of other tracks that have since become classics covered by later groups, such as "Not Fade Away" (the Rolling Stones), "It's So Easy" (Linda Ronstadt), and "Words of Love" (the Beatles). Holly's early death has prompted much speculation about what his music would have sounded like had he lived longer. One indication is provided by two of his last recordings, "It Doesn't Matter Anymore" (p13, 1959) and "True Love Ways." Both employ orchestral accompaniment and suggest that Holly might have joined Presley in moving to a more mainstream pop style.

In many ways, Buddy Holly and Chuck Berry offer an interesting comparison: both were guitarists who wrote most of their own songs and performed them in a distinctive manner. They also wrote music intended for a pop audience that was strongly influenced by country and western and rhythm and blues. The country elements of Berry's music can be heard in his vocals, his penchant for telling stories with his lyrics, and occasional upbeat tempos (as heard in "Maybellene," for instance). However, Berry's guitar playing is derived strongly from the electric blues tradition, often relying on muted, low-register chords for rhythm playing and distorted string bends and double stops for leads. Holly, by contrast, tends to strum full chords energetically with an open, clean tone on his electric guitar, much the way traditional country guitarists do on an acoustic guitar. Combined with a clear country twang in his voice and the vocal hiccups that came to be his trademark, Holly's west-Texas musical roots are perhaps the most obvious feature of his style. But Holly was also fascinated by Elvis's assimilation of rhythm and blues singing, and with the records of Clyde McPhatter and others who influenced Elvis. The development of Holly's distinctive sound, using the same styles that had influenced so many other early rockers, offers a fascinating musical case study.

Much of the distinctiveness of Holly's stylistic approach can be heard in his recording of "Oh, Boy!" (one of the few Holly hits not from his own pen). A very open, country-style guitar accompanies Holly's eager and excited delivery of the lyrics. A closer listen reveals that the song is in AABA form with verses based on a 12-bar blues structure, showing the influence of both country and western and rhythm and blues. "Peggy Sue" is perhaps the best example of Holly's vocal technique. Holly never delivers any of the verses in exactly the same way. To vary them, he changes not only the notes and rhythms but also the timbre of his voice, producing the sound either back in his throat and chest or very forward and through his nose. This manipulation of timbre is an extension of Presley's approach. (Holly's direct tribute to Elvis can be heard on his "Rock around with Ollie Vee.") The drums on "Peggy Sue" are also noteworthy: Crickets drummer Jerry Allison employs only tom-toms in the drum set—no cymbals or snare drum are heard.

As engaging as his recorded performances may be, Buddy Holly was most influential among later rockers as a songwriter. While his lyrics are not exceptional in the way that Chuck Berry's are, the fact that Holly wrote his own songs served as a model for many rock musicians in the 1960s and '70s. If Berry's songs were more lyrically accomplished, Holly's were much more adventurous in terms of formal design. Holly employed 12-bar blues, AABA, simple verse-chorus, and contrasting verse-chorus forms in his songwriting, thereby avoiding the impression that a song was simply poured into a preexisting mold. In addition, his stylistic range was broader than most rock and roll songwriters of the time. Comparing the excitement

Hailing from Lubbock, Texas, Buddy Holly blended country twang with R&B rhythm to become an important songwriter and performer during rock's first wave. Shown here with the Crickets, Holly died in a plane crash in February 1959—an event singer-songwriter Don McLean would later describe as "the day the music died."

of "That'll Be the Day" or "Maybe Baby" with the gentle pop lyricism of "Words of Love" or "True Love Ways" clearly illustrates his range. Buddy Holly and Chuck Berry were definitive examples of the successful songwriter-performer—a model that would come to define much rock music after the Beatles used it to shake up the music industry in early 1964.

THE DAY THE MUSIC DIED

The Misfortunes of Many in Rock and Roll's First Wave. The 1950s ended with rock and roll suffering a series of setbacks that removed some of its principal figures from the music business. At the height of his success in 1957, Little Richard believed he received a calling to go into the ministry. He promptly quit music and began a course of study that led to his ordination as a minister in the Seventh Day Adventist Church. Elvis received his draft notice in December 1957, and after a deferment and boot camp at Fort Hood, he was on his way to Germany by late September 1958. In May 1958, the British press broke the story of Jerry Lee Lewis's marriage to his thirteen-year-old cousin—a scandal that sent his career on a steep decline. Buddy Holly's plane went down on February 3, 1959, a date singer-songwriter Don McLean dubbed "the day the music died." Fellow rock and roll singers Ritchie Valens and the Big Bopper were also killed in the crash. Also in 1959, Chuck Berry was charged with violating the Mann Act (transporting a minor across state lines for immoral purposes). He was convicted, but the verdict was overturned on appeal. He was tried again and convicted in February 1961, receiving a three-year sentence (of which he served less than two years). By the end of 1959, many of rock and roll's most important figures were out of the pop-music picture, and rock and roll seemed to be a played-out fad, fading away just as many of its biggest critics had predicted it would.

The Payola Investigations. A series of legal and political proceedings fed a nationwide scandal over payola in the record business beginning in late 1959. As mentioned earlier, record labels and distributors often paid disc jockeys to play records on the radio—sometimes the payment was cash; other times it was in goods or services. This practice of paying to get your song heard goes back to the nineteenth century in the American popular-music business. In the early twentieth century, singers received payola to include particular songs in their acts; during the big band era, bandleaders received payment to play and record certain numbers; and during the 1950s, disc jockeys were paid to play records on the radio. In each era, certain professionals were "gatekeepers"—they had the power to expose a song to a broad audience and hoped to increase record or sheet music sales by doing so. In the first half of the century, there were periodic squabbles over this, either because the publishers resented having to pay the fees or because they paid the fees and did not get the song played as much as they wanted. So from inside the music business, there was nothing new about payola.

By the end of the 1950s, however, a major shake-up had occurred in the music business. Early in the decade, most hit pop records were recorded and released by major labels. By 1958, because of rock and roll's breakthrough to the pop mainstream, a significant portion of the hit pop records were on independent labels. From the perspective of major-label executives, these new indies presented a substantial competitive threat that had to be eliminated. In addition to the record company money at stake in this shake-up, there was also a struggle between the two organizations that collected public performance royalties for songwriters. ASCAP (the American Society of Composers, Artists, and Performers) represented the traditional pop-song composers. They were very selective about who could be a member, and composers of rhythm and blues or country and western songs were not welcome to join their ranks. BMI (Broadcast Music Incorporated) was a newer organization that embraced the kinds of songwriters ASCAP was proud to reject. The majors and ASCAP therefore represented music's powerful and well-entrenched old guard (Tin Pan Alley and Hollywood songwriters, mainstream pop performers and their record companies), while the indies and BMI represented rock and roll. Clearly the musical establishment had much to gain by attacking both the indie labels and the songwriters who provided their material. The payola scandal was the means by which the old guard attempted to win back its market share.

It is important to understand just how little respect rock and roll had in the minds of many seasoned musical professionals in the late 1950s. Most music executives had come up in the business during the 1930s and '40s, achieving their greatest success promoting the music of big bands and song stylists. They considered rock and roll—and the rhythm and blues and country and western from which it developed—to be crude and unrefined. Of course, most listeners over the age of thirty felt the same way, and many people had a tough time understanding how rock and roll could have become so popular so fast. Many adult listeners questioned this new music's quality given its ubiquity on the radio. One explanation made particular sense to opponents of rock and roll: these ragamuffin indie labels were buying their time on the air—paying the disc jockeys to play that primitive musical garbage—and *that's* why people were buying it. The argument was presented in just such terms to the listening public as the industry began creating controversy over payola. As it happened, a congressional committee was just winding up its investigation into television quiz shows (some of which were rigged, they discovered) and now decided to turn its attention to payola in the music business. In November 1959, the House Special Subcommittee on Legislative Oversight, chaired by Oren Harris (an Arkansas Democrat), began taking testimony.

From the start, the committee's investigation focused on radio stations that played rock and roll. The testimony offered no significant acknowledgment that payola had existed in the music business for decades and that both majors and indies, marketing rock and roll as well as other styles, were involved. The committee manipulated deeply ingrained stereotypes that people involved in rhythm and blues were likely to be dishonest, bringing the cultural struggle over the segregation of black and white cultures to a new field of conflict. The Federal Trade Commission (FTC) and Federal Communications Commission (FCC) eventually got involved, causing most stations to take action, if only for show: disc jockeys were fired and formats were changed. Strangely enough, there was nothing illegal about taking money or gifts in exchange for playing a record on the radio. There were two catches, however: by FCC rules, the gift had to be acknowledged on the air, and any money received had to be claimed on the recipient's income tax form. The problem for many of the disc jockeys under scrutiny was not that they took gifts, but that they never declared them. For most of the radio stations involved in the investigation, it was a matter of public perception and trying to guard against losing their broadcast license with the FCC.

The two highest profile subjects in the payola investigations were Alan Freed and Dick Clark. Clark was extremely cooperative and emerged from the proceedings with his reputation intact, even being praised as a hardworking young businessman. However, he was forced to divest himself of a number of financial holdings that might have created a conflict of interest with his broadcast activities. Freed, on the other hand, resisted the idea that there was anything wrong with his activities. He argued that he would never take money to play a record he didn't like, but if he'd played a record and a company wanted to show its appreciation, he was happy to accept the gift. Such honest but rebellious declarations made him a liability to his broadcast employers, and he lost both his radio job at WABC and his television show on WNEW-TV. There is little doubt that Freed took a wide variety of payments; he was even credited as one of three writers of Chuck Berry's "Maybellene," even though he had no role in its composition. (The practice of sharing publishing rights was common within the business; Norman Petty's name, for instance, appears on a number of songs that Buddy Holly composed alone.) But as a "gatekeeper," Freed was in the position to promote songs in which he had a financial interest, and the investigating committee considered this a questionable practice. In December 1962, Freed pleaded guilty to a charge of taking bribes. While he received only a six-month suspended sentence and a $300 fine, the damage had been done. The payola scandal had driven Alan Freed out of the music business. With the severe shake-up in both the personnel and the business of rock and roll, by 1960 it seemed to many that the Golden Age of rock and roll was over.

The U.S. government hearings on payola in the radio business were the undoing of many in radio, including Alan Freed. However, Dick Clark (center) emerged from the investigation relatively unscathed and went on to become one of the most powerful figures in pop-music broadcasting.

Rock and roll emerged in 1955 following a series of significant events: "Rock around the Clock" became a pop hit associated with juvenile delinquency; Alan Freed's radio show rose

Sound Check

Artist	Song	Sound
Fats Domino	Blueberry Hill (1956)	Form: ABBA Loping New Orleans feel Repeated high chords and rolling low line in piano Horn lines support vocal melody
Chuck Berry	Johnny B. Goode (1958)	Form: simple verse-chorus Famous double-stop guitar introduction Drums use a shuffle rhythm and guitar does not Constantly changing piano fills
Little Richard	Tutti Frutti (1956)	Form: simple verse-chorus Form begins with chorus Double entendre in lyrics Verse and chorus are slightly different in form, but still considered Simple verse-chorus
Bill Haley and His Comets	(We're Gonna) Rock Around the Clock (1954, 1955)	Form: simple verse with introduction Lyrics employ clock countdown Verses based on 12-bar blues structure Classic guitar solo
Elvis Presley	That's All Right (Mama) (1954)	Form: simple verse Drum sound created by slapping bass Swooping vocal line Vocal improvisation in final verse
Gene Vincent and His Blue Caps	Be-Bop-a-Lula (1956)	Form: contrasting verse-chorus Both chorus and verse sections based on 12-bar blues structure Verses expand 12-bar blues structure by employing stop-time Use of strong echo on lead vocal and guitar are a rockabilly trademark

to prominence in New York; and Fats Domino, Chuck Berry, and Little Richard enjoyed their first crossover hits, all on independent labels. By the end of the year, Elvis Presley was signed to RCA and on his way to becoming the most commercially successful entertainer in rock and roll. His popularity launched a major-label search for rock and roll singers that led to recording deals for figures such as Gene Vincent and Buddy Holly. As exciting as rock and roll was, it also represented a serious threat to established music-business interests, which pulled political strings to shut down the upstarts, and by 1960 the first wave of rock and roll was all but over.

The big record companies and music publishers were not about to let this new market in youth music fade away, however, because it was now a lucrative aspect of the business. In the years that followed, big companies took control of American popular music, primarily producing music for middle-class teens that would not offend their parents. In the next chapter, we will explore how popular music returned to its Tin Pan Alley ways, with a wide variety of artists hoping to duplicate the success of Elvis Presley and other rock and roll artists.

For Additional Online Resources, visit:
digital.wwnorton.com/whatsthatsound5

FURTHER READING

Chuck Berry, *The Autobiography* (Faber & Faber, 2001).

Rick Bragg, *Jerry Lee Lewis: His Own Story* (Harper, 2015).

Howard A. DeWitt, *Chuck Berry: Rock 'n' Roll Music* (Pierian Press, 1985).

Ahmet Ertegun, *What'd I Say: The Atlantic Records Story* (Welcome Rain, 2001).

Colin Escott, with Martin Hawkins, *Good Rockin' Tonight: Sun Records and the Birth of Rock 'n' Roll* (St. Martin's, 1991).

Mark Fisher, *Something in the Air: Radio, Rock, and the Revolution That Shaped a Generation* (Random House, 2007).

Ben Fong-Torres, *The Hits Just Keep on Coming: The History of Top 40 Radio* (Backbeat, 2001).

Charlie Gillett, *Making Tracks: Atlantic Records and the Growth of a Multi-Billion-Dollar Industry* (Dutton, 1974).

Peter Guralnick, *Sam Phillips: The Man Who Invented Rock 'n' Roll* (Little, Brown, 2015).

John A. Jackson, *Big Beat Heat: Alan Freed and the Early Years of Rock & Roll* (Schirmer, 1995).

Ernst Jorgensen, *Elvis Presley: A Life in Music* (St. Martin's, 2000).

Myra Lewis, with Murray Silver, *Great Balls of Fire: The Uncensored Story of Jerry Lee Lewis* (St. Martin's, 1982).

Craig Morrison, *Go Cat Go! Rockabilly Music and Its Makers* (University of Illinois, 1998).

Philip Norman, *Rave On: The Biography of Buddy Holly* (Simon & Schuster, 1996).

Kerry Segrave, *Payola in the Music Industry: A History, 1880–1991* (McFarland, 1994).

Wes Smith, *The Pied Pipers of Rock 'n' Roll: Radio Deejays of the 50s and 60s* (Longstreet, 1989).

Albin J. Zak, *I Don't Sound Like Nobody: Remaking Music in 1950s America* (University of Michigan Press, 2010).

CHAPTER 3

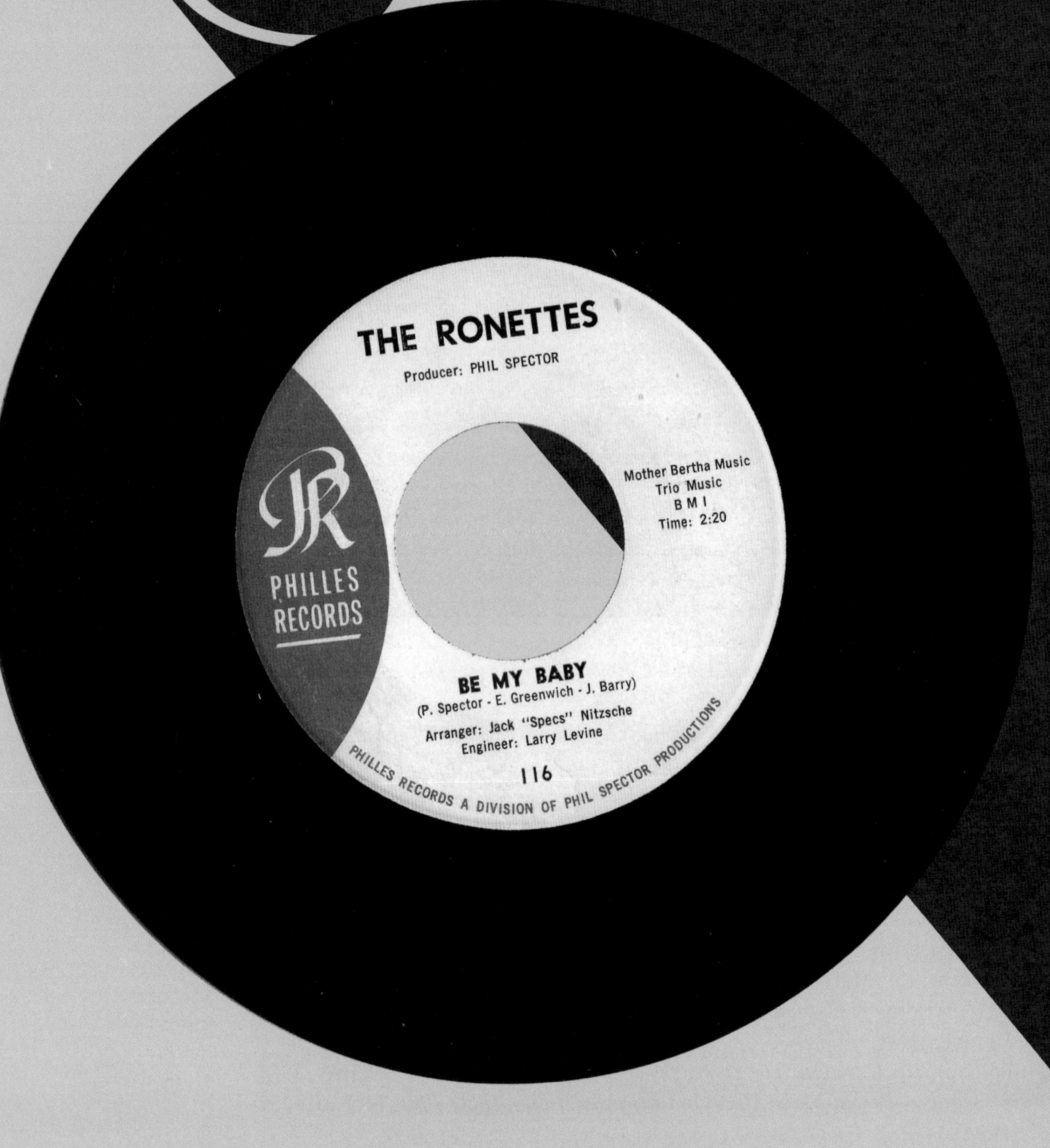
THE RONETTES
Producer: PHIL SPECTOR
PHILLES RECORDS
Mother Bertha Music
Trio Music
B M I
Time: 2:20
BE MY BABY
(P. Spector - E. Greenwich - J. Barry)
Arranger: Jack "Specs" Nitzsche
Engineer: Larry Levine
116
PHILLES RECORDS A DIVISION OF PHIL SPECTOR PRODUCTIONS

THE DEMISE OF ROCK AND THE PROMISE OF SOUL

CHAPTER PREVIEW

- In the early 1960s, record labels targeted the youth market. Many styles emerged as labels attempted to find the "next Elvis."

- While the folk music of the Kingston Trio appealed to college students, younger listeners popularized such teen idols as Frankie Avalon and Fabian.

- On television, *American Bandstand* fueled a 1960s dance craze.

- Producers such as Lieber and Stoller and Phil Spector gained influence in defining a song's particular sound.

- Sam Cooke, the Drifters, and Ben E. King became known for sweet soul, while the Everly Brothers, Ricky Nelson, and Roy Orbison developed pop-oriented rockabilly.

- The Beach Boys and Jan and Dean emerged as important artists in surf music.

- Singles called "death discs" or "splatter platters" often blended teen love with violent death in melodramatic fashion.

An original pressing of the Ronettes' "Be My Baby," produced by Phil Spector in 1963. Although early 1960s rock and roll is seen by some as a mere pause between Elvis and the Beatles, others cite the period's many musical innovations. Spector was one of the most important producers of this era—drawing influence from Leiber and Stoller before him and influencing the Beatles and Brian Wilson after. Spector demanded total control over the music and was famous for his "Wall of Sound," which was created through a combination of his arrangements, the small size of the spaces in which he recorded, and a large group of (sometimes exotic) instruments. This complex, richly textured sound was often complemented by strong vocals from female singers like Darlene Love and Veronica Bennett (Ronnie Spector). "Be My Baby," featuring Ronnie Spector, is representative of Phil Spector's Wall of Sound.

B y the end of the 1950s, many important figures in rock and roll's first wave were out of the music business, and radio stations and independent labels that supplied rock records had been shaken by the payola scandal. Rock and roll not only posed a cultural challenge to the values of many Americans but also threatened the old guard music business. The basic problem, as some older hands saw it, was that the wrong people controlled rock and roll: musicians, disc jockeys, and independent label owners. According to the old pros, all this hustling led to a market for youth music that was destined to run into trouble because these small-time operators could not be depended on to act responsibly. Too much free choice resulted in too many unpredictable variables, and the entire enterprise fell apart. Despite these seeming failures, rock and roll *had* accomplished something important: it demonstrated convincingly that youth culture provided a significant and profitable market. Now seasoned professionals were needed to pick up the pieces and bring some order to the chaos. A lot of money could be made if the processes of creating and selling music to a youth market were more tightly organized and controlled. As we saw in the last chapter, however, rock and roll did not collapse entirely on its own; the music-business establishment played a significant role in hastening the demise of the first wave.

The period after the first wave and before the arrival of the Beatles is a source of controversy among rock historians. For some, the perspective outlined here explains why rock music was so mediocre during these years: corporate types tried to domesticate rock, turning it into a slick, cynically produced commercial product that was a shadow of its former self. Teen idols, girl groups, and songs composed and produced by professionals—exemplified by New York's Brill Building—are often seen to represent the severe decline of rock that was reversed only with the "British invasion" in 1964. However, some writers and historians take a more positive view of this period, arguing that it was filled with important music and musical accomplishments. They cite the music of Leiber and Stoller, Phil Spector, and the rise of sweet soul as marking an important maturation in rock and roll that was cut short by the British invasion.

This chapter surveys the variety of pop styles that comprised the youth market in the early 1960s. As we will see, the period between 1959 and 1963 was indeed filled with a wide variety of music. Rock and roll had brought an audience (and a market) together, but many considered it a fad that now seemed to be over. Nearly everyone in the music business was on the lookout for the "next big thing" that would seize the attention of youth culture the way Elvis and the early rock and rollers had done. As it turned out, the next big thing was the Beatles, but the Fab Four did not become popular in the United States until early 1964. In the interim, a number of styles vied for center stage—a spot that none would ultimately win.

SPLITTING UP THE MARKET: TEENYBOPPERS AND THEIR OLDER SIBLINGS

The period from 1959 to 1963 was a time of transition in the history of rock. Music executives took advantage of the opportunities provided by the youth market, noticing that by 1960 it was no longer a single entity. Many of the kids who had been excited by Little Richard, Chuck Berry, and Elvis in the mid-1950s had graduated from high school by the end of the decade and were now eager—in time-honored fashion—to be treated as adults. This meant that there were at least two distinct markets: one focused on the new generation of teenagers (the younger siblings of first-wave rock and roll fans) and another directed at former rock and rollers. Teen idols and dance music, concerned with nonsexual romance and dancing, were directed at the younger set. Folk, a style that grappled with social, cultural, political, and economic issues, had the greatest appeal for older fans.

The Adults in the Room: Brill Building and Aldon Publishing.
The return of pre–rock and roll practices in teen pop music can be seen clearly in the Brill Building music of the early 1960s. The Brill Building is an actual place, but "Brill Building" is also a stylistic label and refers to a set of business practices (much like "Tin Pan Alley"). Located in midtown Manhattan, the building housed many of the most important and established music publishers. The business practices of Aldon Music, run by Al Nevins and Don Kirshner, provide an example of how Brill Building pop worked. The Aldon offices (located nearby at 1650 Broadway) contained a number of small rooms equipped with pianos, where songwriters or songwriting teams would work all day writing new pop songs. Carole King and Gerry Goffin, Cynthia Weil and Barry Mann, and Neil Sedaka and Howard Greenfield were some of the best-known professional songwriters at Aldon, turning out a new song every day or so and competing to have their song recorded next. (Jeff Barry and Ellie Greenwich worked in a similar manner for Trio Music, while Doc Pomus and Mort Shuman wrote for Hill and Range Songs.) Once a song was selected by Aldon, it was then matched to the appropriate performing group, who were almost never the songwriters themselves. A professional producer organized the session and professional studio musicians would record the tune, which might be released on any of a number of record labels. This was a very methodical way of producing pop music, with duties assigned to specialists and songs cranked out with machine-like efficiency and precision. In such a situation, the actual recording artist was not at the center of the process. The Brill Building approach—which extended to many other publishers—was one way that professionals in the music business established more control after rock and roll's first wave. In the Brill Building practice, there were no unpredictable or rebellious singers, and none of the songs had lyrics that might offend middle-class sensibilities. Brill Building songs were written to order by professionals who could customize music and lyrics for the targeted teen audience. In many ways, the Brill Building approach was a return to typical business practices before rock and roll: it returned power to the publishers and made the performing artists more peripheral to the music's production. The public, however, focused on these performers, with teen idols and girl groups (discussed later) becoming the principal means of delivering Brill Building tunes to the pop audience. (See What's That Source? for more about the Brill Building.)

Teen Idols for Idle Teens.
The rise of Pat Boone and Elvis during the first wave established two distinct types of teen idol: the "good boy"—a clean-cut and respectable young man middle-class parents would allow their daughters to date—and the "bad boy"—a tough, sex-obsessed hoodlum whom parents tried hard to keep their girls away from. (These good- and bad-boy roles would be reworked in the 1960s, with the Rolling Stones cast as troublemakers and the Beatles as the

WHAT'S THAT SOURCE?

The rise of rock and roll in the mid-1950s led to many changes in the infrastructure of the music industry. Still, there was a strong core of songwriting and publishing in the music business, situated mainly in large urban areas such as New York City. The Brill Building (at 1619 Broadway) and its lesser-known sibling at 1650 Broadway were at the center of popular music publishing on the East Coast of the United States. This selection from Ken Emerson's *Always Magic in the Air* helps depict the inner workings of this industry center, the relationship between the Brill Building model and Tin Pan Alley, and the differences between the music created in these two buildings.

In the late 1950s, the Brill Building retained a certain raffishness. A bookie would interrupt songwriting sessions to retrieve the betting slips he stashed in a piano. Enterprising writers continued to start on the top floor and work their way down. "If they had a song that was so-so but they could sell," recalled Ed Cramer, an attorney who became head of BMI, "they'd get $25 for an advance, and they'd sell it five times before they hit the first floor. It was like *The Producers*. The song wasn't going to make it so no one would ever know the difference." Still, by now the Brill Building had settled into stodgy semi-respectability. One major publisher nearly fired a young secretary for wearing a sweater to work. "It could just as well have been an insurance company," she recalled.

"The Brill Building was the real old-timers," one reporter observed, "the 'Shine On, Harvest Moon' guys." Many of them belonged to ASCAP, the oldest and most exclusive performing rights organization, whose membership requirements and old-boy network strongly favored traditional Tin Pan Alley, Broadway, and Hollywood composers. "They never let country songwriters in, and rock 'n' roll neither," said one record company executive. "It had nothing to do with 'artistic.' They didn't want to share the pie." Gene Autry once complained that it was easier to get into the White House than into ASCAP. BMI, on the other hand, had been founded by radio broadcasters, and its open-door policy made it a haven for writers of country-and-western

charming, good boys.) During his stint in the army, Elvis's image was carefully reformed, suggesting that the strict discipline of army life had made a respectable man out of him. By 1957, it was clear that preteen and younger teenage girls were very eager to buy—or have their parents buy—records by young, handsome men singing songs about love. These "good-boy" teen idols were cast as ideal boyfriends: well-groomed and attractive, sensitive, and absolutely not interested in anything more than holding hands and an occasional kiss. It was another indication of how poorly regarded rock and roll was within the music business that record companies figured anybody could be a rock singer; if the songs were written by pros and the backing music was played by experienced studio musicians, all that was needed was somebody who could carry a tune, or be coached to do so. The crucial thing was that these teen idols look and act the part effectively.

Teen idols recorded for both independent and major labels with almost equal success between 1957 and 1963 (although the indies involved were usually not those that had previously released rock and roll). Philadelphia produced an especially high number of teen idol hits in this period, including Frankie Avalon's "Dede Dinah" (p7 r8, 1958) and "Venus" (p1 r10, 1959), Bobby Rydell's "Wild One" (p2 r10, 1960), and Freddy Cannon's "Palisades Park" (p3 r15, 1962). Other teen idols with hits included Bobby Vee ("Take Good Care of My Baby"; p1, 1961), Bobby Vinton ("Roses Are Red"; p1 r5, 1962), and three singers who wrote many of their

music (like Autry) and rhythm and blues and rock 'n' roll (like Leiber and Stoller). The competition between the two organizations regularly spilled over into Congress and the courts. At one point Sinatra's lawyer, Mickey Rudin, sued BMI on behalf of thirty-three ASCAP songwriters. The wrangles pitted generation against generation, genres against genres. While the Brill Building was a bastion of ASCAP writers and publishers, BMI probably represented a greater percentage of the tenants at 1650 Broadway, two blocks uptown and across the street, just past the Winter Garden, where *West Side Story* opened on September 26, 1957.

Many of 1650's occupants then were as young as the musical's Sharks and Jets. Built in 1922, 1650 Broadway was nearly a decade older than the Brill Building and a couple of stories taller, but many of the Brill Building writers looked down on it. Nameless and opening on Fifty-first Street rather than Broadway, it appeared as if it had been "dropped in by helicopter," one songwriter recalled, contrasting its anonymity to the "very plush and regal" Brill Building.

Like the Brill Building, 1650 was a model of what one music historian called "vertical integration." Among its warren of offices you could find publishers to buy a song, arrangers to arrange it, and musicians and singers to record on cheap acetate in a bare-bones studio a "demo," or demonstration record, that served as the song's calling card and blueprint. A demo could cost as little as $60 and became increasingly valuable with the rise of rock 'n' roll, whose impresarios, producers, and performers were often unable to read music.

"Sixteen-fifty to me was the hip building," recalled Hank Medress, a founding member with Neil Sedaka of the Tokens. "The Brill Building was really holding on to the past of Tin Pan Alley. The Brill Building is always depicted as *the* place, but actually it was the cornier. Sixteen-fifty was cool, more progressive." Singer Tony Orlando, who worked in 1650 but married a Brill Building secretary, said there "was a little bit of a competitive thing" between the two addresses. "They were much like two high schools. It was like 'The people in that building aren't as contemporary as the people in *our* building.'" Sixteen-fifty saw the Brill Building as old-line publishers.

The youthfulness and glitz of 1650 Broadway made it more receptive, by and large, to rock 'n' roll. According to Jay Siegal, another member of the Tokens, "Sixteen-fifty was a little easier to get access to. . . . At the Brill Building you needed an appointment. You had to know the secretary to get in. At Sixteen-fifty, you banged on the door and most people would let you in and say, 'Well, whaddya got?'"

Source: Ken Emerson, *Always Magic in the Air* (Penguin, 2005), 20–23.

own songs: Paul Anka ("Diana"; p1 r1, 1957), Bobby Darin ("Dream Lover"; p2 r4, 1959), and Neil Sedaka ("Breaking Up Is Hard to Do"; p1 r12, 1962). Although teen idols were usually white (many were from Italian descent), they often found popularity among black audiences, with Bobby Rydell, Freddy Cannon, and Neil Sedaka all scoring Top 20 R&B hits during this period. Fabian Forte's "Turn Me Loose" (p9, 1959), a product of Bob Marcucci's Philadelphia-based Chancellor label, is a good example of the musical problems that the teen-idol adaptation of rock and roll could produce for first-wave rock fans. The song was written by Brill Building songwriters Doc Pomus and Mort Shuman and the backup playing is proficient but nondescript—another day at the office for these musicians. Fabian's vocals are tenuous, creating the impression that he can just barely sing the tune. For many listeners who had experienced the excitement of the first recordings of Elvis and Little Richard, this was discouragingly tame stuff. Like many teen idols, Fabian's appearances on television and in films allowed him to appeal visually to audiences and were central to his success as a recording artist.

The emergence of the teen idols in the late 1950s inaugurated a segment of the market that has since been termed "bubblegum music." Despite the cynical system in which this strategically accommodating music was produced, there were some genuine highlights. Paul Anka, Neil Sedaka, and Bobby Darin all got their starts as teen idols, and each later translated that success into a career in songwriting and

Teen idols Fabian (left) and Frankie Avalon (right) are shown here with cheerleaders from Fairleigh Dickenson University. After the controversy that surrounded Elvis, Jerry Lee Lewis, and the payola scandal, record labels promoted clean-cut teen idols who were unlikely to offend. These singers projected the image of the "perfect boyfriend"—well groomed, attractive, and sensitive—and embraced a smooth, tame vocal style.

performing for a broader audience. Though their packaging would transform to follow changing fashions, ideal boyfriends would continue to be marketed to young girls for decades afterward. In the early 1960s, teen idols were marketed on the radio and special television shows devoted to teen pop, the most important of which was *American Bandstand*.

The Dance Craze, *American Bandstand,* and "The Twist."

By the early 1960s, many American teenagers were in the habit of heading straight home from school to watch a new television show developed especially for them. The idea of *American Bandstand* was simple: get a bunch of teenagers together in the studio, play current hit records as they dance, and have a few musical guests "performing" their most recent hits. *Bandstand* was another instance of the migration of entertainment from radio to TV. The show was essentially a rock and roll radio program adapted for television. Although he made it famous, Dick Clark was not the first host of the program. Bob Horn was the host when the show debuted on Philadelphia's WFIL in 1952, but was fired in 1956 after a series of personal problems. *Bandstand* was not the only television rock and roll show, but it was the one that survived and succeeded. Debuting nationally on the ABC network in 1957, the show was broadcast every weekday afternoon and on Saturday nights. In his first years of network broadcast, Dick Clark had almost every important rock and roll performer on his show. Unlike Jerry Lee Lewis on *The Steve Allen Show* or Elvis on *Toast of the Town, Bandstand* appearances were almost always lip-synched—another symptom of the industry's perceived need to control the music. There was no throwing of piano benches or provocative hip swiveling—just good clean fun and dancing. Of course, the lip-synching practice worked out well for the teen idols who were often featured performers on Clark's show, many of whom looked the part and could dance, but had less public performance experience than many of the first-wave performers.

Most of the focus of *American Bandstand* was not on these controlled "performances," however; it was on dancing. Dancing had never been absent from rock and roll, especially since dancing was the crucial substitute for references to sex in the original rhythm and blues that so much rock and roll appropriated. But during the first wave, dancing was often secondary, as the performance itself was the focus of the experience. The high profile of Clark's show created heightened interest in dancing to pop music. For example, in 1960 Clark introduced a cover version of Hank Ballard's "The Twist" by a young singer named Ernest Evans, who went by the stage name Chubby Checker (compare with Fats Domino). The record quickly rose to number one on the pop charts (r2) and initiated a craze for named dances: the fly, the fish, and the mashed potato were among those that would be demonstrated by the teens on Clark's show. The popularity of the twist reached far beyond youth culture, as even affluent Manhattan socialites began frequenting the

Peppermint Lounge in New York City to do the twist—prompting a hit spin-off song, Joey Dee's "Peppermint Twist" (pl r8, 1962). Hoping to re-create the previous year's success, Checker released "Let's Twist Again" in 1961, which rose as high as number eight. "The Twist" then returned to the number-one slot for a second time in 1962 (r4), a feat that had been accomplished only by Bing Crosby's "White Christmas."

While *American Bandstand* was responsible for igniting the early 1960s dance craze, its greater importance is the role it came to play in representing America's youth. Having a network television show dedicated to young people reinforced the idea that there was a national youth culture, and while there might be regional differences in the way people spoke and acted, when it came to music most teens were united by a common bond. Movies featuring well-known musicians also played a role in building this sense of community and shared concern. Elvis—at this point as much a teen idol as anything else—was making family-oriented films, and Frankie Avalon (among many other teen idols) made the jump to movies, appearing in a series of music- and dance-filled, teen-targeted beach movies with Annette Funicello (who had been a Mouseketeer on the original *Mickey Mouse Club* television show). As commercially successful as movie and television exposure was for pop music in the early 1960s, it also prepared the way for the Beatles—a group as charming as they were musically talented, who would become the darlings of television and movie audiences. *American Bandstand* also helped make rock and roll more acceptable to adults. Although the show had been designed to appeal to teens, Clark soon discovered that adults were tuning in too. He has remarked that he considers "The Twist" to be one of the most important songs in the history of rock and roll because its reception constituted the first time that most adults could freely admit that they liked rock and roll. Hardliners might reply that this is precisely the problem: rock and roll should be about resistance to adult culture, not assimilation into it. But like "(We're Gonna) Rock around the Clock" appearing in *Blackboard Jungle* and Elvis achieving mainstream success, the popularity of "The

Dick Clark, host of *American Bandstand*, 1959. Unlike Elvis's performance on Ed Sullivan's show or Jerry Lee Lewis's performance on Steve Allen's, *Bandstand* was just good, clean fun: lip-synched performances by current pop stars with teenagers dancing. Clark's show featured both black and white artists and was seen as a force for racial integration.

Twist," *American Bandstand*, and teen movies clearly indicated that rock and roll was becoming firmly established within American culture.

Folk Music and the Putting Away of Childish Things. While teens and their parents were enjoying *American Bandstand*, many college-age listeners were looking for music more consistent with their new standing as adults. They may have consigned rock and roll to their high school past, but many were not quite ready to enter the cultural world of their parents. Some remained devoted to first-wave rock, others assimilated into adult culture, but many—college students especially—began to enjoy music that seemed more "real" than the mainstream commercial music. As different as it sounded, folk music shared with early rock an "alternative" mindset that preferred music *not* embraced by the mainstream. Some older listeners were attracted to jazz, blues, or classical music, but folk became the most popular style of alternative music among these former rock and rollers.

Folk had enjoyed a certain amount of popular appeal throughout the 1940s, with traditional performers such as Pete Seeger and Woody Guthrie reaching larger audiences, both as soloists and then together in the Almanac Singers. During the first half of the 1950s, the Weavers (with Pete Seeger) had a series of pop hits, including "Good Night Irene" (p1, 1950), "So Long (It's Been Good to Know Ya)" (p4, 1951), and "On Top of Old Smoky" (p2 c8, 1951). Folk had a long history of addressing the problems faced by the less fortunate in American society, and folk singers often advocated social change from a markedly left-wing political position. As a consequence, many folk artists ran into problems during the Red Scare of the early 1950s, as the U.S. government vigorously attempted to identify communists within its borders. The Weavers' career, for instance, was cut short when they were

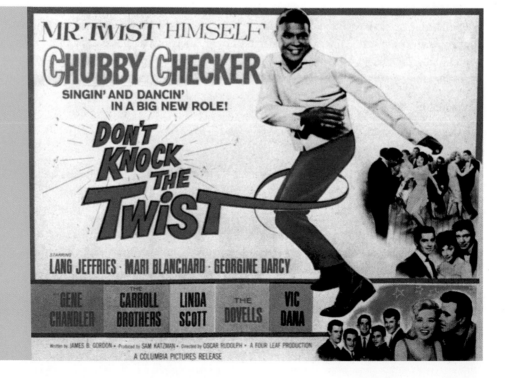

Chubby Checker is shown here dancing the twist on a 1962 film poster. Dick Clark, host of *American Bandstand*, said that "The Twist" was one of rock and roll's most important songs: it swept the nation (and reached into Europe), and everyone, young, old, black, and white, could all do the dance with ease.

One of the most important groups in American folk was the Weavers: (from left) Ronnie Gilbert, Pete Seeger, Lee Hayes, and Fred Hellerman. Characterized by its focus on social issues and musical and instrumental simplicity, folk appealed to a college (and decidedly nonteen) audience. After many hits, the Weavers' career was cut short when they were blacklisted for reportedly being sympathetic to the Communist Party.

blacklisted for reportedly being in sympathy with the Communist Party. By the mid-1950s, politically engaged folk music was forced out of mainstream pop. Only a few years later, however, fueled largely by its appeal to college audiences and down-playing any overt political connections, folk music experienced a revival that pushed it back into the pop mainstream. By the early 1960s, some folk artists were once again openly political, as many aligned themselves with the civil rights movement and, later, the opposition to the Vietnam War.

One of the key components of folk that attracted many listeners was its marked populist character. Folk seemed to be devoted to a greater sense of community than commercial pop: to its adherents, it was music for regular people, performed by regular people. Folk performers were not perceived to be above their audience; they were thought to be in some sense representative of it. Virtuosic or theatrical performance practices were rejected in favor of unpretentious and direct musical expression. Folk lyrics frequently told stories that illustrated various kinds of societal problems, and the meaning of the lyrics was much more important to folk listeners than the musical prowess of the folk singer, or his or her good looks. No matter how accurate such a description of folk-music culture during the original folk song movement (1935–48) might be, much of the untutored quality of folk singers and their audiences in the later folk revival period (1958–65) was studied and self-conscious. To college-age people who were drawn to it, a big part of folk culture's appeal was its break with the norms of middle-class life. The music itself was in many cases not new to these young people; they had been humming and strumming folk tunes on camping trips and in school music classes almost all their lives. Its democratic ethos, combined with a seriousness of purpose and cultural distinctions from adult culture, made folk music very popular on college campuses by the turn of the decade. One index of the popularity of folk is the steep increase in the number of acoustic guitars that were sold in the United States as collegiate folkniks were popping up throughout the country. Equipped with a passable singing voice and the ability to strum a few easy guitar chords, almost anyone could play it, which reinforced the idea that folk was "for the people and by the people."

The rise of folk was preceded by a brief fascination with calypso music. Harry Belafonte's "Jamaica Farewell" (p14, 1957) and "Banana Boat (Day-O)" (p5 r7, 1957) are the best examples of this easygoing, soft-pop style featuring Caribbean folk inflections that seemed exotic at the time. Inspired by a Pete Seeger performance they heard while auditioning in a San Francisco club, Dave Guard, Bob Shane, and Nick Reynolds began performing folk to collegiate audiences and adopted a name inspired by Belafonte's Jamaican-drenched hits. The Kingston Trio's version of the traditional "Tom Dula"—which they called "Tom Dooley"—began to climb the pop charts in late 1958, hitting number one in early 1959 (r9) and initiating the folk revival in the mainstream pop market. This recording serves as a representative example of the group's easygoing and polished approach, with a carefully scripted verbal introduction to the tune, followed by an elegant arrangement. The Kingston Trio's pop-sensitive approach to folk proved to be a winner; the group placed ten singles in the pop Top 40 between 1958 and 1965, all of which were recorded for Los Angeles–based Capitol, including "Where Have All the Flowers Gone" (p21, 1962) and "Reverend Mr. Black" (p8 r15, 1963).

While pop singles give us some picture of an artists' success in the youth market, a better measure of pop success for folk artists among other listeners is album sales. Long-playing 33-rpm records were only a secondary concern for teen-oriented pop acts, but they were the primary format for two other "serious" styles of music at the time: jazz and classical. It suited the cultural aspirations of folk listeners to be part of the more sophisticated, album-buying—as opposed to singles-buying—public. Accordingly, the Kingston Trio had a series of nineteen Top 40 albums through 1964; thirteen of these reached the Top 10, including five number-one albums. The group's first album, *The Kingston Trio* (1958), stayed on the pop-album charts for 195 weeks. In the early 1960s, the Kingston Trio was among the most consistently

The Kingston Trio—(from left) Bob Shane, Nick Reynolds, and Dave Guard—at a recording session. The group was the most popular of the "folk revival" of the late '50s and early '60s. Their first album, *The Kingston Trio* (1958), stayed on the pop-album charts for 195 weeks.

Listening Guide

The Kingston Trio, "Tom Dooley" Capital 45-CL 14951

Words and music by Frank Warner, John Lomax, and Alan Lomax, produced by Voile Gillmore. Released in 1958 as a single and on the album *The Kingston Trio*. Reached #1 on the *Billboard* "Hot 100" chart and #9 on the "Hot R&B Sides" chart in 1959.

FORM: Simple verse-chorus, beginning with the chorus. The entire song repeats the same 8-bar music for verses and choruses. The verses are presented the same way each time, with the lead vocal supported by two-part backups. The chorus is presented first in unison (all three voices sing the same notes), then in three-part harmony, and then in a more complicated arrangement for three voices that introduces a new melody over the chorus melody. The last 2 bars of the chorus are repeated three times, a technique often used to close out a tune and called a **"tag."**

TIME SIGNATURE: 12/8, a gently rolling four-beat feel.

INSTRUMENTATION: Acoustic guitar, banjo, acoustic bass, lead vocal, and two backup vocals.

0:00–0:28	**Introduction**, 16 mm.	Spoken introduction, banjo plays melody.
0:28–0:46	**Chorus**, 8 mm.	Choral unison vocal, strummed rhythm kicks in, "Hang down your head . . ."
0:46–1:01	**Verse 1**, 8 mm.	Solo vocal w/ backup vocals, "I met her on the mountain . . ."
1:01–1:16	**Chorus**, 8 mm.	Three-part harmony vocal introduced, "Hang down your head . . ."
1:16–1:32	**Verse 2**, 8 mm.	Solo vocal w/ backups as before, "This time tomorrow . . . Tennessee."
1:32–1:47	**Chorus**, 8 mm.	Energetic new solo melody against two-part harmony, music gets much louder, "Hang down your head . . ."
1:47–2:02	**Chorus**, 8 mm.	New texture continues, "Hang down your head . . ."
2:02–2:17	**Verse 3**, 8 mm.	Music gets quiet again, solo vocal w/ backups as before, "This time tomorrow . . . tree."
2:17–2:32	**Chorus**, 8 mm.	Three-part harmony vocal as in first chorus presentation, "Hang down your head . . ."
2:32–3:00	**Chorus**, 14 mm.	Music gets louder, energetic 8-bar chorus is extended by tag.

successful acts in popular music and in many ways defined folk music for most general listeners.

In the years that followed the first hit records of the Kingston Trio, two sides of the folk revival developed. Listeners interested in folk's roots and tradition began exploring the rich literature of folk that had already begun to be documented by musicologists and folklorists such as Charles Seeger and Alan Lomax in the preceding decades. Singers such as Joan Baez and Bob Dylan emerged from this side of the folk revival, gaining popularity and respect among the folkniks; neither produced a hit single during this period, but both had Top 40 albums. To the discriminating fan, singers like Baez and Dylan were the real thing. The Kingston Trio, and other groups that followed in their wake such as the Highwaymen ("Michael Row the Boat Ashore"; p1, 1961), the Rooftop Singers ("Walk Right In"; p1 r3 c23, 1963), and the New Christy Minstrels ("Green Green"; p14, 1963), were oriented much more toward the pop market. Other pop-oriented groups that had successful albums but no hit singles were the Chad Mitchell Trio and the Limelighters. But however much uncompromising folk fans disparaged the Kingston Trio and other commercially successful folk groups, by music-business standards these acts were enormously successful and many within the business sought to stoke the fire that was now burning under folk music.

Formed in New York's Greenwich Village in 1961, the group known as Peter, Paul, and Mary eventually eclipsed the Kingston Trio as the most successful folk-pop group of the 1960s. After the success of "Lemon Tree" (p35, 1962), they followed up with "If I Had a Hammer" (p10, 1962), "Puff the Magic Dragon" (p2 r10, 1962), and a cover of Bob Dylan's "Blowin' in the Wind" (p2, 1963). The group released ten Top 40 albums during the decade: two hit number one, and their first album, *Peter, Paul, and Mary* (1962), stayed on the album charts for 185 weeks. The members of the group all had different musical backgrounds: Peter Yarrow had been a solo folk artist, Paul Stookey had played in a rock and roll band, and Mary Travers had sung in the chorus of an unsuccessful Broadway musical. While he was a full-fledged folkie, Yarrow was working as a stand-up comic when the group formed, and Travers was just getting back into singing. Manager Albert Grossman was responsible for bringing the group together, and the idea from the start was to capitalize on the folk revival ignited by the Kingston Trio. Peter, Paul, and Mary were assembled much the way other pop acts were put together. One might suspect that an act born of such music-business calculating would be rejected by the folk community, which often made a show of denouncing commercialism. But even though part of their fame rested on slick, pop-flavored cover versions of Bob Dylan originals, Peter, Paul, and Mary were mostly well received by die-hard folkniks, perhaps owing to their strong commitment to the civil rights protest movement. Their lasting popularity was a result of the group's ability to represent both strains of the folk revival, maintaining a believable sense of authenticity and an approachable performance style.

A comparison of Peter, Paul, and Mary's version of "Blowin' in the Wind" with Dylan's illustrates important differences between the folk music of this period. While Dylan makes no concessions to pop sensibilities, the Peter, Paul, and Mary version is professionally sung, played, and arranged (by Milton Okun)—increasing its likelihood of appealing to a pop audience. At the time, Dylan's performance would have seemed too rough and amateurish for pop radio. Of course, such perceptions of Dylan's marketability would change dramatically later in the decade when American folk rock emerged as a response to the music of the Beatles and other British bands (see Chapter 5). For now, it is enough to point out that folk's image of sincerity and authenticity—as it was perceived by pop audiences in the early 1960s—was largely constructed by the music industry. Like the old adage—"sincerity: if you can fake that you've got it made"—folk performers worked carefully to project a homespun image. (This parallels the "construction of authenticity" discussed in Chapter 1

Peter, Paul, and Mary—(from left) Paul Stookey, Mary Travers, and Peter Yarrow—was a group constructed not for the small coffeehouses that had been the traditional home of folk, but for larger concert halls. Even though their music was decidedly more polished than that of many folk artists, die-hard folkniks embraced the group—in part because of their passionate involvement in the civil rights movement.

regarding the development of the *Grand Ole Opry* and the country music business.) Such constructions of authenticity bear out the notion that no matter what sort of image a performer projects, he or she is still part of the entertainment business. Even if a performer actually is sincere and homespun in his or her everyday personal manner, it will never be enough simply to show up and be oneself; these qualities must be projected from the stage, and most performers must learn how to do this. The issue of authenticity will return in later chapters, since later rock musicians (the singer-songwriters especially) used the perceived authenticity of the folk revival as a model of artistic integrity.

The similarities between folk music and Brill Building pop are striking; these styles were indeed two faces of the same music business in the early 1960s. Each was carefully crafted to appeal to a distinct age group within the youth culture. The images of the two styles contrasted strongly—pop was superficial and cute, folk was serious-minded and intellectually engaging—but the business mechanisms that marketed the music were often the same. Both folk and Brill Building pop were strikingly polite in comparison to the first wave of rock and roll, and much of this family orientation can be attributed to the control being exercised within the music business during this period.

AMBITIOUS POP: THE RISE OF THE PRODUCER

Some of the most enduring pop songs of this period were created by well-known producers such as Leiber and Stoller and Phil Spector. To understand this aspect of early 1960s music, we must understand just what a "producer" is. During the early years of rock and roll, many performers brought their own fully worked-up arrangements of songs from the country and western and rhythm and blues repertoires into the recording studio. Less often, as with Chuck Berry and Buddy Holly, the songs were written by the artists. But regardless of who wrote the songs, many early rock and roll artists had a strong voice in the recording process, deciding what would be recorded and how the song would be arranged. In mainstream pop, by contrast, artists used songs written and arranged by professionals. Most record companies employed A&R (artists and repertoire) people whose job was to organize and coordinate the various professionals involved in making the record, including hiring the musicians who played on the tracks. This was an early version of the record producer. The mainstream pop approach put more of the crucial decision-making authority in the hands of the A&R man, leaving the artists relatively powerless. For example, Buddy Holly's unsuccessful sessions for Decca were the result of an A&R man who had no feel for Holly's strengths and weaknesses. As the business took greater control of rock and roll, the mainstream pop model became the norm for making rock and roll records. But as this aspect of the business was changing, the role of the A&R man/producer also shifted, and the role of the record producer began to develop. Replacing the mostly organizational role of the label's A&R man, the producer became a specialist in charge of shaping the sound of a record, from the details of arranging to fine points in the recording process, such as microphone placement or equalization. In some cases, the record became the result of the producer's vision rather than that of the artist or songwriter. In most cases, the producer, not the performing artists, was responsible to the record company for how a record turned out.

The first important production team was Jerry Leiber and Mike Stoller. Their success with a variety of artists was imitated by others such as Carole King and Gerry Goffin, Shadow Morton, and, perhaps most important, Phil Spector. As the role of the producer in pop developed, there was parallel growth in the ambition with which song ideas were executed. Producers increasingly experimented with ways to make their records more musically sophisticated, some establishing a trademark "sound" that distinguished their records. Drawing from classical music and musical theater, as well as sounds available only in the recording studio, early 1960s teen pop records initiated an important shift away from the idea that a record should represent a recorded version of a live performance (as it had been until then) to the concept of a record as a kind of performance in its own right. This increased focus on the recording studio and the sounds it could produce would resonate in almost all rock music that followed.

Leiber and Stoller with the Coasters. During the early 1950s Jerry Leiber and Mike Stoller were the most important songwriting team in rock and roll. They had roots in the West Coast rhythm and blues scene and enjoyed hits on the R&B charts such as Charles Brown's "Hard Times" (r7, 1952), Big Mama Thornton's original version of "Hound Dog" (r1, 1953), and the Robins' "Smokey Joe's Cafe" (r10, 1955). In 1956, Elvis Presley's version of "Hound Dog" went to number one on the pop charts (r1 c1), prompting the team to write more songs for Presley, including "Jailhouse Rock" (p1 r1 c1, 1957) and "Don't" (p1 r4 c2, 1958). Almost from the beginning, Leiber and Stoller wanted more control over the recording process than songwriters were typically allowed. In 1953, they formed their own label in Los

Angeles, Spark Records, and began "producing" their songs in what would soon become the standard sense of the term. The pair has often said, "We don't write songs, we write records." In many ways, Leiber and Stoller already had a clear idea of how a record should sound before the performers entered the studio, and the artists' task became more a matter of realizing Leiber and Stoller's concept for the song rather than finding their own interpretation of the tune.

Leiber and Stoller had already produced three rhythm and blues hits with the Robins on Spark when they got an offer to produce records for Atlantic. The duo had found the business end of running an independent label to be unrewarding, so they welcomed the chance to move to a bigger label and leave the bookkeeping chores behind. The arrangement they made with Atlantic was exceptional for its time: rather than become A&R men working exclusively for the label, as was the industry norm, Leiber and Stoller retained the right to work with other artists and labels, making them among the first independent producers in pop music. They had had great success working with the Robins and wanted to take the group with them to Atlantic, but disagreement over the move meant only two members went with Leiber and Stoller. Two new members were added and the new group was called the Coasters; this group became the focus of Leiber and Stoller's most creative work over the next several years.

The Coasters recorded "playlets": short songs that often told a humorous story. In writing for the Coasters, Leiber and Stoller were inspired by Broadway and radio play traditions. As Jerry Leiber has remarked, the very first song they wrote for the Robins, "Riot in Cell Block #9," was inspired by a radio show called *Gangbusters*. The Coasters would frequently act the lyrics out in performance, sometimes using costumes, emphasizing the similarity to the Broadway stage. There were clear connections to older forms of vaudeville and minstrelsy in these playlets. Some Coasters' records also deal with teen life, like the songs of Chuck Berry, the Everly Brothers, or Ricky Nelson, discussed later in this chapter. Of these, "Yakety Yak" (p1 r1, 1958)—about household chores and teenage disputes with parents—and "Charlie Brown" (p2 r2, 1959)—about a kid who always gets in trouble at school—were the most

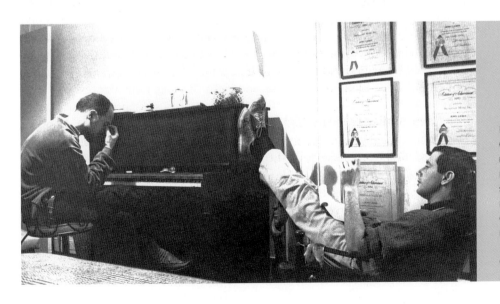

Mike Stoller (left) and Jerry Leiber (right) helped define the important role producers would play in the music of the early 1960s. Their songs were characterized by strong rhythm and blues influences and complex arrangements, often recounting mini-dramas (called "playlets"), as in "Smokey Joe's Cafe" and "Down in Mexico."

The Coasters were important collaborators with Leiber and Stoller. This team produced a number of hits, including the playlets "Smokey Joe's Cafe" (when the Coasters were still the Robins) and "Down in Mexico."

popular. Mostly, however, the playlets dealt with topics in black culture and were directed at a black audience (even if they also became popular with white audiences). Original Coasters member Carl Gardner has marveled at how two white songwriters so expertly captured aspects of black culture. Leiber and Stoller responded, "We thought we were black—we were wrong, but that's what we thought." The producers had considerable control over their records with the Coasters, though group members were free to change things or reject entire numbers they didn't like. Nevertheless, many aspects of the arrangements were composed in advance. Stoller, who was trained as a classical composer, even wrote out many of the saxophone lines played by Atlantic session man King Curtis that became closely associated with hits like "Yakety Yak," "Charlie Brown," and "Along Came Jones" (p9 r14, 1959).

"Smokey Joe's Cafe" and "Down in Mexico" are early examples of playlets by the Coasters. "Smokey Joe's Cafe" was recorded when the Coasters were still the Robins, and was initially released on Spark in 1955. After Leiber and Stoller signed with Atlantic, the song was rereleased on the Atlantic subsidiary Atco and rose to number ten on the rhythm and blues charts (but only as far as number seventy-nine on the pop charts). The lyrics proceed in an AABA formal pattern: two verses develop the story, a bridge brings the action to a climax, and a return of the verse forms a kind of epilogue. In this case, the singer is sitting in Smokey Joe's Cafe when a sexy woman sits next to him and starts to flirt. Other patrons warn him about the woman's jealous boyfriend just as the boyfriend emerges from the kitchen, wielding a knife and telling the singer to finish his meal and get out. In the last verse the singer explains that he'll never go into that café again. "Down in Mexico" reached number eight on the rhythm and blues charts in 1956 but missed the pop charts entirely. This song takes the barroom action south of the border; in the first two verses, we hear about a "honky tonk, down in Mexico." A guy named Joe who works at the bar "wears a red bandana" and "plays a blues piana." The bridge narrates how a scantily clad dancer enters the bar to the accompaniment of Joe's piano playing; she grabs the singer and dances with him, doing "a dance I never saw before." The last verse advises listeners to visit the bar if they're ever in the neighborhood. Both of these songs are clear extensions of the hokum blues discussed in Chapter 1 in connection with Big Joe Turner's "Shake, Rattle, and Roll," complete with themes of seduction that were hardly the kind of thing that would sell to white listeners in the mid-1950s. Leiber and Stoller's production makes the south-of-the-border theme more vivid through the use of Mexican-sounding nylon-string guitars and percussion. The bridge is sung to music the dancer might have performed to, a kind of Latin striptease with emphasis on the conga drums.

As unsuited as these two early playlets might have been for white radio, it is interesting to compare them to "Little Egypt (Ying Yang)," a number-sixteen rhythm and blues hit that reached number twenty-three on the pop charts. Here,

Listening Guide

The Coasters, "Down in Mexico" Atco 6064

Words and music by Jerry Leiber and Mike Stoller, produced by Leiber and Stoller. Reached #8 on the *Billboard* R&B "Most Played in Juke Boxes" chart in 1956.

FORM: AABA form. Each 16-bar verse is divided into an 8-bar section with lyrics that change from verse to verse, and a refrain that begins with the lyrics "He wears a red bandana" (most refrains are not as lengthy as this one). The bridge repeats a 2-bar section eight times, building to the song's comic punchline. Note the dramatic introduction and the spoken fade-out, both of which heighten the comedy of this classic playlet.

TIME SIGNATURE: 4/4. There are three distinct Latin-tinged feels on this track, one with the first half of the verse, another with the second half of the verse (refrain), and a third with the bridge. These changes of feel are unusual in pop music of the time, and reinforce the influence of Broadway stage numbers, in which such changes are common.

INSTRUMENTATION: Piano, bass, electric guitar, nylon-string guitar, percussion, lead and backup vocals. Mike Stoller plays piano on this (and most) Coasters tracks. Famous jazz guitarist Barney Kessel plays guitar on this track.

0:00–0:21	**Introduction**, 6 mm., 2 mm.	Rubato (sax and guitar), and then 4 mm. in time to begin sultry Latin feel.
0:21–0:57	**A-Verse 1 with refrain**, 16 mm., 8 mm. verse + 8 mm. refrain	The verse uses the sultry Latin feel, while the refrain uses a brighter Latin feel employing nylon-string guitar and castanets, "Down in . . ."
0:57–1:32	**A-Verse 2 with refrain**, 16 mm.	As before, "The first time . . ."
1:32–2:06	**B-Bridge**, 16 mm., eight 2 mm. phrases	Employing a more violent Latin feel to suggest a sensual dance show, building to the song's dynamic high point, "All of a sudden . . ."
2:06–3:13	**A-Verse 3 with refrain**, 16 mm.	As before, then fade on intro material, "If you're . . ."

the Mexican scene is shifted to a carnival, and the seductress is a belly dancer. The first two verses describe this dancer, Little Egypt, who wears "nuttin' but a button and a bow" and does "the hootchie-kootchie real slow." The bridge pulls back from being too suggestive, describing instead an acrobatic performance during which she reveals a picture of a cowboy tattooed on her back. The last verse says that Little Egypt no longer dances because now she and the singer are married and she is busy taking care of their seven children. The final verse also features the singing of high, speeded-up voices (similar to those of Alvin and the Chipmunks from the same period), meant to be those of the children, and creating an almost irresistible comic effect. Despite its clear connections to songs with a more adult theme, this playlet represents both literally and figuratively a domestication of the topic and thus serves as another instance of the changes needed for a crossover to be possible for a rhythm and blues song. Like the Chuck Berry lyrics discussed in Chapter 2, Leiber and Stoller's lyrics can also be read on more than one level. "What About Us" from 1959 (p47 r17) is a thinly veiled comment on racial inequality. "Run Red Run" hit number thirty-six on the pop charts in early 1960 (r29) and tells the story of a monkey whose owner, Red, teaches him how to play poker. When the monkey learns to play, he also learns that Red has been cheating him. The monkey grabs a gun and chases Red until he catches him, takes his keys, watch, hat, and suit, and heads back into town. While the lyrics seem to focus the listener's attention on the comedy of a man being chased around town by a gun-toting monkey, the deeper message addresses the exploitation of blacks in American culture. Leiber and Stoller claim to have many more socially motivated songs that were never recorded, partly because the Coasters were not interested in becoming controversial.

The Important Collaboration between Songwriter/Producers and Performers.
Leiber and Stoller had considerable control over their records with the Coasters, though group members were free to change things or reject entire numbers they didn't like. Many aspects of the arrangements were composed in advance. Stoller, who was trained as a classical composer, even wrote out many of the saxophone lines played by King Curtis that became so closely associated with the pop hits "Yakety Yak," "Charlie Brown," and "Along Came Jones" (p9, 1959). As important as the unprecedented degree of control that Leiber and Stoller exercised in producing these records, was the close and long-lasting relationship the duo formed with the Coasters; both were essential elements in the success of those records.

In composing playlets such as "Smokey Joe's Cafe," "Down in Mexico," "Shoppin' for Clothes," and "Little Egypt," Leiber and Stoller drew from a broad range of music styles, often blending these within a single track. In 1959, they recorded "There Goes My Baby" with the Drifters (featuring Ben E. King at the time), and the song's arrangement employed the orchestra in a manner reminiscent of classical music. This blending of easygoing rhythm and blues with orchestral backing would soon be dubbed "sweet soul" and will be discussed in more detail later in this chapter. Such a stylistic blending was unusual for its time, prompting Atlantic's Jerry Wexler to remark that "There Goes My Baby" sounded like a radio stuck between two stations.

Taking on Social Issues.
Leiber and Stoller had shown that rock and roll could aspire to greater sophistication: their playlets were carefully crafted to tell a story, and their arrangements employed elements drawn from a wide range of styles. This would seem to make girl-group music a poor prospect for ambitious production, focused as it is in most cases on teen love. But as it turns out, some of the most ambitious pop music during this time came from girl-group records. One of the first records to approach a subject that might have been considered provocative was the Shirelles' "Will You Still Love Me Tomorrow?" (p1, 1960). Produced by Aldon's Carole King and Gerry Goffin (two young songwriter/producers strongly influenced by Leiber and Stoller), this song dealt with a topic many teenage girls

were likely to face during the course of their dating: whether or not to engage in sexual intimacy. While such a topic seems mild by today's standards, in 1960—just as payola and the struggle against the negative influences of rock and roll were beginning to subside—lyrics dealing with teenage sex posed a commercial risk. But King was especially dedicated to this song, at one point taking the mallets and playing the tympani part herself when the professional percussionist could not get it just the way she heard it. Becoming a number-one hit that further fueled the public's enthusiasm for girl-group music, the song addressed the topic with enough thoughtful sensitivity to quell any parental fears. With its serious-minded lyrics and orchestral accompaniment, the song extended the ambition of Leiber and Stoller's productions.

Producers in the Brill Building: The Rise of the Girl Groups. By the late 1950s, Leiber and Stoller's approach to record production had spread throughout the music business. At Aldon Music, the songwriting teams of Neil Sedaka and Howie Greenfield and Carole King and Gerry Goffin began making demonstration records (demos) of their songs, which were sometimes so nicely done that they were released without even being rerecorded. Like Leiber and Stoller, other Brill Building songwriting teams such as Cynthia Weil and Barry Mann and Jeff Berry and Ellie Greenwich were increasingly working in the studio supervising the recording process. By the early 1960s, these producers were directing many female vocal groups, often referred to as "girl groups." The Chantels, Shirelles, Crystals, Chiffons, Cookies, Dixie Cups, and Ronettes were among the many girl groups that appeared during the first half of the 1960s. These groups were mostly composed of black teenagers with little professional experience. (There were some exceptions: Claudine Clark was a singer who had an undergraduate degree in music composition and wrote much of her own music.) A few groups included one male (the

The Brill Building approach to music making involved songwriting teams including Gerry Goffin (left) and Carole King (right). Strongly influenced by Leiber and Stoller, King and Goffin also exerted a great deal of control over the production of their songs.

Exciters) or were made up of white teens (the Angels). Like the teen idols discussed earlier, girl groups provided the performance and image to go with a song. Unlike the teen idols, however, most girl group vocalists were strong singers. Still, in most cases the producer made crucial musical decisions at the session; as a result, the performing talent was almost completely interchangeable. Girls were regularly changed out between recordings and tours and sometimes, as in the case of the Crystals, the entire group could be replaced.

Female singers had not been completely absent from teen pop before the girl groups. Connie Francis enjoyed a string of thirty-nine hit records between 1958 and 1964 (including Neil Sedaka and Howie Greenfield's "Stupid Cupid," which hit number fourteen in 1958), while Connie Stevens ("Kookie, Kookie [Lend Me Your Comb]"; p4, 1959) and Annette Funicello ("Tall Paul"; p7, 1959) also had Top 10 hits. These singers were more or less the female counterparts to the male teen idols. After 1960, many female solo singers such as Little Eva ("The Loco-Motion"; p1 r1, 1962), Mary Wells ("My Guy"; p1 r1, 1964), and Lesley Gore ("It's My Party"; p1 r1, 1963) fit well into the girl-group stylistic category, since most of their records featured backup vocals and thus differed from girl-group records only in terms of image. This easy crossing of the stylistic border between teen-idol and girl-group music underscores the principal similarity between the styles: the Brill Building approach.

More than any other style of music discussed in this chapter, girl-group music was dominated by the industry's drive to control the music. There was no way a performer could rock the boat since so little depended on her. The creative control had shifted from the performer (who, to the public at least, still seemed to be important) to the producers and songwriters (who worked behind the scenes with multiple groups, often having more than one record on the charts at the same time). This system was tremendously successful. Girl groups were responsible for dozens of hit records between 1960 and 1965, including the Shirelles' "Will You Love Me Tomorrow" (p1 r1, 1960) and "Soldier Boy" (p1 r3, 1962), the Crystals' "He's a Rebel" (p1 r2, 1962), the Chiffons' "He's So Fine" (p1 r1, 1963) and "One Fine Day" (p5 r6, 1963), the Angels' "My Boyfriend's Back" (p1 r2, 1963), and the Dixie Cups' "Chapel of Love" (p1, 1964). The combination of mostly African American singers and accessible pop music also helped the girl-group movement achieve consistent crossover success between the pop and rhythm and blues charts.

Phil Spector and the Wall of Sound. Phil Spector was the most ambitious producer of the early 1960s and the most important producer of girl-group pop. While still a teenager in Los Angeles, he had a number-one hit as both a performer and songwriter with the Teddy Bears in 1958 (r10). The idea for the song, "To Know Him Is to Love Him," is reported to have come from the inscription on Spector's father's gravestone. Having tasted national success but being unable to repeat it with subsequent releases, Spector began to work under Leiber and Stoller, helping at sessions and learning how to produce records. More than any other producer during the early 1960s, Spector demanded total control of the recording process. He wanted his records to have a signature sound. While it took him a while to achieve such control, when he did, he developed an approach to production that he called the "Wall of Sound." Most groups, of course, have a distinct sonic identity, often resulting from the singing voices involved. But for Spector, the production was the star of the record, not the group. His trademark sound came from several sources. He often recorded an enormous number of instruments in a relatively small space. Several guitars, pianos, basses, and drum sets could be crammed into one room at Gold Star Studios in Los Angeles. The sound from one instrument would spill into the microphone of the next, and all of this would be mixed together into a monophonic backing track. Moreover, Spector's arrangements supported this wash of sound by including interesting cases of "doubling," a technique that requires two or more instruments (sometimes contrasting in sonic character) to play exactly the same notes, creating a novel combination of instrumental color. Finally, Spector relied on heavy amounts of reverb to thicken up the record's "sound" and blend the instruments and voices. Like the ingredients in a fine sauce, the idea was for a single sonic "taste" to emerge that could not easily be broken down into its component parts. Vocals were layered over this mono backing track, with strings added to finish it off.

The most important Wall of Sound hits are the Crystals' "Da Doo Ron Ron" (p3 r5, 1963) and "Then He Kissed Me" (p6 r8, 1963), featuring the lead vocals of Darlene Love, and the Ronettes' "Be My Baby" (p2 r4, 1963). Written with Jeff Barry and Ellie Greenwich, "Be My Baby" featured the distinctive voice of Ronnie Bennett (who would later become Ronnie Spector). As with almost all his Gold Star sessions, Spector utilized a cast of Los Angeles's top studio musicians, nicknamed the Wrecking Crew and often including drummer Hal Blaine, pianist Leon Russell, bassists Larry Knechtel and Carol Kaye, and guitarists Glen Campbell and Tommy Tedesco. The recording was done on a three-track machine that allowed each track to be recorded separately. The usual procedure was to record the guitars, basses, pianos, and percussion on the first track, all the vocals on the second track, and add the strings on the third track. This three-track version was then mixed down to the mono version that would appear on the record. By the time "Be My Baby" was recorded, Spector had developed a reputation as a perfectionist, asking for multiple playbacks and rerecording until the sound was exactly as he imagined it in his

Phil Spector defined the role of the dominant producer. He ferociously controlled his music—both the songwriting and production. Spector was also an innovator in recording techniques. His "Wall of Sound" was built by packing many instruments into a small room and recording them as they all played together.

head. This method produced some tremendously successful records that were very expensive to make.

"Be My Baby" opens with a heavy drumbeat from Blaine, delivered with plenty of reverberation that establishes a bigness of aural space. Bennett delivers the first two lines of the verse to the accompaniment of the rhythm section. At the lyrics "So won't you say you love me," the background vocals enter with the low saxophone, building to the chorus ("Be my baby"), in which the sound opens up as Bennett's lead vocal is set in call-and-response to the backup vocals and the drum beat changes to create a sense of greater forward drive. After a return to the verse, the second chorus adds another brick to the Wall of Sound by bringing in the strings, which then perform the melody for the abbreviated third verse. After this, the entire ensemble plays out two statements of the chorus, interrupted only by Blaine's drumbeat from the introduction, before beginning the fade-out. The form is simple and the song is short (less than three minutes). But somehow the track created an aural impression of grandness of scale that made it stand out from other songs on the radio.

In addition to their great popularity, Wall of Sound records like "Be My Baby" made an enormous impression on music-industry professionals. Spector referred to these singles as "teenage symphonies," and comparisons to great classical composers and conductors abounded. As a producer, he was characterized as an eccentric genius who followed nothing but his own artistic impulses in creating innovative and ambitious records. Some characterized him as a Wagner-like figure (a reference to the German opera composer, Richard Wagner). The fact that Spector had blended instruments into a single timbral entity made the records almost impossible to cover and added to the mystery of his technique. In the face of the British invasion, Spector continued to have hits, though by the end of 1964 the girl-group sound in which he played such a crucial role began to fade (or at least to migrate to Detroit, as we will see later). However, Spector had yet another production innovation up his sleeve, and the Righteous Brothers' "You've Lost That Lovin' Feelin'," written by Barry Mann, Cynthia Weil, and Spector, was the result. Topping the pop charts in early 1965 (r2), the record was longer and more musically ambitious than anything Spector had tried to that point. After two statements of the verse and chorus sections, the music moves into a bridge section with a contrasting rhythmic feel. It was considered unwise to change the feel of a tune like this because delaying the return of the chorus could prevent listeners from remembering it. Mann, Weil, and Spector may have had similar middle sections from Coasters records in mind when they wrote this song, and the gamble paid off as the record became enormously successful.

Girl-group pop in the early 1960s might be thought of as a study in opposites. It was blatantly commercial: the songs were formulaic and written by pros who tried almost cynically to project a kind of "wholesome" teen lifestyle. But in the hands of producers such as Carole King and Phil Spector, girl-group records became the most artistically ambitious music that rock and roll had yet produced. As innocent and frivolous as some of these records seemed at the time, many would have a lasting impact on the music that followed. The ambitious experimentation that became so characteristic of psychedelic rock of the later 1960s can be traced directly back to groups like the Shirelles and the Ronettes, and we will pick up this story in the chapters that follow.

Listening Guide

The Ronettes, "Be My Baby" Philles 116

Words and music by Phil Spector, Ellie Greenwich, and Jeff Barry, produced by Phil Spector. Reached #2 on the *Billboard* "Hot 100" chart and #4 on the "Hot R&B Singles" chart in 1963.

FORM: Contrasting verse-chorus. Note how verse 1 builds, starting with only the lead vocal for the first 8 bars, then adding backup vocals and saxes for the second 8 bars, and finally bringing all the instruments and vocals in for the chorus, which is clearly the "hook"—the part of the song that sticks in the listener's memory. Verse 2 pulls back again, but not all the way back to the level of verse 1, before building to the chorus. The orchestral strings take the melody in the instrumental verse, though only the first 8 bars are used before breaking into the chorus again. Just when it seems like there's not much more the tune can do, Spector brings back the catchy drum intro and launches once more into the chorus before the track fades out.

TIME SIGNATURE: 4/4. Note the way hand claps and percussion are used to build excitement and drive toward the chorus.

INSTRUMENTATION: Piano, bass, electric guitar, drums, horns, orchestral strings, percussion, hand claps, lead and backup vocals.

0:00–0:08	**Introduction**, 4 mm.	2 mm. drum intro and then 2 mm. in time. Note the heavy reverb on the drums.
0:08–0:37	**Verse 1**, 16 mm.	Solo vocal in first 8 mm., then backup vocals; saxes added in second 8 mm., "The night we met . . ."
0:37–0:52	**Chorus**, 8 mm.	Lead and backup vocals, this is the song's hook, "Be my baby."
0:52–1:22	**Verse 2**, 16 mm.	Mostly as before, though first 8 mm. are fuller than before, "I'll make you happy . . ."
1:22–1:37	**Chorus**, 8 mm.	As before, "Be my baby . . ."
1:37–1:52	**Instrumental verse** (partial), 8 mm.	Violins play first half of melody with vocal backups.
1:52–2:07	**Chorus**, 8 mm.	As before, "Be my baby . . ."
2:07–2:10	**Reprise of intro**, 2 mm.	Drum intro returns to relaunch the chorus.
2:10–2:25	**Chorus**, 8 mm.	As before, with lead vocals improvising over top.
2:25–2:36	**Chorus**, 8 mm.	As before, with fade-out.

SWEET SOUL ON THE RISE

Sam Cooke at a recording session. Like many artists, including Ray Charles, Cooke was strongly influenced by gospel. Cooke combined this sensibility with a sweet soul style to create his own sound. After a string of hits, including "You Send Me," Cooke's career came to a tragic end when he was murdered at a motel in 1964.

Sam Cooke Turns to Pop. In the late 1950s, a new and softer approach to black pop emerged that turned out to have tremendous crossover potential. Working with the Drifters and Ben E. King, Leiber and Stoller produced a long series of hits in a style that came to be called "sweet soul." In addition to the rhythm and blues and rock and roll artists we have discussed thus far, other black singers had already appeared regularly on the pop charts since the mid-1950s. Nat King Cole scored a number of soft-pop hits, including "Send for Me" (p6 r1, 1957) and "Looking Back" (p5 r2, 1958). Johnny Mathis was also a familiar artist on the pop Top 40, with such releases as "It's Not for Me to Say" (p5, 1957), "Chances Are" (p1 r12, 1957), and "Misty" (p12 r10, 1959). Neither of these singers were rock and rollers, since they tended to record easy-listening pop ballads that were similar to other mainstream-pop song stylists such as Al Martino, Eddie Fisher, and Dean Martin. It would also be difficult to find much rhythm and blues influence in their music.

Singing in a light pop style that *did* have marked elements of black music, however, was Sam Cooke, who placed twenty-nine singles in the pop Top 40 between 1957 and 1965, including "You Send Me" (p1 r1, 1957), "Chain Gang" (p2 r2, 1960), "Twistin' the Night Away" (p9 r1, 1962), and "Another Saturday Night" (p10 r1, 1963). Cooke came to the pop side of the business from gospel, where he had sung with the Soul Stirrers. In many ways, Cooke's transition from gospel to pop was preceded by Ray Charles, who had a number-two rhythm and blues hit in 1955 by setting a gospel tune to secular lyrics with "I Got a Woman." Charles went on to have a number of important hits outside of rhythm and blues, surprising many in the music business with pop- and country and western–influenced records such as "Georgia on My Mind" (p1 r3, 1960), "Hit the Road Jack" (p1 r1, 1961), and "I Can't Stop Loving You" (p1 r1, 1962). With the success of "I Got a Woman," record companies began to consider gospel artists as potential rhythm and blues hit-makers. These artists were deeply conflicted about turning to pop, since gospel was "the Lord's music," and many considered pop the Devil's music. Cooke's first record was released under the name Dale Cooke, to test his marketability without adversely affecting his gospel reputation. What Cooke brought to pop from gospel was a clear tenor voice and a penchant for frequent melodic embellishment that often sounded improvisatory.

The Drifters and Ben E. King. As one of the most successful groups on the Atlantic roster, during the 1950s the Drifters recorded many important examples of sweet soul. At first featuring Clyde McPhatter, the group scored a series of rhythm and blues hits in the mid-1950s. But by 1958, the Drifters were floundering, and Atlantic was reluctant to let the group dissolve since the name had become strongly associated with a string of hits. Manager George Treadwell found another vocal group, the Crowns, to take over as the Drifters. In fact, the Drifters and the Crowns appeared together on the same bill at the Apollo Theater in Harlem one evening in 1958, after which the Crowns became the Drifters. To rebuild the group's career, Atlantic brought in Leiber and Stoller. "There Goes My Baby" (p1 r2, 1959) was the first fruit of this new combination, and it was followed by a string of hits, including "Save the Last Dance for Me" (p1 r1, 1960) with Ben E. King singing lead, and "Up on the Roof" (p5 r4, 1962) and "On Broadway" (p9 r7, 1963) with Rudy Lewis singing lead ("On Broadway" features an uncredited electric guitar solo by Phil Spector). Atlantic staff producer Bert Berns took over from Leiber and Stoller in 1963. His "Under the Boardwalk" reached number four in 1964 with Johnny Moore on lead vocals (r1).

The influence of Cooke's singing can be found throughout Ben E. King's performance on "There Goes My Baby." While the song was written by King (aka Benjamin Nelson), it is credited to Benjamin Nelson, Lover Patterson, George Treadwell, Jerry Leiber, and Mike Stoller. With the deals that were typically made on publishing rights, it is possible that everyone credited was not involved in the song's composition but were included as compensation for their services. At any rate, it is certain that the lead singer is Ben E. King and the record hit number one on the rhythm and blues charts (number two on the pop charts) in the summer of 1959. As mentioned earlier, fellow producer Jerry Wexler was initially so confused by the sound of the record that he thought it sounded like a radio stuck between two different stations. This comes from the fact that orchestral strings had not been used on rhythm and blues records much before this song was released, and the classically oriented strings (and tympani) combined with a relatively square-cut doo-wop introduction would have seemed incongruous to many listeners.

The track begins with a male vocal-harmony passage led by bassist Elsbeary Hobbs, who sings a pattern outlining a chord progression common to much doo-wop. But set against this are tympani, followed by an ascending flourish from the strings (four violins and a cello, according to Mike Stoller). Finally, King enters with the chorus, as his melody is accompanied by the rest of the Drifters and a countermelody played by the violins. When King gets to the verse lyrics, "I want to know, did she love me," the strings introduce a melodic figure with resonances of nineteenth-century orchestral music in a call-and-response exchange that sounds like it could have come from the gospel tradition. This track encapsulates the eclectic

The new lineup of the Drifters had formerly been the Crowns. This publicity shot from 1959 features (left to right) Charlie Thomas, Ben E. King, Dock Green, and Elsbeary Hobbs. Leiber and Stoller produced a series of hits for the group, as did Bert Burns. When King left the group to pursue a solo career, Leiber and Stoller also produced a series of hits for him, including "Stand by Me."

Listening Guide

The Drifters, "There Goes My Baby" Atlantic 2025

Words and music by Benjamin Nelson, Lover Patterson, and George Treadwell, produced by Jerry Leiber and Mike Stoller. Released in 1959 as a single. Reached #1 on the *Billboard* "Hot R&B Sides" chart and #2 on the "Hot 100" chart in 1959.

FORM: Simple verse-chorus. The same 8-bar pattern is used for the entire song, underpinning the introduction, verses, and chorus. The song begins typically enough, with a doo-wop inflected vocal intro, two verses, and a chorus. Verse 4 introduces what sounds like an improvised verse over a melodic figure in the cellos that might have been borrowed from a classical composer (Stoller has suggested the line resembles Russian composer Rimsky-Korsakov). The rest of the song continues to create this impression of improvising over the repeated 8-bar progression, with the background vocals from the introduction returning, as well as the chorus, before the song fades out.

TIME SIGNATURE: 12/8.

INSTRUMENTATION: Acoustic guitar, electric guitar, bass, tympani, orchestral strings, lead and backup vocals.

0:00–0:15	**Introduction**, 8 mm.	Doo-wop vocals led by bass voice.
0:15–0:30	**Verse 1**, 8 mm.	Lead vocal enters, along with backing string melody, "There goes my baby . . ."
0:30–0:45	**Verse 2**, 8 mm.	String melody continues, backup vocals enter, "I broke her heart . . ."
0:45–0:59	**Chorus**, 8 mm.	Main melody sung in backup vocals, with lead vocal improvising over top, "There goes my baby . . ."
0:59–1:14	**Verse 4**, 8 mm.	Classical-style cellos enter, improvised lead vocal melody, tympani can be heard clearly in this section, "I want to know . . ."
1:14–1:29	**Verse 5**, 8 mm.	Cellos continue, backup vocals added, "I wonder why . . ."
1:29–1:44	**Verse 6**, 8 mm.	String melody replaces cellos, no backup vocals, "I was going to tell her . . ."
1:44–1:59	**Verse/Intro**, 8 mm.	String melody continues, backup vocals reenter, "Where am I . . ."
1:59–2:08	**Chorus**, 8 mm.	Backup vocals take melody as before, lead vocal improvises over top, "There goes my baby . . ."

musical influences that fed Leiber and Stoller's songwriting and producing. It is unlikely that many other producers could have gotten away with releasing such a record at the time, but by 1959 Leiber and Stoller had an established record of success, giving them the influence they needed to get the track issued.

Ben E. King was fired from the Drifters in May 1960, reportedly because he complained to Treadwell that the members of the group were not being paid enough to live on, despite their chart success. Leiber and Stoller quickly stepped in and offered to produce King as a solo act for Atlantic. At the first session, King recorded four tracks, "Spanish Harlem," "First Taste of Love," "Young Boy Blues," and at the last minute, a song King had begun writing himself called "Stand by Me." Out of this first session, both "Spanish Harlem" (p10 r15, 1961) and "Stand by Me" (p4 r1, 1961) reached the pop Top 10, initiating a series of five Top 40 hits for King in the 1961–63 period. (Illustrating the interconnectedness of figures and styles in the early 1960s, "Spanish Harlem" was written by Jerry Leiber and Phil Spector because Mike Stoller was out of town one weekend.) Taken together, the music of the Drifters and Ben E. King established sweet soul as a style characterized by a fluid lead vocal melody often supported by doo-wop backup vocals, counter melodies in the strings, and a rhythm section laying down a medium-tempo beat, sometimes influenced by Latin music (remember that Harry Belafonte had just had several hits employing a calypso sound).

After the first few successful records from the Drifters, other performers had hits with similarly styled releases. Jerry Butler scored with "He Will Break Your Heart" (p7 r1, 1960), and Chuck Jackson hit with "Any Day Now (My Wild Beautiful Bird)" (p23 r2, 1962). While the string of hits from the Drifters and Ben E. King was mostly over by the end of 1964, other artists took some of the elements of sweet soul into the British invasion years and beyond. Pop song-stylist Dionne Warwick was first noticed by composer Burt Bacharach while singing backup at a Drifters session. She became the most important performer of songs by Burt Bacharach and Hal David, hitting the charts in 1964 with "Anyone Who Had a Heart" (p8 r6) and "Walk on By" (p6 r1)—two of many hits that would follow. Motown artists were also influenced by sweet soul, while rhythm and blues singers with a more strongly pronounced gospel element—such as Solomon Burke, Otis Redding, and Wilson Pickett—emerged early in the 1960s and paved the way for soul music later in the decade. Motown and southern soul are covered in Chapter 6.

ROCKABILLY POPSTERS

While Brill Building pop tended to dominate pop music in the early 1960s, other styles also vied for attention. We have already seen how folk defined itself in opposition to the commercialism of Brill Building offerings, even if its careful construction and marketing of its anticommercial image did parallel teen pop. And while rockabilly is not usually associated closely with Brill Building pop, perhaps because the style is seen to have its roots in the South, its development after the first wave was very much influenced by Brill Building practices. The wilder music of early Elvis, Carl Perkins, and Jerry Lee Lewis became the sweeter country-inflected pop of the Everly Brothers, Roy Orbison, and Ricky Nelson. The development of rockabilly, however, does not fit into neat chronological divisions, with significant overlap between the first-wave artists and their successors. By 1959, Presley, Perkins, Lewis, and Buddy Holly were no longer playing a role in rockabilly. However, the Everlys and Nelson continued to develop without losing a step on the pop charts, and Roy Orbison was just beginning to make his mark in 1960. So there was a dovetailing between these two groups of musicians, as well as a stylistic tendency of the second group of artists (the Everlys, Nelson, and Orbison) to soften the rockabilly sound by incorporating a more marked pop component, under the general influence of the Brill Building approach. After 1958, and perhaps in reaction to the controversy surrounding first-wave performers due to the payola scandal, this second group of rockabilly popsters seemed eager to please a teen audience without offending parents or other authorities.

The Everly Brothers. Coming from a strong background in the traditional country music of the southeast—their father, Ike, was a professional musician who had the brothers performing together from an early age—the Everly Brothers' easygoing rockabilly sound emerged in 1957 when their first single, "Bye Bye Love," raced up all three charts. Like Carl Perkins's "Blue Suede Shoes" and Elvis Presley's "Heartbreak Hotel," "Bye Bye Love" reached the Top 10 on each chart, hitting number one on the country and western charts, number two on the pop charts, and number five on the rhythm and blues charts. The duo had signed with Columbia in 1955 but were dropped after only one release and subsequently rejected by a number of labels. In 1957, their manager Wesley Rose (an important song publisher in Nashville whose father had managed Hank Williams) convinced Archie Bleyer at the New York–based independent Cadence to sign the brothers, even though he had declined to do so the previous year. After their hit with "Bye Bye Love," the Everlys went on to score fifteen additional Top 40 hit singles on Cadence through 1960, and seven more through 1964 after moving to Warner Brothers.

Don and Phil Everly each wrote songs that became hits: Don wrote "('Til) I Kissed You" (p4 r22 c8, 1959), "Cathy's Clown" (p1 r1, 1960), and "So Sad (to Watch Good Love Go Bad)" (p7 r16, 1960), while Phil wrote "When Will I Be Loved" (p8, 1960). But in the first few years of their success, the Everlys depended on the well-crafted songs of Boudleaux and Felice Bryant and the backup of top Nashville studio musicians under the direction of Bleyer. The Everly Brothers released a consistent stream of hits under this system, two of which went to number one on all three of the most important charts ("Wake Up, Little Susie" in 1957 and "All I Have to Do Is Dream" in 1958); "Bird Dog" hit number two on the rhythm and blues chart in 1958 and reached the top slot on the other two. A country influence is readily evident in the earlier hits, where the energetic strumming on jumbo acoustic guitars by both brothers provides the rhythmic drive. Both "Bye Bye Love" and "Wake Up, Little Susie"

The Everly Brothers used lush harmonies, combining them with elements of country to create a sweet, seemingly simple vocal sound. Their hits include the up-tempo "Bye Bye Love" and the ballad "All I Have to Do Is Dream."

Listening Guide

The Everly Brothers, "All I Have to Do Is Dream" Cadence 1348

Words and music by Boudleaux Bryant, produced by Archie Bleyer. Reached #1 on *Billboard* pop, country and western, and rhythm and blues charts in 1958. In mid-1958 there were two active *Billboard* charts ("Disc Jockey" and "Sales") in each of the three major markets (pop, R&B, and C&W). This single went to #1 on all six of these charts.

FORM: AABA, with partial reprise. The "Dream" refrain from the introduction returns just before the repeat of the bridge and then again at the end as the song fades.

TIME SIGNATURE: 4/4, with a slightly Latin feel.

INSTRUMENTATION: Electric guitars, acoustic guitar, acoustic bass, drums, and two-part harmony vocal throughout.

Time	Section	Description
0:00–0:12	**Introduction**, 4 mm.	Guitar chord, and then vocals enter, "Dream . . ."
0:12–0:30	**A-Verse**, 8 mm.	"When I want you . . ."
0:30–0:49	**A-Verse**, 8 mm.	"When I feel blue . . ."
0:49–1:07	**B-Bridge**, 8 mm.	"I can make you mine . . ."
1:07–1:31	**A-Verse**, 10 mm. (8 mm. + 2 mm. drawn from intro)	"I need you so . . ."
1:31–1:49	**B-Bridge**, 8 mm.	"I can make you mine . . ."
1:49–2:18	**A-Verse**, 8 mm. and fade on intro	"I need you so . . ."

reveal the influence of rhythm and blues in their respective guitar introductions, played here—as in much Everly Brothers music—on the steel-string acoustic guitar. The lyrics address teenage love life, the best example being "Wake Up, Little Susie," which deals with a young couple who go to a drive-in and fall asleep during the movie. Waking up after the film has ended, they worry that their reputations will be shot because their parents will suspect them of engaging in sexual activity.

The most distinctive feature of the Everly Brothers' music is the duet singing of Don and Phil. Much like the "brother duets" popular in bluegrass music, their songs are often sung in harmony throughout, their voices tending toward the high end of the male vocal range and using a relatively straight tone, free of vibrato. Arguably their best duet singing occurs on "All I Have to Do Is Dream," a soft ballad that the brothers treat with a gentle touch, blending their voices in close-knit harmony in a very controlled manner. This high, light vocal quality gives their music its distinctive sound, and was very influential on later artists, especially Simon and Garfunkel, the Hollies, and the Beatles, who covered several Everly Brothers songs in their early years. The Everlys' tendency toward a softer style brought a

Roy Orbison in concert. While usually associated with rockabilly, Orbison's music spans a range of influences and styles: country and western ("Ooby Dooby" and "Rockhouse"), doo-wop (his trademark use of falsetto), pure pop ballads ("Running Scared" and "Crying"), and rhythm and blues ("Candy Man" and "Mean Woman Blues").

more pronounced mainstream-pop influence to rockabilly. Unlike the recordings that Jerry Lee Lewis was making for Sun at about the time of the Everlys' first chart success and much more like the teen-idol music discussed earlier, this music is neither dangerous nor out of control.

Roy Orbison. Hailing from Wink, Texas, Roy Orbison toured the west Texas region with the Wink Westerners before ending up at the University of North Texas (called North Texas State at the time) as a fellow student of Pat Boone. Orbison's first release, "Ooby Dooby," was written by two of his North Texas school buddies and was chosen because it was a crowd favorite with Orbison's band. The song was initially recorded in Fort Worth by Columbia (which rejected it) and then again by Norman Petty in Clovis (this second version was released on Je-Wel). On the advice of Johnny Cash, who Orbison met when Cash was touring west Texas in 1955, Orbison sent the record to Sam Phillips at Sun, who subsequently rerecorded and released it in 1956. None of Orbison's four Sun releases were significant hits ("Ooby Dooby" reached number 59), nor were the songs he did in the late 1950s for RCA with Chet Atkins producing. Orbison then signed with a new independent label, Monument, and released "Only the Lonely (Know How I Feel)," which rose as high as number two on the pop chart in 1960 (r14). He followed with a string of nineteen hit records for Monument through 1965, including "Running Scared" (p1, 1961), "Crying" (p2, 1961), "Dream Baby (How Long Must I Dream)" (p4, 1962), "In Dreams" (p7, 1963), and his biggest hit, "Oh, Pretty Woman," which occupied the number-one slot for three weeks in the fall of 1964 at the height of the British invasion.

Like Buddy Holly, Orbison wrote most of his own material and his music incorporates a wide range of styles. Orbison's "Ooby Dooby" and "Rockhouse" singles for Sun are squarely in the up-tempo, country-influenced rockabilly style of Presley and Perkins. With the Monument releases, however, his west Texas roots in country and western are less perceptible, replaced with a haunting ballad singing style that features both Elvis-like low chest singing and frequent, almost operatic passages in which

falsetto

Orbison flips into his **falsetto** voice. The verses of "Oh, Pretty Woman"—beginning "Pretty woman, walkin' down the street"—present an example of the lower, Presleyesque delivery; the "mercy" and growl that follow are reminiscent of Presley's mannerisms in "Don't Be Cruel." The stop-time sections of "Only the Lonely (Know How I Feel)" are a good example of Orbison's characteristic falsetto; in the second verse, after delivering a pair of lines in his chest voice and beginning with the lyrics "maybe tomorrow," Orbison builds to the song's expressive climax on the words "but that's the chance you gotta take." His trademark use of falsetto is an adaptation of doo-wop practice, and the backup vocals—"dum dum dum dum de doo wah"—are clearly drawn from doo-wop and help make the stylistic derivation clear. Orbison's next two hits, "Blue Angel" (p9 r23, 1960) and "I'm Hurtin'" (p27, 1960), follow

Listening Guide

Roy Orbison, "Only the Lonely (Know How I Feel)" Monument 421

Words and music by Roy Orbison and Joe Melson, produced by Fred Foster. Released in 1960 as a single and on the album *Lonely and Blue*. Reached #2 on the *Billboard* "Hot 100" chart and #14 on the "Hot R&B Sides" chart.

FORM: This song has an interesting structure derived from AABA form. The first 11-bar verse takes the place of the first two A-section verses usually found in AABA forms, and is followed by an 8-bar B-section bridge, before a return to the A-section verse, here 6 bars in length. The first 11-bar verse is tricky to count, since Orbison flips the regular accent on beat one over to beat three to create bars of 2/4 time. If you keep counting in four, however, everything will work out, though you may feel you are off for a couple of measures. A 10-bar interlude connects the two presentations of this special AABA-derived form, and this music is taken directly from the introduction. The second time through, the structure is similar to the first time except that the end of the bridge is much more dramatic, and the return to the verse is shorter and more melodically and lyrically connected to the bridge.

TIME SIGNATURE: This song is 4/4 throughout, though there are measures of 2/4 created in the verse sections. Challenge yourself to hear the measures of 2/4 and create a metric scheme that maps the entire verse section.

INSTRUMENTATION: Piano, bass, electric guitar, acoustic guitar, orchestral strings, vibraphone, lead and backup vocals.

0:00–0:21	**Introduction,** 10 mm.	Doo-wop style backup vocals, "Dum dum dum . . ."
0:21–0:43	**Verse 1,** 11 mm.	Lead vocal enters, backups continue, "Only the lonely . . ."
0:43–0:59	**Bridge,** 8 mm.	Dramatic solo vocal with stop-time string orchestra and vibraphone chords to add musical emphasis, "There goes my baby . . ."
0:59–1:11	**Verse,** 6 mm.	Added string melody in dialogue with lead vocal, "But only the lonely . . ."
1:11–1:30	**Interlude,** 10 mm.	Repeat of introduction, "Dum dum dum . . ."
1:30–1:52	**Verse 2,** 11 mm.	As before, "Only the lonely . . ."
1:52–2:14	**Bridge,** 8 mm.	Solo vocal with stop-time chords as before, but now driving to the song's dramatic high point on highest vocal notes, "Maybe tomorrow . . ."
2:14–2:24	**Verse,** 4 mm.	Tempo resumes to end, "If your lonely heart breaks . . ."

the same general pattern, using the standard pop practice of succeeding a hit with another, very similar record. By contrast, "Runnin' Scared" and "Crying," are pure pop ballads without a hint of Presley leads or doo-wop backups. Orbison's delivery is very similar in these songs, building to a dramatic climax in each case. Orbison's vocal style influenced several later rockers, including Bruce Springsteen, and his songs have been covered in well-known versions by artists as diverse as Linda Ronstadt ("Blue Bayou"; p3 c2, 1977) and Van Halen ("Oh, Pretty Woman"; p12, 1982).

Ricky Nelson. Ricky Nelson's music from 1957–64 draws together a number of themes that have been discussed thus far. The son of bandleader Ozzie Nelson and singer Harriet Hilliard, Ricky played himself in the Ozzie and Harriet radio show *The Adventures of Ozzie and Harriet* from 1949, moving with the show to television in 1952. Inspired by his girlfriend's enthusiasm for Elvis, seventeen-year-old Nelson boasted that he was also making a record. Nelson's father, Ozzie, was quickly convinced of the commercial possibilities of Ricky singing rock. Growing up in a family of professional musicians, Nelson had a knack for singing from the very start of his career. His first single was a cover version of Fats Domino's "I'm Walkin'," which went to number four in 1957 (r10), followed by the B-side "A Teenager's Romance," which climbed to the number-two slot. Suspecting that there would be problems collecting royalties from the Verve label on which these hits appeared, Ozzie signed Ricky to the Los Angeles–based Imperial (Fats Domino's label). Starting with "Be Bop Baby" (p3 r5, 1957), Nelson scored a series of twenty-six Top 40 singles for Imperial through 1962, and a few more after switching to Decca in 1963. Nelson's good looks and clean-cut image made him one of the first teen idols.

Musically, Nelson's records are well crafted, although he did not write his own music and depended on songwriters for material, especially Baker Knight, Johnny Burnette, and Dorsey Burnette. Nelson's music is clearly patterned after that of Elvis Presley. He even used some of the same musicians on his records that Elvis did during his RCA period, with guitarist James Burton featured on lead guitar in most cases (Burton would later play in Presley's band). Presley's influence is clear on "Stood Up" (p2 r4 c8, 1957), "Believe What You Say" (p4 r6 c10, 1958), and "Just a Little Too Much" (p9, 1959), songs that sound like Elvis's up-tempo rockers on RCA like "Too Much," "All Shook Up," and "Teddy Bear," all of which preceded Nelson's first hit for Imperial. Other influences are clearly audible in Nelson's music, too. Gene Vincent's "Be-Bop-a-Lula" may have been the initial inspiration for "Be-Bop Baby," though Nelson's record is bouncier and has none of Vincent's swagger. Nelson's "Waitin' in School" (p18 r12 c12, 1958), which deals with going through the school day in anticipation of dancing later, seems inspired by Chuck Berry's "School Day"; the lyrics and vocal delivery on the chorus of "Waitin' in School" ("one-two, buckle my shoe, three-four, get out on the floor") are also reminiscent of Bill Haley's "Rock around the Clock." The lyrics to "It's Late" (p9 r30, 1959) describe how the singer gets in trouble for bringing his girlfriend home too late and parallel the Everly Brothers' "Wake Up, Little Susie." Far from being overly derivative, however, Ricky Nelson's music emerges as a rich product of its time. Stylistically, Nelson combines the pop rockabilly approach of the Everly Brothers with the good-boy image of Pat Boone to imitate the music of Elvis Presley.

In the development of rockabilly music during the early 1960s, we can clearly see the influence of Brill Building practice, especially in regard to the rise of teen idols. But there is also a distinct connection with the first wave of rock and roll. The songs

Known as "the French Elvis," Johnny Hallyday enjoyed hit singles in France during the early 1960s, even appearing on a telecast of The Ed Sullivan Show taped in Paris. Hallyday went on to have continued success in the French-speaking world, with singles topping the French charts into the new millennium and sales exceeding 80 million records worldwide.

of the Everly Brothers and Ricky Nelson were as much continuations of Elvis and Carl Perkins as they were parallels to Frankie Avalon and Fabian. Unlike the teen idols, however, rockabilly artists sometimes wrote their own music, though they often depended on professional songwriters for hits. As we will see in Chapter 8, these later rockabilly artists were a more controlled and polite first wave of southern rock, filtering the original rockabilly sound through a Brill Building sensibility.

European Elvises. As the American music business searched of the next Elvis, Some European countries found their next Elvis much closer to home. In Germany, Ted Herold was known as the German Elvis, releasing a series of German-language covers of Elvis hits and modeling his appearance very much on Presley's. In France, Johnny Hallyday earned the title of the French Elvis, initially scoring a number-four hit in France with "*T'Aimer follement.*" Hallyday then hit the top of the charts in France with his cover of Chubby Checker's "Let's Twist Again," titled "*Viens danser le twist.*" As we'll see in Chapter 4, Elvis and the first wave of rock and roll had an even more dramatic impact in England, producing numerous Elvis-inspired singers and singles and paving the way for the emergence of the Beatles.

SURFIN' USA: IT'S JUST GOOD, CLEAN, WHITE-SUBURBAN FUN

The Beach Boys, Jan and Dean, and Vocal Surf Music. Aside from a handful of labels that were based in Los Angeles (majors MGM and Capitol and indies Modern, Imperial, and Specialty), most of the rock music business in the first half of the 1960s was located east of the Mississippi (primarily in New York and Philadelphia). Elvis and a few other teen idols were in Hollywood making movies, and Ricky Nelson was in Southern California, but they were in many ways a long way from the pop-music action. *American Bandstand* was broadcast from Philadelphia, and many of the important songwriters and producers worked from the Brill Building in Manhattan. This may explain why the influences that came together in the

Beach Boys' music seem so eclectic. Growing up in suburban Los Angeles in the late 1950s, this quintet of three brothers, a cousin, and a high school friend were influenced by black doo-wop groups, mainstream white vocal groups like the Four Freshmen, Chuck Berry's driving rock and roll, and Phil Spector's Wall of Sound. Along with their fellow Los Angelenos Jan and Dean, the Beach Boys created a style of music that seemed devoted to the ideal teenage world of summer fun: surf music.

The Beach Boys first enjoyed success in late 1961 with a regional hit single, "Surfin'," written by group leader Brian Wilson and released on the small Candix label. The group signed with Capitol in 1962 and released a series of Top 40 hits—twenty-six by the end of the decade—including "Surfin' Safari" (p14, 1962), "Surfin' U.S.A." (p3 r20, 1963), "Surfer Girl" (p7 r18, 1963), "Be True to Your School" (p6 r27, 1963), and "Fun, Fun, Fun" (p5, 1964). While the British invasion was taking American pop by storm in the first half of 1964, the Beach Boys enjoyed their first number-one hit, "I Get Around," the B-side of which, "Don't Worry Baby," rose as high as number twenty-four. The tremendous popularity of the Beatles only made Wilson and the Beach Boys work that much harder. We will take up that aspect of the Beach Boys in Chapter 5, but note that in the period between the Beatles' arrival in the United States in early 1964 and the psychedelic summer of 1967, the Beach Boys had fourteen Top 40 singles, ten of which were in the Top 10 and two of which hit number one.

Until 1964, the Beach Boys' music held fairly close to the same surf-music formula that was also followed by Jan and Dean. Song lyrics are usually about three topics: cars, girls, and surfing. At times lighthearted (as in Jan and Dean's 1964 number-three hit, "Little Old Lady from Pasadena," which tells the story of a hot-rod granny), the lyrics hardly ever deal with adult sexuality. The vocals seem to draw in equal parts from the doo-wop, girl-group, and glee-club traditions, with some perceptible vocal jazz elements. The instrumental accompaniments lean heavily on Chuck Berry's music. In fact, "Surfin' U.S.A." is an obvious reworking of Berry's "Sweet Little Sixteen," and Berry sued the Beach Boys for copyright infringement

The Beach Boys—(from left) Dennis Wilson, Al Jardine, Carl Wilson, Brian Wilson, and Mike Love. While the Beach Boys' music seemed like simple, catchy pop, their harmonies and arrangements were very complex. Influenced by Phil Spector, Brian Wilson wrote and produced many of the Beach Boys' songs and was an innovator of recording techniques.

Listening Guide

The Beach Boys, "Surfin' U.S.A." Capital 4932

Words and music by Brian Wilson and Chuck Berry, produced by Nik Venet. Based on Chuck Berry's "Sweet Little Sixteen." Reached #3 on the *Billboard* "Hot 100" chart and #20 on the "Hot R&B Singles" chart in 1963.

FORM: Simple verse form. Each verse ends with the refrain "surfin' U.S.A.," though verses 2 and 4 feature the high falsetto "everybody's gone surfin'," making these verses seem to function like choruses, even though they are not actually choruses. The song ends with an instrumental verse shared by organ and guitar; the refrain here is sung as in verses 2 and 4, with a tag made up of four repetitions of the refrain.

TIME SIGNATURE: 4/4, with stops during verses 1 and 3. Note the constant bass drum during stops.

INSTRUMENTATION: Electric guitars, bass, drums, organ, lead and backup vocals.

0:00–0:03	**Introduction**, 4 mm.	Chuck Berry–style guitar intro, note the heavy reverb.
0:03–0:27	**Verse 1 with refrain**, 16 mm.	Lead vocal with "oo" backups; note the stop time with bass drum beats that continue, "If everybody had an ocean . . ."
0:27–0:50	**Verse 2 with refrain**, 16 mm.	Backup vocals sing lyrics as lead vocal continues, band plays in regular time to add rhythmic drive, "You can catch 'em at Del Mar . . ."
0:50–1:15	**Verse 3 with refrain**, 16 mm.	As verse 1, in stop time, "We'll all be plannin' out a route . . ."
1:15–1:39	**Verse 4 with refrain**, 16 mm.	As verse 2, regular time, "At Haggarty's and Swami's . . ."
1:39–2:04	**Instrumental verse with refrain**, 16 mm.	Organ solo, guitar solo, and then sung refrain.
2:04–2:24	**Tag (refrain)**, 16 mm.	Repeat of refrain and fade.

(modern copies of this song list the songwriters as Berry and Wilson). Nevertheless, the song is a good example of the band's early surf style. Wilson's new lyrics list all the hot surf spots in Southern California, while the back-up vocals alternate between "ooo" and "inside, outside, U.S.A.," all sung in multivoice harmony. Wilson's ringing falsetto on "everybody's gone surfin'" provides the song's hook, while the instrumental solos provide a slice of early 1960s beach music, featuring a very "electronic" organ followed by a clean, Berryesque electric guitar solo soaked in electronic reverb.

In addition to using Berry as a model, Brian Wilson and the Beach Boys drew heavily on the music and production techniques of Phil Spector. While the band was initially assigned a producer in what was then typical music-business fashion, Brian soon demanded that he produce the records. A good example of the audible connection between the Beach Boys and Spector can be found in the Wilson-produced

"Don't Worry Baby." Describing the first time he heard "Be My Baby" on the radio, Wilson recalls that while he was fascinated by the first verse, he was so captivated by the chorus that he had to pull his car over to avoid an accident. His enthusiasm for the Ronettes/Spector record was so great that, together with Los Angeles disc jockey Roger Christian (who is mostly responsible for the lyrics), he wrote a song especially for the Ronettes to record. When Spector rejected "Don't Worry Baby," Wilson and the Beach Boys recorded it. Wilson's song is modeled closely on "Be My Baby," featuring a similar form and series of chord progressions. The similarity can be heard right from the start, as the tune begins with a drumbeat strongly reminiscent of the Spector tune. This beat is played by drummer Hal Blaine, who had performed the instrumental accompaniment for "Be My Baby" with other members of the Wrecking Crew. After Wilson sings the first two lines of the verse, the backup vocals enter on the third line at the lyrics "but she looks in my eyes," building the texture to drive toward the chorus, where Wilson's voice and the backup vocals work together in a call-and-response relationship. All of this is in direct imitation of "Be My Baby."

But there are also some notable differences between the songs. For example, "Don't Worry Baby" does not use strings and features male voices. Rather than dealing with romantic longing as in "Be My Baby," Christian's lyrics describe the singer's reluctant involvement in a drag race. As Wilson tells the story, he was concerned he would never be able to equal Spector's achievement and his wife reassured him with the phrase, "Don't worry, baby." Perhaps the drag race described in "Don't Worry Baby" is a metaphor for Wilson's sense of competition with Spector. In any case, "Don't Worry Baby" is closely related to "Be My Baby."

As formulaic as the early singles can often be, the Beach Boys were also capable of great musical subtlety and sophistication; the slow ballads "Surfer Girl" and "In My Room" are elegant Wilson compositions that, despite their teen themes, are compositionally innovative and reveal the group's prowess as a vocal ensemble. Jan and Dean also had a series of surf-music hits; in addition to "Little Old Lady from Pasadena," the duo hit with "Surf City" (co-written by Brian Wilson; p1, 1963), "Honolulu Lulu" (p11, 1963), "Drag City" (p10, 1963), and "Ride the Wild Surf" (p16, 1964). In the early years of surf music, Jan and Dean worked closely with the Beach Boys until their respective record companies objected. An important element in the Beach Boys' success was the writing and production of Brian Wilson. Under the strong influence of Phil Spector's most ambitious records, Brian worked to create the biggest recorded sound for the band that he could muster, increasingly emphasizing innovation. Wilson's records with the Beach Boys are a clear continuation of the ambitious producer story this chapter has been tracing, though his most creative and ambitious work would not be done until 1965 and 1966.

Dick Dale, King of the Surf Guitar.
While the Beach Boys and Jan and Dean were placing one single after another on the Top 40 charts, another group of Southern California surf records was focused almost exclusively on instrumental music featuring the guitar. Dick Dale and the Del-Tones were pioneers in this style of guitar-based surf music and spent the autumn of 1961 (the season of the first Beach Boys single) at the lower reaches of the national pop charts. While only one of the Beach Boys (Dennis Wilson) ever spent any time surfing, Dale's music grew straight out of surf culture; Dale recalls that it was normal for him to come in from

the beach, dry off, and step directly onstage to play. Dick Dale and the Del-Tones' "Misirlou" (1962) features his trademark rapid tremolo picking on the guitar set to a tune that had been a Greek pop standard in the 1940s. His most commercially popular single was "Let's Go Tripping," which hit number sixty in 1961. Dale's tendency to slide his hand down the guitar strings (from high to low) while picking rapidly created an effect he thought sounded like a wave crashing around a surfer. That trademark sound can be heard in many of the surf hits of the time, including the Chantay's instrumental hit, "Pipeline" (p4 r11, 1963), the Duals' "Stick Shift" (p25, 1961), and the Surfaris' "Wipe Out" (p2 r10, 1963).

Duane Eddy and the Ventures. While Dale and the surfers developed a particular form of guitar-band instrumental, in many ways these groups were building on the success of guitarist Duane Eddy, whose "Rebel Rouser" hit number six in 1958 (r8) and was followed by a series of instrumental hits through 1962. Eddy's distinctively twangy guitar records also inspired the Seattle-based Ventures, who hit number two with "Walk, Don't Run" in 1960 (r13). Driven by two guitars, bass, and drums, the group had placed five hits in the Top 40 by 1964. The instrumental records by Dale, Eddy, and the Ventures were considered a novelty, which indicates how much the music business had changed in the fifteen years since the end of World War II. Instrumental records had been quite popular during the big band era, but the rise of the singers (led by Sinatra) had changed all that, and most rock and roll focused on vocal performances. In the period after 1964, however, increased attention would be given to instrumental playing as young guitarists inspired by electric blues and jazz made accomplished instrumental playing as much a feature of rock music as the vocals.

NARRATIVE LYRICS RUN AMOK: THE SPLATTER PLATTER

Teenage Romanticization of Death. The 1959–64 period saw the release of a number of songs dramatically portraying teenage death. Most of these records are maudlin at best and downright tasteless at worst. Mark Dinning's "Teen Angel" (p1, 1960), for instance, tells the story of a young couple whose car stalls on the railroad tracks just as a train is approaching. They escape the car, but the girl goes back to the car to retrieve the boy's class ring and is killed. The song is cast as a prayer by the boy to the girl, who is now a "teen angel." Similarly gruesome and hypermelodramatic stories were taken up by Ray Peterson's "Tell Laura I Love Her" (p7, 1960), the Everly Brothers' "Ebony Eyes" (p8, 1961), and J. Frank Wilson and the Cavaliers' "Last Kiss" (p2, 1964). Perhaps the most infamous of these records— sometimes called "death discs" or "splatter platters"—is the Shangri-Las' "Leader of the Pack." One might expect that such records only warrant a brief mention in a study of the era, but splatter platters are far more emblematic of teen pop during the early 1960s than they first appear. To understand how these strange records, especially "Leader of the Pack," pull together a number of threads we have been following in this chapter, it is important to know a bit about the history of the song and the people involved in making and releasing the record.

In perhaps the first move that spelled the end of the Brill Building domination of teen pop, Aldon Music was sold to Columbia Pictures–Screen Gems in the summer of 1963 (at about the same time that the Beatles were enjoying their first overwhelming success in England). Aldon founder Don Kirshner joined the corporation, running its Colpix label, while his associate Al Nevins was hired as a consultant (we will hear from Kirshner and some of his Brill Building colleagues again in Chapter 5). At about the same time, Leiber, Stoller, and George Goldner founded Red Bird Records (one reason Leiber and Stoller turned production of the Drifters over to Bert Berns was to concentrate on developing the new label). Jeff Barry and Ellie Greenwich had begun writing and producing for Red Bird, having a number-one hit in 1964 with the Dixie Cups' "Chapel of Love," a song they had written with Phil Spector and that he had recorded with both the Crystals and the Ronettes but never released. An old acquaintance of Greenwich's, George "Shadow" Morton, worked with Barry and Greenwich on a new single by the Shangri-Las, "Remember (Walkin' in the Sand)," which was released on Red Bird and rose to number thirteen in August of 1964. The trio then began writing the follow-up, "Leader of the Pack," produced by Barry and Morton.

True to the death-disc genre, "Leader of the Pack" chronicles the untimely demise of a teenager, in this case a motorcycle hoodlum named Johnny (paralleling Marlon Brando's character in *The Wild One*). Johnny's violent motorbike death is represented by taped crash sounds and screams, a feature that caused some consternation among parents. This Shangri-Las splatter platter is perhaps best viewed as a death-disc playlet. The involvement of Leiber and Stoller further underscores this. The verses set up the middle section, which provides the climax (the bike crash), and a final verse offers an epilogue. The sound-effect technique had also been employed in their first Coasters single, "Riot in Cell Block #9" (released as the Robins on Spark), which featured taped gunshots and police siren noises to represent the jailbreak. In a strange way, "Leader of the Pack" brings the Leiber and Stoller story back to where it began, incorporating a number of elements of their careers. "Leader of the Pack" would be among the last records to come out of the Brill Building establishment, since by 1964 the British invasion had arrived on American shores, causing yet another shake-up of the American popular-music business.

A far more tragic epilogue to the splatter-platter genre is the true story of Jan and Dean. In 1964, Jan and Dean also had a teenage tragedy hit, "Dead Man's Curve," which rose to number eight. The song chronicles a car crash on a stretch of road so treacherous that it had earned the nickname "dead man's curve." On April 19, 1966, Jan Berry was involved in an auto accident in which three passengers were killed and he was critically injured, effectively ending his career.

The quintessential "splatter platter": Jan and Dean's "Dead Man's Curve." Splatter platters, or "death discs," told the stories of teenagers meeting gruesome deaths, usually in a car or motorcycle crash. This record reveals the strong storytelling style of Leiber and Stoller.

Sound Check

Artist	Song	Sound
Kingston Trio	Tom Dooley (1959)	Form: simple verse-chorus Form begins with chorus Spoken introduction Music has changing dynamics, getting louder and softer throughout
Coasters	Down in Mexico (1956)	Form: AABA A dramatic form called a "playlet" Three different Latin-tinged rhythmic feels No repeat of the AABA
The Ronettes	Be My Baby (1963)	Form: contrasting verse-chorus Heavy reverb throughout the track Dense orchestration Reprise of introduction at the end
The Drifters	There Goes My Baby (1959)	Form: simple verse-chorus Note the lack of a drum set Doo-wop vocals in chorus Prominent strings
The Everly Brothers	All I Have to Do Is Dream (1958)	Form: AABA Two-part vocal harmony throughout the song Partial reprise of AABA form, repeating B and A sections only Slight Latin feel to rhythm
Roy Orbison	Only the Lonely (Know How I Feel) (1960)	Form: AABA (modified) Doo-wop-style backing vocals Stop-time chords in bridge Dramatic high vocals in second bridge
Beach Boys	Surfin' U.S.A. (1963)	Form: simple verse Chuck Berry–style introduction Note the difference between a refrain (included) and a chorus (not included) Intricate backing vocals

As mentioned at the beginning of this chapter, the period between the first wave of rock and roll and the arrival of the Beatles is viewed by some as a period of decline—a kind of "dark age" in rock history—while others see it as an important era filled with a lot of great music. For those who champion early 1960s pop, the British invasion was an unfortunate turn of events that snuffed out a number of pop styles prematurely. For those who view the early 1960s as dark days, Brill Building pop was rock and roll without its vitality, cynically neutered for crass commercial purposes. Whatever position one takes, it is clear that these years saw the music business gain control of a youth market that was cultivated during the first wave. Almost no aspect of pop during the early 1960s was completely immune from the influence of Brill Building practices, which were themselves merely a return to the practices that had dominated mainstream pop before rock emerged. If teens generally thought the new, more controlled pop constituted a decline, they certainly did not abandon pop music as a result. With business booming, it must have been enormously frustrating to the music-business establishment to face another serious challenge to their control of youth music: just when they thought they had it all figured out, a band arrived from England in February 1964 and radically changed the business again.

For Additional Online Resources, visit:
digital.wwnorton.com/whatsthatsound5

FURTHER READING

Alan Betrock, *Girl Groups: The Story of a Sound* (Delilah Books, 1982).

Hal Blaine with David Goggin, *Hal Blaine and the Wrecking Crew: The Story of the World's Most Recorded Musician* (MixBooks, 1993).

Robert Cantwell, *When We Were Good: The Folk Revival* (Harvard University Press, 1996).

Ron Cohen, *Rainbow Quest: The Folk Music Revival and American Society, 1940–1970* (University of Massachusetts Press, 2002).

Ken Emerson, *Always Magic in the Air: The Bump and Brilliance of the Brill Building Era* (Penguin Books, 2005).

Peter Guralnick, *Dream Boogie: The Triumph of Sam Cooke* (Little, Brown, 2005).

Kent Hartman, *The Wrecking Crew* (St. Martin's, 2012).

John A. Jackson, *American Bandstand: Dick Clark and the Making of a Rock 'n' Roll Empire* (Oxford University Press, 1997).

Jerry Leiber and Mike Stoller with David Fitz, *Hound Dog: The Leiber and Stoller Autobiography* (Simon & Schuster, 2009).

Mark Ribowsky, *He's a Rebel: The Truth about Phil Spector—Rock and Roll's Legendary Madman* (Dutton, 1989).

Ronnie Spector with Vince Waldron, *Be My Baby* (HarperCollins, 1990).

Jacqueline Warwick, *Girl Groups, Girl Culture: Popular Music and Identity in the 1960s* (Routledge, 2007).

Timothy White, *The Nearest Faraway Place: Brian Wilson, the Beach Boys, and the Southern California Experience* (Henry Holt, 1994).

Brian Wilson with Todd Gold, *Wouldn't It Be Nice? My Own Story* (HarperCollins, 1991).

Although the 1960s in America began with great hope, it was a decade that saw tremendous turbulence and war. The true spirit of the time was reflected in the rise and fall of President John F. Kennedy. Some historians say the sixties ethos began with Kennedy's election—that his youthfulness and passion for grand ideas epitomized the growing influence of youth culture. Others say the sixties truly began with Kennedy's assassination in 1963, and the resulting despair and conspiracy theories foreshadowing the many social movements that were deeply critical of government and traditional economic, social, and religious institutions. Wherever one places the beginning of the 1960s, it is clear that both themes are present in these chaotic years: youth culture presented itself more forcefully than ever, and social movements became more vigorous, critical, and violent. The music of this time—revealing and heightening these trends—provided the appropriate soundtrack. The world was exploding, and rock musicians were listening more closely than ever.

Among the issues that divided Americans, none loomed larger than the Vietnam War and the civil rights movement. Although the struggle for the rights of African Americans began when the first blacks were brought to America (1619) and continued through the landmark desegregation case, *Brown v. Board of Education of Topeka, Kansas*, the intensity and organization of the movement increased greatly in the 1960s. To protest the racial segregation that lingered after *Brown*, four young African Ameri-

can students "sat in" at a segregated lunch counter in 1960 at Woolworth's in Greensboro, North Carolina. Their protest set off many more across the country and caused Woolworth's to integrate its lunch counters. The movement for African American civil rights continued in many locales, with major protests in Birmingham and Montgomery, Alabama.

A watershed moment in the movement came on August 28, 1963, when 250,000 Americans—black and white—took part in the "March on Washington." At this historic event, Martin Luther King Jr. delivered his "I Have a Dream" speech, which vocalized the movement's goals and spirit to all Americans. Following the March, Congress passed the Civil Rights Act (1964), making discrimination based on race illegal. Despite this, racial tensions remained high in some big cities. Race riots erupted in the Watts neighborhood of Los Angeles in 1965, in Newark and Detroit in 1967, and in many cities following the assassination of King in 1968. As the decade rolled on, the movement became more militant, and earlier calls for integration and nonviolence gave way to "Black Power"—promoted by the Black Panthers, among others.

The antiwar movement paralleled the civil rights movement. By mid-decade, America had combat troops in Vietnam and the number of American casualties began to increase. Many young Americans questioned the wisdom of the war, and dissent became increasingly vocal and organized, especially on college campuses. Students—white and

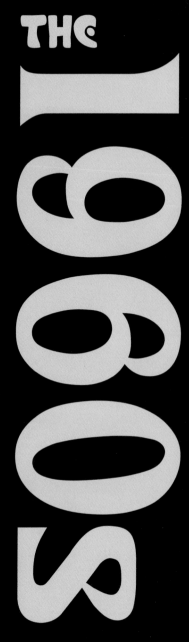

movements, many other movements first appeared on the radar of national awareness in the 1960s. The feminist movement was nurtured significantly by Betty Friedan's 1963 best-selling book *The Feminine Mystique*, which argued that women were constrained by the traditional role of homemaker. In 1966, the National Organization for Women (NOW) was founded with Friedan as its first president. Environmentalism grew when Rachel Carson's *Silent Spring* (1962) drew the country's attention to the dangers resulting from the indiscriminate and persistent use of pesticides such as DDT. Similarly, the consumer protection movement got its spark from Ralph

status quo with militant passion.

The entertainment business was also going through important, and in some cases turbulent, changes. By the beginning of the decade, network programming had almost entirely migrated from radio to television. Driven by advertising demographics, AM radio continued to be mostly a regional or local affair, devoted to hit records and old favorites. FM radio, however, initially an undeveloped wilderness of college lectures, religious programming, and classical music, became the musical home of the hippie counterculture after 1967.

On television, ideas of the 1950s "normalcy" reinforced by shows such as *Leave*

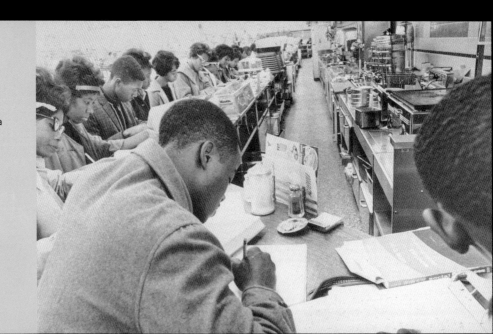

African American students were particularly active in initial public acts connected to the civil rights movement during the early 1960s. Here, a group of students demand service by "sitting in" at a Woolworth counter in Little Rock, Arkansas, in 1963.

Sons. The first show to challenge this sense of domestic normalcy was *The Beverly Hillbillies* (1962), which placed a Tennessee backwoods family in the center of Beverly Hills. At first, the hillbillies seemed to be the target of the show's humor, but it became clear that a better strategy was to use the hillbillies to make the "normal" folks look foolish. This soft critique of 1950s normalcy continued in *My Favorite Martian*, *Bewitched*, and *I Dream of Jeannie*—all shows based on the idea that unique, supernatural powers needed to be concealed from public view, lest the one who had them be considered "abnormal." The youth counterculture of the second half of the 1960s would be far less playful in its critiques of 1950s values.

Movies in the 1960s reflected the pressure of the Cold War and the emergence of the elegant "jet set." Beginning with *Dr. No* in 1962, James Bond (Agent 007) fought communist secret agents in a continuing series of feature films, jetting around the globe, while James Bond might represent the West's confidence in foiling its Cold War enemies, some filmmakers were much more skeptical. Stanley Kubrick offered a stinging critique of the Cold War arms race in *Dr. Strangelove, or: How I Learned to Stop Worrying and Love the Bomb* (1964). And though some saw Kubrick's *2001: A Space Odyssey* (1968) as a celebration of space travel, others saw it as posing a fundamental question regarding man's reliance on technology.

The 1960s drew to a close the same way they began: with a mixture of hope and fear. On July 20, 1969, the United States was unified in celebration: astronauts Neil Armstrong and Buzz Aldrin had realized President Kennedy's challenge to put a man on the moon by the end of the decade. However, this brief moment of unity did nothing to heal the country's wounds over Vietnam and civil rights. Wars and riots raged on, and rock was raging with them.

Anti–Vietnam War protesters taunt military police during a demonstration at the Pentagon in Washington, D.C., October 21, 1967. Throughout the 1960s antiwar sentiment increased, especially among students, as more and more young American soldiers died in battle.

153

CHAPTER 4

THE BEATLES AND THE BRITISH INVASION

CHAPTER PREVIEW

- The Beatles' performance on Ed Sullivan's television show in early 1964 launched Beatlemania in the United States, which led to the "British invasion."

- Performing in Hamburg, Germany, and in Liverpool's Cavern Club the Beatles covered many American rock and roll hits from 1955 to 1963.

- During the 1964–66 period, the Beatles' music gets increasingly ambitious, as they make the shift from craftsmen to artists.

- The Rolling Stones were deeply influenced by American, Chicago-style electric blues. The Animals and the Yardbirds also share strong blues roots.

- In the mid-1960s, the Kinks and the Who focused on original songwriting and raucous performance styles.

- The popularity of the Beatles and other UK bands caught the American pop music business by surprise.

This photo was used on the cover of the Beatles' extended-play single (EP), *Twist and Shout*. Released in the UK in July 1963, this collection of four songs was never released in the United States, though the songs did appear on *Introducing the Beatles* in early 1964. That album was released in the United States by Chicago-based Vee-Jay Records because Capitol Records, the American subsidiary of the Beatles' British label EMI, was confident that a British act could never sell enough records in the U.S. to make it worth their while. After declining to release the British hit singles "Love Me Do," "Please, Please Me," and "She Loves You" in the U.S., however, Capitol finally decided to release "I Want To Hold Your Hand" in the last week of 1963. By early 1964, the single had gone to number one on the U.S. charts, but the other three singles (on Vee-Jay and Philadelphia–based Swan) were also climbing the charts. Scrambling to recover from rejecting these tracks, Capitol quickly put together an album for American release, combining tracks from the first two British albums with both sides of the "I Want to Hold Your Hand" single. The resulting album, *Meet the Beatles!*, differs somewhat from the similar British release called *With the Beatles* and battled Vee-Jay's *Introducing the Beatles* at the top of the U.S. album charts. Capitol continued carving up Beatles albums through the first few years of the band's career in the U.S., creating several albums that have no direct British counterpart, such as *The Beatles' Second Album* (1964), *Something New* (1964), *Beatles VI* (1965), and *Yesterday and Today* (1966).

The early 1960s offered a wide variety of musical styles to American youth, from the simple teenybopper love songs of the teen idols to the more worldly traditionalism and social consciousness of the folk revival. In the music-stylistic space between these opposing poles were girl-group music, rockabilly, surf music, and sweet soul. All these styles seemed to be competing to be the "next big thing" in rock and roll; following the overwhelming popularity of rock's first wave with teen listeners, musicians and businesspeople were hoping to duplicate the enormous success of Elvis Presley. In early 1964, the American music business was taken entirely by surprise when the "new Elvis" turned out to be four young men from Liverpool, England. On February 9, 1964, the Beatles appeared on Ed Sullivan's Sunday evening variety show, just as Elvis Presley had done eight years earlier in 1956. The Beatles reached a record-breaking 73 million viewers, making them a household name practically overnight. This performance was so popular that it was reported later that the crime rate in the United States went down during the time the show was on the air. (See What's That Source? for more reactions.)

The Beatles' success created a fad, and during most of 1964 American fans had a voracious appetite for music performed by young men with British accents, long hair, and matching suits. This "British invasion" of American pop, and the enormous success of the Beatles in particular, altered the music business in several significant ways, affecting both musical style and music-business practice. The Beatles first became popular in the United Kingdom, and the British popular-music scene during the late 1950s and early '60s was also transformed by the music and musicians that would invade the colonies only slightly later. The story of the British invasion is therefore not one, but rather two interdependent stories: the first is a chronicle of British pop before 1964 and British musicians' fascination with American pop, country, jazz, folk, and rhythm and blues; the second is an account of how British music strongly affected American pop after the arrival of the Beatles.

BRITISH POP IN THE LATE 1950S AND EARLY 1960S

The Music Business in the UK. Prior to 1964, American listeners viewed Britain as a secondary force in popular music. Likewise, listeners in the UK consumed a lot of American music, importing far more popular music than it exported. A comparison of the pop hits in Britain during the late 1950s and early '60s with those in the United States reveals that many of the same records, performed in many cases by white American artists, were popular in both countries. British artists were far more likely to achieve success at home than in the States, with occasional exceptions. Orchestra leader Mantovani, for instance, placed twenty-six albums in the American Top 40 between 1955 and 1963, and two singles in the U.S. pop Top 40—the movie themes from *Around the World in Eighty Days* (p12, 1957) and *Exodus* (p31, 1961)—but this was a level of American success unmatched by other British artists. This American dominance in popular music was largely a product of the differences between British and American society. After the end of World War II in 1945, there was tremendous enthusiasm in Britain for American popular culture. American armed forces had taken their culture overseas with them during the war, and many Britons had developed a taste for American pop. Many areas in Britain, and London especially, were devastated by German bombing, and the postwar years were marked by struggle and rebuilding in the UK. Many Britons looked to America as a country full of hope and confidence, affluent and unburdened by the scars of war or the weight of history and tradition. When rock and roll began to emerge in the United States, teens in Britain enthusiastically embraced the new style. The idea of the "teenager" was seen as an American innovation. To many young people in Britain, teens in the United States led lives filled with rock and roll, dancing, cars, and drive-in movies. In the sometimes dreary rebuilding years of the 1950s, British teens found such images enormously attractive and rock and roll became the music of teenage rebellion.

Big companies influenced the music business in Britain much more than in the United States, and this affected the way rock and roll was understood by listeners in the UK. Britain had four major record labels—EMI, Decca, Pye, and Philips—and two radio stations—the BBC and Radio Luxembourg. These major labels licensed music from American majors and indies for release in the UK, Decca and EMI being the most active. The BBC was government-owned and featured three channels, only one of which played rock and roll. Beginning in 1958, the BBC's two-hour radio show *Saturday Club* (hosted by Brian Matthew) became an important weekly source of rock and roll music and information. Radio Luxembourg was a commercial station broadcast from the European continent. Rock and roll was mostly played on shows financed by the major labels, which used these broadcasts to promote their own records. Unlike the United States, Britain had no independent radio stations before 1964, and very few successful independent labels.

Running an indie label in the UK was a tough business: since radio access was controlled by the government or wealthy major labels, an independent stood little chance of ever getting a record played. While rock and roll records that appeared on the American pop charts were mostly available in stores, rhythm and blues was much more difficult to find, as was country and western music. Information about such music was even scarcer, though newspapers such as *Melody Maker*, *New Musical Express*, and *Record Mirror* increasingly devoted attention to rock and roll. Movies became an important resource for young people interested in rock and roll; films made to capitalize on the first wave that featured performances (the Freed movies and *The Girl Can't Help It*) and Elvis films were very popular. British tours by performers such as Bill Haley, Buddy Holly, and the Everly Brothers were important events for young rock and roll fans as well, giving them a chance to see some of their favorite artists perform in person.

These rock and roll enthusiasts were not the first to seek out American pop music. The British had a long-standing infatuation

Regarded as the most important figure in the late-1950s skiffle movement in Britain, Lonnie Donegan and his band blended American folk music with a traditional jazz beat. This photo shows Donegan (second from left) playing banjo while other group members play stand-up bass, tambourine, and the type of hollow-body electric guitar commonly used in jazz.

Music business professionals took notice when the Beatles arrived on American soil in February 1964 to appear on the *Ed Sullivan Show* and perform several concerts in the United States. These three articles appeared simultaneously on the cover of *Variety* magazine shortly after "Beatlemania" came to New York City. They offer contrasting perspectives on the implications of the Beatles' newfound popularity in the United States: "Britain Exports a Mania" provides an overview of the Beatlemania phenomenon from the perspective of the music press; "Pincus Swings" tells the story of a music publisher who is pleased with the Beatles' success; and "Promoter Fears" explains why concert promoters do not see much financial potential in organizing Beatles performances.

"Britain Exports a Mania"

Yank showmen knifed their memories this week to recall a parallel to the four mad youths from Liverpool, England, the Beatles. None came to mind. Elvis Presley is the nearest comparison during the first orgiastic-hysteric reaction to his unique swivel-hip brand of song. More moderate examples of teenage madness were connected with Frank Sinatra in his Dorsey era, with Dean Martin–Jerry Lewis when they hit the kids with a rare blend of sexy lullaby and uninhibited adolescent showoff comicking. It hardly makes sense to go back to Rudy Vallee, circa 1931, with his heigh-ho megaphoning since teenagers were then more or less under parental control.

The Beatles are being much explained, but none of the explanations quite suffice. They are creatures of the phonograph boom, of the Brittanicized rock 'n' roll. There is some of the wild young thing exuberance of Jerry Lewis and more than a trace of precocious sex thrust. Their mad hair-dos are symbolic both of youth's rebellion against barbers and love of "fad."

If there was some surprise after the Ed Sullivan telecast Sunday night that the boys are really something new in rock 'n' roll, this in no way slowed the momentum of their whirlwind tour of the United States. Their press conference Monday morning at the Plaza Hotel bore the classic marks of a White House press conference. There were ground rules. Each reporter had to

with American folk and jazz that dated back to before World War II. After 1945, both of these styles experienced a resurgence in the UK and, in many ways, the British infatuation with rock and roll was a continuation of this interest in earlier American forms. Traditional jazz ("trad"), which stuck very close to the early twentieth-century New Orleans style, was championed by bandleader Ken Colyer and was later broadened to include other jazz styles by Chris Barber, Kenny Ball, and Acker Bilk. Barber's band featured banjo player Tony Donegan, who later began to use the first name "Lonnie." Donegan recorded a version of the traditional folk song "Rock Island Line" in a new style called "skiffle" that blended folk music with an up-tempo rhythmic feel. Credited to Lonnie Donegan and His Skiffle Group (Donegan on vocals and guitar, Barber on bass, and Beryl Bryden on washboard), the single rose to the number-eight slot on the UK charts in 1956, igniting a pop craze for skiffle music. Parallel to the folk boom that took hold in the United States slightly later, this tuneful yet easy-to-play music encouraged the participation of many British teenagers. "Rock Island Line" crossed the Atlantic to hit number eight on the U.S. pop charts in 1956. Donegan followed up this success by placing thirty-one hits on the UK charts by 1962, including a version of "Tom Dooley," which rose to number three in the UK in 1958. By the late 1950s, however, the skiffle fad had been replaced by a preference for trad on the British charts, with Ball, Barber, and Bilk each scoring a series of hits. Some of these even crossed the Atlantic,

raise his hand, rise and identify himself and medium, confine himself to a single question.

What accounts for their sudden burst to prominence, which has, among other things, given them just about the fastest selling disks in history with the exception of Vaughan Meader's "First Family"? Timing, the boys said. They were just in the right place at the right time. Any advice for would-be stars? "Be unique."

"Pincus Swings on String of Beatles Clicks"

Gil Music, George Pincus' company, has turned into a very hot operation by way of a publishing tie-in with The Beatles, the ubiquitous combo from Britain. Pincus' British firm, Ambassador Music, has wrapped up the American rights to a flock of Beatle hits, all of which are written by two members of the combo, John Lennon and Paul McCartney, and published through Northern Music of London, a partnership deal with Dick James.

Pincus has nabbed "I Saw Her Standing There," which is the flip side to the Capitol Records smash, "I Want to Hold Your Hand." The former song is also starting to step out on its own. In addition, Gil Music owns the rights to "She Loves You," on the Swan label, and "From Me to You" on the Veejay label.

"She Loves You" is also shaping up as a solid sheet music seller. It has already gone over 15,000 copies and is heading for 50,000. The Beatles' album for Capitol also contains a Gil Music number, "I Wanna Be Your Man," and has five songs in the Veejay album.

"Promoter Fears about Economics of the Beatles"

Some American promoters aren't too keen on booking the Beatles during their present American tour. Reasoning is that the Beatles' asking price is such that auspices cannot start making any money in any of the large shops unless they gross upwards of $25,000 for a single evening.

The Beatles' asking price for a single evening is $7,000 against 60% of the gross. In addition, the promoters must supply a band and a surrounding show for the entire half of the evening. In addition, the promoter has to lay out an advertising budget, pay for the hall, also pay stagehands, electricians, printing tickets, and sundry other items. The promoters feel that under these circumstances, it will be extremely difficult to make a buck.

The staple prices in a promotion of this kind, based on a $25,000 gross, would be $15,000 for the Beatles. The arena rental for a gross of that kind would be 15% of the gross or $3,750. Already, they say the mathematics of the scheme becomes too frightening, and therefore as much as someone would like to latch onto this hot British import, the possibilities of making money in this deal would be virtually nonexistent.

Source: Selections from *Variety*, February 12, 1964: 1, 87.

such as Barber's "Petite Fleur" (p5 uk3, 1959), Ball's "Midnight in Moscow" (uk2, 1961; p2, 1962), and Bilk's "Stranger on the Shore" (uk2, 1961; pl r7, 1962).

The most pressing challenge facing the UK music business in the late 1950s and early 1960s, however, was not how to place more British records on the American charts. It was how to place more domestic records on the British charts, which, despite the success of homegrown artists like Donegan, Barber, Ball, and Bilk, were still dominated by Americans. British companies had already begun to produce teen-idol singers modeled on Elvis Presley. The first was Decca's Tommy Steele, who hit in 1956 with "Rock with the Caveman" (uk13) and followed later the same year with the number-one British hit, "Singin' the Blues," and sixteen more hits through 1961. The most successful British rocker was EMI's Cliff Richard. From 1958 to 1963, Richard scored twenty-seven UK hit singles. His backup band, the Shadows, was the English equivalent of the Ventures and placed a series of instrumental hits on the UK charts, beginning with "Apache" (uk1, 1960). For all the domestic success that Richard and the Shadows enjoyed, however, only one record crossed the Atlantic before 1964: "Living Doll," which went to number thirty on the U.S. charts in 1959. Like Bob Marcucci's star-making machinery in Philadelphia discussed in Chapter 3, London's Larry Parnes managed a stable of teen idols. Building on his success managing Tommy Steele, Parnes developed Marty Wilde, Billy Fury, Georgie Fame, and Joe Brown, each of whom had a series of hits in

The most successful of the British teen idols that arose in the wake of Elvis Presley, Cliff Richard was one of Britain's top performers in the late 1950s and early 1960s. Despite his star status in the UK, Richard was not able to make much of an impact in the United States, where there was little interest in British groups until the arrival of the Beatles.

the UK. Despite the increased success of British artists, in 1962 the UK charts were still full of Americans: four Elvis Presley records hit number one, along with one each by Ray Charles and B. Bumble and the Stingers. The turn-around for British performers would occur in 1963 with the emergence of what Britons called the "beat boom"—a style led by a group from Liverpool.

THE BEATLES AS STUDENTS OF AMERICAN POP, 1960–1963

Formation and First Gigs. The Beatles formed in Liverpool in 1957, playing as a skiffle band and calling themselves the Quarry Men, then moving on to rock and roll as the popularity of skiffle waned. John Lennon was born in 1940 and Paul McCartney in 1942, so they were fifteen and thirteen years old, respectively, when rock and roll broke out on both sides of the Atlantic. They were among the first generation of musicians for whom rock was the music of their youth. Elvis Presley, by contrast, was fifteen in 1950 and twenty-one when he hit nationally in 1956. Coming along a few years after the first wave, young British musicians learned to play by imitating these older American rock and rollers, and the music of the first wave left an indelible imprint on British rock in the 1960s. It is not surprising that the first recording of the Beatles from 1958 (as the Quarry Men and now including a fifteen-year-old George Harrison on lead guitar) features Buddy Holly's "That'll Be the Day," performed in close imitation of Holly's record. The group also recorded an original song that emulated Holly's style, written by Harrison and McCartney, called "In Spite of All the Danger."

After performing locally with some success and winning a talent contest under the name Johnny and the Moondogs, in 1960 Lennon, McCartney, and Harrison auditioned for manager Larry Parnes. Parnes decided not to sign them as a feature act, but to use the group (now known as the Silver Beetles, after Holly's Crickets) to support one of his singers (Johnny Gentle) on a brief tour of Scotland. Earlier that year Lennon's art-college buddy Stuart Sutcliffe had joined the band on bass, and by summer Pete Best had joined on drums. It was this lineup, with Lennon, McCartney, and Harrison all playing guitar and singing, that later set out to play a four-month stint in the red-light district of Hamburg, Germany.

Hamburg and Liverpool (1960–1962). Between August 1960 and May 1962 the group traveled to Hamburg for three extended stays (playing 106, 92, and

48 nights) and then returned for two shorter periods in late 1962. The Beatles' first regular gig in Hamburg was at the small Indra Club, and they later moved to the larger Kaiserkeller. The group had been booked through agent Allan Williams, who had already sent another Liverpool band, Derry and the Seniors, to Hamburg. Other bands in the city at the time included the Jets, from London, and Liverpudlians Rory Storm and the Hurricanes, featuring drummer Ringo Starr. The Beatles played six-hour sets in which they were constantly being prompted to "make a show." In order to fill the time, the group learned every song they could find, especially high-energy rock and roll numbers that excited German patrons. During their second stint in Hamburg, at the Top Ten Club, the band played from 7 P.M. until 2 A.M. with a fifteen-minute break each hour. Conditions improved greatly by the time of their third visit, when they played the Star Club, at one point sharing the bill with Little Richard. These long nights in tough German bars refined the Beatles' performance skills, making professionals out of the aspiring rock and rollers. The Beatles also became regulars at Liverpool's Cavern Club during this period. Their first appearance was in February 1961, two months after their first stay in Hamburg and only a few weeks after a tremendously successful dance gig at the Litherland Town Hall in Liverpool. Arranged by Cavern Club DJ Bob Wooler, the band played almost 300 shows at the Cavern through early 1962. Many of these were lunchtime affairs, with the crowd and the band eating during the performance. Between shows at the Cavern and stints in Hamburg, the Beatles were performing frequently and continually developing their skills while building an enthusiastic following.

There were advantages and disadvantages to being a Liverpool group. An important advantage was that the city was a seaport, and seamen who traveled the Atlantic regularly brought back American records. Some experts believe that this gave the young Beatles greater exposure to American pop than they might have had even in London. That exposure continued in Hamburg (also a port city) and added to the band's knowledge of American pop, rhythm and blues, and country and western music. The major disadvantage to being based in Liverpool was that the entire British music business was centered in London. It was very difficult for groups outside the capitol to gain acceptance by the most important players in the business, especially bands from the more working-class north.

Before they became worldwide stars, the Beatles regularly played the Cavern Club in their hometown of Liverpool. The photo on the left shows the band at the Cavern in 1961, clad in leather and with Pete Best on drums. The image on the right shows them in 1963 with Ringo Starr on drums and wearing the matching suits suggested by manager Brian Epstein.

In November 1961, Brian Epstein first saw the Beatles perform at the Cavern. Epstein was running a family-owned record store and sought out the group partly through customers' requests for a rocked-up version of "My Bonnie Lies over the Ocean" (1961) performed by Tony Sheridan (backed by the Beatles), a record that had been a hit in Germany. Epstein soon became the Beatles' manager, and immediately set to work on cleaning up the band's stage appearance. In addition to their new "Beatle haircuts," the band also donned matching tailored suits. Epstein's efforts to change the group's image and his efforts at promotion helped the group get better jobs for more money. Epstein then set his sights on a recording contract. Using his contacts inside the British record industry, he was able to secure a recording audition at Decca's London studios. Based on this fifteen-song session (January 1, 1962) and after months of consideration, Decca's Dick Rowe chose to sign Brian Poole and the Tremeloes rather than the Beatles. The Beatles were allowed to keep the demo tape, however, and while the group was in Hamburg in early May 1962, Epstein made the rounds of record companies in London. After being turned down by several labels, Epstein was introduced to George Martin, head of a small EMI label called Parlophone. Martin heard promise in the Decca tape and set up an EMI recording audition for the group in June 1962. By September, he was producing the group's first release for Parlophone, Lennon and McCartney's "Love Me Do." The Hurricanes' Ringo Starr had joined the band in August (replacing Best), but Martin was wary of Starr's unsure playing at the audition and hired a session drummer for the recording date. Martin also had the group record "How Do You Do It?" written by Mitch Murray, although the band successfully lobbied to release an original song as the first single. "Love Me Do" rose to number seventeen on the UK charts by late 1962, and in 1963, "How Do You Do It?" hit number one when it was released by another Epstein-managed Liverpool group, Gerry and the Pacemakers.

By the end of 1962, the Beatles had done what no Liverpool band had done before: gone to London, signed a recording contract, and placed a single on the UK charts. As a result, more bands from Liverpool, Manchester, and Birmingham made their way south and were welcomed by record companies eager to capitalize on the success of the "Mersey Beat" (pop music originating in the mid-1960s around Liverpool and northwest England).

A Performance That Launched a Career.

In the waning weeks of 1960, the Beatles must have thought their fortunes seemed dim. Just weeks after their first exhausting stint in Hamburg, which ended discouragingly with some members of the band being ejected from the country, the group played a local dance at the Litherland Ballroom in Liverpool on December 27. Sharing the bill with two other bands, the Beatles—now experienced performers from their long hours playing in Germany—hit the stage with a ferocity that stunned and then delighted the audience. The Beatles were billed as "from Hamburg" and the crowd must have assumed this was some new German pop phenomenon. (John Lennon was amused that these fans had praised him for his fluent English.) Though it would be more than a year before Ringo would join the band, that night in Liverpool established the group's reputation in their hometown and was the first clear indication of their exceptional future sucess.

BEATLE INFLUENCES

A survey of the songs the Beatles played during the Hamburg and Liverpool period provides valuable insight into their influences and allows us to trace their development as songwriters. Young songwriters often learn their craft by modeling new songs on ones they know. Live recordings provide documentation of what the Beatles played during those years, songs that likely served as models for their later hits. Perhaps the richest source for this repertoire are tapes the band made for a variety of BBC radio broadcasts, including Brian Matthew's *Saturday Club*, in the first years of their British success (1963–65). *The Beatles Live at the BBC* reveals the extent of the band's fascination with American rock and roll. The tapes feature four Elvis Presley covers, including McCartney performing a close copy of "That's All Right (Mama)," and nine Chuck Berry covers, including Lennon singing the lyrically sophisticated "Memphis." Among the other first-wave rockers, Little Richard and Carl Perkins are also represented multiple times. The band also shows an appreciation for Leiber and Stoller's Coasters records, as well as Phil Spector's "To Know Him Is to Love Him." The first of the *Anthology* CD sets, released in 1995, provides five selections from the band's audition tape for Decca (including two Coasters tunes) and an excerpt from Ray Charles's "Hallelujah I Love Her So" recorded at the Cavern Club. Finally, their first two British albums, *Please Please Me* and *With the Beatles* (both 1963), contain several cover versions, including girl-group numbers ("Chains" and "Baby It's You"), Motown tracks ("You Really Got a Hold on Me," "Please Mr. Postman," and "Money"), and a movie theme ("A Taste of Honey"). Based on these early recordings, it is clear that Lennon and McCartney were experienced students of American pop by the time they entered the EMI Abbey Road studios with Martin to make their first hit record in the fall of 1962.

BEATLEMANIA, 1963–1966

Success in England. The success of "Love Me Do" was a sign of things to come for the Beatles, but nobody expected the level of success the group achieved in the UK in 1963, which spread to the rest of the world the next year. They began the year by recording and touring in support of their first album, *Please Please Me*. By August, they had three more hit singles in the UK—"Please Please Me" (uk2), "From Me to You" (uk1), and "She Loves You" (uk1)—as well as a chart-topping album. That summer, the British press coined the term "Beatlemania" to describe the tremendous excitement created among fans at the band's live performances. The group's breakthrough in Britain occurred in mid-October when they performed on *Sunday Night at the London Palladium*, a national television broadcast similar to Ed Sullivan's *Toast of the Town*. This was followed in early November by another high-profile television appearance on the *Royal Variety Performance* in the presence of the Queen Mother, Princess Margaret, and Lord Snowdon. By late November, the group's second album, *With the Beatles*, entered the UK charts at number two on its way to the top spot (which it held until the end of April 1964). In December,

"I Want to Hold Your Hand" hit number one on the UK charts, where it replaced "She Loves You" and became the band's fourth consecutive hit. In late December, the *Times'* music critic William Mann named Lennon and McCartney the "outstanding English composers of 1963."

The Beatles' tremendous success opened the British popular-music business to dozens of other groups. Most of the number-one hits on the UK charts in 1963 were by domestic artists, many of whom made their debuts that year. If the first goal of the British music business had been to place more homegrown acts on the UK charts, 1963 had been an important year. Despite Beatlemania and all that followed in its wake, however, none of this success and excitement made any impact across the Atlantic. Capitol Records, EMI's American subsidiary, declined the right to issue the first Beatles hits in the United States. George Martin was forced to license these singles to American indies—"Please Please Me" and "From Me to You" appeared on Vee-Jay, while "She Loves You" was released by Swan. None of the three records had much chart impact. As strange as it seems today, Capitol was reluctant because they were sure that the Beatles would fail in the United States. This was logic based on experience: most British artists, even Cliff Richard, had been unable to establish themselves as consistent hit-makers in America. In fact, the Beatles were so afraid of failing in America that they told Brian Epstein they did not want to go to the United States until they had a number-one hit there. Despite their reluctance, Epstein tried to get the band booked in the United States. In November 1963, he visited New York and worked out a deal for three appearances on Ed Sullivan's variety show in February 1964. Sullivan had agreed that the Beatles would get top billing on the show, so Epstein and Martin were able to convince Capitol to release "I Want to Hold Your Hand" in late December 1963. By the beginning of February 1964, the single had hit number one in the United States, just in time for the first Sullivan performance on February 9.

The American Experience. With the breakthrough success of the first Sullivan appearance, the Beatles became the hottest act in the American entertainment business almost overnight. Still, everyone involved with the band expected that their success might dry up just as quickly as it had appeared, as had happened with the first wave of rock and roll. Laboring under the idea that they had to make the most of their brief moment of opportunity, the Beatles worked at a furious pace, touring and recording almost without a break. The result was one of the most impressive runs of hit records ever posted in popular music. Of course, success had not come to the group as easily as it seemed to Americans in 1964. Few fans knew of the long, grueling hours in Hamburg or the many shows at the Cavern and across Britain that had filled the previous four years. The Beatles followed the success of "I Want to Hold Your Hand" with more than thirty Top 40 U.S. hits through 1966 (including the records that had been rejected by Capitol), with twelve going to number one, including "Can't Buy Me Love" (1964), "A Hard Day's Night" (1964), "Ticket to Ride" (1965), "Help!" (1965), and "Paperback Writer" (1966). The week after the first Sullivan show, *Meet the Beatles!* hit the top of the American album charts, staying at number one for almost three months, only ceding its spot to *The Beatles' Second Album.* All the group's studio albums would go to number one in both the UK and the United States, although the U.S. albums often featured different titles and songs from the British releases. In July 1964, the band

The Beatles' first performance on the Ed *Sullivan Show*, February 9, 1964, is legendary. Millions tuned in to watch the British invasion storm the home shores.

was featured in their first full-length movie, *A Hard Day's Night*, and followed up with *Help!* in August 1965. Both were tremendous box-office successes, taking advantage of a lucrative market for teen movies that had been established by Alan Freed, Elvis, and others.

Things turned sour for the band in 1966, when controversy erupted in the United States over remarks that John Lennon had made in a UK interview. Asked about the role religion played in the lives of British youth, Lennon replied that "Christianity will go," and that in British society the Beatles were more popular than Jesus Christ. These comments were made in the context of a larger debate in the UK about youth and the church—prompted in part by the changes brought by the Roman Catholic church through the Vatican II reforms. Lennon's words were taken out of context by American reporters, and he was cast as having claimed that the Beatles were more important than Jesus. An uproar in the American South resulted, with Beatles records and other merchandise being burned in large bonfires in major cities. The Ku Klux Klan threatened violence at Beatles concerts, and the band began to fear for their lives. As a result of this controversy, and the toll taken by constant work, the Beatles played their last public concert at San Francisco's Candlestick Park on August 29, 1966.

The Beatles' Music Develops: From Craftsmen to Artists. A clear development can be heard in the Beatles' music during the 1964–66 period. Early on the band seemed content to imitate U.S. models, combining diverse but nonetheless identifiable elements from earlier American music. This derivative music often took American pop of the late 1950s and early '60s, blended it with some hallmark stylistic elements, and sold it back to Americans as British pop. The sources employed by the group tell us that much of the Beatles' music extends American traditions, and these surprising juxtapositions begin to mark the distinctive ways the band

ROCK FILM IN THE 1960S: THE BEATLES IN *A HARD DAY'S NIGHT*

Viewing Rock

After the establishment of rock films during the late 1950s, the Beatles were perfectly poised to release a movie upon their rise to international stardom in early 1964. The result was *A Hard Day's Night*, a film directed by Richard Lester, released in both the UK and the United States later that summer. *A Hard Day's Night* featured the Beatles playing themselves, and furthered stereotypes of the band including their childish nature, a rock-like unreliability,

In private, group members playfully disrespect the authority of their managers and handlers. And on stage, the band performs perfectly to audiences full of screaming female fans. As a vehicle for promoting the group's international stardom, this film certainly blurred the lines between reality, fiction, and corporate marketing. Although Beatles songs are used throughout the film soundtrack, the songs are not integrated into the plot, there are

limited instances of the group actually miming performance, and all performances are lip-synched. One performance occurs early in the film on a train, when a card game inexplicably turns into a musical rendition of "I Should Have Known Better" (2).

The plot of the film, which involves losing and finding Ringo, leads up to a musical performance on a television variety show. The last ten minutes of the film consist of a mini-Beatles concert, providing the perspective of the production crew, as if the film audience was present at the filming of the final television special (3) and (4).

Even though it was a thinly veiled promotion tool with little-to-no plot value, *A Hard Day's Night* still stands up as an interesting film. It places the Beatles in the context of Beatlemania (even if on the terms of the filmmakers), allows us to see them in a quintessentially British environment, and provides several noteworthy video performances.

and the group's knack for exposing a cultural gap between rock listeners and an older generation. The action of the film is based entirely on the Beatles in the context of Beatlemania. In public, the group is constantly chased by rabid female fans (1).

reinterpreted American rock and roll. The Beatles' first American hit, "I Want to Hold Your Hand," is a good example. The driving guitars, playing Chuck Berry–like chords in the low register, recall "Johnny B. Goode" or "Roll Over Beethoven," while the hand claps could have come from girl-group tunes of the early 1960s (such as "My Boyfriend's Back"). The duet singing in the song's bridge is reminiscent of the Everly Brothers, while the "ooo's" that became one of the Beatles' trademarks are lifted directly from Little Richard. The form of the song is AABA with abbreviated reprise—a structural design common in the music of Tin Pan Alley.

Much of the Beatles' music recorded in 1963 to 1964 relies heavily on reworking a limited number of musical elements, most of which can be traced back to the band's earlier music. The group can hardly be faulted for this, since they anticipated their success would be fleeting and wrote and recorded quickly. In this context, it is impressive how much variety they achieved early on. The practice of producing songs according to a "formula" is an aspect of the craft of songwriting. Brill Building songwriters worked in precisely the same manner, as had the Tin Pan Alley songsmiths before them. Another approach employed by the Beatles is usually associated with classical-music composers from the nineteenth and twentieth

Listening Guide

The Beatles, "I Want to Hold Your Hand" Parlophone R-5084 (UK), Capitol 5112 (U.S.)

Words and music by John Lennon and Paul McCartney, produced by George Martin. Reached #1 on UK charts in late 1963 and #1 on the *Billboard* "Hot 100" in early 1964.

FORM: AABA, with partial reprise. The bridge and verse sections are repeated after the complete verse-verse-bridge-verse structure has been presented. Each verse ends in a 4-bar refrain, employing the song's title in the lyrics and featuring two-part vocal harmony; the previous bars in the verse are sung in two-part unison. Note that the first bridge is sung in unison (except at the very end), while the repeated bridge is sung in two-part harmony. The introduction is built from the last 4 bars of the bridge, while the song's ending is created by tagging the last bars of the refrain.

TIME SIGNATURE: 4/4. This lighthearted, driving pop feel with accents on beats 2 and 4 was called "Mersey beat" in the UK.

INSTRUMENTATION: Electric guitars, bass, drums, hand claps, and two-part lead vocal (with sections in unison and in harmony).

0:00–0:08	**Introduction**, 4 mm.	Instrumental with lots of driving rhythm guitar, derived from bridge.
0:08–0:29	**A-Verse with refrain**, 12 mm.	Mostly unison vocals, hand claps enter, "Oh yeah I'll tell you . . ."
0:29–0:51	**A-Verse with refrain**, 12 mm.	As before, "Oh please, say to me . . ."
0:51–1:11	**B-Bridge**, 11 mm.	Unison until end, quieter to provide contrast, but building at end, "And when I touch you . . ."
1:11–1:33	**A-Verse with refrain**, 12 mm.	As before, hand claps return, "Oh you got that somethin' . . ."
1:33–1:54	**B-Bridge**, 11 mm.	New two-part harmony vocals, quiet until the end as before, "And when I touch . . ."
1:54–2:22	**A-Verse with tag**, 15 mm.	As before, 3 bars added at ending, "Yeah you got that . . ."

Listening Guide

The Beatles, "Tomorrow Never Knows" Parlophone PMC-7009 (UK), Capitol T-2576 (U.S.)

Words and music by John Lennon and Paul McCartney, produced by George Martin. Included on the album *Revolver*, which rose to #1 on the U.S. and UK album charts in 1966.

FORM: Simple verse, with each verse built on the same 8-bar structure. The droning of the bass makes the harmonic dimension of the music sound static, suggesting the influence of Indian music, while the tape loops, backward guitar, and processed lead vocals create an otherworldly atmosphere.

TIME SIGNATURE: 4/4. Notice the constant repeated notes in the bass, which interact with the repeated drum pattern, creating a rhythmic feel that seems unrelenting.

INSTRUMENTATION: Bass, sitar, drums, organ, backward guitar, tape loops, piano (at end), and electronically processed lead vocal.

Time	Section	Description
0:00–0:12	**Introduction**, 4 mm.	Opens with sitar, then other instruments and tape loops enter. Note persistent but catchy drumbeat and drone bass.
0:12–0:26	**Verse 1**, 8 mm.	Vocals enter, tape loops slip in and out, "Turn off your mind . . ."
0:26–0:42	**Verse 2**, 8 mm.	As before, "Lay down all thoughts . . ."
0:42–0:56	**Verse 3**, 8 mm.	As before, "That you may see . . . "
0:56–1:12	**Instrumental verse**, 8 mm.	Tape loops and then backward guitar prominently featured.
1:12–1:27	**Instrumental verse**, 8 mm.	Continues loops and backward guitar.
1:27–1:42	**Verse 4**, 8 mm.	Vocals return, as before, "That love is all . . ."
1:42–1:57	**Verse 5**, 8 mm.	As before, "That ignorance and hate . . ."
1:57–2:13	**Verse 6**, 8 mm.	As before, "But listen to the color . . ."
2:13–2:55	**Verse 7 with tag and fade**, 20 mm.+	Fades out with piano, "Or play the game . . ."

centuries. Composers such as Beethoven, Brahms, and Schoenberg avoided solving the same musical problem in precisely the same way. Rather than finding a formula, these composers sought novel solutions for each piece of music. For the purposes of this discussion, we can therefore place craft and art in opposition and reveal something crucial about the Beatles' music and its effect on popular music. From 1964 to 1966, the Beatles increasingly moved away from the formulaic approach to songwriting and toward the artistic one. This transition began in very small ways, but by the time the band entered the studio in early 1966 for the sessions that produced *Revolver*, they had begun experimenting with studio effects, stylistic juxtapositions, and novel timbral and structural elements.

"Tomorrow Never Knows" is a good example of how far the Beatles had come in just over two years. The song is in simple verse form, built on a single 8-measure structure played nine times with no chorus. Lennon draws his lyrics from the *Tibetan Book of the Dead*, an ancient spiritual text that offers advice to those who will soon die (Lennon found the verses adapted in Timothy Leary's *The Psychedelic Experience*). The music creates a kind of static meditative drone, using a repetitive drumbeat and a limited number of chords. The strange sounds that occur throughout the work and especially during the instrumental verse include repeating fragments of prerecorded material created by looping a small piece of tape. These tape loops were manipulated to suggest an otherworldly sonic landscape and mixed into the final recording in real time. Because of the randomness of this procedure, the same result cannot have been easily duplicated either in the studio or in live performance. "Tomorrow Never Knows" is a one-time solution to the challenges presented by the ideas behind this particular track: the band did not repeat this exact approach in subsequent tracks (though other tape techniques were often employed). In this way, "Tomorrow Never Knows" is more art than craft.

The Growing Importance of Lyrics. The Beatles' tendencies toward a more artistic approach are also evident in their song lyrics. The words for "She Loves You," "I Want to Hold Your Hand," and "A Hard Day's Night" typify the band's early lyrics in their dedication to teenage love, and are no more suggestive than the songs by contemporary teen idols. The lyrics for songs like "Help!" and "Norwegian Wood," however, are far more unconventional. In "Help!" Lennon confesses that he has lost his confidence and needs to be reassured, looking back on his youth, when his own naiveté provided a self-confidence that maturity has stripped away. The story of "Norwegian Wood" concerns a one-night stand that leaves the singer sexually frustrated. In a surprising turn (like the one found in Chuck Berry's "Memphis"), the singer then burns the apartment down, sarcastically admiring the quality of the wood as it goes up in flames. Most of the more ambitious lyrics came from Lennon, though McCartney's "Eleanor Rigby" paints a dark picture of alienation, perhaps influenced by the existentialist German students the band befriended in Hamburg. McCartney would follow this song with "She's Leaving Home" on *Sgt. Pepper's Lonely Hearts Club Band* (1967), proving any characterization of Lennon as the "lyric man" and McCartney as the "music man" to be overly facile and misleading. The Beatles' fascination with increasingly complex lyrics led them to print the complete lyrics on the album sleeve of *Sgt. Pepper*, a move that was uncommon among pop acts but has since become standard. The band's focus on lyrics was clearly influenced by folk music, especially the music of Bob Dylan. Dylan, whom the band met in 1964, was the first to challenge Lennon and McCartney to move past teenage love tunes. The folksinger is also perhaps responsible for introducing the Beatles to marijuana (though this claim has been disputed)—an event that would have tremendous influence on pop culture by 1967.

Developing Greater Stylistic Range. The Beatles' early songs incorporated American styles such as rhythm and blues, country and western, and girl-group pop, but this began to change in 1965. The easiest way to observe this expansion of range is by looking at instrumentation. On *Help!* (1965), for example, Lennon's "You've Got to Hide Your Love Away" incorporates a flute and is clearly influenced by Dylan and the folk revival, while McCartney's "Yesterday" features string accompaniment that evokes classical chamber music. On *Rubber Soul,* the folk influence became even more pronounced, with Harrison also introducing a sitar into the band's sound on "Norwegian Wood." *Revolver* ranged even more widely, from McCartney's "Eleanor Rigby" to Lennon's "Tomorrow Never Knows" and from the children's song "Yellow Submarine" to the Stax-style horns of "Got to Get You into My Life." Being the most successful band in the world brought with it a certain freedom not usually extended to young pop musicians, and the Beatles were able to experiment much more than other bands. In taking advantage of this opportunity, they established a model for the rock musician as recording artist. The Beatles' progression from craft to art in this period marks a shift to greater seriousness and self-consciousness among rock musicians and their listeners, paving the way for something that would have seemed like an oxymoron earlier in the decade: rock culture. The next stage of the band's career, when the group's ambition extended even further, will be taken up in our discussion of psychedelia in Chapter 7.

THE BRITISH INVADE

Haircuts, Accents, and Guitars. In the wake of the Beatles' overwhelming American success in early 1964, a number of British bands flooded the U.S. charts. After the Beatles, the most prominent band was the Rolling Stones, a group that positioned itself as the bad boys of the British invasion. If the Beatles were charming, cute, and friendly, the Stones were sensual, dangerous, and often rude—in short, they were the anti-Beatles. In reality, the Stones and the Beatles were good friends and the individual members of these groups shared more similarities than differences. Other British bands of the time can be roughly divided into Beatles-type and Stones-type groups. Beatles-type bands such as Gerry and the Pacemakers and the Dave Clark Five were more pop and vocally oriented, while Stones-type groups like the Animals and the Yardbirds were more blues oriented. This split did not apply to all popular British bands in the United States, and bands such as the Who and the Kinks do not fit well into either category.

The term "British invasion" refers to UK groups who played guitars and, initially, wore long hair. Stylistically, there is a broad range of music within the British invasion, so while the term is useful as a general stylistic marker (these bands did have a number of things in common musically), it is most useful in terms of marketing and image. As discussed later in this chapter, the British invasion was clearly a fad at first. It hardly seemed to matter whether the music was influenced by the slick production of Motown or the direct expressiveness of Chess recordings. Initially, the Beatles and the British-invasion bands that followed in their wake drew a large portion of their audience from teenagers who, just a few years earlier, were listening to the teen idols of the early 1960s.

Gerry and the Pacemakers, the Dave Clark Five, and Other Beatles-type Bands.

In retrospect, we can see that the Beatles' success overshadows that of almost every other British band in the 1960s, but this was less obvious at the time. In the UK, Gerry and the Pacemakers were nearly as popular as the Beatles. The Pacemakers followed their 1964 number one, "How Do You Do It?" with two more chart-topping British singles that year: "I Like It" and "You'll Never Walk Alone." While the band eventually scored seven Top 40 hits in the United States through 1966, with "Don't Let the Sun Catch You Crying" rising as high as number four in summer 1964, they were never as popular in America as they were in Britain. London's Dave Clark Five was a Beatles-type band that fared better in the United States, with seven Top 40 American hits in 1964 alone, and nearly as many in 1965, including "Glad All Over" (p6 uk1, 1964) and "Over and Over" (p1 uk45, 1965). The success of the Dave Clark Five led some in the business to predict that they would topple the Beatles. (By the end of the 1964, however, the Beatles had nineteen Top 40 hits.) Two other Liverpool bands, Billy J. Kramer and the Dakotas and the Searchers, also did well in the United States, respectively placing four and five singles in the Top 40 in 1964. The fact that the music business was on the lookout for the next big thing while the Beatles were enjoying their first success reveals how widely rock music, or at least particular rock acts, were still viewed as passing fads. Many music business professionals at the time saw all these bands as pretty much the same act. In many ways, these professionals were right.

Herman's Hermits, Freddy and the Dreamers, and the Hollies.

A second wave of Beatles-type Manchester bands began to hit U.S. shores in 1965. They were led by Herman's Hermits, whose "I'm into Something Good" went to number thirteen in late 1964. The group followed this success with seventeen more Top 40 hits through 1968, including "Mrs. Brown You've Got a Lovely Daughter" (p1, 1965), "I'm Henry VIII, I Am" (p1, 1965), and "Listen People" (p3, 1966). The boyish good looks of singer Peter Noone made him an immediate teen heartthrob just when the Beatles were moving away from their mop-top haircuts and pop image. Another Manchester group, Freddie and the Dreamers, topped the U.S. charts early in 1965 with "I'm Telling You Now," following with three more Top 40 hits that year. Singer Freddie Garrity took a cue from the Beatles' flair for comedy by performing a silly dance while singing "Do the Freddie" (p18, 1965). The Hollies also found popularity in America with the "Manchester sound," placing six hits in the U.S. Top 40, including "Bus Stop" (p5, 1966). The Hollies' music emphasized and expanded the precise harmony singing heard on many Beatles records, a feature that their lead vocalist, Graham Nash, would further develop with the group Crosby, Stills, and Nash at the end of the decade.

During the first year of the Beatles' success, fellow Liverpudlians Gerry and the Pacemakers rivaled the Fab Four's chart success in the UK. This poster is from a June 1963 "Mersey beat" showcase concert that took place in New Brighton, just outside Liverpool. At the time, both of these groups had records in the UK Top 10.

THE ROLLING STONES AND THE BRITISH BLUES REVIVAL

Bad Boys, Blues, and Rhythm and Blues. Following the lead of the Rolling Stones, another group of British bands projected a more brash, nonconformist, and rebellious image. These groups depended less on the vocal- and song-oriented pop styles of the late '50s and early '60s. Instead, they drew on the 1950s Chicago electric blues tradition, featuring slide guitar, harmonica, and styles of vocal delivery that were indebted to Muddy Waters, Elmore James, and Little Walter. These blues-oriented bands emerged from a blues revival scene in the UK that flourished during the early 1960s and gained popularity in the United States after the Beatles broke into the American market. Despite the differences in musical style between the Beatles- and Stones-type bands, they were all packaged in the matching suits and haircuts ushered in by Beatlemania—even if some groups loosened their ties a bit more or lost parts of their outfits from time to time.

Blues Enthusiasts. The UK blues revival was mostly centered in London and was fueled by the same British enthusiasm for American folk styles that had launched trad and skiffle. The catalysts for this scene were guitarist Alexis Korner and harmonica player Cyril Davies, who began playing blues during breaks at performances of Chris Barber's trad band. Korner and Davies soon began regular blues sessions in London's Marquee Club (which Barber owned) and later in the Ealing Club. Aspiring blues musicians would generally play cover versions of American electric blues, trying to emulate the sounds on the records as closely as possible. Recordings from 1962 of the Korner-Davies group, Blues Incorporated, demonstrate how faithful these cover versions were. American blues records were not easy to find in the UK, and the scarcity of these recordings led to trading and borrowing among members

Eric Burdon (center) stands at the microphone, with the rest of the Animals backing him. Though strongly influenced by American blues, the Animals emerged from northern England and did not play much of a role in the London blues revival scene that nurtured the Stones and the Yardbirds. Bassist Chas Chandler (left) would go on to manage Jimi Hendrix later in the 1960s.

Listening Guide

The Animals, "House of the Rising Sun" Columbia OB 7301 (UK), London 45-LON 9766 (U.S.)

Also known as "Rising Sun Blues," the music and text of this song are based on a traditional ballad, which dates back at least to the early nineteenth century. Early recordings exist by Clarence "Tom" Ashley (1932) and Lead-belly (1948). The Animals version was arranged by Alan Price and produced by Mickie Most. It reached #1 on the U.S. *Billboard* "Hot 100" and UK *Record Retailer* charts in 1964.

FORM: Simple verse.

TIME SIGNATURE: 6/8. Throughout the song each chord change is held for two "big" beats.

INSTRUMENTATION: Electric guitar, bass guitar, drums, electric organ, lead vocals.

0:00–0:11	**Introduction**, 8 mm.	Featuring the guitar and bass, the introduction comes from the last 8 mm. of the verse structure.
0:11–0:46	**Verse 1**, 22 mm.	Each verse consists of a pattern of chords that seems to continually rise and then stabilize twice, forming two phrases. The first phrase is 8 mm. ("There is a house . . .") and the second 14 mm. ("It's been the ruin . . ."). Note how the second phrase seems to "skip" 2 mm., beginning the 8-mm. instrumental interlude and introduction music 2 mm. early.
0:46–1:20	**Verse 2**, 22 mm.	The story of the song recalls a myth of gambling and prostitution in New Orleans, showing the Animals' interest in American folklore.
1:20–1:53	**Verse 3**, 22 mm.	This verse emphasizes the difficulty of a gambler's lifestyle, reflecting on (and arguably glorifying) an unstable upbringing.
1:53–2:27	**Verse (Instrumental)**, 22 mm.	Solo section featuring the organ playing of Alan Price.
2:27–3:00	**Verse 4**, 22 mm.	A confessional verse, during which the protagonist takes on a type of religious fervor. Is this an invitation to the "House," or an admonition to stay away?
3:00–3:34	**Verse 5**, 22 mm.	Note the intensity created by the strumming guitar at the opening of the verse, which parallels the decision to return to New Orleans in the text.
3:34–4:04	**Verse 6**, 22 mm.	The repeated lyrics from verse 1 help to depict circularity in both the gambling lifestyle, to which addicts return again and again, and a cycle of abuse that passes from parents to their children. Note the intensity

(continued)

of the music at the end. As a song in simple verse form, the growing dynamic levels help to define the action.

4:04–4:30	**Postlude**, 16 mm.	Just after the most intense part of the song, the postlude helps "wind down" the intensity level almost to a halt.

of the London-based blues culture—which further reinforced the subculture aspects of the UK blues revival. Many important musicians in the history of rock came up through the London blues scene, including John Mayall, Steve Winwood, Eric Clapton, Jack Bruce, and John McLaughlin. Among those who attended Davies and Korner's jam sessions were a pair of teenagers from London's Dartford suburb, guitarist Keith Richards and singer Mick Jagger. Hailing from Newcastle, the Animals were another blues-based band that enjoyed success in the UK and United States. Fronted by the powerful blues singing of Eric Burdon, the group initially played clubs in the north of England and even did a two-month stint at Hamburg's Star Club before moving to London in early 1964. The Animals got a crucial break when they were chosen to play on a UK tour featuring Chuck Berry as headliner. Figuring that they needed to make a strong musical impression on this important tour, the band closed their set with a slow traditional American folk-blues number, "House of the Rising Sun," calculating that it would be unwise to try to outrock Chuck Berry. Produced by Mickey Most (who would also produce Herman's Hermits), the single hit number six in the UK and number seven in the United States during the summer of 1964. The group followed with a string of international Most-produced hits, including a cover of Nina Simone's "Don't Let Me Be Misunderstood" (p15 uk3, 1965), Barry Mann and Cynthia Weil's "We've Gotta Get Out of This Place" (p13 uk2, 1965), and "It's My Life" (p23 uk7, 1965). After switching to producer Tom Wilson, the band continued to enjoy hit singles, including the traditional prison blues song "Inside Looking Out" (p34 uk12, 1966) and the Gerry Goffin–Carole King song "Don't Bring Me Down" (p12 uk6, 1966). By September, the original Animals lineup had dissolved, although Burdon continued with new musicians as Eric Burdon and the Animals, while bassist Chas Chandler went on to manage Jimi Hendrix.

The Rolling Stones. While our current image of the Rolling Stones tends to focus on Jagger and Richards, in its first years the group was led by guitarist Brian Jones, a talented and dedicated student of American blues. The Rolling Stones were formed by Jones (and modeled after Blues Incorporated) to cover American blues records in the clubs of the London underground blues scene. Jagger and Richards were also enthusiastic fans of Chuck Berry, although this music was viewed with some suspicion by dedicated blues aficionados like Jones. The group got its start in July 1962 filling in for Blues Incorporated at the Marquee and later played regularly at the Ealing Club. By January 1963, bassist Bill Wyman and drummer Charlie Watts had joined forces with Jones, Jagger, Richards, and pianist Ian Stewart. Excitement for the band's live performances started to build when they established

In contrast to the Beatles, who dressed in matching suits during the years following the British invasion, the Rolling Stones often sported more casual styles of dress. The group is pictured here in 1965 performing on the British television show *Thank Your Lucky Stars*.

a regular weekly gig at the Richmond Crawdaddy Club in February. The club's manager, Giorgio Gomelsky, managed the group during its early days and helped the Stones build a strong following at the Crawdaddy. In May 1963, Andrew Loog Oldham and Eric Easton took over management of the band. Easton was experienced in the recording industry and Oldham had worked as a publicist for Larry Parnes and Brian Epstein (he had helped promote Gerry and the Pacemakers and Billy J. Kramer).

The Stones turned toward a more mainstream, pop-oriented style in the wake of the Beatles' first UK success in mid-1963. The two groups knew one another and were friendly, although the Beatles were by far the more successful and experienced group. The Stones recorded for Decca and were signed by Dick Rowe, "the man who turned down the Beatles." Before they were signed, Rowe was judging a talent contest in Liverpool on a panel that included George Harrison. After apologizing to Harrison about not signing the Beatles, he asked whether Harrison knew any up-and-coming groups. Harrison enthusiastically endorsed the Stones and Rowe immediately sought them out at the Crawdaddy. Oldham and Easton negotiated an unprecedented deal with Decca, specifying that while the label would have exclusive rights to distribute the band's recordings, the Stones would retain ownership of their recordings. Oldham got the idea of retaining these rights from a conversation with Phil Spector when the American producer was in the UK. Although he had no experience in the recording studio, Oldham immediately assumed the additional role of producer for the band. With Oldham in charge of the group's recording sessions, the Rolling Stones relied on engineers for technical support and enjoyed extensive creative freedom in the studio. This led to the group cultivating a rough sound on record, which matched their brash style of performance.

Initially, the Stones did not write their own music. Their first single was a cover version of Chuck Berry's "Come On" (uk21, 1963) and their third was a cover of Buddy Holly's "Not Fade Away" (uk3, 1964). The band's second single was a song Lennon and McCartney wrote for them, "I Wanna Be Your Man" (uk12, 1963), which both groups recorded. (Comparing the two versions reveals an interesting contrast between these two bands in their early years: the Stones version shows much more of a blues influence, with a loose arrangement that prominently features the slide guitar, and the Beatles' version is tightly arranged and focuses on the vocals.) Quickly understanding the financial advantages that writing music could provide, Oldham decided that Jagger and Richards, who had become the leaders of the group, should try their hand at songwriting, reportedly locking them in a room until they wrote a song. "The Last Time" was the first of many Jagger-Richards hits, reaching number one in the UK in 1965 (p9). The budding songwriting team also had an international hit in 1964 with Marianne Faithfull's recording of "As Tears Go By" (p22 uk9). While the Stones would increasingly record more Jagger-Richards songs, their first six albums contain more cover versions than originals, and reveal the band's dedication to American rhythm and blues artists such as Muddy Waters, Jimmy Reed, and Bo Diddley, among others. Two early singles show the band's range of influences: "It's All Over Now" (p26 uk1, 1964) was originally recorded by African American vocalist Bobby Womack, and the Stones give it a country and western feel, while Chicago bluesman Willie Dixon's "Little Red Rooster" (uk1, 1964) is a slow blues tune.

The Stones enjoyed great popularity in the UK in late 1963 and through 1964, but this success did not extend to the United States, where the Beatles, Gerry and the Pacemakers, and the Dave Clark Five were much more warmly received. Late in 1964, things began to improve, with "Time Is on My Side" hitting number six in the United States and "The Last Time" reaching number nine in spring 1965 (r19). The Stones' slow start in the United States was partly due to the group's bad-boy image. Oldham had bought the Stones matching outfits when he took over, but the band soon lost or hopelessly soiled parts of these stage clothes—and not entirely by accident. The Stones rode to fame in the UK as the antithesis of the Beatles, sporting scruffier clothing, longer hair, and rebellious attitudes that shocked adults. This, of course, was the key to the Stones' appeal for many young people in Britain. That appeal would soon spread to the United States, starting with an American tour in late 1964 that generated several stories portraying the band as rock and roll troublemakers.

The Stones solidified their image as rock's bad boys with the single "(I Can't Get No) Satisfaction," which, driven by Richards's fuzz-guitar introduction, hit number one in the United States and the UK in summer 1965 (r19). Although the song's lyrics clearly express a general dissatisfaction with the superficiality of daily life, a rumor circulated that the topic of the song was masturbation, perhaps owing to the last verse, which refers to menstruation and a resultant sexual frustration. Jagger and Richards did little to calm the storm over the record, since the rumor fit well into the anti-Beatles image the band was now cultivating. What could be better, after all, than a thin, swaggering Mick Jagger singing a song about something many American kids and their parents regarded—publicly at least—as a forbidden pleasure? The Stones followed with "Get Off of My Cloud" (p1 uk1, 1965), "As Tears Go By" (p6, 1966), "19th Nervous Breakdown" (p2 uk2, 1966), and "Paint

The pandemonium of rock shows could sometimes turn violent. This photo shows a Zurich crowd getting out of hand in April 1967 at a Rolling Stones concert. Considering the manic quality of many of these events, it seems remarkable that such chaos did not break out more often.

It Black" (pl uk1, 1966). As the group's popularity rose in the United States, they appeared on American television and toured with increasing success. Unfortunately, as an outgrowth of the band's rebellious image, their shows were often marked by fan riots and police interventions. After experiencing what was becoming the standard fan mania during the band's first appearance on his show in 1965, Ed Sullivan vowed the Stones would never return. By 1967, however, Sullivan had changed his mind, but in a situation reminiscent of Elvis Presley's appearances, the group was asked to change the chorus of "Let's Spend the Night Together" to "let's spend some time together."

The Stones and the Blues Tradition. Considering the importance of blues music for the Stones, it is somewhat surprising that the majority of 12-bar blues in their mid-1960s repertoire consists of cover versions. ("19th Nervous Breakdown," which does employ the 12-bar pattern, is one important exception.) Jagger-Richards originals tend to be influenced more by Chuck Berry and Motown than by Muddy Waters or Howlin' Wolf. This may reflect Jagger's opinion, expressed during the band's first years of success, that the idea of a blues song being written by a white Brit was preposterous. Whatever the reason, "Satisfaction" illustrates an approach used often by Jagger and Richards. The strong riff and Jagger's improvisation during the song's final seconds are clearly reminiscent of the blues, but the song's complex form is more indebted to non-blues popular styles. While the Beatles employed mostly AABA forms of Brill Building pop, Jagger and Richards preferred the contrasting verse-chorus form found in Chuck Berry and Buddy Holly's music. "Satisfaction" is the same contrasting verse-chorus form as Holly's "That'll Be the Day" and Berry's "Rock and Roll Music."

Listening Guide

The Rolling Stones, "(I Can't Get No) Satisfaction" Decca F12220 (UK), London 45-LON 9766 (U.S.)

Words and music by Mick Jagger and Keith Richards, produced by Andrew Loog Oldham. Reached #1 on the U.S. *Billboard* "Hot 100" and UK *Record Retailer* charts in 1965.

FORM: Contrasting verse-chorus. Each chorus is followed by two measures that repeat the opening riff and lead back to the next verse, except at the end, where this riff is used to create the ending of the song. Note that the song features a reprise of the introduction at the end, similarly to The Ronettes' "Be My Baby" (see Listening Guide in Chapter 3).

TIME SIGNATURE: 4/4 throughout, with each beat punctuated by a snare hit.

INSTRUMENTATION: Electric and acoustic guitars, bass guitar, tambourine, drums, lead and backing vocals.

Time	Section	Description
0:00–0:15	**Introduction**, 8 mm.	Focused on the main riff of the chorus. Note the way the instruments enter one at a time in this order: electric guitar, bass, drums, acoustic guitar, and tambourine.
0:15–0:42	**Chorus**, 16 mm.	The multisection chorus begins with a calm 8-mm. statement and is followed by two shorter 4-mm. group vocal sections ("Cause I try . . ." followed by "I can't get no . . .").
0:42–1:16	**Verse** 1, 18 mm.	"When I'm driving in my car . . ." Each multisection verse begins with 10 mm. explaining a frustrating situation, followed by two 4-mm. refrains ("I can't get no . . ." followed by "No, no, no . . .").
1:16–1:42	**Chorus**, 16 mm.	The chorus section seems to project less energy in this song, which is the opposite of its usual role. This is especially evident at the beginning of each chorus, when the intensity drops.
1:42–2:15	**Verse** 2, 18 mm.	"When I'm watching my TV . . ."
2:15–2:43	**Chorus**, 16 mm.	Notice how Jagger changes the lyrics from "satisfaction" to "girl reaction."
2:43–3:16	**Verse** 3, 18 mm.	"When I'm riding 'round the world . . ."
3:16–3:41	**Coda**, 16 mm.	This repeated section reveals the rhythm and blues influence on the Stones. Jagger improvises over the main riff, accelerating the intensity while the song fades out.

The Yardbirds and Other UK Blues Revivalists. When the Stones gave up their regular date at the Crawdaddy Club in Richmond in 1963, the Yardbirds took their place, and also took on Gomelsky as a manager. The group initially consisted of Keith Relf on vocals and harmonica, Paul Samwell-Smith on bass, Jim McCarty on drums, and Chris Dreja and Tony Topham on guitar, but Topham was soon replaced by lead guitarist Eric Clapton. Clapton earned his nickname "Slowhand" during these early years because he often broke guitar strings and had to change them on-stage, as audience members joked with him about it by providing slow applause. Initially, the group was even more devoted to the blues tradition than the Stones had been, and Clapton was especially uncompromising in his resistance to pop music at the time. The Yardbirds developed long, improvisatory passages at the end of songs that they called "rave-ups"; these emphasized the instrumental prowess of band members (Clapton especially) and were forerunners to the instrumental jam sessions that would characterize much rock music later in the decade. An example of this can be heard at the end of the band's version of Howlin' Wolf's "Smokestack Lightning," recorded at the Marquee and released on the album *Five Live Yardbirds* in December 1964.

Gomelsky had hopes that the Yardbirds could follow the Stones' model as hit-makers, but the band's first two UK singles performed disappointingly: "I Wish You Would" failed to chart, and "Good Morning Little Schoolgirl" rose only as high as number forty-four. Deciding that the group needed a sure-fire pop hit, Gomelsky (who was not only managing but also producing the band, with Samwell-Smith acting as musical director), acquired songwriter Graham Gouldman's "For Your Love" for the Yardbirds. The verses of the tune primarily use studio musicians, with the band playing as a whole only during the middle bridge section. While session musicians often played on pop records, this concession was more than Clapton

This photo from January 1965 shows Keith Relf, the lead singer of the Yardbirds, with Paul Samwell-Smith and Chris Dreja (background) during a gig at Woolwich.

could bear. After "For Your Love" was finished, the guitarist left the Yardbirds to join John Mayall and the Bluesbreakers. The Yardbirds' single rose to number six in the United States and number three in the UK in the first half of 1965. Jeff Beck replaced Clapton on lead guitar, and his more experimental nature can be heard on the group's follow-up single, "Heart Full of Soul" (p9 uk2, 1965). Beck uses a fuzztone to create the tune's distinctive guitar **lick**, a technique Keith Richards would use on "Satisfaction." ("Heart Full of Soul" was recorded on April 20, 1965, while "Satisfaction" was recorded three weeks later on May 12, 1965.) "Heart Full of Soul," also written by Gouldman, reached number nine in the United States and number two in the UK in the summer of 1965.

lick

While Clapton felt the band had not remained true to its blues roots, the other members of the Yardbirds might not have agreed. The band was especially excited to record their first original single, "Shapes of Things" (p3 uk11, 1966), at the Chess studios in Chicago, where they also recorded a cover of Bo Diddley's "I'm a Man." At Sam Phillips's new recording studio (the successor to Sun Studios) in Memphis, the Yardbirds recorded a version of "Train Kept a Rollin'," a Memphis rockabilly track most often associated with the Johnny Burnette Rock and Roll Trio version of 1956. In spring 1966, Simon Napier-Bell and Paul Samwell-Smith took over production duties from Gomelsky, resulting in the band's last hit single, "Over, Under, Sideways, Down" (p13 uk10). In June, Samwell-Smith left the band to devote himself to producing, and session guitarist Jimmy Page was brought in. Page initially played bass, but by the fall Dreja switched to bass, leaving Beck and Page to share the lead-guitar spot. In October, Beck left the Yardbirds, going on to form the Jeff Beck Group, while Page, Dreja, Relf, and McCarty kept the Yardbirds alive until the summer of 1968, when they disbanded. Page formed a new group to fulfill the remaining dates the Yardbirds had booked: Led Zeppelin.

Not all the blues-based bands playing the London clubs achieved chart success. Perhaps the busiest band on the London scene was Georgie Fame and the Blue

The Beatles' success extended far beyond North America and the UK, and the band toured many parts of the world as Beatlemania spread. In July of 1966, the Beatles performed at the Nippon Budokan in Tokyo. The Budokan had historically been reserved for Japanese martial arts and wrestling events, and there were protests from those opposed to having rock music in the venue. While the Beatles were the first rock band to perform there, many live albums would be recorded there in the years following, including records from Bob Dylan, Cheap Trick, and Ozzy Osbourne.

Listening Guide ᴵᴵᴵᴵᴵ

The Kinks, "You Really Got Me" Pye 7N 15673 (UK), Reprise 0306 (U.S.)

Words and music by Ray Davies, produced by Shel Talmy. Reached #1 on the UK *Record Retailer* and #7 on the *Billboard* "Hot 100" in the United States in 1964.

FORM: Simple verse form, with repeated 20-bar verses built on a two-chord pattern that is repeated progressively higher on the guitar providing a sense of growing tonal intensification as the verse proceeds. This two-chord pattern is not transposed during the guitar solo, and a comparison of that partial verse with the other complete ones highlights this tonal difference.

TIME SIGNATURE: 4/4. Note the use of repeated piano chords and tambourine to underscore the beat and its division in two parts (simple time).

INSTRUMENTATION: Electric guitars, piano, bass, drums, tambourine, lead and backup vocals. While this track is professionally produced, the backup vocals give it a wild and almost amateurish quality, an impression reinforced by the manic but relatively primitive guitar solo.

0:00–0:07	**Introduction**, 4 mm.	Starts with 1-bar guitar figure played twice, then band enters. Note the distorted tone in the guitar.
0:07–0:42	**Verse 1 with refrain**, 20 mm.	Vocals enter. Note how the verse builds, first with solo vocal, then with added piano, then with added backup vocals, also getting increasingly louder to drive to the refrain, "Girl, you really got me . . ."
0:42–1:17	**Verse 2 with refrain**, 20 mm.	As before, "See, don't ever set . . ."
1:17–1:34	**Instrumental verse** (partial), 10 mm.	Guitar solo as the music breaks into a controlled frenzy.
1:34–2:12	**Verse 2 with refrain**, 20 mm.	Repeats lyrics of second verse, last 2 bars changed to create ending.

Flames—which at various times featured guitarist John McLaughlin and drummer Mitch Mitchell, who would later play with Jimi Hendrix. Fame, who was born Clive Powell but renamed by Larry Parnes in the early 1960s, scored several UK hits, including two number ones: "Yeh Yeh" (p21) in 1965 and "Get Away" in 1966. Other bands on the scene included the Graham Bond Organization, featuring Jack Bruce, future Cream drummer Ginger Baker, and McLaughlin; and Zoot Money's Big Roll Band, featuring future Police guitarist Andy Summers. The Spencer Davis Group, with organist Steve Winwood, scored two chart-topping UK hits, "Keep

Led by brothers Ray and Dave Davies, the Kinks blended elements of the Beatles and the Rolling Stones. This photo from December 1965 shows Dave Davies (left), Pete Quaife (back), Mick Avory (front), and Ray Davies (right) performing on television.

On Runnin'" (1965) and "Somebody Help Me" (1966), before hitting internationally with "Gimme Some Lovin'" (p7 uk2, 1966) and "I'm a Man" (p10 uk9, 1967).

The Kinks and the Who: Raw Power and Ambitious Lyrics. The Beatles- and Stones-type labels obviously cannot be applied to all British bands from the 1960s. The most important among the bands that defy such strict categorization are the Kinks and the Who. The Kinks emerged from the same rhythm and blues roots as the Stones-type groups but performed mostly with package tours that featured more pop-oriented acts. The Who claimed no real roots in the blues but played the London rhythm and blues clubs regularly. Like the Beatles, both bands depended on members' strong songwriting for their best material (Ray Davies for the Kinks and Pete Townshend for the Who); and like the Stones, both groups emphasized the raw power and rhythmic drive of American rhythm and blues.

Formed in 1963, the Kinks featured brothers Ray and Dave Davies on guitar and vocals, with Peter Quaife on bass and Mick Avory on drums. Both Davies brothers had played in various blues-oriented groups around London, while Avory had been one of the first drummers for the Rolling Stones. The Kinks benefited early on from an aggressive management team and the production talents of Australian Shel Talmy. The band's first two singles, released in the first half of 1964, did not chart. Their third single, "You Really Got Me," went to number one in the UK and number seven in the United States in fall 1964. The Kinks' aggressive pop approach can be heard in the opening guitar chords of "You Really Got Me," and in the wild

The Who were embraced by the British Mod movement in the mid-1960s. This live shot from a March 1966 television shoot shows the snappy fashion so typical of Mods. Band members are (from left to right) John Entwistle, Roger Daltrey, Keith Moon, and Pete Townshend.

Listening Guide

The Who, "My Generation" Brunswick 05944

Words and music by Pete Townshend, produced by Shel Talmy. Rose to #2 in the UK "Record Retailer Singles" chart in late 1965.

FORM: Simple verse, each verse includes a refrain. The verses are quite similar and are built up from 4-bar phrases. Later verses expand in 4-bar increments to 24 and 28 measures, with the coda running to 36 measures plus the final bar (37 mm.). A distinctive feature of this song is the use of key changes, always moving upward (in this case, G, A, B♭, and C). This has the effect of driving the song toward its explosive climax at the end.

TIME SIGNATURE: 4/4, moderately fast tempo.

INSTRUMENTATION: Lead and backup vocals, two electric guitars, bass, drums. During the aggressive coda the band would often destroy the guitar and drums. Something of that manic energy is projected through the use of driving drums and guitar feedback at the end in this studio recording.

0:00–0:05	**Introduction**, 4 mm.	Guitar, bass, and drums establish driving main riff.
0:05–0:30	**Verse (with refrain)**, 20 mm.	Vocal enters, stuttering and alternating with backup vocals, "People try . . ."
0:30–0:55	**Verse**, 20 mm.	As before, notice the provocative stutter on the word "fade," "Why don't you all . . ."
0:55–1:20	**Verse (instrumental)**, 20 mm.	Bass solo featuring John Entwistle.
1:20–1:54	**Verse**, 28 mm.	Key change for new verse, with another new key established in last four bars, "Why don't you all . . ."
1:54–2:24	**Verse**, 24 mm.	As before, but in new key established at end of previous verse, "People try . . ."
2:24–3:16	**Coda**, 37 mm.	Yet another key change as drums become much more active and guitar gets wilder, based on refrain.

guitar solo in the middle of the track. A series of original songs followed, including "All Day and All of the Night" (p7 uk2, 1964), "Tired of Waiting for You" (p6 uk1, 1965), and "Till the End of the Day" (p50 uk6, 1965). As the Beatles grew more serious and ambitious with their lyrics in 1965, so did Davies: his "A Well-Respected Man" (p13, 1965) and "Dedicated Follower of Fashion" (p36 uk4, 1966) offered clever and biting critiques of 1960s culture.

Initially formed in 1962 as the Detours, the Who combined the guitar playing and songwriting of Pete Townshend with the singing of Roger Daltrey, the assertive bass playing of John Entwistle, and the manic drumming of Keith Moon. Although they eventually became one of the most important bands in the history of rock music, the Who did not exert much influence in America until the late 1960s. Their series of UK hit singles during the mid-1960s never made the U.S. Top 40, and the band's success was restricted to Britain until the release of "I Can See for Miles," which went to number nine in the United States in the fall of 1967. Like the Kinks, the Who's early singles were produced by Shel Talmy. Their first single, "I Am the Face," was released under the name the High Numbers in summer 1964 and failed to chart. In 1965, now performing as the Who and recording Townshend's songs, the band scored a series of top UK hits, including "I Can't Explain" (uk8, 1965), "Anyway, Anyhow, Anywhere" (uk10, 1965), "My Generation" (uk2, 1965), "Substitute" (uk5, 1966), "I'm a Boy" (uk2, 1966), and "Happy Jack" (uk3, 1966; p24, 1967). Appearing every Tuesday for six months at the Marquee Club during 1964–65, the group billed its music as "maximum R&B" and quickly became popular among the Mod subculture in London.

The Mod movement never made it to the United States, although "the Mods" were a significant faction within the London youth culture of the mid-1960s. Mods listened to American rhythm and blues and Jamaican ska and Blue Beat, dressed in very particular ways, worked but disdained advancement, often rode motorscooters, and danced late into the night—frequently under the influence of amphetamines—at select London clubs such as the Scene. Mods often conflicted with "Rockers," who rode motorcycles and wore leather jackets after the style of Marlon Brando in *The Wild One* (1953). The animosity between these two factions was serious enough for riots to break out, with Mods and Rockers fighting openly in the streets of Brighton, a quiet seaside resort town, in the summer of 1964. The Mod scene and lifestyle is captured in the Who's 1973 album *Quadrophenia*, a concept album in which the Brighton Beach rumble plays a crucial role, and in the 1979 movie of the same name. By the late 1960s, Townshend's songwriting had become increasingly ambitious, and this progression through *Tommy* and on to *Quadrophenia* will be taken up in Chapter 8.

THE MOP TOPS THREATEN THE BIG WIGS

The rise of the Beatles transformed popular music in at least two significant ways. First, it opened doors for British acts within the UK, allowing British artists to reclaim their own popular-music charts and reap the benefits of domestic success. This revitalized British popular music in a fundamental way. Second, the success of the Beatles in America—and indeed, the world—opened new opportunities for British acts outside the UK. Considering the broad stylistic range of the British bands that succeeded in the United States in the wake of the Beatlemania, it is clear that for many young Americans the British invasion was as much about fashion as it was about music. Strictly in terms of musical style, a Beatles concert and a Yardbirds concert were quite different. But in the eyes of the American fans, the groups were

Sound Check

Artist	Song	Sound
The Beatles	**I Want to Hold Your Hand (1964)**	Form: AABA Each verse ends in a 4-bar refrain Two-part vocal alternates between unison (or singing the same thing) and harmony Mersey Beat: Emphasis in beats two and four (listen in hand claps)
The Beatles	**Tomorrow Never Knows (1966)**	Form: simple verse Atmosphere created by droning bass, tape loops, sitar, and processed lead vocals Influence of Indian music Guitar sound created by playing recorded guitar backward
The Animals	**House of the Rising Sun (1964)**	Form: simple verse Odd, 22-measure verse structure (8 + 14) The song becomes more intense throughout, echoing the story Based on a traditional American ballad
The Rolling Stones	**(I Can't Get No) Satisfaction (1965)**	Form: contrasting verse-chorus Two-measure riff is the basis for the song's musical structure Instruments enter one at a time Chorus has multiple sections
The Kinks	**You Really Got Me (1964)**	Form: simple verse Two-measure riff is the basis for the song's musical structure Frenzied guitar solo Amateurish background vocals
The Who	**My Generation (1965)**	Form: simple verse Stuttering lead vocal Virtuosic bass solo Key changes increase energy Aggressive ending

part of the same trend. The British invasion was initially a fad in which music was only one factor. For our purposes, distinguishing between pop-oriented (Beatles-style) groups and blues-oriented (Stones-style) groups helps organize the music of the British invasion along music-stylistic lines that can be placed within the broader context of music before 1964 and after 1966. The most important aspect of the British invasion is that it established a more equal footing within American popular music for U.S. and British artists. The musical cross-fertilization between the United States and the UK has been a prominent feature of popular music in both countries ever since.

Rock historians often emphasize the impact of the Beatles on the American scene in early 1964 and the subsequent flood of British bands. While it is clear that the UK bands pushed many American groups off the charts, the 1964 *Billboard* pop charts show that domestic music continued to enjoy success even after the British arrived, including records by Phil Spector, the Beach Boys, and a host of Motown artists. While the dividing line of February 1964 is convenient for articulating changes within popular music at the time, it is only a rough boundary. In the next chapter, we will see how American musicians reacted to the Brits and what the American music business did to gain back its lost market share.

For Additional Online Resources, visit:
digital.wwnorton.com/whatsthatsound5

FURTHER READING

Tony Bacon, *London Live* (Miller-Freeman Books, 1999).

Alan Clayson, *Beat Merchants: The Origin, History, Impact, and Rock Legacy of the 1960s British Pop Groups* (Blandford, 1995).

Walter Everett, *The Beatles as Musicians:* Revolver *through the* Anthology (Oxford University Press, 1998).

Walter Everett, *The Beatles as Musicians: The Quarry Men through* Rubber Soul (Oxford University Press, 2001).

Spencer Leigh and John Firminger, *Halfway to Paradise: Britpop, 1955–1962* (Finbarr International, 1996).

Mark Lewisohn, *Tune In: The Beatles—All These Years, Vol. 1* (Crown Archetype, 2013).

Dave McAleer, *The Fab British Rock 'n' Roll Invasion of 1964* (St. Martin's, 1994).

Chas McDevitt, *Skiffle: The Definitive Inside Story*, rev. ed. (Roller Coaster Books, 2012).

Barry Miles, *The British Invasion: The Music, The Times, The Era* (Sterling, 2009).

Paul Myers, *It Ain't Easy: Long John Baldry and the Birth of British Blues* (Greystone, 2007).

Philip Norman, *Shout! The Beatles in Their Generation* (Simon & Schuster, 2006).

Philip Norman, *The Stones* (Penguin, 1993).

James E. Perone, *Mods, Rockers, and the Music of the British Invasion* (Praeger, 2008).

Terry Rawlings, *Mod: A Very British Phenomenon* (Omnibus, 2000).

Keith Richards, *Life* (Little, Brown, 2010).

Roberta Freund Schwartz, *How Britain Got the Blues: The Transmission and Reception of American Blues Style in the United Kingdom* (Ashgate, 2007).

Harry Shapiro, *Alexis Korner: The Biography* (Bloomsbury, 1996).

Gordon Thompson, *Please, Please Me: Sixties British Pop, Inside Out* (Oxford University Press, 2008).

Bill Wyman with Ray Coleman, *Stone Alone: The Story of a Rock 'n' Roll Band* (Da Capo, 1997).

CHAPTER 5

AMERICAN RESPONSES

CHAPTER PREVIEW

- A wide range of American bands and artists responded to the "British invasion" by the summer of 1965.

- Prompting the uproar of folk purists, Bob Dylan picked up an electric guitar and helped launch a folk-rock style.

- The Byrds' use of the twelve-string electric guitar gave folk rock a jingle-jangle sonic signature that can be heard on their first hit, "Mr. Tambourine Man," a song written by Dylan.

- As producer of the Beach Boys' *Pet Sounds* album, Brian Wilson pushed the limits of surf music.

- Los Angeles became more central to the American rock scene in the mid-1960s.

- Inspired by British invasion groups, garage bands across the United States produced a variety of "one-hit wonder" rock music artists.

- Through network television series, Paul Revere and the Raiders, the Monkees, and other American groups broadened the base of U.S. pop music fans.

The Byrds' distinctive version of Bob Dylan's "Mr. Tambourine Man," frequently cited as the first folk-rock hit, was part of an American response to the British invasion. While the Byrds were steeped in the music of the American folk revival, they were also influenced by the Beatles' early music. After seeing *A Hard Day's Night*, the group added an electric twelve-string guitar to their already refined vocal harmonies, blending the Beatles, Dylan, the Kingston Trio, and a touch of surf music to create a trans-Atlantic number-one hit in the summer of 1965. Although the Byrds played as a band on subsequent releases, the only member of the group to play an instrument on this first single was Roger McGuinn, who played the electric twelve-string. With the Byrds providing the vocals and McGuinn adding his jingle-jangle guitar sound, the rest of the music was performed by Los Angeles studio musicians—a group of top professionals who went by the nickname "the Wrecking Crew."

The reaction of American teenagers to the music of the Beatles in early 1964 is easy to document. Although the term "Beatlemania" had been coined in the UK in 1963 to describe the reaction of British fans to the Beatles' music, it is an even more apt description of the reaction in the United States. Chapter 4 described the enormous commercial success enjoyed by the Beatles, the Rolling Stones, and a host of other British groups during 1964–66. This chapter will focus on the response of American musicians and the American popular music business to the competition offered by the Brits, showing that this reaction was not nearly as immediate as the one found among fans. In fact, British bands did not erase all American pop acts from the charts, and many groups who had hit records during 1963 continued to have success, seemingly undiminished by the enormous popularity of the Beatles and other British groups. Phil Spector, the Beach Boys, the Four Seasons, and most artists on the Motown label, for instance, vied neck-and-neck with the foreign invaders for top chart positions and radio airtime.

By the summer of 1965, new musical styles in American pop were emerging as a result of the cross-fertilization of American styles with the Mersey beat. Folk rock is perhaps the most obvious example. Led by the Byrds and Bob Dylan, folk rock took the easy strumming-and-singing texture of folk and added electric guitars, bass, drums, and (occasionally) keyboards to create an American music-stylistic reaction to the British invasion. It is easy to see how and why this happened. Many young American musicians had learned to accompany themselves (usually on guitar) during the folk revival. Moreover, during their early years on the charts the Beatles were essentially a guitar-oriented vocal group. Many performers who sang and harmonized about social injustice to the accompaniment of the acoustic guitar or banjo made an easy transition to the electric guitar and bass. Emulating the Beatles' and Stones' guitar-dominated sound, a slew of garage bands formed across the country, most with only minimal musical skills that tended not to impede their enthusiasm.

New York was the center of the American pop music scene in the early 1960s, but after 1964, much of the most popular new music emerged from Los Angeles (on New York–based record labels). Many folk rockers made their way from New York's Greenwich Village to Los Angeles, and by 1965 the Hollywood-based television industry was becoming a factor in the music business, with several pop-music variety shows aimed at America's teens. These included a show hosted by Paul Revere and the Raiders, who underlined the idea of an American response by donning Revolutionary War costumes. The American response was heightened in 1966, when the industry put forward its most direct answer to the Beatles: the Monkees. The music business may have been surprised in 1964 by the overwhelming success of the Brits, but by mid-1965 American bands were again scoring significant chart successes by imitating British bands, revamping American styles, and adapting tried-and-true music-business practices.

FOLK ROCK

Dylan Plugs In. In December 1960, a young folksinger arrived in New York from Minnesota, where he had been playing gigs in folk clubs and coffeehouses. Within a few months, Bob Dylan was performing in Greenwich Village and becoming increasingly active in the city's burgeoning folk scene. By the beginning of 1964, he was among the most respected young folksingers in the United States. Dylan was not particularly well known outside the folk community, since the general pop audience associated "folk" with the music of the Kingston Trio or Peter, Paul, and Mary. Some pop listeners might have known that Dylan wrote "Blowin' in the Wind" and "Don't Think Twice It's Alright" (both hits in 1963 for Peter, Paul, and Mary), but most would not have heard Dylan's own versions, which appear on his second album, *The Freewheelin' Bob Dylan* (p22 uk16, 1963). Like many folk artists, he enjoyed success mostly on the album charts in absense of hit singles, with sales fueled by appearances in folk clubs and on college campuses. By 1964, his albums *The Times They Are A-Changin'* (p20 uk20, 1964) and *Another Side of Bob Dylan* (p43 uk8, 1964) did well enough on both sides of the Atlantic to make him one of the most emulated folksingers of this period.

Dylan was a skilled performer and an even more accomplished songwriter. It was common for folksingers to write their own music, often creating new songs from tunes drawn or adapted from traditional folk melodies. Dylan's idol Woody Guthrie frequently reworked familiar music with new lyrics that chronicled social injustice. Dylan initially followed this model, creating topical songs such as "Blowin' in the Wind," which addressed civil rights, and "Masters of War," which challenged the Vietnam conflict. Dylan's songs, however, became increasingly focused on his own feelings and attempts to understand the world, prompting some in the folk world to remark that he had a tendency to replace the "we" in folk with "me." Early songs such as "Girl from the North Country" and "Don't Think Twice It's Alright" display his exceptional gifts as a songwriter. The personal lyrics of these songs are crafted with the painstaking aesthetic attitude more common among poets than musicians.

After an enormously successful tour of the UK in 1965 (documented in the D. A. Pennebaker film *Don't Look Back*), Dylan made a break with the folk tradition that would have tremendous consequences for popular music. Contrary

Bob Dylan first made his name as a folksinger, strongly influenced by the music and image of Woody Guthrie. As a folk revivalist who addressed issues of social, economic, and political injustice, Dylan developed a reputation for delivering "finger-wagging songs" that brought attention to such issues. In this picture, a young Dylan is shown performing at a voter registration drive in 1963.

Listening Guide

Bob Dylan, "Positively 4th Street" Columbia 43389

Words and music by Bob Dylan, produced by Bob Johnston. Rose to #7 on the *Billboard* "Hot 100" (uk8) in the fall of 1965.

FORM: Simple verse. Like many Dylan songs, this song has a lot of lyrics. In this case, Dylan delivers 12 verses over the same 8-bar structure, without much change in the accompaniment. In contrast to the technique of building an arrangement by adding instruments or vocal parts as the song progresses, this track remains static, leaving the listener to focus on the lyrics.

TIME SIGNATURE: 4/4. Note the finger cymbals on beat 4 of each measure.

INSTRUMENTATION: Piano, organ, electric guitars, drums, finger cymbals, lead vocal. Pay particular attention to Al Kooper's organ playing, which came to be much imitated despite Kooper's insistence that he was not really an organist.

0:00–0:09	**Introduction**, 4 mm.	Organ melody featured.
0:09–0:26	**Verse 1**, 8 mm.	Vocals enter, organ adds melodic interest, while the other instruments keep a low profile, supporting the vocal, "You got a lot of nerve . . ."
0:26–0:44	**Verse 2**, 8 mm.	As before, "You got a lot of nerve . . ."
0:44–1:01	**Verse 3**, 8 mm.	As before, "You say I let you down . . ."
1:01–1:19	**Verse 4**, 8 mm.	As before, "You say you lost your faith . . ."
1:19–1:36	**Verse 5**, 8 mm.	As before, "I know the reason . . ."
1:36–1:53	**Verse 6**, 8 mm.	As before, "Do you take me . . ."
1:54–2:11	**Verse 7**, 8 mm.	As before, "You seen me on the street . . ."
2:11–2:28	**Verse 8**, 8 mm.	As before, "When you know . . ."
2:28–2:46	**Verse 9**, 8 mm.	As before, "Now I don't feel . . ."
2:46–3:03	**Verse 10**, 8 mm.	As before, guitar and piano get a little busier, but not much, "And now I know . . ."
3:03–3:21	**Verse 11**, 8 mm.	As before, "I wish that for just one . . ."
3:21–3:38	**Verse 12**, 8 mm.	As before, "I wish that for just one . . ."
3:38–3:51	**Instrumental verse** (partial), 4 mm.+	Organ featured again, as track fades out.

to the folk revival orthodoxy, he had long been interested in using electric instruments in his music, and a few sessions for his second album had been recorded with what was essentially a rock band; he even tried out a version of "That's All Right (Mama)." Dylan was not satisfied with the results of these sessions and only one of the resulting tracks ("Corrina, Corrina") was used on the album. (Another of these songs, "Mixed Up Confusion," became his first single, but it did not chart when released in 1962.) Dylan's interest in rock instrumentation was also evident on his album *Bringin' It All Back Home* (p6 uk1, 1965), half of which used electric instruments, including his first hit single, "Subterranean Homesick Blues" (p39 uk9, 1965). The folk community did not express an overwhelmingly negative reaction to Dylan's electrified music when the album was released perhaps because of the strong acoustic-based material. It was not until he played the Newport Folk Festival in July 1965 that the controversy began. Dylan's electric numbers met with resistance among the more traditionally minded folkies in attendance, and while accounts of the events vary, it seems clear that many senior members of the folk establishment who had strongly supported Dylan up to this point (including Pete Seeger of the Weavers, who was a key player in the folk revival—see Chapter 3) felt betrayed by his turn to electric instruments. Many felt that Dylan had sold out to pop; as a result, he became the target of very strong criticism within folk circles.

A week before the 1965 festival, Columbia Records released Dylan's single "Like a Rolling Stone," one of the electric songs he performed at Newport, and the song rose to number two in the United States (uk4) in the summer and fall of 1965. He followed with the album *Highway 61 Revisited* (p3 uk4, 1965) and the angry hit single, "Positively 4th Street" (p7 uk8, 1965). The folk-music establishment continued to react negatively to Dylan's use of electric instruments, and he felt betrayed by their response. As a traditional folksinger, he had written songs like "Masters of War," which attacked those who exploited others to gain unfair social or economic advantage. Dylan referred to such tunes as "finger pointing" songs, and after his 1965 Newport performance he used "Positively 4th Street" to point his finger at the folk establishment he felt had unfairly criticized him. The fervor of Dylan's obsession on this issue can be seen in the song's structure, which is a simple verse form employing twelve verses. After a short four-measure introduction, Dylan plows away at verse after verse, all based on the same eight-measure harmonic pattern. The song concludes with part of a thirteenth time through the chord progression, with vocals absent and the focus on Al Kooper's organ part, until the song fades out.

Dylan followed up with the single "Rainy Day Women Nos. 12 and 35" (p2 uk7, 1966), and using most of the Hawks (later known as the Band), he recorded *Blonde on Blonde* (p9 uk3, 1966). In July 1966, Dylan was almost killed in a motorcycle accident in upstate New York and his injuries kept him out of the spotlight for months afterward. Even while Dylan was out of commission, his records continued to influence other musicians, and his lyrics were especially important. Dylan's songs showed

Bob Dylan shocked the folk establishment by shifting his focus to nontopical songs backed by an electric band in 1965. Dylan appears here on July 25, 1965, with his Fender Stratocaster electric guitar at the Newport Folk Festival, a performance that is legendary for the manner in which Dylan challenged the expectations of the folk revival audience.

that pop music could address serious social issues rather than just teenage romance or frivolous concerns, and this seriousness of purpose became a model for many other songwriters in the 1960s and later. And while the folk traditionalists may have believed Dylan's music had become too commercial, it was not nearly as commercial as much of the folk rock that followed in its wake.

The Byrds and the Jingle-Jangle of the Electric Twelve-String Guitar.

Dylan's importance in the rise of American folk rock is evident in the fact that the first international number-one folk-rock single was a song he wrote. In the summer of 1965, the Byrds' recording of "Mr. Tambourine Man" hit the top of both the U.S. and the UK charts. The Byrds formed in Los Angeles in 1964. The band's leading members had been active in the folk-music scene for several years. Roger McGuinn had studied folk music as a teenager at Chicago's Old Town School of Folk Music before working with the Limelighters and the Chad Mitchell Trio on the folk circuit. He was also part of the early 1960s music scene in New York's Greenwich Village, playing in folk clubs by night while working as a Brill Building songwriter for Bobby Darin during the day. In 1964, he went to Los Angeles for a stint at the Troubadour Club, where he played sets mixing folk numbers with Beatles songs. At the Troubadour, McGuinn met songwriter and singer Gene Clark, who had been a member of the New Christy Minstrels, and they began writing songs together. Soon singer-guitarist David Crosby joined the group and bluegrass mandolin player Chris Hillman was recruited to play bass, while Michael Clarke joined on drums. The band rehearsed under the direction of manager Jim Dickson, who taped the rehearsals and insisted that the group listen to themselves. Surviving tapes from that period document the band's progression from a folk vocal-harmony act to a rock band. The distinct jingle-jangle guitar sound played a key role in that development, inspired by a viewing of *A Hard Day's Night*, during which band members noticed that George Harrison was playing an electric twelve-string guitar. The instrument was not widely used in pop at that time, and Harrison was playing the second one ever made. McGuinn traded in his acoustic twelve-string for a Rickenbacker electric

The Byrds are joined onstage by a harmonica-playing Bob Dylan. Note that Roger McGuinn (right) is playing his signature Rickenbacker electric twelve-string guitar, while David Crosby (left) plays a Gretsch Tennessean similar to the one George Harrison used on *Beatles for Sale*.

Listening Guide

The Byrds, "Mr. Tambourine Man" Columbia 43271

Words and music by Bob Dylan, produced by Terry Melcher. Rose to #1 on the *Billboard* "Hot 100" (uk7) in the summer of 1965.

FORM: Contrasting verse-chorus, beginning with the chorus. Dylan's original alternates the chorus with multiple verses, but the Byrds use only one of the original verses. The resulting form looks a little strange, but the band had to fit the arrangement into the two-minute format of AM radio at the time.

TIME SIGNATURE: 4/4, with a feel borrowed from "Don't Worry Baby."

INSTRUMENTATION: Electric twelve-string guitar, electric six-string guitar, bass, drums, solo and duet vocals.

0:00–0:08	**Introduction**, 4 mm.	Electric twelve-string begins with a lick inspired by J. S. Bach, then sliding bass enters, followed by the entire band.
0:08–0:41	**Chorus**, 17 mm.	Duet vocals, then 2-bar link to verse; note the jingle-jangle picking on the electric twelve-string guitar, "Hey Mr. Tambourine Man . . ."
0:41–1:30	**Verse**, 25 mm.	Solo vocal; note the short, sharp chords played high on a second electric guitar, "Take me for a trip . . ."
1:30–2:00	**Chorus**, 15 mm.	Duet vocals as before; "Hey Mr. Tambourine Man . . ."
2:00–2:15	**Coda**, 6 mm. and fade	Music is the same as in the introduction.

twelve, and the distinctive jingle-jangle sound of that guitar, heard on the introduction to "Mr. Tambourine Man," became a Byrds hallmark.

The Byrds initially made their mark with rock versions of folk songs. The group's first album, *Mr. Tambourine Man* (p6 uk7, 1965), featured three additional Dylan covers, including "All I Really Want to Do," which hit number four in the UK but stalled at number forty in the United States when a version by Cher went to number fifteen. The Byrds' second number-one U.S. hit, "Turn, Turn, Turn" (uk26, 1966), was a version of a Pete Seeger song that McGuinn had played on a Judy Collins album years before. The album that contained this single, also called *Turn, Turn, Turn* (p17 uk11, 1966), included other Dylan covers and Byrds originals, mostly written by Gene Clark. When Dylan met with success performing rock versions of his own songs, the Byrds were forced to rely on their own songwriting, and Clark, McGuinn, and Crosby wrote the band's next hit, "Eight Miles High" (p14 uk24, 1966). The guitar introduction invokes jazz, employing a melodic figure borrowed from legendary saxophonist John Coltrane's "India." The lyrics refer both to the cruising altitude of a transatlantic jet (actually six miles high) and to drugs, and when an American radio tip sheet listed it as a "drug song" in summer 1966, stations immediately stopped playing it.

The Byrds, Dylan, the Beach Boys, and the Music Business.

The Byrds' recording of "Mr. Tambourine Man" represents a point of convergence for several elements of the music business that are often thought of as mutually exclusive. The seriousness of the Byrds' brand of folk rock seemed to set this music apart from manufactured Brill Building music and carefree surf songs. On this first hit single, however, separating the authenticity of folk music (Dylan especially) from the calculated aspects of teen pop is more difficult than might be expected. All the members of the Byrds do not actually play on this record: McGuinn plays the electric twelve-string guitar and he and David Crosby sing, but the rest of the music is provided by the Wrecking Crew—a loose group of studio musicians who played on many Phil Spector hits (the Byrds played on their own records after this). Wrecking Crew musicians had provided the musical backing for the Beach Boys' "Don't Worry Baby," and they used the same rhythmic feel to back the Byrds' "Mr. Tambourine Man" at the suggestion of producer Terry Melcher. Thus, "Mr. Tambourine Man" brings together the folk revival (Dylan's song), girl groups (Phil Spector), surf music (the Beach Boys) and, with the use of the electric twelve-string inspired by *A Hard Day's Night*, the British invasion as well.

The Byrds adapted the tune from an acoustic folk version that Dylan had decided not to release. As the Listening Guide shows, the song is in a contrasting verse-chorus form. The Byrds use only one of Dylan's three verses to keep the song at the two-minute length typical of pop singles in 1965. The odd number of measures in the verse and chorus arise because these sections are expanded (and in the case of the second chorus, contracted) from what would typically be sixteen-measure sections. As you listen, see if you can detect where the extra measures are added or dropped (this is especially obvious in the verse section).

Simon and Garfunkel Go Electric.

Perhaps no song better illustrates the transformation of folk into folk rock than Simon and Garfunkel's "The Sounds of Silence" (p1, 1965). Paul Simon and Art Garfunkel began their professional careers as high school students in the late 1950s under the name Tom and Jerry. Modeling their act on the Everly Brothers, Tom and Jerry had a minor hit in late 1957/early 1958 with "Hey Schoolgirl," and even appeared on *American Bandstand*. The duo turned to folk in the early 1960s, recording the album *Wednesday Morning, 3 A.M.* (1964). When the album sold poorly, the pair went their separate ways. Simon went to London to perform solo, and Garfunkel went to graduate school. After "Mr. Tambourine

Modeling themselves on the Everly Brothers, Paul Simon (left) and Art Garfunkel (right) enjoyed modest success in the late 1950s as Tom and Jerry. When folk rock became popular in mid-1965, electric guitar, bass, and drums were added to an earlier recording to create the duo's first hit single, "The Sounds of Silence."

Man" and "Like a Rolling Stone" became hits for the Byrds and Bob Dylan, somebody at Columbia Records remembered the Simon and Garfunkel album. Without their knowledge, Tom Wilson, who had produced Dylan's albums and *Wednesday Morning, 3 A.M.*, was brought in to augment the acoustic version of "The Sounds of Silence" that appears on the album—the same master tape was used—with jangly guitar, electric bass, and drums in the style of the Byrds. The resultant folk-rock single topped the charts in the United States in January 1966. Simon rushed home from the UK and the duo released an album, *Sounds of Silence* (p21 uk13, 1966), to capitalize on their newfound and unexpected success as rock stars. Subsequent singles, "Homeward Bound" (p5 uk9, 1966), "I Am a Rock" (p3 uk17, 1966), and "Hazy Shade of Winter" (p13, 1966) continued in the folk-rock style. By late 1966, however, the album *Parsley, Sage, Rosemary and Thyme* (p4), which contains the delicate "Scarborough Fair/Canticle" (p11, 1968) made it clear that the duo were still pursuing traditional folk revival material. Later in the 1960s, Simon and Garfunkel would enjoy their greatest commercial and aesthetic success with *Bookends* (p1 uk1, 1968), the single "Mrs. Robinson" (p1 uk4, 1968) from the soundtrack to the film *The Graduate*, and *Bridge over Troubled Water* (p1 uk1, 1970).

California Dreamin': Barry McGuire, the Turtles, and the Mamas and the Papas.
While many of the first folk-rock records simply set preexisting folk songs to a rock beat and instrumentation, new songs were soon written specifically as folk-rock numbers. Perhaps the first of these—aside from those Dylan wrote and recorded after he went electric—was P. F. Sloan's "Eve of Destruction." Recorded by Barry McGuire, another former member of the New Christy Minstrels who had made his way to Los Angeles from Greenwich Village, this song ascended to number one on the U.S. charts (uk3) in fall 1965. Producer Lou Adler had given Sloan the task of writing a batch of Dylan-like songs, and the songwriter did his best to mimic the earnest sense of social protest found in much folk.

Updating the polished folk approach of Peter, Paul, and Mary with a folk-rock beat, the Mamas and the Papas focused on sophisticated vocal arrangements by John Phillips (second from left).

Meanwhile, groups continued to cover Dylan songs with hopes of scoring folk-rock hits as the Byrds had done. The Los Angeles–based Turtles worked this trick successfully with "It Ain't Me Babe" (p8, 1965) before moving on to a more mainstream pop style and a series of non-Dylan hits including "Happy Together" (p1 uk12, 1967). The Turtles' arrangements often showcased the polished dual lead vocals of Howard Kaylan and Mark Volman, who went on to work with Frank Zappa and the Mothers of Invention and later performed as the duo Phlorescent Leech (Flo) and Eddie.

Formed in New York in 1965, the Mamas and the Papas also followed the folk migration westward and moved from Greenwich Village to Los Angeles, where they first enjoyed commercial success in the wake of Dylan, the Byrds, and Simon and Garfunkel. Three of the group members had worked previously in vocally oriented pop or folk acts. Led by singer/songwriter/arranger John Phillips and including Michelle Phillips, Denny Doherty, and Cass Elliot, the group showcased John Phillips's sophisticated four-part vocal arrangements. The group's sound was influenced by the close harmony singing found in early 1960s folk (especially Peter, Paul, and Mary and the Kingston Trio) and doo-wop (they had a hit with a cover of the 5 Royales' "Dedicated to the One I Love"), and these distinctive vocals were often accompanied by a rock rhythm section of drums, electric bass, guitars, and keyboards. The Mamas and the Papas had nine hit singles, most written by John Phillips, including "California Dreamin'" (p4 uk23, 1966), "Monday Monday" (p1 uk3, 1966), "I Saw Her Again" (p5 uk11, 1966), and the autobiographical "Creeque Alley" (p5, 1967), the lyrics of which mention both Roger McGuinn and Barry McGuire. This run made the quartet one of the most successful acts of the era. See What's That Source? about folk rock.

AMERICAN POP ON BOTH COASTS

L.A.: Spector and His Legacy. Phil Spector was another American record producer and songwriter to have tremendous success in the Beatles' wake. Spector was a favorite of the Fab Four, to the extent that he flew with the band from London to New York on February 7, 1964. However, he was yet to experience some of his greatest successes when the Beatles stormed the U.S. charts. The Crystals' "Doo Doo Ron Ron" (p3 r5 uk5, 1963) and "Then He Kissed Me" (p6 r8 uk2, 1963), and the Ronettes' "Be My Baby" (p2 r4 uk4, 1963), were all Spector-produced hits in the months before the Fab Four landed. After the onset of the British Invasion, Spector produced one of his most enduring songs, the Righteous Brothers' "You've Lost That Lovin' Feeling," which went to number one in both the United States and the UK in early 1965, and hit number three on the U.S. rhythm and blues charts. The group followed with "Unchained Melody" (p4 r6 uk14, 1965) and "Ebb Tide" (p5 r13 uk48, 1966) before Spector began to lose his hit-making touch. During this time, Spector could have produced the Young Rascals and the Lovin' Spoonful, but he declined offers from both bands. Instead, he pinned everything on what he hoped would be his greatest record yet, Tina Turner's "River Deep, Mountain High." Written by Spector with Jeff Barry and Ellie Greenwich, the song failed in the United States, rising only as high as number eighty-six in mid-1966. The record did hit number three in the UK (mostly through airplay on pirate stations), but Spector was crushed by the failure in America

WHAT'S THAT SOURCE?

The Folk Rock Revolution

Mainstream rock began to incorporate elements previously associated with the folk revival during the summer of 1965, forming a hybrid style that is often called "folk rock." This piece, oriented toward teen readers in Los Angeles, tracks the rise of folk rock, providing an insider's perspective on why mainstream listeners began to value folk elements in a rock context.

What's happening to rock 'n' roll? It's proving what I have always contended—that teenagers are smarter and more idealistic than most people give them credit for. Because suddenly rock 'n' roll has something to say.

"The eastern world it is explodin'; violence flarin' bullets loadin'. You're old enough to kill but not for votin' . . . But what's that gun you're totin' . . ." Of course you know the song—all teens do. It's "The Eve of Destruction"—which teens kept high up on the record charts for months! It was written by the 19-year-old Phil Sloan and sung by Barry McGuire, who became an overnight celebrity as a result of it.

"I wait all day to get up on that stage and sing that song," says Barry. "I want people to think about those things."

What are those things you hear in "folk rock" today? They're anti-war, they're anti-prejudice, they're anti-poverty and anti-injustice. They're rock with a cause and, as such, they express perfectly the teenage mystique today: involvement with the world, but involvement on their own terms, and in their own style.

It all started with Bob Dylan—the original poet of protest, a writer of contemporary folk songs, a rebel with many causes—some personal, some social.

Bob Dylan is almost an archetype of the way-out teen pace-setter: he has always been a kind of Pied Piper to folkniks. With his wild hair, his offbeat clothes, his high, really strange voice, he had a kind of high priest quality to all those who really appreciated pure folk music. But Dylan was not to be pigeonholed. When his fans were shocked and disappointed at the new rock beat he put behind his songs (you can hear it on his album "Highway 67 [sic] Revisited"), Dylan's reply was "It's all music," and went his own way.

A lot of music went along with him. The Byrds made their reputation with Dylan's "Tambourine Man." Today folk rock gets bigger and bigger. Sonny and Cher are wildly popular both here and in England—pulling in teens by the thousands to their concerts. In fact, teens are not only listening to this young married couple but dressing like them. At another point is Johnny Rivers playing

"folk rock-a-billy" which is rock 'n' roll, hillbilly style.

And now even those classics The Beatles have succumbed. They've come from the opposite pole to rock-folk. In "Help," John Lennon and Paul McCartney have written a rock folk tune called "You've Got to Hide Your Love Away"—and their new album "Rubber Soul" has even more influences of this kind of folk rock. Let's face it, folk rock is big because the teens love it. And the teens love it because it has the rhythm that is theirs, and has something to say—something besides "I love you" and "moon, June, spoon." The old trite ballads are just not real enough for today's teens . . . not while nuclear bombs are around! Folk rock and protest rock are the teens' way to sing out—and speak up! Where do you stand on current teen music? Who best represents the music you like? Write and let me know!

Source: Sylvie Reice, "Why Teens Switched to Folk Rock," *Los Angeles Times*, January 6, 1966.

and retired from the music business. He would return to producing a few years later, enjoying the success of several Beatles-related projects in the early 1970s, including number-one albums for the Beatles (*Let It Be*, 1970), George Harrison (*All Things Must Pass*, 1970), and John Lennon (*Imagine*, 1971).

The Beach Boys: Brian Stays Home. Like Spector, the Beach Boys continued to produce hits in 1965 and 1966. In 1964, the group released "Fun, Fun, Fun," which reached number five in the United States during the height of Beatlemania. That summer, the Beach Boys had their first number-one U.S. hit (uk7), "I Get Around," while the world was also celebrating *A Hard Day's Night*. Contending with the Beatles' success was tougher for the Beach Boys than most other American pop acts, however, because both groups were signed to Capitol Records. This meant that the Beach Boys had to fight for the attention of both pop listeners and their record company. In December 1964, the band's music began to change when songwriter and producer Brian Wilson decided to stop touring. Instead, he stayed in California writing new music and recording backing tracks. During breaks from touring, the other band members added vocal tracks that Wilson had carefully worked out for them. On the road, Glen Campbell and then Bruce Johnston replaced Brian, so he could focus entirely on making records.

The Beach Boys' next two albums, *The Beach Boys Today!* (p4, 1965) and *Summer Days (and Summer Nights!!)* (p2, 1965) reflected Wilson's increasingly sophisticated approach to songwriting, arranging, and production. "Help Me Rhonda" (p1 uk27, 1965) and especially "California Girls" (p3 uk26, 1965) began to explore more complicated musical structures and employed a broader palette of instrumentation, including orchestral instruments.

In late 1964, Brian Wilson (bottom right) decided not to tour with the Beach Boys, opting to stay at home working on new material while the band hit the road. While Brian clocked in long hours in the recording studio experimenting with new sounds, Bruce Johnston (just above Wilson on right) replaced him on the road.

After *Beach Boys' Party!* (p6 uk3, 1966), a quickly recorded and informal taping of the band jamming and singing with friends (which produced the hit single "Barbara Ann" [p2 uk3, 1966]), Brian set to work on a much more musically ambitious project. Named after some of his favorite studio sounds, *Pet Sounds* (p10 uk2, 1966) set a new standard for record production and musical sophistication within rock music. On the single released in advance of the album, "Sloop John B." (p3 uk2, 1966), you can hear the clear combination of Spector's Wall of Sound with Wilson's lush vocal-harmony arrangements. The echo-drenched harp introduction of the first track, "Wouldn't It Be Nice," announces that what follows moves beyond the surf music that had brought the band its early success. "God Only Knows," which Paul McCartney once called the perfect pop song, is the best illustration of how far Wilson's music had come during this period. Although not as commercially successful as previous Beach Boys' albums, *Pet Sounds* would become one of the most influential records of the 1960s, prodding the Beatles to experiment more radically while recording *Sgt. Pepper's Lonely Hearts Club Band*. In Chapter 7 we will return to the friendly competition that developed between the bands, and consider the Beach Boys' music after *Pet Sounds*.

Listening Guide

The Beach Boys, "California Girls" Capitol 5464

Words and music by Brian Wilson, produced by Brian Wilson. Rose to #3 on the *Billboard* Pop charts in fall 1965 (uk26).

FORM: Contrasting verse-chorus, with a 10-bar intro leading into a 2-bar vamp that prepares the arrival of the first-verse vocals. The verse and chorus are both 8 bars in length. Wilson builds his arrangement by employing solo lead vocals in the first two verses, then introducing a call-and-response scheme in the harmony vocals of the chorus, and using doo-wop-inspired backup vocals in the third and fourth verses. As Phil Spector does in "Be My Baby," Wilson uses a short instrumental break late in the song to allow a fresh return of the chorus: a brief 2-bar organ and glockenspiel passage based on the "Happy Trails" bass line that prepares the way for the song's hook, "I wish they all could be . . ."

TIME SIGNATURE: 4/4 (with a shuffle). Note that the repeated figure in the bass sounds like the old cowboy song, "Happy Trails," giving the track a bouncy, easygoing rhythmic feel.

INSTRUMENTATION: Electric twelve-string guitar, organ, bass, drums, glockenspiel, horns, percussion, lead and backup vocals.

0:00–0:26	**Introduction**, 12 mm.	10-mm. intro using harp and twelve-string guitar, then bass and cymbals, and then horns, followed by a 2-mm. lead-in to verse 1 using the "Happy Trails" bass line.
0:26–0:43	**Verse 1**, 8 mm.	Solo lead vocal enters, "Well, east coast girls . . ."
0:43–0:59	**Verse 2**, 8 mm.	As before, "The midwest farmers' daughters . . ."
0:59–1:16	**Chorus**, 8 mm.	Arrangement gets fuller and louder, with call-and-answer harmony vocals, "I wish they all could be . . ."
1:16–1:32	**Verse 3**, 8 mm.	Doo-wop vocals, lightly doubled by horns, now backup solo lead vocal, "The west coast . . ."
1:32–1:49	**Verse 4**, 8 mm.	Texture continues as in verse 3, "I've been all 'round . . ."
1:49–2:06	**Chorus**, 8 mm.	Louder, fuller, with call-and-answer vocals, as before.
2:06–2:27	**Coda**, 10 mm. and fade	2-mm. interlude drawn from intro, and then 4 mm. drawn from chorus repeated as track fades.

Ride the Ambitious Surf: Brian Wilson as Producer. When Brian Wilson retired from touring, he began devoting his energies to increasingly complex and ambitious arrangements for the band. The introduction to "California Girls" is an early example of Wilson's blending of a symphonic sensibility with surf music. While the harmonies Wilson employs in this song are interesting and innovative, the formal

Musically, Sonny and Cher drew on the legacy of Phil Spector to create lush pop arrangements. They were also known for a flamboyant style of dress, and were pioneers of hippie fashion.

design is the kind of straightforward contrasting verse-chorus design that is almost identical to Spector's "Be My Baby" (especially with the instrumental break after the second chorus and before the chorus fade). The introduction is the exceptional element in this song, and this short section builds from a brief two-measure figure played quietly at first and then repeated as new instruments enter. Finally, a growing series of chords in the horns drive this eight-measure introduction to the rhythmic two measures that lead into the first verse. There are other subtle touches throughout the rest of the song that signal Wilson's increased interest in expanding rock's musical vocabulary. Notice, for instance, how the drums during the chorus break from a steady four-beat pattern to provide an almost symphonic background, or the lushness of the backup vocals during the second verse. These relatively minor features in "California Girls" point the way to the more intensely experimental quality of the later *Pet Sounds* and "Good Vibrations."

Sonny and Cher: Dylan Meets the Wall of Sound.
By the mid-1960s, Sonny Bono had been working in the music scene around Los Angeles for a decade. A sometime songwriter, he worked at Specialty Records and was designated to deal with Little Richard when the singer decided to give up rock and roll for the ministry. Bono eventually began handling promotion for Phil Spector's Philles label and became one of the producer's most trusted aides. Present at many of the important Los Angeles recording sessions at Gold Star Studios, Bono often sang backup or played percussion on tracks, and thus had ample opportunity to soak up Spector's methods in the studio. He frequently brought his girlfriend, Cher (Cherilyn La Piere), to sing backup. A failed Spector project that attempted to cash in on Beatlemania had Cher singing a song called "Ringo I Love You" under the name Bonnie Jo Mason. Sonny and Cher began performing together in 1963 under the name Caesar and Cleo and released three singles that did not chart. In late 1964, Sonny produced and wrote "Baby Don't Go" and "Just You," and both singles enjoyed regional success in Southern California in the first half of 1965. When the Byrds' "Mr. Tambourine Man" became a hit, Sonny produced a Cher cover of Dylan's "All I Really Want to Do"—which eclipsed the Byrds' version—and wrote and produced the duo's signature song, "I Got You, Babe." In fall 1965, "I Got You, Babe" hit number one on both the U.S. and the UK charts (r19). Although the couple got their start by capitalizing on the folk-rock boom, Sonny and Cher's later recordings moved into a more traditional brand of pop, including the Bono-written song "The Beat Goes On" (p6 uk29, 1967).

While Sonny extended the Spector legacy and Sonny and Cher followed in the husband-and-wife tradition of Les Paul and Mary Ford, one of the duo's most important contributions was in the arena of hippie fashion. The pair wore deliberately outlandish clothes, both onstage and off, which drew nearly as much comment as their music. A few years later, Sonny and Cher hosted a very successful network television variety show, but during the 1965–67 period they were considered subversive by establishment culture. They were frequently refused accommodation at hotels in the United States and abroad because of their appearance. Sonny's "Laugh at Me" (1966) is a response to a specific incident when he was ridiculed for his clothing and haircut at one of the couple's favorite restaurants. While this became a common experience for hippies a few years later, in the rebellious spirit of rock and roll, Sonny and Cher were among the first to insist that they had the right to dress any way they chose.

Gary Lewis and the Playboys, Johnny Rivers, and Nancy Sinatra.

Gary Lewis and the Playboys, led by the son of comedian Jerry Lewis, was another Los Angeles group that enjoyed tremendous chart success. Like Ricky Nelson, Gary started as an actor in family projects, and had appeared in his father's 1957 film *Rock-a-Bye Baby*. By 1964, he formed a band that was booked as regular entertainment at Disneyland and earned a cameo appearance in the Raquel Welch film *A Swingin' Summer*. The group's first hit was "This Diamond Ring" (p1, 1965), which Lewis performed with his father in the film *The Family Jewels*. The song was produced by veteran Snuff Garrett and featured arrangements by Wrecking Crew pianist Leon Russell (the song was co-written by Al Kooper, who played on Dylan's "Like a Rolling Stone" and "Positively 4th Street"). Gary Lewis and the Playboys followed with eleven more U.S. hits including "Count Me In" (p2, 1965), "Save Your Heart for Me" (p2, 1965), "She's Just My Style" (p3, 1965)—clearly influenced by the Beach Boys' records of the same period—and "Green Grass" (p8, 1966). Lewis and the band broke up when he was drafted into the U.S. Army in 1967.

Like Sonny Bono, Johnny Rivers had been in the music business for several years before he scored a hit record. Born John Ramistella, he took the stage name Rivers on the advice of Alan Freed in 1958. That same year, Ricky Nelson recorded Rivers's "I'll Make Believe," though it proved unpopular. After playing with Louis Prima's band in Las Vegas and Lake Tahoe, Rivers made his way to Los Angeles, where he established himself as a live act. He became a regular at the Whiskey-a-Go-Go, where he played mostly rock oldies and drew a star-studded crowd. His popularity at the Whiskey led to a contract with Imperial Records. Rivers was signed by Lou Adler, who made the strange but inspired decision to record a live album, *Johnny Rivers at the Whiskey-a-Go-Go*, which went to number twelve on the U.S. album charts. His first two hit singles were covers of Chuck Berry tunes, "Memphis" (p2, 1964) and "Maybellene" (p12, 1964). Rivers placed eleven more singles in the U.S. Top 40 during the 1960s and released eight Top 40 albums. Although not aligned with the folk movement, Rivers also experimented with folk rock. In 1965, before the Byrds or Dylan had hit with folk rock, Rivers released covers of the Weavers's "Midnight Special" (which became the theme song of the early 1970s music-variety show of the same name), and the Kingston

Johnny Rivers's first album was recorded live, and its success prompted him to release a string of live albums during the 1960s—an unusual practice for pop music during that time. In 1966, Rivers released his famous song "Secret Agent Man."

Trio's "Where Have All the Flowers Gone." In late 1966, his ballad "Poor Side of Town," written with Adler, hit number one in the United States, although Rivers is perhaps best known for the song "Secret Agent Man" (p3) released earlier that year. "Secret Agent Man" was written in part by P. F. Sloan ("Eve of Destruction") and became the theme song of a popular television spy program. In 1966, Rivers started his own label, Soul City, signing songwriter Jimmie Webb and singing group the Fifth Dimension. He produced the Fifth Dimension's version of Webb's "Up, Up, and Away," which won multiple Grammy awards in 1967.

Another famous family name reached the pop charts in the U.S. and UK in 1966 when Nancy Sinatra's "These Boots Are Made for Walkin'" went to number one on both sides of the Atlantic. The daughter of Frank Sinatra, Nancy had appeared on her father's 1960 television special welcoming Elvis Presley back from his stint in the army. Signed to her father's Reprise label, she had some success in Europe and Japan but did not make many waves in the States. She teamed up with songwriter and producer Lee Hazelwood, who helped Sinatra recraft her image and reignite her career. Following up on the sultry singing of "Boots" (which also featured the studio backing of the Wrecking Crew), "Sugar Town" (p5 uk8, 1966) was much more pop-oriented. "Something Stupid" featured a duet with her father and again topped the charts in the U.S. and Britain in 1967. Interestingly, Sinatra's "Boots" was the top single of the year 1966 in Australia, where the charts included not only British and American artists but also many homegrown pop stars such as Normie Rowe and the Easybeats.

Meanwhile Back in New York: The Lovin' Spoonful and the Rascals.

There was a steady migration of folk musicians from Greenwich Village to Southern California in 1964 and 1965. Most of the folkies who headed west did so because they felt neglected by record labels in New York. Ironically, many of the Los Angeles acts who signed recording contracts in summer 1965 (when the folk-rock style emerged) were signed by New York–based labels. The Byrds, for instance, were on Columbia, and Sonny and Cher were on Atlantic. One Greenwich Village folkie who stayed in New York was John Sebastian, who had played on several folk albums (including an early version of Dylan's "Subterranean Homesick Blues") and performed with the Even Dozen Jug Band. Sebastian met guitarist Zal Yanovsky at a recording session and, inspired by the Beatles, they formed the Lovin' Spoonful with bassist Steve Boone and drummer Joe Butler. The new band became a popular attraction at the Night Owl Coffee House in Greenwich Village, but was not signed by a major New York label. Instead, the newly formed independent Kama Sutra Records released "Do You Believe in Magic" in summer 1965, and the single rose to number nine on the U.S. charts. This easygoing melodic hit was followed by a string of catchy, playful, and mostly upbeat hit singles written by Sebastian and produced by Erik Jacobsen, including "Daydream" (p2 uk2, 1966), "Did You Ever Have to Make Up Your Mind" (p2, 1966), and "Summer in the City" (p1 uk8, 1966).

Normie Rowe was among the top-hit makers in Australia during the second half of the 1960s. His 1965 cover of "Que Sera Sera," a rocked up version of the 1956 hit by Doris Day, was backed by "Shakin' All Over," originally recorded in 1960 by Johnny Kidd & the Pirates, to make a double-sided hit that was one of the biggest selling records in Australia of the 1960s. Rowe went on to have a performing career that included television acting and musical theatre.

Formed in New York in early 1964 but emerging from rhythm and blues clubs rather than the Greenwich Village folk scene, the Young Rascals (later simply the "Rascals") are better seen as American cousins to British blues bands like the Spencer Davis Group than as an answer to the Beatles. Nevertheless, they caught the attention of New York promoter Sid Bernstein, who became their manager, booking them as the opening act for the Beatles' 1965 performance at Shea Stadium. The group was led by the funky Hammond organ of Felix Cavaliere and the soulful vocals of Eddie Brigati, and backed by Gene Cornish's guitar and Dino Danelli's drums. The Rascals first hit with a hard-rocking cover of the Olympics' 1965 rhythm and blues hit, "Good Lovin'," which went to number one on the U.S. charts in spring 1966. Allowed to produce themselves with oversight from Atlantic's experienced house producers, the band followed with a series of rhythm and blues–inspired hits written by Cavaliere and Brigati, including "I've Been Lonely Too Long" (p16, 1967), "Groovin'" (p1 r3 uk8, 1967), "How Can I Be Sure" (p4, 1967), "A Beautiful Morning" (p3, 1968), and "People Got to Be Free" (p1 r14, 1968).

The Old Guard Hangs On: New York.
By mid-1963, Don Kirshner had left New York's Brill Building for the Los Angeles–based Colpix label. Brill Building veterans Leiber and Stoller continued to place hit records on the pop charts through 1965 on their newly formed Red Bird label. The Ad Libs' "The Boy from New York City," for instance, hit number eight in the first half of 1965 (r6), while Red Bird releases such as the Dixie Cups' "Chapel of Love" and the Shangri-Las' "Leader of the Pack" also enjoyed chart

Lovin' Spoonful vocalist and guitarist John Sebastian in a 1966 photo. Based out of New York, the Lovin' Spoonful created pop music that was indebted to their folk revival roots. Here, Sebastian is seen performing on the autoharp, an instrument associated more with folk than with rock.

success. When Leiber and Stoller formed Red Bird, they turned production of the Drifters over to Bert Berns. In 1965, Berns formed Bang! Records with his bosses from Atlantic, Ahmet and Neshui Ertegun and Jerry Wexler. In the fall of 1965, Berns produced an Indiana-based band, the McCoys (featuring guitarist Rick Derringer), doing a version of "Hang On Sloopy" that reached the top of the *Billboard* "Hot 100" (uk5) in October 1965. The McCoys followed with two more Top 40 hits for Bang!: "Fever" (p7 uk44, 1965) and "Come On Let's Go" (p22, 1966). Berns had the most success with singer-songwriter Neil Diamond, who began his hit-making career on Bang!, scoring first with "Cherry, Cherry" (p6, 1966), and following with eight more hits before leaving the label. Diamond's song "I'm a Believer" would also soon be a hit for the Monkees.

The Four Seasons, featuring lead vocalist Frankie Valli, was another New York–based act that didn't seem to be affected by the British invasion. The group's first success came in 1962 with successive crossover number-one singles produced by Bob Crewe, "Sherry" and "Big Girls Don't Cry." The Four Seasons would release

Emerging in the mid-1960s, the Young Rascals developed a reputation for a hard-driving, rhythm and blues–inspired approach to rock. The New York group's aggressive sound was driven by Felix Cavaliere on the Hammond organ and drummer Dino Danelli.

twenty-five more U.S. Top 40 hits during the 1960s, including "Walk Like a Man" (p1 r3, 1963), "Rag Doll" (p1, 1964), "Let's Hang On" (p4, 1965), and "Workin' My Way Back to You" (p9 uk50, 1966) (the last was recorded under the name the Wonder Who?). In early February 1964, "Dawn (Go Away)" rose to the top of the *Billboard* chart in the United States alongside the Beatles' "She Loves You" and "I Want to Hold Your Hand." The Four Seasons recorded for Vee-Jay, which had also released the Beatles' first album, and the label released a double album late in 1964 called *The Beatles vs. the Four Seasons*, which was a rerelease of *Introducing the Beatles* combined with a Four Seasons greatest hits compilation. The Four Seasons' doo-wop vocal style was very different from the music of the Beatles and other British invasion groups, however. Perhaps their closest musical parallel is the Beach Boys, who also depended on tight vocal harmonies and the high falsetto of Brian Wilson. Frankie Valli's distinctive falsetto was much raspier and more aggressive than Wilson's, and while similar in many ways, one group would hardly be mistaken for the other. But despite the success of the Four Seasons and a handful of other New York–based groups, the British invasion, and the music-stylistic changes in American rock that it caused, spelled the end of New York's domination of pop.

GARAGE BANDS: NO EXPERIENCE NECESSARY

From the Northwest: Garage Bands, the Kingsmen, and "Louie Louie."
Almost immediately after the Beatles landed in the United States, bands composed of male teenagers with more enthusiasm than musical training sprang up across the country. These bands gained regional popularity playing at dances and clubs,

and local record labels attempted to cash in by releasing records for small markets. These "local hero" bands often rehearsed in basements or garages on inexpensive instruments, and their records were frequently recorded on very simple equipment. Like the doo-wop groups of the preceding years, garage bands often had only one hit, and many of these were songs that only achieved regional popularity. When a garage band did have more than one hit, the music almost always became more refined as the band migrated away from the charming but amateurish sound of their first success. There are hundreds of garage-band singles from the 1960s, records that have spawned an entire culture of collectors. Much of this interest grew out of a collection assembled in the early 1970s by writer and guitarist Lenny Kaye. Called *Nuggets*, this compilation brought together rare recordings that collectively told a story of a thriving rock underground during the 1960s. Many bands of the early punk movement took their inspiration from the rough-and-tumble, amateurish character of these 1960s garage bands.

The first important national garage-band hit was the Kingsmen's "Louie Louie." This song was a live staple for many early garage bands in the Pacific Northwest. The Kingsmen's recording went to number two on the *Billboard* "Hot 100" at the same time Beatlemania was reaching a fever pitch in the United States (r1). The song was written by Richard Berry and originally recorded in 1956 as a calypso-flavored rhythm and blues tune. The Kingsmen's version was recorded for $50 in a small studio in Portland, Oregon. This rendition is notably amateurish: at one point vocalist Jack Ely comes in at the wrong place and abruptly corrects himself. The song's difficult-to-discern lyrics led to a rumor that it contained foul language. At one point in early 1964, the governor of Indiana declared "Louie Louie" to be pornographic and called for an FCC investigation. In fact, the lyrics did not contain any profanity or overt sexual references, and the FCC ultimately concluded that the lyrics were indecipherable. Even though another Portland group, Paul Revere and the Raiders, recorded their version of "Louie Louie" soon after and in the same studio, it was the Kingsmen's version that took off, as controversy stoked the curiosity of young listeners across the country.

After the success of the Kingsmen in 1964, record companies licensed records by many unknown American bands, and in the summer of 1965, a series of mostly one-time garage-band Top 40 hits appeared on the U.S. pop charts. Among these groups and their hits were: Cannibal and the

Hailing from Portland, Oregon, the Kingsmen rose to national attention in 1963 with "Louie Louie." Though the song was famously rumored to contain obscene language, an FCC investigation pronounced the passage in question to be unintelligible.

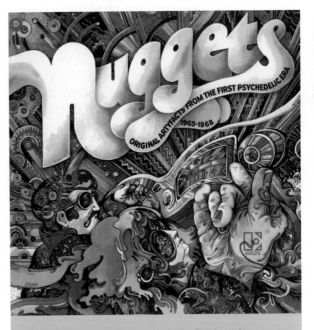

Garage rock emerged in the wake of the Beatles, when amateurish bands across the United States began recording singles, some of which achieved regional and national popularity. The compilation *Nuggets*, first released in 1972, documented the garage rock movement for the emerging punk generation.

Listening Guide

The Kingsmen, "Louie Louie" Wand 14

Words and music by Richard Berry, produced by Ken Chase and Jerry Dennon. Reached #2 on the *Billboard* "Hot 100" (r1 uk26) in late 1963.

FORM: Simple verse-chorus, with the entire song built on the famous four-chord sequence that opens the song. In the first half of the song, the choruses precede the verses, but after the guitar solo, the order is flipped and verse 3 precedes the final chorus. The guitar solo was likely meant to be 16 bars in length (twice that of a verse or chorus). When the vocal enters at the end of these 16 measures, however, singer Jack Ely stops abruptly as if he's made a mistake, and then starts again 2 bars later. This "mistake" was left in the released version, and creates a section of 18 bars. The final chorus is extended by 5 bars, with the last of these extra measures simply being the last chord of the song.

TIME SIGNATURE: 4/4.

INSTRUMENTATION: Electric piano, electric guitar, bass, drums, and lead vocals.

0:00–0:08	**Introduction**, 4 mm.	The famous four-chord sequence is played on the electric piano, then the band joins in.
0:08–0:24	**Chorus**, 8 mm.	Lead vocal enters. Note the cross between blues and Jamaican singing styles. "Louie, Louie . . ."
0:24–0:40	**Verse 1**, 8 mm.	Lead vocal continues, as music remains the same. The lyrics are hard to decipher at times. "A fine little . . ."
0:40–0:55	**Chorus**, 8 mm.	As before. "Louie, Louie . . ."
0:55–1:11	**Verse 2**, 8 mm.	As in verse 1, hard-to-discern lyrics could be selectively interpreted as profanity. "Three nights . . ."
1:11–1:27	**Chorus**, 8 mm.	As before, with an increase in energy leading into the guitar solo. "Louie, Louie . . ."
1:27–2:02	**Guitar solo**, 18 mm.	Blues-based guitar solo for 16 mm., followed by 2 bars that prepare the next verse.
2:02–2:17	**Verse 3**, 8 mm.	As in the previous verses, though lyrics are here even more garbled. "See Jamaica . . ."
2:17–2:41	**Chorus**, 13 mm.	One last time through the chorus, with a 4-bar extension and a final chord stretching the section to 13 mm. "Louie, Louie . . ."

Headhunters, "Land of 1000 Dances" (p30, 1965); the Count Five, "Psychotic Reaction" (p5, 1966); ? & the Mysterians, "96 Tears" (p1, 1966); the Seeds, "Pushin' Too Hard" (p36, 1966); Shadows of Knight, "Gloria" (p10, 1966); the Standells, "Dirty Water" (p11, 1966); and the Syndicate of Sound, "Little Girl" (p8, 1967). Some bands followed up with additional hits. Tommy James and the Shondells initially recorded their version of the Jeff Barry and Ellie Greenwich song "Hanky Panky" in 1963 at a studio in their hometown of Niles, Michigan. A few years later, a Pittsburgh DJ began playing it, and the song took off. Released on Roulette, it rose to number one in the second half of 1966. James then formed a new bunch of Shondells and followed with thirteen Top 40 hits over the next few years, including "Mony Mony" (p3, 1968), "Crimson and Clover" (p1, 1968), and "Crystal Blue Persuasion" (p2, 1969). Dallas-based Sam the Sham & the Pharaohs hit nationally with "Wooly Bully" (p2, 1965) and followed with five more hits through 1967, including "Little Red Riding Hood" (p2, 1966).

TV ROCK: THE INDUSTRY TRIES TO TAKE CONTROL ONCE MORE

One if by Land, Two if by Sea: Paul Revere and the Raiders. Part of the Pacific Northwest garage-band scene in the early 1960s, Paul Revere and the Raiders had initially formed in Idaho and made their commercial mark mid-decade after relocating to Los Angeles. After their single "Like, Long Hair" hit number thirty-nine on the national charts in 1961, the group moved to Portland, Oregon. When their version of "Louie Louie" failed to break out of the regional market, lead singer Mark Lindsay and organist Paul Revere parted ways. Revere and Lindsay would later rejoin and, with the help of *American Bandstand* impresario Dick Clark, Paul Revere and the Raiders debuted in 1965 as musical hosts of Clark's new rock variety show on CBS, *Where the Action Is.* Clark's show was launched in response to ABC's *Shindig,* which had debuted earlier that year under the production of Jack Good, who had produced innovative shows in the UK during the late 1950s. NBC also joined the TV-rock race with *Hullabaloo.* Together, these three shows targeted America's teenagers, providing wide exposure for British invasion and American acts. Regular television exposure on *Where the Action Is,* combined with a Columbia Records recording contract and the production talents of Terry Melcher (who was also producing the Byrds), helped Paul Revere and the Raiders score a series of hit singles on the American charts. They became the most successful of all the garage bands, scoring hits with "Just Like Me" (p11, 1966), "Kicks" (p4, 1966), "Hungry" (p6, 1966), and "Good Thing" (p4, 1966). "The Great Airplane Strike" (p20, 1966) marked the first Paul Revere and the Raiders single written by members of the group (Lindsay and Melcher). The band continued to enjoy chart success through the rest of the decade, scoring their first number-one hit with "Indian Reservation" in 1971. Singer Mark Lindsay also had a solo hit with "Arizona" in 1970.

A Collision of the Old and New: The Monkees' Tale. No group benefited more from television exposure than America's most commercially successful answer to the Beatles: the Monkees. Initially, the Monkees were formed as a band to make records

Paul Revere and the Raiders (from left to right): Drake Levin, Phil Volk, Mark Lindsay, Mike Smith, Paul Revere on a television set. As the house band for Dick Clark's *Where the Action Is*, the Raiders grew out of the garage-band movement to help define the growing presence of rock on television in the mid-1960s.

in support of a weekly television series. The brainchild of television producer Bert Rafelson and media executive Bob Schneider, *The Monkees* was a clear response to the Beatles' *A Hard Day's Night* and *Help!* Its intent was to reproduce the spirit of fun and wit that Richard Lester had captured with these two Beatles films. In forming the band, Rafelson and Schneider sought four unknowns who could be trained primarily as an on-camera acting team, but could also play music. In August 1965, auditions were held and eventually four young men who had never worked together were selected. Guitarist and songwriter Michael Nesmith had played professionally in Texas and the Los Angeles folk clubs, while Peter Tork had been part of the Greenwich Village folk scene. Davy Jones and Mickey Dolenz both had professional backgrounds in acting, Dolenz as star of the TV series *Circus Boy*, and Jones as a star of the musical *Oliver!* in London and New York (Jones performed in a selection from the show on the same Ed Sullivan broadcast that featured the Beatles' debut).

Since Rafelson and Schneider were mainly concerned with the success of the television show, not the records that might be released by the band, they focused the group's efforts on building their rapport and acting skills. As a result, the musical aspect of the group's training was neglected, and when the show was ready to begin production, Rafelson and Schneider needed songs. They turned to the songwriting-production team of Tommy Boyce and Bobby Hart (who had auditioned to become band members themselves), and to former Brill Building publisher Don Kirshner, who had relocated to Los Angeles. The Monkees' music was created according to a distinctively old-school music-business procedure: songs were written by professionals (Boyce and Hart, Goffin and King, Neil Diamond), backing tracks were performed by studio musicians, and the records were produced by Boyce and Hart. Initially, the Monkees did little more than sing on their records, and when word of this leaked out, many in the rock community used the information to discredit

Listening Guide

The Monkees, "Last Train to Clarksville" Colgems 1001

Words and music by Tommy Boyce and Bobby Hart, produced by Tommy Boyce and Bobby Hart. Rose to #1 on the *Billboard* "Hot 100" chart in fall 1966 (uk23, early 1967).

FORM: Modified simple verse, with verses of different lengths and two interludes not derived from the verses. While the first verse is 14 bars in length, the second is 2 measures longer, owing to a closing line that extends the verse, "and I don't know . . ." The third verse is like the first, except that it is preceded by the 2-bar guitar figure from the introduction, while the fourth verse is like the second, with the extra concluding bars. The last verse repeats the lyrics of the first, while using the ending of the second. In the middle of all this, two instrumental interludes are inserted. These interludes are actually based on similar material, but differ enough to sound new when they appear in the arrangement.

TIME SIGNATURE: 2/4, with a hint of a country two-step feel, which is a lively one-two, one-two rhythm.

INSTRUMENTATION: Electric guitars, acoustic guitar, bass, drums, tambourine, lead and backup vocals. Note that the guitar lick employed here seems influenced by similar figures in the Beatles' "Ticket to Ride," "Day Tripper," and "I Feel Fine." Note as well that the background vocals imitate a train whistle in various ways throughout the track, picking up on the song's title.

0:00–0:10	**Introduction**, 8 mm., 2 mm.	Beatles-style guitar lick played (w/bass and tambourine) 4 times.
0:10–0:27	**Verse 1**, 14 mm. (last 2 mm. truncated)	Lead vocal enters, "Take the last . . ."
0:27–0:47	**Verse 2**, 16 mm.	As verse 1 (with 2 mm. ending added), train-whistle background vocals added, "'Cause I'm leaving . . ."
0:47–1:08	**Verse 3**, 18 mm.	4 mm. of guitar from intro, then 14 mm. verse, lead vocal with train-whistle backup vocals, "Take the last . . ."
1:08–1:18	**Interlude 1**, 8 mm.	Vocal melody without words, quieter, pulsating bass guitar.
1:18–1:38	**Verse 4**, 16 mm.	As in verse 2, new train-whistle backup vocals, "Take the last . . ."
1:38–1:57	**Interlude 2**, 16 mm.	No vocal melody, based on the harmonies from interlude 1 but louder and brighter, verse 4 backup vocals enter toward end of this section.
1:57–2:17	**Verse 1**, 16 mm.	Same lyrics as verse 1, same ending as verse 2, "Take the last . . ."
2:17–2:42	**Coda**, 20 mm.	Repetition of same four-measure phrase, with Beatles-inspired guitar lick and another variation of the train-whistle backup vocals.

Modeled on the witty and fun-loving Beatles of *A Hard Day's Night and Help!*, the Monkees were originally formed as an acting troupe, with the music intended to help promote their weekly television show. Written by professional songwriters and using a studio band, the music proved much more popular than the producers anticipated, and the band enjoyed a string of hit singles and albums.

the group. None of this affected the band's popularity, however. While Rafelson and Schneider may have hoped their series would be a hit (which it was), they could not have imagined how successful the music would be. After the show debuted on NBC in fall 1966, the Monkees' "Last Train to Clarksville" rose to the top of the U.S. charts. Soon the success spread to Britain, when "I'm a Believer" went to number one in the States and the UK at the end of 1966. The Monkees followed with "A Little Bit Me, a Little Bit You" (p2 uk3, 1967), "Pleasant Valley Sunday" (p3 uk11, 1967), and "Valleri" (p3 uk12, 1968). The band's first four albums went to number one in the United States and placed in the UK top five. The first two Monkees albums together occupied the U.S. top slot for thirty-one consecutive weeks from late 1966 through the summer of 1967.

While the Monkees were clearly modeled on the Beatles, their music was produced according to the established Brill Building pattern, and this association has led many to dismiss the Monkees' hits. With the exception of guitarist Michael Nesmith, the Monkees did not play on their early records, and Mickey Dolenz or Davy Jones mostly sang songs written by professional songwriters to the accompaniment of studio musicians. "Last Train to Clarksville," however, gives some indication of the kinds of musical complexities that often resided behind the band's bubblegum image. This song is generally in simple verse form, presenting a series of five verses (the fifth repeats the lyrics of the first) with no real chorus. These verses are built on a sixteen-measure pattern, although the first and third verses come to only fourteen measures, owing to the truncation of what would have been the final two measures. Musical contrast is provided by two interludes, the first featuring a wordless vocal melody sung on the syllable "dooo." The second interlude is based **arpeggios** on the first, but now guitar **arpeggios** and high background vocals rework the musical material and expand it to encompass sixteen measures.

The Monkees themselves soon came to resent the entertainment-business machine. This was especially true of Nesmith, who felt that the band should be able to write its own material and perform on recordings. This struggle clearly illustrates how the new approach to popular music initiated by the Beatles conflicted with the older approach represented by the Brill Building. Taking their cue from the Beatles, the Monkees wanted to exercise control over the music they recorded. Eventually, the band did gain control, although its popularity quickly slipped away. The fact that the Monkees did not initially play on their own records does not set them apart from most Beach Boys records or the Byrds' "Mr. Tambourine Man." Rather, the Monkees'

Sound Check

Artist	Song	Sound
Bob Dylan	Positively 4th Street (1965)	Form: simple verse Finger cymbals played on beat four of each measure Organ featured throughout Repetitive 8-bar verse puts the focus on lyrics
The Byrds	Mr. Tambourine Man (1965)	Form: contrasting verse-chorus Uses only one verse from the Dylan original Guitar enters first, followed by bass and then the full band 12-string guitar has a "jangly" sound often associated with the Byrds
The Beach Boys	California Girls (1965)	Form: contrasting verse-chorus Ambitious instrumentation and arrangement for a rock group Full doo-wop background vocals Short interlude at the end, followed by a return to the chorus
The Kingsmen	Louie Louie (1963)	Form: simple verse-chorus Four-chord riff defines the musical structure Extended guitar solo may have been a mistake Unintelligible lyrics
The Monkees	Last Train to Clarksville (1966)	Form: simple verse (modified) Clear Beatles influence Backing vocals imitate a train whistle Verse is modified with slightly different lengths and interludes

eagerness to play and write is an indication of how deeply the idea that band members should exert greater control had infiltrated rock record production.

In the mid-1960s, there was a clear division in the rock market between young teens who listened to the pop-oriented music of the Monkees and older teens who were drawn to the increasingly more serious-minded and self-conscious rock of the Beatles. Music aimed at younger listeners was called "bubblegum" or "teenybopper" music, and continued to be played on AM radio stations nationwide. After the Monkees, Don Kirshner went on to promote a group made up of cartoon characters that also had a TV show, the Archies. After hitting number twenty-two in the United States with "Bang Shang a Lang" in 1968, the fictitious Archies (whose music was written by Jeff Barry and played by studio musicians) had a chart-topping hit in America and the UK with "Sugar Sugar" (1969). Other make-believe bands directed at young teens populated television in the late 1960s, including the Banana Splits (characters in fuzzy costumes) and Lancelot Link and the Evolution Revolution (a band of chimpanzees). Even episodes of the Hanna-Barbera cartoon *Scooby-Doo Where Are You!* featured obligatory chase scenes to the accompaniment of pop tunes. By the early 1970s, the Partridge Family would become America's foremost make-believe television band, with David Cassidy (Keith Partridge) sharing space in teen magazines with Bobby Sherman and members of the *Brady Bunch*.

While the younger teens listened to bubblegum pop, their older brothers and sisters were turning to psychedelia—a style of music that eschewed singles in favor of albums and was more likely to be heard on FM instead of AM radio. We will turn to psychedelia in Chapter 7. In the next chapter, we explore the rise of soul music in the 1960s and the story of an American company that benefited from the British invasion: Motown.

For Additional Online Resources, visit:
digital.wwnorton.com/whatsthatsound5

FURTHER READING

Glenn A. Baker, with Tom Czarnota and Peter Hogan, *Monkeemania: The True Story of the Monkees* (Plexus, 1997).

Sonny Bono, *And the Beat Goes On* (Pocket Books, 1991).

Marc Eliot, *Paul Simon: A Life* (Wiley, 2010).

Bobby Hart, with Glenn Ballantyne; *Psychedelic Bubblegum: Boyce & Hart, the Monkees, and Turning Mayhem into Miracles* (Select Books, 2015).

Clinton Heylin, *Bob Dylan: The Recording Sessions, 1960–1994* (St. Martin's, 1997).

Christopher Hjort, *So You Want to Be a Rock 'n' Roll Star: The Byrds Day-by-Day, 1965–1973* (Jawbone, 2008).

Dave Laing, Karl Dallas, Robin Denselow, and Robert Shelton, *The Electric Music: The Story of Folk into Rock* (Methuen, 1975).

Michelle Phillips, *California Dreamin': The True Story of the Mamas and the Papas* (Warner Books, 1986).

Rich Podolsky, *Don Kirshner, the Man with the Golden Ear* (Hal Leonard Books, 2012).

Johnny Rogan, *Timeless Flight Revisited: The Sequel* (Rogan House, 1998).

Andrew Sandoval, *The Monkees: The Day-By-Day Story of the 60s TV Pop Sensation* (Thunder Bay, 2005).

Robert Shelton, *No Direction Home: The Life and Music of Bob Dylan* (Da Capo, 2003).

Richie Unterberger, *Turn! Turn! Turn! The '60s Folk-Rock Revolution* (Backbeat Books, 2002).

Ritchie Unterberger, *Urban Spacemen and Wayfaring Strangers: Overlooked Innovators and Eccentric Visionaries of '60s Rock* (Backbeat Books, 2000).

Sean Wilentz, *Bob Dylan in America* (Doubleday, 2010).

Brian Wilson with Todd Gold, *Wouldn't It Be Nice* (HarperCollins, 1991).

DANCING IN THE STREET
MARTHA & THE VANDELLAS

MOTOWN POP AND SOUTHERN SOUL

CHAPTER PREVIEW

- Based in Detroit and led by Berry Gordy Jr., Motown released a series of hit records by artists such as the Supremes, the Temptations, and the Miracles.

- Motown employed a system that included in-house songwriters, producers, and studio musicians, and the company's artists often took instruction in dance and etiquette.

- Chicago continued to be an important location for the development of rhythm and blues during the 1960s via record labels such as Chess and Vee-Jay, and performers such as the Impressions.

- New York–based Atlantic Records, often in conjunction with Stax in Memphis, released hit records by Sam and Dave and Otis Redding, helping to define southern soul—a style that included hits recorded in Muscle Shoals by Wilson Pickett and in New York by Aretha Franklin.

- James Brown continued to be an important force in black pop, with hits during the '60s such as "Papa's Got a Brand New Bag, Pt. 1" and "I Got You (I Feel Good)."

While Motown was best known in the 1960s for its politely restrained pop music, Martha and the Vandellas represented the more soulful side of the Detroit-based label. Lead singer Martha Reeves (center) was a secretary at Motown before being tapped at the last minute to replace Mary Wells for a recording session. "Dancing in the Street" is probably the group's best-known record, and this Holland-Dozier-Holland–written single rose as high as number two on the *Billboard* "Hot 100" in the summer of 1964. Martha and the Vandellas' style displayed more gospel influence than that of their Motown rivals the Supremes, though the looser quality of their music did not translate into considerations of image. As exemplified in this "picture record," the dress and image projected by Motown and its artists was usually polished and controlled, regardless of the musical style explored in the recording. Here, Reeves and company wear evening dresses, presenting an image of sophistication and elegance. One could imagine them performing for the president or the queen of England as easily as in front of 10,000 screaming teenagers.

During the 1950s, many African American musicians were less successful in mainstream markets than white artists covering their records. A lot of African American recording artists were signed to independent labels, and the popularity of their recordings was sometimes eclipsed by artists with better access to mainstream outlets. Attitudes toward covering changed radically at the end of the 1950s, however, and by the beginning of the next decade there were many more recordings by African American artists achieving popularity in both the R&B and pop markets. Similar to artists like Elvis Presley and Pat Boone, British invasion bands took much of their early inspiration from African American popular music. While some black artists from the early 1960s remarked that the British invasion had a disastrous effect on the girl-group movement and sweet soul, by the middle of the decade the youth-music market began to thoroughly embrace recordings by black artists. It was a time when crossover became so prevalent that between December 1963 and January 1965 *Billboard* stopped tracking R&B charts separately.

Between 1960 and 1970, music by black musicians from regional centers—such as Detroit, Chicago, Memphis, Muscle Shoals (Alabama), and Atlanta—made a huge impact on the pop charts and interacted heavily with emerging rock styles. Among the most important developments was the music that came out of Motown Records—an independent company whose most important era of success paralleled that of the Beatles. A slew of record companies and artists operating out of Chicago also created important crossover R&B during the 1960s. During the last half of the decade, southern soul became wildly popular with mainstream listeners. Other legendary performers also established themselves during the 1960s, including James Brown, who had his first success as early as 1956 and remained popular in the R&B market with notable crossover success throughout the 1960s and 1970s.

In light of these varying companies and artists who achieved popularity with mainstream audiences during the 1960s, there were important musical trends that mirrored national attitudes toward race. This was a decade that emerged out of postwar 1950s conservatism. In 1964 and 1965, historic legal and social changes were evidence of an emerging movement for civil rights. During the last half of the decade, race relations reflected a move farther into chaotic political and social territory, mostly surrounding the growing presence of the United States in Vietnam. As attitudes toward blackness changed throughout the decade, elements encoded into crossover R&B appealed differently to pop audiences. Some of these included regional associations, the manner in which an artist dressed and moved on stage, orchestration and manner of recording, vocal style, and lyrical references to black life or themes that came out of gospel traditions. When white audiences accepted African American performers more fully into the mainstream, perceptions of racial authenticity

Berry Gordy (left) was the figurehead behind Motown records. In this photo he is engaged in backstage discussion with Levi Stubbs (right), lead singer of the Four Tops. Gordy handled all aspects of his artists' careers, including their recordings, publishing, and management.

became extremely important to the reception of black pop for both listeners and industry professionals. We begin our study of black pop with Motown—a label that enjoyed enormous commercial success in the 1960s.

BERRY GORDY JR. AND BLACK MUSIC FOR WHITE AUDIENCES

Adapting a Brill Building Production Model. In the years after World War II, Berry Gordy Jr., a professional boxer in the Detroit area, worked for his father's construction company, owned a record store, and worked on the Ford assembly line. He spent a lot of time in Detroit's jazz clubs, although his experience with the record store taught him that—financially, at least—jazz was not the key to success in the music business. Gordy began writing material for fellow Detroiter Jackie Wilson. Working with his sister Gwen Gordy and Roquel "Billy" Davis (a.k.a. Tyran Carlo), Gordy wrote several songs that became hits for Wilson, including "Reet Petite" (1957), "Lonely Teardrops" (p7 r1, 1958), and "That's Why (I Love You So)" (p13 r2, 1959). Gordy also wrote and produced songs for other singers and groups, leasing these recordings to labels in New York and Chicago.

In 1959, Gordy formed Motown records with a loan from a family trust. His first hit record for Motown was Barrett Strong's "Money (That's What I Want)" (p23 r2), a song he had also leased to his sister's record company, Anna Records. During his first few years in business, Gordy often modeled his releases on already successful records. The Marvelettes' "Please Mr. Postman" (p1 r1, 1961) resembles the girl-group hits of the Brill Building, while the grittier "Do You Love Me" (p3 r1, 1962) by the Contours is similar to the Isley Brothers' style of the early '60s. Gordy knew that there was enormous commercial potential in producing records that could cross over from the rhythm and blues charts onto the pop charts. Adopting Chuck Berry's strategy to prevent covers of his songs by white artists, Gordy hoped to make Motown singles acceptable to mainstream listeners in their original versions.

Motown was groundbreaking in many ways, but Gordy's production method was derived from Brill Building practices. He gave songwriting and production duties to a collection of specialized individuals and teams, using a model that had been established by Leiber and Stoller a few years earlier. From 1960 to 1964, Gordy, William "Mickey" Stevenson, and William "Smokey" Robinson handled many of the songwriting and production duties. The first consistently successful Motown group was the Miracles, fronted by Robinson as lead vocalist. Gordy and Robinson wrote the first Miracles hit, "Shop Around" (p2 r1, 1960),

The Funk Brothers: Behind the Scenes

The 2003 documentary film *Standing in the Shadows of Motown* chronicles the contributions of the studio musicians behind the Motown sound. Most listeners tend to focus their attention on singers, and perhaps songwriters or producers. Few are aware of the crucial role that backup musicians play on a given record. Candid and intelligent interviews with surviving Motown studio musicians bring these players out of the shadows and into the spotlight.

while Robinson wrote and produced the group's "You've Really Got a Hold on Me" (p8 r1, 1962). Robinson was among Motown's most successful early producers, handling songwriting and production for singer Mary Wells, whose string of hits included "The One Who Really Loves You" (p8 r2, 1962), "You Beat Me to the Punch" (p9 r1, 1962), "Two Lovers" (p7 r1, 1962), and "My Guy" (p1, 1964). The years between 1964 and 1967 at Motown were dominated by the tremendous success of the Brian Holland, Lamont Dozier, and Eddie Holland team. "H-D-H" were responsible for a string of hits by the Supremes, the Four Tops, and Martha and the Vandellas, among others. H-D-H left Motown and stopped producing music in late 1967 over a royalty dispute. Following the departure of H-D-H, Norman Whitfield emerged as the label's most successful producer, with a series of singles by the Temptations through the early 1970s. In the late 1960s, the team of Valerie Ashford and Nick Simpson also had tremendous success at Motown, beginning with a series of Marvin Gaye and Tammi Terrell duets, and Frank Wilson collaborated with the Supremes and the Four Tops.

The Studio, the Band, and Quality Control.

Through most of the 1960s, Motown productions were recorded in the company studio at 2648 West Grand Boulevard in Detroit—called "Hitsville, USA." This studio, and several other offices in converted houses on the same block, made up the business headquarters for the company. The studio was busy around the clock, as artists and producers moved in and out working on various releases. Like Phil Spector in Los Angeles, Motown producers had a gifted and experienced group of studio musicians to help them craft their arrangements. Drawn from Detroit's lively jazz scene, these players were adept at creating their parts on the spot, often without the benefit of scored-out parts or even a completed formal design. Many musicians were employed at Motown sessions throughout the decade, but the key players were pianist Earl Van Dyke, drummer Benny Benjamin, and electric bassist James Jamerson. One key to the "Motown Sound" was that most of the records featured this studio band, referred to as the Funk Brothers.

Gordy promoted competition within the ranks of Motown performers, songwriters, and producers. Once a week, he gathered the staff together for "quality control" meetings, which served as the final test for each song, its arrangement, and its recorded sound. A number of freshly recorded potential releases were presented for Motown employees, and sometimes members of the community, to vote on which songs would be released that week. These meetings were generally a good barometer of a song's potential success, although the initial vote occasionally went against a now-classic song. Perhaps the most famous example is Marvin Gaye's version of "I Heard It through the Grapevine" in 1967. Only after Gladys Knight and the Pips recorded a new version of the song, which climbed to the top of the charts in late 1967 (p2 r1), did local disc jockeys begin to play Gaye's recording. Realizing that quality control had made a rare mistake, Gordy eventually released Gaye's version of "Grapevine" as a single in 1968, which sold several million copies and went to number one on both the "Hot 100" and the "Best Selling Rhythm & Blues Singles" charts.

Artist Development and Professional Choreography.

According to Gordy's philosophy, Motown artists had to project an image of class and sophistication. He wanted the dance movements that accompanied singing in live performance to be refined and graceful, so he hired choreographer Cholly Atkins, who carefully honed every onstage movement and dance step. For what Motown performers playfully called "the charm school," Gordy hired Maxine Powell, who had run a finishing school within Detroit's black community since the early 1950s. Powell was charged with teaching both women and men how to move and speak with grace. Gordy's goal was to prepare his acts for the highest echelons of success in the music business and to book his best acts into elegant supper clubs such as the Copacabana in New York or the big hotel stages of Las Vegas. In light of these ambitious goals, Powell told her charges that she was preparing them to perform and socialize in two places: the White House and Buckingham Palace.

Motown Girl Groups. The Supremes were the quintessential Motown girl group during the mid to late 1960s. Working out of the Phil Spector and Brill Building traditions, the Supremes extended the girl-group format to the highest reaches of commercial success. The group formed in Detroit in 1959, when Diana Ross, Mary Wilson, Florence Ballard, and Betty McGlown started a quartet called the Primettes—a sister group to the Primes (later known as the Temptations). McGlown soon left the group, and the remaining trio hung around the Motown headquarters hoping to sing backup and convince Gordy to sign them (he once told them to go home and finish school). They were eventually signed, although their first singles were so unsuccessful that other Motown artists jokingly called them the "no-hit Supremes." Holland-Dozier-Holland took over production and songwriting duties for the group, and they hit in 1964 with "Where Did Our Love Go?" (p1). Although Ballard was considered the most accomplished singer, H-D-H experimented during the sessions for this single with both Wilson's and Ross's voices, deciding that Ross's was the more evocative. Once they found the formula, the team chalked up a string of five consecutive number-one pop hits, following up with "Baby Love" (r1, 1964), "Come See about Me" (r2, 1964), "Stop! In the Name of Love" (r2, 1965), and "Back in My Arms Again" (r1, 1965). Showing the interchangeability of

Motown artists performed regularly on television shows during the 1960s. In this photo Motown founder Berry Gordy (seated left) and the Supremes—Mary Wilson and Diana Ross seated to his left and Florence Ballard seated behind—rehearse for *Hullabaloo*. Intense preparation and attention to detail gave Motown acts a sense of professionalism lacking from many other pop performances during the period.

The Supremes were known as much for their elegant style as for their ubiquitous records during the mid-1960s. Here the trio, wearing stunning green gowns, performs "I Hear a Symphony" with an orchestra in 1965 on the NBC television program *Hullabaloo.*

Motown artists in groups like the Supremes, Ballard was asked to leave the group in 1967 after a series of personal issues, and was replaced by Cindy Birdsong. The group continued its success with "Reflections" (p2 r4, 1967) and, after the departure of H-D-H, "Love Child" (p1 r2, 1968). Ross left the group in late 1969 to focus on her solo career. "Someday We'll Be Together" (p1 r1, 1969), an ironic title in retrospect, was her last hit single with the group, which had changed its name to Diana Ross and the Supremes amidst Ross's growing stature as the leader of the group. Ross became a very successful solo artist, and was replaced in the Supremes by Jean Terrell as the group went on to score several more pop hits in the 1970s, including "Stoned Love" (p7 r1, 1970).

From 1964 to 1967, the teaming of the Supremes with Holland-Dozier-Holland produced a series of hit singles that made H-D-H one of the most successful writing and production teams in popular music and placed the Supremes among the top recording artists of the decade. A number-one hit in the fall of 1964, "Baby Love" is a prime example of a Supremes hit written and produced by H-D-H during the mid-1960s. The track begins with an introduction that features a series of pulsating piano chords accompanied by drums. Notice that the rhythm of the piano and drums is supported by what sound like handclaps or marching. This sound was produced by slapping together wooden two-by-fours, making the song's beat unmistakable. Also present is the sound of the vibraphone (or "vibes"), a percussion instrument similar to the xylophone but featuring a sustained sound with vibrato. Notice from the Listening Guide that the song is a simple verse form. The repeated verses are performed with little change in the accompaniment, which includes electric guitar and bass after the introduction. The other Supremes provide backup vocals as Ross works her way through seven verses. There are a few twists to the arrangement: in the third verse, a saxophone takes over for the lead vocal for the last eight measures, making the vocal return for verse 4 sound fresher than it might otherwise. Verse 5 introduces a change of key (up a half-step from D-flat to D) that also propels the song forward. The pronounced rhythmic stomping in this tune is a continuation from the previous single, "Where Did Our Love Go?," as is the repetition of the word "baby"—showing that H-D-H were trying to repeat a winning formula with this second single.

Motown had other important girl groups. Formed in Detroit in 1962 by former members of the Del-Phis, who had recorded for Chess Records, Martha and the Vandellas also had many hits for the company. Martha Reeves had been performing in a Detroit club when she was spotted by Motown producer Mickey Stevenson, who hired her not as a singer but as his secretary. When the backup singers hired for a Marvin Gaye recording session failed to show up for one session, Reeves and her friends provided backup vocals on "Stubborn Kind of Fellow" (p46 r8, 1962), impressing Gordy enough that he had them record "I'll Have to Let Him Go" as Martha and the Vandellas. By early 1963, the group consisted of Reeves on lead

Listening Guide

The Supremes, "Baby Love" Motown 1066

Words and music by Brian Holland, Lamont Dozier, and Edward Holland Jr., produced by Brian Holland and Lamont Dozier. Reached #1 on the *Billboard* "Hot 100" chart in the fall of 1964. (Note that the *Billboard* R&B charts did not run from December 1963 to late January 1965.)

FORM: Simple verse. A 12-bar verse structure is repeated relatively unchanged throughout. The only significant alterations are in verse 3, where the saxophones take over the melody after 4 bars, and in verse 5, which introduces a change of key via a 2-bar transition. The arrangement builds by adding instruments: the guitar enters in verse 2, as do call-and-response phrases between the lead and backup vocals, and saxophones are added in verse 3. The change of key gives the song a lift after verse 4. The song structure is nevertheless very simple, relying heavily on the vocal performance of Diana Ross.

TIME SIGNATURE: 4/4 (shuffle in four). Note how the sounds of feet stomping on boards pound out the beat throughout the song.

INSTRUMENTATION: Piano, vibes, electric guitar, bass, drums, saxes, foot stomping, lead and backing vocals.

0:00–0:09	**Introduction**, 5 mm.	Stomping boards, vibes, piano, and drums prepare the way for the vocals.
0:09–0:30	**Verse 1**, 12 mm.	Vocals enter, and Ross sings solo with only a little backup. "Ooo, baby love . . ."
0:30–0:51	**Verse 2**, 12 mm.	Add guitar, as backup vocals add call-and-response to second half of verse. "'Cause baby love . . ."
0:51–1:13	**Verse 3**, 12 mm.	4 mm. of vocals with sax backup, and then saxes take melody, "Need ya . . ."
1:13–1:34	**Verse 4**, 12 mm.	As verse 3, without the saxes, "Baby love . . ."
1:34–1:58	**Verse 5**, 14 mm.	2 mm. key change peps up arrangement and then the regular 12 mm. verse follows, as the saxes return. "Need to hold you . . ."
1:58–2:20	**Verse 6**, 12 mm.	As verse 5, ". . . of me my love . . ."
2:20–2:40	**Verse 7**, 12 mm.	Fade out on second half of verse, "'Til it's hurtin' me . . ."

vocals, backed by Rosalyn Ashford and Annette Beard (Betty Kelly replaced Beard in 1964). The group had its first hit during the winter of 1963, when the Holland-Dozier-Holland–produced "Come and Get These Memories" hit number twenty-nine on the *Billboard* "Hot 100" (r6). After their first hit with H-D-H, the group followed up with "Heat Wave" (p4 r1, 1963) and "Quicksand" (p8 r7, 1963) before

The songwriting team of Holland-Dozier-Holland was responsible for some of the biggest hits of the 1960s. Working with the Supremes, the Four Tops, and Martha and the Vandellas, H-D-H produced a string of hits that kept Motown records at the top of the pop charts from 1963 to 1967.

Mickey Stevenson took over production duties for what would become the group's most successful and best known single, "Dancing in the Street" (p2 r8, 1964). Martha and the Vandellas continued their success through 1967 with singles produced by H-D-H, including "Nowhere to Run" (p8 r5, 1965) and "Jimmy Mack" (p10 r1, 1967). Despite their popularity, the group certainly suffered because of the Supremes' success and the attention Motown gave to cultivating Diana Ross. Moreover, roots in gospel and rhythm and blues were more apparent in the recordings of Martha and the Vandellas than those of the Supremes, who sounded somewhat controlled by comparison. This was largely due to Martha Reeves's full-throated, soulful vocal style, which reflected a rise in southern soul and set the stage for Aretha Franklin later in the decade.

Motown Guy Groups. A typical Motown guy group known for their athletic dance moves, the Temptations were among the label's top acts between 1964 and 1972. The group formed in 1961 in Detroit when Otis Williams, Melvin Franklin, and Al Bryant of the Distants joined forces with Eddie Kendricks and Paul Williams (no relation to Otis) of the Primes. In 1963, after a few unsuccessful releases for Motown, Bryant left the group and David Ruffin joined, completing the classic Temptations lineup that would remain intact until 1968. The group hit the pop charts in early 1964 (when the Beatles were making their first splash), with "The Way You Do the Things You Do" (p11), a tune written and produced by Robinson that showcased Kendricks's high tenor lead vocal. This catchy track is an example of the early Temptations style, and highlights Robinson's clever approach to writing lyrics. While lines such as "You got a smile so bright, you know you could've been a candle" may sound a bit corny in isolation, when combined with Robinson's sunny music, they come to life in a distinctive and broadly appealing way. On the basis of this song's success, subsequent Temptations releases were produced by Robinson, including "My Girl" (p1 r1, 1965) and "Get Ready" (p29 r1, 1965). Perhaps disappointed that Robinson could not duplicate the enormous success of "My Girl," Gordy gave Norman Whitfield a chance to produce the group in 1966. Beginning with "Ain't Too Proud to Beg" (p13 r1, 1966), he delivered a string of hits for the group, including "I Know I'm Losing You" (p8 r1, 1966) and "You're My Everything" (p6 r3, 1967).

Formed in 1954 by Levi Stubbs, Obie Benson, Lawrence Payton, and Duke Fakir, the Four Tops were older and more experienced than most Motown groups of the mid-1960s. The group released an early single on Chess Records, but signed to Motown in 1963 and recorded a jazz album for Gordy's Workshop label. They soon teamed up with Holland-Dozier-Holland, who had begun working with the Supremes a few months earlier. Led by the vocals of Stubbs, the Four Tops were in many ways the male counterparts to the Supremes, enjoying a string of H-D-H–produced hits, including "Baby I Need Your Loving" (p11, 1964), "I Can't Help Myself (Sugar Pie, Honey Bunch)" (p1 r1, 1965), "It's the Same Old Song" (p5 r2,

The Temptations were one of Motown's most successful guy groups. Known for their dense vocal harmonies and striking choreography, this photo depicts the group's classic lineup (left to right: Eddie Kendricks, David Ruffin, Otis Williams, Melvin Franklin, Paul Williams) performing in tandem at New York's famous Apollo Theater in 1964.

1965), "Reach Out I'll Be There" (p1 r1, 1966), and "Standing in the Shadows of Love" (p6 r2, 1966). Like the music of the Supremes, most of the Four Tops' songs have a pronounced pop orientation, with frequent use of orchestral strings and other instrumentation drawn from classical music. "Reach Out I'll Be There" illustrates this blend of rhythm and blues and classical music in the use of winds in its orchestral introduction and its harmonic progressions, which are combined with a strong beat and soulful vocals.

Marvin Gaye and Stevie Wonder. Motown was also home to many important solo singers during the 1960s, including Mary Wells, Kim Weston, and Brenda Holloway. Two of the company's most important solo vocalists were Marvin Gaye and Stevie Wonder (known for much of the decade as "Little" Stevie Wonder). Originally, Gaye sought a career as a pop crooner in the vein of Frank Sinatra or Nat "King" Cole, but he found the Motown environment more suitable to creating dance-oriented R&B hits. In 1962, he had a hit with "Stubborn Kind of Fellow," and continued this success throughout the decade with sixteen more singles in the pop Top 40, and another ten duets with Mary Wells, Tammi Terrell, and Kim Weston. Gaye worked with most of the Motown producers, recording upbeat soul hits like "Pride and Joy" (p10 r2, 1963) with Mickey Stevenson, pop hits like "How Sweet It Is to Be Loved by You" (p6 r4, 1965) with Holland-Dozier-Holland, and "Ain't That Peculiar" (p8 r1, 1965) with Smokey Robinson. He also recorded classic duets like "Ain't Nothing Like the Real Thing" (p8 r1, 1968), sung with Tammi Terrell and produced by Ashford and Simpson. In 1968, Gaye continued his solo success with the Norman Whitfield and Barrett Strong song "I Heard It through the Grapevine." By the end of the decade, he was also writing and producing for other artists, and the Originals, a male vocal quartet, became his charges in the studio. The combination produced the hits "Baby I'm for Real" (p14 r1, 1969) and "The Bells" (p12 r4, 1970).

Stevie Wonder followed a path similar to Marvin Gaye's. Signed to Motown in 1961 at the age of eleven, Wonder was blind from birth and promoted as a musical prodigy in the manner of Ray Charles. At the age of thirteen, he scored a surprise

DANCE SHOWS IN THE 1960S: TEMPTATIONS, "MY GIRL"

Viewing Rock

Dance variety shows were extremely popular during the 1950s and 1960s. In addition to dances performed by a studio full of teens, many of these programs contained feature performances, during which a popular group would appear on the show and lip-synch to their latest hit record. *American Bandstand* is the most famous of these programs, but there were dozens of other local and regional dance programs. Among their many television appearances during the mid-1960s, the of the group's 1965 hit "My Girl." The performance style of the Temptations offers an example of a typical rhythm and blues vocal group, in which choreography and physical movement are the vital elements. The group appears with a single lead singer, in this case David Ruffin, staged to the viewer's right, while the remaining four members form a collective backup group on the left of the screen. Echoing their vocal roles, Ruffin is able to move freely, while the group must remain synchronized. Although it is hard to know the origin of the choreography, it was most likely developed by group member Paul Williams and Motown staff choreographer Cholly Atkins. Some of the moves are literal readings of the lyrics, such as "I've got sunshine" (1) and "when it's cold outside" (2). Other steps are more abstract. As per the vocal roles, the camera often focuses on Ruffin depicting the lead vocal line (3). All the while, it is important to remember that the group is performing for a studio full of dancing teenagers, who are often visible in the broadcast (4). Performances such as "My Girl" were extremely popular during the earliest decades of rock, offering artists the opportunity to show physical depictions of their music and giving listeners entrée to dance around the living room.

Detroit-based Temptations appeared several times on the local, Windsor, Ontario, program *Swingin' Time*. One of the most compelling of these appearances is a 1966 performance

number-one hit on both the pop and rhythm and blues charts with "Fingertips, pt. 2" (1963). The record captures an impromptu moment during a live Motown Revue concert when Wonder launches into an extended improvisation without warning (bass player Larry Moses can be heard asking "What key? What key?"). The spontaneous and exuberant quality of that moment transferred well to vinyl, and Motown ended up with one of its most successful releases up to that time. After this initial success, Wonder floundered a bit—his voice changed and Motown seemed unsure how to advance his career. By early 1966, however, his "Uptight

(Everything's Alright)" hit number three on the pop charts (r1), beginning a string of hits that included "I Was Made to Love Her" (p2 r1, 1967), "For Once in My Life" (p2 r2, 1968), and "My Cherie Amour" (p4 r4, 1969). Wonder earned partial songwriting credit for "I Was Made to Love Her" and "My Cherie Amour," and in 1970 he produced "Signed, Sealed, Delivered, I'm Yours" (p3 r1), helping Motown to make the transition out of the 1960s. The music of Gaye and Wonder, and their role as producers, will be considered further in Chapter 9.

Listening Guide

The Temptations, "The Way You Do the Things You Do" Gordy 7028

Words and music by William "Smokey" Robinson and Robert Rogers, produced by Smokey Robinson. Reached #11 on the *Billboard* "Hot 100" chart in 1964.

FORM: Simple verse. After an introduction based on a two-chord vamp, the first two verses follow the same lengthy structure: a 16-bar section that leads into a 4-bar refrain and then a 3-bar ending subsection (based on the two-chord vamp from the introduction). This extended structure is truncated after the second verse, first in an 8-bar instrumental verse, then in the third verse, which pares the structure down to 12 measures. The arrangement builds by adding horns in verse 2, changing key for the saxophone solo, and scoring the horns in a higher register in verse 3.

TIME SIGNATURE: 4/4 (shuffle in four).

INSTRUMENTATION: Electric guitar, piano, bass, drums, horns, lead and backup vocals.

0:00–0:08	**Introduction**, 4 mm.	Two-chord vamp featuring guitar with treble tone.
0:08–0:53	**Verse 1 w/refrain**, 23 mm.	Harmony vocals take first part of each phrase ("You got a smile so bright . . ."), which is answered by Kendricks's high tenor ("You know you could have been . . .").
0:53–1:37	**Verse 2 w/refrain**, 23 mm.	Vocals continue call-and-response, though now the harmony parts add some supporting "ooo's" derived from doo-wop. Horns are added. "As pretty as you are . . ."
1:37–1:52	**Instrumental verse** (partial), 8 mm.	Verse is shortened, change of key, sax solo.
1:52–2:16	**Verse 3 w/refrain** (partial), 12 mm.	Horns are higher than before, and this gives the song an increased intensity, "You made my life so rich . . ."
2:16–2:38	**Coda**, 12 mm.	Vamp on chords from introduction, lead vocal improvises over repeated backup vocals.

Marvin Gaye (right) and Stevie Wonder (left) were two of Motown's most successful male singers. In this photo, a young Wonder shares a harmonica with Gaye behind the microphone in 1965.

CHICAGO R&B

Chess Legacies. Chicago was an important regional center for R&B during the 1960s, boasting many important independent labels, writers, producers, and artists. Styles of black music produced in Chicago during this time were varied, and included music inflected by rising trends in vocal harmony groups and the city's historic connection to the electric blues. Chicago R&B music was also connected to a rising trend in gospel-oriented soul music during the mid-1960s. Many of the production techniques employed at Motown during this time were also prevalent in R&B created in Chicago.

Professional songwriters and producers were active in this scene, and they often created tightly wound arrangements with high production qualities that featured "sweetening" elements like backing vocalists and orchestral instruments. Known mostly for releasing electric blues and early rock and roll during the 1950s by artists like Muddy Waters, Howlin' Wolf, and Chuck Berry, Chess Records was still active a decade later. On subsidiaries such as Cadet, Checker, and Check-Mate, Chess released a broad range of black pop during the 1960s by artists such as Etta James, Sugar Pie DeSanto, and Jackie Ross. The company also released several noteworthy crossover records, which showed the manner in which R&B connected still to the pop market a decade after the rise of rock and roll. Little Milton was known best for his stereotypical Chicago blues song "So Mean to Me" (r14, 1962) before releasing the upbeat "We're Gonna Make It" (p25, r1) in 1965, a song that featured sophisticated production and an extensive horn arrangement. At the end of the decade, Chess also had several hits on the Cadet imprint by the Dells, a vocal harmony group that had their first hit during the doo-wop era with "What a Nite" (r4) in 1956. The Dells released two popular crossover records in the late 1960s that were both remakes of their own previous songs. One of these was "Stay in My Corner" (p10 r1, 1965), which had been in a hit in 1965 on Vee-Jay, and the other was "What a Night" (p10 r1, 1969), a reworked version of their 1950s hit. The most popular Chess crossover hit of the decade, however, was "Rescue Me" by Fontella Bass (p4 r1, 1965). This record was produced in part by Billy Davis, who had been Berry Gordy's songwriting partner in Detroit during the late 1950s and was now working full time at Chess. Unsurprisingly, despite its strong Chicago origins "Rescue Me" includes many elements in common with Motown's most popular music of the time.

Vee-Jay, Okeh, and Brunswick. Vee-Jay Records was formed in 1953 by the husband-and-wife team of Vivian Carter and James Bracken. Vivian's brother Calvin Carter was the company's main producer. The company specialized in electric blues and doo-wop in the 1950s, releasing recordings by the Spaniels, the El Dorados, and Jimmy Reed. One of the company's first crossover hits was "For Your Precious Love," a doo-wop recording by Jerry Butler and the Impressions (p11 r3, 1958). The company achieved even greater sales during the early 1960s, however. After leaving the Impressions, Butler enlisted the help of former band mate Curtis Mayfield to write and perform "He Will Break Your Heart" (p7, r1 1960), a duet that incorporated a light Latin arrangement with shuffling snare and upright bass. Dee Clark was another successful performer for Vee-Jay. His 1961 single "Raindrops" (p2 r3) was stylistically similar to "He Will Break Your Heart," but also used a prominent string arrangement. Gene Chandler's "Duke of Earl"

Marvin Gaye performing on the British television show *Thank Your Lucky Stars* in November 1964. Originally interested in crooning songs like Frank Sinatra or Nat "King" Cole, Gaye eventually turned to upbeat rhythm and blues. A staple of Motown, Gaye scored many solo hits, sang duets with Tammi Terrell and Mary Wells, and wrote songs for other Motown artists.

(p1 r1 1962) was one of the most best-known Vee-Jay releases of the time. A doo-wop group called the Dukays that included both Chandler and a man named Earl Edwards recorded this song, but it was credited to Chandler as a solo artist on the single. Vee-Jay also released music by white groups, including the early 1960s music of the Four Seasons (discussed in Chapter 5), which crossed freely between pop and R&B markets in 1962 and 1963. The most auspicious holdings by the company were several early singles by the Beatles. When Capitol Records in the United States declined distribution rights to several early Beatles singles, Vee-Jay was one of the companies that took hold of these records, eventually releasing five singles by the group in 1964 on the Vee Jay and Tollie imprints. In the wake of the Beatles' success, two important singles by black artists appeared on Vee-Jay in 1964. Betty Everett's "The Shoop Shoop Song (It's in His Kiss)" (p6 r1, 1964) explored the girl-group style through active backing vocals and a tightly arranged backing track that featured xylophone, cello, and horns. Everett also teamed with Butler to record a successful version of the ballad "Let It Be Me" (p5 r1, 1964), which had been a hit for the Everly Brothers in 1960.

Okeh Records had been the "race" imprint of Columbia from the mid-1920s to the mid-1930s but was discontinued during a downturn in the record business. After another short stint in the late 1940s, Okeh was revived yet again in the early

1950s, this time to explore the new crossover R&B market. The company released music by many artists in the 1960s, but none was as successful as Major Lance. Lance worked closely with songwriter Curtis Mayfield on several hit singles during this period, including "The Monkey Time" (p8 r2, 1963) and "Um, Um, Um, Um, Um, Um" (p5 r1, 1963). One of the major creative forces at Okeh was producer Carl Davis, who left the company in 1966. Davis quickly aligned himself with the Brunswick label, and produced two important hits for Jackie Wilson, "Whispers (Gettin' Louder)" (p11 r5, 1966) and "(Your Love Keeps Lifting Me) Higher and Higher" (p6 r1, 1967). Brunswick also released music by one of the most important Chicago vocal harmony groups at the turn of the 1970s, the Chi-Lites. Their "Have You Seen Her" (p3 r1, 1971) and "Oh Girl" (p1 r1, 1972) became staples of pop and R&B radio, and offered a connection to earlier doo-wop styles of the 1950s. Davis later started a record company called Dakar, also based in Chicago, releasing popular singles by Tyrone Davis that included "Can I Change My Mind" (p5 r1, 1968) and "Turn Back the Hands of Time" (p3 r1, 1970).

The Impressions. Curtis Mayfield was involved with a lot of Chicago's most important R&B in the 1960s. Mayfield took the reins of the Impressions after Jerry Butler left for a solo career in the late 1950s. After several lineup changes, the group signed to ABC-Paramount, a major label based in New York, and settled as a trio that included Mayfield, Sam Gooden, and Fred Cash. ABC-Paramount was actively exploring the R&B market at the time, having recently signed Ray Charles, and the company opened a Chicago office in the early 1960s headed by producer and arranger Johnny Pate. The Impressions released about two-dozen singles during the 1960s, most of which sold well in the R&B market. Mayfield wrote all of these songs, in addition to music for other Chicago artists like Major Lance and Jerry Butler. In the first half of the decade, the group's music was also very popular with mainstream audiences. During the most crucial early years of the civil rights movement, songs like "It's All Right" (p4 r1, 1963), "Keep On Pushing" (p10 r1, 1964), "Amen" (p7 r1, 1964), and "We're a Winner" (p14 r1, 1967) combined slick,

The Impressions in the recording studio during the mid 1960s. Led by guitarist and songwriter Curtis Mayfield (left), the Chicago-based Impressions released a number of popular songs that combined sophisticated arrangements with lyrical references to the civil rights movement and other aspects of black life at the time.

Listening Guide

The Impressions, "People Get Ready" ABC-Paramount 10622

Words and music by Curtis Mayfield, produced by Johnny Pate. Reached #14 on the Billboard "Hot 100" chart and #3 on the "Hot Rhythm and Blues Singles" chart in the spring of 1965.

FORM: Simple verse. An 8-bar verse structure is constructed of two 4-bar phrases. Within this structure, a 2-bar harmonic pattern repeats three times, and the fourth iteration is different. In the verse, notice how the lead vocal melody rises at the end of measures 2 and 6 ("com-in" and "hum-min" in verse 1), creating tension, and maintains its pitch in measures 4 and 8 ("get on board" and "thank the lord" in verse 1), providing closure. The chords and vocal harmonies at the ends of measures 4 and 8 are especially evocative of gospel music. This type of phrase ending is sometimes called an "Amen" cadence.

TIME SIGNATURE: 4/4. A light snare hits on the fourth beat of every measure.

INSTRUMENTATION: Drums, bass, guitar, horns, xylophone, strings, lead and backing vocals.

0:00–0:12	**Introduction**, 4 mm.	Vocal humming is accompanied by prominent horns, strings, and xylophone.
0:12–0:40	**Verse 1**, 8 mm.	Mayfield begins as lead vocalist, but alternates phrases in call-and-response with Cash and Gooden. The group also sings several phrases as a unit. "People get ready . . ."
0:40–0:47	**Instrumental interlude**, 2 mm.	Guitar and xylophone provide a contrast of texture, performing over a section that uses the first 2-bar phrase of the verse.
0:47–1:14	**Verse 2**, 8 mm.	Notice the horn accompaniment, xylophone, countermelody, and strings entering in the last phrase. "So, people get ready . . ."
1:14–1:28	**Interlude**, 4 mm.	This section doubles the length of the interlude, and changes key upward to create a sense of drive.
1:28–1:56	**Verse 3**, 8 mm.	Mayfield sings lead, with more traditional backing vocals provided by Gooden and Cash. Note how the guitar plays sharp, offbeat hits. "There ain't no room . . ."
1:56–2:26	**Verse 4**, 8 mm.	All three vocalists perform in unison until the end, repeating the lyrics of the first verse. Strings accompany these vocals throughout the verse. "People get ready . . ."
2:26–2:37	**Postlude**, 2 mm.	Full orchestration is used in this appearance of the interlude (with strings performing the vocal melody) to provide closure.

professional arrangements by Pate with empowering lyrics and overt black consciousness. Although it wasn't the group's most popular single at the time, "People Get Ready" (p14 r3, 1965) has since become an iconic Impressions song. The song evokes lyrical and musical tropes of gospel music and connects the civil rights movement to a larger, historic African American struggle. Musically, the song's harmonic progression, call-and-response vocals among all three singers, and thick vocal harmonies also connect to African American spiritual sources. All these elements are supported by an eloquent orchestral element arranged by Pate, which incorporates xylophone, strings, and horns. In 1968, Mayfield and band manager Eddie Thomas formed Curtom Records. The company's main producers were Pate and Donny Hathaway, a native Chicagoan who would later become a popular recording artist. Curtom released popular music by Mayfield as a solo artist and the Impressions (with replacement vocalist Leroy Hutson). The music of the Impressions represents well the essence of the Chicago R&B scene of the 1960s, a time and place in which African American artists on mostly independent labels released music that achieved notable popularity in the mainstream market. The northern, industrial setting of Chicago inspired approaches to production similar to those found at Motown in the first half of the decade but connected differently with African American identity, exploring freely messages of uplift and gospel in a more forward manner than the most popular crossover hits released by Motown.

SOUTHERN SOUL

Atlantic in the Early 1960s. As discussed at the end of Chapter 3, New York–based Atlantic Records enjoyed considerable success in the early 1960s with hits from the Drifters, the Coasters, and Ben E. King. During this period, the highly produced and often relaxed style of sweet soul was the most public face of the label's activity. Later in the decade, Atlantic invested heavily in a new stylistic direction—a harder-edged brand of black pop that became known as southern soul.

Along with the label's co-founder Ahmet Ertegun, producer Jerry Wexler was responsible for much of Atlantic's success in the late 1950s. With the emergence of other producers at the label, most notably Leiber and Stoller, Wexler soon found himself focused on directing the label's business affairs. His interest in producing was rekindled, however, when Atlantic signed gospel-influenced singer Solomon Burke in 1961. Working with Bert Berns, Wexler produced a series of successful singles for Burke in the southern soul style, including "If You Need Me" (p37 r2, 1963), "Everybody Needs Somebody to Love" (p58 r4, 1964), "Got to Get You off My Mind" (p22 r1, 1965), and "Tonight's the Night" (p28 r2, 1965).

There were important stylistic differences between Atlantic's approaches to sweet and southern soul. The Drifters' "Under the Boardwalk" and Ben E. King's "Stand by Me," examples of sweet soul from the early 1960s, tended to include vocals and arrangements that were more restrained. Southern soul incorporated enthusiastic emotional expression, often associated with gospel music. As was apparent in the reception of southern soul as it emerged in the mid-1960s, expectations of both black and white listeners often perceived the pronounced gospel influence in southern soul as truer to the African American heritage than softer, more pop-oriented styles of black music. Wexler was quick to hear this quality and realize the potential for sales in the mainstream market. While black listeners were searching for music that expressed a growing consciousness of racial identity in the context of the civil rights movement, white listeners were fascinated with "real" black culture and wanted to hear unadulterated sounds from the South. Wexler played a crucial role in developing southern soul throughout the decade, either by signing artists directly to Atlantic or by licensing their recordings from other, smaller labels.

Soulsville, USA: The Memphis Connection.

Larger record companies often licensed music from smaller labels, pressing new copies or simply distributing a record for smaller companies. This was a mutually beneficial relationship: it relieved the smaller company of the significant financial commitment of pressing large numbers of records while providing access to listeners that would otherwise be out of reach. Larger companies benefited from sharing in the profits of records that were proven regional hits, and were often more innovative than those produced within an established company. Atlantic and Memphis-based Stax formed a very successful partnership through this type of agreement. Founded in 1960 by Jim Stewart and his sister Estelle Axton, Stax Records came to the attention of Atlantic's Jerry Wexler with the early single "Cause I Love You." Written by Memphis DJ Rufus Thomas and sung as a duet with his daughter Carla, it became a regional hit in the South. Atlantic leased the national rights to the record, and then secured the rights to "Gee Whiz," a second single written and sung by Carla Thomas, which rose to number ten on the *Billboard* "Hot 100" chart and number five on the "Hot R&B Sides" in early 1961. With right of first refusal on the Stax catalog, Atlantic scored success on both the pop and R&B charts with several Stax singles, including the instrumentals "Last Night" (p3 r2, 1961) by the Mar-Keys and "Green Onions" (p3 r1, 1962) by Booker T. & the MG's, as well as Rufus Thomas's dance hit "Walkin' the Dog" (p10 r5, 1963). The leasing of rights worked out well for both labels, and led to a closer relationship between them.

Isaac Hayes (left) and David Porter (standing right) working at Stax Records. Hayes and Porter wrote songs for many artists, working consistently with a "house band"—in this case Booker T. & the MG's. Stax recordings were generally less regimented and more relaxed than Motown sessions, and the classic Stax sound is often less polished than Motown's.

In the early 1960s, Stax was a much smaller operation than Motown. Like Motown, however, Stax often depended on its studio band, Booker T. & the MG's, to pull together backing tracks on the spot, often without music or prepared arrangements. The band's membership changed a bit, but by the time of the classic recordings by Otis Redding, Wilson Pickett, and Sam and Dave in the mid-1960s, the core members of the band were: Booker T. Jones on organ, Steve Cropper on guitar, Donald "Duck" Dunn on bass, Al Jackson Jr. on drums, Andrew Love on saxophone, and Wayne Jackson on trumpet. Unlike Motown, where roles were mostly kept distinct, production duties and credits at Stax were shared among the studio musicians, Stewart, and other singers and producers present at the sessions. Cropper worked closely with Otis Redding, co-writing songs and playing the role of producer at many sessions. The closest thing Stax had to the songwriting and production specialists at Motown was the team of David Porter and Isaac Hayes. Porter and Hayes wrote and produced material for the Astors, Carla Thomas, and the Soul Children, but their greatest success was with Sam and Dave. Despite the differences between Stax and Motown, the Hitsville and "Soulsville" approaches were quite similar. In reality, at both companies, music often emerged spontaneously during recording sessions. This was not as common at larger companies located in New York and Los Angeles.

Otis Redding. One of the most important Stax artists during the 1960s was Otis Redding, who recorded for the company's Volt label. As early as 1963, Redding released "These Arms of Mine," which scored moderately on the R&B charts (r20). A series of crossover hits followed during 1965, including "Mr. Pitiful" (p41 r10), "I've Been Loving You Too Long" (p21 r2), and "Respect" (p35 r4). Redding's gospel-influenced vocals, combined with the driving accompaniment of Booker T.

This poster advertises three Redding performances at the Fillmore (San Francisco) in 1966, each night with a different local band opening—including the Grateful Dead!

& the MG's, produced a style of southern soul that seemed less polished but more heartfelt and urgent than the slicker records coming out of Motown. Redding followed up his earlier chart success with "Try a Little Tenderness" (p25 r4, 1966) and "Sittin' on the Dock of the Bay" (p1 r1, 1968), which became a hit after he was killed in a plane crash in December 1967. Before his tragic death, Redding made significant inroads with hippie rockers when he appeared (backed by Booker T. & the MG's) at the Monterey Pop Festival in spring 1967. Although present-day audiences might not consider it strange for a southern-based rhythm and blues singer to perform at a mainstream pop festival in Northern California, at the time the band was extremely apprehensive. As it turned out, the flower children who attended the festival warmly embraced Redding and his music, encouraging white audiences to further explore the southern soul movement.

Sam and Dave. As part of Wexler's agreement with Stax, he sent the vocal duo Sam and Dave to Memphis. They were under contract to Atlantic, but Stewart maintained creative control over the duo, making records with them as if they were Stax artists. Stewart joined Sam and Dave with Stax songwriters David Porter and Isaac Hayes, and the team produced a series of successful singles, starting with "You Don't Know Like I Know" (r7) in early 1966, and crossing over to the pop charts in mid-1966 with "Hold On, I'm Comin'" (p21 r1). Sam and Dave's best-known song was "Soul Man," which hit number two on the pop charts and number one on the rhythm and blues charts in fall 1967. In 1979, the song achieved even wider popularity with a cover version by the Blues Brothers (led by *Saturday Night Live* comedians John Belushi and Dan Aykroyd), who were in

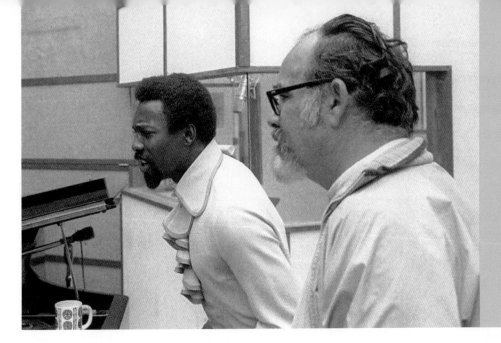

Wilson Pickett (left) working with Atlantic Records producer Jerry Wexler in the Fame Studios in Muscle Shoals, Alabama. Pickett's hit "In the Midnight Hour" displays the "delayed backbeat" feel that Wexler and the Stax band developed, and which became a regular element in the southern soul sound.

part modeled on Sam and Dave. Working in tandem with successful Stax artists like Otis Redding and Booker T. & the MG's, Sam and Dave brought soul music to a national audience through their hit records and energetic stage performances.

Wilson Pickett. After singing with a Detroit-based vocal group called the Falcons, Wilson Pickett came to the attention of Jerry Wexler in 1963 under unlikely circumstances. Pickett had sung on the original demo recording from which Wexler, Bert Berns, and Solomon Burke worked while recording "If You Need Me." In a strange error of omission, Atlantic bought the rights to the song but not the original demo, and Pickett's version, released on the Double L label, competed directly on the rhythm and blues charts with Burke's recording. In 1964, Pickett came to Atlantic looking for a record deal, and Wexler was happy to sign him as a solo act. After a few unsuccessful releases produced by Berns and recorded in New York, Wexler decided to take Pickett to the Stax studios, where he hoped to capture the more relaxed quality heard in Otis Redding's music. During the recording sessions for Pickett's "In the Midnight Hour," Wexler described to the musicians a dance he had seen in New York featuring a movement that seemed to delay beats two and four until the last possible moment. Trying to imitate this movement musically, the band discovered a "delayed backbeat" feel that became a regular element in the southern soul sound. Recorded in May 1965, "In the Midnight Hour" hit number one on the rhythm and blues charts and number twenty-three on the pop charts around the time that Bob Dylan and the Byrds were introducing listeners to folk rock.

Stax became known for a house style during the mid-1960s, which included a prominent organ, distinctive horn arrangements that became associated with Memphis, a funky bass, and a clean, biting guitar sound. Wilson Pickett's "In the Midnight Hour," released by Atlantic and recorded at Stax, is representative of this Stax sound. The track begins with a four-measure introduction featuring horns, followed by two measures of a simple two-chord pattern that forms the basis for the tune. Between the horn intro and the entrance of Pickett's voice, listen to the character of the rhythmic feel: notice that the guitar and snare drum play together

Listening Guide

Wilson Pickett, "In the Midnight Hour" Atlantic 2289

Words and music by Wilson Pickett and Steve Cropper, produced by Jerry Wexler. Rose to #23 on the *Billboard* "Hot 100" chart and #1 on the *Billboard* "Top Selling Rhythm and Blues Singles" chart in the summer of 1965.

FORM: Simple verse, with an instrumental interlude. After an instrumental introduction featuring the horns, the band falls into a repeated figure, often called a "vamp." In this case, the vamp is made up of two chords played over one measure, and this measure is repeated. Two 17-bar verses featuring Pickett's lead vocal are followed by an instrumental interlude with the horns playing over new material based on the intro vamp. Pickett's vocals then return, and he delivers only the first part of a verse before seeming to improvise over the intro vamp as the song fades out.

TIME SIGNATURE: 4/4, with an accent on the second beat of each measure that is so late it is almost out of time. This is the Stax "delayed backbeat."

INSTRUMENTATION: Electric guitars, bass, drums, horns, lead vocals.

0:00–0:13	**Introduction**, 6 mm.	A 4-mm. harmonized line in horns leads into the 2 mm. vamp.
0:13–0:50	**Verse 1**, 17 mm.	Vocals enter. Note the low horn (baritone sax) that helps propel the song's groove, and how the rhythm guitar and snare drum lock in on beats 2 and 4. "I'm gonna wait . . ."
0:50–1:27	**Verse 2**, 17 mm.	As before, but horns added to the first part of the verse. "I'm gonna wait . . ."
1:27–1:44	**Instrumental Interlude**, 23 mm.	Horns play over a new melody loosely based on the introduction.
1:44–2:31	**Verse** (partial), 20 mm.	Pickett seems to start a final verse as the horns play a new line underneath, but the vamp continues without changing in the usual place, as Pickett improvises and the song fades out. "I'm gonna wait . . ."

on beats 2 and 4, which occur so late that they are almost out of time. (This is the delayed backbeat rhythm mentioned earlier.) Comparing "In the Midnight Hour" to the Supremes' "Baby Love" clarifies the differences between stereotypical music from Stax and Motown during the mid-1960s. Both songs are in simple verse form and use instrumental introductions and interludes featuring horns to create a sense of formal variety. Typical of the Stax sound, however, there are no backup vocals on the Pickett track, making his vocal delivery the focus of the song. Pickett's performance makes it seem as if his vocalizing is spontaneous and only loosely planned, leaving the listener to imagine that another performance could differ greatly.

After clashes between Pickett and the Stax studio musicians, Stax founder Jim Stewart began denying outside productions in the Stax studio in late 1965. Wexler's response was to find another studio to use for his productions. He turned to another southern location, the musically fertile region of Muscle Shoals, Alabama. Atlantic had recently distributed two songs connected to this area: the 1965 hit "Hold What You've Got" (p5 r2), recorded at Fame Studios by Dial artist Joe Tex, and Percy Sledge's "When a Man Loves a Woman," which was recorded at a small studio called Quinvy. In 1966 Wexler took Pickett to Fame, which was owned and operated by local musician Rick Hall. Pickett recorded some of his best-known tracks at the studio, including "Land of 1000 Dances" (p6 r1, 1966), "Mustang Sally" (p26 r6, 1966), and "Funky Broadway" (p8 r1, 1967). Like Memphis and Detroit, Muscle Shoals had a core of fine studio musicians, the most important of whom were guitarist Jimmy Johnson, keyboardist Spooner Oldham, and drummer Roger Hawkins. The success of "When a Man Loves a Woman" and Pickett's hits was attributed by many in the music business to the "Muscle Shoals sound," which made the area a popular place to record.

Aretha Franklin. Known as the Queen of Soul, Aretha Franklin was born in Memphis, raised in Detroit, and recorded most of her hits in New York. Franklin is the daughter of the Reverend C. L. Franklin, who led one of the most prominent African American congregations in the United States at New Bethel Baptist Church in Detroit. C. L. Franklin was known throughout the country for his rousing sermons, which were regularly broadcast on the radio and released on record. Aretha grew up hearing some of the best gospel singers in the world at close range. She credits Clara Ward's performance of "Peace in the Valley" at a Franklin family funeral with inspiring her to devote herself to a career as a singer. When she turned eighteen and with her father's blessing, Franklin left Detroit for New York to pursue a singing career. In the early 1960s, she was signed to Columbia Records, and released several records of traditional pop songs in a mainstream setting. These early records did not make much of a commercial impact. When the Columbia contract expired in 1966, Jerry Wexler moved in, trying to get Stax to sign Franklin, but eventually signing her directly to Atlantic. In early 1967, in the wake of his fallout with Stax, Wexler brought Franklin to Fame to record her first tracks for Atlantic.

The sessions at Fame started well. The first track completed was the hit "I Never Loved a Man (The Way I Love You)" (p37 r9, 1967), which abandoned the supper-club, easy-jazz character of Franklin's Columbia work to showcase the gospel roots of her singing. After completing this first track, however, the session fell apart when a dispute

Aretha Franklin in a recording session at Fame Studios in 1967. After recording smooth pop songs for Columbia, Franklin signed with Atlantic. Jerry Wexler encouraged her to be more expressive, drawing on the passion of gospel. The session pictured here was Franklin's first for Atlantic, and it yielded some of her biggest hits, including "I've Never Loved a Man (The Way I Love You)." While other hits, like "Respect," were recorded in New York, Franklin and Wexler continued to pursue the "southern sound" that first surfaced in Muscle Shoals.

Listening Guide

Aretha Franklin, "Respect" Atlantic 2403

Words and music by Otis Redding, produced by Jerry Wexler. Reached #1 on the *Billboard* "Hot 100" and "Top Selling R&B Singles" charts.

FORM: Modified simple verse. Beginning with a 4-bar introduction, this track continues by presenting three very similar 10-bar verses. It then moves into an 8-bar instrumental bridge, which provides a brief contrast before returning to the fourth verse. Perhaps the most notable formal feature of this track is the coda, which begins with Franklin's famous passage ("R-E-S-P-E-C-T"). As distinctive as these measures are, they really only help launch the song's ending and are built on the same two-chord vamp that is used for the entire coda and fade-out.

TIME SIGNATURE: 4/4. This is Wexler's attempt to capture the Stax rhythmic feel in Atlantic's New York studios.

INSTRUMENTATION: Electric guitar, organ, piano, bass, drums, tambourine, horns, lead and backup vocals. Note that while Franklin's lead vocals are much more relaxed than most other female lead singers of the 1960s, the backup vocals are more restrained, in the girl-group tradition.

0:00–0:09	**Introduction**, 4 mm.	Horns and guitar play in call-and-response
0:09–0:30	**Verse 1**, 10 mm.	Vocals enter. Note the backup vocals, which blend girl-group support with a strong gospel element. "What you want . . ."
0:30–0:51	**Verse 2**, 10 mm.	As before. Note that the guitar and snare are not locked in with the same precision as "In the Midnight Hour," and that the low notes in the piano here take over the role played by the baritone sax in the Pickett song. "I ain't gonna do you wrong . . ."
0:51–1:12	**Verse 3**, 10 mm.	As before, "I'm about to give ya . . ."
1:12–1:28	**Instrumental Bridge**, 8 mm.	Sax solo offers contrasting material in a new key.
1:28–1:50	**Verse 4**, 10 mm.	As before and back in the original key, though harmonic shift back is somewhat awkward. "Your kisses are . . ."
1:50–2:22	**Coda**, 16 mm.	Famous "R-E-S-P-E-C-T" stop-time passage, and then vamp, as Stax-style baritone sax enters just as the song fades out.

broke out between Franklin's husband and somebody else in the studio. Soon thereafter Franklin and Wexler were back in New York working on more tracks with the Muscle Shoals rhythm section, who had been flown in without Rick Hall's knowledge. These and later New York sessions—southern soul recorded in the Big Apple—produced a series of hits for Franklin, including a reworking of Otis Redding's "Respect" (p1 r1, 1967), as well as "Baby I Love You" (p4 r1, 1967), "(You Make Me Feel Like) A Natural Woman" (p2 r2, 1967), "Chain of Fools" (p2 r1, 1968), and "Think" (p7 r1, 1968). "Respect" illustrates the power of Aretha Franklin's soul music from the late 1960s. By changing the perspective of the song from male to female, she turned Redding's arguably sexist rant into a feminist anthem. Her performance of "Respect" is so powerful that, although Redding wrote it and recorded it first, Franklin's performance has become the cultural standard.

The Reverse Invasion. Many bands associated with the British invasion were especially interested in R&B records from America, forging strong connections in both Europe and North America between British groups and firms like Atlantic, Stax, and Motown. In the United States, R&B firms welcomed British groups with open arms. Otis Redding recorded a popular version of the Rolling Stones'

The Supremes deplane at London's Heathrow Airport in March 1965 in preparation for Motown's historic tour of the UK. Many British listeners were first exposed to American R&B during this period, leading to a long and significant reception history.

"Satisfaction," Motown's Brenda Holloway toured America with the Beatles in 1965, and the Supremes recorded an entire album of songs made popular by British artists called *A Bit of Liverpool*. British bands often traveled to R&B recording studios in America after they had achieved fame. The Rolling Stones recorded at Chess and Muscle Shoals and the Beatles were rumored to have interest in recording at both Motown and Stax. American R&B companies also sent their artists to the UK during the mid-1960s, exposing many African American acts to the British public for the first time. Perhaps the most important of these was Motown's 1965 tour of the UK (with one stop in France), which the company hoped would create a "reverse invasion." After months of planning, and many trips to Britain by Motown artists to promote the tour, the Motortown Revue flew across the Atlantic in March 1965 for three weeks of dates up and down the British Isles. Although the tour was seen by many at the time as a financial failure, it turned out to be the beginning of a relationship between Motown and Britain that lasted for decades, making the UK one of the most important sites for American R&B reception in the world during the 1970s and 1980s.

JAMES BROWN: ON THE WAY TO FUNK

From Doo-Wop to Soul. In light of his tremendous importance and stylistic distinctiveness during the 1960s, it is strange to think that James Brown started his career as a stand-in for Little Richard. Born in South Carolina and raised in southern Georgia, Brown had gained some regional attention in the mid-1950s as a member of the Famous Flames. At a show just before Little Richard hit with "Tutti Frutti," Brown and his group delivered an uninvited, impromptu performance that impressed Richard's manager, Clint Brantley. Brantley booked the Flames for a

James Brown, live at the Apollo. Brown worked with top-notch musicians and rehearsed them tirelessly. His live shows were equally tiring, with Brown passionately dancing, belting out lyrics, and directing the band.

Listening Guide

James Brown, "Papa's Got a Brand New Bag, Pt. 1" King 5999

Words and music by James Brown, produced by James Brown. Rose to #1 on the *Billboard* "Top Selling Rhythm and Blues Singles" chart and #8 on the *Billboard* "Hot 100" chart in fall 1965.

FORM: Simple verse with bridge. The 12-bar verses return without alterations (except for new lyrics), and are based on the 12-bar blues structure. The 8-bar bridge enters after two verses, which might indicate an AABA form, especially since a verse returns right after the bridge. However, the bridge is static, vamping on a single chord and not driving toward the return of the verse, as in an AABA form. The structure of this song is perhaps best understood as a verse-verse-bridge structure that is repeated, with the bridge serving as the ending while the song fades. The form of this track is closest to a simple verse form, though one might also see it as a hybrid of simple verse and AABA forms.

TIME SIGNATURE: 4/4. Note the precise interplay between the instruments and how they work together to project an intricate rhythmic background over which Brown delivers his lead vocal.

INSTRUMENTATION: Electric guitar, bass, drums, horns, and lead vocal.

0:00–0:26	**Verse 1**, 12 mm.	After opening upbeat chord, vocal enters and verse locks in based on the 12-bar blues, "Come here sisters . . ."
0:26–0:48	**Verse 2**, 12 mm.	As before. Note the use of the baritone sax, playing the same role here as it does in Pickett's "In the Midnight Hour." Similarly, the rhythm guitar and snare are locked in on beats 2 and 4 throughout. "Come down brother . . ."
0:48–1:03	**Bridge**, 8 mm.	Lead vocals over vamp on single chord, with horn backups. "He did the jerk . . ."
1:03–1:26	**Verse 3**, 12 mm.	As before, "Come down sister . . ."
1:26–1:48	**Verse 4**, 12 mm.	As before, "Oh and father . . ."
1:48–2:06	**Coda** (Bridge), 8 mm. +	Based on single-chord vamp from bridge and then fade out, "c'mon, hey hey . . ."

series of performances across the South. When "Tutti Frutti" became a hit, Richard left Georgia to capitalize on his success, and Brown stepped in to perform as Little Richard for a series of appearances that Brantley had already scheduled. James Brown and the Famous Flames enjoyed moderate success with Brown's impassioned delivery on "Please Please Please" (r6, 1956), his first record released by Cincinnati-based King Records, run by Syd Nathan. King would release all but a handful of Brown's records until Brown signed with Polydor in 1971. Brown hit again in 1958 with "Try Me," his first number-one rhythm and blues hit, which also enjoyed moderate crossover appeal (p48).

Debates about "Blackness" during the Mid-1960s

As music from the rhythm and blues market became more popular among mainstream listeners during the mid-1960s, there were accompanying debates about the black community that crossover R&B represented. The first of these selections comes from a review written by LeRoi Jones (later Amiri Baraka) published in *DownBeat* about new avant-garde jazz, a scene that Jones felt had lost touch with a "black reality" that was exhibited in music of contemporaneous R&B artists that found favor with mainstream audiences. In his *Urban Blues*, Charles Keil offered a rejoinder to Jones, questioning the manner in which these artists represent "nasty" ideas. While both Jones and Keil acknowledge the existence of a wide range of African American class identity, they differ in their views of how contemporary R&B represents this divide.

Does anybody really think it's weird that all these English "pop" groups are making large doses of loot? It's simple actually. They take the style (energy, general form, etc.) of black blues, country, or city, and combine it with the visual image of white American nonconformity, i.e., the beatnik, and score heavily.

These English boys are hipper than their white counterparts in the United States, hipper because, as it is readily seen, they have actually made a contemporary form, unlike most white U.S. "folk singers," who are content to imitate "ancient" blues forms and older singers, arriving at a kind of popular song, at its most hideous in groups like Peter, Paul, & Mary, which has little to

Brown's early hits remained within the stylistic range of 1950s doo-wop, as he sang lead vocal supported by the backup vocals of the other Flames. With "Think" (p33 r7, 1960), however, Brown began to develop the soul style for which he would become so well known. The song's tight accompaniment features horns and a driving rhythm section. While much pop music of the time focused on lyrics, harmony, and background vocals, Brown's aggressive singing and the rhythmic groove created to support it are the clear focal points of the music.

By the early 1960s, Brown was known on the R&B circuit for his stage show, which featured athletic dancing and a famous closing routine in which he was led off stage exhausted, only to vault back into the spotlight with fresh energy. Hoping to capture on record the excitement of James Brown and the Famous Flames in concert, Brown and manager Ben Bart decided to release a live album recorded during a 1962 performance at the Apollo Theater in New York. Except for jazz, folk, and classical, albums were not the focus of record sales in the early 1960s. Despite this, Brown's *The James Brown Show* (now called *Live at the Apollo*) went to number two on the pop album charts in the summer of 1963, showcasing both his energetic performance and stylistic range. While "Think" had already anticipated Brown's turn toward a domination by tight rhythmic grooves, "Out of Sight" (p24, 1964) went even further in this direction, introducing the hard-driving soul style that continued with "Papa's Got a Brand New Bag, Pt. 1" (p8 r1, 1965), "I Got You (I Feel Good)" (p3 r1, 1965), "It's a Man's Man's Man's World" (p8 r1, 1966), and "Cold Sweat, Pt. 1" (p7 r1, 1967).

do with black reality, which would have been its strength anyway—that reference to a deeper emotional experience. As one young poet said, "At least the Rolling Stones come on like English crooks."

I say this as one way to get into another thing, namely that even the avant-garde music suffers when it moves too far from the blues experience.

All the young players now should make sure they are listening to the Supremes, Dionne Warwick, Martha and the Vandellas, the Impressions, Mary Wells, James Brown, Major Lance, Marvin Gaye, Four Tops, Bobby Bland, etc., just to see where contemporary blues is. All the really nasty ideas are right there, and these young players are still connected with that reality, whether they understand why or not. Otherwise, jazz—no matter the intellectual bias—having moved too far away from its most meaningful sources, and resources, is weakened and becomes, little by little,

the music of another emerging middle class.

Source: LeRoi Jones, *DownBeat* 32 (March 25, 1965), 34.

**

With the exceptions of Bobby Bland, James Brown (a great performer if there ever was one), and possibly the Impressions, the singers listed by Jones all peddle variations on the so-called Detroit Sound engineered by Berry Gordy for the massive teenage audience, Negro and white. They appear frequently on those joyous and wholesome television shows *Shindig and Hullabaloo*, and this is not exactly "where contemporary blues is," in my opinion. Are "all the really nasty ideas" really there? Diana Ross, lead vocalist with the Supremes, contends: "It's less wild than most of the big beat music you hear today, but it still has feeling to it. We call it sweet music." "Sweet" and "nasty" are not necessarily contradictory terms, as

used by Negroes, and most Negroes would agree that all these performers have "soul," that is, the ability to communicate something of the Negro experience. The bands of Bland and Brown do have something to offer the avant-garde jazzmen, and the Vandellas have done some "tough" things; but the Detroit sound is a soft-spoken, refined, polished soul music for the most part; the lyrics are usually pleasant, sometimes innocuous; the supporting beat is firm, simple, four to the bar, and highly danceable. Ironically, the Detroit sound is the one Negro-produced style that comes closest to being "the music of another emerging middle class" and a culturally integrated American middle class at that, at least to the extent that white teenagers are committed to it.

Source: Charles Keil, *Urban Blues* (Chicago: University of Chicago Press, 1991), 42–43.

Unlike most of the other artists in this chapter, James Brown exerted almost total control over his music from the beginning of his career. He wrote and produced most of his hits, and after the death of King Records' Syd Nathan and his manager Ben Bart in 1968, he also made most of his own business decisions. Brown uniquely combined an aggressive style of vocal and dance performance, songwriting and production skills, and astute business acumen. In his artistic and musical independence, he parallels Brian Wilson, Bob Dylan, and the Beatles, who also took significant control over their music and careers during the 1960s. As a bandleader, Brown hired great musicians and rehearsed them vigorously. He even fined players who made mistakes during performances. Although some of his musicians found this work environment too difficult, Brown's rigorous approach produced some of the best ensemble playing in popular music during the 1960s and 1970s.

"Papa's Got a Brand New Bag, Pt. 1" is an example of the instrumental precision achieved in performances by James Brown and his band. The track opens with a sustained chord, and soon falls into the first verse (the verses employ the 12-bar blues structure). Listen to how the ensemble works together rhythmically to create the groove that drives the song. The stops at the end of the verses help distinguish this track from a Stax arrangement, and exhibit the cohesiveness of Brown's band. The form of the song mixes verses with a bridge, which is sung once and then used as the basis for the vamp in the coda. Note the absence of background vocals—a feature that helps distinguish Brown's approach from that of Motown and highlights the contrast with his music in the 1950s, which often featured doo-wop backup vocals.

Black Pride and the Birth of Funk. In the late 1960s, James Brown and his music were increasingly valued within the black community for his apparent racial pride. To many, Brown's hard-edged musical style, political lyrics, and outward interest in arranging his own affairs seemed uncompromised in comparison to the necessary concessions made by Motown and Atlantic artists to appeal to white audiences. While this perception was not entirely accurate, Brown was counted among the most important figures in black popular music when "Say It Loud, I'm Black and I'm Proud" (p10 r1) climbed the charts in the fall of 1968. Brown's music would soon turn toward funk, making him one of the principal influences on 1970s black pop. We will continue our consideration of Brown and his influence on funk in Chapter 9, and the issues of race addressed in this chapter will return in our discussions of the rise of black pop, disco, and the emergence of rap.

CROSSOVER R&B

Assimilation and Issues of Blackness. Despite origins in the R&B market, much of the music in this chapter achieved popularity in the mainstream. The different styles of R&B that achieved this type of popularity are closely related to larger movements of African American assimilation during the 1960s. In light of this, much like members of the emerging black middle class of the time, Motown's urbanity and Berry Gordy's desire to appeal to white audiences have frequently prompted criticisms that Motown sold out to white America. Sophisticated musical arrangements, carefully choreographed movements, and charm-school training were important signals of an assimilationist attitude on Gordy's part. In defense of the company, black American listeners never really tuned out Motown. In fact, even if the pop charts are not taken into account, Motown remains one of the most important and successful rhythm and blues labels of the 1960s. The R&B originating in Chicago complicated this view of northern, urban black communities producing music that pandered to white audiences. While the arrangements of music by groups like the Impressions and Little Milton were often as refined as those coming out of Motown, the lyrics forwarded by these groups showed a growing acceptance of black consciousness in the mainstream. Southern soul music was easy to view as a counterexample that more fully embraced regional attributes closer to the roots of northern black culture. Yet, the manner in which rock communities embraced southern-based R&B as the "real thing," coupled with the record companies intentionally producing this music for crossover audiences, shows that African American stereotypes were sometimes used deliberately to invoke authenticity among mainstream listeners. Whatever position you take, all of these examples were pivotal to the development of black pop music, and each interacted significantly with emerging rock styles.

1968: A Pivotal Year for Black Popular Music. On April 4, 1968, the Reverend Dr. Martin Luther King Jr. was assassinated on the balcony of his Memphis hotel room. It would be difficult to exaggerate the importance of this event for race relations in America at the end of the 1960s. King had been an important leader in

Sound Check

Artist	Song	Sound
The Supremes	Baby Love (1964)	Form: simple verse Stomping on boards used in introduction to establish beat Key change in verse 5 Arrangement builds by adding instruments: guitar and backing vocal (verse 2), saxes (verse 3)
The Temptations	The Way You Do the Things You Do (1964)	Form: simple verse Structure based on a two-chord vamp 4-bar refrain: "Well, you could have been . . ." Horns added in verse 2
The Impressions	People Get Ready (1965)	Form: simple verse Call-and-response vocals Gospel attributes Prominent strings and xylophone
Wilson Pickett	In the Midnight Hour (1965)	Form: simple verse Instrumental interlude that features a horn melody Low, baritone saxophone propels the groove Listen for the delayed second beat of each measure
Aretha Franklin	Respect (1967)	Form: simple verse (modified) Famous R-E-S-P-E-C-T line comes in the coda Based on a two-chord vamp Backing vocals from the girl-group tradition
James Brown	Papa's Got a Brand New Bag, Pt. 1 (1965)	Form: simple verse (modified) Bridge added to simple verse form 12-bar blues Intricate rhythmic background

the civil rights movement, and he was perhaps the most respected and widely known advocate for racial equality in the United States. King's approach to social protest was markedly nonviolent. The reaction to his death, however, led to an escalation of protest violence that had begun months earlier in black neighborhoods in some of the country's major cities.

King's death had a palpable impact on black music. It hit especially hard at Stax, which was plagued with business problems and was located only minutes away from the hotel where Dr. King was killed. In late 1967, Atlantic had been sold to Warner Brothers–Seven Arts, leaving Stax with a six-month option to continue or terminate its distribution agreement with Atlantic. During the sale, Jim Stewart learned that the agreement he had signed with Atlantic some years before was not a simple distribution contract. The Atlantic attorneys had inserted a clause assigning ownership of the master tapes for all Stax recordings to Atlantic. Stewart was also reminded that Sam and Dave were on loan to Stax, and if the contract were not renewed they would revert to Atlantic. With the death of his best artist, Otis Redding, in late 1967, Stewart was left with few choices. Disgusted with the Atlantic negotiations, he and his sister eventually opted to sell the company to Gulf and Western, a conglomerate that once produced metal bumpers. Stax continued as a very different company under the leadership of Al Bell and Detroit-based record producer Don Dixon, who once competed with Berry Gordy for the local Detroit market. The label was soon back on the charts with Johnnie Taylor's "Who's Makin' Love" (p5 r1, 1968), but the original community of Stax musicians, writers, and producers began to pull apart.

In July 1967, a series of riots broke out in Detroit, which made many at Motown uncomfortable about working in the city's downtown area. By April 1968, Holland-Dozier-Holland had departed and Norman Whitfield was the label's most successful writer and producer. Berry Gordy was set on moving the label to Los Angeles in order to become more involved with the film industry, and he turned over much of the day-to-day operation to others. In the wake of King's death, Motown Records began to deal more directly with issues facing black America: the Supremes' "Love Child" (p1 r2, 1968), for instance, confronts the realities of urban life from the perspective of an illegitimate child, a growing issue in the black community. By the early 1970s, Whitfield and the Temptations, Marvin Gaye, and Stevie Wonder would all focus on issues in black urban life in unmistakable terms.

For Additional Online Resources, visit:
digital.wwnorton.com/whatsthatsound5

FURTHER READING

Rob Bowman, *Soulsville, U.S.A.: The Story of Stax Records* (Schirmer, 2006).
James Brown with Bruce Tucker, *James Brown, the Godfather of Soul* (Da Capo, 2003).
Gerald Early, *One Nation under a Groove: Motown and American Culture* (University of Michigan Press, 2004).
Andrew Flory, *I Hear a Symphony: Motown and Crossover R&B* (University of Michigan Press, 2017).

Jon Hartley Fox, *King of the Queen City: The Story of King Records* (University of Illinois Press, 2009).

Nelson George, *Where Did Our Love Go? The Rise and Fall of the Motown Sound* (University of Illinois Press, 2007).

Robert Gordon, *Respect Yourself: Stax Records and the Soul Explosion* (Bloomsbury, 2013).

Berry Gordy, *To Be Loved: The Music, the Magic, and the Memories of Motown* (Warner Books, 1994).

Peter Guralnick, *Sweet Soul Music: Rhythm and Blues and the Southern Dream of Freedom* (Back Bay, 1999).

Charles L. Hughes, *Country Soul: Making Music and Making Race in the American South* (University of North Carolina Press, 2015).

Robert Pruter, *Chicago Soul* (University of Illinois Press, 1991).

Mark Ribowsky, *The Supremes: A Saga of Motown Dreams, Success, and Betrayal* (Da Capo, 2009).

David Ritz, *Respect: The Life of Aretha Franklin* (Back Bay, 2015).

Brian Ward, *Just My Soul Responding: Rhythm and Blues, Black Consciousness, and Race Relations* (University of California Press, 1998).

Jerry Wexler and David Ritz, *Rhythm and the Blues* (St. Martin's, 1994).

Otis Williams with Patricia Romanowski, *Temptations* (Cooper Square, 2002).

CHAPTER 7

PSYCHEDELIA

CHAPTER PREVIEW

- During the 1960s, some listeners of psychedelic music thought LSD would lead to a "higher consciousness" while others felt the music was a trip of its own.

- In both composition and production the Beatles and the Beach Boys expanded the boundaries of rock music.

- San Francisco psychedelia began as an underground scene over a year before the summer of 1967. Important bands were the Grateful Dead, Jefferson Airplane, and Big Brother and the Holding Company.

- British psychedelia started as an underground scene in London and resembled the San Francisco scene in general, though with many distinctive differences. Important bands were Soft Machine, Pink Floyd, Tomorrow, Cream, and the Jimi Hendrix Experience.

- Eric Clapton and Jimi Hendrix were pioneers of virtuosity in rock music.

- The Los Angeles scene produced the Doors and Love, while New York yielded Vanilla Fudge from the city, and the Band from upstate.

- Large crowds at the Monterey Pop Festival and Woodstock proved the commercial potential of "hippie rock."

- Beginning in 1967, FM radio's album-oriented rock offered an alternative to AM's hit singles.

The Beatles' *Sgt. Pepper's Lonely Hearts Club Band* played a critical role in making the album into an art form. The band's hit single during the Summer of Love, however, was "All You Need Is Love," which did not appear on the album. The lyrics to this song capture the positive hippie philosophy of the moment, while the music eclectically begins with the French national anthem and ends by superimposing a horn break from Glenn Miller's "In the Mood," a contrapuntal passage by baroque composer J.S. Bach, the traditional song, "Greensleeves," and the chorus to the band's "She Loves You." The Beatles are shown here performing this song live on a special worldwide satellite broadcast, *Our World*, in June of 1967, just weeks after the release of *Sgt. Pepper's*. The performance was not entirely live, however, since the band used a backing track. The festive and colorful counterculture atmosphere in the Abbey Road studio was enhanced by the presence of rock luminaries such as Mick Jagger, Keith Richards, Eric Clapton, Marianne Faithful, Keith Moon, and Graham Nash.

June, July, and August of 1967 are frequently referred to as the Summer of Love, a time when Scott McKenzie's "San Francisco (Be Sure to Wear Flowers in Your Hair)" played on radios across the United States and England. The song, written by John Phillips of the Mamas and the Papas, celebrates the emerging hippie culture and flower power movement centered in San Francisco. At the same time in London, the Beatles released *Sgt. Pepper's Lonely Hearts Club Band*—perhaps the most important album in the history of rock music. The summer of 1967 also saw an American guitarist fronting a British band and emerging as an international sensation at a rock festival in Monterey, California. When Jimi Hendrix set his guitar aflame at the climax of his virtuosic and outrageous performance, it was an important signal that rock music was heading down a new path in 1967: "psychedelia." Psychedelic music and culture began in the regional underground scenes of London and San Francisco in the 1950s and were well established by the end of 1965. Thus, the Summer of Love does not mark the beginning of psychedelia per se, but rather its breakthrough into mainstream popular culture.

In early 1966, only hints of psychedelic music were found on the records of major rock artists. Instead, relatively unknown musicians were developing the new style. Some of these bands became commercially successful (the Grateful Dead, Pink Floyd, Jefferson Airplane), though others did not (Soft Machine, Tomorrow, the Charlatans). Psychedelia emerged from its origins in the London and San Francisco underground movements (consisting of regional bands, clubs, shops, and newspapers) into mainstream pop culture and became a pervasive influence on rock culture by the end of the 1960s. It is important to examine the development of psychedelic music on two fronts, exploring the underground scenes in London and San Francisco and considering how this music infiltrated the pop charts. But before we trace its history, we need to define it: What is psychedelia and what makes music psychedelic?

DRUGS AND THE QUEST FOR HIGHER CONSCIOUSNESS

The Doors of Perception: Ken Kesey, Timothy Leary, and LSD. The psychedelic movement was concerned with exploring new ways of experiencing the world. Young adults in the mid-1960s felt that the cultural values of the 1950s were too focused on being "normal," and they challenged these values by seeking out alternative approaches to life and culture. Influenced by the civil rights movement and a growing public resistance to the Vietnam War, many young people in the 1960s were suspicious of institutions in American life: government, schools, churches, big business, the military, and the police. Teens in the 1950s were the first to experience a youth culture that could be clearly distinguished from adult culture, but the counterculture that emerged in the 1960s was much more assertive in this separation.

Drugs generally—but marijuana and LSD especially—played a central role in the new worldview many young people were seeking. Led by author Ken Kesey and ex-Harvard professor Timothy Leary, two older men who had publicly rejected "the establishment," many young people came to see hallucinogenic drugs as essential to unlocking "the doors of perception" (a reference to Aldous Huxley's essay of the same name, in which the author describes his experience with the hallucinogenic drug mescaline). Leary's advice to "turn on, tune in, and drop out" became a slogan of the counterculture, as many young adults earnestly explored drug use, radical philosophy, and Eastern religion.

LSD (lysergic acid diethylamide) was developed accidentally by Swiss scientist Albert Hoffmann in 1943 while he was working on a cure for migraine headaches. Along with mescaline, LSD was tested by the CIA during the 1950s as a truth serum and was considered as a potential treatment for alcoholism. LSD was also used recreationally by a relatively small group of people in the United States and the UK. The young adults who discovered it in the mid- to late 1960s thought LSD allowed the user to suppress the false and misleading modes of understanding imposed by school and society and to perceive the world and life itself as they really were. "Dropping acid" supposedly allowed one to see new possibilities, opening the mind to new knowledge and modes of understanding. In short, LSD was viewed as a kind of magic drug that led to a "higher consciousness" that had previously been available only to mystics and visionaries.

A Journey to the East. Until the summer of 1967, most counterculture activity was restricted to large cities like New York, San Francisco, and London. As discussed in Chapter 5, the Byrds' "Eight Miles High" hit the U.S. charts in 1966 and was one of the first public signs that drug use was becoming a central part of rock music and youth culture. The unlikely blend of Eastern spirituality and drug use that "Eight Miles High" evoked had been advocated by Timothy Leary in his 1964 book *The Psychedelic Experience*. Co-written with Harvard colleagues Ralph Metzner and Richard Alpert (who would later change his name to Ram Dass and play an important role in popularizing Eastern religion among the hippies), the book offered a guide to acid use based on the ancient Tibetan Book of the Dead. The association of drugs with Eastern philosophy was further reinforced somewhat unintentionally by the Beatles, who became students of transcendental meditation with the Maharishi Mahesh Yogi around the time that they released *Sgt. Pepper's Lonely Hearts Club*

The Beatles were leaders in the popularization of Eastern religion during the psychedelic era. Band members are pictured here with their wives, Mike Love from the Beach Boys, and many others at the Rishikesh in India with the Maharishi Mahesh Yogi in March 1968.

Band. While drug use is not part of the practice of yoga in most Eastern traditions, it became linked with Eastern religion and higher consciousness in the eyes of the burgeoning hippie culture via the quest for higher consciousness. As Eastern gurus sought truth through spiritual discipline, the hippies sought truth through the use of LSD. In the late 1960s, a variety of lifestyle philosophies emerged that blended aspects of Eastern spirituality and drug use, sometimes including avant-garde art, and both radical and utopian politics. Taken together, these sometimes contradictory approaches make up what is generally called the 1960s counterculture—a hippie worldview committed to cultural change with music at the center.

Two Psychedelic Approaches to Music. There are two general ways music might reflect a growing interest in higher consciousness. The first is to use music to enhance a drug trip. According to this approach, the focus is the drug experience itself, and the music is a soundtrack that may provoke a response with novel and unfamiliar sounds, but does not provide a trip itself. We will encounter instances of this tendency in our discussions of both the San Francisco and London underground scenes and groups like the Grateful Dead and Pink Floyd. A second approach is to understand the music as the trip. In this case, the artist must craft music that acts as an aesthetic drug, taking the listener on an aural journey that may or may not be enhanced by the use of drugs. This approach is demonstrated by the music of the Doors and the Beatles, discussed later. In both instances, the trip and the quest for higher consciousness are essential; the difference is in whether music is primary or secondary. In either case, musicians became more experimental and ambitious about writing, performing, and recording music. For music to enhance or provide a trip, however, it had to move beyond the two- or three-minute radio format that was standard for AM radio in the mid-1960s.

PSYCHEDELIC AMBITION: THE BEACH BOYS AND THE BEATLES

Two Bands, One Label. The cultural rise of psychedelia coincided with a tendency toward more ambitious approaches to rock songwriting, arranging, and recording. For example, once firmly within the domain of teen interests, the music of both the Beatles and the Beach Boys became increasingly complicated as the '60s progressed. Lyrics addressed more serious topics, a wider range of instrumentation was used, harmonic language became more innovative, standard formal types were often modified or abandoned, and more time was taken in the studio to record tracks that were often not reproducible in live performance. The Beatles gradually moved away from the model of professional craftsmen (best exemplified by the Brill Building songwriters) and toward a more self-consciously "artistic" stance (akin to that of a classical-music composer or artist). With the Beach Boys, a quest to match and surpass the accomplishments of Phil Spector seemed to drive Brian Wilson to an increasingly experimental approach. In the United States, the Beatles and the Beach Boys were on the same record label, Capitol. This meant that they competed not only for the public's attention but also for the attention of their own record company. The combined effect of the increased artistic ambitions of both bands and a commercial rivalry produced a sequence of records that exhibit the transformation of rock from dance music to listening music.

We have already considered the Beatles' music through *Revolver* and the Beach Boys' music through *Pet Sounds* (Chapters 4 and 5). Here we consider how these bands influenced and even inspired one another. Brian Wilson has remarked, for instance, that he admired the way the songs on *Rubber Soul* all worked together as an album. This inspired Wilson to think of *Pet Sounds* as an album of related songs. Paul McCartney remembers that he listened to *Pet Sounds* constantly after its release, admiring the production and songwriting. With *Revolver*, and especially "Tomorrow Never Knows," the Beatles pushed the limits of studio experimentation, producing a track that many consider the introduction of psychedelia into the mainstream.

"Good Vibrations." Not to be outdone by the ambition of "Tomorrow Never Knows," Wilson and the Beach Boys released "Good Vibrations" (p1 uk1, 1966)—a single that consumed more studio time and budget allocation than any other pop single ever had before. Wilson called it his "pocket symphony," and many consider this single to be his finest achievement. As the Listening Guide shows, "Good Vibrations" begins by using a contrasting verse-chorus approach. But after the second time through the chorus, the track continues with a sequence of three sections of new material. In a sense, "Good Vibrations" takes the listener on a "trip," through unfamiliar musical territory. Each section of the song was recorded separately and spliced together later, cutting and pasting tape with scotch tape and a razor blade. Each of the three sections introduces new musical material. Section 1 employs a tack piano (an upright piano with tacks stuck in the hammers to create a sharper attack), a Jew's harp (a small instrument held against the teeth or lips and plucked with the fingers), bass harmonica and sleigh bells in addition to voices, bass, tambourine, and organ. The splice into section 2 can be heard clearly, as the music immediately gets quieter, starting only with a low organ and percussion. After the vocals, a higher organ, and bass enter, the passage works its way toward a beautiful harmony on "ah" to end the section (listen carefully for the echo as the vocals die out). The third section then begins as if it might be another chorus, only to introduce a new three-part vocal passage before resuming the chorus music for the fade-out. While "Good Vibrations" starts out as a contrasting verse chorus form, the addition of these three sections and the way they introduce new sounds and material represented an important departure for pop music. Wilson spent a great deal of time experimenting with the order of these sections before arriving at the final version. Capitol later released some of the alternate versions and studio rehearsals of "Good Vibrations" and these tapes illustrate the centrality of studio techniques and the sense of experimentation in the creation of this song. The rehearsal tapes reveal how diligently Wilson worked at finding the precise instrumental sounds he employed, providing a rare glimpse of his working method. "Good Vibrations" marked a high point in the musical ambition of the Beach Boys that they would never again equal.

Rising Rock Ambitions

Beatles, *Rubber Soul* (late 1965)

Beach Boys, *Pet Sounds* (early to mid-1966)

Beatles, *Revolver* (late summer 1966), "Tomorrow Never Knows"

Beach Boys, "Good Vibrations" (late 1966)

Beatles, "Penny Lane/Strawberry Fields Forever" (early 1967)

Beach Boys, *SMiLE* (late 1966/early 1967; not released)

Beatles, *Sgt. Pepper's Lonely Hearts Club Band* (June 1, 1967)

Beach Boys, *Smiley Smile* (August 1967)

Listening Guide

The Beach Boys, "Good Vibrations" Capitol 5676

Words and music by Brian Wilson and Mike Love, produced by Brian Wilson. Reached #1 on the *Billboard* "Hot 100" chart in late 1966 (uk1).

FORM: The first half of the song uses contrasting verse-chorus form, which breaks off after the second statement of the chorus (1:41). At that point, a series of three sections begin, the last of which uses music from the chorus to help round the song off as it fades out. Taken as a whole, the song does not fit neatly into any conventional pop formal pattern, except in the most general sense that contrasting material often follows the second statement of the chorus.

TIME SIGNATURE: 4/4.

INSTRUMENTATION: Organ, guitar, bass, drums, woodwinds, cellos, slide theremin, bass harmonica, Jew's harp, tambourine, sleigh bells, maracas, lead and backing vocals.

0:00–0:25	**Verse 1**, 16 mm. (8-mm. phrase with repeat)	Lead vocals enter immediately, note repeated chords in the organ, orchestral-style drumming, and subtle use of woodwinds in second 8 mm. "I love the colorful clothes . . ."
0:25–0:50	**Chorus**, 16 mm. (four 4-mm. phrases)	Multipart vocals in counterpoint, note entrance of cellos low in the texture and there min melody on the top. "I'm pickin' up . . ."
0:50–1:15	**Verse 2**, 16 mm.	As before. Note that verse is quieter than chorus—this dynamic contrast can be heard clearly in this shift back to the verse. "Changed my mind . . ."
1:15–1:41	**Chorus**, 16 mm.	As before, end leads into section 1. "I'm pickin' up . . ."
1:41–2:13	**Section 1**, 20 mm.	New music. Piano, bass harmonica, sleigh bells, Jew's harp enter, "Excitations . . ." Listen for tape splice to section 2.
2:13–2:57	**Section 2**, 24 mm.	More new music, quieter now, starting with organ and ending with vocal "ah." Listen again for tape splice into section 3. "Gotta keep . . ."
2:57–3:35	**Section 3**, 22 mm.	Based on chorus, with new vocal counterpoint. Starts louder, gets quieter and then louder again before fade-out. "I'm pickin' up . . ."

Sgt. Pepper's Lonely Hearts Club Band. After the release of *Revolver*, the Beatles abandoned touring and devoted their energies to recording. There were several reasons for this drastic change. Some of the group's recent songs were nearly impossible to perform live as a quartet, and fan noise made performances generally

Most of the Beach Boys' creative songwriting and production came from Brian Wilson (pictured here in the studio, 1966). Like his hero Phil Spector, Wilson demanded total control of the musical production and experimented with nontraditional instruments and recording technology. Wilson was constantly pushing himself to outdo the Beatles and their legendary producer, George Martin.

unpleasant. In the wake of the controversy surrounding John Lennon's remarks about Christianity, live appearances had also become too dangerous. Perhaps more important, working on recordings that the group knew did not need to be reproduced in a live setting allowed for an immense amount of freedom in the recording studio, satisfying the creative ambitions of an emerging psychedelic movement.

In the fall of 1966, the Beatles began working on *Sgt. Pepper's Lonely Hearts Club Band*, seeking to use the full resources of a recording studio and London's musical community. At first, the idea was to unite all the songs on the album around a central theme—their memories of growing up in Liverpool. But by early 1967, EMI was eager to at least release a single, since the label knew it was never good for a pop act—even the Beatles—to be away from the pop charts for too long. The band's next release was a double-A-sided single of "Penny Lane" and "Strawberry Fields Forever." The lyrics to "Penny Lane" describe a variety of scenes that McCartney felt captured a cross-section of everyday life in his hometown, while "Strawberry Fields Forever" recalls a neighborhood park where Lennon played as a child.

The group's growing musical ambitions can be heard in the piccolo trumpet solo in "Penny Lane," inspired by a Bach concerto McCartney heard while they were working on the track. "Strawberry Fields Forever" is more adventurous in terms of recording. It uses a wide variety of sounds including cellos, inside-the-piano playing, reversed-tape, and the Mellotron, an early **sampling** keyboard that uses taped sounds to create orchestral strings, choral voices, and an ensemble of recorders (simple wooden flutes). This keyboard can be heard at the very beginning of the song using its recorder-ensemble setting. The final version of "Strawberry Fields Forever" is actually a spliced together combination of two versions that had been recorded at different tempos and in different keys. Producer George Martin varied the tape speed so the recordings could be joined without the listener noticing the splice. "Strawberry Fields Forever" also includes a novel feature: after the song fades at the end, there is a moment of silence and then a brief passage of new music fades back in. This must have surprised disc jockeys the first time they played the song: just as the jock talked over the end of the song, the music marched back in!

sampling

The idea of creating an album based on childhood in Liverpool was dropped when the "Penny Lane"/"Strawberry Fields Forever" single was released. Paul McCartney then hit on the idea of the Beatles assuming the role of the fictional Sgt. Pepper's Lonely Hearts Club Band. The album would be a recorded performance of various acts, hosted by the made-up band. Thus, the album begins with "Sgt. Pepper's Lonely Hearts Club Band," in which the group introduces itself and announces singer "Billy Shears" (played by Ringo) to sing "With a Little Help from My Friends." The plan breaks down after these first tracks, however, returning only at the very end with a reprise of the first track before "A Day in the Life" concludes the album. Because of the Sgt. Pepper idea, the fact that there were no gaps between songs, and the way the album packaging participates in the charade (the original album came in a gatefold cover, complete with pictures of the band dressed in uniform), *Sgt. Pepper's Lonely Hearts Club Band* is often cited as rock's first "concept album"—an album that is organized around some central idea or story. John Lennon resisted thinking of *Sgt. Pepper* this way, claiming that his songs could have appeared on any Beatles album. However, Lennon's objections did little to discourage rock fans from lauding, and musicians from imitating, this aspect of *Sgt. Pepper*, and in the wake of its release concept albums seemed to pop up everywhere.

Sgt. Pepper's Lonely Hearts Club Band is one of the most important albums in the history of rock music. In the weeks after its release, most of the important figures in rock music and millions of listeners were listening to it carefully. There are many aspects of the album that marked a fundamental change in rock music. In addition to the elaborate photographs intimately bound up with the "concept," the complete lyrics were printed on the album cover, signaling that they were central to the experience and perhaps worth reading on their own. Stylistically, the album ranges widely, bringing together British music hall, Indian music, chamber music, and rock and roll. The use of techniques borrowed from avant-garde music is central to "Being for the Benefit of Mr. Kite," which uses taped organ sounds randomly assembled to create a kaleidoscopic aural background. "A Day in the Life" also incorporates experimental techniques with two passages in which the orchestral string players start from a low note on their instrument and gradually play higher notes until given a cue to play an E-major chord closest to wherever they happen to end. Such chance techniques, called "aleatoric" in classical music, were very much a part of avant-garde music in the 1960s. The Beatles were well aware of the connection, as they included avant-garde composer Karlheinz Stockhausen on the cover of the album. The use of such techniques further underscores the seriousness with which the Beatles now approached their music.

Perhaps one of the most important and influential aspects of *Sgt. Pepper* is that it created a new focus on the album as opposed to the single. In the years following *Sgt. Pepper*, single-oriented pop would be directed at a teen audience via AM radio, and album-oriented rock (AOR) would be directed at older teens and college-age listeners on FM. While the Beatles would continue to have hit singles after *Sgt. Pepper*, the new album-as-basic-unit idea served as a model for rock for several decades after 1967.

Collapse and Retreat: *SMiLE* and *Smiley Smile*. While the Beatles were recording "Penny Lane" and "Strawberry Fields Forever," Brian Wilson was at work on perhaps the most famous album never released. Working from the idea that laughter and "good vibes" were what made the world a better place, Wilson planned to call

Listening Guide

The Beatles, "A Day in the Life" Parlophone PMC-7027 (UK), Capitol MAS-2653 (U.S.)

Words and music by John Lennon and Paul McCartney, produced by George Martin. Included on the album *Sgt. Pepper's Lonely Hearts Club Band*, which hit #1 on the *Billboard* "Top LPs" chart in the summer of 1967 (uk1).

FORM: Compound ABA form, with both the A and B sections using a simple verse scheme. The A section is an incomplete song by John Lennon, while the B section is an incomplete song by Paul McCartney. The two songs are stitched together by an interlude that leads from the A section to the B section, and by a bridge that returns to the A section. In the interlude, the Beatles employ the strings in an avant-garde manner, creating a strange growing rush of sound that is repeated at the end of the song.

TIME SIGNATURE: 4/4 in both sections.

INSTRUMENTATION: Acoustic guitar, piano, bass, drums, maracas, strings, brass, alarm clock, lead vocal.

A	0:00–0:12	**Introduction**, 8 mm.	Strummed acoustic guitar, with bass, drums, and percussion joining in second 4 mm.
	0:12–0:44	**Verse 1**, 20 mm.	Vocal (Lennon) enters. Note the echo on the voice. Starts with guitar, piano, and maracas only. "I read the news . . ."
	0:44–1:11	**Verse 2**, 20 mm.	As before. Drums enter, played in an orchestral manner, with a lot of fills in dialogue with vocal line. "He blew his mind . . ."
	1:11–1:41	**Verse 3**, 19 mm.	As in verse 2, but last measures overlap with beginning of interlude, "I saw a film . . ."
	1:41–2:16	**Interlude**, 23 mm.	Orchestral sound builds up, creating an enormous crescendo that cuts off abruptly, forming a transition to the second big section. "I'd love to turn you on . . ."
B	2:16–2:21	**Introduction**, 4 mm.	Repeated chords on acoustic piano help establish a quieter contrasting mood. Note the alarm clock.
	2:21–2:36	**B Verse 1**, 9 mm.	Vocal (McCartney) enters. Note how little reverb there is on the vocal. Bass plays a happy walking line on the second half, "Woke up . . ."
	2:36–2:49	**B Verse 2**, 9 mm.	As before, "Found my coat . . ."
	2:49–3:18	**Bridge**, 20 mm.	10-mm. phrase occurs twice, sung by Lennon and soaked in reverb. Note the ominous orchestral backdrop.

(continued)

A'	3:18–3:46	**Verse 4**, 19 mm.	As in verse 3 of the A section, with last measures overlapping with ending section. "I read the news . . ."
	3:46–4:57	**Interlude** as ending,	Orchestral crescendo as in the previous occurrence of the interlude, but with a giant chord played on the piano to end at 4:21. This chord is sustained for almost 40 seconds using electronic means to keep the sound audible.

his new concept album *SMiLE*. After a planned release date of December 1966 was missed, he continued working through the first months of 1967 before eventually abandoning the project, with more than 70 percent of the album finished according to some reports. The Beach Boys did release *Smiley Smile* (p41 uk9, 1967), a significantly different album from what *SMiLE* would have been (and turned out to be). In the years since, many myths about *SMiLE* have arisen. Some writers speculate that it would have been Wilson's masterpiece, while others claim that his high intake of drugs left him confused and unable to manage the complexity of the music. Scholars now have a good idea of how the album might have sounded from studio material released by Capitol in the 1990s and from bootleg recordings. One track was released at the time and provides a sample of the original *SMiLE*. Much like "Good Vibrations," "Heroes and Villains" is a product of the recording studio, with separately recorded and highly produced sections spliced together to create a sequence of musical episodes. While a version was released officially during the summer of 1967 (p14 uk8), several alternative versions released later exist that are much more experimental—one runs over ten minutes. Wilson's rerecorded version from 2004 maintains the spirit of the original, although his vocal energy is less active, and the musical tracks betray a twenty-first century sheen.

Since it was abandoned, *SMiLE* has achieved considerable status, so it may seem surprising that the project created controversy within the band when Wilson was working on it. The other Beach Boys spent a lot of time on the road performing the band's earlier hits. When they encountered Brian's newest music in late 1966, they thought it would never be popular with fans. To a certain extent this was true: *Pet Sounds* had not sold as well as previous albums. On *Smiley Smile* and subsequent albums through the rest of the decade, the Beach Boys made an effort to simplify their sound, although the group never again achieved the kind of commercial success they had enjoyed in the mid-1960s. Wilson was still writing for the band and performing on the recordings, but the albums were now listed as "produced by the Beach Boys."

And in the End: The Beatles after *Sgt. Pepper*. John Lennon may have insisted that *Sgt. Pepper* was not a concept album, but much of what the Beatles did after *Sgt. Pepper* was driven by organizing themes, often dreamed up by Paul McCartney. *Magical Mystery Tour*, for instance, was built around the concept of the band traveling the English countryside by bus, making a movie as they went. In early 1968, the band traveled to India to study meditation at the ashram of the Maharishi Mahesh Yogi and brought back dozens of songs, many of which would appear on *The Beatles* (often called the "White Album"). The band was also approached about making an animated film that would use them as characters in a surrealist adventure in Pepperland. The result, *Yellow Submarine*, could be described as a kind of psychedelic *A Hard Day's Night*. After this, McCartney devised a plan to make a documentary film of the Beatles writing, rehearsing, and recording an album, concluding with a performance of the finished music. The "Get Back" project went badly, with producer George Martin walking out (he was later replaced by Phil Spector), and the camera frequently captured arguments among band members. The film and album were scrapped and the Beatles reunited with Martin to record what would become their last studio album, *Abbey Road* (1969). The film and studio tracks from "Get Back" were later salvaged and released as *Let It Be* in 1970. (In 2003, the Beatles rereleased these same recordings as *Let It Be Naked*, which erased much of Spector's production to return the music to a more elemental and raw sound.)

The period after *Sgt. Pepper* also saw major changes in the business side of the Beatles: in the summer of 1967, their manager Brian Epstein died of a drug overdose. The band eventually decided to take over their business affairs themselves, renting offices and forming Apple Records (the Beach Boys formed Brother Records at about the same time). Apple was launched with much fanfare: the Beatles would not only run their own careers but would also promote the work of deserving artists who might otherwise be turned away by mainstream commercial backers. It was based on a generous idea, but Apple was soon losing money and professionals had to be called in to stem the losses and reorganize the group's finances. By late 1969, all four Beatles were ready to disband, and in April 1970, the Beatles officially broke up. In the years that followed, each band member went on to a successful solo career.

In the late 1960s, the Beatles' interest in the culture of India translated into using the Indian sitar on several tracks. Here George Harrison plays sitar for the Maharishi as John Lennon and Ringo Starr look on.

Despite some failed projects and the Apple fiasco, the Beatles' success never lagged during the 1967 to 1970 period: every album and single they released placed high on the pop charts, most at number one in both the United States and the UK. In many ways, the band's later music would prove to be more influential for future rock musicians than their early releases. In terms of the development of psychedelic music, the friendly competition between the Beach Boys and the Beatles had important consequences. The ways these bands applied themselves to developing the stylistic, timbral, and compositional range of rock music was a model for other groups. *Pet Sounds*, "Good Vibrations," "Strawberry Fields Forever," and *Sgt. Pepper* demonstrated that rock could stand on its own as music and be taken seriously. Rock music was no longer simply dance music about teen romance. Because these bands were so successful, Capitol and EMI gave them a certain freedom to experiment. When these experiments produced hit singles and albums, other groups were given greater license as well.

THE SAN FRANCISCO SCENE AND HAIGHT-ASHBURY

Between the summers of 1966 and 1967, the Beatles and the Beach Boys were dominating American rock with increasingly ambitious music, but a local psychedelic scene had been developing since mid-1965 in San Francisco. One of the first important signs to the greater public that something new was burgeoning in the city was the Human Be-In, held in Golden Gate Park in January 1967. Posters advertising the event called it a "gathering of the tribes," and it brought together thousands of hippies from Northern California for a day of poetry, spirituality, and music provided by local bands such as Quicksilver Messenger Service and Jefferson Airplane. The Be-In drew media attention to San Francisco's growing hippie culture, and within a few months the event was imitated in New York and Los Angeles. A local San Francisco bus-tour company began offering a "Hippie Hop Tour." In many ways, the San Francisco psychedelic scene grew out of the area's Beat movement of the late '50s and early '60s—with gatherings at Lawrence Ferlinghetti's City Lights Bookstore in North Beach, this bohemian scene celebrated the poetry of Allen Ginsberg and the prose of Jack Kerouac. Ginsberg and fellow Beats Michael McClure and Gary Snyder mentored the emerging hippie movement, even helping to organize the Human Be-In. Despite the many parallels between the Beats and the hippies, however, there were also significant differences, the most crucial being music: the jazz of be-bop musicians Charlie Parker and Dizzy Gillespie was the choice of most Beats, while hippies favored the music of the Rolling Stones, Bob Dylan, and the Beatles.

The Red Dog, the Family Dog, and Kesey's Acid Tests. During the mid-1960s, counterculture scenes developed rapidly in many areas of the United States, with important bands, newspapers, and clubs emerging in New York, Detroit, Los Angeles, and Northern California. San Francisco, and the old Victorian neighborhood of Haight-Ashbury especially, soon became the center of the American psychedelic scene. However, the first stirrings of psychedelia actually took place in Virginia City, Nevada, at a restored western-style bar called the Red Dog Saloon. In June 1965, San Francisco musicians the Charlatans became the house band at the Red Dog. Evenings of free-form music-making and acid tripping increasingly drew young people out to Virginia City for psychedelic happenings that would serve as the model for later ones in the Bay Area. By the fall of 1965, a group of friends calling themselves the Family Dog began organizing psychedelic dances at local San Francisco ballrooms. The first was held in October at the Longshoremen's Hall under the title "A Tribute to Dr. Strange" and featured the Charlatans, the newly formed Jefferson Airplane, and the Great Society. The second dance, "A Tribute to Sparkle Plenty," was held several days later with the Charlatans and the Lovin' Spoonful (a New York band).

Around the time of the psychedelic dances, novelist Ken Kesey organized a series of events that he called "acid tests." Since 1964, Kesey and a band of vigorously bohemian friends who called themselves the Merry Pranksters had been traveling the country in a brightly painted schoolbus emblazoned with the destination FURTHUR. Like Timothy Leary, Kesey celebrated the liberating effects of LSD and wanted to share the drug as broadly as he could. But Kesey was not seeking spiritual wisdom through methods of quiet contemplation and revelation. Instead, he and the Pranksters wanted to provide an environment rich in unpredictable stimulation to those who paid a dollar to enter the acid tests and experience LSD. In addition to a dose of the drug, participants were treated to light and slide shows, bizarre sound effects, and rock music, all in hopes of intensifying the effects of the acid. Kesey first offered his acid tests to the public in November 1965 in Santa Cruz, and they quickly caught on. In January 1966, 2,400 people attended one of Kesey's acid tests at San Francisco's Fillmore Auditorium. The house band for the evening was a group called the Grateful Dead, who had recently changed their name from the Warlocks.

This poster announces a series of shows by San Francisco's Charlatans at the Red Dog Saloon in Virginia City, Nevada. These shows took place in June 1965, two years before psychedelia went mainstream during the Summer of Love in 1967.

It Takes a Village to Raise a Ruckus: Concerts, News, the Psychedelic Shop, and FM Radio.
The multiple-bill dances combined with the unpredictable and multimedia aspects of Kesey's acid tests became the model for psychedelic events in San Francisco for the next few years. Soon psychedelic evenings of LSD and rock music were a regular feature in the Bay Area. Promoter Bill Graham began organizing shows at the Fillmore, while Chet Helms promoted shows at the Avalon Ballroom. Ron and Jay Thelin opened the Psychedelic Shop in the Haight-Ashbury district to meet the countercultural needs of the hippies, and local bands rented large Victorian houses in the neighborhood that also served as rehearsal spaces.

WHAT'S THAT SOURCE?

Birth of the Rock Press: Opening Editorials for *Crawdaddy* and *Rolling Stone*

During the late 1960s, a new type of publication surrounding rock music and culture emerged in the United States. Closely related to the underground press movement, rock-oriented publications like *Rolling Stone, Crawdaddy, Cheetah,* and *Creem* supported a new style of journalism, mostly featuring writing by rock fans for rock fans that reflected the social underpinnings of youth culture during this time. The opening editorials for *Rolling Stone* and *Crawdaddy* reflect common goals and a shared perspective despite the fact that the former emerged out of the San Francisco scene and the latter at Swarthmore, a liberal arts college in Pennsylvania. Representative of a growing national movement, both of these publications viewed themselves against trade magazines like *Billboard,* in addition to other teen-oriented fan publications, and sensed a need for intelligent writing about rock music that adequately reflected the seriousness of the youth counterculture.

You're probably wondering what we are trying to do. It's hard to say: sort of a magazine and sort of a newspaper. The name of it is ROLLING STONE, which comes from an old saying: "A Rolling Stone gathers no moss." Muddy Waters used the name for a song he wrote; the Rolling Stones took their name from Muddy's song, and "Like a Rolling Stone" was the title of Bob Dylan's first rock and roll record.

We have begun a new publication reflecting what we see are the changes

(The Grateful Dead lived at 710 Ashbury.) By September 1966, the *San Francisco Oracle* joined the *Berkeley Barb* as the area's most important counterculture newspaper, and they were joined by *Rolling Stone* magazine in November 1967. While many outside the hippie subculture may have first learned about it in 1967 with news of the Human Be-In and the summer of love, the hippie underground in San Francisco was already firmly established in the fall of 1966.

One place where psychedelic music was absent, however, was on the radio. Pop music radio was still entirely on the AM dial and oriented toward short hit singles. Clearly the new, lengthier psychedelic rock would not fit that format. The FM dial had been available for some years and mostly featured public-service programming—university lectures, classical music concerts, and foreign-language shows. Many radios did not even have an FM dial. San Francisco radio veteran Tom Donahue, a member of the psychedelic scene, became disgruntled with the AM radio business and developed a new, free-form approach to programming. His format featured longer tracks placed back-to-back, with more freedom given to the disc jockey and less in-your-face between-song chatter. Donahue's wife, Rachel, reports that he phoned a number of FM stations in the local phone book until he found one where telephone service had been disconnected. Figuring that any radio station that could not pay its phone bill might be receptive to new ideas, Donahue eventually came to terms with KMPX-FM. Starting with an evening slot in April 1967, Donahue and

in rock and roll and the changes related to rock and roll. Because the trade papers have become so inaccurate and irrelevant, and because the fan magazines are an anachronism, fashioned in the mold of myth and nonsense, we hope that we have something here for the artists and the industry, and every person who "believes in the magic that can set you free."

ROLLING STONE is not just about music, but also the things and attitudes that the music embraces. We've been working quite hard on it and we hope you can dig it. To describe it any further would be difficult without sounding like bullshit, and bullshit is like gathering moss.

Source: Jann Wenner, "A Letter from the Editor," *Rolling Stone*, November 9, 1967, 2.

**

You are looking at the first issue of a magazine of rock and roll criticism. *Crawdaddy* will feature neither pin-ups nor news-briefs; the specialty of this magazine is intelligent writing about pop music. *Billboard*, *Cash Box,* etc., serve very well as trade news magazines; but their idea of a review is: "a hard-driving rhythm number that should spiral rapidly up the charts just as (previous hit by same group) slides." And the teen magazines are devoted to rock and roll, but their discussion is a string of superlatives below a fold-out photograph. *Crawdaddy* believes that someone in the United States might be interested in what others have to say about the music they like.

This is not a service magazine. We fully expect and intend to be of great use to the trade: by pushing new 45's that might have otherwise been overlooked, by aiding radio stations in deciding on their playlists, by giving manufacturers some indication of response to a record other than sales, by providing buyers with critiques of new lps so that they'll have some idea of what they're getting before they buy, and, most importantly, by offering rock and roll artists some sort of critical response to their work. But we are not a service magazine.

The aim of this magazine is readability. We are trying to appeal to people interested in rock and roll, both professionally and casually. If we could predict the exact amount of sales of each record we heard, it would not interest us to do so. If we could somehow pat every single pop artist on the back in a manner calculated to please him and his fans, we would not bother. What we do want to do is write reviews and articles that you will not want to put down, and produce a magazine that you will read thoroughly every week. And we think we can do it.

Source: Paul Williams, "Get Off of My Cloud!" *Crawdaddy*, February 7, 1966.

a growing staff soon took over the full day's programming, mostly playing records from their own collections. While Donahue was not the first to launch a free-form FM radio show—a New York station had briefly run one in 1966 and another DJ had tried one at KMPX just a month before Donahue went on the air—he was the first person to make the format successful. Within months, he was also running a station in Los Angeles, and FM rock stations popped up across the country in the wake of the breakthrough of psychedelia in the summer of 1967.

The Grateful Dead. Music was at the center of San Francisco psychedelia, and the group at the center of psychedelic music in the Bay Area was the Grateful Dead. The band had its roots in the folk movement of the early 1960s. Guitarist Jerry Garcia started out as a folk, bluegrass, and jug-band musician, playing traditional music on guitar and banjo. Like many young American musicians of his generation, he was introduced to American electric blues by the Rolling Stones. By the spring of 1965, Garcia was playing a combination of blues covers, folk-based traditional songs,

This multicolor bus was used by Ken Kesey and his Merry Pranksters to take their acid tests on the road. The destination sign on the front of the bus read simply: Furthur.

and original music with the Warlocks. Based in the Bay Area, the Warlocks also included Ron "Pigpen" McKernan (organ, harmonica), Bob Weir (guitar), Bill Kreutzmann (drums), and eventually Phil Lesh (bass). The band soon changed its name to the Grateful Dead and, as the house band for the Kesey acid tests, began to develop a highly improvisational approach in which single songs could last longer than most albums. While the group's free-form style worked well in the context of the acid tests and in subsequent performances at the Fillmore and Avalon, capturing it in the recording studio posed significant difficulties. Signed by MGM in 1966, the band and the label parted ways after several months without a record ever being released. The band then signed with Warner Brothers and in March 1967 it released a debut album, *The Grateful Dead*, containing short tunes that give no real indication of the improvisatory nature of the band's live shows.

The group's second album, *Anthem of the Sun* (1968), did not solve the problem of how to record a representative portrayal of their live act, but it provided an important instance of the band's improvisational bent. Made up of segments drawn from live and studio recordings, the album consists of two sides that were each assembled via multiple tapes in real time. Just as the Beatles had mixed tape loops in real time on "Tomorrow Never Knows," Garcia and Lesh "mixed" each side of their album on the fly with a considerable amount of studio improvisation subject to the element of chance. According to Garcia, the album was mixed with the goal of intensifying the acid experience. Lesh, a former composition student, was familiar with electronic avant-garde music, and has remarked how impressed the band was when they heard "Tomorrow Never Knows." The parallels between Lennon's lyrics (drawn from Leary's *The Psychedelic Experience*, which counsels one during an acid trip) and the psychedelic aesthetic of *Anthem of the Sun*, combined with the similarities in the manipulation of taped sounds, make the Grateful Dead album a clear extension of the Beatles track. The Dead had still not captured their

The Grateful Dead were at the center of the San Francisco psychedelic scene and their heavy emphasis on improvisation has made them one of the foundational jam bands in rock history. The strong focus on improvisation meant that the band's live shows could differ significantly from one performance to the next. While fans loved this, it made it difficult to capture the full spirit of the group's music in the studio.

live show on record, however, although the 1970 album *Live/Dead* would go a good way toward achieving that. *Live/Dead* was recorded before a group of friends live in the studio, and it contains a twenty-five-minute version of "Dark Star," a song written with poet Robert Hunter (a friend of Garcia's from his army days) that had become a staple of the band's live set. This track is representative of the band's extended improvised instrumental solos, which frequently occur over simple chord progressions and feature the use of modal scales (as opposed to the more common major and minor scales), as might be found in jazz of about the same period. Released later in 1970, *Working Man's Dead* and *American Beauty* return to shorter, more country- and folk-oriented tracks and, taken with *Live/Dead*, form a trio of albums that launched the Grateful Dead as one of the most successful live bands in the 1970s and '80s. While they struggled at times to create commercial recordings in the studio, during the 1970s their fans began a long-standing tradition of recording live concerts. Subverting conventional methods of studio recordings, Grateful Dead fans have always felt more connected to this form of listening, as evidenced by the vast networks trading these "bootleg" recordings, and the prominence of many noncommercial live recordings.

Jefferson Airplane. Formed by singer Marty Balin and guitarist Paul Kantner in mid-1965, Jefferson Airplane established themselves on the San Francisco scene slightly earlier than the Dead. Formed to play in Balin's Matrix club, the band's performance at the club opening in August 1965 garnered a positive review from *San Francisco Chronicle* critic Ralph Gleason (who was to mentor young editor Jann Wenner in the early years of *Rolling Stone*) and led to a recording deal with RCA. Along with original members Jorma Kaukonen (guitar) and Signe Anderson (vocals), bassist Jack Cassady and drummer Spencer Dryden rounded out the band lineup that recorded *Jefferson Airplane Takes Off*. Recorded in late 1965, it was not released until late 1966. By October 1966, however, Anderson had been replaced by Grace Slick, who had been a member of another San Francisco group, the Great Society. Slick brought two songs with her, both of which became hit singles: "Somebody to Love" (p5, 1967) and "White Rabbit" (p8, 1967). Jefferson Airplane's second album, *Surrealistic Pillow* (1967), which contained both of these songs, featured Slick and rose to number three on the American album charts. This lineup subsequently recorded a series of successful and often innovative albums, including *After Bathing at Baxter's* (p17, 1967), *Crown of Creation* (p6, 1968), the live *Bless Its Pointed Little Head* (p17 uk38, 1969), and the politically inspired *Volunteers* (p13

A San Francisco Timeline

June 1965: Charlatans begin at Red Dog Saloon

October 1965: Family Dog's "A Tribute to Dr. Strange," Longshoremen's Hall, Charlatans, Great Society, Jefferson Airplane

October 1965: Family Dog's "A Tribute to Sparkle Plenty," Charlatans, Lovin' Spoonful

November 1965: Kesey's first public acid test

December 1965: Acid test draws 400 in San Jose after Rolling Stones concert

January 1966: Acid test at the Fillmore Auditorium draws 2,400, Grateful Dead

January 1966: Three-evening Trips Festival, Longshoremen's Hall, Grateful Dead, Big Brother

Early to mid-1966: Psychedelic Shop opens

September 1966: First issue of *Oracle*

January 1967: Human Be-In draws 20,000, Quicksilver, Jefferson Airplane, Big Brother

April 1967: KMPX-FM goes on the air

November 1967: First issue of *Rolling Stone*

Listening Guide

Jefferson Airplane, **"White Rabbit"** RCA Victor 47-9248

Words and music by Grace Slick, produced by Rick Jarrard. Reached #8 on the *Billboard* "Hot 100" chart in the summer of 1967.

FORM: AABA form, with the last verse expanded to create a musical climax. The entire piece builds gradually, beginning quietly and ending loudly.

TIME SIGNATURE: 4/4, with the drums suggesting a Spanish flavor in imitation of a bolero rhythm.

INSTRUMENTATION: Electric guitars, bass, drums, lead vocals.

0:00–0:28	**Introduction**, 12 mm.	Bass guitar and snare drum suggest "bolero" rhythm, as the guitar enters with winding lines that evoke Spanish music.
0:28–0:55	**A-Verse**, 12 mm.	Vocals enter quietly, with only bass, guitar, and snare drum accompaniment. "One pill makes you . . ."
0:55–1:23	**A-Verse**, 12 mm.	Just a little louder and more forceful, "And if you go . . ."
1:23–1:42	**B-Bridge**, 8 mm.	Second guitar now enters, drums go into a more traditional rock beat, and the music gains intensity, getting markedly louder. "When men on . . ."
1:42–2:27	**A-Verse** (expanded), 21 mm.	Vocal now much more forceful, as rhythm in the accompaniment gets much more insistent, driving toward the climax at the end. "Go ask Alice . . ."

uk34, 1969), all of which became staples of late 1960s progressive FM radio. The group's early influences were American folk and blues, but elements of modal jazz and Indian music can be found throughout their music, especially in their extended instrumental solos.

The single "White Rabbit" shows how Jefferson Airplane was able to blend musical ambition with the AM single format. The song is in AABA form, with an introduction. The first two verses are followed by a bridge and then an expanded verse, which also includes a dramatic ending. The lyrics of the song refer to Lewis Carroll's *Alice in Wonderland* stories, although the clear reference in lines like "feed your head" is to the use of psychedelic drugs. Slick's surreal images resonate with those of many other psychedelic songwriters, especially John Lennon, whose "Lucy in the Sky with Diamonds" was also inspired in part by *Alice in Wonderland*. Jefferson Airplane modeled the music in "White Rabbit" on the Spanish bolero, heard especially in Kaukonen's Spanish-sounding guitar lines in the introduction. Slick recalls listening to the Miles Davis and Gil Evans orchestral jazz album *Sketches of*

Spain for inspiration, but the overall dynamic shape of the piece closely resembles a well-known orchestral work by the French composer Maurice Ravel titled *Boléro* (1927–28). Often used by music educators to illustrate the wide variety of tone colors available to the master orchestrator, Ravel's *Boléro* employs a single Spanish-tinged melody that is repeated several times, but contextualized differently at each repetition to exploit the full range of available orchestral colors. More important to our discussion of "White Rabbit," however, *Boléro* is constructed as a single long crescendo—it continually and gradually builds toward its violent musical climax. This is precisely what "White Rabbit" does, although on a more compressed time scale (the Ravel piece lasts almost fifteen minutes). As with the Grateful Dead's *Anthem of the Sun* and the Beatles' "Tomorrow Never Knows," we again find a song dealing with the acid experience and employing ambitious techniques borrowed from classical music. In the case of "White Rabbit," however, the classical music involved is not avant-garde music, but early twentieth-century orchestral music.

Big Brother and the Holding Company and Janis Joplin. Like the Grateful Dead and Jefferson Airplane, Big Brother and the Holding Company experimented with classical and avant-garde music. At one point, the band regularly performed a version of Edvard Grieg's "Hall of the Mountain King" from *Peer Gynt*, and contemplated an experimental piece called "Bacon," which would last as long as it took to fry a plate of bacon on stage. The band enjoyed its greatest acclaim and success, however, backing up singer Janis Joplin on electric blues numbers. Joplin had left her hometown of Port Arthur, Texas, in the early 1960s to sing in Austin night clubs. By mid-decade, she had made her way to San Francisco, where she sang for a brief period before giving up music to return to Port Arthur. Big Brother and the Holding Company was formed in part by concert promoter Chet Helms, who convinced her to return to San Francisco to join the band. The band's self-titled first album was released in the fall of 1967. Their second album, *Cheap Thrills*, became an enormous commercial success, hitting number one on the U.S. album charts in the fall of 1968, while the single "Piece of My Heart" rose to number twelve. Joplin soon left Big Brother to embark on a solo career, and by the fall of 1969 her debut album, *I Got Dem Ol' Kozmic Blues Again Mama!*, went to number five

The Jefferson Airplane was one of the leading bands on the San Francisco psychedelic scene. Here we can see the kind of stage lighting that was often a part of many bands' performances at the time. Lead singer Grace Slick stands at the microphone, with Marty Balin playing tambourine to her right.

Janis Joplin (left) singing with her group Big Brother and the Holding Company at a 1967 concert at Winterland in San Francisco. Joplin's aggressive, passionate blues style drew inspiration from singers like Bessie Smith and Ma Rainey. Their hard lives proved a model for Joplin, who died of a drug overdose in 1970, just months before her album *Pearl* was released and quickly climbed the charts to number one.

on the U.S. pop chart. Throughout her adult life, Joplin struggled with drug and alcohol abuse, and on October 4, 1970, she was found in a hotel room dead from an overdose. Her posthumously released album *Pearl* became her most popular release, rising to number one in early 1971, while her version of Kris Kristofferson's "Me and Bobby McGee" hit the top of the U.S. singles charts. Joplin's powerful blues style and hard-living image were reminiscent of the earlier blues singers like Ma Rainey, Bessie Smith, and Big Mama Thornton whom she emulated. She was a central figure in the Haight-Ashbury scene leading up to the summer of 1967, and her blues-based singing style offers an important example of the connection between psychedelia and African American music. The musicians in Big Brother were more in step with other aspects of the psychedelic aesthetic, and while acknowledging the importance of blues in their music, also stressed how they were striving to find something new—a style they called "blues in Technicolor."

Country Joe and the Fish. Led by singer-guitarist Joe McDonald from Washington, D.C., and Barry "The Fish" Melton from New York, Country Joe and the Fish were active in radical politics in Berkeley, California. While the politics of the Berkeley radicals and the counterculture of the San Francisco hippies are typically thought of as different aspects of the same local scene, the two communities often had difficulty agreeing on issues of cultural and political change. Music was important to both groups, but to many of the radicals, the hippies seemed spacey and generally detached from the political issues that most concerned them. To many hippies, the radicals seemed too intense and hung up on political action. Country Joe and the Fish were something of a bridge between the two communities. In 1965, for instance, the band issued an extended-play (EP) recording that was included in an issue of *Rag Baby*, a radical magazine founded by McDonald that circulated in the San Francisco area. Two years later, the band released a markedly psychedelic debut album, *Electric Music for the Mind and Body* (p39, 1967). While this album clearly displays the band's origins in acoustic blues and folk, it is most noteworthy for its many moments influenced by the band's use of LSD. The atmospheric and experimental "Section 43" is the best example of this. According to band accounts, the entire record was designed, like the Grateful Dead's *Anthem of the Sun*, to enhance the listener's acid trip. The group's next album, *I-Feel-Like-I'm-Fixin'-to-Die* (p67, 1968), featured the title song, originally recorded in 1965 as an outspoken denouncement of the Vietnam War, and the "Fish Cheer," which the band made famous by inserting the word "fuck" in place of "Fish" at live performances, most notably at Woodstock. While *Together* (p23, 1968) brought the group's greatest commercial success, it already marked the musical decline of the band.

THE LONDON SCENE

The Rise of the British Underground. In 1965, while the Grateful Dead were turning to electric blues and Jefferson Airplane were rehearsing for their debut performance, Beat poet Allen Ginsberg was in London helping bookstore owner Barry Miles organize a poetry reading that featured several American and European Beats, including Lawrence Ferlinghetti and Gregory Corso. Convinced that Miles's Better Books was far too small to contain the crowd they were hoping to draw, the organizers rented the Royal Albert Hall. In June 1965, "Poets of the World/Poets of Our Time" drew over 5,000 people—many under the influence of pot or acid—and inaugurated the London psychedelic underground. The following September, British researcher Michael Hollingshead (who had introduced Timothy Leary to LSD), opened the World Psychedelic Center in London, which would soon become the English center for psychedelic music and culture.

Drugs were not entirely new to rock culture in the UK. The Beatles had been introduced to marijuana in late 1964, and John Lennon and George Harrison had already experienced LSD in the spring of 1965 (it was secretly slipped into their coffee after dinner at the home of an acquaintance). But similar to San Francisco, a community of young people in London was beginning to form around drugs, Eastern philosophy, radical politics, and experimental music. By the end of January 1966, a series of weekly events called the Spontaneous Underground were initiated that combined poetry, music, and avant-garde performance art. Held in the Marquee Club on Sundays, these events were akin to Kesey's acid tests, although on a smaller scale. In February, a bookstore and gallery called the Indica was launched by Barry Miles, John Dunbar (the husband of Marianne Faithfull), and Peter Asher (of the musical duo Peter and Gordon and brother of Paul McCartney's girlfriend, Jane). The Indica, similar to the Psychedelic Shop, specialized in counterculture items, and it was here that John Lennon first encountered *The Psychedelic Experience*. Unlike the San Francisco scene, the London underground boasted a kind of countercultural night school where students could study topics such as housing problems, race relations, mental health, and law. Called the London Free School, it began to hold meetings in March 1966.

Despite the many parallels, the San Francisco and London scenes were quite different. Members of the early London psychedelic underground had only a few descriptions of the San Francisco scene as a guide. In the late 1960s, when air

In the spring of 1966, *Time* magazine proclaimed London "the swinging city." But while tourists and the media were focused on Swinging London, a psychedelic underground was developing in the British capital, mostly out of view of anyone except those in the know. This photo captures a UFO Club audience during a Pink Floyd show in late 1966.

travel was far less commonplace than it is today, there were few people in London who had actually experienced the San Francisco underground, and since the San Francisco scene remained underground until mid-1967, published reports were very scarce. From Ginsberg and a few others, psychedelic Londoners knew the main points of San Francisco psychedelia but were forced to work out the specific applications according to their own imaginations. The result was a London scene that was at once very similar to but also very distinct from the one in California.

Underground Clubs in Swinging London.

In April 1966, just as the London psychedelic scene was gaining momentum and remained unknown to anyone outside of it, *Time* magazine ran a cover story on "Swinging London," focusing on what the editors in New York perceived as a refreshing urban lifestyle filled with glamorous nightspots attended by hip stars adorned in daring and colorful fashions. The summer of 1966 saw young tourists flocking to London to catch some of the excitement, but the psychedelic scene developed mostly out of their sight. In October, the *International Times* began publication, providing the burgeoning scene with a newspaper devoted to its concerns, and before the end of the year the UFO Club was established. Unlike the Fillmore or the Avalon in San Francisco, the UFO was more of an organization than a place. UFO evenings occurred in a spot that was an Irish pub during the rest of the week. When using that bar became a problem, the UFO simply relocated. While other clubs also featured psychedelic music (even some of the same bands, such as Pink Floyd, Soft Machine, Tomorrow, and the Crazy World of Arthur Brown), for most of 1967, the UFO was the most prominent gathering of the psychedelic underground in London. Larger events occurred during this period as well. In late April 1967, an evening of psychedelia brought 10,000 London hippies together. Called "The 14-Hour Technicolor Dream," the all-night event was held at Alexandra Palace, a Victorian palace overlooking London. Avant-garde happenings (one supervised by Yoko Ono), a light show, and a long roster of bands were meant to intensify the chemically enhanced experiences of those in attendance. A month later, Pink Floyd sponsored a similar event, "Games for May," which was held in Queen Elizabeth Hall, and in July, a "Love-In" back at Alexandra Palace featured Pink Floyd, Tomorrow, the Crazy World of Arthur Brown, and the Animals. By August, when the Middle Earth Club was established for evenings similar to those hosted by the UFO, little about psychedelia was underground anymore: in the wake of *Sgt. Pepper's Lonely Hearts Club Band*, it seemed that psychedelia was everywhere.

Musical Notes from the Underground: Pink Floyd, Soft Machine, and Tomorrow.

There were generally two types of bands on the London scene during the 1966 to 1969 period: those who enjoyed commercial success (the Beatles, the Stones, Cream, Jimi Hendrix, Donovan), and those whose success was limited to the London underground. The first band to make its name on the underground scene formed in 1965 and took its name from American bluesmen Pink Anderson and Floyd Council. Initially calling themselves the Pink Floyd Sound, then the Pink Floyd and eventually simply Pink Floyd, the band became regulars at Spontaneous Underground events, and later at the UFO Club.

The band took its name from the blues, but much of its approach was more indebted to avant-garde art music. The group's extended improvisations would often dispense with chord patterns and scales and wander into exploratory noise-making, produced by playing their instruments in unconventional ways or feeding their electric guitars and keyboards through tape-echo devices. While leader and guitarist Syd Barrett, bassist Roger Waters, organist Richard Wright, and drummer Nick Mason could play songs like "Interstellar Overdrive" for half an hour, they also had a pair of radio-friendly hit singles in mid-1967, written by Barrett. "Arnold Layne," a song about a transvestite who steals women's clothing off other people's clotheslines at night—which somehow avoided being banned by the BBC—reached number twenty on the UK charts. The follow-up, "See Emily Play," hit number six. The band refused to play these songs live, however, preferring to perform their extended improvisations instead. Pink Floyd's first album, *Piper at the Gates of Dawn* (uk6, 1967), was recorded around the same time and at the same Abbey Road facility as the Beatles' *Sgt. Pepper* (Paul McCartney is reported to have visited at least one of the sessions). Barrett, however, soon began to show signs of mental illness, and during an American tour in 1967, he became unable to perform reliably. Guitarist and Barrett friend David Gilmour was brought in to cover, but eventually replaced Barrett entirely. In light of the tremendous success the band enjoyed worldwide in the 1970s (discussed in Chapter 8), it is surprising that their success before *The Dark Side of the Moon* (1973) was limited to the UK. The group scored a string of hit albums in Britain, including *A Saucerful of Secrets* (uk9, 1968), *More* (uk9, 1969), *Ummagumma* (p74 uk5, 1969), and *Atom Heart Mother* (p55 uk1, 1970), but they could never break the Top 40 of the album charts in the States. Their concert performances in London during 1966 to 1968, often accompanied by elaborate light shows

A London Timeline

June 1965: "Poets of the World/Poets of Our Time," Royal Albert Hall

September 1965: Michael Hollingshead opens World Psychedelic Center

January 30, 1966: Spontaneous Underground weekly events begin (Marquee Club)

February 1966: Indica Bookshop and Gallery opens

March 1966: London Free School is launched

April 1966: *Time* cover story on Swinging London

October 1966: *International Times* begins publication

December 1966: UFO evenings begin

April 1967: "The 14-Hour Technicolor Dream," Alexandra Palace

May 1967: "Games for May," Pink Floyd, Queen Elizabeth Hall

July 1967: "Love-In," Pink Floyd, Tomorrow, the Animals, Arthur Brown, Alexandra Palace

August 1967: Middle Earth evenings begin

Led by guitarist and singer Syd Barrett (center), Pink Floyd developed an experimental and free-form approach to improvisation that drew as much from avant-garde sources as from blues or jazz. They are shown here performing at the "Love-In" at London's Alexandra Palace in July 1967—one of the festivals that defined the London psychedelic scene.

and played for audiences tripping on acid, made them one of the most important bands in the London psychedelic underground.

Soft Machine also performed regularly for the UFO Club and other psychedelic events in London. They blended a passion for experimental weirdness with a penchant for the free jazz of Ornette Coleman and John Coltrane. Unlike Pink Floyd, the group never had a hit single and had only modest success with their albums. *The Soft Machine*, a 1968 U.S.-only release, did not chart (the band was touring America at the time, opening for Jimi Hendrix). In 1966 to 1968, the band alternated short song-like sections with avant-garde improvisations. After this, in a series of numbered albums (*Volume Two*, *Third*, *Fourth*, and so on), the band tended toward jazz fusion and became pioneers of the British jazz fusion called Canterbury progressive rock. Tomorrow was another band that became regulars at UFO events and around the London scene. Featuring guitarist Steve Howe (who would later play in the progressive rock band Yes) and vocalist Keith West, the band released a pair of singles that were popular around London but failed to chart. One of these, "My White Bicycle," exhibits many of the psychedelic features found on other records: backward tape sounds, exotic Eastern-sounding melodies, and simple pop lyrics.

The Rolling Stones: Psychedelic Rhythm and Blues?
While Pink Floyd, Soft Machine, and Tomorrow were important components of the burgeoning London psychedelic scene in 1966 to 1967, other British bands and artists enjoyed a much higher profile, especially after June 1967. First among these was certainly the Beatles. The Rolling Stones also continued to score hit singles and albums throughout the second half of the 1960s. New bands such as Cream, the Jimi Hendrix Experience, and Traffic emerged in the months leading up to the Summer of Love, building on the Stones' passion for electric blues. Folksinger Donovan Leitch also turned to flower power and provided a lighter take on British psychedelia.

By late 1966, Brian Jones's contribution to the Rolling Stones' music had diminished considerably, and the Jagger-Richards songwriting partnership began to dominate the band's music. Their seventh album, *Aftermath*, was the first to contain only Jagger-Richards songs, securing their role as group leaders. Despite their well-established position as one of rock music's leading bands, however, the

Stones remained junior colleagues of the Beatles, which was evident in the second half of 1967, as the band prepared *Their Satanic Majesties Request* in response to *Sgt. Pepper*. Jagger had been present at sessions for *Sgt. Pepper* and appeared with the Beatles on their worldwide broadcast of "All You Need Is Love" in July 1967. Jagger had also accompanied the Beatles when they traveled to Wales to study with the Maharishi later that summer. The summer and fall of 1967 had been difficult for Jones, Jagger, and Richards. Each was convicted on drug possession charges and faced the possibility of serving a prison sentence. The single "We Love You" was the band's way of thanking fans for their support during the trials. It hit number eight in the UK in the fall of 1967 and provided a somewhat darker echo of the Beatles' "All You Need Is Love." Released in December 1967, *Their Satanic Majesties Request* (p2 uk3) featured a holographic cover image of the band dressed in wizard outfits—if the Beatles were a happy-go-lucky brass band, the Stones would pose as menacing magi of the occult. The single "She's a Rainbow" illustrates the *Sgt. Pepper* influence on the Stones: the tune employs orchestral instruments and a classical-sounding piano figure that recurs frequently, each time breaking the steady beat of the music.

This album remains a source of disagreement among rock writers. Some consider it to be the Rolling Stones' low point—a project that fails by attempting to imitate the Beatles too closely. Others think it is an interesting and perhaps necessary step in the band's development. Most writers agree, however, that the Rolling Stones came into their own as a band when they stopped worrying about what the Beatles were doing and turned back to their rhythm and blues roots. The hard-driving rhythm of "Jumpin' Jack Flash" (p3 uk1, 1968) gives the first indication of this new stylistic orientation, and the band's next album, *Beggar's Banquet* (p5 uk3, 1968), confirmed it. As discussed in Chapter 4, the Stones' manager Andrew Loog Oldham had marketed the band as bad boys beginning in 1964. By the end of 1967, Oldham was no longer managing the group, but this did not keep the Stones from amplifying the outlaw image that had been crystallized by the scandal over "(I Can't Get No) Satisfaction." In the wake of their widely publicized legal issues, and at a time when the counterculture shifted to include the riots and antiwar protests of 1968, the Stones' "Street Fighting Man" was banned from the radio because authorities thought it might fuel violence. When Jagger adopted the role of Lucifer to sing "Sympathy for the Devil" in 1968, it was clear the band's involvement with flower power was over.

Cream: British Blues on Acid with Pop on the Side.

The first rock band to be billed as a "supergroup" was formed in July 1966 when Eric Clapton (formerly of the Yardbirds), bassist Jack Bruce, and drummer Ginger Baker formed Cream. Individually, they had played in British blues bands with Alexis Korner, John Mayall, and Graham Bond, and the initial idea was that the trio would focus on traditional blues. The band eventually covered several traditional blues numbers, including Robert Johnson's "Crossroads" and Muddy Waters's "Rollin' and Tumblin'." But Clapton had helped develop the instrumental "rave-up" sections that had been a feature of the Yardbirds' live shows, and these became an important element in Cream's blues adaptations. The live version of Willie Dixon's "Spoonful" found on *Wheels of Fire* (1968) is typical. It includes a lengthy instrumental

Cream are shown here during their farewell concert at London's Royal Albert Hall in November 1968. Bassist Jack Bruce (left), drummer Ginger Baker (center), and guitarist Eric Clapton (right) blended a pop sensibility with psychedelia and extended blues-based jams to firmly establish the power trio in rock music, and Clapton's virtuosic playing helped develop the idea of the guitar hero.

rave-up and runs to almost seventeen minutes. While the focus of the music was often on Clapton's guitar playing, Bruce and Baker were also accomplished players who would solo from time to time. Baker's drum solo on "Toad," for example, became a model for many rock drummers. Clapton was widely celebrated in England as guitar "god," and helped popularize distortion and the wah-wah pedal among guitarists. Although the blues were a central element in Cream's music, the band also had a knack for pop singles, demonstrated by the success of "I Feel Free" (uk11, 1966) and "Strange Brew" (uk17, 1967) in the first year of their career.

Initially, the band's success was greater in the UK, where the band members were already well known. *Fresh Cream*, the group's first album, hit number six on the UK charts at the beginning of 1967. In the wake of the Summer of Love, the new passion for trippy music sent *Disraeli Gears* to number four on the U.S. charts (uk5) in the fall, and *Wheels of Fire* rose to number one (uk3) a year later. Whereas the focus of the Beatles' and Beach Boys' music was on expanding the limits of rock songwriting and recording techniques, Cream relied more on virtuosic playing. Cream's penchant for instrumental soloing parallels that of the San Francisco bands, many of whom were inspired by the Rolling Stones' and Yardbirds' adaptations of American electric blues. While the San Francisco guitarists were known more for the bands they played in, Clapton and Hendrix became famous as individuals, ushering in the idea of the "guitar hero." For all the excitement generated by Cream, the band stayed together for only about two years. In November 1968, the band performed a farewell concert in London's Royal Albert Hall. All three members went on to solo careers, although Clapton was the most successful, scoring hit singles and albums in the 1970s, '80s, and '90s.

Six Albums That Changed Rock Guitar Forever

When Chas Chandler asked Hendrix to go with him to London, Hendrix asked Chandler if he could introduce him to Clapton. Clapton was immediately impressed with Hendrix's playing, and a friendly rivalry began. The Jimi Hendrix Experience and Cream brought out an alternating sequence of albums that progressively raised the bar on rock-guitar virtuosity.

Band: *Album*	Release date UK/US
Cream: *Fresh Cream*	Dec 1966/Jan 1967
Hendrix: *Are You Experienced?*	May 1967/Aug 1967
Cream: *Disraeli Gears*	Nov 1967
Hendrix: *Axis: Bold as Love*	Dec 1967/Feb 1968
Cream: *Wheels of Fire*	Aug 1968/Jul 1968
Hendrix: *Electric Ladyland*	Nov 1968/Oct 1968

Listening Guide

Cream, "Sunshine of Your Love" Polydor 56286 (UK), ATCO 45-6544 (U.S.)

Words and music by Eric Clapton, Jack Bruce, and Pete Brown, produced by Felix Pappalardi. Reached #5 on the *Billboard* "Hot 100" chart in early 1968 (uk25).

FORM: Simple verse, with each verse employing the same 24-bar pattern, created by doubling each measure in the standard 12-bar blues structure so that each single measure becomes two measures. The song draws on the "lick blues" tradition of building a tune around a repeating riff or lick. Note the expansion of the 24-bar pattern that occurs in the last verse.

TIME SIGNATURE: 4/4.

INSTRUMENTATION: Electric guitar, bass, drums, and lead vocal.

0:00–0:16	**Introduction**, 8 mm.	2-mm. riff stated four times in guitar and bass. Note that the drum part employs no cymbals.
0:16–1:06	**Verse 1**, 24 mm.	Vocal enters as riff continues. Clapton and Bruce trade off singing vocal phrases. "It's gettin' near dawn . . ."
1:06–2:00	**Verse 2**, 26 mm.	A 2-mm. link precedes a repetition of the 24-mm. verse. Vocal trade-off continues and the verse is performed as before. "I'm with you my love . . ."
2:00–2:50	**Instr. Verse**, 24 mm.	Clapton blues-based guitar solo. After laying off the cymbals in the previous verses, Baker employs them heavily now.
2:50–4:08	**Verse 3**, 32 mm. and fade-out	This last verse is much more forceful, owing to the now copious use of cymbals carried over from the solo. The verse proceeds as before until "I've been waiting so long," where the 24-mm. structure is expanded by repeating this line to create a dramatic ending before the fade-out. "I'm with you my love . . ."

Cream's Blues Adaptations. One of Cream's best-known tracks is "Sunshine of Your Love," written by Clapton, Bruce, and lyricist Pete Brown (p5 uk25, 1968). The song is built around a central guitar figure (sometimes called a "riff" or "lick") that is repeated in the guitar and bass throughout much of the song. (The technique of building a blues number around a central riff is common in American electric blues.) In "Sunshine of Your Love," this central riff is combined with the 12-bar blues structure to create verses that repeat throughout the tune according to the simple verse formal design. The 12-bar pattern is doubled to twenty-four measures, although the proportions remain the same—the first 4-bar phrase is now 8 bars, and the second and third phrases are expanded in the same manner. The third phrase departs somewhat from the standard blues version, but is clearly derived from that pattern. By modifying elements within the 12-bar blues structural framework, Cream creates an original blues-rock song that builds on and expands traditional blues techniques and patterns.

The Jimi Hendrix Experience: Psychedelic Blues Meets the Avant-garde.

Seattle-born Jimi Hendrix is one of the most influential guitarists in the history of rock music. Hendrix spent the first half of the 1960s (with the exception of a short term of service in the U.S. Army) playing in various bands, including stints with Little Richard and the Isley Brothers. In 1964, he moved to New York, where he worked with soul singer Curtis Knight before forming his own band, Jimmy James and the Blue Flames. In July 1966, Animals bassist Chas Chandler saw Hendrix's act at Café Wha? in Greenwich Village and offered to manage the guitarist. Chandler brought Hendrix to London in September, where he formed the Jimi Hendrix Experience with Hendrix, drummer Mitch Mitchell, and bassist Noel Redding. Despite being an American, Hendrix first made his mark on the London psychedelic scene. By early 1967, the Experience's rendition of "Hey Joe" was number six on the UK charts, followed by "Purple Haze" (uk3) in May. The band's first album, *Are You Experienced?* (p5 uk2, 1967), was a tremendous success in the UK during the second half of 1967. It rose to the number-two spot behind *Sgt. Pepper*. Hendrix's success in the United States followed his appearance at the Monterey International Pop Festival in the summer of 1967 (discussed later). His first album was not released in the United States until August, and while it did well, "Purple Haze"

Jimi Hendrix was an innovative and explosive rock guitarist. His music displays a strong blues influence mixed with psychedelic elements and catchy lyrics and melodies. Hendrix used his guitar to produce a wide range of sounds, including his signature fuzz and feedback. His stage shows were exciting, improvisational, and often destructive.

reached only number sixty-five and "Foxey Lady" stalled at number sixty-seven on the American singles charts. By early 1968, *Axis: Bold as Love* was at number three in the United States (uk5), and the band followed up with *Electric Ladyland* (p1 uk6, 1968) and the compilation *Smash Hits* (uk4, 1968; p6, 1969). In the summer of 1969, just weeks before his legendary Woodstock performance, the Experience parted ways after Hendrix began to explore different material more based in blues. For the next year, Hendrix performed and recorded widely with many different musicians, including the group Band of Gypsys. On September 18, 1970, Jimi Hendrix died of a drug overdose, cutting short a career of less than four years in the mainstream spotlight.

"Purple Haze" and "Foxey Lady" from *Are You Experienced?* are good examples of Hendrix's distinctive blend of blues and pop. Both tracks employ chord progressions and melodic materials derived from electric blues to form effective pop "hooks." In "Purple Haze," the line, "S'cuse me while I kiss the sky," is followed by a catchy response in the guitar, just as the titular line "foxey lady!" is answered in a parallel manner by the guitar.

There are many examples of Hendrix's experimental music. "If 6 Was 9," from *Axis: Bold as Love*, runs more than five minutes, with three minutes of instrumental play-

Listening Guide

The Jimi Hendrix Experience, "Purple Haze" Reprise 0597 (U.S.), Track 604001 (UK)

Words and music by Jimi Hendrix, produced by Chas Chandler. Reached #65 on the *Billboard* "Hot 100" in 1967 (uk3). Contained on the album *Are You Experienced?*, which rose to #2 in the UK and #5 in the United States.

FORM: Simple verse, with contrasting instrumental bridge. The introduction plays an important role in the track, and it returns after the instrumental bridge, serving to relaunch the tune. The practice of using an instrumental bridge and returning to the introduction to set up the last verse are features that will become commonplace in later rock music.

TIME SIGNATURE: 4/4.

INSTRUMENTATION: Electric guitars, bass, drums, lead vocal, and extra spoken voices.

0:00–0:32	**Introduction**, 14 mm.	The first 2 mm. introduce the famous dissonant riff in the guitar and bass, followed by 8 mm. of blues-based melodic phrases on the guitar. The introduction concludes by setting up the chord progression that will follow in the verse.
0:32–0:52	**Verse 1**, 9 mm.	Vocal enters. Note call-and-response between the vocal ("S'cuse me") and the lead guitar at the end of the verse. "Purple haze all in my brain . . ."
0:52–1:12	**Verse 2**, 12 mm.	The first 9 mm. are as before, but then a 3-mm. transition ("Help me") leads into the guitar solo. "Purple haze all around . . ."
1:12–1:35	**Instrumental bridge**, 8 mm.	Guitar solo. While based on the blues, this solo also invokes sitar-like lines. Note speaking voices in the background.
1:35–1:53	**Return of introduction**, 8 mm.	A repetition of the melody from the intro.
1:53–2:12	**Verse 3**, 9 mm.	As before, "Purple haze all in my eyes . . ."
2:12–2:49	**Coda**, 17 mm. and fade	Music is drawn from the instrumental bridge.

ing featuring novel guitar sound effects and some counterculture narration. Perhaps Hendrix's most ambitious experimental track, "1983 (A Merman I Should Turn to Be)" from *Electric Ladyland*, clocks in at just under fourteen minutes. After about four minutes of the song proper (which is filled with backward tape effects), the band launches into a series of loose atmospheric instrumental sections that allow Hendrix, Mitchell, and Redding ample opportunity to shine individually before ending with a reprise of the song. Immediately following the track is the short electronic piece, "Moon, Turn the Tides . . . Gently, Gently Away," which adds a clear avant-garde final touch to "1983." Hendrix's experimentation in the recording studio (he often worked very closely with engineer Eddie Kramer) clearly extends the work done by others, especially the Beatles and the Beach Boys. His virtuosity as a guitarist served as a model for many important rock musicians who followed, and his sonic innovations employing feedback and the vibrato bar on the electric guitar were much imitated. His performances were flamboyant and often sexually suggestive or physically destructive—setting the guitar on fire or otherwise destroying it—and became the stuff of rock legend.

Performances That Launched a Career. While Jimi Hendrix is frequently remembered for his festival performances at the Monterey and Woodstock festivals, the first shows the Experience played were quite different. The band's first series of gigs were as the opening act for singer Johnny Hallyday (mentioned in Chapter 3 as the "French Elvis"). Halliday's brief tour of France in October of 1966 ended with a big show at L'Olympia in Paris. The Experience were allotted fifteen minutes playing time for each show. Mitch Mitchell has remarked that he was taken aback by the French audiences: "They don't clap. You'd finish off a number and . . . silence." The band played a private showcase gig in London immediately after the French tour, but then headed off the Germany for a few shows in Munich. The first show in the series of London performances that established the band's reputation was at the Bag O' Nails in Soho on November 25, 1966. Performances on the popular television programs *Ready Steady Go!* And *Top of the Pops* the next month helped push the band's first single "Hey Joe" (recorded directly after the French tour) into the UK top ten in early 1967.

Traffic and Van Morrison. At the beginning of 1967, the Spencer Davis Group was enjoying great success. In the previous six months, the band had two top-ten singles in both the United States and the UK. During that time, however, rumors had also circulated that eighteen-year-old Stevie Winwood would leave the group. The tremendous success of the Spencer Davis Group brought with it musical limitations that Winwood was eager to abandon in favor of exploring more "musicianly" concerns. Winwood quit the band and formed Traffic in April 1967 with drummer Jim Capaldi, guitarist Dave Mason, and flutist/saxophonist Chris Wood. The band's first single, "Paper Sun" (p94 uk5) was released in May 1967 and captured the whimsical character of emerging British flower power with its opening measures of sitar and upbeat vocal melody. The band's next single, "Hole in My Shoe" did even better, going to number two in the UK. By the end of 1967, the band had released its first album, *Mr. Fantasy*, which rose to number eight in the UK. With their second album, *Traffic* (p17 uk9, 1968), the group finally scored success in the United States, which increased with the release of *Last Exit* (p19, 1969). While the Spencer Davis Group had been rooted securely in rhythm and blues, Traffic experimented with a broad range of styles. Tracks from the first album blend psychedelic pop and blues ("Heaven Is in Your Mind") with Latin rhythms ("Dealer"), classical instrumentation ("No Face, No Name, No Number"), and jazz soloing ("Coloured Rain"). The group disbanded in early 1969, and Winwood went on to play with Clapton and Baker in Blind Faith before reforming Traffic with Wood and Capaldi in early 1970 (Traffic's music from the 1970s is discussed in the next chapter).

Irish singer-songwriter Van Morrison first hit the charts as a member of the band Them, whose "Baby Please Don't Go" (uk10, 1964) and "Here Comes the Night" (p24 uk2, 1965) enjoyed success in the UK. The band's recording of "Gloria"—the B-side of "Baby Please Don't Go"—became a garage-band classic and was covered most famously by Patti Smith (1976). By 1967, Morrison had set out on a solo career, and this move was given a substantial boost by the commercial success of "Brown Eyed Girl" (p10), a song that has been a staple of American radio ever since. As catchy as his hit songs could be, Morrison also had a more experimental side, which showed itself clearly on the 1968 album *Astral Weeks*. Recorded in New York in less than two days, the album's raw looseness influenced many later singer-songwriters, though it was more a critical than a commercial success. The tracks on *Astral Weeks* bring together a wide variety of styles, including acoustic folk music, jazz, classical, and rhythm and blues, and many of the tracks were recorded with top-notch studio players improvising in support of Morrison. This highly improvised dimension of the music has a certain aleatoric (chance) quality that was popular in both jazz and avantgarde performances of the 1960s. There are also connec-

Although Van Morrison may be better known for his more catchy pop songs, his psychedelic *Astral Weeks* (1968) is an influential album. Recorded in less than two days, this highly improvisational collection brings together many styles, including acoustic folk music, jazz, classical, and rhythm and blues. Here Morrison performs at New York's The Scene night club in 1969.

tions to the experimental aspects of performances by Pink Floyd or the aleatoric studio practices found on the Grateful Dead's *Anthem of the Sun*. The music is loose and improvisatory, but rarely dissonant or angular—it is impressionistic, jazzy, and filled with a sense of poetic mysticism. Morrison went on to be an important singer-songwriter in the 1970s, and we will consider his music further in Chapter 8.

Donovan and Psychedelic Folk. Born Donovan Philips Leitch, Donovan first attracted international attention as a traditional folksinger and songwriter with his 1965 hit single "Catch the Wind" (p23 uk4). Much like the music of Bob Dylan, Donovan's early folk music was strongly influenced by Woody Guthrie. As folk rock developed in mid-1965, Donovan adapted his music to the new style by using electric guitars, keyboards, bass, and drums in his arrangements. Among the many studio musicians who played on Donovan's recordings were future Led Zeppelin members Jimmy Page and John Paul Jones. Donovan enjoyed a series of hit singles in the UK and United States, including "Sunshine Superman" (p1 uk2, 1966) and "Mellow Yellow" (p2, 1966; uk8, 1967). When psychedelia and flower power emerged from regional underground scenes into mainstream culture in 1967, Donovan's gentle melodic sense, eclectic stylistic range, and often mystical lyrics made him a leading figure for hippie pacifism. His success continued with more hit singles including "Wear Your Hair Like Heaven" (p23, 1967) and "Hurdy Gurdy Man" (p5 uk4, 1968), the second of which features the playing not only of Page and Jones but also future Led Zeppelin drummer John Bonham.

With "Atlantis" (uk23, 1968; p7, 1969), Donovan reached the edge of counter-culture utopianism, reciting the tale of the lost continent in a manner suggesting that its lost wisdom might help rebuild Western culture. The song concludes with a long sing-along section similar to the end of the Beatles' "Hey Jude." Donovan remained active in the 1970s, releasing albums such as *Cosmic Wheels* (p25 uk15, 1973) and providing music for films, including Franco Zeffirelli's *Brother Sun, Sister Moon* (1973).

LOS ANGELES AND NEW YORK

The Byrds and Buffalo Springfield. The most important psychedelic subcultures were based in San Francisco and London, but other American cities also participated in the growth of the psychedelic movement. Along with the Mamas and the Papas and the Beach Boys, the Byrds were among the most successful bands to come out of Los Angeles in the mid-1960s. After the controversy over "Eight Miles High" in the summer of 1966, the group released *Fifth Dimension* (p24 uk27, 1966), which contained "Eight Miles High" and "Mr. Spaceman" (p36, 1966), the band's first attempt to mix rock with country music. While this was more the exception than the rule for the Byrds in 1966, by 1968 they had released *Sweetheart of the Rodeo*, often cited as a pivotal album in the development of country rock. By the end of 1967, David Crosby had left the group to join Hollies vocalist Graham Nash and guitarist Stephen Stills. Stills had enjoyed moderate success with Buffalo Springfield, whose single "For What It's Worth" had hit number seven on the U.S. charts in early 1967. Crosby, Stills, and Nash (sometimes joined by ex-Buffalo Springfield guitarist Neil Young) became one of the first supergroups of the 1970s. Their music will be considered in Chapter 8. As these established artists were heading off in new musical directions, other musicians were emerging from the Los Angeles scene.

Shown here performing in Germany in 1968, the Doors' music tended to focus on the darker side of psychedelia. Lead singer Jim Morrison (far right) was a student of poetry and literature and brought that sensibility to many of his lyrics with the band. While the band included a studio bassist on their recordings, during live performances keyboardist Ray Manzarek (second from the left) played the bass parts on a dedicated keyboard (note the topmost of the two keyboards in the photo).

The Doors and Jim Morrison: Turning to the Dark Side.

The Doors were formed in Los Angeles in 1965 by singer and lyricist Jim Morrison and keyboardist Ray Manzarek, taking their name from eighteenth-century British poet William Blake (via Aldous Huxley's book *The Doors of Perception*). Rounding out the lineup were guitarist Robbie Krieger and drummer John Densmore. The Doors first attracted attention with their hit single "Light My Fire" (p1 uk49, 1967). The foursome produced an often-moody brand of late 1960s blues-based psychedelia with a tendency to linger over the darker aspects of emotional life, perhaps best exemplified by "The End," a dramatic and shocking piece in which Morrison recites and then shouts his Oedipal desires. If most psychedelia in 1967 seemed to focus on the positive side of drug use—the path to higher consciousness and liberation—the Doors seemed determined to explore avenues opened up by the "bad trip," beginning with the first track on the first album, "Break on Through." Morrison's lyrics are filled with grotesque and unsettling images of alienation and repression, and his onstage antics took to a new level the bad-boy, nonconformist, overtly sexual image cultivated by Elvis Presley and Mick Jagger. With the band's third album, *Waiting for the Sun* (p1 uk16, 1968), Morrison introduced an alter ego, the Lizard King. The idea of a rock singer assuming an onstage persona would influence many other performers, including Alice Cooper, David Bowie, Peter Gabriel, and Madonna. While the group's music became increasingly refined over the course of the six studio albums from *The Doors* (p1, 1967) to *L.A. Woman* (p9 uk26, 1971), their style remained relatively stable as the band produced several hit singles, including "Hello, I Love You" (p1 uk15, 1968), "Touch Me" (p3, 1969), and "Love Her Madly" (p11, 1971). *L.A. Woman*, however, would be their last album, as Morrison died under mysterious circumstances in 1971.

Love, Iron Butterfly, and Vanilla Fudge.

Formed in 1965 by singer and guitarist Arthur Lee, Love played an important role in the Los Angeles psychedelic scene, although they never achieved the level of success enjoyed by groups like the Byrds or the Doors. Love was actually signed to Elektra before the Doors, and recommended the Doors to the record label. Love's first single, "My Little Red Book" (1966), was a rock cover version of a Burt Bacharach and Hal David song, and much of the group's other early music shows strong Byrds and Rolling Stones influences. In the wake of *Sgt. Pepper*, Love released their third and most celebrated album, *Forever Changes* (1967), which featured ambitious tracks, at times employing orchestral accompaniment, heady lyrics, and dense vocal harmonies.

As dark as the Doors could get, the heaviest band of the late 1960s was Iron Butterfly. Formed in San Diego in 1966, they bounded onto the scene with their second album, *In-a-Gadda-Da-Vida*, which hit number four in the United States during the summer of 1968. The seventeen-minute title track to this album is filled with extended organ, guitar, bass, and drum solos that would serve as the model for almost every live rock show in the following few years. The song's heavy, menacing opening riff and references to classical organ music (perhaps purposefully overdone for a melodramatic effect similar to a bad horror movie), established some of the characteristics that would develop into the early heavy metal music of Black Sabbath, Deep Purple, and even Led Zeppelin (see Chapter 8).

Back in New York, Vanilla Fudge developed a reputation for taking simple pop songs and turning them into elaborate and often lengthy cover versions. "You Keep Me Hangin' On" (p6 uk18, 1967) is a representative example: the band takes a two-minute song by the Supremes and Holland-Dozier-Holland and turns it into a five-minute psychedelic movement complete with dramatic dynamic shifts and sitar lines. The musical ambition exemplified by these psychedelic-symphonic cover versions made Vanilla Fudge, like many other groups discussed in this chapter, a significant, early influence for many of the progressive rock bands that would emerge in the 1970s.

Upstate Americana: Dylan and the Band.

Just as the Byrds were turning to country music, Bob Dylan made a similar turn in his music. Sidelined by a motorcycle crash in 1966, Dylan retreated to Woodstock, New York, where he continued his recording work with the Band. Drummer Levon Helm (the lone American), guitarist Robbie Robertson, bassist Rick Danko, pianist Richard Manuel, and organist Garth Hudson (all Canadian) had played the Ontario bar circuit behind rockabilly singer Ronnie Hawkins in the early 1960s and, without Helm, backed Dylan on his world tour in 1965 and 1966. The extensive sessions from this period between Dylan and the Band were released in 1975 as *The Basement Tapes* (p7 uk8). Albums released by these musicians in 1968, the Band's *Music from Big Pink* (p30) and Dylan's *John Wesley Harding* (p2 uk1), were collaborations that became important records for the emergence of country rock. It might seem strange that a band mostly made up of Canadians could play such a central role in redefining American rock, but the members of the Band were experienced students of rural American musical styles. Just as it took a loose collection of British bands to introduce many Americans to their own electric blues during the mid-1960s, a group of Canadians helped introduce American audiences to musical Americana during the latter part of the decade.

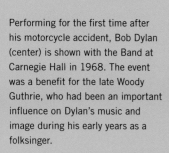

Performing for the first time after his motorcycle accident, Bob Dylan (center) is shown with the Band at Carnegie Hall in 1968. The event was a benefit for the late Woody Guthrie, who had been an important influence on Dylan's music and image during his early years as a folksinger.

A WOODSTOCK NATION: FESTIVALS, AUDIENCES, AND RADIO

Do You Know the Way to Monterey? Large, open-air music festivals became an important element of rock culture for the first time in the late 1960s. In the spring of 1967, John Phillips of the Mamas and the Papas and record-company executive Lou Adler organized the Monterey International Pop Festival, modeling it on the already established Monterey Jazz Festival. Monterey Pop was the first important international rock festival, and it brought together bands from San Francisco, Los Angeles, and London to perform on June 16–18 at the Monterey County Fairgrounds in California. Jefferson Airplane, the Grateful Dead, Big Brother and the Holding Company, the Byrds, the Mamas and the Papas, the Animals, the Who, and many others played for free, receiving only travel expenses. Jimi Hendrix's appearance introduced him to musicians and businessmen in the United States and was crucial to his subsequent success. The Mamas and the Papas performed for the last time in their original lineup. The Beach Boys' decision not to play was widely thought to have hurt their reputation within the burgeoning counterculture. Otis Redding, backed by Booker T. & the MG's, wowed the hippie audience with the Stax brand of southern soul. While attendance figures for any outdoor event often vary widely, most responsible accounts agree that between 55,000 and 90,000 people attended the festival. In many ways, Monterey was simply an extension of the regular hippie concert events in San Francisco that began in 1965. While the San Francisco events featured mostly local and regional acts, the Monterey Festival placed a broad range of international acts on the same bill. This provided a model for the open-air rock festival that would be followed by major concert events staged in Newport (1968 and 1969), Miami (1968), Toronto (1969), Atlanta (1969), Denver (1969), and many other locales. Monterey Pop was filmed by D. A. Pennebaker, and the release of the *Monterey Pop* film in December 1968 (as well as a not-very-representative album) further added to the importance of the festival.

Good Trip, Bad Trip: Woodstock and Altamont. If Monterey marked the beginning of the era of large outdoor rock festivals, Woodstock was its peak. Held on a large patch of farmland in Bethel, New York, August 15–17, 1969, the Woodstock Music and Art Festival drew at least 400,000 hippies. The roadways in upstate New York were so unexpectedly crowded that many had to be closed to avoid large-scale regional gridlock. Tickets had been offered for sale in advance, but most fans turned up at the event expecting to get in for free. The meager security forces were overwhelmed—all in the spirit of hippie fellowship—and most people ended up crashing the event without paying. In addition, heavy rain stopped the show and created muddy conditions and other issues. Despite these potentially devastating financial and logistical setbacks, the event was tremendously successful, turning the festival's slogan, "Three Days of Peace and Music," into an ideal that represented the power and influence of the hippie counterculture. Many important American and British bands performed (the Grateful Dead, Jimi Hendrix, Jefferson Airplane, Janis Joplin, the Who), while performances by Santana; Crosby, Stills, and Nash;

1970S LIVE-PERFORMANCE FILM: JIMI HENDRIX AT WOODSTOCK

Viewing Rock

As rock became oriented toward more ambitious, lengthy performances in the late 1960s, documentary films provided an appropriate forum to display visual performances. Among the most important rock documentaries from this time is *Woodstock*, a film released in 1970 depicting the famous August 1969 festival in upstate New York. Of the many iconic performances associated with *Woodstock*, perhaps the most famous is that of Jimi Hendrix, which

mances of the Hendrix segment have also been released independently of the larger film.) Hendrix's appearance in the "director's cut" begins with a rendition of "Voodoo Chile (A Slight Return)," which segues into his famous rendition of "The Star-Spangled Banner," and then transitions into "Purple Haze." In some instances, Hendrix is shown as a guitar virtuoso, performing tricks such as placing his right hand over top of the strings or playing the instrument with his teeth (1 and 2).

Yet, there are many instances when the sound of the film includes blistering guitar performances, while the video focuses solely on Hendrix as a person, highlighting his body movements and facial expressions (3).

This is especially evident during the rendition of "The Star-Spangled Banner," when the pink, white, and turquoise of Hendrix's outfit form an interesting correlation to the red, white, and blue of the American flag. In the context of the film, however, Hendrix's performance is used to signal the aftermath of the three-day festival, showing various efforts to clean up the mess of more than half-a-million hippies camping on

occurred at the end of the festival and also serves as the finale to the film. Performing on Monday morning after much of the crowd had dispersed, Hendrix led a makeshift group called Gypsy Suns and Rainbows. Much of the footage focuses on Hendrix performing without accompaniment. (Complete perfor-

the mud-soaked farmland (4).

As more than half of the crowd had left before this performance, the video footage is an important record of Hendrix's historic part of this program, exhibiting the growing importance of documentary films in the reception of rock during the 1970s.

Joe Cocker; and Sly and the Family Stone effectively introduced these acts to a much wider audience. The 1970 release of Michael Wadleigh's documentary film, *Woodstock*, and a multidisc live album helped make the event a financial success and, like the Monterey film and album, added to the event's significance.

After large-scale gatherings in Monterey and Woodstock, the era symbolically ended on December 6, 1969, with a festival organized by the Rolling Stones at the Altamont Speedway in Livermore, California. The original plan was that the Grateful Dead would sneak the Stones into San Francisco's Golden Gate Park for a free surprise show for the hippie faithful. The Stones saw the show as a way to thank loyal fans and announced the concert at a press conference a few days beforehand. The original plans were canceled when San Francisco city officials got word of the event, but a venue was located out of town at an old racetrack. Two decisions seem to have led to the disaster that followed: a motorcycle gang, the Hells Angels, was used to provide security; and the Stones waited until nightfall to begin their portion of the show, leaving an open spot in the day's program that left concertgoers with nothing to do. The Stones waited until dark because they had planned a light show and were filming a movie, later released as *Gimme Shelter* in 1970. The Hells Angels were without some of their senior members, and a few confrontations got out of control, with fans being beaten if they got too close to the stage (Jefferson Airplane's Marty Balin was knocked out cold at one point). When Meredith Hunter, an eighteen-year-old black fan, allegedly pulled a gun at the front of the stage, he was beaten and stabbed to death—the events were captured on film and took place in front of the band's eyes as they tried to perform. Many writers have since pointed out that the sometimes haphazard organization of these events meant it was only a matter of time before something tragic occurred. Nevertheless, Hunter's murder has caused many to view Altamont as the event that marked the end of the hippie era.

Richie Havens performing at Woodstock. Although the event was dominated by rock-oriented groups, Havens was the festival's first act. Due in part to travel delays and scheduling issues, Havens kept the large crowd captivated for several hours with a stunning solo performance.

Festivals in the UK and Europe. As Monterey had expanded on Family Dog events and outdoor gatherings like the Human Be-In, so too did the August 1967 Festival of Flower Children at Woburn Abbey expand the 14-Hour Technicolor Dream for British hippies. This three-day outdoor event included performances by Jimi Hendrix, Tomorrow, the Jeff Beck Group, and the Small Faces, among others. (The Duchess of Bedford attended, mistakenly believing it would be a flower show.) Rock acts also appeared on the bill of the National Jazz and Blues Festival, an annual event that had begun in 1961. In August 1967, the festival was held in Windsor and included Cream, Tomorrow, Donovan, and the Crazy World of Arthur Brown. Other large-scale concerts followed in France, Italy, and Switzerland. The most important later British festivals were held in London's Hyde Park in July 1969 (organized by the Rolling Stones to honor the recently deceased Brian Jones), and the Isle of Wight Festival in August 1970. The Isle of Wight festivals began in 1968, when about 10,000 people enjoyed a one-day bill that included the Crazy World of Arthur Brown and Jefferson Airplane. The 1969 festival was a far more ambitious enterprise: expanded to two days and including Bob Dylan and the Band on a roster along with the Who, the Moody Blues, and the Nice, it drew about 150,000 attendees. Conservative estimates place the attendance of the enormous 1970 Isle of Wight Festival at 500,000, and this festival remains among the largest ever to take place in Great Britain. The program included a mix of established artists and emerging acts that would make their name in the years that immediately followed. The Doors, Donovan, and Jimi Hendrix (in his last public performance) were joined by Emerson, Lake & Palmer, Jethro Tull, and Chicago.

While Woodstock reinforced the positive side of the hippie ideal, the concert at Altamont seemed to reveal a darker side of the psychedelic experience. As the Rolling Stones performed, violence erupted between a fan and members of the Hells Angels, resulting in a tragic stabbing death.

The Fracturing of the American Radio Audience: AM versus FM.

Psychedelic music was never meant to appeal to young teens or preteens. Like folk, it was music targeted at college-age listeners. With the development of free-form FM radio in 1967 and its spread to radio markets across the country, an important distinction between single-oriented AM pop and album-oriented FM rock began to develop: younger listeners tended toward the AM dial, while their older siblings listened to FM. By the end of the decade, the free-form format was becoming somewhat more organized, and by the mid-1970s the increasing constraints of the album-oriented rock (AOR) format sparked great debate within the rock community. In the late 1960s, however, it was possible to tune in an AM station and hear the Monkees, the Fifth Dimension, the Association, and many other hit-oriented artists, while the FM dial might play longer album tracks by groups that did not have hit singles. There was some crossover: the Doors' "Light My Fire" charted as a pop single, for instance, in an edited version that removed much of the instrumental soloing from the center section.

This separation by age group within the rock market foreshadowed the even greater fragmentation of that market in the 1970s, even among FM rock stations. As we will see in Chapter 8, rock music in the 1970s took the psychedelic era as a

Sound Check

Artist	Song	Sound
The Beach Boys	**Good Vibrations (1966)**	**Form: contrasting verse-chorus, three new sections** **Unconventional formal design** **"Space age" theremin sound on chorus** **Form achieved by splicing together tape from different performances**
The Beatles	**A Day in the Life (1967)**	**Form: compound ABA** **Two separate songs stitched together with an interlude** **Interlude is avant-garde string performance, starting with lowest note and ending with highest** **Reverb used to depict a dream state**
Jefferson Airplane	**White Rabbit (1967)**	**Form: AABA** **Bolero rhythm** **Last verse expanded to create a musical climax** *Alice in Wonderland* **theme**
Cream	**Sunshine of Your Love (1968)**	**Form: simple verse** **12-bar blues doubled to make 24 measures for each verse (with some extensions)** **Two measure riff** **Lead vocals trade between Jack Bruce and Eric Clapton**
The Jimi Hendrix Experience	**Purple Haze (1967)**	**Form: simple verse (modified)** **Introduction music also serves as basis for the bridge** **Virtuosic blues-based guitar throughout** **Extra spoken vocals add to the psychedelic aura**

point of departure, taking musical features that coexisted within psychedelia and separating them out for further development. It is to this expansion and fragmentation of psychedelia that we turn next.

For Additional Online Resources, visit:
digital.wwnorton.com/whatsthatsound5

FURTHER READING

Doug Bradley and Craig Werner, *We Gotta Get Out of This Place: The Soundtrack of the Vietnam War* (University of Massachusetts Press, 2015).

Nick Bromell, *Tomorrow Never Knows: Rock and Psychedelics in the 1960s* (University of Chicago Press, 2002).

Ray Coleman, *Clapton! An Authorized Biography* (Pan Books, 1995).

Jim DeRogatis, *Kaleidoscope Eyes: Psychedelic Rock from the '60s to the '90s* (Citadel, 1996).

James Henke and Parke Puterbaugh, eds., *I Want to Take You Higher: The Psychedelic Era 1965–1969* (Chronicle Books, 1997).

Michael Hicks, *Sixties Rock: Garage, Psychedelic, and Other Satisfactions* (University of Illinois Press, 2000).

Sarah Hill, *San Francisco and the Long 60s* (Bloomsbury, 2016).

Jerry Hopkins and Daniel Sugerman, *No One Here Gets Out Alive* (Grand Central Publishing, 2006).

Jesse Jarnow, *Heads: A Biography of Psychedelic America* (Da Capo, 2016).

Michael Lang, with Holly George-Warren, *The Road to Woodstock* (HarperCollins, 2009).

Timothy Leary, Ralph Metzner, and Richard Alpert, *The Psychedelic Experience: A Manual Based on the Tibetan Book of the Dead* [1964] (Citadel, 2000).

Ray Manzarek, *Light My Fire: My Life with the Doors* (Century, 1998).

John McDermott with Eddie Kramer, *Hendrix: Setting the Record Straight* (Warner Books, 1992).

Jon Savage, 1966: The Year the Decade Exploded (Faber & Faber, 2016).

Gene Sculatti and Davin Seay, *San Francisco Nights: The Psychedelic Music Trip, 1965–68* (St. Martin's, 1985).

Joel Selvin, *Summer of Love: The Inside Story of LSD, Rock and Roll, Free Love, and High Times in the Wild West* (Cooper Square, 1999).

Grace Slick with Andrea Cagan, *Somebody to Love? A Rock-and-Roll Memoir* (Warner Books, 1998).

Derek Taylor, *It Was Twenty Years Ago Today* (Simon & Schuster, 1987).

Chris Welch with Steve Winwood, *Steve Winwood: Roll with It* (Perigee, 1990).

Tom Wolfe, *The Electric Kool-Aid Acid Test* [1968] (Picador, 2008).

By the early 1970s, the counterculture of the late 1960s had become mainstream. The peace signs, long hair, tie dye, incense, and hippie values that had been found mostly on college campuses were now popular in middle-class suburbs and shopping malls across the country. This commodification of counterculture might have been a signal that some of the problems that had divided America in the 1960s were "solved" in the 1970s. However, people continued to question these solutions and expose new problems that kept the country in a state of turmoil throughout the decade.

In the first years of the 1970s, Richard Nixon reached an agreement with the North Vietnamese, effectively ending the Vietnam War, which had been one of the most divisive issues of the 1960s. Though its real horrors were over, the scars from Vietnam ran deep. Many called it the first war America lost and questioned the government's attention to "the people" in matters of policy. This skepticism exploded in 1974, when a Republican break-in to the Democratic offices at the Watergate office complex in Washington, D.C., was covered up by members of the Nixon White House. As a result of the ensuing scandal, Nixon became the first president in history to resign his position.

Jimmy Carter promised America a brighter future and was elected in 1976, but his presidency was plagued with problems. In the last few years of the decade, the American economy was stagnant and inflation was high, a situation so pronounced that economists coined a new term to describe it: "stagflation." Part of the problem was a fuel shortage, leading to long lines at gas stations and a general sense of an "energy crisis." Nuclear power seemed to offer a viable alternative, but a 1979 accident at the Three Mile Island nuclear power plant in Harrisburg, Pennsylvania, raised public fears about the safety of such facilities. Finally, a political revolution in Iran resulted in the taking of American hostages—a situation that gave more than a hint of political problems to come in the Middle East.

As mentioned earlier, the hippie values of the 1960s became mainstream in the 1970s. Feminism became known as "women's liberation"—or simply "women's lib"—in popular culture. Gloria Steinem established Ms. magazine in 1972, providing a high-profile media forum for feminist issues. In a long-running series of advertisements beginning in 1969, Virginia Slims promoted a cigarette made especially for women with the slogan, "You've come a long way, baby." Women's lib also found its way into sports and mainstream music. Tennis pro Bobby Riggs challenged Billie Jean King to a "Battle of the Sexes" match in 1973, claiming that a man could easily beat a woman (he lost), and in 1972 Helen Reddy won a Grammy for the feminist anthem, "I Am Woman."

Advocates for gay rights also became more visible in pop culture. After the 1969 "Stonewall Riots" erupted in reaction to a police raid on a New York City gay club, the movement organized and worked to change state laws prohibiting homosexual activity. An important step forward occurred when the American Psychological Association removed homosexuality from its list of diseases in 1973.

debuted in 1971 and addressed many of the burning issues of the time. Set in the home of a working-class New York City family, the show's central character was Archie Bunker, a middle-aged, poorly educated bigot. Archie frequently, and humorously, locked horns with those around him, including his liberal, college-educated son-in-law, Michael (whom he called "Meathead"), his women's lib–inspired daughter, Gloria, and even his bighearted but somewhat dim-witted wife, Edith. Archie sometimes tangled with neighbor George Jefferson on issues of race. Jefferson was Archie's black counterpart—just as bigoted but markedly more successful in his career. In 1975, *The Jeffersons* became the first *All in the Family* spin-off, followed by *Maude*, whose central character was a strong-willed woman who had also traded barbs with Archie.

for themselves without the support of a husband was *The Mary Tyler Moore Show*. From its first episode in 1970, the show consistently dealt with issues that women faced in the workplace, though these were usually handled in a light-hearted manner. By mid-decade, *Chico and the Man* was raising the country's awareness of Hispanic life, making television programming more diverse than it had ever been.

The 1970s also saw the rise of rock-music television, a step forward from 1960s teen-oriented shows such as *American Bandstand*. Brill Building mogul Don Kirshner produced a new series in 1972, *In Concert* (later called *Rock Concert*), that featured live performances by leading rock bands and artists. *The Midnight Special* debuted the next year, featuring famous radio disc jockey Wolfman Jack. R&B found

Originating as a spin-off of the popular *All in the Family* television series, *The Jeffersons* portrayed an upwardly mobile black family led by George Jefferson. Played by Sherman Hemsley, George was as much a bigot as Archie Bunker had been in *All in the Family*, with much of the humor based on Jefferson's absurdly racist and otherwise foolish outbursts and proclamations, frequently deflated by wife, Louise, played by Isabel Sanford.

each city fighting for listeners (and advertising revenue). As FM developed, AM radio was increasingly the home of preteen pop, oldies, and what was left of traditional network-style programming. As the decade progressed, FM rock radio became more tightly formatted, allowing the disc jockeys less control over what was played and reducing their influence on music and culture.

Outer space remained a fascination for American moviegoers, though it now had a definite hippie tinge. When George Lucas's *Star Wars* appeared in 1977, record crowds

Throughout the 1970s, blacks struggled with whites, men struggled with women, and gays struggled with straights. However, these groups were standing closer to each other than ever before. If the '60s was about the problems of segregation (or division), the '70s was about the problems of diversity. As we will see, this diversity was reflected in the music of the time. Folk and progressive rock, disco and punk, rhythm and blues, and funk all fought for—and received—attention. Every social group, it seemed, had a band. And every band had an audience.

The trio of principal actors for the first *Star Wars* trilogy included Mark Hamill (Luke Skywalker), Harrison Ford (Han Solo), and Carrie Fisher (Princess Leia), shown here. While Ford went on to many other notable roles (including the intrepid archeologist Indiana Jones), the roles of Skywalker and Leia defined the careers of Hamill and Fisher. The trio reprised these roles nearly forty years later in 2016's *Star Wars: The Force Awakens*.

291

THE GROWING ROCK MONSTER

CHAPTER PREVIEW

- Rock music styles of the mid-1970s traced their influences to the psychedelic music of the late '60s. Other distinct styles emerged from the eclectic blend of 1960s rock.

- The hippie aesthetic denotes an attempt by rock musicians to make their music as artistically and musically ambitious as possible.

- British blues-based music, blended with folk and classical elements, fueled Led Zeppelin and Deep Purple. The Allman Brothers and Lynyrd Skynyrd added elements from America's southern culture to their blues-driven rock.

- Progressive rock bands like Yes, Jethro Tull, and ELP combined rock with classical music to develop an ambitious style that is often virtuosic.

- Steely Dan's jazz-rock style was influenced by jazz artist Miles Davis. The jazz-rock of Steely Dan developed out of the combination of rock with late 1960s jazz, pioneered by Davis. Jazz-oriented horn sections were featured in the music of Chicago and Blood, Sweat & Tears.

- David Bowie and Alice Cooper created unique personae for their dramatic stage shows.

- Singer-songwriters James Taylor and Carole King made the song and the singer the central focus of their music, as did British artists such as Elton John and Cat Stevens.

- Late '60s artists the Byrds, Bob Dylan, and the Band influenced the Eagles, who also blended elements of country music with slick vocals and potent pop songs.

Though Led Zeppelin is usually considered primarily a blues-based band, their music at times incorporates classical elements as well. "Stairway to Heaven" uses a quasi-classical guitar introduction accompanied by a recorder ensemble, while "The Rain Song" and "Kashmir" both employ (sometimes simulated) orchestral strings.

The late 1960s provided fertile music-stylistic ground for rock musicians in the 1970s. Most of the styles that we will explore in this chapter grow out of some aspect of '60s rock, though elements that coexisted within psychedelia in the '60s get increasingly separated out and developed as distinct styles in the '70s. The first half of the 1970s is characterized by bands still experimenting musically and testing the limits of the rock style. The second half of the decade, however, is somewhat more controversial. As the stylistic range of rock music was expanding over the course of the decade, the business of rock music was also growing and transforming from a business owned and run mostly by entertainment companies into a business owned and run by multinational corporations with little previous involvement in music. For some writers, the stylistic and corporate expansions are linked, such that one way of telling the story of rock in the 1970s is to cast it as a chronicle of rock music in decline (similar to one view of the early 1960s as described in Chapter 3). According to this interpretation, most of what's best about music in the late 1960s gets progressively corrupted by big money and even bigger egos, all motivated by the corporate bottom line, resulting in the much-despised corporate rock of the late 1970s, which is dismissed as a formulaic exploitation of rock designed only to make money—music that has sold its rock and roll soul. One problem with this interpretation of rock history is that the music of many of the bands these writers tend to hate—Led Zeppelin, Deep Purple, and Jethro Tull from earlier in the decade, for instance, and Bad Company, Boston, Kansas, and Foreigner from later—has become the core of "classic rock" radio format as it developed throughout the 1990s. For many young listeners, the rock music of the 1970s that we will consider in this chapter and Chapter 10 is not seen as a decline from anything, and in fact, its connection to 1960s rock is often forgotten or only dimly acknowledged.

As we consider rock in the 1970s then, we are faced with at least two interpretations of this music: one that sees much classic rock as a corruption, and thus tends to celebrate the underground punk scene during the first half of the decade and the emergence of punk and new wave in the second half; and another view that understands classic rock almost entirely in terms of the way it has been recast by FM radio and cable television in the period since about 1990. Both these perspectives have their problems: in the first case, the connection to the 1960s is acknowledged but misunderstood, and in the second, the music that has come to represent the 1970s via the classic rock radio often leaves important music out, mostly because some tracks are too long to be accommodated within current radio formats. This chapter will explore rock music in the first half of the 1970s with an eye toward the ways in which this music develops out of the psychedelic music we studied in Chapter 7. Chapter 10 focuses on the second half of the decade, charting the growth of the business side of rock and examining the development of punk and new wave music during the 1970s. Chapter 9 will focus on black pop, disco, and reggae during the same period. In this chapter, we will track each 1970s style out of its '60s roots and follow its development during the decade. After studying this chapter and the next two, you can decide for yourself if either of the interpretive positions briefly outlined here should be rehabilitated, incorporated into another view, or abandoned entirely.

THE HIPPIE AESTHETIC

Psychedelic Legacies. One of the most important changes brought about in the 1966 to 1969 period by artists such as the Beach Boys, the Beatles, and Bob Dylan was to change the focus of rock music from the single to the album, and from dancing music to listening music. While hit singles did not go away—in fact, as we've already seen, some psychedelic groups had hit singles—there was a growing sense that singles were a distinctly different part of the business. The focus of bands in the years after *Sgt. Pepper's Lonely Hearts Club Band* was increasingly fixed on creating albums that provided a musically provocative listening experience—in short, an album was a "trip."

As discussed in Chapter 7, musicians expanded rock's stylistic range by incorporating elements drawn from classical music, electronic music, and jazz. Musicians also came to depend increasingly on the recording studio as a creative tool, producing records that would have been difficult to reproduce live in many cases (at least back then). By the early 1970s, this focus on musical and technological craft, combined with a distinctly artistic approach to music-making (even among those groups who cultivated a no-nonsense, hard-rocking image), led to an aesthetic approach to rock that will be called the "hippie aesthetic." The basic idea behind the hippie aesthetic is that the rock musician is an artist who has a responsibility to produce sophisticated music using whatever means are at his or her disposal. The music should stand up to repeated listening and the lyrics should deal with important issues or themes. Musical prowess is especially valued, and fans begin voting in annual polls sponsored by music magazines according to categories like Best Guitarist, Best Keyboardist, Best Drummer, Best Bassist, and Best Vocalist (in addition to typical categories like Best Album and Best New Act). Polls like this had been common for years in jazz publications (*DownBeat* especially), where musical virtuosity and improvisatory fluency were often highly valued. Now rock musicians and their fans began taking themselves and their music just as seriously.

The hippie aesthetic is central to understanding what connects a wide variety of 1970s rock styles; as strange as it may sometimes seem, artists as diverse as Yes, the Eagles, the Allman Brothers Band, Steely Dan, and even Alice Cooper share elements of a common aesthetic approach. The hippie aesthetic also helps us realize that seventies rock is a clear development of psychedelia, making the period from about 1966 to 1979 seem much more unified than it is typically assumed to be. When we consider music in the 1980s in later chapters, we will also see how aspects of the hippie aesthetic surface even in the work of artists who seem to be soundly rejecting it. For now, however, we will begin by considering how sixties roots and the hippie aesthetic influence the music of the British blues rockers.

BLUES-BASED BRITISH ROCK

The Rolling Stones, Cream, and the Yardbirds. Blues-based rock music coming out of Britain in the 1970s was an important extension of earlier blues-influenced rock. Blues music, especially the Chicago electric blues of musicians like

Muddy Waters and Howlin' Wolf, was central to much rock music of the 1960s, especially in the UK. As discussed in Chapter 5, groups like the Rolling Stones brought this style back to America, or perhaps more specifically, they introduced blues to white American teenagers. In the wake of the Stones came the Yardbirds, a group that at various points featured Eric Clapton, Jeff Beck, and Jimmy Page. In the early 1970s, British bands like Deep Purple, Led Zeppelin, and Black Sabbath built on this stylistic foundation established by the Stones, the Yardbirds, and Cream. The Stones themselves enjoyed tremendous commercial success during this period by returning to their blues roots after a brief foray into psychedelia. Albums such as *Sticky Fingers* (p1 uk1, 1971), *Exile on Main Street* (p1 uk1, 1972), and *Goat's Head Soup* (p1 uk1, 1973) were wildly popular on both sides of the Atlantic, bringing the Stones out of the Beatles' shadow and positioning them as one of the most important groups to make the transition from the 1960s to the 1970s. Yardbirds alumni also remained active: Clapton continued as a solo artist after his stints with Cream and Derek and the Dominoes, emerging with the hit single, "I Shot the Sheriff" (p1 uk9, 1974), and Jeff Beck led a succession of bands, including the Jeff Beck Group and Beck, Bogert & Appice, that tended toward a jazz-fusion approach. Mixing blues roots with psychedelic sounds and heavy rock volume, Jimmy Page played an important role in continuing the guitar virtuosity and showmanship standards set by Clapton and Hendrix during the 1960s. Drafted into the Yardbirds toward the end of the band's career, Page was the only band member left by 1969. In order to fulfill a series of performance obligations, Page called on bassist John Paul Jones, a seasoned session musician, and two newcomers: vocalist Robert Plant and drummer John Bonham. After working for a short time under the name the New Yardbirds, the band changed their name to Led Zeppelin.

Led Zeppelin: Blues, Folk, and Psychedelia Take the Next Step. With a string of eight number-one albums in the UK and six number ones in the United States, Led Zeppelin was among the most successful new British groups of the 1970s. Page co-wrote most of the group's music (often with Robert Plant providing the lyrics), and, deeply devoted to the album format, the band was resistant to releasing tracks as singles. When Page first approached Plant about forming a band, he described his vision as a blend of traditional electric blues, acoustic folk, and a fair amount of experimentation. Over the years, listeners and critics have focused on the heavier elements of the group's music, forgetting other aspects of their catalog. For example, a blend between electric and acoustic instrumentation is clear on the group's first two albums, *Led Zeppelin* (p10 uk6, 1969) and *Led Zeppelin II* (p1 uk1, 1970). On the first record, "Babe I'm Gonna Leave You" is a reflection of the band's acoustic tendencies, while "Good Times, Bad Times" shows off a harder edge. The more psychedelic side comes out in "Dazed and Confused," a staple of the band's live shows that featured Page playing his guitar with a violin bow. A blend of the harder elements and psychedelia can also be found in "Whole Lotta Love."

This blend of acoustic, blues, and psychedelic elements can also be found in what is arguably Led Zeppelin's best-known track, "Stairway to Heaven," from their fourth, untitled album (p2 uk1, 1972). The song begins with an acoustic guitar passage and introduces a chorus of recorders followed by Robert Plant's vocals. This texture continues for the first two minutes of the song. As the arrangement slowly builds, electric twelve-string guitar, electric piano, bass, and drums are added. The

Led Zeppelin's Robert Plant (vocals) and Jimmy Page (guitar) in performance. The band combined complex arrangements with guitar mastery, and Page's playing displayed strong blues and folk roots. Although they were known for their harder, electrified music, Led Zeppelin often used acoustic instruments and produced quieter, simpler songs.

final section of the song moves into heavy rock, featuring a blues-influenced electric guitar solo from Page and Plant's distinctive high wailing vocals. The lyrics to "Stairway to Heaven" deal with the topic of spiritual enlightenment, a perennial concern among hippies of the late 1960s, and a recurrent theme in 1970s rock. The band would later return to themes of spirituality and the wisdom of the ancients and the East, most famously in "Kashmir" from *Physical Graffiti* (pl uk1, 1975).

Led Zeppelin lyrics often focus on sexual themes as well. Plant's swaggering on "Whole Lotta Love" and "Black Dog" take the playful hokum blues lyrics of songs like "Shake, Rattle, and Roll" beyond metaphor, making direct references to sexuality. Page produced all of the band's albums and was especially masterful at creating a thick sonic palette by double-tracking vocals, creating deep reverb for Bonham's drum tracks, and layering electric guitars—adding one after another, each playing distinct parts. Led Zeppelin continued to perform widely throughout the 1970s, releasing albums such as *Houses of the Holy* (pl uk1, 1973), *Presence* (pl uk1, 1976), and *In Through the Out Door* (pl uk1, 1979). The group disbanded after the tragic alcohol-related death of John Bonham in September 1980.

As we saw in our discussion of Cream's "Sunshine of Your Love" in Chapter 7, adapting blues practices to rock often resulted in tracks that strayed far from the aesthetic of traditional blues. Led Zeppelin's 1969 track "Whole Lotta Love" provides another chance to see this transformation at work and gives a sense of how British bands combined the blues with other elements. Originally credited to Jimmy Page and Robert Plant, the song is an adaptation of a Willie Dixon number called "You Need Love." (After some legal wrangling, it is now credited to Dixon and all four members of Led Zeppelin.) While blues is clearly a central component of "Whole Lotta Love," elements of psychedelia, and features that anticipate later 1970s rock, can be found in the song. It begins as a simple verse-chorus form, presenting two verse-chorus pairs based on the same music after the brief guitar-riff introduction. A long central section follows—longer, in fact, than all the music that precedes it. This section uses panning across the stereo field to make it seem as if the sound is swirling in circles. Vocal moaning from Plant creates a distinctively psychedelic flavor, while Page's aggressive guitar solo continues the psychedelic blues-rock

Listening Guide

Led Zeppelin, "Whole Lotta Love" Atlantic 2690

Words and music by Jimmy Page, Robert Plant, John Paul Jones, John Bonham, and Willie Dixon; produced by Jimmy Page. Released as a single that rose to #4 on the *Billboard* "Hot 100" chart in late 1969.

FORM: Compound AABA. The A sections follow simple verse-chorus form, with verse and chorus based on the same musical material. An extended central section forms the B section, leading to a return of the A section and a coda, which begins with a vocal "cadenza" in free time before the riff kicks back in and the song fades out.

TIME SIGNATURE: 4/4.

INSTRUMENTATION: Electric guitars, bass, drums, lead and backup vocals.

	0:00–0:11	**Introduction**, 4 mm.	Begins with guitar alone, playing 2-bar blues-derived riff. Bass joins for the second time through this riff.
A	0:11–0:35	**Verse 1**, 9 mm.	Lead vocal enters, riff continues in guitar and bass. "You need coolin' . . ."
	0:35–0:47	**Chorus**, 4 mm.	Drums enter, as backup vocals provide vocal hook. Note sliding guitar effect in call-and-response to vocal. "Got a whole lotta love . . ."
A	0:47–1:10	**Verse 2**, 9 mm.	As before, except that drums now continue from previous section. "You been learnin'. . ."
	1:10–1:21	**Chorus**, 4 mm.	As before, but the fourth bar of the chorus serves as the first bar of the central section that follows.
B	1:21–3:22	**Central section**, 45 mm.	39 bars of spacey psychedelia. Drums keep a light beat, as guitar sounds and vocal wails move from side to side, amid avant-garde sound effects. An aggressive 6-bar guitar break concludes this section.
A	3:22–3:50	**Verse 3**, 11 mm.	As in verse 2, but extended by 2 bars at the end. "You've been coolin' . . ."
	3:50–4:00	**Chorus**, 4 mm.	As before. "Got a whole lotta love . . ."
	4:00–5:30	**Coda**, 24 mm.	Vocal "cadenza" in free time begins this final section, and then the song's riff returns as Plant improvises vocally and the song fades out.

virtuosity associated with Eric Clapton and Jimi Hendrix. The song then returns to the verse-chorus pair, presented a third time with only slight alterations. The track ends with a coda, which moves from a free-form Plant vocal phrase (a kind of vocal "cadenza" in which the music stops and Plant provides a solo flourish), to a return of the tune's guitar riff and fade-out.

The overall formal structure of "Whole Lotta Love" follows a pattern that became common among rock bands in the 1970s. After two verse-chorus pairs, a contrasting section occurs: this section might be a guitar, sax, or keyboard solo over the verse material, or it may consist of entirely new material. A return to the verse-chorus pair or the verse often concludes this pattern. If the verse-chorus pairs are thought of as A sections and the contrasting section is considered the B section, a large-scale AABA pattern emerges. When an AABA section is made up of verse-chorus components, the term compound AABA is used (reserving "AABA" for the song forms discussed earlier). "Whole Lotta Love" provides a bridge from the 1960s into the 1970s, with its blues roots, psychedelic central section, aggressive guitar virtuosity, and use of compound AABA form. The combination of elements looks both forward and backward in the development of rock.

Deep Purple: Blues, Classical, and Psychedelia.

Like Led Zeppelin, Deep Purple had its origins in late 1960s rock. Formed in London in 1968, the group had a number-four U.S. hit single that year with a version of Joe South's "Hush." From its inception, the band mixed blues-based rock with classical music, releasing one of the first albums to combine a rock band with a symphony orchestra, *Concerto for Group and Orchestra* (uk26, 1969). After three relatively unsuccessful albums ("Hush" notwithstanding), founding members Jon Lord (keyboards), Ritchie Blackmore (guitar), and Ian Paice (drums) replaced original singer Rod Evans and bassist Nick Simper with singer Ian Gillan and bassist Roger Glover. This lineup stormed the rock charts in the first half of the 1970s. *Deep Purple in Rock* went to number four in the UK in 1970, followed by *Fireball* (p32 uk1, 1971) and *Machine Head* (p7 uk1, 1971), albums that showed increasing popularity in the United States. *Machine Head* contains "Smoke on the Water" and "Highway Star," two songs that have become staples of rock radio.

"Highway Star" is often cited as one of the songs that most influenced the development of heavy metal in the late 1970s and early 1980s, but in the context of the hippie legacy, it illustrates how Deep Purple blended rock music and classical idioms. The song features two long instrumental sections—one each for guitar and keyboard solos. Both solos make use of harmonic and melodic practices more often associated with the European baroque music of Bach and Vivaldi than with the blues of Muddy Waters

Deep Purple's Ritchie Blackmore in concert. Deep Purple was innovative in mixing its blues-based rock with classical music. Like Led Zeppelin, the band focused on instrumental solos, often displaying strong blues and classical influences.

or Elmore James. While the earlier *Concerto for Group and Orchestra* had merely juxtaposed the band with a classical orchestra, here classical music compositional techniques are integrated much more effectively (though no orchestra is used). Another track from *Machine Head*, "Lazy," is a blend between psychedelic trippiness and blues-rock style. The track begins with a moody organ solo, which seems to combine church music, blues, and a bit of *Phantom of the Opera*–style organ playing. Both Lord and Blackmore provide blues-oriented solos, and Gillan delivers falsetto screams, which became common in rock singing during the late '70s and early '80s. (Gillan's vocal style also became well known in the context of musical theater through his performance as Jesus on the 1970 Tim Rice/Andrew Lloyd Webber concept album, *Jesus Christ Superstar*.) The classic lineup folded by 1974, and singer David Coverdale and bassist Glenn Hughes joined the band for several albums, most notably *Burn* (p9 uk3, 1974). By the end of the decade, members had formed other bands, including Rainbow (Blackmore), Whitesnake (Coverdale), and Gillan (Gillan).

Black Sabbath: British Rock Meets Boris Karloff and the Gothic Beginnings of Metal. Consisting of guitarist Tony Iommi, bassist Geezer Butler, drummer Bill Ward, and singer John "Ozzy" Osbourne, Black Sabbath began as a blues band in the late 1960s, but quickly turned to the darker elements of rock. Early on, the band changed its name from "Earth" to "Black Sabbath," after a Boris Karloff horror movie. "Black Sabbath," the first track on their first album, *Black Sabbath* (p23 uk8, 1970), begins with the tolling of distant church bells, followed by a sinister riff using the musical interval of the tritone, a dissonant and unstable combination of notes known among classical-music aficionados for its association with Satan. The band's next album, *Paranoid* (p12 uk1, 1970), contains "Iron Man," which begins with the low-pitched tolling of guitars to accompany Osbourne's distorted voice intoning "I am Iron Man." Instrumentally, Black Sabbath songs often convey a dark texture because the guitar, bass, and vocals all perform variants of the same riff simultaneously ("Iron Man" is a good example of this). Despite these gothic touches, however, Black Sabbath's music is mostly based on blues riffs and common rock structures. The group's first four albums, including *Master of Reality* (p8 uk5, 1971) and *Black Sabbath, Vol. 4* (p13 uk8, 1972), were great commercial successes and laid the foundation for the use of music and images that would become central to the emergence of heavy metal a few years later. By the end of the decade, the original lineup parted ways and Ozzy went on to a solo career as one of the most prominent practitioners of heavy metal in the 1980s and 1990s.

AMERICAN BLUES ROCK AND SOUTHERN ROCK

Southern Rock: The Allman Brothers Band, Lynyrd Skynyrd, and the Charlie Daniels Band. The influence of 1960s British blues rock was not restricted to UK bands. Many aspiring young rockers from the United States were drawn to electric blues in the 1960s, and by the early 1970s a strong blues influence could be heard in rock associated with the American South. During the late 1960s, Nashville-born guitarist Duane Allman became a studio favorite of Rick Hall at Fame Studios in Muscle Shoals, adding his blues-drenched playing to numerous sessions for Hall and Atlantic's Jerry Wexler, including Wilson Pickett's version of the Beatles' "Hey Jude" (p23 r13, 1968). Through his playing at Muscle Shoals, Allman came to the attention of Phil Walden, who had managed several southern rhythm and blues singers during the 1960s, including Otis Redding. By the end of the decade, Walden was managing Allman, and the young guitarist formed the Allman Brothers Band. By 1969, Allman had enlisted bassist Barry Oakley, guitarist Dickey Betts, and drummers Jai Johnny Johnson ("Jaimoe") and Butch Trucks. Duane's brother Gregg was the last to join, and his blues-influenced vocals and organ playing rounded out the group. Walden, who founded Capricorn Recording Studios in Macon, Georgia, signed the band to his label. In short order, the Allman Brothers Band became the most important band playing "southern rock."

The Allman Brothers Band drew their influences from the blues and rhythm and blues that they heard growing up in the South, and the British blues rockers of the 1960s. Their live shows featured extended improvised solos, a practice drawn from San Francisco psychedelia. Like Led Zeppelin and Deep Purple, the Allman Brothers Band developed and extended methods of blending blues and rock that began in the 1960s, and the embracement of both their musical and cultural heritage served as a model for many other southern bands. After modest commercial success with their first two studio albums, the Allman Brothers released a double live album, *At Fillmore East*, which rose to number thirteen in the United States in 1971. The album contains the band's signature song from their first studio album, "Whipping Post," written by Gregg Allman and perhaps the best example of the band's strong blues influences and penchant for extended soloing.

Despite the death of Duane Allman in a 1971 motorcycle accident, the band's next album, *Eat a Peach*, hit number four on the U.S. album charts in early 1972. Slightly more than a year after Allman's death, Oakley was killed in a similar accident. Now depending much more on Betts, the group also added Lamar Williams on bass and Chuck Leavell on piano. The album *Brothers and Sisters* hit number one in the United States in the fall of 1973, and yielded the hit single "Ramblin' Man" (p2). This Dickey Betts track brings the band's country influences to the fore. Much of the band's early music was produced by veteran engineer and producer Tom Dowd, who had worked on recordings for Atlantic (including sessions at Stax and Muscle Shoals) since the early 1950s.

Among other rock groups from the South, perhaps the greatest beneficiaries of the Allmans' success were a group of rockers from Florida who named their band after a high school teacher. Like the Allman Brothers, Walden and Capricorn also

Brothers Gregg (organ) and Duane (guitar) Allman shown together on stage. Duane was a popular studio musician before devoting his full energies to the Allman Brothers Band. He played on important recordings in Muscle Shoals, Alabama. Gregg's bluesy lead vocals and organ playing were key elements of the band's sound, which blended rock virtuosity, a rhythm and blues sensibility, and psychedelic elements to create southern rock.

Listening Guide

The Allman Brothers Band, "Whipping Post" Capricorn 2476-124

Words and music by Gregg Allman, produced by Adrian Barber. Contained on *The Allman Brothers Band*, released in 1969. A much longer version that represents the development of this song in a live context is included on *At Fillmore East* (1971).

FORM: Contrasting verse-chorus. Each verse consists of two 4-bar phrases over the same repeating 2-bar chord progression, followed by a 2-bar buildup to the chorus. Each chorus consists of three 1-bar phrases followed by a stop-time phrase, and then a bar of instrumental response that echoes the vocal. Note the instrumental interlude that follows the second instrumental verse. It creates a passage that dramatically builds up to the final statement of the chorus in an almost symphonic manner, using an ascending scale and stop-time lead-guitar blasts. Also note how the final chord shows some of the band's jazz influences.

TIME SIGNATURE: 12/8, with sections in 11/8 as indicated. In this case, 11/8 can be counted as 1 & uh, 2 & uh, 3 & uh, 4 &, as if it were 12/8 with the last element lopped off. It is also possible to count this song in 6/8, in which case all measure numbers below can simply be doubled and the 11/8 sections would be counted as a measure of 6/8 followed by a measure of 5/8.

INSTRUMENTATION: Two electric guitars, bass, organ, drums (featuring two drummers), and lead vocals.

0:00–0:26	**Introduction**, 8 mm. (in 11/8 time)	This section begins with the bass, adding drums, guitars, and organ one by one to provide a gradual buildup that leads to the first verse.
0:26–1:04	**Verse 1**, 10 mm. (in 12/8)	Lead vocal enters singing two 4-bar phrases and then a 2-bar phrase that leads to the chorus. "I've been run down . . ."
1:04–1:38	**Chorus**, 9 mm.	Music gets louder and more dramatic as 1-bar vocal phrase is repeated, leading to stop-time climax. Guitars then echo vocal phrase, and then lead into a 4-bar transition in 11/8 based on the introduction. ". . . tied to the whipping post . . ."
1:38–2:07	**Instrumental verse**, 8 mm.	Guitar solo over the first 8 bars of the verse.
2:07–2:45	**Verse 2**, 10 mm.	As in verse 1. "My friends tell me . . ."
2:45–3:19	**Chorus**, 9 mm.	As before, once again leading to a guitar solo. ". . . tied to the whipping post . . ."
3:19–3:49	**Instrumental verse**, 8 mm.	A second guitar solo, structured just like the first one.
3:49–4:31	**Interlude**, 10 mm.	This instrumental buildup consists of 4 bars of an ascending scale that leads to 4 bars of dramatic stop-time. The music then stops, as Allman introduces the 2-bar buildup to the chorus found in the previous verses ("Sometimes I feel"), which drives headlong into the final statement of the chorus.
4:31–5:18	**Chorus**, 5 mm.	As before, but with more energy and a tremendous sense of arrival. The final echo of the vocal presented previously by the guitars is replaced with a gentle and mysterious jazz-influenced ending. ". . . tied to the whipping post . . ."

courted Lynyrd Skynyrd. Figuring that they might get more attention from a label that did not already have a southern rock band, however, Skynyrd signed with Al Kooper's label, Sounds of the South, based in Atlanta. Several years after the All-man Brothers had made their mark nationally, Lynyrd Skynyrd released a series of successful albums, beginning with *Pronouced Leh-nerd Skin-nerd* (p27, 1973) and peaking with *Street Survivors* (p5 uk13, 1977). Kooper was a veteran in the record-ing studio who had played organ on most of the Dylan sessions from 1965 to 1966. As a result of his experience, Skynyrd's tracks were somewhat more radio-friendly than those of the Allmans. Skynyrd also associated itself with the South much more directly than the Allman Brothers Band. Lynyrd Skynrd's songs provided images of everyday life in the South, and they scored hits with "Sweet Home Alabama" (p8, 1974), "Saturday Night Special" (p27, 1975), and "What's Your Name?" (p13, 1977). The song "Free Bird" has been a staple of rock radio playlists since its release on the live album, *One More from the Road* (p9 uk17, 1976). A plane crash in late 1977 killed singer Ronnie Van Zant and two other band members—Steve and Cassie Gaines—only days after the release of *Street Survivors*. While this tragic event raised the band's profile and prompted radio stations to play more of their older music, the remaining members found it difficult to go on and split up soon after, although the band eventually regrouped years later.

Another important southern rock artist was guitarist, singer, and fiddle player Charlie Daniels. Daniels started as a studio musician in Nashville, playing on a wide variety of records (including Dylan sessions in the late 1960s), and formed his own band in the early 1970s. He had five Top 40 albums between 1975 and 1982, including *Million Mile Reflections* (p5 c1, 1979) and *Full Moon* (p11 c5, 1980). "The Devil Went Down to Georgia" (p3 c1 uk14, 1979), a song about a young fiddler making a deal with the devil, became his trademark. Daniels's style is some-times thought of as more country than rock, although he moved in southern rock circles during the 1970s. His early music shows strong connections to the hippie movement and since he was an older musician, members of the other southern rock bands looked upon him as a mentor.

Although the three bands discussed here were wildly popular at the time, the connotations associated with the term "southern rock" can be misleading. This label stemmed partly from writers in the North and on the West Coast describ-ing bands from the South. A "southern rock" category allowed music executives to market this music through connections with stereotypical images of the South (hard-drinking men, pickup trucks with gun racks, and Confederate flags) fostered by northern media outlets. These southern musicians were certainly proud of their geographical heritage, and often embraced this label, even if they felt conflicted about being identified with the politics of the old South. Some of these artists were extremely progressive in their political views, were accepting of racial integration, and were more closely aligned with the legacy of psychedelia. As we see and hear in the images and music of these groups, southern culture is more complex than the simple stereotypes conjured by the label "southern rock."

Texas and South of the Border: Santana and ZZ Top. As we have seen, the term southern rock usually referred to bands from the southeastern United States who emerged in the wake of the Allman Brothers Band. But the influence of electric blues extended further, and can be heard clearly in the music of Texas-based ZZ Top and the Mexican-influenced sounds of Santana. Led by Mexican-born guitarist

Led by virtuoso guitarist Carlos Santana (pictured here), Santana took influences from psychedelia (their performance at Woodstock is legendary) and combined them with Latin rhythms and percussion. Carlos Santana's improvisations put him in the same league as guitar greats Duane Allman, Jimi Hendrix, Eric Clapton, and Jimmy Page.

Carlos Santana and featuring the organ playing and singing of Greg Rolie (who would later form Journey), Santana emerged from the San Francisco psychedelic scene in 1969. The band's success was fueled in part by their inspired performance at Woodstock. *Santana* (p4 r13, 1969) featured the band's trademark blend of jazz- and blues-influenced improvisation set to the accompaniment of Latin rhythms and percussion. "Evil Ways" (p9, 1970), the band's first hit, is an example of Santana's style from the early 1970s. The group built on the success of its first album with *Abraxas* (p1 r3 uk7, 1970), which contained "Black Magic Woman" (p4, 1970) and "Oye Como Va" (p13, 1971). Later albums included *Santana III* (p1 r5 uk6, 1971) and *Caravanserai* (p8 r6 uk6, 1972). If Duane Allman was the South's answer to Eric Clapton, Carlos Santana's smooth soulful playing was the Latino response to the electric blues explosion of the 1960s.

ZZ Top became a staple of rock radio by the end of the 1970s and enjoyed success into the 1980s. In the early 1970s, however, Texas electric blues was not yet an influential force, and guitarist Billy Gibbons, bassist Dusty Hill, and drummer Frank Beard struggled for recognition. While *ZZ Top's First Album* (1971) did not chart, *Tres Hombres* fared much better, hitting number eight on the U.S. charts in 1973. *Fandango!* (p10, 1975) contained the track "Tush" (p20, 1975), an up-tempo 12-bar blues tune. While Santana's music is often referred to as "Latin rock," and ZZ Top is considered Texas blues, neither is typically thought of as southern rock (much less country rock). Stylistically, however, the music of both bands is similar to that of the southern rock bands. Santana most closely parallels the Allman Brothers with an emphasis on improvisation, while the tighter arrangements in ZZ Top's music are more similar to Lynyrd Skynyrd. The key element in the music of both groups is a significant stylistic debt to the electric blues.

American Bands: Steppenwolf, Three Dog Night, Grand Funk Railroad, and Aerosmith.

The musical impact of the blues in American rock in the early 1970s was not restricted to the South. Bands such as Steppenwolf, Grand Funk Railroad, and Aerosmith were all influenced strongly by the blues tradition. German-born singer and guitarist John Kay spent time in many of the important musical hot spots of the 1960s. He visited the folk scene in New York, experienced San Francisco psychedelia, and hung around Los Angeles in the months before Love and the Doors burst onto the scene. Together with organist Goldy McJohn and drummer Jerry Edmunton—whom he had worked with in Canada—Kay formed Steppenwolf (named after the Hermann Hesse novel) in Los Angeles in 1967. The band's first album, *Steppenwolf* (p6, 1968), contained the hit single "Born to Be Wild" (p2 uk30, 1968), and "Magic Carpet Ride" (p3, 1968) was released on the next album, *Steppenwolf the Second* (p3, 1969). Either single can be taken as repre-

Listening Guide

Santana, "Evil Ways" Columbia 4-45069

Words and music by Sonny Henry, produced by Brent Dangerfield and Santana. The song reached #9 on the *Billboard* "Hot 100" chart in early 1970.

FORM: Simple verse, based on a two-chord vamp that remains constant except for the last bars of each verse. Each verse is based on a 16-measure structure, though the last measures can be repeated to create an 18-bar verse, as in verses 1 and 3. The solos are built on the two-chord vamp and unfold in 4-bar units. Note that the organ solo is 24 bars in length, which is simply six times through the 4-bar unit. Heading into the third verse, the band plays a 4-bar interlude that sets the scene for this final verse and closes out the organ solo.

TIME SIGNATURE: 4/4, with a strong emphasis on Latin rhythms, especially during the guitar solo at the end.

INSTRUMENTATION: Electric guitar, Hammond organ, bass, drums, various Latin percussion, lead and background vocals.

0:00–0:18	**Introduction**, 8 mm.	After a brief lead-in from the drums, the entire band enters with the two-chord vamp that forms the basis for the song.
0:18–0:54	**Verse 1**, 18 mm.	Vocals enter, sung mostly in unison by multiple voices. The 16-bar structure is extended by two measures to create an 18-bar section. "You got to change . . ."
0:54–1:27	**Verse 2**, 16 mm.	Very similar to verse 1, except that the section is not extended by 2 bars and is thus 16 bars in length. "When I come home . . ."
1:27–2:17	**Organ solo**, 24 mm.	Solo begins slowly, developing more activity and energy as it unfolds, leading to a climax in the closing measures.
2:17–2:25	**Interlude**, 4 mm.	Band comes together on the two-chord vamp to mark the end of the organ solo and the beginning of verse 3.
2:25–3:01	**Verse 3**, 18 mm.	Similar to verse 2, except that the 2-bar extension at the end serves to launch the guitar solo. "When I come home . . ."
3:01–3:54	**Guitar solo**, 24 mm. + fade	High-energy guitar solo, as the rhythm section becomes much more active and drives the music forward before the song eventually fades out.

sentative of Steppenwolf's approach to blues rock: Kay's gruff vocals are supported by driving guitars and drums, with McJohn's distorted organ often coming to the front of the texture. The band continued into the 1970s but disbanded after a special concert played on Valentine's Day in 1972. Three Dog Night was also based in Los Angeles, and Brian Wilson produced their early music. The group's blue-eyed soul featured three lead singers, and focused on the song and vocals with an AM-friendly approach. The band had a series of hit records, many written by songwriters who would later establish themselves as performers. Successful singles included

Harry Nilsson's "One" (p5, 1969), Laura Nyro's "Eli's Coming" (p10, 1969), and Randy Newman's "Mama Told Me (Not to Come)" (p1 uk3, 1970). Often overlooked by rock writers, Three Dog Night enjoyed enormous success until their breakup in the mid-1970s.

Hailing from Flint, Michigan, Grand Funk Railroad also had roots in 1960s pop. As members of Terry Knight and the Pack, guitarist and vocalist Mark Farner and drummer and vocalist Don Brewer had a minor hit in 1967 with "I (Who Have Nothing)" (p46). Soon they brought in bassist Mel Schacher to form Grand Funk Railroad, and Knight managed the new band. The group enjoyed success almost immediately, as *On Time* hit number twenty-seven on the U.S. charts in 1969, and the band's next nine albums charted in the *Billboard* Top 10. Among these, *We're an American Band* (p2, 1973) was the most successful, and the single of the same name went to number one in 1973. The band followed with *Shinin' On* (p5, 1974), which contained a version of Little Eva's 1962 hit "The Loco-Motion" (p1, 1974), and they later released a version of the old rhythm and blues number "Some Kind of Wonderful" (p3, 1975). Grand Funk's music is deeply rooted in 1960s soul, and Farner's singing shows these influences at almost every point. The band's sustained success during the early 1970s made them one of the most popular acts in rock music at the time.

Although their first album, *Aerosmith* (1973), did not chart and the track "Dream On" rose only as high as number fifty-nine in the U.S. charts, Aerosmith's music became much more popular by the middle of the decade. Led by singer Steven Tyler and guitarist Joe Perry, the Boston-based band was often compared to the Rolling Stones. Tyler's appearance and stage performance style were reminiscent of Mick Jagger, and Perry's stoic, tough-guy demeanor paralleled that of Keith Richards. With the success of *Toys in the Attic* (p11, 1975) and *Rocks* (p3, 1976), the group's music saturated American FM radio with songs such as "Same Old Song and Dance" (1974), "Train Kept a Rollin'" (1974), "Sweet Emotion" (p36, 1975), and "Walk This Way" (p10, rereleased in 1976). Aerosmith's success has continued into the present, and "Walk This Way" helped rap cross over to the rock audience in the mid-1980s, which will be considered in Chapter 12.

Taken together, American blues rockers from the Allman Brothers to Aerosmith balanced their British counterparts. Stylistically, both American and British groups extended the blues rock of the 1960s into the 1970s and forged a mainstream rock style that enjoyed tremendous commercial success. Most of these groups subscribed to the hippie aesthetic that developed in the psychedelic era: some bands blended in classical, folk, or country elements, while others focused on virtuosic soloing influenced by blues and jazz. The blues tradition was just one influence on 1970s rock, and for British progressive bands the traditions and practices of classical music played a greater role.

PROGRESSIVE ROCK: BIG IDEAS AND HIGH AMBITION

Philosophical Lyrics and Concept Albums. Following the release of *Sgt. Pepper's Lonely Hearts Club Band*, many bands on both sides of the Atlantic recorded concept albums. A heightened sense of concept, however, became the hallmark of a new type of "progressive rock" that emerged from the UK. The idea of turning an album into a self-contained artistic statement was already a few years old by the 1970s, but progressive rock bands turned the practice into an obsession within rock music. These groups also took a cue from *Sgt. Pepper* in lavishing attention on album covers. The bizarre covers Hipgnosis designed for Pink Floyd and Roger Dean's fantasy landscapes for Yes, for example, are integral to the album-listening experience. These new concept albums also featured lyrics dealing with philosophical issues such as religion and spirituality, politics and power, the forward march of technology, and existential angst. Some fans devoted to the emotional aspects of rock were repelled by such ambitious topics in the context of the hippie aesthetic, and critics often dismissed progressive rock as pretentious. Yet, these elaborately packaged concept albums were clearly an extension of the idea that music should provide a trip. Progressive rockers may have taken themselves and their music very seriously, but the style was a logical development of the increasingly lofty ambitions that rock had adopted over the course of the 1960s.

The Use of Classical Music with Rock. A primary element of British progressive rock in the 1970s was the clear and self-conscious use of classical music. The Beatles were the most obvious source of this practice, although many other psychedelic groups employed elements drawn from classical music (as we saw in Chapter 7). For example, Procol Harum's best-known track, "A Whiter Shade of Pale" (p5 uk1, 1967), combines the feel of Percy Sledge's "When a Man Loves a Woman" with a chord progression drawn from a cantata by J. S. Bach. Among the earliest attempts to blend classical music into a concept album is the Moody Blues' *Days of Future Passed* (p3 uk27, 1967). The band already had a hit single with "Go Now" (p10 uk1, 1965) when their label, Decca, asked them to record a rock version of Dvořák's *New World Symphony* as a demonstration record to help sell stereo units. Instead, the group came up with a song suite, and a professional arranger was brought in to compose the orchestral interludes between tracks, eventually creating *Days of Future Passed*. The Moody Blues went on to place a string of albums high on the charts, including *A Question of Balance* (p3 uk1, 1970), *Every Good Boy Deserves Favor* (p2 uk1, 1971), and *Seventh Sojourn* (p1 uk5, 1972).

The Who: Townshend's Big Projects. Although they are not usually considered a progressive rock band, the Who were tremendously influential in the development of rock ambition at the end of the 1960s. Made up of guitarist Pete Townshend, vocalist Roger Daltrey, bassist John Entwistle, and drummer Keith Moon, the band was managed by Kit Lambert, the son of a well-known classical-music composer in Britain. The younger Lambert was well acquainted with the structure of classical music, and encouraged Townshend to borrow classical-music ideas in his writing for the Who. Townshend's first attempts were relatively short pieces, "A Quick One While He's Away"

During the 1970s, the Who's music resisted classification into any one of the many styles that developed early in the decade. Led by Pete Townshend's ambitious ideas and songwriting along with John Entwistle's virtuosic bass playing, the group might be viewed as progressive rock. But the manic drumming of Keith Moon and the energetic vocal and performance style of Roger Daltrey—not to mention Townshend's on-stage leaping and sliding—made the band seem much more visceral than cerebral at times.

(1966) and "Rael" (1968). These laid the groundwork for a much larger work, *Tommy* (p4 uk2, 1969). *Tommy* tells the story of a deaf, dumb, and blind boy who gains spiritual enlightenment through playing pinball. When Tommy is relieved of his disabilities, he is cast as a guru, possessing the great wisdom of the ages. The story is a parable about the superficiality of much hippie spirituality. When Tommy tells his followers that to gain spiritual insight they will need to renounce smoking pot and drinking, mute their senses, and play pinball, the crowd soundly rejects him. Through *Tommy*, Townshend sent a message that spiritual pursuits require effort and sacrifice. Ironically, many of the hippies who were the intended targets of this album never understood its message. Musically, Townshend employed a variety of recurring material that is reintroduced during important moments of the album, a practice that occurs often in opera.

The Who followed *Tommy* with two more concept albums, *Who's Next* (p4 uk1, 1971) and *Quadrophenia* (p2 uk2, 1973). *Who's Next* began as a project called *Lifehouse*, which sought to merge the band and its listeners through a series of concert experiences that would be captured on record. When this didn't work out, the band recorded much of the music as the *Who's Next* collection. With *Quadrophenia*, Townshend returned to his Mod past, crafting a story about a young Mod seeking meaning in his life. The Who had continued success throughout the 1970s, although they moved away from large conceptual projects.

In the Beginning: King Crimson and Emerson, Lake & Palmer. While the Beatles, the Moody Blues, Procol Harum, and the Who were clear influences on 1970s progressive rock, the album that created the stylistic template for the progressive rock that followed was King Crimson's *In the Court of the Crimson King* (p28 uk5, 1969). The band was led by guitarist Robert Fripp, who was joined by bassist and vocalist Greg Lake, drummer Michael Giles, and multi-instrumentalist Ian McDonald on keyboards and woodwinds. King Crimson blended the harder, more dissonant aspects of twentieth-century music, the softer more consonant elements of nineteenth-century classical music, and a modern jazz influence into a rock context. The group's first album opens with "21st Century Schizoid Man," which features Lake belting out aggressive vocals and a virtuosic middle section filled with odd rhythmic syncopations and angular melodic riffs. The group endured a number of personnel changes, although the lineup that settled in for several albums in the early 1970s, featuring Fripp with drummer Bill Bruford, bassist and vocalist John Wetton, and violinist David Cross, produced some of the band's finest music, including *Larks' Tongues in Aspic* (p61 uk20, 1973) and *Red* (p66 uk45, 1974).

King Crimson enjoyed far less commercial success than the bands centered on multi-keyboardist Keith Emerson. As early as 1967, Emerson was well known on the London scene as a member of the Nice, which enjoyed two hit albums in Britain, *The Nice* (uk3, 1969) and *Five Bridges Suite* (uk2, 1970). During his time with the Nice, Emerson built a reputation for virtuosic playing and destroying (or seeming to destroy) keyboards during shows—an idea he got from Jimi Hendrix (the Nice toured with the Jimi Hendrix Experience in the late '60s). Emerson also became known for his clever rock adaptations of classical-music favorites. While touring the United States with King Crimson during late 1969, Emerson and Lake decided to form their own band together, drawing in Carl Palmer, who had played drums with Arthur Brown. Emerson, Lake & Palmer (ELP) picked up where the

Nice had left off, and the band's self-titled debut album rose to number four in the UK in 1970 (p18). For their second album, the band considered releasing a double album consisting of one record of original material and a second containing a live version of nineteenth-century Russian composer Modest Mussorgsky's piano suite, *Pictures at an Exhibition*. The dual-release plan was scrapped and the albums were released separately as *Tarkus* (p9 uk1, 1971) and *Pictures at an Exhibition* (p10 uk3, 1971). These two records illustrate the two key characteristics of ELP's approach to progressive rock. The original music on *Tarkus* features long tracks that alternate lyrical songs with Emerson's versatile playing on organ, piano, and synthesizer. *Pictures* provides an example of the band reworking classical music, dropping some parts and adding newly composed ones, to produce a new work in its own right. The band followed up with *Trilogy* (p5 uk2, 1972) and *Brain Salad Surgery* (p11 uk2, 1973) and remained successful on both sides of the Atlantic through the 1970s.

Hippie Spirituality: Jethro Tull and Yes. Just as *Tommy* had touched on the role of spirituality in hippie culture, Jethro Tull and Yes focused their most ambitious works on religious institutions and traditions. Unlike most other progressive rock bands, Jethro Tull began as a blues band. On early albums such as *Stand Up* (p20 uk1, 1969), group leader Ian Anderson played more harmonica than his trademark flute (in addition to singing lead vocals). By the beginning of the 1970s, however, Anderson became increasingly focused on issues of spirituality, and like Townshend, was highly suspicious of religious and political institutions. The first album to express these ideas was *Aqualung* (p7 uk4, 1971), which deals with society's treatment of the poor and is, in part, a bitter indictment of the Church of England. The band's next album, *Thick as a Brick* (p1 uk5, 1972), is an attack on bourgeois values, while *A Passion Play* (p1 uk13, 1973) takes on the topic of life after death and reincarnation. While *Aqualung* is divided into separate tracks, the other albums are divided only by the obligatory break required to turn the record over and are essentially single tracks of about forty minutes' length. The band's personnel shifted over the decade, although the lineup of Anderson, Martin Barre (guitar), John Evans (keyboards), Barrie Barlow (drums), and Jeffrey Hammond (bass) played on most of the more conceptual albums.

Led by singer and flautist Ian Anderson (shown here), Jethro Tull emerged as one of the top progressive rock bands of the early 1970s. The group had formed as a blues outfit, and those influences can be heard in their later music, especially the long instrumental solos on *Thick as a Brick* (1972) and *A Passion Play* (1973).

Led by vocalist Jon Anderson (no relation to Ian), Yes was also concerned with issues of spirituality inspired by the hippie mélange of Eastern religious ideas. Although the group had released three albums, *Fragile* (p4 uk7, 1971) marks the first release by the band's definitive lineup, consisting of Anderson, guitarist Steve Howe, bassist Chris Squire, drummer Bill Bruford, and multi-keyboardist Rick Wakeman. In terms of instrumental prowess, Yes was perhaps the most accomplished group in all of progressive rock, with Howe, Squire, Wakeman, and Bruford consistently winning awards for their playing in magazine polls on both sides of the Atlantic. While

Yes were perhaps the most virtuosic of the early-'70s progressive rock bands. In 1977 keyboardist Rick Wakeman rejoined Yes, and by 1978 the band were touring "in the round," employing a rotating stage that was positioned in the center of the venue to allow more fans to be closer to the group. Shown here are (left to right) Steve Howe, Jon Anderson, Chris Squire, and Wakeman.

spiritual themes can be found on *Fragile*, they are much more obvious on *Close to the Edge* (p3 uk4, 1972). Based in part on Hermann Hesse's novel *Siddhartha*, the eighteen-minute title track is inspired by the quest for spiritual wisdom with very little of the caustic critique found in the music of Jethro Tull. (If any band from the 1970s perfectly captures the optimistic innocence of psychedelia, it is Yes.) The concept for the band's follow-up, *Tales from Topographic Oceans* (p6 uk1, 1973), was inspired by Eastern scripture (drawn from a footnote in Paramahansa Yogananda's *Autobiography of a Yogi*, a hippie favorite) and consists of four tracks on two albums. After the release of *Tales*, Wakeman left to pursue a solo career and the band drafted Swiss keyboardist Patrick Moraz for *Relayer* (p5 uk4, 1974), featuring the epic track "The Gates of Delirium," inspired by Leo Tolstoy's *War and Peace*. The band's heady blend of instrumental virtuosity and spiritual subject matter proved to be a winning combination. Together with ELP and Jethro Tull, Yes was one of the most commercially successful rock bands during the first half of the 1970s.

Symphonic Expansion. Most progressive rock bands were eager to integrate classical-music influences to create longer, more intricate musical arrangements, but the elements of these more symphonic rock tracks are drawn from common pop-music forms. Yes's "Roundabout" illustrates how a long track—it is almost nine minutes—can be constructed out of shorter, more familiar components. The piece uses the same compound AABA form that we saw in Led Zeppelin's "Whole Lotta Love."

"Roundabout" is filled with many musical features that show classical-music influences, including the idea of reusing melodic material in new ways, which is a central feature of much classical music. The piece also incorporates a number of inventive rhythmic ideas. Notice how the bridge sections cannot be counted according to a simple four-beat pattern. This kind of rhythmic patterning (called

Listening Guide

Yes, "Roundabout" Atlantic 2854

Words and music by Jon Anderson and Steve Howe, produced by Yes and Eddie Offord. Reached #13 on the *Billboard* "Hot 100" chart in early 1972.

FORM: Compound AABA form. The A sections consist of verse and bridge sections, but no chorus. The B section falls into three parts: new verses based on a repeating riff, a return of the introduction and bridge section, and a series of solos on the organ and guitar. Note how the return of the introduction (marked by asterisks) restarts the song—a formal strategy that became common in the 1970s, especially in longer and more complicated songs.

TIME SIGNATURE: Mostly in 4/4, with measures of 2/4 and 3/4 occurring along the way.

INSTRUMENTATION: Acoustic and electric guitars, bass, organ, piano, synthesizer, mellotron, drums, percussion, lead and backup vocals.

*	0:00–0:44	**Introduction**	Rubato, acoustic guitar free rhythm, punctuated by tape effect created by playing tape-recorded grand-piano bass notes backward.
A	0:44–1:18	**Verse 1**, 20 mm.	Entire band plays 8 bars to prepare for the entrance of lead vocals, which then present a 2-bar verse. "I'll be the roundabout . . ."
	1:18–1:45	**Verse 2**, 16 mm.	4 bars now prepare the return of the vocals, which present the 12-bar verse as before, but with backup vocals added and leading to the bridge. "The music dance . . ."
	1:45–2:15	**Bridge**, 18 mm.	Starts with guitar, high hat, and vocal only, then organ and finally bass enter. "In and around the lake . . ."
A	2:15–2:49	**Verse 3**, 20 mm.	8 bars prepare vocal return, then the 12 mm. verse as before with slight changes in instrumentation. Note the use of synthesizer here, as well as the new fast melodic figure that occurs just before the singing returns. "I will remember . . ."
	2:49–3:25	**Bridge**, 21 mm.	As before, without staggered entrance in bass and drums, but adds new backup vocal part. Fast melodic figure returns to create transition to middle section. "In and around the lake . . ."
B	3:25–4:57	**Middle section**, 50 mm.	Twelve times through a 4-bar phrase based on a riff in the bass and guitar. Choral vocals present melody, with some instrumental interludes along the way. The end of the section reintroduces the verse melody to transition back to the introduction. "Along the drifting cloud . . ."
*	4:57–5:50	**Reprise of introduction and bridge**	Rubato during intro and then 9 bars that reinterpret the music from the bridge. "In and around the lake . . ."

(continued)

	5:50–7:05	**Instrumental solos,** 45 mm.	The organ and guitar alternate solos based on music drawn from the bridge. An ascending scale passage creates a transition to the return of the verse.
A	7:05–7:26	**Verse 4**, 12 mm.	The verse returns varied somewhat, but using the lyrics from verse 1. "I'll be the roundabout . . ."
	7:26–7:53	**Bridge**, 17 mm.	The fullest presentation of the bridge so far, leading directly into the coda. "In and around the lake . . ."
	7:53–8:30	**Coda**, 20 mm.	Layered harmony vocals over a strummed acoustic guitar, as the song ends with a guitar phrase drawn from the end of the introduction.

"changing meter") is standard in much twentieth-century classical music and some jazz, but is not often a feature in earlier rock (the Beatles' "All You Need Is Love" is a notable exception—try it using three- and four-beat counting). A similar use of changing meter can be heard in in the Allman Brothers' "Whipping Post."

With its formal patterning drawn from simpler pop forms and its manipulation of melodic and rhythmic material drawn from classical music, "Roundabout" demonstrates how progressive rock depended on both pop and classical traditions. While formal patterns within progressive rock vary considerably, the pattern found in "Roundabout" recurs regularly (although with some variation) in Yes's music from the 1970s. The Listening Guide also shows that the track is separated into two big parts, marked by the classical guitar introduction and its return at 4:57 (shown by asterisks). This division does not however line up with the AABA form, revealing a formal structure that is operating on multiple levels (two in this case), another feature common in classical music.

Bizarre Tales and Progressive-Rock Theater: Genesis and Pink Floyd.

During the first half of the 1970s, Genesis was among the most creative and bizarre bands in progressive rock. The band included singer Peter Gabriel, drummer and backup vocalist Phil Collins, Michael Rutherford on bass, Steve Hackett on guitar, and Tony Banks on keyboards. Musically, Genesis focused on lengthy, carefully worked out arrangements, while Gabriel's lyrics spun fantastic tales that delivered stinging, if sometimes obscure, criticisms of British life and values. Onstage, while the other band members were absorbed in their playing, Gabriel acted these stories out. Using costumes and props to create a new kind of rock theater, Genesis extended the rock-opera ambitions of the concept album into the concert hall. For example, during live performances of "The Musical Box" from *Nursery Cryme* (1971), Gabriel donned a mask to help him act out the role of a reincarnated spirit who has aged seventy years and built up decades of unsatisfied sexual longing. *Foxtrot* (uk12, 1972), includes the twenty-minute track "Supper's Ready," live performances of which featured Gabriel in the role of the returning Messiah, lifting him from the stage via wires to increase the effect of divine presence. In *The Lamb Lies Down on Broadway* (p41 uk10, 1974), much as in Jethro Tull's *A Passion Play*, we follow the main character, Rael (like the Who piece mentioned earlier), after death and before rebirth. Gabriel's costumes for performances of *The Lamb* became so elaborate that he sometimes found it difficult to hold the microphone close enough to his mouth to sing.

Gabriel's penchant for the bizarre was paralleled by Roger Waters's fascination with madness—which is evident on many Pink Floyd albums from the 1970s. After their success on the London psychedelic scene late in the 1960s, Pink Floyd—featuring Waters on bass and vocals, Rick Wright on keyboards, Nick Mason on drums, and guitarist David Gilmour—scored a series of successful albums in the UK, including *Ummagumma* (uk5, 1969), *Atom Heart Mother* (uk1, 1970), and *Meddle* (uk3, 1971). True to the psychedelic ethos, these albums were markedly experimental, depending more on interesting electronic timbres and compositional devices than instrumental virtuosity. *The Dark Side of the Moon* (p1 uk2, 1973) firmly established the band in the United States: the album was enormously successful and many of its tracks have been staples of FM rock radio since its release. Barrett was forced to leave the group in the late 1960s by the onset of mental illness, and Waters seemed obsessed with Barrett's illness and the death of his own father during World War II. Many Pink Floyd lyrics can be traced to these two themes: *Wish You Were Here* (p1 uk1, 1975), for instance, directly deals with Barrett's madness, especially in the track "Shine On You Crazy Diamond." While Genesis made Peter Gabriel the focus of its live show, Pink Floyd chose to extend the idea of the psychedelic light show to include a variety of elaborate stage effects, such as a crashing airplane and a flying pig. The complex stage show for the band's two-record concept album *The Wall* (p1 uk3, 1979) featured a wall being slowly built onstage between the band and the audience, and projected animations (akin to the famous album art) by artist Gerald Scarfe.

Impressive lighting and prop effects were a part of almost all progressive rock shows, although some bands took this idea further than others. Concept albums and rock operas first developed in the late 1960s, as did the notion of addressing

In the early days of Genesis, lead singer Peter Gabriel hit on the idea of donning costumes for performances of the band's lengthy numbers. Here Gabriel is shown performing the "Willow Farm" section from the ambitious "Supper's Ready," an epic that engages in sexuality and surrealistic images, and ends with the Second Coming. It is one of the group's signature tracks from the early 1970s and was often the climax of their live shows.

WHAT'S THAT SOURCE?

Pink Floyd Gets Panned

Pink Floyd's *Dark Side of the Moon* is an iconic rock statement, and one of the best-selling albums of all time. At the time of its release, however, the album's place among the rock canon was not at all apparent. This review from the British music weekly *Melody Maker* chronicles the premiere of *Dark Side* as it was presented to critics in 1973 at the London Planetarium with an accompanying light show. Reviewer Roy Hollingsworth depicts a mediocre reception of the work, which contrasts sharply with the album's later reception.

Heartbeat

The thick thump, the staggered bumping of a heartbeat filled the blackness, gaining in volume and intensity until it packed against your whole body. Such a glorious feeling.

That feeling of being immersed in music that is so very sacred to Floyd. The heartbeats faded to blend into a gushing stream of noise, and colour that split the room open. Imperial Floyd.

Black bag darkness gave way to the warmth of starlight as the Planetarium sky winked and twinkled into life. "'Ere look there's the Plough . . . And . . . and . . . there's the Bear," we were all quite moved. I was moved enough to fumble in the darkness for a light ale, smuggled in. It fell over.

Now as I say—it was all very moving, being slumped back in a chair surrounded by stars and heavy, dribbling, gurgling, rushing music . . . climaxes, and quiet periods, and fiddly bits.

There were a lot of fiddly bits, and as they fiddled onwards, they fiddled into nothing. Oh dear.

Yes, ten minutes from blast-off the music became so utterly confused with itself that it was virtually impossible to follow. It wasn't just a case of that either. It was becoming less and less attractive, and after 15 minutes diabolically uninteresting.

This was a dreadfully disappointing moment, and only coloured by the fact that shooting stars appeared, and shot out of the room into Baker Street.

Over Notting Hill a squad of stars so intense with white light baffled winos lying in the gutters. And then, from the West in magnificent procession came Patrick Moore, clothed in gold followed by a host of angels in white samite and Marks and Spencer tights. Patrick picked up a star-shaped guitar and jammed in the sky.

To the left, near the Post Office Tower skyline, 40 meteors sped across the sky. The sight was indeed amazing, but less amazing as the projectors showed the same movement eight times over—and Floyd fell into a jungle of nothing.

Quite a few people were beginning to chatter, and light cigarettes. A naughty thing to do.

You see, when you light a cigarette in the Planetarium a blinding light fills the hall when the match is struck—thus ruining every pattern in the sky.

A dozen fags were lit within seconds—and for a moment we were given insight into what 40 Heinkels could do over London. Flash . . . flash . . . flash . . . It was the Blitz.

And there, as people found more fun in being funny, the shape of a bunny rabbit appeared on one wall. This was done by holding a lighted match behind a hand, and performing tricks with the fingers.

Later, after several other attempts at rabbits, I witnessed a swan in strangled flight, and brace of doves. Then some enterprising fellow scooped the impromptu magic lantern show with an enormous portrayal of a naughty thing.

With Capricorn rising and hearts falling, the first side plunged to a halt. Oh what a waste of wonderful talent.

I mean, the heartbeat thing was just magnificent. Thought I was really going to witness another "Ummagumma"—something so incredible that you couldn't move or think of anything else while it was playing.

Mild applause greeted the completion of the first side, and the houselights were turned on to reveal a horde of faces. They looked slightly bored. They had every right to be.

Cosmic Ripples and Spaceship Icebergs on sticks failed to arrive.

The lights dimmed again, and the sound of coins entering a cashbox, or telephone money box, pierced the air in rhythmic ways. Sonata for the cash-box, something like that, and it was good. It became more intense, clashy, and clangy, and spirited by God—as did the whole of Side Two. It was fabulous.

Although the Planetarium sky became increasingly boring—the music

lifted, as did my head and heart. The songs, the sounds, the rhythms were solid and sound. Saxophone hit the air, and the band rocked and rolled, and then gushed, and tripped away into the night.

One song in particular was extremely Sydbarrettsian to the point of being a straight lift from any of The Lost Hero's songs.

Yes, Sydbarrettsian. A well-spoken lank voice, well echoed, and sad, with wonderfully obvious rhyming to the lyrics. Barrett still exists you know, and it was pleasing that the best track on this album is 80 per cent plus influenced by him. And I'll back that up in argument with anybody.

This track, and what followed presented Floyd as Floyd should be, enormous, and massive, and overwhelmingly impressive. It was here that quadraphonic finally hit upon me.

Here it became valid, and not some expensive toy.

I can assure you that in stereo Side Two is equally fabulous. The title track faded into the heartbeat, and the music left the room. I remember sitting, laying back, and breathing out. Nice one. But whatever happened to Side One? Nine months in the making . . . And only one good side? But draw your own conclusions when you buy this album.

Which you should do, 'cause like The Stones and The Beatles, The Floyd were also what was—and hopefully still is—all right.

Source: Roy Hollingworth, "The Dark Side of Floyd," *Melody Maker*, March 10, 1973, 19, 54.

important and serious-minded issues. Progressive rock in the 1970s extended and refined these psychedelic tendencies, and had roots that extend as far back as the playlets of Leiber and Stoller. Of all the music of the 1970s, progressive rock was most faithful to the hippie aesthetic, making it the prime target against which punk rebelled later in the decade (more about that in Chapter 10).

Roger Waters (left) and David Gilmour (right) were key to the '70s version of Pink Floyd. Waters was responsible for the big ideas that dominated the band's albums over the decade, while Gilmour's emphasis on the music (along with keyboardist Rick Wright) helped produce some of the most atmospheric music in rock. Waters and Gilmour are shown here in 1972, with drummer Nick Mason in the background.

Among the Italian progressive rock bands of the '70s, Premiata Forneria Marconi (PFM) was probably best known in the UK and the United States, partly owing to the support of members of ELP, who helped the band get signed to English and American labels. The band's 1975 album, *Chocolate Kings*, was the first to feature lyrics in English and lead singer Bernardo Lanzetti, who had lived in Austin, Texas as a college student and spoke fluent English. Pictured here in a 1976 performance are (left to right) Mauro Pagani, Patrick Djivas, Lanzetti, Franco Mussida, and Flavio Premoli.

Progressive Rock in Italy. Something about progressive rock's blending of classical music with rock and pop made the style extremely popular in Italy during the 1970s. British bands such as Genesis, Van der Graaf Generator, Gentle Giant, and Emerson, Lake & Palmer were received with great enthusiasm by Italian music fans, and sometimes more enthusiastically than they were at home. One result of prog's popularity in Italy was the emergence of several homegrown prog bands. The most successful of these groups was Premiata Forneria Marconi (PFM), whose debut album, *Storia di un minute*, hit the top of the Italian charts within its first week of release in early 1972. PFM subsequently enjoyed moderate success in the UK and United States, releasing English-language versions of much of their music. Other important Italian prog bands of the 1970s include Le Orme, Banco del Mutuo Succorso, Area, and Goblin.

JAZZ-ROCK FUSION AND JAZZ-INFLUENCED ROCK

Jazz and the Studio Musician. As rock musicians became increasingly ambitious about their music, they also focused more on achieving technical mastery on their instruments. Jazz, in particular, provided a model that many musicians embraced. For decades, jazz had been revered for the musical prowess of its players, with artists such as Charlie Parker, Dizzy Gillespie, John Coltrane, and Art Tatum setting high standards with their technical and aesthetic achievements. As solos assumed a more central role in rock music, it was natural that many artists would look to jazz as a source for new ideas. Jazz players had been involved in popular music for years, and it is a style that encourages musicians to develop their improvisatory skills. In addition to playing clubs at night, many jazz artists made a living by playing at pop recording sessions by day. The Funk Brothers who played the Motown sessions, for instance, were all gifted and experienced jazz players, as were Los Angeles studio musicians like guitarist Barney Kessel, who played on everything from Phil Spector records to those by the Monkees. In the 1970s, the "studio musician" came to mean a player who was fluent in all styles, could read music well, and could be counted on to play expertly in any musical situation. Many of the studio musicians came from the jazz tradition. Jazz-schooled players such as drummer Steve Gadd, bassist Tony Levin, and guitarists Lee Ritenour and Larry Carlton played on many rock records and their high level of professionalism served as a model for many aspiring rock musicians.

Jazz-Rock Fusion: Miles and Beyond. Already one of the most important figures in jazz during the late 1960s, trumpeter Miles Davis began noticing that the extended jams of Cream and Hendrix were not all that different from what a lot of jazz players were doing. What impressed Davis most, however, was that rock audiences would sit and listen to this kind of music. Jazz audiences were generally much smaller than those for even a moderately well attended rock show, and Davis decided that he wanted to play for festival-sized crowds. He began experimenting in live performance and in the recording studio with jazz musicians whom he thought could fuse rock with jazz, including guitarist John McLaughlin, keyboardists Joseph Zawinul, Chick Corea, and Herbie Hancock, and saxophonist Wayne Shorter. The most famous result of these experimentations was the double album *Bitches Brew*, which rose to number thirty-five on the U.S. album charts in 1970 (r4), and introduced rock audiences to jazz-rock fusion.

Following the success of *Bitches Brew*, and with a rising appreciation for technical virtuosity triggered by the progressive rock bands, members of Davis's band formed their own groups and enjoyed commercial success on the pop album charts. John McLaughlin formed the Mahavishnu Orchestra, bringing rock, jazz, and Eastern mysticism together on the debut album *Inner Mounting Flame* (1972) and subsequently enjoyed moderate success with *Birds of Fire* (p15, 1973). Herbie Hancock hit with *Head Hunters* (p13 r2, 1974), while Chick Corea's band, Return to Forever, appeared on the album charts several times with *Romantic Warrior* (p35 r23, 1976), which owed a clear debt to progressive rock. Shorter and Zawinul formed Weather Report and scored later in the decade with *Heavy Weather* (p30 r33, 1977). Violinist Jean-Luc Ponty left McLaughlin's band to pursue a solo career and released *Enigmatic Ocean* (p35, 1977). Taken together these fusion bands were only moderately successful in pop terms, but compared with typical jazz sales and audiences they were enormously popular. Instrumental music had not enjoyed such commercial success since the days of the big bands.

Frank Zappa: Satire and Complexity. Beginning with the Mothers of Invention's *Freak Out!* (1966), Frank Zappa's music blended

Pictured here during a 1973 concert in Copenhagen, Miles Davis was the most influential artist of the jazz-rock style. Although Davis was a key player in jazz from the late 1940s, in the late 1960s he began to incorporate funk and rock influences, drawing inspiration from the music of Jimi Hendrix, James Brown, and Sly and the Family Stone. Davis's album *Bitches Brew* (1970) was very influential in jazz-rock fusion and included many artists who formed important fusion groups. Among these were Chick Corea of Return to Forever, John McLaughlin of the Mahavishnu Orchestra, and Joseph Zawinul and Wayne Shorter of Weather Report.

satire, compositional sophistication, and musical virtuosity that at times pressed the bounds of good taste. Zappa's penchant for cynicism can be seen in the 1968 album sending up *Sgt. Pepper* called *We're Only in It for the Money* (p30). After the moderate success of *Money*, Zappa, with the support of a long line of band members, chalked up eight more Top 40 albums in the United States. His most successful album in the UK was *Hot Rats* (uk9), while *Apostrophe* (p10, 1974) was his biggest American success. "I'm the Slime" from *Overnite Sensation* (p32, 1973) displays Zappa's blend of jazz-fusion style playing with cartoonish vocals and satirical lyrics that offer a critique of television. Although Zappa clearly took his music-making seriously, he was vigilant in deflating any effort to interpret his music according to the usual categories, insisting that he didn't care whether it was "commercial," "artistic," or "relevant." Zappa also composed a number of pieces for small and large ensembles (or adapted rock band pieces) that are best classified as twentieth-century classical music, despite often-goofy titles such as "Mo and Herb's Vacation."

Low Sparks and Pretzel Logic: Traffic and Steely Dan. The second incarnation of the British group Traffic flourished in the 1970s on the jazz-rock scene, which was dominated by American acts. After their hiatus in the late 1960s, Steve Winwood (keyboards and vocals), Jim Capaldi (drums), and Chris Wood (flute and sax) teamed up again to release *John Barleycorn Must Die* (p11 uk5, 1970). Capaldi soon left and the band released its signature album of the 1970s, *The Low Spark of High-Heeled Boys* (p7, 1971) with drummer Jim Gordon, bassist Rick Grech, and percussionist Reebop Kwaku-Baah. The title track provides a good example of how Traffic blended Winwood's bluesy vocals with Wood's Coltrane-inspired sax soloing. After more personnel changes, the band released more successful albums, including *Shoot Out at the Fantasy Factory* (p6, 1973) and *When the Eagle Flies* (p9 uk31, 1974). Winwood left the band in 1975 to embark on a successful solo career.

Back in the United States, Steely Dan emerged with their debut album *Can't Buy a Thrill* (p17, 1972), which contained two hits, "Do It Again" (p6, 1972) and

Featuring Walter Becker (bass and guitar, second from left) and Donald Fagen (vocals and piano, right), Steely Dan used jazz elements and virtuoso studio musicians to create a winning jazz-rock sound. Every one of their seven albums in the 1970s charted in the *Billboard* Top 40. Although they did perform concerts, Becker and Fagan focused their attention on the studio, where they wrote carefully organized arrangements punctuated with improvised solo sections.

"Reelin' in the Years" (p11, 1972). Led by Donald Fagen (keyboard and vocals) and Walter Becker (bass and guitar), the band's initial lineup also included guitarist Jeff "Skunk" Baxter. After some initial success as a traditional touring band, Becker and Fagen began to focus on recording, using studio musicians to provide the instrumental tracks and virtuosic solos. For much of Steely Dan's late work, the band's only regular members were Fagen and Becker. Perhaps the best album showing this arrangement at work is *Aja* (p3 uk5, 1977), which included three hit singles: "Peg" (p11, 1977), "Deacon Blues" (p19, 1978), and "Josie" (p26, 1978). Steely Dan arrangements, like those of Zappa and other jazz rockers, were often written out before recording began. Solos, however, were left open and became showcases for some of the best studio musicians in the business. In "Peg," for example, the horns and rhythm section play mostly worked-out parts, while Jay Graydon's guitar solo was improvised live in the studio. Steely Dan placed seven albums in the American Top 40 during the 1970s, in addition to scoring ten Top 40 singles.

Horn Bands: Blood, Sweat & Tears and Chicago.

The music of Miles Davis, Frank Zappa, Traffic, and Steely Dan often relied on horns to provide a jazz element, but two bands from the early 1970s are most often identified as the jazz-rock "horn bands": Blood, Sweat & Tears and Chicago. After playing sessions with Bob Dylan and before he became Lynyrd Skynyrd's producer, keyboardist Al Kooper formed Blood, Sweat & Tears, releasing *Child Is Father to the Man*, which hit number forty in the UK in 1968 (p47). Kooper soon left the band and teamed with guitarists Michael Bloomfield and Stephen Stills to record *Super Session* (p12, 1968). With Kooper's departure from Blood, Sweat & Tears, singer David Clayton-Thomas joined and the group enjoyed enormous success in the United States with its next album, *Blood, Sweat & Tears* (p1 r15 uk15, 1969), which contained three hit singles—"You've Made Me So Very Happy" (p2, 1969), "Spinning Wheel" (p2, 1969), and "And When I Die" (p2, 1969). The album also won the Grammy Award for Album of the Year in 1970. Their follow-up *Blood, Sweat & Tears 3* (p1 uk14, 1970) contained Goffin and King's "Hi-De-Ho" (p14, 1970) and Clayton-Thomas's own "Lucretia MacEvil" (p29, 1970). Their use of a small horn section was certainly nothing new in the history of rhythm and blues or pop: Stax and Motown arrangements often used horns to "sweeten" the accompaniment. But Blood, Sweat & Tears made the horns more central to the arrangements, even providing instrumental showcases for both solo and ensemble playing that were influenced by the big band tradition in jazz. An example of this is the group's arrangement of the Rolling Stones' "Sympathy for the Devil," which Blood, Sweat & Tears titled "Symphony for the Devil/Sympathy for the Devil." Similar to a Vanilla Fudge symphonic-psychedelic cover version, Blood, Sweat & Tears created an almost eight-minute epic out of the Stones tune, including long instrumental passages that employ both traditional jazz and avant-garde practices. Although their most popular music was released at the beginning of the decade, Blood, Sweat & Tears continued to release successful music until the middle of the 1970s.

Another band to place increased focus on a horn section was Chicago. Beginning with their debut album, *Chicago Transit Authority* (p17 uk9, 1969), the band released thirteen Top 40 albums in the United States during the 1970s (five in the UK) and five of these went to number one. The band also scored twenty-two Top 40 singles (three in the UK) with its blend of melodic pop vocals and sophisticated, horn-dominated accompaniments. "If You Leave Me Now," sung by bassist Peter

Blood, Sweat & Tears employed a horn section to further develop the blending of rock and jazz. The group was formed by Al Kooper in the late 1960s, although he soon left the band and was replaced by singer David Clayton-Thomas, who sang hits like "Spinning Wheel" and "You've Made Me So Very Happy." The band is shown performing here in the early 1970s.

Cetera, rose to number one in both the U.S. and UK charts in 1976, and is a good example of the band's softer side. "Does Anybody Really Know What Time It Is?" (p7, 1970) from their first album features the singing of keyboardist Robert Lamm and demonstrates how they blended Beatles-influenced pop with jazz-influenced horn arrangements. The track begins with an instrumental introduction focusing on rhythmic ensemble playing and breaks into a brief trumpet solo from Lee Loughnane. The horns then retreat to the accompaniment as Lamm delivers the verses and chorus, supported by Beatle-esque backup vocals. A final flourish at the end is provided by a jazzy trombone lick courtesy of James Pankow.

As popular as jazz rock was during the 1970s, it was also the source of enormous controversy within the jazz community, especially later in the decade. Some jazz musicians and fans welcomed the blending of rock and jazz elements, but many traditionalists hated it, labeling the style a sell-out to the pop-music industry. Some rock purists also rejected jazz rock because it seemed too concerned with instrumental virtuosity and lacked the visceral punch that they felt was essential to rock. Similarly, these same rock purists often rejected progressive rock as too complex and pretentious, while most classical-music listeners found progressive styles too pop-oriented to be taken seriously. Thus, jazz rock and progressive rock often found themselves in an in-between situation with some listeners—"neither fish nor fowl," stylistically speaking. The psychedelic approach was to blend styles freely and delight in the new combinations; and since the first half of the 1970s was dominated by the hippie aesthetic, most rock listeners and critics embraced jazz rock and progressive rock as an extension of hippie musical values.

GLAM ROCK AND ROCK THEATER: SHOCKING CHARACTERS

Dressing Up and Acting Out. In our discussion of Genesis, we touched on Peter Gabriel's use of costumes, makeup, and props in performance and linked this to Pink Floyd's growing fascination with highly visual stage shows. In the early 1970s, big rock shows were mostly staged in arenas and stadiums rather than theaters and ballrooms, as they had been in the late 1960s. This led to a growth in production standards across the rock-music industry. Increasingly, audiences expected a show with professional stage lights and some kind of special effects. Genesis and Pink Floyd stand out in the context of many bands that offered elaborate extra-musical excitement. Amid this new attention to the more theatrical elements of rock performance, it was perhaps inevitable that certain artists would come to specialize in portraying fictional characters onstage. In the 1970s, two of the most important figures in this regard were David Bowie and Alice Cooper. Both adopted distinct onstage personas that most audiences understood as characters they were portraying. The roots of this practice go back to the Beatles and the "concept" of the Beatles portraying the Lonely Hearts Club Band. With the growth of the theatrical side of the concert business in the 1970s, it became possible to put on and tour a sophisticated show with elaborate props and effects—a kind of rock theater with increasingly higher production values.

Ziggy Played Guitar: David Bowie.

A style of theatrical rock called "glam rock" was particularly important in the United Kingdom in the early 1970s. Popular glam rock groups, such as T. Rex and Mott the Hoople, dressed in androgynous clothing and sang songs that often discussed the aspects of glam culture, including themes of science fiction, alienation, and typical characters associated with the glam scene. Of all the British glam stars who stormed the UK charts, however, the most important was David Bowie. His first important success in the UK came with the single "Space Oddity" (uk5, 1969; p15, 1973), a song inspired by the Stanley Kubrick film adaptation of Arthur C. Clarke's *2001: A Space Odyssey.* By the early 1970s, Bowie had formed the Spiders from Mars, a band with shifting personnel that featured Mick Ronson on guitar. He also created the character of Ziggy Stardust for the album *The Rise and Fall of Ziggy Stardust and the Spiders from Mars* (uk5, 1972), which contained "Suffragette City" (uk10, 1972). The release of *Aladdin Sane* (p17 uk1, 1973) and *Pin-Ups* (p23 uk1, 1973) reinforced Bowie's stature in the UK, while helping him become the only UK glam artist to achieve significant success in the United States. The album that made Bowie's reputation in America was *David Live* (p8 uk2, 1974), which featured a generous selection of songs from earlier albums that had topped the charts in the UK. The success of *Young Americans* (p9 uk2, 1975), which contained the single "Fame" (p1 uk17, 1975), and *Station to Station* (p3 uk5, 1976) solidified Bowie's star status in America.

Alice Cooper: Welcome to My Nightmare.

It is perhaps a measure of how far hippie androgyny had developed by the early 1970s that a band of hard-drinking, tough-looking rock and rollers could have a front man named Alice. On stage, Vincent Furnier became Alice Cooper and led his audiences

David Bowie performing in 1973 as his alter ego, Ziggy Stardust. Like Alice Cooper and Peter Gabriel, Bowie pushed the boundaries of sexual and gender identity, although in a more mysterious, fashion-conscious manner. Ziggy Stardust emerged on the album *The Rise and Fall of Ziggy Stardust and the Spiders from Mars* (1972), and Bowie continued to reinvent the character throughout the decade.

Kiss took the idea of onstage personae further than any band before them, creating four distinct characters (prompting the sale of action figures) and never being seen (at least in the 1970s) without their makeup. The band's show was bombastic, setting a new standard for live production. Years earlier, bands had simply stood and played, but a Kiss show was theater, extending the approaches developed by Genesis, Alice Cooper, and David Bowie.

into the darkest parts of the imagination, often ending the show in a gruesome way. On different tours, Cooper was hanged, executed in an electric chair, and beheaded by a guillotine. His obsession with such ghoulish topics was influenced by his admiration for Jim Morrison, who befriended the young Cooper in the late 1960s. After two commercially unsuccessful records produced by Frank Zappa and released on Zappa's label, Cooper and his band released *Love It to Death* (p35, 1971), which contained the single "I'm Eighteen" (p21, 1971), an almost gothic study in teenage depression and anger. Bob Ezrin (who later produced *The Wall*) produced this album and continued to work with the group. Cooper enjoyed rising success with *Killer* (p21 uk27, 1971); *School's Out* (p2 uk4, 1972), which contained the single "School's Out" (p7 uk1, 1972); and *Billion Dollar Babies*, which hit number one on both sides of the Atlantic in 1973. Cooper's often-dramatic music had just enough self-satire in it to keep things from getting too heavy. For example, in "Be My Lover," Cooper and the band go into the kind of bump-and-grind ending found in strip clubs, prefaced by an "oh" spoken in the manner of movie sex goddess Mae West. By the middle of the decade, the original band had split up and Cooper went solo, enjoying more success with *Welcome to My Nightmare* (p5 uk19, 1975).

It is important to recognize the similarities and differences between Bowie and Cooper. Each adopted a stage persona that was based in fantasy and both pushed the boundaries of sexual and gender identities. But while Cooper enjoyed his greatest commercial success in the UK when glam was at its peak, he did not share Bowie's interest in the world of urbane fashion. Bowie also tended to change characters, while Cooper stuck with his Alice character for his entire career. Despite their differences, Cooper and Bowie shared a common aesthetic goal that had its roots in psychedelia: making the music a trip—even if the trip ended up being weird, campy, or ghoulish.

KISS and Makeup. Taking the theatrical element even further, all four member of KISS—bassist Gene Simmons, drummer Peter Criss, and guitarists Paul Stanley and Ace Frehley—cast themselves as distinct characters onstage, rather than only the lead singer donning makeup and costumes. The band wore elaborate face makeup that kept their countenances secret for years. From the beginning, KISS provided a bombastic live show using lights, flames, and explosions to create a high-energy rock spectacle. Stylistically, KISS was essentially a blues-rock band. "Rock and Roll All Nite" illustrates their approach, blending verses not unlike those of Bad Company or Foghat with an anthemic sing-along chorus that works well as the song's hook. The group's first few albums—*KISS* (p87, 1974), *Hotter Than Hell* (p100, 1974), and *Dressed to Kill* (p32, 1975)—did not do particularly well. When the band released a live version of "Rock and Roll All Nite," however, it went to number twelve in the United States (1975) and prepared the way for the success of

Destroyer (p1 uk22, 1976). The live album *Alive* (p9, 1975) contained songs from their earlier albums, which saw increased sales and playing time on rock radio. By the end of the decade, KISS had masterfully exploited the marketing opportunities provided by their success, starring in their own feature film and even selling action figures.

THE SINGER-SONGWRITERS

The Importance of Being Earnest. The singer-songwriter style of the 1970s arose in part from the folk revival of the 1960s, and from the acoustic music of the Beatles. When Bob Dylan delivered a song from behind his acoustic guitar, or Paul McCartney sang while at the piano, it was understood that each was sincerely expressing the results of his own personal reflection and experience. The singer-songwriter movement was especially appealing to audiences that had left college and moved into adulthood. In a famous 1976 *New York* magazine article, writer Tom Wolfe referred to the 1970s as the "Me Decade," which is particularly fitting in the context of the "self"-oriented singer-songwriter movement. The singer-songwriters stood as the direct antithesis to Bowie and Cooper: rather than playing characters, these artists seemed to reveal their unmediated personal perspectives. Much of this, it is important to understand, is only an ideal. No matter how authentic a performance or recording seems, show-business concerns for projecting the proper image almost always mediate it. The aural impression of sincerity and intimacy created by most singer-songwriter records was achieved by placing the singer front and center, with the accompaniment in a secondary and supporting role. In the 1970s, Dylan continued his career as a singer-songwriter, as did John Lennon. Lennon enjoyed several hit singles and albums in the first half of the decade, perhaps most notably *Imagine* (p1 uk1, 1971), which featured a title single that went to number three in the United States. In the case of both these artists, the focus was always the singer and the song.

1960s Connections: James Taylor, Carole King, and Paul Simon. One of the important new singer-songwriters to emerge out of the late 1960s was James Taylor. Taylor was among the first acts signed to the Beatles' record label, Apple, in 1968. His debut on Apple, *James Taylor* (1968), did not chart, although it contained "Carolina in My Mind," which would become internationally popular over time. Taylor soon signed to Warner, and hit in 1970 with "Fire and Rain" (p3 uk4) and *Sweet Baby James* (p3 uk6,

After a productive decade as a top songwriter in the 1960s, Carole King stepped into the spotlight to become one of the most important singer-songwriters of the '70s and eventually one of the most successful female songwriters of the twentieth century. Her 1970 album *Tapestry* sat at the top of the album charts for more than three months and remained on those charts for almost six years. She is shown here in a performance for the BBC in 1970.

Listening Guide

Carole King, "You've Got a Friend" Ode SP-77009

Words and music by Carole King, produced by Lou Adler. Contained on *Tapestry* (1970).

FORM: Compound AABA form. The A section is based on contrasting verse-chorus form, and consists of a 16-bar verse and a 14-bar chorus. The 10-bar bridge section is followed by a partial return of the A section, consisting of only the chorus. The song ends with a quiet coda.

TIME SIGNATURE: 4/4.

INSTRUMENTATION: Acoustic piano, acoustic bass, acoustic guitar, congas, string quartet, lead and backup vocals.

	0:00–0:12	**Introduction**, 4 mm.	Solo acoustic piano sets the intimate tone of the song.
A	0:12–0:58	**Verse 1**, 16 mm.	Vocal enters, as piano continues but with the support of the acoustic bass. "When you're down . . ."
	0:58–1:49	**Chorus**, 18 mm.	Congas and harmony vocal are added. James Taylor's acoustic guitar playing can just barely be heard in the background. The chorus consists of 14 bars, to which 4 bars are added, drawn directly from the additional introduction. "You just call . . ."
A	1:49–2:34	**Verse 2**, 16 mm.	As before, but now with acoustic guitar continuing and string quartet added. "If the sky . . ."
	2:34–3:13	**Chorus**, 14 mm.	All instruments continue, as harmony vocal and congas return. "You just call . . ."
B	3:13–3:42	**Bridge**, 10 mm.	Same instrumentation as verse 2, "Now ain't it good . . ."
A'	3:42–4:21	**Chorus**, 14 mm.	As in the first chorus, string quartet drops out until the very end. Note how the guitar gets busy toward the end. "You just call . . ."
	4:21–5:05	**Coda**, 15 mm.	Repeat of vamp drawn from first 2 bars of the introduction, with King improvising vocal lines on top. "You've got a friend . . ."

1970), which established his popularity on both sides of the Atlantic. He enjoyed continued success with albums like *Mud Slide Slim* (p2 uk4, 1971) and *One Man Dog* (p4 uk27, 1972). Taylor's single "You've Got a Friend" (p1 uk4, 1971) was written by a familiar name in American popular music, Carole King. By the end of the 1960s, King had decided to step out from behind the scenes, becoming one of the most important and influential female artists of the 1970s. She scored a string of successful albums, beginning with *Tapestry* (p1 uk4, 1970), which contained the hit "It's Too Late" (p1 uk6, 1971) as well as her own version of "You've Got a Friend" and a reinterpretation of "Will You Love Me Tomorrow?" Later King albums included *Music* (p1 uk18, 1972) and *Rhymes and Reasons* (p2, 1972).

Another familiar name among the singer-songwriters was Paul Simon. In the wake of his tremendous run of hit records with Art Garfunkel, Simon decided to strike out on his own, updating his 1960s approach and releasing *Paul Simon* (p4 uk1, 1972). The album contained "Mother and Child Reunion" (p4 uk5, 1972)—a song that featured Jamaican musicians before reggae was well known. He often employed studio musicians to play on his tracks and expanded the singer-songwriter style. Simon increasingly incorporated jazz elements in his music with a series of albums and singles including *There Goes Rhymin' Simon* (p2 uk4, 1973), "Koda-chrome" (p2, 1973), *Still Crazy after All These Years* (p1 uk6, 1975), and "50 Ways to Leave Your Lover" (p1 uk23, 1975). A clear example of this is "Still Crazy after All These Years." The lyrics reflect on meeting an old lover by chance and reassessing the course his life has taken. The backup playing is subdued but sophisticated during the verses, while the middle section features a soaring and melodic jazz-tinged saxophone solo.

American Poets Society.
Carly Simon (no relation to Paul) first came to the attention of most rock listeners with "That's the Way I Always Heard It Should Be" (p10, 1971) and "Anticipation" (p13, 1971). Similar to the music of Carole King, Simon's confessional songs focus on her vocals, piano, acoustic guitar, and strings. Simon's lyrics frequently discuss life changes facing the post-college generation. Her album *No Secrets* (p1 uk3, 1973) stands as the peak of her popular appeal, and contains the single "You're So Vain" (p1 uk3, 1972). The song features backup vocals by Mick Jagger and was rumored to refer to Simon's romantic relationship with Jagger, actor Warren Beatty, or many other dominant male characters in her life at the time. After nearly forty years of remaining secretive about the subject of the song, in 2010 Simon revealed "You're So Vain" was written about music executive David Geffen. Harry Chapin was another important singer-songwriter from the period. His "Taxi" (p24, 1972) and "Cat's in the Cradle" (p1 1974) both reflect on life's twists and turns while highlighting his emotive baritone voice and acoustic guitar. Don McLean also used piano, acoustic guitar, and nostalgic lyrics to create music aligned with this movement. His "American Pie" (p1 uk2, 1972) attempts to summarize the previous two decades of rock and roll history, while his song "Vincent" (p12 uk1, 1972) offers a portrait of the painter Vincent Van Gogh. Jim Croce was at the height of his popularity in 1973 when he was killed in an airplane crash. His song "Bad, Bad Leroy Brown" (p1, 1973) was at the top of the U.S. charts at the time of the accident. The release a few months later of his "Time in a Bottle" (p1, 1974), a reflection on the unwelcome approach of death, recorded just months before the crash, gave the song an eerie poignancy.

British Singer-Songwriters: Van Morrison, Cat Stevens, and Elton John.
The singer-songwriter style was not restricted to Americans, as Van Morrison, Cat Stevens, and Elton John all enjoyed considerable success during the early and mid-1970s. Morrison continued his 1960s success into the new decade, bringing his blend of jazz and rhythm and blues influences to albums like *Moondance* (p29 uk32, 1970) and *Tupelo Honey* (p29, 1971). Cat Stevens first stormed the U.S. charts with

Elton John, pictured here in a 1975 concert, was the most successful singer-songwriter of the early 1970s. He blended folk and rhythm and blues influences (he performed on the black dance show *Soul Train*) with some of David Bowie's glam-rock sensibility. John's worldwide popularity continues to this day.

his single "Peace Train" (p7, 1971). A string of successful albums made him a regular on the charts on both sides of the Atlantic, including *Teaser and the Firecat* (p2 uk3, 1971), *Catch Bull at Four* (p1 uk2, 1972), and *Buddha and the Chocolate Box* (p2 uk3, 1974). Perhaps the most successful of the singer-songwriters was Elton John. John was introduced to American audiences with the single "Your Song" (p8 uk7, 1971), and followed with a series of hugely successful albums: *Honky Chateau* (p1 uk2, 1972), *Don't Shoot Me I'm Only the Piano Player* (p1 uk1, 1973), *Goodbye Yellow Brick Road* (p1 uk1, 1973), and *Caribou* (p1 uk1, 1974). He wrote most of his songs with lyricist Bernie Taupin, forming a songwriting team that rivaled the success of Lennon and McCartney. Taupin's images are clever and compelling, and John's melodic-harmonic sense draws on a wide range of influences. Except for the fact that John performs the tunes, the partnership is strongly reminiscent of the Tin Pan Alley and Brill Building songwriting teams of previous decades, owing to the fact that they wrote their respective parts completely separately. John began employing a backup band in the early 1970s (most often drummer Nigel Olsson, bassist Dee Murray, and guitarist Davey Johnstone), and the idea of the singer-songwriter as front man became the model for many others later in the decade. Elton John's move into rock prepared the way for the next batch of harder-rocking singer-songwriters, including Billy Joel, Bob Seger, and Bruce Springsteen (discussed in Chapter 10).

Canadian Voices: Joni Mitchell and Neil Young. Joni

Mitchell's music in the 1960s was very much indebted to the folk revival, and like Paul Simon, she began experimenting with the use of jazz in the 1970s. Mitchell first climbed the pop charts as a songwriter when Judy Collins recorded "Both Sides Now" (p8 uk14, 1968). Mitchell's albums, including *Ladies of the Canyon* (p27 uk8, 1970) and *Blue* (p15 uk3, 1972) did not achieve popularity to match their critical success. Her music developed further into the mid-1970s, as she made a practice of using very talented and sometimes well-known musicians to back her. *Court and Spark* (p2 uk14, 1974), which contained the single "Help Me" (p7), was her biggest commercial success and featured the playing of Tom Scott's LA Express. A year later, she experimented with new, sometimes avant-garde stylistic territory with *The Hissing of Summer Lawns* (p4 uk14, 1975), and later explored esoteric jazz with *Mingus* (p17 uk24, 1979). Mitchell was probably the most musically eclectic and experimental singer-songwriter of the decade, and her influence extended directly into the Lilith Fair movement of the 1990s (discussed in Chapter 13).

Also with roots in the 1960s, Neil Young enjoyed success as a member of Buffalo Springfield, and in his on-again, off-again relationship with Crosby, Stills, and Nash.

As a solo artist, Young placed a string of albums high on the charts. He began the 1970s with *After the Gold Rush* (p8 uk7, 1970), containing "Southern Man," a song that directly confronted slavery and the question of reparations. The track never charted, but received enough airplay that Lynyrd Skynyrd felt they had to answer it in the lyrics to "Sweet Home Alabama" (the entire second verse responds to Young's sharp criticism of racism in the South). Young enjoyed his greatest commercial and critical success with *Harvest* (p1 uk1, 1972), which featured the hit "Heart of Gold" (p1 uk10). Performing in a style in which voices are often pretty and controlled, Young's singing voice is frequently thin, somewhat out of tune, and seemingly unsure. But like Bob Dylan, Young showed that in the rock context imperfect vocal qualities could be deeply expressive and evocative.

With music ranging from folk to avant-garde rock to jazz, Joni Mitchell (pictured here in a 1974 concert) is probably the most musically eclectic and experimental singer-songwriter of the decade. She combined her own strong songwriting skills with a unique style of acoustic guitar performance and several very talented backup bands.

COUNTRY ROCK

The Gift to Be Simple. Like the singer-songwriter movement, the country-rock style that emerged in the early 1970s was in many ways the result of a reaction against the growing excesses of psychedelic rock. The impulse that made rock listeners interested in blues or folk also attracted many rockers to country music. The apparent simplicity of country music seemed more honest and authentic to the American experience than most pop music. As we saw in Chapter 1, this was partly because the genre projected a perception that it was down-home music. Nashville and Bakersfield, California, became destinations for many rock musicians to connect with the country side of the music business. The Byrds were among the first rockers to record in Nashville in the new country rock style. By 1968, most of the original Byrds had left the band and Roger McGuinn brought guitarist Gram Parsons on board. Parsons knew the country style well, and this is evident in the band's influential *Sweetheart of the Rodeo* (1968). Bob Dylan also headed to Nashville to record *Nashville Skyline* (p3 uk1, 1969) during this period, which contains a duet version of "Girl from the North Country" sung with Johnny Cash.

Now out of the Byrds, David Crosby teamed up with Buffalo Springfield's Stephen Stills and the Hollies' Graham Nash to record *Crosby, Stills & Nash* (p6 uk25, 1969). Their next album, *Déjà Vu* (p1 uk5, 1970), included Neil Young (who had been in Buffalo Springfield with Stills), followed by the live album, *4 Way Street* (p1 uk5, 1971). Crosby, Stills, and Nash (with or without Young) blended the folk rock of the Byrds with touches of jazz, country, and blues. "Suite: Judy Blue Eyes" (p21, 1969) provides a good example of the band's blend of acoustic and electric instruments, close vocal harmony, and catchy pop songwriting. The family narrative of "Teach Your Children" (p16, 1970) (in addition to a prominent pedal steel guitar performed by Jerry Garcia) also shows strong connections to country music.

While working with Dylan in upstate New York, the Band recorded its first album, *Music from Big Pink* (p30, 1968). Led by drummer Levon Helm and guitarist Robbie Robertson, this group of mostly Canadian musicians had a deep love for the music of the American South, including country music. A series of successful albums, including *The Band* (p9 uk25, 1970), *Cahoots* (p21, 1971), and *Rock of Ages* (p6, 1972), established them among American listeners. Their first single was "The Weight" (uk21, 1968), a great example of a song that went largely unnoticed in the U.S. at the time of release, but has since become a fixture in the standard rock repertoire. The group's next release, "Up on Cripple Creek" (p25, 1970), had as its B-side "The Night They Drove Old Dixie Down." "Dixie" chronicles the fall of the South during the Civil War and draws on both folk and country styles.

Poor Boys Make Good: Creedence Clearwater Revival.

Most listeners in the late 1960s were surprised to learn that the band made up of brothers John and Tom Fogerty on guitar, Stu Cook on bass, and Doug Clifford on drums were from the San Francisco Bay area. Their music was an eclectic blend: stylistically they had a country sound, John Fogerty sang like a rhythm and blues vocalist, and they came from the home of psychedelia. Recording for the small Fantasy label, Creedence Clearwater Revival (CCR) placed a long string of singles on the charts, beginning with "Suzie Q" (p11, 1968), and extended their success to Britain with "Proud Mary" (p2 uk8, 1969) and "Bad Moon Rising" (p2 uk1, 1969). John Fogerty wrote most of the band's music, delivering commercially successful albums like *Green River* (p1 uk20, 1969), *Willy and the Poor Boys* (p3 uk10, 1970), and *Cosmo's Factory* (p1 uk1, 1970). The hippie component was not entirely missing from CCR's music. *Willy and the Poor Boys* showed the influence of *Sgt. Pepper*, as the members of CCR became the jug band pictured on the cover and named in the title. From the first track, "Down on the Corner," to "Poor Boy Shuffle" and "Fortunate Son," the tracks seem to be generated from the central "concept" of the album. Yet, much like the Canadian members of the Band, the southern themes of this music aligned CCR most closely with country rock.

The Avocado Mafia.

By the early 1970s, Los Angeles, Woodstock, and San Francisco became centers for country rock in the United States. In Southern California, the Eagles were the leading band working in this style. Guitarist Glenn Frey and drummer Don Henley got to know one another while playing in the touring band for singer Linda Ronstadt. They decided to form their own band and recruited bassist Randy Meisner and guitarist Bernie Leadon, recording their debut album in London—not sunny California—under the production of Glyn Johns. This album, called *Eagles* (p22, 1972), was followed by a country-rock concept album about the Old West called *Desperado* (p41, 1973). Guitarist Don Felder joined the group after the second album, and they subsequently released *On the Border* (p17 uk28, 1974) and *One of These Nights* (p1 uk8, 1975). Beginning with "Take It Easy" (p12, 1972), the band placed eight singles in the American Top 40 by 1975, including "Best of My Love" (p1, 1974) and "One of These Nights" (p1, 1975). By mid-decade, Leadon was replaced by ex–James Gang guitarist Joe Walsh, and the band moved away from its country rock sound to become even bigger stars.

The Eagles were the leaders of the California country-rock scene, placing eight singles in the U.S. Top 40 by 1975 by blending a strong pop sensibility with often rich vocal harmonies and driving guitars with a country twang. Shown here in a 1973 performance in the Netherlands are (left to right) Randy Meisner, Don Henley, Glenn Frey, and Bernie Leadon.

The Eagles' "Take It Easy." The Eagles brought together many elements of previous rock styles, and their first hit, "Take It Easy," is a good example of the group's country-rock approach. The first seventeen seconds of the tune tell the listener a lot about where the band is coming from musically. Opening with big, brilliant electric guitar chords reminiscent of folk rock, another electric guitar soon enters with a lick that is meant to imitate the sound of the steel guitar, characteristic of country music. As the song continues and the lead vocal enters, Glenn Frey sings with a southern accent. When the backup vocals enter, they show a marked Beatles and Beach Boys influence (notice how the harmonies are set high in the male voice register). In the second verse, a high harmony is added to make it a duet, much in the style of the Everly Brothers. The guitar continues to emulate a steel guitar during the solo, and banjo is added in the accompaniment to reinforce the country connection. In the third verse, a new vocal part is added above the lead vocal to create interest and keep the arrangement fresh. In the coda, the banjo comes to the front of the mix, and the band showcases their harmony vocals. The song is in simple verse form—there is no clear chorus or bridge—but the verse structure is more complicated than is usual for a simple verse form. In this case, it consists of three 8-bar sections to total 24 bars. Notice that only the first two 8-bar sections are used in the instrumental verse.

A Performance That Launched a Career. Glenn Frey and Don Henley did much of the planning for their new band while touring with Linda Ronstadt. In fact, Ronstadt and her manager, John Boylan, were helpful bringing Randy Meisner and Bernie Leadon into the group. And while all four Eagles would appear on the singer's 1972 album, *Linda Ronstadt*, this entire foursome backed Ronstadt in only one performance. The show was at Disneyland on July 15, 1971, almost a year before the band's debut album would appear. Leadon has remarked that the group had rehearsed together once before this show, but this otherwise routine show did indeed mark the first public performance of one of the top bands in rock history.

Listening Guide

The Eagles, "Take It Easy" Asylum 11005

Words and music by Jackson Browne and Glenn Frey, produced by Glyn Johns. Reached #12 on the *Billboard* "Hot 100" chart in the summer of 1972.

FORM: Simple verse form. The verse structure is complicated, with three distinct 8-bar phrases. The middle phrase sounds like it might be a chorus, and the last phrase has a refrain. The song cycles through the verse four times, with the third time (instrumental verse) consisting of only two repetitions of the verse.

TIME SIGNATURE: 4/4.

INSTRUMENTATION: Acoustic and electric guitars, bass, banjo, drums, lead and backup vocals.

0:00–0:17	**Introduction**, 10 mm.	8 bars of big-sounding guitars, then 2 bars with the entire band, setting the country-flavored mood of the song.
0:17–0:58	**Verse 1**, 24 mm. (8 + 8 + 8)	Lead vocal enters, joined by rich vocal harmonies in the second 8-bar phrase. "Well I'm runnin' . . ."
0:58–1:44	**Verse 2**, 26 mm.	2-bar country guitar riff from introduction is followed by the 24-bar verse, performed mostly as in verse 1, with the addition of a second backup vocal part in the first and third 8-bar phrases. "Well I'm standin' . . ."
1:44–2:13	**Instrumental verse**, 16 mm.	Guitar solo based on first two phrases of the verse. Note the addition of banjo to the accompaniment.
2:13–2:55	**Verse 3**, 24 mm.	As before, but with the addition of even more backup vocals. The banjo continues in the background. "Well I'm runnin' . . ."
2:55–3:31	**Coda**, 19 mm.	10 bars of vamp with choral vocals on top and the banjo moving to the front of the mix, then a new 9-bar melody based on the verse that ends with a surprise chord.

This chapter has followed the development of several rock styles of the first half of the 1970s, tracing their roots in the psychedelic era. Surveying the music of the first half of the 1970s, it is clear that aspects of psychedelia became the impetus for the formation of new styles. Country rock focused on the integration of country music into rock, for instance, while progressive rock refined the use of classical music, and jazz rock experimented with infusing jazz into the rock tradition. The close connections found in rock music between 1966 and 1976 might raise questions about the usefulness of these stylistic divisions. It is probably best to view the music discussed in Chapters 7 and 8 as more unified than divided, and to look for connections between stylistic categories. What unifies the music is the hippie aesthetic, and until

Sound Check

Artist	Song	Sound
Led Zeppelin	Whole Lotta Love (1969)	Form: compound AABA Riff-based Psychedelic central section Vocal cadenza
The Allman Brothers Band	Whipping Post (1969)	Form: contrasting verse-chorus Jazz influence Rhythmic fluctuation Dramatic build to final chorus
Santana	Evil Ways (1970)	Form: simple verse Two-chord vamp Emphasis on Latin rhythms Lengthy organ and guitar solos
Yes	Roundabout (1972)	Form: compound AABA Extended B section Extended instrumental solos Layered harmony vocals
Carole King	You've Got a Friend (1970)	Form: compound AABA No drum kit or electric instruments Intimate tone Close vocal harmony
The Eagles	Take It Easy (1972)	Form: simple verse Country mood Active banjo Extended vamp at the end

about 1975 there was nothing to deter the idea that rock music would continue to develop the subgenres that emerged under the banner of psychedelia. However, three things happened in the mid-1970s that changed the course of rock history: (1) corporate conglomerates became involved in the music business, (2) the punk movement began to form, and (3) disco music produced to accompany dancing at large-scale clubs became widely popular. The reaction within the rock community caused by the rise of disco will be explored in Chapter 9, and the challenge of punk's return-to-simplicity approach will play an important role in Chapter 10.

For Additional Online Resources, visit:
digital.wwnorton.com/whatsthatsound5

FURTHER READING

Mark Blake, *Comfortably Numb: The Inside Story of Pink Floyd* (Da Capo, 2008).

Hank Bordowitz, *Bad Moon Rising: The Unofficial History of Creedence Clearwater Revival* (Schirmer, 1998).

Marley Brandt, *Southern Rockers: The Roots and Legacy of Southern Rock* (Billboard Books, 1999).

David Buckley, *Strange Fascination: David Bowie, the Definitive Story* (Chicago Review, 2017).

Henry Edwards and Tony Zanetta, *Stardust: The David Bowie Story* (McGraw-Hill, 1986).

John Einarson, *Desperados: The Roots of Country Rock* (Cooper Square, 2001).

Mark Eliot, *To the Limit: The Untold Story of the Eagles* (Little, Brown, 1998).

Susan Fast, *In the Houses of the Holy: Led Zeppelin and the Power of Rock Music* (Oxford University Press, 2001).

Billy James, *An American Band: The Story of Grand Funk Railroad* (SAF Publishing, 1999).

Bob Kealing, *Calling Me Home: Gram Parsons and the Roots of Country Rock* (University Press of Florida, 2012).

Carole King, *A Natural Woman: A Memoir* (Grand Central Publishing, 2012).

Edward Macan, *Rocking the Classics: English Progressive Rock and the Counterculture* (Oxford, 1997).

Dave Marsh, *Before I Get Old: The Story of the Who* (St. Martin's, 1983).

Barry Miles, *Zappa: A Biography* (Grove, 2005).

Stuart Nicholson, *Jazz Rock: A History* (Schirmer, 1998).

Philip Norman, *Sir Elton: The Definitive Biography* (Carroll & Graf, 2001).

Alan Paul, *One Way Out: The Inside History of the Allman Brothers Band* (St. Martin's, 2014).

Simon Reynolds, *Shock and Awe: Glam Rock and Its Legacy, from the Seventies to the Twenty-First Century* (Dey Street, 2016).

Linda Ronstadt, *Simple Dreams: A Musical Memoir* (Simon & Schuster, 2013).

Carlos Santana, *The Universal Tone: Bringing My Story to Light* (Little, Brown, 2013).

Marc Shapiro, *The Long Run: The Story of the Eagles* (Omnibus, 1995).

Paul Stump, *The Music's All That Matters: A History of Progressive Rock* (Quartet Books, 1997).

Brian Sweet, *Steely Dan: Reelin' in the Years* (Omnibus, 2000).

Dave Thompson, *Alice Cooper: Welcome to My Nightmare* (Omnibus, 2012).

Sheila Weller, *Girls Like Us: Carole King, Joni Mitchell, Carly Simon—and the Journey of a Generation* (Washington Square, 2008).

Dave Zimmer, *Crosby, Stills, and Nash: The Authorized Biography* (Da Capo, 2000).

CHAPTER 9

BLACK POP, REGGAE, AND THE RISE OF DISCO

CHAPTER PREVIEW

- During the first half of the 1970s, rock and black pop were supported by relatively separate markets, though they often shared important musical characteristics.

- Sly and the Family Stone was among the first groups to cross over to white rock audiences, establishing a funkier style of black pop that was developed by bands like Kool and the Gang; Earth, Wind, and Fire; and Tower of Power.

- Motown artists gained more control in the recording studio, led by concept-driven albums from Marvin Gaye and Stevie Wonder.

- Kenny Gamble and Leon Huff developed the Philadelphia sound, often adding smooth string lines to catchy grooves in arrangements for the O'Jays and the Spinners.

- Isaac Hayes and Curtis Mayfield composed music for important blaxploitation films of the 1970s such as *Shaft* and *Superfly*.

- Building on the funk grooves of James Brown, George Clinton developed an approach that mixed psychedelia and concept-album features to create music for both Parliament and Funkadelic.

- Originating in Jamaica, reggae began to attract listeners after Eric Clapton covered "I Shot the Sheriff," helping artists such as Bob Marley to become important figures during the second half of the decade.

- Disco emerged into mainstream mid-decade as a kind of novelty style, but soon grew to become a dominant force in pop, fueled by the success of *Saturday Night Fever* and the music of artists such as KC and the Sunshine Band, the Bee Gees, and Donna Summer.

Released in 1971, Marvin Gaye's *What's Going On* signaled an important change in direction for Motown. Departing from the traditional Motown formula, which featured singles over albums, it was a concept album. Gaye's songs were linked together, flowing seamlessly from one to the next, creating the feeling of a larger, complete artistic work. Diverging from the traditional Motown stance against controversy, Gaye focused his lyrics on important social issues like the Vietnam War ("What's Going On" and "What's Happening Brother"), the environment ("Mercy Mercy Me [The Ecology]"), and urban blight ("Inner City Blues [Make Me Wanna Holler]"). Popular and influential in its own time, *What's Going On* is still cited by industry professionals as one of the most important albums ever made. The photo shown here is from the same session that produced the shot featured on the album's cover.

When rock and roll emerged in the mid-1950s, it was controversial for a number of reasons. One of the ways rock and roll challenged white middle-class values was in its blending of rhythm and blues and country and western. For many in America, the increased emphasis on musical elements clearly drawn from black music elicited the strongest reaction.

Early rock and roll, it is often claimed, acted as a force for breaking down racial and cultural barriers during the 1950s. In the context of rock's history, it is ironic that by the end of the 1970s fans of mainstream rock were overwhelmingly white, as were most of the musicians and others involved with making, performing, and selling rock. During the 1970s, black pop was still contained in a market separate from the mainstream (which included rock). Despite their separate markets, however, there were many musical similarities between styles originating in the "soul" market and the most popular rock at the time. Black pop in the 1970s deserves a much fuller treatment than can be provided here—one that sets this music primarily in the larger context of the African American pop traditions. We will consider this music in terms of how it relates to the history of rock. In the context of the 1970s, we will also explore how black pop in the 1970s inspired the rise of reggae and disco.

BLACK POP IN THE 1970S

Sylvester Stewart is shown here at the keyboards, surrounded by his band. With his racially mixed group, Stewart combined James Brown–like bass patterns with aspects of psychedelia. As a result, Sly and the Family Stone appealed to both black and white audiences. While influencing many black artists, the group also put on an incendiary performance at Woodstock (in front of a largely white audience) and got significant airplay on rock radio.

Sly and the Family Stone: Sly Crosses Over. It is difficult to exaggerate the influence of Sly and the Family Stone on the course of black pop at the end of the 1960s. The changes brought about by Sly's music inspired an entire generation of funk and pop, ranging from groups like the Temptations to the Jackson 5 and the Osmonds. Beginning with "Dance to the Music," which went to number eight on the pop charts (r9, 1968), Sly and the Family Stone released a series of crossover hit singles that rose to number one on both the pop and rhythm and blues charts: "Everyday People" (1969), "Thank You (Falettinme Be Mice Elf Agin)" (1970), and "Family Affair" (1971).

Sly Stone (Sylvester Stewart) was born in Texas but moved to the San Francisco area as a child. During the mid-1960s, he was a disc jockey and record producer, working with artists like the Beau Brummels and the Great Society (the band Grace Slick left to join Jefferson Airplane). In 1967, Sly and the Family Stone began playing in the Bay Area and circulating in the San Francisco psychedelic music scene. Bassist Larry Graham, drummer Gregg Errico, and guitarist Freddie Stone laid down rhythmic backdrops strongly influenced by James Brown's bands, and Sly and his sister Rose Stone Banks provided catchy vocals and solid keyboard playing (topped off by the trumpet and sax playing of Cynthia Robinson and Jerry Martini). The band stood out not only for its distinctive blend of white and black musical styles but also because it was one of the few racially and sexually integrated bands of the era. Early Family Stone tracks were optimistic and dance-oriented, such as "Stand" (1969) and "I Want to Take You Higher" (1969). "Thank You (Falettinme Be Mice Elf Agin)" is representative of the

Listening Guide

Sly and the Family Stone, "Thank You (Falettinme Be Mice Elf Agin)" Epic 10555

Words and music by Sylvester Stewart, produced by Sly Stone. Hit #1 on the *Billboard* "Hot 100" and "Best Selling Soul Singles" chart in 1970.

FORM: Simple verse-chorus. The entire song is based on the groove laid down in the introduction. Twice in the song the bass drops out to create an instrumental interlude after each chorus, allowing the bass to reenter sounding fresh. After the third verse-chorus pair, a contrasting verse occurs providing further contrast.

TIME SIGNATURE: 4/4.

INSTRUMENTATION: Electric guitars, bass, drums, horns, and vocals.

0:00–0:18	**Introduction**, 8 mm.	Groove established first with guitar, bass, and high-hat only, with drums and horns entering for second 4 bars.
0:18–0:54	**Verse 1**, 16 mm.	Unison vocals, music continues as in introduction. "Lookin' at the devil . . ."
0:54–1:12	**Chorus**, 8 mm.	Harmony added to vocal part. "Thank you . . ."
1:12–1:21	**Interlude**, 4 mm.	Bass drops out and leaves guitar and drums only.
1:21–1:57	**Verse 2**, 16 mm.	As before, but with horns fading in and out to create a train-whistle effect. "Stiff all in the collar . . ."
1:57–2:15	**Chorus**, 8 mm.	As before, with horn line added. "Thank you . . ."
2:15–2:24	**Interlude**, 4 mm.	As before.
2:24–3:01	**Verse 3**, 16 mm.	As in verse 2, with slightly busier accompaniment filling in the spaces between vocal phrases. "Dance to the music . . ."
3:01–3:19	**Chorus**, 8 mm.	As before, with horns. "Thank you . . ."
3:19–3:37	**Contrasting verse**, 8 mm.	A new verse is presented over the same music. Note the treble tone of the vocals, which adds timbral contrast. "Flamin' eyes . . ."
3:37–3:55	**Chorus**, 8 mm.	As before, with horns. "Thank you . . ."
3:55–4:13	**Chorus**, 8 mm.	As before, with horns.
4:13–4:32	**Chorus**, 8 mm.	As before and fade-out.

group's musical approach. The entire song is built over a repeating riff in the bass, which established the song's rhythmic feel or "groove." It is the catchiness of this groove that is central to the song's effectiveness, which can be said for much of the Family Stone's music.

With the 1971 album *There's a Riot Goin' On* (p1 r1 uk31), the band's music began to adopt a more militant stance, at times focusing on controversial racial and political issues. The album *Fresh* (p7 r1, 1973), which contained the hit single "If You Want Me to Stay" (p12 r3), was the last major commercial success for the group. By 1973, the overwhelming crossover appeal of the band was already much imitated among black artists. From the beginning, CBS subsidiary Epic Records had marketed the band as if they were a rock act, emphasizing both singles and albums, and creating a hybrid category of "psychedelic soul." This cross between San Francisco hippie culture and heavy funk music helped introduce a new style of African American pop music that drew on the crossover success of Motown and southern soul acts during the mid-1960s.

In Sly's Wake: Ohio Players; Kool and the Gang; and Earth, Wind, and Fire.

The funk element of the Family Stone's music paved the way for many dance-oriented African American groups in the early 1970s. Hailing from Dayton, the Ohio Players began as Robert Ward and the Untouchables in 1959. Over the course of the 1960s, the band—subsequently called the Ohio Untouchables and then the Ohio Players—released a series of singles without much commercial success. In 1973, their novelty number, "Funky Worm," hit number one on the rhythm and blues charts and rose as high as number fifteen on the pop charts. The Ohio Players followed up with a string of number-one rhythm and blues albums, all of which placed high on the pop charts as well, including *Skin Tight* (p11, 1974),

Kool and the Gang, shown here in a live performance. The group first achieved popularity as a funk band strongly influenced by Sly and the Family Stone. As the 1970s wore on, however, their sound became smoother and they became major players in disco, scoring hits with "Ladies' Night" and "Celebration."

Anchored by Maurice White's compositions and led by Philip Bailey's soaring voice, Earth, Wind, and Fire often combined funk with smoother sounds and the complex disco production process.

Fire (p1, 1975), *Honey* (p2, 1975), and *Contradiction* (p12, 1976). The band is perhaps best known for the singles "Fire" (p1 r1, 1974) and "Love Rollercoaster" (p1 r1, 1975), both of which incorporated funk musical elements, such as heavy riff-bass and sing-along refrains.

Another Sly-influenced band was Kool and the Gang, who started out as the Jazziacs and developed their musical skills in Jersey City, New Jersey. By the late 1960s, the group had turned from jazz to a more commercial sound, enjoying modest success on the soul charts with singles like "Let the Music Take Your Mind" (r19, 1970) and "Funky Man" (r16, 1970). The band emerged as an important crossover act in 1973 with the album *Wild and Peaceful*, which developed the pop funk of Sly Stone and hit number six on the *Billboard* "Soul LPs" chart (p33), while spawning three crossover hit singles, "Funky Stuff" (p29 r5), "Jungle Boogie" (p4 r2), and "Hollywood Swinging" (p6 r1). Both the Ohio Players and Kool and the Gang built on Sly's blending of funky rhythms with catchy vocal hooks. While the Ohio Players' popularity peaked in 1975 with "Love Rollercoaster," Kool and the Gang enjoyed even greater success after disco became popular, hitting with "Ladies' Night" (p8 r1 uk9, 1979) and "Celebration" (p1 r1 uk7, 1980), two songs that have since become staples of the party-band repertoire.

Maurice White was a studio drummer at Chess Records during the mid-1960s, performing on recordings by many Chess artists. In 1966, White joined the Ramsey Lewis Trio, a group that had formerly been a fixture of the Chicago jazz scene, but had begun exploring more pop-oriented instrumental tracks, including "Wade in the Water" (p19 r3, 1966). In 1969, White moved to Los Angeles and formed Earth, Wind, and Fire, soon adding lead singer Philip Bailey to the lineup. Operating with a large, shifting cast of top performers during the 1970s, Earth, Wind, and Fire scored a series of crossover hits with catchy pop hooks and sophisticated horn arrangements. "Shining Star" (p1 r1, 1975) is a prime example of the band's approach. The tune begins with a hard-driving funk groove in the style of Sly and the Family Stone, setting up vocals that alternate between sophisticated vocal harmonies and gritty solo singing, all complemented by rhythmic horn shots and held down by a catchy chorus.

The Rock Connection: Tower of Power and War. The Oakland-based band Tower of Power was also part of the Bay Area hippie scene, counting among its first important supporters Fillmore concert promoter Bill Graham and record producer David Rubinson. A band made up of white, Latino, and black musicians, Tower of Power was celebrated for its hard-driving funk grooves and a high caliber horn section, which often performed on other artists' records, including Elton John, the Rolling Stones, and Rod Stewart. Recording for Warner Brothers, the band had a series of moderately successful albums during the first half of the 1970s, including *Bump City* (r16, 1972), *Tower of Power* (r11, 1973), and *Back to Oakland* (r13, 1974), almost always finding more success on the soul charts than in the pop market.

Another notable rock connection in 1970s black pop came via Eric Burdon, who had been lead singer for the Animals. While Burdon was a major player in the British invasion, the members of War were based in the Los Angeles rhythm and blues scene during the 1960s. As the Nightriders, they had been hired to back up Deacon Jones, a famous football player who made a failed attempt to build a new career in music. While backing Jones, the band was spotted by Burdon, Danish harmonica player Lee Oskar, and producer Jerry Goldstein. With Burdon and Oskar, War recorded *Eric Burdon Declares War*, which hit number eighteen on the pop album charts in 1970 and contained the number-three pop single "Spill the Wine" (1970). Burdon soon left the group, although this did nothing to weaken its popularity. War's *All Day Music* (p16 r6, 1971) began a string of highly successful albums and singles for the group, who often blended Latin styles with its rhythm and blues roots. *The World Is a Ghetto* (p1 r1, 1973) was the band's most commercially successful album, containing the crossover hit singles "The World Is a Ghetto" (p7 r3, 1972) and "Cisco Kid" (p2 r5, 1973). War's 1975 single "Low Rider" (p7 r1 uk12) is probably its most enduring track, and has come to symbolize the large, often-customized automobiles of the mid-1970s.

Motown in the 1970s. Motown was quick to absorb the changes in black pop that characterized the late 1960s. According to the Temptations' Otis Williams, "Cloud Nine" (p6 r2 uk15, 1968) was recorded as a direct response to the Family Stone's "Dance to the Music." The Temptations had recently suffered the departure of lead singer David Ruffin, who was replaced by Dennis Edwards in the summer of 1968. Now sharing songwriting duties with Motown veteran Barrett Strong, Norman Whitfield's production style created a more aggressive, groove-oriented, and psychedelic sound for the Temptations. This new stylistic turn would prove even more successful with "I Can't Get Next to You," which hit the number-one slot on both the *Billboard* "Hot 100" and the recently renamed "Best Selling Soul Singles" chart during the summer of 1969 (uk13). A string of funk-oriented hits continued with "Psychedelic Shack" (p7 r2 uk33, 1970) and "Ball of Confusion" (p3 r2 uk7, 1970), followed by the gentle lyricism of "Just My Imagination (Running Away with Me)," which topped both the pop and R&B charts in the spring of 1971 (uk8). In the context of psychedelic soul, the throwback style of "Just My Imagination" shows how much Motown's sonic palette had grown since the mid-1960s. Whitfield and the Temptations addressed

Listening Guide

The Temptations, "Papa Was a Rolling Stone" Gordy 7121F

Words and music by Norman Whitfield and Barrett Strong, produced by Norman Whitfield. Hit #1 on the *Billboard* "Hot 100" chart in 1972, and #5 on the "Best Selling Soul Singles" chart (uk14).

FORM: Simple verse-chorus. Like Sly Stone's "Thank You (Falettinme Be Mice Elf Agin)," the entire song is built over the same repeating bass line. Perhaps the most striking feature of this track is its drama and scope, running to almost seven minutes, employing orchestral strings, harp, and jazz trumpet to establish a menacing atmosphere.

TIME SIGNATURE: 4/4.

INSTRUMENTATION: Electric guitars (one with wah-wah), electric piano, bass, drums, hand claps, trumpet, orchestral strings, harp.

0:00–1:57	**Introduction**, 60 mm.	Lengthy and atmospheric introduction, beginning with bass and high-hat, but then adding orchestral strings, wah-wah guitar, jazzy trumpet improvisation, hand claps, and harp.
1:57–2:28	**Verse 1**, 16 mm.	Lead vocal enters, counterpointed by bluesy guitar lines and wah-wah guitar. "It was the third . . ."
2:28–3:00	**Chorus**, 16 mm.	Choral vocals share melody with lead vocal. Note the double-time hand claps that begin with the second 8-bar phrase. "Papa was a rolling stone . . ."
3:00–3:31	**Interlude**, 16 mm.	Jazzy trumpet and wah-wah guitar return, along with orchestral strings.
3:31–4:03	**Verse 2**, 16 mm.	Melody now traded between singers, "Hey mama . . ."
4:03–4:35	**Chorus**, 16 mm.	As before, but hand claps begin immediately, doubled by the wah-wah guitar. "Papa was a rolling stone . . ."
4:35–4:59	**Interlude**, 12 mm.	Trumpet returns, now with pronounced echo effect and supported by electric piano, bass, and drums, and wah-wah guitar.
4:59–5:30	**Verse 3**, 16 mm.	This verse mostly features the high tenor voice of Damon Harris. "Hey mama . . ."
5:30–6:02	**Chorus**, 16 mm.	As before, but without hand claps. "Papa was a rolling stone . . ."
6:02–6:18	**Chorus**, 8 mm.	Hand claps kick in with partial repeat of the chorus.
6:18–6:52	**Coda**, 16 mm.	Strings enter as vocals fade and double-time hand claps continue, then track fades out.

more serious social issues with "Papa Was a Rolling Stone" (p1 r5 uk14, 1972). A dramatic and atmospheric track focusing on problems within black urban life, it featured a haunting string arrangement by Motown arranger Paul Riser and ranks among Whitfield's finest achievements as a producer. Extending to a length of almost seven minutes, "Papa Was a Rolling Stone" was based on a single repeated bass line, much like the Family Stone's "Thank You."

As a new Motown group in the 1970s, the Commodores were among the most commercially successful black pop bands of the decade. The group started in 1968 as a party band in Tuskegee, Alabama, where the members met as freshmen at the prestigious Tuskegee Institute. In 1971, the band was signed to Motown and opened for the Jackson 5. The Commodores' roots in funk can be heard in tracks such as "Brick House" (p5 r4 uk32, 1977), but it was the band's ballads, written by singer Lionel Richie, that yielded the greatest commercial success. "Easy" (p4 r1 uk9, 1977) and "Three Times a Lady" (p1 r1 uk1, 1978) illustrate the Commodores' smooth, pop-ballad style, featuring Richie's polished lead vocals and refined horn arrangements.

By the early 1970s, Motown was mostly run from Los Angeles after Berry Gordy had left Detroit to pursue a broader range of possibilities for his company in Southern California. While many consider the 1960s to be the "golden age" of Motown, Gordy's company continued to record an impressive roster of successful artists. Diana Ross continued her hit making during the 1970s, though no longer at quite the level she had achieved with the Supremes. Ross also made the move into film after Motown moved to Los Angeles, receiving an Oscar nomination for her portrayal of jazz singer Billie Holiday in the 1972 film *Lady Sings the Blues*.

The company maintained its presence in the teen market during the early 1970s with a group of brothers from Gary, Indiana. The Jackson 5, featuring the high

The Jackson 5 performing on television (Michael is holding the microphone in the foreground). While Marvin Gaye and Stevie Wonder were demanding control over their music, the Jackson 5 developed in the traditional Motown mold: Berry Gordy controlled most aspects of their sound, style, and look. The group's tight arrangements and short, catchy songs, combined with Michael Jackson's powerful voice and charismatic performances, made the brothers enormously successful worldwide.

prepubescent vocals of younger brother Michael, scored a string of top bubble-gum hits, starting with "I Want You Back" (p1 r1 uk2, 1969) and continuing with "ABC" (p1 r1 uk8, 1970), "The Love You Save" (p1 r1 uk7, 1970), and "I'll Be There" (p1 r1 uk4, 1970)—all of which hit number one on both the pop and rhythm and blues singles charts. The funk-oriented dance music of the Jackson 5, and the group's Technicolor psychedelic wardrobe, showed how Motown reacted to the crossover success of Sly and the Family Stone. The Jackson 5 as a group, and Michael as a solo artist, placed over a dozen more hits on the charts before leaving Motown for Epic in the mid-1970s. In the second half of the decade, the Jacksons (as they were now called, since Gordy owned the Jackson 5 name), continued to enjoy success, and Michael began a solo career that made him one of the most successful artists in the history of popular music.

Motown Matures: Stevie and Marvin.

As Berry Gordy set up shop on the West Coast during the early 1970s, two Motown artists in particular were allotted freedom to work outside of the traditional system. One of the most successful African American male vocalists of the 1960s, who had also married into the Gordy family, Marvin Gaye experimented as a songwriter and producer by helping create music for the Originals, whose "Baby, I'm for Real" and "The Bells" achieved notable popularity. With his 1971 album *What's Going On* (p6 r1), Gaye produced one of the first concept albums in black pop, reflecting yet another link with rock-music practice while remaining faithful to his Motown roots. Containing the crossover hit singles "What's Going On" (p2 r1), "Mercy Mercy Me (The Ecology)" (p4 r1), and "Inner City Blues (Make Me Wanna Holler)" (p9 r1), Gaye's album confronted problems of black urban life and issues of environmentalism in modern society, and questioned the U.S. presence in Vietnam. In the wake of his success with *What's Going On*, Marvin Gaye continued to be a fixture of black pop with his albums *Let's Get It On* (p2 r1, 1973) and hits such as "Trouble Man" (p7 r4, 1972) and "Got to Give It Up, Pt. 1" (p1 r1 uk7, 1977).

After his twenty-first birthday in early 1971, Stevie Wonder was also given complete artistic control over his records and produced a series of albums that each cohered in a similar manner to album-oriented rock. Unlike any other Motown artist of the time, Wonder often wrote, produced, and played many of the instruments on his albums. While Wonder was a leading force in African American dance music and balladry, his experiments with new sounds and timbres (including extensive use of the synthesizer) and studio techniques were highly indebted to rock. Blending cutting edge aspects of rock and rhythm and blues, his complex arrangements, inventive musical material, intense vocal style, and topical lyrics were among the most original of the decade.

Wonder's albums showed the effects of his self-produced approach beginning with *Music of My Mind* (p21 r6, 1972) and *Talking Book* (p3 r1 uk16, 1972). Throughout the remainder of the decade, he continued to release chart-topping albums that explored a variety of musical styles and ambitious approaches, including *Innervisions* (p4 r1 uk8, 1973), *Fulfillingness' First*

Stevie Wonder, one of Motown's most successful artists, in performance. In the 1960s Wonder was a staple of Motown's lineup of pop stars. He broke with Motown tradition in the 1970s and took total control of his music—writing, producing, and playing a variety of instruments. Wonder combined the driving, danceable funk of Sly and the Family Stone with Marvin Gaye's social consciousness to create albums of lasting influence, including *Music of My Mind* (1972), *Talking Book* (1972), and *Songs in the Key of Life* (1976).

Listening Guide

Stevie Wonder, "Living for the City" Tamla 326L

Words and music by Stevie Wonder, produced by Stevie Wonder. An edited single version (Tamla 54343F) rose to #1 on the *Billboard* "Hot Soul Singles" chart and #8 on the "Hot 100" in 1973 (uk15).

FORM: Modified compound AABA. The A sections are made up of two verses and one instrumental bridge each. The verse contains the "Livin' just enough for the city" refrain, while the instrumental bridges make clear references to classical music through their use of more complicated harmony, melody, and rhythm. The B section is not really a musical section, but rather a mini-drama that has some musical accompaniment. The compound AABA form is modified in the use of a third A section before the B section (though this A section is itself a modified version). The repetitions of the bridge section at the end of the track help create a strong sense of ending and are not exceptional in such larger forms. The closest formal comparison among the pieces we have studied would be "Roundabout" by Yes.

TIME SIGNATURE: 4/4 in the 12-bar verses, with a 9-bar section made up of 6 bars of 3/4, one of 2/4, and then 2 bars of 4/4 used in the instrumental bridges.

INSTRUMENTATION: The rhythm section is made up of synthesizer bass, electric piano, hand claps, and drums. Wonder's lead vocal is featured with sparing use of backup vocals, and multiple synthesizers are employed to lend a symphonic quality to the track. All instruments on this track are played by Wonder.

	0:00–0:11	**Introduction**, 4 mm.	Electric piano and synthesizer bass establish the song's basic chord progression.
A	0:11–0:40	**Verse 1**, 12 mm.	Lead vocals added, along with bass drum. "A boy is born . . ."
	0:40–1:09	**Verse 2**, 12 mm.	Drumbeat kicks in. "His father works . . ."
	1:09–1:26	**Bridge**, 9 mm.	Synthesizers enter, playing a classical-sounding passage with lead vocal on the syllable "la." Time signature changes to 3/4, with the final bar in 2/4 before returning to 4/4.
A	1:26–1:56	**Verse 3**, 12 mm.	As before, though the vocal may now be a little more urgent. "His sister's black . . ."
	1:56–2:30	**Verse 4**, 14 mm.	As before, with new synthesizer line added. Two extra bars are added to end of verse. "Her brother's smart . . ."
	2:30–2:47	**Bridge**, 9 mm.	As before.
A'	2:47–3:56	**Vamp**, 28 mm.	A vamp drawn from the verse is played as Wonder provides vocal improvisations supported by gospel-flavored backup vocals and hand claps. Synthesizer lines weave in and out, and synthesizer bass gets busier.
	3:56–4:13	**Bridge**, 9 mm.	As before, and then vamp and fade create transition.

B	4:13–5:19	**Central drama**	"Bus for New York City . . ." with spoken dialogue portraying story of deception, arrest, trial, and prison. The music continues to play underneath, and then breaks down to synthesizer incidental music (with some drumming), and verse music fades back in.
A	5:19–5:47	**Verse 5**, 12 mm.	Lead vocals become bitter and gruff, backup vocals added, as synthesizer lines continue to weave in and out. "His hair is long . . ."
	5:47–6:21	**Verse 6**, 14 mm.	Lead vocals are still gruff, as second vocal part is added and synthesizers play in harmony. Two bars added to end of verse as music seems to break down briefly. "I hope you hear . . ."
	6:21–6:38	**Bridge**, 9 mm.	As before, but now with more elaborate counterpoint in the synthesizer part.
	6:38–6:54	**Bridge**, 9 mm.	Repeat of previous 9 bars.
	6:54–7:24	**Bridge**, 16 mm.	As before, but here extended to create majestic ending. Note that this section is all in 3/4, with no time signature change at the end as in previous statements.

Finale (p1 r1 uk5, 1974), *Songs in the Key of Life* (p1 r1 uk2, 1976), and *Journey through the Secret Life of Plants* (p4 r4 uk8, 1979). "Living for the City" (p8 r1 uk15, 1973), from *Innervisions*, demonstrates these traits in Wonder's music. The track tells the tale of a poor, black country youth whose family scrimps and saves to send him to the city to seek his fortune. He is duped into carrying drugs and summarily convicted and jailed. In the last verse, Wonder's gravelly voice testifies to the suffering undergone by this young man and his family. The full version of the track (there is a shorter radio edit) provides a spoken vignette over Wonder's synthesizer accompaniment, telling of the youth's arrival, duping, arrest, and conviction. The song's tone is not confrontational, and seems to indict society at large rather than pit black society against the white power structure. It is easy to see in this track a general thematic kinship with "Papa Was a Rolling Stone," *What's Going On*, and *There's a Riot Goin' On*. In its extended length (over seven minutes) and with its harmonic and melodic sophistication, "Living for the City" even shows a connection to progressive rock. The relationship of Wonder's music to white rock in the 1970s was strong: he received a significant amount of rock-radio airplay, reviews of his work appeared in rock magazines, and his records sold well among rock-oriented listeners.

The Philadelphia Sound: Gamble and Huff.

During the second half of the 1960s, Kenny Gamble and Leon Huff were independent producers in Philadelphia, writing songs and producing records for the rhythm and blues market. They released some of these records themselves, such as the Intruders' "(We'll Be) United" (r14, 1966), which appeared on the Gamble label. Other records were released through major labels, including Archie Bell's "I Can't Stop Dancin'" (p9 r5, 1968) and Wilson Pickett's "Don't Let the Green Grass Fool

Don Cornelius on the set of *Soul Train*. As the soul market became more popular, dance shows like *Soul Train* featured African American performers, fashion, and dance styles.

You" (p17 r2, 1971), both of which appeared on Atlantic. Independents like Atlantic, Motown, and Stax had dominated black music sales during the 1960s, and major labels began to take note of the potential for increased sales in the new soul market in the early 1970s. In 1971, CBS reacted to this market potential by providing the money for Gamble and Huff to establish their own label, Philadelphia International, devoted specifically to their records but distributed through the well-established CBS network.

Philadelphia International became quickly known as the home of the "Philadelphia sound," a style that blended lyric vocals and a driving rhythm section with elegant string arrangements. In 1972, the label began a series of hit releases that put them on top of the charts through the end of the decade. Some acts had one or two hit singles, such as Billy Paul, MFSB, the Three Degrees, McFadden and Whitehead, and Lou Rawls. But Gamble and Huff's most consistently successful acts were Harold Melvin and the Blue Notes (featuring Teddy Pendergrass), whose hits were often limited to the rhythm and blues charts, and the O'Jays, whose singles regularly crossed over to the pop charts.

The O'Jays' "Back Stabbers" (p3 r1 uk14, 1972) is a representative example of the Philadelphia sound. After a dramatic solo piano opening, a Latin-flavored groove begins, which is then overlaid with strings and brass. As the O'Jays enter singing the hook-oriented chorus, it is easy to hear the Motown influence of the Temptations or the Four Tops. A happy, up-tempo groove is also central to "Love Train," which hit number one on both the "Hot 100" and soul charts in 1973 (uk9), and may be the best-known Gamble and Huff song. A major part of the success of Gamble and Huff productions was their house band, MFSB (or Mother Father Sister Brother). MFSB had a hit of their own when they provided the theme music to *Soul Train*, a television show devoted to black pop hosted by Don Cornelius. This song, "TSOP (The Sound of Philadelphia)," hit number one on both the pop and rhythm and blues charts in 1974 (uk22).

Thom Bell, the Spinners, and the Stylistics. Thom Bell was another important purveyor of the Philadelphia sound, producing artists for Gamble and Huff in addition to his own freelance work for other labels. Bell had notable success with the Spinners, who had a history in Detroit going back to the late 1950s and had been signed to Motown in the 1960s. Although the group had scored a handful of hits for Motown, including "It's a Shame" (p14 r4 uk20, 1970), they left the company in 1972 and were picked up by Atlantic. With Bell producing them, the Spinners stormed the charts with a string of records that helped establish the Philadelphia sound, including "I'll Be Around" (p3 r1, 1972), "Could It Be I'm Falling in Love" (p4 r1 uk11, 1972), "They Just Can't Stop It (The Games People Play)" (p5 r1, 1975), and "The Rubberband Man" (p2 r1 uk16,

1976). Bell had similar results with the Stylistics, a Philadelphia group signed to Avco Records. Along with lyricist Linda Creed, Bell wrote many of the Stylistics' hits, including "Betcha by Golly, Wow" (p3 r2 uk13, 1972) and "You Make Me Feel Brand New" (p2 r5 uk2, 1974). With both groups, he continued to work in the polished Philadelphia style, emphasizing upbeat themes and elegant string arrangements.

"Blaxploitation": Isaac Hayes and Curtis Mayfield.

Drawing on the increasingly cinematic sound of African American pop music in the 1970s, a new genre of film (with supporting soundtracks) rose to prominence at the beginning of the 1970s—a genre often called "blaxploitation." Arguably, the first of these films was Melvin Van Peebles's 1971 independent feature *Sweet Sweetback's Baadasssss Song*, which offered a rare African American perspective on urban life. *Sweet Sweetback's* was made entirely outside the usual Hollywood establishment, and the film's unexpected success indicated to the major studios that there was money to be made in movies that cast strong main characters in tough urban situations. Musically, *Sweet Sweetback's* featured a soundtrack on Stax by Earth, Wind, and Fire, recorded just after the group moved to Los Angeles. Blaxploitation films and soundtracks were closely linked, and many of these films, often stereotyped today as campy black-oriented action films, are now remembered mostly for their music.

In 1971, *Shaft* became the first widely popular blaxploitation movie, and Isaac Hayes's music for the film earned him an Oscar. Hayes had been part of a team at Stax with David Porter during the 1960s, writing and producing a series of hits for Sam and Dave. After the sale of the company (as discussed in Chapter 6), the opportunity arose for Hayes to record as a solo artist. His first album, *Hot Buttered Soul* (p8 r1, 1969), was the first in a series of seven number-one Hayes albums to appear on the soul album charts. Hayes also crossed over to the pop charts with "Theme from *Shaft*" (p1 r2 uk4, 1971) and the accompanying soundtrack album. His ultra-cool vocal delivery on this track—part spoken and part sung—served as a model for many black artists. The text of the song is concerned with the stereotypical "private dick that's a sex machine to all the chicks," and the accompaniment prominently features the wah-wah effect on the electric guitar. The wah-wah had been a staple in rock music since psychedelic guitarists such as Jimi Hendrix and Eric Clapton popularized the sound in the late 1960s. As early as 1968, "Cloud Nine" introduced the wah-wah as a part of Motown's psychedelic soul, and Family Stone singles such as "Family Affair" relied heavily on this sound. While many examples exist, "The Theme from *Shaft*" has become especially associated with the rhythmic sound of the wah-wah guitar in black pop.

Like Hayes, Curtis Mayfield also had deep roots in 1960s rhythm and blues. Throughout the decade,

Isaac Hayes performing in Los Angeles as part of the Wattstax Festival in 1972. Hayes was one of the most popular recording artists for Stax Records during the 1970s. His "Theme from *Shaft*" was a crossover hit and won an Academy Award for Best Original Song. Hayes was also known for a flamboyant sense of fashion, which was on display during this performance.

Curtis Mayfield performing on television. Although Mayfield started his career as a songwriter and singer for the rhythm and blues group the Impressions, he struck out on his own at the beginning of the 1970s, forging a successful solo career. Much of Mayfield's music tackled social issues with an optimistic outlook. The soundtrack to the 1972 film *Superfly* contained some of Mayfield's biggest hits, including "Superfly" and "Freddie's Dead."

he had been a member of the Chicago-based vocal group the Impressions, who scored a long series of rhythm and blues hits, including crossovers such as "It's All Right," "People Get Ready," and "We're a Winner" (also discussed in Chapter 6). Inspired by Hayes's success with *Shaft*, Mayfield enthusiastically accepted the challenge of writing music for the 1972 film *Superfly*. His high tenor voice soars above the rhythmic wah-wah guitar and elegant strings on songs like "Freddie's Dead" (p4 r2, 1972), showing the influence of Hayes and Stone alongside the smooth production values of Philadelphia and Motown. The title track "Superfly" (p8 r5, 1972) similarly reveals his funk proclivities. To white audiences of the early 1970s, Mayfield was one of the most powerful voices speaking about the problems of black urban life. He performed frequently on prime-time network television shows and became a cultural ambassador to the white community.

JAMES BROWN, GEORGE CLINTON, AND PARLIAMENT/FUNKADELIC

Soul Brother Number 1. In the first half of the 1970s, a style that came to be called funk was closely associated with black culture in the minds of both black and white listeners. Much of the success of funk before the 1970s can be attributed to the work of James Brown. As discussed in Chapter 6, Brown's career began in the 1950s, and by the mid-1960s, his groove-oriented music made him one of the most important figures in black pop. Brown's success in both the mainstream and soul markets continued into the first half of the 1970s, with hits such as "Get Up (I Feel Like Being a) Sex Machine (Part 1)" (p15 r2, 1970), "Super Bad" (p13 r1, 1970), and "Hot Pants" (p15 r1, 1971). After the 1968 assassination of Martin Luther King Jr., Brown became an important voice within the black community, encouraging black pride. Although it became an anthem of Black Power, the 1968 song "Say It Loud, I'm Black and I'm Proud" was a top-ten hit on the pop charts. Brown also made statements against drug abuse with songs like "King Heroin" (p40 r6, 1972) and "Public Enemy #1" (a B-side from 1972), both of which contain strong antidrug messages and are delivered more like sermons than songs. Many of his 1970s tracks put more emphasis on the rhythmic interlocking of guitar, bass, and drums than his '60s records had, although horns still played an important role in these later tracks. Brown's music influenced and served as a model for many of the acts discussed already in this chapter. Sly Stone, Stevie Wonder, and Norman Whitfield all drew on Brown's characteristic emphasis on the rhythmic groove and tight ensemble playing as well as his flamboyant approach to live performance.

James Brown and Muhammad Ali in 1974. As black pop became popular outside of the United States, American musicians increasingly performed abroad. This event was a festival in Zaire called "Zaire 74" that featured music by Brown, the Spinners, Bill Withers, and several Afro-Cuban and salsa acts like Celia Cruz and the Fania All Stars.

Mothership Connections: George Clinton and Company. Despite Brown's influence on a wide range of black pop bands and artists, it was an ambitious musician and songwriter based in Detroit, George Clinton, who was most closely associated with the extensive development of funk in the 1970s. Beginning in the late 1960s, Clinton combined the approaches of James Brown and Berry Gordy to establish one of the most successful music-business operations in the second half of the 1970s. Originally from New Jersey, Clinton moved to Detroit during the Motown boom of the 1960s. He sang, wrote, and produced songs for a vocal group called the Parliaments, who performed in the manner of the Temptations or Four Tops. Although he worked for a short time as a songwriter at Motown, Clinton also collaborated with Motown's cross-town rivals Golden World and Revilot, the latter releasing Parliaments' number-three rhythm and blues hit "(I Wanna) Testify" in 1967 (p20). Due to a dispute over the name of the group, Clinton began recording with his backing musicians under the name Funkadelic to avoid legal complications. When the legal wrangling ended, Clinton used both group names for contracts with different record companies. Parliament's first record was released on Holland-Dozier-Holland's label Invictus. Funkadelic records were first released on the Detroit-based funk label Westbound, then, beginning in 1976, on Warner Brothers. From the beginning, Parliament was considered the more commercial act, while Funkadelic was more avowedly experimental. The first few Funkadelic albums blended heavy psychedelic rock with soul, showing diverse influences such as Jimi Hendrix, Sly Stone, Miles Davis, and James Brown. The group also developed a reputation for dressing outrageously during performances, as well as for wild onstage antics.

By 1974, Clinton had convinced Neil Bogart of Casablanca Records to sign Parliament, and the band released *Up for the Down Stroke* (r17, 1974), the first in a series of successful releases for Clinton and crew under the Parliament moniker. The next year, Clinton exposed his political side with the release *Chocolate City*

Parliament in concert. George Clinton was strongly influenced by James Brown's high musical standards. In fact, many of Clinton's musicians had come directly from Brown's band, including bassist Bootsy Collins, saxophonist Maceo Parker, and trombonist Fred Wesley. Clinton, however, drew influence for his stage shows from rock bands like KISS (who were also on the Casablanca label). His shows had an otherworldly, comic-book feel, with a spaceship—"the mothership"—landing on stage, ready to take the band away.

(r18, 1975), which contained a title track that empowered citizens of black ghettoes or "chocolate cities" (focusing on Washington, D.C.) and reminding the white establishment "we're gaining on ya." The band's important breakthrough record was *Mothership Connection* (p13 r4, 1976), which contained the hit "Tear the Roof Off the Sucker (Give Up the Funk)" (p15 r5). For the tour to support this album, Clinton developed an elaborate stage show that featured a spaceship descending onto the stage, from which he would emerge as a character called Dr. Funkenstein. Casablanca was to fund this elaborate show, and considering that Bogart also had KISS on his label, it is no surprise that he supported the idea. *Mothership Connection* brought a surreal quality to Parliament shows and albums, and Clinton liked to emphasize this aspect of the music. He borrowed and adapted considerably from audacious rock acts such as Alice Cooper and Genesis. Subsequent albums such as *The Clones of Dr. Funkenstein* (p20 r3, 1976) and *Funkentelechy vs. the Placebo Syndrome* (p13 r2, 1977) continued to develop the concept-album idea, bringing funk to the masses along with healthy doses of irony and humor. During the string of successful Parliament albums in the later 1970s, Funkadelic also released albums that enjoyed considerable success on the rhythm and blues charts. *One Nation under a Groove*, for instance, went to number one on the "Soul LPs" charts in 1978 and *Uncle Jam Wants You* hit number two in 1979.

Clinton led the songwriting and producing on these records, which used a large stable of musicians, including many who had previously played in James Brown's bands, such as sax player Maceo Parker, trombonist Fred Wesley, and bassist Bootsy Collins. Because of his success with Parliament and Funkadelic after 1975, Clinton was able to negotiate deals for other artists within his "Parliafunkadelicment Thang" collective, and albums were released by Bootsy's Rubber Band (led by bassist Collins), the Horny Horns (the horn section), the Brides of Dr. Funkenstein (female backup singers), and Parlet (more female backup singers), among others. By building on the examples set by Brown and Gordy, George Clinton became one of the most influential figures in black pop during the second half of the 1970s as both a performer and businessperson, and he has remained the prime exponent of funk in the years since.

Average White Band: The Funk Band That Did Get Airplay on White Rock
Radio. Despite the popularity of Parliament and Funkadelic among black listeners and the positions on the pop charts earned by some of their albums, white rock listeners heard very little Parliament or Funkadelic on the radio. Ironically, the funk band that many rock listeners would have known best was a group from Scotland, formed in London, and called the Average White Band. Their first American album, *AWB*, hit number one on both the pop and soul charts in the fall of 1974 (uk6), propelling the single "Pick Up the Pieces" to number one on the pop singles chart

Listening Guide

Parliament, "Tear the Roof Off the Sucker (Give Up the Funk)" Casablanca NB 856

Words and music by George Clinton, Bootsy Collins, and Jerome Brailey, produced by George Clinton. Rose to #5 on the *Billboard* "Hot Soul Singles" chart and #15 on the "Hot 100" chart in 1976.

FORM: Modified contrasting verse-chorus. This track employs two choruses rather than a verse and chorus, and each uses music that is different enough for it to be considered contrasting. The form is built up generally through an alternation of these two choruses. The first time through, chorus 2 is expanded, creating an 8-bar interlude. The second time through this interlude itself is expanded by four measures. The third time through presents the most extensive expansion: chorus 1 is repeated once and then chorus 2 occurs seven times. The track ends with a fourth time through chorus 1 and chorus 2, returning them to the texture and length found at the beginning of the tune.

TIME SIGNATURE: 4/4. Note especially how bass and electric guitar weave complicated rhythmic patterns against the more straightforward patterns in the drums.

INSTRUMENTATION: Drums, bass, and guitar form rhythmic background throughout. Horns employed for emphasis and embellishment, and vocals throughout are sung in a choral, sing-along style. Note the use of synthetic orchestral strings, a keyboard sound more often associated with mainstream rock and disco.

0:00–0:19	**Introduction**, 8 mm.	Low male voice intones "Tear the roof off the mutha . . ." to the accompaniment of the drums, and then to the rest of the band.
0:19–0:37	**Chorus 1**, 8 mm.	Choral, sing-along vocals; note syncopated bass line and sustained keyboard chords. "You've got a real type of thang . . ."
0:37–0:56	**Chorus 2**, 8 mm.	Choral vocals continue, but notice change in bass line and keyboard part, and sparer texture in the rhythm section. "We want the funk . . ."
0:56–1:14	**Interlude**, 8 mm.	This section employs the music from chorus 2. "La la la . . ."
1:14–1:33	**Chorus 1**, 8 mm.	As before, but now with bass voice at the front of the mix. "You've got a real type of thang . . ."
1:33–1:51	**Chorus 2**, 8 mm.	As before. "We want the funk . . ."
1:51–2:09	**Interlude**, 8 mm.	As before. "La la la . . ."
2:09–2:19	**Interlude extension**, 4 mm.	New vocal added over same music, as sustained keyboard chord returns. "We gotta turn this mutha out . . ."
2:19–2:54	**Chorus 1**, 16 mm.	Length is doubled by repetition of 8-bar section, "You've got a real type of thang . . ."

(continued)

2:54–3:30	**Chorus 2**, 16 mm.	Length is also doubled here, as the texture builds up by adding layers, "We want the funk . . ."
3:30–5:00	**Chorus 2**, 40 mm.	Extension here comprises five times through the 8-bar pattern, beginning by returning to a simpler texture and then building up again, adding the material from the interlude extension. "We want the funk . . ."
5:00–5:18	**Interlude**, 8 mm.	"La la la . . ." Note that chorus 1 melody enters early.
5:18–5:35	**Chorus 1**, 8 mm.	As at the beginning, "You've got a real type of thang . . ."
5:35–5:44	**Chorus 2**, 8 mm.	As at the beginning, with fade-out. "We want the funk . . ."

(r5 uk6). *Cut the Cake* (p4 r1, 1975) and *Soul Searching* (p9 r2, 1976) also did well and received significant airplay on rock radio. It is some measure of how far apart white and black audiences had grown that many white listeners who enjoyed the Average White Band had little awareness of funk in the first half of the 1970s. This lack of familiarity with funk—and with black pop generally—would contribute significantly to the furor that later developed in the rock community over the rise of disco.

Rediscovery: Northern Soul and the Remarkable Case of Rodriguez. Beginning in the late 1960s, a scene devoted to dance music developed in the north of England. The Twisted Wheel in Manchester began to feature evenings filled with American black pop of the mid-1960s, especially Motown records and anything that imitated the Motown sound. In fact, readily accessible hits were soon discouraged, as DJs took great pride in finding obscure records to spin for the enthusiastic dancers. By the early 1970s, this northern soul dance scene had spread to the Catacombs in Wolverhampton, the Wigan Casino in Lancashire, and the Mecca in Blackpool, with dancers spending entire evenings moving to a pop style that was no longer on the charts, and grooving to records that had never charted anyway. While initially an underground scene very much off the music-industry radar, enthusiasm for northern soul caused old records to be reissued, helped a handful of records become hits in the UK, and even reinvigorated the performing careers of a few 1960s singers. The lack of new "old" records to be rediscovered, combined with the rise of funk and disco, spelled the end for the original northern soul movement in the second half of the 1970s.

Another story of obscure music with Detroit origins is the career of Sixto Rodriguez. In the late 1960s, Rodriguez recorded and released several tracks that were commercial flops in the United States. The album *Cold Fact* was recorded in late 1969 at a Detroit studio with Motown guitarist Dennis Coffey co-producing. The album sold poorly in the United States, as did the follow-up, *Coming from Reality* (1971). It seemed Rodriguez's career was over, except that his music became very popular in South Africa, where he was celebrated as a star. Various stories of his death circulated until researchers discovered that the singer had been living in Detroit all along, completely unaware of his fame on the other side of the globe.

The story of Rodriguez's surprising rediscovery is the topic of the documentary *Searching for Sugar Man* (2012).

REGGAE COMES ASHORE

New Orleans and New York. During the 1970s, the Jamaican form of popular music called reggae entered the mainstream in the United States and Britain. Reggae had roots in American rock and rhythm and blues, and produced aftershocks in many later pop styles, especially punk and rap. Jamaican music had played a peripheral role in mainstream popular music in the United States since the 1950s. In Chapter 3, we mentioned the late 1950s craze for calypso music, the popularity of songs such as "Jamaica Farewell," and the fact that the Kingston Trio took its name from a town in Jamaica. As a result of British imperialism, the music of Jamaica also played an important part in the popular culture of the UK, especially after World War II. While many Americans enjoyed Jamaican music during the late 1950s, however, Jamaicans were also listening to American pop. For years, Jamaican radio stations had been quite conservative, based on the model of the BBC. But when portable radios become more affordable, Jamaicans tuned in to American radio stations, especially those broadcasting from New Orleans and Florida. As a consequence, many Jamaicans developed a taste for artists such as Fats Domino and the rolling feel of New Orleans–based rhythm and blues.

The scarcity of American rhythm and blues records on the island led to the appearance of the "sound system man"—an entrepreneur who assembled a powerful sound system on the back of a truck and drove it from town to town, stopping to play records for public gatherings. Competition soon arose among these mobile music promoters, leading some to scratch the labels off their records so that competitors would not know the identity of the artist. It also led sound system men to begin featuring disc jockeys who would talk over records, often inventing rhyming verses to display their cleverness and verbal dexterity.

In the early 1960s, a Jamaican form of popular music called "ska" emerged, which emphasized an upbeat tempo reminiscent of American rhythm and blues and featured an offbeat "skank" rhythm pattern. As the 1960s progressed, ska was replaced by a newer style called "rock steady," which was popular from about 1966 to 1968. Reggae developed out of this second style. The leaders of the reggae movement in the 1970s had backgrounds in Jamaican pop that stretched back into the early 1960s. The most important figure among these musicians was Bob Marley. With Peter Tosh and Bunny Livingston, Marley had been a member of a vocal trio in the 1960s called the Wailers. The Wailers were signed by Jamaican producer Lee "Scratch" Perry, who recorded the group backed by his band, the Upsetters. The Wailers' records did well regionally, and Perry convinced them that they needed to play instruments to be successful. In 1970, Marley and the Wailers released their first recordings in Jamaica.

Chris Blackwell's Island Records was an important outlet for Jamaican music in the UK. Beginning in the early 1960s Blackwell released Jamaican records to the British market such as Millie Small's "My Boy Lollipop" (p2 uk2, 1964). The demand for such records was stronger in England than it was in America, due to the large Jamaican population living in the UK that was eager to hear music from home. The homesick Jamaicans enjoyed this music, but so did British kids, and the availability of reggae in the UK influenced many English musicians who would later end up in punk and new wave bands. In the early 1970s, Island released music by rock acts like Free, Traffic, and Cat Stevens. Blackwell also signed the Wailers to Island during this period and advanced them enough money to record an album. In the spring of 1973, *Catch a Fire* was released internationally on Island, followed by *Burnin'* at the end of the year. "Get Up, Stand Up" appeared on the second of these records, and exemplified Bob Marley's approach to reggae. Like much funk-influenced rhythm and blues of the early 1970s, the track is built on a bass and drum groove that remains steady throughout the tune and demonstrates the reggae rhythmic feel that emphasizes upbeats. While the verse and chorus are built on different bass lines, they are similar, and contrast is provided by the use of group vocals on the chorus and solo vocals during the verses. Showing the development from ska, which was often called "rude boy" music because of its youth-oriented subject matter, the focus in "Get Up, Stand Up" is topical, containing lyrics that advocate political freedom.

While Marley and the Wailers were popular among reggae fans, their music remained mostly underground until the mid-1970s. Two events helped bring a broader audience to reggae after this time. The first was the independent film *The Harder They Come*, which chronicled the rise and fall of a fictional pop singer in Jamaica. Released in the United States in 1973, the movie became a cult hit. A soundtrack album was released by Island and featured tracks by Jimmy Cliff (who had starred in the movie) and other Jamaican artists, including Toots and the Maytals. Reggae also garnered attention with the successful Eric Clapton cover of Marley's "I Shot the Sheriff," which had originally appeared on Marley's *Burnin'*. Clapton's version topped the U.S. pop charts during the summer of 1974 (r33 uk9) and Clapton fans soon sought out Marley's music. About this time, both Tosh and Livingston left the Wailers to pursue solo careers, but Marley's career was the one that really took off. A year later, *Burnin'* surfaced for the first time on the *Billboard*

Bob Marley, the world's most famous reggae musician, in a 1976 concert. Here, Marley performs in front of the image of Haile Selassie, the leader of the Rastafarian religion, which preached salvation for African people all over the world. Marley's lyrics focused on political and social freedom, making him an icon for social justice movements around the world.

Listening Guide

Bob Marley and the Wailers, "Get Up, Stand Up"

Island ILPS 9256 [Tuff Gong 422-846 200-4]

Words and music by Bob Marley and Peter Tosh, produced by Chris Blackwell and the Wailers. Contained on *Burnin'*, which was released in 1973.

FORM: Contrasting verse-chorus, with verse and chorus based on similar but distinct bass lines. Choruses and verses alternate regularly with no interludes between. Like "Papa Was a Rolling Stone" and "Thank You (Falettinme Be Mice Elf Agin)," this track is driven by the bass part and drumbeat, even if it does not use the same bass line all the way through.

TIME SIGNATURE: 4/4. Note how every second measure features a stress on beat 3. This is sometimes referred to as the "one-drop" rhythm.

INSTRUMENTATION: Electric guitar, clavinet (an electric keyboard similar to a harpsichord, but sounding more like an electric guitar), electric piano, bass, drums, percussion, lead and backup vocals.

0:00–0:08	**Introduction**, 4 mm.	After drum lead-in, clavinet, guitar, bass, and drums enter, setting up entrance of the voices.
0:08–0:32	**Chorus**, 16 mm.	Unison, sing-along vocal melody. "Get up, stand up . . ."
0:32–0:57	**Verse 1**, 16 mm.	Lead vocal takes over; note the change in the line played by the bass and guitar. "Preacher man . . ."
0:57–1:21	**Chorus**, 16 mm.	Choral vocals return. Note the percussion in the background. "Get up, stand up . . ."
1:21–1:46	**Verse 2**, 16 mm.	Lead vocal takes over again. Note wah-wah guitar lines in background. "Most people think . . ."
1:46–2:11	**Chorus**, 16 mm.	Choral vocals return, but now Marley improvises over the melody. "Get up, stand up . . ."
2:11–2:35	**Verse 3**, 16 mm.	New lead singer, Peter Tosh, changes the melody somewhat. "We're sick and tired . . ."
2:35–3:00	**Chorus**, 16 mm.	Choral vocals return, and both Marley and Tosh improvise over the melody. "Get up, stand up . . ."
3:00–3:13	**Chorus**, 8 mm.	As before, as song fades out.

album charts (two years after it was originally released), sparking a wave of hits in both the pop and soul markets that peaked in the United States with *Rastaman Vibration* (p8 r11 uk15, 1976) and *Exodus* (p20 r15 uk8, 1977). By the end of the decade, Marley was revered as a musician, cultural hero, and fighter for political and social justice. His albums sold well, especially in the UK, and he played to sold-out audiences around the world. Late in the 1970s, Marley developed cancer, and in 1981 he died at the age of thirty-six. After his death, both Tosh and Livingston (as Bunny Wailer) continued their solo careers, and Marley's son Ziggy enjoyed success with his band, the Melody Makers.

As a crossover form of music that grew out of the African diaspora, reggae was similar in many ways to 1970s black pop. Although not a style of black pop in the strict sense, reggae can be seen as a parallel consequence of crossover during the 1950s and 1960s. When 1950s rock and roll and electric blues went out of style in the United States, it continued to develop in the UK, returning to the States—with a distinctive accent—via the Beatles and the Rolling Stones. New Orleans rhythm and blues and 1960s soul had a similar effect in Jamaica, returning to the mainland transformed into reggae.

THE RISE OF DISCO

I Should Be Dancin': A New Dance Craze. In the late 1970s, dance-oriented "disco" music became extremely popular in the United States. Like many forms of music that suddenly achieve mainstream popularity, disco had a long history as an underground style. The popularity of disco, beginning largely in 1977, can be attributed to an interest in enjoying music through physical movement (dancing) rather than cerebrally (stationary listening). By the mid-1970s, rock had become music that was meant primarily for listening. Although people could dance along with much rock music, and many did, dancing was not the driving force behind most music associated with rock culture. In rock clubs and bars, live bands were considered preferable to disc jockeys, who were thought to be budget alternatives to live music. Within black pop, however, dancing was still a central element. Early in the 1970s, dancers began to frequent small clubs that specialized in spinning dance records late into the night. According to many accounts, this practice first began within urban gay communities, especially in New York at small dance clubs like 12 West, the 10th Floor, the Loft, and Paradise Garage. Until it hit the mainstream in 1977, disco was mostly an underground style that occasionally popped up into greater visibility. Among the first hits to arise from

Saturday Night Fever (1977) featured the story of Tony Manero (John Travolta), a young man from Brooklyn caught between his friends—who are content with their lives—and the dream of something more. Much of the film centers on Tony's disco dancing. The film and its wildly popular soundtrack (featuring the Bee Gees' "Stayin' Alive") epitomized disco culture and music, and set off a craze for both.

the disco subculture were George McCrae's "Rock Your Baby" (p1 r1, 1974) and Van McCoy's "The Hustle" (p1 r1 uk3, 1975). These songs blended a direct dance beat with a catchy pop hook. Barry White's Love Unlimited Orchestra also scored with "Love's Theme" (p1 r10 uk10, 1973), which added lush strings to the disco mix. Another series of early hits came from Florida's KC and the Sunshine Band, whose best known song was "That's the Way I Like It" (p1 r1 uk4, 1975). Rock listeners would have known all of these songs, but viewed them as novelty tunes rather than serious threats to the rock world order. Moreover, many disc jockeys created special extended versions of dance songs, which were not available to the record-buying public. Other extended versions formed a new "dance" market. These records were often called "12 inch" releases, a reference to the larger disc size needed to hold their longer tracks.

Disco emerged onto the national scene in 1977 with the release of *Saturday Night Fever*, a film starring John Travolta. A gifted dancer, Travolta became the model for the macho disco dancer, establishing a markedly heterosexual context for disco. The soundtrack to *Saturday Night Fever* featured tracks by the Bee Gees that became disco staples: "Stayin' Alive" (p1 r4 uk4, 1978) and "Night Fever" (p1 r8 uk1, 1978) both topped the pop charts and fueled a national craze for disco music. Amid the excitement of Travolta, *Saturday Night Fever*, and the Bee Gees, many hippies cut their hair, put on sleek polyester shirts, and headed out to dance clubs. Suddenly, many major artists were turning out disco-flavored tracks: rockers Rod Stewart ("Do You Think I'm Sexy?"), the Rolling Stones ("Miss You"), and even KISS ("I Was Made for Loving You") jumped on the disco bandwagon. Disco versions of well-known songs began popping up everywhere, including a popular disco version of the first movement of Beethoven's Fifth Symphony!

The Return of the Producers. By the mid-1970s, the music industry had given over much of the production authority in rock to the musicians themselves. Bands used producers to help run recording sessions, but often retained a significant amount of say in how the record sounded. The popularity of disco represented a return to the authority of producers. Following their roots in the R&B market, disco records were made according to the Brill Building or Motown models, with producers and engineers taking a central role in the creative process. Two of the most important producers in commercial disco were Jacques Morali and Giorgio Moroder, who both produced American acts using a European style of disco (often called Eurodisco). Eurodisco differed from the underground dance music of urban clubs in America because it was more rhythmically precise and not as funk-based. Along with the Bee Gees, one of the first disco acts to emerge in the mainstream was the Village People, a group whose music often exemplified Eurodisco. Assembled by producer Jacques Morali as a kind of "gay Monkees," the group specialized in songs that took a playful slant on life in the gay underground, with references that most listeners missed entirely. The group's 1978 hit "YMCA" (p2 r32 uk16) depicts the YMCA as a place to meet young gay men. Even today, this song is regularly played at sporting events, with crowds getting up and dancing to the chorus, most of them unaware of the song's original context.

The Black Side of Disco

Disco emerged in the mainstream during the mid-1970s, but drew heavily on dance-oriented styles popular in the soul market. In this article published in the important New York black-oriented newspaper *Amsterdam News*, Nelson George discusses the manner in which African American performers and producers interacted with the disco craze after the music began to regularly cross over into mainstream markets. George confronts criticisms of disco as noncreative music, acknowledging tensions between disco as mindless dance music alongside other ambitious elements of the form.

In 1974, "Rock Your Baby" by George McRae, "Rock Your Boat" by the Hues Corporation and "Express" by B. T. Express pioneered a new way of reaching the record-buying public. The success of these records didn't depend on record company promotion or on personal appearances by the performers, but on being played in establishments that called themselves discotheques.

Now, discos were not new. Discotheque is a French word which has been used in France since the early 1960s, and for a time in the mid-60s Americans used it to describe clubs like the Cheetah, Electric Circus and Trude Heller's. Such clubs not only played recorded music, but were great places for upcoming rock bands to play—this, because in the 60's there was really no music designed specifically for discos. Whatever music was danceable was played, so young bands like the Young Rascals found these clubs excellent for testing their skills.

Way back then, discos were considered to be just another fad. People patronized them, of course, but the public eye had turned elsewhere. Nevertheless, this sudden explosion of good, danceable Black music began to attract attention and interest grew. Accordingly, the disco became one of the most discussed, promoted and enjoyed social institutions in American history, and Blacks have been involved in all aspects of it.

The question, then, is how has the disco phenomenon affected Black folks? Are Blacks benefitting from something we played the major role in revitalizing?

The answer is yes and no. Where one places one's emphasis depends on one's point of view. To break it down, let's look at disco in three ways: as a business, as an art form and as entertainment.

The Disco Business

Disco has definitely put money in the pockets of many Blacks. Black-owned discos proliferate throughout the New York area, from chic Manhattan spots to working class hangouts in Queens. Moreover, the D.J.'s and other personnel at these discos are usually Black. Discos have also formed a contemporary "chitlin' circuit" wherein Black performers can work before Black audiences.

Hit disco records that "crossed over" to the pop market (a nice way of saying, caught the fancy of white people) have lifted bands like the T-Connection, B. T. Express and the Gary Toms Empire from being little known bar bands to being widely recognized musical aggregations. For Black songwriters and arrangers, disco has increased their workload and, in turn, their take-home pay. Bunny Sigler, a Philadelphia-based singer/songwriter/producer/arranger, who has worked with the South Shore Commission (remember "Free Man"?), Archie Bell and the Drells, the Tramps and other disco groups, is a perfect example. He is prolific and, though perhaps not too original, knows how to get those feet moving on the dance floor. His disco work is so well regarded that

Sigler has managed to do several solo albums (his latest is on Salsoul Records and is called "Let Me Party with You"). However, his greatest talent lies in writing and arranging.

Producers like Van McCoy, Norman Harris and Jeff Lane have been very busy since the advent of the disco boom. Lane, for example, has turned successful recordings with B. T. Express and Brass Construction into lucrative production deals with Arista Records. Lane recalled that before B. T. Express's success, "All I had working for me was me. Now I employ ten people in my office, plus I have other Blacks across the country helping me promote my records."

Some people, like Norby Walters, a prominent disco booking agent, feel that disco has made it easier for Black performers to reach the pop market. But, unfortunately, that isn't necessarily so.

A look at *Billboard* magazine's top 100 pop records of 1973 shows that 36 of them crossed over from Black stations. This was the year before the disco explosion. Skipping 1974, which was the year the phenomenon took root, we move to 1975 to gauge disco music's impact on the Black music crossover. That year, 28 of the top 100 records came over from Black stations, while in 1976 there was a slight recovery to 30 out of 100.

Last year, with disco firmly established on the music scene, only 23 records moved from Black stations to Billboard's top 100, and that includes Meco's "Theme From Star Wars" which began in discos and was then picked up by Black stations. If these figures are correct (they were supplied courtesy of Robert Ford at *Billboard* magazine), they refute the idea that the disco rage has helped Black performers.

In fact, disco music has opened up Black stations to penetration by white artists. Leo Sayer, the Bee Gees, Cerrone and others all made it onto Black radio through the *disco route.*

The Art of Disco

Disco D.J.'s can be creative artists if they have the touch and the right equipment. The successful selection, ordering and mixing of disco music requires an artistic temperament. A wrong move by the D.J. can clear the dance floor and give the club a bad reputation, so a good D.J. can mean success or failure for a club.

Now comes a touchy subject: The music itself. The negative adjectives applied to disco music are legion. Even some of those people involved in making the music will knock it. Jeff Lane, for example, feels "There's nothing in it that could help a person mentally. It's just dance, dance, dance. Blacks aren't accomplishing much by dancing." Lane even discerns the development of a backlash against the up-tempo disco sound. "Music," he says, "is getting back to the early 60s—the Sam Cooke days. Then, when a singer stepped up to the microphone he had to be able to sing and had to be singing about something."

Most of those who attack disco music are really speaking about "formula" disco music, the kind that features that stereotyped, hi-hat drum sound and inane lyrics. But there is also really good R&B and jazzy disco music to be found in the disco section of record stores. The dance music of L.T.D., the Blackbyrds, T-Connection, Dr. Buzzard's Savannah Band and any Gamble and Huff production also make for very enjoyable listening. And a little known band called Morning, Noon and Night put out a 12-inch disco disc called "Bite Your Granny," which features a mix of jangling rhythm guitars, tambales and synthesizer, that is simply brilliant.

So not to worry: The Afro American tradition of making dance music that is musically interesting hasn't died with disco. In many cases, aided by modern recording facilities, Black musicians have advanced the style.

Disco Is Dance Fun

Be it at house parties, wedding receptions or disco clubs, Black people do like to dance and take almost every opportunity to do so. There are few more enjoyable scenes than a swinging, uninhibited Black disco, and the long cuts made to accommodate dancing are perfect tools for dancing fools.

But there is a small problem. When the recorded music stops and a performer comes on, all of the material he/she presents isn't danceable. Often, in fact, the performer—especially a singer—will do a night club act. The dancers generally don't mind because it gives them a chance to cool off and relax.

However, as Carol Douglass, famous for her early disco smash "Doctor's Orders," notes, "When you perform before a night club or concert hall audience, it's often hard to reach them." So although Ms. Douglass inserts ballads into her repertoire to showcase her all-around talent, when she performs her disco selections she finds herself in front of a band that's playing long instrumental passages, and all she can do is stand there.

The extended length of disco pieces is, then, a hindrance to disco singers when they perform in non-disco settings. Instead of being the focus of the music, they are often playing second fiddle to the arrangement.

As with most things, disco is a mixed bag. The music has brought success to many Blacks and will help many aspirants who've yet to reach stardom. But disco is no magic door to the bigtime; it can also be a trick bag leading nowhere.

Source: Nelson George, "The Disco Boom and Blacks," *Amsterdam News*, January 28, 1978, 36.

Donna Summer, shown here in concert in 1979, was one of disco's biggest stars. Her hits "Love to Love You Baby," "Hot Stuff," and "Bad Girls" are disco classics. Summer's music exemplifies the style of Eurodisco.

By contrast, it would be difficult to mistake what Donna Summer was singing about on "Love to Love You Baby" (p2 r3 uk4, 1976). Produced by Munich-based Moroder and Pete Bellotte, Summer moans and groans her way through a seventeen-minute extended mix that underscores the sensual aspects of disco dancing. A song like "Love to Love You Baby" shows the manner in which disco often relied on repetitive chorus refrain material instead of narrative verses. The song's allusions to classical music through melodic development and orchestration, in addition to a large-scale dynamic build (even in the five-minute version edited for the singles market), show the manner in which disco connected to the more intricate aspects of progressive rock. After disco broke into the mainstream, Summer became one of its biggest stars, hitting the top of the charts with "Hot Stuff" (p1 r3 uk11, 1979) and "Bad Girls" (p1 r1 uk14, 1979), both contained on the album *Bad Girls*, which could be considered a disco concept album. Michael Jackson also took advantage of the disco craze in 1979, releasing the album *Off the Wall*, which contained the hit "Don't Stop 'Til You Get Enough" (p1 r1 uk3). *Off the Wall* began Jackson's collaboration with producer Quincy Jones—a partnership that would enjoy overwhelming success in the 1980s.

Disco Sucks? The rise of disco after the release of *Saturday Night Fever* caused a violent reaction within parts of the rock-music community. Perhaps the clearest instance of this can be seen in the anti-disco rally held by Chicago rock DJ Steve Dahl in 1979 between games of a Tigers–White Sox doubleheader. Dahl arranged to have a large crate of disco records placed in the outfield and ceremoniously blown up. The resulting rioting was so extreme that the second game had to be canceled. This hatred of disco was widespread among rock fans, who popularized the slogan "disco sucks." There are many misconceptions about the source of this hostility toward disco. A common fallacy is that rockers were reacting against

Listening Guide

Donna Summer, "Love to Love You Baby" Oasis 401

Words and music by Giorgio Moroder, Pete Bellotte, and Donna Summer, produced by Pete Bellotte. Reached #2 on the *Billboard* "Hot 100" chart and #3 on the "Hot Soul Singles" chart in early 1976. An extended version (Unidisc Spec-1574), often called a 12-inch, went to #1 on the *Billboard* "Disco Action" chart in late 1975.

FORM: Modified simple verse with bridge. There is no real verse (!), only a chorus section repeated and modified throughout the song. The only lyrical variation occurs in the short, contrasting bridge sections. Musical variation occurs in the middle of the song through a long "breakdown" section inserted between the instrumental bridge and chorus, which includes a large-scale buildup by adding instruments cumulatively and leading into a melodic interlude. After a reprisal of the chorus and bridge complex, the song ends with a one-minute coda, which introduces a new melodic and harmonic approach to the lyrical phrase "love to love you, baby."

TIME SIGNATURE: 4/4. The kick drum that enters at 0:15 plays each beat of the measure. Like a lot of disco, the beats are emphasized in a fairly even manner, leading to a sense of mechanization.

INSTRUMENTATION: Drums, bass, guitar (both plucked and wah-wah), strings, piano, synthesizer, horns, lead vocals, and backing vocals.

0:00–0:25	**Introduction**, 10 mm.	Starts with voice and high-hat, adds harmony vocal (:05), wah-wah guitar (:09), kick drum (:15), groans (:20). "I love to love . . ."
0:25–0:32	**Bridge**, 3 mm.	The only section that contains harmonic movement, bass guitar enters. "When you're laying . . ."
0:32–0:47	**Chorus**, 6 mm.	Strings enter.
0:47–0:55	**Bridge**, 3 mm.	"Do it to me . . ."
0:55–1:11	**Instrumental**, 6 mm.	Like the chorus, but with a string melody.
1:11–1:17	**Instrumental bridge**, 3 mm.	
1:17–2:17	**Breakdown**, 24 mm.	At the beginning of this section, the instrumentation is scaled back to high-hat (like the introduction), and builds cumulatively, adding groans and vocals in a lower register than the chorus (1:23), kick drum (1:37), bass (1:47), guitar and strings (1:57), and wah-wah guitar (2:07).
2:17–3:03	**Melodic interlude**, 18 mm.	A doubled piano and synth perform a simple 4-mm. melody supported by drums, which use a more open beat pattern incorporating the snare drum (2:17). The entire melodic phrase is then repeated, up a whole step (2:28). Then the phrase occurs again in the original key area, this time with string accompaniment (2:37). A fourth iteration of this melody then occurs (slightly extended), performed by a synth with a more biting tone, while the band plays staccato hits (2:47).

(continued)

3:03–3:18	**Chorus**, 6 mm.	The full band performs and a large chorus of vocals sing; "I love to love . . ."
3:18–3:25	**Instrumental bridge**, 3 mm.	As before.
3:25–3:40	**Chorus**, 6 mm.	As before. "I love to love . . ."
3:40–3:49	**Instrumental bridge**, 3 mm.	As before.
3:49–3:58	**Chorus**, 4 mm.	As before. "I love to love . . ."
3:58–4:57	**Coda**, 20 mm.	A new melody and harmonic progression is introduced, and repeated as the song fades. Horns appear for the first time. The arrangement and a chorus of backing vocals harmonize the main lyrical theme. "Love to love you . . ."

the origins of disco in the gay community. There may be some truth in this, but remember that most rock fans had no idea that disco originated in gay night spots. For most American listeners, disco originated in the very heterosexual context of John Travolta and *Saturday Night Fever*. Moreover, rock fans had traditionally tolerated many different forms of androgyny without a similar reaction, and by the end of the decade many rock musicians happily admitted nonheterosexual orientations. Another specious explanation is that disco was largely music that facilitated meeting members of the opposite sex at bars for quick, one-night stands, and rockers were offended by this blatant promiscuity. Sexual practices may have been different within disco culture, but it is difficult to square such puritanical attitudes with rock and roll since swaggering braggadocio was hardly foreign to rock culture.

In retrospect, there are several more plausible reasons why rock fans hated disco with such a passion. One important explanation requires us to question the ways in which disco was viewed as a threat within the rock community. In many ways, disco stood in direct confrontation to the hippie aesthetic that had been developing in rock music since the mid-1960s. Disco was not about listening to music but dancing to it. Instead of being concerned with important spiritual or social issues, disco was about fun. And perhaps most important to the musicians involved, disco was not about the specific artists but about the beat in general—which was sometimes provided by a machine. It took the production authority away from the artist and returned it to the producer. Disco threatened the very foundation of the rock subculture established with albums like *Sgt. Pepper's Lonely Hearts Club Band*, which had made rock a more serious-minded, "listening" music. While homophobia and racism may have played a role in how some rock fans reacted to disco, more often, many of these fans also rejected the anti-hippie aesthetic of disco. In other words, this was a reaction against a genre that catered to the tastes of the mainstream, which prefaced newer dance-oriented

Sound Check

Artist	Song	Sound
Sly and the Family Stone	**Thank You (Falettinme Be Mice Elf Agin) (1970)**	Form: simple verse-chorus Riff-based Slightly altered "contrasting verse" Mostly group vocals
The Temptations	**Papa Was a Rolling Stone (1972)**	Form: simple verse-chorus Riff-based Expansive drama and scope Alternation between lead singers and group vocals
Stevie Wonder	**Living for the City (1973)**	Form: compound AABA (modified) All instruments performed by Wonder AABA form augmented by improvised vocal section (A') Central drama (B section) offers a contrast
Parliament	**Tear the Roof Off the Sucker (Give Up the Funk) (1976)**	Form: contrasting verse-chorus Two separate chorus sections, but no verse Bass and guitar weave complicated patterns against strict drums Choral, sing-along vocals
Bob Marley and the Wailers	**Get Up, Stand Up (1973)**	Form: contrasting verse-chorus Riff-based Emphasis throughout on beat three ("one-drop" rhythm) Verse and chorus built on different (but similar) bass lines
Donna Summer	**Love to Love You Baby (1976)**	Form: modified simple-verse with bridge No narrative verse section A large-scale dynamic build in the interlude Lengthy coda with a new harmonic foundation

Taking advantage of many rock fans' hatred for disco, Chicago disc jockey Steve Dahl arranged a Disco Demolition Night between games of a Tigers–White Sox doubleheader. When disco records were blown up on the field, the resulting riot caused the second game to be canceled by the umpires, who declared the field unfit for play.

developments in the pop market during the coming decades. The inflexibility of rock listeners to adhere to changing tastes in the mainstream offered early signs of a growing distance between rock and pop. Thus the "disco sucks" movement is an early instance of what we will later call "rockism," a belief that some forms of popular music are less important because of a perceived lack of authenticity or connection to the core values of rock listeners. Strangely enough, disco was united with the emerging punk movement in its rejection of the hippie aesthetic. Many rock fans, whether they could articulate it precisely or not, sensed that their approach to music was under attack from the widespread popularity of disco and punk. As things turned out, neither disco nor punk displaced rock. Both did have a marked effect on rock, however, and in the next chapter we chart punk's assault on "corporate rock" and, more important, on the hippie aesthetic.

For Additional Online Resources, visit:
digital.wwnorton.com/whatsthatsound5

FURTHER READING

Lloyd Bradley, *This Is Reggae Music: The Story of Jamaica's Music* (Grove, 2000).

George Clinton and Ben Greenman, *Brothers Be, Yo Like George, Ain't That Funkin' Kinda Hard on You?: A Memoir* (Atria, 2014).

Anne Danielsen, *Presence and Pleasure: The Funk Grooves of James Brown and Parliament* (Wesleyan University Press, 2006).

Alice Echols, *Hot Stuff: Disco and the Remaking of American Culture* (Norton, 2011).

Nelson George, *The Death of Rhythm and Blues* (Penguin, 2004).

John Jackson, *A House on Fire: The Rise and Fall of Philadelphia Soul* (Oxford University Press, 2004).

Arthur Kempton, *Boogaloo: The Quintessence of American Popular Music* (University of Michigan Press, 2005).

Tim Lawrence, *Love Saves the Day: A History of American Dance Music Culture, 1970–1979* (Duke University Press, 2003).

Dave Thompson, *Funk* (Backbeat Books, 2001).

Michael Veal, *Dub: Soundscapes and Shattered Songs in Jamaican Reggae* (Wesleyan University Press, 2007).

Rickey Vincent, *Funk: The Music, the People, and the Rhythm of the One* (St. Martin's Griffin, 1996).

Timothy White, *Catch a Fire: The Life of Bob Marley* (Henry Holt, 2000).

10

The Clash

LONDON CALLING

MAINSTREAM ROCK, PUNK, AND NEW WAVE

CHAPTER PREVIEW

- In the middle to late 1970s, FM radio matured as a business and large corporations invested in record companies.

- The success of mega-albums like *Frampton Comes Alive* and *Rumours* seemed to cause record companies to limit their risk in launching new acts.

- In the mid-1970s, New York's underground punk scene included the Ramones, Talking Heads, and Blondie, whose musical roots can be traced to late-1960s bands like the Velvet Undergound.

- Influenced, in part, by the New York punk scene, the Sex Pistols led the English punk movement that also included groups like the Clash and the Jam.

- The American music business recast punk as new wave, distancing its artists from more controversial groups like the Sex Pistols and shifting the message from social protest to mainstream observations.

- New York's Blondie, Talking Heads, and Patti Smith successfully transitioned to new wave, joined by the Cars and Devo. New wavers Elvis Costello and the Police invaded from Britain.

I n many ways, the spirit of psychedelic music continued well into the 1970s. By the middle of the decade, various manifestations of hippie rock had become the status quo. Punk and new wave also began to challenge mainstream rock's commercial domination. Rock music had become big business, and some critics and fans argued that this was beginning to have a negative effect on the musical substance of rock. According to this view, which was based on a growing need for authenticity in

The cover of the Clash's *London Calling* (1980) illustrates that punk was about rebellion: political, social, and musical. Government and traditional moral values were the focus of punk's political and social attacks, while disco and concert rock were the focus of its musical attacks. *London Calling* was a landmark punk album, and the Clash's first success in the United States. Punk started in the New York underground, and later developed and gathered steam in London. With the success of the Sex Pistols, the Clash, the Buzzcocks, and others, punk soon broke into the mainstream in both the UK and the United States. The movement culminated in new wave, which many saw as a more radio-friendly version of punk.

rock, musicians were designing their music for the greatest popular appeal rather than as sincere musical expressions.

While the first half of the 1970s was mostly a time of emerging new styles that developed aspects of psychedelic music, the second half can be seen largely as a consolidation of earlier styles. Commercial rock continued to develop in the mainstream, while the punk movement flourished in underground scenes in New York and London, eventually emerging into the mainstream in the form of new wave. Punk and new wave both positioned themselves in opposition to mainstream rock: they rejected the highly produced and sophisticated sounds of hippie bands in favor of simplicity, which they believed had been central to pre-hippie rock. To understand what the punks were rebelling against, we must explore how the rock music business grew over the course of the 1970s.

MAINSTREAM ROCK: 1975–1980

FM Radio Goes from Late 1960s Free Form to AOR. The radio industry saw tremendous growth in the 1970s. By the beginning of the decade, FM stations were broadcasting rock music and focusing on album cuts, following the model established by Tom Donahue in San Francisco. This format developed into what is now called "album-oriented rock," or AOR. The change was accompanied by a decrease in the freedom of disc jockeys to choose their own music. By the end of the decade, most AOR stations were heavily formatted, with program directors or consultants programming the music. By this time, extended tracks and rock symphonies were no longer considered "radio friendly." Moving toward the commercial tendencies of AM, programmers felt that long rock songs did not leave enough time for commercials or prompted listeners to change the station. Musicians and record companies understood that there was an ideal length for an FM radio track (about four to five minutes), and bands that did not conform would have a hard time breaking into the growing AOR market.

Young people were increasingly tuning in to these stations, which translated into growing sources of advertising revenue. Since listeners tuned in for free, commercial radio stations had to look to advertising to provide profits. In general, advertising rates are based on how many people are expected to listen to a station, and radio stations do extensive research to determine listener demographics. As AOR radio grew, this information figured heavily into how much stations could charge their advertisers, and since the kind of music played on the station directly influenced who listened, advertising concerns often affected what music was programmed. When rock radio became increasingly profitable in the mid-1970s, major corporations invested in the music business, buying radio stations. Because the corporations were interested in only the financial bottom line, and programming decisions were made to maximize profits, there was a growing perception that AOR had abandoned the rebelliousness once central to the rock movement, and it was often called "corporate rock" by its detractors.

Show Me the Way: The Advent of the "Big Album." Corporations that prompted concern among mainstream rock's critics were not restricted to radio. Fueled by the steady growth of hippie culture, the entire record business experienced a transformation during the 1970s. The psychedelic rock culture celebrated at Woodstock in the summer of 1969 had become the hippie rock culture that flourished across the country in the first few years of the 1970s. By the middle of the decade, it became clear that more money could be made in rock music than anybody had ever imagined.

A significant factor in this realization was the emergence of the "big album." Generally, before the mid-1970s most bands and their record labels would be thrilled if an album sold five hundred thousand copies, achieving what the Record Industry Association of America (RIAA) called a "Gold" album award. However, as more records began to achieve this level, the RIAA launched a "Platinum" award for sales of one million copies. A good example of a million-selling album from the 1970s is Peter Frampton's live album *Frampton Comes Alive!* (1976). Frampton had been a member of Humble Pie but left to go solo after the *Rockin' the Fillmore* album in 1971. Stylistically, Frampton's music exemplified approachable, middle-of-the-road rock from the period that focused on his guitar solos and melodic songwriting. After releasing four moderately successful solo albums, *Frampton Comes*

Shown playing his trusty Les Paul Custom guitar, Peter Frampton enjoyed spectacular commercial success in the mid-1970s. Frampton was the poster boy for the "big album" and "corporate rock." His album *Frampton Comes Alive!* set a benchmark by selling over thirteen million copies, while he consistently played to huge, sell-out crowds.

Alive! was a blockbuster hit, reaching number one on the U.S. album charts (uk6) and producing the singles "Show Me the Way" (p6 uk10), "Baby, I Love Your Way" (p12 uk43), and "Do You Feel Like We Do" (p10 uk39).

The substantial financial returns of albums such as *Frampton Comes Alive!* helped transform the record business into an attractive possibility for investment. Large multinational corporations with no previous experience in music—Phillips Petroleum, for instance—bought up record labels in hopes of cashing in on the "big album." The concert circuit had also changed, as venues became larger and national and international tours became the norm for bands signed to major labels. Theaters and ballrooms were too small for major acts, so shows moved into stadiums and sports arenas, and attendance records were regularly broken. Important benchmarks of the rock live circuit were the scope of and venues played in tours by the Rolling Stones in 1969 and 1972, and Bob Dylan's return to live touring with the Band in 1974. The growth in record and concert revenues meant musicians began to enjoy the fruits of increased profits, leading to the use of private jets, long stays in expensive recording studios, and the ingestion of significant quantities of expensive—and illegal—drugs.

Life's Been Good to Me So Far: More Big Albums.
Among the albums that followed *Frampton Comes Alive!* in the big money sweepstakes was the Eagles' *Hotel California*, which hit number one in the United States (uk2) in early 1977 and included three hit songs: "New Kid in Town" (p1 uk20), "Hotel California" (p1 uk8), and "Life in the Fast Lane" (p11). Guitarist Joe Walsh replaced Bernie

Listening Guide

Peter Frampton, "Show Me the Way" (Live) A&M 1795

Words and music by Peter Frampton, produced by Peter Frampton. As a single, the song hit #6 on the *Billboard* "Hot 100" chart in 1976. The song was also released on the album *Frampton Comes Alive!,* which topped the "Top LPs & Tape" chart.

FORM: Contrasting verse-chorus. The verses consist of an 8-bar phrase, its repetition, and a 4-bar phrase that leads to the chorus, and the chorus is based on a contrasting 4-bar phrase that occurs two to four times. Note the false ending at 3:49, probably provided to fool the audience into thinking the song was ending so as to charge back into the chorus by surprise. Since this version is taken from a live recording, timings may differ among CD reissues.

TIME SIGNATURE: 4/4.

INSTRUMENTATION: Acoustic guitar, electric guitar, bass, drums, lead and backup vocals.

0:00–0:33	**Introduction**, 16 mm.	Strummed acoustic guitar opens the song as the band comes in after first 4 bars, first in stop time and then in regular time. Note the use of the voice box on the lead guitar, which makes the guitar seem to speak.
0:33–1:09	**Verse 1**, 20 mm.	Lead vocal enters with two 8-bar phrases, followed by 4 bars that drive toward the chorus. "I wonder how . . ."
1:09–1:30	**Chorus**, 12 mm.	Backup vocals enter to sing two 4-bar phrases, followed by a 4-bar transition drawn from the introduction, again featuring voice-box lead guitar. "I want you . . ."
1:30–2:07	**Verse 2**, 20 mm.	As before, "Well I can see no reason . . ."
2:07–2:29	**Chorus**, 12 mm.	As before, but now the 4-bar phrase is sung three times and then goes right into the guitar solo. "I want you . . ."
2:29–2:58	**Instrumental verse**, 16 mm.	Twice through the 8-bar phrase, featuring a solo on the voice-box lead guitar.
2:58–3:20	**Verse 3**, 12 mm.	Only once through the 8-bar phrase, then to the 4-bar phrase leading to the chorus. The sung verse is shortened here because we have just heard an instrumental verse and a full sung verse following that might become too repetitive. "I wonder if . . ."
3:20–3:49	**Chorus**, 16 mm.	As before, but four times through the 4-bar phrase. "I want you . . ."
3:49–3:56	**False ending**, 4 mm.	Song sounds as if it will end, but comes charging back.
3:56–4:18	**Chorus**, 12 mm.	As before, but three times through the 4-bar phrase. "I want you . . ."
4:18–4:32	**Coda**, 5 mm.	Once through the 4-bar progression from the introduction, plus one last bar on the final chord, provide the real ending for the tune.

Leadon on this album, and the band abandoned their easygoing country rock approach for a harder rocking, more mainstream style. The Eagles followed with *The Long Run* (p1, uk4), which was among the top albums of 1979.

While Frampton and the Eagles produced hit albums during this period, Fleetwood Mac soon took the big album phenomenon even further. Fleetwood Mac had started out as a British blues band in the late 1960s, led by guitarist Peter Green and including guitarist Jeremy Spencer, drummer Mick Fleetwood, and bassist John McVie. The band enjoyed some success in England with *Peter Green's Fleetwood Mac* (uk10, 1968) and a number-one single the same year with "Albatross." By 1971, Green and Spencer had left the group and keyboardist and vocalist Christine McVie had joined, followed in 1975 by guitarist and vocalist Lindsay Buckingham and singer Stevie Nicks. The style of the revamped lineup changed significantly, focusing on mainstream rock and ballads led by Buckingham, Nicks, and Christine McVie, the group's newcomers and principal songwriters. The new quintet released *Fleetwood Mac* in 1975, which slowly rose up the *Billboard* album chart, reaching number one in the United States in 1976. The album contained several popular singles, including "Rhiannon" (p11) and "Say You Love Me" (p11 uk40). *Rumours*, the group's next release, was even more successful. It spent thirty-one weeks at number one on the *Billboard* charts in 1977 and contained the hit tracks "Go Your Own Way" (10p), "Dreams" (1p), and "Don't Stop" (p3). No album had ever sold so many copies and dominated pop music in this way. Fleetwood Mac would never duplicate the success of *Rumours*, though they continued to release successful albums into the 1980s, including *Tusk* (p4 uk1, 1979), *Mirage* (p1 uk5, 1982), and *Tango in the Night* (p7 uk1, 1987).

Fleetwood Mac's Stevie Nicks (left) and Lindsay Buckingham (right). Building on the success of other "big albums" like *Frampton Comes Alive!*, Fleetwood Mac's *Rumours* stayed on the *Billboard* charts for thirty-one weeks in 1977, helping make the band one of the most popular groups of the 1970s.

One effect of the quest for the mega-hit album within the recording industry was to encourage a conservative attitude. In looking for the next Frampton, Eagles, or Fleetwood Mac, record companies were less willing to take chances on bands that might be interesting but were likely to sell only 350,000 records—a figure that had been acceptable only a few years before. Every new band was an entry in the big-album lottery, and record company staff increasingly seemed to ask themselves: Why waste a chance on a group that can't win? When modern critics lament the late 1970s, it is often because they feel that record companies killed the spirit of rock music when they became obsessed with the big album. Music became just another way to make money and it didn't seem to matter how the music sounded or what it stood for, as long as financial benefits could be realized.

It's Still Rock and Roll to Me. In Chapter 8, we saw how the wide range of rock styles in the 1970s emerged from the primordial rock soup of psychedelia. Rock in the early 1970s was teeming with competing stylistic approaches that are relatively easy to distinguish from one another. By mid-decade, however, these styles began to

Though successful in the first half of the decade with a harder, straight-ahead rock style, later in the 1970s the Doobie Brothers turned to a more laid-back, jazz-influenced rock, with the help of lead singer and songwriter Michael McDonald and ex–Steely Dan guitarist Skunk Baxter (left).

blend, reducing the usefulness of the old stylistic labels. Instead, mainstream rock moved back toward a more unified style in which elements of earlier styles could be easily detected but combinations of features were less predictable. This "evening out" of the earlier styles is sometimes attributed to the conservative attitude that became pervasive in the record company decision-making processes, a charge leveled by critics of banal "corporate rock." While we saw early 1970s rock through the lens of stylistic expansion, mainstream rock in the second half of the decade will be viewed in this chapter as a process of stylistic consolidation. It is important to understand how mainstream rock continued and *extended* earlier styles, while also pulling together elements that had previously been used to *distinguish among* styles.

Like Fleetwood Mac, many groups that were active in the early 1970s became more popular later in the decade, creating a strong relationship among earlier styles. This situation was new to rock music: rock musicians could sustain active careers after the age of thirty (or even forty, in some cases). The Rolling Stones, for example, continued active recording and touring schedules in the second half of the 1970s, hiring in ex-Faces guitarist Ron Wood to replace Mick Taylor and releasing *Black and Blue* (p1 uk2, 1976), *Some Girls* (p1 uk2, 1978), and *Emotional Rescue* (p1 uk1, 1980). Only a few years after the breakup of the Beatles, Paul McCartney formed Wings with his wife Linda, guitarist Denny Laine, and drummer Denny Seiwell. Considering the popularity of the front man, it was no surprise when the band's second album, *Red Rose Speedway*, hit number one on the U.S. charts (uk5) in 1973, and the ballad "My Love" topped the American singles charts (uk9). Wings' most successful album, commercially and aesthetically, was *Band on the Run* (p1 uk1, 1974), on which McCartney successfully updated his style to create an album of well-crafted tracks. Wings continued to enjoy success with a string of chart-topping albums and singles before the group disbanded in 1981. Unlike the Stones and McCartney, who had maintained popularity since the early 1960s, the Steve Miller Band enjoyed much more success in the 1970s than they ever had in the 1960s. Beginning with *The Joker* (p2, 1973), which contained an eponymous number-one single,

Miller and company were regular entrants on the American album and singles charts. *Fly Like an Eagle* (p3 uk11, 1976) is perhaps the band's best-known album, containing the tracks "Fly Like an Eagle" (p2), "Rock 'n' Me" (p1 uk11), and "Take the Money and Run" (p11). In all of these cases, artists who were popular (or active) in the 1960s extended their careers into the late 1970s while maintaining the essence of their musical style.

In addition to bands with roots in the 1960s, many groups that first achieved success in the early 1970s continued to build on their success during the remainder of the decade. Faced with the departure of Tom Johnston due to illness, the Doobie Brothers brought pianist and singer Michael McDonald on board and adopted a stylistic approach that laid more emphasis on jazz influences. The resultant records *Takin' It to the Streets* (p8, 1976) and *Livin' on the Fault Line* (p10 uk25, 1977) reestablished the band, but *Minute by Minute* (p1, 1979) pushed the group to new levels of commercial success. The album contained the hit track "What a Fool Believes" (p14, 1979), which quickly became a staple of FM radio. KISS also reached its commercial peak in the United States during this same period with the live albums *Alive!* (p9, 1975), which contained the more popular live version of the single "Rock and Roll All Nite" (12p), and *Alive II* (p7, 1977) and the studio albums *Love Gun* (p4, 1977) and *Dynasty* (p9, 1979).

Rethinking Previous Approaches: New Arrivals in the Late 1970s.

A number of mainstream bands that emerged in the second half of the 1970s also seemed to adopt features of earlier music, shaping them to fit the new, more restricted radio formats. The band Boston, for instance, blended blues rock with aspects of progressive rock to produce music that sold well and received generous radio play. Their first album, *Boston*, was released in early 1977 and quickly climbed to number three on the album charts (uk11). As a compact rock song with several highly organized instrumental sections, "More Than a Feeling" is representative of the group's approach. Boston's next album, *Don't Look Back* (p1 uk9, 1978) seemed to ensure their continued success, but a dispute with their record label kept the highly anticipated *Third Stage* (1p) from being released until 1986.

If any late 1970s band showed that radio success could come from merging popular styles from the early 1970s, it was Foreigner. Formed by guitarist Mick Jones and featuring the lead vocals of Lou Gramm, the band's debut, *Foreigner* (p4, 1977), and the tracks "Feels Like the First Time" (p4) and "Cold as Ice" (p6) quickly established them with American audiences. The next album, *Double Vision* (p3, 1978), contained the hit singles "Hot Blooded" (p3) and "Double Vision" (p2). Gramm's vocal approach was clearly derived from an interest in rhythm and blues, while Jones's blues-rock guitar hooks drove the songs forward. Differing from the traditional

As an MIT grad working for Polaroid, Tom Scholz also pursued his musical ambitions, writing and recording much of the music that would ultimately be featured on his band's debut album, *Boston* (1976). Scholz (left) is shown here in a trademark harmony-guitar live moment with bandmate Barry Goudreau.

Listening Guide

Boston, "More Than a Feeling" Epic 50266

Words and music by Tom Scholz, produced by John Boylan and Tom Scholz. Reached #5 on the *Billboard* "Hot 100" chart in September 1976. Contained on the album *Boston*, which reached #3 on the *Billboard* "Top LPs & Tape" chart.

FORM: Compound AABA, with each A section based on contrasting verse-chorus form, while the bridge offers new material employing lead guitars playing in harmony. Note that the verse and chorus lengths are different in each presentation of the A section, giving some indication of the variety employed when these sections reappear.

TIME SIGNATURE: 4/4.

INSTRUMENTATION: Electric and acoustic guitars, bass, drums, handclaps, lead and backup vocals.

	0:00–0:18	**Introduction**, 6 mm.	Acoustic guitar fades in, as electric guitar and bass join in.
A	0:18–0:42	**Verse 1**, 11 mm.	Vocals and drums enter, music remains quiet, ending gets louder and transitions into chorus via lead guitar melody. "I looked out . . ."
	0:42–1:17	**Chorus**, 16 mm.	Louder, with backup vocals and handclaps added to create excitement. Again, ending provides a transition, this time back to the verse. "It's more than a feeling . . ."
A	1:17–1:51	**Verse 2**, 15 mm.	Quieter again, with 4 bars of interlude before singing returns. Transition to verse gets louder, as before. "So many people . . ."
	1:51–2:30	**Chorus**, 18 mm.	As before, but now a new transition leads to the instrumental bridge. "It's more than a feeling . . ."
B	2:30–2:55	**Instrumental bridge**, 11 mm.	Melodic guitar solo featured, frequently doubled in harmony. The feel in this section is symphonic, similar to earlier progressive rock.
A	2:55–3:48	**Verse 3**, 24 mm.	Quieter again, with 4 bars of acoustic guitar preparing the introduction of the lead vocal. This time the verse is extended by repeating the end of the last phrase before beginning the transition to the chorus. "When I'm tired . . ."
	3:48–4:41	**Chorus**, 20 mm.	As before, and then fade out. "It's more than a feeling . . ."

blues-rock approach, however, was the prominent use of keyboards, clearly influenced by progressive rockers like Yes and Emerson, Lake & Palmer, but pared down to radio-friendly dimensions.

Musicians who were active in other bands during the previous decade also formed many of the most popular new groups of the late 1970s. For example, each member of Foreigner, save Lou Gramm, had performed professionally before teaming up in the mid-1970s. Journey is another example of a new group formed by older members. Formerly of Santana, guitarist Neal Schon and organist Greg Rolie teamed up with bassist Ross Valory (ex-Steve Miller) and drummer Aynsley Dunbar (ex-Zappa) to form the band's instrumental core. Journey experienced only moderate success until they added singer Steve Perry for their fourth album, *Infinity* (p21, 1978). The album contained such radio staples as "Lights" (a good example of the band's power ballad style) and "Feelin' That Way" (an example of their harder-rocking approach). With Perry's soaring tenor voice and the group's heavy, guitar-driven sound, Journey's style in many ways drew on the legacy of progressive rock. As the decade closed, Journey's popularity grew, with *Departure* (p8, 1980) becoming the group's first Top 10 album and *Escape* hitting the top spot in 1981.

Emerging from Los Angeles and featuring the virtuosic guitar playing of Eddie Van Halen and the antics of singer David Lee Roth, the music of Van Halen provided a mainstream glimpse of the emerging California-based metal scene, which explored older forms of rock in extremely new ways. The band stormed the charts in the late 1970s with a style that blended hard-driving rock with blues-based vocals and futuristic guitar performance. Their album *Van Halen* (p19, 1978) contains a cover version of the Kinks' "You Really Got Me" (p36), and arguably their best-known track, "Runnin' with the Devil." Van Halen quickly became a radio favorite, and the albums *Van Halen II* (p6 uk23, 1979) and *Women and Children First* (p6 uk15, 1980) clearly established the band as one of the most promising new mainstream rock groups. In many ways, Van Halen's approach owes much to the earlier British blues rockers, especially Deep Purple, and we return to them in our discussion of heavy metal in Chapter 12.

Mick Jones (left) and Lou Gramm of Foreigner, in concert. Foreigner took guitar and vocal influences from rhythm and blues and combined them with a progressive rock keyboard style to create a winning combination for radio and record sales. Their hits "Feels Like the First Time" and "Cold as Ice" made Foreigner megastars in America.

Progressive Rock Revamped. For the most part, the progressive rock movement had expended its energies by mid-decade: King Crimson had broken up, Peter Gabriel had quit Genesis, and many of the other bands were winding down. Yes was the exception, as 1977's *Going for the One* went to number one on the U.S and UK charts (in the same year that punk began to make its mark in Britain). In many ways, it fell to two American bands to revamp the progressive rock style for late-1970s radio: Kansas and Styx. Kansas enjoyed only moderate success until its fourth album, *Leftoverture* (p5, 1977), which contained the hit "Carry On Wayward Son" (p11). Powered by the songwriting of guitarist/keyboardist Kerry Livgren and the singing of Steve Walsh, Kansas pruned away some of the extravagance associated with

Listening Guide

Foreigner, "Feels Like the First Time" Atlantic 3394

Words and music by Mick Jones, produced by John Sinclair and Gary Lyons. Reached #4 on the *Billboard* "Hot 100" chart in the United States in mid-1977. Contained on the album *Foreigner*, which reached #4 on the *Billboard* "Top LPs & Tape" chart.

FORM: Modified compound AABA, with A sections based on contrasting verse-chorus form. The second A section includes a bridge, based on the chorus, inserted between the verse and the chorus. The last A section is abbreviated, using only the chorus section.

TIME SIGNATURE: 4/4, with bridge 1 in 2/2.

INSTRUMENTATION: Electric guitars, bass, drums, synthesizer, organ, lead and backup vocals.

	0:00–0:27	**Introduction,** 12 mm.	Begins with distorted guitar, then stop-time bass and drums enter, with sparkling progressive rock synthesizer above. Full band and drumbeat enter at m. 9.
A	0:27–1:02	**Verse 1**, 16 mm.	Vocals enter, as music builds from quiet to loud, first adding distorted guitars, and then backup vocals, as chords get higher and higher. "I would climb . . ."
	1:02–1:21	**Chorus**, 8 mm.	Loud, with choral vocals, with sparkling synthesizer on top. "It feels like . . ."
A	1:21–1:56	**Verse 2**, 16 mm.	As before, but now with rhythmic guitar underneath during the quiet part, and backup vocals entering earlier. "I have waited . . ."
	1:56–2:38	**Bridge 1**, 18 mm.	Change of meter to 2/2, change of key to minor, with classical-music references in the synthesizer part and in the accompanying harmony. "It feels like . . ."
	2:38–2:56	**Chorus**, 8 mm.	As before, but now with improvised lead vocals playing off the choral-vocal statement of the melody. "It feels like . . ."
B	2:56–3:14	**Bridge 2**, 8 mm.	Virtuosic guitar solo, with stop in the bass and drums, and improvised vocal interjections. "Open up the door . . ."
A'	3:14–3:32	**Chorus**, 8 mm.	As in the second statement of the chorus. "It feels like . . ."
	3:32–3:49	**Chorus**, 8 mm.+	Repeat of chorus and then fade out.

progressive rock, getting their tracks down to the four-minute range encouraged by radio. The band's most successful album was *Point of Know Return* (p4, 1978), which contained the ballad "Dust in the Wind" (p6). Like Kansas, Chicago's Styx recast progressive rock grandeur in a more economical manner. Although Styx often sang about progressive topics, such as space, the future, and science fiction, and the group created lengthy tracks, their music was not nearly as complex as the progressive rock of Yes or Genesis. After scoring a hit with "Lady" (p6, 1975), it was not until their seventh album that they had significant commercial success. *The Grand Illusion* rose to number six on the U.S. charts in 1977, containing "Come Sail Away" (p8), a track that blends Wakemanesque keyboards with a simpler pop-rock approach. Styx continued to enjoy hit albums into the 1980s with *Cornerstone* (p2, 1979), *Paradise Theater* (p1 uk8, 1981), and *Kilroy Was Here* (p3, 1983).

Perhaps the most enduring of the progressive rock–influenced bands to emerge in the second half of the 1970s was the Canadian power trio Rush. The band first made its mark in 1976 with its fourth release, the concept album *2112*, and followed with a string of records that were increasingly more popular. In 1980, *Permanent Waves* hit the number-four spot in the United States (uk3) when most bands were turning away from ambitious concept albums. Because the band depended on Alex Lifeson's guitar playing rather than keyboards for its harmonic color, their sound avoided some of the classical pretension that generated so much criticism of the original progressive rock bands. Bassist Geddy Lee's high-pitched vocals were reminiscent of both Yes and Led Zeppelin. Neil Peart's virtuosic drumming and ambitiously poetic lyrics also made it clear that there was no return-to-simplicity to be found in Rush's music. The Canadian trio has remained commercially successful to the present day, with top-selling albums and sold-out tours, long after most other progressive bands had split.

North American acts were not the only ones reworking the progressive-rock style. Electric Light Orchestra (ELO) was originally formed out of the ashes of the British psychedelic band the Move. Soon it became the vehicle for the singing and songwriting of guitarist Jeff Lynne, whose stylistic indebtedness to *Sgt. Pepper*–era Beatles is unmistakable. ELO took the idea of the rock band with chamber strings accompaniment, developed by the Beatles on tracks such as "Strawberry Fields

Rush drummer Neal Peart, shown here surrounded by an arsenal of percussion instruments. Rush was one of the most enduring of the prog-influenced bands. They produced top-selling albums and performed to sell-out crowds in the late 1970s, continuing their popularity for decades.

Forever" and "I Am the Walrus," and made it their trademark. After moderate success in the UK during the first half of the decade, ELO broke through in the United States with their fifth album, the conceptually driven *Eldorado* (p16, 1975), which contained the hit "Can't Get It Out of My Head" (p9, 1975). The band followed with a series of hit singles, including "Evil Woman" (p10 uk10, 1976), "Telephone Line" (p7 uk8, 1977), and "Don't Bring Me Down" (p4 uk3, 1979).

The stylistically eclectic aspects of the late Beatles output and the later British progressive movement also inspired Queen. Featuring the singing of Freddie Mercury and the guitar of Brian May, the band scored its first success in the UK with *Queen II* (uk5, 1974). *Sheer Heart Attack* (p12 uk2, 1975) brought Queen to the attention of listeners in America, while *A Night at the Opera* (p4 uk1, 1976), featuring the extravagant "Bohemian Rhapsody" (p9 uk1), established the band as a cross between the glam aspects of David Bowie and the classical ambitions of progressive rockers. Queen continued their success into the late 1970s with *A Day at the Races* (p5 uk1, 1977) and *News of the World* (p4 uk3, 1977), the latter of which contained the anthemic one-two punch "We Will Rock You" and "We Are the Champions." More success followed in the early 1980s with the release of *The Game* (p1 uk1, 1980), which contained "Another One Bites the Dust" (p1 uk7). While many fans were convinced that he was gay, perhaps prompted by his use of flamboyant stage costumes, Mercury himself never fully disclosed his sexual orientation to the public. However, his death from AIDS in 1991 raised public awareness of a disease that had been devastating the gay community for several years. As a prominent rock star, Mercury's death also forced many rock fans to confront sexual stereotypes, opening the door for many gay musicians to feel comfortable revealing their sexual orientation to the public.

Freddie Mercury of Queen, live in concert. Queen combined the "glam" tendencies of David Bowie with the scope of classical-influenced prog rock, exemplified in the ambitious song "Bohemian Rhapsody." Mercury died in 1991, a day after announcing he had AIDS—solidifying his position as an icon in the gay community.

Singers, Songwriters, and Bands. By the mid-1970s, singer-songwriters were often fronting bands, keeping the intimate bond created by soul-searching lyrics but exploring harder rock styles in their music. In most cases, this meant that the bands themselves, though now more prominent, were still not the focus of the act. The dean of American singer-songwriters, Bob Dylan, returned to touring in support of the hit album *Planet Waves* (p1 uk7, 1974). After a successful tour with the Band in 1974, Dylan released the stripped-down *Blood on the Tracks* (p1 uk4, 1975), which has since become a critical favorite. The end of 1975 saw Dylan back on the road with a large group of musicians that he called the Rolling Thunder Revue, followed by several more critically acclaimed albums, including *Desire* (p1 uk3, 1976) and *Street Legal* (p11 uk2, 1978). Famous for career shifts that confused and confounded his followers and critics, Dylan began espousing a relatively fundamentalist brand of Christianity in the late 1970s with *Slow Train Coming* (p3 uk2, 1979) and *Saved* (p24 uk3, 1980).

Elton John was another singer-songwriter who increasingly explored a rock band backing in the late 1970s, continuing his string of hit albums and singles. A cover version of "Lucy in the Sky with Diamonds" (p1 uk10, 1974) and his own "Philadelphia Freedom" (p1 uk12, 1975) both reached the top of the charts, and his 1975 album *Captain Fantastic and the Brown Dirt Cowboy* (p1 uk2) was one of the top albums of the year. John's most popular song from the late 1970s was "Don't Go Breaking My Heart" (p1 uk1, 1976), a single recorded with singer Kiki Dee. As John explored rock and other popular forms less typical of singer-songwriters, Paul Simon's music in the late 1970s highlighted his interest in jazz, rhythm and blues, and gospel. His *Greatest Hits, etc.* (p18 uk6, 1977) blended a best-of package with new tracks, including "Slip Slidin' Away" (p5 uk36), in which jazz and gospel influences are pronounced. Simon then embarked on an album and movie, *One-Trick Pony*, bringing on a band of studio pros including bassist Tony Levin, guitarist Eric Gale, pianist Richard Tee, and drummer Steve Gadd. While the movie received mixed reviews, the accompanying album *One-Trick Pony* (p12 uk17, 1980) was the most musically complex of Simon's career. The album's single "Late in the Evening" (p6) is not representative of this complexity, but tracks like "Jonah" and "How the Heart Approaches What It Yearns" showcase Simon and his band at their most musically sophisticated.

Pianist, singer, and songwriter Billy Joel illustrates the merging of piano-based singer-songwriter music and rock by performing while standing on top of his piano. Joel produced a string of popular songs and albums from the mid-1970s through the 1990s that centers on his strong piano playing and easy-to-follow, catchy lyrics.

By mid-decade, other artists were building on the idea of the singer-songwriter fronting a band. Among these was Billy Joel, whose second album, *Piano Man* (p27, 1973), the title track of which went to number 25 on the pop chart, helped launch his career in early 1974. After several years of disappointing records, Joel released *The Stranger* (p2 uk25, 1977), which contained "Just the Way You Are" (p3 uk19), "Movin' Out" (p17), "Only the Good Die Young" (p24), and "She's Always a Woman" (p17). Joel continued this string of hit albums and singles into the 1980s. His *52nd Street* hit number one in 1978 (uk10), buoyed by the popularity of "My Life" (p3 uk12) and "Big Shot" (p14, 1979). Joel's music from this period incorporates his piano and vocals as the center of attention on both ballads and up-tempo rock songs backed by his band. With the arrival of new wave on the scene at the end of the decade, it was especially relevant when Joel released *Glass Houses* (p1 uk9, 1980), which engaged earlier rock and pop styles. A particularly strong connection with older music can be found in "It's Still Rock and Roll to Me" (p1 uk14), which discussed older forms and was musically modeled on late 1950s rock.

Jackson Browne was another singer-songwriter from the period whose music featured rock band accompaniment. Browne had been part of the early 1970s country-rock scene in Southern California, and in addition to cowriting the Eagles' "Take It Easy," he scored a hit single with "Doctor My Eyes" (p8) in 1972. Browne released his most memorable music during the late 1970s, with a series of albums and singles that included *The Pretender* (p5 uk26, 1976), *Runnin' on Empty* (p3 uk28, 1978), and *Hold Out* (p1, 1980). Similarly, Detroit-native Bob Seger fronted a hard-rocking group called the Silver Bullet Band, but still fell squarely in the singer-songwriter mold of the late part of the 1970s. After nearly a decade of moderate success, Seger broke into the rock mainstream in 1977 with the album

Night Moves (p8) and the singles "Night Moves" (p4) and "Mainstreet" (p24). For the remainder of the 1970s and well into the 1980s, Seger maintained a consistent style featuring folksy lyrics about everyday problems, distinctive gravelly vocals, and memorable rock hooks. A fixture of classic rock radio into the 1990s, later Seger "classics" included "Old Time Rock & Roll" (p28, 1979) and "Against the Wind" (p5, 1980).

Bruce Springsteen also emerged in the context of the late 1970s singer-songwriter movement. Backed by the E-Street Band, Springsteen established himself as an important new voice in rock music with his third album, *Born to Run* (p3 uk17, 1975). Much like the others discussed here, Springsteen wrote lyrics that were understood to be largely autobiographical and frequently confessional. He also embraced rock's past, and the single "Born to Run" (p23) seemed inspired equally by the narrative style of Bob Dylan, Phil Spector's Wall of Sound, and the energetic performance style of the Rolling Stones. Albums such as *Born to Run* and *Darkness on the Edge of Town* (p5 uk16, 1978) provided only a glimpse of Springsteen's future work (discussed in Chapter 11).

Form or Formula?

We have stressed how mainstream (or "corporate") rock developed out of the music of the first half of the 1970s. In some cases, late-1970s mainstream rock streamlined musical elements, combining them to create new forms of stylistic synthesis. One way to examine how bands of the late 1970s recast music from earlier in the decade is through formal design. For example, the lengthiest tracks by earlier artists often employed multiple sections, organized so that at least a part of the music from early in a track would return later in the tune. In Chapter 8, we looked at Led Zeppelin's "Whole Lotta Love" and Yes's "Roundabout," noting that both employed a compound AABA formal scheme, with verses, choruses, or bridges used within the A sections. In this chapter, there are also several instances of AABA form that exhibit how groups in the last half of the decade compressed large-scale formal designs commonly associated with adventurous progressive music into the length of a radio-friendly single. Boston's "More Than a Feeling" squeezes a level of organizational complexity comparable to "Roundabout" into a track about half as long. The Boston track uses a compound AABA design, with a verse-chorus pair making up each A section and an instrumental guitar solo (actually two guitars playing in harmony) as the B section. Note that each verse and chorus varies in length, with no two being exactly the same. This creates a more complicated arrangement than simply repeating the material. Foreigner's "Feels Like the First Time" offers another interesting twist on the compound AABA design. It begins as if the A sections will consist of verse-chorus pairs like those found in the Boston track. However, in the second A section a bridge is inserted between verse two and the chorus. In a more conventional formal design, this bridge would occur after the second iteration of the chorus. "Feels Like the First Time" incorporates a second bridge in this spot, however, featuring a guitar solo. The final A section contains only a chorus, with no return to the verse, and the entire track clocks in at under four minutes—perfect for radio.

Instrumentation is another parameter that we may use to observe the ways rock from the late 1970s incorporates aspects of earlier rock. While both songs feature the distorted guitar sounds that are a central feature in blues-based rock (both American and British), there are a few progressive rock touches as well. With Foreigner, these are found mostly in the use of the high synthesizer arpeggios in the introduction and choruses, as well as in the synthesizer melody in the first chorus. In the Boston example, the harmony guitar parts throughout (and especially in the bridge) are carefully coordinated—"composed" in the classical sense—showing a concern for matching them with the parts being played by the other instruments. Both Boston and Foreigner condense qualities of earlier rock, blending them together and fitting them into shorter tracks. This can be seen as a culmination of earlier musical practices. However, it could also be seen as applying a kind of formula. The first interpretation suggests that late 1970s mainstream rock is a synthesis of earlier music, refining and recombining musical elements. The second interpretation suggests that the music was homogenized and simplified in order to reach the broadest possible audience.

THE ROOTS OF PUNK IN THE UNITED STATES, 1967–1975

Safety Pins and Leather. To an FM-rock radio listener in the 1970s, music did not change very drastically during the course of the decade. Many of the same bands remained popular, and most of the newer groups that emerged did not depart too radically from established acts. Listeners might have noticed that the playlists were becoming slightly more restricted, and certain albums were in heavy rotation, but there was not much else that signaled the big changes on the horizon for rock music. By the fall of 1977, however, American rock fans began to hear about a movement in the UK called "punk," spearheaded in large part by the Sex Pistols, whose outrageous antics were often the focus of news reports. Punk first rose to mainstream attention in the UK, where groups like the Sex Pistols, the Buzzcocks, and the Clash became popular in the later 1970s, placing singles and albums high on the British charts. However, because of the sometimes aggressive and dangerous images associated with punk, American record labels were quick to tone down the style, endorsing more fully a style they dubbed "new wave." Until the early 1980s, the mainstream American market barely registered the punk movement. Yet, punk actually had its most important roots in an American underground scene that goes back to the mid-1960s and was centered mostly in New York. Like American rhythm and blues in the early 1960s, punk was exported from the United States to the UK, only to return and be reintroduced as new wave.

Punk Roots: The Velvet Underground, the Stooges, and the MC5. Between 1967 and 1975, when most of the rock world was focused on psychedelia and mainstream rock, punk was brewing underground. Among the most important early influences on this music was the Velvet Underground. The group emerged when Lou Reed, who had studied creative writing in college and then worked as a professional songwriter, and John Cale, who had studied avant-garde composition and was playing with a performance ensemble led by avant-garde composer LaMonte Young, came together in the mid-1960s. The Velvet Underground were closely associated with pop artist Andy Warhol, who had included the group in some of his pop-art happenings, including his *Exploding Plastic Inevitable* multimedia show that ran in various cities during 1966 and 1967. Warhol was among New York's leading young artists at the time, championing a style that adapted elements from everyday American culture, refocusing them in an artistic context. (You may be familiar with Warhol's multicolor prints of Campbell's Soup cans, Elvis, and Marilyn Monroe.) It is easy to see how pop music would fit into Warhol's project, and considering the experimental aspirations of Reed and Cale, Warhol was a valuable ally. Reed's lyrics focused on the darker side of urban life, while Cale was eager to employ avant-garde ideas in a pop context. With Reed on guitar and vocals, Cale on bass and viola, Sterling Morrison on guitar, and Maureen Tucker on drums, the band recorded *The Velvet Underground and Nico* in late 1966. The singer Nico was added at Warhol's insistence, and Warhol produced the album. In the summer of 1967, when much of rock culture was focused on the fantastic images of *Sgt. Pepper*, the Velvets' first album, containing tracks such as "Heroin" and "Venus in Furs," went largely unnoticed. The group split from Warhol soon thereafter and continued performing and recording until membership changes effectively ended their tenure. The band performed its last shows under the leadership of Reed at the Warhol hangout Max's Kansas City during the summer of 1970.

While the Velvets were experimenters obsessed with dark downtown reality, Detroit-based Iggy Pop made his mark in the late 1960s underground as an outrageous performer. Pop seemed to challenge the audience at every show, sometimes walking on the audience's hands and smearing peanut butter all over his body. The band's raw sound, characterized by loud guitars, heavy drumming, and Pop's screaming vocals, is best captured on its second release, *Fun House* (1970). Another Detroit band, the MC5, were also important to the later punk scene. The band's *Kick Out the Jams* (p30, 1969) is representative of the aggressive sound of the band, especially the title track, which contained profanities (anticipating the vulgarity of later punk). All three bands have an aspect of confrontation: with the Velvets it's an aesthetic confrontation, with the Stooges it's a performance confrontation, and with the MC5 it's a confrontation with the sheer aggressiveness of the music. All this would prove influential for the New York punk rockers who would soon follow.

From left, Lou Reed, John Cale, and Nico of the Velvet Underground in concert. While hippies and "flower power" were dominating rock in the late 1960s, the Velvet Underground often looked at the darker side of life. Many of the creative artists of the punk and glam scenes—Patti Smith and David Bowie, among others—often cite the Velvet Underground as a major influence.

The Beginnings of the New York Scene. The Velvet Underground had performed frequently in New York, but in the early 1970s the most important band to connect the late '60s with the mid-1970s was the New York Dolls. Fronted by the flamboyant David Johansen, the band incorporated elements of British glam into their performances of gritty, hard-driving rock music. The Dolls used makeup and costumes, although they nevertheless projected an image of toughness, danger, and reckless disdain for convention that would become central to punk music. Their two albums, *The New York Dolls* (1973) and *Too Much Too Soon* (1974), sold poorly and the group never gained national popularity. Nevertheless, the band was an important step between the art-based experimental music of the Velvet Underground and the New York punk scene to follow. Alongside the New York Dolls, many others in New York began to develop an approach that drew on the underground music of the late 1960s.

In November 1973, poet Patti Smith teamed up with guitarist and rock critic Lenny Kaye. The two had performed together years before, with Smith usually reciting poetry while Kaye accompanied on guitar. Smith had already begun to develop a reputation as a poet, so initially these performances were less musical events than literary ones. But soon the duo added pianist Richard Sohl and by August 1974 had released "Hey Joe," a cover version of the song made famous by Jimi Hendrix. The Patti Smith Group, which eventually included Ivan Krahl on bass and Jay Dee Daugherty on drums, became the first band from the developing New York punk scene to sign a major-label record deal. Late in 1975, the band released *Horses*, which rose to number forty-seven on the American charts. The band's version of "Gloria" provides an example of how their numbers would often unfold: Smith begins with a recitation that seems unrelated to the tune itself but eventually builds in intensity and winds its way to an energetic rendering of the chorus.

At about the same time Smith and Kaye were beginning to work together, school friends Richard Hell and Tom Verlaine formed Television. The two were interested in literature and had even published a collection of poetry under an assumed name. In early 1974, Hell and Verlaine began searching around New York for someplace their new band could perform. In March 1974, they landed a regular Sunday evening spot at a deserted bar in lower Manhattan called CBGB (the name is an acronym for Country, Bluegrass, and Blues). Shortly thereafter, Television and the Patti Smith Group were sharing the bill and attracting attention. CBGB became the home of the New York punk scene, joining a relocated Max's Kansas City as the most prominent clubs of the New York underground.

Singer Iggy Pop is shown here in performance. Pop's outrageous onstage antics at shows were notorious and earned him a reputation as a dangerous and somewhat eccentric rebel. He was the perfect model for the punk musicians who would follow him.

The Ramones and Blondie. Among the other bands to play CBGB in its earliest days as punk headquarters were the Ramones. Playing under the stage names of Joey (vocals), Johnny (guitar), Dee Dee (bass), and Tommy (drums) Ramone, the Ramones produced a stripped-down, high-energy style of rock that focused on short, simple songs played very fast. The band signed with Sire Records—an important New York

Patti Smith in concert at CBGB in New York. Though Smith started her career as a poet, she formed a band, calling it the Patti Smith Group. Smith's group and Television (another punk band) began performing at CBGB in 1974, and the club quickly became the center of the U.S. punk rock scene. Smith's vocal style continued to be strongly influenced by poetic recitation.

label—and released *Ramones* (1976), which contained "Blitzkrieg Bop." Because of the resurgence of interest in the Ramones' music years later, many are surprised to learn that the band never had any significant success in the United States. Despite the group's importance in the history of punk, no Ramones album ever reached the Top 40 of the *Billboard* album charts, even during the late 1970s when many of their CBGB colleagues were topping the charts. Perhaps owing to the Ramones musical style, the band's music was consistently received more warmly in the UK.

In May 1974, the Stillettos—a band influenced by the early '60s girl groups—played CBGB. At that time, the band included singer Debbie Harry and guitarist Chris Stein. Soon, however, the band reconfigured itself and became Blondie. By 1976, the group featured Harry, Stein, keyboardist Jimmy Destri, guitarist Frank Infante, drummer Clem Burke, and bassist Nigel Harrison, and this line-up released *Blondie* on the small Private Stock label. The track "X Offender" provides an aural glimpse of the early girl-group influences, with the spoken introduction, happy driving beat, back-up vocals, '60s combo organ sounds, and Ventures-like guitar solo. The first Blondie album did not do well, however, at that point there was not much indication that the band would eventually become one of the most commercially successful of the CBGB bands. The band's rise would occur only after the Sex Pistols brought punk to the attention of the mainstream rock audience in the United States; for now, punk was an underground scene in the United States.

New York was by no means the only city in the United States to maintain a growing punk music scene, especially after the emergence of the Sex Pistols. Cleveland, Detroit, Los Angeles, Boston, and many other towns saw a rise of this style and related fashion and art subcultures. Still, as home to bands such as the Dictators, Richard Hell and the Voidoids, the Dead Boys, the Cramps, and the Misfits, New York was the national center of the scene, even as other New York punk groups like Blondie, Talking Heads, and Patti Smith enjoyed commercial success as new wave acts (discussed later in this chapter). During the late 1970s, the punk subculture became a national movement. Punks often dressed in radical clothing, including intentionally ripped jeans, leather jackets, and safety pins. Another important aspect of punk fashion was hairstyle, as punks experimented with outlandish hair color and often adopted the Mohawk. The overriding aesthetic of punk was strongly connected to the mantra "do it yourself" (or DIY). Punks often took on all aspects of musical production, including recording, distribution, album art, and concert promotion. Hence a desire for professionalism was often avoided in favor of a product (album notes, concert flyers, sound recordings, etc.) that showed some evidence of being homemade. While this approach had obvious drawbacks in regard to maintaining quality, the punk aesthetic—much like the garage band movement of the 1960s—led many amateur musicians to experiment with rock music. In turn, many of these untrained musicians made an important impact in an area of rock that had

WHAT'S THAT SOURCE?

Record Charts, Hardcore Style.

Touch and Go was a Michigan-based hardcore zine published between 1979 and 1983. In a play on the teen-oriented Top 40, these charts clearly reflect the attitudes of punk musicians and listeners toward elements of the mainstream during this time. The cut-and-paste do-it-yourself production quality was common in many punk-oriented publications, and became a hallmark of countercultural approaches to music in the early 1980s. The content of these charts, which include bands and many other elements, humorously situates this Midwestern hardcore scene against the backdrop of corporate rock, new wave, and the continuing legacy of the hippie aesthetic.

Source: Tesco Vee and Dave Stinson, *Touch and Go: The Complete Hardcore Punk Zine '79–'83*, edited by Steve Miller (Brooklyn, NY: Bazillion Points, 2010); Issue 1 (November 1979): 17.

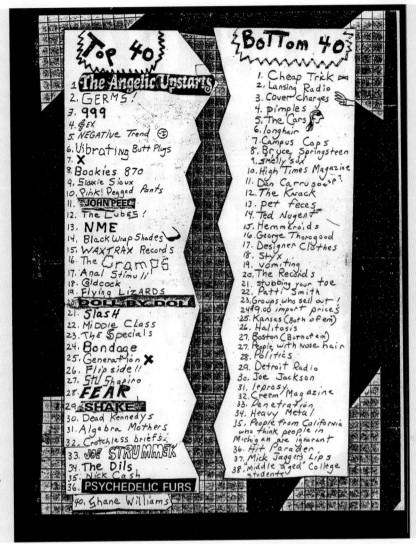

expanded to an international audience. Although punk music was largely united by the DIY aesthetic, it was hardly a monolithic musical style. With artists ranging from the loud and fast Ramones to the extended instrumental jams of Television and the angular vocals of the Voidoids, American punk music was only united by what it *wasn't*, which was corporate rock.

THE RISE OF PUNK IN THE UK, 1974–1977

No Hope: Malcolm McLaren, British Punk, and the Sex Pistols. Unlike the situation in the United States, the rise of punk in the UK can be linked to specific socioeconomic circumstances. Britain in the mid-1970s was suffering a crushing economic recession. For Britain's youth, this meant jobs were hard to find, and those that were available offered no significant opportunity for advancement. Whether or not their feelings were justified by the country's economic troubles, many British teens were prone to despair. That despair soon turned into anger, and punk became the music that best represented this angry spirit. British manager and shop owner Malcolm McLaren became a central character in helping this socioeconomic frustration find its voice in punk music and culture in the UK. In the early 1970s, McLaren ran a clothing store in London called Let It Rock. He was interested in early rock and roll, and his shop specialized in biker jackets and other 1950s clothes. By 1973, McLaren relaunched his shop as Too Fast to Live, Too Young to Die and befriended members of the New York Dolls, who had wandered into the shop while in London to perform. McLaren provided matching red leather suits for the band, which they sported during performances in New York in early 1975. He was impressed by the underground punk scene in New York, and especially with Richard Hell's manic performing style and sense of punk fashion. McLaren helped manage the Dolls during the first months of 1975, but returned to London after the group dissolved amid bitter disputes among band members. McLaren then renamed his clothing shop Sex, specializing in leather clothing and fetish wear.

In the meantime, guitarist Steve Jones and drummer Paul Cook started a band, playing mostly on equipment that Jones had stolen from other London-based groups. Soon Glen Matlock, who worked at Sex part-time, joined on bass, followed by John Lydon. The band pressured McLaren to manage them, and his first move was to change Lydon's name to Johnny Rotten. With McLaren now calling the shots, the Sex Pistols began playing gigs in late 1975, and by November 1976 they had signed with EMI, releasing their first single, "Anarchy in the UK" (uk34). In early December, the band filled in at the last minute for Queen on a British television show. Provoked by the host, they uttered a few forbidden words, causing a scandal

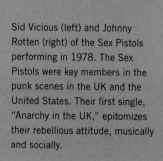

Sid Vicious (left) and Johnny Rotten (right) of the Sex Pistols performing in 1978. The Sex Pistols were key members in the punk scenes in the UK and the United States. Their first single, "Anarchy in the UK," epitomizes their rebellious attitude, musically and socially.

and becoming notorious overnight. Embarrassed by their punk behavior, EMI dropped the band but paid their promised advance money, and McLaren quickly helped them sign to A&M. A&M then got cold feet and released the band as well, also paying off a healthy advance. The band then signed to Virgin Records. In other words, before their first album was released in late 1977, the Sex Pistols had already collected advances from three record companies, a fleecing of the music-business establishment that only enhanced their reputation as troublemakers. When *Never Mind the Bollocks, Here's the Sex Pistols* was released, it went straight to the number-one slot in the UK. The band eventually placed seven singles in the UK Top 10 during the late 1970s, including the highly controversial "God Save the Queen," the cover of which featured a picture of the queen with a safety pin through her face. The scandals surrounding the Sex Pistols lasted just over a year, and by early 1978 the band had broken up (with Sid Vicious replacing Matlock on bass during the final months). Although there was a related punk scene forming in the United States, the Sex Pistols were the catalyst for punk in the UK. In every spot the band played, it seemed, new punk bands would start up, inspired by the experience. McLaren, Rotten, and company made punk a dirty word—in the American music industry at least—and no label wanted to sign a new punk band if this meant they would go through what EMI and A&M had experienced with the Sex Pistols.

A Performance That Launched a Career.

By the summer of 1975, Malcolm McLaren had assembled Jones, Cook, and Matlock, but lacked a singer to round out the Sex Pistols. John Lydon had frequented McLaren's shop and Malcolm noticed Lydon's shirt: it was a Pink Floyd T-shirt with "I hate" written above the band name. A conversation ensued, and it was suggested Lydon might be a possibility as the band's lead singer. According to Glen Matlock, everybody gathered in McLaren's shop and Steve Jones chose Alice Cooper's "I'm Eighteen" from a jukebox in the room for Lydon to sing along to. "He stood there, shouting along and flapping his arms round like an over-excited seagull. He looked *just* like he did when we played real gigs. He was John Rotten from that very first moment. . . . 'This guy is the one,' Malcolm said."

The Clash, the Buzzcocks, the Jam, and Siouxsie and the Banshees.

Based on the widespread popularity of the Sex Pistols, punk bands seemed to spring up all over England, giving British punk a greater stylistic range. Early in the history of British punk, for instance, a familiar relationship was forged between the Sex Pistols and the Clash. Managed by Bernard Rhodes, the Clash adapted a positioning strategy that had worked for the Rolling Stones: if the Sex Pistols were the nihilists of punk, the Clash would be its political protesters. Thus with Joe Strummer (vocals and guitar), Paul Simonen (bass), Mick Jones (guitar), and Tory Chimes (drums), the band released *The Clash* in April 1977 (uk12), which contained the single "White Riot" (uk38). After the demise of the Pistols and with Topper Headon on drums, the Clash did even better in late 1978 with *Give 'em Enough Rope* (uk2). In 1980, the band entered the American market with the release of *London Calling* (p27 uk9, 1980), which contained the radio favorite "Train in Vain (Stand by Me)" (p27). In addition to their political stance, it became evident by the turn of the 1980s that the Clash were interested in a wide range of musical styles. As the 1980 triple-album *Sandinista!* revealed, the group was comfortable incorporating American R&B,

Listening Guide

The Sex Pistols, "Anarchy in the UK" EMI 2566

Words and music by Paul Cook, Steve Johns, Glen Matlock, and Johnny Rotten, produced by Chris Thomas and Bill Price. Reached #38 in the UK in late 1976. Contained on the album *Never Mind the Bollocks, Here's the Sex Pistols*, which went to #1 in the UK in late 1977.

FORM: Modified simple verse, with instrumental bridges inserted. Each verse ends with an 8-bar refrain.

TIME SIGNATURE: 4/4.

INSTRUMENTATION: Electric guitars, bass, drums, lead and backup vocals.

0:00–0:14	**Introduction**, 8 mm.	Music derived from the refrain sets the stage for the entrance of the vocals.
0:14–0:43	**Verse 1 with refrain**, 16 mm.	Vocals enter, raw and urgent. "I am an antichrist . . ."
0:43–1:11	**Verse 2 with refrain**, 16 mm.	As before, with no significant changes. "Anarchy for the UK . . ."
1:11–1:31	**Bridge 1**, 11 mm.	Simple guitar solo over new musical material. Note occasional rude vocal sounds throughout.
1:31–1:59	**Verse 3 with refrain**, 16 mm.	As before, but now with repeated note on the guitar. "How many ways . . ."
1:59–2:14	**Bridge 2**, 8 mm.	New musical material, melodic but driving, as repeated note in guitar becomes sustained note, with feedback throughout the first half of the following verse.
2:14–2:42	**Verse 4 with refrain**, 16 mm.	As before. "Is this the M.P.L.A. . . ."
2:42–2:57	**Refrain**, 8 mm.	Repeat of refrain to create ending. "I want to be . . ."
2:57–3:11	**Refrain**, 8 mm.	Repeat; note guitar licks in the background throughout the ending.
3:11–3:29	**Refrain**, 8 mm.	Repeat; ends with menacing vocal on the word "destroy" and guitar feedback.

reggae and ska, and a varied assortment of other musical influences into their brand of UK punk.

Among the groups to emerge in the excitement caused by the success of the Sex Pistols and the Clash, the Buzzcocks adopted a pop-influenced approach to punk. Led by Pete Shelley, the group released a series of successful albums, including *Another Music in a Different Kitchen* (uk15, 1978) and *Love Bites* (uk13, 1978). Similarly, the Jam drew their distinctive look from mods and their musical influences from the mid-1960s Kinks and Who, even though these two groups had since embraced ambitious 1970s styles. Comprised of Paul Weller (guitar and vocals), Bruce Foxton (bass), and Rick Buckler (drums), the Jam signed with Polydor and released *In the City* (uk20) in May 1977. The band followed up later that year with *This Is the Modern World* (uk22), the title track of which demonstrates the band's blend of hard-driving rhythm with catchy pop hooks. The group's success built through the end of the decade and into the 1980s with the albums *All Mod Cons* (uk6, 1978), *Setting Sons* (uk4, 1979), and *Sound Affects* (uk2, 1980). The Jam grew to extreme popularity in the UK during the early 1980s, releasing four number-one singles before disbanding in 1982.

Before joining the Sex Pistols, Sid Vicious had played drums for the debut concert of a band fronted by Siouxsie Sioux, who had created with bassist Steven Severin a group called Siouxsie and the Banshees. The band signed with Polydor and released "Hong Kong Garden" (uk7) in the fall of 1978, followed by *The Scream* (uk12, 1978), a dark, brooding album that contained a gothic cover of the Beatles' "Helter Skelter." The band enjoyed continued success into the 1980s with several albums and singles, the most popular of which was a cover version of "Dear Prudence" (uk3, 1983). Siouxsie was by no means the only woman in British punk in the late 1970s. X-Ray Spex, fronted by Poly Styrene, enjoyed brief success with *Germ Free Adolescents* (uk30, 1978) and the Slits, an all-female punk trio that opened for the Clash on their spring 1977 tour and released *Cut* (uk30) in September 1979.

The groups discussed here were quite successful in the British market during the late 1970s, but none enjoyed American success except the Clash, who broke into the American market in 1980. In general, British punk music did not make the Atlantic crossing until much later, when record aficionados became interested in the style. At the time, however, other British acts did become popular in America. Rather than "punk," these groups were categorized under a new label: "new wave."

Punk Poetics—Organization or Anarchy? Punk fashion attacked the status quo and punk lyrics often advocated social or political change. Moreover, the sound of punk—which often featured difficult-to-discern vocals, sloppy distorted guitars, and loud drums—broadcast the movement's antagonistic stance toward authority. In spite of these seemingly out-of-control features, punk music is often fairly conventional in its structure. This is partly because of punk rock's "return-to-simplicity" aesthetic—the idea of eliminating the complexity and expansiveness that hippie rock had developed. For example, the Sex Pistols' first single, "Anarchy in the UK," provides an interesting example in terms of musical structure. Overall, the song employs a simple verse structure. Each verse is sixteen measures in length, with the last eight measures in each verse carrying the same lyrical refrain. This eight-bar refrain is repeated three times at the end of the track, creating a coda that drives home the song's catchiest line (its "hook"). The exceptions

The influence of the Sex Pistols was not restricted to male musicians. Fronted by Siouxsie Sioux (Susan Dallion), Siouxsie and the Banshees enjoyed success on the UK punk scene. The connections between the two bands were further reinforced when Sid Vicious left the Banshees and replaced original bassist Glen Matlock in the Sex Pistols.

are the two bridges inserted along the way, the first between verses two and three, and the second between verses three and four. Ironically, the insertion of bridge sections into a typical formal design is similar to the Foreigner example explored earlier in this chapter. Unlike the bridge sections found in the Foreigner and Boston examples, however, this track features no elaborate guitar solos or synthesizer riffs. In fact, the return-to-simplicity approach is perhaps most obvious in the driving guitar, bass, and drums accompaniment and the self-consciously untrained and amateurish character of Johnny Rotten's singing. The fast tempo and driving, steady eighth notes in the guitar, bass, and drums are also clear features of early punk. The use of simple verse form—inserted bridges notwithstanding—links this music with early rock and rhythm and blues, as well as with much traditional folk music, and contrasts strongly with the examples from Yes, Boston, and Foreigner discussed earlier. While punk disrupted the rock status quo, the music itself had strong connections with earlier rock traditions and practices.

THE RISE OF NEW WAVE, 1977–1980

The Next Big Thing. As late as the fall of 1977, most mainstream rock fans in America were largely unaware of either British or American punk. CBGB was popular among some people in New York, but punk had virtually no presence on the increasingly restricted playlists of FM rock radio. In late 1977 and early 1978, the Sex Pistols toured the United States, but instead of playing rock clubs in the northeast and on the West Coast, the band toured the South—a move designed, it seemed, to invite trouble and provoke yet more headlines (which it did). In December 1977, Elvis Costello appeared on *Saturday Night Live* (filling in for the Sex Pistols, who had trouble getting into the country), marking a significant breakthrough for punk into the American mainstream. During the mid-1970s, rock magazines like *Rolling Stone, Crawdaddy,* and *Creem* were giving significant coverage to punk rock. Punk, however, had built a reputation for being dangerous and potentially embarrassing within the music business. For much of the commercial music business, relabeling punk as "new wave" was a solution to this problem. This new term tamed the more aggressive elements of punk, making it more of an artsy aesthetic statement than a statement of nihilism or protest. If punks were angry, new wavers were ironic. Punk's answer to frustration was to lash out, perhaps break a window and form a band. New wave's was to reflect on urban alienation, have a cup of coffee, and write a clever lyric. Since many of the CBGB bands had backgrounds in the arts, industry interest in new wave worked to their advantage. Blondie and Talking Heads, both regulars at CBGB, became stars under this banner, leaving the Ramones and the punks behind. Strangely enough, Television seemed as poised as any of the other CBGB bands to achieve broad commercial success, but Hell left the group in 1975 and Verlaine took over the band. Having signed with Elektra, the band's debut album, *Marquee Moon* (uk28), flopped in the United States in the first half of 1977. The next album, *Adventure* (uk7), was released in April 1978 and did no better in the States. It was a different story for the Patti Smith Group, who scored on both sides of the Atlantic with *Easter* (p20 uk16, 1978), which contained the hit single "Because the Night" (p13 uk5) (co-written with Bruce Springsteen), and followed with *Wave* (p18 uk41, 1979).

CBGB Goes New Wave. In early 1978, Blondie had signed with Chrysalis, but it still seemed as if the band might be in for the same fate as Television—successful in England and unknown at home. Released in February 1978, Blondie's *Plastic Letters* (uk10) did well in the UK, in part on the strength of the hit singles "Denis" (uk2) and "(I'm Always Touched by Your) Presence, Dear" (uk10). But in the fall of that year, the band released *Parallel Lines* (p6 uk1, 1978), which contained a single that hit number one on both sides of the Atlantic, "Heart of Glass." Blondie followed with several smash hit singles in America, including "Call Me" (p1 uk1, 1980), "The Tide Is High" (p1 uk1, 1980), and "Rapture" (p5 uk1, 1981). In a few short years, Blondie had gone from a band many at CBGB thought was the least likely to make any headway in the business to the most successful of the lot. Moreover, modeling the industry change from punk to new wave, the musical style of each of Blondie's singles had little resemblance to American stereotypes of punk. This is especially evident in "Rapture," which is dance-oriented and even contains a rapped section that reveals a connection to the rising hip-hop movement in New York.

Made up of students from the Rhode Island School of Design, Talking Heads was led by songwriter David Byrne, and featured Jerry Harrison (guitar), Chris Frantz (drums), and Tina Weymouth (bass and vocals). Talking Heads debuted at CBGB in May 1975, gaining recognition in New York almost immediately. Eventually the band signed with Sire and released *Talking Heads: 77* in September 1977. The track "Psycho Killer" provides an example of the early Talking Heads approach, with spare instrumental accompaniment and Byrne's spastic vocal delivery. The next album, *More Songs about Buildings and Food* (p29 uk21), was released in the summer of 1978 and enjoyed moderate success, although interest began to heat up considerably when "Take Me to the River," written by R&B singer Al Green and guitarist Teenie Hodges, was released as a single in October (p26). The next two releases, *Fear of Music* (p21, 1979) and *Remain in Light* (p19 uk21, 1980), established the band as one of new wave's leading groups, especially since they were well liked by many music critics, who praised the intellectual and artsy character of Byrne's songs. Another important aspect of the recordings of Talking Heads was the production of Brian

Talking Heads at CBGB as a foursome (left to right: Jerry Harrison, David Byrne, Chris Frantz, and Tina Weymouth) in 1977. Like many so-called new wave groups that would follow, Talking Heads took punk's rebellion in a new, "artsy" direction. If punk turned passion into violence, new wave turned it into introspective vocals and more complex music.

Eno, who had performed with Roxy Music during the early 1970s but had become an important voice in experimental approaches to recording rock music.

New Wave in the American Mainstream. While New York was central to the development of American punk and new wave, many of the most successful of the new wave bands in the late 1970s did not arise out of CBGB or Max's Kansas City. The Boston-based Cars, led by guitarist and vocalist Ric Ocasek and drummer David Robinson, were among the first new wave bands to break onto the FM rock radio playlists. Signed to Elektra, the band's debut release, *The Cars* (p18, 1978), contained two tracks that got significant airplay on mainstream rock radio stations beginning in late 1978: "My Best Friend's Girl" (p35 uk3, 1978) and "Just What I Needed" (p27, 1978; uk17, 1979). The band followed with *Candy-O* (p3, 1979), which contained "Let's Go" (p14), and continued to top the charts well into the 1980s with perennial radio favorites such as "Shake it Up" (4p, 1981). The Cars were well versed in early rock styles, and these references pervaded their music, reinforcing cover art images redolent of the 1950s used on their albums.

Florida's Tom Petty and the Heartbreakers adapted the 1960s folk-rock style of Dylan and the Byrds, so much so that the Byrds' Roger McGuinn joked that the first time he heard "American Girl" from *Tom Petty and the Heartbreakers* (uk24, 1977), he thought it was one of his own songs. As new wave was gaining in popularity in the second half of 1978, Petty and company released *You're Gonna Get It* (p23), which contained "I Need to Know." When the band's label, Shelter, was sold, they ended up recording for MCA, releasing *Damn the Torpedoes* (p2, 1979), which rose to number two in the United States on the strength of several tracks, including "Don't Do Me Like That" (p10) and "Refugee" (p15, 1980), which became staples of FM rock radio. From a contemporary perspective, the Heartbreakers hardly seem like a new wave act. Yet during the late 1970s, the group was certainly marketed among the new wavers. Part of this connection was visual, as the group often donned the colorful suits and thin ties associated with new wave. But there was also a sonic connection in the group's return to the 1950s roots of rock, which was at the heart of both punk and new wave.

Led by the songwriting of guitarist and vocalist Ric Ocasek (second from right), the Cars were likely the first new wave band that many '70s hippie rockers could identify with. Bassist Benjamin Orr (second from left) also sang some of the band's most memorable songs.

Listening Guide

The Cars, "My Best Friend's Girl" Elektra 45537

Words and music by Ric Ocasek, produced by Roy Thomas Baker. Reached #35 on the *Billboard* "Hot 100" chart and #3 in the UK in mid-1978.

FORM: Compound AABA, with A sections based on contrasting verse-chorus form. The B section is instrumental, featuring a guitar solo and based on the music from the chorus.

TIME SIGNATURE: 4/4.

INSTRUMENTATION: Electric guitars, bass, synthesizer, organ, drums, hand claps, lead and backup vocals.

	0:00–0:16	**Introduction,** 8 mm.	Clean guitar for 4 bars, and then handclaps enter at 0:09.
A	0:16–0:48	**Verse 1**, 16 mm.	Vocals enter, with full band joining in after 4 bars, along with backup vocals. "You're always dancin' . . ."
	0:48–1:08	**Chorus**, 10 mm.	Choral vocals, as organ enters. Ends with 4 mm. rockabilly guitar that leads to next verse. "She's my best friend's . . ."
A	1:08–1:40	**Verse 2**, 16 mm.	As before, but now with "96 Tears" organ and lightly arpeggiated guitar in first half and rockabilly pattern in second half. "You got your nuclear boots . . ."
	1:40–2:00	**Chorus**, 10 mm.	As before, 4 mm. link leads to instrumental chorus this time. "She's my best friend's . . ."
B	2:00–2:20	**Instrumental chorus**, 10 mm.	6-bar guitar melodic solo, then 4-bar link leads back to last verse.
A	2:20–2:51	**Verse 3**, 16 mm.	Repeat of verse 1 lyrics with verse 3 accompaniment.
	2:51–3:11	**Chorus**, 10 mm.	As before, 4 mm. link leads to coda.
	3:11–3:43	**Coda**, 10 mm.	New melody based on chorus with chords from verse. Synthesizer strings enter in the background at 3:19, and handclaps at 3:27, as fade-out begins, "My best friend's girlfriend."

Perhaps the most ironic of all new wave bands was Devo, led by brothers Bob and Mark Mothersbaugh. Using costumes, space-aged keyboard and guitar sounds, and alienated vocals, the band adopted the image of futuristic beings from 1950s science-fiction movies. The Ohio band's first album, *Q: Are We Not Men? A: We Are Devo!* (uk12, 1978), produced by Brian Eno, contained a mechanistic cover of

Devo took new wave to the peak of irony, often employing hightech sounds in their music and a 1950s space-movie look in their videos and live performances. Their robot-like version of the Rolling Stones' "(I Can't Get No) Satisfaction" and the pseudosexual "Whip It" epitomize the detached humor of the band's music and videos.

"(I Can't Get No) Satisfaction" and their theme song "Jocko Homo." In spite of poor sales in America, this album became popular in England when released in September 1978. The band did not enjoy commercial success in the United States until *Freedom of Choice* (p22, 1980), which contained the single "Whip It" (p14). Devo's northern take on new wave was echoed from a southern perspective by the Georgia group the B-52s. Led by singer Fred Schneider and featuring singers Kate Pierson and Cindy Wilson, the band made its first significant showing in the UK with *The B-52s* (uk22, 1979), which contained "Rock Lobster," a track that has since become closely associated with the new wave movement. Performing at Max's in New York in 1978 and on *Saturday Night Live* in 1980 brought the band a national following, which led to broader commercial success with the release of *Wild Planet* (p18, uk18) in 1980. Like the Cars, the music of the B-52s was full of references to prepsychedelic music, including frequent surf-style guitar riffs, a prominent electric organ sound popular in the mid-1960s, and vocals from Pierson and Wilson that played with girl-group stereotypes. The group even recorded a cover of Petula Clark's "Downtown." As new wave icons, the B-52s did not achieve their greatest success until the late 1980s, after nearly more than a decade of recording and touring.

During the late 1970s, the Knack was another popular new wave group that was calculating in the use of musical styles and images drawn from rock's history. Based in Los Angeles and led by guitarist Doug Feiger, the band signed with Capitol. The first album, *Get the Knack* (p1, 1979), was a smash hit and was supported by a hit single, "My Sharona" (p1 uk6). The front cover of the record featured the band in early 1960s Beatle-esque attire, and the back cover was meant to suggest the Beatles' appearance on the *Ed Sullivan Show*. The group wore these same outfits in promotional videos and television performances. The band even had Capitol revert to using the same logo on the record labels as it had back in the mid-1960s. All this worked only briefly, as their next album, *But the Little Girls Understand* (p15, 1980), was the last Knack album to climb the charts.

British New Wavers in America. Besides the Sex Pistols and the Clash, most of the British punk bands that dominated the charts in England never made an impact in the United States. Those acts that fit the American new wave profile, however, did enjoy success. First among these was Elvis Costello. Signed with Stiff in the UK but distributed by Columbia in the United States, Costello's releases were among the first British new wave records to make the U.S. Top 40 in the first half of 1978. While *My Aim Is True* (p32 uk14, 1977) contained the ballad "Alison," Costello became much better known for aggressive and clever attacks on the status quo. This was especially true after his performance on *Saturday Night Live* in late 1977. His second album, *This Year's Model* (p30 uk4, 1978)—recorded with a new backup band called the

Attractions—contained "Pump It Up" (uk24), which is a good example of Costello's more raucous side, as is the single "Radio, Radio" (uk29, 1978). Elvis Costello and the Attractions followed with *Armed Forces* (p10 uk2, 1979), completing a trio of albums that would establish Costello as one of rock's most heralded songwriters.

The Police also debuted in America in the context of new wave. Their first album *Outlandos d'Amour* (p23) from early 1979 contained both "Roxanne" (p32 uk12) and "Can't Stand Losing You" (p42 uk2). Initially blending a strong reggae influence into their style, the Police became well known for the complex drumming of Stewart Copeland, the literary lyrics of Sting, and the atmospheric guitar of Andy Summers. A series of successful albums followed, including *Regatta de Blanc* (p25 uk1, 1979) and *Zenyatta Mondatta* (p5 uk1, 1980). Although Police songs from this period, such as "So Lonely" (uk6) and "Message in a Bottle" (uk1), are known well in the United States, the group did not achieve much success in the singles market until late 1980. The Police became one of the most important bands of the early 1980s, and will be discussed further in Chapter 11.

Pangs of Rock History? One aspect of new wave sets it apart from the hippie rock that preceded it: new wave bands had a clear fascination with earlier musical styles and—perhaps more important—with the visual images associated with those styles. Thus it's *Elvis* Costello who wears horn-rimmed glasses like Buddy Holly, straight leg pants, and short hair in an era of bellbottoms and shoulder-length hair. Why this dimension of new wave was important to these musicians and their fans is discussed later, but for now we will focus on the music itself. Spotting the references to rock history in the visual aspect of new wave is easy, but how can we hear stylistic references to earlier rock *in the music itself*? The Cars' "My Best Friend's Girl" offers an example rich in new wave references to past styles. Notice first the handclaps that enter during the introduction, reminiscent of early 1960s girl-group recordings ("My Boyfriend's Back") or early Beatles tracks ("I Want to Hold Your Hand"). The rockabilly guitar lick that occurs in the passages linking the choruses to the verses seems inspired by Carl Perkins, Elvis Presley, or Gene Vincent records from the late 1950s. The repeated organ chords that enter with the second verse bring to mind the mid-1960s garage-band sound. Ocasek's vocal delivery is full of vocal hiccups that imitate those of Buddy Holly and the naive innocence of much teen music before the mid-1960s. These many references to pre-hippie rock are not particularly well reinforced by the form, which follows a compound AABA design not too different from Boston's "More Than a Feeling," employing verse-chorus pairs for A sections and a guitar solo for the bridge. Yet the Cars material here is far simpler in its harmonic content than the harmonies in the Boston track, and all the sections are repeated without much structural change. Like much new wave, this song is less an attempt to duplicate earlier rock styles than an eclectic view of earlier rock taken in through a late 1970s "lens."

New wave's relationship to past rock music styles is the key to understanding how it differentiated itself from mainstream rock. Rock music from psychedelia through late 1970s mainstream rock was founded on the hippie aesthetic: the idea that rock music should take the listener on a kind of trip and use all the possibilities of technology—in terms of both equipment and instrumental and compositional skill—to do so. Rock should deal with important issues, not teen love, and should reflect on man's place in the universe. New wave musicians moved away from these governing principles. They scaled back the musical complexities and shortened the tunes, returned to topics of teenage romance, and no longer paraded their musical prowess. Thus the music-stylistic and visual references in new wave were almost always to rock before *Sgt. Pepper*. The new wave haircuts, clothes, album art, music, and lyrics all seem to reject hippie culture and music. But in rejecting the hippie present, were new wavers advocating a return to rock's past? The answer is no; instead, new wave musicians were making ironic references to earlier music—they were not embracing past styles but rather using them to offer a critique of the present and a vision of the future.

Mainstream versus New Wave. One way to see the contrast between the mainstream rock and new wave approaches in the late 1970s is to compare bands and artists with obvious similarities but also with telling differences. American Gary Wright had been a member of Spooky Tooth (along with Mick Jones in his days before Foreigner), but set out on a solo career. He released *The Dream Weaver* (p7) in late 1975 and his music caught on in 1976 with two hit tracks, "Dream Weaver" (p2) and "Love Is Alive" (p2). Englishman Gary Numan was originally a member of Tubeway Army, whose second album *Replicas* was number one in the UK in the summer of 1979 with the help of the hit single, "Are We 'Friends' Electric?" (uk1). Numan went solo as well, releasing *The Pleasure Principle* (p16 uk1) in September 1979, which contained the hit "Cars" (p9 uk1). Comparing "Dream Weaver" with "Cars" reveals that both tracks rely almost exclusively on synthesized sounds. Wright's warm timbres, saturated with reverb and echo, are similar to the broad textures used by progressive-rock keyboardists such as Rick Wakeman and Keith Emerson, while Numan's sounds are much harsher, creating a drier, more focused sound. Wright's vocals show a blues influence and Numan's are clipped and almost mechanical. Both Wright and Numan employ futuristic images on their respective album sleeves. Yet Wright's future seems optimistic and utopian, while Numan's seems cold and mechanical, dominated by machines. Despite similarities to "Dream Weaver," Numan's "Cars" makes its mark by rejecting the hippie dreams of fantastic voyages into the bright technological future—Numan rejects the trip, or at least suggests a very different kind of trip.

Another comparison can be drawn between the music of Heart and Blondie. Led by sisters Anne and Nancy Wilson, Heart's debut album, *Dreamboat Annie* (p7, 1976), rose on the U.S. charts with the help of the tracks "Crazy on You" (p35) and "Magic Man" (9p). The group's music from the late 1970s has both a harder edge, in which Anne Wilson belts out her vocals with power and authority, and a softer, more acoustically oriented side, often showcasing Nancy's guitar. Anne Wilson adopted the stage persona of the tough, hard-driving woman. Her singing was often forceful and technically schooled, filled with bluesy melodic twists and turns. Debbie Harry (of Blondie), in contrast, had a vocal approach that was much more limited, far less free rhythmically, and devoid of any blues influence. This is immediately evident in comparing Heart's "Straight On" (15p, 1978) with Blondie's "Heart of Glass."

Though Elvis Costello is often thought of as an innovative but still relatively traditional pop songwriter and performer, his early image embraced punk anger and rebellion. At a time when rock performers were wearing flowing clothes and long hair, Costello's appearance here harkens back to the mid-1960s look of bands like the Rolling Stones and the Animals.

Listening Guide

Elvis Costello and the Attractions, "Pump It Up" Radar ADA 10

Music and lyrics by Elvis Costello, produced by Nick Lowe. Released as a single in 1978 in the UK and rose to #24. Also included on the album *This Year's Model*, which hit #4 in the UK and #30 on the *Billboard* "Top LPs & Tape" chart in 1978.

FORM: Contrasting verse-chorus. The chorus might alternatively be thought of as a refrain, creating an overarching verse structure consisting of verse, refrain, and organ hook (reinforced by the shading below) that is repeated four times with a tag at the end. Under this alternative analysis, the form is simple verse. Deciding between the two depends on how one hears the chorus/refrain: if it is heard as structurally independent of the verse, it is a chorus; if it is seen as structurally dependent on the verse, it is a refrain. Note the small but interesting changes that occur in the verses: the second one is shortened (with the following organ hook extended); the third verse returns to the structure of the first while the fourth introduces a variation in underlying harmony.

TIME SIGNATURE: 4/4, with strong groove in the bass and drums that drives the song throughout. Note how the opening bass line anchors the verse sections that follow but is transposed. Despite constant returns in the verse sections, that bass line never returns exactly as in the introduction.

INSTRUMENTATION: Lead vocal, backup vocals, electric guitar, bass, drums, organ, and percussion. The clearest mark of the new-wave style in this song is the use of a mid-1960s organ tone prominently throughout, especially in the organ hook.

0:00–0:20	**Introduction**, 12 mm.	8 bars anchored by drums and bass, leading to 4 bars of "organ hook."
0:21–0:34	**Verse**, 8 mm.	8 bars of verse, "I've been on tenterhooks . . ."
0:35–0:48	**Chorus**, 8 mm.	4 bars adding backup vocals followed by 4 bars of organ hook, "Pump it up . . ."
0:49–0:58	**Verse**, 6 mm.	Shortened to 6 bars, "Down in the pleasure center . . ."
0:59–1:19	**Chorus**, 8 mm.	As before but now with 8 bars of organ hook, "Pump it up . . ."
1:19–1:33	**Interlude**, 8 mm.	4 bar drum break, followed by 4 bars of organ hook.
1:34–1:47	**Verse**, 8 mm.	As in the first verse, "She's been a bad girl . . ."
1:47–2:00	**Chorus**, 8 mm.	As in first chorus, "Pump it up . . ."
2:01–2:14	**Verse**, 8 mm.	As in first verse, but with change in harmony during first 4 bars, "Out in the fashion show . . ."
2:15–2:28	**Chorus**, 8 mm.	As in first chorus, "Pump it up . . ."
2:29–2:42	**Chorus**, 8 mm	As in first chorus (could be heard as tag), "Pump It up . . ."
2:42–2:56	**Chorus**, 8 mm	As in first chorus, 4 bars of organ hook blend into the Coda, "Pump it up . . ."
2:57–3:15	**Coda**, 11 mm.	Based on organ hook, with fade-out at end.

Wilson belts out the vocals of "Straight On," performing forcefully, often on the verge of screaming, featuring a noticeable thick vibrato. Harry's style is motivated by a rejection of hippie technical virtuosity. It is based on an amateurish quality common among many new wave performances. Harry's singing in this regard is similar to that of David Byrne and Ric Ocasek, neither of whom would be considered "polished" vocalists in a traditional sense. That was part of new wave's return-to-simplicity charm, and central to its rejection of rock's hippie legacy.

In the second half of the 1970s, mainstream rock continued many of the stylistic practices of the first half of the decade. It made adjustments in response to the tremendous growth of the record and radio businesses, as big albums came to dominate the charts and radio preferred shorter, less expansive tracks. Fans of late 1970s rock argue that it was the culmination of hippie rock, while critics contend that it was cynically created to make as much money as possible for the corporations that came to dominate the music business during this time. Punk reacted against what it saw as an indulgent rock music industry, challenging its pomposity with a return to rock and roll basics. As powerful as the punk challenge was, however, it was commercially co-opted into a style called new wave. New wave kept much of punk's return-to-simplicity attitude and rejection of the hippie aesthetic (a rejection shared by disco). Yet, by the early 1980s, most new wave was incorporated within the mainstream rock playlists of FM radio, attesting to the influence of new wave, but also revealing underlying similarities between new wave and mainstream rock. When mainstream rock and new wave came together during the early 1980s, it seemed as if hippie rock had run its course and an era had ended. Although elements of the hippie aesthetic would reemerge innumerable times over the course of the 1980s and 1990s—especially in heavy metal and music videos—the era of ambitious rock devoted to the idea of music as a trip was over.

The music-stylistic contrast between Heart's Anne Wilson (left) and Blondie's Debbie Harry (right) is shown in these live images. Wilson belts a rock anthem, while Harry offers a simpler new wave sophistication.

Sound Check

Artist	Song	Sound
Peter Frampton	**Show Me the Way (Live) (1976)**	Form: contrasting verse-chorus Voice box changes the sound of the lead guitar part Extended guitar solo False ending helps to regain listener attention
Boston	**More Than a Feeling (1976)**	Form: compound AABA Each A section includes a verse and a chorus Vast dynamics, going from soft to loud Doubled guitar solo
Foreigner	**Feels Like the First Time (1977)**	Form: compound AABA (modified) Second A section modified by added bridge with references to classical music Second bridge features guitar solo Lyrics offer a thinly veiled commentary on "romance"
Sex Pistols	**Anarchy in the UK (1977)**	Form: simple verse (modified) Form modified by inserted bridge sections Refrain at the end of each verse Intentional guitar feedback throughout the first half of verse 4
The Cars	**My Best Friend's Girl (1978)**	Form: compound AABA A sections based on contrasting verse-chorus Different musical styles highlighted in guitar (rockabilly) Handclaps reminiscent of girl groups
Elvis Costello and the Attractions	**Pump It Up (1978)**	Form: contrasting verse-chorus Use of mid-1960s organ sound marks the song as new wave Form might be understood alternatively as simple verse Verses feature small but interesting changes in structure

For Additional Online Resources, visit:
digital.wwnorton.com/whatsthatsound5

FURTHER READING

Victor Bockris, *Transformer: The Lou Reed Story* (Simon & Schuster, 1994).

David Bowman, *This Must Be the Place: The Adventures of Talking Heads in the 20th Century* (HarperCollins, 2001).

Craig Bromberg, *The Wicked Ways of Malcolm McLaren* (Harper & Row, 1989).

Theo Cateforis, *Are We Not New Wave? Modern Pop at the Turn of the 1980s* (University of Michigan Press, 2011).

Elvis Costello, *Unfaithful Music and Disappearing Ink* (Blue Rider, 2015).

Jerome Davis, *Talking Heads* (Vintage, 1986).

Toby Goldstein, *Frozen Fire: The Story of the Cars* (Contemporary Books, 1985).

Debbie Harry, Chris Stein, and Victor Bockris, *Making Tracks: The Rise of Blondie* (Da Capo, 1998).

Will Hermes, *Love Goes to Buildings on Fire: Five Years in New York That Changed Music Forever* (Faber & Faber, 2011).

Clinton Heylin, *From the Velvets to the Voidoids: The Birth of American Punk Rock* (A Cappella, 2005).

Brian Hinton, *Let Them All Talk: The Music of Elvis Costello* (Sanctuary, 1999).

Glen Matlock with Pete Silverton, *I Was a Teenage Sex Pistol* (Omnibus, 1990).

Legs McNeil and Gillian McCain, *Please Kill Me: The Uncensored Oral History of Punk* (Penguin, 1996).

Thurston Moore and Byron Coley, *No Wave: Post Punk. Underground. New York. 1976–1980* (Abrams Image, 2008).

John Savage, *England's Dreaming: Anarchy, Sex Pistols, Punk Rock, and Beyond* (St. Martin's Griffin, 2002).

Patti Smith, *Just Kids* (Ecco, 2010).

The 1980s began with the defeat of incumbent president Jimmy Carter and the election of Ronald Reagan, a Hollywood actor turned politician. Reagan's presidency marked a new conservative attitude throughout much of the country and in popular culture. In his speeches and public remarks, Reagan evoked images of America's idyllic past, and his amiable, "grandfatherly" style helped many regain their confidence in government after Watergate and the Iran hostage crisis.

Reagan's economic policy was driven by "supply-side economics"—lower taxes on wealthy Americans that would, arguably, inspire everyone to work harder (because they'd be keeping more income). His foreign policy embraced building up American military forces and weapons systems. Reagan believed that an arms race would cripple the Soviet Union (which he referred to as the "evil empire"), whose economy could not afford to keep pace with American advances. However, in the midst of this Cold War buildup, Mikhail Gorbachev became leader of the Communist Party in 1985, advocating policies of glasnost (openness) and perestroika (restructuring of Soviet government along Western lines). Historians differ on who gets credit for it, but in November 1989 (almost a year after Reagan left office), the Berlin Wall—a symbol of the division between the Soviet Union and the Western powers—fell, signaling an end to a cold war that had lasted almost half a century. By 1991, the Soviet Union had broken apart and the United States emerged as the world's leading superpower.

The 1980s also marked the emergence and growth of the AIDS epidemic, with more than 150,000 cases diagnosed and more than 90,000 AIDS-related deaths reported in the United States from 1981 to 1989.* AIDS was made most publicly visible by movie star Rock Hudson, who died from the disease in 1985. Hudson had been a leading man in romantic comedies for years, and his homosexuality came as a surprise to many of his fans. Despite the sensationalism following the disclosure of Hudson's sexuality, many Americans learned about AIDS for the first time, leading to an increased awareness of the disease and its seriousness. In 1991, Queen frontman Freddie Mercury succumbed to the disease, further raising the music world's awareness of AIDS.

The American economy grew in many ways during the 1980s, but no sector advanced as impressively and publicly as high tech. The space program had provided many spin-off benefits and technologies, and the development of ever-smaller, more powerful computers made it possible for home computers to be useful and affordable to most Americans. The earliest Apple computers from the mid-1970s were made from kits. By the early 1980s, however, Steve Jobs and Steve Wozniak were marketing a more refined home unit, while Microsoft founders Bill Gates and Paul Allen were offering the MS-DOS operating system for the IBM PC. In 1984, a now-famous commercial during the Super Bowl announced the arrival of the Macintosh computer, and by 1985, the first version of Windows was available for the PC. These years also marked the beginning of Internet

*Statistics compiled from AVERT: www.avert.org/usa-statistics.htm

use by the general public; CompuServe offered home email in 1979 and real-time chat in 1980, and the number of users increased throughout the decade, though the real Internet explosion would not occur until the 1990s.

While many benefited from technologies developed by NASA, the space agency also experienced one of its greatest disasters in 1986. The space shuttle *Challenger* exploded minutes after taking off, killing all the astronauts aboard, including Christa McAuliffe. McAuliffe was a high school teacher who was making the journey in order to bring aspects of the space program into more direct contact with schoolchildren.

Another technology that experienced dramatic growth during the decade was cable television. By mid-decade, many American homes were wired to receive premium movies, news, and sports from channels like HBO, CNN, and ESPN. Most important for the history of rock music, MTV was launched, creating competition for FM radio, which had been the central way to expose the music to a large body of listeners. And just as it was forced to share its audience with MTV, FM was also losing sponsors to a new kind of radio emerging on the AM band: talk radio. Taking advantage of the neglect into which many AM stations had fallen, entrepreneurial broadcasters such as Rush Limbaugh began offering hours of daily political and cultural commentary, sometimes from the left of the political spectrum, but most often from the right. Soon Limbaugh and others built up syndication networks, in a sense reinventing the radio networks of the '30s and '40s, as millions of listeners heard the same programming across the country (though National Public Radio had also been doing the same thing on the FM band for years).

Television reflected America's renewed fascination with money and power. Perhaps no show captured this more vividly than *Dallas*, which debuted in 1978 and focused on a rich Texas oil family led by the shifty J. R. Ewing. Viewers got caught up in the cliffhanger ending to the show's second season, and during the summer of 1980 the phrase "Who shot J. R.?" saturated the media. *Family Ties* also reflected this new conservative trend, featuring a middle-aged liberal couple bantering with their conservative and financially astute son, Alex.

If *Family Ties* underscored the changes taking place in the white middle class, *The Cosby Show* reinforced shifts occurring in the black community. The show's main

AIDS victims and activists in the March on Washington for Lesbian and Gay Rights, 1987. More than 150,000 cases of AIDS were diagnosed between 1981 and 1989. Many AIDS activists did not think the Reagan administration sufficiently supported their cause.

the black middle class during the decade. Middle-class values were in for a completely different treatment, however, when *The Simpsons* debuted in 1989. This animated prime-time comedy irreverently lampooned almost every dimension of American life; playing no political favorites and pulling few punches, it established the model for many animated series in the 1990s.

As the hippies got older, the general cultural middle-class transformation from 1970s idealistic dreamers into well-appointed 1980s Yuppies (young urban professionals) created a cultural crisis for some. Such hand-wringing over identity and authenticity is captured effectively in *The Big Chill*. In this 1983 film, set to the beat of late 1960s rock and soul, a group of thirty-something college friends reunite for the funeral of a friend. While there, each takes in the changes that have occurred in

professionals. Epitomized by the phrase "greed is good," the film provided a glimpse into the dark side of the Reagan years and illustrated how the conservative 1980s were viewed by those with 1960s sensibilities. For the generation that came of age in the 1980s, youth-oriented films like *The Breakfast Club* and *St. Elmo's Fire* grappled with the social issues of young adult life and helped define new cultural attitudes free from the baggage of the 1960s and 1970s ideologies.

Likewise, though rock music benefited from the wealth and technology of the times, it still often displayed the critical stance of the 1960s and 1970s. Hyper-marketed pop stars competed with musicians critical of the growing divide between rich and poor, and the continued gaps between black and white, straight and gay, and male and female.

While shows like *Family Ties* and *The Cosby Show* reflect some of the cultural changes of the 1980s, *The Simpsons* updated the idea of the animated situation comedy in a markedly ironic and irreverent way. Shown here are (clockwise from left) Lisa, Homer, Marge, Maggie, and Bart Simpson.

CHAPTER 11

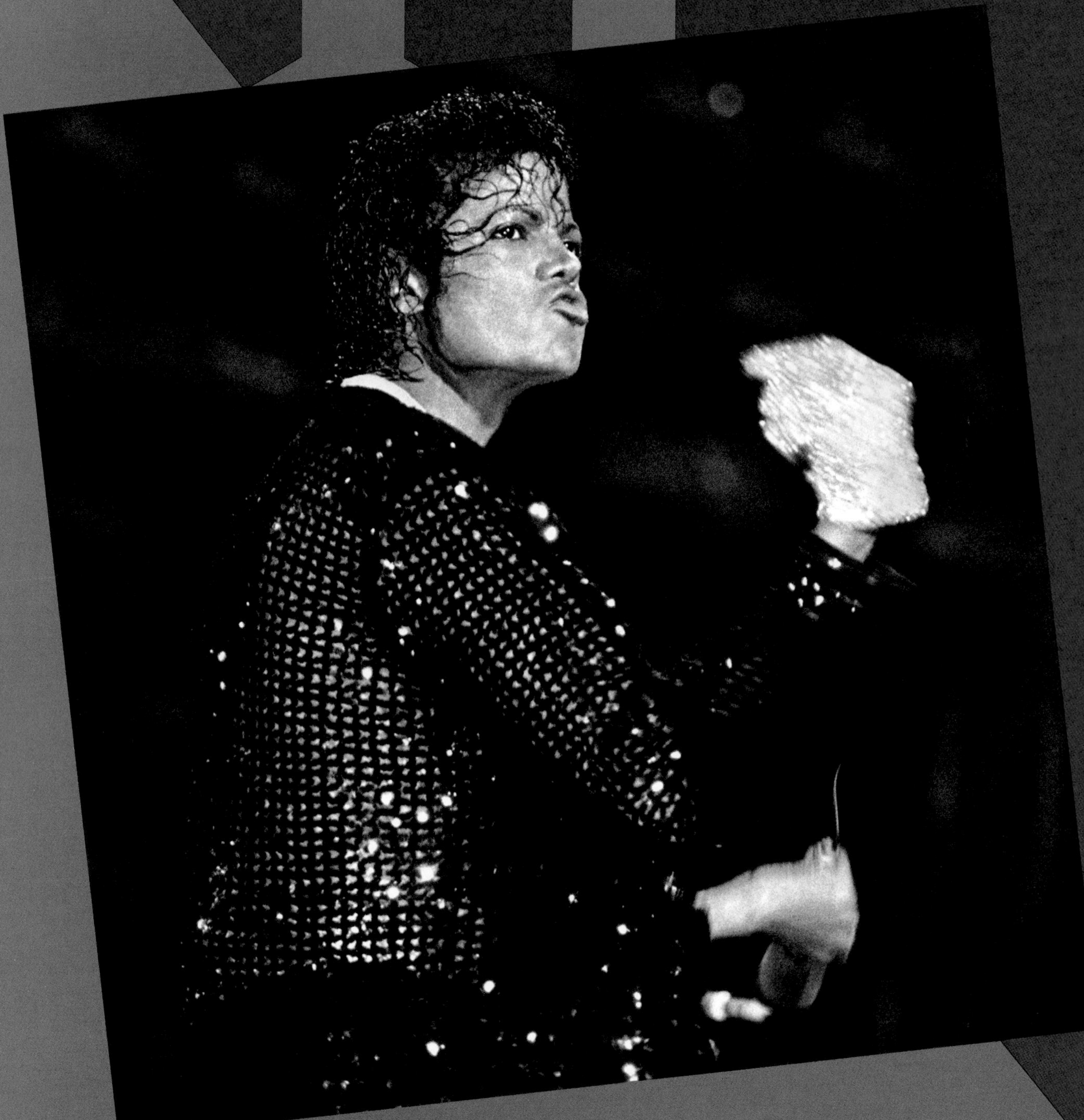

I WANT MY MTV

CHAPTER PREVIEW

- Launched in 1981, MTV's influence grew over the decade, eventually challenging radio as an important way to break new music and build careers.

- MTV has its roots both in the development of the cable television industry and in rock movies and teen-oriented broadcast TV.

- The music, dancing, and artistry of Michael Jackson and Madonna capitalized on the rise of music video. Prince and Janet Jackson also became leading acts on MTV.

- As new wave began to blend into mainstream rock in the early 1980s, many bands embraced a return to rock's earlier styles. Tom Petty and Bruce Springsteen were among these new traditionalists, while the Police and U2 extended the new wave approach.

- Musicians from rock's earlier decades continued to enjoy success in the 1980s. Members of Genesis, Yes, and Emerson, Lake & Palmer had hit albums with a new, leaner, more radio-friendly rock style. The Rolling Stones and Paul McCartney also continued to release top albums.

During the late 1970s, rock became increasingly influenced by the idea of the smash album, and disco, punk, and new wave challenged the rock status quo. Although it seemed as if these styles would eclipse mainstream rock during the 1980s, neither punk nor disco became important in the 1980s pop music mainstream. By the start of the decade, punk had retreated into an underground scene, replaced in the limelight by new wave, which quickly blended into mainstream rock radio playlists. After reminding musicians that music was not only for listening but also for dancing, the craze for disco music ended almost as quickly as it had begun. Although punk and disco fell out of favor, the musical and cultural legacies of both of these styles continued into the 1980s.

Soon after its release in 1982, Michael Jackson's *Thriller* became the best-selling album of all time. It contained several major hits, including "Billie Jean," "Beat It," and "Thriller." Jackson took full advantage of MTV to help promote his talents as both a musician and a performer. His innovative videos became instant classics. Jackson teamed up with film director John Landis to make the video for "Thriller," a short film featuring Jackson as a lovable boyfriend who turns into a gruesome monster. Despite the monster-movie aesthetic, the video provided Jackson ample time to show off his exquisite dancing. Jackson was one of the first performers in the MTV era to successfully combine hit music with artistic visuals. He is shown here performing in 1983.

Big changes were in store for rock music during the 1980s. Music Television (MTV) began to challenge radio as the most important medium for popular music, and heavy metal and rap emerged from the underground by the end of the decade. The rise of MTV led to the emergence of many visually oriented acts during the 1980s, and dance music eventually formed the core of early MTV programming. The decade also saw the continued development of mainstream rock and new wave, and punk fueled the development of hardcore and indie rock.

MTV IS ON THE AIR

The Roots of MTV in Promotional Video. Even though rock musicians had used short films and video performances to promote their music for decades, the idea of a television station devoted to nothing but promotional videos was not at all feasible until the 1980s. In fact, even in the early 1980s the idea seemed strange to many broadcasters. Rather than a music industry initiative, the emergence of MTV was closely aligned with the development of cable television. Initially, cable was seen as necessary in areas where antenna transmission was unsatisfactory. For people who lived in hilly or mountainous areas, for example, cable television provided a reliable way to deliver programming. Like any industry, cable television looked for ways to expand during the 1980s, even in areas where over-the-air transmission was perfectly viable. In order to develop new markets, cable had to offer something the networks and local stations could not, and at first the focus was on recent movies broadcast without commercial interruptions. Because there were no commercials, customers were required to pay for the service. Soon, cable channels such as Home Box Office (HBO) became quite successful, and cable providers looked for more specialty channels to add to their roster. Channels dedicated to sports, news, and weather were devised to bolster cable packages. MTV became the cable channel that focused on music.

Rock music was no newcomer to American television in the early 1980s. Going back to *American Bandstand* in the late 1950s, teenagers had proved that they would happily tune in to listen to new music and watch (often lip-synched) performances. The question for the people who developed MTV was not whether teens would tune in, but whether they would watch music television around the clock on a specialty channel. In the early days of planning MTV, two models were proposed. The first was to show nothing but promotional videos provided by the record companies at their expense. Critics of this approach pointed out that it would make MTV nothing more than an advertising mechanism for record labels. This critical faction, led by former Monkees guitarist Michael Nesmith, pushed for a more artistic approach. They argued that the videos should be experimental

MTV debuted on August 1, 1981, and its first video was, appropriately, "Video Killed the Radio Star" by the Buggles. The song and the visuals associated with it—exploding radios replaced by televisions—signaled the industry impact that MTV would have in the coming decades.

and innovative, not simply commercials. They saw great potential in music videos for expanding the artistic range of pop music by bringing filmmaking and music together in a symbiotic relationship. In the end, the corporate model was used, and it would be several years before artists explored the more creative aspects of music videos. On August 1, 1981, MTV went on the air with the Buggles' "Video Killed the Radio Star," which followed in the tradition of the promotional videos of the 1960s.

On the Air, but Who's Watching? MTV faced enormous challenges in its earliest days, the first of which was having enough videos to fill the broadcasting hours. Videos had been growing in importance in Australia, New Zealand, and the United Kingdom, so many groups popular in these regions had material to offer. In the United States, videos had also appeared on shows such as *Saturday Night Live* and *Video Concert Hall* (on the USA network). However, MTV needed material to fill the cycle of an entire day. Initially, record companies were not entirely convinced that investing money in music videos would pay off in additional sales, and many of the first music videos were shot on shoestring budgets. One reason for the record companies' reservations was that cable television was not widely available in America in the first half of the 1980s. As viewers learned about the benefits of cable, however, more and more communities added the service, and by the end of the decade it was much more accessible. Initially, MTV had its biggest audience wherever HBO and other premium cable movie services had enjoyed success—mainly in the Midwest. Unlike HBO, MTV did sell advertising, so their programming choices were driven by this Midwest target audience, which consisted mainly of white teenagers. To appeal to these viewers, MTV played videos by mainstream rock artists who were, with only rare exceptions, white as well. However, as more new material was created in the early 1980s, dance-oriented styles also became central to the MTV lineup.

An important challenge to these stereotypes occurred in early 1983, with Michael Jackson's "Billie Jean." By some accounts, MTV refused to play Jackson's video because he was black (or because they believed their white viewers would not want to watch black artists). The legend in the music business is that Jackson's label, Epic, threatened to pull all of their artists off MTV if the video was not aired, although this story has been disputed. Jackson's video first played on MTV in March 1983, and the enormous success of "Billie Jean" greatly increased the popularity of the network. Before long, record companies considered music videos to be crucial promotional tools for their artists, and MTV began to rival FM radio as the place to make or break hit records. With the struggle to represent nonwhite performers coupled with the growing importance of music videos, by the late 1980s MTV became a source of controversy in the rock community. Clearly, music videos privileged visual features over musical ones, and the look of an artist became paramount. Thus MTV provided the perfect platform for artists who used the visual dimension as an important part of their act, while sometimes neglecting those who were not young, stylish, or physically attractive. For artists such as Michael Jackson and Madonna, who took full advantage of this new set of artistic and promotional tools, MTV allowed an entirely new way to project both music and image.

WHAT'S THAT SOURCE?

MTV Controversy

MTV emerged in the early 1980s as an industry force that shifted audience focus from listening to viewing. There were vigorous debates among industry insiders about the images presented, and *not* presented, during the network's early years. On one hand, violence and sexism were rampant in many early videos, which reflected a strong connection to misogynist elements of mainstream rock. Alignment with album-oriented rock (AOR) led to another area of concern, the lack of African American artists supported by MTV. In this piece, *Billboard* video editor Laura Foti takes on both of the issues, reflecting the industry voices that challenged MTV, which eventually led to more balanced and inclusive programming.

I see quite a bit of video music programming and talk to many people about this area, both in production and cable television. Unfortunately, for a fast-changing field, I've found that too many outdated ideals exist. To put it bluntly, the video/cable industry has much of which it should be embarrassed.

The relative newness of video/cable production makes it all the more appalling that such age-old problems as sexism, racism, sellout standard and lack of creativity are so rampant. We've all felt the effects of these problems in the film, television and record industries. It is not possible to learn from their mistakes?

First, let's examine promotional video clips, so many of which show a cavalier disregard for taste, ethics and originality. When one considers that more clips are being made now than ever, the situation seems more discouraging.

Props such as French maids, mirrors, beds, highly glossed lips and cheap rip-offs of famous paintings abound, along with violent and sexist themes. Even clips in which the featured artist is a woman portray the female in a subordinate or frivolous role.

The slick negativity of what—and should—be esthetically pleasing (especially considering the astronomical costs!) is depressing to anyone who cares about the effect on those who watch this programming. And, it must be pointed out, the blame lies not only with the creators but with the programmers of such product. Just because it exists and fills a time slot doesn't mean we can't do any better.

This brings up the subject of MTV, Music Television, the number one programmer of these clips. The channel's stated policy to air only AOR—and, consequently, virtually nothing but white artists—means the majority of its 24-hour-a-day programming is made of clips such as those described above. MTV's programming executives have defended themselves by comparing MTV to typical AOR radio stations, but this argument avoids the real issues. The fact is it's more the wave of the future than the present. MTV appears to be using the term to hide behind the fact that, for whatever reason, it does not want to air clips by black artists.

Of the clips shown at Billboard's Video Conference this year, those by black artists—Kool and the Gang, Stevie Wonder, Odyssey, Tina Turner (and Rod Stewart), the Whispers and, especially, the Pointer Sisters—were standouts in terms of quality and positive attitude. These clips were done with such a sense of fun, and with such energy, that they put most of the others to shame.

Another comparison: "Night Flight" is the most successful show on the USA Network. It combines rock music with jazz, black and other forms, as well as some non-music segments like the "Video Artists" series. Mail comes in from 12-year-olds, and from 60-year-olds.

The show has proven it is possible to satisfy all of the people most of the time. Imagine if that philosophy were put into effect 24 hours a day!

For MTV to dismiss black artists as not fitting its "format" is an insult to the artists and to MTV's viewers. A young friend attending the video showcases at Billboard's recent conference asked, "Why don't I ever see any of this stuff on MTV?" Good question.

This person is an avid rock'n'roll fan, but he's not so narrow-minded that he doesn't want to know what's going on in other forms of music. At least until this type of programming is available elsewhere on the cable dial, why can't MTV bend a little and give black artists a chance? Their own research shows a high interest in R&B among their viewers. Must cable TV repeat the racist history of baseball, television, and so on? Please, MTV, don't underestimate your audience. You may be the only game in town now, but when that changes, cable viewers with wide-ranging interests will turn elsewhere for their sustenance.

Source: Laura Foti, "Taste and Fairness on Video," *Billboard*, December 11, 1982, 10.

DANCE MUSIC OF THE 1980s

Music Video's New Elite: Michael Jackson and Madonna. As discussed in Chapter 9, Michael Jackson's career began during the early 1970s at Motown with the Jackson 5. Known for bubblegum pop hits, the group increasingly turned to disco-oriented dance music in the mid-1970s, such as the popular "Dancing Machine" (p2 r1, 1974). Jackson left the group and Motown in 1975, signing to Epic Records as a solo artist. As disco increased in popularity during the late 1970s, Jackson teamed with veteran producer Quincy Jones to record the album *Off the Wall* (p3 r1 uk3, 1979), which contained four Top 10 pop hits. Jackson and Jones teamed again to record *Thriller* (p1 r1 uk1, 1982), which was released with enormous anticipation. Jackson was at the height of his fame, and the music video era, which suited him perfectly, was on an upswing. *Thriller* contained seven Top 10 singles, which included two number-one crossover hits, "Billie Jean" and "Beat It." "The Girl Is Mine," a duet with Paul McCartney, hit number two on the pop charts. To date, *Thriller* is the best-selling album in the history of the music business, with more than 100 million copies sold. Jackson's next album, *Bad* (p1 r1 uk1, 1987), continued this success, containing four songs that hit the number-one slot on both pop and rhythm and blues charts during 1987 and 1988: "Bad," "The Way You Make Me Feel," "I Just Can't Stop Loving You," and "The Man in the Mirror." Throughout this incredible run on the charts, Jackson not only sold tens of millions of records for Epic but also won numerous awards. He was arguably the biggest star in popular music during the 1980s and earned the title King of Pop. Jackson's music in the 1980s was almost always driven by a strong beat, showing not only his roots in 1970s black pop but also his experience with disco. "Billie Jean" is representative, beginning with a groove laid down in the bass and drums, which serves as the musical foundation for the song. Jackson's vocals project a sense of restrained emotional urgency during the verses, and the chorus provides the more open and catchy melodic hook. Jackson's famous high-voiced "ooo" can be heard scattered throughout the track, which features a Quincy Jones arrangement that builds continuously as the song unfolds.

Jackson was the perfect artist to take advantage of the emerging video age. As a performer, he continued the tradition of slick and sometimes athletic choreography made famous by the Temptations, updated with his silver glove and patented "Moonwalk" dance step. His video performances provided an opportunity to showcase his enormous dancing skill, making his videos stand out during the mid-1980s. Infusing unprecedented creative energy into his video productions, Jackson produced highly ambitious music videos. The first of these was the extended twelve-minute video for "Thriller," directed by Hollywood's John Landis and employing state-of-the-art special effects. The popularity of this video on MTV was buttressed by an hour-long documentary titled *Making Michael Jackson's Thriller*, which aired nearly as frequently as the video itself.

Although his album *Thriller* was a hit for Epic at the time, Michael Jackson agreed to perform on "Motown 25"—a tribute to the Jackson 5's longtime label. Jackson's performance at this event became legendary. It was here he first performed the "Moonwalk." Jackson brought down the house with this performance and further solidified his status as the world's most popular entertainer.

Listening Guide

Michael Jackson, "Billie Jean" Epic ES-823

Words and music by Michael Jackson, produced by Quincy Jones. Rose to #1 on the *Billboard* "Hot 100" and "Black Singles" charts, as well as on the UK charts, in 1983. Contained on the album *Thriller*, which also topped the album charts.

FORM: Simple verse-chorus. Most of the song is built over a repeating bass line (heard in the introduction) and a simple four-chord progression. Both the verse and the chorus use this material, making the form a simple verse-chorus type. This song also features a **pre-chorus.** A pre-chorus is a section that is no longer the verse but not yet the chorus and functions as a way of intensifying the arrival of the chorus. In this case, the pre-chorus contrasts with the material used in the verse and chorus, making the form as a whole a simple verse-chorus with contrasting pre-chorus. The arrangement is constructed traditionally, adding new elements along the way and becoming increasingly busy as the song unfolds.

TIME SIGNATURE: 4/4.

INSTRUMENTATION: Drums, electronic percussion, synthesizers, electric piano, guitar, lead and backup vocals. Notice that all the voices are Jackson's and that he frequently doubles the melody an octave higher than the main voice.

0:00–0:28	**Introduction**, 14 mm.	10 mm. of drums and bass set up the song's groove, and then the synthesizer enters playing a repeating 4-chord pattern.
0:28–0:53	**Verse 1**, 12 mm.	Lead vocal enters; note the heavy reverb on Jackson's voice and the use of vocal octaves at the end, "She was more like a beauty queen . . ."
0:53–1:10	**Verse 2**, 8 mm.	As before, "She told me her name . . ."
1:10–1:26	**Pre-chorus**, 8 mm.	Contrasting musical material, as arrangement builds through the addition of new synthesizer melody, electric piano, and splash cymbal. "People always told me . . ."
1:26–1:50	**Chorus**, 12 mm.	Harmony vocals enter. Note rhythmic octaves in the guitar, "Billie Jean is not my lover . . ."
1:50–2:15	**Verse 3**, 12 mm.	As before, with added string melody in the synthesizer part and more activity between voice parts, "For forty days . . ."
2:15–2:32	**Verse 4**, 8 mm.	As verse 3, "She told my baby . . ."
2:32–2:48	**Pre-chorus**, 8 mm.	Builds as before, but now with new string melody, "People always told me . . ."
2:48–3:05	**Chorus**, 8 mm.	As before, but now with new string melody at end of phrase, "Billie Jean . . ."
3:05–3:28	**Chorus**, 12 mm.	Guitar line and synthesizer trumpet line are added.

3:28–3:54	**Interlude**, 12 mm.	Rhythmic guitar line highlighted, with vocals at end.
3:54–4:18	**Chorus**, 12 mm.	As before, but with guitar line mixed forward and more vocal interjections. "Billie Jean . . ."
4:18–4:50	**Coda**, 16 mm.	Various improvised singing along with harmony vocals as song fades out.

Although Jackson's records after the mid-1970s no longer appeared on Motown, he continued Berry Gordy's practice of straddling the line between rhythm and blues and pop. Two of *Thriller*'s top hits featured white musicians who were well known to mainstream rock fans at the time. The duet with Paul McCartney, "The Girl Is Mine," paired Jackson with the most publicly visible Beatle, and Eddie Van Halen's guitar solo on "Beat It" brought a rising guitar icon into the picture. This was all smart business, and it certainly reflected Jackson's musical interests. Yet Jackson's crossover practices drew the ire of many critics who accused him of selling out his blackness. Of course, Jackson's close association with Motown during the first half of the 1970s made him an especially inviting target. Jackson, however, never backed down from his efforts to bridge the gaps he saw between white and black culture, and he continued to extend his musical range until the end of his career.

Like Michael Jackson, Madonna depended as much on the visual aspect of her music as the sonic dimension. She had worked as a professional dancer in New York, appearing at various points with the Pearl Lange and Alvin Ailey dance companies. Her first recordings enjoyed success within the New York dance-club scene, and she signed to Sire records, one of the most important labels to release New York–based new wave. Her 1984 debut album *Madonna* (p8 r20) contained two hit singles, "Borderline" (p10) and "Lucky Star" (p4 uk14), and the videos for these songs provided an early glimpse of one of the most controversial figures of the video age. By early 1985, Madonna's *Like a Virgin* (p1 r10 uk1) was climbing the pop album charts, while four singles from the album hit the top five, including "Like a Virgin" (p1 r9 uk3) and "Material Girl" (p2 uk3). *True Blue* did even better, reaching number one on the pop album charts in 1986 (uk1) and producing three number-one pop singles that same year—"Live to Tell," "Papa Don't Preach," and "Open Your Heart."

Like Jackson, Madonna's music is often driven by a dance beat, drawing from her dance-club background and a close association with many of the most important instrumentalists and producers to work in the New York dance scene. "Like a Virgin" provides an interesting comparison with Jackson's "Billie Jean." The tracks start out in a similar manner. Yet while the repeating bass line in Jackson's song is somewhat menacing, the bass in Madonna's song is buoyant and celebratory. Madonna also seems to borrow Jackson's high-voiced

Madonna was one of the earliest dance-oriented artists from the United States to receive heavy exposure on MTV. Her music was influenced by her dance-club background and a close association with many of the most important instrumentalists and producers to work in the New York dance scene. Here, she dances and sings during a 1985 concert.

MUSIC VIDEOS IN THE 1980s: MICHAEL JACKSON, "THRILLER"

Viewing Rock

With the establishment of MTV in the early 1980s, music videos became an important way for performers to reach audiences visually. The video for Michael Jackson's "Thriller" was the most important music video of the early 1980s. A collaborative effort between Jackson and filmmaker John Landis, "Thriller" exceeded the scope of early music videos in length, depth, and creativity. Based loosely on Landis's film *An American Werewolf in Lon-*

1950s horror movie with music by veteran film composer Elmer Bernstein. After being exposed to a full moon, Jackson's character transforms into a werewolf, using dramatic special effects more common in movies than in music videos (1).

The audience perspective then shifts to Jackson and the same girlfriend in the setting of a modern movie theater, revealing that the werewolf scene was actually a film-within-the-film (2).

After Jackson's date is frightened to the point of leaving the theater, the music of "Thriller" begins. Jackson presents the verses of the song in a famous two-minute sequence while walking down a dark street (3).

A spoken interlude by horror-film actor Vincent Price provides the backdrop for a scene reminiscent of *Night of the Living Dead,* where zombies rise out of their graves and surround Jackson and Ray. An extended dance interlude follows, in which Jackson, now in the form of a zombie himself, leads the group in a groundbreaking two-minute sequence choreographed by Jackson and Michael Peters (4).

As the best example of an early music video that highlights the artistic possibilities of the new form, "Thriller" had a dramatic effect on the creativity employed in music videos that followed.

don, the fourteen-minute "Thriller" begins by casting Jackson and an on-screen girlfriend (performed by Ola Ray) in the context of a

"ooo" which can be heard in her chorus as "hey." "Like a Virgin" also betrays a dance-club influence in the layers of synthesizers that create an accompanimental backdrop for Madonna's singing. Later tracks expanded her stylistic range to include moodier songs such as "Papa Don't Preach" and sensual songs like "Justify My Love" (the video for which was banned on MTV). Madonna did not write or produce many of her early hits, but she began to take a more active role in the creative aspects of her music as her career developed, earning songwriter and production credits beginning with *True Blue* in 1986.

Madonna's albums and singles in the mid-1980s established her as one of the most important figures in pop music, and she remains among the most successful acts

Listening Guide

Madonna, "Like a Virgin" Sire 29210

Words and music by Billy Steinberg and Tom Kelly, produced by Nile Rodgers. Hit #1 on the *Billboard* "Hot 100" and #9 on *Billboard* "Hot Black Singles" charts in 1985 (uk3). Also contained on the album *Like a Virgin*, which went to #1 on the *Billboard* "Top Pop Albums" and #10 on the "Hot Black Albums" charts (uk1).

FORM: Compound AABA. The A sections are based primarily on simple verse-chorus form, except that the chorus is built on the first part of each verse only. The second part of each verse differs from the first in that its last 6 bars break off the pattern set by the first part, creating a section that functions similarly to the pre-chorus in "Billie Jean." The bridge presents contrasting material drawn from the last 6 bars of the second part of the verse, but developed and changed. The return of the final A section brings back only the second part of the verse, but the repetition of the chorus helps balance the end of the song.

TIME SIGNATURE: 4/4.

INSTRUMENTATION: Layers of synthesizers, drums, guitar, lead vocals.

	0:00–0:08	**Introduction**, 4 mm.	Synthesizer bass and drums begin, with synthesizer chords added in last 2 bars.
A	0:08–0:24	**Verse 1** (first part), 8 mm.	Vocals enter, as drumbeat locks in. "I made it through . . ."
	0:24–0:44	**Verse 1** (second part), 10 mm.	Note how the first 4 bars repeat the first part of the verse, but then add new material that propels the song toward the chorus. "I was beat . . ."
	0:44–1:00	**Chorus**, 8 mm.	Added synthesizer lines and rhythmic guitar. "Like a virgin . . ."
A	1:00–1:16	**Verse 2** (first part), 8 mm.	As before, with added synthesizer interjections. Note how this verse emerges directly out of the chorus. "Gonna give you . . ."
	1:16–1:36	**Verse 2** (second part), 10 mm.	As before, "You're so fine . . ."
	1:36–1:52	**Chorus**, 8 mm.	As before, but note Michael Jacksonesque high-voiced "hey." "Like a virgin . . ."
B	1:52–2:08	**Bridge**, 8 mm.	Material derived and developed from second part of verse, with vocals on "Whoa."
A	2:08–2:29	**Verse 3** (second part), 10 mm.	As verse 2, "You're so fine . . ."
	2:29–2:45	**Chorus**, 8 mm.	As before, with extra background parts added. "Like a virgin . . ."
	2:45–3:01	**Chorus**, 8 mm.	Repeat, but with a sensual vocal variation at the end.
	3:01–3:09	**Chorus**, 4 mm.	Repeat, with vocal improvisation as song fades out.

in the music business. She has continually challenged aspects of what she perceives to be some of society's most troubling issues and practices. Early on, her "boy toy" image cast her as a sex object, although this was done with great irony—Madonna put on the role of sex object in order to call it into question, and a link can be made to previous figures who adopted personae, such as Jim Morrison and David Bowie. In this way, Madonna has explored the boundaries of sexual conduct, racial issues, women's roles, and spirituality. Detractors have accused her of seeking publicity by titillating and shocking audiences, while her supporters have praised her methods of raising important social issues for debate. Whatever position you take on Madonna's place in popular culture, video images clearly played a central role in her music. Her videos are rich in symbolism and striking juxtapositions—a factor that has caused many academics to offer extended interpretations of their deeper meanings.

Dirty Minded? Prince and Janet Jackson.

In addition to Michael Jackson and Madonna, Minneapolis-based Prince deserves credit for asserting racial difference and sexuality in the MTV lineup during the mid-1980s. Prince's video for "1999" actually predated "Billie Jean," and his practice of using blatant sexual images, both in his songs and in live performance, goes back to the late 1970s, when Madonna was still in college. Born Prince Rogers Nelson, he was one of the most prolific artists of the 1980s, writing and producing a long string of hit records under his own name—often playing all the instruments on his records—and writing and producing other artists, such as the Time, Vanity 6, and Sheila E. Prince's musical roots were in the black pop and funk of the 1970s, and his careful control of both his music and that of satellite projects was modeled on the practice of George Clinton, while his one-man-band approach was reminiscent of Stevie Wonder. Prince's first four albums did well in the rhythm and blues market, with both *Prince* (1979) and *Controversy* (1981) reaching number three and containing several singles that became especially popular on the *Billboard* "Hot Soul Singles" charts. During this early period, Prince developed his image as a sexually charged and somewhat androgynous figure, and songs such as "Head" and "Jack U Off" provided ample opportunity for him to project this image in live performance.

Like Marvin Gaye and Stevie Wonder before him, Prince had total control over his music (and, like Wonder, often played all the instruments). However, Prince demanded this arrangement from the beginning of his career. He combined Michael Jackson's crossover appeal with Madonna's blatant sexual imagery, and with this mixture scored hits throughout the 1980s and 1990s.

While he had enjoyed modest crossover success earlier, the 1982 release of his album *1999* (p9 r4) made Prince a star in the pop world, fueled by the singles "1999" (p12 r4) and "Little Red Corvette" (p6 r15) and his exposure on MTV. The title track finds Prince employing a synthesizer-heavy backdrop, driven hard by a strong beat in the drums. His technique of using different voices for each line in the verse goes back to doo-wop groups like Clyde McPhatter and the Drifters, but here the most immediate influences are probably Sly and the Family Stone or the Temptations. At the very end of "1999," you can hear the strong funk influences that supported Prince's music.

In 1984, Prince released the semi-autobiographical feature film *Purple Rain*, which was greeted with critical acclaim and accompanied by a soundtrack album that quickly hit the top spot on both pop and rhythm and blues charts. Two singles from the album, "When Doves Cry" and "Let's Go Crazy," also went to number one on both singles charts. More hit albums and singles followed over the next few years, including *Around the World in a Day* (p1 r4, 1985), *Batman* (p1 r5 uk1, 1989), and *Diamonds and Pearls* (p3 r1, 1991), each of which sold more than two million copies. Prince's blending of the funk grooves and outrageousness of George Clinton with a strong pop sensibility made him one of the most influential artists of the decade, and among black artists he was rivaled only by Michael Jackson.

As Prince was developing his musical style in the late 1970s, Michael Jackson's younger sister Janet was a regular guest on the television sitcom *Good Times*. During the early 1980s, Janet released albums and singles on the side while continuing to act in television shows such as *Diff'rent Strokes* and *Fame*. In 1986, however, she teamed with the Minneapolis-based production and songwriting team of Jimmy Jam and Terry Lewis, two musicians who had been in the Prince-produced band the Time. Under their direction, Janet's 1986 album *Control* shot to the top of the pop and rhythm and blues charts (uk8), containing six crossover hit singles. She projected an image of confidence and independence with *Control,* and the hard-driving beats behind this new music showed the

Originally a teen star on television, Janet Jackson remade herself as a woman in charge of her own life and career with the album *Control* (1986). Her performances often featured flamboyant costumes and extensive dancing, similar to those of her brother Michael and not unlike those of another self-determined female singer, Madonna.

influence of hip hop and funk. With the music of Jackson, Jam and Lewis became progenitors of a dance-based style of hip-hop and pop called New Jack Swing, which created dense, stark musical textures from drum machines and samples. The team of Jackson with Jam and Lewis followed with *Rhythm Nation 1814* (1989), which also topped both charts (uk4) and surpassed *Control* by producing seven singles to reach the top five of the "Hot 100." While *Rhythm Nation 1814* took on a more serious, socially conscious tone than its predecessor, the original plan had been for it to project a sexier and more seductive image for the singer. It would be her next release, *janet.* (p1 r1 uk1, 1993), that launched Jackson's more adult-oriented image. This was underscored by an infamous *Rolling Stone* cover photo released in September 1993 that featured a topless Jackson with her breasts covered only by a pair of hands from an unseen person. Of the six hit singles on *janet.*, the chart-topping "That's the Way Love Goes" illustrates the production approach taken by Jackson, Jam, and Lewis. In stark contrast to the choppy New Jack Swing of her previous albums, "That's the Way Love Goes" uses music sampled from the recording of James Brown's "Papa Don't Take No Mess," creating a more laid-back and sultry sound. Throughout her career, video played a central role in Janet Jackson's musical presentation. As with her famous brother, dancing was as important as singing in Janet's performances (Paula Abdul choreographed many of Janet's early videos), and the musical dimension of her videos certainly takes a backseat to the visual one. As we have seen with both Madonna and Michael Jackson, during the early MTV era this balance was especially difficult for visually stimulating performers.

Listening Guide

Prince, "1999" Warner Brothers GWB-0468

Words and music by Prince, produced by Prince. Originally released in late 1982, hitting #44 on the *Billboard* "Hot 100." Rereleased in summer 1983 (after the success of "Little Red Corvette"), it hit #12 on the *Billboard* "Hot 100" and #4 on the "Black Singles" charts. Contained on the album *1999*, which went to #9 on the *Billboard* "Top LPs and Tape" and #4 on the "Black LPs" charts in 1983.

FORM: Contrasting verse-chorus (with extended coda). Notice how extra measures are added to the end of each chorus: first 4 measures, then 8 measures, and then the final extended coda. It is also interesting to note that the repeating chord progression in the synthesizer part is based on the Mamas and the Papas' hit single "Monday, Monday."

TIME SIGNATURE: 4/4.

INSTRUMENTATION: Electric guitar, bass, drums, synthesizer, synthesized percussion, and lead all provided by Prince, plus female backup vocals.

0:00–0:50	**Introduction**, 16 mm.	Begins with electronically modified voice, as drumbeat enters, and then synthesizer.
0:50–1:22	**Verse 1**, 16 mm.	Vocal enters; notice exchange of voices, perhaps influenced by Sly or the Temptations. "I was dreaming when I wrote this . . ."
1:22–1:39	**Chorus**, 8 mm.	Harmony vocals, no extension added yet, "Two thousand zero zero . . ."
1:39–2:12	**Verse 2**, 16 mm.	As before but with new synthesizer and guitar lines, "I was dreaming when I wrote this . . ."
2:12–2:37	**Chorus**, 12 mm.	As before, but now extended by 4 mm., "Two thousand zero zero . . ."
2:37–3:10	**Verse 3**, 16 mm.	Now sung in harmony, with small variations in the accompaniment. "If you didn't come to party . . ."
3:10–3:25	**Chorus**, 8 mm.	As the first time, "Two thousand zero zero . . ."
3:25–3:58	**Chorus**, 16 mm.	As the second time, but now extended by 8 mm., with plenty of vocal improvisation.
3:58–4:13	**Chorus**, 8 mm.	One more time through the coda, before heading into the extended ending.
4:13–6:14	**Coda**, 60 mm.	Extension of chorus now becomes a lengthy coda. Note that the last 16 mm. are quieter, with a sudden stop in the last measure. The funk influence comes out especially in these last measures.

Brit Pop Hits MTV: Duran Duran and Culture Club. Due to the shortage of usable videos in the early years of MTV, an entire crop of British pop acts received disproportionate airplay on MTV, prompting what many critics have called a "second British invasion." Bands and artists such as Bow Wow Wow, Adam and the Ants, A Flock of Seagulls, Howard Jones, Thomas Dolby, and ABC, who might otherwise have never cracked the American market, profited handsomely from the exposure their music received on MTV. Among the most successful of these groups was Duran Duran, whose synthesizer- and guitar-heavy new wave sound was driven by infectious dance beats. Their visual dimension was marked by a concern for style and rebellious elegance. The band first made its mark in the United States with *Rio* (p6 uk2, 1982), containing "Hungry like the Wolf" (p3 uk5), and the video for this song went into regular MTV rotation. The success of *Rio* spurred American interest in the band's 1981 album, *Duran Duran* (p10, 1983), which had risen to number three in the UK when it was originally released. Appearing in late 1983, *Seven and the Ragged Tiger* (p8 uk1) continued Duran Duran's run on the international charts, spawning three Top 10 hits, including "The Reflex" (p1 uk1). Keeping in line with the band's reliance on MTV, the video for "The Reflex" was groundbreaking in its use of special effects, as it depicted a waterfall pouring over the audience of a Duran Duran concert.

Culture Club was another British group that exploited the visual side of their act through heavy exposure on MTV during the early 1980s. Singer George "Boy George" O'Dowd, who dressed in women's clothes and sported long dreadlocks, was the band's lead singer and most visible member. One of the group's first appearances on British television prompted one critic to write, "It's a bird, it's a bloke, it's Boy George." *Kissing to Be Clever* (p14 r24 uk5, 1982) featured three Top 10 hits, including the easygoing "Do You Really Want to Hurt Me" (p2 uk1), which was played heavily on both MTV and radio. The group's next album, *Colour by Numbers* (p2 r7 uk1, 1983), brought three more Top 10 hits, among them the ubiquitous "Karma Chameleon" (p1 uk1). Culture Club's music was unabashedly pop-oriented in the Brill Building sense: catchy tunes and hooks established a generally happy tone, while Boy George's fluid and laid-back singing style was influenced by black pop singers of the 1960s and 1970s. Moreover, while Boy George's looks may have seemed like a detriment, the cultural space between the UK and the American Midwest placed a comfortable distance between his obviously androgynous style and the often-conservative values of the American Heartland.

The striking style of dress and soul-influenced vocals of Boy George helped Culture Club become popular in the U.S. market during the mid-1980s. Here, Boy George performs on stage in 1984 at London's Wembley Stadium.

Thinking Person's MTV: Eurythmics and Tears for Fears. Eurythmics took advantage of the synthesizer-pop sound that had emerged in the UK at the end of the 1970s and combined it with an innovative approach to music video. Combining the soul-influenced vocals of Annie Lennox, the synthesizer wizardry of David Stewart, and a penchant for intellectual experimentation, the duo released *Sweet Dreams (Are Made of This)* (p15 uk3, 1983), the title song of which hit number one in the United States (uk2). The song was supported by a surreal music video that featured a cow circling a boardroom table, several odd scenes in a pasture, and Stewart accompanying Lennox using a computer-turned-synthesizer. During a period in which many videos were relatively inane depictions of performance, the sophisticated "Sweet Dreams" video became must-see MTV. Following with *Touch* (p7 uk1, 1984) and *Be Yourself Tonight* (p9 uk3, 1985), Eurythmics were able to remain successful in America through the mid-1980s. The group continued a string of successful albums and singles in Britain through the end of the decade before embarking on a long hiatus.

Influenced by the primal scream therapy of Arthur Janov, keyboardist Roland Orzabal and bassist Curt Smith called their UK-based band Tears for Fears. Basing their stylistic approach in British synthesizer-pop, the duo released its debut album, *The Hurting* (uk1), in 1983. The album barely created a ripple in the United States, but their follow-up, *Songs from the Big Chair* (p1 uk2, 1985), became an international sensation. Fueled by two number-one American hits, "Everybody Wants to Rule the World" (uk2) and "Shout" (uk4), the record was also bolstered by heavy video rotation on MTV. In many ways, *Songs from the Big Chair* shows the more ambitious side of British pop from the 1980s: the lyrics deal with serious topics, the music is sometimes complicated, and tunes run into one another to create long tracks. Perhaps owing to their seriousness of purpose, the duo was not able to produce a timely third album, and while *The Seeds of Love* (p8 uk1, 1989) enjoyed success, it was the last big record for the band.

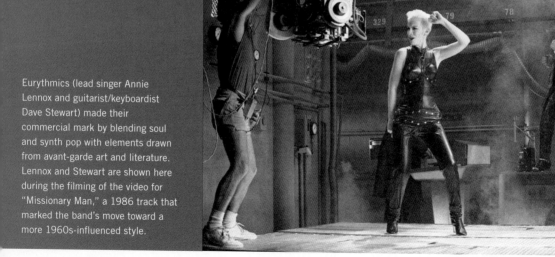

Eurythmics (lead singer Annie Lennox and guitarist/keyboardist Dave Stewart) made their commercial mark by blending soul and synth pop with elements drawn from avant-garde art and literature. Lennox and Stewart are shown here during the filming of the video for "Missionary Man," a 1986 track that marked the band's move toward a more 1960s-influenced style.

Girls Just Wanna Have Fun: Olivia Newton-John, the Go-Go's, Cyndi Lauper, and the Bangles. The late 1970s had ushered in a new era for women in rock music, as artists such as Blondie, the B-52s, and Heart had all nurtured more aggressive and sensual female images. Among the highest-profile women in pop music during the early 1980s was the Australian-born singer Olivia Newton-John, whose image by the start of the decade had become much more aggressive and sensual than it had been in the '70s. This transformation was powered by the success of *Totally Hot* (p7, 1979) and *Physical* (p6, 1981), which contained "Make a Move on Me" (p5) and the dance-beat driven, synthesizer inflected "Physical" (p1). In the wake of this important line of female representation in rock, the Go-Go's became the first successful all-female new wave band. Fronted by singer Belinda Carlisle, the band's *Beauty and the Beat* hit the top of the U.S. charts in 1981, powered in part by the single "We Got the Beat" (p2), which offered a no-frills musical approach that featured a memorable sing-along chorus. The Go-Go's worked pre-hippie 1960s images to the hilt: the band name is derived from "go-go girls," while the *Beauty and the Beat* cover featured a shot of the band clad in bath towels, seemingly in the middle of a slumber party. Their success was fleeting, although Carlisle returned to the charts regularly as a solo artist. Her second album, *Heaven on Earth* (p13 uk4, 1987), contained three hits including "Heaven Is a Place on Earth" (1987), which topped both the American and British charts.

Cyndi Lauper, seen here in a 1986 concert, capitalized on woman-focused new wave groups like the Go-Go's and produced the girl-power rock anthem "Girls Just Want to Have Fun." Lauper projected an image of a strong and fiercely independent woman, and this was supported by her powerful voice, woman-focused lyrics, creative dress, and video production.

Capitalizing on the girl-specific images of the Go-Go's, Cyndi Lauper emerged into the mainstream spotlight with the hit album *She's So Unusual* (p4 uk16, 1984), which featured a hit that could be considered an anthem for female power in rock, "Girls Just Want to Have Fun" (p2 uk2). The video for this song quickly became an MTV classic, featuring the energetic spirit of Lauper rebelling against the wishes of her parents. The album also included hits that showed other aspects of Lauper's musical personality. "Time after Time" (p1 uk3) is a haunting ballad, while "She Bop" (p3) is a thinly veiled engagement with the topic of female masturbation. Lauper continued her success with the album *True Colors* (p4, 1986), which codified her worldwide fame and produced two singles, including the title track (p1) and "Change of Heart" (p3).

In the wake of the wild success of many female rock musicians, the Bangles emerged from California with *Different Light* (p2 uk3, 1986). The album was propelled up the charts by "Manic Monday" (p2 uk2, 1986), a song written by Prince, and the tongue-in-cheek "Walk Like an Egyptian" (p1 uk3, 1986). Building on the long legacy of women in rock music provided by Heart, Fleetwood Mac, the Pretenders, the Talking Heads, and the Go-Go's, the Bangles coolly projected feminine identity into rock, blending the jingle-jangle of 1960s folk rock with smooth vocal harmonies.

THE NEW TRADITIONALISTS

No Irony, Just a Healthy Love for Earlier Styles. During the first years of new wave in the late 1970s, the fact that a band or an artist made use of features associated with pre-hippie rock was enough to include them under a general banner of "new simplicity." The rejection of hippie values—even if only on the surface in some cases—was such an overriding characteristic that it tended to eclipse important differences within the first cluster of new wave bands. But as the 1980s began and hippie rock started to recede into history, it became increasingly clear that there were two distinct approaches to appropriating earlier rock music styles and features. The first was to employ these sounds and images in an ironic manner, not so much to endorse earlier rock as to reject the corporate rock of the 1970s—Devo offers the clearest example of this tendency. A second approach was to employ such sounds and images in earnest. That is, bands used elements of earlier rock music because they were genuinely interested in revisiting older styles. These bands and artists were not exploiting earlier music to create a pastiche but rather were "new traditionalists" concerned with returning rock to what they considered to be its core aesthetic values.

I Won't Back Down: Tom Petty, with and without the Heartbreakers. Initially received in the context of new wave, during the early 1980s Tom Petty became more closely aligned with the new traditionalism approach. Ironically, Petty's music always had a strong connection to the 1960s, and he didn't change his style throughout the 1970s and 1980s. He hadn't come to new wave as much as new wave had come to him. As the 1980s began, however, Petty and the Heartbreakers continued their successful practice of blending jangly guitar sounds with catchy melodies and poetic lyrics. *Hard Promises* (p5, 1981) contained the radio favorite "The Waiting" (p19), while *Southern Accents* (p7, 1985) featured "Don't Come Around Here No More" (p13). Petty's music had tended to enjoy more success in the United States than in England, although his first solo album, *Full Moon Fever* (p3 uk8, 1989), cracked the UK Top 10, and produced the hits "Free Fallin'" (p7) and "I Won't Back Down" (p12) in the States. His position as keeper of the rock and roll flame was further solidified with the formation of the Traveling Wilburys in 1988, led by ex-Beatle George Harrison and including Petty, Bob Dylan, Roy Orbison, and Electric Light Orchestra front man Jeff Lynne. This all-star band released *Traveling Wilburys Volume 1* (p3, 1988), containing the single "Handle with Care" (p45). Displaying a Beatle-esque sense of humor—itself a throwback to those carefree mop-top days—the band named their second album *Traveling Wilburys Volume 3* (p11 uk14, 1990).

New Jersey Nostalgia: Bruce Springsteen and the E-Street Band. Unlike Tom Petty, Bruce Springsteen was never lumped in with the new wavers of the 1970s. Springsteen's songs and fashion put him in the category of a colorful, New Jersey–based singer-songwriter who drew earnestly on older traditions of rock. The dense, almost symphonic instrumentation of his third album with the E-Street Band, *Born to Run* (p3 uk17, 1975), showed more than a hint of Phil Spector's influence and its success marked Springsteen as an important force for the voice of rock traditionalists. Springsteen's greatest success would come in the 1980s, however, beginning with his fifth album, *The River* (p1 uk2, 1980), featuring the hit "Hungry Heart" (p5), and continuing with the more introspective and stripped-down *Nebraska* (p3 uk3, 1982). Springsteen's landmark release was 1984's *Born in the U.S.A.*, which topped the charts in both the United States and Britain and produced six Top 10 American hits, including "Glory Days" (p5 uk17) and "Born in the U.S.A." (p9 uk7). The boxed set *Live 1977–1985* (p1 uk4, 1986) was released at the height of Springsteen's popularity in the mid-1980s, introducing his many new fans to his older material and sparking renewed sales and radio play for his music from the 1970s. Springsteen followed up with *Tunnel of Love* (p1 uk1, 1987) and the simultaneous release of two albums in 1992: *Human Touch* (p2 uk1) and *Lucky Town* (p3 uk2).

Springsteen's image relied on the idea that he was the voice of that average working-class guy, and his lyrics reflected on common emotional and social problems. "Born in the U.S.A.," for instance, paints a vivid picture of the decay of American values in the industrial heartland, all seen from the perspective of someone who is powerless to effect change. (In a strange turn of events, "Born in the U.S.A." was mistakenly appropriated by Ronald Reagan's presidential campaign as a paean to traditional values and American pride, until Springsteen eventually asked them to stop using the song.) The song's form seems simple: it employs the same eight-bar progression and two-bar melody, both of which are unrelentingly repeated. But formally, the song threatens to lose its way in the middle, as verses break off, incomplete. The constant repetition of the music, combined with the formal wandering of the song's midsection, creates a sense that the Vietnam veteran in the lyrics is not sure which way to turn. Throughout much of his career, Springsteen has projected an image reminiscent of a late 1950s or early 1960s white rock and roll singer, although the topicality of his lyrics hark back to Dylan in the 1960s.

Bruce Springsteen belts out "Born in the U.S.A." in Washington, D.C., the first stop on his 1986 concert tour. This song, although used briefly by Ronald Reagan in his 1984 campaign, was deeply critical of American involvement in Vietnam and the subsequent treatment of veterans after the war. Springsteen's music is marked by a big, seemingly traditional rock and roll sound combined with poetic, socially conscious lyrics reminiscent of Bob Dylan's.

Listening Guide

Bruce Springsteen, "Born in the U.S.A." Columbia 04680

Words and music by Bruce Springsteen, produced by Bruce Springsteen, Jon Landau, Chuck Plotkin, and Steven Van Zandt. Rose to #9 on the *Billboard* "Hot 100" in 1984 (uk7). Contained on the album *Born in the U.S.A.*, which topped the pop album charts in the United States and the UK.

FORM: Simple verse-chorus. A 2-bar melodic figure permeates this track, which is further built on almost identical repeating 8-measure sections for both verse and chorus sections. After breaking the verse-chorus pattern after verse 3, notice how verses 4 and 5 also break off lyrically. The overall effect is to drive to verse 6 and toward the final statements of the chorus. Springsteen wants to parallel the sense of abandonment portrayed in the lyrics by allowing the music to wander somewhat. At certain points the song seems unsure of where it wants to go, but is nevertheless pushed forward by the nagging 2-bar melody.

TIME SIGNATURE: 4/4.

INSTRUMENTATION: Drums, guitar, bass, piano, synthesizers, lead vocal.

0:00–0:16	**Introduction**, 8mm.	Snare drum, piano, and synthesizer playing repeated 2-mm. melody.
0:16–0:33	**Verse 1**, 8 mm.	Vocal enters over this stark music of the intro, "Born down in a dead man's town . . ."
0:33–0:49	**Chorus**, 8 mm.	Lead vocal doubles the 2-mm. melody that has been repeating since the beginning of the song. "Born in the U.S.A. . . ."
0:49–1:05	**Verse 2**, 8 mm.	Guitars and bass enter and drums break into a beat, as the song gets louder and more intense. "Got in a little hometown jam . . ."
1:05–1:21	**Chorus**, 8 mm.	As before, but with new parts added in verse 2 continued. "Born in the U.S.A. . . ."
1:21–1:36	**Verse 3**, 8 mm.	As in verse 2, "Come back home to the refinery . . ."
1:36–1:52	**Interlude**, 8 mm.	Music continues without vocal melody, Springsteen improvises quietly in the background.
1:52–2:07	**Verse 4**, 8 mm.	Partial verse, as last phrase is broken off, "I had a brother . . ."
2:07–2:23	**Verse 5**, 8 mm.	Partial verse, broken off even sooner, "He had a woman . . ."
2:23–2:39	**Verse 6**, 8 mm.	Music goes back to spare texture of verse 1. "Down in the shadow . . ."
2:39–2:55	**Chorus**, 8 mm.	Spare, as in chorus 1. "Born in the U.S.A. . . ."
2:55–3:10	**Chorus**, 8 mm.	Music gets fuller again, as in chorus 2. "Born in the U.S.A. . . ."
3:10–4:28	**Coda**, 40 mm.	Vocal melody drops out, as Springsteen improvises and screams in the background. The music goes through the 8-bar pattern five times, with a dropout in the fourth one.

A Performance That Launched a Career. When Bruce Springsteen performed at Cambridge's Harvard Square Theater in May 1974, many might consider that to be a performance that marked a turning point in his career. In the audience that night was journalist and aspiring producer Jon Landau, who would write a review of the show in which he famously claimed, "I saw rock and roll future and its name is Bruce Springsteen." But a more crucial performance for Springsteen took place more than two years earlier under far less glamorous circumstances. In early 1972, Springsteen's manager secured him an audition at Columbia Records with John Hammond—the legendary figure who had signed Bob Dylan, Aretha Franklin, and Billie Holiday, and supervised recordings by Bessie Smith. Springsteen was close to penniless at the time and performed in Hammond's New York office on a borrowed guitar. According to Springsteen, "I sat directly across from him and played 'Saint in the City.' When I was done I looked up . . . and I heard him say, 'You've got to be on Columbia Records.' One song—that's what it took." Not long after, Springsteen was signed and began recording his debut album, *Greetings from Asbury Park, N.J.* (p60 uk41, 1973).

Americana on Both Sides of the Pond: John Mellencamp and Dire Straits. Emerging in 1979 with the radio hit "I Need a Lover" under the name John Cougar, John Mellencamp made his commercial and critical mark with his third album, *American Fool* (1982). The album topped the U.S. charts and contained the hits "Hurts So Good" (p2) and "Jack and Diane" (p1). Mellencamp followed up with *Scarecrow* (p2, 1985), featuring "Small Town" (p6). Like Springsteen's constant depiction of working-class New Jersey, Indiana-born Mellencamp embraced an image of a small-town Midwesterner. His songs show an interest in characters who are plainspoken, not fancy, and interested in social justice and emotional self-understanding. This homespun image was also projected musically through the use of traditional rock instrumentation and no-frills songwriting, making Mellencamp a foundational figure in the strain of new traditionalism commonly called Americana.

The English band Dire Straits, on the other hand, represented America through a much different lens. Led by singer-songwriter-guitarist Mark Knopfler, the band emerged during the first excitement of new wave in late 1978 with *Dire Straits* (p2 uk5), which featured the single "Sultans of Swing" (p4). The song celebrates the virtues of anonymous jazz virtuosos and features Knopfler's accomplished guitar playing, rendered without the usual amplifier distortion characteristic of 1970s mainstream rock. In the early 1980s, Dire Straits had markedly better luck in the UK than in America. The band's reemergence as international chart-toppers came with *Brothers in Arms* (p1 uk1, 1985), containing the hit "Money for Nothing" (p1 uk4). Sting (from the Police, discussed next) provided background vocals on the song and it was supported by an innovative music video that went into heavy rotation on MTV, despite its critique of that station. Like the other new traditionalists, Dire Straits employed a no-nonsense approach in their music, with a strong respect for older styles and a simpler, more transparent approach to production.

Keepers of the Wave: The Police and U2. Another successful band to emerge into the rock mainstream from the new wave movement was the Police. Formed in England by Brits Andy Summers (guitar) and Sting (bass and vocals), and American Stewart Copeland (drums), the band's first hit single, "Roxanne" (p32 uk12, 1979),

Featuring bassist and lead singer Sting, guitarist Andy Summers, and drummer Stewart Copeland, the Police were one of the most popular rock bands of the 1980s. They combined the hard-driving guitar sound of punk, reggae's rhythmic complexity, and serious-minded lyrics to create eight Top 10 hits in the United States during the early 1980s.

showed a strong reggae influence. Although the group's first album, *Outlandos d'Amour* (p23 uk7, 1979), picked up on the return-to-simplicity approach of punk, the group clearly were interested in creating sophisticated musical arrangements along with self-consciously poetic lyrics. The title of the band's fifth album, *Synchronicity* (p1 uk1, 1983), for instance, is drawn from the psychological writings of Carl Jung. The music of the Police dominated rock in the first half of the 1980s. Eight singles placed in the American Top 20 during that time, and while only one of these ever went to number one ("Every Breath You Take" in 1983), the band's music was a staple of FM rock radio. "Don't Stand So Close to Me" illustrates the band's musical approach. The music is spare and skillfully executed, creating a mysterious atmosphere to go with Sting's lyrics, which tell of a teacher's unhealthy romantic attraction to his young student. Andy Summers's guitar playing is more focused on creating washes of sound than soloing, and Copeland's drumming lays down an often complex rhythmic grid beneath the other instruments. There is a sense of agitation in this song that reflects the uneasiness of the teacher who, according to the lyrics, ends up being publicly accused.

As the Police's active career was coming to a close in the mid-1980s, Ireland's U2 was just getting started. The band's first five albums made good showings, including *War* (p12 uk1, 1983) and *The Unforgettable Fire* (p12 uk1, 1984). With 1987's *The Joshua Tree* (p1 uk1, 1987), however, U2 began a string of enormously successful albums that continues to the present day. U2 built on the sophisticated approach of the Police: both bands wrote simple songs but arranged them in innovative ways. Lead singer Bono's lyrics often strive for a poetic quality, while lead guitarist the Edge layers sound behind Bono's voice to create a rich backing texture. The band often composed their songs by improvising in the studio, then leaving producers such as Brian Eno and Daniel Lanois to collate and reassemble the most compelling material. "Pride (In the Name of Love)" illustrates some of the musical features of U2's music from the middle of the decade. The Edge plays repeated-note figures on the guitar, soaked in echo, that provide one of the band's most recognizable sonic signatures. During the verses, Bono delivers accounts of people who have given their lives in the name of love, including Dr. Martin Luther King Jr., while his wailing on the chorus underscores the passion of the cause for which their lives were given. U2 has remained an important band, with a string

Listening Guide

The Police, "Don't Stand So Close to Me" A&M AMS-7564

Words and music by Sting, produced by the Police and Nigel Gray. Rose to #1 on the UK charts and #10 on the *Billboard* "Hot 100" in the United States in 1981. Also contained on the album *Zenyatta Mondatta*, which also hit #1 in the UK and #5 in the United States.

FORM: Contrasting verse-chorus. Notice how each verse builds up a bit more, adding new parts with each occurrence—an arranging approach we have seen often. The timbre-rich instrumental verse thus arrives as a natural extension of this process. The lyrics describe a teacher who is attracted to an underage student. The agitation in the music, and perhaps the central instrumental verse, attempt to capture this sense of uneasiness.

TIME SIGNATURE: 4/4.

INSTRUMENTATION: Drums, bass, guitars, synthesizer, lead and backing vocals.

0:00–0:37	**Introduction**	Free-form synthesizer and guitar sounds establish a mysterious texture to open the track, and then drums usher in 4-bar reggae-inspired vamp as groove locks in.
0:37–1:04	**Verse 1**, 16 mm.	Lead vocal enters, accompanied by a quiet repeating guitar line, two-part harmony on second half of verse, "Young teacher . . ."
1:04–1:19	**Chorus**, 9 mm.	Harmony vocals, as music gets fuller and louder, "Don't stand so close . . ."
1:19–1:46	**Verse 2**, 16 mm.	As before, but sung higher and with added guitar parts. Harmony vocals on second half of verse are also sung higher, creating a sense that the song is getting more intense. "Her friends are so jealous . . ."
1:46–2:02	**Chorus**, 9 mm.	As before, "Don't stand so close . . ."
2:02–2:29	**Verse 3**, 16 mm.	As in verse 2, "Loose talk in the classroom . . ."
2:29–2:48	**Chorus**, 11 mm.	As before, "Don't stand so close . . ."
2:48–3:15	**Instrumental verse**, 16 mm.	Synthesizer sweeps added. Are these sounds meant to capture the emotional confusion of the main character in the song?
3:15–3:29	**Chorus**, 8 mm.	As before, but with counter line added in vocals. "Don't stand so close . . ."
3:29–3:42	**Chorus**, 8 mm.	Repeated with counter line.
3:42–3:56	**Chorus**, 8 mm.	Repeated again as song fades out.

Bono (left) and the Edge (right) of U2, performing in California in 1983. Based on the often-topical lyrics of Bono and layers of guitar produced by the Edge, U2 produced hard-driving rock hits that often tackled serious social issues.

of successful albums and sold-out tours, while Bono has become an outspoken advocate for humanitarian issues.

Old School Newcomers: AC/DC and Huey Lewis and the News. While older, more established bands continued to thrive and a host of new styles arrived on the scene, it was still possible for new acts to enjoy success playing music that seemed more suited to an earlier time. Neither AC/DC nor Huey Lewis was aligned with the new traditionalists or new wavers, and both of these groups harkened back to earlier music. Thus these two vastly different groups offer an interesting comparison of bands that drew on earlier music in very different ways. The music of AC/DC is strongly influenced by the British blues rock of bands like Led Zeppelin and Deep Purple. This Australian group did not make its first important mark on the U.S. charts (and on American radio) until the 1970s were almost over. AC/DC had formed in 1973—during the salad days of British blues rock—and established themselves at home in Australia. But with the release of *Highway to Hell* (p17 uk8) in 1979, the band's music broke in the United States, driven by the powerful lead guitar playing of Angus Young and the raspy vocals of Bon Scott. Scott died tragically in 1980, and did not live to enjoy the band's American success. He was replaced by Brian Johnson, and the band did not skip a beat on the charts, as *Back in Black* (p4 uk1, 1980) and the rereleased *Dirty Deeds Done Dirt Cheap* (p3, 1981) further established AC/DC's position as old-school rockers and influenced the heavy metal bands that were beginning to assemble in places like Southern California.

Unlike AC/DC, who were earnestly interested in classic rock, Huey Lewis and the News made a trademark of being somewhat out of step with the times, perhaps best exemplified by their 1986 hit "Hip to Be Square" (p3). Veterans of the San Francisco rock scene of the 1970s, the band formed in 1980 and scored their first chart success in 1982 with "Do You Believe in Love" (p7 uk9). The albums *Sports* (1983) and *Fore!* (1986) topped the U.S. album charts and the song "The Power of Love" hit number one in 1985 after it appeared in the film *Back to the Future*. Huey Lewis and the News videos ran in regular rotation on MTV, and their songs became fixtures of FM rock radio. The easy-rockin', sunny, and wholesome feel of much of

Listening Guide

U2, "Pride (In the Name of Love)"   Island 99704

Words and music by U2, produced by Brian Eno and Daniel Lanois. Single rose to #3 in the UK and #33 on the *Billboard* "Hot 100." Also contained on the album *The Unforgettable Fire*, which went to #1 in the UK and #13 in the United States in 1984.

FORM: Compound AABA. The A sections employ simple verse-chorus structure that is based on the same chord pattern, while the B section presents a new melody in the guitar, supported by a new chord progression, as well as a return to the introduction.

TIME SIGNATURE: 4/4.

INSTRUMENTATION: Electric guitars, bass, drums, lead and backing vocals. Notice the use of the repeated-note guitar sound throughout, and how avoiding that repeated-note sound in verses 2 and 3 adds excitement to its return.

	0:00–0:28	**Introduction**, 12 mm.	Rhythmic guitar with echo featured with drums before bass enters and song begins the repeated progression that will form the basis of the verse and chorus.
A	0:28–0:46	**Verse 1**, 8 mm.	Vocal enters over music established in the introduction, sung in the middle register. "One man come in the name of love . . ."
	0:46–1:04	**Chorus**, 8 mm.	Vocal continues over same music, but now sung higher and with more urgency. "In the name of love . . ."
A	1:04–1:23	**Verse 2**, 8 mm.	As before, but rhythmic guitar gives way to broad arpeggios to create a sense of contrast. "One man come on a barbed-wire fence . . ."
	1:23–1:41	**Chorus**, 8 mm.	As before, as rhythmic guitar returns, "In the name of love . . ."
B	1:41–1:58	**Bridge** (instrumental), 8 mm.	Contrasting music featuring a repeated guitar melody consisting of a three-note figure repeated as an echo, but in tempo.
	1:58–2:26	**Re-intro**, 12 mm.	Same material as intro, last 4 mm. hummed. The technique of restarting a song by returning to the introduction can be traced back to "Purple Haze" and can be seen in much 1970s music.
A	2:26–2:44	**Verse 3**, 8 mm.	As in verse 2, with broad guitar arpeggios. "Early morning, April 4 . . ."
	2:44–3:02	**Chorus**, 8 mm.	As before, as rhythmic guitar returns. "In the name of love . . ."
	3:02–3:21	**Chorus**, 8 mm.	As before, but backup vocals add countermelody.
	3:21–3:47	**Coda**, 8 mm. + fade-out	Same material as verse, chorus, and intro, as Bono improvises on the song's melody.

their music stood in stark contrast to some of the edgier music of the decade, and made them favorites for listeners who yearned for the days when pop music was more often fun than scandalous.

Blue-Eyed Soul, '80s Style: Hall and Oates, George Michael, and Michael Bolton.

A strain of traditionalism emerged in the 1980s among white artists who were strongly influenced by 1960s black pop styles. Daryl Hall and John Oates can probably claim the most direct connections to late 1960s and early 1970s rhythm and blues, since Hall grew up in Philadelphia and had worked with Leon Huff, Kenny Gamble, and Thom Bell. Hall and Oates's soul-drenched singing fueled their first American hits, "Sara Smile" (p4 r23, 1976) and "Rich Girl" (p1, 1977), and developed into a more mainstream sound with the release of *Private Eyes.* The album rose to number five on the U.S. charts in 1981 (r11 uk8), and contained two number-one hits, "Private Eyes" and "I Can't Go for That." Hall and Oates later released *Big Bam Boom* (p5 uk28, 1984), which featured another number-one hit, "Out of Touch," and established the duo as the most important American "blue-eyed" soul act of the early 1980s.

The British duo Wham! (George Michael and Andrew Ridgeley) were stylistically similar to Hall and Oates, and emerged at the height of Hall and Oates's popularity. Michael produced the albums and wrote much of the material, as Wham! scored first in the UK with *Fantastic* (uk1, 1983). The next year, the duo reached number one on both sides of the Atlantic with the aptly titled *Make It Big,* which had three U.S. number-one hits—"Wake Me Up before You Go-Go" (uk1), "Careless Whisper" (r8 uk1), and "Everything She Wants" (r12)—and a single that rose to number three: "Freedom" (uk1). Despite the success of Wham!, Michael decided to go solo, releasing the chart-topping *Faith* (p1 r1 uk1, 1987), fueled by four number-one hits and two Top 5 hits in the

Hall and Oates found success throughout the 1980s performing a style of "blue-eyed" soul that drew from their connection to Philadelphia. Here, the duo performs in 1985 at New York's famous Apollo Theater.

George Michael and Andrew Ridgeley of Wham! in concert, 1984. Michael's singing had roots in 1960s rhythm and blues, and he enjoyed hits with Wham! ("Wake Me Up before You Go-Go" [1984]) and as a solo artist ("Faith" [1987]). Like Madonna, Boy George, and Prince, Wham! often projected images of androgyny, and became icons in the gay community.

United States, with three of these scoring in the British Top 10 as well. Michael's music, both with Wham! and as a solo act, is deeply indebted to the soulful singing of 1960s black pop, continuing a tradition established by earlier British singers such as Joe Cocker and Steve Winwood. In the wake of George Michael's international success, American Michael Bolton emerged with two moderately successful singles, "That's What Love Is All About" (p19, 1987) and a cover version of Otis Redding's classic "(Sittin' on) the Dock of the Bay" (p11, 1988). Bolton escorted blue-eyed soul into the 1990s with his *Soul Provider* (p3 uk4, 1990), which ascended the charts on both sides of the Atlantic powered by three Top 10 American hits, including "How Am I Supposed to Live without You" (p1 uk3). Bolton soon became one of the most successful singers of the first half of the 1990s, further reinforcing his strong debt to 1960s soul by covering Percy Sledge's "When a Man Loves a Woman" (p1 uk8, 1991). Unlike Wham! and Michael, however, Bolton never found success with African American audiences, showing an interesting difference in reception between two of the most popular blue-eyed soul singers during the 1980s.

ADAPTING TO NEWER STYLES: OLDER MUSICIANS IN THE 1980s

The Dinosaurs Adapt. Even though the progressive rock style had died out by the end of the 1970s, the musicians associated with this movement remained active and in many cases enjoyed far more commercial success in the 1980s. By streamlining their sound and making it more accessible and radio friendly, members of Yes, Genesis, and Emerson, Lake & Palmer remained in the mainstream rock limelight with chart-topping albums and sold-out tours. While many had predicted the extinction of these progressive rock dinosaurs, the musicians instead adapted to changes in the pop climate and revitalized their careers. The success of these older musicians made it apparent that the rock mainstream was no longer confined to young artists, and that rock musicians could have careers that lasted decades.

From Genesis to Corporation. When Peter Gabriel left Genesis in the middle of the 1970s, drummer Phil Collins took over the lead vocal duties, and initial predictions were that the group would probably lose some of its popularity. However, a series of albums in the early 1980s solidified the band's shift to a poppier style, as *Duke* (p11 uk1, 1980), *Abacab* (p7 uk1, 1981), and *Invisible Touch* (p3 uk1, 1986) went to the top of the charts, with the single "Invisible Touch" hitting the number-one spot in the United States (uk15). At the same time, individual members of Genesis enjoyed success outside the band. As a solo artist, Phil Collins released *Face Value* (p7 uk1) in 1981, which contained the single "In the Air Tonight" (p19 uk2)—a track that received significant radio play. Collins followed up in 1985 with *No Jacket Required*, which topped the charts in both the United States and the UK, producing the hits "One More Night" (p1 uk4) and "Sussudio" (p1 uk12). He scored again in 1989 with . . . *But Seriously* (p1 uk1), which contained "Another Day in Paradise" (p1 uk2). Collins's solo music eschewed the philosophical lyrics, sophisticated harmonies, and extended forms of earlier Genesis music in favor of direct lyrics, simple harmonies, and tight, radio-friendly arrangements. Collins was not the only member of Genesis to achieve popular success during the 1980s. Bassist Michael Rutherford led Mike + the Mechanics, whose first album did moderately

Peter Gabriel's classic "Sledgehammer" video used many types of animation and creative camera techniques to produce a stunning visual effect. The ambitious impulse of these videos suggests that some elements of the hippie aesthetic were still viable in the 1980s.

Listening Guide

Peter Gabriel, "Sledgehammer" Geffen 28718

Words and music by Peter Gabriel, produced by Daniel Lanois and Peter Gabriel. Rose to #1 on the *Billboard* "Hot 100" in 1986 (uk4). Contained on the album *So*, which reached #2 in the States (uk1).

FORM: This track falls into two large sections, consisting of a contrasting verse-chorus form in the first half followed by a simple verse form in the second. The influence of southern soul is obvious throughout the track, and this two-part form may be modeled on tracks like Aretha Franklin's "Respect," which have a high-energy ending filled with vocal improvising. The lyrics mark the song as a tribute to hokum blues songs such as Big Joe Turner's "Shake, Rattle, and Roll."

TIME SIGNATURE: 4/4.

INSTRUMENTATION: Drums, bass, guitar, piano, synthesizers, brass, percussion, lead and backup vocals.

A	0:00–0:30	**Introduction**, 12 mm.	Rhythm and blues horns play a repeated melodic line, propelled by a driving beat.
	0:30–1:00	**Verse 1**, 12 mm.	Vocals enter, as the lyrical allusions remain fairly innocent. Organ comes in. "You could have a steam train . . ."
	1:00–1:20	**Verse 2**, 8 mm.	As before, the allusions get a little sexier. "You could have a big dipper . . ."
	1:20–1:40	**Chorus**, 8 mm.	Backup vocals are added, "I want to be your sledgehammer . . ."
	1:40–1:51	**Interlude**, 4 mm.	Accompanimental groove continues.
	1:51–2:11	**Verse 3**, 8 mm.	Horn line added, as lyrics push a little further. "Show me 'round your fruit cage . . ."
	2:11–2:31	**Chorus**, 8 mm.	As before, "I want to be . . ."
	2:31–2:51	**Chorus**, 8 mm.	As before, "I'm gonna be . . ."
	2:51–3:01	**Interlude**, 4 mm.	Creates transition to second section.
B	3:01–3:21	**Verse**, 8 mm.	Spacey synthesizer melody, based on new musical material.
	3:21–3:41	**Verse**, 8 mm.	Vocal enters, note the gospel-style call-and-response backup vocals, "I kicked the habit . . ."
	3:41–4:00	**Verse**, 8 mm.	Vocal harmony added to lead vocal, "Show for me . . ."
	4:00–4:21	**Verse**, 8 mm.	Lead vocal improvisation begins, as arrangement builds, "Show for me . . ."
	4:21–4:40	**Verse**, 8 mm.	Vocal improvising continues, influenced by southern soul, as song seems to fade out. "Show for me . . ."
	4:40–4:49	**Interlude**, 4 mm.	Drumbeat continues alone until snuffed out electronically.

well (p26, 1985) and produced two Top 10 hits, "Silent Running" and "All I Need Is a Miracle" (p6, 1986). The next release, *The Living Years* (p13 uk2, 1988), did even better, producing the hit single "The Living Years" (p1 uk2). Former Genesis frontman Peter Gabriel had a commercial breakthrough in 1986 with *So* (p2 uk1), featuring the hits "Sledgehammer" (p1 uk4) and "Big Time" (p8 uk13), both of which were the subject of innovative videos that received lots of MTV airplay. "Sledgehammer" offers an opportunity to see the roots of rock and roll in what may be considered an unlikely place. The lyrics to this track are Gabriel's tribute to the double entendre discussed in Chapter 1 with Big Joe Turner's "Shake, Rattle, and Roll," as Gabriel playfully alludes to sexuality throughout. The two-part form seems to hark back to southern soul, where the end of the song becomes a kind of loose jam of a groove, as occurs in Aretha Franklin's "Respect." Gabriel's follow-up to *So*, *Us* (p2 uk2, 1992), established him as one of the most influential songwriters of the 1990s.

Going for the One: Yes and Asia.
By the end of the 1970s, singer Jon Anderson and multikeyboardist Rick Wakeman had left Yes, replaced by Trevor Horn and Geoff Downes, who existed separately as the synth-pop band the Buggles (it was their "Video Killed the Radio Star" that inaugurated MTV). The band released *Drama* (p18 uk2, 1980), which would prove to be the last gasp of '70s prog, and then Downes, Horn, and guitarist Steve Howe left the group. Yes recruited Trevor Rabin, a South African singer-songwriter-guitarist who had regional success with Rabbitt in the mid-1970s and had since released a couple of solo albums. With Anderson back in the band and with Horn now producing, Yes released *90125* (p5 uk16, 1983), an album full of Rabin rockers, one of which, "Owner of a Lonely Heart," gave the band its first-ever number-one single in the United States (uk 28). Howe and Downes had also been busy after leaving Yes, forming Asia with drummer Carl Palmer and King Crimson bassist–lead vocalist John Wetton. The band's first album, *Asia* (uk11), topped the charts in the United States in 1982, spawning the hit singles "Heat of the Moment" (p4) and "Don't Cry" (p10). The next album, *Alpha* (p6 uk5, 1983), continued the band's success, though Howe left to form G.T.R. with former Genesis guitarist Steve Hackett. That band's only album, *G.T.R.* (p11, 1986) produced an American hit single, "When the Heart Rules the Mind" (p14) in the same year that keyboardist Keith Emerson and bassist–lead vocalist Greg Lake regrouped, this time with veteran drummer Cozy Powell aboard, to release *Emerson, Lake & Powell* (p23, 1986).

I Will Survive: Rock Bands Continue to Thrive.
If progressive rock musicians maintained a central role in rock long after their predicted demise, they were not alone. Many bands and artists from the 1960s and 1970s remained active during the 1980s without changing their stylistic approach. Foreigner, for instance, continued to dominate mainstream rock with albums such as *4* (p1 uk5, 1981) and *Agent Provocateur* (p4 uk1, 1984), the latter of which had the hit ballad "I Want to Know What Love Is" (p1 uk1). Styx continued their interest in science fiction themes with *Kilroy Was Here* (p3, 1983), including "Mr. Roboto" (p3), while Boston contributed *Third Stage* (p1, 1986), with the hit "Amanda" (p1). David Bowie's *Let's Dance* (p4 uk1, 1983) saw him returning to the rhythm and blues orientation of earlier

Sound Check

Artist	Song	Sound
Michael Jackson	Billie Jean (1983)	Form: simple verse-chorus (modified) Pre-chorus offers contrasting material Jackson performs all vocal parts Repeating bass line is central to the form
Madonna	Like a Virgin (1985)	Form: compound AABA Intricate synthesizer work (bass, horns, strings, electric piano) Verse 3 is a partial repeat of verse 2 Contrast between acoustic drums and synthesized sounds
Prince	1999 (1982)	Form: contrasting verse-chorus Prince performs all instruments Lead vocals alternate between several members of the Revolution The last two minutes are an extended coda
Bruce Springsteen	Born in the U.S.A. (1984)	Form: simple verse-chorus Based on important two-bar melodic figure Lyrics to verses 4 and 5 are incomplete, depicting abandonment Extended coda
The Police	Don't Stand So Close to Me (1981)	Form: contrasting verse-chorus Gradual dynamic increase in introduction leading directly into verse 1 Verse 2 more intense because vocals are delivered in a higher octave Reggae influence in rhythm
U2	Pride (In the Name of Love) (1984)	Form: compound AABA Rhythmic guitar with echo Vocal range changes intensity; verses sung lower, choruses sung higher Lyrics address social issues
Peter Gabriel	Sledgehammer (1986)	Form: contrasting verse-chorus/simple verse Two large sections (A and B), that use different formal structures Sexual innuendo in lyrics Influence of rhythm and blues in horns, rhythmic groove, and vocal improvisation

records while enjoying a number-one hit on both sides of the Atlantic. Billy Joel's *An Innocent Man* (p4 uk2, 1983) featured some of his strongest material to date, including "Tell Her about It" (p1 uk4) and "Uptown Girl" (p3 uk1). He continued his success with *Storm Front* (p1 uk5, 1989), which contained "We Didn't Start the Fire" (p1 uk7). The Rolling Stones seemed not to be slowed much by age, as *Tattoo You* (p1 uk2, 1981) produced the classic "Start Me Up" (p2 uk7), and subsequent albums like *Undercover* (p4 uk3), *Dirty Work* (p4 uk4, 1986), and *Steel Wheels* (p3 uk2, 1989) topped charts worldwide. Paul McCartney achieved notable success in the 1980s as well, hitting the number-one slot in both Britain and America with 1982's *Tug of War*. In many ways, the 1980s made it clear that rock artists need no longer think of their careers as only a few years in the sun. Rock careers could in fact span decades, and acts could successfully continue even after the style with which they were originally associated had passed from popular favor.

During the 1980s, MTV and the video age challenged some of rock's deeply held values. The centrality of video images seemed to take attention away from the music itself. Viewed from a broader historical perspective, however, the ambitious scope of some music videos—and especially those of Michael Jackson, Madonna, and Eurythmics—clearly reinterpreted and redirected at least one aspect of the musical ambition that developed in the decade after *Sgt. Pepper*. Just as concept albums in the 1970s pushed at the boundaries of rock by exploring a variety of musical styles while pursuing serious-minded themes, music videos in the 1980s followed a similar path. However, the focus in the 1980s shifted to making music and image work together to create a compelling synthesis. In this case, there was certainly a strong element of artistic ambition. The music videos of the 1980s provide an important aesthetic connection to rock's past that is often missed by critics who focus more on the differences between 1970s and 1980s music than on the underlying continuities.

In addition to MTV, a generation of "new traditionalists" emerged during the early 1980s, earnestly employing the sounds and images of older forms of rock. These groups revisited older styles at face value with a concern for returning rock to its core aesthetic values. While some aspects of the punk movement developed into commercial forms of new wave, the 1980s also saw an emerging underground hardcore movement in various locations across the United States. In the next chapter, we explore how heavy metal, rap, and alternative rose from their respective underground scenes during the 1980s to emerge as important styles by the end of the decade.

For Additional Online Resources, visit:
digital.wwnorton.com/whatsthatsound5

FURTHER READING

Saul Austerlitz, *Money for Nothing: A History of the Music Video from the Beatles to the White Stripes* (Continuum, 2007).

Stewart Copeland, *Strange Things Happen: A Life with the Police, Polo, and Pygmies* (It Books, 2009).

Jason Draper, *Prince: Chaos, Disorder, and Revolution* (Hal Leonard, 2011).

Bill Flanagan, *U2 at the End of the World* (Delacorte Press, 1995).

Thomas Harrison, *Music of the 1980s* (Greenwood, 2011).

Michael Jackson, *Moonwalk* (Harmony Books, 2009).

Craig Marks and Rob Tannenbaum, *I Want My MTV: The Uncensored Story of the Music Video Revolution* (Dutton, 2011).

Dave Marsh, *Born to Run: The Bruce Springsteen Story, Volume 1* (Thunder's Mouth Press, 1996).

Dave Marsh, *Glory Days: Springsteen in the 1980s* (Thunder's Mouth Press, 1996).

Tom McGrath, *MTV: The Making of a Revolution* (Running Press, 1996).

June Skinner Sawyers, *Racing in the Street: The Bruce Springsteen Reader* (Penguin, 2004).

Bruce Springsteen, *Born to Run* (Simon & Schuster, 2016).

Joseph Vogel, *Man in the Music: The Creative Life and Work of Michael Jackson* (Sterling, 2011).

Warren Zanes, *Petty: The Biography* (Henry Holt, 2015).

Paul Zollo, *Conversations with Tom Petty* (Omnibus, 2005).

CHAPTER 12

HEAVY METAL, RAP, AND INDIE ROCK

CHAPTER PREVIEW

- Heavy metal developed out of a return-to-heavy-rock movement in the late 1970s in northern England and Los Angeles, remaining largely out of the mainstream except for a few acts such as Ozzy Osbourne, Black Sabbath, and Van Halen.

- Heavy metal began to break into the mainstream in the mid-1980s with the tremendous success of Bon Jovi and Guns N' Roses. Bands like Metallica took metal in a more ambitious direction in the late 1980s.

- Rap developed out of the hip-hop culture of New York, with roots in Jamaican music party traditions. DJs such as Grandmaster Flash and Afrika Bambaataa developed techniques for extending songs and scratching.

- Def Jam, led by Russell Simmons and Rick Rubin, helped rap cross over to a rock audience by employing electric guitar hooks and enlisting Aerosmith to record with Run-DMC.

- As rap became more mainstream, groups such as Public Enemy, KRS-One, and N.W.A become more political, challenging the status quo and reflecting on the problems of urban life.

- By the end of the 1980s, heavy metal and rap both emerged into the mainstream, as reflected by the popularity of MTV shows such as *Yo! MTV Raps* and *Headbangers Ball*.

- Extending the late-1970s punk scene, hardcore music developed in underground regional scenes around the country, including Los Angeles, Minneapolis, and Washington, D.C.

- With the help of college radio, a national indie rock scene developed outside of the mainstream, giving listeners an alternative to FM radio and MTV. Indie and hardcore paved the way for the alternative rock of the 1990s.

Run-DMC's *Raising Hell* (1986) was the first rap album to have a major impact on white audiences. This crossover appeal was driven by Run-DMC's sound, which featured strong lyrics mixed with samples from rock music. Their version of Aerosmith's "Walk This Way" exemplified this blend, and the video "duel" between Run-DMC and Aerosmith's Steven Tyler and Joe Perry brought the mix to MTV. The strong sales of *Raising Hell* to both white and black audiences and the consistent airplay of "Walk This Way" on MTV proved to industry professionals that they could make money selling rap, which in turn caused the style to explode into the mainstream.

During the first half of the 1980s, while new wavers, new traditionalists, revamped progsters, and mainstream rockers were sharing the FM radio waves and MTV was transforming the visual aspects of rock music, two underground scenes were developing that would emerge into the pop-music spotlight later in the decade. As happens with most new styles, both rap and heavy metal had their roots in previous music, and this chapter will trace the ways each drew on these earlier musical styles and practices throughout the decade. In the case of both styles, MTV played a crucial role first in exposing the music to a broader audience, and second in marking the success rap and metal artists began to enjoy as these styles began to assume increasingly central positions in popular music in the second half of the decade. Emerging out of late 1970s punk, hardcore and indie developed in underground scenes across the country and mostly off the radar of the mainstream music business during the 1980s. Fueled by fanzines, independent record stores, and college radio, these styles would emerge into the mainstream after heavy metal and rap had already become big business, ultimately playing an important role in the emergence of alternative rock in the early 1990s. The styles discussed in this chapter all developed in underground scenes, emerging later to enjoy tremendous commercial success. In some sense, each of these styles positioned itself as the voice of some disenfranchised segment of the culture. Interestingly, each style was able to keep that sense of identity even in the midst of overwhelming popularity.

HEAVY! DUTY!
HEAVY METAL IN THE 1980S

Heavy Metal Thunder. It is unclear exactly where heavy metal got its name. The phrase *heavy metal thunder* appeared in the lyrics of Steppenwolf's "Born to Be Wild," which became popular in the summer of 1968. Beat writer William Burroughs had also used the phrase in his 1962 novel *The Soft Machine*. Although the origins of the label are unclear, heavy metal's stylistic forebears are much easier to identify. Heavy metal developed out of the harder, more aggressive aspects of rock from the 1960s and 1970s. The garage band music of the Kingsmen and the early punk of the MC5 and the Stooges were early models. Progressive psychedelic songs like Iron Butterfly's "In-A-Gadda-Da-Vida" were also precursors. However, most writers cite the music of Black Sabbath as the earliest form of heavy metal. The gothic character of Sabbath's early music—driving riffs, dark themes, extended guitar solos—was an important source for later metal bands, as was the heavier side of Led Zeppelin's music. Deep Purple's blending of these same musical features with aspects of classical music also served as a model, as did the extravagant showmanship of Alice Cooper and KISS. Yet there are aspects of the music of Led Zeppelin, Alice Cooper, and Deep Purple that heavy metal musicians did not typically adapt and, until the early 1980s, the stylistic features that would prove inspirational to metal musicians existed in music that was not set apart from other rock. Heavy metal as a separate stylistic category did not emerge in a significant way until several bands, developing as part of close-knit musical communities in England and Los Angeles, began to break out of underground venues with the help of successful albums and constant touring.

Blue-Collar Man: Image and Class. It is common to refer to heavy metal musicians and fans as "headbangers," in part owing to fans' tendency to bang their heads in the air while listening to the music. This term captures the sense, shared by many in the music world (however unfairly), that heavy metal music is primitive and its adherents are simple-minded and generally unsophisticated. This image is often compounded by a view of heavy metal as music that appealed specifically to blue-collar white audiences. Stereotypes of heavy metal listeners are prevalent throughout popular culture. More innocent characteristics, such as honesty, loyalty, and unselfish devotion to partying, are exhibited by actors Mike Myers and Dana Carvey in the *Wayne's World* movies (1992 and 1993). More negative metal stereotypes—ignorance, vulgarity, and laziness—are lampooned in the *Beavis and Butthead* cartoon series. In contrast to the general flashiness that characterized successful MTV acts during the early to mid-1980s, it is easy to see how heavy metal bands used their ragged image to oppose the status quo. Even when metal bands portrayed glamour, it was a tawdry, seedy form of glitz more closely associated with strip clubs than the various movements toward high fashion found in mainstream pop music. In any case, metal fans saw this rejection of the commercial status quo as a mark of authenticity and embraced it with enthusiasm, situating metal music as a form of cultural defiance.

The New Wave of British Heavy Metal. During the late 1970s in the UK, punk and new wave were the most visible reactions against mainstream rock released on major labels. Instead of the return-to-simplicity solution offered by punk and new wave, however, musicians that formed the nucleus of the metal scene opted for what might be termed a "return to heavy rock and roll." Many of these bands were from working-class sections of England, north of London. The various members of Black Sabbath, for example, were an important force in the growing heavy rock scene at the end of the 1970s. By 1977, Ozzy Osbourne had quit Black Sabbath to pursue a solo career. The group continued on with Ronnie James Dio taking over lead vocals (he was followed by a series of lead singers throughout the 1980s), while Osbourne recruited virtuoso guitarist Randy Rhoads and released a pair of successful solo albums, *Blizzard of Ozz* (p2 uk7, 1980) and *Diary of a Madman* (p16 uk14, 1981).

While Osbourne and Sabbath became high-profile acts, playing for stadium crowds and enjoying the benefits of past success, other English bands developed their music under the pop-industry radar. Judas Priest had formed in Birmingham in 1970, but it wasn't until 1979 that their album *Hell Bent for Leather* (uk32, 1979) earned them a broader audience in England. The group's next album, *British Steel* (p34 uk4, 1980), achieved success in the United States on the strength of tracks like "Breaking the Law" and "Living after Midnight." Iron Maiden formed outside of London in 1976, and became popular in their home country after the release of *Iron Maiden* (uk4, 1980), breaking into the American market with *The Number of the Beast* (p33 uk1, 1982). Sheffield-based Def Leppard also started from within the emerging British heavy metal scene and became internationally popular after the release of *High 'n' Dry* (p38 uk26, 1981). The group's next album, *Pyromania* (p2 uk18, 1983), showed an increasing interest in venturing into the pop field. This is apparent in the single "Photograph" (p12 uk66), which became more popular in the United States than any of the group's prior releases due, in part, to a video that became an early staple of MTV. Each of these bands, referred to collectively as the "new wave of British heavy metal," emerged into rock's mainstream in the early 1980s and continued to record and tour successfully throughout the decade. Their music was primarily guitar-driven, following the early 1970s model of Black Sabbath and Deep Purple, and often featured pyrotechnical soloing and unrelentingly heavy drumbeats.

Early Los Angeles Bands and the American Heavy Metal Underground.

While a new brand of heavy metal was developing in the north of England, American metal bands were forming their own underground networks. Although metal was not confined to a single place in America, during the 1980s the most prominent metal scene emerged in Los Angeles. In the decade before this scene emerged, Los Angeles had increasingly become the place to "make it" in the music business. As a result, musicians from all over the country migrated to Southern California seeking rock stardom and fame. The hopes and dreams of metal aspirants in Los Angeles were fed by the late 1970s success of Van Halen, who had worked their way up through the scene and enjoyed a series of hit albums. By 1984, however, the relationship between virtuoso guitarist Eddie Van Halen and lead singer David Lee Roth had gone sour. Roth's last album with the band was *1984* (p2 uk15, 1984). After this, Sammy Hagar joined the band as lead singer for the album *5150* (p1 uk16, 1986), and performed with the group for the remainder of the decade.

As the Van Halen personnel saga was playing out, other bands from Los Angeles began to emerge into the mainstream. Quiet Riot was among the first, as their *Metal Health* reached the top spot on the *Billboard* album charts in 1983. The album contained a version of "Cum on Feel the Noize," a hit for the British heavy rock band Slade a decade earlier. Although Quiet Riot did not like the tune and thought they turned in a poor performance, the track went to number five on the singles charts and became a staple of FM radio. Ratt was another Los Angeles metal group that entered the mainstream during the early 1980s. The group's first commercial success, *Out of the Cellar* (p7, 1984), included the hit single "Round and Round" (p12). Mötley Crüe, featuring singer Vince Neil and drummer Tommy Lee, also emerged from the Los Angeles club circuit in 1983 with *Shout at the Devil* (p17) and increased in popularity throughout the decade before releasing *Dr. Feelgood* (p1 uk4, 1989), which became their best-selling album. Mötley Crüe's "Shout at the Devil" is a good example of the kind of guitar-driven, pop-oriented metal that came out of Los Angeles in the mid-1980s. Vince Neil's singing is high, almost screaming, showing the influence of Led Zeppelin's Robert Plant, while the drumming is loud and assertive. The sing-along vocals on the chorus give the song an anthem-like quality, and the band drops out late in the track, allowing the listener to focus on the vocal hook (in live performance, audience members sing along and clap their hands).

In addition to being talented songwriters and musicians, singer David Lee Roth (left) and guitarist Eddie Van Halen (right) were consummate showmen. Onstage, Roth projected a sense of wild, party-animal energy, while Van Halen delivered high-intensity guitar virtuosity.

Spectacular stage shows and outrageous costumes were a central part of 1980s heavy metal. Building on the approach of Alice Cooper, David Bowie, and Kiss from the 1970s, 1980s metal bands regularly used fiery explosions, as seen in this 1986 performance of Mötley Crüe, who often sported spandex clothes and teased hair.

The Rise of the Metal Megastars and Hair Bands. Although Def Leppard had enjoyed significant commercial success in the first half of the 1980s, no American heavy metal band had reached megastar status. The group that broke through this barrier was Bon Jovi, a group based in New Jersey and led by singer Jon Bon Jovi. The group's *Slippery When Wet* topped the U.S. album charts in 1986 (uk6), containing a handful of hit singles, including "You Give Love a Bad Name" (p1 uk14) and "Livin' on a Prayer" (p1 uk4). The band's 1988 follow-up, *New Jersey*, did even better, topping the album charts on both sides of the Atlantic and producing several hit singles, including "Bad Medicine" (p1 uk17) and "I'll Be There for You" (p1 uk18). The group's style was based on the high, soaring vocals of Jon Bon Jovi and virtuosic (but often restrained) guitar work of Ritchie Sambora. Lyrically, Bon Jovi strayed from heavy metal topics of parties and defiance, focusing instead on themes of working-class youth and Americana, revealing a close kinship with the songs of Bruce Springsteen. Despite their origins, by the late 1980s, it was clear that both Def Leppard and Bon Jovi had become too pop-oriented to be considered heavy metal. Both of these groups embraced a more mainstream style, a move that ultimately helped Bon Jovi survive the demise of metal in the 1990s.

Los Angeles–based Guns N' Roses was another American group to emerge from the metal scene as mainstream stars. Singer Axl Rose and lead guitarist Slash fronted the quintet, releasing *Appetite for Destruction* (p1 uk5) in 1987. Guns N' Roses' music often focused on the seedier side of life in Los Angeles, singing openly about drug and alcohol abuse and urban chaos. The group's music featured Rose performing in both a low baritone register and contrasting high, screaming vocals more akin to metal, along with lengthy, melodic guitar solos performed by Slash. Although *Appetite for Destruction* did not achieve success immediately, by the fall of 1988 the singles "Welcome to the Jungle" (p1 uk24) and "Sweet Child o' Mine" (p7 uk24) caught fire on the charts, making Guns N' Roses one of the most successful rock acts of the year. Relationships within the band tended to be stormy even during the best of times, however, and while the group simultaneously released two enormously successful albums in 1991, *Use Your Illusion I* (p2

Listening Guide

Mötley Crüe, "Shout at the Devil" Elektra 60289

Words and music by Nikki Sixx. Produced by Tom Werman. Contained on the album *Shout at the Devil*, which went to #17 on the *Billboard* "Hot LPs and Tape" chart in 1983.

FORM: Compound AABA. The A sections are made up of a verse-chorus pair, while the middle B section features a guitar solo and employs a melodic figure drawn from the introduction. The intro itself begins with 8 measures of guitar, bass, and drums, followed by a statement of the chorus, leading to 4 measures of lead guitar melody. This melody returns not only during the bridge, but also during the coda. In the last A section, the chorus occurs three times, once with only vocals and drums. This repetition places strong emphasis on the anthemic chorus, which is the song's hook. It's easy to imagine a crowd singing along to this chorus during live shows. Notice that the arrangement does not really build much, with verses and choruses throughout the song presented mostly the same way each time.

TIME SIGNATURE: 4/4.

INSTRUMENTATION: Electric guitar, bass, drums, lead and background vocals.

	0:00–0:41	**Introduction,** 16 mm.	Powerful figure played by guitar, bass, and drums in the first 8 bars, then 8 mm. that return as the song's chorus.
A	0:41–1:01	**Verse 1,** 8 mm.	Lead vocals enter. Note the high, almost screaming quality of Neil's voice, reminiscent of Led Zeppelin's Robert Plant. Note also the stops between vocal phrases. "He's a wolf screaming lonely . . ."
	1:01–1:11	**Chorus,** 4 mm.	Catchy backup vocals added. This is the material that appeared in the introduction. "Shout! Shout! . . ."
A	1:11–1:31	**Verse 2,** 8 mm.	As before. "He'll be the love in your eyes . . ."
	1:31–1:41	**Chorus,** 4 mm.	As before. "Shout!"
B	1:41–1:57	**Instrumental bridge,** 6 mm.	Lead guitar solo over material based on the chorus.
A	1:57–2:17	**Verse 1,** 8 mm.	Repeat of first verse, done as before, "He's a wolf . . ."
	2:17–2:27	**Chorus,** 4 mm.	As before, "Shout!"
	2:27–2:37	**Chorus,** 4 mm.	Lead and backup vocals with drums only. This is where the crowd sings along in a live setting. "Shout!"
	2:37–2:47	**Chorus,** 4 mm.	Guitar and bass return. "Shout!"
	2:47–3:12	**Coda and fade,** 8 mm. +	Backup vocals continue, but music changes feel and lead guitar enters after 4 mm. with melody from introduction.

uk2) and *Use Your Illusion II* (p1 uk1), they split up just a few years later.

By the end of the 1980s, the use of costumes and stage makeup by a certain segment of metal groups prompted many listeners to designate these groups as "hair bands." Following the models of Alice Cooper, KISS, David Bowie, and many others, groups like Mötley Crüe wore makeup, outrageous clothes, and heavily teased hair, as did many other metal bands. Poison is one group that took this approach to the extreme. In an interesting contradiction to gender positioning, hair bands often attracted a disproportionate number of female fans. The Poison single "Talk Dirty to Me" (p9, 1987) represents musical and textual stereotypes of Los Angeles hair metal, with its compact form and quick but virtuosic guitar solos and sexist lyrics. Poison's 1986 album *Look What the Cat Dragged In* hit number three in the United States, and *Open Up and Say . . . Ahh!* (p2 uk18, 1988) was even more successful. The latter album contained the hit single "Every Rose Has

Guns N' Roses guitarist Slash and lead singer Axl Rose performing in concert. Guns N' Roses was one of the most popular heavy metal groups in the 1980s emerging from the Los Angeles scene to become worldwide stars. The band's sound featured Rose's multifaceted vocals and melodic guitar work from Slash.

Its Thorn" (p1 uk13), which is a prime example of the "power ballad" genre that became popular in the context of metal during the late 1980s. Power ballads give the singer—in this case, Bret Michaels—a chance to display his sensitive side, as they often begin with a quiet expressive section before the heavy guitars and drums enter, intensifying the arrangement. Other late-1980s hair bands of note are Warrant, who scored with *Dirty Rotten Filthy Stinking Rich* (p10, 1988) and *Cherry Pie* (p7, 1990); Winger, who hit with *Winger* (p21, 1988) and *In the Heart of the Young* (p15, 1990); and Skid Row, who enjoyed success on both sides of the Atlantic with *Skid Row* (p6 uk30, 1989) and *Slave to the Grind* (p1 uk5, 1991).

Poison's C. C. DeVille (left), Bret Michaels (center), and Bobby Dall (right) in a 1987 concert. As representatives of what many people called "hair metal," Poison performed sexist party anthems and power ballads while wearing feminine costumes and makeup.

Metal Ambition. There was clearly a significant amount of empty showmanship in the pop-oriented sector of heavy metal toward the end of the 1980s. However, metal also had its more serious-minded, musically earnest, and ambitious practitioners during this period. Perhaps no metal band fits this description better than Metallica. The band began in Los Angeles but moved to the San Francisco area, where they felt that metal fans had a deeper appreciation of their approach. Like other metalheads, Metallica was influenced by Black Sabbath, Led Zeppelin, and Deep Purple. But the band was also influenced by some of the more serious groups associated with the new wave of British heavy metal, such as Motörhead. Formed by Lemmy Kilmister in the mid-1970s after the bassist had done a stint with Hawkwind, Motörhead brought together the guitar-dominated sound of British blues rock, the hectic tempos of punk, and a love for biker culture. Though influential, Motörhead never enjoyed marked commercial success in the United States, although albums such as *Motörhead* (uk43, 1977), *Ace of Spades* (uk4, 1980), and *Iron Fist* (uk6, 1982) were popular with audiences in England.

Metallica embraced a form called speed metal, which refers to the fast tempos and blazing guitar passages featured in the music of a growing sector of metal bands. Groups such as Metallica, Megadeth, Anthrax, and Slayer explored both speed and thrash metal, the latter allowing for a broader range of musical textures and tempos. Metallica's music indeed displays a wide variety of textures, and this can be found on their early records, such as *Master of Puppets* (p29 uk41, 1986). The band's breakthrough album, . . . *And Justice for All* (p6 uk4, 1988), contains the track "One," a representative example of their music from the late 1980s. Cast in a large-scale two-part form, "One" begins quietly, but gains intensity and speed in its second section. Not to be confused with a power ballad, the complex formal design and ambitious instrumental sections in "One" are far beyond the stylistic confines of pop-oriented music made popular by hair bands, drawing more from the prog-rock influences on 1980s metal. The follow-up album, *Metallica* (p1 uk1, 1991), often called the "black album," marked the group's arrival as one of the most important bands in heavy metal.

Megadeth was another important thrash metal band, whose music combined metal styles and socially conscious themes. Led by former Metallica guitarist and singer Dave Mustaine, Megadeth emerged with the album *Peace Sells . . . but Who's Buying?* (1986). Later releases such as *Countdown to Extinction* (p2 uk5, 1992) and *Youthanasia* (p4 uk6, 1994) were more popular, and marked the band's move into the upper echelon of the *Billboard* charts. New York's Anthrax was another thrash metal band that developed alongside both Metallica and Megadeth. The band's 1987 album *Among the Living* (p62 uk18) also showed an interest in social themes with the song "Indians," and experimented with mixing rap and metal on "I Am the Man." The Los Angeles group Slayer was also an important presence on the thrash metal scene. *Reign in Blood* (p94 uk47, 1986) was the group's first notable

Metallica in concert, 1984. Though their guitar-driven style might seem to connect them with '80s hair bands, Metallica, led by guitarist and singer James Hetfield (right), brought a more musically complex style to heavy metal. Pictured with Hetfield is bassist Cliff Burton (left), who died tragically in a bus crash in 1986.

Listening Guide

Metallica, "One" Elektra 69329

Words and music by James Hetfield and Lars Ulrich. Produced by Metallica with Flemming Rasmussen. Single rose to #35 on the *Billboard* "Hot 100" (uk13) in 1989.

FORM: In the largest sense, this track is in two-part form, and these sections are marked "A" and "B" below. After a lengthy introduction, the A section is in contrasting verse-chorus form, with the addition of the instrumental interlude that appears three times and acts as an instrumental refrain. The fourth time this interlude occurs, it is developed and expanded musically. The second section begins as a simple verse form, but then breaks off into a through-composed instrumental composition.

TIME SIGNATURE: This track begins in 4/4, but the last 9 bars of the introduction shift to 3/4, and the A section stays in 3/4, though extra bars of 2/4 are added throughout, often at the ends of phrases. The chorus is the exception in the first section, as it mixes 4/4 and 2/4. The B section is entirely in 4/4.

INSTRUMENTATION: Two guitars, bass, drums, and lead vocal.

A	0:00–0:20	**Taped war sounds**	Machine-gun fire, helicopter sounds establish the mood.
	0:20–1:31	**Introduction**, 25 mm.	Three 8-bar phrases (the last extended by a measure) then a 9-bar anticipation of the verse using quiet, clean guitar sounds.
	1:31–1:46	**Instrumental interlude**, 8 mm.	This music returns as refrain several times. Music remains quiet and this passage is sunny and might be mistaken for '70s prog-rock.
	1:46–2:13	**Verse 1**, 16 mm.	Lead vocal enters, as mood turns back to quiet and mysterious. "I can't remember anything . . ."
	2:13–2:20	**Chorus**, 4 mm.	Backup vocals enter, music contrasts strongly with verse, turning much heavier and more aggressive, using distorted guitar sounds, "Hold my breath . . ."
	2:20–2:34	**Instrumental interlude**, 8 mm.	Sunny, quiet music from the first interlude returns.
	2:34–3:02	**Verse 2**, 16 mm.	Mysterious, as before. "Back in the womb . . ."
	3:02–3:09	**Chorus**, 4 mm.	Heavy and aggressive, as before. "Hold my breath . . ."
	3:09–3:37	**Instrumental interlude**, 16 mm.	Twice through the returning quiet and sunny interlude music.
	3:37–3:54	**Chorus**, 10 mm.	The heavier and more aggressive 4-bar chorus is repeated once and then extended by 2 bars. "Now the world . . ."

(continued)

	3:54–4:38	**Instrumental interlude (developed)**, 27 mm.	Mostly in 3/4 and in 4-bar phrases, based on the earlier interlude but now much heavier, though still melodic. Toward the end (4:20), a machine-gun rhythm begins in the drums, preparing the way for the next section, while also recalling the taped sounds that began the track.
B	4:38–4:55	**Instrumental transition**, 8 mm.	"Machine-gun" rhythm now played by entire band. This is the most aggressive and angular music so far in the track, and it sets up the mood for the second half of the song.
	4:55–5:13	**Verse 1**, 8 mm.	Lead vocal enters, as the mostly pastoral mood of the first half of the song is shattered by angry aggression. "Darkness imprisoning me . . ."
	5:13–5:22	**Verse 2**, 4 mm.	As before, "Landmine has taken my sight . . ."
	5:22–7:25	**Instrumental finale**, 57 mm.	Mostly in 4/4, this long section can be broken into sections of 12, 13, 14, and 19 mm. Note the tight playing among band members, as well as virtuosic guitar soloing.

album, and spawned a series of moderately successful releases during the 1990s and 2000s, showing the lasting legacy of thrash metal after the 1980s.

Scandinavian Metal. While the rise of heavy metal in the 1980s influenced rock musicians in various locations around the globe (inspiring Brazil's Sepultura), perhaps the most noteworthy region to embrace the style was Scandinavia, where dozens of bands have emerged and a wide variety of metal styles have developed since the early 1980s. In Denmark, Mercyful Fate formed in 1981, while Bathory (named after a song by Venom about a murderous countess) formed in Sweden in 1983. The 1984 Monsters of Rock concert in Stockholm, featuring Van Halen, Mötley Crüe, and AC/DC, was an important moment for Scandinavian heavy metal, bolstering the scene and its devotees. In Norway, Mayhem and Darkthrone emerged in the second half of the 1980s and At the Gates formed in Gothenburg, Sweden, in 1990. The Scandinavian metal scene also made headlines for activities beyond the music when a series of Norwegian churches were set aflame in the 1990s by a significant minority of metal fans who took the dark themes in some of the music far too literally.

The Role of Virtuosity and the Hippie Aesthetic. Many metal bands embraced instrumental virtuosity, and technically demanding instrumental performance is closely associated with the genre. Virtuosic guitar was an especially important element of metal, and many metal guitarists actively cited influential players from hard rock in the 1970s. Some traced their musical pedigree back to Deep Purple's Ritchie Blackmore, for example, whose solo during "Highway Star" is a prime example of proto-metal virtuosity. Eddie Van Halen was a later influence who had developed a distinctive two-hand tapping technique, which can be heard on his solo "Eruption" from Van Halen's eponymous first album. Randy Rhoads was another important originator of guitar technique associated with the metal guitar tradition. Rhoads's style can be heard during the solo section of "Mr. Crowley," from Ozzy Osbourne's *Blizzard of Ozz*. Blackmore, Van Halen, and Rhoads became foundational figures in metal guitar during the late 1970s, inspiring a generation of performers who often took their levels of virtuosity to the extreme. Perhaps the best example of a self-consciously virtuosic metal guitarist from the generation following these leaders was Yngwie Malmsteen. Originally from Sweden, Malmsteen moved to California in 1982, where he played the Los Angeles clubs with Steeler and then Alcatrazz before forming Rising Force. The track "Black Star," from the band's 1984 debut album, showcases Malmsteen's formidable technique, and provides an example of what many fans consider to be virtuosity gone awry.

In many ways, heavy metal—or at least the more technically oriented strain of it—clearly continues the propagation of the hippie aesthetic, and as such, constitutes a direct continuation of late 1960s and '70s sensibilities into the 1980s. In its elevation of classical music models, extended forms, virtuosic solos, and even concept albums devoted to serious-minded issues, heavy metal can be seen as perhaps the most "traditional" style of rock music in the 1980s—an aspect of the music that seems strange for a style that features plenty of leather, chains, hair spray, and makeup.

THE EMERGENCE OF RAP

Rap Music and Hip-Hop Culture. The form of music that we now loosely call rap had its origins in New York's African American and Latino communities during the late 1970s. As a musical form, rap was one element of a larger hip-hop culture, alongside graffiti art, street dance styles such as breaking and popping, and trends in fashion surrounding this movement. Graffiti artists became widespread in New York during the mid-1970s, with artists splashing their names across the city on buildings and subway cars. Subway trains were an especially effective way to broadcast graffiti, since they traveled throughout the city, reaching a wide range of residents along the way. At the same time, a style of creative movement called break dancing became extremely popular. Breaking involved performing athletic movements on a piece of cardboard or hard plastic, a style of artistic movement suited perfectly for urban dwellers. The first break dancers were black and Hispanic teens, whose exciting displays brought the form to the attention of the general public.

The origins of rap music are best understood within this mix of urban art and dancing. The first

As depicted in this image from the early 1980s in the Bronx, New York, the popularity of rap and hip-hop culture crossed racial lines. Early rap heroes like Run-DMC and LL Cool J defined the hip-hop look epitomized here: gold chains, a focus on "name brand" style, and the ubiquitous "boom box"—the portable radio/tape deck combination that allowed people to carry their music with them and share it at a party, or even in public (whether that public wanted to hear it or not).

Views on Metal

Metal emerged from an underground movement to become internationally recognized by the late 1980s. This 1987 *Washington Post* article by music journalist Gerri Hirshey tries to make sense of the metal scene. Like many nonmetal fans from the time, Hirshey is struck by the fashion, gender attitudes, and sheer volume of metal music. She finds striking connections to older forms of rock and seeks to align the "metal urges" of the time with adolescence. Parsing subgenres and mentioning groups that are still discussed by many fans and critics, Hirshey's piece gives us a sense of what many people experienced when they encountered metal for the first time.

Metal is Major in sub-voting-age America, most popular among young males in hormonal crisis. Metal albums are selling millions; metal acts pack big urban arenas and suburban clubs like the Copa in Springfield, Va., where there are enough metal maniacs to support megadecibel bills every Wednesday and Thursday night. You will not hear much heavy metal on the radio; presumably the sound is too much like a diesel wreck to be played during drive time. It is fast, often raunchy, and above all *loud*. The sound is so evocative of industrial-age Armageddon that horror-meister Stephen King—himself an avowed metal head— got the metal band AC/DC to score his recent film "Maximum Overdrive," in which amok appliances and tractor trailers terrorize the Earth. Hollywood has also spoofed metal in Rob Reiner's "This Is Spinal Tap," a hilarious mockumentary about a band with Cro-Magnon esthetics and songs like "Smell the Glove."

It's no accident that metal is big in a decade that supports "Chainsaw Massacre" remakes and folk heroes like Jason, the horror in the hockey mask of "Friday the 13th." Like the slice-and-dice fare pouring out of Hollywood, metal imagery is not pretty: Most album covers look like stills from "Nightmare on Elm Street," heavy on skulls, snakes, insects, chain mail and vague mythic allusions to dungeons, dragons, warlocks—and Old Nob himself.

Here's where some confusion seems to exist. Most metal heads wouldn't think of actually worshipping Satan. But they'd give a month's lawn-cutting money to copy his look. Face it—adolescence can be the ultimate gross-out, all cracked voices, gangly limbs and Clearasil death masks. Intentional Ugly—screaming, atonal vocals, destroyed clothing, heavy makeup—is the perfect camouflage for what nature has temporarily wrought. If you've got to feel hideous for a couple of years, why not make it a ritual affair with thousands of other pimpled pilgrims?

Break dancing, which developed in the late 1970s was, along with graffiti art, a major part of hip-hop culture. As seen here, break dancers choreographed elaborate routines that showed off the acrobatic nature of the style. Like rival rap groups, break dance teams challenged each other to put on the best routine— and put down the competition at the same time.

Live in the head-banger trenches, metal seemed pretty tribal to me. At a Quiet Riot show, I saw thousands of boys in denim and leather. They stood on the arms of the seats (metal heads never sit). They hollered themselves hoarse. Only a few butted heads—and gently, so as not to unglue the 'do. Over and over, they flashed the metal-head descendant of the '60s peace sign—a raised pinkie and forefinger, thrust forward like horns. As one adherent explained, it means "Solid, death-to-conformity, *loud and ugly outrageousness.*"

Peace and love it ain't. But we'd do well to remember that many metal heads are the progeny of Dead Heads. The Grateful Dead are about as menacing as Mister Rogers, but their late-'60s logo was a grinning skull.

Like '60s psychedelia, metal has its roots in California—fittingly, in L.A. rather than San Francisco. Bands like Van Halen, Ratt, Mötley Crüe, Metallica and Slayer were spawned in two-car garages nestled in the Hills of Hype. Now there are metal bands from all over the United States, England, Australia, Japan. Some heavy-metal bands spit stage blood at their audiences; a Christian metal group called Stryper hurls Bibles. There are metal record labels, metal fanzines, metal boutiques and opposing metal camps. The war is mainly over wardrobe.

Semi-ugly, occasionally melodic music sung by pretty boys in spandex and makeup is called Glam metal. Revolting music churned out at hyperspeed and volume by self-proclaimed "maximum disgusto, major uggo" leather mutants is called Thrash or Speed Metal.

The Thrashers are about as attractive as sea slugs. But I will admit to a grudging fascination with the Glam Boys, guys who depend, as a recent MTV special reported, on "Big Hair and Makeup." Mötley Crüe has declared that it simply could not rock without adequate supplies of FlexNet, a spray compound that molds the members' manes into sweat-resistant haystacks.

Members of another Glam group called Poison wear feather boas in their hair; their album is called "Look What the Cat Dragged In." The boys of Sybil, an up-and-coming Glam group, wear women's lingerie.

Since metal is such a macho subgenre, this may still seem puzzling. But listen to the highly hetero lyrics and check out the ideal females pictured on metal men's album covers and tattoos. They, too, are cartoons, with cleavage far deeper than their minds and teensy leatherette wardrobes that would fit inside an album sleeve. Metal men are to the right of Bluebeard when it comes to feminism; they only mess with "chicks" and "old ladies."

Whatever one might think of these retro-politics and Visigoth styles, Ugly is beautiful to many fashion entrepreneurs. Metal magazines carry ads for "explosive rock fashions" featuring "leather, stud and spike work." In Valley Stream, Long Island, there is even a heavy-metal "supermarket" called Slipped Disc. Besides carrying hard-to-find records like "Accused" by Martha Splatterhead and metal literature like *Mega Metal Kerrang!*, owner Mike Schutzman stocks a full line of T-shirts, patches, buttons and stickers. Big spenders can enjoy the "full leather department" featuring bullet, handcuff and demon belts, and leather gauntlets, hand shields, gloves. For in-store appearances by bands like Ratt and Motorhead, says Schutzman, "we get anywhere from 200 to a thousand kids on a Saturday afternoon. Most of them dress up. Which is *down*, if you get what I mean."

Source: Gerri Hirshey, "Metal Urges," *The Washington Post*, January 4, 1987: w30.

hip-hop DJs played records at neighborhood parties, often in city parks or recreation rooms. Adapting a practice from Jamaican DJs, hip-hop DJs would often carry their own sound systems and employ an MC, or "master of ceremonies," to comment on the music and encourage the partygoers. One of the most popular early hip-hop DJs was Kool Herc, who made a practice of bringing his powerful sound system to a local park, using a city power source for electricity, and spinning records loud enough for everyone in the neighborhood to hear. Herc was perhaps the first to use an MC (Coke La Rock). These early MCs would soon develop into rappers, blending this new role with the clever patter of black radio disc jockeys.

Early hip-hop DJs such as Kool Herc and Grandmaster Flash claim credit for technical innovations that would spawn important developments in modern rap. For years, radio stations and dance clubs had used at least two turntables, one for the record being played and a second for the record that would follow. Using a pair of turntables, DJs were able to transition seamlessly from one record to the next, employing a mixing board or a cross-fader to decrease the volume of one record while increasing the volume of the other. Kool Herc and Grandmaster Flash employed portable turntables and mixers based on this set-up. In addition to

Grandmaster Flash was an important figure in the New York hip-hop scene's early years. Here, Flash performs at London's Wembley Arena in 1985.

transitioning from song to song, however, they developed techniques such as "break spinning," in which a DJ repeats a short phrase by spinning one record backward while the other is playing. "Punch phrasing" was another early technique that DJs used to feature short bursts from one record while the other was holding down the beat. The instrumental accompaniment of rap music began to feature "breaks," the catchiest instrumental breaks or passages (often drawn from disco or Latin-music recordings). This was done to incite the dancers to greater excitement, but it also began a technique of creating new music out of recorded "samples"—an idea that would form the aesthetic basis for the rap that followed. Grandmaster Flash also popularized "scratching," a technique in which the record is rotated in the reverse direction and then forward, quickly and repeatedly while manipulating the record's volume, to create a distinctive rhythm.

In addition to the technological expansions of Kool Herc and Grandmaster Flash, another early DJ, Afrika Bambaataa, expanded the range of source recordings employed within hip-hop. Bambaataa had founded Zulu Nation in the early 1970s, a gang-like organization devoted to building a sense of fraternity among hip-hop artists and de-emphasizing the role of fighting and crime in the urban neighborhoods of New York. Known in the community as the "master of the record," Bambaataa incorporated obscure or unlikely tracks such as the Mohawks' "Champ" and Kraftwerk's "Trans-Europe Express" into his mixes.

From the Park to the Radio: The First Rap Records. During the

early years of hip-hop, there were no hip-hop records—mixing records and MCing was strictly a live affair, something you had to experience in person. In 1979, a new label called Sugar Hill Records released "Rapper's Delight," arguably the first hip-hop single. Credited to the Sugar Hill Gang, the record went to number four on the rhythm and blues charts (p36). Before this unexpected success with Sugar Hill, label owners Joe and Sylvia Robinson had run an indie label called All Platinum. Sylvia had enjoyed hit records as half of Mickey and Sylvia ("Love Is Strange," 1957) and as a solo performer ("Pillow Talk," 1973). As the story goes, Sylvia heard guests at a Harlem party chanting rhymes over the instrumental passages in disco records. Thinking this might be catchy enough to sell some records, she rounded up several young men and they "rapped" over a rhythm track drawn from Chic's "Good Times" to produce "Rapper's Delight." The success of this single demonstrated that the live hip-hop experience could indeed be transferred to vinyl. Soon after the success of "Rapper's Delight," Kurtis Blow scored with a hit for Mercury Records, "The Breaks (Part 1)," which went to number four on the rhythm and blues charts in 1980. Meanwhile, Sugar Hill developed into the most important rap label of the early 1980s, signing an impressive roster of rappers and DJs, and releasing a series of classic old-school tracks, including Grandmaster Flash and the Furious Five's "The Message" (p62 r4, 1982).

Russell Simmons and Rick Rubin: Crossing Over to White Audiences.

Russell Simmons and Rick Rubin, two college students at New York University, formed another important early hip-hop label called Def Jam Records. In the mid-to late 1980s, Def Jam released music by the decade's leading rappers, including LL Cool J, the Beastie Boys, and Public Enemy. Simmons's management company, Rush Entertainment, also handled some of rap's top acts, including Run-DMC, Kurtis Blow, and DJ Jazzy Jeff and the Fresh Prince. Through management, label ownership, and production, Simmons and Rubin presided over the most impressive stable of talent on any indie label devoted to rap. Using a basic texture made up of beats generated by an electronic drum machine, highlighted scratching, and the occasional sample or punch phrase, the music of Def Jam artists defined a new style of mainstream hip-hop during the mid-1980s. Moreover, Simmons and Rubin were instrumental in helping popularize rap music in the mainstream.

One of the first successful artists at Def Jam was LL Cool J, whose career was jump-started in 1985 by an appearance in the movie *Krush Groove* and a hit single, "I Can't Live without My Radio" (r15). The song made reference to the growing practice of youth broadcasting music publicly using large portable "boomboxes" (also called "ghetto blasters"). The album *Radio* rose to number six on the rhythm and blues charts in 1986, hitting number forty-six on the pop charts. LL Cool J crossed over in 1987 with "I Need Love" (p14 r1), a track that is perhaps the first rap ballad, while the album *Bigger and Deffer* hit number one on the rhythm and blues album chart (p3).

About the same time, another act associated with Rubin and Simmons was crossing over in an even more direct way. Signed to Priority records but produced and managed by the Def Jam stable, Run-DMC consisted of rappers Joseph Simmons ("Run," Russell's younger brother) and Darryl McDaniels ("DMC"), and DJ Jason Mizell ("Jam Master Jay"). The group enjoyed some crossover success with the single "Rock Box" (r22, 1984), in part because the video for the song was played on MTV. Run-DMC often rapped over breaks from rock records, and this influence can be heard clearly throughout "Rock Box." The band's first album, *Run-D.M.C.* (p53 r14, 1984), is often cited as among the most influential releases of early rap. Two years later, *Raising Hell* (p6 r1, 1986) became a mainstream hit, thrusting Run-DMC into the center of the American music scene.

Another break Run-DMC used frequently was the opening drumbeat from Aerosmith's "Walk This Way." Rick Rubin, a big fan of hard rock and heavy metal who would later go on to produce Slayer and Danzig, invited Steven Tyler and Joe Perry to rerecord tracks for the tune rather than sampling them from the record. The resulting Run-DMC version thus featured both the rappers and the rockers. By using Aerosmith and their music, Rubin and Run-DMC brought rap to many white rockers who probably would have ignored it otherwise, and "Walk This Way" (p4 r8, 1986) became an important record for bringing rap into the pop mainstream.

Def Jam also produced a popular group made up of white rappers. The Beastie Boys had originally been active in the New York hardcore punk scene but transitioned into the emerging hip-hop scene in the early 1980s. After releasing a series of singles that appeared on

Hip-hop pioneer Afrika Bambaataa performing during the early 1980s. Note the two turntables and mixer in the photo. Bambaataa is "scratching" with his left hand and manipulating the mixer with his right.

Listening Guide

Run-DMC, "Rock Box" Profile 5045

Words and music by Larry Smith, Joseph Simmons, and Darryl McDaniels. Produced by Russell Simmons and Larry Smith. Rose to #22 on the *Billboard* "Black Singles" chart in 1984. Contained on the album *Run-D.M.C.*, which hit #14 on the *Billboard* "Black LPs" chart.

FORM: Simple verse. This track features 2-measure vocal phrases played over a repeating 1-measure riff in the accompaniment. In the first verse sections, eight of these 2-bar vocal phrases occur, while in the second verse section twenty such phrases are heard. The last verse section is shorter than either of the previous two, containing only four 2-bar phrases. Interludes 1 and 2 create contrast by focusing the listener's attention on the background music. The coda features segments of relatively free verse, delivered over the same accompaniment found throughout the track.

TIME SIGNATURE: 4/4.

INSTRUMENTATION: Electric guitars, bass, drums, electronic percussion, vocals.

0:00–0:33	**Introduction**, 13-1/2 mm., 1-1/2 mm. pick up, then 12 mm.	Using a sampled beat and multiple distorted, hard-rock guitar melodies.
0:33–1:11	**Verse 1**, 16 mm.	Rapping begins, using eight 2-bar vocal phrases over the repeating guitar riff and beat from the introduction. "For all you sucker MCs . . ."
1:11–1:30	**Interlude 1**, 8 mm.	No vocal, focus on guitars and drums, as repeating guitar riff goes into stop time and multiple guitar melodies cascade.
1:30–3:01	**Verse 2**, 40 mm.	Twenty 2-bar phrases, the first two over only the drumbeat, then the repeated guitar riff returns. The last phrase employs scratching but no rapping. "Because the rhymes I say . . ."
3:01–3:16	**Interlude 2**, 4 mm.	No vocal, with emphasis on drumbeat as music breaks down.
3:16–3:35	**Verse 3**, 8 mm.	Four 2-bar phrases, guitar riff occurs in stop time. "We got all the lines . . ."
3:35–5:27	**Coda and fade**, 44 mm. +	Repeated guitar riff returns and is interrupted with stop time, then continues as lead guitar solos and rappers improvise, creating a long, atmospheric ending section. "Jay, Jay, Jay . . ."

the R&B and dance charts, the group's first mainstream single, "(You Gotta) Fight for Your Right (to Party)," hit number seven on the pop charts in 1987. Their album *Licensed to Ill* became the first rap record to hit number one on the pop album charts (r2, 1986). The Beastie Boys were also among the first bands to take advantage of the new digital sampling technology—instead of working with records and turntables, passages were recorded digitally and looped with far more precision than turntables would allow. By the end of the 1980s, digital sampling was a widespread practice among rappers, beginning a long history of lawsuits over music copyright connected to hip-hop's creative practices.

Challenging the Status Quo. Although Def Jam was a dominant force during the second half of the 1980s, other labels and artists also enjoyed success. Ice-T was born in New Jersey (as Tracy Morrow) but moved to Los Angeles as a child; he became one of the most important representatives of West Coast rap in the late 1980s and early 1990s. "I'm Your Pusher" (r13, 1988) explores the same themes of urban life that had been addressed by black musicians decades earlier, although often in a more graphic and angry manner. The music of Ice-T and other West Coast artists that depicted these stark themes was known as "gangsta rap." Consistent with its influences from the 1970s, the track employs samples drawn from Curtis Mayfield's "Pusherman." While the 1988 album *Power* (p35 r6) did well commercially, Ice-T would enjoy much greater crossover success in the 1990s with *O.G. Original Gangster* (p15 r9, 1991) and *Home Invasion* (p14 r9, 1993).

N.W.A (Niggaz With Attitude) brought an even angrier approach to rap, creating much controversy in the process. The group's 1989 album, *Straight Outta Compton* (p37 r9), contained a track titled "Fuck Tha Police," which earned its record company a warning letter from the FBI. In an interesting historical instance of crossover appeal, this penchant for depicting dangerous urban life appealed strongly to white listeners, many of whom were from the American Midwest. With this support, the 1991 album *EFIL4ZAGGIN* hit number one on the pop album charts (r2), much to the consternation of many parents and community leaders. While Run-DMC used spare musical accompaniment and the Beastie Boys often incorporated samples from the rock repertoire, the music of N.W.A, created in large part by Dr. Dre, often used samples based in harder forms of funk such as Parliament and Kool and the Gang.

In addition to the stark realities explored in gangsta rap, other rap artists began to engage in social and political criticism. Boogie Down Productions (BDP), led

Run-DMC—(from left) MC Darryl McDaniels ("DMC"), DJ Jason Mizell ("Jam Master Jay"), and MC Joseph Simmons ("Run"). Run-DMC combined traditional rap lyrics with rock breaks and samples. They were among the most important innovators in rap, influencing rap and hip-hop throughout the 1980s.

The original line-up of N.W.A included (from left to right): MC Ren, Yella, Eazy-E, and Dr. Dre. By the time this 1990 picture was taken, Ice Cube had left the group and N.W.A's music was driven by Eazy's sometimes exaggerated lyrics and Dre's masterful production.

by KRS-One (Kris Parker), is often cited as the most significant of these artists. The band's first album, *Criminal Minded* (r73, 1987), influenced many rappers who followed in its sometimes uncompromising and harsh depictions of urban life. After the death of rapper Scott La Rock in 1987, the tone of BDP's music changed drastically. In contrast to the anarchistic leanings of N.W.A, KRS-One began to portray himself as an intellectual on songs such as "My Philosophy," from the 1988 album *By All Means Necessary* (p75 r18), whose title and album cover referred directly to Malcolm X. BDP reached the peak of its crossover success with *Ghetto Music: The Blueprint of Hip-Hop* (p36 r7, 1989) and *Edutainment* (p32 r9, 1990).

Building on the rhythmic style of Run-DMC and the social and political approach of BDP, Public Enemy first stormed the rhythm and blues charts in 1988 with *It Takes a Nation of Millions to Hold Us Back* (p42 r1), containing the single "Don't Believe the Hype" (r18). "Fight the Power" (r20, 1989), which also makes direct reference to the black power movement, was featured in Spike Lee's film *Do the Right Thing.* This growing black consciousness resonated with listeners, and the group's next album, *Fear of a Black Planet* (p10 r3, 1990), sold extremely well in pop markets. Led by Chuck D and Flavor Flav, Public Enemy became one of the most influential groups in rap, enjoying their greatest crossover success with *Apocalypse 91—The Enemy Strikes Back* (p4 r1, 1991). Much like the social disarray depicted in their lyrics, Public Enemy's music is often chaotic, featuring heavy layers of samples, drum beats, the "hype man" calls of Flavor Flav, and the deep, sanctified tone and phrasing of Chuck D's vocals.

While many popular rappers during the 1980s were male, Queen Latifah emerged as an important female voice in hip-hop with her 1989 debut, *All Hail the Queen* (r6). Born Dana Owens in Newark, New Jersey, Latifah started out in a hip-hop group called Ladies Fresh before signing as a solo artist with Tommy Boy Records. While *All Hail the Queen* was only a moderate commercial success, it made a large impact

Listening Guide

Public Enemy, "Don't Believe the Hype" Def Jam 652833

Words and music by Carlton Ridenhour, Hank Shocklee, Eric Sadler, and Charles Drayton. Produced by Hank Shocklee and Carl Ryder. Single rose to #18 on the *Billboard* "Hot Black Singles" chart in 1988. Also contained on the album *It Takes a Nation of Millions to Hold Us Back*, which rose to #1 on the "Top Black Albums" chart (p42).

FORM: Simple verse-chorus. The verses are made up of 4-bar vocal phrases; the first verse uses four such phrases, the second uses five, and the third employs ten. The first chorus is also a 4-measure phrase, as is the third. The second and fourth choruses employ an 8-bar structure in which a 4-bar phrase is followed by a contrasting 2-bar phrase and a return to the first phrase. Note how the rhyme schemes and rhythms change often and sometimes cross over from one phrase to the next.

TIME SIGNATURE: 4/4.

INSTRUMENTATION: Vocals, guitar, bass, drums (likely sampled and looped to create a constant and repetitive backdrop). An electronic whistle sound also recurs regularly.

Time	Section	Description
0:00–0:10	**Introduction**, 4 mm.	Electronically sampled and altered sounds over looped groove.
0:10–0:49	**Verse**, 16 mm.	Rapping enters in four 4-bar phrases, as looped groove continues underneath. "Bang, caught you lookin' . . ."
0:49–0:58	**Chorus**, 4 mm.	Recited two 2-bar phrases with nonverbal vocal interjections, "Don't believe the hype . . ."
0:58–1:47	**Verse**, 20 mm.	Rapping now presents five 4-bar phrases, with loop continuing with occasional stop time. "Yes was the start . . ."
1:47–2:07	**Chorus**, 8 mm.	First two 2-bar phrases as before, then one contrasting phrase, followed by a return to first 2-bar phrase.
2:07–3:44	**Verse**, 40 mm.	Rapping now presents ten 4-bar phrases, with loop continuing uninterrupted. Note the exchange of rapped phrases. "Don't believe the hype, it's a sequel . . ."
3:44–4:04	**Chorus**, 8 mm.	The first 4 mm. are without vocals, followed by two 2-bar vocal phrases.
4:04–5:00	**Verse**, 23 mm	Rapping uses five 4-bar phrases, then one 3-bar phrase, "I got flavor . . ."
5:00–5:19	**Chorus**, 8 mm.	As before, two 2-bar phrases, one contrasting phrase, then return to first 2-bar phrase.

Public Enemy's Chuck D (left) and Flavor Flav (center) during the filming of the video for "Fight the Power," directed by Spike Lee. As seen in the bodyguards on stage, Public Enemy forwarded themes of militancy in rap during the late 1980s. Calling attention to underserved communities, Public Enemy railed against racism in the Los Angeles police department with "Burn, Hollywood, Burn" (1990) and decried attitudes toward public services in black neighborhoods in "9-1-1 Is a Joke" (1990).

by establishing a strong female voice in hip-hop. This is exemplified on the single "Ladies First," in which Latifah shares the rapping with Monie Love. The lyrics of this track extol the pleasures of womanhood, dismiss any prejudice that women can't rap, and defiantly assert, "stereotypes, they gotta go." Latifah was nominated for a Grammy and was named Best Female Rapper by *Rolling Stone* in 1990.

Emerging from the male-dominated hip-hop industry in the late 1980s, Dana Owens (a.k.a. Queen Latifah) challenged the stereotype that women couldn't rap. She continues to enjoy a successful recording and acting career.

Fear of a Black Planet? The Flap over Rap. Much like rock and jazz in their early years, rap faced a steady stream of controversy during the 1980s. One strain of criticism surrounded the complaint that rap was not really "music," since most rappers do not play instruments or sing. Even the lyrical content of rap music came under fire. Although it is easy to equate rap with poetry, the offensive words and images employed in some rap, which can be misogynistic, homophobic, vulgar, and violent, have sparked social and legal debate. In the context of our study of rock music, rap again trips the wires of race and class distinctions among some white listeners—a phenomenon that has emerged with many of the most important styles of popular music during the twentieth century. In the 1980s, however, this tension was often portrayed as a conflict between rock and rap, in which rock is seen as the "old guard" and rap as the newcomer.

The video for Run-DMC's "Walk This Way" displays a caricature of the racial tension between rock and rap during the mid-1980s. During the first half of the video, neither Run-DMC nor Aerosmith has much patience with the other, and it is hardly a happy moment of reconciliation when rocker Steven Tyler breaks down the wall that physically separates the two groups. While issues of race and class may have accounted for some of the tension over rap, they also accounted for some of its appeal. Many young white rap fans in the late 1980s and early 1990s were clearly fascinated by the worlds of urban violence and struggle that played a role in much of the harder-edged rap—worlds that were very different from the often affluent and mostly white suburban environment in which they lived (though perhaps not as different as is often imagined). Contrary to claims that rap is not really music, it is worth noting that rap musicians often take preexisting music and refashion it into something new, which has been an accepted aesthetic approach in the visual and musical arts at least since World War II. Many listeners might object to the music of contemporary composers such as John Cage or Karlheinz Stockhausen, but few would go so far as to say that they are not musicians. Anyone who has ever tried to compose hip-hop music can certainly attest to the artistic merits of this form, reminding us that refashioning preexisting material—even if it comes from records—can be just as "musical" as working with new material.

In many ways, rap and heavy metal might have appeared to be in opposition to one another during the second half of the 1980s, but they developed commercially along parallel paths. For example, both styles established devoted followings on MTV as the network gained a foothold as a mainstream tastemaker. *Headbangers Ball* premiered in 1987, playing metal videos exclusively, while *Yo! MTV Raps* debuted in August 1988 and quickly became one of the most popular shows on the network. Both styles also maintained a kind of "outsider" status, depending in large part on class differences—and in the case of rap, race issues. Both styles became emblematic of the lower end of the class spectrum and used this class distinction as part of their appeal, often drawing in middle- and upper-class fans as well.

PUNK GOES HARDCORE

Regional Hardcore. By the end of the 1980s, both heavy metal and rap had emerged from mostly underground scenes to become important forces in rock music. Other scenes remained largely underground and out of the mainstream. Hardcore was one of these styles, developing out of late 1970s punk. This new form of independent music was most closely associated with the Ramones and the UK punk bands, rather than the more conceptual music of first-wave New York punk bands such as Talking Heads or Blondie. Moreover, unlike the more accessible new wave styles that grew from punk and became commercially successful, hardcore continued the raw punk traditions of loud, fast, and aggressive music grounded in the DIY aesthetic. Hardcore bands were usually associated with a major city (or region) and released their music on independent labels. By the end of the 1980s, the hardcore movement had become a national underground movement, with a vast network of performance venues, record labels, and dedicated fans. Although hardcore punk never appeared on national charts, this music was partly responsible for the infrastructure that supported the alternative movement of the 1990s, which will be discussed in Chapter 13.

Los Angeles. One of the epicenters for hardcore music in the United States during the 1980s was Los Angeles. Chronicled in the historic Penelope Spheeris documentary *The Decline of Western Civilization* (1980), a growing discontent among the youth of Los Angeles translated perfectly into a hardcore scene. Although dozens of bands were important contributors to the independent punk-based music of Los Angeles, among the most important were Fear, X, the Germs, the Circle Jerks, and Black Flag. Formed in 1977, Fear was a fixture of the Los Angeles scene that, like so many hardcore bands, performed fast, loud, and distorted music to support the mostly screamed vocals of guitarist and singer Lee Ving. The group is perhaps best known for a 1981 performance on *Saturday Night Live* that went awry. Controversy resulted from several things that occurred on live television, which were perfectly representative of the hardcore scene. First, the group antagonized the New York–based studio audience by performing a song called "New York's Alright if You Like Saxophones," which discussed some of the less-appealing aspects of the Big Apple. Afterward, members of the band openly screamed "New York sucks." Second, the form of physical dancing enjoyed by the fans (called moshing or slam dancing) consisted of listeners running into one another and diving off the stage, which was generally consensual among participants, but seemed chaotic and violent to observers. While these aspects of audience interaction and dancing were common in hardcore clubs, this display was frightening for a nationally televised program, and NBC faded to commercial during the musical performance.

Formed in 1976 by guitarist Greg Ginn, Black Flag was another seminal Los Angeles hardcore band. After several years of name and membership changes (the group's lineup was never stable), Black Flag slowly ingratiated itself to the Los Angeles scene through constant self-promotion and the formation of the SST record label, which became one of the most important independent companies associated with the hardcore movement. Beginning with the 1978 four-song EP, *Nervous Breakdown*, the music of Black Flag represented the burgeoning hardcore movement with rough production values, fast tempos, heavily distorted guitars, screaming vocals, and profane lyrics that exposed youthful alienation. Another feature of this release that became commonplace in hardcore was its brevity. The combined playing time of all four songs was just over five minutes, with the shortest song clocking in at fifty-five seconds. After several lead singer changes, the band settled on Henry Rollins, who became the longest-lasting vocalist for the group. The 1981 album *Damaged* is perhaps the best document of the Rollins-era incarnation of Black Flag, and has since become an icon of the Los Angeles hardcore movement of the early 1980s.

While Fear and Black Flag represented a stereotypical form of hardcore, with music that was loud, fast, and irreverent, the Minutemen, based in San Pedro (the port district of Los Angeles), offered a slightly different take on the movement. Consisting of guitarist and vocalist D. Boon, bassist Mike Watt, and drummer George Hurley, this trio performed music that was loud and fast but lacked the distortion and anarchistic attitude of typical hardcore. Their slogan was "we jam econo." This mantra grew directly out of the DIY movement, signifying that the Minutemen were interested in shedding the excesses of corporate rock. Yet, "econo" also spoke to the group's interest in community and a back-to-basics philosophy that sometimes seemed closer to the hippie aesthetic than hardcore punk. Like other hardcore groups, the music of the Minutemen changed substantially in the mid-1980s, infusing a wider range of musical styles. An interesting take on the group's more developed sound can be found in the song "History Lesson, Part 2," from the 1984 double-album *Double Nickels on the Dime*. While the lyrics of this song recall the formation of the Los Angeles hardcore movement from the direct experience of the band, the musical accompaniment consists of a light, mid-tempo arrangement supporting a spoken-word vocal element.

D.C. Hardcore. At the same time the Reagan administration came to Washington, D.C., the nation's capital became the center of an intense hardcore scene, fueled by bands such as Bad Brains, Teen Idles, and Minor Threat. While this music was often stylistically similar to hardcore found in other locales, the D.C. hardcore scene featured several unique aspects: doctrinaire attitudes toward substance abuse, racial tolerance, and a stance toward politics and government grounded in intellectual debate rather than anarchistic diatribes. Bad Brains, for example, was a hardcore group composed entirely of African Americans who infused elements of funk and reggae into their music. Drawing on the close connection between British punk and West Indian forms, as found in the music of the Clash, the ethnic heritage of Bad Brains fit perfectly into the D.C. hardcore scene. The group was formed in 1977 and made an initial mark in Washington, but relocated to New York in the late 1970s amid a growing anti-hardcore sentiment among club owners. After an initial single release, "Pay to Cum" (1980), the group released a self-titled full-length record (1982), which became a foundational release of the hardcore movement.

Certainly the most important figure in the D.C. hardcore scene was guitarist, vocalist, songwriter, and label owner Ian MacKaye. MacKaye's first band was the short-lived Teen Idles, formed by MacKaye and drummer Jeff Nelson. Although the group was active for only a little more than a year, they released an extended-play album called *Minor Disturbance* (1981), the first offering by MacKaye and Nelson's new label, Dischord. After the Teen Idles disbanded in 1980, MacKaye and Nelson formed Minor Threat, which became arguably the most important group on the D.C. hardcore scene. In 1981, the band released *Minor Threat* and *In My Eyes*, two extended-play records that took musical cues from the same brand of UK punk rock that inspired Fear, Black Flag, and the Minutemen. However, MacKaye and company took a radically different social course than much of the punk rock that came before, swearing off drugs and alcohol and advocating a clean lifestyle. This philosophy was at the heart of the song "Straight Edge" (included on *Minor Threat*), which became the moniker for a new movement of unencumbered, drug-free hardcore musicians and fans. While Minor Threat was at the heart of D.C. hardcore until the group disbanded in 1983, the Dischord label became one of the most prominent independent companies of the hardcore movement. Sticking to a community-based philosophy of releasing no-frills music to fans at a reasonable price, the company had no connection to corporate interests.

Twin Cities Punk. In opposition to the movements in Los Angeles and Washington, D.C., which were closely related in style, a Minnesota-based strain of hardcore developed in the late 1970s that shied away from aggressive rants in favor of a melodic foundation, producing some of the most accessible music of the independent punk legacy. Two bands emerged in the early 1980s as representative of the Minnesota scene: the Replacements and Hüsker Dü. Fronted by singer, guitarist, and songwriter

Listening Guide

Minor Threat, "Straight Edge" Dischord 3

Words by Ian MacKaye, music by Minor Threat (Ian MacKaye, Lyle Preslar, Brian Baker, and Jeff Nelson). Produced by Minor Threat. Included on the 1981 EP *Minor Threat*, which did not chart. [The two EP releases *Minor Threat* and *In My Eyes* were later combined into a single LP with the title *Minor Threat*.]

FORM: Simple verse-chorus. Reflecting a no-frills hardcore approach to songwriting and performance, this song packs an introduction and two verse-chorus pairs into less than a minute. There are two refrain-like sections. The first begins each verse proclaiming, "I'm a person just like you," and the second utters the theme of the song "I've got the straight edge." Due to the expansion of the "straight edge" phrase at the end of the song, it is considered a chorus here. Notice how each verse mounts tension by progressing through a harmonic pattern closely related to many standard rock songs. (Musicians know this as a I – IV – V progression.)

TIME SIGNATURE: 4/4.

INSTRUMENTATION: Drums, bass, guitar, and lead vocals.

0:00–0:05	**Introduction**, 8 mm.	The song is in a very fast 4/4 time. Each guitar chord represents a whole measure of music. A solo guitar performs for 4 mm. before the band enters.
0:05–0:18	**Verse 1** (with opening refrain), 20 mm.	The verse starts with a 4-mm. refrain ("I'm a person just like you"), before entering into a more free narrative section ("Than sit around . . .").
0:18–0:23	**Chorus and interlude**, 8 mm.	The chorus is similar to a refrain. Only a single line is presented here followed by an interlude that parallels the introduction.
0:23–0:35	**Verse 2** (with opening refrain), 20 mm.	Uses the same opening refrain followed by narrative verse. Notice the standard, high-energy hardcore instrumental texture under the verse, in which the guitars and drums perform relentlessly on each beat and the snare drum hits on beats two and four. "I'm a person . . ."
0:35–0:45	**Chorus**, 12 mm.	In this iteration, the chorus repeats the line "I've got the straight edge" three times, ending abruptly at the end of the last presentation.

Paul Westerberg, the Replacements emerged in 1981. The group's first album, *Sorry Ma, Forgot to Take out the Trash* (1981), was released on the local Twin/Tone label, which became an important arbiter of Minnesota-based independent music. The music of the Replacements certainly had connections to the loud, fast, and distorted styles popular on the West Coast and in Washington and New York, but Westerberg's penchant for striking melodic and harmonic material set it apart. While most of the material recorded by Black Flag or Minor Threat was based on simple chord progressions and screamed melodies, the Replacements were quite ambitious in these areas, creating memorable melodic hooks in the context of hardcore punk. Also unlike many hardcore groups, the Replacements remained active throughout the decade, becoming more accessible to the average rock listener as the 1980s unfolded.

A good example of the typical Replacements style is the song "Color Me Impressed" from 1983. While it contains the fast, distorted, and sloppy style that many listeners might associate with punk rock, the compact song structure is deeply indebted to the pop tradition. Musical use and reuse in the song show Westerberg's highly economical songwriting, as verse and bridge sections appear in multiple contexts. Perhaps most important, the song is quite melodic and memorable, and contains a single chorus section, showing the band's ability to create a hook, but an unwillingness to repeat it throughout the song. Albums such as *Hootenanny* (1983) (which contains "Color Me Impressed") and *Let It Be* (1984), also released on Twin/Tone, included less screaming and more singing. Later albums, including *Tim* (1985) and *Pleased to Meet Me* (1987), were released on the major label Sire, which reflected the group's growing commercial appeal. Still, the Replacements never found success on the *Billboard* charts. In light of their connection to the punk movement, and the simultaneous rise of MTV, it is not surprising that the video for "Bastards of Young" (1985) consisted of nothing more than a live depiction of a stereo playing an album.

Hüsker Dü formed in St. Paul in 1979 in the wake of the growing Minnesota hardcore movement. Led by guitarist, vocalist, and songwriter Bob Mould, the group released several singles and albums beginning in 1981 before signing to SST records for the 1984 album *Zen Arcade*. Much like the Replacements, Hüsker Dü began exploring more accessible music in the mid-1980s, becoming popular with the growing college rock market. This was apparent in the group's choice to release a cover version of the Byrds' "Eight Miles High" as a single in 1984, but translated especially in the group's 1985 single "Makes No Sense at All," from the album *Flip Your Wig* (1985). Like the Replacements' "Bastards of Young," the music video was featured on MTV's alternative rock show "120 Minutes." In another connection to pre-punk popular culture, Hüsker Dü's video for "Makes No Sense at All" included an ironic punk version of "Love Is All Around," the theme from the 1970's sitcom *The Mary Tyler Moore Show*. In 1986, the group signed with Warner Brothers, releasing two more albums before disbanding a year later. Unlike the hardcore bands from Los Angeles and Washington, D.C., both the Replacements and Hüsker Dü showed a penchant for popular appeal, and eventually embraced a more approachable style, signing to major labels. Yet all three of these scenes, as well as important hardcore music from Boston, San Francisco, and New York, continued the tradition of underground punk in the United States throughout the 1980s. These underground movements paved the way for the alternative movement that would enter the mainstream a decade later.

Listening Guide

The Replacements, "Color Me Impressed" Twin/Tone 8332

Words and music by Paul Westerberg, produced by Paul Stark, Peter Jesperson, and the Replacements. Included on the 1983 album *Hootenanny*, which did not chart.

FORM: Contrasting verse-chorus, with instrumental bridge sections.

TIME SIGNATURE: 4/4.

INSTRUMENTATION: Drums, bass, guitar, and vocals.

0:00–0:11	**Introduction**, 8 mm.	A loud and fast rhythm guitar begins the tune. This might sound like punk rock, but listen to the speed at which the chords change (every two beats) and the melody created in the chords. Drums and bass enter at the end of the first chord cycle. The squeaking sound in the second half of this introduction is the sound of a guitarist sliding his pick against the guitar strings.
0:11–0:22	**Verse 1**, 8 mm.	The introduction becomes the basis for the verse sections. "Everybody at your party . . ."
0:22–0:33	**Interlude**, 8 mm.	The repeat of the introduction material (now called an interlude) creates an expectation of a scheme that will alternate between instrumental and sung sections. Notice how you can hear vocalist Paul Westerberg humming throughout this section, adding a bit of amateurism.
0:33–0:44	**Verse 2**, 8 mm.	The lyrics continue to describe the people at the "party" (or the people associated with the scene), a typical construction in later college and alternative rock. "Staying out late tonight . . ."
0:44–0:55	**Instrumental bridge**, 8 mm.	This section continues the alternating scheme between instrumental and vocal sections, but provides a different material from the verse/interlude. Notice how the mood of the chord progression is "darker" than the bright verse section.
0:55–1:07	**Verse 3**, 8 mm.	This verse makes a reference to drug use, which the group seemed to celebrate in their music. "Put the monkey on the mirror . . ."
1:07–1:17	**Chorus**, 8 mm.	Although not repeated, we should think of this section as a chorus. A common method of delivery in the very economical hardcore (and later indie) styles was to present a melodic chorus section only once, enticing the listener with the most appealing section but not repeating it too many times. "Can you stand me . . ."

1:17–1:28	**Instrumental bridge**, 8 mm.	Another presentation of the contrasting bridge material. Listen to the vocal line Westerberg adds to this progression.
1:28–1:39	**Solo**, 8 mm.	The instrumental bridge becomes the basis for a short guitar solo by Bob Stinson.
1:39–1:50	**Verse 4**, 8 mm.	A varied repeat of verse 1, except now the party revelers *don't* look depressed. "Everybody at your party . . ."
1:50–2:01	**Interlude (with refrain)**, 8 mm.	The interlude and verse material is now repeated several times as a type of coda for the song, with the addition of the vocal refrain used at the end of each verse. "Color me impressed . . ."
2:01–2:12	**Interlude (with refrain)**, 8 mm.	Coda continues. "Color me impressed . . ."
2:12–2:24	**Interlude**, 4 mm.	The final tag section of the song. Notice how the first part of this section alludes to the chorus chord progression, creating a very subtle reprise before a typical chaotic rock ending.

INDIE AND COLLEGE ROCK

College Rock Underground: R.E.M. The return-to-simplicity credo was also the working principle for a scene that would develop on U.S. college campuses in the late 1980s, known as "college rock." As an outgrowth of hardcore, this scene celebrated its lack of affiliation with major labels and corporations, with music circulating through small independent labels (or sometimes by the bands themselves), airplay on college radio stations, and live performances at clubs that formed a circuit of the country's most important college towns. In many ways, college rock got its start in Athens, Georgia, home of the University of Georgia and a local band called R.E.M. Led by guitarist Peter Buck and vocalist Michael Stipe, R.E.M. emerged from Athens to have a string of successful albums in the second half of the 1980s, marking what is perhaps the most significant instance of independent rock success in the mainstream during the decade. The band's fifth album, *Document*, rose to the number-ten position on the U.S. charts in 1987 (uk28), while the single "The One I Love" hit number nine on the American charts. While many R.E.M. fans were displeased with the success of the group after "The One I Love," the driving simplicity included in this song is an example of the widespread appeal of the group. Consisting of little more than a single verse and chorus section, each repeated several times, the basic rock formula of "The One I Love" exhibited the core of R.E.M.'s aesthetic: moderately cryptic, energetic rock and roll performed by a classic rock band lineup. R.E.M. had much more chart success in the United States than in Britain, but with 1991's *Out of Time*, they finally reached the number-one spot on both sides of the Atlantic, fueled in part by the success of the singles "Losing My Religion" (p4 uk19) and "Shiny Happy People" (p10 uk6).

Listening Guide

R.E.M., "The One I Love" I.R.S. 53171

Words and music by Bill Berry, Peter Buck, Mike Mills, and Michael Stipe. Produced by Scott Litt, Bill Berry, Peter Buck, Mike Mills, and Michael Stipe. Rose to #9 on the *Billboard* "Hot 100" in late 1987. Also contained on the album *Document*, which rose to #10 on the *Billboard* "Top Pop Albums."

FORM: Simple verse-chorus. The material for the introduction, the core of the verses, and the chorus uses the same music. The verse sections are made of a compact AABA form, with 4 measures used for each of the subsections. The single, contrasting B section within each verse acts as a mini bridge. It seems as if the verses might strictly use AABA form, while the chorus sections follow an AA pattern. Yet an interesting derivation occurs with the instrumental solo, which uses a BA pattern, completing the AABA form started by the preceding chorus. Moreover, the final chorus is doubled in length to 16 measures. Perhaps the most fascinating aspect of the form is that there is almost no derivation in lyrics in the verse sections, creating a large-scale alternation between two sections (a verse and a chorus).

TIME SIGNATURE: 4/4.

INSTRUMENTATION: Electric guitars, bass, drums, auxiliary percussion, lead and backing vocals.

0:00–0:16	**Introduction**, 8 mm.	The track opens with a featured guitar that alternates between a low, melodic figure and a jangly rhythm guitar pattern associated closely with guitarist Peter Buck.
0:16–0:46	**Verse 1**, 16 mm.	Each verse is like a small AABA section, with each subsection lasting 4 mm. The A sections uses the music presented in the introduction, while the B begins with the lyrics "A simple prop . . ."; "This one goes out . . ."
0:46–1:01	**Chorus**, 8 mm.	A simple, one-word chorus, supported by the guitar melody presented in the introduction and a distorted rhythm guitar. "Fire . . ."
1:01–1:31	**Verse 2**, 16 mm.	The lyrics and music repeat verse 1 verbatim.
1:31–1:46	**Chorus**, 8 mm.	A backing vocal melody is added. "Fire . . ."
1:46–2:01	**Instrumental verse**, 8 mm.	This section completes the AABA form initiated by the chorus, featuring Peter Buck's solo guitar.
2:01–2:31	**Verse 3**, 16 mm.	The lyrics and music repeat verse 1 nearly verbatim. Notice the subtle vocal effects added to Michael Stipe's voice, which create an eerie ambiance.
2:31–2:46	**Chorus**, 16 mm.	Listen closely for the multiple guitar layers in the chorus section and the added percussive shaker placed in the left speaker. "Fire . . ."
3:01–3:18	**Coda**, 2 mm.	The song's momentum ceases, revolving around the guitar melody that plays throughout.

R.E.M. performing at the Rat in Boston in 1983. As a group that began in the Athens, Georgia, indie rock scene, R.E.M. successfully made the transition into the major-label mainstream during the late 1980s.

Massachusetts Indie: Dinosaur Jr. and the Pixies. The independent rock movement that grew out of hardcore cultivated musical scenes in many unlikely places. While we have seen the growth of regional scenes in places like Los Angeles, Minneapolis, and Washington, D.C., another regional indie center was Western Massachusetts, centered on Amherst and Northampton. These quintessential college towns became home to a thriving independent music scene in the late 1980s. Perhaps the best-known group from this area is Amherst's Dinosaur Jr. Led by guitarist J. Mascis and bassist Lou Barlow, the band released several albums on independent labels Homestead and SST in the late 1980s, including *You're Living All over Me* (1987). Soon after this album, they signed to a major label (Sire) and Barlow departed, with the group becoming a vehicle for Mascis. Although the group's tenure was relatively short, Dinosaur Jr. has held a solid place in the alternative rock pantheon, with characteristic heavy guitar, melodic vocal hooks, and atmospheric guitar solos. In Boston, another independent scene was thriving, with bands such as Galaxie 500 and Morphine. The most important independent group to emerge from Boston was the Pixies, who recorded for the independent British 4AD label and then Elektra. The band was fronted by guitarist Frank Black and bassist Kim Deal, and featured catchy songs that often alternated between soft, driving verses and loud, anthemic choruses. Their albums *Surfer Rosa* (1988) and *Doolittle* (uk8, 1989) were successful in England and became landmarks of the American indie scene in the late 1980s.

No Wave Know-How: Sonic Youth. Formed in New York under the influence of punk, avant-garde art, and composer Glenn Branca, Sonic Youth developed a style that blended together pop and art sensibilities, much as the Velvet Underground had done fifteen years earlier though with very different stylistic results.

Led by guitarist Thurston Moore, the band's first recordings employed dissonance, noise, and novel guitar approaches, making them one of the leaders in New York's noise rock scene as well as representatives of "no wave," a punk reaction against the commercial rise of new wave. *Daydream Nation* (uk99, 1988) is often considered a watershed album for the band, with the song "Teen Age Riot" considered particularly iconic and receiving considerable college radio play. Sonic Youth signed with a major label in 1990 (DGC), gaining them greater exposure, especially in the wake of Nirvana's *Nevermind* (discussed in Chapter 13). Even in the midst of arena tours in the 1990s, Sonic Youth retained an underground aesthetic and their music remained experimental, with few concessions made to increase popular appeal.

UK Indie: The Smiths and the Cure.
In the UK at about the same time, the Smiths become the darlings of the British underground, becoming popular on college radio in the United States as well. (The Irish band U2, discussed in Chapter 11, was also a fixture on American college playlists in the 1980s.) Combining the songwriting talents of guitarist Johnny Marr and vocalist Morrissey, the band first tasted success outside the British underground scene in 1984 with *The Smiths* (uk2, 1984), containing the single "What Difference Does It Make?" (uk12); the band's UK chart success never led to mainstream success in America, making college radio one of the few ways listeners could hear the band's music. Back home in England, the Smiths again topped the charts with *Meat Is Murder* (uk1, 1985) and *The Queen Is Dead* (uk2 us70, 1986). Morrissey went on to further UK success as a solo artist, beginning with *Viva Hate* (uk2 us48, 1988).

Another college radio favorite was the Cure, led by guitarist, vocalist, songwriter Robert Smith, whose tendency to moping lyrics has led critics to dub him the "messiah of melancholy." After a series of albums such as *Kiss Me Kiss Me Kiss Me* (p35 uk6, 1987) that did well in the UK and became staples of college radio, the Cure enjoyed mainstream success late in the decade, breaking through with *Disintegration* (p12 uk3, 1989), which included the single "Lovesong." Other important UK bands on college radio playlists during the 1980s included Depeche Mode, Joy Division, Siouxie and the Banshees, the Jesus and Mary Chain, and the Stone Roses.

College radio did not play only music that was outside the mainstream; commercially successful artists such as the Police, David Bowie, Talking Heads, and Peter Gabriel were popular on campus playlists as well. College radio stations across the country did provide an alternative to FM radio and MTV for rock fans, however. Combined with regional hardcore and indie scenes, record labels, and fanzines, a new rock culture was developing underground, one that would eventually become alternative rock. As heavy metal and rap had done by the end of the 1980s, alt rock would emerge from underground in the early 1990s.

Sound Check

Artist	Song	Sound
Mötley Crüe	Shout at the Devil (1983)	Form: compound AABA High metal vocals without speed or virtuosity Audibly multitracked guitars and background vocals Anthemic chorus
Metallica	One (1989)	Form: contrasting verse-chorus (modified) / simple verse Highly complex two-part form Virtuosic guitar soloing Instrumental interlude that develops each time it appears
Run-DMC	Rock Box (1984)	Form: simple verse Mainstream rock musical track with rap vocals Vocalists alternate solos and simultaneous rapping Riff-based, which becomes similar to sample-based hip-hop
Public Enemy	Don't Believe the Hype (1988)	Form: simple verse-chorus Much of the musical material is drawn from samples Chuck D performs vocals for verses, while Flavor Flav performs each chorus Politically charged lyrics
Minor Threat	Straight Edge (1981)	Form: simple verse-chorus Fast hardcore style Refrain before each verse Chorus expanded in second presentation
The Replacements	Color Me Impressed (1983)	Form: contrasting verse-chorus (modified) More intricate chord changes than stereotypical punk rock Characteristic rough vocals Only one presentation of the chorus
R.E.M.	The One I Love (1987)	Form: simple verse-chorus Each verse is a small AABA form Listen for several different guitar parts No changing lyrics for verses

For Additional Online Resources, visit:
digital.wwnorton.com/whatsthatsound5

FURTHER READING

Michael Azerrad, *Our Band Could Be Your Life: Scenes from the American Indie Underground, 1981–1991* (Back Bay, 2002).

Matthew Bannister, *White Boys, White Noise: Masculinities and 1980s Indie Guitar Rock* (Ashgate, 2006).

Steven Blush, *American Hardcore: A Tribal History* (Feral House, 2010).

Jeff Chang, *Can't Stop Won't Stop: A History of the Hip-Hop Generation* (Picador, 2005).

Ian Christie, *Sound of the Beast: The Complete Headbanging History of Heavy Metal* (Harper, 2003).

Wendy Fonarow, *Empire of Dirt: The Aesthetics and Rituals of British Indie Music* (Wesleyan University Press, 2006).

Nelson George, *Hip-Hop America* (Penguin, 1998).

Marcus Gray, *It Crawled from the South: An R.E.M. Companion* (Da Capo, 1997).

David Konow, *Bang Your Head: The Rise and Fall of Heavy Metal* (Three Rivers Press, 2002).

Alan Light, ed., *The Vibe History of Hip Hop* (Three Rivers, 1999).

Keith Morris, *My Damage: The Story of a Punk Rock Survivor* (Da Capo, 2016).

Glenn Pillsbury, *Damage Incorporated: Metallica and the Production of Musical Identity* (Routledge, 2006).

Tricia Rose, *Black Noise: Rap Music and Black Culture in Contemporary America* (Wesleyan University Press, 1994).

Joseph Schloss, *Foundation: B-boys, B-girls, and Hip-Hop Culture in New York* (Oxford University Press, 2009).

Russell Simmons, with Nelson George, *Life and Def: Sex, Drugs, Money, and God* (Crown, 2001).

Robert Walser, *Running with the Devil: Power, Gender, and Madness in Heavy Metal Music* (Wesleyan University Press, 1993).

Deena Weinstein, *Heavy Metal: The Music and Its Culture* (Da Capo, 2000).

The fall of the Berlin Wall in 1989 marked the end of the Cold War and left the United States as the world's only superpower. Clear military superiority came with responsibilities, however. In the decades that followed the Cold War, several important armed conflicts arose, and the world often looked to the United States to take the lead in both war and peacemaking efforts. In 1991, Iraq invaded oil-rich Kuwait, and American troops intervened, pushing Iraq's army back across the Kuwait border. This first Gulf War was seen as a major victory for President George Bush, but as he and his son George W. Bush would find out, this was not the last conflict the United States would have in the Middle East.

Although the Cold War was over and America was riding high after the victory in the Gulf, Bush's reelection hopes were dashed by Bill Clinton (and a recession economy) in 1992. The election of the youthful Clinton and his running mate Al Gore seemed to bring a fresh, new spirit to government. Clinton had many policy setbacks (losing a battle to reform America's health care system, most notably), but the economy boomed during his presidency and he was easily reelected in 1996. Clinton's presidency, however, was marred by one of the most public scandals since Watergate. Clinton was accused of, and finally admitted to, having a sexual affair with a White House intern and lying to Congress about it under oath. Even though Congress impeached him, Clinton (the self-proclaimed "comeback kid") stayed in office, and his approval ratings grew as the economy continued to surge.

The economy was driven by the explosion of the high-tech industry. Computer sales soared as more people used the Internet to communicate, shop, date, and do research. In the late 1990s, businesses rushed to tap into the awesome power they believed the Internet held. Companies associated with the computer industry, often called dotcoms, seemed to come and go with each passing day, some making huge profits as their stock prices skyrocketed. Wall Street professionals seemed to care less about a company's ability to sell goods and services than about how well it appeared to take advantage of new technologies. High-tech innovators like Bill Gates (co-founder of Microsoft) and Steve Case (co-founder of America Online) achieved rock star status, and many investing novices became serious day traders, seeking the quick bucks the market yielded every day. Eventually, cooler heads began to outnumber irrational ones, and the market dropped nearly as quickly as it had risen.

One of the most contentious segments of the Internet economy was in the music industry. In 1999, twenty-year-old Shawn Fanning created Napster, a file-sharing service that allowed users to exchange music, free of charge, over the Internet. Napster made music available to all, and cut record labels and artists out of the process. The Record Industry Association of America

THE 1990s

eventually reborn as a legal music company). As Napster proved, many Internet users felt that anything on the Web should be free—including artistic material. The music industry continues to struggle with issues of ownership to this day.

Although the American military dominated international affairs and the economy boomed in the 1990s, all was not well at home. In 1992, four white police officers in Los Angeles stopped Rodney King for speeding and beat him senseless before arresting him. This was surely not the first instance of white police officers' brutality toward an African American, but it was the first to be caught on videotape and broadcast around the country. Public outcry became public rage when the police officers in the case were acquitted on nearly all charges. To many, this confirmed the racism of white America and the Los Angeles Police Department. When the verdict was issued, riots ensued, and several neighborhoods in Los Angeles were destroyed.

themselves. No one will ever know the true intentions of the perpetrators, but many speculated that the boys saw themselves as social outcasts who were often harassed by the more "popular" students. Some parents blamed "grunge" and heavy metal music, gothic clothing, video games, and violent television and movies. What was clear to everyone, however, was that young people, for whatever reason, were angry at the establishment to the point of violence, and that guns in schools were a serious and widespread problem. All of this—and many of the decade's news events—was captured by twenty-four-hour cable news channels, led by CNN. The worlds of violence, entertainment, and cable news came together most noisily in the high-profile trial of football-star-turned-actor O. J. Simpson. Simpson was accused (and eventually acquitted) of the murder of his ex-wife and her friend. The country followed every moment of the proceedings on television: from the car chase, through the trial, to the verdict.

Shawn Fanning (with guitar) and Sean Parker founded Napster, the first important Internet resource to make downloading of music files possible. Napster became so popular in the late 1990s that the major record companies believed the site was hurting sales of new CDs. Lawsuits were brought against Napster, as teens and college students across the country debated the ethics of file sharing. Napster was eventually converted to a law-abiding music-downloading service, but the genie was out of the bottle, and the practice of illegal file sharing remains widespread.

Movies in the 1990s tapped into America's high-tech and (perceived) violent culture. One of the most popular movies of the decade was Quentin Tarantino's *Pulp Fiction* (1994), which featured John Travolta and Samuel L. Jackson as thugs who would rather kill than see their boss's valuables stolen. Another innovative film was *The Blair Witch Project* (1999), which was marketed as actual footage recovered from three student filmmakers who disappeared into the Maryland woods. The seemingly amateur camera work and true story made *Blair Witch* one of the scariest movies of the decade. To promote the myth surrounding the movie, the producers used the Internet to form an underground community, spurring the movie's popularity and making websites standard movie advertising tools. Mainstream films also combined fiction and reality. *Jurassic Park (1993), Forrest Gump* (1994), and *Titanic* (1997) topped the decade's list of box-office smashes, each exploiting quickly developing forms of digital technology to produce stunning special effects.

Television also blurred the line between fiction and reality in the 1990s. In 1992, MTV launched *The Real World*, which took young people from diverse backgrounds and made them live together, with cameras following their every move. As the network expected, the cast fought over many issues, from roommate dating to racism. CBS's hit "reality" show, *Survivor* (2000), placed strangers on a tropical island, where they fought, backstabbed, and negotiated while competing for a $1 million prize. Though viewers of *The Real World, Survivor,* and their imitators felt like voyeurs in these strangers' lives, others felt that "reality" TV was as contrived as any soap opera.

Computer-oriented technology drove major economic and social changes during the 1990s. Tim Berners-Lee, pictured here, was the scientist who devised much of the programming language that made the Internet broadly accessible to the public.

ALTERNATIVE ROCK AND ROCK ALTERNATIVES

CHAPTER PREVIEW

- Nirvana's *Nevermind* launched the alternative rock movement into the mainstream in 1991. Alternative was a reaction to the excesses of much mainstream pop and rock of the 1980s.

- Initially thought of as a Seattle style described as grunge, bands from other parts of the country also had success with this return-to-simplicity style, including the Red Hot Chili Peppers and Green Day.

- Alternative emerged out of the indie rock and hardcore scenes of the 1980s. When bands from those scenes went mainstream in the wake of *Nevermind*, a new generation of bands emerged within the indie underground and college rock scenes, including Pavement, Liz Phair, and Beck.

- Several bands such as Rage Against the Machine and Korn blended the straightforward approach and punk attitude of alternative with other styles, developing extensions of metal that blended in elements of rap.

- The industrial music of Nine Inch Nails and Marilyn Manson blended noise and avant-garde elements to produce a successful concept-driven but often disturbing new approach.

Nirvana (left to right, Dave Grohl, Kurt Cobain, Krist Novoselic) combined simple but intense guitar work with poetic, sometimes disturbing, longing lyrics to create a new sound: "grunge." This sound appealed especially to young, white suburbanites who felt alienated from mainstream American values.

In the fall of 1991, an unknown band from Seattle released an album that featured a naked baby chasing a dollar bill underwater. Nirvana's *Nevermind* would go on to become one the most important releases of the 1990s, launching the alternative rock boom and opening the door not only for Seattle bands but also for groups across the country that embraced a return-to-simplicity approach. As sudden as the emergence of alternative seemed at the time, the music had its origins in the hardcore and indie rock scenes that had been simmering underground for most of the 1980s. It was also in many ways reminiscent of the rise of punk in the 1970s. While '70s punks were reacting against the big labels and what they believed was the overproduced rock of Jethro Tull, Pink Floyd, and Led Zeppelin, the 1990s alternative rockers were reacting against the visually oriented MTV artists and the flashy (and often virtuosic) heavy metal bands. Alt rockers dressed very casually (no spandex or teased hair), projected themselves as amateur instrumentalists (no long guitar solos!), and often rejected—at least initially—the idea of recording for a major label, opting instead to work with smaller indie labels. This do-it-yourself (DIY) aesthetic was one way of rejecting the crass commercialism of popular music, as well as most of the trappings of fame. Alt rockers and their fans became rock's new bohemians—self-consciously scruffy and full of attitude.

As we have seen many times already in the history of rock, the emergence of one important group or record can trigger a kind of music-business feeding frenzy, as labels scramble to get in on the next big thing. In the early 1990s, alternative seemed like the next big thing, and alt-rock bands were signed to lucrative deals with major labels, became staples of FM radio and MTV, and played to large concert audiences. Ironically, by the middle of the decade, alternative was mainstream. The movement of so many bands out of the indie underground and into the mainstream did not eliminate the indie rock scene, however. A new generation of bands emerged on college radio, which played releases from a host of indie labels featuring musicians who were committed to the DIY aesthetic and sometimes even proud to have only limited commercial potential. In many ways, indie rock became the alternative to alternative.

Nirvana's lead singer Kurt Cobain performing in England, 1992. Cobain's suicide two years later helped turn him into an icon of "alternative" music and culture.

THE RISE OF ALTERNATIVE

Seattle's Grunge Scene: Nirvana. When Nirvana's second album *Nevermind* (p1 uk7) was released in late 1991, it rose to the top of the pop charts on both sides of the Atlantic, partly with the help of the single "Smells Like Teen Spirit" (p6 uk7). Although they played their first shows in Olympia, Washington, Nirvana was perhaps the most significant of the "grunge" bands that came out of Seattle in the first half of the 1990s. Led by singer, songwriter, and guitarist Kurt Cobain, the band quickly became stars, despite Cobain's dedication to the idea that Nirvana's music rejected the rock star apparatus in show business. Accordingly, Cobain and Nirvana projected an image of amateurism, but Cobain was in fact a gifted songwriter and a tasteful guitarist. The two albums that followed *Nevermind* further solidified the band's status as one of the hottest acts in rock. *In Utero* (1993) and *Unplugged in New York* (1994) both hit the number-one slot in the United States and the UK.

"Smells Like Teen Spirit" provides a representative example of Nirvana's music. The tune features a simple, catchy guitar pattern played on the low strings that repeats throughout most of the song. The lyrics are delivered with calculated carelessness, creating a sense of tortured spontaneity in the verses while driving toward the intense and aggressive chorus. The contrast between the mellow verses and the frenetic chorus sections echoes the bipolar nature of alternative music, which evolved from often-energetic hardcore, but had gained widespread commercial appeal. Despite the rejection of commercialism that was central to alternative rock, Cobain was clearly skilled at working with the traditional elements of pop songwriting and arranging, as this and many other Nirvana tracks demonstrate. Moreover, bassist Krist Novoselic, drummer Dave Grohl, and the group's main producers, Butch Vig and Steve Albini, provided Cobain with expert support. Nirvana's career, however, was cut tragically short by Cobain's suicide in April 1994, and it would be left to others to carry the alternative torch.

A Performance That Launched a Career. While Nirvana is commonly associated with Seattle, the band's origins are actually in rustic Aberdeen, Washington. On October 30, 1988, the group played a Halloween party at an Evergreen State College dormitory in nearby Olympia. Nirvana shared the bill that night with a couple of other bands. Charles R. Cross writes that "when Nirvana finally took the stage, or more accurately moved to the corner of the room acting as a stage, they played only a 25-minute set, but it was a show that was to transform them from Aberdeen hicks to Olympia's most beloved band." A few weeks later the band's first single, "Love Buzz," was released and Cobain heard it on the University of Washington's KCMU—after he had dropped a copy off there and then phoned in the request himself.

Pearl Jam. In Nirvana's wake, a host of alternative rock bands began to enjoy a level of commercial success that had mostly eluded post-punk and hardcore bands in the 1980s. Also from Seattle was Pearl Jam, led by singer Eddie Vedder. The albums *Ten* (p2 uk18, 1992), *VS.* (p1 uk2, 1993), and *Vitalogy* (p1 uk6, 1994) established them as mainstream stars by mid-decade. Pearl Jam's music was in many ways closer to the heavy metal that had immediately preceded it, which made it easy to program on the mainstream rock radio stations of the mid-1990s. The group was central to the alternative rock scene, but they were also important to the anticommercial aesthetic of the alt-rock lifestyle. The band battled with Ticketmaster, a national service that handled ticket sales for many large rock concerts, because the agency was forcing

Pearl Jam's Eddie Vedder is shown here performing at London's Finsbury Park in 1993. Along with Nirvana, Pearl Jam represented Seattle "grunge" to the nation—a scene that had its own rebellious music and fashion sense. Pearl Jam also publicly opposed Ticketmaster over ticket prices, establishing the band's credibility within the anticommercial alternative community.

Listening Guide

Nirvana, "Smells Like Teen Spirit" DGC 19050

Words and music by Kurt Cobain, Krist Novoselic, and Dave Grohl. Produced by Butch Vig. Single rose to #7 on the *Billboard* "Hot 100" (uk6) in early 1992. Also contained on the album *Nevermind*, which rose to #1 on the *Billboard* "200" (uk7).

FORM: Simple verse-chorus (modified). The 16-bar introduction is made up of two 2-bar phrases played solo on the guitar, then four 2-measure phrases played loudly by the entire band, followed by the same phrase played twice more but quietly and arranged differently. This last "quiet" 2-bar phrase returns again as a lead-in to the second verse and is abbreviated to 2 bars to lead into the third verse. Each verse and chorus is built on the same 2-bar phrase heard in the introduction. The 16-bar verses cycle through the phrase eight times; the first 8 bars in each case employ new lyrics, while the second 8 bars repeat the "Hello/how low" lyric. The 16-bar choruses contain the 2-bar phrase six times each, with a contrasting 4 bars added to the end in each case. After the second verse-chorus pair, the verse is played instrumentally, as the guitar plays the vocal melody. The song ends with a chorus containing ten statements of the basic 2-bar phrase.

TIME SIGNATURE: 4/4.

INSTRUMENTATION: Guitars, bass, drums, vocal. Notice the contrast between the clean sounding guitar at the beginning of each sung verse and the heavily distorted guitars heard in the choruses.

0:00–0:33	**Introduction**, 16 mm.	Solo guitar plays 2-bar phrase twice through relatively quietly, then the entire band comes in playing the same music for 8 bars, followed by a return to a quiet, but differently arranged version of the same music.
0:33–1:06	**Verse 1**, 16 mm.	Lead vocal enters to the accompaniment of the "quiet" music in the first 8 bars, and to the "loud" music in the second 8 bars. "Load up on guns and bring your friends . . ."
1:06–1:47	**Chorus**, 20 mm.	Played and sung at its most aggressive, plus 4 bars of contrasting music, then a 4-mm. lead-in to the next verse using the "quiet" music, "With the lights out it's less dangerous . . ."
1:47–2:20	**Verse 2**, 16 mm.	As in verse 1, "I'm worse at what I do best . . ."
2:20–2:53	**Chorus**, 16 mm.	As before, but without the "quiet" music lead-in to the next verse. "With the lights out it's less dangerous . . ."
2:53–3:34	**Instrumental verse**, 20 mm.	16 mm. guitar solo plays the melody almost exactly as it is sung in the verses, then the 4-mm. "quiet" music serves to lead into the verse, though this time it is a little different, allowing space for the lead guitar to die out.
3:34–4:05	**Verse 3**, 16 mm.	As in verses 1 and 2, "And I forget just why I taste . . ."
4:05–4:58	**Chorus**, 21 mm.	As before, but extended to include ten times through the 2-bar phrase, plus a last chord added to create an ending. Cobain's vocals become the most frenzied toward the end.

WHAT'S THAT SOURCE?

Nirvana Shuns Success

After working for several years as an under-the-radar band on the Seattle independent label Sub Pop, Nirvana became extremely popular in early 1992 after the release of their second album, *Nevermind*. Contrary to their background as ne'er-do-well slackers from the Pacific Northwest, the group launched a national craze for "grunge," which contrasted in many ways with the metal-oriented styles that had been so popular in the late 1980s. This 1992 profile of the band by Pleasant Gehman (printed in *Spin*) portrays the national excitement over Nirvana and the band's apathy toward their newfound fame. The article highlights perfectly the "alternative" paradox: What happens when a band that defines itself against the mainstream becomes the most popular group in the world?

I'm on my way up to Seattle, which is currently to the rock'n'roll world what Bethlehem was to Christianity, and the only thing the passengers on the plane seem to be talking about is the movie *Singles*. I'm grateful to be sitting next to a serene-looking woman in a coral sweater and Bermuda shorts, a string of cultured pearls around her neck, her upturned nose buried in a paperback. An hour and a half into the flight, the turbulence starts. It's bad. She's white-knuckling it. In an attempt to take her mind off the frantic bouncing around, I engage her in small talk. She's a 24-year-old mother of three, going to Seattle to visit her father, whom she hasn't seem in five years. A devout Catholic, she's worried that if the plane crashes, her kids won't be raised Catholic. She, in turn, asks me questions. I'm going to Seattle to interview a band, I tell her. She asks about rock writing politely, almost disinterestedly. Finally she asks which band.

"They're called Nirvana," I say.

"Oh my gawwwd!" she screams in a 15-year-old's ecstatic falsetto. *"No way! How awesome!"* She looks at me hard for a second, and then in a conspiratorial tone, whispers, "Do they know you're coming?"

As with all situations of an underground band or artist coming up with an across-the-board crowd-pleaser, a backlash seems inevitable. Hip kids are already dissing the entire grunge scene, snickering about sellouts. Record companies are in a feeding frenzy for the next Nirvana. The pressure is on.

"Everything happened so quickly," says Grohl. "I don't think anyone knows what's gonna happen next."

"Every time somebody says the word 'Seattle,' you have to say 'Nirvana.' People are sick of us," sighs Novoselic. "More people probably hate us in Seattle than anywhere else in the country."

Though Novoselic still tools around Seattle in his battered Volkswagen van, and the band still practices in a weathered, unfinished warehouse space where, until recently, squatters were hydroponically growing marijuana in the basement, Nirvana can feel its own fame breathing down its neck. Though Grohl still dresses like an outdoorsy ragamuffin—hunting caps and saggy-assed long johns—he admits to giving Madonna prank calls from Europe. Now, *that's* budding rock star decadence at its finest.

"It's not that great being on MTV 20 times a day," Cobain says, not in a bratty way, but earnestly. "It's great for record sales, but I wish there was some kind of contract you could draw up where there was only a certain amount of time they could play you in a week."

"And when people write about you, everything gets screwed up," Novoselic says.

"I don't believe anything that's written about anyone anymore," Grohl adds. "You just have to read it and form your own perspective."

Source: Pleasant Gehman, "Artist of the Year: Nirvana." *Spin*, December 1992: 51–53.

individual tickets to sell for more than $20, making it difficult for some fans to attend the band's shows. (Ticketmaster merged with the concert promotion company Live Nation to become Live Nation Entertainment in 2010.) Although Pearl Jam eventually lost a long legal battle with Ticketmaster, their willingness to fight corporate interests—and lose the revenue they would have earned through concert appearances during this time—made them heroes within the alternative movement. By the end of the decade, *Yield* (1998) hit number two on the U.S. charts, and the band scored a surprise single with "Last Kiss" (p2, 1999), an unlikely cover of a 1964 splatter platter by J. Wilson and the Cavaliers.

Other Seattle Bands: Soundgarden and Alice in Chains.

Led by the vocals of Chris Cornell and the guitar playing of Kim Thayil, Soundgarden also emerged from Seattle. Formed in the late 1980s and expected by many in Seattle to be the band that would first break onto the national scene, Soundgarden's blend of heavy metal, 1970s blues rock, and 1960s psychedelia achieved national commercial success in 1994 with the release of *Superunknown* (p1 uk4). Initially signed by Columbia Records as a metal band, Alice in Chains was formed by singer Layne Staley in the late 1980s. Staley's penchant for dark lyrics dealing with drug addiction and death are similar to those of speed metal bands like Metallica or Megadeth, and the group's 1990 debut album, *Facelift*, was initially directed to metal fans. In the wake of Nirvana's success, however, Alice in Chains were promoted as a "Seattle band," which helped the sales of *Facelift* and pushed the next album, *Dirt* (1992), to number six in the United States. In 1994, the acoustically oriented *Jar of Flies* became the first extended-play release ever to top the *Billboard* album charts, while 1995's *Alice in Chains* debuted at number one in the United States.

California Bands.

Although Seattle is often thought of as the home of the alternative movement, a number of bands farther down the West Coast were developing along parallel lines. The wildly eclectic Faith No More was formed in San Francisco in 1982, and after the addition of singer Mike Patton, the band released *The Real Thing* (p11, 1990), which included the number-nine single "Epic." *Angel Dust* (p10) followed in 1992 and further established the band's reputation. In many ways, Faith No More's musical approach may be more akin to the comic irreverence of Frank Zappa than to the angry rebelliousness of the Sex Pistols.

The Red Hot Chili Peppers also did not fit neatly into the alternative template. Formed in 1983 in Hollywood, the group seemed just as influenced by funk as by punk, and this is especially evident in the playing of the band's bassist, Flea. Their second album, *Freaky Styley* (1985), was produced by George Clinton, while 1989's *Mother's Milk* contained a cover version of Stevie Wonder's "Higher Ground." The band enjoyed its first commercial success with the Rick Rubin–produced *Bood Sugar Sex Magik*, which rose to number three in 1991. Following with hit

Shown here performing in New Jersey in 1991, the Red Hot Chili Peppers blended a strong funk element into their music. Formed in early 1983 and originally named Tony Flow and the Miraculously Majestic Masters of Mayhem, the Los Angeles–based band went on to be one of the most commercially successful groups to emerge from the alternative rock movement.

Listening Guide ▚

Red Hot Chili Peppers, "Give It Away" Warner Bros. 9 40261-2

Words and music by Flea, John Frusciante, Anthony Kiedis, and Chad Smith, produced by Rick Rubin. Reached #1 on the *Billboard* Modern Rock chart in 1991. Contained on the album *Blood Sugar Sex Magic*, which reached #3 on the *Billboard* Hot 200 album chart.

FORM: Compound AABA (modified). This song employs regular 4-bar phrases played at a moderate tempo. Combined with the quickly delivered lyrics of the verses, this produces a long series of sections based almost entirely on the groove established by the drums, bass, and guitar. The overall AABA form is augmented by a repeat of the B and A sections before moving to a coda to end the track. Each A section is composed of three verses combined with a contrasting chorus.

TIME SIGNATURE: 4/4, with the entire song built on a repeating rhythmic groove driven by the drums and bass.

INSTRUMENTATION: electric guitars, bass, drums, lead vocal, jaw harp.

	0:00–0:11	**Introduction**, 4 mm.	Drums and guitar
A	0:11–0:21	**Verse**, 4 mm.	Groove established by drums, bass, and guitar, vocal enters, "What I got . . ."
	0:21–0:31	**Verse**, 4 mm.	As before, "What I got . . ."
	0:31–0:42	**Verse**, 4 mm.	As before, "Realize . . ."
	0:42–0:53	**Chorus**, 4 mm.	Bass and guitar offer contrast, while drum drive beat forward, "Give it away . . ."
A	0:53–1:03	**Verse**, 4 mm.	As before, "Greedy little . . ."
	1:03–1:14	**Verse**, 4 mm.	As before, "I'm lowbrow . . ."
	1:14–1:24	**Verse**, 4 mm.	As before, "Bob Marley . . ."
	1:24–1:34	**Chorus**, 4 mm.	As before, "Give it away . . ."
	1:34–1:45	**Chorus**, 4 mm.	Bass and guitar drop out, "Give it away . . ."
B	1:45–2:06	**Bridge (instrumental)**, 8 mm.	Contrasting music, backward guitar melody
A	2:06–2:16	**Verse**, 4 mm.	As before, "Lucky me . . ."
	2:16–2:27	**Verse**, 4 mm.	As before, "My mom . . ."
	2:27–2:37	**Verse**, 4 mm.	As before, "There's a river . . ."
	2:37–2:48	**Chorus**, 4 mm.	As before, bass and guitar drop out, "Give it away . . ."
B	2:48–2:58	**Bridge (instrumental)**, 4 mm.	As before, but abbreviated.
A	2:58–3:09	**Verse**, 4 mm.	As before, "What I got . . ."
	3:09–3:19	**Verse**, 4 mm.	As before, "What I got . . ."
	3:19–3:29	**Verse**, 4 mm.	As before, "Realize . . ."

(continued)

3:29–3:40	**Chorus**, 4 mm.	Guitar and bass parts varied, guitar recalls intros "Give it away . . ."
3:40–3:51	**Chorus**, 4 mm.	Vocal now also varied, "Give it away . . ."
3:51–4:12	**Coda**, 8 mm.	Guitar varies line from verses, "Give it away . . ."
4:12–4:40	**Coda continues**, 10 mm.	Heavy guitar enters, an extra 2 bars end the song, "Give it away . . ."

albums such as *One Hot Minute* (p4, 1994) and *Californication* (p3, 1999), the Red Hot Chili Peppers also developed a reputation for innovative videos, many of which became staples on MTV.

Formed in 1987 even farther south in San Diego, Stone Temple Pilots drew heavily on the style of Seattle bands like Alice in Chains and Pearl Jam, while drawing in elements of 1970s guitar-oriented mainstream rock. The band was dismissed by some critics for being too derivative, but Stone Temple Pilots' first three albums— *Core* (1992), *Purple* (1994), and *Tiny Music* (1996)—all cracked the top five on the U.S. charts. After the group disbanded in 2003, singer Scott Weiland went on to form Velvet Revolver with former members of Guns N' Roses and Wasted Youth, showing the lasting connections between punk, hair metal, and alternative rock.

Alternative Impulses: Live, Lifehouse, and Creed. In the years after the emergence of grunge, the "alternative" style and indie roots of bands such as Nirvana and R.E.M. was (ironically) fully imbedded in the mainstream. Pennsylvania-based Live is an example of a group from this period that emerged through mainstream channels but was marketed as alternative. With records on a major label subsidiary and sales of over eight million copies for their 1994 album *Throwing Copper* (p1), Live was a mainstay of radio and concert venues until the turn of the millennium. Similarly, the California-based trio Lifehouse created a sonic texture that drew heavily from the grunge movement. In the band's breakout single "Hanging by a Moment" (p2 uk25, 2001), there are clear allegiances to Nirvana, which are made even clearer in the music video for the song, which includes several segments that resemble the video for "Smells Like Teen Spirit." However, the transgressive nature of Nirvana and many other grunge bands was not present in the lyrics of Lifehouse songs, reflecting the band's history of playing in churches. Although not exclusively a Christian band, the lyrics for "Hanging by a Moment" can certainly be interpreted as devotional, creating a fascinating cultural combination of grunge and Christianity. With songs that alluded to Christian theology, Creed was another post-grunge band that was extremely successful in the mainstream using the heavy sound of alternative rock. Songs such as "Higher" (p7, 1999) and "My Sacrifice" (p4, 2001) clearly refer to religious themes, while the band's best-known song, "With Arms Wide Open" (p1, uk13, 2000), depicts the perspective of a new father. Although neither of these groups officially espoused the enormous side of the music industry that deals in Christian music, the conservative themes explored by both Lifehouse and Creed point to the emergence of Christian rock in the American mainstream during the 1990s.

Irony and Self-Awareness: Foo Fighters and Weezer. Although the grunge scene influenced many bands during the mid-1990s, Foo Fighters are a band that actually grew out of the ashes of two important Seattle groups, Nirvana and Sunny Day Real Estate, after the death of Kurt Cobain in 1994. Fronted by guitarist Dave Grohl, who played drums for Nirvana, Foo Fighters has released a series of albums since the mid-1990s that placed them consistently in the upper reaches of the pop charts. Unlike Nirvana, the music of Foo Fighters is less angry and internal, perhaps owing to the personable Grohl, who served initially as the band's main songwriter and set the aesthetic tone for later releases. Also in contrast to the seriousness of Nirvana's music is the group's often-humorous tone in their music videos. "Big Me" (p13 uk19, 1996) featured the group in a pseudo-commercial for breath mints, while "Learn to Fly" (p19 uk21, 2000) showcased several band members in costume playing multiple roles. Although the band's music is rarely this slapstick, the comedic self-awareness included in these videos shows a lighter, more-accessible side of musicians who were once associated with contemplative angst. With albums such as *One by One* (p3 uk1, 2002), *In Your Honor* (p2 uk2, 2005), and *Echoes, Silence, Patience and Grace* (p3 uk1, 2007), Foo Fighters have become rock music mainstays during the past decade.

Emerging on the national scene in late 1994, the often-comedic music of Weezer embodied the self-awareness of the intelligent alternative slacker. This attitude can be found in the group's first Top 40 hit, "Buddy Holly" (p18 uk12, 1995), which depicts the song's protagonist as a geek facing threats against his girlfriend. Using slang associated with hip-hop, lead singer and songwriter Rivers Cuomo draws attention to his frailty, asking "What's with these homies dissin' my girl?" The video for the song takes the 1950s references even further, portraying the band on the set of the sitcom *Happy Days* as the entertainment at Al's Diner. Incredibly productive since their debut, the group has released a number of albums that scored very high on the *Billboard* charts, while maintaining a heavy guitar-oriented sound over a steady, danceable groove.

Pop Punk and Ska Revival. Several bands widely influenced by punk music entered the mainstream in the early 1990s, creating a style often given the ironic label pop punk. Many of these bands were from California, showing the long lineage of heavier forms of rock in both the northern and southern parts of the state. San Francisco's Green Day, led by singer, songwriter, and guitarist Billie Joe Armstrong, enjoyed its first significant commercial success in 1994 with *Dookie* (p2 uk13) and followed in 1995 with *Insomniac* (p2 uk8). The band's music is often hard driving and aggressive, marking their stylistic debt to 1970s punk. The song "When I Come Around" from the *Dookie* album provides a good example of how the energy of power-chords on the guitar can be blended with a strong pop melodic sensibility in the band's music. A softer side can be heard in the ballad "Good Riddance

Green Day guitarist Billie Joe Armstrong in a 1997 concert. The most popular band to emerge from the California pop punk scene. Green Day combined the speed, distortion, and style of punk with catchy pop hooks.

Listening Guide

Green Day, "When I Come Around" Reprise 7-17941-A

Lyrics by Billie Joe Armstrong, music by Billie Joe Armstrong, Mike Pritchard, and Frank E. Wright. Produced by Rob Cavallo and Green Day. Released on the album *Dookie* (p2 uk13) in 1994; also released as a single, reaching #1 on the *Billboard* "Modern Rock Tracks" chart (uk27) in 1995.

FORM: Contrasting verse-chorus. Most of the song is built over a repeated sequence of four chords; the chorus provides the only harmonic contrast in the song. Note how the instrumentation drops out at the end of the chorus to emphasize the song's title, creating a memorable hook for the song.

TIME SIGNATURE: 4/4, with drums, bass, and guitar driving the same rhythm throughout except in the guitar solo in the abbreviated verse.

INSTRUMENTATION: Electric guitars, bass, drums, lead and backing vocals. No building of the arrangement occurs in this track; instead all instruments are in from the start and the texture remains mostly consistent, with some background vocals added as the song progresses and brief contrast during the guitar solo.

0:00–0:14	**Introduction**, 6 mm.	3 times through a 2-bar chord sequence, introduced by guitar, then with bass and drums added.
0:15–0:34	**Verse**, 8 mm.	Based on 2-bar chord sequence from intro, 4 vocal phrases of 2 mm. each, "I heard you . . ."
0:34–0:53	**Verse**, 8 mm.	As before, "Well, don't get . . ."
0:53–1:03	**Chorus**, 4 mm.	Contrasting 2-chord sequence, backing vocals and stop at end to emphasize vocal hook (title), "No time . . ."
1:03–1:13	**Interlude**, 4 mm.	Lead vocal absent after chorus hook, as section prepares arrival of the next verse.
1:13–1:32	**Verse**, 8 mm.	As before, "I heard it . . ."
1:32–1:52	**Verse**, 8 mm.	As before, with backing vocal added at end. "So go do what . . ."
1:52–2:02	**Chorus**, 4 mm.	As before, "No time . . ."
2:02–2:12	**Interlude**, 4 mm.	As before.
2:12–2:22	**Verse**, 4 mm.	Instrumental, abbreviated to 4 mm. with guitar solo featured.
2:22–2:31	**Chorus**, 4 mm.	As before, "No time . . ."
2:31–2:55	**Coda**, 8 mm.	Extended by repeating 2-bar sequence and tagging the vocal hook. "When I . . ."

(Time of Your Life)" (p11 uk11), which was played during the final episode of the enormously successful television show *Seinfeld*. Green Day has had the most longevity of these pop punk groups, especially after their critically acclaimed 2004 album *American Idiot* (p1 uk1), a political rock opera that has since been converted to a Broadway show. The Offspring also emerged in 1994, releasing records on the independent Epitaph label before signing to Columbia in 1997. The group's breakthrough album was *Smash* (p4 uk21, 1994), which contained the single "Come Out and Play" (p38). This single mixes heavy riff-based punk with a simple surf guitar line during the verses, connecting to the groups' Southern California roots. San Diego's Blink-182 hit the mainstream later in the decade with the albums *Enema of the State* (p9 uk15, 1999) and *Take Off Your Pants and Jacket* (p1 uk4, 2001). A trio similar to Green Day in many ways, this group showed their comedic side in several music videos. In "What's My Age Again" (uk17, 1999), they appeared for the duration of the video running through various scenes with no clothing, while in "All the Small Things" (p6 uk2, 2000), the group parodied the video style and dress of many pop and hip-hop acts from the period.

Several years after the emergence of pop punk in the mainstream, there was a similar ska revival, which produced several notable bands. Fronted by Brad Nowell, Sublime emerged in 1996 with an eponymous album (p13) that contained the single "What I Got" (p29). Containing elements of laid-back beach music, hip-hop, and traditional Jamaican music, Sublime's music revealed an interesting Southern California subculture of tattooed punks that were interested in West Indian roots music. Hailing from Cambridge, Massachusetts, the Mighty Mighty Bosstones also received mainstream attention during the mid-1990s. The group had been active for nearly a decade before releasing *Let's Face It* (p27 uk40, 1997), which contained the single "The Impression That I Get" (p23 uk12). Presenting a much more energetic mix of ska and punk (often called ska-core), the Mighty Mighty Bosstones featured a full horn section, and even employed a full-time dancer to help energize the audience. No Doubt was the mid-1990s ska revival band that made the largest impression on the American mainstream. On the strength of the single "Don't Speak" (p1 uk1), the group's *Tragic Kingdom* (p1 uk3, 1996) sold more than ten million copies, making lead singer Gwen Stefani into a household name and a fashion icon. Later releases, such as *Return of Saturn* (p2 uk31, 2000) and *Rock Steady* (p9, 2002), explored various forms of dance music, exposing connections between American pop, Jamaican dancehall, reggae, American electronic dance styles, and even hip-hop. Stefani has also shown a wide range of musical interest, collaborating on successful singles with Moby, Eve, and Akon, in addition to releasing the multifaceted solo album *Love.Angel.Music.Baby* (p5 uk4, 2005).

METAL EXTENSIONS

Rap and Rock: Rage Against the Machine. As rap was expanding into many substyles during the early 1990s, it was also gaining a firmer foothold in the world of white rock. In the years following Run-DMC's crossover cover of "Walk This Way," many rock musicians took an interest in employing aspects of rap in their music. Rap and heavy metal rose to mainstream popularity at about the same time,

Rage Against the Machine, pictured here in concert, was one of the first groups to successfully combine a rap vocal style with rock. Zack de la Rocha's (right) often political lyrics shared the spotlight with Tom Morello's innovative guitar playing, which often imitated the sound of DJ scratching. Bassist Tim Commerford is pictured left.

and cross-pollination between the two played an important role in the second half of the 1980s. Eclectic bands like Anthrax and Faith No More began to employ rapped passages in a heavy-rock context. Taking their cue from Faith No More and the Red Hot Chili Peppers, the Los Angeles–based band Rage Against the Machine blended hard-driving rock with mostly rapped vocals to establish a stylistic model many later bands would follow. Their first album, *Rage Against the Machine* (p45 uk17, 1992), evinced the group's dedication to political causes while musically drawing much from the Chili Peppers' blend of funk grooves and heavy metal riffs. Zack de la Rocha's vocals shared the spotlight with Tom Morello's innovative guitar playing, which blended metal, blues rock, and jazz, and at times imitated the sound of DJ scratching. *Evil Empire* (p1 uk4, 1996) followed and established the band as an important force in the rap-rock style, while *The Battle of Los Angeles* (p1 uk23, 1999) served to confirm this. By the end of the decade, de la Rocha had left the group and the remaining members reorganized as Audioslave, with Soundgarden's Chris Cornell performing lead vocals.

Getting Heavy: Korn, Limp Bizkit, System of a Down, and Kid Rock. Hailing from Bakersfield, California, Korn brought the sound of the seven-string guitar into rap-rock. The electric seven-string had been used by a handful of jazz guitarists over the years to make a wider range of notes available on the instrument. In most configurations, the seventh string was added below the bottom string of a conventional guitar, not only making more bass notes possible but also providing for a greater range within the grip of the guitarist's left hand. Heavy metal virtuoso Steve Vai had introduced the instrument into rock, but Korn guitarists James "Munky" Shaffer and Brian "Head" Welch practically made it into a brand name, using the low strings for heavy, angular, distortion-soaked riffs. The band's first album, *Korn* (1994), introduced the group's trademark sound, while *Life Is Peachy* (p3 uk32, 1996) and *Follow the Leader* (p1 uk5, 1998) established their reputation. As with Rage Against the Machine, Korn's lyrics are most often rapped, but also sometimes screamed, and together with the pronounced influence of heavy metal, create a more menacing stylistic blend.

Florida's Limp Bizkit picked up Korn's use of the seven-string guitar, added more screaming in the vocal dimension, and produced *Three Dollar Bill Y'all* (p22, 1997), which included a cover of George Michael's "Faith," and *Significant Other* (p1 uk26, 1999). Led by charismatic vocalist Fred Durst and guitarist Wes Borland, the band received considerable airtime on MTV. System of a Down also brought together many features of these rap-rock groups. With *System of a Down* (1998) and *Toxicity* (p1 uk13, 2001), the group continued the political and social commitment of Rage Against the Machine while blending in the heavy, gothic tones of Korn and Limp Bizkit. Their producer was Rick Rubin, who had produced the Run-DMC records that first brought rock and rap together. Starting out as a rapper in the style of the early Beastie Boys, Detroit's Kid Rock extended the rap-rock of earlier bands by employing a wide range of styles in his music during the late 1990s. *Devil without a Cause* (p4, 1998), his major label breakthrough, uses fewer heavy metal guitar riffs and more sounds drawn from traditional blues rock. Kid Rock's vocals are both rapped and sung (at times in a very conventional manner), showing a stronger flair for pop hooks and a broad range of stylistic references, including country rock. Kid Rock's lyrics are rarely gothic or politically ambitious; instead, they are much more playful and at times ironic and comic. Unlike Korn, Limp Bizkit, and System of a Down, who were incredibly consistent in their blend of rap and metal, Kid Rock has branched out into more mainstream forms of pop.

The Menacing Sounds of Industry: Nine Inch Nails and Marilyn Manson.
While bands like Rage Against the Machine and Korn were extending 1980s heavy metal by blending in rap elements, other musicians were exploring a style often called "industrial." The roots of industrial can be traced to British bands of the mid-1970s such as Throbbing Gristle and Cabaret Voltaire, as well as to Skinny Puppy, a Canadian band from the 1980s. The genre was heavily imbued with concept art and anti-conformity, resulting in music that blended electronic sources with live performance and was decidedly avant-garde and disturbing. Mixing heavier strains of metal with industrial, Nine Inch Nails is often considered the premier 1990s group in the style, and the band's 1994 album *The Downward Spiral* (p2 uk9, 1994) brought industrial to a mainstream rock audience for the first time. In the recording studio, Nine Inch Nails is San Francisco–based composer Trent Reznor, who writes the music and performs all the parts himself, while a rotating cast of backing musicians perform with Reznor in a live setting. Nine Inch Nails' music is moody, with frequent shifts in atmosphere, and the lyrics are often concerned with the darker side of the human psyche. *The Downward Spiral*, for instance, was recorded in the house where Charles Manson and his followers committed the famous (and hideous) murders of actress Sharon Tate and her friends.

A similar fascination with the grotesque can be found in the music of Marilyn Manson. Much like Alice Cooper, Marilyn Manson is the name of the band and the lead singer (who is male). Each member of the group adopted a stage name that combined the name of a glamorous female celebrity with that of a famous

Trent Reznor of Nine Inch Nails is seen performing here at Woodstock '94 in Saugerties, New York. Like Stevie Wonder and Prince, Reznor is capable of playing all instruments on his recordings himself, and like Velvet Underground, the Doors, and Alice Cooper, he often focuses on the darker side of the human psyche.

Listening Guide

Nine Inch Nails, "Hurt" Nothing/Interscope 92346

Words by Trent Reznor. Produced by Trent Reznor. Included on the 1994 LP *The Downward Spiral*, which reached #2 on the "Billboard 200" in 1994.

FORM: Contrasting verse-chorus (with connective bridge). The bridge acts as a pre-chorus, and uses the same harmonic progression as the chorus. Unmetered, soft ambient noise is used as an introduction, and the song devolves into a louder, distorted noise after the final chorus before moving abruptly to a softer noise section as the song concludes (both also unmetered). An altered version of the chorus, with changed lyrics, is presented after the second verse-bridge-chorus composite.

TIME SIGNATURE: 4/4.

INSTRUMENTATION: Acoustic guitar, programmed synthesizers, piano, drums, ambient noise (soft and loud), bass, electric guitar, backing vocals, lead vocals.

0:00–0:22	**Introduction**	Low noise
0:22–1:10	**Verse**, 16 mm.	"I hurt myself . . ."
1:10–1:35	**Interlude**, 8 mm.	Instrumental
1:35–1:59	**Bridge**, 8 mm.	"What have I become . . ."
1:59–2:23	**Chorus**, 8 mm.	"You could have it all . . ."
2:23–2:35	**Interlude**, 4 mm.	Instrumental
2:35–3:23	**Verse**, 16 mm.	"I wear this crown . . ."
3:23–3:47	**Bridge**, 8 mm.	"What have I become . . ."
3:47–4:11	**Chorus**, 8 mm.	"You could have it all . . ."
4:11–4:35	**Chorus** (altered), 8 mm.	"If I could start again . . ."
4:35–6:14	**Coda**, unmeasured	Noise (changes at 5:53)

serial killer (the keyboardist, for instance, is Madonna Wayne Gacy). Emerging from Florida, the band made its first commercial mark with its Trent Reznor–produced third album, *Antichrist Superstar* (p3, 1996), following with the even more successful *Mechanical Animals* in 1998 (p1 uk8). Like other shock-rockers before him, Manson did all he could to outrage the more conservative segment of middle America: he dressed outrageously (as a kind of ghoulish transvestite) and included vulgar and satanic content on the albums, practically begging to be banned from the radio. And mirroring the appeal of earlier outrageous bands to previous generations of youngsters, the band's attraction was largely that it misbehaved so proudly and unabashedly.

INDIE ROCK

In the last several chapters, we have followed the indie-rock underground, which began to develop during the early 1980s supported by a circuit of clubs and bars (often in college towns), college radio stations, and several magazines that chronicled the movement, including *College Music Journal* (*CMJ*). After the rise of alternative music in the pop mainstream during the early 1990s, indie rock continued to thrive as underground music. A series of important independent record labels played an important role in the scene during this time, furthering the ideals of the punk and hardcore movements. For example, the New York–based Matador label was extremely successful during the 1990s, releasing seminal music by groups such as Yo La Tengo, Pavement, and Guided by Voices. Other important labels were Merge in Chapel Hill, North Carolina, a label run by two members of the band Superchunk, and Sub Pop in Seattle, which released early records by Nirvana, Soundgarden, and Mudhoney. In Olympia, Washington, K Records had the band Beat Happening, while Kill Rock Stars Records released material by bands such as Sleater-Kinney, Elliott Smith, and Bikini Kill. Despite the popularity of alternative music in the early 1990s, college radio stations were still the main source of radio exposure for indie rock, and *CMJ* tracked which stations were playing which records, much as *Billboard* did for mainstream pop styles. Several annual festivals that showcased live indie rock performances also emerged during the 1990s as important industry events, including the *CMJ* Music Marathon hosted in New York City and Austin's South by Southwest festival. After withstanding major label pilfering, during the 1990s indie rock was still small and off the beaten path, culturally speaking. For those who loved it, that was its charm.

Against the backdrop of a corporate machinery used to create and promote mainstream rock, perhaps the most prominent feature of indie rock in the 1990s was its do-it-yourself aesthetic: the idea that a band didn't need the machinery of a major record label to make good music. Most indie bands recorded for small labels and didn't get much mainstream attention or sell in large numbers compared to major label acts. However, with a growing infrastructure and fan base, many indie bands, even those who had the opportunity to record for major labels, found that they were happy to make a living playing music on their own terms. Even though the alternative movement grew out of the indie rock scene, with most Seattle bands moving from independent labels to major labels almost overnight, the indie scene outside of Seattle continued to thrive. In fact, many indie rock bands viewed the transformation of the Seattle scene as a negative example, and further evidence of the dangers of dealing with mainstream music conglomerates. Despite the small scale on which most of the bands enjoyed success, music critics often warmly praised indie bands and the indie scene generally. For such critics, indie music offered a purer and more direct style of rock music—a style uncorrupted by concerns about marketing and audience demographics.

Lo-Fi: Pavement, Guided by Voices, and Elliott Smith. Before the digital revolution of the late 1990s made high-quality recording facilities accessible to a much wider range of musicians, one of the drawbacks to working as part of the indie scene was the lack of good recording facilities. Moreover, as aspects of musical "professionalism" were often perceived as mechanistic and inauthentic, many indie bands celebrated a recording style that revealed the impulsive nature of their music.

Nowhere was this better exemplified than in the widespread "lo-fi" aesthetic that pervaded much indie rock during the early 1990s. In many ways, Pavement represented both the continuation of the indie scene during the 1990s and the celebration of the lo-fi aesthetic. Formed by childhood friends and classmates at the University of Virginia, the band eventually coalesced after moving to Hoboken, New Jersey, in the early 1990s. Among the most heralded indie bands of the 1990s, Pavement's take on lo-fi can be found in their physical and lyrical embodiment of the slacker lifestyle, in addition to the loose sound on their recordings. With albums released on Matador such as *Slanted and Enchanted* (1992) and *Crooked Rain, Crooked Rain* (uk15, 1994), Pavement's style featured characteristic half-sung, half-spoken vocals from singer Stephen Malkmus, heavy distorted guitar, and a loose backing groove. Hailing from Dayton, Ohio, Guided by Voices offered another take on lo-fi, piecing together albums from amateur recordings that included audible mistakes, eclectic instrumentation, and haphazard songwriting. As older musicians from a remote location, Guided by Voices were unlikely rock musicians, which fit the indie rock profile perfectly. Led by songwriter and lead vocalist Robert Pollard, the band and its many collaborative offshoots have released hundreds of albums since emerging on the Scat and Matador labels in the early 1990s with releases such as *Bee Thousand* (1994) and *Alien Lanes* (1995), both of which have become indie classics. Portland, Oregon–based Elliott Smith approached lo-fi in yet another manner, as an intimate window into the musical world of an inward-focused solo artist. Smith recorded his first solo record while part of the group Heatmiser, which was for a time signed to a major label. Far outweighing the reception of his rock-oriented work with Heatmiser, acoustic-based albums such as *Roman Candle* (1994), *Elliott Smith* (1995), and *Either/Or* (1997) featured Smith playing all the instruments by himself, often with primitive equipment, creating a homemade atmosphere that accompanied often existential lyrics. After several of his songs were featured on the soundtrack to the film *Good Will Hunting*, Smith was nominated for an Academy Award, and appeared in an incongruous setting on national television at the annual ceremony in Los Angeles backed by a full orchestra—a rare mainstream appearance for an indie rocker.

Merge: Magnetic Fields, Neutral Milk Hotel, and Superchunk. Although some indie labels cultivated a particular type of music, others highlighted a broad range of styles. In this way, it is often difficult to speak of "indie rock" as a musical style. Focusing on several of the most important bands to record for North Carolina's Merge records during the 1990s can highlight the wide range of styles proffered by a single label. Perhaps the most stereotypical group that recorded for Merge during this time was Superchunk, whose singer and guitarist Mac McCaughan and bassist Laura Balance started the label while recording several records for Matador. A high-energy group with clear roots in the punk movement, Superchunk is perhaps best known for their 1991 Matador album *No Pocky for Kitty* and the anthemic "Slack Motherfucker." Released on Merge, the single regales listeners with the story of a lowly, unmotivated employee, a typical character in the indie scene. Far from the high-energy style of Superchunk, the Louisiana-based group Neutral Milk Hotel espoused a lo-fi aesthetic to support the songwriting of group leader Jeff Mangum. Featuring cryptic instrumentation and lyrical references, and supported by styles that range from intimate acoustic settings to avant-garde noise experiments,

Jeremy Barnes (drums) and Jeff Mangum (guitar) of Neutral Milk Hotel. Using a lo-fi recording approach, unorthodox instrumentation, and vivid lyrical subject matter, Neutral Milk Hotel created some of the most heralded music of the 1990s indie scene.

the 1998 album *In the Aeroplane over the Sea* is considered one of the finest indie releases of the 1990s. A third Merge band, the Magnetic Fields, highlights the presence of perspectives from within indie rock that defy traditional male-dominated viewpoints. The group is the creative outlet for songwriter Stephin Merritt, and the music highlights songs rather than performance, featuring inventive instrumental accompaniment provided by cellist Sam Davol and multi-instrumentalists John Woo and Claudia Gonson. Merritt's music often includes themes of gender, punctuated by his lethargic baritone voice. His crowning achievement is the three-volume collection *69 Love Songs* (1999) (twenty-three songs per disc), which showcases his prodigious songwriting abilities.

Noise Pop: Yo La Tengo and My Bloody Valentine.

Through the lo-fi movement, we have seen that experimenting with sound was an important element of indie rock in the 1990s. While artists such as Guided by Voices and Elliott Smith often created intimate textures, other bands went to the opposite extreme, investigating the possibilities of noise, volume, repetition and droning in the recording studio and in live performance. New Jersey's Yo La Tengo offers a good example of this approach from the American indie scene. After recording a series of records for various independent labels in the late 1980s and early 1990s, the group signed to Matador and released iconic noise-rock albums such as *Painful* (1993) and *I Can Hear the Heart Beating as One* (1997). The latter contains several songs that exemplify the band's mid-1990s style. "Moby Octopad" shows the band's repetitive nature. It is built over a bass and drum groove that repeats for the length of the tune, overlaid with vocals and swaths of sound. A cover version of the Beach Boys' "Little Honda"

Georgia Hubley (drums) and Ira Kaplan (guitar) are the core members of Yo La Tengo, one of the most successful indie rock bands of the 1990s. Indie rock centered around a DIY (do-it-yourself) method of production: many bands had their own labels or used small ones (Matador produced many important indie groups, including Yo La Tengo), and the music often incorporated experiments in fidelity and noise.

Listening Guide ▪▪▪

Neutral Milk Hotel, "In the Aeroplane over the Sea"

Merge 136 (also released as Blue Rose 10192 and Domino 21)

Music by Jeff Mangum. Produced by Robert Schneider. Contained on the album *In the Aeroplane over the Sea*, which did not chart.

FORM: Simple verse, with bridge. After a short introduction, a 16-measure verse is presented. In the second verse, a series of instruments enter to enhance the musical texture. The instrumental bridge uses very similar musical material, but changed enough to offer contrast. The second bridge incorporates vocals, and repeats the musical material of the instrumental bridge, but presents the chords half as fast. This turns an 8-measure section into a 16-measure section. The interlude also presents this contrasting music at the same rate. A final 16-measure verse ends the song, with no fade out or postlude.

TIME SIGNATURE: 6/8.

INSTRUMENTATION: Acoustic guitar, drums, fuzz bass, singing saw (L and R), flugelhorn.

0:00–0:07	**Introduction**, 4 mm.	Multitracked acoustic guitar.
0:07–0:40	**Verse 1**, 16 mm.	Vocals and guitar. Notice how the form of the verse is 8 + 8, with two distinct parts. "What a beautiful face . . ."
0:40–1:12	**Verse 2**, 16 mm.	Drums and bass enter. Notice the multitracked "singing saws," which create an ethereal sound that reflects the subject matter. "And one day . . ."
1:12–1:28	**Instrumental bridge**, 9 mm.	Solo featuring a flugelhorn. Note how a basic 8-mm. phrase adds an additional measure to prepare for the entrance of the next verse.
1:28–2:00	**Verse 3**, 16 mm.	As before with active singing saws. "What a curious life . . ."
2:00–2:32	**Bridge**, 16 mm.	The flugelhorn performs multiple parts. "Now, how I remember . . ."
2:32–2:47	**Interlude**, 8 mm.	The squeaking sounds in each speaker are the saws!
2:47–3:22	**Verse 4**, 16 mm.	The flugelhorn has been added to the final verse. "What a beautiful face . . ."

provides an excellent example of the group's use of noise. Supported throughout by a heavy bed of distorted guitar, the formal guitar solo section consists of the band playing through the chord changes, while guitarist Ira Kaplan plays a single distorted guitar chord throughout. Although bands like Yo La Tengo often infused noise experiments into their music, other bands were known for working more thoroughly with this technique. Among these was the Irish band My Bloody Valentine, whose 1991 album *Loveless* (uk24) has become a fixture of indie-rock playlists. Led by guitarist Kevin Shields and featuring the vocals and guitar of Bilinda Butcher, My Bloody Valentine produced a dense sonic palette of noisy guitars supporting strong melodic material, producing what has often been called "shoegazing" music. Drawing on the 1980s legacy of groups like Sonic Youth, experiments with noise were by no means confined to Yo La Tengo and My Bloody Valentine, and were central to the work of many indie-rock groups during the 1990s.

Female Perspectives: Liz Phair, Ani DiFranco, and Sleater-Kinney.

Although overwhelmingly white and upper middle class, the indie-rock movement was arguably more open than the mainstream in terms of embracing varying gender perspectives. Chicago-based Liz Phair, for example, was known for her *Girly Sound* tapes, which spread as bootlegs through the indie community. She later released the Matador album *Exile in Guyville* (1993), which is a response to the Rolling Stones' *Exile on Main Street*. Containing provocative songs like "Fuck and Run," this album and the follow-up *Whip-Smart* (p27, 1994) propelled Phair's lo-fi female perspective into the center of the indie community. New York–based Ani DiFranco made a mark as a female songwriter, performer, and businesswoman,

Ani DiFranco performing in the Netherlands in 2001. DiFranco was staunchly independent and acted as songwriter, performer, and producer on her numerous releases beginning in the 1990s. DiFranco also ran her own record company, Righteous Babe, which put her in control of the business aspects of her music.

resisting major label offers and releasing her music on her own indie label, Righteous Babe. Her 1995 album, *Not a Pretty Girl*, garnered critical acclaim and mainstream media attention, while *Little Plastic Castle* (1998) rose as high as number twenty-two on the pop charts. Frank and confrontational, DiFranco has been prolific as a songwriter, releasing nearly twenty studio albums since her debut in the 1990s. Portland, Oregon-based Sleater-Kinney also provided a loud female voice among the indie underground. Composed of all female musicians, Sleater-Kinney was an integral part of the riot grrrl movement of feminist punk musicians in the Pacific Northwest, which was supported by a wide variety of self-produced zines and concert promotions. Releasing albums on seminal indie labels like Chainsaw, Kill Rock Stars, and Sub Pop, Sleater-Kinney is best known for the albums *Call the Doctor* (1996) and *Dig Me Out* (1997), which are cited consistently as important contributions to the indie scene.

Alt-Country: Uncle Tupelo and Ryan Adams.

The idea of blending country music with rock goes back at least to the second half of the 1960s with the Byrds' *Sweetheart of the Rodeo* and Dylan's *Nashville Skyline*. By the early 1970s, the Eagles and others had developed sophisticated country-rock styles, and these groups would influence not only a generation of rock musicians but also a new generation of country musicians, such as Garth Brooks. By the late 1980s, country music was undergoing a stylistic shift under the influence of rock that would lead to chart-topping albums throughout the 1990s, and a pair of friends from Belleville, Illinois, returned to the idea of blending rock and country from an indie-rock perspective, forming the band Uncle Tupelo. Jeff Tweedy and Jay Farrar named the band's debut album *No Depression* (1990), after an old Carter Family song they covered as the album's opening track. Released on the small label Rockville, the album would spawn a movement within indie rock called "alt-country," as college radio stations began playing the band's music. Like many indie bands, Uncle Tupelo created the impression of musical informality and seemed to project a lack of concern for commercial appeal. But Tweedy and Farrar were highly skilled songwriters and performers, and their talent became increasingly clear as the band continued to record albums such as *Still Feel Gone* (1991), *March 16–20, 1992* (1992), and *Anodyne* (1993). The group split up in 1994, as Farrar went on to form Son Volt and Tweedy formed Wilco. Both of these bands would enjoy success and critical acclaim well into the next decade. While alt-country bands like the Old-97s and the Bottle Rockets prospered in the indie scene during the 1990s, North Carolina's Ryan Adams offered a different take on the alt-country movement. With his group Whiskeytown, Adams joined fiddle player and vocalist Caitlin Cary on albums such as *Faithless Street* (1997) and *Stranger's Almanac* (1999) to replicate a pop-country sound through the palate of a former punk musician. After breaking from the group, however, Adams signed with Universal's Nashville subsidiary Lost Highway and released a string of albums including *Heartbreaker* (2000) and *Gold* (uk20, 2001) that showed his ability to perform in a wide range of styles.

Indie Music in the Mainstream: Beck.

Considering the aversion to major labels within the indie world, fans were especially wary of indie bands or artists who signed with big record companies. Among the acts who successfully managed this transition was Beck Hansen, a Los Angeles–based singer-songwriter who recorded several lo-fi records on independent labels in the early 1990s. These early releases included *Golden Feelings* (1993), *Stereopathic Soulmanure* (1994), and *One Foot in the Grave* (1994), which grew out of the "anti-folk" movement in New York, a group of like-minded musicians who were shunned by the folk establishment. During the same period, Beck's single, "Loser" (1993), appeared on the indie label

Singer, songwriter, and producer Beck, in concert, 1997. For years, Beck has successfully straddled the indie–major label divide. His music blends the do-it-yourself feel of indie rock with elements of hip-hop, country rock, 1970s soul, and even classical music.

Listening Guide

Beck, "Loser" Bong Load Custom Records BL5 and DGC DGCS7-19270

Lyrics by Beck Hansen, music by Beck Hansen and Carl Stephenson. Produced by Beck Hansen, Carl Stephenson, and Tom Rothrock. Initially released in 1993 by Bong Load and then rereleased by DGC, the song reached #10 on the *Billboard* "Hot 100" (uk15) in 1994.

FORM: Simple verse-chorus. The entire song is based on a single chord, with the principal contrast being that the verses are rapped while the choruses are sung. Subsections are organized into 4-bar units. Note how the acoustic guitar, electric guitar, bass, and sitar move in and out of the texture following the structure of the 4-bar phrase structure.

TIME SIGNATURE: 4/4.

INSTRUMENTATION: Lead and backup vocals, acoustic guitar (with slide), electric guitar, sitar, bass, drums, percussion. The sitar part is likely played on an electric sitar, a guitar fitted with a bridge that reproduces the "buzzy" sound of a real sitar. Note as well the use of the tremolo effect on the electric guitar, creating a sound that seems to pulsate quickly in volume.

0:00–0:22	**Introduction**, 8 mm.	1-bar pattern introduced first in acoustic guitar, then repeated with drums then bass.
0:22–1:07	**Verse**, 16 mm.	Lead vocal is rapped. Sitar and electric guitar enter. Four 4-bar phrases. "In the time . . ."
1:07–1:29	**Chorus**, 8 mm.	Sung vocal, employing two 4-bar phrases. "Soy un perdedor . . ."
1:29–2:03	**Verse**, 12 mm.	Accompaniment varied from first verse, with 4-bar structure retained. "Forces of evil . . ."
2:03–2:26	**Chorus**, 8 mm.	As before, "Soy un perdedor . . ."
2:26–2:59	**Interlude**, 12 mm.	Based on the verse structure, 4-bar structure retained.
2:59–3:22	**Chorus**, 8 mm	As before, "Soy un perdedor . . ."
3:22–3:49	**Chorus**, 8 mm.	As before, with fade. "Soy un perdedor . . ."

Bong Load to much acclaim within the Southern California indie scene. He then signed with a major label (Geffen) and the single was rereleased, going to number ten in the United States (uk15, 1994). Geffen then released *Mellow Gold* (p13, 1994) and *Odelay* (p16 uk17, 1996). Beck's music blends the lo-fi approach of bands like Guided by Voices with hip-hop, country rock, 1970s soul, and even classical music. Combined with a keen sense for pop hooks ("Loser" is a good example), he produced a dizzying succession of styles and stylistic references, often within the same song. Beck's music is often full of samples and rapid shifts created by editing, like much beat-based music from earlier in the decade. Beck continued to enjoy

Sound Check

Artist	Song	Sound
Nirvana	Smells Like Teen Spirit (1992)	Form: simple verse-chorus (modified)
		Contrast between verse and chorus (instrumentation and vocals)
		2-bar phrase in the instruction is the basis for the song
		Short, contrasting 4-measure section added to choruses as transition
Red Hot Chili Peppers	Give It Away (1991)	Form: compound AABA (modified)
		Recurring rhythmic groove establish by drums, bass, and guitar
		Built on 4-bar phrases throughout
		Use of backward guitar effect on bridge sections
Green Day	When I Come Around (1995)	Form: contrasting verse-chorus
		Based mostly on a repeating 2-bar chord sequence
		Instrumental texture remains relatively constant throughout
		Instrumental stop at end of chorus creates emphasis on vocal "hook"
Nine Inch Nails	Hurt (1994)	Form: contrasting verse-chorus
		Unmeasured noise used as introduction and coda
		Altered lyrics in final chorus
Neutral Milk Hotel	In the Aeroplane over the Sea (1998)	Form: simple verse (modified)
		Interlude and bridge share a chord progression, but bridge moves half as fast
		Listen for musical saws
		Flugelhorn featured as solo instrument
Beck	Loser (1993)	Form: simple verse-chorus
		Entire song built on one chord
		Use rapped vocals In verses and sung vocals in chorus to establish contrast
		Instrumental parts come in and out of texture according to 4-bar structure

success on the charts and with critics during the second half of the decade with *Mutations* (p13 uk24, 1998) and *Midnite Vultures* (p34 uk19, 1999) and into the new century with *Sea Change* (p8 uk20, 2002) and *Guero* (p2 uk15, 2005). Much like R.E.M. in the late 1980s and Nirvana in the early 1990s, Beck maintained an indie aesthetic while transitioning into the mainstream. As we will see, many more bands began to cross this divide after the turn of the millennium, as distribution of indie records became more sophisticated and fans gained greater access to music from outside the mainstream.

While alternative rock began the 1990s as the next big thing, it was not the only style of importance in the decade. Already in this chapter, we have seen how indie reacted against alternative while other bands extended metal by integrating elements of rap, among other elements. One of the most important elements binding all of this music together is the shared wariness of the mainstream music business. Even for those bands signed to major labels and receiving mainstream attention, it was important to be perceived as independent of the influence of commercial pressure. This attitude of defiance goes back to the first days of rock and roll in the mid-1950s, though in this case the more direct link is to late-1970s punk. In the next chapter, we will explore how a wide variety of styles continued to develop out of other pop and rock legacies from the 1960s, '70s, and '80s, creating a broad range of styles during the 1990s.

For Additional Online Resources, visit:
digital.wwnorton.com/whatsthatsound5

FURTHER READING

Michael Azerrad, *Come as You Are: The Story of Nirvana* (Broadway Books, 1993).

Scott Becker, ed., *We Rock So You Don't Have To* (Incommunicado, 1998).

Peter Blecha, *Sonic Boom: The History of Northwest Rock, from "Louise Louie" to "Smells Like Teen Spirit"* (Backbeat Books, 2009).

Carrie Brownstein, *Hunger Makes Me a Modern Girl: A Memoir* (Riverhead, 2015).

Charles R. Cross, *Heavier Than Heaven: A Biography of Kurt Cobain* (Hyperion, 2001).

Rob Javanovic, *Nirvana: The Recording Sessions* (Soundcheck Books, 2012).

Jeff Kitts, Brad Tolinski, and Harold Steinblatt, eds., *Alternative Rock: They Launched a Revolution—and Won!* (Hal Leonard, 1999).

Kim Neely, *Five against One: The Pearl Jam Story* (Penguin, 1998).

Kaya Oakes, *Slanted and Enchanted: The Evolution of Indie Culture* (Holt, 2009).

Pearl Jam, *Pearl Jam Twenty* (Simon & Schuster, 2011).

Dick Porter, *Rapcore: The Nu-Metal Fusion* (Plexus, 2003).

Marc Spitz, *Nobody Like You: Inside the Turbulent Life, Times, and Music of Green Day* (Hyperion, 2006).

14

WIDENING GAPS

CHAPTER PREVIEW

- The rise of the classic rock radio format, combined with the popularity of the CD and the emergence of rock documentaries, kept 1960s and '70s rock in demand among listeners.

- New bands emerged that made use of earlier rock traditions, such as Phish leading the jam band movement and Radiohead engaging elements of psychedelia.

- Feel-good, guitar-driven rock of artists like Sheryl Crow, Hootie and the Blowfish, and Matchbox 20 became staples of FM radio.

- The female singer-songwriter movement became prominent in the 1990s, led by artists such as Tori Amos and Sarah McLachlan and promoted via concert events such as Lilith Fair.

- Artists such as *NSYNC and the Spice Girls reinvented the teen idol approach, while singers Britney Spears and Christina Aguilera became pop sex symbols.

- Rap continued to develop into the 1990s, with a strong division emerging within gangsta rap between East Coast (Puff Daddy) and West Coast (Snoop Doggy Dog, Dr. Dre) artists. Eminem emerged as an often-controversial artist.

- Electronic dance music developed out of late-1970s disco and 1980s regional dance-club scenes.

Today, most college-age students who are fans of rock music from the 1960s and 1970s were born decades after this music was first popular. In many ways, it is the music of their parents'—or even their grandparents'—generation. Considering the role that rock music still plays in establishing a generation's sense of identity, it is fascinating that large numbers of teens still listen to decades-old rock music, in some cases even preferring it to newer and more current rock. Many of these fans of "classic rock" are first exposed to this music through their parents (or their parents' record collections), while others first encounter classic rock on the radio, on cable television, or in record stores.

Britain's Radiohead emerged as one of the most popular and innovative bands of the 1990s. The group's 1997 record, *OK Computer,* was groundbreaking in a number of ways. It was received favorably by critics and propelled the band to international stardom. Many of the themes on *OK Computer* are abstract, but the more narrative sections display an earnest—often called "anxious"—quality, with self-reflective lyrics. The music mixes heavy rock sounds with complicated rhythms and forms. The soundscape of the record shows an attention to detail missing from many rock records, with avant-garde electronic sounds and a drone-oriented feel that appealed to many listeners. Sometimes chided for their seriousness and sentimentality, the group is representative of a more overtly virtuosic, intellectual strain of rock's history that used recording in novel ways.

This chapter will consider new industry developments in the 1990s such as the rise of the classic rock radio format and birth of the CD reissue. Musically, most of the music we will cover was indebted in some way to the rock of the past. Jam bands, the feel-good rock of Hootie and the Blowfish, female singer-songwriters associated with the Lilith movement, and even a new breed of teen idol groups all had strong connections to previous movements in rock music. Other forms considered in this chapter, such as new styles of electronic-based music, point to newer developments that unfolded over the course of the decade, leading to important musical developments in the new millennium.

THE RISE OF CLASSIC ROCK

The Age of the CD Reissue: Selling the Same Music Again. A slow change in the standard format of the record business from records to compact discs, which began in the 1980s, was complete by the early 1990s. Compact disc technology was first introduced by Sony and Philips in 1980, and the first commercial CD was issued in late 1982. By the mid-1980s, record companies offered a small number of albums in this new format, which gradually grew over the course of the decade, as sale of cassettes and long-play records dwindled. CDs had become the industry standard by the beginning of the 1990s, with almost one-third of all American households using them in one form or another. From a music lover's point of view, the CD constituted a major advance. Compact discs were much more portable than records, and unlike tapes, you could go directly to the song you wanted to hear without having to fuss with rewind or fast-forward buttons. And while records and tapes showed signs of wear with each use, CDs were marketed to last forever, with no appreciable degradation in audio fidelity no matter how many times you played them. (We now know that this is not true!) Add this to claims by audio experts that the digital sound of CDs was far superior to the analog sound of records or tapes—a claim that is still hotly debated—and CDs seemed to be the perfect format. Since the CD had a reputation for superior audio quality, many middle-class baby boomers—now entering middle age and with plenty of disposable income—revisited the music of their youth in a new format.

The changeover to compact discs was just the financial shot in the arm the sagging music business needed during the second half of the 1980s. Although production of CDs was limited by a small number of available pressing plants in the early 1980s, once manufacturing began to shift toward these new digital discs, companies were able to manufacture CDs in large enough volume to reduce production costs. The age of the CD reissue was in full swing in the late 1980s, often advertising features such as "digital remastering" and "bonus tracks" to tempt buyers and further sweeten the deal. Companies began to put together

A CD player from 1983 made by Philips of Holland. The CD was developed by Philips in conjunction with the Japanese manufacturer Sony, and was first released in 1982. The rise of the CD reissues in the late 1980s and early 1990s was a boon to the record industry. At the time, these units were cutting-edge technology, lauded for their compact size and audio fidelity.

multi-CD boxed sets for the most serious-minded and dedicated fans, often with extensive and detailed liner notes, previously unreleased tracks or mixes, and endorsements from the original artists. The price of CDs, however, stayed higher than it had been with vinyl, and these extra profits went right into record-company coffers. Older rock albums had long ago covered their initial costs of production, so reissuing them produced easy money for the major labels.

Radio Killed the Video Star: The Classic-Rock Radio Format.

About the same time record companies were beginning the compact disc switchover, radio formatting also began to reflect listener interest in a format that came to be called classic rock. Detroit radio consultant Fred Jacobs helped create this format, which courted baby boomers to tune in to stations playing nothing but the biggest rock hits from 1966 to 1978. Since the rapid-growth years of the mid-1970s, radio stations had relied increasingly on outside consultants like Jacobs to program their playlists. Lee Abrams, for instance, is widely credited (or blamed) for developing the stricter album-oriented rock format that characterized rock radio in the late 1970s. Like most consultants, Abrams sold his format to stations across the country as a prepackaged product—a tried-and-tested recipe for radio ratings success. Jacobs was trying to do the same thing when he came up with his classic-rock format. In 1985, the first classic-rock station went on the air in Lansing, Michigan, and dominated its market. As word of this early success spread, so did the format. By 1990, classic rock had become one of the most successful formats in radio and led the business of radio through the rest of the decade, sometimes with multiple stations in a single market competing against one another.

Classic-rock radio succeeded because it appealed to the same people who were buying CD reissues and, as this group aged in the 1990s, they stuck with classic rock. Programmers tweaked the format, adding songs that were less well known ("deep tracks") or recently released tracks ("fresh tracks") by the original '60s and '70s bands. The format was initially popular with record companies, since it seemed to support their rerelease of older rock. When classic rock continued to dominate in most markets and the playlists showed little change, however, the record labels began to see classic rock as squeezing out their new artists and releases. This became compounded by the fact that many younger listeners preferred classic rock to new music. Although there were many other popular radio formats, classic rock was one of the most common types of stations between the mid-1980s and a large-scale radio industry transformation in 1996, when a Telecommunications Act was passed in the U.S. Congress that allowed station owners much more flexibility in ownership.

Behind the Music: The Rise of VH-1 and the Rockumentary.

For the first few years of its existence, MTV was the only mainstream cable channel specializing in music videos. The MTV audience was young, however, and in 1985 MTV's parent company MTV Networks began broadcasting a new channel called VH-1, which targeted an older demographic—the same baby boomers who bought CD reissues and listened to classic-rock radio. Originally, the channel did not play much classic rock, preferring adult-oriented "light rock," rhythm and blues, and jazz. VH-1 did not succeed as quickly as CDs and classic-rock radio, however, and the channel struggled for over a decade until the development of several new types of shows. One of these was *Pop-Up Video*, which began in 1996. Featuring videos with onscreen facts about the music (sometimes very clever and humorous), this program drew many viewers who might not have had the patience for music videos otherwise. Many people found the factoids more fun and entertaining than the music. VH-1 then developed two quasi-historical series in 1997, *Behind the Music* and *Legends*. Both of these focused on famous rock musicians and their careers, following a predictable rags-to-riches template (with disaster sprinkled in along the way) and placing far more emphasis on the sensational aspects of their subjects' personal lives than their musical or stylistic development. Despite this, VH-1 gave viewers the sense that they were learning about rock's history, and it provided a video angle to complement CD reissues and classic-rock radio. Far from anomalous, the rise of VH-1 documentaries accompanied a large-scale international interest in rock history during the mid-1990s. In 1995, the ten-episode Time-Life series *A History of Rock and Roll* debuted, as did the ten-episode PBS series produced by Quincy Jones, *The History of Rock 'n' Roll*. By focusing on rock as a historical entity rather than a new form, VH-1 participated in a growing appreciation for rock as an important American art form. Moreover, through sales of reissued CDs, the classic-rock radio format, and new video channels focused on adult audiences, it was clear that there was big money in old music.

Eric Clapton proved that artists from rock's past could forge successful careers decades later. His album *Unplugged* (1992), with the somber hit "Tears in Heaven," was one of the 1990s' biggest releases. Clapton's success in the 1990s was matched by other classic rockers, including Santana and Paul McCartney.

You're Never Too Old to Rock and Roll. While the classic-rock movement celebrated rock's past, many of the bands and artists featured in this revival enjoyed great success in the 1990s. Less than two years before VH-1 developed *Behind the Music* and *Legends*, the *Beatles Anthology* video documentary aired for the first time on ABC, featuring two unfinished John Lennon sessions completed by Paul, George, and Ringo. "Free as a Bird" hit the Top 10 of the "Hot 100" in late 1995, and "Real Love" reached the Top 5 of the UK charts. The Beatles also hit the top of the album charts in 1995 and 1996 with three *Anthology* collections of rare tracks and alternative takes. Their British-invasion compatriots, the Rolling Stones, also had big albums in the 1990s with *Voodoo Lounge* (p2 uk1, 1994) and *Bridges to Babylon* (p3, uk6, 1997), and ex-Yardbird and Cream guitarist Eric Clapton released one of the decade's biggest-selling albums, *Unplugged* (p2 uk2, 1992), drawn from his performance on the MTV show of the same name. The album featured the tender ballad "Tears in Heaven" (p2 uk5), written for his young son, who had been killed in a tragic accident. Acts from the 1970s also stormed the charts: the reunited Eagles hit the top spot in 1994 with *Hell Freezes Over*, Peter Gabriel steamed back with *Us* (p2 uk2, 1992), and Santana hit later in the decade with *Supernatural* (p1 uk1, 1999), featuring the hit single "Smooth" (p1). Stars from the 1980s also scored big, with Sting's *Ten Summoner's Tales* (p2 uk2, 1993) and *Mercury Falling* (p5 uk4, 1996), Tom Petty's Rick Rubin–produced *Wildflowers* (p8, 1994), and Bruce Springsteen's *Greatest Hits* (p1 uk1, 1995). Perhaps most impressive, U2 hit the top spot on both sides of the Atlantic with *Zooropa* (1993) and *Pop* (1997), establishing themselves among rock's most enduring acts.

Bands without popular new material also benefited from a resurgence of older groups. As classic-rock stations focused on hits from previous decades, many bands that had been famous in the 1960s and 1970s regrouped and toured outdoor theaters during the summer months. Bands such as Chicago, Yes, Foreigner, Styx, Kansas, and others never returned to the charts with the same force, but they were once again capable of filling large venues, especially if they shared the bill with other vintage acts. Like jazz, blues, or country, it was now possible to grow old in rock and roll—as an artist and as a fan. Moreover, the success of older groups in record stores and on concert tours reinforced the idea that rock had an important past with senior figures to act as standard-bearers.

NEW ROCK TRADITIONS

The Return of Jamming. As a younger generation of listeners embraced rock traditionalism, a new breed of younger roots rockers began to emerge. One place that traditionalism flourished during the 1990s was the "jam band scene," which had become an important underground movement across the country. The jam band phenomenon revived the idea that live performances were the central focus of the music and that highly developed musical skill—especially in improvisation—was an important element of rock performance. While jam bands regularly released studio versions of their material, fans often considered live performances by these groups to be the most definitive. Many of these bands allowed (and even encouraged) fans to record and trade live performances. It was not uncommon for concert promoters to designate specific "taper" sections at shows, where technological savvy was apparent in a sea of tall microphone stands. Jam band performances often revealed how night after night a track could change through improvisation, heading off in any number of stylistic directions.

The heroes of the 1990s jam bands were primarily the Grateful Dead and the Allman Brothers Band, both legendary for their sprawling live shows and die-hard cultural followings. Although many new jams bands had gained regional popularity in the early 1990s, a collective summer tour in 1992 called H.O.R.D.E. (Horizons of Rock Developing Everywhere) marked the first important step toward a new generation of jam bands reaching a national audience. Among the most prominent of these was Vermont-based Phish, who arguably became the torchbearers of the jam band movement after the death of Jerry Garcia in 1995. Creating music that incorporated jazz improvisation, children's fairy tales, silly rituals (like jumping on trampolines and vacuum-cleaner solos), and high-energy rock solos, Phish garnered a huge following in the mid-1990s.

Phish performing live in 1995. After the death of Grateful Dead guitarist Jerry Garcia, Phish became one of the most important and popular groups in the jam band scene. Like the Dead, they allowed taping, and many fans followed the band from town to town during their sellout tours. The music of Phish expanded the jam band style in a number of ways, often stretching performances into long, experimental journeys while using a varied repertoire of cover songs and maintaining a quirky sense of humor.

Listening Guide

Phish, "Chalkdust Torture" Electra 61274

Words by Tom Marshall and music Trey Anastasio. Produced by Phish. Included on the album *Picture of Nectar*, which was released in mid-1992 and made no significant showing on the national charts.

FORM: Contrasting verse-chorus. The nucleus of the song is a 2-bar riff, which is presented in pairs throughout. This jam serves as the basis for the verse, interlude, vamp, and solo sections. Despite the regularity of this simple kernel of an idea, there are many instances of phrase extension and playfulness with the small-scale elements of the form. Examples of this are the second vocal section in each verse (5 measures) and the second phrase of the chorus (7 measures). In keeping with Phish's quirky identity, this song vacillates between virtuosic, screaming rock sections and cartoonish precomposed melodies. (Be sure to count 2 measures of rest after the guitar solo.) Notice the use of dynamics throughout, ranging from a relatively docile vamp beginning each verse to the height of the guitar solo. This type of ecstatic "arrival" is a common feature of jam-oriented music. (Also note that this is the original studio version of the song, and there are many live versions available, which are usually extended. Studying the places in the form that lead to this sort of flexibility can be an interesting exercise!)

TIME SIGNATURE: 4/4.

INSTRUMENTATION: Drums, bass, electric guitars, piano, organ, lead and backing vocals.

0:00–0:28	**Introduction**, 8 + 8 mm.	The song starts with a driving, distorted guitar riff and drums, and during the first 8 mm. drums, bass, and piano enter progressively. The band plays full tilt as a unit during the second group of 8 mm.
0:28–1:01	**Verse 1**, 4 + 3 + 4 mm., 4 + 5 + 8 mm.	A 4-mm. vamp begins the first verse, during which the band plays with a much softer dynamic. The first vocal section is 3 mm., followed by a 4-mm. presentation of the main riff. After another 4-mm. vamp, the second vocal section is extended to 5 mm., creating a sense of instability. A longer, 8-mm. presentation of the riff follows. Notice the spacializing effect on the lead vocals. "Come stumble my mirth . . ."
1:01–1:28	**Verse 2**, 4 + 3 + 4 mm., 5 + 4 mm.	Like verse 1, without a vamp before the second vocal section, and with a shorter presentation of the riff at the end. "Confuse what you can . . ."
1:28–1:55	**Chorus**, 4 + 7 + 4 + 4 mm.	Organ enters and the drumbeat incorporates the ride cymbal during the first two phrases. The anthemic "can't I live while I'm young" section is a dynamic high point, followed by a driving iteration of the main riff. "But who can unlearn . . ."
1:55–2:22	**Verse 3**, 4 + 3 + 4 mm., 5 + 4 mm.	Uses the same structure of verse 2. "But no peace . . ."
2:22–2:47	**Chorus**, 4 + 7 + 4 + 4 mm.	As before. "But who can unlearn . . ."

(continued)

2:47–3:52	**Solo**, 50 mm.	The solo section begins with a wailing guitar, which leads much of the activity throughout. Notice how the ideas presented throughout this section occur in groups of eight and how the guitar gets higher and higher, leading to a climax. During the last two 8-mm. sections the band performs a composed melody that leads to a complete stop. This serves as both a letdown from the solo and a bridge to the chorus.
3:52–4:19	**Chorus**, 4 + 7 + 4 + 4 mm.	As before. The "Can't I live while I'm young" section is doubled. "But who can unlearn . . ."
4:19–4:31	**Postlude**, 5 mm.	The time signature changes during this instrumental postlude, which is disorienting, leading to a cartoonish ending of an otherwise intense, driving song. The 4 mm. of 8 beats divided in a 3 + 3 + 2 scheme (count one, two, three, one, two, three, one, two) are followed by a single measure of 6 beats, divided into three groups of two (count one, two, one, two, one, two).

Phish took control over many aspects of their concert promotion and recording efforts. Perhaps the best example of this control came in the form of the many large-scale festivals the group organized, beginning with the "Clifford Ball" in 1996. Held in remote locations such as rural Maine or the swamps of Florida, the band would create an entire town of followers for an entire weekend. Although Phish recorded many studio albums, their 1995 live album *A Live One* (p18) and the many official live concerts released through the group's Live Phish series give the best idea of how the band sounded in concert. Showing how the jam band movement and commercial radio were often disconnected, Phish consistently put together one of the highest-grossing concert tours during the late 1990s with little radio play and no hit singles. In many ways, the business practices of Phish were closely aligned with those of indie rock, as both jam bands and indie rockers worked largely outside of the mainstream music industry.

Another important group on the first H.O.R.D.E. tour was Widespread Panic, based out of Athens, Georgia. If Phish was considered an East Coast version of the Grateful Dead, Widespread Panic had a lot in common musically and culturally with the Allman Brothers. Not only was Widespread Panic from the Allmans' adopted state of Georgia, they were also the first group to sign with the newly resuscitated Capricorn Records (now based in Nashville). Featuring the swirling guitar of Michael Houser and the gritty vocals of John Bell, Widespread Panic's music embodied their southern roots, while exhibiting that the range of rock culture in the American South defied stereotypes. The group's early albums *Widespread Panic* (1991) and *Everyday* (1993) became widely known in jam band circles. Hailing from the New York metropolitan area, both Blues Traveler and the Spin Doctors also built their reputations on live performance, and anchored the H.O.R.D.E. scene in the urban mid-Atlantic region. The Spin Doctors and Blues Traveler were among the few jam-oriented groups to enjoy commercial success during the early 1990s. Featuring the offbeat vocal style of Chris Barron, the Spin Doctors' *Pocketful of Kryptonite* (1991) hit number three on the *Billboard* "Top Albums" chart in 1992 (uk2), while the single "Two Princes" rose into the Top 10 of the "Hot 100" (uk3). Two years later, Blues Traveler's harmonica-laden "Runaround" also reached the Top 10, and has since become a staple of light-rock radio and television commercials.

While Phish and Widespread Panic found success mostly in touring, and Blues Traveler and the Spin Doctors enjoyed brief stints on the pop charts, Dave Matthews Band emerged out of the jam band scene as a group that combined grass-roots touring with widespread commercial success. With an unorthodox instrumental lineup consisting of drums, bass, saxophone, violin, and acoustic guitar, Dave Matthews Band combined elements of jazz, funk, bluegrass, and the singer-songwriter movement to create memorable songs to serve as the basis for large-scale improvisation. The group built a strong regional following during the early 1990s working out of Charlottesville, Virginia, and emerged on the national stage in late 1994 after the release of *Under the Table and Dreaming* (p11). The group established several connections to the jam band movement, with Blues Traveler's John Popper playing harmonica on their hit "What Would You Say" (p22, 1994). Moreover, on several occasions in 1994 they performed as an opening act for Phish, a rare occasion in itself. Unlike their jam band brethren, however, Dave Matthews Band became fixtures on the *Billboard* charts, releasing chart-topping albums such as *Crash* (p2, 1996), *Before These Crowded Streets* (p1, 1998), *Everyday* (p1, 2001), *Busted Stuff* (p1, 2002), and *Stand Up* (p1, 2005). In early 2000, Matthews and several associates formed the ATO record label, which has released recordings by groups such as Alabama Shakes, My Morning Jacket, Drive-By Truckers, and Widespread Panic.

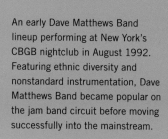

An early Dave Matthews Band lineup performing at New York's CBGB nightclub in August 1992. Featuring ethnic diversity and nonstandard instrumentation, Dave Matthews Band became popular on the jam band circuit before moving successfully into the mainstream.

Oasis, Radiohead, and Smashing Pumpkins.

The jam band scene was certainly not the only musical movement of the 1990s to freely reference rock music from the 1960s and 1970s. Led by singer-songwriter-guitarist Billy Corgan, Chicago's Smashing Pumpkins became one of the most successful acts of the 1990s by reworking aspects of progressive rock, psychedelia, and early heavy metal. The band is often thought of as an alternative band, though the conceptual nature of the music makes them much more similar to Radiohead than to Nirvana or Pearl Jam. After a couple of relatively successful album releases, including *Siamese Dream* (p10 uk4, 1993), *Mellon Collie and the Infinite Sadness* topped the U.S. charts in 1995 (uk4).

Radiohead's Thom Yorke performing live in Belgium in 1997. Emerging out of the Britpop scene of the early 1990s, Radiohead went on to become international superstars and one of the most innovative and popular rock bands of their generation. Often mixing references to classic rock and progressive tendencies with modern electronic sounds and approaches to musical creation, Radiohead became a model of a new form of intellectual rock in the twenty-first century.

Similarly, a group of bands from the UK who became popular during this time, often under the label Britpop, drew heavily on British invasion music of the 1960s. In the United States, the most popular of these groups was Oasis, a band heavily influenced by the Beatles. Oasis reached the top of the British charts in 1994 with *Definitely Maybe*, scored a transcontinental hit the next year with *(What's the Story) Morning Glory?*, and reached the peak of their success in the United States in 1997 with the album *Be Here Now* (p2 uk1). Within the UK, the success of Oasis was more overwhelming than it was in the States, and many other groups who were virtually unknown to American audiences rose to the top of the charts in Britain, including Suede, Pulp, Supergrass, and Blur.

Perhaps the most important band to come out of England during this time was only marginally related to the Britpop movement. Drawing heavily on the atmospheric music of Pink Floyd and later British progressive rock, Radiohead first scored with *Pablo Honey* (p32 uk22, 1993), which contained the Top 40 single "Creep," and followed up with *The Bends* (p88 uk4, 1995), which sold only marginally in the United States. Their next effort, *OK Computer* (p21 uk1, 1997), made the band international critical darlings, and they won the Grammy Award for Best Alternative Album in 1998 despite not even reaching the Top 20 of the *Billboard* album charts. Often dealing with lyrical themes of isolation and alienation, Radiohead's music incorporated avant-garde noise, electronic effects, and wide dynamic shifts. Later Radiohead albums were commercially successful in the United States, including *Kid A* (p1 uk1, 2000), *Amnesiac* (p2 uk1, 2001), and *Hail to the Thief* (p3 uk1, 2003). In October 2007, the band made headlines for releasing their album *In Rainbows* to the public through their website on a pay-as-you-wish basis. Much like the jam bands, who advocated tape trading as a means of maintaining a loyal and knowledgeable fan base, Radiohead's experiment with *In Rainbows* was a legal way to expose hesitant album buyers to their newest music. And just as groups such as Phish and the Dave Matthews Band used free music to increase concert and album sales, *In Rainbows* hit the top slot on the album charts in both the United States and the UK upon its physical release in December 2007.

Listening Guide

Radiohead, "Airbag" Electra 61274

Music and words by Thom Yorke, Jonny Greenwood, Phil Selway, Ed O'Brien, and Colin Greenwood. Produced by Radiohead and Nigel Godrich. Included on the album *OK Computer*, which was released in mid-1997 and reached #21 on the "Billboard 200" chart and #1 in the UK.

FORM: Simple verse with refrain. This record shows the potential complexity of a song using three main parts: a verse, a refrain, and a composed instrumental melody. The majority of the track is based on (what seems to be) a looped drum performance. Although the musical style is quite different, the form of each verse works much like a 12-bar blues, making up a statement, a restatement, and a contrasting statement. In this case, the contrasting statement is a refrain, which appears in multiple contexts throughout the song. The composed melody that begins the track also plays an important role throughout, as an introduction, an interlude between verses, and a conclusive section at the close of the record. The "extension" section provides an example of Radiohead flirting with more experimental electronic music.

TIME SIGNATURE: 4/4.

INSTRUMENTATION: Drums, bass, electric guitars, various keyboards and synths, lead and backing vocals.

0:00–0:26	**Introduction**, 9 mm.	The song starts with a driving riff and a tambourine, bass, electric guitar, and drums all enter sequentially, leading to a short vamp.
0:26–1:18	**Verse 1 (with refrain)**, 6 + 6 + 4 + 2 mm.	Two verse phrases are followed by a refrain and a vamp. Notice the active bass and ethereal instrumental melody. "In the next . . ."
1:18–1:32	**Interlude**, 5 mm.	A short presentation of the riff that opened the song with a new guitar melody (mostly without bass and drums), returning to the texture of the introduction.
1:32–2:18	**Verse 2 (with refrain)**, 6 + 6 + 4 mm.	Like verse 1, without the extended vamp at the end. A guitar countermelody enters at the beginning. "In a deep . . ."
2:18–2:58	**Solo**, 2 + 6 + 6 mm.	After 2 mm. of relative repose, an instrumental section ensues that mirrors the structure of the verse phrases, featuring a fast-picked guitar melody supported by bass and drums, then electric guitar.
2:58–3:27	**Refrain**, 10 mm. (6 + 4)	The refrain resolves in a new way, then repeats in its more normal form. "In an interstellar burst . . ."
3:27–4:12	**Extension**, 8 + 8 mm.	The beat continues but is accompanied by experimental sounds. The drums enter for the second half.
4:12–4:44	**Postlude**, 8 mm.	The introductory riff enters, creating a summative statement, and then resolves into the record's final chord. Notice the high-pitched ringing and other sound effects throughout.

ROCK IS STILL POP

Feel-Good Rock: Sheryl Crow and Hootie and the Blowfish.

Several groups emerged in 1994 that offered a lighter form of "feel good" rock music, seemingly as a reaction to the intensity that characterized grunge. Like the jam bands and Britpop, much of this music was clearly indebted to earlier styles. Created for the pop music market and live performances that featured literal presentations of studio recordings (and little jamming), the music of Sheryl Crow and Hootie and the Blowfish capitalized on a mainstream interest in back-to-basics rock. Based out of Los Angeles, Crow worked as a professional backing vocalist in the 1980s, appearing on a string of records and touring with Michael Jackson and Don Henley. Her 1993 album *Tuesday Night Music Club* (p3 uk8) contained the hits "All I Wanna Do" (p2 uk5, 1994) and "Strong Enough" (p5, 1995), and eventually ranked among the best-selling records of the decade. Her subsequent releases included *Sheryl Crow* (p6 uk5, 1996), *The Globe Sessions* (p5 uk2, 1998), and *C'mon C'mon* (p2 uk2, 2002). Unlike many of her roots-rock contemporaries from the mid-1990s, Crow's longevity has persisted into the 2000s as she has experimented with styles ranging from country to rhythm and blues. She has been a mainstay on the American album charts with each of her releases—including *Wildflower* (p2, 2005), *Detours* (p2, 2008), and *100 Miles from Memphis* (p3, 2010)—rising to the top of the *Billboard* album charts.

Sheryl Crow's *Tuesday Night Music Club* (1993) was one of the best-selling albums of the decade. Her style often combines the rootsy jingle-jangle guitars and vocal approach of the Byrds and Tom Petty with strong hooks and clever lyrics.

Based in the university town of Columbia, South Carolina, Hootie and the Blowfish projected a good-time, roots-rock style that featured Darius Rucker's soulful vocals (with occasional gospel influences) accompanied by happy, strummed acoustic guitar along with drums, bass, and 1970s-oriented electric guitar. Hootie and the Blowfish emerged into the mainstream in 1994, and were in the limelight for only a few years. Nevertheless, the band was among the most popular groups of the 1990s, with album sales that reached into the stratosphere. Their breakthrough album, *Cracked Rear View* (p1 uk12, 1994), contained the hits "Hold My Hand" (p10), "Let Her Cry" (p9), and "Only Wanna Be with You" (p6) and made the band's music a staple of mainstream rock radio in the mid-1990s. To date, *Cracked Rear View* has sold more than 15 million copies, making it one of the best-selling albums of the decade. The group followed with *Fairweather Johnson* (p1 uk9, 1996) and *Musical Chairs* (p4 uk15, 1998), but did not regain the popularity of their first commercial release. Subsequently, lead singer Darius Rucker remade himself as a country performer. His albums *Learn to Live* (p5 c1, 2008) and *Charleston, SC 1966* (p2 c1, 2010) both rose to the top of the country album charts and spawned several top-selling singles.

Counting Crows and the Wallflowers.

Coming out of the San Francisco area and led by songwriter and lead vocalist Adam Duritz, Counting Crows also emerged on the national stage in early 1994 during the mainstream peak of the alternative movement. The 1993 album *August & Everything After* established the band, going to number four in the United States (uk16) and containing the

Listening Guide

Sheryl Crow, "All I Wanna Do" A&M 0702

Words and music by Wyn Cooper, Sheryl Crow, Bill Bottrell, David Baerwald, and Kevin Gilbert. Produced by Bill Bottrell. Rose to #2 on the *Billboard* "Hot 100" chart in 1994 (uk4).

FORM: Simple verse-chorus, with pre-chorus. The verse and chorus are built on the same 3-chord, 4-bar chord progression, though the chorus diverges from that progression in the last 2 bars each time. The verses lead into a pre-chorus section, which drives the song forward to the chorus. This pre-chorus material is first heard as the introduction to the song. After the first time through the chorus, an instrumental interlude leads to the second verse; after the second chorus, that interlude—which is based on the song's 3-chord progression—is stretched to 8 bars, as a low guitar line that was first introduced during the verse sections comes to the fore. This creates a section that might be considered an instrumental verse, especially since the section leads right into the pre-chorus and forward to the final chorus. The last chorus repeats the final 4 bars—a "tag"—before heading into the ending, which is a 13-bar section that could be heard as an instrumental version of the chorus (note the ending) with an extra bar added for the last chord.

TIME SIGNATURE: 4/4. Note how the percussion and handclaps work with the drums to create a variety of rhythmic feels that help distinguish the song's sections.

INSTRUMENTATION: Electric guitar, slide guitar, acoustic guitar, electric piano, synthesizer strings, bass, drums, percussion, handclaps, lead and backing vocals.

0:00–0:14	**Introduction,** 6 mm.	This music becomes the pre-chorus later in the song, as Crow speaks over rhythmic and jazzy guitar, synthesizer strings, and handclaps. "This ain't no disco . . ."
0:14–0:54	**Verse 1,** 20 mm.	Full band kicks in, as slide guitar weaves in and out of the solo vocal, a low guitar melody enters toward the middle. "All I wanna do . . ."
0:54–1:06	**Pre-chorus,** 6 mm.	Synthesizer strings return with intro music, now without jazzy guitar but with full band. "They drive their shiny . . ."
1:06–1:38	**Chorus,** 16 mm.	Harmony vocal and acoustic guitar enter, as slide guitar comes back for 12-bar chorus, which is followed by a 4-bar instrumental interlude. "All I wanna do . . ."
1:38–2:02	**Verse 2,** 12 mm.	As in verse 1, though shorter this time. Note Crow's conversational delivery of the lyrics, which don't rhyme and enhance the sense of a story told in free prose. "I like a good . . ."
2:02–2:14	**Pre-chorus,** 6 mm.	Synthesizer strings return as before, "And a happy couple . . ."
2:14–2:54	**Chorus,** 12 + 8 mm.	Harmony vocal and acoustic guitar enter as before, but this time the instrumental interlude stretches to 8 bars, focusing on a guitar melody first introduced in the verses but now functioning almost as an instrumental verse. "All I wanna . . ."

(continued)

2:54–3:10	**Pre-chorus**, 8 mm.	As before, but a little more rhythmically active. "Otherwise the bar is ours . . ."
3:10–3:58	**Chorus**, 20 + 4 mm.	Harmony vocal and acoustic guitar return as before, but this time the chorus is stretched to 20 bars and is followed by a 4-bar tag. "All I wanna do . . ."
3:58–4:32	**Coda**, 13 mm.	This ending is a 12-bar chorus, played instrumentally, with some of the instruments dropping out in the last couple of measures.

hit singles "Mr. Jones" (p2) and "Round Here" (p7). *Recovering the Satellites* topped the charts in 1996 (uk6) and contained two hit singles, "Angels of the Silences" (p3) and "A Long December" (p5). The band's music-stylistic debts to earlier artists can be heard especially in Duritz's vocal style, which has often been compared to Van Morrison. At a time when electronic music was prevalent, it was also notable that the band employed vintage instrumentation (clearly visible in the music video for "Mr. Jones"), including an organ, classic Gibson and Fender guitars, and an old-fashioned large diaphragm microphone. These elements contributed directly to the band's "alternative" identity in the marketplace.

Interestingly, both Hootie and the Blowfish ("Only Wanna Be with You") and Counting Crows ("Mr. Jones") make prominent references to Bob Dylan in their hit songs during this period. Certainly, this was a time of rekindled mainstream interest in Dylan, as he had just released his first all-acoustic album since 1964, *Good as I Been to You* (1992). Yet both of these references seem to point to the "old" Dylan, establishing deep connections between 1990s pop and music from decades before. The connection to Bob Dylan in mainstream rock during the 1990s was even more pronounced with the success of the Los Angeles–based Wallflowers, led by singer and songwriter Jakob Dylan (son of Bob). The band splashed on the rock scene with *Bringing Down the Horse* (p4, 1996), which featured the hits "6th Avenue Heartache" (p10), "One Headlight" (p1), and "The Difference" (p3). Despite the media's desire to focus on Jakob's family ties, the younger Dylan avoided exploiting his father's fame as much as he could. However, the band's traditional rock sound would likely have led to comparisons even if there had been no blood relation.

Matchbox 20 and Third Eye Blind. By the second half of the 1990s, a wave of music became popular that merged the pop aspects of guitar-driven roots rock with the harder driving, edgier sounds of alternative rock. Florida's Matchbox 20 found a blend that combined the elemental energy of grunge with a Beatle-esque sensibility, creating a model for much of the modern guitar pop that followed in the late 1990s. The band's debut album, *You or Someone Like You* (p5), was released in 1996 and sold steadily for years after its release, making it one of the best-selling albums of the decade. Several of its tracks became staples of rock-radio playlists, including "Push" (p5), "3 A.M." (p3), and "Real World" (p9). Led by singer Rob Thomas (who sang on Santana's 1999 hit "Smooth"), the band followed up with *Mad Season* (p3, 2000).

Several other groups that created similar blends of traditional simplicity with heavier alternative sounds (and even some hip-hop influence) joined Matchbox 20 on the charts during the late 1990s. San Francisco–based Third Eye Blind enjoyed success in 1997 with "Semi-Charmed Life" (p4) and "How's It Going to Be" (p9) from the album *Third Eye Blind* (p25). Hailing from Los Angeles, Sugar Ray softened a hard-edged approach to score hits with "Fly" (p1, 1997), "Every Morning" (p3 uk10, 1999), and "Someday" (p7, 1999). Similarly, the Goo Goo Dolls morphed from a Buffalo-based post-punk band in the mid-1980s to purveyors of pop ballads such as "Name" (p5, 1995) and "Iris" (p1, 1998). Train continued the trajectory of these groups into the new millennium with the song "Drops of Jupiter" (p5 uk10, 2001), which has remained a staple of FM rock radio.

FEMALE SINGER-SONGWRITERS

Tori Amos and many female singer-songwriters of the period (Ani DiFranco and Sarah McLachlan, among others) were the antithesis of the mass-marketed pop diva. Amos, a classically trained pianist, wrote, produced, and sang songs about highly personal, intimate moments. She was also known for covering male-oriented classic rock songs in concert, injecting them with a female perspective. Although her music was originally produced on a small scale, Amos proved that such music could sell in large numbers: she had several successful albums through the 1990s and beyond.

Both Sides Now: Women's Perspectives in the Pop Mainstream. In the discussion of the singer-songwriters of the 1970s (Chapter 8), we traced the development of the style back to artists in the 1960s who wrote their own songs and delivered them with relatively simple accompaniment. Often featuring acoustic guitar and piano, this style focused heavily on the vocal element and the importance of the lyrics. The singer-songwriter style grew throughout the 1970s to include many artists, sometimes using simple acoustic accompaniment and at other times, as in the case of Paul Simon, Bob Seger, or Joni Mitchell, fronting bands and using more elaborate and sophisticated accompaniment. Although the initial folk revival instrumentation often merged with standard rock and jazz ensembles, the core of the singer-songwriter movement continued to thrive in mainstream pop during the 1990s. This core is based on what popular music scholars often call a perception of "authenticity." In this case, the listener has to believe the artist is singing about his or her own experiences, or reflecting his or her own thoughts and feelings. A crucial sense of authenticity is based on this projection of sincerity, and sometimes even vulnerability. Many artists from the 1970s, such as Bob Dylan and Billy Joel, thrived in the 1980s and 1990s by projecting this perception of authenticity. Perhaps the most significant development for the style in the 1990s was the emergence of a new generation of female singer-songwriters—artists whose lyrics dealt with issues that are important to women generally, and with specifically feminist issues. Influenced by well-known singer-songwriters like Carole King, Joni Mitchell, and Carly Simon as well as lesser-known but critically celebrated artists such as Kate Bush, Tracy Chapman, and others, the music of this new generation of younger women ranged from quiet and contemplative to angry and aggressive.

Listening Guide

Tori Amos, "Crucify" Atlantic 82358

Words and music by Tori Amos, produced by Davit Sigerson. Contained on the album *Little Earthquakes*, which rose to #54 on the *Billboard* "Pop Album" chart in 1992 (uk14).

FORM: Compound AABA. The A sections are interesting in that they consist of a verse, a pre-chorus, a chorus, and an "after-chorus." (The last A section, marked A', omits the verse.) We have already seen how a pre-chorus can serve to prepare the chorus, but here we have an 8-bar passage that grows out of the chorus to become a distinctive section. If this section were shorter, we might simply think of it as an extension of the chorus, but in this case the after-chorus earns a label of its own. Note how the ending blends the chorus and after-chorus together by combining the melodies.

TIME SIGNATURE: 2/4. Most of the song can be counted in groups of 4 measures (note the 16- and 8-bar sections), except the end of the chorus, where the 4-bar pattern breaks down on the way to the after-chorus, creating a 19-bar section.

INSTRUMENTATION: Piano, bass, drums, percussion, mandolin, ukulele, lead and background vocals.

A	0:00–0:23	**Verse 1**, 16 mm.	Lead vocals enter quietly with minimal accompaniment. "Every finger . . ."
	0:23–0:46	**Pre-chorus**, 16 mm.	Note how the increased activity in the piano begins to open up the texture. "I've been looking . . ."
	0:46–1:13	**Chorus**, 19 mm.	The drums come to the fore here, along with a reverb-drenched percussion sound. "Why do we . . . "
	1:13–1:25	**After-chorus**, 8 mm.	The voice and piano join forces in a descending melody. "Chains . . ."
A	1:25–1:48	**Verse 2**, 16 mm.	The music gets quiet again, contrasting with the end of the previous section. "Got a kick . . ."
	1:48–2:11	**Pre-chorus**, 16 mm.	The music begins to build, as it did before. "I've been looking . . ."
	2:11–2:39	**Chorus**, 19 mm.	As before, but now with background vocals added. The 4-bar pattern is broken. "Why do we . . ."
	2:39–2:50	**After-chorus**, 8 mm.	As before, but now opening into the bridge. "Chains . . . "
B	2:50–3:14	**Bridge**, 16 mm.	Note the interweaving vocal melodies that create an almost churchlike atmosphere. "Please . . ."
A'	3:14–3:37	**Pre-chorus**, 16 mm.	Music gets quiet again, though building to lead to the pre-chorus. "Looking for a . . ."

(continued)

3:37–4:04	**Chorus**, 19 mm.	As before. "Why do we . . ."
4:04–4:16	**After-chorus**, 8 mm.	As before, but leading to ending. "Chains . . . "
4:16–4:57	**Ending**, 26 mm.	Combines chorus and pre-chorus, with new background vocal parts added. "Why do we . . ."

Lilith Fair, a festival devoted to women's music, was initiated in 1997. The fair toured North America in 1997, 1998, and 1999. Sarah McLachlan was among the founders of Lilith Fair, and a long list of female artists performed during its three seasons. The poster shows the highlights of the 1998 lineup.

Assertive Female Voices: Tori Amos and the Indigo Girls.

Among the first of this new group of singer-songwriters to emerge in the 1990s was Tori Amos. Growing up in Baltimore, Amos had been a piano prodigy who studied at the prestigious Peabody Conservatory. She eventually made her way to Los Angeles, and after a brief stint fronting a rock band, recorded her singer-songwriter debut, *Little Earthquakes* (p54 uk14, 1991). Amos's classical training is audible in her use of harmony and melody as well as in her masterful piano playing. The first track on *Little Earthquakes*, "Crucify," provides a good example of her early style. The most striking song on the album, however, is an unaccompanied vocal track called "Me and a Gun," an intimate and gripping portrayal of a rape experience. After an extended play recording consisting of cover versions of songs by Nirvana, Led Zeppelin, and others, Amos released *Under the Pink* (p12 uk1) in 1994, and *Boys for Pele* (p2 uk2) in 1996. The success of these albums established her as one of the most talented and innovative songwriters of her generation.

The Atlanta-based Indigo Girls were a duo of female singer-songwriters from Athens, Georgia, who represented another facet of the rise of authentic female artists in the 1990s. The two women at the core of the group, Amy Ray and Emily Saliers, were openly gay from the group's inception, and supported various political movements. They broke into the mainstream in 1989 with the song "Closer to Fine" (p52), winning a Grammy Award for Best Contemporary Folk Album. Later albums enjoyed further chart success, including *Swamp Ophelia* (p6, 1994), which showcased the often-contrasting songwriting styles of Ray and Saliers. The duo's music often features duet singing and acoustic guitar accompaniment, with Ray evincing more rock influence and Saliers projecting a gentler, folk-influenced style.

Northern Contrasts: Sarah McLachlan, Jewel, and Alanis Morissette.

Hailing from Nova Scotia, Sarah McLachlan was a female pianist who contrasted sharply with the often-harsh tone of Tori Amos. With a soft vocal delivery and lilting melodies, McLachlan's specialty became heartfelt ballads. She enjoyed moderate chart success in 1993 with *Fumbling Towards Ecstasy* (p50, 1993), but it was not until her 1997 release *Surfacing* that McLachlan broke into the pop mainstream. Popular singles like "Building a Mystery" (p13), "Adia" (p3 uk18), and

This photo shows several of the performers from the 1998 lineup of Lilith Fair onstage during a San Francisco show. From left to right: Sarah Bettens (K's Choice), Amy Ray (Indigo Girls), Erykah Badu, Sarah McLachlan, and Tara Maclean. Dozens of female artists performed on the 1998 tour, with many others included in the 1997 and 1999 lineups.

"Angel" (p4) cemented McLachlan as a fixture of pop radio during the late 1990s. Her music was consistently produced by (and often written with) notable Canadian musician Pierre Marchand. As organizer of a music festival called Lilith Fair from 1997 to 1999 devoted to music by women, McLachlan became a figurehead in the female singer-songwriter movement. While initially seeming partial to white, acoustic songwriters, the festival soon included a wide range of artists and styles, including Liz Phair, the Indigo Girls, Sheryl Crow, Tracy Chapman, and Queen Latifah. Lilith Fair was relaunched in 2010, featuring a new generation of female singer-songwriters, many of whom drew inspiration from the movement in the 1990s.

Raised in Alaska, Jewel offered a pop-oriented singer-songwriter style similar to Sarah McLachlan during the last half of the 1990s. With four albums in the *Billboard* Top 10 between 1996 and 2002, Jewel was one of the best-selling artists of the period. A texture featuring acoustic guitar was used for her first two singles, "Who Will Save Your Soul" (p11, 1996) and "You Were Meant for Me" (p2, 1997). Later songs, including "Foolish Games" (p7, 1997) and "Hands" (p6, 1998) were backed by an instrumental combination that, due to a prominent piano, more closely resembled McLachlan's signature sound. This change in sonic presentation was accompanied by a move toward more adult images projected in Jewel's later music videos. Efforts to "clean up" her sound were evident in attempts to rerecord "You Were Meant for Me" after the success of her debut album *Pieces of You* (p4, 1996). As a result, the version of the song featured in the music video was much more restrained than the recording included on the album. In a fascinating reversal, Jewel abandoned her singer-songwriter roots in 2003 with the dance-oriented album *0304* (p2).

Canadian Alanis Morissette's debut album *Jagged Little Pill* (p1 uk1, 1995) was neither gentle nor delicate. Her enormously successful album contained the hits "Ironic" (p4 uk11), "You Learn" (p6), and "Head Over Feet" (p3 uk7). The album's first single, "You Oughta Know" (p13) captures the sense of anger, frustration, and outrage experienced after a romantic breakup. Although there is certainly an autobiographical element to the album's lyrics, the project was largely a collaboration with songwriter and producer Glen Ballard, an industry veteran who had written music for Michael Jackson, Paula Abdul, and Wilson Phillips. (The most famous of Ballard's songs from the earlier era is Jackson's "Man in the Mirror.") Morissette's later albums *Supposed Former Infatuation Junkie* (p1 uk3, 1998) and *Under Rug Swept* (p1 uk2, 2002) also rose to the top of the pop album charts, making her one of the most successful female singer-songwriters in the second half of the decade.

TEEN IDOLS

The Return of Classic Motown: Boyz II Men. While old rockers kept vintage sounds alive, a new cast of young rockers returned to these traditional approaches, and as a generation of women were exploring the singer-songwriter aesthetic, a fresh sense of traditionalism was also assuming a more central place in rhythm and blues. The most commercially successful of the many rhythm and blues artists to return to earlier styles was the Philadelphia-based vocal quartet, Boyz II Men. The band signed with Motown at the beginning of the decade, reinvigorating a label that had struggled during the 1980s. Like the Drifters or the Temptations before them, Boyz II Men's music featured highly crafted and nuanced harmony-vocal arrangements, putting the focus on the rich blending of their voices as well as on solo passages by the band's members. They depended on others for songwriting, accompaniment, and production, returning to the Brill Building model of the early 1960s. The group's more immediate influences included New Edition and New Kids on the Block, two Boston-based vocal groups developed by songwriter-producer Maurice Starr. Both of these earlier groups enjoyed considerable chart success in the late 1980s, especially among teenage girls, and New Edition's Michael Bivens was instrumental in getting the Philadelphia band signed with Motown.

The debut Boyz II Men album, *Cooleyhighharmony* (p3 r1 uk7, 1991), contained several crossover hit singles, including "Motownphilly" (p3 r4) and "It's So Hard to Say Goodbye to Yesterday" (p2 r1). The group topped both the "Hot 100" and "Hot R&B Singles" charts for the first time with "End of the Road" (uk1,

Boyz II Men in concert, 1995. Like the Temptations or the Drifters before them, Boyz II Men featured highly choreographed stage shows and a polished, richly harmonized vocal style. Their album *Cooleyhighharmony* (1991) was a crossover hit and helped revitalize Motown Records, which had struggled in the 1980s.

Listening Guide

Boyz II Men, "End of the Road" Motown 2178

Words and music by L. A. Reid, Babyface, and Daryl Simmons. Produced by Babyface. Rose to #1 on the *Billboard* "Hot 100" and "Hot R&B Singles" charts in 1992 (uk1).

FORM: Simple verse-chorus, with pre-chorus. The verse and chorus sections are based on the same 8-bar chord progression as the introduction. The pre-chorus section introduces contrasting material and drives toward the chorus each time. The pre-chorus acts as a bridge section that links the verse with the chorus and offers the only strong structural contrast, not only driving toward the chorus but also helping make the return of the same material seem fresh. Each verse features a solo voice, which shifts to a different singer in the pre-chorus, while harmony vocals characterize the chorus sections. The song begins with a voice speaking over the background music, and the voice-over returns in the third verse. This last verse is the most complicated vocally, featuring 8 bars spoken, with a solo voice entering in the next 8 bars as the speaking continues and choral vocals, speaking, and solo vocals present in the pre-chorus. The song ends with four times through the chorus, the last two eventually breaking down to nothing but vocals and handclaps.

TIME SIGNATURE: 6/8. Note the strong accent on beat 4 during the chorus sections. This beat arrives just a little late and has the effect of creating a strong groove that helps distinguish the chorus from the verse sections.

INSTRUMENTATION: Electric guitar, electric piano, bass, drums, synthesizer strings, French horn, hand-claps, solo and backup vocals.

0:00–0:20	**Introduction**, 8 mm.	The song's 8-bar chord progression is introduced here, with voice-over. "Girl, you know . . ."
0:20–0:59	**Verse 1**, 16 mm.	Twice through the 8-bar progression, with solo lead vocal featured throughout. Note the Motown-style guitar melody in the background. "We belong together . . ."
0:59–1:18	**Pre-chorus**, 8 mm.	Contrasting material with new voice singing solo vocal, as French horn enters. "When I can't sleep . . ."
1:18–1:56	**Chorus**, 16 mm.	Twice through the 8-bar progression, with a new melody sung by harmony vocals with handclaps emphasizing beat 4 of each measure. "Although we've come . . ."
1:56–2:36	**Verse 2**, 16 mm.	As before, note the virtuosic vocal technique, with many melodic twists and turns (melismas). Horn sound enters on second 8 bars this time. "Girl, I know you really . . ."
2:36–2:55	**Pre-chorus**, 8 mm.	New lead vocal enters, now fuller than before and supported by synth strings along with horn sound. "Will you love me . . ."
2:55–3:34	**Chorus**, 16 mm.	As before, but now with lead vocal improvising over the backup vocals, adding a sense of urgency and intensity. "Although we've come . . ."

(continued)

3:34–4:12	**Verse 3**, 16 mm.	First 8 bars are spoken, as the second 8 bars add a solo vocal part behind the voice-over. "Girl, I'm there for you . . ."
4:12–4:31	**Pre-chorus**, 8 mm.	Voice-over continues, now with new backup harmony vocals, then the urgent solo vocal reenters. "Lonely . . ."
4:31–5:48	**Chorus**, 32 mm.	Four times through the 8-bar progression, with the first two times through as before in the second chorus, but with the accompanying instruments dropping out toward the end of the third time and the fourth time performed with only vocals and handclaps. "Although we've come . . ."

1992), a song recorded for the movie *Boomerang* (starring Eddie Murphy) and the first to match the vocal quartet with songwriter and producer Kenneth "Babyface" Edmunds. Boyz II Men followed up in 1994 with their second album, *II*, which hit the number-one spot on both the pop and R&B album charts with the help of the hit singles "I'll Make Love to You" (p1 r1 uk5) and "On Bended Knee" (p1 r2). Boyz II Men's tremendous success with a traditional vocal-harmony approach made them a model for many groups to follow in the second half of the decade, especially the Backstreet Boys and *NSYNC.

If You Build It, They Will Come: Boy Bands, Girl Groups, and Pop Divas.

From Fabian to the Monkees to David Cassidy, the history of pop music can claim a series of teen idols—performers whose images and music are carefully crafted to appeal to teenage and preteen girls. The late 1990s experienced a resurgence of acts designed specifically for this audience, though their musical style was more indebted to the traditionalist rhythm and blues of Boyz II Men, Babyface, and Mariah Carey than the bubbly but stiff bubblegum pop of previous decades. The two most important "boy bands" during these years were the Backstreet Boys and *NSYNC: both all-male vocal groups were modeled on Boyz II Men and managed by business mogul Lou Pearlman, who specialized in groups of this type. In 1997, Pearlman and the Backstreet Boys released *Backstreet Boys* (p4 uk12), mostly a collection of tracks that had already been successful overseas. The album was a success, and the singles "Quit Playing Games (with My Heart)" (p2 uk2) and "As Long as You Love Me" (p4 uk3) made the Backstreet Boys teenage heartthrobs. The band's next two albums, *Millennium* (p1 uk2, 1999) and *Black & Blue* (p1 uk13, 2000), and a string of Top 10 singles made the group mainstays of Top-40 radio, although by 1999 the group had officially split with Pearlman and his organization.

One factor that caused the split between the Backstreet Boys and Pearlman was Pearlman's attention to a new group he was developing—one that would compete directly with the Backstreet Boys as teen idols. Among the members of *NSYNC were JC Chasez and Justin Timberlake, two young men who were already familiar to the teen crowd as regular members of the Disney Channel's *The New Mickey Mouse Club*. The new group's first album, *NSync* (p2, 1998), did well, producing the hit single "God Must Have Spent a Little More Time on You" (p8, 1999), but the band did not come close to challenging the Backstreet Boys with this first outing. The second album, *No Strings Attached* (p1 uk14, 2000), was *NSYNC's blockbuster, generating the hits "Bye Bye Bye" (p4 uk3), "It's Gonna Be Me" (p1 uk9), and

*NSYNC performing on their 2000 world tour. Drawing on a long history of teen-oriented boy bands, *NSYNC became one of the most popular groups in the world during the late 1990s, releasing albums that sold by the millions and selling out huge concert venues around the world. After a 2002 breakup, group members such as Joey Fatone, Lance Bass, and Justin Timberlake have continued to have successful careers, confirming a longstanding trend in which boy-band artists have transitioned into adult-oriented entertainers.

"This I Promise You" (p5 uk21), placing them side by side with the Backstreet Boys in the boy-band sweepstakes. Both bands worked from the stylistic model established earlier in the decade by Boyz II Men. As the Backstreet Boys and *NSYNC became more popular, many other boy bands enjoyed immense success, including 98° and O-Town.

At about the same time the Backstreet Boys were enjoying success in Europe, an all-girl vocal quintet was also topping the charts in the UK. The five original Spice Girls were each experienced in show business when they answered the same 1993 ad placed by a manager forming a singing group. The manager selected the girls, but they rejected him, heading off to organize the act themselves and to be managed by Simon Fuller, who had managed Annie Lennox. By the fall of 1996, the debut album, *Spice*, and the single "Say You'll Be There," were both at the top of the UK charts, making the band into stars in Britain. Each Spice Girl had a special name (Ginger Spice, Baby Spice, Scary Spice, Posh Spice, and Sporty Spice), and the group quickly began exploiting their newfound fame by endorsing products of all kinds. Their catchy music, fun-loving image, and distinctive good looks made them not only successful pop stars but also high-profile celebrities. In early 1997, they worked on breaking into the United States, at roughly the same time as Pearlman was pushing the Backstreet Boys. The American release of *Spice* (1997) went to number one, powered by the hit singles "2 Become 1" (p4), "Say You'll Be There," and the catchy "Wannabe" (p1), featuring the rapped line "I tell you what I want." The band's next album, *Spiceworld* (p3, 1997), was released in conjunction with their feature film of the same name. At the height of their success, the group separated from their manager and Ginger Spice quit. The group carried on for a while longer, but had split up by late 2000. Like the Backstreet Boys and *NSYNC, the Spice Girls' music owed much to R&B, combined in the up-tempo numbers with the beat of European dance music. The group projected an image of "girl power," by which they meant that they

MUSIC VIDEO IN THE 1990s: WEEZER, "BUDDY HOLLY"

Viewing Rock

As the music video entered its second decade as the primary medium of visual promotion, many groups worked creatively within the genre. One of the most popular directors of this period was Spike Jonze. Unlike "Thriller" director John Landis, Jonze was from a generation of young filmmakers who used the music video as a means to assert their creative voice before gaining entrance into the big-budget Hollywood feature. The video for Weezer's 1990s retro-hipster fashion, Jonze set "Buddy Holly" in the context of *Happy Days*, a 1970s television sitcom about the 1950s. Using the actual *Happy Days* set and actor Al Molinaro, who portrayed a character named Al on the show, Jonze alternated modern shots of Weezer with actual footage from the original show. Although the video is only four minutes long, it offers a condensed *Happy Days* episode, beginning with opening credits and ending with Al closing up the restaurant for the night (1).

The band, outfitted with 1950s hairstyles and matching cardigan sweaters, performs for dancing teenagers from the diner's stage (2). Throughout the video, Jonze uses editing to make it seem as if band members are interacting with audience members. As in many *Happy Days* episodes, the video pauses before the song's bridge as a caption informs viewers that the episode is "to be continued" (3).

In the final section of the video, Fonzie, the show's "coolest" character, enters and begins an aggressive dance that borders on absurd (4).

As a statement of Weezer's self-consciousness and Jonze's creative reading of the song, "Buddy Holly" offers a wonderful depiction of the place of the music video in early 1990s rock.

"Buddy Holly," directed by Jonze, was one of the most popular videos of late 1994. Taking a cue from the song's self-aware depiction of

---

were themselves in charge of what they were doing and were not powerless pawns being pushed around by the music business. They shared writing credits on many of their tracks—including the hits—though they often teamed with professional songwriters such as Matt Rowe and Richard Stannard. In terms of their projection of independence, the Spice Girls credited Madonna as an important influence.

Late in 1998, female vocalist Britney Spears entered this scene, and soon became the most important artist in the burgeoning preteen movement. Like JC Chasez and Justin Timberlake, Spears had also appeared on *The New Mickey Mouse Club*, so she was an experienced performer by the time she emerged as a solo artist. In fall 1998, Britney released her debut album, *. . . Baby One More Time* (p1 uk2), produced by Swedish songwriter Max Martin. The Martin-penned single ". . . Baby

One More Time" hit the number-one spot on the pop charts in America and the UK, and Spears's video for the song featured her dancing suggestively in a skimpy schoolgirl outfit. A later hit, "You Drive Me Crazy" (p10 uk5), further established her as the next big thing, and her second album, *Oops . . . I Did It Again* (p1 uk2, 2000), confirmed it. Another ex-Mouseketeer, Christina Aguilera, debuted in 1999 with a more uncompromisingly sexy image, and *Christina Aguilera* topped the pop charts, featuring the hits "Genie in a Bottle" (p1 uk1) and "What a Girl Wants" (p1 uk3). The next year, Aguilera released *Mi Reflejo*, sung in Spanish and intended to capitalize on the boom in Latin pop, led by Ricky Martin's ubiquitous hit single "Livin' La Vida Loca" (p1 uk1, 1999) and Santana's "Smooth." The album topped the Latin charts and hit number twenty-seven on the pop charts. Aguilera was a skilled and versatile vocalist—a feature that was easy to miss in the hype over the sensual image she projected—and her approach to singing owed much to the melismatic stylings of Mariah Carey and Whitney Houston.

Critics of Britney Spears and Christina Aguilera charged them with making themselves into sexual objects, reinforcing unhealthy images of young women that are considered the source of a wide range of sociocultural problems. Proponents of this music point out that these were strong role models for women who retained significant control of their careers and provided a positive feminine image. With the simultaneous rise of female singer-songwriters and teen idols, it is certainly easy to see that there is a big difference between Tori Amos singing "Me and a Gun" and Britney Spears singing ". . . Baby One More Time." However, no matter what conclusion you draw from this disparity, by the end of the 1990s, women were playing a central role in popular music, as both the singer-songwriters and the teen idols were back.

BEAT-BASED POP

Making Beats. During the 1980s, programmable and computer-based methods of making music were widespread in a variety of popular music styles. Listening closely to the teen pop discussed earlier, for example, reveals that the nonvocal elements of

One of the most successful recording teams in hip-hop history, Snoop Doggy Dogg (left) and Dr. Dre (standing). Dre was a key player in West Coast rap, where he came up with Eazy-F and Ice Cube in the group N.W.A (Niggaz with Attitude). Snoop and Dre teamed up to create *The Chronic* (1992), which became the model for West Coast gangsta rap. These two are seen here in the studio during the creation of Snoop's 1993 album *Doggy Style*.

WHAT'S THAT SOURCE?

Biz Markie Gets Sued

Hip-hop music changed dramatically in the early 1990s, when artists stopped freely sampling previously recorded works without permission. The case that established legal precedent for sound sampling was *Grand Upright Music Ltd. v. Warner Bros. Records, Inc.*, in which Biz Markie was challenged for using a sample of Gilbert O'Sullivan's 1972 recording of "Alone Again (Naturally)." The following selections from a law journal article, published in 1994, describe the legal significance of the case, and reflect on the ways in which hip-hop creative practices did not fit into existing copyright law.

Digital sound sampling, the borrowing of parts of sound recordings and the subsequent incorporations of those parts into a new recording, continues to be a source of controversy in the law. Part of the controversy stems from a lack of legal standards against which to assess its legitimacy. Because music sampling is such a recent phenomenon, Congress did not address the practice in the Copyright Act of 1976 and has not addressed it in amendments to the Act. Thus far, there are no legislative criteria governing sampling. Furthermore, disputes involving music samplers have largely remained out of the courts; as a result, no judicial standards have been established.

On December 17, 1991, the United States District Court for the Southern District of New York decided the first music sampling case to proceed through trial, *Grand Upright Music Ltd. v. Warner Bros. Records, Inc.* In *Grand Upright Music,* plaintiff was the copyright owner of the song "Alone Again (Naturally)," made famous in a 1972 recording by singer-songwriter Raymond "Gilbert" O'Sullivan. Plaintiff brought suit to enjoin the "improper and unlicensed" use of the song by rap artist Biz Markie in "Alone Again," a track appearing on the artist's album *I Need a Haircut.* In the song, Biz used a digital sample of ten seconds of music from "Alone Again (Naturally)." In a terse four-page opinion, United States District Court Judge Kevin Thomas Duffy granted the injunction and referred the defendants—Biz, his publisher, his producers, and his record label, among other entities—to the United States Attorney for possible criminal prosecution.

Reaction in the performing arts community to *Grand Upright Music* has taken most of these tracks were carefully constructed using a variety of electronic instruments, including drum machines, synthesizers, and samplers. Even when traditional rock instruments were employed in these tracks, such as guitars or the electric bass, the performances were recorded to mesh with the prevailing electronic texture. This process of creating a musical track, or "making beats," was often completed independently from the vocalist or rapper before the lyrics and melodies were constructed. Beat-based production techniques were used during the 1990s to create a wide variety of popular music, including most teen pop, rap and hip-hop, and electronic dance music. While this manner of creation may at first seem to be the antithesis of the rock tradition, which valued recordings of live performance, beat-based production techniques became influential in many forms of hybrid rock in the 1990s. Moreover, by the end of the decade most rock musicians who performed live in the studio with traditional instrumentation used digital audio workstations that grew largely out of the beat-based recording movement, adding much more flexibility to the recording process.

Hip-Hop in the 1990s. In the 1990s, hip-hop culture was pervasive internationally, as rap grew into one of popular music's dominant styles both in the United States and the UK. This growth was so dramatic that hip-hop deserves to be

several forms. One effect of the ruling has been a noticeably more hostile climate for samplers. This climate was manifested by a renewed round of litigation. Four days before the *Grand Upright Music* decision, perhaps in anticipation of an adverse ruling, dance music producer Jellybean Benitez filed suit over an unauthorized sample. Four days after the ruling, Tuff City Records, a New York–based independent label, sued Sony Music Inc. and the Sony-distributed label Def Jam Records over a drum sample. About a month later, Bridgeport Music, a publishing company, brought suit to enjoin the manufacture and sale of a hit record containing a sample of a recording to which it owned the copyright. A group calling itself "The Association of Parliament/Funkadelic Members 1971–83" filed a massive suit alleging that it owns copyrights to recordings created by George Clinton that have been sampled by at least sixty-two recording acts. Most recently, Bridgeport Music and label Westbound Records have sued over the use of a sample.

Had the court in *Grand Upright Music* squarely confronted the issue, much of this subsequent litigation could have been avoided. Rather than assuming that sampling was copyright infringement from the beginning, the court should have examined what interests are at stake when a sampler samples, in order to decide when samples rise to the level of actual infringement. The decision rendered *all* unauthorized sampling legally suspect; no distinction seemingly could be made between small bites and large cuts, between instantly recognizable "trademarks" and impossibly obscure and mundane banalities. Instead the inquiry became cut and dried: Does someone else own the copyright? If so, then any unlicensed sample is an infringement.

Predictably, the court's overly broad decision in *Grand Upright Music* has made sampling a hazardous occupation. Recordings featuring samples must spend more time in limbo while every sample is cleared. In some cases, rappers have eschewed samples entirely, preferring to use live musicians rather than suffer the potential consequences of an adverse judgment. These difficulties suggest a future in which the risks of sampling are so great that the technique will virtually perish as an art form.

On the other hand, the facts of *Grand Upright Music* are such that subsequent litigants would be hard-pressed to rely on it as precedent. Performers will rarely ask permission to use a sample and then release the album without authorization to use the sample; in so doing, Biz made it easy for the court to throw the book at him. Furthermore, "Alone Again" did not involve the use of a mere drum beat or shout lifted from an obscure recording; the sample was instantly recognizable, and it constituted the entire musical accompaniment to Biz's rap. Without use of the sample, there would have been no music at all.

The significance of *Grand Upright Music,* however, cannot be denied—a judge in one of the most important trial courts in the federal system has declared unauthorized sampling to be against the law. Moreover, as of this date, *Grand Upright Music* is the only source of legal standards with regard to sound sampling in existence.

Source: Carl A. Falstrom, "Thou Shalt Not Steal: *Grand Upright Music Ltd. v. Warner Bros. Records, Inc.* and the Future of Digital Sound Sampling in Popular Music," *Hastings Law Journal,* January 1994.

considered as the focal point of its own history and not as one facet of the history of rock music. Yet just as much of the popular music during the 1990s reflected heavily on earlier styles, rap music (which we will consider as part of a larger hip-hop culture that included aspects such as dancing, art, and fashion) championed eclecticism with references to older music. Early DJs like Kool Herc and Afrika Bambaataa had used a wide range of sources to create their live music in the 1970s, and the ability to combine disparate prerecorded pieces became even easier with the growth of the sampler in the late 1980s. Samplers allowed beat makers to record small sections of commercial recordings and create repetitive "loops" or present them at opportune points in a musical arrangement. Favorite early sources of music mirrored those used by live DJs in the 1980s, including artists such as James Brown and Parliament/Funkadelic. Yet, throughout the decade, sample sources were often taken from sources not usually associated with hip-hop culture, such as classical music and rock. While focused on African American culture, most hip-hop in the 1990s was extremely popular with white suburban teenagers, a demographic group that dramatically increased record sales for rap artists and created a generation of listeners who were equally familiar with Snoop Dogg and Led Zeppelin. The use of preexisting material in hip-hop challenged notions of ownership and copyright throughout the 1990s. One of the most important cases

Listening Guide

Dr. Dre, featuring Snoop Doggy Dogg, "Nuthin' but a 'G' Thang" Death Row 53816

Words and music by Cordozar Broadus, Andre Young, Leon Haywood, and Frederick Knight. Produced by Dr. Dre. Rose to #2 on the *Billboard* "Hot 100" (#1 on "R&B Singles Sales") in 1993; contained on the album *The Chronic*, which rose to #3 on the "Billboard 200" pop album charts (#1 on the *Billboard* "Top R&B Albums").

FORM: Simple verse. The verses in almost every case are built on 4-bar phrases, producing either 12- or 16-bar sections. The only exception is verse 1, which is 10 measures in length. Verses 1 and 2 are followed by a 4-bar refrain, as are verses 3, 4, and 5, and this forms a relatively regular and symmetrical formal pattern. Once the groove is set up in the accompaniment, the focus is on the rapping, which is done by both Snoop Doggy Dogg and Dr. Dre. While the rhymes are clever, the ways in which the delivery of these lines flow alternately with and against the rhythmic grouping in the accompaniment is where Snoop and Dre really display their skills. Notice how lines do not always begin or end where you might expect them to—sometimes beginning late or ending early, other times seeming to blur over the underlying 4-bar pattern. To keep the accompaniment interesting, synthesizer lines come and go throughout the track.

TIME SIGNATURE: 4/4.

INSTRUMENTATION: Electric guitars, bass, synthesizers, drums, percussion, vocals, and samples drawn from Leon Haywood's "I Wanna Do Something Freaky to You" and Kid Dynamite's "Uphill (Peace of Mind)."

0:00–0:11	**Introduction,** 4 mm.	This instrumental section establishes the laid-back groove. Note the female sighs that saturate this track and the signature synthesizer melody.
0:11–0:36	**Verse 1,** 10 mm.	Snoop begins the rapping, with a brief contribution from Dre. This verse consists of a 4-bar phrase, then a 2-bar phrase, followed by another 4-bar phrase. "One, two, three . . ."
0:36–1:07	**Verse 2,** 12 mm.	Snoop takes a verse solo. "Back to the lecture at hand . . ."
1:07–1:18	**Refrain,** 4 mm.	This refrain, rapped by Snoop and Dre together, signals the end of this portion of the track, setting up the next verse and introducing Dre. The synthesizer melody from the intro returns. "It's like this . . ."
1:18–1:48	**Verse 3,** 12 mm.	Dre now takes a verse solo. "Well I'm peepin' . . ."
1:48–1:58	**Refrain,** 4 mm.	The refrain again signals the end of this section. Return of synthesizer melody from intro and refrain as before. "It's like this . . ."
1:58–2:07	**Interlude,** 4 mm.	This instrumental section parallels the introduction, as synthesizer melody continues amid vocal samples and scratching.
2:07–2:38	**Verse 4,** 12 mm.	Snoop returns for another solo verse, calling on Dre at the end. "Fallin' back on that . . ."

(continued)

2:38–3:19	**Verse 5**, 16 mm.	Dre again takes a solo verse. "Here's where it takes place . . ."
3:19–3:29	**Refrain**, 4 mm.	This time the refrain signals the end of the track, as the signature synthesizer melody returns as before. "Like this . . ."
3:29–3:56	**Coda**, 8 mm. and fade	As in the introduction, this section is instrumental and fades out during the third time through the 4-bar pattern. Signature synthesizer melody continues, as vocal samples and scratching from interlude return.

was a ruling against rapper Biz Markie in 1991, which set a strict precedent requiring hip-hop producers to attain various levels of permission to use sampled sources (see What's That Source?). In effect, this ruling changed the way many producers approached their work and limited access to the multitude of samples available during the 1980s.

With its growth and commercial success, rap fractured into many substyles, much as rock did during the first half of the 1970s. Within gangsta rap early in the 1990s, a rivalry developed between Southern California and New York, and this feud became the source of much controversy in the music press and eventually ended in tragedy. The West Coast faction was led by Death Row Records, owned and controlled by aspiring impresario Suge Knight. Knight signed N.W.A member Dr. Dre, whose 1993 album, *The Chronic* (p3 r1, 1993), included the rapper Snoop Doggy Dogg. The track "Nuthin' but a 'G' Thang" (p2 r1) provides a famous example of the album's approach. The track employs two samples: "Uphill (Peace of Mind)," a 1976 track by Kid Dynamite, and "I Wanna Do Something Freaky to You" (1979) by Leon Haywood, both drawn from late 1970s soul music. Both Snoop and Dre rap, and rather than being cast in a sing-song and predictable rhyme pattern, the lines weave in and out against the accompanying groove, often employing sophisticated rhythms and phrase groupings.

The East Coast faction of gangsta rap was led by producer, businessman, and future rap artist Sean Combs, who went by the name Puff Daddy (later changed to P. Diddy, then just Diddy). Combs had been in A&R for Uptown Records, working with artists such as Father MC and Mary J. Blige. Fired from Uptown, Combs formed his own record label, Bad Boy, and the Notorious B.I.G. was among the first to score a top crossover success for the label. B.I.G.'s *Ready to Die* reached number fifteen on the pop charts in 1995 (r3), and *Life after Death* topped the pop and rhythm and blues charts in 1997. Another group based on the East Coast (but not necessarily purveyors of the East Coast style) was the New York–based Wu-Tang Clan, a collective of nine artists. The idea of Wu-Tang Clan was to produce a smash album that would allow each of the members to spin off his own solo career. The first album, *Enter the Wu-Tang (36 Chambers)*, was released in 1993 and went to number eight on the rhythm and blues charts (p41). The next release, *Wu-Tang Forever* (1997), topped the

Notorious B.I.G.—"Biggie"—was born Christopher Wallace in Brooklyn. He was associated with the East Coast scene, and fell victim to the East Coast–West Coast feud in 1997 when he was gunned down in Los Angeles.

Dr. Dre discovered Eminem (Marshall Mathers, pictured here at a live concert) in 1997 and soon helped him produce his first album. Eminem had a distinctive vocal style and his lyrics focused not on "gangsta life" or politics, but on his personal experiences growing up as a poor white kid in Detroit. Eminem's mother and his wife, Kim, were only two of many targets of his aggressive and often violent rhymes.

pop and rhythm and blues charts in the United States and the pop album charts in the UK. Later spin-off projects produced ten Top 10 albums in the United States, with several more charting in the Top 40.

Emerging at the end of the decade, Eminem challenged many of the assumptions about race that the mainstream media had placed on hip-hop. Born Marshall Mathers, Eminem grew up as a poor white kid in an urban Detroit neighborhood. After establishing a reputation locally, he won a 1997 freestyle rap competition in Los Angeles and as a result, a copy of his demo tape was heard by Dr. Dre. While Dre was surprised that Eminem was white, he was soon won over by the rapper's wit and talent and produced his breakthrough album, *The Slim Shady LP* (p2 r1 uk12, 1999). While Eminem had sometimes rapped on positive themes on his first album, *Infinite* (1997), for this album he adopted the persona of Slim Shady, a character who could express his deepest emotional pain and hostility. The lead single from the album, "My Name Is" (p36 r18 uk2), provides a good example of Eminem's aggressive approach, and the rapper soon provoked widespread controversy for the violent content of his lyrics, making him rap music's preeminent bad boy. With *The Marshall Mathers LP* (p1 r1 uk1, 2000), Eminem turned his attention to the problems of his own life. The portrayal of his wife in "Kim" created a storm of public and private controversy, and his mother filed a lawsuit against him for defamation of character. The negative reaction to Eminem's music only seemed to make him more successful, partly because many fellow artists—and unlikely ones such as Elton John—strongly defended his talent and intelligence. Eminem's *Recovery* (p1 r1 uk1, 2010) provides an about-face for the successful rapper, chronicling his years of substance abuse, which surely added to his often-erratic behavior.

In addition to "hardcore" artists like Dr. Dre and the Wu-Tang Clan, many others who participated in the hip-hop tradition were less militant and linked more closely to the rock tradition. Often employing samples from more familiar rock and soul songs, records by these artists have been consistently praised by rock critics in spite of their origins in the hip-hop community. New York's Beastie Boys are emblematic of this category of "rock approved hip-hop." Through a series of albums in the 1990s, including *Paul's Boutique* (p14 r24, 1989), *Check Your Head* (p10 r37, 1992), *Ill Communication* (p1 r2 uk10, 1994), and *Hello Nasty* (p1 uk1, 1998), the band matured from a rowdy fraternity group into socially conscious politicos who advocated Eastern religion. With samples from a wide variety of sources, including jazz and classic soul, De La Soul became critical darlings after the release of their first album *3 Feet High and Rising* (p24 r1 uk13, 1989). Through subsequent efforts, including *Stakes Is High* (p13 r4, 1996) and *Art Official Intelligence: Mosaic Thump* (p9 r3 uk22, 2000), the group focused on positive, introspective lyrics, which set them apart from the violent depictions of the ghetto used in gangsta styles. Although many hip-hop groups featured the occasional vocal melody, the Fugees were a trio that mixed two male rappers, Wyclef Jean and Pras Michel (both of Haitian origin), and female singer Lauryn Hill. Often featuring reggae-tinged accompaniments, the group's breakout single was a version of the 1971 Roberta Flack single "Killing Me Softly" (p2 r1 uk1, 1996), which was also included on *The Score* (p1 r1 uk2, 1996). Two years later, Hill's solo album *The Miseducation of Lauryn Hill* (p1 r1 uk2, 1998) became a pop sensation on the strength of the single "Doo Wop (That Thing)" (p1 r2 uk3). The video for this song shows a particular interest in connecting with the past, as it features a split screen with Hill depicted simultaneously as a performer from 1967 (on the left side of the screen) and in modern dress (on the right side of the screen).

Electronic Dance Music. Although hip-hop was popular for dancing, an important strand of beat-based electronic dance music also entered the mainstream during the 1990s. Like other styles we have discussed so far, dance music had gone underground after its time in the pop limelight during the 1970s, and regional dance scenes developed in major cities like New York, Chicago, and Detroit. Throughout the 1980s, dance music developed away from the mainstream, as devoted dancers populated specialized clubs and DJs crafted sets designed to keep the dance floor full. By the late 1980s, America's underground dance music had made its way to England, where a dance craze began to build. The UK scene then spread back across the Atlantic to New York, San Francisco, and Los Angeles, forming the basis for the rise of electronic dance music throughout the decade. By the late 1990s, many observers of pop-music trends were predicting that electronic dance music—often referred to broadly as "techno"—would be the next big thing, replacing rock as the music of America's youth.

Much of the electronic dance movement stemmed from 1970s clubs like the Paradise Garage in New York's SoHo district, where Larry Levan established himself as one of the city's top dance DJs while disco was still popular. Employing a spectacular sound system and often controlling the lighting as well, Levan combined a wide range of music to create his sets, sometimes blending records together and at other times moving abruptly from one to another. The New York approach to dance music is often called "garage," and the New York City Peech Boys' "Don't Make Me Wait" (1982) provides a representative example of the style. However, New York was

One of the most important DJs in post-disco dance music was Larry Levan, pictured here in 1990 performing at Mars, an important club in the New York City house music scene. With his innovative use of multiple records, lighting, and sound effects, Levan controlled all aspects of the dance club experience. He proved that in this new genre it was not the records that were important—it was the DJ.

In many ways, rave culture combined the psychedelic culture of the late 1960s with the disco dance culture of the late 1970s. All-night dancing under the influence of drugs was commonplace, and a dance club's light and sound systems were often designed to enhance the "dance trip." DJs controlled the flow of the music, as dancers gave themselves over to the electronic beats and sounds.

not the only city in America where dance music thrived. Frankie Knuckles, who had worked with Levan, brought the techniques and practices of the New York scene to Chicago in the late 1970s. By the early 1980s, he and other Chicago DJs were developing a style that would soon be called "house," after a Chicago club. Remixes became increasingly complex, as passages from various records were spliced together and new parts were added on top, often with inexpensive synthesizers and drum machines—all in an attempt to provide a full night's worth of fresh-sounding dance music. The first recorded example of house music is probably Jesse Saunders's "On and On" (1983). In Detroit, a group of aspiring DJs, often called the Belleville Three, began blending their love for the European synthesizer music with their passion for Parliament/Funkadelic. Juan Atkins, Derrick May, and Kevin Saunderson began producing a refined, futuristic, and sonically sophisticated version of dance music that many originally called "Detroit house." The Detroit approach tends not to employ traditional instruments, but rather emphasizes the drum machine, synthesizers, and sequencers. A representative example is Juan Atkins's "No UFOs" (1985), released under the name Motel 500.

By the summer of 1988, all-night rave parties began to get so large they would sometimes be held outdoors, often at secret locations to avoid police intervention. The drug Ecstasy became an important part of the experience for many dancers, leading some to refer to 1988 as the "Second Summer of Love" because of the blend of trippy music, altered consciousness, and tribal sensibilities. British musicians were soon producing their own version of electronic dance music, and by the early 1990s, dance records were becoming hits on the UK pop charts. In 1990, for instance, Orbital scored with "The Chime" (uk17) and the American musician Moby hit with "Go" (uk10, 1991)—a track that samples a theme from the *Twin Peaks* television show. Other hits included the Prodigy's "Everybody in the Place" (uk2, 1992), Shut Up and Dance's "Raving I'm Raving" (uk2, 1992), and SL2's "On a Ragga Tip" (uk2, 1992). In the early 1990s, dance made its way back to the United States, as British rave culture was transplanted to New York, San Francisco, and Los Angeles. In each case, these newly founded rave scenes were driven by DJs who had experienced British rave, and each local scene had its own distinctive musical and cultural profile. In the second half of the decade, dance music became more popular as more and more local scenes sprang up and major labels began to invest in the style. The mainstream success of electronic dance music in America was driven primarily by album sales rather than singles, as had been the case in the UK earlier in the decade. MTV also played an important role, airing dance videos that were often innovative and spacey. Important hit electronic dance albums were released by the Chemical Brothers, whose *Dig Your Own Hole* (p14 uk1, 1997) made an early mark, and the Prodigy's *The Fat of the Land* (1997), which topped

Sound Check

Artist	Song	Sound
Phish	Chalkdust Torture (1992)	Form: contrasting verse-chorus Based on a two-measure riff Listen for "ecstatic" section of guitar solo Contrasts between driving rock and playfulness
Radiohead	Airbag (1997)	Form: simple verse-chorus (with refrain) Uses three recurring sections: verse, refrain, and instrumental melody A recurring riff opens the songs and returns several times Experimental sounds and noise are examples of modern experimentation
Sheryl Crow	All I Wanna Do (1994)	Form: simple verse-chorus (modified) The music for the introduction becomes the music for the pre-chorus Strings in introduction sound like "disco" strings Verses tell stories about Los Angeles from Crow's perspective
Boyz II Men	End of the Road (1992)	Form: simple verse-chorus (modified) Verses feature solo vocals and chorus sections highlight group vocal texture Virtuosic, melismatic vocals throughout Spoken vocal section reminiscent of 1950s ballads
Tori Amos	Crucify (1992)	Form: compound AABA Piano enters in first pre-chorus and vocals add echo Odd, electronic sounds during the chorus Stark bass chords to accompany verses
Dr. Dre (featuring Snoop Doggy Dogg)	Nuthin' but a 'G' Thang (1993)	Form: simple verse-chorus Note that the rapped vocals are sometimes double-tracked High keyboard sound characteristic of Dr. Dre "g-funk" Main sample taken from Leon Haywood's "I Wanna Do Something Freaky to You"

both the U.S. and UK charts. Moby became an important figure during these years, as every track of his 1999 album *Play* (p38 uk1, 1999) was licensed for either commercials or movie soundtracks.

Covering a wide range of music at the end of the twentieth century, this chapter has focused on several important strains. Much of the music discussed here has an outward relationship with music of the past, from the jam bands that incorporated the cultural and musical developments of the Grateful Dead and the Allman Brothers Band, to female singer-songwriters and teen idols, who extended the traditions of the 1970s and the Motown guy and girl groups. Not only did much of the music of the 1990s refer to older music, but classic-rock radio formatting and reissue sales also celebrated music of the past. The vast influence of beat-based music was reflected in rock styles during the 1990s, mostly through popular rap-rock groups, which were in tune with both heavy metal and hip-hop. In the previous chapter, we saw how the alternative movement that emerged in the early 1990s inspired a series of mainstream rock acts, which were sometimes less alternative than popular. We also saw how the indie-rock movement made great strides during the decade, establishing a variety of styles and aesthetic approaches to rock, such as lo-fi and experimental noise recording techniques. Although it seemed that the musical styles and approaches under the umbrella of rock were ever expanding and limitless, large-scale changes in the music business in the new millennium brought into question many of the practices used to connect popular music to its fans. The digital revolution will be the subject of the next chapter.

For Additional Online Resources, visit:
digital.wwnorton.com/whatsthatsound5

FURTHER READING

Tori Amos and Ann Powers, *Tori Amos: Piece by Piece* (Broadway Books, 2005).

Bill Brewster and Frank Broughton, *Last Night a DJ Saved My Life: The History of the Disk Jockey* (Grove, 2000).

Mark J. Butler, *Unlocking the Groove: Rhythm, Meter, and Musical Design in Electronic Dance Music* (Indiana University Press, 2006).

Nelson George, *Hip Hop America* (Penguin, 1998).

Bruce Haring, *Off the Charts: Ruthless Days and Reckless Nights inside the Music Industry* (Birch Lane, 1996).

Alan Light, ed., *The Vibe History of Hip Hop* (Three Rivers, 1999).

Lucy O'Brien, *She Bop II: The Definitive History of Women in Rock, Pop, and Soul* (Continuum, 2002).

Simon Reynolds, *Generation Ecstasy: Into the World of Techno and Rave Culture* (Little, Brown, 1998).

The new millennium began with widespread anxiety that the world's computer networks would fail at midnight on January 1, 2000. Even though this invisible threat (nicknamed Y2K) never came to fruition, the fear it prompted raised to unparalleled heights societal concerns over our reliance on technology. Ironically, less than a year after the Y2K scare, issues stemming from old-fashioned paper-based voting machines marred the U.S. presidential election contest between Democrat Al Gore and Republican George W. Bush. The election was one of the closest in the history of the United States, with the final tally hinging on results from the state of Florida. Only after a Supreme Court decision in December of that year was George W. Bush named president.

Cultural, religious, and economic differences between the United States and radical terrorist groups boiled over during the early 2000s, stunning the world on September 11, 2001, when the terrorist network al-Qaeda completed a large-scale attack on the United States, intentionally crashing hijacked airplanes into several landmark buildings. One attacked the U.S. Pentagon building, killing nearly two hundred people and severely damaging the center of U.S. military operations. The two airplanes that crashed into the World Trade Center's twin tower buildings, causing them to collapse from the impact and killing nearly three thousand people, completed the most devastating portion of the attack. These events sent the entire country into a period of mourning, and incited military reactions from the United States that are still unresolved. In October 2001, U.S. forces entered Afghanistan, and in May 2003 troops invaded Iraq. While this "war on terrorism" became a divisive issue in the United States and abroad, several important outcomes helped mark the progress of the international effort to challenge terrorist groups, including the capture and execution of Iraqi leader Saddam Hussein in 2003 and the death of al-Qaeda leader Osama bin Laden in 2011.

While troops were fighting terrorism in the Middle East, a devastating natural disaster raised important issues of domestic preparedness and race relations in America. In August 2005, Hurricane Katrina ravaged the Gulf Coast of the United States, causing damage from Texas to the Florida Keys. The city of New Orleans was in the direct path of the storm, and was particularly overwhelmed. The failure of a major levee caused massive flooding in the city and destroyed thousands of homes. Public debate ensued almost immediately over local and federal preparedness for such a disaster, and how the large, mostly poor, African American community of the Gulf Coast was treated in the aftermath of the storm. Many people from both American and international communities came to the aid of the Gulf Coast, seeking to help this ravaged area. The steadfastness of the region's citizens became a major rallying cry to help rebuild.

Television programming changed dramatically during the first decade of the new millennium. Reality shows became extremely popular with American audiences and were increasingly favored by networks. The reality formula expanded to include entertainment competitions like *American Idol* and *Dancing*

the 2000s

..m the Stars, family-based shows like _Jon & Kate Plus 8_, and travel contests such as _The Amazing Race_. Even _The Apprentice_ gained notoriety as audiences anticipated the phrase "You're fired!," delivered at a contestant by host and producer, Donald Trump. An important group of more ambitious television programming moved to cable networks like HBO, Showtime, and AMC, and the appeal of season-long series sustained immensely popular shows like _Game of Thrones_, _The Walking Dead_, and the highly anticipated _Westworld_. Today, streaming services like Netflix and Amazon Prime have become the dominant forces in visual media, revolutionizing the manner in which people watch television. Once mere service providers, both of these companies are now major players in the creation of cutting-edge content.

After the dot-com boom of the 1990s, a computer-savvy society began to experiment with new avenues of communication during the 2000s. Video-based chatting over computer networks became common in the middle of the decade, aided greatly by programs like Skype, which was released to the public in 2003. Perhaps more important was the concept of social media, which was strongly embraced and led to the use of services like Facebook, which became popular in 2004. Originally used as a method of facilitating communication between college friends, Facebook grew to become a corporate giant used for interaction between businesses and potential customers. More people ditched their "land lines" and turned to cellular phones for communication, often through the ever-growing act of text messaging. And Twitter became a popular social medium after its release in 2005, allowing users to broadcast constant updates, and follow the "tweets" of friends, celebrities, and even presidential candidates.

The U.S. economy grew sharply after a technology-bust low point in early 2003.

Much of this financial boom was based on speculative housing sales and "subprime" lending, or loaning large amounts of money to risky borrowers. These economic practices weakened several large financial institutions and a global panic ensued, proving that American financial practices can impact the international economy. To save the American economy, the government released two massive stimulus packages in an effort to prevent a complete collapse. Regardless, millions of Americans lost their jobs, housing values plummeted, and home foreclosures increased when borrowers could not maintain (often unfair) lending agreements.

Barack Obama's decisive election as the forty-fourth, and first African American president, in November 2008 represented for many the culmination of the civil rights movement of the 1960s. Inheriting a financial crisis and two wars put Obama into a difficult position, and his first two years in office were marred by low approval ratings, especially after his strong endorsement of a comprehensive healthcare reform act in early 2010. In the years leading up to the 2016 election, Americans faced homefront attacks dedicated to ISIS, increasingly strained race relations and controversy related to police power, and discomfort with gender-related political policies that resulted in cancellations and boycotts by music performers and corporations. After a contentious national election in late 2016, Donald Trump was elected president of the United States. The real estate mogul used social media very effectively, and his unconventional political tactics galvanized the support of a less visible working class, shocking many voters who assumed Hilary Clinton was the easy bid for the White House. As political and cultural developments continue into the second decade of the new millennium, there are certain constants that seem to be part of the fabric of the America...

experience. Issues such as technological change, race relations, class struggles, financial swings, and changing entertainment brokers have been constant since the birth of rock music. As all of these factors combined to form a rich culture during the twentieth and twenty-first centuries, rock music lived on, reacting to change, inspiring ideas, and reflecting immense changes in American society.

Bruce Springsteen ✔
@springsteen

👤+ **Follow**   ⌄

Bruce Springsteen & the E Street Band's April 10th show is canceled. Tickets will be refunded at point of purchase.

brucespringsteen.net

RETWEETS	LIKES
1,351	3,248

12:40 PM - 8 Apr 2016

↩ 617   🔁 1.4K   ♥ 3.2K

Bruce Springsteen ✔
@springsteen

👤+ **Follow**   ⌄

Voice your opposition of discriminatory legislation like #HB2 by contacting your elected officials. Find them here:

act.commoncause.org/site/PageServe …

RETWEETS	LIKES
3,034	4,968

2:42 PM - 8 Apr 2016

↩ 871   🔁 3.0K   ♥ 5.0K

The 2010s have unquestionably become one of the most politically contentious decades of the last century. Mostly associating with the left and more liberal viewpoints, rock musicians have often shared their views on matters of politics and used the stage as a means to forward these perspectives. Here we see two tweets from Bruce Springsteen cancelling a North Carolina concert in protest of a statewide law preventing transgender individuals from using public bathrooms that correspond to their gender identity.

15

ALABAMA SHAKES

BOYS & GIRLS

ROCK TRADITIONS AND THE BUSINESS OF CHANGE

CHAPTER PREVIEW

- Technology dramatically changed the manner in which rock music was distributed after 2000, first with digital downloads and then through cloud-based streaming.

- There were many forms of mainstream rock in the new millennium, including pop-oriented music that was connected closely to R&B, pop punk, blues, metal, jazz, and folk.

- Country musicians like Taylor Swift and Carrie Underwood also incorporated rock styles and were popular with mainstream audiences.

- Many musicians associated with hip-hop, such as Kanye West and the Roots, also made music that incorporated rock elements.

- Despite origins as industry outsiders, indie rock labels became very popular after 2000, and indie-oriented artists were often popular with mainstream audiences.

- Once considered music for youthful degenerates, many important institutions after 2000 accepted rock as an important element of modern culture.

We have reached a point in our survey when it becomes increasingly difficult to gain a reliable historical perspective on the development of rock music. Historians often need at least twenty years to pass before an era settles enough for them to determine what the really important elements are—or at least to begin critical and scholarly debate. In this chapter, then, we will survey a variety of styles that made their mark after the turn of the twenty-first century and consider how these styles fit with some of the themes we have been following throughout this book. Rather than provide a comprehensive survey of the period up to the present, this chapter will consider selected examples of recent rock

The Alabama Shakes released their debut album *Boys and Girls* on the ATO label in 2012. Aligned with the contemporary indie rock market, the Alabama Shakes music explored older styles associated with the classic rock of the 1960s. This was not surprising, given that several of the group's members were from the area surrounding the Muscle Shoals recording studios that were most active in the R&B scene of the 1960s and 1970s. Groups like the Alabama Shakes helped to show that indie rock could be extremely popular in the mainstream. The single "Hold On" garnered wide radio support, *Boys and Girls* eventually rose to the Top 10 of the *Billboard* album charts, and the group was nominated for several Grammy awards.

music and related styles. The focus will be the ways the events and performers in the 2000s extended, repeated, or reacted against musical styles or other elements relating to rock's past. While there were clear stylistic and cultural demarcations between mainstream rock, the indie community, beat-based practices, and the country industry, there were also many important instances of crossover between these styles. The music industry saw extreme changes as digital media became the preferred method of acquiring and listening to music. On par with the rock revolution of the 1950s, a shift in the way bands reached audiences and listeners enjoyed music shook the business to its very core, causing many to question the entire infrastructure of the recording industry. It became increasingly clear during the 2000s that rock music, once considered degenerate noise by cultural gatekeepers, had become an integral part of American culture. Acceptance into academic fields and publications like the *New York Times* and the *New Yorker*, the creation of museums and large-scale cultural institutions, and the "canonization" of rock music in Broadway shows and other venues all showed how deeply rooted this music had become in the American national identity.

TECHNOLOGY AND ROCK

Changing Systems of Production and Consumption. The development of digital technology had broad and far-reaching effects on popular music. Like the wave of independent labels in the 1950s and the DIY revolution of the 1970s, during the 1990s digital recording made it possible for almost any artist or band to record inexpensively. Techniques associated with digital tools such as sampling and sequencing revolutionized how music was created. The technological creation of music became commonplace by the turn of the millennium. The next frontier was electronic distribution. The first important method of Internet distribution was the online sale of physical merchandise. Rather than traveling to a retail space, consumers began using online stores to purchase CDs and have them shipped directly to a home or an office. Harkening back to the days of catalog retail, which existed as far back as the late nineteenth century, this form of distribution became popular in the second half of the 1990s after the dot-com boom in the earlier part of the decade. Although this practice is widespread in today's economy, online retail took some time to gain ground, as consumers questioned the security of this form of commerce. After years of losing money, for example, the popular online shopping company Amazon turned a profit for the first time in 2001. Today, Amazon is the largest online retailer in the world, with sales of more than $128 billion in 2016.

As the Internet facilitated online sales of physical CDs, an entire generation of listeners also began to experiment with sharing music in the form of electronic files. Encoding music into digital file formats had been possible for some time, but several technological developments in the 1990s helped facilitate the easy transfer of music. The widespread use of the MP3, a highly compressed format that greatly reduces the size of a music file, allowed users to send music through email or create collections of data files with hundreds of songs on a single CD. File-sharing services emerged, allowing users to easily trade these smaller, more manageable music files. The most popular and notorious of these services was Napster, a peer-to-peer file-sharing program that allowed users to download files quickly and easily from other users. The use of Napster and other peer-to-peer file sharing services such as Limewire and Gnutella grew dramatically at the turn of the millennium, causing a massive free-for-all of music trading and changing the relationship between the music industry and its customers. There were clear advantages and disadvantages to the Napster revolution. On one hand, listeners gained access to more music than ever, easily suggesting music to friends and sampling songs that they might not have considered buying. In this way, peer-to-peer networking was a democratizing force that decentralized the power of major labels, placing distribution at the fingertips of listeners. We can read evidence of this viewpoint in a widely distributed lecture-turned-article by Courtney Love called "Courtney Does the Math" from 2000, which is based on an earlier essay by indie-rock producer Steve Albini called "The Problem with Music." The perspectives of both Love and Albini reflected common claims of musicians who distrusted the music business, citing specific examples of how the industry mistreated artists.

There were also tremendous drawbacks to these networks. For one, trading music through Napster and other peer-to-peer services was illegal, and a decade of litigation proved that both users and those who developed these systems violated copyright laws. Several important issues arose from this widespread illegal activity. Musicians, songwriters, and record companies lost a tremendous amount of revenue. While many groups certainly received great exposure from peer-to-peer trading, they were not being paid for their services. Bands spoke out publicly against the practice and filed lawsuits to challenge Napster's activities. The most famous of these, Metallica, faced a public relations nightmare when their actions were perceived as evidence of music industry greed. When Napster was forced to shut down in July 2001, the die had already been cast. Although illegal trading continued to flourish, mostly through difficult-to-monitor decentralized networking protocols such as BitTorrent, this accounted for a much smaller share of revenue than when Napster was at its peak. In just two short years of activity, Napster challenged the very fabric of the music industry business model. The most important result of this revolution was a large-scale decline in sales of physical media. Throughout the first decade of the 2000s, sales of compact discs decreased by almost two-thirds from the peak years at the end of the 1990s. Today, CDs account for about 15 percent of total revenue of the recording industry.

As digital files became an important method of consuming music, a new sector of the music business developed to support listeners' technological needs. A variety of portable music players flooded the market in the late 1990s and early 2000s, allowing users to access an immense amount of music using an extremely small device. Consumers began to use computer software to organize their files on a computer. In January 2001, in

A Google Home device in 2016. As listeners embraced new forms of streaming, music became a more central component of new "smart speaker" systems that allow users to interact with a variety of media.

the midst of the controversy surrounding Napster, the computer company Apple launched a new application called iTunes. Like competitors Musicmatch and Winamp, iTunes was originally designed as Apple-only "jukebox software," which assisted users in managing their digital music files. Later that year, the company introduced the first of its revolutionary iPod music players. In 2003, Apple opened its "iTunes Store," which allowed users to purchase music files, downloading them directly through iTunes software, and place them on the iPod, which had become the industry-leading portable device. Other companies sold products to do all of these things, but Apple quickly became the most popular technological music retailer, selling twenty-five million downloads through the iTunes Store before the end of 2003. What seemed to be a fringe industry exploded during the 2000s, as Apple integrated video, gaming, and other computer applications into its iTunes Store and various handheld devices. As a result of this change in purchasing, in 2005 *Billboard* began to publish digital download charts, and incorporate these figures into its data for the "Hot 100" chart. Moreover, iTunes charts became the best place to find the pulse of the current music industry. Offering music, television and films, podcasts, audiobooks, educational initiatives, social networking, and a wide variety of apps, Apple is now the largest music retailer in the United States. As of 2014, the company had sold more than 35 billion music downloads through the iTunes Store, and sales of digital singles dwarfed sales of compact discs.

Digital distribution in the form of purchasing downloadable files quickly morphed into streaming as the dominant form of consumption. Grooveshark launched in 2007 with a model similar to peer-sharing sites like Napster: listeners were charged with uploading songs to a server and then shared in the profits when these songs were purchased and downloaded. Like Napster, the legal status of Grooveshark was murky, with many significant lawsuits challenging the site's business model. Major agreements between record companies and newer sites, however, allowed users to freely stream songs without paying for downloads. Services in this manner—such as Spotify, Rdio, and Beats Music—became popular in the wake of a turn toward streaming as a primary method of consumption. Most of these companies allowed users to maintain free accounts and charged small monthly fees to eliminate advertising or for access on mobile devices. Although endorsed through legal agreements with record companies, the "micropayments" offered to artists for streaming caused great controversy among artists. Later "cloud"-based models became popular in 2011, with technology giants such as Google (Google Play), Apple (iCloud and Apple Music), and Amazon (Cloud Drive) launching subscription services that would allow listeners to buy music, store previously owned files, and access a single collection using mobile devices, home entertainment units, desktop computers, and even car stereos. Apple made industry news by purchasing Beats in 2014 and Jay-Z invested in Tidal in 2015, making both of these services industry leaders. As the music business slowly embraced digital distribution during the decade between the rise of Napster and development of streaming models, independent musicians used similar technological advances to reach listeners. CD Baby opened in 1997 as an online retailer focused on selling music of independent artists. Sites such as MySpace proliferated in the early 2000s, allowing independent bands to create profiles and offer images, audio, and video examples of their work. Social networking giants like Facebook also catered to independent musicians with specific

PHYSICAL MEDIA

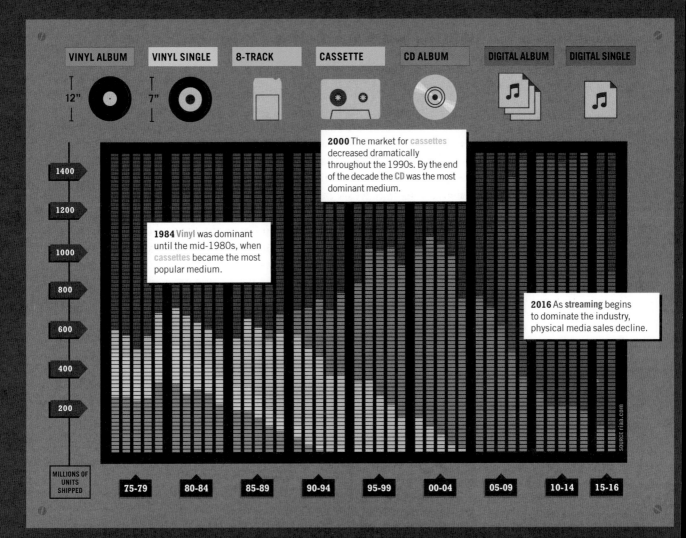

VINYL ALBUM — 12"
VINYL SINGLE — 7"
8-TRACK
CASSETTE
CD ALBUM
DIGITAL ALBUM
DIGITAL SINGLE

2000 The market for cassettes decreased dramatically throughout the 1990s. By the end of the decade the CD was the most dominant medium.

1984 Vinyl was dominant until the mid-1980s, when cassettes became the most popular medium.

2016 As streaming begins to dominate the industry, physical media sales decline.

1400
1200
1000
800
600
400
200

MILLIONS OF UNITS SHIPPED

75-79   80-84   85-89   90-94   95-99   00-04   05-09   10-14   15-16

SOURCE riaa.com

A RISE IN SUBSCRIPTION SERVICES

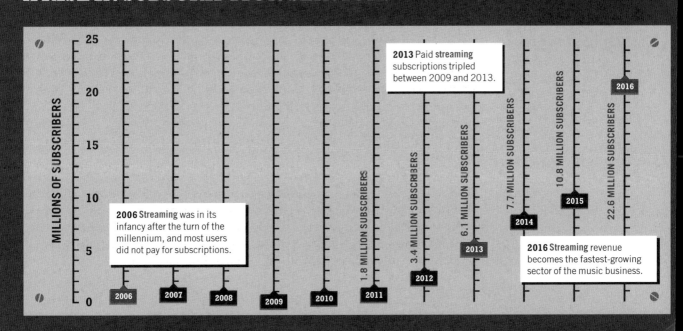

MILLIONS OF SUBSCRIBERS

25
20
15
10
5
0

2013 Paid streaming subscriptions tripled between 2009 and 2013.

2006 Streaming was in its infancy after the turn of the millennium, and most users did not pay for subscriptions.

2016 Streaming revenue becomes the fastest-growing sector of the music business.

1.8 MILLION SUBSCRIBERS
3.4 MILLION SUBSCRIBERS
6.1 MILLION SUBSCRIBERS
7.7 MILLION SUBSCRIBERS
10.8 MILLION SUBSCRIBERS
22.6 MILLION SUBSCRIBERS

2006   2007   2008   2009   2010   2011   2012   2013   2014   2015   2016

audio tools, and specialized sites such as Soundcloud and Bandcamp launched in the late 2000s and became portals for a variety of artists (both signed and unsigned) to connect with listeners.

In direct opposition to the overwhelming use of digital technologies in the 1990s, there was a fascinating return to analog-oriented creation and distribution in several sectors of the rock market. Moribund during the early 1990s, by the turn of the millennium new music by indie-rock, hip-hop, and dance music artists was increasingly offered for purchase on 45-rpm singles and long-play records in addition to CD and digital download formats. In concert with the digital revolution, LP purchases were often bundled with digital downloads, allowing listeners with a single purchase to have the tangibility and artwork of old-school records for occasional listening along with a more pragmatic set of digital files to accompany twenty-first century listening habits. In a similar way, as digital tools began to dominate the industry, some artists became vocal about their preference for tape-based recording and older forms of production. Foo Fighters leader Dave Grohl was one advocate, using his acceptance speech for Best Rock Performance at the Grammy Awards in 2012 to promote "human elements" and "imperfections" in music performed on old-fashioned instruments and recorded in a garage with a tape machine. The next year, Grohl released a film he directed called *Sound City*, which called further attention to the use of older technology in rock recording. Featuring commentary and performances by Stevie Nicks, Trent Reznor, Paul McCartney, Josh Homme, and many others, *Sound City* reflected a generational stance toward digital production by arguing that older rock performance techniques and analog recording technology inspired musicians to create better music. Sales of LPs now account for nearly a quarter of the value of all physical sales.

Changing Conceptions of Media: Rock Is Nowhere, but It's Also Everywhere.
When rock and roll first became popular in the 1950s listeners encountered the new form through AM radio, local dances, and record stores. Sixty years later, it is hard to find rock music in any of these places. Terrestrial radio has changed dramatically since the addition of FM, moving further into the concept of format radio that created classic-rock radio in the 1980s. Commercial rock stations now follow formats such as "classic hits" and "hot adult contemporary" and are often nationally syndicated and out of touch with local communities. Many listeners have turned to Internet and satellite radio as sources for rock music. At the beginning of the 2000s, a more advanced commercial-free system of satellite radio also became available to listeners in the United States through both XM and Sirius (which have since merged into a single company). Offering more breadth and fewer commercials than traditional commercial radio, these stations found immediate success with fans of rock music. Shows like Little Steven's "Underground Garage" and Bob Dylan's "Theme Time Radio" and channels featuring extended jam band performances by the Grateful Dead and Phish were features of satellite programming that showed the possibilities of this new form. The Internet now allows traditional stations to stream online to anywhere in the world, and has provided a forum for thousands of new Internet-only stations. Perhaps the most interesting manifestation of the Internet radio community has been the emergence

of Pandora, a service that works from data collected through a large-scale encoding initiative called the Music Genome Project. Working from a starting point entered by the user (an artist, song, or genre) and the user's taste, Pandora provides personalized radio stations and suggestions for potential new music purchases. Many streaming and cloud-based services have also ventured into similar forms of suggestion-based radio.

Rock concert promotion has come a long way from the local sock hop or senior prom. Now a multibillion-dollar business, tickets to see a mainstream rock act are priced well beyond the budget of the average teenager, targeting instead the expendable resources of the baby boomer generation. Large conglomerate corporations such as Live Nation have become the industry standard, signing artists to lucrative long-term contracts, commanding huge profits from concert tours, and purchasing (or merging with) other powerful industry players like Ticketmaster and House of Blues. Even the indie-rock circuit has become more industry savvy in the last decade, with a series of lucrative reunion tours by bands like the Pixies, Guided by Voices, Pavement, the Replacements, and the Jesus and Mary Chain. We might view the October 2010 Matador Records twenty-first birthday celebration in Las Vegas as a bellwether of this change in indie values. Although it was marketed as an ironic venue for an independent powerhouse, a concert such as this, which featured a $400 VIP ticket option, shows the maturation and financial reach of the modern indie community. More and more, as concert promotion becomes big business, rock shows are becoming less accessible to the average fan. Rather than seeing bands live, rock listeners often make contact with their favorite groups through digital means. Social networking sites and the growth of YouTube has drastically changed how bands interact with listeners. Official music videos are now archived for instant access. Listeners participate in the artistic process by creating their own videos and combinations of existing songs (often called mashups) or their own performances. Historic live concert footage is now widely available, new shows are often uploaded within days (or even hours) after live events, while special video broadcasts are streamed live over the Internet.

Large-scale music festivals became big business during the first decade of the new millennium in the United States, offering listeners the chance to see scores of bands on a variety of stages, sometimes in multiday events that encompassed multiple venues. There is a long history of the destination festival, dating to the Newport folk and jazz gatherings in the 1950s and 1960s and later rock-oriented shows that grew out of hippie culture such as Monterey Pop and Woodstock. Long-standing festivals such as Glastonbury in England, Rock in Rio in Brazil, and Roskilde in Denmark were popular throughout the world during the 1970s and 1980s. Festival gatherings were less popular in the United States during this time.

Several styles of festival emerged in the United States during the 1980s and 1990s, changing the way that concertgoers experienced live music. One of these was the industry showcase model. Founded as an outgrowth of

South by Southwest (SXSW) started during the mid-1980s as a small industry showcase. It slowly grew into a major yearly event, exemplifying the new type of rock festival that became popular after the turn of the millennium.

the alternative industry magazine *College Music Journal*, the CMJ Music Marathon started in 1980 in New York City to connect college radio representatives and other industry professionals with bands popular in the "college" market, which later became associated with alternative and indie rock genre labels. Based in Austin, Texas, South by Southwest (SXSW) started as a similar industry showcase festival during the mid-1980s and later swelled into a behemoth multiday event that far surpassed its original music-oriented focus. In addition to music, SXSW now includes large gatherings for film and interactive media professionals. Traveling festivals also became popular in the 1980s and 1990s. Monsters of Rock was an early example that focused on heavier forms of rock and metal. Jane's Addiction lead singer Perry Farrell started Lollapalooza in 1991, concentrating on bands associated with the rising "alternative" movement. Formed in 1995, the Vans Warped Tour combined sports like skating with dozens of musical acts performing in metal, ska, and pop punk styles often favored by extreme sports fans. Lilith Fair and H.O.R.D.E. were other examples of the carnival-like music showcases that became popular during the 1990s.

During the 2000s, destination festivals in the United States led the widespread popularization of multiday events that supported large audiences. First organized in 1999, Coachella became an annual event located in Indio, a Southern California desert town midway between Los Angeles and San Diego. Located in rural Tennessee, Bonnaroo began in 2002 with an original focus on jam bands that later diffused into much broader bookings. While reminiscent in certain ways of hippie festivals of the 1960s, gatherings like SXSW, Coachella, and Bonnaroo reflected the corporate-led nature of rock after the turn of the millennium. Travel, accommodations, logistics, and staggering ticket prices marked these festivals as destinations for a new breed of rock enthusiasts who were far removed from the teenagers who attended package tour dances during the 1950s. Perhaps the most notorious of these was Desert Trip, which was first held in 2016 on the same site as Coachella. Nicknamed "Oldchella" by many in the industry, this festival included performances by septuagenarian musicians like the Rolling Stones, Bob Dylan, Paul McCartney, Neil Young, Roger Waters, and the Who. Single-day tickets started at several hundred dollars, and the most elaborate VIP packages cost nearly $2000. It is not surprising that these older musicians commanded such ticket prices. Even though new creative works by classic rock musicians rarely make an impact on popular culture, concert tours by these acts are still among the most lucrative in the music business.

Roger Daltrey (left) and Pete Townshend (right) of the Who performing at Desert Trip in 2016. An amalgamation of the rising festival movement and the continued popularity of "classic" rock musicians, this festival commanded ticket prices that were outside the means of most younger listeners. Dubbed "Oldchella" by many, the average performer age was 72 and no women were on the bill. Over two weekends, festival attendance was estimated at 150,000, most of which were baby boomers.

WHAT'S THAT SOURCE?

An Artist Confronts Pandora

David Lowery is a songwriter, guitarist, and singer. He fronted the 1980s band Camper van Beethoven, and the 1990s band Cracker. Lowery has operated a recording studio, a label, and a publishing company. He has also worked in investing, taught music business courses at the University of Georgia, and testified before the U.S. Congress on issues of intellectual property from a musician's perspective. This piece discusses Lowery's shockingly low quarterly royalties from Pandora for use of the song "Low," Cracker's hit from 1994. As streaming services and Internet services like Pandora continue to proliferate, issues like this will surely become central to discussions between musicians, lawmakers, and the music industry.

As a songwriter Pandora paid me $16.89[1] for 1,159,000 plays of "Low" last quarter. Less than I make from a single T-shirt sale. Okay that's a slight exaggeration. That's only the premium multi-color long-sleeve shirts and that's only at venues that don't take commission. But still.

Soon you will be hearing from Pandora how they need Congress to change the way royalties are calculated so that they can pay much, much less to songwriters and performers. For you civilians, webcasting rates are "compulsory" rates. They are set by the government (crazy, right?). Further since they are compulsory royalties, artists cannot "opt out" of a service like Pandora even if they think Pandora doesn't pay them enough. The majority of songwriters have their rates set by the government, too, in the form of the ASCAP and BMI rate courts—a single judge gets to decide the fate of songwriters (technically not a "compulsory" but may as well be). This is already a government-mandated subsidy from songwriters and artists to Silicon Valley. Pandora wants to make it even worse. (Yet another reason the government needs to get out of the business of setting webcasting rates and let the market sort it out.)

Here's an idea. Why doesn't Pandora get off the couch and get an actual business model instead of asking for a handout from Congress and artists? For instance: Right now Pandora plays one minute of commercials an hour on their free service. Here's an idea! Play two minutes of commercials and double your revenue! (Sirius XM often plays 13 minutes and charges a subscription.)

I urge all songwriters to post their royalty statements and show the world just how terrible webcasting rates are for songwriters.

The revolution will not be webcast.

Source: David Lowery, "My Song Got Played on Pandora 1 Million Times and All I Got Was $16.89, Less Than What I Make from a Single T-Shirt Sale!," *The Trichordist*, http://thetrichordist.com/2013/06/24/my-song-got-played-on-pandora-1-million-times-and-all-i-got-was-16-89-less-than-what-i-make-from-a-single-t-shirt-sale.

1. I only own 40% of the song, the rest of the band owns the other 60% so [for the actual] amount paid to songwriters multiply by 2.5 or $42.25.
*I am also paid a separate royalty for being the performer of the song. It's higher but also what I would regard as unsustainable.

[For frame of reference compare Sirius XM paid me $181.00. Terrestrial (FM/AM) radio US paid me $1,522.00.]

Traditional music retail changed greatly during the 1990s and 2000s. Once the center of rock culture, teeming with knowledgeable (and sometimes conceited) experts in the history of popular music, the independent record store saw a slow and painful decline beginning in the early 1990s. Mall chains, big-box stores such as Best Buy and Walmart, and the rise of Internet commerce had a crippling effect on independent record stores. The few surviving relics of this bygone age are located in college towns and large urban environments, and are mostly geared toward an indie-rock audience. Even these markets have had a difficult time supporting independent music retailers because streaming is so easy and the prices of digital

The few remaining record stores are often found in college towns and urban areas. Here, Denver Public Art Program manager Michael Chavez poses for a story about "record store day," a national event that occurs every April. These events seek to draw attention to the continued viability of physical media and to celebrate the independent record store as a place to browse, interact with other collectors, and purchase music.

downloads and CDs at large retail outlets are invariably cheaper than those offered at small record shops. Most listeners now use streaming services rather than physical media or downloaded digital files. Those who show an interest in cassettes, CDs, or vinyl singles and albums often use these media in addition to various forms of digital streaming.

All of this might lead us to believe that rock music is on the decline. Sales of rock music have certainly slowed, but it is also easy to see how exposure to rock music is increasing. Mirroring the digital revolution at the end of the twentieth century that challenged delivery methods for most forms of entertainment media, rock music has become the center of a burgeoning industry that sells music as intellectual property. Synchronization royalties, or payments paid for the use of music in other media like film and television, now form a substantial part of the annual revenue for record companies. Commercial advertising has come to value rock music as a means to sell products to a variety of demographics. Whether it is the Rolling Stones selling Microsoft products, Bob Dylan selling Victoria's Secret underwear, or Sting selling Jaguar automobiles, older rock musicians have grown increasingly tolerant of using their most famous songs in advertising. More modern artists have used television advertising to cross-promote their newest music. In 2009, for example, the Train song "Hey, Soul Sister" was featured in Samsung television commercials while also appearing on the record charts. This practice is by no means limited to classic rock or mainstream, as indie music has been incredibly popular with advertisers and television networks seeking a hip edge. At the beginning of the 2000s, a burgeoning cellular telephone ringtone market exposed listeners to rock music in unconventional places, as audible ringtones pervaded public spaces and ringback tones (the sound you hear when you are waiting for someone to pick up the phone) allowed fans to share their favorite music with friends. Perhaps the most fascinating new market for rock music has been in the gaming industry, as new and old music alike have become soundtracks for the latest video games for the Xbox, PlayStation, or Wii. Games such as Grand Theft Auto, Madden NFL, FIFA, the Tony Hawk Series, Rayman Legends, Portal, and many others have used popular music to great effect in their soundtracks. Beginning in the early 2000s, "machine dance" games such as Dance Dance Revolution became especially important venues for new music. Perhaps the most popular video game to incorporate rock was Guitar Hero, which was first released in 2005. An interactive game requiring players to simulate guitar performance, Guitar Hero and the later Rock Band (which expanded instrumentation to include bass, drums, vocals, and keyboards) became extremely popular methods of exposure for old and new rock alike. Through the addition of downloadable content, the library of available songs for Rock Band extended into the thousands, and several of the largest marketing deals of the decade surrounded content for these interactive video games. The largest Rock Band release was The Beatles: Rock Band in 2009, which accompanied a long-awaited set of the group's remastered recordings.

MAINSTREAM ROCK IN THE NEW MILLENNIUM

From Sk8ers to Idols: Avril Lavigne, P!nk, Lady Gaga, and Kelly Clarkson.

Many popular styles of rock pervaded the American mainstream during the 2000s. Unlike rock's early years, which often featured the voices of women filtered through a male production team, the unadulterated female perspective became common after the turn of the millennium. There was a wide range of important female performers during the decade, reflecting an increasingly diverse listenership that viewed femininity from a variety of perspectives through the medium of rock music. At one end of the musical spectrum was the Canadian teenager Avril Lavigne, who emerged in the summer of 2002 with the album *Let Go* (p2 uk1) and the single "Complicated" (p2 uk3). Lavigne wrote and performed her own music (often with the songwriting team of the Matrix), which echoed early 1990s California pop punk music. A series of number-one pop albums in the United States and UK followed, including *Under My Skin* (2004) and *The Best Damn Thing* (2007), producing hit singles like "Sk8er Boi" (p10 uk8, 2002), "I'm with You" (p4 uk7, 2002), and "Girlfriend" (p1 uk2, 2007). In light of her status as a teen sensation, Lavigne was also notable for her style of dress, often wearing dark, baggy clothing that cloaked her body. This stance served as a pillar of Lavigne's self-promotion and flew in the face of the age-old tradition of sensual female teenage artists.

While Lavigne displayed an early interest in a popular style of music indebted to the punk tradition, vocalist and songwriter P!nk became popular at the beginning of the decade with music from the beat-based community. As a protégé of R&B pioneer L. A. Reid, P!nk's debut album, *Can't Take Me Home* (p26 r23 uk13, 2000), was firmly in the tradition of pop divas and R&B girl groups like TLC and Destiny's Child. Yet, as the decade wore on, P!nk became more involved in her musical output, infusing a distinct rock element into her later albums. Singles such as "Get the Party Started" (p4 uk2, 2001) and "Don't Let Me Get Me" (p8 uk6, 2002) show a much harder vocal style, distorted guitars, and autobiographical lyrics that describe her desire to move away from cookie-cutter pop into more adventurous material. Even the title of P!nk's second album, *Missundaztood* (p6 uk2, 2002), supports this position. Later singles such as "So What" (p1 uk1, 2008), "Sober" (p15 uk9, 2008), and "Raise Your Glass" (p1 uk13, 2010) continue this powerful sense of lyrical ownership based on authenticity and stylistic diversity. Like Lavigne, P!nk's outward ownership of her music also encapsulated the treatment of her image and her stance on femininity in popular music, while still maintaining a strong connection to fashion. Perhaps the best example of her perspective can be found in the song "Stupid Girls" (p13 uk4, 2006) and its accompanying music video, which cite an "epidemic" of young women who lack individuality and ambition.

Lady Gaga performing during the 2017 Super Bowl halftime show. Among a large group of women who performed in rock styles after the turn of the millennium, Lady Gaga is among the most spectacular, often assuming different identities through her music and fashion.

Another important new female performer during the post-millennium period was Lady Gaga. Born Stefani Germanotta, she worked her way through the New York City club scene after starting college at NYU and moving to music full time. Her debut album as Lady Gaga, *The Fame* (p2 uk1, 2008) was a *tour de force* that produced singles like "Just Dance" (p1 uk3, 2008) and "Poker Face" (p1 uk1, 2008). Later albums like *Born This Way* (p1 uk1, 2011), *Artpop* (pi uk1, 2013), and *Joanne* (p1 uk3, 2016) solidified her as one of the most important performers of her generation. Far more than recitations of her music, Gaga's television and live performances often include outlandish sets and costumes in addition to large groups of musicians and dancers. Like David Bowie, Madonna, and Michael Jackson, her image and persona are part and parcel with her music. One of Gaga's most high-profile performances occurred during the halftime show of the 2017 Super Bowl. After years of being perceived as eccentric and mysterious, in part due her constantly changing looks, this was a particularly mainstream opportunity for Gaga, one with the potential to move her even further into popular acceptance. Against the backdrop of a continually fragmented visual culture, the Super Bowl halftime show still represents one of the biggest stages in popular music, its collective audience harkening back to the age of the family variety show of the 1950s. Gaga did not disappoint. Beginning with a medley of two well-known vernacular songs, "God Bless America" and "This Land Is Your Land," she then entered Houston's NRG stadium from the rafters and performed a series of her own popular hits. Debates over the political stance of the performance raged in the press the next day, providing a sense of the still far-reaching nature of this annual musical performance event in American life.

An autobiographical theme of being trapped in the music industry machine is also present in the output of Kelly Clarkson. As the winner of the first season of the television show *American Idol*, Clarkson was immediately thrust into the industry limelight, releasing her first album, *Thankful*, in the summer of 2002. Much like the diverse vocal styles required of a successful *American Idol* contestant, the music contained on *Thankful* was chock full of mainstream pop songs and covers that highlighted Clarkson's vocal acrobatics. Her next album, *Breakaway* (p3 uk3, 2004), highlighted her move away from the beat-based pop music of *American Idol* toward a more decidedly rock sound drenched with heavy drums, distorted guitars, and anthemic vocals. Singles such as "Since U Been Gone" (p2 uk5, 2004), "Behind Those Hazel Eyes" (p6 uk9, 2005), and "Because of You" (p7 uk7, 2005) highlighted Clarkson's new approach. The lead single on the album, "Breakaway" (p6 uk22, 2004), was co-written with a group of songwriters that included Avril Lavigne, who had hoped to record the song for her own debut album. Clarkson's single "Stronger (What Doesn't Kill You)" (p1 uk8, 2008) moved back to the dance realm, but continued the theme of female independence found in so many of her songs.

As we see in the music of these artists, the female voice thrived in mainstream rock music during the 2000s, as women found new avenues to assert their perspectives in a historically chauvinistic musical style. Moreover, comparing their perspectives with the typical female image proffered during the 1950s, we can see how dramatically different female voices have become in American society during the rock era.

Men at Work: Maroon 5, John Mayer, and Coldplay.

Among the increasingly crowded field of female rockers, several middle-of-the-road male artists rose to popularity after the 2000s performing traditional brands of rock. Male artists such as Maroon 5, John Mayer, and Coldplay were among the many musicians who found success during the decade by exhibiting clear debts to earlier rock styles. Maroon 5 emerged from Los Angeles in the early part of the decade after an unsuccessful stint as the band Kara's Flowers. Mixing strains of R&B and funk with heavier rock, the group featured lead singer and songwriter Adam Levine. Maroon 5's first album, *Songs about Jane* (p6 uk1), was released in the summer of 2002, along with the funk-rock single "Harder to Breathe" (p18 uk13). It took several years of incessant touring before the group achieved national popularity in early 2004 with the singles "This Love" (p5 uk3) and "She Will Be Loved" (p5 uk4). *Songs about Jane* would go on to sell more than four million copies in the United States and, despite the fact that the album was released two years earlier, the group won the Best New Artist Grammy Award in 2005. Debuting at the top of the *Billboard* pop album charts, the group's later albums, *It Won't Be Soon before Long* (p1 uk1, 2007) and *Hands All Over* (p2 uk6, 2010), departed from the harder edge of *Songs about Jane*, focusing instead on dance influences. This change is apparent in the singles "Makes Me Wonder" (p1 uk2, 2007) and "Moves Like Jagger" (p1 uk2, 2011), which subdue heavier rock elements to focus on Levine's vocals and a more beat-based approach. Levine has parlayed his Maroon 5 success into many other entrepreneurial efforts, including a longstanding role as judge on the NBC reality show singing competition *The Voice*.

Kelly Clarkson moved on from a contestant on *American Idol* to a successful solo career. Her sometime rebellious image often merged with rock styles in a series of songs and albums that rose to public and critical acclaim.

John Mayer released his first album, *Room for Squares*, through the independent Aware label in 2001 before signing to Columbia. A former student at Boston's Berklee School of Music, Mayer was no stranger to the history of rock, becoming proficient as a songwriter and guitarist in a number of styles during his studies. With all four of his studio albums reaching the *Billboard* Top 10, and a long string of Top 20 singles, Mayer's traditional approach to pop writing and performing made him one of the best-selling rock artists of the decade. Songs such as "No Such Thing" (p13, 2003), "Daughters" (p19, 2004), and "Waiting on the World to Change" (p14, 2006) featured some of the most intricate and audible guitar heard on mainstream radio during the 2000s, often drawing heavy influences from the blues tradition. The sonic space left on many of Mayer's recordings, which lack the layers of instruments that have become standard in twenty-first century production, makes his style seem old-fashioned. Mayer is open about his interest in older forms of rock,

Coldplay, fronted by lead singer Chris Martin, performing in Brisbane, Australia, in 2016. One of the most successful rock bands of the decade, Coldplay emerged from the Britpop tradition in the mid-2000s.

collaborating with blues musicians like B. B. King and Buddy Guys as well as Dead and Company, a modern offshoot of the Grateful Dead.

While Mayer is clearly a student of the blues, the British group Coldplay came out of the Britpop tradition. Fronted by singer and multi-instrumentalist Chris Martin, Coldplay broke into the American market in mid-2000 with the single "Yellow" (p48 uk4). Drawing heavily on the style of Radiohead and Jeff Buckley, the group's debut album, *Parachutes* (p51 uk1, 2000), became a smash hit in the UK, and slowly sold more than two million copies in the United States. Increasing in popularity throughout the 2000s, the band released five more albums, the third of which, *Viva La Vida or Death and All His Friends* (p1 uk1, 2008) contained the hit single "Viva La Vida" (p1 uk1, 2008) and won 2009 Grammy Awards for Best Album and Best Song, respectively. The group's style changed slowly throughout the decade, morphing from a focus on Radiohead-like experimental Britpop to more mainstream concerns, all the while featuring the vocal presence of Martin, the group's leader and most visible member. Coldplay is now one of the biggest rock bands in the world. More recent records like *Mylo Xyloto* (p1 uk1, 2011) and *Ghost Stories* (p1 uk1, 2014) have reached the top of the charts in as many as a dozen countries.

Listening Guide

Coldplay, "Viva La Vida" Capitol 509992 27024

Words and music by Guy Berryman, Jonny Buckland, Will Champion, Chris Martin, and Phil Harvey. Produced by Markus Dravs, Brian Eno, and Rik Simpson. Reached #1 on the *Billboard* "Hot 100" chart and #1 in the UK in 2008. Also included on the album *Viva La Vida or Death and All His Friends*, which also rose to #1 on the "Billboard 200" and in the UK.

FORM: Compound AABA. There is a simple relationship between verse and chorus and sections within each A section. (The chords of the verse and chorus are similar, but not the same.) The initial 8-measure idea is presented in the introduction and serves as the basis for each section of the song except for the bridge. Notice how this germ of an idea seems to get more complex as different melodic lines are presented over it. The use of this figure for multiple sections creates a sense of tension at the end of the bridge: in one way this figure represents a return—the use of the familiar 8-measure string figure—but a memorable new vocalese melody also makes this section more than a simple interlude. Instrumentation, dynamics, and effects are used throughout to create a sense of arc. This is especially evident at the song's conclusion, when a potentially large and dramatic climax is thwarted by a strong decrescendo and simplified texture.

TIME SIGNATURE: 4/4.

INSTRUMENTATION: Strings, kick drum, timpani, cymbals, synthesized piano sounds, bass, piano, lead and background vocals.

A	0:00–0:14	**Introduction**, 8 mm.	The record starts with a driving string part that repeats a 4-chord sequence two times.
	0:14–0:30	**Verse 1**, 8 mm.	Vocals and an insistent dance-like bass drum enter. "I used to rule the world . . ."
	0:27–0:41	**Interlude**, 8 mm.	Accompanying strings continue with a new higher string melody that alternates between two notes and a series of tremolos, accompanied still by the kick drum.
	0:41–1:09	**Verse 2,** 16 mm.	The verse is doubled in length, with more variation in the second half. The strings contain a new countermelody, which moves faster than the vocal melody. "I used to roll the dice . . ."
	1:09–1:37	**Chorus**, 16 mm.	The vocals are double-tracked here, a stronger string melody accompanies this section, and timpani and cymbals are also used. A bass enters for the first time. "I hear Jerusalem . . ."
	1:37–1:51	**Interlude**, 8 mm.	A harpsichord-like figure enters, with another unidentifiable reverb-drenched instrument.
A	1:51–2:19	**Verse 3**, 16 mm.	Notice the fewer effects on the vocals (in comparison to the chorus), which adds a sense of intimacy and a dynamic return to the initial texture. A piano, string melody, and backing vocal figure enters in short succession during the second half. "It was the wicked and wild . . ."
	2:19–2:47	**Chorus**, 16 mm.	As before with timpani and cymbals. "I hear Jerusalem . . ."
B	2:47–3:01	**Bridge**, 8 mm.	The harmonic pattern changes for the first time, now alternating mostly between two tones and arriving at a tense chord at the end.
A	3:01–3:15	**Interlude**, 8 mm.	The chords match the verse (or the first half of the chorus), but a different vocal melody (using "ohs") has been added, creating a sense of contrast.
	3:03–3:42	**Chorus**, 16 mm.	The "oh" melody continues, but the instrumental texture diminishes rapidly during the final phrase of the melody, subverting the ending. "I hear Jerusalem . . ."
	3:42–4:01	**Postlude**, 10 mm.	The looped "oh" figure and a distant organ melody fade, creating a sense of resolution.

Roots Run Deep: Folk Styles Return to the Mainstream. In 2001, the

soundtrack to the film *O Brother, Where Art Thou?* (p1, 2001) became a runaway
success, eventually earning the Grammy Award for Album of the Year. Featuring
modern recordings of old-time and bluegrass music performed by artists like Ralph
Stanley, Alison Krauss, John Hartford, and Gillian Welch, the soundtrack was
situated in a fascinating middle ground between country, folk, and popular interests
at the beginning of the new millennium. The success of *O Brother* foreshadowed a
series of popular releases exhibiting a renewed interest in music with a strong acoustic base during the following decade. The Norah Jones album *Come Away with Me*
(r1 uk1, 2002) was similarly situated between classic song, jazz, and album-oriented
pop, and was also well received by critics and garnered many important awards.
Jones's success showed a noticeable split between the modern pop market and music
made according to older production and songwriting techniques. This was evident
in the heavy critical praise and multiple Grammy awards for her song "Don't Know
Why" (p30 uk59, 2002) despite the mediocre success of this single in the pop market. Later popular albums by Jones, including *Feels Like Home* (p1, 2004) and *Not
Too Late* (p1, 2007) also contained music produced by decidedly nonelectric means.

Several acoustic-oriented artists had success later in the decade. One of the most
popular acts in this vein during the 2000s was Jack Johnson. Raised in Hawaii,
Johnson's easygoing music was marketed strongly against his brief background as
a professional surfer. His debut album *Brushfire Fairytales* (34p, 2002) emerged
slowly, staying on the national album charts for over a year. Later albums such as
On and On (p3, 2003), *In Between Dreams* (p2 uk1, 2005), a soundtrack to the
children's film *Curious George* (p1 uk15, 2006), and *Sleep through Static* (p1 uk1,
2008) showed Johnson's increasing popularity during the decade. Like Jones,
Johnson's albums sold in the millions, but his singles were not very successful in
the pop market. Instead, Jones, Johnson, and the many other acoustic-oriented
artists of the time were more prone to find success in other market segments such
as "Triple A" (Adult Album Alternative), "Adult Pop," "Alternative Songs," and
"Adult Contemporary," the latter of which was a new name for a chart once called
"Easy Listening." These market segments had been used for decades, especially in
radio, but took new life during the 2000s as singles charts that helped show the
popularity of rock-oriented music by essentially filtering out the beat-based music
that dominated the more broadly situated "Hot 100."

The popularity of artists like Jones and Johnson was followed by a popular trend
at the end of the 2000s that fused old-time, acoustic musical textures with modern pop songwriting. The group at the forefront of this movement was Mumford
and Sons, who came out of a small "folk underground" scene in London. There
were many fascinating elements of hybridity in the music and performance style
of Mumford and Sons. The group used fashion that evoked the depression era, a
lyrical style that often used forwardly literary construction and referred to authors
like Shakespeare and Steinbeck, and instrumentation that encompassed both rock
norms (drums, electric keyboards, electric bass) and old-time styles (banjo, acoustic guitar, accordion, washboard, upright bass, mandolin). This mix proved to be
extremely successful. Their 2009 album *Sigh No More* (p2 uk2) became an international sensation, and *Babel* (p1 uk1, 2012), which featured the single "I Will Wait"
(p12 uk12, 2012), won Album of the Year at the 2013 Grammy Awards. Other contemporaneous groups echoed similar hybrid styles that incorporated heavy elements

Mumford and Sons performing in New York City in 2013. Among a larger wave of folk-oriented acts, Mumford and Sons became successful in 2009 with a hybrid style that combined elements of old-time, bluegrass, and rock.

of folk, old-time, or acoustic textures. The Lumineers released the popular single "Ho Hey" (p3 uk8, 2012) and an eponymous album (p2 uk8, 2012). *American Idol* 2012 winner Phillip Phillips clearly evoked this style as well, which was evident on his album *The World from the Side of the Moon* (p4, 2012). With a number of records produced by industry titan Rick Rubin, the Avett Brothers incorporated the long tradition of country music brother duets into the pop mainstream in a series of extremely popular albums, including *The Carpenter* (p4, 2012), *Magpie and the Dandelion* (p5, 2013), and *True Sadness* (p3, 2016). While these albums and singles were genuinely popular, the ways in which they contrasted with heavier styles of rock and beat-based styles that were dominant in the mainstream was no fluke. The revival of old-time, folk, and Americana after the turn of the millennium was for many listeners—especially the Record Industry Association of America (RIAA) voters that decide Grammy Award winners—a glimmer of hope that styles of performance related to rock would maintain mass appeal during the hip-hop era.

Heavy Legacies: Evanescence, Linkin Park, Hoobastank, and Nickelback. Heavier forms of rock also thrived in the 2000s, drawing on the legacies of pop punk, rap rock, and alternative. Fronted by vocalist Amy Lee and guitarist Ben Moody (who departed the group in 2003), Arkansas-based Evanescence offered a blend of heavy music, piano-based balladry, rap, and gothic metal. The group's first album, *Fallen* (p3 uk1, 2003), sold more than seven million copies in the United States, and contained two hit singles that differed drastically in style, showing the band's musical range. "Bring Me to Life" (p5 uk1, 2003) was based on a heavy distorted guitar riff and background rapping, and at times approached the sonic quality of Korn or System of a Down. A notable difference between Evanescence and these heavier groups, however, was the vocal style of Lee, who sang full-voiced with none of the characteristic Nu Metal growl popular among other heavy bands of the time. The group's next single, "My Immortal" (p7 uk7, 2003), could not have been more different. It was a ballad that featured the piano and vocals of Lee.

Amy Lee of Evanescence performs "My Beloved" in 2004 at the Billboard Music Awards. Incorporating elements ranging from metal to the singer-songwriter movement, Evanescence released several wildly successful albums during the 2000s.

Until the full band accompaniment enters nearly three-quarters of the way through the track, the song resembles Sarah McLachlan more than Limp Bizkit, showing the immense diversity of the group's influences. Evanescence continued their success in 2006 with the release of *The Open Door* (p1 uk2), which included the hit single "Call Me When You're Sober" (p10 uk4).

Linkin Park was a group fully enmeshed in the Nu Metal style. The group achieved popularity alongside groups like Korn and System of a Down at the turn of the millennium, but they persisted longer than any of these groups at the highest level of the music business, maintaining a steady career after the release of their debut album *Hybrid Theory* (p2 uk4, 2000). This was probably due to their more accessible sound, which featured less aggressive rapping by Mike Shinoda and melodic vocal parts performed by Chester Bennington. This mix can be found on the group's best-known single "In the End" (p2 uk8, 2001). Later albums *Meteora* (2003), *Minutes to Midnight* (2007), and *A Thousand Suns* (2010) rose to the top of the *Billboard* album charts, producing hits such as "Numb" (p11 uk14, 2003) and "New Divide" (p6 uk19, 2009). Formed in Agoura Hills, California (the same town as Linkin Park), Hoobastank worked in a similar mainstream style of rap metal. After touring with Linkin Park in 2004, their single "The Reason" (2004) became an international hit, rising to the number-two spot on the *Billboard* "Hot 100" (uk12).

The Canadian group Nickelback was another popular band that focused on heavier forms of rock. Employing traditional rock instrumentation and vocal styles, Nickelback released two albums in Canada before reaching the international mainstream. The first successful Nickelback album, *Silver Side Up* (p2 uk1), appeared in stores on September 11, 2001, and included the single "How You Remind Me" (p1 uk4), which went on to become one of the most popular songs of the year. Each of the group's later albums, from *The Long Road* (p6 uk5, 2003) to *No Fixed Address* (p4 uk12, 2014), rose to the upper echelons of the American charts, while consistently topping Canadian sales marks. Similar to Nu Metal bands that mined connections between rock and hip-hop, Nickelback began to explore country influences as the decade progressed. Singles such as "Rockstar" (p6 uk2, 2006) achieved this by including spoken vocal interludes by ZZ Top guitarist and vocalist Billy Gibbons. Country traditions were also apparent in the 2005 single "Photograph" (p2 uk18). Although the musical language of the song was purely mainstream rock, the subject matter drew heavily on the country tradition, reminiscing about youthful pleasures and bygone memories of high school. Filmed in Hanna, Alberta, hometown of band members Chad and Mike Kroeger, the video reinforced the sentimental quality of the song, revealing many of the actual spaces recalled in the lyrics.

In late 2004, a news story surfaced about Nickelback that is particularly revealing for our study of rock. A Canadian fan named Mikey Smith noticed similarities between the Nickelback songs "How You Remind Me" and "Someday," and after combining the two tracks into a single audio file, noticed that they shared strikingly similar musical traits. The new audio track, affectionately called "How You Remind Me of Someday," became an Internet sensation, causing many listeners to question the group's creative integrity. Reports followed accusing Nickelback of cheating fans by recycling the same song. As students of rock, we might use the tools of analyzing song form, instrumentation, and recording techniques to delve further into this controversy. What traits do these songs share, and what is original about each? Moreover, can you find other examples of songs by the same artist that follow similar patterns of form and instrumentation? Members of Nickelback have attributed these likenesses to a "distinct style," similar to other classic-rock bands. Given the similarities within the catalogs of artists such as Little Richard, Chuck Berry, and the Rolling Stones, is it right to vilify a band like Nickelback for reproducing a song in their own style? If not, we may want to consider what kinds of cultural forces inspired this attack.

Like popular acoustic styles, heavy rock was increasingly marginalized in radio and sales marketing during the 2000s. Although artists Evanescence and Nickelback released singles that achieved popularity in mainstream markets, the majority of bands that pursued heavier styles relied on album sales. Few hard-rock singles achieved success on the "Hot 100," and industry magazines like *Billboard* used radio and sales categories such as "Modern Rock," "Mainstream Rock," and "Active Rock" to track popular singles in this style. Looking closely into these markets, it is clear that hard rock flourished after the turn of the millennium. These bands were most often associated with major record companies, and used traditional marketing techniques such as music videos and large package tours to promote their music. Stylistically, this form of rock abounded with riff-oriented, distorted guitars and basses, growling vocals, and dense drum performances under lyrics that often highlighted themes of alienation and aggression. Godsmack achieved considerable success in this "modern rock" market during the 2000s, releasing a string of albums that reached the top of

Featuring former Nirvana drummer Dave Grohl as frontman, Foo Fighters have become important torchbearers for modern rock during the 2000s. Here, the group performs at a 2012 benefit in New York's Central Park.

the "Billboard 200," including *Faceless* (p1, 2003), *IV* (p1, 2006), and *The Oracle* (p1, 2010). Disturbed released a similar series of chart-topping records that included *Believe* (p1, 2002), *Indestructible* (p1, 2008), and *Immortalized* (p1, 2015). Similarly, Three Days Grace and Alice in Chains, who reformed with a new vocalist in 2008, were extremely popular among fans of hard rock.

Several notable bands deftly navigated the space between this hard rock market, the mainstream, and markets that catered to indie rock. After their kooky music videos from the late 1990s, Foo Fighters became a much more serious band that relied on heavy styles oriented to the modern rock market, while maintaining Dave Grohl's well-known association with the indie pioneer band Nirvana. The group's *Wasting Light* (p1, 2011), which featured the single "Rope," offers an example of popular heavy rock from this period, while *Sonic Highways* (p2 uk2, 2014) was the result of sessions filmed for an HBO documentary series that were recorded in (and largely about) a group of important American recording studios. Grohl worked closely with another band that maintained a similar middle ground, Queens of the Stone Age. Fronted by singer and guitarist Josh Homme, Queens of the Stone Age released several popular albums, including *Lullabies to Paralyze* (p5, 2005) and . . . *Like Clockwork* (p1, 2013). Homme and Grohl showed their connection to earlier forms of hard rock by forming the group *Them Crooked Vultures* with former Led Zeppelin bassist John Paul Jones. This trio's live performances were received enthusiastically, the album *Them Crooked Vultures* (p12, 2009) was Jones's first popular recording as a bassist in decades, and the group won a Grammy Award for the song "New Fang" in 2011.

Listening Guide

Foo Fighters, "Rope" RCA 88697-84493

Words and music by Dave Grohl, Taylor Hawkins, Nate Mendel, Chris Shiflett, and Pat Smear. Produced by Butch Vig. Reached #68 on the *Billboard* "Hot 100" chart as a digital single in 2011. Also included on the album *Wasting Light*, which rose to #1 on the "Billboard 200" chart.

FORM: Compound AABA. The A sections contain contrasting verse-chorus pairs connected by an interior bridge (often called a pre-chorus). The song is in common time, and consistent 4-measure phrase lengths are very predictable. However, rhythmic irregularities throughout the song make it difficult to perceive the beginning of phrases. The exception to this is the entrance of each chorus. (Listeners who keep counting steady measures in 4/4 time will find this meter is used consistently throughout the song.) The sections also overlap at times, and the chorus melody consistently finishes on the same beat as the sections that follow.

TIME SIGNATURE: 4/4.

INSTRUMENTATION: Drums, bass, guitars, lead vocals.

| 0:00–0:28 | **Introduction**, 16 mm. | Begins with a guitar with delay effect. (Counting should start right away!) The full band enters for the last 8 mm. |

A	0:28–0:56	**Verse 1**, 16 mm.	Vocals enter. Notice the multiple vocal parts. Each new phrase (every 4 mm.) is anticipated in the last beat of the preceding measure, making it difficult to count a steady rhythm. If you keep counting, the measures will come out even. "This indecision . . ."
	0:56–1:09	**Bridge** (connective), 8 mm.	Over the same verse riff, the vocal melody and texture changes, leading into the chorus section. "Choke on a kiss . . ."
	1:09–1:37	**Chorus**, 16 mm.	The chorus occurs in two parts. Two phrases (8 mm.) make up one section, followed by a parallel section of two subsequent phrases (8 mm.). "Give me some rope . . ."
	1:37–1:51	**Solo interlude**, 8 mm.	The music under this guitar solo is based on the verse section, and the instrumental melody is based on the verse melody.
A	1:51–2:05	**Verse 2**, 8 mm.	This iteration of the verse is half the length of verse 1. "These premonitions . . ."
	2:05–2:19	**Bridge** (connective), 8 mm.	As before. "Choke on a kiss . . ."
	2:19–2:47	**Chorus**, 16 mm.	As before. "Give me some rope . . ."
B	2:47–3:28	**Bridge** (sectional), 24 mm.	There are two notable sections in the bridge. The first section (8 mm.) begins with stark guitar chords alternating with drum fills, offering some sonic space in the otherwise dense track. In the second section (16 mm.), the full band enters, followed by a 12-mm. guitar solo that relies heavily on the wah-wah effect.
A	3:28–4:03	**Chorus**, 20 mm.	The chorus is slightly extended in this restatement. This occurs in the first chorus section, which adds an extra 4-mm. phrase to enlarge from 8 to 12 mm. "Give me some rope . . ."
	4:03–4:19	**Coda**	The opening delay-drenched guitar chords return for 4 mm. in contrast to the dense texture of the song. The technique of overlapping sections is exposed in the second part of the coda, in which Grohl sings the last word of the lyrical statement that ends the chorus, ". . . loose."

COUNTRY AND BEAT-BASED STYLES

Country Rocks. The complex relationship between rock and country continued well into the new century. Like the rockabilly of the 1950s and the 1970s music created by the avocado mafia, the years following the turn of the millennium offered several important examples of rock especially indebted to country music. Not only did many rock groups draw loosely from the country tradition but many country artists also incorporated rock styles into their songs. As beat-based styles dominated the pop charts in the 1990s and 2000s, country music was the bearer of many musical traditions that had fallen out of favor in mainstream rock. The extended guitar solo, for example, was common in country hits and rare in the pop-oriented rock of the 2000s. During a period when much of the rock heard on the radio incorporated dark themes, heavy distortion, rappers, and DJs, the country mainstream was closer to classic rock than ever before. This was aided by a movement in country culture that accepted artists who did not conform to traditional western dress styles. Many country artists who performed pop songs supported by electric guitars and loud drum kits didn't wear cowboy hats and looked and sounded a lot like rock performers. Country music crossed into the mainstream regularly during the 1990s, when artists such as Shania Twain and Garth Brooks had sold millions of records to fans outside of the traditional outlets in the country demographic. A new generation of country crossover artists in the 2000s forged even greater connections between country and rock styles, becoming some of the most popular artists in the American music business.

New Zealand born Keith Urban is an example of a country artist who has been extremely popular among rock fans. In addition to his dashing good looks (and rare cowboy hat), Urban is a talented and flashy guitarist who performs in a high-energy rock style. After moving to Nashville in the early 1990s and working his way through the business, he became a mainstay on the country charts in the early 2000s, releasing more than twenty Top-10 singles in the last decade. His first exposure to a mainstream audience came at the end of 2004, with the song "You'll Think of Me" (p24 c1), which rose to the top of the *Billboard* "Adult Contemporary" chart. Urban continues to release songs that sell solidly in the country market while also extending into the Top 40 of the "Hot 100," and his stint as a judge on *American Idol* further increased his mainstream appeal.

The two most popular singing competition shows in the United States, *The Voice* and *American Idol,* have both had a long history of supporting country singers. Featuring well-known judge Blake Shelton as its "voice" for country music, *The Voice* has launched the careers of artists like Danielle Bradbery and the Swon Brothers. *American Idol* 2010 winner Scotty McCreery also went on to a successful career, while singers like Kellie Pickler and Lauren Alaina similarly used the show to move into the country market. By far the most important country singer to emerge from either of these shows is Carrie Underwood. After winning *American Idol* in 2005, Underwood thrived in Nashville, and became one of the most successful country crossover artists of the decade. In addition to her three albums—*Some Hearts* (p2 c1, 2005), *Play On* (p1 c1, 2009), and *Storyteller* (p2 c1, 2015)— she has placed more than a dozen singles at the top of the country charts, and (like Urban) her music often crosses into the pop Top 40. Underwood's biggest single, "Before He Cheats" (p8 c1, 2006), offers a great example of a crossover country song from the 2000s. The song is performed from the perspective of a woman who has caught her significant other with someone else; her reaction, naturally, is to destroy one of the cheater's most-prized possessions—his pickup truck. Taken in the context of country music, this song offers a strong female perspective, criticizing the "other woman" for her noncountry ways, which include singing karaoke, not knowing how to play pool, and drinking a fruity cocktail instead of whiskey. Musically, the song offers heavy instrumentation featuring dark electric guitar timbres, Underwood performing in the lower part of her range, and a chord progression (in a minor key) that highlights the severity of the lyrical perspective.

Urban and Underwood saw several country compatriots make a similar mark in the pop market in the 2000s. One of the most prominent country crossover artists of this period was singer and guitarist Taylor Swift, who took the entire music industry by storm in the last half of the decade. Releasing her Nashville debut in 2006 as a young teenager, Swift successfully asserted herself as a songwriter in one of the most cutthroat creative environments in the music industry. While her debut album *Taylor Swift* (p5 c1, 2006) produced six singles that rose to the Top 10 of the country singles charts (and Top 40 pop), it was *Fearless* (p1 c1 uk5, 2008) that brought her music to the masses. Singles such as "Love Story" (p4 c1 uk2, 2008) and "You Belong with Me" (p2 c1 uk30, 2009) became staples of pop radio, projecting a strong, young female voice and infectious melodic hooks. Swift continued her chart reign with the release of *Speak Now* (p1 c1 uk6, 2010) and *Red* (p1 c1 uk1, 2012), which both rose immediately to the top of the album charts, amid a bevy of mainstream promotion. In 2014, Swift made the transition from country to pop with *1989* (p1 uk1), which was created in collaboration with Swedish creative insiders like Max Martin and Shellback. A singer who writes incisive

Taylor Swift performing at the Grammy Awards in 2016. After an early career as a country star, Swift quickly crossed into the pop market to become one of the most important songwriters and performers of her generation.

country songs and performs in a pop style, Swift is the perfect package for country crossover, bridging the sounds of both contemporary country and mainstream rock. "Love Story" offers a perfect example of the manner in which Swift blended country and pop in her early hit records. Like much pop music of the time, it is based on a rock-oriented rhythm section of drums and electric bass and guitars and tells the story of a forbidden relationship from a female perspective using a compound AABA form that relies heavily on repeated (and altered) chorus sections. Evidence of Swift's alignment with the country market persists in a number of ways, including featured fiddle, banjo, guitar swells (that sound like steel guitar), and a climactic key change that supports that apotheosis of the narrative structure, the point when "Romeo" proposes marriage.

As the music business continues to evolve during the 2010s, Nashville has become a locus for the entire industry. Far more than the "Country Music Capital of the World," this Tennessee city is now the center for many songwriters, backing musicians, record companies, publishing houses, and artists who aren't explicitly associated with the country market. This proximity has filtered into a lot of current music, making connections between country, rock, and Americana central to the work of a number of artists. Chris Stapleton is a good example of a performer who mixes styles and approaches relating to these different markets. For more than a decade he worked as a Nashville-based songwriter catering to country artists,

Listening Guide

Taylor Swift, "Love Story" Big Machine BMRTS0201

Words and music by Taylor Swift. Produced by Taylor Swift and Nathan Chapman. Reached #4 on the *Billboard* "Hot 100" chart and #1 on "Hot Country Songs" in 2008. Also included on the album *Fearless*, which rose to #1 on the "Billboard 200" and *Billboard* "Top Country Albums" charts.

FORM: Compound AABA, with a compound relationship between verse and chorus sections. (The chords of the verse and chorus are similar, but not the same). Like many pop songs, the content of the A sections becomes more efficient in each iteration, eventually using only the chorus section, whose lyrics change to reflect the development of the song's narrative. Note the difference between the "connective" bridge (what many would call a pre-chorus) and the "sectional" bridge, which functions as a reprieve from the intensity of the chorus. The return to the final A section is obscured at 3:03 by presenting the chorus with a stripped-down instrumentation. Formally, this is the "return" to A material, but dynamically the return does not occur until 3:19. Overall, the track presents a set of three dynamic builds (during each A section), each beginning with a similar, exposed instrumentation and ending with a full-blown presentation of the chorus. Recycling the first line of the song at the end of the song allows this repetition cycle to end.

TIME SIGNATURE: 4/4.

INSTRUMENTATION: Drums, bass, acoustic guitar, electric guitar, banjo, fiddle, lead and background vocals.

	0:00–0:17	**Introduction**, 8 mm.	The record starts with country-oriented instrumentation, including acoustic guitar, pizzicato fiddle (in the left speaker), two guitars using volume swells (in both left and right), and banjo (right).
A	0:17–0:30	**Verse 1**, 8 mm.	Vocals enter. "We were both young . . ."
	0:30–0:49	**Verse 2**, 8 mm.	Drums and bass enter. Electric guitar (R) enters at the end of the section. "See the lights . . ."
	0:49–1:05	**Bridge** (connective), 8 mm.	The drums and bass establish a steady beat in this section that resembles "Be My Baby," creating a sense of anticipation for the chorus. "You were Romeo . . ."
	1:05–1:21	**Chorus**, 8 mm	The drums and bass intensify, the fiddle plays fully bowed notes, and the electric guitar expands the sonic palette. "Romeo take me . . ."
	1:21–1:25	**Vamp**, 2 mm.	Resembles the introduction.
A	1:25–1:41	**Verse 3**, 8 mm.	Drums and bass both play a driving beat. Two harmony vocals enter, one higher than the main melody and the other lower. Guitars swell both left and right. "So I sneak out . . ."
	1:41–1:58	**Bridge** (connective), 8 mm.	As before with harmony vocals in the second half. "'Cause you were Romeo . . ."

	1:58–2:13	**Chorus**, 8 mm.	As before. "Romeo take me . . ."
	2:13–2:30	**Chorus**, 8 mm.	Lyrics change slightly. "Romeo save me . . ."
	2:30–2:45	**Solo**, 8 mm.	Instrumental solo over chorus music, with fiddle and guitars playing mostly in unison.
B	2:45–3:03	**Bridge** (sectional), 8 mm.	The driving rhythm breaks down and the instrumentation reduces to a texture resembling the introduction. "I got tired . . ."
A	3:03–3:19	**Chorus**, 8 mm.	Texture resembles the first verse but uses the chords, lyrics, and melody of the chorus. Intensity builds at the end for a climactic move into the final set of chorus sections. "Romeo save me . . ."
	3:19–3:35	**Chorus**, 8 mm.	An upward key change adds a sense of intensity. (This is often called a "truck driver" key change, due to its popularity in country music.) The lyrics change, resolving the song's narrative conflict. "Marry me Juliet . . ."
	3:35–3:56	**Chorus**, 8 mm.	Mostly instrumental, with vocal improvisation. The song ends by repeating the original first line, a narrative trick often used in country songwriting.

writing hit songs for people like Kenny Chesney, George Strait, and Steel Magnolia while also working in various bands. He then released a solo album in 2014, *Traveller* (p1 c1), which was marketed heavily to both country and mainstream rock listeners. Sturgill Simpson and Jason Isbell are two other singer-songwriters who have emerged similarly, maintaining popularity with both country and rock fans. Simpson's *A Sailor's Guide to Earth* (p3 c1, 2016) and Isbell's *Something More Than Free* (p6 c1, 2015) were notable releases that highlighted this form of crossover.

Beat-Based Rockers: Merging Hip-Hop, Dance, and Rock.

Beat-based music ranging from hip-hop to dance-oriented R&B became the most popular music in the world during the 1990s. The legacy of this approach was important into the 2000s, when dozens of artists used beat-based techniques to create music that reached audiences far beyond the dancers and partygoers of early New York–based hip-hop in the late 1970s. A solo artist such as Beyoncé Knowles is one example of a wildly successful beat-based performer during the 2000s. Beyoncé worked with many of the most important producers in the beat-oriented music community, first as the lead member of the girl group Destiny's Child then as a solo artist. Since her first solo album, *Dangerously in Love* (p1 r1 uk1, 2003), Beyoncé has consistently placed both albums and singles at the top of the R&B and pop charts. In addition to her consistently popular musical releases, she starred in the 2006 motion picture *Dreamgirls*, has appeared regularly in commercial advertising, and is a fixture on awards shows. Representing a far different area of hip-hop culture is Louisiana's Lil Wayne, who achieved success both as a member of the group Hot Boys and as a solo artist. As a rapper who extols his southern roots, Lil Wayne released his first solo

Beyoncé performing at the 2016 MTV Video Music Awards. Her album *Lemonade* was released that year as multi-media project, including an hour-long musical film that streamed on Tidal prior to its official release.

album, *Tha Block Is Hot*, in 1999 (p3 r1), and followed with a long string of albums under his name (in addition to many other collaborative efforts), which all rose to the upper reaches of the pop and R&B charts. Like many active hip-hop artists, he has also released more than a dozen unofficial "mixtape" releases.

Another mainstream hip-hop artist who has achieved immense success as both a producer and a performer is Kanye West. Emerging as a solo artist with the album *College Dropout* (p2 r1 uk12, 2004), West continued to release albums that rose to the top of the R&B and pop album charts. He achieved notoriety for his actions at the 2009 MTV Video Music Awards, when he upstaged winner Taylor Swift to defend the work of Beyoncé. After a noticeable hiatus, West returned with *My Beautiful Dark Twisted Fantasy* (p1 r1 uk16, 2010), which debuted at the top spot on the *Billboard* "Top 200" album chart. His *Watch the Throne* (p1 r1 uk3, 2011), a collaboration with Jay-Z, and *Yeezus* (p1 r1 uk1, 2013) were similarly successful. In light of the styles of Beyoncé and Lil Wayne, West's music and persona represent a strain of hip-hop that has been especially appealing to rock listeners. Some of this may be due to his clear projection of middle-class values, which differs sharply from the glamour of Beyoncé and the gritty, working-class identity created by Lil Wayne. The son of a photojournalist and a college professor, West's fashion sense favors a more clean-cut image, his vocal style lacks the growl of many southern rappers, and his lyrics have often taken an openly intellectual stance. Moreover, in songs such as "Gold Digger" (Ray Charles; p1 r1 uk2, 2005), "Stronger" (Daft Punk; p1 r30 uk1, 2007), and "Good Life" (Michael Jackson; p7 r3 uk23, 2007), West's music features audible samples from sources familiar to rock listeners. West has also collaborated with rock artists such as Adam Levine, Chris Martin, and indie-folk artist Bon Iver. West later became a pioneer in streaming releases. His *Life of Pablo* (p1 r1, 2016) was first revealed through a live stream from Madison Square Garden, and the album underwent several changes after its official release on Tidal, a type of flexibility possible only in the streaming era.

Within the hip-hop community, West has been one of the most visible agents of beat-based music that appealed to both ardent hip-hop fans and rock listeners. Yet, as we have seen in previous chapters, there has been a long tradition of rock-oriented crossover from the hip-hop community, which continued throughout the 2000s. One of the most notable groups of this type was the Roots. Formed in Philadelphia during the late 1980s, the Roots quickly became the most famous hip-hop group to perform using traditional rock instrumentation. The group released several noteworthy records in the 1990s, culminating with *Things Fall Apart* (p4 r2, 1999). This album contained the most popular Roots single to date "You Got Me" (p39 r11, 1999), which was co-written with R&B singer Jill Scott and featured neo-soul artist Erykah Badu. Similar to West, the widespread appeal of the Roots surrounded the group's thoughtful lyrics, which were concerned with middle-class themes, and the musical support of instruments that sound as if they were performed (often with a heavy jazz emphasis) rather than programmed. Group leader Questlove also worked as a member of the Soulquarians, a neo-soul collective behind the creation of D'Angelo's *Voodoo* (p1 r1, 2000) and Common's *Like Water for Chocolate* (p16 r5, 2000). Five more albums by the Roots released in the 2000s rose to the Top 10 of both the R&B and pop album charts, cementing them as one of the most consistent album-oriented hip-hop crossover acts of the decade. Further exposure for the group came in 2009, when they became the house band for the NBC program *Late Night with Jimmy Fallon*, a role that allowed group members to display their range of musical ability outside of the hip-hop tradition. Fallon moved into an earlier late-night slot on NBC in February 2014 with the Roots as a vital part of many episodes, giving the group even more exposure among mainstream listeners and viewers.

As we have seen, Lil Wayne represented a growing strain of southern rap that became popular in the mainstream during the 1990s. While many of these acts were among the most hardcore hip-hop artists, and had little interest in infusing rock styles or exploring crossover connections, this community—rappers who came from Atlanta, in particular—also produced some of the most interesting and popular hybrid forms of rock and hip-hop during the 2000s. A particularly good example of this strain is Cee-Lo Green, a rapper from Atlanta who extensively explored hybrids of rock, rap, and traditional R&B that appealed to a wide listenership. As a founding member of the Goodie Mob, Cee-Lo contributed to several popular albums during the 1990s, including *Soul Food* (p64 r31, 1995). He achieved breakthrough popularity in the 2000s as a solo vocalist and member of the duo Gnarls Barkley with DJ and producer Danger Mouse. Their debut album, *St. Elsewhere* (p4 r4 uk1), was released in 2006, yielding the hit single "Crazy" (p2 r53 uk1, 2006). Although created by a DJ in a beat-based setting, the spare instrumental backing of the song featured heavy strings and lush backing vocals, and Cee-Lo's expressive vocals were more reminiscent of classic soul than modern hip-hop. Moreover, the song took the core of its musical materials from a song called "Nel Cimitero Di Tucson," which came from an Italian spaghetti western soundtrack. Cee-Lo's later solo album, *Lady Killer* (p9 r1 uk3, 2010), was lauded for a similar infusion of classic soul sensibilities, which were at times ironic given the frank nature of the material. This conflict is most evident in the hit single "F**k You" (p2 r57 uk1, 2010), which, over a happy-go-lucky instrumental track, offered the candid perspective of a man toward

MUSIC VIDEO IN THE 2000s: OUTKAST, "HEY YA"

Viewing Rock

The music video became decentralized in the 2000s, as Internet sites such as YouTube replaced cable-based stations as the most convenient portals for video performances. Thus, documentaries, interviews, and official music videos (in addition to unofficial fan-created ones) all became available on demand in the same Internet spaces, blurring the line between historic and new performances, in addition to genres that had previously been separated on

members of OutKast. "Hey Ya" depicts a live television performance by André 3000 on a 1960s-type British television show, offering a reversal of the typical British invasion appearance on television in the United States. André 3000 performed all of the instruments on "Hey Ya," and through video trickery he also performs as every member of the band in the clip. The contrast provided between a black-and-white television monitor and the live band in vivid green-hued color offers a statement on the difference between classic and modern popular music (1).

Like many films that show older television shows being viewed in the home, "Hey Ya" frequently cuts to a family viewing the program in their living room and dancing along (2).

To make the British invasion connection even more clear, each member of the band is introduced through captions, drawing from the famous appearance of the Beatles on the Ed Sullivan variety show when John Lennon's photo was accompanied by the phrase "Sorry girls, he's married" (3).

Eventually, the studio audience plays an important role in the video, especially during the part of the song when the lyrics encourage dancers to "shake it like a Polaroid picture" (4).

television. Yet artists still made important contributions to the music video genre, showing the staying power of the three- to four-minute promotional clip that had become standard in the previous twenty years. One of the most interesting examples of the early 2000s was Out-Kast's video for "Hey Ya," directed by Bryan Barber, who would later write and direct the 2006 feature film *Idlewild*, which also featured

Although the music video has become decentralized from its former MTV home, it has clearly not lost the potential to portray artists in a vivid manner, provide creative commentary on current music, and situate current music in a historical context.

his former lady friend. Green's crossover potential was highlighted further when he became a coach on the popular NBC singing competition *The Voice* in 2011.

As part of a collective called the Dungeon Family, Cee-Lo (through his work with the Goodie Mob) worked closely with OutKast, another Atlanta-based hip-hop group that had a large crossover appeal with rock listeners. Composed of Big Boi and André 3000, two multi-instrumentalists, rappers (and vocalists), and producers, OutKast similarly explored hip-hop life from a southern viewpoint, while infusing its music with a wide range of source material. Although the group released popular albums throughout the 1990s, its breakthrough came in late 2000 with the single "Ms. Jackson" (p1 r1 uk2), which chronicled André 3000's breakup with Erykah Badu. (Ms. Jackson is Badu's mother.) Revealing a quirky sense of fashion and humor, OutKast's next album *Speakerboxxx/The Love Below* (p1 r1 uk8, 2003) contained two wildly popular singles, "Hey Ya" (p1 r9 uk3, 2003) and "The Way You Move" (p1 r3 uk7, 2003), and became one of the most popular albums of the year. While the vocal harmony and horn arrangements of "The Way You Move" sounded like the 1970s group Earth, Wind, and Fire, "Hey Ya" was a deceptively simple, driv-ing pop song. Based on a six-measure chord progression that repeats throughout, the song contains playful key-board work and an infectious chorus. The instrumental elements of the song sound more like rock than hip-hop, and the imagery included on the album sleeve (pictur-ing André 3000 as a cartoonish 1950s family man) and the later music video confirm the song's connection with music outside of the hip-hop tradition. The video fea-tures André 3000 playing each role in an eight-piece band in a setting that mirrors the Beatles' *Ed Sullivan Show* appearance. André 3000 delved further into the rock world when be played the role of Jimi Hendrix in the 2014 biographical film, *Jimi: All Is by My Side.* It was clear after the turn of the millennium through the work of West, the Roots, Cee-Lo, OutKast, and Beyoncé that a significant strain of the hip-hop community was com-fortable embracing elements of rock, and that rock listen-ers were just as happy to support these artists with media attention and album sales.

The rise of a beat-based style often labeled "neo-soul" in the 2000s also connected rock audiences with musical and cultural themes popular among the R&B and hip-hop communities. The music of groups like the Fugees and Lauryn Hill sparked a movement that led to a variety of African American artists working out of the R&B market to create music that was connected closely to the rock and soul of the 1970s. Instrumentation, album concepts, cover art, and textual themes all helped forge these links. One of the most important of these artists was D'Angelo, whose *Voodoo* (p1 r1, 2000) was a formative neo-soul release. After a protracted recording hiatus, D'Angelo released

D'Angelo performing in San Francisco during the summer of 2015. Originally aligned with neo-soul, D'Angelo's later music increasingly embraced rock elements.

Listening Guide

D'Angelo and the Vanguard, "Really Love" RCA 888875-05655

Words by D'Angelo and Kendra Foster and music by D'Angelo. Produced by D'Angelo. Included on the album *Black Messiah*, which rose to #5 on the "Billboard 200" chart and #1 on the "Top R&B/Hip-Hop Albums" chart in early 2015.

FORM: AABA with full reprise. The record also contains a lengthy spoken introduction and a postlude. The first minute and a half of the recording sets the scene, with a female voice (Gina Figueroa) speaking in Spanish over a string and guitar accompaniment. Beginning at about 1:30, the song proper cycles through an AABA form twice, with slight alterations throughout. Much like a Tin Pan Alley song, there is a refrain presented at the end of each verse, which is then used as the final presentation of the A section (minus any new verse material). Following the last iteration of the song form, several solo sections ensue, each following a scheme in which an instrument performs a featured melody during the verse sections, and vocals enter to reiterate the refrain. Notice the small variations in phrase organization throughout, which cause odd measure counts but seem to make sense within the overall context of the track. The harp is sampled from the 1970 Curtis Mayfield track "We Are the People Darker Than Blue."

TIME SIGNATURE: 4/4.

INSTRUMENTATION: Drums, bass, handclaps, acoustic guitars, strings, harp sample, horns, organ, electric guitar.

	0:00–1:32	**Spoken prelude**	The record starts with spoken section in Spanish, during which a woman discusses love and relationship. This is accompanied by strings and a nylon string guitar, connoting Spanish cultural stereotypes.
	1:32–1:48	**Introduction,** 6 + 4 mm.	A beat enters with a crisp drum kit, a walking bass, and a guitar melody, announcing the beginning of the song.
	1:48–2:02	**Introduction,** 6 + 4 + 2 mm.	As before, with a small extension. Small bits of vocalizing are audible, giving the listener a sense that the singer is waiting in the wings. Also notice the manner in which the harp moves between the left and right field of the stereo image.
A	2:02–2:22	**Verse 1** (with refrain), 6 + 4 mm.	Vocals enter. The first line sounds like a solo vocal, but multiple layers of overdubs are slowly revealed, both doubling the main melody and providing harmony vocals. "When you call my name . . ."
A	2:22–2:41	**Verse 2** (with refrain), 6 + 7 mm.	A notable call-and-response backing vocal part is included after the first line and a low horn melody enters. At the end of the refrain woodwinds and strings enter. "When you look at me . . ."
	2:41–2:47	**Interlude,** 4 mm.	Strings take the melody for this section.

B	2:48–3:00	**Bridge**, 8 mm.	The vocal element is now presented as a large composite of voices singing in harmony. "All night beside you . . ."
A	3:00–3:12	**Refrain**, 7 mm.	As before. "Doo doo wah . . ."
A	3:12–3:26	**Verse**, 6 + 4 mm.	The delicate nature of D'Angelo's falsetto sets the tone for this section. "When you touch me . . ."
A	3:26–3:41	**Verse**, 6 + 4 mm.	Notice how the vocal delivery becomes more direct as D'Angelo incorporates a more full-voiced technique. "I'm not an easy man . . ."
	3:41–3:46	**Interlude**, 3 mm.	A slightly shortened interlude keeps the listener attentive.
B	3:46–3:58	**Bridge**, 8 mm.	As before, with slightly different lyrics. "All night . . ."
A	3:58–4:04	**Refrain**, 4 mm.	As before, but shortened. Notice the high screeching strings at the end. "Doo doo wah . . ."
	4:04–4:19	**Solo** (with refrain), 6 + 4 mm.	A guitar solo playing the main verse melody with response vocals, followed by a full vocal refrain.
	4:19–4:34	**Solo** (with refrain), 6 + 4 mm.	A guitar solo performing a new melody with response vocals, followed by a full vocal refrain.
	4:34–4:40	**Interlude vamp**, 4 mm.	Two guitars continue to solo over this short interlude.
	4:40–4:56	**Solo** (with refrain), 10 mm	A horn solo, backing and spoken vocals. The refrain is not as pronounced as before.
	4:56–5:08	**Interlude**, 8 mm	Sound effects punctuate this part, possible a tape loop, creating a wash of sound.
	5:08–5:44	**Solo** (with refrain), 20 mm.	A more focused instrumental group with an electric solo organ emerges out of the interlude, initiating a long fadeout.

Black Messiah (p5 r1) in 2014, an album that included a variety of topical themes related to the Black Lives Matter movement in addition to a group of songs about intimacy, all underscored by guitar-heavy tracks, extensive vocal composites, and dense instrumental textures seemingly performed by musicians in the studio. Often mentioned in the same breath as *Black Messiah* was Kendrick Lamar's *To Pimp a Butterfly* (p1 r1 uk1, 2014). Lamar's rapping places this record outside of the range of neo-soul, but its track and production recall 1970s soul in a number of ways. From the opening crackles meant to simulate the sound of an LP to the liberal use of instruments like saxophone and electric piano and the use of topical themes, this release was closely connected to music and textual elements popular among rock fans. A variety of other records from the 2010s, including releases by Frank Ocean and Solange, created similar connections among rap, R&B, and rock, establishing this wing of beat-based music as an important movement that evoked themes from the past within current hits.

INDIE ROCK SELLS

Indie Roots: Wilco, Vampire Weekend, and Bright Eyes. Rock music produced and released independent of large corporations has always been an important part of American popular music. This history extends from the independent rock and rhythm and blues labels that helped to establish rock in the 1950s, through garage rock in the 1960s, punk in the 1970s, hardcore in the 1980s, and the indie scene from the 1990s to the present. In each of these cases, the intermingling of independent music with the mainstream has become a significant element in rock's history. At times, artists have been thrilled to be given the opportunity to work with large companies, while in other instances there were movements against this interaction. After a period in the 1990s when the indie scene grew wary of working with major labels, during the 2000s it seemed that it was no longer necessary to worry about the risks associated with signing with a major company in order to achieve mainstream success. Although the demise of traditional music distribution channels was devastating for some parts of rock culture, including the independent record store, the move toward Internet sales and digital downloading became a democratizing force in the music business, allowing independent artists to reach fans without the need for major label channels. Moreover, as major label sales suffered, the indie community faithfully supported their favorite acts. All of these factors led to an interesting phenomenon during the 2000s that had not been present in the rock industry since the 1960s: independent rock achieved record sales that regularly placed its acts at the top of the *Billboard* album charts.

Wilco front man Jeff Tweedy (right) performing in 2007 at the Montreux Jazz Festival. Combining elements of country, mainstream rock, folk, and noise, Wilco emerged during the 2000s as an important indie rock band that achieved mainstream success.

A bellwether for this change came at the beginning of the decade from the band Wilco. Formed by singer, guitarist, and songwriter Jeff Tweedy after the breakup of Uncle Tupelo in the mid-1990s, Wilco maintained an affiliation with the Reprise label, which was owned by Warner Brothers. After completing the album *Yankee Hotel Foxtrot* in 2001, the group was released from its Reprise contract and negotiated to keep the rights to the recording. In September 2001, after a series of Internet leaks, the band decided to stream the album free of charge. Meanwhile, they had entered negotiations to sign with Nonesuch, another label owned by Warner, which eventually re-bought *Yankee Hotel Foxtrot* and released it in April 2002. Even though they were associated with Warner, the indie community had long supported Wilco and cheered what seemed to be an example of a band's triumph over a major record company (namely that a company paid for, rejected, and then repurchased the same material after realizing the error of its ways). Despite giving the music away to fans, *Yankee Hotel Foxtrot* sold remarkably well for a band on Nonesuch, rising to #13 on the "Billboard 200" album chart (uk40) and becoming the most successful Wilco album to date. One reason that Wilco maintained such a loyal indie following was the innovative quality of their music, which combined elements of alt-country, the singer-songwriter tradition, and experiments with sonic atmospheres and noise. A good example of this is the song "Ashes of American Flags" from *Yankee Hotel Foxtrot*.

Listening Guide

Wilco, "Ashes of American Flags" Nonesuch 79669

Words by Jeff Tweedy. Music by Jeff Tweedy and Jay Bennett. Produced by Wilco. Not released as a single. Album *Yankee Hotel Foxtrot* rose to #13 on the *Billboard* "Top Albums" chart.

FORM: Contrasting verse-chorus, with unmeasured interlude. A 4-measure vamp is used throughout the song to slow the action and introduce each verse. The complete verses (verse 1 and 2) are constructed of two 4-measure sections. The third abbreviated verse uses only the first of these sections. The second half of the verse structure is also used independently as a pre-chorus. The song's chorus is rather short, consisting of only two phrases and totaling 4 measures. An unmeasured interlude that features atmospheric noise is used as a type of contrasting bridge, and returns at the end of the song to act as a segue into the next song on the album. Note how there are many familiar small segments used and recycled throughout the form, but rarely presented in the same order.

TIME SIGNATURE: 4/4.

INSTRUMENTATION: Various auxiliary percussion, a piano vamp, electric guitars, drums, bass, acoustic guitar, synthesized strings, lead vocals, many other electronic sounds and instruments creating a sonic wash.

0:00–0:17	**Vamp**, 4 mm.	Bell tree percussion, a piano vamp, sustained guitar and strings open the track, getting louder in anticipation of the first verse.
0:17–0:45	**Verse 1**, 8 mm.	Melodic guitar, acoustic guitar, drums and bass enter. "The cash machine . . ."
0:45–1:00	**Vamp**, 4 mm.	Notice how the melodic guitar plays a call-and-response in the left and right speakers. Listen also for the sonic "wind" sounds.
1:00–1:14	**Pre-chorus**, 4 mm.	"I wonder why . . ."
1:14–1:28	**Chorus**, 4 mm.	Listen to the irregular snare drum pattern, which is odd for a chorus section. "All my lies . . ."
1:28–1:43	**Vamp**, 4 mm.	Back to acoustic guitar, wind, and sustained electric guitar.
1:43–2:11	**Verse 2**, 8 mm.	The instrumentation of this verse is completely different. Now featuring flute sounds, before the entrance of a rhythmic acoustic guitar for the second 4 mm. "We want a good life . . ."
2:11–2:25	**Chorus**, 4 mm.	Much smaller instrumental combination for this presentation of the chorus. "All my lies . . ."
2:25–2:40	**Interlude**, unmeasured	The rhythmic element stops, leaving only special sounds.
2:40–2:54	**Pre-chorus**, 4 mm.	Now with a new piano melody in the right speaker. "I'm down on my hands and knees . . ."

(continued)

2:54–3:09	**Chorus**, 4 mm.	With a new chorus of synthesizers harmonizing the vocal melody. "All my lies . . ."
3:09–3:23	**Vamp**, 4 mm.	Presented without the piano.
3:23–3:38	**Verse 3** (abbreviated), 4 mm.	A presentation of the first half of the verse structure. "I would like to salute . . ."
3:38–4:44	**Interlude**, unmeasured	Now the special element takes over, evolving into an experiment with avant-garde noise. (This leads seamlessly into the next track on the album.)

Supporting Jeff Tweedy's lonesome vocal performance are sections that vary greatly in their instrumental backing and wild atmospheric elements throughout the song.

Vampire Weekend and Connor Oberst also added to the indie flood in *Billboard*. An American rock combo that emphasizes Afro-pop influences, Vampire Weekend's infectious dance rhythms and witty lyrics made them a staple of the indie scene. After their 2008 self-titled debut slowly gained popularity, the release of *Contra* in 2010 saw a rare debut at the top slot on the *Billboard* album chart by an independent release. The 2013 album *Modern Vampires of the City* (p1 uk3) continued the group's success. Nebraska-based Conor Oberst is another example of an indie musician who developed a mainstream following. Oberst recorded mostly with the Omaha-based Saddle Creek Records, a company he ran with his older brother, but he also worked with Merge, Rough Trade, and several other important indie labels. He released several solo albums, but was best known for his group Bright Eyes, which issued its first release (a collection of older recordings) in 1998 on Saddle Creek. Slowly gaining popularity through the 2000s, two Bright Eyes albums released on the same day in 2005, *I'm Wide Awake, It's Morning* (p10 uk23) and *Digital Ash in a Digital Urn* (p15) drew national attention. The group's later release, *Cassadaga* (uk13, 2007) rose to number four on the *Billboard* album charts. Oberst was also a member of the indie "supergroup" Monsters of Folk, along with Jim James, Mike Mogis, and M. Ward, whose eponymous debut album (2009) also charted in the Top 20.

Merge in the New Century: Arcade Fire and Spoon. One of the most important indie labels of the 1990s was Merge Records, which had a stocked roster of indie artists at the end of the decade and was poised for success during the indie explosion of the new millennium. Among the Merge bands that saw greater popularity in the 2000s was Arcade Fire. Based in Montreal and performing songs in both English and French, Arcade Fire was a newcomer to the company and an unlikely band to propel Merge into the mainstream. Nevertheless, the group's 2004 album *Funeral* slowly gained popularity, eventually selling more than a half-million copies. Later releases *Neon Bible* (p2 uk2, 2007) and *The Suburbs* (p1 uk1, 2010) were immediately successful, and the latter album shocked many in the music business by winning the Grammy Award for Album of the Year in 2011. The group's 2013 release, *Reflektor* (p1 uk1), was a dance-oriented effort produced by LCD Soundsystem front man James Murphy. With the success of groups like Arcade Fire, Merge had to adapt its business model to keep up with demand. This change was aided by the demise of independent distributor Touch and Go in 2009, which had supported indie labels for decades. Aligned since then with the Alternative Distribution Alliance (which is mostly owned by the major Warner Music Group), Merge saw a different level of distribution but lost some of its indie credibility. Merge recordings were now widely available in big-box stores like Target and Best Buy, allowing those outside of the indie community easy access to its products, and groups like Arcade Fire benefited immensely from this larger market. Another Merge group that launched mid-decade was Spoon. Spoon released its first album on Matador in 1996 (*Telephono*) before signing to Elektra, which was also part of the Warner family of labels. The 1998 Elektra album *A Series of Sneaks* was the source of a major label horror story similar to Wilco, but without the immediate happy

Tim Kingsbury (left) and Regine Chassagne (right) of Arcade Fire perform at California's Shoreline Amphitheater in 2007. A Canadian group that incorporates both English and French lyrics, Arcade Fire won a Grammy for Album of the Year in 2011 despite its indie-rock origins.

ending. Only after signing to Merge at the beginning of the 2000s did Spoon find a happy music-industry home, releasing five albums on Merge during the decade, each of which was more commercially successful than the one before. Released in the same year as Arcade Fire's *The Suburbs* and Vampire Weekends' *Contra*, Spoon's 2010 album *Transference* reached number four on the *Billboard* pop album chart, helping to mark the year that indie rock stormed the mainstream. Featuring the songwriting, vocals, and guitar of Britt Daniel, Spoon's music is often stark and direct, with danceable, repetitive grooves. With an intimate and sometimes experimental production quality favored by the indie rock community, both Arcade Fire and Spoon have proven that independent bands no longer have to trade an independent aesthetic for higher sales.

Emo Rising: Dashboard Confessional and Jimmy Eat World.
Many of the independent labels discussed thus far were known best for releasing music that was popular among college-aged audiences and their older contemporaries. After the punk revolution of the 1980s, however, a new breed of independent communities flourished—using similar networks of radio, clubs, and marketing—which were targeted to, and popular with, audiences of a demographic outside of the standard indie-rock market. The "emo" community is a good example of a largely independent-based network of bands that shared an audience markedly younger than the average indie-rock crowd. Although most bands shied away from the emo label, viewing it as a derogatory classification, the emo aesthetic that emerged in the mid-1980s grew dramatically in popularity during the 2000s, providing another example of independent music that began to make important inroads into the commercial mainstream.

Closely related to pop punk bands like Green Day and Blink-182, the emo tradition drew heavily on high-energy punk indebted to 1970s and 1980s American hardcore. However, while Blink-182 songs such as "All the Small Things" or "First Date" (and their accompanying videos) were fun and sophomoric, popular emo bands relished a more serious personal perspective and often featured heartfelt vocals. Most commentators point to the D.C. hardcore scene of the mid-1980s as the launching point for this movement. Led by vocalist and guitarist Guy Picciotto, the short-lived band Rites of Spring explored the combination of hardcore and heartfelt lyrics, as did Fugazi, Picciotto's later group founded with Ian MacKaye. Emo became popular with younger audiences in more regional scenes during the early 1990s. Moving between New York, Los Angeles, and San Francisco, Jawbreaker was one local favorite that released albums and extended-play releases on several small independent labels before signing to Geffen in the mid-1990s. Sunny Day Real Estate was based in Seattle, amid the growing grunge scene, and released its most important material on Sub Pop records, the same label that held Nirvana's early releases. Milwaukee, Wisconsin, was the home of the Promise Ring, a quartet signed to the small Jade Tree label. Kansas City's the Get Up Kids, Champaign-Urbana's Braid, and Long Island's Thursday were among the many popular regional emo bands to emerge during the mid-1990s.

Independent labels such as Vagrant and Drive-Thru, in addition to a growing number of interested major companies like Interscope, drove emo into the mainstream in the late 1990s and early 2000s. Known more for marketing than music, Drive-Thru aggressively sold merchandise at mall stores such as Hot Topic and signed an agreement with MCA that helped bands such as New Found Glory reach teenage listeners nationwide. Vagrant was even more aggressive, supporting groups such as the Get Up Kids and Dashboard Confessional with lavish tours and Internet marketing. While the Get Up Kids became underground emo icons, Dashboard Confessional went on to release extremely successful albums such as *A Mark, A Mission, A Brand, A Scar* (p2, 2003) and *Dusk and Summer* (p2, 2005). A typical Dashboard Confessional song, "Vindicated" (2005), opens with the line "hope dangles on a string like slow spinning redemption," revealing the sensitive character typically associated with emo. The most popular band of the emo movement was the Arizona-based quartet Jimmy Eat World, whose initially unsuccessful *Clarity* (1999) has since become an emo cult classic. It was not until the album *Bleed American* (p31, 2001), later retitled *Jimmy Eat World* after September 11, 2001, that the group reached a national audience. The most successful single from the album, "The Middle" (p5 uk26, 2002), uses a typical emo formula that appealed particularly to teenagers going through life changes. Over a chunky, pop punk musical groove, singer Jim Adkins advises, "it just takes some time . . . everything will be alright." After the success of "The Middle," Jimmy Eat World continued to release popular albums throughout the decade, including *Futures* (p6 uk22, 2004) and *Chase This Light* (p5 uk27, 2008). Although the emo movement was most popular with teenagers, issues of self-exploration commonly associated with this music echoed other movements related to the history of rock, such as the folk revival of the 1950s and 1960s, the singer-songwriter repertoire of the 1970s, and European pop of the 1980s released by bands like the Smiths. Thus, emo's blend of heavy guitars and introspective lyrics reflects the youth culture of the 1990s and 2000s while connecting with older forms of rock music and textual delivery.

Michigan Calling: The White Stripes and Sufjan Stevens.

One of the calling cards of indie-rock during the 2000s was to reveal cutting-edge local rock from unlikely places. Although Michigan was once home to internationally popular R&B and garage rock, the most notable music to emerge from Michigan in the new millennium was hip-hop and electronic dance music. Yet the indie community also helped popularize several important rock groups from Michigan during the 2000s, offering another example of how the grass-roots efforts of dedicated listeners could transcend the dominance of major labels. Emblematic of Detroit's new garage rock scene was the duo the White Stripes, who recorded their first three albums on the independent Sympathy for the Record Industry label around the turn of the 2000s. The White Stripes went on to sign with the less-independent V2 for the more popular releases *Elephant* (p6 uk1, 2003) and *Get Behind Me Satan* (p3 uk3, 2005). The music of the White Stripes was striking for several reasons. As a drums and guitar duo, with fuller instrumentation sometimes used on later releases, the group's sound included a wealth of sonic space for drummer Meg White to explore unconventional beat patterns that might have otherwise been lost in a cluttered rock band sound. Moreover, Jack White used this arrangement to highlight his virtuoso blues guitar style, a throwback to 1970s arena rock. Although associated more closely with the major label system than many in the indie community, the White Stripes maintained a significant presence in independent music. Beginning in the early 2000s, guitarist and vocalist Jack White promoted the music of indie bands through production efforts and with his own Third Man record company. Perhaps his most famous production effort was the heavily praised 2004 Loretta Lynn album *Van Lear Rose* (p24 c2), released on the major label Universal, which won several Grammy awards in 2005. (Resurrecting the careers of forgotten roots music artists was a running theme of indie rock during the decade.) Reflecting the aesthetic interests of indie rockers, much of the music released on Third Man, including special versions of White Stripes albums, was available only in vinyl form. Also notable were Jack White's many side projects, including the Raconteurs and the Dead Weather.

Meg White (drums) and Jack White (guitar) of the White Stripes performing in 2003. Aligned in many ways with the indie-rock scene, the White Stripes were known for their use of red and white stage design, costumes, and instruments.

The vast catalog of Detroit-born Sufjan Stevens shows another side of the indie community in Michigan. Originally based in the small college town of Holland, Stevens embodied aspects of the singer-songwriter movement, thematic releases akin to concept albums, and a surreal performance style that incorporated unorthodox costumes. Releasing music on Asthmatic Kitty, a label he helped to start while living in Michigan, Stevens's output often tackled large-scale projects or themes. Two of his albums, which form the basis of a rumored 50-states project, were called *Greetings from Michigan, the Great Lake State* (2003) and *Come on Feel the Illinoise* (2005), exploring various locations and aspects of these two Midwestern states. As a Brooklyn transplant, Stevens later released a multimedia project (including a CD and DVD of nonperformance footage, booklet, and View-Master reel) called *The BQE* (2009), which was a meditation on New York's Brooklyn-Queens Expressway. Although his music was often intimate, featuring a trademark banjo, Stevens also worked with nonconventional rock instrumentation ranging from simple string arrangements to large-scale orchestral textures. His 2010 release *The Age of Adz* (p7 uk30) even ventured into electronic beat-based production, while still including the lush choral and orchestral elements that became associated with his own brand of indie music. Like many of the marquee indie releases of 2010, *The Age of Adz* also reached a high position on the *Billboard* pop album charts, reflecting a growing listenership for once-obscure independent artists.

Indie Still Sells.

The releases discussed earlier (and many others) show that many artists affiliated with independently owned companies, which were once considered "alternative," became thoroughly mainstream after the year 2000. Two decades after the term "alternative" entered industry parlance, styles and artists associated with indie rock were among the most popular in rock. Records by groups like the National's *High Violet* (p3 uk5, 2010) and *Trouble Will Find Me* (p3 uk3, 2013), and Grizzly Bear's *Veckatimest* (p8, 2009) and *Shields* (p7, 2012) were extremely popular despite a thorough investment in intellectually driven mixtures of pop and classical chamber music. Less upbeat than the folk of Mumford and Sons and the Lumineers, Bon Iver's *Bon Iver, Bon Iver* (p2 uk4) connected to the larger modern folk revival, and became one of the most popular albums of 2011. Other groups, such as the guitar and drum duo the Black Keys, connected to a riff-oriented classic rock style. After releasing lo-fi records during the early 2000s, the group signed to Nonesuch in the middle of the decade and released *Brothers* (p3, 2010) and *El Camino* (p2 uk6, 2011), hook-oriented records that became ubiquitous in commercial advertising. Despite their status as a steadfast indie band, the Black Keys launched a massive stadium tour

Sufjan Stevens in a 2006 performance in Vancouver, Canada. Often donning odd costumes, Stevens's blend of folk guitar and banjo with album-long themes helped him become one of the most popular indie artists during the 2000s.

in 2012 with the Arctic Monkeys, a British group whose *AM* (p6 uk1, 2013) had become another indie release that crossed into mainstream popularity. Examples of artists using the indie market to establish themselves before negotiating a favorable major label deal are now too numerous to count. Recent instances range from underground groups like the War on Drugs, who went on to sign with Atlantic Records after the critical success of the indie release *Lost in the Dream* (26p 18uk, 2014), to Ed Sheeran, who self-released a half-dozen EPs over the course of five years before also signing to Atlantic and becoming one of the most popular artists in the world.

Alabama Shakes was another indie band to become popular in the mainstream during the 2010s. In contrast to the heady experiments of Grizzly Bear, the ethereal textures created by Bon Iver's Justin Vernon, and the heavy riffs of the Black Keys, Alabama Shakes performed in a style that was more redolent of their eponymous home state, and connected to the Muscle Shoals style that was popularized by rock and soul groups in the 1960s and 1970s. With a voice reminiscent of Janis Joplin, who had, in turn, patterned her style after singers like Tina Turner, Alabama Shakes lead singer Brittany Howard incorporated a wide range of rock history strains. The song "Hold On," from the 2012 album *Boys and Girls* (p6 uk3), released on Dave Matthews's ATO label, connects lyrically to southern gospel themes of perseverance, blues-oriented guitar work reminiscent of 1960s blues rock, and electronic noise associated with modern indie rock. The group's second full-length release, *Sound & Color* (p1 uk6, 2015), was even more popular despite the simultaneous rapid decline of the music industry. It debuted at the top of the "Billboard 200," received many end-of-year accolades, and won a number of Grammy awards, showing the resilience of independent rock during a time when beat-based styles dominated the pop charts.

Brittany Howard of Alabama Shakes performing in England. Alabama Shakes emerged from the indie scene in 2012 with a classic-rock style that emphasized the group's southern roots.

Listening Guide

Alabama Shakes, "Hold On" ATO 0142

Words and music by Zac Cockrell, Heath Fogg, Brittany Howard, and Steve Johnson. Produced by Alabama Shakes (Cockrell, Fogg, Howard, and Johnson) and Adrija Tokic. Reached #93 on the *Billboard* "Hot 100" chart as a digital single in 2012. Also included on the album *Boys and Girls*, which rose to #6 on the "Billboard 200."

FORM: Compound AABA with partial reprise. The song is based on consistent 2-bar units throughout. (The main guitar melody used in the introduction and verse sections lasts two measures.) There are few chord changes in the entire song, which provides a static harmonic nature. The compound AABA is based on a simple verse-chorus. The vocal melody and guitar riffs provide contrast between verse, chorus, and bridge sections. Dynamically, the song builds in a slow, dramatic fashion, which is evident through careful comparison of the first three chorus sections. The final chorus provides a release from tension created throughout.

TIME SIGNATURE: 4/4.

INSTRUMENTATION: Drums, bass, guitars, piano, distorted guitar, and lead vocals.

	0:00–0:28	**Introduction,** 10 mm.	Two measures of solo drums are followed by two repetitions of a persistent, four-measure guitar riff that is used throughout the song under verse sections.
A	0:28–0:50	**Verse 1**, 8 mm.	The vocals enter, and are affected slightly by a vintage microphone sound that gives them an old-fashioned type of distortion. "Bless my heart, bless my soul . . ."
	0:50–1:12	**Chorus**, 8 mm.	The guitar plays a new figure that also is used for subsequent chorus sections. "You got to hold on . . ."
A	1:12–1:33	**Verse 2**, 8 mm.	Notice how the intensity of the melody increases throughout each verse section. "So, bless my heart and bless yours too . . ."
	1:33–1:54	**Chorus**, 8 mm.	As before. "You got to hold on . . ."
B	1:54–2:15	**Bridge**, 8 mm.	The sound field becomes very dense during the bridge, which allows for a dramatic return to the next verse section. "Yeah, you got to wait . . ."
A	2:15–2:37	**Verse 3**, 8 mm.	A piano is audible for the first time during this verse (2:27). "So, bless my heart, bless my mind . . ."
	2:37–3:03	**Chorus**, 8 mm.	A new droning and distorted guitar is now present at the bottom of this chorus. "You got to hold on . . ."
B	3:03–3:18	**Bridge**, 8 mm.	The distortion is now more audible as it explores higher ranges. "You got to wait . . ."
A	3:18–3:25	**Chorus**, 12 mm.	Only the guitar and bass remain, exposing the vocals and distortion. The tempo slows as the song comes to an end. "You got to hold on . . ."

ROCK AS DISCOURSE

School of Rock. As we draw to the end of this survey, it is useful to discuss some examples that illustrate the cultural impact of rock music in contemporary society. Racial mixing, uncouth bodily movements, and teenage rebellion—elements that originally fueled the cold reception of rock during the 1950s—have become among rock's most heralded qualities. Once considered nonintellectual music of the body, rock has since seen a parallel movement as "music for listening," while still maintaining a quality that makes listeners "feel good"—a magical combination of thinking music for dancing feet. The rebellious heart of rock music has become a romanticized hallmark of nearly every teenage movement since rock's emergence in the mid-1950s, and rock continues as a soundtrack for an international tradition of each generation finding the means for its own independence. Perhaps most significantly, after more than sixty years of slow change in societal attitudes toward civil rights, we can now view rock music as a driving force in this process.

These large-scale indicators of rock's acceptance have been accompanied by institutional recognition in a variety of ways. Just as jazz became known as "America's classical music" during the 1980s, rock is now becoming similarly institutionalized. Depending on your outlook, this type of institutional support might be seen as a realization of the importance of the form or a detriment to the future of the art. As a college textbook used in dozens of schools internationally, this book itself is an indication of rock's acceptance into fields of higher learning. Academics have been studying the social and communicative effects of rock music since the late 1960s, and a wide variety of academic fields have slowly accepted this form of music as a worthy subject of study. Courses on rock music are offered as a general education option in most colleges and universities and have increasingly grown in importance for students majoring in cultural studies, communications, gender studies, history, and music. With student interest growing in the serious study of rock music, university professors also have begun to specialize in various aspects of rock music in their research. Decades ago, courses and research on rock were limited to professors who specialized in other fields while dabbling in rock as a secondary area. Now, a growing number of doctoral programs in a wide variety of subject areas have accepted topics in rock (and popular music more generally) as cutting-edge research, and graduate students are engaged in the study of rock as a primary discipline. An extreme example of the extent to which colleges and universities have fully accepted rock music is the creation of a master's program at Liverpool Hope University titled "The Beatles, Popular Music and Society." While most colleges and universities have not risen to this level of acceptance, it is safe to say that rock music has generally become a universal addition to the many subjects available for study at institutions of higher learning.

Rock as Culture. Educational institutions are only one facet of the widespread acceptance of rock music in twenty-first-century society. Important photographers such as Alfred Wertheimer, Linda McCartney, Jim Marshall, Bob Gruen, and many others have seen their work shown at museums internationally, making the visual documentation of rock a noble field in itself. In addition to traveling exhibitions

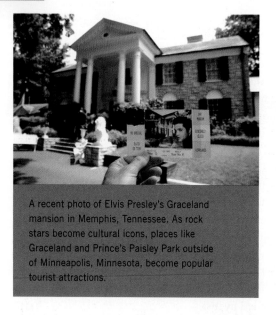

A recent photo of Elvis Presley's Graceland mansion in Memphis, Tennessee. As rock stars become cultural icons, places like Graceland and Prince's Paisley Park outside of Minneapolis, Minnesota, become popular tourist attractions.

of photography and instruments, and growing additions to permanent collections, several museums devoted exclusively to rock music opened in the late twentieth century. In the mid-1980s, a group of rock industry officials began a foundation called the Rock and Roll Hall of Fame, which inducted its first members in 1986. After a decade of development and fundraising, the group opened a Cleveland-based museum in 1995, which serves today as the foremost cultural institution to promote public awareness of rock's history. With more than 600 inductees, including musicians, songwriters, and executives, the museum holds a wealth of cultural capital, confirming the importance of well-known artists, calling attention to influential figures who have been largely forgotten, and placing record company work alongside artistic endeavors. Opened in 2000 with a Frank Gehry–designed building in the shape of an electric guitar, Seattle's Experience Music Project (EMP) offers a similar institutional nod to rock with an emphasis on interaction and participation. With permanent and temporary exhibitions dedicated to many aspects of rock, a variety of public programs, and an annual conference of rock critics and scholars, EMP is another important example of the cultural institutionalization of rock. Graceland in Memphis and Prince's Paisley Park studio complex in Minneapolis are other examples of this widespread practice of opening rock-oriented museums to spur tourism and engage with public history. Moreover, artists like Bob Dylan and Bruce Springsteen are but a few of the rock artists who have donated or sold their personal papers to libraries and archives, further institutionalizing and preserving aspects of rock's history for future study.

It is understandable that baby boomers who have worked in or been influenced by rock would go on to start museums and curate exhibitions about the history of rock. Yet there are other instances in which we can see rock music's acceptance by an even larger public, showering rock musicians with the highest levels of cultural praise in modern society. For example, each year the Kennedy Center in Washington, D.C., honors several individuals for a lifetime of achievement in the cultural arts. Attended by the president of the United States, this ceremony is televised nationally and serves as one of the greatest cultural honors offered in the United States. In addition to famous actors, dancers, comedians, and musicians associated with the classical and jazz traditions, an increasing number of rock musicians have been among the honorees. Ray Charles (1986), Aretha Franklin (1994), Bob Dylan (1997), Elton John (2004), Led Zeppelin (2012), Billy Joel (2013), Carole King (2014) and many others have enjoyed this honor. In 2007, the Library of Congress created a special governmental award specifically for lifetime achievement in popular song called the Gershwin Prize. The first three honorees—Paul Simon, Stevie Wonder, and Paul McCartney—were all closely associated with rock music. Bob Dylan's 2016 Nobel Prize in Literature is perhaps the most notable of these awards, cutting across cultural lines and proclaiming rock as a viable form of arts and letters.

The sounds of rock have also come a long way from their humble origins of traveling hundreds of miles over AM superstations to reach the bedrooms of teenagers late at night under the cover of darkness and behind closed bedroom doors. Now, rock music fills some of the most hallowed halls of the world, including an increasing presence on Broadway stages. While musicals such as *Hair* and *Godspell* were unique in presenting rock styles to Broadway audiences in the late 1960s and early 1970s, musicals based on rock themes have become dominant on theatrical stages in the 2000s. Shows weaving the music of Abba, Billy Joel, and Fela Kuti into loose plots have become extremely popular, and historical shows such as *Smokey Joe's Café*, *Memphis*, *Million Dollar Quartet*, and *Jersey Boys* have romanticized the rock music of the 1950s and 1960s. Other performances, such as *Rock of Ages* and *American Idiot* have brought hair metal and pop punk to the Broadway stage, while the hip-hop oriented musical *Hamilton* recently became the most popular Broadway musical in decades.

The Canonization of Rock. Discerning readers will find that writing about rock took a very serious turn in the late 1960s. The British press had a long tradition of covering popular music, often sensationalizing rock news for teenage fans, American magazines such as *Rolling Stone*, *Crawdaddy*, *Creem*, and a wide variety of underground publications like New York's *Village Voice*, only began to take rock music very seriously at the end of this decade. These publications produced fine commentary and criticism from legendary writers such as Jon Landau, Lester Bangs, Paul Williams, Richard Meltzer, and Robert Christgau. Although important and insightful, this commentary was often limited to a very small and focused readership, and in many ways these writers were simply writing for other devotees. In the last several decades, however, rock criticism has achieved mainstream acceptance in many American

Bob Dylan speaking at the MusiCares Person of the Year award ceremony in 2015. As rock music becomes recognized as a form of arts and letters, musicians are increasingly recipients of humanitarian awards.

The cast of *Hamilton* accepting the 2015 Grammy Award for Best Musical Theater Album. Pop-oriented shows like *Hamilton* have become important to the economic vitality of American musical theater.

publications. Prominent space is reserved for rock and other forms of popular music in esteemed publications like the *New York Times* and the *New Yorker*. Similarly, widely available anthologies of popular music criticism have become commonplace in the last decade, focusing on historical pieces, best-of-the-year collections, and conference proceedings. Moreover, with the digital revolution having similar effects on print media and the record industry, a growing number of highly skilled rock critics are maintaining blogs to document their writing.

Important themes have emerged from the explosion in rock criticism in the last decade, which are helpful to explore as currents of "rock thought" in the early twenty-first century. With the acceptance of rock music on the rise, cultural institutions and critics alike have slowly created a "rock canon," or a loose collection of the most important works in the history of rock. We see this most literally in "best of" lists like the *Rolling Stone* "500 Greatest Albums of All Time" and the myriad countdowns aired on television stations like VH-1. The list of Rock and Roll Hall of Fame inductees offers another concrete example of individuals who have been accepted into a canon of rock history. While we treasure the albums, artists, and songs that most often appear on these lists, the process of creating such a body is necessarily exclusionary. Far more than a simple popularity contest, not including certain music in this constructed history can have detrimental effects on the availability of music for purchase, dramatically changing the lives of forgotten musicians and arguably altering history. A growing number of music critics have been instrumental in fighting the canonization of rock. One of the most powerful tools that has emerged to combat this trend is the concept of "rockism," or understanding how the history of popular music has often been viewed as if rock has been the central form of pop music since 1954. Although many readers may question whether this book falls into the rockism trap, it is helpful to understand that the preceding survey has clearly named rock as the center of our study (not the entire field of popular music), and that we have been careful to consider the music in these pages as mere representations of various forms of rock. Nevertheless, as rock moves further into the twenty-first century and rock writing moves from a means of entertainment to a form of organizing history, it will become essential to continually revisit and reevaluate the music of the past, forcing ourselves to stay as objective as possible about how our place in history affects our perception in the present.

In looking at these issues, this book ends much like it began, with the struggle to define rock. If we have learned anything from studying this form of music and its various manifestations over the last six decades, we should understand that rock music is in a constant state of change, and to define it—to place borders around what is, and what is not, rock—requires us to account for ourselves as much as the music. Rock is intertwined with social, political, and cultural issues. Defining rock depends on who we are, where and when we live, and what we know. Rock has been presented to listeners very specifically by a complex and multifaceted music industry, which has drastically shaped the creation of music and how fans understand it. As a movement dependent on mass media, rock has been formed and reformed again and again through changing technologies. These new developments have altered the ways in which we make music, enjoy it through listening and viewing, document musicians, and facilitate interaction between musicians and fans. No

Sound Check

Artist	Song	Sound
Coldplay	Viva La Vida (2008)	Form: Compound AABA Initial 8-measure idea used throughout most of the song Use of orchestral percussion Thwarted ending
Foo Fighters	Rope (2011)	Form: Compound AABA Syncopation and anticipated phrasing make counting difficult Use of connective bridge and sectional bridge Chorus extended in final presentation
Taylor Swift	Love Story (2008)	Form: Compound AABA Several large-scale dynamic builds create tension and release throughout Repeated and altered chorus sections align with pop Banjo, fiddle, "truck driver" key change, and circular narrative connect with country practices
D'Angelo and the Vanguard	Really Love (2015)	Form: AABA (full reprise) Includes a Curtis Mayfield sample AABA form sits between a lengthy introduction and a postlude jam Extensive background vocal tracks
Wilco	Ashes of American Flags (2002)	Form: Contrasting verse-chorus (modified) Highly modified form that includes a pre-chorus, a floating vamp, and an interlude Verses often feature different arrangements Electronic noise is present throughout the track, and is featured in the final interlude
Alabama Shakes	Hold On (2012)	Form: Compound AABA (with partial reprise) Few chord changes Partial reprise of bridge and chorus Distorted guitar adds tension at dramatic peak

matter how we define this music and its many styles and sounds, it is safe to say that rock has been a dominant musical force during the last half-century. Through close study, intent listening, and broad cultural understanding, readers of this text are now poised to better understand rock as a historical subject, a developing field, and a lifelong pursuit.

For Additional Online Resources, visit:
digital.wwnorton.com/whatsthatsound5

FURTHER READING

Dean Budnick and Josh Baron, *Ticket Masters: The Rise of the Concert Industry and How the Public Got Scalped* (ECW, 2001).

John Cook, Mac McCaughan, and Laura Ballance, *Our Noise: The Story of Merge Records, the Indie Label That Got Big and Stayed Small* (Algonquin, 2009).

Matthew David, *Peer to Peer and the Music Industry: The Criminalization of Sharing* (Sage, 2009).

Andy Greenwald, *Nothing Feels Good: Punk Rock, Teenagers, and EMO* (St. Martin's Griffin, 2003).

Barry Kernfeld, *Pop Song Piracy: Disobedient Music Distribution since 1929* (University of Chicago Press, 2011).

Greg Kot, *Wilco: Learning How to Die* (Broadway, 2004).

Katherine L. Meizel, *Idolized: Music, Media, and Identity in American Idol* (Indiana University Press, 2011).

Kiri Miller, *Playing Along: Digital Games, YouTube, and Virtual Performance* (Oxford University Press, 2012).

Ben Ratliff, *Every Song Ever: Twenty Ways to Listen in an Age of Musical Plenty* (Farrar, Straus, and Giroux, 2016).

Roni Sariq, *Third Coast: OutKast, Timbaland, and How Hip-Hop Became a Southern Thing* (Da Capo, 2007).

John Seabrook, *The Song Machine: Inside the Hit Factory* (W.W. Norton, 2015).

Stephen Witt, *How Music Got Free: A Story of Obsession and Invention* (Viking, 2015).

AABA form. A song form that uses two verses (A A), a bridge (B), and a return to the verse (A) as its basic organizational pattern. Once the complete AABA pattern is presented, a song may repeat all of the pattern (full reprise) or only part of it (partial reprise). AABA form is strongly associated with the Tin Pan Alley popular song style, though it also occurs frequently in rock music.

Ambience. The overall affect of a recording's sound. Ambience can be manipulated in a number of ways, the most popular of which is reverb.

Arpeggio. When the individual notes of a chord are played separately, an arpeggio results. While any instrument can play an arpeggio, they are frequently found in guitar and piano parts as a way of providing variety in the accompaniment.

Bar. Musicians often count out a song, saying "1, 2, 3, 4." This is a bar of music, and the numbers represent beats. These bars usually have the same number of beats in them throughout a song (though not always). The term "bar" is synonymous with "measure." See also, "meter."

Beat. A regular rhythmic pulse in music is called a "beat." Beats are organized into "measures" or "bars" to create "meter."

Blues (as in "blues-based"). The blues is an important style in popular music that displays a series of musical features. When such features occur in rock, we use the term "blues-based" to highlight the influence of this style. Blues-based features might include the use of the "12-bar blues" pattern, string bends on the guitar, or bluesy inflections of pitch in any lead instrument or voice.

Bridge. The bridge is a section in a song that provides contrast to other, more salient sections of the same song, such as the verse or the chorus. While bridge sections can be quite interesting musically, they are almost never the focal section of a song.

Call-and-response. When an instrumental or vocal line is immediately answered or repeated by other instruments or vocals, we refer to this as "call and response."

Chords. A chord is a combination of three or more notes played simultaneously. A limited number of such combinations make up the majority of chords heard in rock music. Musicians classify these combinations, using such terms as "major," "minor," "dominant seventh," "minor seventh," among others.

Chorus. The chorus is usually the most important or easily remembered section of a song, containing the title and the catchiest musical material. Not all songs have a chorus, but when one is present, it is usually the focus of the song.

Coda. Some songs contain an ending section called the "coda." The coda often uses musical material from earlier in the song to provide an ending, which is sometimes a fade-out. Some musicians refer to the coda as an "outro," paralleling the beginning section in a song, which is often called the "intro."

Compound (meter). When we subdivide the basic beat into three equal parts, this creates a compound feel, which is notated using compound meters such as 6/8, 9/8, or most commonly, 12/8. See the Introduction for an explanation of simple and compound meters.

Compound AABA form. In a compound AABA form, each A section contains at least one verse and a chorus section (these can be contrasting or not). After two presentations of this verse-chorus unit (A A), a contrasting bridge section occurs (B), followed by a return to some version of the verse-chorus pair (A). Sometimes this return can consist only of the chorus and repetitions of it.

Contrasting verse-chorus form. In contrasting verse-chorus form, the verse and chorus sections employ contrasting musical material. The form consists of these contrasting verses and choruses presented in alternation, though more than one verse may occur before the chorus.

Digital audio workstations. A category of software that allows computers to serve as recording and editing devices for musical creation. Common DAWs include GarageBand, Pro Tools, and Logic.

Doo-wop progression. The doo-wop progression is a structure that can form the basis for verse, chorus, and bridge sections in rock music. It is a repeating pattern of four chords: I – vi – IV – V. In the key of C major, these chords would be C major – A minor – F major – G major. As per its name, the pattern was common in youth-oriented vocal harmony music during the 1950s, but was also employed widely after this period in a variety of contexts.

Duple (meter). When there are two beats in a bar (or measure) of music, the meter is classified as duple. Duple meter is commonly notated as 2/4 if it is a simple feel, or 6/8 if it is a compound feel. See the Introduction for an explanation of meter classifications.

Echo. An effect often created through tape manipulation (or digital means) in which multiple copies of a sound are layered in quick succession.

Equalizers. Effects that change the quality of sound by increasing or decreasing certain frequencies. Often used to enhance or reduce treble, midrange, or bass sounds in recordings and live performances.

Falsetto. When a male singer uses his highest vocal register, this is referred to as the falsetto. The highest vocal parts on Beach Boys records, for example, are often sung in falsetto. A good example is the line "everybody's gone surfing" in the song "Surfin' U.S.A." Frankie Valli has a more aggressive sounding falsetto, as can be heard in "Big Girls Don't Cry."

Formal diagram. A formal diagram, such as the ones used in the Listening Guides throughout this book, provides an overview of the formal design of a song, or how the different parts of the song fit together to create what is often a familiar pattern. These familiar patterns are organized into the five song forms described in the Introduction.

Full reprise. In an AABA form, playing once through the AABA structure often does not create a song that is long enough. When the entire AABA structure is repeated, this is called a "full reprise." Some songs may use more than one repeat of the entire AABA structure.

Instrumental verse. A verse section that repeats the music of the verse, without the singing and with an instrument soloing, is an instrumental verse. Guitar, saxophone, and keyboard solos are common, though any instrument can solo in an instrumental verse.

Interlude. An interlude is a brief instrumental passage in a song that separates the other sections (verse, bridge, or chorus) from one another. Frequently the musical material of such interludes is drawn from the Introduction.

Introduction. An introduction is a section of a song that precedes the start of the first verse or chorus (when the chorus appears before the verse). Introductions are frequently instrumental, but may also contain singing. Some musicians refer to this section as the "intro."

Key. Most rock songs are in a specific key. This refers to the fact that all of the notes in the song bear a subordinate relationship to some central note. The actual note that is central is identified using a note name (A, B♭, F♯) and the way in which the other notes relate to that central note is identified using terms such as "major" or "minor." When musicians refer to the key of D major, for instance, they mean that the note D is the central note and that the other notes relate to it in a specific way that we hear as major.

Lick. A lick is a short and distinctive melodic figure. A lick is not a complete melody, but it may be employed as part of a melody, either vocally or instrumentally. A lick may also be used anywhere in the accompaniment, often as part of a repeated pattern, but not necessarily. The guitar lick from the beginning of the Rolling Stones' "(I Can't Get No) Satisfaction" is a famous example. For the purposes of this book, "lick" and "riff" are synonymous.

Measure. Musicians often count out a song, saying "1, 2, 3, 4." This is a measure of music, and the numbers represent beats. These measures usually have the same number of beats in them throughout a song (though not always). The term "measure" is synonymous with "bar." See also, "meter."

Meter. A meter establishes how we will notate music within a certain meter classification. Each of the meter classifications discussed in the Introduction can be represented with several meters, but some meters are far more common than others, especially in rock music. Of the simple meters, 2/4, 3/4, and 4/4 are most common, and among the compound meters, 6/8, 9/8, and 12/8 are most common. See "meter classification" and the Introduction.

Meter classification. A meter classification classifies how we feel the organization of the rhythm for a particular song or passage. In this book, meters are classified as either simple or compound, and then as either duple, triple, or quadruple. A meter classification can be notated using a specific meter, and though there are several meters than can be used with each classification, there are six meters that are most common. See "meter," and the Introduction.

Mix down. A creative stage of recording when multiple tracks are combined into mono or stereo masters. Volume levels are manipulated and effects are often added during this stage.

Mono. A method of sound reproduction that produces only one discreet sound signal. AM radio is broadcast in mono, and due to dominance of mono, older cars and record players used only one speaker. Many early rock recordings were conceived in mono.

Octave. An interval (or space) of eight notes. Playing a note with the same name (A, for instance) seven steps apart on a keyboard produces the sound of an octave. In rock instrumentation, the bass is normally tuned an octave below the guitar, allowing it to assume a lower position in the sonic space.

Overdubbing. Overdubbing is a recording process in which new recorded parts are added to previously recorded ones. One benefit to overdubbing is that it allows parts of a song to be recorded at different times, and even makes it possible for the same person to perform multiple parts in a way that would be impossible in real time.

Partial reprise. In an AABA form, playing once through the AABA structure often does not create a song that is long enough. When only a portion of AABA structure is repeated, this is called a "partial reprise." Most partial reprises repeat the BA or the ABA sections of the AABA structure.

Phrase. A phrase is a short passage of music; often in rock music, phrases are four measures in length (sometimes eight measures). A phrase is akin to a sentence in spoken language and divides the music into units that make it easier to comprehend. Vocal phrases often correspond to obvious points of division and articulation in the lyrics being sung.

Pre-chorus. Some songs employ a pre-chorus, which is a section that connects the verse to the chorus. The purpose of a pre-chorus is to build up the musical movement toward the chorus, and in that way it is a special kind of bridge. Many times, the lyrics on each occurrence of the pre-chorus are the same or only slightly varied.

Quadruple (meter). When there are four beats in a bar (or measure) of music, the meter is classified as quadruple. Quadruple meter is commonly notated as 4/4 if it is a simple feel, or 12/8 if it is a compound feel. See the Introduction for a fuller explanation of meter classifications.

Refrain. A refrain is a subsection that often occurs in a verse. It functions much as a chorus does except that it is too brief to be considered a separate section and is otherwise clearly part of a larger section. The refrain will often occur as the last phrases or phases of a verse, but may also constitute the opening phrase or phases of a verse. A song that employs a refrain will most often not also employ a chorus. Refrains are thus most commonly found in the verses of AABA forms, since an AABA form does not employ a chorus.

Reprise. Generally speaking, a reprise is simply a repeat of music that has already been heard; the reprise of "Breathe" on Pink Floyd's *Dark Side of the Moon* or of the title track on *Sgt. Pepper's Lonely Hearts Club Band* are famous examples. In this book, "reprise" is routinely used to describe an aspect of return that occurs within an AABA form. See "full reprise" and "partial reprise."

Reverb. A spacial effect added to recordings and live performances to create an artificial sense of sound happening in reverberant spaces.

Rhythm. In the broadest sense, the word "rhythm" refers to the organized patterning of the temporal dimension in music. More specifically, we can refer to a rhythmic figure in the music, which is usually a short segment with a clearly defined profile of some kind. Meter and meter classification are aspects of the broader aspect of rhythmic organization and are discussed at greater length in the Introduction.

Rhythm section. An instrumental ensemble that accompanies vocal and instrumental soloists. Instruments in the rhythm section may vary. In rock, the ensemble commonly comprises drum kit, electric bass, and several guitars. Keyboard instruments may also be used in a rhythm section. Although all of these instruments may also perform in a "lead" role, when they provide accompaniment they are part of the rhythm section.

Riff. A riff is a short and distinctive melodic figure. A riff is not a complete melody, but it may be employed as part of a melody, either vocally or instrumentally. A riff may also be used anywhere in the accompaniment, often as part of a repeated pattern, but not necessarily. The guitar riff from the beginning of the Rolling Stone's "(I Can't Get No) Satisfaction" is a famous example. For the purposes of this book, "riff" and "lick" are synonymous.

Roman numerals. Roman numerals are used by music theorists to identify chords within a key. The chord based on the first note of the scale in a major key is labeled "I," while the chord built on the fifth note of the same scale is labeled "V." Some theorists use upper-case Roman numerals for major chords and lower-case numerals for minor chords. Thus, the chord built on the first note of a minor key is "i." Once one learns the way chords are formed in major and minor keys, the Roman numerals help to generalize how the chords work in any major key or in any minor key. See Interlude One for further discussion.

Sampling. Sampling is a practice, perhaps most prominent in hip-hop, in which a segment of some existing recording is excerpted and mixed into a new recording. Such samples can be quite long, or they can be much shorter segments. Sometimes shorter segments are made to immediately repeat numerous times, creating a loop. The advent of digital recording made sampling very easy, though the growth and development of this practice gave rise to a series of lawsuits over claims of copyright infringement.

Scale. In the simplest sense, a scale merely takes the notes that are available for use in any given key and puts them in order, starting and ending on the most important note. In the key of C major, for instance, the notes available are A, B, C, D, E, F, and G (these are the white keys on the piano). A C-major scale arranges these notes in relation to C, so that the scale is C D E F G A B C.

Shuffle. A shuffle rhythm is often a way of playing 4/4 that transforms it into something closer to 12/8. The four beats in a measure of 4/4 are each divided into two equal parts, making for a scheme that goes 1 & 2 & 3 & 4 &. In 12/8, the same measure would divide the beats into three equal parts, resulting in 1 & ah 2 & ah 3 & ah 4 & ah. A shuffle uses the second of these schemes, but the & is often silent, so we get 1 (&) ah 2 (&) ah 3 (&) ah 4 (&) ah. This sounds somewhat like the first scheme (4/4), since it has two elements per beat, but unlike the first scheme, the elements do not evenly divide the beat.

Sectional chorus and sectional verse. In the decades before rock music, popular songs often featured two large sections. The first of these was a kind of lengthy introduction to the song proper, employing lyrics that set the scene for the song itself. The second large section was the song itself. Through the years, many of these introductions have been all but forgotten, while the songs themselves have remained familiar. Writers who work in Tin Pan Alley-style pop often call the first section of such songs the "verse," and the second section the "chorus." This usage conflicts with the established use of these terms in rock music, however, and can lead to great confusion. To address this, we will call these introductory sections "sectional verses" and the song proper "sectional chorus," reserving the use of "verse" and "chorus" for use as they are defined in this Glossary and in the text.

Simple (meter). When we subdivide the basic beat into two equal parts, we create a simple feel, which is notated using simple meters such as 2/4, 3/4, or most commonly, 4/4. See the Introduction for a fuller explanation of simple and compound meters.

Simple verse-chorus form. In simple verse-chorus form, the verse and chorus sections employ the same underlying musical material, though the lyrics and sung melodies of each section are different. The form consists of these verses and choruses presented in alternation, though more than one verse may occur before the chorus.

Simple verse form. A simple verse form consists of a series of verses, all of which use the same underlying music. A simple verse form contains no chorus or bridge sections, though the verses may contain a refrain.

Stereo. A method of sound reproduction that produces two discrete sound signals, allowing listeners to create a sense of horizontal space. FM radio is broadcast in stereo and it became a popular playback form during the late 1960s.

Tag. A tag usually occurs at the end of a song or large section and consists of repeating the last few measures of the concluding section up to two times.

Timbre. The quality of a particular sound. Timbre is the character that differentiates one instrument from another. Effects such as reverb and equalization can change an instrument's timbre.

Tracks. Discrete sections of an audio recording that may be recorded, manipulated, and played back in isolation. The development of multi-track tape machines after WWII allowed musicians to record music in stages, or manipulate sections of recordings independently, without changing other parts. Common configurations were four-track, eight-track, sixteen-track, and twenty-four-track machines. Tracks are still used commonly, and are the basis for modern digital recording.

Triple (meter). When there are three beats in a bar (or measure) of music, the meter is classified as triple. Triple meter is commonly notated as 3/4 if it is a simple feel, or 9/8 if it is a compound feel. See the Introduction for a fuller explanation of meter classifications.

Twelve-bar blues. The twelve-bar blues is a structure that forms the musical basis for many verses, choruses, and even bridges in rock music. It can be divided into three 4-bar phrases. The lyrics to the first phrase are frequently repeated in the second phrase, with new lyrics appearing in the third phrase, creating a kind of question/question repeated/answer model as the words unfold. The twelve-bar blues also employs a specific arrangement of chords, and this is explained in greater detail in the Introduction. In the history of rock, the twelve-bar blues is strongly associated with 1950s rock and rhythm & blues. Even when this structure arises in later rock, the reference to the 1950s is often clear.

Verse. A verse is a section that most often features new lyrics with each repetition within a song, unlike a chorus, which tends to repeat the same lyrics with each recurrence. The verse is often used to tell a story or describe a situation. In an AABA form, the verse is the focal point of the song, and may also include a refrain. In a verse-chorus type form, the verse sets up the chorus, which is the focus of the song.

PHOTOS

Introduction

p. 2: John Tefteller at BluesImages.com; **p. 3 (top):** Douglas Kent Hall; **p. 3 (bottom left):** Mark Metcalfe/Getty Images; **p. 3 (bottom right):** Bettman/Getty Images; **p. 6:** Michael Ochs Archives//Getty Images; **p. 8:** Michael Ochs Archives/Getty Images; **p. 19:** Photo courtesy of Michael Inns; **p. 20:** Fin Costello/Redferns/Getty Images; **p. 21:** Kevin Cummins/Getty Images; **p. 26 (left):** Ray Avery/Redferns/Getty Images; **p. 26 (top right):** Photo by Barrie Wentzell; **p. 26 (bottom right):** Courtesy AVID; **p. 31:** From *Motown: The DVD* © 2009 Historic Music, Inc. under exclusive license to Universal Music Enterprises.

Chapter 1

p. 34: Library of Congress; **p. 35:** Bettman/Getty Images; **p. 36:** © 1940, 1942 by Irving Berlin; **p. 39:** Bettman/Getty Images; **p. 40:** Bettman/Getty Images; **p. 41:** Pictorial Press Ltd/Alamy; **p. 44:** *The Wizard of Oz* © 1939 Victor Fleming Metro-Goldwyn-Mayer (MGM); **p. 46:** Photo by Visual Studies Workshop/Getty Images; **p. 47:** GAB Archives/Redferns/Getty Images; **p. 48:** Bettmann Archive/Getty Images; **p. 49:** John Springer Collection/Getty Images; **p. 53:** Michael Ochs Archives/Getty Images; **p. 54 (left):** REUTERS/Benoit Tessier; **p. 54 (right):** Justin Lane/EPA/REX/Shutterstock; **p. 58:** Yale Joel/Time Life Pictures/Getty Images; **p. 59:** Michael Ochs Archives/Getty Images; **p. 62:** GAB Archive/Redferns/Getty Images; **p. 63:** Pictorial Press Ltd/Alamy; **p. 64:** Robert Johnson Estate/Hulton Archive/Getty Images; **p. 66:** Michael Ochs Archives/Getty Images; **p. 69:** Bettman/Getty Images.

Chapter 2

p. 76: J. R. Eyerman/Life Magazine/Time & Life Pictures/Getty Images; **p. 77:** Bettman/Getty Images; **p. 78:** John Tefteller at BluesImages.com; **p. 81 (top):** *The Wild One* © 1953 László Benedek Stanley Kramer Productions Distributor: Columbia Pictures; **p. 81 (middle):** *Rebel Without a Cause* © 1955 Nicholas Ray Warner Brothers; **p. 81 (bottom):** *Blackboard Jungle* © 1955 Richard Brooks Metro-Goldwyn-Mayer (MGM); **p. 83:** GAB Archive/Redferns/Getty Images; **p. 87:** ABC Photo Archives/Getty Images; **p. 89:** Michael Ochs Archives/Getty Images; **p. 91:** GAB Archive/Redferns/Getty Images; **p. 94:** GAB Archive/Redferns/Getty Images; **p. 95:** Michael Ochs Archives/Getty Images; **p. 98:** from DVD: *Elvis: The Ed Sullivan Show, the Classic Performances* © Sofa Entertainment, Inc. All Rights Reserved. © 2009 Image Entertainment; **p. 99:** Time Life Pictures/Getty Images; **p. 100:** AP Image; **p. 101:** Michael Ochs Archives/Getty Images; **p. 102:** Photo by David Redfern/Redferns/Getty Images; **p. 105:** CBS Photo Archive/Getty Images; **p. 107:** Bettman/Getty Images.

Chapter 3

p. 110: John Tefteller at BluesImages.com; **p. 116:** Photo by Hulton Archive/Getty Images; **p. 117:** Michael Ochs Archives/Getty Images; **p. 118:** GAB Archive/Redferns/Getty Images; **p. 119:** Photo by Charles Peterson/Getty Images; **p. 120:** Michael Ochs Archives/Getty Images; **p. 123:** PhotoQuest/Getty Images; **p. 125:** Michael Ochs Archives/Getty Images; **p. 126:** Michael Ochs Archives/Getty Images; **p. 129:** Michael Ochs Archives/Getty Images; **p. 131:** Ray Avery/Getty Images; **p. 134:** Michael Ochs Archives/Getty Images; **p. 135:** Photo by Michael Ochs Archives/Getty Images; **p. 138:** Michael Levin/Corbis Historical/Getty Images; **p. 140:** David Redfern/Getty Images; **p. 143:** Photo by Tony Frank/Sygma via Getty Images; **p. 144:** Michael Ochs Archives/Getty Images; **p. 148:** Capitol/EMI.

Chapter 4

p. 152: Bettmann/Getty Images; **p. 153:** Bob Adelman; **p. 154:** Fiona Adams/Redferns/Getty Images; **p. 157:** CA/Redferns/Getty Images; **p. 160:** Photo by GAB Archive/Redferns/Getty Images; **p. 161 (top):** Michael Ochs Archives/Getty Images; **p. 161 (bottom):** Keystone Pictures USA/Alamy Stock Photo; **p. 165:** Photo by Bernard Gotfryd/Getty Images; **p. 166:** From DVD: *Miramax Films Collector Series: A Hard Day's Night*. Distributed by Buena Vista Home Entertainment; **p. 171:** GAB Archive/Redferns/Getty Images; **p. 172:** John Drysdale/Hulton Archive/Getty Images; **p. 175:** David Redfern/Getty Images; **p. 177:** Bettman/Getty Images; **p. 179:** Val Wilmer/Redferns/Getty Images; **p. 180:** Photo by Robert Whitaker/Getty Images; **p. 182 (top):** Redferns/Getty Images; **p. 182 (bottom):** Michael Ochs Archives/Getty Images.

Chapter 5

p. 188: Columbia Records/Sony; **p. 191:** RB/Redferns/Getty Images; **p. 193:** Michael Ochs Archives/Getty Images; **p. 194:** Michael Ochs Archives/Getty Images; **p. 196:** David Redfern/Getty Images; **p. 197:** Michael Ochs Archives/

Getty Images; **p. 200:** GAB Archive/Redferns/Getty Images; **p. 202:** Jan Olofsson/Redferns/Getty Images; **p. 203:** Michael Ochs Archives/Stringer/Getty Images; **p. 205:** Henry Diltz/Getty Images; **p. 206:** Michael Ochs Archives/Getty Images; **p. 204:** Photo by Chris Ware/Keystone Features/Getty Images; **p. 207 (top):** Michael Ochs Archives/Getty Images; **p. 207 (bottom):** Elektra Records; **p. 210:** Everett Collection Inc/Alamy; **p. 212:** Michael Ochs Archives/Getty Images.

Chapter 6

p. 216: John Tefteller at www.tefteller.com; **p. 218:** Michael Ochs Archives/Getty Images; **p. 221:** Michael Ochs Archives/Getty Images; **p. 222:** Michael Ochs Archives/Getty Images; **p. 224:** Michael Ochs Archives/Getty Images; **p. 225:** Michael Ochs Archives/Getty Images; **p. 226 (all):** From DVD: *The Temptations: Get Ready. Definitive Performances 1965–1972.* (2006) Universal Music Group International; **p. 228:** Redferns/Getty Images; **p. 229:** Redferns/Getty Images; **p. 230:** Michael Ochs Archives/Getty Images; **p. 233:** Michael Ochs Archives/Getty Images; **p. 234:** GAB Archives/Redferns/Getty Images; **p. 235:** Michael Ochs Archives/Getty Images; **p. 237:** Michael Ochs Archives/Getty Images; **p. 240:** © Chuck Stewart Photography, LLC; **p. 239:** Evening Standard/Hulton Archive/Getty Images.

Chapter 7

p. 248: David Magnus/REX/Shutterstock; **p. 251:** Hulton Archive/Getty Images; **p. 255:** Michael Ochs Archives/Getty Images; **p. 259:** Avico.co.uk; **p. 261:** Courtesy of George Hunter; **p. 263:** wolfgangsvault.com; **p. 264:** Robert Altman/Michael Ochs Archives/Getty Images; **p. 267:** Michael Ochs Archives/Getty Images; **p. 268:** Ted Streshinsky/Getty Images; **p. 270:** Adam Ritchie/Redferns/Getty Images; **p. 272:** Michael Putland/Getty Images; **p. 274:** Susie Macdonald/Redferns/Getty Images; **p. 276:** David Redferns/Redferns/Getty Images; **p. 279:** Donaldson/Michael Ochs Archives/Getty Images; **p. 280:** Gunter Zint/K&K Ulf Kruger OHG/Redferns/Getty Images; **p. 282:** Associated Press; **p. 284:** From DVD: *Woodstock: 3 Days of Peace and Music. The Director's Cut.* © 2009 Warner Bros. Entertainment, Inc.; **p. 285:** Ralph Ackerman/Getty Images; **p. 286:** AP Photo.

Chapter 8

p. 290: CBS Photo Archive/Getty Images; **p. 291:** Sunset Boulevard/Corba via Getty Images; **p. 292:** ZUMA Press, Inc./Alamy Stock Photo; **p. 297:** Robert Knight Archive/Redferns/Getty Images; **p. 299:** Pictorial Press LTD/Alamy; **p. 301:** Peter Tarnoff/MediaPunch; **p. 304:** Richard Upper/CNC Productions; **p. 307:** Michael Putland/Getty Images; **p. 309:** David Redfern/Getty Images; **p. 310:** © James R Anderson; **p. 313:** Photo by Waring Abbott/Getty Images; **p. 315:** Photo by Jean-Claude Deutsch/Paris Match Archive via Getty Images; **p. 316:** Michael Putland/Hulton Archive/Getty Images; **p. 317:** Jan Peterson/Redferns/Getty Images; **p. 318:** Michael Ochs Archives/Getty Images;

p. 320: Michael Ochs Archives/Getty Images; **p. 321:** Pictoral Press Ltd/Alamy; **p. 322:** Tom Hill/Wireimage/Getty Images; **p. 323:** Gijsbert Hanekroot/Redferns/Getty Images; **p. 326:** Anwar Hussein/Hulton Archive/Getty Images; **p. 327:** Henry Diltz/Getty Images; **p. 329:** Gijsbert Hanekroot/Redferns/Getty Images.

Chapter 9

p. 334: Michael Ochs Archives/Getty Images; **p. 336:** Pictoral Press Ltd/Alamy; **p. 338:** Pictoral Press Ltd/Alamy; **p. 339:** Charlyn Zlotnick/Redferns/Getty Images; **p. 342:** Michael Ochs Archives/Getty Images; **p. 343:** RB/Redferns/Getty Images; **p. 346:** Michael Ochs Archives/Getty Images; **p. 347:** Archives d 7eme Art/Photos 12/Alamy; **p. 348:** Pictorial Press Ltd/Alamy; **p. 349:** Photo by Lynn Goldsmith/Corbis/VCG via Getty Images; **p. 350:** Richard E. Aaron/Redferns/Getty Images; **p. 354:** Andrew Putler/Redferns/Getty Images; **p. 356:** *Saturday Night Fever* 1977 John Badham: Paramount Pictures; Robert Stigwood Organization (RSO); **p. 360:** Richard E Aaron/Redferns/Getty Images; **p. 364:** Associated Press.

Chapter 10

p. 366: Sony; **p. 369:** Getty Images/Redferns; **p. 371:** Getty Images/Redferns; **p. 372:** Michael Ochs Archives/Getty Images; **p. 373:** Michael Putland/Getty Images; **p. 375:** Getty Images/Redferns/Ebet Roberts; **p. 377:** Photo by Fin Costello/Redferns/Getty Images; **p. 378:** Denis O'Regan; **p. 379:** Redferns/Richard E. Aaron/Getty Images; **p. 382:** Mick Gold/Redferns/Getty Images; **p. 383:** Denis O'Regan; **p. 384:** Lynn Goldsmith/Corbis Premium Historical/Getty Images; **p. 386:** Lynn Goldsmith/Corbis Historical/Getty Images; **p. 389:** Michael Ochs Archives/Getty Images; **p. 391:** Roberta Bayley/Redferns/Getty Images; **p. 392:** LGI Stock/Corbis Historical/Getty Images; **p. 394:** Lynn Goldsmith/Corbis Historical/Getty Images; **p. 396:** Estate of Keith Morris/Redferns/Getty Images; **p. 398 (left):** Michael Ochs Archives/Getty Images; **p. 398 (right):** Pictorial Press LTD/Alamy.

Chapter 11

p. 402: Bettman/Getty Images; **p. 403:** Everett Collection; **p. 404:** KMazur/WireImage/Getty Images; **p. 406:** The Buggles, "Video Killed the Radio Star" (music video) 1980 From a DVD titled *The Best of Alternative 80s—The DVD Collection* distributed by Universal Music Group; **p. 409:** Everett Collection; **p. 412:** MJJ Productions, LLC; **p. 411:** Photo by Roger Ressmeyer/Corbis/VCG via Getty Images; **p. 414:** Richard E Aaron/Redferns/Getty Images; **p. 415:** REUTERS/Jeff Christensen; **p. 417:** Peter Still/Redferns/Getty Images; **p. 418:** Henry Diltz/Getty Images; **p. 419:** Ebet Roberts/Redferns/Getty Images; **p. 421:** Bettman/Getty Images; **p. 424:** Lynn Goldsmith/Corbis Historical/Getty Images; **p. 426:** Richard E. Aaron/Redferns/ Getty Images; **p. 428:** Lynn Goldsmith/Corbis Historical/Getty Images; **p. 429:** Ian Dickson/Redferns/ Getty Images;

p. 430: "Sledgehammer" (music video) 1986 dir. Stephen R Johnson Production Company: Aardman Animation.

Chapter 12

p. 436: Sony BMG Music Entertainment; p. 440: Michael Ochs Archives/Getty Images; p. 441: Bliss Morris/Getty Images; p. 443 (top): © Joe Giron Photography; p. 443 (bottom): Getty Images/Redferns/Ebet Roberts; p. 444: Pete Cronin /Redferns/Getty Images; p. 447: Jamel Shabazz; p. 448: Michael Ochs Archive/Getty Images; p. 450: David Corio/Michael Ochs Archives/Getty Images; p. 451: David Corio/Michael Ochs Archives/Getty Images; p. 453: Ebet Roberts/Redferns/Getty Images; p. 454: Getty Images/Michael Ochs Archive; p. 456 (top): Al Pereira/Michael Ochs Archive/Getty Images; p. 456 (bottom): Tim Mosenfelder/Hulton Archive/Getty Images; p. 465: Laura Levine/Corbis Premium Historical/Getty Images.

Chapter 13

p. 470: Gail Albert Halaban; p. 471: Catrina Genovese/Hulton Archive/Getty Images; p. 472: Paul Bergen/Redferns/Getty Images; p. 474: Mick Hutson/Redferns/Getty Images; p. 475: Mick Hutson/Redferns/Getty Images; p. 478: Steve Eichner/WireImage/Getty Images; p. 481: Pictoral Press Ltd/Alamy; p. 484: Lindsay Brice/Michael Ochs Archives/Getty Images; p. 485: Ebet Roberts/Redferns/Getty Images; p. 489 (top): Photo courtesy of Jason McQuilliams; p. 489 (bottom): Carey Brandon/Redferns; p. 491: Getty Images/Redferns/Peter Pakvis; p. 492: Jon Super/Redferns/Getty Images.

Chapter 14

p. 496: Harry Borden/Contour By Getty Images; p. 498: Getty Images/SPLL; p. 500: Mick Hutson/Redferns/Getty Images; p. 501: C. Taylor Crothers/Getty Images; p. 504: Steve Eichner/WireImage/Getty Images; p. 505: Paul Bergen/Getty Images; p. 507: Getty Images; p. 510: Frans Schellekens/Redferns/Getty Images; p. 512: Mark Arminski; p. 513: Tim Mosenfelder/Corbis Entertainment/Getty Images; p. 514: © John Atashian; p. 518: From DVD: *Weezer Video Capture Device: Treasures from the Vault 1991–2002*. Geffen Records; p. 517: Kevin Mazur/WireImage/Getty Images; p. 519: Chi Modu/Diverseimages; p. 523: Des Willie/Redferns/Getty Images; p. 524: Getty Images/Redferns/Sal Idriss; p. 525: Tina Paul, fifibear@fifibear.com; p. 526: PYMCA/Universal Images Group/Getty Image.

Chapter 15

p. 531: Twitter; p. 532: Courtesy of Alabama Shakes; p. 535: Michael Short/Bloomberg via Getty Images; p. 539: Robert A Tobiansky/Getty Images Entertainment/Getty Images; p. 540: Frazer Harrison/Getty Images; p. 542: Karl Gehring/The Denver Post/Getty Images; p. 544: Kevin C. Cox/Getty Images; p. 560: From DVD: *Outkast: The Videos*. (2003) Arista Records; p. 545: Photo by SGranitz/WireImage for Lifetime Television LA/Getty Images; p. 546: Photo by Samir Hussein/Redferns/Getty Images; p. 549: Stephen Lovekin/Getty Images; p. 550: John Shearer/WireImage/Getty Images; p. 551: WireImage/Getty Images; p. 555: Kevin Mazur/WireImage/Getty Images; p. 558: Kevin Mazur/WireImage/Getty Images; p. 561: FilmMagic/Getty Images; p. 564: Fabrice Cofrini/AFP/Getty Images; p. 567: Tim Mosenfelder/Corbis Entertainment/Getty Images; p. 569: Lex van Rossen/Getty Images; p. 570: Steven Dewall/Redferns/Getty Images; p. 571: Caitlin Mogridge/Redferns via Getty Images; p. 574: Stephen St. John/National Geographic/Getty Images; p. 575 (top): Michael Kovac/WireImage/Getty Images; p. 575 (bottom): Theo Wargo/Getty Images.

TEXT

p. 50: "Phenomenon: The Voice with the Golden Accessories," by E.J. Kahn, Jr., *The New Yorker*, October 26, 1946. Copyright © The New Yorker Magazine/ E.J. Kahn Jr./ Condé Nast. Reprinted by permission of Condé Nast. p. 71: *Shake, Rattle and Roll*. Words and Music by Charles E. Calhoun. Copyright © 1954 (Renewed) Unichappell Music Inc. and Mijac Music. All rights administered by Unichappell Music Inc. All rights on behalf of Mijac Music administered by Sony/ATV Music Publishing LLC, 242 Church Street, Nashville, TN 37219. All Rights Reserved. Used by permission of Alfred Music and Sony/ATV Music Publishing LLC. pp. 114–115: "A Broadway Divided," from *Always Magic in the Air: The Bomp and Brilliance of the Brill Building Era* by Ken Emerson. Copyright © 2005 by Ken Emerson. Used by permission of Viking Books, an imprint of Penguin Publishing Group, a division of Penguin Random House LLC. All rights reserved. And by permission of HarperCollins Publishers Ltd. pp. 158–159: "Britain Exports a Mania," "Pincus Swings on String of Beatles Clicks," and "Promoter Fears about Economics of the Beatles," from *Variety*, February 12, 1964. Copyright © 1964 by Variety, Inc. Reprinted by permission of Variety Media, LLC. p. 199: "Why Teens Switched to Folk Rock," by Sylvie Reice. Originally published in the *Los Angeles Times*, January 6, 1966. Reprinted by permission of the Estate of Sylvie Reice. pp. 242–243: Excerpt from "Apple Cores" by LeRoi Jones, *DownBeat*, March 25, 1965. Reprinted by permission of DownBeat Archive. pp. 262–263: "A Letter from the Editor," by Jann Wenner, *Rolling Stone*, November 9, 1967. Copyright © Rolling Stone LLC 1967. All Rights Reserved. Used by Permission. p. 263: "Get Off of My Cloud!" by Paul Williams, *Crawdaddy!* February 7, 1966. © Wolfgang's Vault, all rights reserved. Reprinted by permission of Wolfgang's Vault. pp. 314–315: "The Dark Side of the Floyd," by Roy Hollingworth, *Melody Maker*, March 10, 1973. Copyright © Time Inc. (UK) Ltd. Reprinted by permission of Time Inc. (UK) Ltd. pp. 358–359: "The Disco Boom and Blacks," by Nelson George, *New York Amsterdam News*, January 28,